MARRIAGE LICENSE AFFIDAVITS

1861–1921

SONOMA COUNTY, CALIFORNIA

VOLUME I: A–F

(ALPHABETIZED BY SURNAME OF GROOM)

PART ONE: GROOM, BRIDE, DATE OF APPLICATION, COMMENTS

PART TWO: GROOM, BRIDE, AGE, RESIDENCE, PLACE OF BIRTH

Sonoma County Genealogical Society

HERITAGE BOOKS
2011

HERITAGE BOOKS

AN IMPRINT OF HERITAGE BOOKS, INC.

Books, CDs, and more—Worldwide

For our listing of thousands of titles see our website
at
www.HeritageBooks.com

Published 2011 by
HERITAGE BOOKS, INC.
Publishing Division
100 Railroad Ave. #104
Westminster, Maryland 21157

International Standard Book Numbers
Paperbound: 978-0-7884-5357-1
Clothbound: 978-0-7884-8901-3

Contents: Volume 1: A - F
(Alphabetized by Surname of Groom)

Part I

Groom, Bride, Date of Application, Comments

Part II

Groom, Bride, Age, Residence, Place of Birth

Marriage License Affidavits, 1861 to 1921
Sonoma County, California

Introduction

The information contained in this four volume series is taken from Marriage License Affidavits currently housed at the Sonoma County History and Genealogy Library in Santa Rosa, California. These data originated in the office of the Sonoma County Clerk. The information is contained on eight reels of microfilm and contains approximately 14,000 records.

The volumes consist of:

Volume	Data Alphabetized by Groom's Surname
I	A - F
II	G - M
III	N - Z
IV	Index to Bride's Surname

In 1990, the Sonoma County Genealogical Society published *Sonoma County Marriages, 1847 - 1902*, which was an index to marriage records housed at the office of the Sonoma County Recorder. This current publication, unlike the index, in most cases contains the age, residence, and birth place of both the bride and groom. In addition, the consent of a parent or guardian is noted for brides under the age of 18 and grooms under the age of 21. In a few cases, birth dates or other pertinent information is given.

Affidavits are the application for a marriage license and may well include persons who were never actually married. The date may or may not coincide with the actual marriage date of those who did, in fact, get married.

Condition of the Microfilm

In many cases, the condition of the microfilm is exceedingly poor, and the handwritten entries vary from readable to totally unreadable. Forms often varied from year to year, and in some cases, a handwritten note from the parent(s), guardian(s), or a notary was substituted for the form generally in use during that time period. Many of the parental consent forms were handwritten notes and were not always adjacent to the marriage affidavits to which they belonged. Some notes partially obscure the information written on the affidavits.

A clerk apparently filled in the form in most cases, which was then usually signed by the groom, sometimes by both the bride and the groom, occasionally only by the bride, or occasionally by another person. Not infrequently, the spelling of the name made by the clerk did not agree with the spelling of the person who signed the affidavit. In such cases we used the spelling of the person(s) who signed if it was legible. All affidavits were read by at least two persons, and, in some cases, by three persons to try to resolve the correct spelling. If the issue could not be resolved, a question mark (?) appears beside the name, or other information provided.

State of California, County of Sonoma, ss.

[illegible] being duly sworn, says: My name is [illegible] I reside at [illegible] I was born in [illegible] My age is 22 I desire a license to authorize my marriage with [illegible]

She resides at [illegible] she was born in [illegible] and is [illegible] years of age.

And I further swear that there are no legal objections to our marriage.

being sworn, says: My name is the facts contained in the foregoing affidavit are true of my own knowledge. I reside at

Subscribed and sworn to this [illegible] day of [illegible] A. D. 1883, before me, [illegible] County Clerk. By Deputy Clerk.

[illegible]

[illegible] parents ~~and guardians~~ of [illegible] who is under the age of 18, hereby give ~~their~~ his consent to the marriage of [illegible] with [illegible] and the County Clerk is hereby authorized to issue a license for said marriage.

Geo. [illegible] Kendall.

Figure 1: Example of an 1883 marriage affidavit

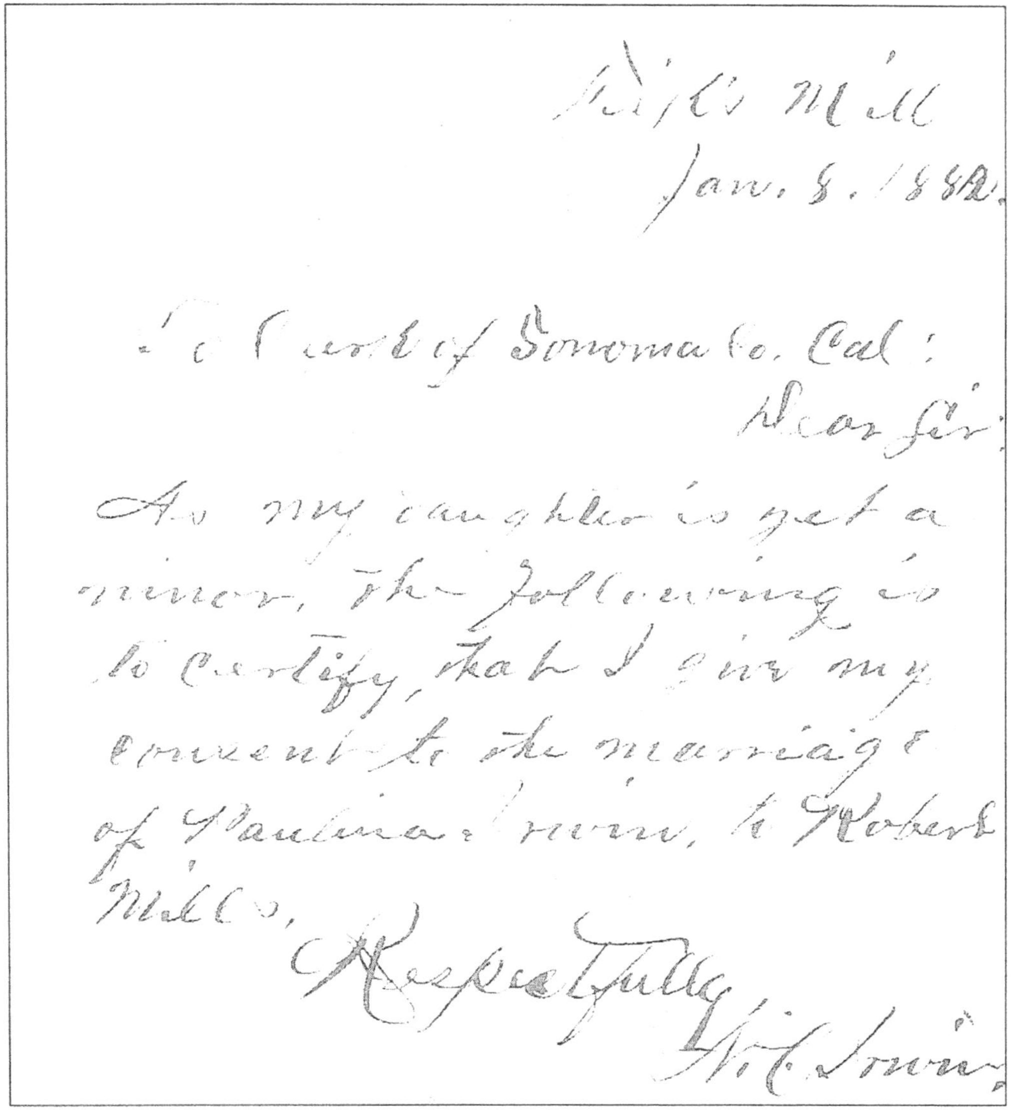

[illegible] Mill
Jan. 8. 1882.

To Clerk of Sonoma Co. Cal:
Dear Sir:
As my daughter is yet a minor, the following is to certify, that I give my consent to the marriage of Paulina Irwin, to Robert Mills,

Respectfully
W. C. Irwin

Figure 2: Example of one of the "better" notes of permission

Description of Data Layout

The data are presented alphabetically by groom's surname in three volumes, each volume having two parts. A fourth volume is an index to the bride's surname.

Part	Data Included
I	Name of groom, bride, date of application, comments (includes name of parent or guardian for males under 21 and brides under 18), and occasionally other notes
II	Detailed information on groom and bride: age, residence, place of birth

Example of Use

If you know the name of the groom, locate the appropriate volume, begin with part I, then go to part II for additional information about both parties. If you know only the name of the bride, go to volume IV and locate the bride's name to find the name of the groom. Then located the groom in parts I and II to find additional detailed information.

For place of residence, the town was most frequently given. The state can be assumed to be California unless otherwise noted (using standard postal codes). State codes may be designated for smaller/lesser known towns in California and other states. State codes are not used for well-known cities (Chicago, New York City, New Orleans, etc.).

Place of birth is most often given as state or country; standard postal codes are used for the USA, as shown in Table 3. A three-character code is used for other nations, as shown in Figure 4. However, some birth places may be given as a city or town, township, county, or region in the USA or in another nation. Those cities or other locations that are most frequently used are also coded to conserve space and are shown in Figure 5.

Table 3: United States Codes

Postal Code	State
AL	Alabama
AK	Alaska
AZ	Arizona
AR	Arkansas
CA	California
CO	Colorado
CT	Connecticut
DE	Delaware
DC	District of Columbia
FL	Florida
GA	Georgia
GU	Guam
HI	Hawaii
ID	Idaho
IL	Illinois
IN	Indiana
IA	Iowa
KS	Kansas
KY	Kentucky
LA	Louisiana
ME	Maine
MD	Maryland
MA	Massachusetts
MI	Michigan
MN	Minnesota
MS	Mississippi
MO	Missouri
MT	Montana
NE	Nebraska
NV	Nevada
NH	New Hampshire
NJ	New Jersey
NM	New Mexico
NY	New York
NC	North Carolina
ND	North Dakota
OH	Ohio
OK	Oklahoma
OR	Oregon
PA	Pennsylvania
PR	Puerto Rico
RI	Rhode Island
SC	South Carolina
SD	South Dakota
TN	Tennessee
TX	Texas
UT	Utah
VT	Vermont
VA	Virginia
VI	Virgin Islands
WA	Washington
WV	West Virginia
WI	Wisconsin
WY	Wyoming

Table 4: International Codes

AFG	Afghanistan
AFR	Africa
ALB	Albania
ALS	Alsace-Lorraine
ARG	Argentina
ASY	Assyria
AUS	Austria
AUT	Australia
AZR	Azores
BAR	Barbados
BAV	Bavaria
BER	Bermuda
BCL	British Columbia
BHS	Bahamas
BLG	Belgium

BOH	Bohemia
BOL	Bolivia
BOR	Borneo
BRA	Brazil
BRG	British Guiana
BUA	Buenos Aires
BUL	Bulgaria
BUR	Burma
BWI	British West Indies
CEN	Central America
CHL	Chile
CHN	China
CLB	Colombia
CLZ	Canal Zone
CND	Canada
COR	Costa Rica
CRT	Croatia
CUB	Cuba
CZH	Czechoslovakia
DEI	Dutch East Indies
DMR	Dominican Republic
DNK	Denmark
EGY	Egypt
EIN	East Indies
ELS	El Salvador
ENG	England
ESI	East India
EUR	Europe
FIN	Finland
FRN	France
FRP	French Polynesia
GAM	Guam
GBR	Great Britain

GER	Germany
GIB	Gibraltar
GRC	Greece
GUA	Guatemala
HAI	Haiti
HIN	Hindustan
HLD	Holland
HND	Honduras
HUN	Hungary
HWI	Hawaiian Islands
ICE	Iceland
IDA	India
IND	Indonesia
IOJ	Isle of Jersey
IOM	Isle of Man
IRL	Ireland
ISR	Israel
ITL	Italy
JAM	Jamaica
JPN	Japan
JVA	Java
KOR	Korea
LAT	Latvia
LEB	Lebanon
LIT	Lithuania
LUX	Luxembourg
MEX	Mexico
MLT	Malta
NAM	North America
NBW	New Brunswick
NRY	Norway
NSC	Nova Scotia
NSW	News South Wales

NTH	Netherlands
NWL	North Wales
NZD	New Zealand
OTT	Ottoman Empire
PAL	Palestine
PAN	Panama
PAR	Paraguay
PEI	Prince Edward Island
PER	Persia
PLD	Poland
PRS	Prussia
PRT	Portugal
PRU	Peru
PUR	Puerto Rico
QUE	Quebec
ROM	Romania
RUS	Russia
SAF	South Africa
SAM	South America
SAX	Saxony
SCT	Scotland
SEA	(born at sea)
SGP	Singapore
SIB	Siberia
SLO	Slovakia
SMI	Santa Maria Islands
SPN	Spain
SRB	Serbia
SWD	Sweden
SWI	Sandwich Islands
SWT	Switzerland
SYR	Syria

TRK	Turkey
URG	Uruguay
VEN	Venezuela
VIE	Vietnam

VRI	Virgin Islands
WIN	West Indies
WLS	Wales

WTS	Western Islands
YUG	Yugoslavia

Figure 5: Cities, Towns, Townships, and Other Areas

Bey	Bayrouth, SYR
Can	Canton Ticino, SWT
Chi	Chicago
Clo	Cloverdale
Clv	Cleveland
Dak	Dakota
Dun	Dundas, Ontario, CND
Hld	Healdsburg
Hon	Honolulu
Lak	Lake Co.
Lon	London, ENG
Mac	Marin Co.
Men	Mendocino Co.
Oak	Oakland
Pet	Petaluma

Pett	Petaluma Twp.
Por	Portland, OR
Saj	San Jose
Sfo	San Francisco
Sab	San Bernardino Co.
Sac	Sacramento
Sar	Santa Rosa
Seb	Sebastopol
Son	Sonoma
Soc	Sonoma Co.
Utt	Utah Territory
Vts	Vallejo Twp., Sonoma Co.
Wat	Washington Territory
Wdc	Washington, D.C.

Acknowledgments

Project Director
Carmen Finley

Data Entry
Maggi Andrews
Kerri Bailey
Kay Clegg
Phyllis Kuehn
Joe Panaro
Helen Strickley

Proofreaders
Anna Conley
Doris Dickenson
Carmen Finley
Lois Nimmo

Editor
Doris Dickenson

Camera Ready Copy
Carmen Finley

Special acknowledgment goes to Anthony Hoskins, head of the History and Genealogy Library in Sonoma County and Sonoma County Archivist who made the microfilm available for abstraction. Also, thanks to Mairi Barsky, Branch Manager of the Guerneville Regional Library for the use of their library facilities.

Groom		Bride			
Surname	Given Name	Surname	Given Name	Date	Comments
?hreeve (?)	Levi	Staggs	Phebe	23 June 1918	
Aanensen	Peider	Downham	Alma N.	21 Nov. 1914	
Aaronson	Phillip V.	Blattenberger	Zoe N.	30 Dec. 1918	
Abbey	Alfred	Bailhache	Ruth	16 May 1883	
Abbey	Alfred B.	Bigsby	Macueleta	22 Mar. 1907	
Abbey	Bert	Lewis	Haltie	29 Oct. 1910	
Abbey	William Newton	Allen	Nellie Angeline	8 Aug. 1908	
Abbott	George Henry	Shire	Maude Frances	24 July 1905	br: Mrs. Frances Shire, mother, gives consent
Abbott	Joel A.	Hendricks	Myrtle	15 Aug. 1899	no previous marriage
Abeel	James Martin	Pepper	Ada Elaine	27 June 1907	
Abels	Ihuk?	Rubben	Helene	16 Feb. 1894	
Ables	Horace T.	Stephen	Mabel Alice	11 June 1898	br: J. I. Stephen, M.D., father; no previous marriage
Abra	Jack W.	Vickery	Nellie G.	14 Sept. 1904	
Abraham	Louis F.	Burston	Francis E.	9 Jan. 1899	no previous marriage
Abraio	William Franklin	Kelton	Alice R.	28 July 1920	br: Mary Ollie Kelton, mother
Abrams	J. William	Florin	Lucile H.	12 June 1901	requested by John Florin
Abrott	Fred Henry	Lyons	Henrietta	9 Oct. 1900	
Abshire	Alfred C.	Laughlin	Myrtle	24 May 1890	br: Mrs. M. J. Cain, mother
Abshire	Farley A.	Crow	Susie E.	2 Oct. 1891	
Abshire	Francis P.	Ross	Vera M.	27 Oct. 1913	
Abshire	Alfred Cecil	Thompson	Maude Elnora	13 Oct. 1915	
Achey	Clarence M.	Fogarty	Ida	28 Mar. 1883	gr: Mary E. Achey, mother; Montesano, WA Territory
Acker	James W.	Pattison	Jean M. O.	23 Feb. 1915	
Ackerman	Charles J.	Petray	Gladys Valentine	10 Aug. 1917	gr: Amelia R. Ackerman, mother
Ackerman	Clarence M.	Ward	Ada L.	10 Sept. 1901	
Ackerman	Oliver Norton	Ranarde	Lina Francis	2 June 1896	
Ackermann	Anton	Weismann	Alvina	6 Jan. 1916	
Acorne	Melville G.	Boman	Marian Beatrice	8 June 1917	
Acquistapace	Amadio	Rossotte	Aurellia	28 Oct. 1914	
Acquistapace	Guiseppe	Piezzi	Sabina	20 Aug. 1910	
Acquistapace	Pietro	Antonietta	Manne	10 June 1908	br: reversal of surname and given name?

Groom		Bride			
Surname	Given Name	Surname	Given Name	Date	Comments
Acuff	Metcalf	Hunt	Luella A.	21 Nov. 1866	
Adair	C. H.	Burckhalter	Agnes	26 Feb. 1887	requested by W. S. Hosmer
Adams	Alfred F.	Thomas	Nettie E.	11 Oct. 1904	
Adams	Arthur Joseph	Munro	Margaret J.	no date	not signed by clerk
Adams	Arthur Miron	Johnson	Ella B.	8 Apr. 1898	not to be published
Adams	Claude W.	Patterson	Bell	2 Aug. 1902	
Adams	Clement Scott	Cartwright	Leta May	9 Aug. 1917	
Adams	Darwin C.	McGowan	Daisy Fedora	27 May 1916	
Adams	Frank	Carlile	Etta	6 Oct. 1880	
Adams	Frank E.	Jones	Carrie E.	29 June 1885	
Adams	Frank T.	Skaggs	Clara C.	28 Dec. 1887	
Adams	George Edward	Fogerty	Annie May	27 Feb. 1883	
Adams	George H.	Green	Una	22 Apr. 1903	
Adams	George William	Richman	Elizabeth Eleanor	1 June 1908	
Adams	J. S.	Greening	Laura A.	1 Aug. 1885	
Adams	John F.	Riley	Gertrude E.	4 Nov. 1893	license requested by Robert C. Rockwitz
Adams	John Henry	Dunkley	Mattie J.	3 July 1884	
Adams	John L.	Halst	Maggie M.	3 Feb. 1896	
Adams	Joseph	Crawford	Harriet Anna	10 Aug. 1889	
Adams	Joseph Walker	Holst	Annie Mary	9 Nov. 1889	br: John J. Holst, father
Adams	Merrit	Murphy	Jennie R.	6 July 1891	gr: W. E. Adams, father; br: William B. Murphy, father
Adams	Robert L.	Morgan	Nellie W.	23 Sept. 1891	
Adams	Robert S.	Keys	Amelia	18 Feb. 1892	
Adams	Ross B.	Lambert	Lotus L.	1 Oct. 1910	
Adams	Wallace A.	Brown	Adelaide M.	22 June 1915	
Adams	William	Calder	Mary Jane	31 Oct. 1888	
Adams	William A.	Hendricks	Mayme E.	23 Oct. 1915	
Adams	William H.	Hillyer	Daisy B.	11 June 1909	
Adams	William J.	Russell	Martha Jane	13 Dec. 1892	
Adamson	Forrest E.	Gregg	Myrtle M.	31 Dec. 1913	
Adamson	Isaac N.	Willson	Nellie, Mrs.	5 Dec. 1887	
Adamson	Isaac Newton	Bell	Lucinda	19 Oct. 1885	br: Henry Bell, father

Groom		Bride		Date	Comments
Surname	Given Name	Surname	Given Name		
Adamson	Isaac Newton	Matthews	Ella, Mrs.	20 Aug. 1900	br: widow
Adamson	John Martin	Adams	Martha	11 Oct. 1875	E. M. Hiatt, Justice of Peace, Anderson Twp.
Adcock	Abe	Francis	Hattie	10 Apr. 1900	do not publish at present
Adcock	George	Dodson	Rosa	20 Oct. 1893	br: Chars Dodson gives consent.
Adcock	Joseph C.	Dodson	Mary Jane	31 Jan. 1903	
Adcock	Samuel W.	Murray	Bertie	5 June 1902	
Adler	Adam Winkle	Quartaroli	Florence M. E.	9 Jan. 1904	br: L. Quartaroli, parent
Adler	Hans	Rohleder	Betti	10 Sept. 1904	
Adolphson	Gustav	Fingahl	Nellie	12 Apr. 1918	
Affonso	Joseph T.	Brazil	Rose Helen	30 Mar. 1918	
Affranchino	Guiseppe	Guglielmini	Rosa	21 Sept. 1907	
Agnew	Asahel Warner	Shaver	Bertha Catherine	16 Feb. 1904	
Agnew	Hugh C.	Barber	Josephine	28 Jan. 1902	
Agnew	James F.	Arnold	Alberta L.	19 June 1897	
Agnew	Newton W.	Cozini	Lottie May	19 Nov. 1895	license requested by S. J. Agnew
Agren	Arthur L.	Pohley	Margaret F.	21 Sept. 1916	
Aguiar	Frank	Silva	Arnicenda Augusta	16 Dec. 1910	
Aguirre	Amadeo	Apodaca	Fermina Saturnina	13 Apr. 1917	
Aguirre	Martin	Archabal	Julia	20 Dec. 1909	
Ahern	George F.	Bones	Hazel Celia	15 Sept. 1917	
Ahern	James B.	Davidson	Sarah E.	17 June 1893	
Ahern	Nicholas	Hardford	Mary	22 Sept. 1888	
Ahl	Harry Jacob	Hiatt	Kate D.	9 Mar. 1912	
Ahl	John	Mayfield	Maud	9 Mar. 1907	
Ahlstedt	Gustave	Nelson	Johanna	18 Feb. 1911	
Ahrens	William M.	Frehe	Annie M.	27 June 1903	
Aiken	Henry S.	Smith	Dollie A.	1 May 1883	
Aiton	Wensley T.	Davis	Anna E.	8 June 1914	
Akers	Austin G.	Cuda	Rose E.	30 June 1913	
Akers	Earl L.	Strickler	Ida Grace	5 Feb. 1912	
Akers	Edward W.	Banks	A. Varde	27 June 1899	
Akers	Lawrence	Parker	Pearl	25 Feb. 1920	
Akers	Stephen	Lawler	Grace	8 Apr. 1904	

Groom		Bride			
Surname	**Given Name**	**Surname**	**Given Name**	**Date**	**Comments**
Alapi	Hans	Szalay	Rosa	14 Jan. 1915	
Albera	Michele	Cabaup	Maria	24 Feb. 1900	
Alberigi	Americo	Ceraille	Jennie	6 Mar. 1911	
Alberti	Francisco	Voletti	Maria	30 Apr. 1900	
Albertson	Iver Magnus	Dahl	Mole Hansen	15 July 1907	
Albini	Abramo	Rossi	Elvera	18 Aug. 1906	
Albini	Charles	Poncia	Maria	14 Aug. 1913	
Albini	Domenico	Furia	Ersilia	29 June 1905	
Albini	John	Pelaccini	Maria	18 Oct. 1909	
Albini	John	Albini	Elvira	29 Sept. 1917	
Albini	John	Barella	Amellia	3 Feb. 1914	gr: John Albini, father
Albini	Paul	Donati	Romilda	10 Sept. 1919	
Albini	Paul, Jr.	Pozzi	Dora	11 Apr. 1911	br: Datobo Albini, witness to mark
Albini	Peter	Barella	Emilia	28 Apr. 1909	
Albini	Pietro	Illia	Adele	30 July 1912	
Albrecht	Asmas	Hoirneche	Mary	11 Sept. 1889	
Albrecht	Charles	Marshall	May	6 Sept. 1898	gr: Golden West Hotel, San Francisco, residence; no previous marriage
Albright	Frederick W. H.	Boyer	Mabel C.	24 Nov. 1899	
Albright	James O.	Matthews	Helen	24 Mar. 1920	
Alderson	Earl Ray	Barnum	Inez Mildred	17 Sept. 1915	br: Elizabeth Barnum, mother
Alessandrini	Charles	Bertoli	Erminia	15 Mar. 1904	
Alessi	Ignazio	Beltrametti	Teodolinda	16 Apr. 1891	
Alexander	David N.	Heald	Sarah E.	28 June 1899	
Alexander	Ernest F.	Garvin	Helen	26 Dec. 1917	
Alexander	George C.	Sarginsson	Nellie Maude	2 May 1900	do not publish until Friday
Alexander	John	Morrow	Jennie	29 Apr. 1884	
Alexander	John	Bill	Lucy A.	5 June 1903	
Alexander	Lawrence	Price	Laura A.	3 Dec. 1879	
Alexander	Lemuel H.	Russell	M. A.	26 Dec. 1885	
Alexander	Rufus	Humphres	Allie L.	16 Dec. 1887	
Alexander	Thomas	Patrick	H. A.	1 Mar. 1897	don't publish
Alexanderson	Philip E.	Cooper	Clara B.	18 June 1902	

Groom		Bride			
Surname	Given Name	Surname	Given Name	Date	Comments
Alfiere	Joseph	Beedle	Addie	12 May 1877	witness: George Beedle
Alford	Charles A., Jr.	Hollar	Viola	29 Oct 1889	
Alford	Erastus	Ward	Elizabeth, Mrs.	25 Oct. 1899	br: widow
Alford	Frederick	Soto	Trinidad	23 Aug. 1904	
Alfrey	Harry K.	Senner	Mabel E.	23 Apr. 1918	
Algeo	Andrew J.	Peterson	Nellie I.	1 June 1892	
Aliphat	Eugene D.	Rafael	Lydia	10 July 1916	
Alison	Archie	Ross	Lucy B.	12 Sept. 1891	
Allan	Frank Walker	Morrison	Katie May	11 Nov. 1911	
Allegrini	Julius	Peruzzo	Jennie	12 June 1893	
Allen	Anderson	Rees	Harriet A., Mrs.	10 Nov. 1891	gr: F. A. Juillard, witness to his mark
Allen	Anthony	Todd	Mary E.	31 Dec. 1887	br: Wm. E. Crigler, guardian
Allen	Charles P.	Smith	Geneva	22 July 1908	
Allen	Chesley M.	Dohl (?)	Effa B.	4 Sept. 1920	
Allen	D. B.	McPeak	Hattie E.	3 Apr. 1895	
Allen	Evan R.	Wright	Olive	5 Feb. 1895	
Allen	Frank	Sylva	Emelia Emma	16 Dec. 1908	
Allen	Frederick William	Warren	Emma Louise	9 Nov. 1905	
Allen	George A.	McPherson	Hazel	25 Aug. 1920	
Allen	George Harrison	Hagan	Mignon C.	5 Nov. 1907	
Allen	George O.	Alten	Anna E.	6 Nov. 1889	gr: license requested by Otis Allen, father
Allen	George P.	Clary	Emma	16 Sept. 1917	
Allen	Gerald M.	Tuttle	Lilla R.	12 Dec. 1914	
Allen	Gilbert W.	Lockman	Ella Ray	5 Apr. 1920	
Allen	Harry R.	Templeman	Agnes M.	26 Nov. 1920	
Allen	Henry C.	Story	Susan	15 Sept. 1879	
Allen	James Edgar	Deuman	Carrie Elizabeth	Mar. 1887	
Allen	James Rodney	Bonham	Rena Lucile	27 Apr. 1912	
Allen	James T.	Bailey	Elma G.	11 Dec. 1916	
Allen	Jay B.	Sherwood	Delphia L.	15 Jan. 1914	
Allen	John F.	Munday	Mabel	18 July 1900	
Allen	John Harvey	Painter	Katie Iowa	25 Apr. 1896	
Allen	John T.	Gray	Lotta L.	9 Aug. 1886	br: G. M. Gray, parent

Groom		Bride		Date	Comments
Surname	Given Name	Surname	Given Name		
Allen	John W.	Wilson	Amy	10 Apr. 1914	
Allen	Leslie Russell	LeWarne	Anna Jean	2 June 1917	
Allen	Maxwell W.	Nicholson	Rose K.	9 Apr. 1919	
Allen	Merton C.	Penrod	Lillie L.	28 Sept. 1891	
Allen	Robert	Graham	Bertha	11 June 1890	
Allen	Thomas Edgar	Booher	Mary Luemma	16 June 1903	do not publish ages
Allenberg	Ferdinand Arthur	Voris	Isabell Alice	8 Oct. 1914	
Allenden	Gerald	Murray	Eva		note from mother objects to granting license, 10 July 1919, Mrs. W. H. Allenden
Allenden	William H.	Young	Myrtle L.	5 July 1899	no previous marriage
Allenwood	Frank	Roehling	Agnes M.	8 May 1920	
Alley	Leonard Samuel	Clark	Ada	1 Feb. 1916	
Alley	Omery Elmo	Dunham	Alta Faye	19 Nov. 1910	
Allis	Edmund C.	Stevens	Louisa E.	2 Aug. 1890	
Allison	Jay J.	Mead	Jenevieve I.	13 June 1915	
Allison	Samuel	Walker	Dasey	21 Mar. 1884	br: L. C. Gearhart, stepfather
Allman	Joe Peter	Minasco	J. Lee, Mrs.	31 Aug 1907	
Almann	John	Patronak	Mamie	4 Nov. 1889	
Alsbarge	Charles A.	Skinner	Mabel A.	25 Jan. 1901	requested by Oliver Skinner, friend
Alten	Henry	Power	Mary E.	26 Oct. 1897	no previous marriage
Alten	John H.	Clayborne	Florence E.	20 Aug 1907	
Alten	Pete	Miller	Maggie E., Mrs.	19 Oct. 1901	
Alten	Wendell	McNeil	Minnie Clara	7 Oct. 1901	
Altenreuther	Leopold C.	Masciorini	Erminia Agnes	20 Nov. 1916	
Alvernaz	Manuel Brum	Norouha (?)	Maria	26 Apr. 1915	
Alves	Frank S.	Clark	Gladys A.	2 May 1917	gr: J. J. Alves, parent
Amann	Wendalin	Koch	Minnie	16 Mar. 1893	
Amanso	Antone	Perry	Rosie	23 July 1913	br: Joe Perry, father; W. E. Saunders, Mildred Mathews, witnesses to father's mark
Amaral	Anthony	Cory	Isabelle L.	29 Oct. 1907	
Ambler	J. Raymond	Bender	Madeleine L.	23 July 1917	
Ambler	John	Dolan	Anna	7 Aug. 1885	
Ambler	Lawrence J.	Stanley	Laura	14 Feb. 1921	

Groom		Bride			
Surname	Given Name	Surname	Given Name	Date	Comments
Ambrose	Frank	Biagi	Lottie	26 Feb. 1912	
Ambrosini	John	Roe	Kate	3 May 1909	
Ameral	Manuel S.	Olivera	Annie	14 Dec. 1909	br: Mary Olivera, mother
Ames	Benjamin J.	Sullivan	Nellie	23 July 1903	
Ames	Charles S.	Jerome	Frances	11 June 1898	
Ames	Earl L.	Gericke	Ethel M.	17 July 1920	
Ames	George Spencer	Skelly	Tessie	7 Sept. 1898	no previous marriage
Ames	Irvin E.	Casmore	Adella L.	22 Nov. 1900	
Ames	Louis	Stone	Ada Myrtle	8 Jan. 1908	
Ames	Lynwood Passen	Kelly	Orpah Grace	29 Aug. 1914	gr: J. S. Ames, parent
Ames	Raymond J.	Doyle	Anna	14 Feb. 1905	
Amesbury	Geo. M.	Snider	Lucy B.	16 Oct. 1894	
Amrhein	John	Nydeffer	Mary, Mrs.	2 Aug. 1900	gr: F. G. Nagle, witness to his mark
Anbucbon	John E.	Pizzotti	Marie R.	3 Aug. 1917	
Ancill	Harold J.	Roe	Martha R.	3 Apr. 1911	
Andersen	Cyril Harry	Beitels	Jewel	31 May 1918	gr: Christian Andersen, parent
Andersen	Henry	Ericksen	Dagmar	10 Aug.1909	
Andersen	Paul	Barnes	Anna M.	25 Jan. 1913	
Andersen	Peter C.	Gale	Marie F.	18 Oct. 1916	
Andersen	Phillip N.	Wessels	Ruth B.	4 Sept. 1915	
Andersen	Rasmus Theodore	Nisson	Lena	23 Oct. 1906	
Andersen	Robert	Furr	Maud E., Mrs.	1 Apr. 1921	
Anderson	A. F.	Cramer	Gladys	5 Nov. 1915	
Anderson	Albert Gustav	Barrass	Mayme Lowery	24 Dec. 1915	
Anderson	Albert S. J.	Martinez	Mollie I.	8 Aug. 1887	
Anderson	Albert V.	Bohn	Edna M.	23 Dec. 1897	
Anderson	Almer Parker	Peterson	Julia C.	4 Jan. 1909	
Anderson	Arthur	Chapman	Helen Edith	19 Mar. 1916	gr: Alfred Anderson, father
Anderson	August	Herman	Laura A.	7 Nov. 1888	
Anderson	Caesar William	Pometta	Florence G.	26 July 1911	
Anderson	Carl	Perry	Clara M.	25 Jan. 1902	
Anderson	Charles F.	Cornelius	Matilda J.	16 Nov. 1901	
Anderson	Chris H.	Green	Lovina D.	15 Sept. 1908	br: E. A. Green, parent

Groom		Bride			
Surname	Given Name	Surname	Given Name	Date	Comments
Anderson	David P.	Reid	Mattie L.	30 Sept. 1891	
Anderson	Ellis R.	Walker	Hazel L.	26 June 1916	
Anderson	George	Haigh	Ethel	21 Nov. 1902	
Anderson	George	Palmsten	Hildur Elvira	28 June 1912	
Anderson	George H.	Ritchie	Mary A., Mrs.	7 Feb. 1910	
Anderson	Haus	Hardt	Mamie	13 Nov. 1896	br: Augusta W. Hardt, mother, gives consent and signs
Anderson	Herbert A.	Dohn	Ella	23 Feb. 1903	
Anderson	Irvine John	Turner	Verona Marie	27 Jan. 1917	
Anderson	J. A.	Leigh	Josephine	6 May 1903	
Anderson	James	Gordon	Edith A.	20 Feb. 1921	
Anderson	James G.	Summerfield	Hattie R.	19 June 1912	
Anderson	James H.	Skaggs	Nellie A.	8 Oct. 1887	
Anderson	James H.	Bidwell	Nancy Jane	10 Nov. 1877	
Anderson	James Orrin	Wilson	Jessie Frances	30 Oct. 1909	
Anderson	Joe	Wise	Goldie	19 Oct. 1914	
Anderson	John G.	Silva	Julia Mendonca	26 May 1917	
Anderson	Joseph A.	Perry	Leonora A.	25 Oct. 1911	
Anderson	Joseph W.	Kellaway	Birdie	8 June 1920	
Anderson	Julius J.	Smith	Effa	25 Mar. 1904	
Anderson	Leroy	Pritchett	Jennie	5 Sept. 1906	
Anderson	Mathew	Brockmon	Elizabeth J.	29 Oct. 1878	
Anderson	Mose A.	Borba	Margaret Genevieve	24 Dec. 1914	
Anderson	Nicols	Perry	Catherine	12 Oct. 1878	
Anderson	Oscar	Messerle	Nellie	3 Dec. 1898	requested by James Cope
Anderson	Oscar E.	Lowrey	Elizabeth F.	30 Oct. 1900	
Anderson	Peter	Pearson	Lena	26 Feb. 1877	
Anderson	Rex A.	Griffin	Lucile	28 Sept. 1917	
Anderson	Robert Marion	Webster	Anna	11 June 1909	
Anderson	Seymour E.	Perry	Theo M.	12 Apr. 1919	
Anderson	Thomas W.	Ames	Clementine	10 July 1890	
Anderson	Victor Henry	Smith	Anna Jessie	19 June 1920	

Groom		Bride			
Surname	Given Name	Surname	Given Name	Date	Comments
Anderson	Vinson	Tebbs	A. L.	26 Feb. 1876	br: I. C. & A. J. Tebbs, parents
Anderson	William F.	Freeman	Clara B.	20 May 1916	
Anderson	William I.	Coombs	Lulu M.	29 July 1901	
Anderson	William J.	Robinson	Jennie M.	24 Feb. 1903	
Anderson	William P.	Hawkins	M. L, Mrs.	24 Nov. 1888	
Anderton	Harry Thomas	Lewis	Alletta C.	16 Apr. 1910	
Andre	Anton	Cabral	Emilia	2 Jan. 1907	
Andreasen	Andrew	Huth	Valenteen	22 July 1915	
Andreasen	James P.	Olstad	Anna	25 July 1908	
Andreini	Pietro	Cardellini	Maria	14 May 1908	br: requested license; Mary Sanguinett witnessed her mark
Andreini	Silvio	Balestracci	Adele	7 Dec. 1908	
Andresen	Carl A.	Peters	Margaret Helen	17 Apr. 1920	
Andrew	Dennis	Francis	Isabella	9 Nov. 1915	
Andrews	A. J.	West	Mary	21 Apr. 1888	br: Mrs. Mary West, mother
Andrews	Admiral Leonadi	Moore	Jessie Marie	14 Apr. 1911	
Andrews	Albert	Walker	Eva	30 Dec. 1904	
Andrews	Geo. Francis	Partington	Lydia H.	21 Nov. 1892	W. W. Madge, witness
Andrews	George	Gordon	Melissa, Mrs.	20 Aug. 1881	
Andrews	George B.	Warren	Ollie A.	12 May1894	
Andrews	Howard	Freeman	M. E.	25 Apr. 1885	requested by C. M. Head
Andrews	Leslie Watson	Morris	Louie Eva	11 Aug. 1914	
Andrews	Robert Shaw	Kline	Eletha Alice	1 July 1914	
Andrews	Vernon	Witherell	Minnie E.	26 Sept. 1891	
Andrews	Walter J.	Archer	Ruth E.	25 Aug. 1917	
Andrews	Walter J.	Maggetti	Carrie	8 Oct. 1904	
Angel	Percy	Raulet	Annyta	23 Sept. 1919	
Angelo	Antonie	Pacini	Ida	7 Apr. 1920	
Angelo	Wallace P.	Welker	Alice	25 May 1912	
Anker	Erik Jessen	Warner	Alma	25 June 1907	
Anker	Neal	Ludwig	Katy	28 Apr. 1877	br: Peter Ludwig, father
Annis	Wm. O.	Melton	Elizabeth A., Mrs.	7 Mar. 1865	
Anthony	Edward Augustus	Dey	Ella Bell	12 May 1887	J. of P. letter gives birth dates

Groom		Bride			
Surname	Given Name	Surname	Given Name	Date	Comments
Anthony	George Francis	Lilja	Olive, Mrs.	29 June 1908	
Anthony	John H.	Horman (?)	Lena Harmon	12 Feb. 1889	
Anthony	M. J.	Hitchcock	Lavina K.	2 Nov. 1878	br: Josepine & J. M. Hitchcock, parents; witness: Thomas Staff
Anthony	William Jas.	Moes	Rosa M.	6 May 1901	
Antognini	Alfred	Antognini	Gabriella	14 Jan, 1915	
Antognini	Carlo	Boradori	Nettie	8 Mar. 1915	
Antrim	Joseph A.	Simpson	Ella	4 Feb. 1902	
Apiarius	Palmer H.	Lottritz	Elizabeth B.	8 Sept. 1916	
Apostle	Arthur	Raymond	Julia M. Ball	25 Dec. 1917	
Appleby	Ray	Prout	Florence G.	7 May 1917	
Appleton	Willington	Moody	Jessie Leona	4 Oct. 1895	
Aquistapace	Louis	Moore	Marguerite	8 May 1913	
Aquisttapace	Giovanni	Aquisttapace	Domenica	5 Jan. 1900	br: became of age 29 Dec. 1899
Arata	John King	Norton	Wilma Mae	29 Oct. 1910	
Arata	Joseph	Foppiano	Louise	22 Oct. 1908	
Arbogast	Ernest	Schilling	Valerie	15 Aug. 1896	
Arbuckle	Cyrus P.	Stone	Prisila M.	5 Jan. 1876	br: James Stone, father; Sonoma County
Archambault	George E.	Owens	Imelda C.	7 Sept. 1918	
Archer	Arthur S.	Gregg	Orbie J.	22 Oct. 1895	
Archer	Claud H.	McCracken	Edna E.	14 Mar. 1911	
Archer	Horace E.	McCracken	Emily G.	18 Feb. 1899	no previous marriage
Archer	James J.	Kennedy	Ann S.	6 July 1894	
Archer	John W.	Austin	Jessie M.	27 Sept. 1890	
Archer	Oliver	Frank	Emilie	11 Dec. 1914	
Archer	Walter M.	Frank	Lydia E.	11 Dec. 1914	
Archibald	Edward Joseph	Modeste	Julia Charlotte	5 May 1917	
Ardis	Livy L.	Snyder	Beula V.	30 Aug. 1904	
Ardoin	Victor	Zurcher	Irma	14 Aug. 1903	
Arfsten	Ben	Kolb	Ola	10 June 1910	
Arfsten	Conrad H.	Bohn	Ida E.	13 June 1906	
Arfsten	Martin Theodore	Jappen	Lena Gerdina	12 June 1914	
Arfsten	William Arthur	Neel	Jennie	12 Jan. 1895	

Groom		Bride			
Surname	Given Name	Surname	Given Name	Date	Comments
Arfsten	Adolph	Avilla	Mary	18 May 1900	
Argoud	Alfred L.	McPike	Edith G.	10 Jan. 1920	
Arguello	Alexander	Mehlhorn	Martha	23 Sept.1904	
Arguello	Henry T.	Freebern	Abbe Gail, Mrs.	5 Dec. 1884	
Ariasi	Peter	Bertossi	Liberata	16 Nov. 1906	
Arlett	George	Stoner	Tessa B.	11 June 1891	
Armello	Manuel	Rafael	Mary	16 Jan. 1897	gr: H. H. Atwater, witness to his mark
Armfield	Tyrus A.	Henry	Amanda B.	14 Oct. 1865	
Armitage	J. D.	Schultz	Ellen A.	20 Feb. 1894	license requested by Gil P. Hall
Armos	Ruel Rogers	Johnson	Wilma Regina	2 Apr. 1898	gr: 1105 Hyde St., San Francisco; br: 43 Beaver St., San Francisco; requested by James E. Montgomery
Armstrong	Alfred E.	Fromm	Martha	7 June 1912	
Armstrong	Benjamin	Faudre	Lusettie	12 Aug. 1889	br: S. W. Faudre, parent; And. Ohlidge [witness?]
Armstrong	Charles Newton	Dennis	Nellie	18 May 1895	
Armstrong	Charley H.	Pedrotti	Lucinda E.	29 May 1916	
Armstrong	Edward J.	Graham	Lola M.	18 Oct. 1898	no previous marriage
Armstrong	Frank L.	Feliz	Cassie	2 Apr. 1910	
Armstrong	Frederic W.	Akers	Malinda C.	5 Apr. 1910	
Armstrong	George R.	Meador	Nannie	4 Aug. 1904	
Armstrong	Harry George	Winkler	Florence Estella	26 Sept. 1905	br: Mrs. M. Winkler, mother
Armstrong	James C.	Ayers	Elise May	4 Aug. 1898	gr: James W. Armstrong, father; no previous marriage
Armstrong	M. V. B.	Menighan	Mary P.	15 Nov. 1865	
Armstrong	Oatie M.	Arnold	Rose L.	17 Feb. 1900	no previous marriage
Armstrong	Roy V.	Lipe	Ina	26 Nov. 1919	
Armstrong	Thos. E.	Thompson	Alice M.	10 Oct. 1888	
Armstrong	Walter Ernest	Crowell	Elizabeth	30 Dec. 1910	
Armstrong	William J.	Munson	Edith O.	30 June 1917	
Arndt	Benjamin F.	Haskell	Vera F.	20 May 1905	
Arnett	Floyd F.	Clark	Wilma S.	21 Aug. 1920	
Arnett	Vivian O.	Lane	Irene J.	27 Sept. 1919	gr: Alice M. Arnett, mother; br: Lotie E. Lane, mother

Groom		Bride			
Surname	Given Name	Surname	Given Name	Date	Comments
Arnold	C. W.	Hoit	Matilda	20 Apr. 1865	
Arnold	Edward	Lewis	Addie	16 Feb. 1886	
Arnold	Floyd Hilton	McCoubrey	Josephine Eva	26 May 1906	gr: Mrs. S. G. Arnold, mother
Arnold	Harry P.	Holland	Elsie	12 Apr. 1919	
Arnold	Hobart Le G.	Gauldin	Mattie A.	6 May 1896	
Arnold	John W.	Kauffman	Minnie I.	19 Nov. 1897	br: Mrs. E. L. Kauffman, mother
Arnold	Richard	Paulson	Anna L.	20 Jan. 1916	
Arrighi	Cesare G.	Guidotti	Emma Agnes	17 Nov. 1915	
Arrowood	Daniel A.	Williamson	Florence E.	24 Apr. 1920	
Arsistide	George	Gilmartin	Josie	6 Oct. 1913	
Arthur	George	Frank	Julia L.	7 Jan. 1909	
Artner	Michael	Weber	Rosa	17 July 1909	
Arville	Archie B.	Mueting	Charlotte Rose	9 Apr. 1917	br: Mary Mueting, mother
Arvold	Louis	Waage	Ollie A.	20 Mar. 1911	
Ascherman	Charles F.	Petersen	Annie M.	2 Nov. 1892	
Ash	Emerson F.	Silvia	Mary E.	21 Dec. 1911	
Ash	Emerson F.	Silvia	Mary E.	10 June 1912	
Ash	Frank E.	Bourras	Catherine	6 Sept. 1918	
Ash	Isador	Goldstein	Sarah	20 Jan. 1912	
Ash	Leroy	Church	Clara Rosa	21 Dec. 1920	
Ashcroft	J. A.	Gregory	M. A., Mrs.	17 Dec. 1866	
Ashe	William W.	Wheeler	Evelyn S.	10 June 1911	
Asher	Charles Lewis	Marin	Hermina	28 May 1914	
Asher	Sidney	Behrens	Henrietta	30 Nov. 1918	
Ashley	David C.	Squyer	Ida E.	7 June 1919	
Ashley	S. Thomas	Garrison	Orletta	30 Oct. 1894	
Ashley	William T.	Waldron	Kate	3 Mar. 1882	
Ashurst	William R.	Patton	Ora Lillian	5 Apr. 1902	
Askins	Samuel M.	Doyle	Mary K.	4 May 1913	
Asplund	John A.	Nielsen	Christine	5 Mar. 1892	
Assenti	Louis	Hillson	Louisa	9 Dec. 1914	
Asti	Erminio	Albini	Victoria, Mrs.	19 Feb. 1904	
Asti	Joseph	Brusa	Julia	22 June 1889	br: Paul & Josephine Brusa, parents

Groom		Bride			
Surname	Given Name	Surname	Given Name	Date	Comments
Asti	Joseph P.	Rossi	Christina	22 May 1915	
Astorg	Louie M.	Shannon	Clara May	9 Nov. 1917	
Astredo	Anthony Dominick	Walsh	Dixie Edith	2 Apr. 1906	
Atchinson	Fred R.	Story	Myrtle J.	24 Dec. 1908	br: requested license
Atherton	Albert W.	Mead	Susie E.	7 Jan. 1884	
Atkins	L. G. F.	Willis	Harrietta T.	27 June 1896	
Atkinson	Joseph	Higgins	Minnie J., Mrs.	21 Apr. 1900	do not publish until Wednesday
Atkinson	Joseph	Miller	Sadie L.	17 Feb. 1913	
Atkinson	Robert Kavanaugh	Gale	Eliza Maude	7 July 1903	
Atkinson	William K.	Moretti	Candeda	17 Nov. 1902	
Atlon	Theodore F.	Wahl	Louisa	24 Feb. 1903	
Atwater	Edwin L.	Millett	Nettie J.	14 June 1897	
Atwood	George C.	Fairchild	Lee	20 Apr. 1921	
Atwood	Joseph C.	DeBow	Sallie	22 Feb. 1914	
Atzeroth	Henry	Scott	Mabel F.	30 June 1903	
Audero	Giovanni	Ferrero	Maria	15 June 1908	
Auerbach	Howell Bidwell	Short	Helen Hutchuis	1 Oct. 1907	
Augustus	Martin	Bonneau	Laura N.	19 Dec. 1898	both widowed
Auld	Royal I.	Hoesch	Margaret C.	29 June 1914	
Ausmus	Delbert	Weyman	Cletys	12 Apr. 1917	
Aussresses	Diderot P.	Herzog	Rosalie	11 Jan. 1899	
Austen	John O.	Oberfell	Clara	21 Feb. 1893	
Austin	Ashton E.	Cummins	Metta H.	30 Mar. 1901	
Austin	Chas.	Bloch	Rosa	11 June 1885	
Austin	George	Paulsch	Susie A., Mrs.	3 Aug. 1896	br: please do not [publish] notice
Austin	Harry C.	Hardisty	Daisy D.	16 May 1898	
Austin	Louis Cecil	Sears	Ethel Matilda	24 June 1908	
Austin	Malcolm O.	Hotaling	Lillian B.	7 Feb. 1889	
Austin	Mervyn Maison	Brand	Katie	26 Nov. 1919	
Austin	Raymond Thomas	Ogan	Mabel Dorothy	16 July 1917	
Austin	Sewell S.	Godman	Ida L.	28 Jan. 1891	
Austin	William G.	Willsie	Lydia	17 May 1890	
Auten	George M.	Casky	Alta M.	4 Nov. 1908	

Groom		Bride			
Surname	Given Name	Surname	Given Name	Date	Comments
Avellar	Jose	Valentine	Frances	15 Sept. 1903	
Avereia	Antonio Silveira	Galinda	Mary M.	24 Oct. 1887	
Averill	Herbert O.	Ober	Bessie I.	26 Sept. 1916	
Avery	Howard	Mason	Lenna	24 May 1911	
Avery	W. J.	Williams	Margaret	6 Dec. 1913	
Avila	Joao Maria	Vieira	Maria Joseph	17 Feb. 1906	br & gr signed with mark, witnessed by J. W. Ford & G. A. Feldmeyer
Avilla	Frank	Joseph	Mary	28 Dec. 1896	br: Flora Joseph, mother, gives consent; Joseph Manill witness to mother's mark
Avilla	Manuel	Cunha	Anna	29 July 1911	
Avilla (?)	A. I.	Bettencourt	Belmera	22 Oct. 1912	gr: W. E. Saunders, S. J. Winans, witnesses to his mark
Avjona	Daniel J.	Velasques	Mary	13 Oct. 1920	
Axley	John R.	Maldonado	Helen	6 Dec. 1919	
Axtell	Asher E.	Hanson	Minnie	26 July 1892	
Ayer	John	Nichols	Vesta	25 Sept. 1876	
Ayers	Andrew M.	Farnsworth	Clara	27 Aug. 1883	
Ayers	Archie	Stewart	Neva	18 May 1903	
Ayers	B. F.	Hitchcock	Ida	22 Jan. 1881	br: S. N. & Josephine Hitchcock, parents
Ayers	Frank	Lawrence	Edith	27 May 1897	gr: resides 1509 Turk St. San Francisco
Ayers	George Lemuel	Talmadge	Hattie May	24 Dec. 1895	not to be published.
Ayers	George Lemuel	Cromwell	Pearl Gertrude	10 Nov. 1906	
Ayers	George W.	Arland	Lela D.	12 June 1909	
Ayers	Omar	McNabb	Jessie I.	1 May 1897	
Ayers	Robert B.	Melehan	Anna E.	22 Nov. 1904	
Ayers	Robert Charles	Earley	Olive J.	26 Jan. 1907	
Ayers	William C.	Gray	May	4 June 1900	
Ayers	William M.	Brown	Maggie	23 July 1881	br: R. B. & S. M. Brown, parents
Aylsworth	Niles W.	Wrottero (?)	Edith	18 Sept. 1879	
Azevedo	Frank Augusto	Lacerda	Mary Augusta	12 Dec. 1906	br: Manuel Viera, guardian
Azevedo	Joseph A.	Brazil	Nellie	30 June 1920	
Azevedo	Manuel Jacinto	D'dasq Noximento	Maria	27 Sept. 1907	gr: G. W. Libby, witness to his mark; br: signed

Groom		Bride		Date	Comments
Surname	Given Name	Surname	Given Name		
Azevedo	Tony Thomas	Augusto	Mary	4 Dec. 1914	
Azevedo	William J.	Ramos	Roselind G.	1 June 1917	
Azveado	John	DeSouza	Katie	16 Jan. 1904	
Azzari	Eriglio	Petri	Annie	14 Feb. 1914	
Baago	Edmund A.	Mendenhall	Lola I.	31 Mar. 1902	
Babbini	Alvise	Asti	Lizzie	10 Apr. 1915	br: Amelia Asti, mother
Babbini	Antonio	Forni	Kate	26 Jan. 1918	
Babbini	Arthur	Babbini	Katherine G.	24 Nov. 1920	
Babbini	Ernesto	Ottoboni	Rosa A.	17 Apr. 1919	
Babbini	Paul	Bologne	Lizzie	17 July 1911	
Babbino	Fred	Werner	Marie	29 May 1909	
Babbino	Thomas	Lagomarsino	Marie	7 Sept. 1901	
Babcock	Albert A.	Riedel	Selma E.	24 July 1917	
Babcock	Joseph L.	Nichalson	Agnes Maye	31 July 1913	
Babcock	Kilbern J.	Monroe	Carrie May	30 Aug. 1902	
Baccala	Antonio	Anselmi	Martini	19 Nov. 1894	Batista Anselmi, witness to his x mark
Baccala	Joseph K.	Finnerty	Mary Alice	26 Sept. 1907	
Bacchini	Romeo	Zanzi	Annie	17 June 1909	br: Louis Zanzi, father
Bacci	Amoto	Pardini	Emma	26 June 1919	
Bacci	Joseph	Pera	Mary	20 Jan. 1912	
Bacci	Vincent	Dinucci	Katherine	21 Aug. 1913	
Bachelder	Horace	Titus	Seba	28 Apr. 1886	
Bachrach	Arthur E.	Donovan	Nadine G.	24 July 1920	
Bacigalupi	Albert C.	Gaddini	Olive	21 Sept. 1914	
Bacigalupi	Giovanni B.	Bacigalupi	Maria	6 Aug. 1901	
Bacigalupi	John E.	Guidotti	Jemella	20 Oct. 1908	
Bacigalupi	Louis	Caulfield	Catherine F.	14 Feb. 1905	
Bacon	Arthur D.	Flesher	L. Maude	19 Oct. 1901	
Bacon	Charles E.	Perry	Marie Jane	1 Apr. 1892	br: Joseph M. Perry, father
Bacon	Charles S.	Johnson	Alice	2 Dec. 1911	
Bacon	George Dudley	Davis	Dora J.	20 Jan. 1899	
Bacon	Herbert Wm.	Migliano (?)	Elizabeth	16 Oct. 1920	
Bacon	Jay S.	Trautner	Frances	3 Nov. 1916	

Groom		Bride			
Surname	Given Name	Surname	Given Name	Date	Comments
Bacon	Mark J.	Walker	Margaret I.	25 Nov. 1907	
Badenhop	Chris	Person	Emma	21 July 1920	
Badenhop	John Henry	Clausen	Dorothy Helen	13 May 1919	
Badger	Albert Neil	Ricketts	Anice Iva	24 June 1908	
Badger	Douglas	Fulkerson	Laura E.		br: S. T. Fulkerson, father; filed between 22 and 26 Dec. 1882
Badger	Henry L.	Peatross	Carrie	2 July 1889	br: William W. Peatross, father
Badger	Joseph J.	Hewitt	Emma M.	31 Dec. 1889	br: widow
Badger	Percy	Staley	Mabel Mae	6 May 1899	
Badgerow	Weston	Preston	L.	2 Aug. 1887	
Badgley	Ira Walter	Isaacs	Dora	21 Aug. 1895	
Badgley	Sherman	Covey	Frances	8 Jan. 1891	
Badgley	Sherman	Ingalls	Lillie, Mrs.	13 July 1897	br: widow
Baer	Geo. B.	Markell	Sarah A.	14 June 1887	
Baer	Reuben E.	Markell	Helen I.	17 Aug. 1896	
Bagley	Carl Elmer	Smaker	Anna Francis	5 June 1902	
Bagley	Donald E.	Shuster	Jessie A.	8 Mar. 1921	br: Elmer L. Shuster, father
Bagley	Herbert L.	Cole	Edna C.	9 Dec. 1889	
Bagley	Weaver T.	Hughes	Georgia A.	2 Apr. 1917	
Bagley	Willard D.	Osborne	Angie L.	30 Nov. 1892	
Baglietto	Ambrogio	Solaro	Ernestina, Mrs.	7 Aug. 1897	not to be published
Bahnsen	Daniel	Springer	Catherine	20 June 1891	license requested by Christopf Springer
Baier	Clemens Loyal	Sillemann	Ruth Augusta	26 Nov. 1915	
Bailey	Allan Leonard	Poehlmann	Marie Dorothy	5 Oct. 1909	
Bailey	Charles M.	Rowland	Maude	25 Nov. 1901	
Bailey	Douglas A.	Kienle	Loretta M.	29 Dec. 1917	
Bailey	Eugene B.	Fischer	Hilda	9 June 1910	
Bailey	Frank R.	Wittkoff ?	Mary A.	7 Jan. 1895	
Bailey	J. E.	Laughlin	Amanda	17 Nov. 1887	
Bailey	Jessie William	Deardorff	Anna M.	12 Jan. 1907	
Bailey	Johnathan J.	Happy	Mary	8 Sept. 1882	
Bailey	Percy D.	Du Commun	Marcelle M.	2 Sept. 1909	
Bailey	T. E. C.	Smyth	Pashie	2 Apr. 1885	

Groom		Bride			
Surname	**Given Name**	**Surname**	**Given Name**	**Date**	**Comments**
Bailey	Terry Elmer	Weir	Mary Gertrude	10 July 1920	
Bailey	Wilson Roy	Drew	Hester	2 Aug. 1916	
Bailhache	Arthur L.	Pickard	Annie H.	20 Aug. 1887	requested by Arthur P. Mulligan
Bailhache	Frederick	Williams	Mattie M.	20 June 1903	
Bailhache	Frederick	Clark	Addie Louise	29 Feb. 1896	
Bailhache	George	Hammond	Eva H.	14 Jan. 1879	
Bailhache	J. Temple	Waterman	Melvina B.	17 Nov. 1902	
Bailhache	Nicholas	Gully	Winona	16 Oct. 1895	
Bailhache	Solon William	Harbin	Amanda	5 Sept. 1901	issued in Solano County
Bailiff	John D.	Tuttle	Edith M.	17 Jan. 1905	
Baillesderr	Joseph C.	Lescure	Julia	16 Dec. 1904	
Bainbridge	Clarence E.	White	Amy F.	13 Dec. 1902	
Baine	Lafayette	Kelley	Virginia Ann	9 June 1908	
Baines	Latin L.	Fay	Anna	20 Apr. 1907	br: Laura Fay, mother
Bains	Gallant	Humphrey	Agnes	18 May 1875	
Baiocchi	Guido F.	Mazzoni	Lena M.	20 June 1916	gr: Frank Baioachi, father; witness Marie Pigoni
Baiocchi	Nello	Giorgetti	Nellie	25 Mar. 1919	
Baird	Fred E.	Marchant	Ethel	17 Nov. 1902	
Baird	J. G.	Humphrey	Marion	5 July 1892	
Baitano	Fortunato	Matteucci	Florence	21 Sept. 1914	
Baker	Albert	Kellogg	Anna	26 Apr. 1886	
Baker	Albert Marion	Andrews	Bernice V.	19 Aug. 1919	
Baker	Asa L.	Jewell	Ida	14 Jan. 1891	
Baker	Charles A.	Peterson	Lillie A.	30 June 1894	br: A. Peterson gives consent, marks with X
Baker	Cicero H.	Fieldler	Mary D.	24 July 1915	
Bakcr	David	Withycombe	Ethel	28 July 1908	
Baker	Fred H.	Flood	Evelyn V.	23 Mar. 1913	
Baker	Fred Lester	Banta	Evalyn F.	24 Sept. 1896	
Baker	George E.	Sharron	Maggie R.	6 Nov. 1879	
Baker	Jesse F.	Martin	Jennette	24 Mar. 1914	br: Rachel B Perkins, mother
Baker	Joel F.	Ball	Sue	10 Aug. 1895	gr: A. M. Baker, parent, gives consent and signs.

Groom		Bride			
Surname	Given Name	Surname	Given Name	Date	Comments
Baker	Louis Alexander	Miller	Emma Estella	3 Nov. 1906	gr: Mrs. Julia Baker, mother
Baker	Peter S.	Smith (?)	?chn (?)	17 May 1884	
Baker	Ralph Weber	Spencer	Genovena Nella	4 Dec. 1910	
Baker	Samuel S.	McClellan	Mary E., Mrs.	3 Nov. 1903	
Baker	Theodore	Farley	Ruby	18 Nov. 1915	
Baker	William J.	Zeiph	Anna Zanona	16 Feb. 1907	
Baker	Wm. M.	Small	Alice	19 Oct. 1894	
Balatti	Peter	Petiti	Maria	7 Jan. 1899	
Baldi	Anselmo	Gambogi	Eda M.	23 Oct. 1915	
Baldizzone	Charles Louis	Fankhausen	Clara	17 Sept. 1919	please do not publish
Baldocchi	Alfred A.	Nighturne	Helen M.	15 Aug. 1916	
Baldocchi	Henry	Canevari	Clara	16 Nov. 1914	
Baldocchi	Lawrence	Brodbeck	Elizabeth	6 June 1915	
Baldwin	C. A.	Alloway	Mary	30 Sept. 1885	
Baldwin	Charles Ellsworth	Peck	Ida Viola	20 Apr. 1904	
Baldwin	Clyde R.	Wheeler	Lela Alpha	31 May 1912	
Baldwin	D. A.	Carr	Mary A.	29 June 1889	
Baldwin	James M.	Howard	Edith V.	8 June 1895	br: John C. Howard of Petaluma gives consent and signs.
Baldy	O. Cass	Judd	Pauline, Mrs.	25 June 1901	br: widow
Bales	Marion	Versell	Carolyn J.	30 Aug. 1919	
Balette	Ernest	Rossi	Mary	23 June 1919	
Baley	George Moses	Meyers	Rose	15 Sept. 1900	
Baley	Joshua	Bargaglotti	Della	16 Feb. 1903	
Ball	Leo Raymond	Gates	Jane Isabell	18 May 1918	
Ball	Raymond Oliver	Ahl	Ruby Ada	20 Dec. 1916	
Ball	Walter E.	Herbert	Ina E.	27 Sept. 1902	
Ball	Wm. P.	Pickle	Mary E.	1 Sept. 1866	written consent
Ballagh	Ehrnest Ellsworth	Campbell	Minnie Lucile	27 Sept. 1907	
Ballard	Augustus Seaton	Farrell	Carmeleta U.	30 Aug. 1909	
Ballard	Benjamin F.	McDaniel	Emma U.	21 Aug. 1893	
Ballard	Hooker	Rodgers	Carrie	21 Aug. 1865	
Ballard	John Henry	Purrington	Marguerite	10 Feb. 1902	

Groom		Bride		Date	Comments
Surname	Given Name	Surname	Given Name		
Ballard	Robert L.	Crane	Catherine H.	17 July 1920	
Ballard	S. E.	Miller	Irena B.	16 Mar. 1888	
Ballestra	Johnie	Ravegno	Mary	27 June 1903	br: Domenico Ravegno, parent; L. A. Pressley, witness to mark
Ballou	Albert L.	McWilliams	Edna Alice	19 June 1897	only signed by County Clerk, not by bride or groom or other witness
Ballou	Arthur M.	Carlyon	Elizabeh	23 Nov. 1898	
Ballou	Miner (?) H.	Relyea	Ida May	31 Jan. 1920	
Balsley	Iven E.	Penrice	Lizzie R.	14 June 1911	
Baltzell	Alfred	Loucks	Kate Myrick	6 Sept. 1886	
BalVelde	Antonio	Bravo	Meri	22 May 1920	witness to marks M. Mathews
Balzari	David	Mignimi	Maria	3 Aug. 1906	
Balzari	J. T.	Nickelsen	Naudine	4 Mar. 1887	
Balzari	James Albino	Ramatici	Lily	8 July 1918	
Banchiero	Antone T.	Basaglia	Amelia E.	25 Oct. 1898	br: Luigi Basaglia, father
Bandiera	Emil	Bertolucci	Liduina	22 Jan. 1914	
Bandieu	Alibrando	Caselli	Angie A.	29 May 1920	
Bane	David A.	Eby	Lucretia	23 Dec. 1902	
Banfield	Frederic H.	Christinsen	Martha B.	10 Mar. 1916	
Banfield	Isaac Newton	Holland	Rosa Ellen	9 May 1882	
Banfield	John T.	Cheney	Sarah E.	19 Nov. 1890	br: David Cheney, father
Banfield	William F.	Gregory	Bertha E.	23 Sept. 1896	
Banks	Ansel W.	Peterson	Gretta M.	24 Jan. 1911	
Banks	Earl Arthur	Van Vicel	Bertha L.	8 July 1910	
Banks	George	Masten	Helen	10 Apr. 1920	
Banks	Herbert John	Sanborn	Etta Leivee (?)	18 Aug. 1911	gr: Adaline Banks, mother
Banks	James A.	Wescott	Mamie	2 Dec. 1890	br: Oliver Wescott, father
Banks	Lester D.	Brians	Ruth E.	28 Nov. 1919	
Banks	Louis Albert	Aiken	Florence	21 July 1920	
Bannon	Peter	Short	Mary	11 Oct. 1895	
Banta	John H.	Bennett	Mary A.	23 Feb. 1880	
Banta	Joseph A.	Harte	Lydia J.	12 Mar. 1888	
Banton	Belva	Love	Lou Donie	8 Oct. 1919	

Groom		Bride			
Surname	Given Name	Surname	Given Name	Date	Comments
Banton	James	Walsh	Nora	27 Nov. 1899	
Banton	James	Hart	Carrie Esther	10 Nov. 1910	
Barangini	Charlie	Mossi	Annie	2 July 1918	
Barbee	Elias W.	La Blanc	Carrie	29 May 1895	
Barber	Lewis R.	Rodd	Dorothy C.	25 Sept. 1913	
Barber	Walter P.	Eberts	Berwin E.	21 Apr. 1917	
Barberie	Joseph	Schiapacape	Antonia Flora	24 Mar. 1866	
Barbier	Harry A.	Cochrane	Evelyn E.	17 Dec. 1920	
Barbier	Howard E. W.	Feige	Mabel A.	30 Dec. 1912	
Barbieri	Peter	Asti	Ersiglia	29 Oct. 1904	br: Mary Asti, mother; Paulo Pigoni, witness to her mark
Barboni	Joseph H.	Dolcini	Irene D.	18 Oct. 1910	
Barbreri	Agostino	Carli	Giudita	8 Sept. 1903	
Barceloux	Henry J.	Tremblay	Laura M.	13 Nov. 1899	no previous marriage; don't publish until Wednesday
Bardell	Luzius	Myer	Mary	7 Apr. 1896	
Bardoni	Charles Costantino	Soldati	Effie Olympia	13 Mar. 1918	
Barela	John	Poncia	Maria	20 Apr. 1911	
Barella	Fred	Crosta	Anna	4 Oct. 1913	
Bargoloti	Louis J.	Maine	Annie	10 June 1911	
Barham	Abwey	Christianson	Minnie	1 Feb. 1887	
Barham	Byrd	Cunningham	Pearl Gertrude	1 Sept. 1905	br: Mrs. Nettie Cunningham, mother, gives consent
Barham	Byrd B.	Flippi	Rose V.	20 July 1918	
Barham	Edwin C.	Fulkerson	Linda V.	2 Nov. 1895	license requested by R. W. Miller
Barham	Fred	Hottinger	Gertrude E.	12 Dec. 1903	
Barham	J. A.	Cook	Mary	11 Feb. 1865	
Barilani	Guglielmo	Trusendi	Laura	12 Feb. 1908	
Barindelli	Charles	DelCarlo	Emma	15 Apr. 1920	
Barisich	Peter	Rodman	Lieuary A.	10 Aug.1909	
Barisione	Baci	Ponzo	Valentina	25 June 1908	
Barker	Ambrose B.	Goodrich	Mamie	6 July 1901	
Barker	Frank E.	Lillard	Dora M.	3 Jan. 1899	gr: 2217 Chestnu St., Oakland; br: Mrs. N. E. Lilland, mother

Groom		Bride		Date	Comments
Surname	Given Name	Surname	Given Name		
Barker	Henry	Cooper	Rachael	5 July 1865	
Barker	Richard, Jr.	Lewis	Edna	28 Sept. 1893	
Barkway	Henry Thomas	Stevenson	May Frances	5 Sept. 1905	
Barkway	Wm M.	Barnes	Marien E.	31 Dec. 1900	
Barlieri	Italo	Albini	Rosie	25 Jan. 1911	br: Vitoria Asti, parent
Barling	Wm. H.	Higson	Dora E.	23 Mar. 1901	
Barlow	Richard Wright	McDonald	Mary	16 Oct. 1893	
Barlow	Thomas E.	Miller	Laura E.	9 Feb. 1891	
Barndt	Julius	Hart	Grace P.	12 Oct. 1901	
Barnes	Aaron	Burk	Jessie	16 July 1885	
Barnes	Aaron H.	Urton	Eunice D.	5 Sept 1893	gr: H. S. Barnes, father gives consent and signs
Barnes	Aaron, Jr.	Ross	Mary E.	1 Dec. 1882	
Barnes	Allen Percival	Mallory	Hazel Florence	20 Dec. 1916	
Barnes	Arthur John	Haddock	Marion T.	15 Oct. 1915	
Barnes	Ben H.	Nichols	Cynthia	5 Nov. 1900	
Barnes	Ben H.	Ferguson	Velma Crawford	12 Dec. 1918	
Barnes	Benjamin Franklin	Robinson	Alice	28 July 1882	br: Fletcher Robinson, father; letter from Lakeport
Barnes	Edward D.	Parks	Tamy (?) H.	31 Dec. 1879	
Barnes	Edwin E.	Soule	Frances	22 June 1891	
Barnes	Ellis James	Craig	Ina Margaret	25 Feb. 1920	
Barnes	George Otis	Parrish	Harriet	24 June 1913	
Barnes	H. G.	Glatfelder	Lulu	9 Jan. 1912	
Barnes	Henry	Risk	Jennie	10 Jan. 1893	
Barnes	Henry L.	Carrillo	Amelia	10 Nov. 1890	
Barnes	Henry L.	Campion	Margaret M.	14 Oct. 1897	gr: widower
Barnes	Henry S.	Siston (?)	Kattie (?) E.	24 Sept. 1880	
Barnes	Jesse W.	Shull	Beulah B.	13 Nov. 1920	
Barnes	John B.	Toney	Ada	19 Apr. 1902	
Barnes	L. J.	Fredrichs	Sophia A.	21 Aug. 1888	
Barnes	Louis G.	Walker	Ella M.	15 Sept. 1896	
Barnes	Millard L.	Clover	Leonora	28 Dec. 1896	

Groom		Bride			
Surname	Given Name	Surname	Given Name	Date	Comments
Barnes	P. D.	Armstrong	Lucy	18 Sept. 1885	
Barnes	Perry S.	Gauldin	Gennevieve	26 Feb. 1903	gr: Mrs. E. A. Barnes, mother
Barnes	Thomas P.	Findley	C. J., Mrs.	8 June 1897	
Barnes	Thomas Sturgis	Berry	Carrie Ella	4 July 1908	
Barnes	Thos. J.	Thing	Sarah J.	7 Sept. 1887	
Barnes	W. P.	Rader	Elizabeth A.	21 Apr. 1866	
Barnes	William A.	Landis	Hattie	24 Oct. 1901	
Barnes	William Julius	Denham	Lena Ethel	26 Mar. 1913	
Barnett	Frank W.	Kirlin	Annie E.	28 June 1902	
Barnett	Garrett C.	Schultis	Julia E.	24 Jan. 1914	
Barnett	Harry J.	Lentz	Grace A.	18 Dec. 1891	
Barnett	Lester H.	Gibbs	Harriet E.	23 Feb. 1915	
Barnett	Marion L. R.	Kirkbride	Blanche Bernice	22 Nov. 1907	
Barnett	Montie	Ward	Jessie M.	24 Dec. 1912	
Barnett	Stanley	Martin	Mathilde	24 Dec. 1910	
Barnett	Walter E.	Gibbs	Evangeline C.	12 Sept. 1914	
Barney	Henry W.	Gauldin	Minnie L.	14 Nov. 1892	
Barnhart	Frank McGowan	Allen	Nina	31 July 1902	gr: Peter D. Barnhart, father, 25 July 1902, Kern, Kern Co., CA
Barnhill	A. F.	Bryan	Susan	30 Aug. 1865	
Barnum	Clarence L.	Fouts	Elsie M.	6 Apr. 1906	gr: Lizzie Barnum, mother; br: Jacob G. Fouts, father
Barnum	Samuel	Covey	Elizabeth	8 Oct. 1885	br: Uriah Covey, parent
Barr	Elmere Roy	De Gassick	Aylene Stewart	15 Dec. 1917	
Barr	John	Zehringer	Adel	4 Nov. 1897	
Barr	William Holt	Van Riper	Catherine	29 Jan. 1915	
Barre	Charles Munson	Smith	Mable Turner	16 Sept. 1915	
Barre	Lyman C.	Tucker	Jessica B.	30 Sept. 1915	
Barrett	Albert	Timme	Ora E.	23 Dec. 1907	
Barrett	Francis E.	Stone	Nora	25 July 1896	
Barrett	John	Hamilton	Lulu	9 Mar. 1891	
Barrett	John J.	Glover	Margaret C.	18 Oct. 1913	
Barricklaw	David George	Gaby	Emma	30 Oct. 1875	

Groom		Bride		Date	Comments
Surname	Given Name	Surname	Given Name		
Barrie	Nelson T.	Barnell	Barbara	13 Apr. 1920	
Barron	Harold	Dollar	Grace E.	10 July 1917	
Barrows	Arthur C.	Hepner	Virginia M.	17 Nov. 1903	
Barry	Garland	Lockard	Ruby	22 June 1909	gr: Lulu Porter, mother: br: Mrs. Ida Lockard, mother
Barry	John J.	Brown	Gertrude E.	4 Nov. 1902	
Barry	Norman J.	Hardin	Etta	30 July 1886	
Barry	William R.	Willis	Margaret M.	21 Jan. 1899	no previous marriage
Barsi	Nichol	Rovai	Carolina	24 Nov. 1906	
Barsi	Nicholas	Dinucci	Clara	23 July 1908	
Barsi	Santi	Motroni	Filomina	14 Nov. 1894	
Barsi	Nichol	Wehrspon	Carrie	30 Dec. 1913	
Barsot	Robert Eugene	Cole	Chrissie V.	9 Oct. 1909	
Barsotti	Antonio	Camiglia	Marssimiglia	29 Mar. 1887	
Barsotti	Frank	Guidotti	Annette Jane	25 Nov. 1916	
Bartalini	Joseph	Pardi	Venice	11 Mar. 1918	
Barth	Adolf	Muller	Babetta	21 Nov. 1891	
Bartlett	Alexander	Delzell	Maggie	26 Mar. 1884	
Bartlett	Fred	Moran	Elenor Elizabeth	24 Sept. 1898	
Bartlett	Frederick D.	Robinson	Marjorie C.	30 Sept. 1906	
Bartoli	Efisio	Zopetti	Vittoria	24 Dec. 1914	
Bartolomei	John	Frugoli	Lena	9 Dec. 1911	
Bartolomei	Salvatore	Cassani	Rica	29 June 1905	
Bartolomei	Victor	Pauluci	Giulia	13 Nov. 1908	gr: T. Bartolomei, witness to his mark
Barton	John W.	Martin	Elizabeth, Mrs.	27 July 1865	
Barton	John W.	Williamson	Cynthia A.	8 Mar. 1866	
Bartosh	William	Heath	Annie M.	29 Sept.1904	
Bartsch	Charles	Wittkowski	Anna	14 Feb. 1910	
Bascom	Elmer	Martin	Leona	16 Aug. 1912	
Basileu	Jordan	Forni	Angeline	29 Nov. 1915	
Bass	Seymour S.	Edringlow	Carrie B.	11 Oct. 1879	
Bassett	Henry F.	Grey	Carrie	23 Dec. 1884	
Bassett	Henry W.	Beattie	Alice M.	9 Jan. 1904	

Groom		Bride			
Surname	Given Name	Surname	Given Name	Date	Comments
Bassett	William David	Nielsen	Marie	19 July 1905	
Bassi	Abramo	Carotta	Catherina	18 Sept. 1901	
Bassi	Amando G.	Tunzi	Geneva M.	12 Aug. 1919	
Bassi	Giatano	LaFranci	Margaret		filed between two other licenses dated 23 Oct. 1880
Bassignani	Cesare	Bellotti	Minnie	3 May 1919	
Bassini	Bernard	Pedrotti	Clara	25 Nov. 1914	
Batchelder	Thaddeus	Stewart	Agnes R.	3 Nov. 1890	
Batchelor	David William	MacFarlane	Susie W.	22 Jan. 1908	
Bates	Alphonzo	Garrett	Phrona E.	9 Mar. 1916	
Bates	Ezekiel F.	Price	Mary	4 May 1881	
Bates	Frank Earle	Wagner	Jessie Adeline	12 Feb. 1916	
Bates	George H.	Delamater	Mary E.	24 Dec. 1904	br: Mrs. E. J. Delamater, mother
Bates	Henry Frederick	Clark	Zoe Ruah	15 Nov. 1894	
Bates	Philip	England	Angeline, Mrs.	9 Mar. 1867	
Bates	Vernon G.	Manion	Edith L.	16 May 1914	
Bateson	Claude William	Clarke	Delia	7 Oct. 1907	
Bath	Thomas	Letterman	Hattie F. A.	31 Oct. 1899	br: Mrs. Frances Letterman, mother
Bathurst	Roland L.	Barker	Bertha B.	18 Oct. 1913	
Batsakis	Nicholas	Appiarius	Victoria B.	7 Jan. 1920	
Batt	Elmer M.	Brown	Elsie I.	17 July 1913	
Batt	Leo F.	Crispin	Hazel M.	6 Aug. 1910	br: I. B. Crispin, parent
Battaglia	Lorance Daniel	Silvia	Mary	3 Nov. 1906	gr: Linto Battaglia, mother; br: Manuel Silvia, father; W. S. Coulter, witness to her mark
Batten	Albert	Fagon	Margaret	23 Nov. 1893	
Batten	George	Simonton	Cora May	7 Aug. 1899	
Battero	Vittorio E.	Coco	Ugolina	14 June 1919	
Batton	John Wesley	Hastings	Sarah A.	26 Aug. 1876	br: J. A. Hastings, father
Bauer	Earl F.	Hindringer	Louisa B.	2 Oct. 1920	
Bauer	Ernest William	Lundholm	Esther Leone	14 June 1911	
Baugh	Clive Evertt	Lee	Rachel Orlena	22 June 1918	
Baugh	Douglas Guy	Potter	Ruby Elizabeth	3 Apr. 1915	
Baugh	Douglas Guy	Doss	Pearl Elizabeth	10 Oct. 1907	

Groom		Bride			
Surname	Given Name	Surname	Given Name	Date	Comments
Baugh	Ernest	Phillips	Letitia R.	6 Aug. 1894	
Baughman	Horace Ray	King	Ruby E.	1 July 1911	
Baum	Alexander R.	Scott	Laulu	17 July 1888	
Baum	John Wesley	Adams	Nellie May	6 Aug. 1894	
Baum	Thomas J.	Arfsten	Emma D.	17 Dec. 1890	
Bauman	Charles Henry	Schmidt	Katherine Francis	7 Apr. 1917	gr: Mrs. Alice E. Bauman, mother
Bauman	Conrad	Haubrich	Clara G.	9 Feb. 1895	br: Peter Haubrich, father, gives consent and signs.
Bauman	Edward	Greer	Lizzie A.	8 Mar. 1921	
Baumann	Charles	Rose	Emma	7 Sept. 1909	
Baumeister	Carl A.	Walker	Hazel E.	30 Oct. 1915	br: Elmer Walker, father
Baumgartner	Leonhard	Wasserfallen	Anna	6 May 1915	
Baumhogger	John C.	Jewell	Mary E.	18 Oct. 1890	license requested by Louis A. Le Febvre
Bauright	Wilson	Odell	Nettie	1 Mar. 1887	
Baxman	Charles F.	Jensen	Ida H.	19 May 1915	
Baxman	Ernest B.	Davis	Rebecca Dorothy	24 June 1916	
Baxman	Fred	Crusher (?)	Eliza	blank	
Baxman	Fred	Crocker	Eliza	30 Sept.	br: Michael & Alice Sichel, stepfather & mother; Fisks Mill
Baxmann	Arthur V.	Johnson	Elvira	16 Feb. 1911	
Baxter	Arthur W.	McCoy	Cora	15 Dec. 1908	
Bay	Edward L.	Howard	Sarah, Mrs.	10 June 1899	gr: divorced three years ago, South Dakota; br: widow
Bayer	Herman Henry	Fick	Hernine D.	3 Jan. 1893	
Bayes	Lou	Dugan	Edith	28 Mar. 1908	gr: signed with his mark
Bayler	John R.	Steiger	Hermina A.	6 Mar. 1894	
Bayler	Joseph Anthony	Lewis	Emma Isabella	22 Dec. 1894	
Baymiller	Fred C.	Rued	Margaret	31 Oct. 1919	
Bayol	Frank P.	Clements	Katherine	31 Aug.1916	
Beach	Alva Frank	Maniz	Cassie	19 May 1906	
Beach	Charles Henry	Smith	Louise Marie	24 Nov. 1915	
Beach	Gordon S.	Blair	Gertie	15 Jan. 1910	
Beach	Riley	Gibbs	Rosa M.	25 Apr. 1914	

Groom		Bride			
Surname	Given Name	Surname	Given Name	Date	Comments
Beagle	William H.	Adams	Emma D.	5 Aug. 1914	
Beal	S. Pryor	Babcock	Edith M.	7 May 1910	
Bealer	George A.	O'Laughlin	May A.	8 Oct. 1902	
Beales	Edmund	Polk	Josephine, Mrs.	8 Nov. 1893	br: widow
Beales	George F.	Wilson	Hannah J.	17 Oct. 1885	
Beall	Asbury	Rippey	Clara E.	6 Dec. 1899	no previous marriage
Bean	Eben D.	Abshire	Laura P.	6 Dec. 1894	
Bean	Oliver F.	Franquelin	Adelaide M.	24 Aug. 1915	
Bean	Ulysses S.	Hodgson	Alice	14 May 1904	
Bearden	James M.	Freeman	Martha E.	4 Sept. 1879	gr: signs with his mark
Beardin	Hubert W.	Delaney	Blanche M.	13 Nov. 1915	
Beardslee	John W.	Hyatt	F. G., Mrs.	12 Apr. 1905	
Beardsley	J. A.	Evans	Eva L.	18 Dec. 1893	
Beasley	Jaba	Southern	Lucy, Mrs.	7 Nov. 1901	
Beasley	Russell L.	Yeager	Cynthia Eleanor	29 July 1905	
Beasom	John Frank	Finley	Willie Camille	16 May 1905	
Beatie	Walter C.	Hite	Eva B.	22 Oct. 1890	
Beattie	John	Barnes	Mary Susannah	6 May 1895	
Beatty	Edward Waldron	Gilbert	Minnie E.	24 July 1896	
Beatty	James H.	Borhinger	Margaret, Mrs.	1 May 1902	
Beaulieu	Charles B.	Hayward	Mary O.	12 Apr. 1915	
Beaurgard	Harry Julius	Pedrotti	Stella Julia	29 Sept. 1906	
Beaver	J. S.	Bigsby (?)	Bell	24 May 1877	br: Mrs. Eliza Reed, mother
Beaver	W. J.	Beaver	Sylvia	6 June 1887	
Bebagliati	Eugene	Angeli	Madalain	19 Aug. 1911	br: Raffaillo Angeli, mother
Beck	Christian Hansen	Bahr	Elsie	13 Apr. 1903	
Beck	Edward H.	Hockins	Lee	17 Nov. 1896	
Beck	Frank Ross	Janssen	Elsie	13 Apr. 1917	
Beck	George N.	Thomas	Vera Jewell	24 Aug. 1918	
Beck	Hans Madison	Kunzler	Della Adele	8 Oct. 1907	
Beck	John E.	Jacobson	Dora E.	8 Oct. 1900	
Beck	Louis	Hansen	Florence	24 May 1902	
Beck	Mads Sorensen	Olsen	Esther Alena	9 June 1917	

Groom		Bride		Date	Comments
Surname	Given Name	Surname	Given Name		
Beck	Niels Anderson	Schelling	Elizabetha	29 Apr. 1896	
Becker	Burton F.	Grassly	Clara H.	25 Feb. 1921	
Becker	Myron B.	Carroll	Virginia E.	11 Oct. 1918	
Becker	Roy D.	Munday	Jessie	6 July 1906	
Becker	W. F.	McNalta	Delia	26 Oct. 1883	
Beckett	Frank E.	Smith	Rhoda	8 Apr. 1912	
Beckman	Albert	Barr	Myrtle	21 Apr. 1914	
Beckman	Louis Henry	Oehlman	Gertrude Clara	30 Mar. 1921	
Beckner	W. S.	Ashcraft	Rebekah, Mrs.	5 Mar. 1888	
Beckner	William S.	Lockwood	Linnie, Mrs.	30 Sept. 1881	
Beckwith	Nelson M.	Catlin	Kate	5 Nov. 1888	
Bedford	Frederick A.	Hammel	Ruth I.	29 May 1919	
Bedwell	S. J.	Brooks	Mattie	14 Feb. 1888	gr: J. C. Bedwell,parent; br: Wm. Brooks, father
Bee	Edward L.	Potter	Edna A.	12 Oct. 1901	
Bee	Louis	Moes	Anna Mary	23 July 1908	
Bee	Milliard F.	Ayers	Alice	12 May 1878	
Beebe	Edward T.	German	Kate, Mrs.	27 July 1899	br:divorced more than one year
Beebe	Elbert E.	Dollar	Alice	15 Nov. 1911	
Beebe	Elijah W.	Hitchcock	Clara G.	9 Oct. 1894	
Beebe	John Franklin	Barnett	Lillian May	9 Oct. 1905	
Beebe	Louis W.	Gisel	Frieda	17-19 Aug. 1904	undated, but document located between others dated 17 and 19 Aug. 1904; not signed by clerk
Beebe	Thomas E.	Pare	Della	25 Aug. 1903	
Beene	Luther Garnett	Patterson	Alma Vivian	10 May 1906	
Beeson	Charles Wesley	Bartle	Fannie Myrtle	27 Sept. 1907	
Beeson	E. I.	Logan	Emma C.	12 Oct. 1886	
Beeson	Isaac R.	Mathews	Salina	24 Oct. 1874	
Beeson	Jesse R.	Nelson	Tekla B.	5 Sept. 1912	
Beeson	Orville W.	Flago (?)	Mary A.	11 Aug. 1883	
Beeson	William I.	Burbank	Emma L.	29 Sept. 1887	
Beeson	William S.	Lafferty	Naoma E., Mrs.	28 Dec. 1895	gr: widower; br: widow.

Groom		Bride			
Surname	Given Name	Surname	Given Name	Date	Comments
Beeson	Willis Lewis	Russell	Ruth	21 Feb. 1911	
Beevers	Robert L.	Smith	Harriet E.	14 Aug. 1920	
Beffa	Caesar F.	Burris	Nellie, Mrs.	14 Oct. 1910	
Beffa	James	Carroz	Mary	20 Aug. 1913	
Beffa	James, Jr.	Elphick	Clytie	8 June 1914	br: Mr. & Mrs E. F. Elphick, parents
Beffa	Joseph Edward	Pool	Elba	15 Jan. 1916	
Beffa	Quillie W.	Paulucci	Marie E.	5 Oct. 1920	
Beffa	Tony	Zamaroni	Jessie	18 Sept. 1915	
Beffa	Tony	Zamaroni	Lillie	6 Dec. 1919	
Beggs	Thomas G.	Burns	Rose A.	18 Feb. 1903	
Beggs	W. H.	Black	Alice	15 Aug. 1887	
Beggs	William John	McCoy	Carrie	3 May 1884	
Beggs	William P.	McBrown	Jenevive	24 Nov. 1900	
Behler	Benjamin J.	Henke	Bertha C.	25 June 1919	
Behler	William	Kunde	Alice	12 Aug. 1908	
Behmer	John	Miller	Rosa A.	13 Oct. 1885	
Behmer	John	Harley	Ella	12 May 1877	
Behrens	Albert Percy	Cole	May	15 Sept. 1914	
Behrns	Carl Nisson	Church	Juanita Sybil	14 Aug. 1915	
Bei	Giulio	Rossi	Mary	3 Feb. 1912	
Belati	John	McCollough	Mary	8 June 1891	gr: signed with mark, no witness
Belden	Ralph Austin	Ungerwitter	M. Gretchen		date blank, filed between 17 and 19 June 1905
Belfils	Ernest	DeCosta	Annie	13 June 1910	
Belford	Frank G.	Radekey	Revia	4 Jan. 1921	
Bell	Edward H., Jr.	Garcia	Margaret M.	22 Dec. 1917	
Bell	Geo. K.	Bice	M. E.	2 Apr. 1866	
Bell	Grant	McCappen	Jennie	21 Sept. 1901	
Bell	Henry	Herbert	Retta	20 Dec. 1895	
Bell	Henry	Linebaugh	Kate, Mrs.	22 Jan. 1896	
Bell	Holly E.	Beguhl	Emma	14 June 1890	
Bell	Luther	Fisher	Ada	30 Dec. 1895	license requested by William Newton
Bell	Noah	Bamber	Elsie	19 Feb. 1894	

Groom		Bride			
Surname	Given Name	Surname	Given Name	Date	Comments
Bell	Raymond C.	Patrow	Clara May	19 Feb. 1919	
Bell	Walter C.	Adams	Lillie D.	19 July 1902	
Bell	Walter C.	Burt	Blanche A.	7 July 1913	
Bell	Warren	Shular	Ella	2 July 1881	
Bell	Wellie Samuel	Fairbanks	Zoe	31 Oct. 1901	
Bella	Angelo	Zanderina	Virginia	8 Jan. 1896	br: Juessepina Zanderina, mother, gives consent, her father being dead; A. H. Pond, witness to her x mark
Bellah	W. M.	Johnson	Vida	27 Apr. 1887	
Bellany	Severino R.	Johnson	Jennie N.	18 June 1898	no previous marriage
Bellazzini	Senio	Bondi	Claudina	3 Feb. 1921	
Bellesi	Achelli	Bellesi	Domenica	25 Feb. 1905	
Bellesi	Nestore	Moretti	Elisa	20 Nov. 1909	
Belli	Albert Joseph	Dogia	Anociata	30 July 1919	
Belli	Angelo	Gerali	Elvira	22 Oct. 1910	
Belli	Harry Alfred	Malpiede	Angeline	26 May 1919	
Belli	Luigi	Domenighini	Maria	27 Sept. 1909	
Belli	Ostaguio	Massoni	Laurina	15 Oct. 1885	
Belli	Sante	Capri	Maria	15 July 1907	
Bello	Frank N.	Rudolph	Elizabeth	21 Dec. 1915	
Bello	Joseph G.	Finnerty	Gertrude F.	25 Apr. 1919	
Bellon	Walter M.	Pomi	Mabel D.	18 Aug. 1919	
Belluomini	Matteo	Lituanio	Marie B.	28 Nov. 1917	
Belluomini	Palmiro	Benedetti	Edith M. (Tela)	14 Apr. 1921	
Beltrami	Lorenzo	Zanoni	Delia	26 May 1915	
Belvail	John H.	Daugherty	Maria Theresa	19 Sept. 1883	
Belvail	John H.	Bierkle	Emma Christine	3 Dec. 1910	
Belvail	Lewis	Phillips	Mae E.	25 Nov. 1903	
Belveal	Otis E.	Howard	Daisy M.	21 Aug. 1919	
Bement	Leighton W.	Slaten	Eva	1 Feb. 1900	no previous marriage
Bemis	Charles G.	Johnson	Estelle M.	30 Oct. 1913	br: W. P. Johnson, parent
Bendorf	Derby	Bartlett	Sibyl	5 May 1917	
Benedetti	Conrad	Zimmerman	Elizabeth	23 Sept. 1910	

Groom		Bride			
Surname	Given Name	Surname	Given Name	Date	Comments
Benedetti	John	Dondero	Katie	17 May 1897	license requested by Katie Dondero.
Benelli	Harry	Albini	Mary	7 Jan, 1915	br: Vittoria Asti, mother
Benelli	Joseph	Martinelli	Mary	21 Aug. 1915	
Benelli	Lucca	Giannecchini	Serofina	26 Jan, 1915	
Benepe	Charles S.	Gilmore	Lizzie E.	20 June 1898	no previous marriage
Benepe	Selden C.	Milne	Laura	1 Oct. 1906	
Benepe	W. Weimer	Blazer	Lena A.	24 Dec. 1904	requested by G. W. Libby
Benepe	Wesley L.	Libby	Martha M.	23 Dec. 1899	
Bengtson	Carl	Hultgren	Emma	30 Mar. 1918	
Benjamin	Frank E.	Brown	Minnie	6 Dec. 1887	gr: G. H. Benjamin,
Benjamin	William E.	Smith	Jennie, Mrs.	6 Nov. 1892	br: widow
Benjegerdes	Carl L.	Rapun	Annie	29 Dec. 1904	
Benkiser	Fred	Mosna	Anna	21 Dec. 1907	
Bennesen	Peter L.	Darling	Nora M., Mrs.	3 Sept. 1919	
Bennett	Charley	Cunningham	May	26 Mar. 1915	gr: Fred Bennett, father; br: Mrs. Eva Hamilton, mother
Bennett	Edwin George	Lewis	Grayce Edna	21 Jan. 1901	
Bennett	George H.	Lee	Emmie H.	19 Oct. 1892	
Bennett	Gilbert Louis	Cullen	Mary Alice	30 Sept. 1915	
Bennett	Glover Henry	Thompson	Fannie Jane	4 Feb. 1895	
Bennett	Grant	Brown	Laura	27 Oct. 188	
Bennett	James	Burns	Sarah, Mrs.	21 Nov. 1898	br: widow
Bennett	John C.	Casey	Katherine	28 Feb. 1905	
Bennett	Joseph	Kane	Catherine	1 Feb. 1909	gr: L. L. Cannon, witness to his mark
Bennett	Ralph	Broback	Naomi	16 July 1915	br: Laura Broback, mother
Bennett	W. J.	Bailey	Annie	8 Sept. 1888	br: James B. Bailey, guardian
Bennett	Warner	Danules (?)	Alice	24 Feb. 1880	witness: E. Stockstill
Bennett	William C.	Ichtertz	Mary Emily	6 May 1918	
Bennett	William Stephan	Northern	Hattie Belle	18 Aug. 1915	
Bennetts	Herbert Franklin	Baker	Jennie Cecelia	18 June 1914	
Benns	Clarence F.	Brake	A. Edith	25 June 1912	
Benson	A. F.	Heisen	Lillian	1 May 1914	
Benson	August	McDermott	Flora A.	1 Oct. 1907	

Groom		Bride			
Surname	Given Name	Surname	Given Name	Date	Comments
Benson	Benjamin James	Mooney	Rachael Bertha	1 Feb. 1910	
Benson	Elwin D.	Lewis	Mabel C.	3 Sept. 1912	gr: Louis E. Benson, father; br: Anna Lewis, mother
Benson	H. Urban	Torr	Agnes Leona	26 Apr. 1913	
Benson	Harry	Leiva	Irene M.	16 Aug. 1920	
Benson	Henry	Braman	Mary	11 July 1895	
Benson	Henry	Hurd	Charlotte	31 Dec. 1886	
Benson	Josiah H.	Hardin	Sarah C.	31 Mar. 1900	
Benson	L. E.	Derby	Cora	13 Nov. 1886	
Benson	Nathaniel W.	Merritt	Ida J.	16 Mar. 1886	br: J. & Mrs. S. E. Merritt, parents
Benson	Roy	Koster	Bertha Josephine	18 Dec. 1909	
Benson	Vernon Henry	Snyder	Sarah Rebecca	15 Apr. 1912	
Benson	William	Sartzer	Augusta	13 Jan. 1909	
Bent	Edwin M.	Farrell	Genevieve M.	14 July 1914	
Bentley	Rufus W.	Thompson	Christie D.	11 Dec. 1903	
Benton	C. C.	Bryant	Mary E.	8 Jan. 1914	
Benton	Henry Benjamin	Atkinson	Laura M.	3 Mar. 1917	
Benton	Louis J.	Snyder	Anna E.	8 May 1883	gr: Eliza Salter, guardian
Bequette	Julian P.	Patton	Bertha V.	21 Nov. 1898	no previous marriage
Beretta	Angelo	Modini	Mary	5 May 1904	
Beretta	Angelo P.	Mazza	Angelina M.	7 Apr. 1920	please omit ages in publishing
Berger	Charles O.	Harris	Maud E.	4 June 1904	license requested by E. D. Harris
Berger	Emil Julius	Haun	Alice Edna	21 Dec. 1918	
Berger	Frederick W.	Pinches	Marie G.	25 Nov. 1917	
Berger	Otto William	Pierce	Edna Langley	25 Sept. 1917	also signed by Frank Quartaroli (?)
Berger	William	Older	Edith M.	12 July 1915	
Bergevin	Alexander M.	Wickersham	Mae S.	23 June 1891	
Berglund	Harvey M.	Forsyth	Mary E.	31 Aug. 1915	
Bering	Edward A.	Farmer	Carrie J.	11 June 1900	gr: 1620 Sutter St., San Francisco
Berizzi	John	Dominechelli	Luigina	6 Dec. 1913	
Berka	F.	Boettcher	Pollie A.	1 Oct. 1887	
Berkman	James H.	McFarling	Eva J.	18 Jan. 1897	br: C. B. McFarling gives consent and signs
Berlin	William Herman	Newell	Flossie Clair	28 Dec. 1908	

Groom		Bride			
Surname	Given Name	Surname	Given Name	Date	Comments
Bernard	Gerardus	Fennell	Mary J.	8 Nov. 1919	
Bernard	John Leo	Equi	Marie	10 Sept. 1902	
Bernard	Robert L.	Weybright	Anna	22 Sept. 1890	
Berndt	Paul	Moldenhauer	Milea	28 July 1893	
Bernhard	Rudolph H.	Bruphacher	Elisabeth	30 Sept. 1911	
Bernhardt	Chas. F.	Fitzgibbon	Helen B.	31 Dec. 1900	signed by S. Wolf
Bernnan	Patrick	Buchanan	Anna	15 Mar. 1913	
Bernstein	David	Greenstein	Mary	10 Apr. 1917	
Berruti	Emilio	Zappa	Mary M.	8 Mar. 1920	
Berry	C. S.	Wilson	Jennie	21 May 1892	
Berry	George H.	England	Susan A.	1 Mar. 1897	
Berry	George Herod	England	Martha Isabel	27 Apr. 1895	
Berry	John E.	Clow	Crystal M.	14 Mar. 1912	
Berry	Joseph P.	Koenig	Lillie F.	26 Oct. 1891	
Berry	S. B.	Purvince	Lew J.	6 Sept. 1876	
Berry	Samuel B.	Miller	Mary J.	6 Jan. 1865	
Berry	Samuel C.	Williams	Willmina	8 Sept. 1903	
Berry	W. P.	Menefee	Emma	2 Apr. 1866	
Berryhill	Archie Tanner	Sawyers	Hazel Marjory	18 Aug. 1919	
Berryhill	Joseph F.	Burright	Retta	9 Aug. 1913	
Berryman	Samuel	O'Laughlin	Maggie	2 Dec. 1915	
Bertellotti	Pio	Nina	Florence Dello	25 Aug. 1920	
Bertholdi	Stephen P.	Orozco	Julia V.	18 May 1915	
Bertino	Thomas	Moore	May T.	3 May 1919	please do not publish
Bertolani	Angelo L.	McCumiskey	Florence	13 Sept. 1902	
Bertolani	Martino	Guirgu	Assunta	18 July 1914	
Bertoli	Paul	Frati	Sarah	14 Apr. 1911	br: Domenice Frati, parent
Bertoli	Paul Pete	Forrest	Agnes May	25 Feb. 1918	br: George A. Forrest, father
Bertoli	Paulo	Bernetti	Lizza	5 June 1894	
Bertoli	Romeo	Gainnini	Della	7 July 1910	
Bertolucci	Guido C.	Picchi	Frances A.	16 Dec. 1920	
Berton	Mars F.	Laughlin	Irene J.	28 Apr. 1920	
Bertoni	Guido	Porta	Mary	9 Aug. 1917	

Groom		Bride			
Surname	Given Name	Surname	Given Name	Date	Comments
Bertossi	Carlo	Mandarini	Guiseppina	27 Dec. 1910	
Bertossi	Joseph	Leonardini	Theresa	7 June 1899	no previous marriage
Bertossi	Louis	Cassani	Nora	24 Feb. 1904	
Bertram	Arthur H.	Spring	Rosenia	5 Dec. 1917	
Bertrand	Paul Emil	Huni	Sophe	20 July 1897	Frieda Biermann of San Francisco, witness
Bertron	Albert	Basford	Ida Ellen	21 June 1883	br: John N. & Sarah J. Ferguson, stepfather & mother
Bertsch	Frank	Brown	Elyda, Mrs.	20 June 1892	br: widow
Bertuccelli	Fabo	Proctor	Gladys C.	21 Feb. 1920	
Bertulucci	Lorenzo	Cassini	Giuseppina	27 Apr. 1886	br: Bartolomeo Cassini, father
Besenthal	Adolph	Kolasa	Stanislaw	31 Oct. 1888	
Bethune	John	Fenwick	Juanita	15 Jan. 1880	
Bettega	Louis	Kelley	Hazel C.	31 Dec. 1920	
Bettencorte	Manuel Martin	Souza	Caroline M.	30 Oct. 1906	
Bettencourt	John M.	Alves	Mary C.	26 Aug. 1915	
Bettencourt	Joseph A.	Frates	Irene	9 Apr. 1917	
Bettencourt	Manuel	Aveil	Maria	11 Sept. 1905	J. W. Ford, witness to her mark
Bettiga	Bruno	Sarzotti	Minnie	23 Nov. 1918	
Bettiga	Pietro	Pinoli	Catherina	25 Jan. 1910	
Bettiga	Vincenzo	Deghi	Prima	11 June 1914	
Bettinelli	Filippo	Pedrelli	Margheritta	24 Dec. 1890	
Bettinelli	Silvio L.	Kuhule	Irene Genevieve	20 Oct. 1907	
Bettini	Alessio J.	Wade	Grace E.	26 July 1919	
Betts	Ross Everett	Dill	Nettie	29 Oct. 1908	
Beukers	Peter Gerard	Berka	Regina	30 July 1920	
Beutel	Christian	Scott	Bertha	5 Dec. 1894	
Beutel	Gottlieb	Spieth	Anna	21 Oct. 1899	no previous marriage
Bever	Thomas J.	Renfrew	Anna L.	28 Dec. 1882	
Bever	Tunis V.	Howard	Martha G.	15 Jan. 1890	
Beveridge	James	Horwege	Loretta C.	10 Oct. 1919	
Beveridge	William, Jr.	Hendrickson	Ida	6 Aug. 1920	
Bevington	Walter Clark	Law	Tammy	22 Apr. 1898	
Bewick	William Young	Torgelson	Anna	21 Dec. 1905	

Groom		Bride			
Surname	Given Name	Surname	Given Name	Date	Comments
Beyer	Edward	Baldrusch	Katie	3 Nov. 1888	
Biagggi	Antony	Tunzi	Albina	11 June 1913	
Biaggi	B.	Nobelli	Philomena	8 June 1885	
Biaggi	John Robert	Bree	Eva	23 Apr. 1917	
Bianchi	Antonio	Ferrari	Edith Margaret	14 May 1917	
Bianchi	Attilio	Lucchesi	Elvira Rosa	2 Feb. 1918	br: Genesio Lucchesi, parent
Bianchi	Peter	Perinoni	Annie	14 Dec. 1903	
Bianchini	Bernardino	Viviani	Maria	26 July 1920	
Bianchini	Fred P.	Rowe	Leona V.	19 Mar. 1913	
Bianchini	Giovanni	Hasnip	Sarah	5 June 1895	
Bianchini	Giovanni W.	Bertino	Rose N.	27 Sept. 1918	gr: Sarah Bianchini, mother; br: Jennie Bertino, mother
Bianchini	Mariano	Allesandri	Elisa	11 June 1902	
Bianchini	Mario	Bianchini	Sarah, Mrs.	2 Dec. 1897	br: widow
Bianconi	Mansueto	Buzzi	Mary	28 Sept. 1912	
Biasotti	Giovanni	Leonardini	Teresa	15 Jan. 1916	
Biasotti	Luigi	Ghiozzi	Marie	17 Jan. 1912	
Biavaschi	Emil	Lemmon	Ethel	28 Apr. 1914	
Bice	Fred L.	Higgins	Adeline	19 June 1895	
Bickford	Elmer Leonard	Putnam	Ada	12 July 1900	gr: born Mar 1872; br: born 4 Aug. 1873
Biddings	Henry A.	Bel	Ida May	20 Feb. 1885	
Bidwell	Albert	Morrill	Mary Francis	23 Dec. 1904	
Bidwell	Charles E.	Combs	Kittie L.	8 Oct. 1901	gr: James Bidwell, father
Bidwell	James	Martin	Lucy	26 May 1879	
Bidwell	James E.	Peck	Annie	23 Nov. 1899	gr: James Bidwell, father;br: M. Peck, father; no previous marriage
Bidwell	John W.	St. Clair	Ellen	12 Oct. 1894	
Bierer	David William	Sutherlan	Grace Elizabeth, Mrs.	17 Aug. 1904	
Bigelow	Calvin	Jones	Louisa	3 May 1887	
Bigelow	Frank L.	Adgate	Nannie	30 Apr. 1895	
Bigelow	George A.	Griffin	Jessie E.	21 Sept. 1907	
Biggs	Frank Leland	Fore	Mable Edith	9 Nov. 1914	

Groom		Bride			
Surname	Given Name	Surname	Given Name	Date	Comments
Biggs	George C.	Veale	Margaret	27 Aug. 1890	
Biggs	George C.	Hardin	Alice M.	24 Aug. 1880	
Bigham	M.	Brooks	Emma	31 Oct. 1887	
Bigham	Ray E.	Dollar	Daisy B.	12 June 1913	
Bignell	James	Blair	Josephine	29 June 1920	
Bigsby	Milton S.	Willis	Mary	28 July 1881	
Bill	Frank B.	Barry	Margaret M.	15 Feb.1915	
Bill	Henry	Gerlach	Elizabetha	3 Feb. 1891	
Bill	Howard	Rodgers	Edna Isabelle	15 Aug. 1910	gr: Arthur C. Bill, father
Bill	Philip C., Jr.	Schuhmann	Johanna	4 Apr. 1912	
Billett	Frank E.	Twitchell	Henrietta Genevia	3 July 1902	gr: Wm. A. Twitchell, father,Veterans Home, CA; br: Anna Joy, guardian, Bodega
Billings	J. F.	Madden	Elizabeth	18 July 1891	
Bills	Lemuel James	Chaffee	Carrie	23 Aug. 1879	
Bilstein	Alfred George	Tenter	Elizabeth Mary	2 July 1902	br: Diedrich Tenter, father
Bindi	Acille	Battaglia	Luisa	7 Mar. 1917	
Bindt	Rudolph	Johnson	Clara Belle	26 June 1900	br: Henry Johnson, father
Bingaman	Joseph Wheeler Dores	Kimball	Edna Genevieve	7 Sept. 1909	
Binggeli	George	Balozs	Rose M.	22 May 1919	
Bink	Conrad	Holst	Annie M.	29 Nov. 1893	
Bino	John	Pedrotti	Annie Teresa	9 Oct. 1907	
Biocca	Louis	Cassina	Margaret	11 Aug. 1920	br: Elizabeth Cassina, mother
Birch	James F.	Wilson	Nellie K.	6 May 1889	
Birch	Russell J.	Schelling	Marie C.	21 Feb. 1913	
Bird	Charles A.	Dewey	Beatrix C.	31 Aug. 1915	
Bird	George Francis	Hale	Mabel	31 Mar. 1904	
Bird	Harry	Sawyer	Jennie L.	3 Mar. 1906	
Bird	Jesse	Thorpe	Louise E.	2 Mar. 1883	
Bird	Seth J.	Jensen	Anna	1 Aug. 1914	
Bird	James				filed between 22 and 24 Oct. 1887
Birkle	Nickolas	Berta	Emma Mengere	9 Feb. 1894	
Birmingham	Winfred W.	Dick	Mayme S.	24 Aug. 1915	
Bisbee	George Marion	Samuels	Pearl Katherine	3 Sept. 1914	br: Robert M. Samuels, father

Groom		Bride			
Surname	Given Name	Surname	Given Name	Date	Comments
Bischof	Martin T.	Pillsbury	Harriet	30 Jan. 1918	
Bish	Lewis M.	Norris	Bertha M.	7 July 1891	br: Martha E. Norris, mother
Bishop	E. L.	Burr	Flora I.	5 Apr. 1915	
Bishop	William A.	Greene	Vilette	26 July 1879	
Bishop	William Raymond	Caughey	Elizabeth Annie	23 Apr. 1896	
Bisinger	Hubert G.	Throckmorton	Margaret M.	11 Feb. 1919	
Bisordi	Frank	Paulinelli	Emma	29 Nov. 1904	
Bisordi	Angelo	Banks	Bertha	11 June 1914	
Bisordi (?)	Pasquale	Gianella	Theresa	22 Apr. 1882	br: Lorenzo Gianella, parent
Bitcon	George	Ingalsbe	Luinie	19 Jan. 1918	
Bizzini	Joseph	Bolla	Domenica	11 Sept. 1893	
Bizzini	Julius	Kuhl	Catharina	27 July 1885	
Bjorman	Henry	Nelson	Christine B.	19 Nov. 1890	
Black	Charles A.	Groshong	Anna E.	3 May 1889	
Black	Charles M.	Bowman	Jessie Z.	8 July 1898	
Black	Claude Henry	Phillips	Pauline	3 Jan. 1906	
Black	George H.	Crew	Minnie M.	20 Feb. 1892	br: F. M. Crew, father
Black	George H.	Ward	Sarah A.	12 Oct. 1877	br: J. ? A. Ward, Cloverdale; B. J. Davis, witness
Black	Harry Edward	Smith	Maude Alma	18 Jan. 1904	license requested by E. F. Woodward
Black	Homer W.	Leard	Bernice Edna	23 Feb. 1906	
Black	Martin L.	McCready	Laura T.	1 May 1918	
Black	Oscar W.	Read	Hazel G.	6 Feb. 1913	gr: Celia A. Black, mother
Black	Samuel	Lowe	Teresa, Mrs.	8 June 1888	
Black	Shirley R.	Leroux	Cora F.	26 May 1899	gr: George H. Black, father
Black	V. D.	Norris	Dalia	30 July 1890	
Black	Walter C.	Terry	Nora L.	20 June 1904	
Black	Wilbur C.	Smith	Belle Anna	19 Oct. 1909	
Black	William Earl	Cooper	Hazel Marguerite	25 June 1908	gr: W. A. Black, father
Black	William H.	Hulbert	Eleonora Agnes	7 Sept. 1910	gr: Annabelle Black, mother
Black	Wm. H.	Hall	Ensima	4 Nov. 1876	
Black	Wm. H.	Easlie	Nora Emma	6 Aug. 1878	
Blackburn	Allen H.	Winquist	Annie S.	1 Sept. 1877	

Groom		Bride			
Surname	Given Name	Surname	Given Name	Date	Comments
Blackburn	Charles Walter	Kyle	Maude	7 Feb. 1903	
Blackburn	Frank L.	Williams	Caroline T. D.	12 Jan. 1904	
Blackburn	George	Thurman	Margaret	27 Oct. 1894	
Blackford	Clyde R.	Schneider	Katherine	30 Apr. 1910	
Blackford	Ernest F.	Lane	Lottie E.	22 Dec. 1919	
Blackly	Frank E.	McCario	Minnie	26 Aug. 1904	
Blackman	Samuel	Williams	Rebecca	22 Sept. 1885	
Blackman	W. S.	Harrow	Frances S.	18 Dec. 1915	
Blackwell	Edward E.	Wilkinson	Leonora F.	15 Sept. 1915	
Blair	Duke	Otis	Flora	5 May 1919	
Blair	F. M. D.	Masey	Vesta, Mrs.	8 Jan. 1867	
Blair	James K.	Monticello	Sylvia C.	17 Apr. 1920	br: Rosline Monticello, mother
Blair	John	Ushman	Frederika	14 Apr. 1894	
Blair	Thomas N.	Gober	Sarah J., Mrs.	24 Sept. 1896	
Blair	William E.	Feltz	Mary S.	17 Aug. 1893	br: Mrs. Auguste Feltz, widow, gives consent and signs
Blaisdell	Harry Lee	Wiswell	Wyima (?) Florence	18 Apr. 1919	
Blake	Frank T.	Askam	Lillian	29 July 1912	
Blake	James B.	Singley	Katherine	11 Jan. 1898	no previous marriage
Blake	Jeremiah Burton	Hockin	Grace Mabel	26 Dec. 1903	
Blake	John R.	Mays	Mattie H.	24 Feb. 1890	
Blake	John R.	Hines	Alice J.	10 Feb. 1881	
Blakeley	Leslie A.	Burns	Jessie E.	8 Jan. 1920	
Blakely	T. M.	Ayers	Rosalie	31 May 1887	
Blakesley	Claude	Teel	Ida	29 Apr. 1901	
Blakesley	Franklin C.	Miller	Hazel	4 Nov. 1914	
Blakeway	Horace	Richardson	Emma	17 Oct. 1903	
Blakley	Albert Edward	Taylor	Junita Eyleen	10 Aug. 1912	
Blakley	James M.	Simpson	Rebecca, Mrs.	31 Jan. 1900	both widowed
Blakley	Jesse E.	Leon	Lupe	14 Apr. 1920	
Blakley	Thomas F.	Woods	Katie	19 July 1917	
Blakley	Thos. S.	Beardon	Martha E.	2 Sept. 1882	
Blanchard	Bowman	Purvine	Olive	8 Apr. 1905	

Groom		Bride			
Surname	Given Name	Surname	Given Name	Date	Comments
Blanchard	D. N.	Edwards	Helen R.	7 Nov. 1885	
Blanchard	Frank	Loyan (?)	Annie	15 Nov. 1880	br: Malissa Garrigus, mother
Blanchard	Frank I.	Glynn	Mamie	1 June 1896	
Blaney	John W.	Zilhart	Ella F.	20 Nov. 1890	
Blank	George	Huber	Emily A.	11 Oct. 1899	no previous marriage
Blank	John	Baker	Amy T.	30 Mar. 1909	
Blank	John	Greist	Leah Agnes	30 Sept. 1876	
Blank	Louis	Baker	Eva M.	31 Mar. 1909	
Blast	Leo A.	Edwards	Evelyn Maud	30 June 1909	
Blazer	C. Lloyd	Gardella	Emily I.	25 Nov. 1914	
Blazer	Charlie	Ottmer	Adelia B.	16 Mar. 1883	
Blazer	John J.	Harbine	Addie	31 Mar. 1888	
Bleakley	William	Richardsen	Sarah Jane	31 Aug. 1874	br: written consent of parents
Bledsoe	A. J.	Woodruff	Clara J.	1 July 1887	
Bledsoe	Henry Thornton	Schulz	Matilda Lucille	14 Feb. 1920	
Bledsoe	Isaac	Michaid	Mary, Mrs.	14 Dec. 1866	
Bledsoe	John H.	Bane	Eleanor, Mrs.	6 Mar. 1893	
Bledsoe	John Henry	Conger	Cornelia Constance	20 Sept. 1883	br: Charles Conger, father
Bledsoe	Linn	Vaughn	Louisa F., Mrs.	21 Mar. 1900	
Bledsoe	Robert R.	Thorton	Thusa	14 Aug. 1885	
Bledsoe	W. O.	Molleston	Catheline	10 Sept. 1887	
Blik	Ell Carl Dunda	Rassmussen	Hazel M.	8 Aug. 1918	
Bliss	Philip P.	LeBaron	Beryl	18 Dec. 1919	
Bloch	Albert	Walker	Carrie Belle	23 Dec. 1903	
Block	George	Ottmer	Lora A.		gr: Geo. Block, father; filed between 15 and 16 Mar. 1883: br: Henry C. Ottmer, father
Block	George Henry	Baines	Irene	4 Aug. 1914	overlays record gr: Diana L Block, mother; George Henry birth 4 Oct. 1894
Block	Walter Ottmer	Guerin	Ella	17 Dec. 1908	
Blogg	Ernest J.	Philkill (?)	Nell M.	9 Dec. 1920	
Blomme	John	Desmue	Ida	20 Jan. 1904	
Blomquist	John	Chapman	Catherine	21 Oct. 1886	
Bloom	Americo James	Filippini	Vivian Mabel	7 Dec. 1908	

Groom		Bride			
Surname	Given Name	Surname	Given Name	Date	Comments
Bloom	Plauso G.	Dado	Irene E.	16 Sept. 1909	
Bloom	Valenti J.	Casarotti	Mary O.	24 Aug. 1909	
Blosser	Thomas G.	Hardwick	Mary	27 Feb. 1892	
Blot	Louis	Gaffney	Madeleine	17 Apr. 1909	
Blow	James	Clark	Susie	10 June 1885	br: A. Comisto, guardian
Blower	Sumner J.	Leininger	Carrie	8 Dec. 1899	
Blum	Jacob	Huber	Helena	24 Nov. 1899	no previous marriage
Blum	Louis	Haas	Theresa	21 June 1900	
Blumenthal	Albert M.	Blumenthal	Valerie	4 Apr. 1918	
Blundell	Vance D.	Acker	Eolim (?)	2 May 1879	
Bly	Albert R.	Quinby	Ella	6 Oct. 1898	gr: divorced over one year; br: widow
Blythe	Frank	Ashmore	Emily F.	20 July 1913	
Board	Horace D.	Ottmer	Ida F.	2 Jan. 1880	
Board	William	Oleven (?)	Azora A.	29 Apr. 1879	
Boardman	Edward Madison	Augeir	Adelia Anna	10 Apr. 1917	
Bobb	H. I.	Galle	Mary V.	2 June 1914	
Bobkiewicz	Louis	Einfeldt	Mary Ellen, Mrs.	21 Oct. 1904	
Bobst	George M.	Button	Flossie	23 Mar. 1904	gr: J. I. Bobst, parent
Bobst	John W.	Harmon	Lilly	8 Aug. 1904	
Bobst	Richard M.	McFarling	Jessie M.	9 June 1902	gr: J. H. Bobst, father; br: Alice V. McFarling, mother
Bock	Walter D.	Parks	Anna M.	6 Oct. 1890	
Boden	Jack	McFarlane	Leonore May	8 Dec. 1920	
Bodin	Walter B.	Wentzy	Bessie F.	18 Sept. 1920	
Boding	Raymond O.	Ward	Gertrude Alice	28 Aug. 1906	
Boerner	Richard F.	Parkins	Tamson	15 Mar. 1910	
Bogale	John	Benedetti	Clarinda	9 Aug. 1902	
Bogard	William J.	White	Julia Emma	3 Aug. 1898	no previous marriage
Boggiono	Antonio	Grambruna	Mary	11 Apr. 1912	
Boggs	Geo. W.	McMeans	Alabama	17 Oct. 1865	
Bogle	Samuel S.	Woodward	Bess Van Alst	3 June 1916	
Bogni	Enrico	Sorio	Annie	7 Sept. 1907	br: G. Sori, parent
Bogusch	Herbert W.	Becker	Alice M.	5 Aug. 1919	

Groom		Bride			
Surname	Given Name	Surname	Given Name	Date	Comments
Bohan	Michael	Miller	Martha E.	18 Sept. 1917	
Bohlin	Bernard	Stagman	Anna C.	11 Aug. 1888	br: Frank A. Bohlin, guardian
Bohlin	Frank Anton	Steigeman	Mary Gertrude	23 Nov. 1886	br: William Steigman, parent
Bohmer	Jacob	Kady	Mary	24 Apr. 1866	
Bohn	Johannes W.	Niquet	Katie	15 Nov. 1920	
Bohni	Frederick	Steiger	Rosa	25 Aug. 1887	
Boice	John Dudley	Chambers	California	25 Sept. 1876	
Boida	G.	Blandini	Armenia	10 Mar. 1903	
Boida	Lorenzo	Goodrich	Rosa Meador	14 Dec. 1893	gr: M.D. after name; br: last name may be hyphenated Meador-Goodrich
Boien	P.	Arfsten	Giene	14 Nov. 1903	
Boitano	Leo	Rosasco	Anna Maria	3 Nov. 1906	
Boivin	Emile Peter	Burns	Elsie Viola	6 Jan. 1913	
Bojorques	John	Young	Adeline	6 Sept. 1919	
Boldi	Giacomo	Rossi	Luigia	9 Aug. 1904	
Boldi	Gioseppe	Gufanti	Rosa	9 Aug. 1904	
Bolla	Olympio G.	Soldate	Louisa, Mrs.	31 Aug 1907	
Bolla	Pacific J.	Gambonini	Emma A.	19 Sept. 1919	
Bolla	Romelio G.	Tognaldo	Elvizia C.	2 Feb. 1909	
Bolles	Walter A.	Greott	Marie (?) F.	24 Dec. 1881	
Bollinger	David K.	Gregson	Ruth Annie	12 June 1909	
Bollinger	Fred	Jones	Susie C.	15 Sept. 1911	
Bolser	Chester Arthur	Campbell	Grace Evelyn	28 May 1909	
Bolton	John F.	Robinson	Sadie L.	4 Sept. 1894	
Bolton	Walter A.	Kline	K. Isabelle	15 Apr. 1891	
Bolton	William L.	Lewis	Faye B.	27 Apr. 1920	
Bolz	Albert W.	Whitlatch	Leila M.	13 Sept. 1920	
Bolz	Francis J.	Petersen	Marie	7 Dec. 1904	
Bolz	Phillip C.	Smith	Mary F.	14 Mar. 1903	
Bomemann	Arthur F.	Mann	Embie (?)A.	22 Oct. 1907	
Bonardi	Guiseppe	Pagani	Katie E.	20 Apr. 1918	
Bond	Charles Allen	Wilcox	Grace E.	9 July 1895	
Bondi	Oreste	Novelli	Clariee	18 Dec. 1917	br: Luigi Novelli, father

Groom		Bride			
Surname	Given Name	Surname	Given Name	Date	Comments
Bondietti	Frank	Mazzolini	Clementina	19 Oct. 1885	
Bondietti	W. J. T.	Fiori	Francis	27 Oct. 1900	gr: W. J. T. Orr applied for license
Bones	Albert E.	Stewart	Lettie May	19 Dec. 1899	
Bones	Benjamin Marcus	Bishop	Nellie M.	28 Jan. 1903	
Bones	Charles H.	Francisco	Emma	5 Aug. 1897	do not publish
Bones	Francis L.	Peters	Gertrude A.	7 July 1919	
Bones	Frank M.	Leggett	Maud Lillian	8 Nov. 1894	
Bones	John F.	Stone	Sardmier ?	19 June 1866	
Bones	John Franklin	Gillett	Kate, Mrs.	20 Sept. 1905	
Bones	Lester	Derrickson	Hila	26 Nov. 1907	br: Anna Derrickson, mother
Bones	R. W.	Duke	Ethel E.	23 Nov. 1914	
Bones	Thomas J.	Foster	Rose S.	25 Sept. 1915	
Bones	William H.	Patterson	Martha	31 Aug. 1886	
Bonetti	Joseph	Tamba	Annetta	19 July1892	
Bonfigli	Alvise	Bathaglia	Lena	20 June 1914	
Bonham	James B.	Rima	Rosa M.	13 Oct. 1879	br: Harriet A. & Arial W. Rima, parents
Bonham	John P.	Johnson	Ada T.	23 June 1900	
Bonham	Melvin	Hulbert	Belle	7 May 1910	
Bonham	Willard C.	Green	Gertrude A.	12 Sept. 1919	
Bonini	Olivero	Alessandri	Dina	6 July 1912	
Bonnard	Constant	Cabaup	Marie G.	2 June 1893	
Bonnecaze	Joseph	Bonnemason	Louise M.	17 Jan. 1913	
Bonner	Chas. D.	Lumsden	Fannie L.	22 Nov. 1887	
Bonnet	Robert A.	McConaghy	Annie N.	8 Apr. 1921	
Bonney	Alfred T.	Staton	Cora W.	19 Sept. 1898	no previous marriage; requested by F. M. Staton
Bonnie	B. F.	Petray	Parthenia	23 Apr. 1865	
Bonugli	Peter	Tocchini	Julia	17 Jan. 1913	
Bonward	P. N.	Lund	Annie L.	23 Dec. 1893	br: nativity, Marysville crossed out and replaced by California
Booth	John	Condon	Ruth	19 Dec. 1912	br: Mrs. R. M. Condon, mother
Boothe	William N.	Norcross	Alice	30 Aug. 1886	
Borba	Emanuel Ignacio	Vier	Angeline Genevieve	26 Dec. 1905	

Groom		Bride			
Surname	**Given Name**	**Surname**	**Given Name**	**Date**	**Comments**
Borba	Frank	Kirsch	Frances Margaret	9 Feb. 1907	
Bordessa	Antonio	Bordessa	Juiliana	4 Feb. 1910	
Bordessa	Davide	Pozzi	Margheritta	20 Nov. 1901	
Bordessa	Dominico	Poncio	Carolina	11 Sept. 1917	gr: Giovanna Poncio, parent, signs with mark
Bordessa	Martin	Maffioli	Catherina	25 Aug. 1913	
Bordges	Joseph S.	Dutro	Josephine	27 Sept. 1915	
Bordwell	Fred Albert	Graves	Georgia	13 Aug. 1903	Alameda form
Borelli	Matteo	Benatti	Italia	22 July 1920	
Borello	Pietro J.	Findley	Ruby F.	15 Mar. 1920	gr: Alassendro Borello, father; br: Charles Findley, father
Borges	George Louis	Marks	Lena	30 Nov. 1906	
Borgess	Antone E.	Simoni	Mary	16 Oct. 1920	
Borgo	Filippo	Marmori	Luigia	11 Feb. 1898	no previous marriage
Borgwardt	August	Stevenson	Grace	7 Mar. 1903	
Bork	Julius	Kopken	Sophia	1 Oct. 1887	
Borland	Lee	Dempsey	Maggie M.	12 Aug. 1865	
Borlini	Augustine	Pozzi	Valeria	13 June 1891	
Borman	Noel	Ullman	Edna	5 Aug. 1918	
Bormolini	Louis	Pedroli	Antonietta	20 Dec. 1920	
Borri	Lodovico Vincenzo	Yancey	Ruby V.	15 July 1915	br: Sophia Baker, mother
Borserini	Zeno	de Cungi	Lina	18 July 1911	
Bortone	Michel	LeCam	Marie C.	1 Feb. 1913	
Borziny	Bob	Milano	Teresa	7 Dec. 1915	
Bosch	Arnold	Huffman	Myrtle	30 June 1898	
Boschetti	Centuria	Furia	Cisara	30 Nov. 1912	
Boschke?	George W.	Smith	Carrie M.	2 Aug. 1890	
Bose	John Edward	McAlpin	Edith S.	2 Sept. 1916	
Boss	George W.	Hale	Laura I.	25 Nov. 1884	
Bostwick	N. W.	Looney	Addie	30 Mar. 1865	
Boswell	Ernest J.	Nelson	Rose B.	17 Dec. 1904	
Boswell	F. C.	Kerrn	Ella R.	25 June 1912	
Boswell	William L.	Earl	Deta	10 Apr. 1912	
Bosworth	Bernard P.	Gabriel	Hazel	2 Aug. 1920	

Groom		Bride			
Surname	Given Name	Surname	Given Name	Date	Comments
Bosworth	Fred E.	Gibson	Margaret E.	3 Dec. 1900	
Bottomley	Thomas H.	Shaw	May Francis	26 Oct. 1907	
Boudin	Lucien Victor	Assenti	Lillian F.	30 Oct. 1916	
Bouhaben	Emil H.	Frary	Adele M.	4 Dec. 1919	
Bouk	Alva Roy	Kircke	Amelia Anna	23 July 1917	
Boulden	Frederick N.	Weymouth	Mae Z.	27 July 1911	
Bound	Joseph	Picknell	Catharini M., Mrs.	20 Mar. 1885	
Bouneau	Louis	Whitaker	Lottie N.	4 May 1885	
Bourbeau	Joseph	Bisordi	Emilia	4 Mar. 1905	
Bousse (?)	Daniel	Burrus	Mary C.	11 Oct. 1875	br: G. M. Burrus, parent; Healdsburg
Bovett	George Harold	Adams	Gladys Eleanor	1 Oct. 1915	
Bowbeer	Benjamin F.	Overton	Mary A.	30 Oct. 1893	
Bowbeer	C. W.	Beeson	Anna	5 Dec. 1885	
Bowbeer	Earl V.	Hall	Mabel G.	8 Nov. 1919	
Bowden	Isaac	Delaney	Elizabeth A.	13 Feb. 1879	requested by H. E. Laurence
Bowden	J. W.	Peterson	Ellen J.	13 Nov. 1883	br: A. Peterson, father
Bowden	John Wesley	Lansdale	Mary Elizabeth	10 July 1905	
Bowen	Arthur R.	Hartley	Nellie Frances	17 Dec. 1917	
Bowen	John Thomas	Irving	Martha	24 May 1911	
Bowen	Lorenzo H.	King	Getrude	21 Nov. 1918	
Bowen	R. Hunt	Starr	Vera L.	17 Aug. 1917	
Bower	Bertram H.	McDaniel	Olive L.	11 Apr. 1917	
Bower	G. N.	Lockwood	Beulah M.	25 Aug. 1915	
Bower	George A.	Churchman	Hattie L.	15 Dec. 1899	
Bower	J. Elmer	McCausland	Amy	7 June 1913	
Bower	William G.	Meyer	Marguerite	18 May 1892	
Bower (?)	Daniel	Hammett (?)	Martha	19 July 1883	
Bowers	Colon R.	Shreve	Guineviere L.	10 Mar. 1913	
Bowers	Edward B.	Rowe	Elizabeth A.	1 Dec. 1897	
Bowers	George	Case	Susie A.	14 Apr. 1920	
Bowers	Henry P.	Jacobs	Stella M.	25 Sept. 1900	
Bowers	Herbert Andrews	Green	Hazel	28 Oct. 1898	gr: J. T. Bowers, father; br: Warren Green, father

Groom		Bride			
Surname	**Given Name**	**Surname**	**Given Name**	**Date**	**Comments**
Bowers	Joseph Ellsworth	Kindler	Amelia L.	18 June 1919	
Bowers	Oliver Clyde	DeLong	Nellie Alice	23 Aug. 1905	
Bowker	William C.	Hanley	Sophie E.	25 Nov. 1916	
Bowles	Frank Herbert	Fowler	Ada Rosella	25 July 1906	
Bowman	James C.	Aced	Pilar S.	18 May 1918	
Bowman	Thomas Franklin	Nunley	Isabelle	8 Sept. 1920	
Bowman	Walter	Shader	Florence	27 Dec. 1913	br: Rebecca Shader, mother
Bowman	William Frederick	Miller	Louise Sunderhouse	2 July 1906	
Bowmer (?)	William	Pool	Abby, Mrs.	3 Dec. 1881	
Boyce	F. O.	Seawell	Bessie	20 Dec. 1888	
Boyd	Alfred Hillis	Powers	Marguerite	31 July 1906	
Boyd	B. C.	Wilfley	Rhoda A.	2 May 1883	requested by John L. Seawell
Boyd	Bennie C.	Shoemake	Ella	18 Aug. 1900	br: H. (Omer), Shoemake, father
Boyd	Dan	Haas	Bertha M.	4 Oct. 1915	
Boyd	Elmer	Newbert	Byrdie Geneva	13 Nov. 1912	
Boyd	George	Lewis	Lucy	26 June 1882	
Boyd	Henry	Ryan	Minnie	22 Jan. 1910	
Boyd	Hugh Coleman	Dunham	Essie	31 May 1904	
Boyd	James K., Jr.	Francisco	Mabel Grace	23 June 1909	
Boyd	John	Macdonald	Helen Gertrude	9 Nov. 1917	
Boyd	John David	Nobles	Adeline May	23 Dec. 1913	br: Mrs. Sarah Nobles, mother
Boyd	Leon G.	Hinman	Mae	15 Jan. 1908	
Boyd	Noah M.	Lubas	Marie J.	8 Dec. 1913	
Boyd	Sloan	Mayfield	Gussie B.	10 Nov. 1901	br: requests that you do not mention ages
Boyd	William M.	Poff	Ella E.	22 Sept. 1892	
Boyer	Ernest D.	Lambert	Elise Mary	15 Dec. 1915	
Boyer	Henry W.	Harmon	Maggie	6 Mar. 1899	br: Mrs. T. B. Binkley, mother; requested by Mrs. M. J. Baker for her son; don't publish
Boyer	Otis J.	Storey	Frieda G.	23 Nov. 1920	
Boyer	Sidney Roswell	Eproson	Addie	27 June 1906	
Boyse	Clarence	Venon	Nora G.	15 June 1918	
Boysen	Charley M.	Wells	Grace Eva	6 May 1909	

Groom		Bride		Date	Comments
Surname	Given Name	Surname	Given Name		
Boysen	Fred B.	Petersen	Annie M.	8 Sept. 1919	
Boysen	William Henry	Wyrick	Blanche Christina	20 June 1913	gr: John Boysen, father
Boysen	William Henry	Krusick	Eva Angelina	24 Feb. 1916	
Boysen	Clarence Constant	Boyes	Lola M.	2 Nov. 1917	
Boyson	Simon C.	Henrickson	Alma I.	17 June 1915	
Brackett	J. B.	Gedney	Della	10 Jan. 1888	
Brackett	Jack H.	Gregory	Joanna	22 Oct. 1866	
Brackett	Raymond Gregory	Gater	Lillian Edith	11 Oct. 1910	
Bradbury	Edward A.	McMillan	Leonora	30 June 1920	
Bradbury	Halta	Piatt	Lela M.	15 Jan. 1901	
Braden	Charley	Pittman	Ada, Mrs.	4 Nov. 1908	
Bradford	Branch Johnson	Badell	Ellen M.	7 Apr. 1875	
Bradford	Christopher W.	Fowler	Irene F.	24 Jan. 1895	
Bradford	Clifford G.	Kirwan	Nellie E.	9 Aug. 1920	do not publish
Bradford	D. J.	Varney	Helen	12 Aug. 1889	
Bradford	Elbert	Baker	Harriet F.	30 Mar. 1895	
Bradford	Frank	Neil	Francis E.	29 Oct. 1900	
Bradford	George W.	Adams	Sarah M., Mrs.	28 Nov. 1902	
Bradford	Robert A.	Robertson	Fannie F.	30 Dec. 1884	
Bradlee	Adelbert S.	Ball	Addie L.	18 Oct. 1890	
Bradlee	Arthur S.	Lukas	Emma M.	19 Oct. 1912	
Bradlee	Arthur S.	Wiseman	Edna O.	18 Apr. 1896	gr: Stephen H. Bradlee, father, gives consent and signs.
Bradlee	Arthur Seawell	Montgomery	Rose Bagley, Mrs.	2 June 1909	
Bradley	A. F.	Bradley	Lydia F.	8 Apr. 1878	
Bradley	Byron B.	Mangis	Lola E.	24 Nov. 1903	br: John W. Mangis, father
Bradley	Henry L.	Ely	Sarah E.	28 July 1885	
Bradley	Hugh	Navins	Mary	18 Sept. 1894	
Bradley	William A.	Smith	Gertrude R.	11 Mar. 1920	
Brady	C. H.	Ross	Mary M.	5 Oct. 1891	
Brady	Howard	Mason	Violet Belle	24 Dec. 1903	
Brady	Jerry F.	Thompson	Josie M.	10 Aug. 1920	
Brady	Thomas M.	Streeter	Emma I.	18 Mar. 1912	gr: Mary M. Brady, mother; br: Nina L. Streeter, mother

Groom		Bride			
Surname	Given Name	Surname	Given Name	Date	Comments
Brady	Thomas M.	Nobles	Pearl E.	20 Aug. 1920	br: Winifred M. Nobles, mother
Brady	William Franklin	Mastrup	Anna Sophia	18 Apr. 1907	
Braga	Joe F.	Dutra	Margarida P.	13 Dec. 1912	
Braga	John	Dambrogia	Mary	8 Jan. 1902	
Braga	Peter	Piezzi	Mary	17 Oct. 1907	
Brain	Herbert Roy	Dillian	Lillian Pearl	2 Aug. 1910	
Brain	Walter Earl	O'Loughlin	Leah Hester	24 Dec. 1909	
Brain	William H.	McFarland	Amelia	3 July 1890	
Brain	William H.	Burgess	Jennie	6 Feb. 1883	
Brainard	W. H.	Bush	Ella M.	21 July 1891	
Brammer	Jochim F.	Greens (?)	Florence (?)	21 Feb. 1883	
Brand	Fenton M.	Bingham	Olga R.	27 Jan. 1914	
Brand	Philip Edward	Delahanty	May Frances	24 Oct. 1908	
Brand	William H.	Lyons	Helen	19 Feb. 1921	
Brandis	William G.	Shortridge	Ethel Mae	31 Dec. 1906	
Brandt	August	Starck	Bertha	7 May 1884	
Brandt	August J.	Mazzucchi	Theresa E.	19 Apr. 1911	br: E. Mazzucchi, parent
Branelenberg	Heinrich	Hasche	Emma M.	26 Aug. 1918	
Branern	William F.	Nelson	Irine Mae	14 Jan. 1911	
Branigan	Charles Floyd	Anderson	Frieda Cecelia	27 July 1910	
Brannan	G. Clark	Krug	Anna Agnes	25 Nov. 1903	
Brannum	Casswell	Priak	Mary Jane, Mrs.	26 Nov. 1902	gr: C. H. Pond witness to his mark
Brannum	Caswell	Linebarger	Marinda, Mrs.	16 Apr. 1908	gr: his mark
Brannum	Leonard B.	Scott	Ethel A.	7 July 1919	
Branson	John	Jacobsen	Dorthea	28 Jan. 1911	
Branstetter	Charles H.	Crow	Charlie Eveline	15 July 1908	
Brantley	Robert L.	Silva	Martha	10 Nov. 1913	
Brassill	James Frederic	Kneller	Emilie Florence	29 Mar. 1906	
Brattain	Arthur Lane	Davis	Edell	2 June 1917	
Braugher	Oscar H.	Sutherland	Ella C.	15 Apr. 1899	requested by W. F. Cowan
Bray	Elisha Jessie	Stevens	Louisa June	9 Apr. 1878	gr: signs with his mark; br: Intha A. Van Buren, mother; Elmer Van Buren, father
Bray	Elyah C.	Urhr	Charla M.	27 Sept. 1884	

Groom		Bride			
Surname	Given Name	Surname	Given Name	Date	Comments
Bray	Frank Jerome	Aldridge	Crystal G.	24 Sept.1904	br: N. T. Aldridge, parent
Bray	Lester F.	Jones	Emma M.	24 Dec. 1911	
Bray	William	Hartman	Hattie	30 May 1891	gr: signed with mark, no witness
Brayer	Geo. H.	Nunes	Mary L.	27 Aug. 1891	
Brayman	Willard V.	Horstmann	Ethel B.	10 Jan. 1918	
Brayton	Leon Conway	Lewis	Mildred Marie	2 Mar. 1914	
Brayton	William H.	Crane	Grace L.	2 July 1904	
Brazil	Anthony	Paula	Maria	3 June 1894	br: Manuel Paula, father, gives consent; witness: Fawkiss? Cain
Brazil	Manuel M.	Matos	Margarete Etelvena	28 Dec. 1901	do not publish until Monday; do not give ages
Breaks	Gent D.	Bryan	Iva May	9 Dec. 1912	
Breeding	Charles	Brune	Anna	29 Aug. 1904	
Breen	John M.	Bohen	Josie	22 Oct. 1907	
Bregal	Manuel S.	Jason	Julia	4 Jan. 1894	gr: signs with an X; br: Joseph Jason, father.
Breiling	Alfred F.	Muller	Louise	14 Oct. 1902	do not publish
Breitenbach	Louis	Fick	Annie S.	17 May 1890	
Brendel	Fred W.	Doran	Mamie J.	14 Oct. 1876	
Brewer	Clyde Clinton	Kendall	Thelma	22 Dec. 1917	
Brewer	Frank F.	Rossi	Louise	6 Nov. 1909	br: Lena Rossi, mother; Louise 18 on 29 May 1910
Brians	Benjamin	Bones	Hattie	7 Sept. 1895	
Brians	Daniel Boone	Pippin	Josie A.	15 July 1879	gr: parents consent given
Brians	James Cameron	Smith	Carrie May	28 May 1910	br: Mrs. Nellie Smith, mother
Brians	John F.	Craig	Henrietta	14 Mar. 1899	
Briard	George H.	Gsobo (?)	Elizabeth	13 Nov. 1878	
Brichetto	Edmund J.	Cassoni	Josephine B.	18 July 1914	
Brick	Joseph V.	Hawkins	Evalyn	2 Oct. 1920	gr: Tony Brick, father; br: R. R. Hawkins, parent
Bridges	Ira T.	Haberman	Gertrude	2 Dec. 1903	
Bridges	Isaac Newton	Wright	Grace Anna	18 Jan. 1904	
Bridgford	Chester Allen	Petray	Laura May	20 Nov. 1906	
Briganti	Angelo	Lei/Sei	Norina	24 Apr. 1920	
Briggs	Albert D.	Thompson	Ione G.	21 Apr. 1917	

Groom		Bride			
Surname	**Given Name**	**Surname**	**Given Name**	**Date**	**Comments**
Briggs	C. A.	Walker	E. L., Mrs.	27 Nov. 1866	
Briggs	E. C.	Suhling	Sophie	24 Nov. 1893	br: her father says she is past 18; Initialled by H. H. Atwater.
Briggs	Edgar W.	Jones	Beulah M.	20 Sept. 1919	
Briggs	Ezra	Hall	Carrie E.	9 Sept. 1916	
Briggs	George S.	Thrift	Laura	26 Feb. 1879	
Briggs	Hanley	Mapes	Leora	5 Aug. 1903	
Briggs	James M.	Keller	Annie	28 Oct. 1901	
Briggs	Lawrence E.	Haynes	Belle	12 June 1918	
Briggs	Paul C.	McClure	Arabelle	2 Nov. 1904	
Briggs	Peter C.	Holler	Elizabeth A.	8 Jan. 1867	
Briggs	Stiles Harlan	Denner	Emily Rose	13 July 1915	
Briggs	William Edward	Denning	California	2 Nov. 1906	
Briggs	William H.	Cooper	Sarah Alice	9 Jan. 1875	witness: John Quincy White
Briggs	William Henry	Owen	Jennie Mabell	29 Nov. 1878	
Brigham	Edward S.	Sparks	Emma L.	28 Oct. 1901	
Brigham	George H., Jr.	McClish	Florence	19 Mar. 1901	
Brighouse	Thomas H.	Heald	Henriette E.	9 Dec. 1890	
Bright	John Farr	Jerome	Theresa	25 Sept. 1903	
Brightenstine	Theodore	Sellers	Annie	5 June 1885	br: James H. Sellars, father
Brikenstock	Evert F.	Hargreaves	Juanita M.	22 Mar. 1920	
Brink	Johannes	Norris	Zona E.	20 June 1914	
Briseno	Ruben C.	Quintero	Annie	9 Oct. 1916	
Brittain	Norris	Mize	Julia	14 Dec. 1895	
Brittian	George McAlpine	Boyd	Viola	18 May 1912	
Brittisigi?	Leo	Bihli	Eliza	11 June 1890	
Britton	Clyde A.	Hulbert	Katherine A.	13 June 1913	
Britton	Leland M.	Underhill	Allene R.	10 Aug. 1920	
Britton	Norris	Catron	Nellie	31 Dec. 1879	
Broaddus	Andrew S.	Ellis	Eva M.	24 Sept. 1892	
Brocco	Emil	Frugoli	Virginia	5 Apr. 1902	br: Orazio Frugoli, parent; W. H. Mobley, witness to his mark
Brockelman	Ernest A.	Moxley	Alta R.	27 Jan. 1921	

Groom		Bride			
Surname	Given Name	Surname	Given Name	Date	Comments
Brockman	Joseph	Brady	Delia	4 Apr. 1865	
Brockmann	Henry	Schicoh (?)	Agnes	15 Aug. 1883	
Brockmann	Henry M.	Menow	Virginia L.	3 Feb. 1915	
Brockowsky	Otto R.	Stein	Nora L.	13 Nov. 1918	
Broder	Lee S.	Nesbitt	Chetanna M.	4 Nov. 1913	
Brodersen	Julius Peter	Kochuke	Margaret Martha	3 Aug. 1917	
Brodie	Louis F.	Belding	Jessica	25 May 1920	
Brody	Sam	Meyer	Doris	18 June 1915	
Bromley	Frank A.	King	May Louisa	11 May 1906	gr: Electa A. Bromley, parent; br: Mary King, mother
Bronnais	Victor	Lafore	Marie	24 Aug. 1910	
Bronson	Harry R.	Wight	Ida M.	19 May 1919	
Bronson	William M.	Tracey	Olive	5 Oct. 1904	
Brooke	Robert	Farmer	Marie G.	9 Nov. 1892	
Brooker	Frank Russell	Gordon	Sarah A.	1 Apr. 1878	
Brooks	Arthur M.	Freshour	Louise M.	12 Nov. 1902	
Brooks	C. E.	Stites	Katheryn I.	25 Apr. 1905	
Brooks	Charles	Hillbrant	Nellie	1 Apr. 1914	gr: Edwin R. Brooks, father; br: Mrs. Ethel Hillbrant, mother
Brooks	Charles W.	Pallady	Bessie	24 Jan. 1902	br: Mrs. S. M. Legg, mother
Brooks	Charles Wesley	McDonald	Mary E.	20 Dec. 1911	
Brooks	Cicero C.	Young	Jennie N.	21 Sept. 1909	br: G. M. Young, parent
Brooks	Elmer E.	Yagemann	Henrietta P.	16 Oct. 1920	
Brooks	George	Miller	Emma	6 Dec. 1899	
Brooks	Henry C.	Runyon	Mary J.	10 June 1884	
Brooks	Henry W.	Bidwell	Antonia P.	11 Oct. 1895	br: S. J. Bidwell, brother and guardian, gives consent and signs.
Brooks	James	Miller	Maud	31 Dec. 1896	br: Ed Miller, father, gives consent and signs
Brooks	James Monroe	Schalchli	Leona	16 Apr. 1915	
Brooks	Joseph F.	Corbett	Hazel M.	21 June 1916	
Brooks	Reginald Charles	Cambra	Mary Roseline	8 May 1906	
Brooks	Silas	Sensebaugh	Rebecca	5 Jan. 1878	
Brooks	Thomas J.	Mordon	Emma S.	12 Nov. 1878	

Groom		Bride			
Surname	Given Name	Surname	Given Name	Date	Comments
Brooks	Walter	Richten	Stella	3 Sept. 1918	
Brooks	Walter	McMahon	Gertrude	18 July 1911	
Brooks	William H.	Zalud	Annie C.	30 June 1898	
Brookshire	Thos. J.	Harris	Margaret A.	15 Jan. 1866	
Broomfield	Byrd	Terry	Annie	29 Sept. 1891	
Brosnahan	Terrance F.	McMahon	Rose	6 May 1897	
Brott	Edward S.	Hockensmith	Mary L.	19 July 1911	
Brovelli	Emilio	Nangeroni	Lettizia	18 Feb. 1911	
Brower	Walter J.	Arfsten	Eva M.	29 Jan. 1916	
Brown	Alenzo Theodore	Drake	Mary Emily	28 Apr. 1877	
Brown	Alfred	Page	Georgiana	27 Apr. 1915	
Brown	Arthur	Dalton	Edna M.	16 Aug. 1918	
Brown	Arthur	Duenwald	Ethyl E.	10 Dec. 1912	
Brown	Ben C.	Howard	Mary Emma	5 June 1918	
Brown	Benjamin F.	Price	Carrie Francis Park	29 May 1917	
Brown	Carl J.	Sherwood	Ivah R.	27 July 1916	
Brown	Charles	Scott	Betsy, Mrs.	25 Apr. 1867	br: colored
Brown	Charles A.	Wise	A. F., Mrs.	2 Jan. 1909	
Brown	Charles A.	McCarthy	Maggie	25 May 1881	
Brown	Charles Alfred	Souza	Anna Clara	6 Nov. 1905	br: Talvania Souza, parent
Brown	Charles D., Jr.	Sharpe	Geneva L.	3 June 1912	
Brown	Charles F.	Sherman	Mary M.	26 Sept. 1892	
Brown	Charles W.	Walds	Jennie	20 Nov. 1903	
Brown	Charley	Maxwell	Ollie V.	12 Aug. 1904	br: Mrs. Nancy L. Jeffers, mother
Brown	Chesney E.	Elphick	Blanche	30 Nov. 1912	
Brown	Chester B.	Von Arx	Emma	27 Dec. 1897	gr: divorced 19 Nov. 1895, Sonoma Co.
Brown	Chester B.	Case	Martha J.	8 Oct. 1890	
Brown	E. W.	Cannon	Julia V.	9 May 1888	
Brown	Earl D.	Copeland	H. Edith	21 June 1913	
Brown	Edgar Allen	Vitonsek	Hazel Peryl	29 June 1920	
Brown	Edward	Martins	Libania Jason	12 Aug. 1905	
Brown	Edward A.	Lockwood	Cora B.	23 Feb. 1892	license requested by Miss Anita Bishop
Brown	Edwin Francis	Downing	Annette Robie	6 June 1908	

Groom		Bride		Date	Comments
Surname	Given Name	Surname	Given Name		
Brown	Frank Cornelius	Sugher	Ida	5 Feb. 1914	
Brown	Frank G.	Wolf	Anna Marie	3 Aug. 1912	
Brown	Frank J.	Bartlett	Ella Lillian	3 Jan. 1910	
Brown	Frank W.	Switzer	Avis V.	14 May 1905	
Brown	Fred H.	Grove	Blanche	22 July 1914	
Brown	George C.	Kellogg	F. E.	5 April (?) 1884	
Brown	George F.	Jensen	Carrie	3 Nov. 1903	
Brown	George G.	Coon	Laura	27 June 1892	
Brown	George L.	Simpson	Edith M.	31 Dec. 1920	
Brown	George W.	Case	Mary E.	10 Dec. 1894	
Brown	H. H.	Bailey	Ethyl A.	9 Oct. 1915	
Brown	Henry B.	Engelund	Marie C.	22 Dec. 1913	
Brown	Henry W.	Teters	Dora G.	24 Feb. 1899	
Brown	Horace E.	Hunkler	Amie L.	13 Nov. 1899	no previous marriage
Brown	Horace Herman	Pons	Bertha	4 Feb. 1914	
Brown	J.	Wright	Angeline	5 May 1866	by her father
Brown	James A. R.	Smith	Hazel M.	12 Mar. 1907	br: Mrs. Luella Smith, mother
Brown	James R.	Gallaway	Ella May	11 Oct. 1918	
Brown	John	Brown	Francis E.	11 Apr. 1899	br: widow
Brown	John	Haltman	Gertrude	12 Aug. 1914	
Brown	John	Whallon	Lielia E.	2 July 1866	
Brown	John McA.	Bullis/Butler?	Mabel Ella	24 Aug. 1891	
Brown	Lawrence Edward	Halverson	Alice Ethelyn, Mrs.	8 June 1906	
Brown	Leo Allyn	Drennan	Hazel Estelle	13 Mar. 1920	
Brown	Lynn R.	Van Vicel	Pauline	8 Sept. 1915	
Brown	M. V.	Butler	Clara L.	5 Nov. 1866	father present & consenting
Brown	Manuel J.	Lockwood	Alice	3 Sept. 1898	no previous marriage
Brown	Marqus	Laughlin	Eliza Jane	30 Dec. 1876	
Brown	Orson Dana	Wilson	Rose Hanhart	21 May 1912	don't publish
Brown	Ralph	Walker	Olive	3 Feb. 1866	
Brown	Raymond E.	Scott	Laura E.	27 May 1899	no previous marriage; requested by Otto O. Scott
Brown	Richard	Stump	Mary C.	19 Nov. 1879	gr: Mrs. Sarah Ward, mother; Joseph Campbell, guardian; Conrad Stump, witness

Groom		Bride			
Surname	Given Name	Surname	Given Name	Date	Comments
Brown	Richard E.	Penn	Caroline L.	27 Dec. 1913	
Brown	Robert	Dabel	Ida	10 Jan. 1895	br: Fred Bell certifies as to age of Dabel.
Brown	Robert Curtis	Brown	Lena May	29 June 1918	
Brown	Robert Henry	Mooney	Mary Ellen	20 Sept. 1898	no previous marriage
Brown	Rudolph M.	Moyer	Carrie S.	10 Sept. 1910	
Brown	Samuel	Scott	Harriett	17 Dec. 1885	
Brown	Thomas Howard	Williams	Carrie	5 Mar. 1878	
Brown	Thomas J.	Hallahan	Elizabeth	14 Oct. 1919	
Brown	Thomas P.	Ridenhour	Emily	13 June 1877	br: Lewis W. & Mary E. Ridenhour, parents
Brown	Thos.	Congleton	Augusta	26 Sept. 1866	
Brown	W. M.	Cox	May M.	18 Mar. 1896	
Brown	William	Bartlett	Clara	11 May 1907	
Brown	William Carl	Farbstein	Anna	2 Aug.1909	
Brown	William E.	Kline	Lena E.	26 Aug. 1902	
Brown	William Herbert	Potter	Charlotte Isabell	1 June 1896	
Brown	William M., Jr.	Trowbridge	Leslie A.	8 Apr. 1905	
Brown	Wilson J.	Olmsted	Helen M.	25 June 1917	
Brown	Wm. M.	Tann	Catharine A.	25 Oct. 1866	
Browne	William Frank	Gaige	Alpha Eunice	9 Mar. 1903	
Browning	Edmond	Beard	Jennie	8 Feb. 1902	
Brownscombe	Travis D.	Thomas	Hazel B.	25 May 1910	
Broyles	Fred H.	Anderson	Anna M.	17 Aug. 1920	
Brubeck	L. S.	DeSart	Florence J.	20 Mar. 1915	
Bruce	Charles L.	Campbell	Jennie L.	2 Oct. 1900	
Bruce	Fred Clarence	Kennedy	Rosa Belle	19 Aug. 1902	br: B. D. Kennedy, parent
Bruce	Willis L.	Harris	Louisa J.	12 July 1888	
Bruce	William	Foster	Caroline	30 Mar. 1916	
Bruch	Calvin C.	Stegmuire	Helen V.	8 Sept. 1919	
Bruck	Ernest	Jenny	Sabilla	19 Oct. 1895	gr: umlatt over the u.
Brucker	Martin	Samuels	Louisa	3 Aug. 1897	license requested by Louisa Samuels; br: Jane Samuels gives consent, her x mark witnessed by R. L. Thompson
Bruening	Charles	Young	Maggie I., Mrs.	12 Aug. 1898	br: divorced in 1895

Groom		Bride		Date	Comments
Surname	Given Name	Surname	Given Name		
Bruer	Fred Matthew	Philpott	Gertrude	24 Nov. 1898	no previous marriage
Brugge	George E.	Maestretti	Dena M.	21 Apr. 1919	
Bruggy	George H. W.	Pool	Mamie	20 Aug. 1891	
Bruhn	Andrew Peter	Bruhn	Mary	28 Apr. 1905	
Bruhn	Nickels	Domenighini	Lettie	29 Aug. 1903	
Brum	Manoel S.	Goulart	Maria E.	25 Sept. 1902	gr: witness to mark M. or W. Simus
Brumbaugh	Raymond	Pedrotti	Estella Belle	18 Sept. 1906	
Brumfield	Chas. A.	Capell	Minnie O.	2 Nov. 1885	
Brundige	A. L.	Daffort	Marie	13 June 1914	
Bruner	Clement M.	McWilliams	Edith T.	29 Oct. 1890	
Bruner	Herman D.	Gates	Leonora V.	3 Dec. 1894	license requested by D. Bruner.
Brunh	Ernest Roy	Magnani	Paulina Zita	25 Mar.1910	not signed by br or gr
Brunings	John H.	Benson	Mabel E.	3 Apr. 1917	
Brunings	John H., Jr.	Barnard	Panchita C.	7 Aug. 1920	
Brunk	Hezakiah	Stevens	I. A., Mrs.	29 Mar. 1865	
Brunk	Hugh Dennis	Benson	Velma Lee	10 Aug. 1916	
Brunner	Robert	Stocker	Dora	3 Nov. 1897	no previous marriage
Brunning	John H.	Marshall	Effie L.	20 Feb. 1907	
Bruns	John Henrich Henry	Semler	Marie Phillipine	26 Aug. 1913	
Bruns	Richard F. C.	Lucas	Edna W.	13 May 1917	
Brunskill	Ralph W.	Parson	Sarah Elizabeth	12 Feb. 1904	br: Mrs. Clara J. Seaman, mother
Brunson	Frank L.	Hall	Florence L.	26 Sept. 1908	
Brusa	Carlos	Frati	Celia	8 Aug. 1893	
Brusco	Henry D.	Erno	Winifred	25 June 1919	
Brush	Charlie W.	Downing	Annie M.	16 June 1879	gr: D. C. Brush, father; br: Mrs. Fannie Downing, mother
Brush	Daniel	Franceski	Nellie	4 Nov. 1907	
Brush	Frank A.	Swain	Lena G.	17 Dec. 1888	
Brush	Fred W.	Cheeks	Lena A.	15 Dec. 1892	
Brush	Samuel	Gobetti	Kate	16 Mar. 1899	
Brush	Wm. T.	Walker	Lucy	13 June 1866	
Bryan	Frederick J.	Freeman	Lulu	19 Mar. 1890	
Bryan	Joseph	Sodergren	Hilda	4 Mar. 1907	

Groom		Bride			
Surname	Given Name	Surname	Given Name	Date	Comments
Bryan	Thomas Welsh	Conniff	Mary Ellen	8 Feb. 1904	
Bryan	William F.	Howells	Jessie	23 Nov. 1901	
Bryan (?)	John Leo	Gustafson	Ellen	8 Sept. 1908	
Bryant	Abner	Harrington	Hattie A.	9 Nov. 1882	
Bryant	Albert James	Treehan	Catherine R.	14 July 1888	
Bryant	Allen	Mynatt	Bettie, Mrs.	14 July 1898	neither party divorced within one year
Bryant	George E.	Armeau	Elisabeth Anne	10 Nov. 1891	
Bryant	George Gilbert	Zuur	Gustine Helen	29 Oct. 1910	
Bryant	Hubert	Dornin	Alice	11 Aug. 1896	
Bryant	Jay	Sinclair	Elizabeth M.	10 Apr. 1916	
Bryant	John I.	Pritchett	Elenor E.		filed between 15 and 17 Nov. 1883
Bryant	John Kenneth	Dexter	Alice B.	1 Mar. 1915	
Bryant	William Henry	Hendricks	Susan E.	19 July 1879	
Buchan	James E.	Poppe	Catherine	24 Aug. 1881	
Buchanan	Frank T.	Tomblinson	Myrtle	28 Nov. 1911	
Buchanan	James A.	Loosley	Bonnis	9 Apr. 1921	
Buchanan	John A.	Nieman	Laura B.	28 Aug. 1920	
Bucher	Conrad	Brien	Laura	16 Nov. 1912	
Buchi	John Henry	Schwarting	Dorothe Magarethe	29 June 1916	
Buchignani	Rizieri	Sbragia	Fanny	11 May 1912	
Buchignani	Victor	Georgi	Eva V.	5 June 1919	br: Giacomo Georgi, mother
Buck	Charles	Ashley	Louisa R.	23 Oct. 1876	
Buckingham	Edwin B.	Parriott	Lois I.	25 July 1920	
Buckingham	T. H.	Holmes	Minnie A.	15 July 1882	br: Walter H. Holmes, father
Buckle	John	Owen	Mary	15 Nov. 1882	
Buckley	Dennis	Staeubli	Bertha	24 June 1914	
Buckmaster	Rlando	Fowler	Gladys M.	22 Nov. 1915	gr: C. F. Buckmaster, parent
Bucknell	Bert Monroe	Levreau	Hattie La Dow	31 Dec. 1917	
Bucknell	Roy	Armstrong	Mabel F.	15 Mar. 1910	
Buckner	E. L.	O'Brien	Ellen	29 Apr. 1913	
Buckner	Zachariah E.	Rector	Zerah	22 Aug. 1891	
Budde	Frederic/Fritz	Kohl	Charlotte	22 Jan. 1878	
Buechler	John	Parks	Clara Adele	17 Sept. 1918	

Groom		Bride		Date	Comments
Surname	Given Name	Surname	Given Name		
Buechler	Lewis	Denehy	Helen	19 Sept. 1910	
Buegge	Harry	Wendte	Felicitas E.	23 June 1911	
Buell	Park A.	Moore	Essie B.	24 Oct. 1919	gr: Lillian Buell, mother
Buell	Robert	Wyatt	Catherine	10 Mar. 1898	
Buffett	Chas. C.	McCray	Amanda	20 Feb. 1885	
Bufford	Lawrence	Warboys	Irene	3 Oct. 1911	
Bufton	Harvey M.	Davis	Marion	18 Mar. 1912	
Bufton	William Arthur	King	Martha Winifred	3 Jan. 1913	
Bugbee	Bert	Von Grafen	Nellie	4 Sept. 1901	
Bugbee	Troby E.	DeBord	Nevada	16 Aug. 1898	br: Mrs. E. A. DeBord, mother; no previous marriage
Buger	Henry Antes	Bruning	Natalie Lucile	2 July 1920	
Buher	Florentin	Miller	Emma	11 Sept. 1907	
Buhs	Henry F.	Hall	Emily H.	21 July 1919	
Buisson	Eugene	Richards	Hannah D.	22 Nov. 1916	
Buleis	Wesley	Wassman	Ida	8 Sept. 1906	
Bullock	Lewis M.	Lambert	Clara V.	26 Apr. 1892	
Bulotti	Alexio	Bulotti	Mary	7 Jan. 1886	
Bulotti	Frederick	Small	Catherine Norine	15 Aug. 1904	
Bulotti	Lee	Bulotti	Gina	29 Jan. 1891	
Bumbaugh	Erle Leroy	Cofer	Lydia May	16 Oct. 1903	
Bunch	John B.	Abshire	Alice	29 July 1881	
Bundesen	Karl	Kolkmeyer	Freda C.	3 Aug. 1917	
Bundesen	Martin	Riewerts	Blanche L.	30 July 1920	
Bundesen	Martin	Peterson	Anna	21 Feb. 1888	
Bundesen	Martin	Bahr	Sophie	21 Oct. 1907	
Bundesen	William	Johnson	Nan	29 Apr. 1916	
Bundesen	William Frederick	Wittkowski	Christine Janette	2 Dec. 1912	
Bundschu	Ralph M.	Geary	Jean L.	27 Feb. 1915	
Bundy	Pete D.	Liebscher	Lucy B.	9 June 1919	
Bunker	Frank	Kameyer	Josie A.	29 July 1914	
Bunney	Alexander, Jr.	Hyde	Cora Lee	24 Dec. 1900	
Burbank	David B.	Burgess	Ella	14 July 1897	gr: Widower

Groom		Bride			
Surname	**Given Name**	**Surname**	**Given Name**	**Date**	**Comments**
Burch	George Alexander	McGregor	Loella Rea	22 June 1893	
Burch	George M.	Chamley	Charlotte E.	22 Nov. 1900	
Burchard	Karl Sieden	Thomsen	Alma Erna (?)	8 Dec. 1917	
Burden	William D.	Grainger	S. Margery	29 June 1897	
Burdette	Charles O.	Chaffee	Maud E.	26 Dec. 1911	
Burdick	O. U.	Pyle	Anna	17 Apr. 1913	
Burdick	Fred E.	Bailey	Emily E.	30 May 1913	
Burger	Calvin	Van Buren	Stella	16 Mar. 1897	br: E. Van Buren, parent, gives consent and signs; gr: C. H. Burger, parent, gives consent and signs
Burgess	Alauson T.	Yeager	Susie	7 Dec. 1901	
Burgess	Edward Homer	Silverthorn	Martha Jane	6 Jan. 1892	
Burgess	James F.	Peter	Jesserah	4 Oct. 1899	gr: he is widower
Burgess	Loiuis L.	Waldorf	Maude, Mrs.	18 Jan. 1914	
Burgett	William	Walker	Elizabeth H.	25 Mar. 1878	
Burghard	G. F.	Valenzuela	Mary	12 Aug. 1884	
Burghardt	Frank A.	Hollenbeck	Nella E.	12 July 1917	
Burginger	John Frank	Weeks	Laura Jane	6 Apr. 1895	
Burk	John C.	Osbam	Susan A.	15 Mar. 1878	requested by David M. Clark; br: consent of her guardian
Burke	Abner L.	Mangis	Nora E.	17 Nov. 1894	
Burke	Benjamin L.	Cotrell	Minnie E.	7 Jan. 1902	
Burke	Claude E.	McCappin	Ruth Olive	30 Dec. 1914	br: Lavina E. McCappin, mother
Burke	Edmund J.	Drake	Edith Martha	16 Sept. 1916	
Burke	James G.	Stump	Margaret A.	13 Mar. 1920	
Burke	John H.	Johnston	Jennie M.	26 Mar. 1902	
Burke	Joseph	Williams	Etta C., Mrs.	3 Jan. 1903	br: widow
Burke	Leo A.	Forster	Lulu L.	16 Sept. 1908	
Burke	Nevel Ross	Shriver	Martha Ann	17 Mar. 1919	
Burke	Sylvester	Christie	Mabel F.	24 Mar. 1909	
Burke	Walter A.	Burke	Lillian M.	12 Aug. 1908	
Burke	Walter A.	Burne	Mary A.	30 Oct. 1893	license requested by L. L. Jewett
Burling	Geo. W.	Holland	Bella	18 Dec. 1883	

Groom		Bride		Date	Comments
Surname	Given Name	Surname	Given Name		
Burling	William B.	Blake	Minerva	2 Oct. 1903	
Burlingam	Raleigh W.	Cornelius	Elizabeth L.	22 Jan. 1921	
Burlingame	Claude	Appleton	Carrie S.	28 June 1893	
Burmann	Adolf	Schultz	Marie	12 Jan. 1891	
Burmeister	Charles H.	Stevens	Intha May	10 June 1909	br: John B. Stevens, father
Burmester	Charles F. D.	Benedetti	Amalia Rosa	9 Nov. 1904	
Burnett	A. J.	World	Dolley	14 May 1887	
Burnett	Horace Malcohm	Roessle	Stella W.	10 Dec. 1906	
Burnett	Thomas B.	Cook	Jennie	6 Apr. 1886	handwritten
Burnett	William	Reid	Alice	24 Nov. 1894	
Burnham	A. E., Jr.	Smith	Annie E.	14 June 1913	
Burnham	Leslie J.	Clayman	Margaret McI.	10 May 1920	
Burns	E. F.	Donahue	May	25 Jan. 1894	
Burns	Eugene	Clairy (?)	Anna	3 Sept. 1883	
Burns	Eugene L.	Snow	Edna N.	25 Aug. 1915	
Burns	Harry David	Gill	Jennie, Mrs.	22 Nov. 1906	
Burns	James F.	Cereghino	Nellie D.	16 Sept. 1911	
Burns	Jas.	Hendren	Lizzie	7 Nov. 1892	
Burns	John M.	Macomber	Pearl A.	11 Oct. 1899	gr: divorced more than one year
Burns	John T.	Donahue	Georgia	5 Jan. 1893	
Burns	Robert A.	Dollar	Mary E.	10 Apr. 1901	
Burns	Robt. W.	McGah	Mary E.		filed between 9 and 14 Nov. 1882
Burr	Robert L.	Lawrence	Mabel M.	6 July 1895	
Burrel	Wesley Jay	Sparks	Mattie Belle	16 Oct. 1895	
Burrier	Edgar V.	Cambra	Mae A.	24 Dec. 1912	
Burris	Luther W.	Mathews	Laura	19 Sept. 1882	requested by L. W. Burris
Burris	Shirley David	Espey	Evelyn Blanche	11 Dec. 1906	
Burroughs	David	Solomon	Hattie C.	1 Dec. 1893	
Burroughs	John	Hayden	Eva	11 Apr. 1894	
Burrows	Robt. K.	Hubbard	Nancy K.	4 Oct. 1865	
Burs	Henry S.	Leland	Maude	24 Oct. 1910	
Burt	Charles Arthur	Prince	Helen M.	9 Dec. 1905	
Burt	Roy J.	Badger	Blanche	22 Dec. 1902	br:Douglas Badger, father; br: Lewis S. Burt, parent

Groom		Bride			
Surname	Given Name	Surname	Given Name	Date	Comments
Burtchaell	George C.	Ward	Henrietta	30 Jan. 1901	
Burtchall	Walter L.	Marvin	Evalyne Lottie	1 July 1904	br: requested license
Burtner	Jesse H.	Armbruster	Marie W.	19 Oct. 1910	
Burtnett	Charles Gordon	Nutter	Josephine Hattie	2 July 1878	br: J. R.? Nutter, father
Burton	Francis A.	Overton	Martha Jane Mildred	12 Oct. 1889	
Burton	George M.	Ponyferrie	Madeline	9 Nov. 1914	
Burton	George Walter	Marango	Verlie Elden	5 June 1918	br:Theresa Snider, mother
Burton	John C.	Smith	Elva Sirena	23 Dec. 1905	
Burton	Oliver F.	Duncan	Susan A.	20 Dec. 1913	
Bury	John F.	Burroughs	Edith A.	16 Aug. 1910	
Bury	Joseph L.	Pasage	Clare	12 Feb. 1914	
Bury	William G.	Goyheneix	Helen M.	31 Aug. 1918	
Bush	Eli F.	Cullum	Alice M.	13 May 1884	
Bush	Giles H.	Ruffner (?)	Anna		filed between 10 and 19 Apr. 1884
Bush	Joe	Calestini	Freida E.	30 May 1919	
Bush	Joe	Heiss	Henrietta	4 Mar. 1920	
Bush	William H.	Phippen	Mary A.	10 Feb. 1921	
Bush	William Herbert	Hunt	Pearl	1 Oct. 1907	
Bush	William P.	Sholes	Pearl J.	20 Jan. 1882	
Busher	Walter H.	Gage	Iva L.	12 Nov. 1913	
Bushnell	Edwin R.	Smith	M.	9 Feb. 1866	
Bushnell	John D.	Norton	Bessie, Mrs.	3 Dec. 1903	
Bushnell	John D.	Scales	Anna	21 Dec. 1877	
Bussman	Frank	Edgewood	Margaret	14 Sept. 1911	
Bussman	Frederick	Fehrensen	Susie Elizabeth	4 Sept. 1915	
Bussman	Peter William	Camp	Eva D.	13 May 1891	
Bussman	William G.	Gibson	Nona M.	2 Sept. 1914	gr: Mrs. Eva D. Bussman, mother
Butchen	W. P.	Small	Nettie V.	22 Dec. 1884	
Butcher	Albert W.	Morrison	Junietta	24 Apr. 1890	
Butcher	Charles Walter	Zweifel	Lulu Rosa	1 Nov. 1909	
Butenop	Wilhelm	Ehlers	Margaretta	28 Feb. 1896	
Butin	Charles J.	Schaumberg	Emma J.	15 Oct. 1896	

Groom		Bride		Date	Comments
Surname	Given Name	Surname	Given Name		
Butler	A. B.	Middleton	Tilly	8 Feb. 1882	
Butler	A. M.	Cox	Anna	3 Nov. 1884	
Butler	Carl Guy	Remer	Frances Effie	15 Nov. 1906	
Butler	Carl Guy	Smith	Ruth Evelyn	2 Oct. 1911	
Butler	Charles H.	Miller	Mary E.	12 Dec. 1887	
Butler	Clyde A.	Gregson	Juanita C.	29 Nov. 1919	br: John N. Gregson, father
Butler	Edmund J.	O' Sullivan	Josephine	18 May 1916	
Butler	Edward H.	Burns	Margaret	23 Oct. 1900	
Butler	H. G.	Taylor	Vivian	3 June 1913	
Butler	Harry Alfred	Rodgers	Mary Ann	2 May 1895	both bride ande groom sign.
Butler	James T.	Murphy	Helen E.	29 Aug. 1902	
Butler	Jesse L.	Schultz	Bertha	11 Dec. 1908	
Butler	John Samuel	Durham	Elizabeth	27 July 1878	
Butler	John Walter	Tullar	Diadama Helen	1 May 1906	
Butler	Osmand W.	Robertson	Myrtle	30 Nov. 1901	gr: T. J. & A. E. Butler, parents
Butler	Samuel Reed	Luebberke	Clara F.	25 Aug. 1906	
Butler	Thomas B.	Wilson	Susan Emily	11 Oct. 1884	
Butler	Thomas B.	Gregsen	Eliza J.	27 Nov. 1876	
Butler	Thomas I.	Page	Yuma L.	5 Jan. 1917	
Butler	Vernon Miller	Boyd	Dorothy Juanita	21 Aug. 1914	br: Ella Boyd, mother
Butler	Willie	De Bolt	Kate	24 Oct. 1903	
Butler	Wm. M.	Hooten	Lillian	18 July 1893	
Butt	George A.	Ball	Mary M.	6 June 1890	gr: Alfred Butt, father, requested license
Butterworth	Thomas C.	Davis	Margaret L.	18 July 1900	
Buttler	Wilmer	Smith	Georgia C.	17 Nov. 1917	
Buttner	Joseph F.	Pickrell	Cordie M.	11 Feb. 1901	
Button	Eugene R.	Mendenhall	Florence	28 May 1907	
Button	Floyd Walter	Kenworthy	Vera	7 Mar. 1914	
Button	H. H.	Pool	Eva A.	7 Dec. 1886	
Button	Horace H.	Pattcson	Adeline G.	7 Aug. 1901	
Button	Ray E.	Baker	Julia J.	5 Dec. 1916	
Butts	Alfred	Martin	Nellie	3 July 1913	
Butts	Charles M.	Greening	Emma R.	25 June 1886	gr: D. C. Butts, father

Groom		Bride			
Surname	Given Name	Surname	Given Name	Date	Comments
Butts	Claude	Jackson	Lula	11 Apr. 1910	
Butts	Raymond L.	Hillhouse	Elsie	9 Apr. 1921	
Butts	Robert Samuel	Thompson	Irene Ethel	31 May 1918	
Butts	Thomas J.	Dean	Jeannie	24 Dec. 1892	br: Baltimore crossed out in residence column and replaced by Santa Rosa
Butts	Thomas Jefferson	Robinson	Amoret Malinda	19 Oct. 1877	
Buxton	Ernest Edward	Derrick	Lulu Maude	13 July 1904	
Buxton	Natt	Smith	Camilla G.	5 Nov. 1903	
Buzzell	Albert A.	Philbrooks	Lucinda	11 Sept. 1876	
Buzzi	Joseph L.	Bertossi	Josie	12 May 1919	
Byce	Gideon A.	Scott	Evaline	23 Nov. 1889	
Byce	L. C.	Gray	Lily C.	26 Oct. 1887	
Byce	Malcolm Lyman	Coggeshall	Catherine	22 July 1912	
Byerly	Frank F.	Warner	Mary E.	25 Oct. 1892	
Byers	Judson A.	Ryan	Clara A.	5 Aug. 1903	
Byers	Thomas Homer	Loe	Dorothy E.	7 July 1897	
Byers	William A.	Mitchell	Emma E.	20 Jan. 1896	
Byington	Charles T.	Ryan	Kate C.	22 Aug. 1893	
Byle	Joseph H.	Samuelsen	Elizabeth Marie	13 Feb. 1912	
Byrd	J. L.	Russ	Dora J.	3 Aug. 1889	br: James R. Russ, father
Byrn	George M.	Pohley	Adelaide C.	21 May 1902	
Byrne	James	Johnsen	Nellie M.	16 July 1872 ?	br: consent of only parent
Byrne	Malachy L.	Hibbitts	Amelia Francis	16 June 1893	
Byrne	Marshal H.	Skaggs	Emma L.	15 Nov. 1877	M. A. & M. F. Wilson, Windsor, give consent
Byrne	William W.	Jelinski	Mary	31 May 1919	
Byron	Chester	Hale	Mabel	4 May 1907	
Cabarrubia	Frank	Watts	May	3 Nov. 1902	
Cabeceira	Henry J.	Schlicker	Ida Bertha	28 Sept. 1906	
Cabeleira	Antonio Silveira	Nunes	Lucy	13 Apr. 1896	br: mother, Emily Nunes gives consent and signs with x, mark witnessed by H H Atwater
Cabral	Fernando	Gomez	Agnes R.	27 Dec. 1912	gr: W. E. Saunders, R. F. Crawford, Agnes R. Gomez, witnesses to his mark
Cadd	Edwin	Galloway	Charlotte	20 May 1904	

Groom		Bride			
Surname	Given Name	Surname	Given Name	Date	Comments
Cadd	Thomas	Enzenauer	Annie	28 Dec. 1896	
Cade	H. C.	Smith	May E., Mrs.	23 July 1879	
Cader	Israel	Lehman	Lilian H.	24 June 1920	
Cadra (?)	Emil C.	Patten	Mary	15 Nov. 1883	
Cahill	James Felix	Wescoatt	Alice Clare	7 Feb. 1906	
Cahill	James Morden	McCann	Eva Theresa	29 Apr. 1905	
Cailleaud	Henry, Jr.	Gaye	Adele	10 Dec. 1910	
Cain	Walter	Hahn	Lena	19 May 1920	
Cake	Charles M.	Williams	Stella Price	23 Nov. 1904	
Cake	Luther B.	Parrott	Elsie E.	4 Dec. 1915	
Calanchini	Emil Phillip	Filippini	Louise Elvezia	24 Apr. 1916	
Calder	Alexander E.	Spotswood	Mary Jane	5 Aug. 1875	
Calderwood	Ambrose	Waterman	Tempy	30 Dec. 1893	
Calderwood	Henry E.	Neil	Bell	17 Aug. 1889	
Caldwell	Edward J.	Shearer	Rena	19 Nov. 1904	
Caldwell	J. G.	Bidwell	Freda M.	30 Dec. 1918	
Caldwell	John Charles	Seely	Martha	23 May 1877	
Caldwell	Samuel T.	Patteson	Mollie D.	4 Aug. 1881	
Caldwell	William Beatty	Oman	Genevieve Ida	24 Apr. 1906	
Cale (?)	Theodore Webster	Partridge	Marion	29 Sept. 1919	
Calhoun	J. W.	Henderson	S. M.	28 June 1865	
Calkins	Charles F.	Hawks	Hazel R.	6 Apr. 1908	
Call	Clyde C.	Medland	Florence F.	3 May 1919	
Call	George B.	Banfield	Ida F.	7 Oct. 1892	
Callahan	Walter H.	Beckner	Lillian E.	4 Feb. 1899	don't publish
Callahan	William Daniel	Finnell	Lurena Hulse	23 Nov. 1906	
Callahan	William H.	Reinhart	Mary J.	17 Dec. 1894	
Callen	S. H.	Bell	Carrie V.	12 Sept. 1887	
Callenberg	Hugo, Jr.	Russell	Cora	16 Apr. 1917	
Calliman	William G.	Lahne	Gerda H.	17 Apr. 1919	
Calzascia	Emilio	Pellascio	Minnie	28 Dec. 1907	
Camarda	Joe	Orlando	Rosa	8 Apr. 1914	
Cambra	Manuel F.	Foyd	Lucy	13 Mar. 1914	

Groom		Bride			
Surname	**Given Name**	**Surname**	**Given Name**	**Date**	**Comments**
Camenzind	Lewis	Yori/Jori	Mary	26 Jan. 1912	
Camerlo	James A.	Anderson	Myrtle	26 Sept. 1912	
Camero	Nathan	Lovejoy	Mary M.	11 Nov. 1890	br: widow
Cameron	Alan F.	Mills	Blanche B.	10 July 1920	
Cameron	Charles Edwin	Enlow	Ada	11 Nov. 1905	
Cameron	Charles L.	Lyttaker	Martha M.	3 July 1893	
Cameron	Donald B.	Morris	Marie L.	31 Dec. 1919	
Cameron	Donald C.	Meacham	Elvira F.	1 Dec. 1892	
Cameron	Fred J.	Barnhardt	Minnie	30 Oct. 1897	no previous marriage
Cameron	George H.	Watson	Mamie	5 Sept. 1916	
Cameron	Henry I.	Squires	Ella, Mrs.	27 Sept. 1899	gr: widower; br: divorced 15 Dec. 1892, Sonoma Co.
Cameron	John Willard	Cladden	Mary Ella	10 Sept. 1883	
Cameron	Russell L.	Murphy	Jennie	16 Feb. 1903	
Cameron	Wallace A.	Welch	Lois L.	18 Sept. 1920	
Camotta	Joe	Donati	Annie	7 Apr. 1910	
Camotta	Laurence	Bartoli	Edith	19 Aug. 1911	
Camozzi	Walter C.	Deal	Dorothy May	19 Apr. 1919	
Campaglia	Domenick	Roux	Anna G.	19 June 1916	
Campana	Joe	Pozzi	Rosalia	17 Sept. 1917	
Campbell	Alexander	Joachim	Bessie	22 Nov. 1906	
Campbell	Arthur B.	Tully	Alice J.	23 Dec. 1920	
Campbell	B. F.	Smith	Essie E.	31 Aug. 1889	
Campbell	Boyd	Martin	Mabel S.	19 Aug. 1908	
Campbell	C. I.	Van Winkle	Lola	25 Apr. 1903	
Campbell	David L.	Richardson	Mabel A.	30 Mar. 1918	
Campbell	Frank	Smith	Mary	8 Nov. 1870	
Campbell	Geo. S.	Adams	Allie	16 Nov. 1880	
Campbell	George	Campbell	Alice	16 Nov. 1914	
Campbell	Harold George	Orr	Marguerite Ellen	11 Dec. 1920	br: S. L. Orr, parent
Campbell	Ira Samuel	Baird	Leona Lovel	24 July 1904	
Campbell	J. Otto	Denham	Ada B.	31 Dec. 1914	
Campbell	James J.	Michaels	Mae A.	11 June 1920	

Groom		Bride		Date	Comments
Surname	Given Name	Surname	Given Name		
Campbell	R. E.	Ruffins (?)	Jessie	31 Jan. 1883	
Campbell	Walter	Jordan	Amy	9 Mar. 1887	
Campbell	Walter G.	Barth	Susie A.	24 Nov. 1886	
Campbell	William A.	Eakin	Mary E.	11 July 1910	
Campbell	William A.	Crickett	Lizzie	23 July 1885	
Campbell	William E.	Rubly	Clara E.	14 Sept. 1900	br: Nancy Jane Rubly, mother; Nettie E. Rubly, witness
Campbell	Wm.	Ayers	Martha J.	27 June 1867	consent step-father
Campi	Lorenzo	Roncalli	Annie	7 May 1896	
Campigli	Albert E.	Mack	Florine	14 Dec. 1906	
Campigli	Albert E.	Steele	Effie M.	26 Nov. 1902	
Campigli	Frank Charles	Koster	Anna D.	8 July 1898	no previous marriage
Campion	George W.	Wallis	Lena, Mrs.	26 Oct. 1901	
Campion	James	Cunningham	Lillie A., Mrs.	3 Sept. 1894	
Campion	Thomas	Samuels	Jennie	6 Dec. 1894	br: Mrs. Jane Samuels consents and her x mark is witnessed by A. S. Luce.
Campion	Thomas	Harris	Eunice Caroline	5 Feb. 1910	
Campodonica	Adolpho P.	Pancrazi	Josephine Florence	18 Nov. 1916	
Camron	John T.	Morton	Carrie	4 Aug. 1888	gr: Margret Quin, mother; father dead
Canada	Alonzo M.	Josephs	Emily H.	1 Jan. 1918	
Canello	Henry G.	Howell	Margaret Lent	13 Dec. 1875	br: L. V. H. Howell, parent; Lowry & Wightman, Commission Merchants, S. F.
Canepa	Ben	Tunzi	Lily B.	23 Oct. 1912	
Canessa	Attilo	Paladini	Amelia	5 May 1906	
Canevara	Don A.	Cooper	Minnie L.	21 June 1916	
Canevari	Adolph	Scaroni	Romilda	15 July 1919	
Canevari	John J.	Spooncer	Letha P.	22 Mar. 1919	
Canevascini	S. J.	McFarland	Margaret	22 June 1889	
Canficld	Albert	Baker	Matilda	17 Mar. 1866	
Cannell	Fletcher	Smalley	Jessic	4 Nov. 1909	
Canney	Edward Phillip	Shane	Mary Gertrude	19 Jan. 1916	
Cannon	Calvin W.	Jensen	Mary	21 Aug. 1912	br: Nels & Ellavena Jensen, parents
Cannon	Chester G.	Marsh	Dora E.	9 Dec. 1919	gr: L. L. Cannon, parent

Groom		Bride			
Surname	Given Name	Surname	Given Name	Date	Comments
Cannon	Earl	Cook	Illiene	29 Dec. 1915	br: L. L. Cannon, parent
Cannon	James P.	Cocknill (?)	Ida J.	6 July 1881	
Cannon	Jerome	Gist	Meda	15 Nov. 1884	br: William Gist, father
Cannon	L. L.	Clark	Nettie	18 Aug. 1886	
Cannon	Louis	Ducker	Mary	14 Dec. 1907	gr: L. L. Cannon, parent
Cannon	R. D.	Bishop	May M.	31 Dec. 1885	
Canobbio	Ferdinando	Toroni (?)	Edith	2 Dec. 1899	no previous marriage
Canobbio	Serafino	Bacigalupi	Lena	31 Mar. 1900	
Cantel	Eugene	Fritsch	Mary Ealie	1 Oct. 1907	
Cantel	Eugene Jean Baptista	Graham	Ida	4 Apr. 1885	
Cantoni	Romeo	Barbarin	Augustine	25 Feb. 1909	
Cantor	Nathan	Bauer	Jennie	15 July 1920	
Cantrell	Joe W.	Steeter	Floretta N.	25 June 1919	
Cantwell	William L.	Niblett	Metta B.	21 Feb. 1911	
Capell	Chas. W.	Johnson	Elizabeth E.	15 Aug. 1885	
Capella	James	Nelson	M. M., Mrs.	25 Feb. 1903	
Capella	James C.	Martignoni	Rosa	24 Jan. 1905	
Capitani	Antonio	Pedrini	Clementina	2 Feb. 1912	
Capitani	Michele	Maroni	Mary	27 July 1914	
Capps	John W.	Holder	Clara M.	1 July 1903	
Capps	Lennie C.	Rubly	Nettie E.	14 Sept. 1900	br: Nancy Jane Rubly, mother; Clara Rubly, witness
Capucetti	L. A.	Gianini	Marie	10 July 1890	
Capucetti	Frank Charles	Pedrotti	Beatrice Margaret	25 Nov. 1913	
Carah	J. H.	Bavricklow	Emma Alice		filed between 6 and 10 September 1883
Carden	Arthur G.	Waugh	Lenna M.	2 Mar. 1920	
Carden	William Joseph	Newman	Marguerite F.	15 July 1905	br: Mrs. N. H. Newman, mother, gives consent
Cardinet	Edward H.	Hegler	Myrtlye	18 Feb.1901	
Cardinet	Ernest H.	Harris	Elva	21 Apr. 1897	
Cardoza	John H.	Burnett	Leonora	8 Oct. 1909	
Cardoza	Joseph S.	Cerini	Nora A.	23 Apr. 1918	
Cardoza	Manuel	Holtslander	Lizzie	8 Feb. 1897	signed by both br and gr

Groom		Bride		Date	Comments
Surname	Given Name	Surname	Given Name		
Cardoza	Thomas	Cardoza	Virginia	31 Jan. 1913	
Cardozo	Joseph S.	Pereira	Clara	16 Dec. 1893	br: Libano Pereira, father, gives consent; Joseph Wedge, witness
Caretto	Pete	Marcucci	Ida	25 Sept. 1911	
Carey	Albert Brock	Somerville	Margaret Rodgers	1 May 1906	
Carey	Charles Edward	Patterson	Mattie A.	27 Aug. 1914	
Carey	Edward J.	Miller	Hattie E.	3 Jan. 1905	
Carey	John	Sabini	Mary	12 Apr. 1912	
Carey	William F.	McCarren	Rita H.	2 July 1919	
Cargile	Charles W.	Kennedy	Rosa M.	25 Nov. 1892	
Cargile	James L.	Shuler	Blanche R.	19 Nov. 1894	br: Mr. and Mrs. George Shuler give consent and sign.
Carico	John W., Dr.	Hill	Effie	27 Dec. 1904	
Carillo	Frank	Enright	Margaret	21 Sept. 1879	br: Denis Enright, parent
Carillo	Joseph	Olbrich	Lou F.	11 May 1885	
Carithers	David N.	Carithers	Mary E.	13 Aug. 1891	
Carithers	William R.	Ewing	Ida B.	9 Sept. 1893	
Carl	William T.	Higgins	Carnelia, Mrs.	11 Mar. 1896	
Carleton	Calvin W.	Dutton	Ada W.	15 Oct. 1889	license requested by H. H. Churchill
Carleton	John M.	Stout	Mary Ellen	11 July 1881	br: J. B. Stout, father; Fishermans Bay, Sonoma
Carlisle	Herbert L.	McLaren	Eugenie	27 Sept. 1910	
Carlsen	Thorval T.	Harrison	Emma Burlington	17 Aug. 1917	
Carlson	Gust	Belin	Agnes	15 Apr. 1913	
Carlton	Thomas	Smith	Sonora	27 Mar. 1867	order from mother
Carman	Cecil C.	Lamb	Laura B.	2 Feb. 1921	
Carman	Harry Vanoy	Blessing	Josephine	19 Oct. 1910	
Carmana	Frederick A.	Johnson	Carinne E.	6 Apr. 1918	
Carmody	Chester Arthur	Kennedy	Ruby Gwendoline	17 Nov. 1909	
Carmody	Fred L.	Kennedy	Nellie	1 Oct. 1913	
Carmody	Thos. B.	Griffin	Annie	14 Feb. 1884	
Carner	Ohmer E.	Roelle	Anna F.	24 July 1920	
Carniglia	Charles A.	Bertoni	Rose I.	28 Mar. 1921	

Groom		Bride			
Surname	**Given Name**	**Surname**	**Given Name**	**Date**	**Comments**
Carothers	John W.	Smith	Lillian C.	10 Oct. 1885	
Carpenter	Charles Thomas	Amstael	Gina Matildos	15 June 1914	
Carpenter	Clair W.	Trondsen	Ruth	15 Apr. 1916	
Carpenter	Jay W.	Stump (?)	Susie	24 Nov. 1919	
Carpenter	Laurence	Northrop	Lenna May	14 Sept. 1914	
Carpenter	Perl R.	Williams	Alice L.	15 Apr. 1907	
Carpenter	S. E.	Monahan	Mamie L.	15 Feb. 1887	
Carr	Arthur C.	Kent	Winifred L.	19 June 1918	
Carr	Charles F.	Brain	Alice P.	23 June 1886	
Carr	Elgin Otto	Nielson	Helen Ione	18 Oct. 1919	
Carr	George David	Davis	Alice	28 Sept. 1915	
Carr	Mark, Jr.	Johnson	Mamie	30 Oct. 1883	
Carr	T. M.	Allaway	Sarah E. (?)	1 May 1880	
Carr	William	Cole	Beatrice	19 Sept. 1913	
Carrico	Charles E.	Anderson	Botella	18 Dec. 1918	
Carrie	Henry C.	Taylor	Jennie E.	17 Dec. 1892	
Carrier (?)	Fred J.	Partlow	Loella M.	23 Mar. 1921	
Carriger	I. C.	Carriger	Emma	18 Mar. 1879	
Carriger	William W.	O'Brien	Katie C.	11 Apr. 1891	
Carrilla	Cassie	Salies	Annie	24 Apr. 1915	
Carrillo	Abraham	Cook	Lydia M.	5 Mar. 1892	br: Louisa Cook, mother
Carrillo	Albert Frank	Enright	Margaret	22 Sept. 1879	br: consent of father
Carrillo	Frank Joseph	Thompson	Mary E.	25 Jan. 1877	gr:Tony & Mary Carrillo, parents
Carrillo	Manuel	Meyer	Elizabeth	18 Dec. 1894	
Carrillo	Paul Abraham	Carrillo	Jennie Rose	11 Sept. 1918	
Carrington	Bartine	Abeel	Lola Elizabeth	26 Apr. 1905	
Carrington	Charles N.	Patterson	Clara	20 Nov. 1890	
Carrington	George	Lamer	Annie, Mrs.	30 Aug. 1902	license requested by Chs. N. Carrington for his son
Carrington	Homer Bennett	Haynie (?)	Annie	21 Feb. 1910	
Carrington	Joseph H.	Gardner	Sarah Cornelia, Mrs.	22 Dec. 1896	
Carrington	Olo Robert	Taylor	Lela Marjorie	6 July 1918	

Groom		Bride			
Surname	Given Name	Surname	Given Name	Date	Comments
Carroll	James P.	Carvey	Mary	4 Nov. 1899	no previous marriage
Carroll	Wm. F.	Woodson	Leona Eleanor	5 Feb. 1907	
Carson	Fred	Isaacs	Myrtle	25 Feb. 1901	
Carstensen	Charlie R.	Geils	Elsie May	12 Sept. 1916	
Carston	Godfrey M.	Jacobs	Flora B.	22 Sept. 1919	
Carter	A. E.	Hitchcock	Lizzie B.	10 Apr. 1894	gr: Mrs. L. W. Carter gives consent and signs and also requests license.
Carter	Albert	Marmori	Katie	1 Oct. 1918	
Carter	Andrew Jackson	Wilson	Mary Mitchell	13 May 1905	
Carter	C. Gilbert	Brodie	Mabel Gray	9 July 1907	
Carter	Geo. W.	Switzer	A. E.	27 Mar. 1865	
Carter	Grant	Snow	Thelma Fay	24 Mar. 1916	br: W. H. Snow, parent
Carter	Harvey H.	Rimmer	Mae	19 Feb. 1921	
Carter	Herbert Eaton	Thorne	Grace G.	20 July 1910	
Carter	Lawrence J.	Ogilvie	Mable L.	8 Sept. 1916	
Carter	Oliver C.	Cathcart	Mary	7 Dec. 1903	
Carter	Raymond	Holcomb	Daisy	5 May 1908	
Carter	Robert L.	Monroe	Dora B.	16 Dec. 1916	
Carter	William A.	Murphy	Florence M.	23 May 1914	
Carter	James W.	Peterson	Hettie	3 Oct. 1894	
Cartwright	Aubrey Badger	Bjornskob	Nicolina Christina	15 Aug. 1906	
Cartwright	Frank	Englebright	Eva	15 May 1901	
Cartwright	George W.	Hembree	Mattie L.	8 June 1901	
Carvalho	J. P.	Costa	Maria L.	2 Nov. 1912	
Carvalho	Joaquin P.	Green	Filomena	11 Jan. 1890	br: Manuel Green, father
Carvalho	Joseph	Gardner	Geneveve	18 June 1908	
Carvey	Dennis	Jones	Mabel	10 Nov. 1900	
Casaday	Fred W.	Renshaw	Myrtle M.	16 Nov. 1902	
Casarotti	Americo E.	Garzoli	Clara Irene	3 Sept. 1909	
Casassa	Dominic, Jr.	Simoncini	Julia	25 Jan. 1913	br: Mabel Simoncini, mother
Casassa	Frank A. J.	Lyttaker	Lenora	29 Sept. 1896	not to be published.
Casassa	Louis	Adams	Pearl	15 June 1911	
Casazza	Ricardo	Ricci	Ottavia	9 Apr. 1921	

Groom		Bride			
Surname	Given Name	Surname	Given Name	Date	Comments
Cascardozo	Frank	Silva	Laura	19 Jan. 1889	br: John M. (stepfathr) & Mary M. Perry
Case	Benjamin B.	Nowlin	Margaret A.	30 Oct. 1911	
Case	Benjamin Bascom	Norton	Philinda	29 Dec. 1905	
Case	Drury G.	Thompson	May I.	16 Oct. 1888	
Case	J. W.	Lockley	Susie	22 May 1875	gr: J. M. Case, parent, Denver, CO
Case	John Wyatt	Lockley	Susie E.	29 June 1875	
Case	Wm. E.	Page	Sarah Jane	9 June 1906	
Caseres	Albert H.	Kricke	Ernestena	21 Apr. 1900	
Caseres	J. O.	Williams	Mary R. M.	1 Oct. 1886	
Caseri	Arthur	Benedetti	Agnes	15 Dec. 1906	
Caseri	Robert A.	Tunzi	Emma M.	31 May 1916	
Casey	Edward C.	Hunt	Anna L.	27 Sept. 1881	br: Chas. Hunt, father, Cloverdale
Casey	John	Murray	Mary	13 Nov. 1907	
Casey	Thurman G.	Bord	Dixie O.	14 Sept. 1915	
Cash	O. P.	Hopkins	Mary E., Mrs.	26 June 1893	br: widow
Casini	Neibo	Foresti	Mollie A.	20 Feb. 1911	
Cassab	Elias Kalile	Englander	Minnie Diana	23 Dec. 1907	
Cassel	Wm. F.	Low	Sarah A., Mrs.	19 July 1865	
Cassiday	Samuel D.	Holland	Helen C.	27 Nov. 1899	
Cassidy	Albert H.	Armstrong	Bessie	2 Mar. 1890	
Cassin	Richard J.	Bray	Mae	31 July 1916	
Cassine	Frank	Barsi	Abbina	1 Sept. 1906	
Cassini	Charley	Buzzi	Carrie	27 May 1907	
Castagnasso	Enrico A.	Chelini	Anita Mary	8 Feb. 1921	br: Americo D. Chelini, father
Casteel	J. C.	Jardelle	Bertha	30 Apr. 1915	
Castiglio	Louis	Baldocchi	Julia C.	2 Oct. 1919	
Castiglioni	Peter	Stroll	Evelyn	12 Mar. 1912	
Castle	Raymond R.	Silvia	Louise A.	6 Mar. 1905	
Castro	Manuel C.	Focha	Isabel	8 June 1907	
Catarina	Antonio	Ananos	Joaquina	13 Aug. 1911	
Catelani	Leonori	Maccano	Mary	28 Mar. 1910	
Catendo	Albert G.	Wright	Elois	12 Apr. 1917	gr: Eveline Catendo, mother
Cathey	C. L.	Fletcher	E. J., Mrs.	2 Feb. 1885	

Groom		Bride		Date	Comments
Surname	Given Name	Surname	Given Name		
Catlin	D. Willis	Lewis	Mabel M.	28 Sept. 1903	
Catlin	Lovel D.	Quigley	Julia M.	20 Dec. 1898	br: W. B. Quigley, parent, she will be 18 on 27 Mar. 1899
Cattanep	Louis P.	Mazza	Louisa	14 Jan. 1908	
Cauckwell	Isaac Newton	Weatherington	Myrtle Alberta	26 May 1906	
Caughey	Alexander	McMichael	Eula	13 Mar. 1907	
Caughey	Chester	Baxman	Alice	16 Mar. 1909	
Caughey	John	Watson	Mary, Mrs.	20 May 1881	
Caughey	Robert	Martin	Millie M.	21 Oct. 1920	
Caulfeild	W. Stafford	Neuman	Maggie	14 July 1915	
Caulfield	Daniel Philip	Cruson	Minnie	24 Sept.1904	
Cautel	Louis	Keller	Fannie	30 Jan. 1905	license requested by Eugene Cautel
Cavagna	Emile	Balemi	Giacomina	17 Dec. 1902	
Cavagna	Joseph	Scaroni	Celestina	28 July 1904	
Cavagnaro	Charles V.	Pope	Elizabeth I.	23 Oct. 1920	
Cavallero	C. L.	Solari	Vittoria	8 Dec. 1913	br: Rosa Solari, mother
Cavalli	Antone	Canevascini	Irene	14 July 1902	br: Peter Canevascini, father
Cavanagh	John Edward	Ingram	Nellie	21 Apr. 1891	
Cavanagh	Stephen Patrick	Sutton	Anna Eliza	19 June 1906	
Cavanagh	William	Flinn	Frances	24 Aug. 1905	
Cavanaugh	William M.	Overton	Harriet L.	12 Aug. 1889	
Cayla	Raymond Marcellin	Asti	Josephine Lucy	20 Aug. 1918	br: Julia Asti, mother
Caylor	John J.	Storenetta	Ida M.	22 Dec. 1916	
Cecchi	Pietro	Bertozzi	Pascuina	16 Aug. 1911	
Cella	Dominick	Paulucci	Celistina	9 Oct. 1913	
Cellarius	William	Henry	Ella Etta	17 June 1912	
Cepernich	Maxin J.	Ferris	Helen M.	25 July 1918	
Cereghino	Nathaniel	Downer	Mae	15 Nov. 1920	
Cereghino	Tony	Frideger	Margaret	23 Dec. 1905	
Cerini	Henry	Cerini	Olga	9 May 1910	
Cerini	Isidaro	Pancio	Domenica	29 Sept. 1914	
Cerutti	Paul	Bettiga	Anna	28 Apr. 1921	
Ceva	Daniele	Sacchaz	Jennie	10 July 1913	

Groom		Bride			
Surname	**Given Name**	**Surname**	**Given Name**	**Date**	**Comments**
Chace	Ernest B.	Buckley	Margaret J.	22 June 1917	
Chadd	George H.	McCombs	Nellie D.	27 Aug. 1904	
Chadwick	James W.	Stevens	Harriet Ann, Mrs.	22 Feb. 1904	
Chaffee	E. S.	Adams	Lucy K.	17 June 1885	
Chaffee	Jarvis	Greening	Lenna	28 Dec. 1886	
Chaffee	Joseph E.	Bryant	Margaret J.	28 Jan. 1888	
Chaffer	Chester C.	Osborne	Grace M.		gr: Mrs. R. O. Chaffer, mother; don't publish; not issued
Chaffie	Weaver S.	Buckbee	Violia	27 Aug. 1915	
Chahon	Gustave Cecil	Adams	Clara Violet	19 Nov. 1916	
Chaix	Emile Adrien	DeSoto	Dorthey Christa	7 Feb. 1916	do not publish
Chamberlain	Albert F.	Young	Corinthia A.	13 Sept. 1892	
Chamberlain	Selah	McDonald	Edith M.	27 Aug 1907	
Chamberlain	W. Warren G.	Hopper	M. Myrtle	30 Apr. 1901	
Chamberlain	William H.	Chaffee	Nellie	blank	
Chambers	Benjamin H.	Boehm	Ella L.	19 Apr. 1920	
Chambers	David M. C.	Moller	Georgine N.	30 June 1915	
Chambers	E. W.	Baker	Bertha H.	8 Sept. 1915	
Chambers	Edward C.	Field	Olive B.	14 Feb. 1882	
Chambers	Joseph A.	Smith	Kate C.	2 June 1909	
Chambers	King	English	Dora	6 Sept. 1880	
Chambers	Peter	Jones	Mattie	16 Jan. 1886	
Chambers	William D.	Bill	Estelle L.	12 Oct. 1914	
Champion	John E.	Paul	Theresa M.	26 Dec. 1918	
Champion	Stanley W.	Seavers	Deborah M.	4 Mar. 1921	
Champlin	Charles V.	Agnew	Lizzie	19 Dec. 1882	
Chance	Glenn I.	Davis	Anna E.	7 May 1910	
Chandler	Ernest R.	Chamberlin	Carrie	17 Dec. 1910	
Chandler	Haven Burwell	Sweetnam	Evelyn Mae	27 July 1915	
Chandler	Leo F.	Lehn	Marguerite	8 Aug. 1914	previous letter overlays part of record
Chandler	W. R.	Curtis	Mary J.	6 Apr. 1885	
Chandler	Joseph	Barnes	Zella	3 Nov. 1882	br: Mrs. Lizzie Barnes, mother; M. Menihan, witness

Groom		Bride			
Surname	Given Name	Surname	Given Name	Date	Comments
Chaney	John W.	Reardon	Mary J.	23 Nov. 1920	
Chaney	Vernon E.	Crain	Hazel M.	18 Oct. 1919	
Chaney	William Henry, Jr.	Vaughan	Jessie A.	12 June 1916	
Chaney	William Levi	Elkerton	Ida May	8 Dec. 1908	
Chanin	Peter	Crivelli	Lizzie	17 Aug. 1914	
Channel	L. M.	Farquar	Mary I.	21 Feb. 1919	
Chapman	Charles M.	Simpson	Alice C.	13 June 1919	
Chapman	Edwin A.	Lunt	Addie R.	30 June 1886	
Chapman	Elliot C.	Peoples	Cora M.	27 Oct. 1891	
Chapman	Frank H.	Nielsen	Violet	22 Apr. 1921	
Chapman	Guy Lee	Huckabay	Ferne Elizabeth	15 Dec. 1917	
Chapman	H. E.	Ayers	Edith	1 Feb. 1889	
Chapman	Lawrence L.	Caldweil	Sarah O.	24 Dec. 1914	
Chapman	Rockwell Jerome	Bailey	Bania ? Mary	23 May 1907	
Chapman	Thomas A.	Yates	Alice D.	12 Sept. 1881	
Chappell	Alfred U.	Knight	Rosetta	22 Dec. 1902	
Chappell	Emmet	Tindall	Frankie	6 Apr. 1908	
Charles	Elbert R.	Rowlett	Virginia, Mrs.	24 Nov. 1865	
Charles	Everett L.	Lewis	Mabel E.	18 Mar. 1896	
Charles	Geo. W.	Richardson	Vernette	22 Apr. 1867	
Charles	Isaiah B.	Lowry	Jennie	23 Jan. 1879	
Chartrand	Louis	Locke	Alice	5 Oct. 1912	
Chase	Charles Edwin	Mathews	Amanda	23 Sept. 1914	
Chase	Frank J.	Bryan	Angie	29 Oct. 1913	
Chase	Gay Henry	Ferguson	Laura Virginia	29 May 1905	
Chase	George M.	Seipp	Maria S.	21 Oct. 1886	
Chase	John W.	Hensley	Vina L.	29 Oct. 1914	
Chase	Louis Walter	McLain	Marjorie Lewis	7 Apr. 1916	
Chase	Ralph Noble	Wallace	May Etta	22 Jan. 1918	
Chatard	Philibert	Goyheneix	Marie E.	1 June 1914	
Chatburn	Joseph L.	Ralston	Alta	29 Sept. 1913	
Chattman	Beverly B.	Crosby	Mary	3 Feb. 1891	
Chauvet	Henry J.	Lounibos	Annie	6 Nov. 1893	

Groom		Bride		Date	Comments
Surname	Given Name	Surname	Given Name		
Checchi	Luigi	Ciabbatini	Serafina	1 Nov. 1906	br: H. Bacigalupi, witness to mark
Check	Elliott E.	Cartwright	Mary M.	12 June 1919	
Chelini	Americo D.	Zampa	Dorotea	6 Apr. 1921	
Cheney	Ansel Colby	Preston	Winifred Wood	13 June 1910	
Cheney	Charles	Durant	Ella	5 Nov. 1896	
Cheney	Edward L.	Martin	Estella M.	20 Feb. 1905	
Cheney	John L.	Cozad	Dora E.	20 Oct. 1915	
Cheney	Thomas W.	Wall	Florence V.	8 May 1899	no previous marriage
Chenoweth	A. Roy	Hickman	Minnie E.	31 Dec. 1898	
Chenoweth	Frank B.	Miller	Henrietta	29 Oct. 1891	
Chenoweth	Hardin Talman	Barnes	Harriet Florence	13 Aug. 1910	
Chenoweth	Warren L.	Rudolph	Mae	6 Sept. 1907	
Cherry	Edwin E.	Morgan	Marguerite M.	18 Aug. 1904	
Cheyney	Earl H.	Williamson	Camella	21 Oct. 1914	
Chiappero	Domenico	Mancini	Liduina	17 Jan. 1912	
Chiaroni	Daniel	French	Meta A.	28 Nov. 1918	gr: Laurence Chiaroni, father: br: Ada French, mother
Chicca	Americo	Bernasconi	Della	24 Sept. 1910	
Chick	D. A.	Brians	Olive May	24 July 1884	br: Sarah H. Brains, mother, signs with her mark; Mrs. Lena Sturgene (?), witness
Childers	Arnold, Jr.	Clark	Linnie P.	14 Aug. 1876	
Childers	Dennis Spencer	Melehan	Ella Gertrude	18 Sept. 1908	
Childers	Eugene Lester	Williams	May E.	17 Mar. 1904	
Childers	George T.	Culligan	Petronilla	2 Mar. 1906	
Childers	J. S.	Bryant	Ida E.	1 June 1887	
Childers	William E.	Forrest	Annie	25 Aug. 1891	
Childs	George B.	Ellis	Carrie E.	14 Apr. 1892	
Chinn	Joseph M.	Grohs (?)	Jennie	12 Nov. 1878	
Chiotte	Giovanni	Reinero	Catterina	3 Dec. 1904	br: Amary Reinero, mother; L. A. Pressley, witness to mark; Erminia Asti; Lucy Pasero
Chiotti	James	Vanina	Tilly	19 Aug. 1911	
Chisholm	Donald	Adam	Catherine M.	8 June 1886	
Chisholm	William	Coul (?)	Annie	25 Sept. 1880	

Groom		Bride			
Surname	Given Name	Surname	Given Name	Date	Comments
Chisholm	William C.	Barnes	Nettie A.	12 Feb. 1900	no previous marriage
Chittenden	Justin L.	Graham	Violia M.	22 Sept. 1920	
Chittenden	Louis F.	Hapkal	Mary A.	22 Mar. 1917	
Chitwood	James M., Jr.	Matthews	Jerenia E.	24 Oct. 1881	
Chitwood	John F.	Brooks	Mary	11 Sept. 1883	
Chitwood	Joseph Andrew	Chitwood	Anna Eliza	16 May 1887	
Chitwood	Joseph I.	Runyan	Sarah E.	26 Nov. 1889	
Chodrow	Samuel	Ochsenreiter	Helen L.	18 Sept. 1915	
Choney	Lawrence	Crutchen	Virginia	8 Apr. 1911	
Choquette	Stephen	Garrison	Ora M.	27 Feb. 1920	br: Charlotte S. Garrison, mother
Choquette	Stephen A.	Brown	Myrtle M.	3 Nov. 1915	
Christansen	John	Veasne (?)	Anna	6 Sept. 1883	
Christensen	Christian	Nicol	Harriet J.	19 Oct. 1911	
Christensen	Clarence	Barnes	Etta	24 Sept. 1915	gr: Andrew Christensen, father
Christensen	Harry Edward	Maritzen	Florence Otilla	15 May 1914	
Christensen	Martin Petersen	Larsen	Laura Christina	11 Aug. 1915	
Christensen	Wm. E.	Noble	Ada	2 Nov. 1892	
Christenson	James Rasmussen	Cole	Mary Violet	7 Aug. 1896	
Christian	Charles E.	Tracey	Amy M.	21 Dec. 1912	
Christian	Harry E.	Ragan	Mary C.	10 Mar. 1879	br: George & Mary Ragan, parents; witness: Thos. C. Ragan
Christian	Harry Henry	Hood	Alzina Rose	4 Feb. 1918	
Christian	Herman B.	Fallon	Ruth	5 Mar. 1915	
Christiansen	Christian	Schienmann	Ida	3 Nov. 1920	
Christiansen	Walter	Whitehead	Florence Estella	6 Sept. 1905	
Christie	Frank B.	Thompson	Kate	12 Oct. 1895	br: M. L. Thompson gives consent by x mark; witness: F. G. Nagle
Christie	Wilfred A.	Wilkie	Grace E.	21 Jan. 1908	
Christiensen	Ernest	Hinricksen	Mary	1 Aug. 1898	no previous marriage
Christoffel	Jacob	Kling	Christine	26 July 1909	
Christopher	Irvine T.	Masvik	Hanna	30 Sept. 1913	
Christopher	Jas. C.	Tully	Catharine	13 Mar. 1865	
Christy	Henry Alfred	Campbell	Leonore Francorce (?)	20 Dec. 1920	

Groom		Bride			
Surname	Given Name	Surname	Given Name	Date	Comments
Chrones	Lebertus	Silva	Elizabeth	5 July 1915	
Chuny ?	J. M.	McHeary ?	Tammy A.	9 Oct. 1866	
Church	Charlie	Hare	Lillie	15 May 1874	br: Mr. & Mrs. E. Hare (?), parents; Valley Ford
Church	Claude Leslie	Winn	Rosa Clara	17 Feb. 1910	
Church	Douglas	Fowler	Margaret A.	31 Mar. 1865	
Church	Jessie Raymond	Shaw	Maude May	2 Oct. 1900	
Church	John L.	Evans	Rose	2 June 1885	
Church	Royal Ira	Linebaugh	Mae Olivia	15 Oct. 1906	gr: Walter Church, father; don't publish ages
Church	William Thomas	Marcucci	Jennie Mary	14 Aug. 1906	
Churchill	H. Harry	Wright	Emma A.	29 Oct. 1888	
Churchill	Jabez F.	Howell	Elva C.	1 Dec. 1919	
Churchill	William F.	Huffman	Bessie J.	27 Nov. 1914	
Churchman	George	Wilson	Sarah Maria	29 Apr 1865	
Churchman	John W.	Thomas	Rachel A.	20 Dec. 1898	
Churchman	John William	Poe	Ina Alma	27 Jan. 1917	
Churchman	Schuyler	Wilson	Eliza Ann	29 Apr 1865	
Cia	Domenico	Guera	Henrietta	3 Feb. 1885	
Cia	Silvio	Giannecchini	Crotilde	30 Oct. 1915	br: Demetrio Giannecchini, father
Ciancio	Charles	Brightenstine	Nettie E.	23 Mar. 1911	
Ciancio	Giuseppe	Guidi	Ida	28 Sept. 1888	br: Carlo Guidi, father
Ciavarelli	Nello	Bondi	Mary	13 Feb.1915	
Ciezere	Lavagino	Lavagnino	Mary	22 Oct. 1888	
Cills	Rudolph F.	Gann	Gladys G.	23 Aug. 1919	
Cinquini	D.	Giusti	Eda	6 Oct. 1904	br: Angelo Giusti, father
Cirimele	Angelo	Arnold	Philippina	27 Nov. 1917	
Civa (?)	Joseph	?atorce (?)	Anna	5 Dec. 1883	
Clanton	George	Haase	Bertha K.	26 Mar. 1914	
Clanton	Samuel B.	Davies	Florence C.	20 Mar. 1886	
Clanton	Thomas D.	Millsap	Amanda Jane	3 Aug. 1887	
Clare	George A.	Clough	Julia M.	3 Apr. 1916	
Clark	A. N.	Black	Harriet Isabel	27 Jan. 1885	
Clark	Albert Earl	Skinner	Goldie B.	25 Feb. 1909	

Groom		Bride		Date	Comments
Surname	Given Name	Surname	Given Name		
Clark	Alfred Churchill	Amons	Susannah	23 Oct. 1915	
Clark	Benjamin Henderson	Brown	Carrie	30 Oct. 1900	gr: A. W. Clark; note from Alexander Valley
Clark	Charles A.	Ketcham	Agnes Grace	20 Nov. 1919	
Clark	Charles E.	Millington	Anna E.	24 Dec. 1889	
Clark	Charles Preston	Keller	Nevada	7 Nov. 1889	
Clark	Charles Raymond	Andrews	Alice May	15 Apr. 1912	
Clark	Charles Raymond	Doughty	Lula Amelia	30 Dec. 1918	
Clark	Doane	Court	Caroline	8 Dec. 1906	
Clark	Duval L.	Skinner	Minnie M.	16 June 1900	br: Mrs. S. J. Skinner, mother; Mrs. W. M. Flewelling, witness
Clark	Edwin Curtis	Hendrickson	Etta Pearl	14 Sept. 1907	
Clark	Frank	Wonacott	Esther B.	27 Feb. 1920	
Clark	Frank A.	Brown	Georgia A.	19 Mar. 1903	
Clark	Fred L.	Judkins	Alice M.	11 June 1892	
Clark	Geo. C.	Evans	Catherine J.	25 Sept. 1886	
Clark	Geo. C.	Guill	Elizabeth	31 July 1901	
Clark	George F.	Talbot	Allena	20 Nov. 1888	
Clark	Grant Guildford	Rilf	Marie	31 Jan. 1914	
Clark	H. O.	West	Nellie G.	1 May 1886	
Clark	Harry A.	Vier	Clara	9 Apr. 1902	
Clark	Harry H.	Watt	Chrissie L.	14 Oct. 1893	
Clark	J. W.	Howe	Catharine, Mrs.	18 Sept. 1865	
Clark	James E.	Denner	Bessie K. (?)	13 Nov. 1901	
Clark	James H. H.	Michelsen	Agusta	20 Oct. 1888	
Clark	James H. H.	Copple	Annie	12 May 1881	
Clark	James M.	Hill	Nellie	26 June 1879	
Clark	James R.	Weinreich	Ann, Mrs.	12 Nov. 1895	br: divorced.
Clark	James Wesley	Marshall	Jennie S.	7 July 1900	
Clark	John Thomas	Mallon	Bridget P.	22 May 1886	
Clark	Joseph B.	Cameron	Maggie	17 June 1879	
Clark	Joseph H.	Spotswood	Hattie B.	18 Apr. 1899	
Clark	Leonard P.	Freshour	Marie A.	18 July 1914	gr: Mrs. Lena Clark, mother; br: Mrs. Kate Freshour, mother

Groom		Bride		Date	Comments
Surname	Given Name	Surname	Given Name		
Clark	Leslie D.	Overton	Laurene	8 Dec. 1917	
Clark	Mathew	Stemple	Henrietta E.	4 Jan. 1882	
Clark	Richard L.	Cummings	Olive	16 Dec. 1899	neither party has been divorced within one year
Clark	Richard R.	Pedranti	Estelle V.	7 Aug. 1920	
Clark	Robert F.	Rima	Estella	2 Feb. 1907	
Clark	Samuel Berry	Franz	Minnie L.	25 June 1883	
Clark	Stephen D.	Clark	Jennie B.	4 Feb. 1893	
Clark	Terrence	Fitzpatrick	Mary Ann	2 May 1878	
Clark	William D.	Hudspeth	Alice S.	18 Oct. 1915	
Clark	Willie L.	Jewett	Emma L.	12 Nov. 1890	
Clark	Winfred P.	Duncan	Gemma E.	8 May 1909	
Clark	Wm. E.	Thompkins	Carrie	10 June 1887	
Clarke	Leslie Albert	Wright	Ruth Irene	30 Dec. 1916	gr: Lenna Clarke, parent
Clarke	P. F.	Stradling	Julia	3 July 1915	
Clary	Clarence H.	Imbler	Elsie	11 June 1919	
Clary	Dennis G.	Mulvehill	Margaret	6 Sept. 1897	
Clary	Paul Dennis	Temple	Christie		filed between 13 & 15 Jan. 1906
Clary	Thomas Peter	Temple	Rosamond	23 May 1916	
Clasby	Michael M.	Brush	Jennie M.	9 Jan. 1902	
Clasquin	Emil	Cames	Justine	7 Jan. 1904	
Clattenbury	Alexander	Robinson	Mary	21 Nov. 1906	
Clausen	Dietrich	Geertz	Josephine	25 Nov. 1898	
Clawson	Ardent Benjamin	Murray	Lola	15 Dec. 1905	br: J. C. Murray, father
Clawson	Charles D.	Reimer	Jessie	24 Apr. 1909	
Clawson	Chas.	Kennedy	Mary Jane	28 Feb. 1866	
Clawson	Cyrus R.	Beatty	Maggie	15 Nov. 1898	
Clay	E. W.	Monroe	Lois	13 Oct. 1911	
Claypool	Jerry W.	Dearborn	Mollie Theresa	17 Feb. 1903	
Claypool	Stephen B.	Riddle	Sue Frances	5 Apr. 1902	
Clayton	Capius Henry	Smith	Ann Elizabeth	24 Nov. 1875	
Clayton	Howard B.	Seavers	Ida Ruth	17 Nov. 1915	
Clayton	S. A.	Hennigan	Ida J.	31 Mar. 1891	

Groom		Bride		Date	Comments
Surname	Given Name	Surname	Given Name		
Cleary	Edward	Riley	Mary	15 Feb. 1911	
Cleaveland	H. J.	Cordingly	Lila H.	24 Dec. 1913	
Cleaveland	Robert Fuller	Langhlin	Ida, Mrs.	9 June 1909	
Cleek	Samuel P.	Snow	Ruby E.	11 Sept. 1915	
Clegg	Frances L.	Egli	Emma	30 July 1914	
Clement	Jesse Edward	McGimsey	Marie M.	9 Mar. 1907	
Clement	Walter L.	Branick	Mary P.	8 Nov. 1913	
Clement	Walter L.	Weber	Josephine E.	6 Jan. 1921	
Clements	T. H.	Dolan	Mary	7 Sept. 1904	
Clements	Edgar J.	Porter	Nell W.	30 Sept. 1919	
Clementz	Fred A.	Wright	Violet E.	12 May 1920	
Clemo	William H.	Dahlmann	Eunice F.	6 Mar. 1920	
Clemons	William L.	Mulgew	Josephine	1 Oct. 1898	no previous marriage
Clerici	August	Castagnasso	Annie	29 Aug. 1904	
Clevenger	Thomas P.	Williams	Ellen, Mrs.	4 May 1866	
Clewe	William F.	Smith	Harriet Porche	12 May 1909	
Cliff	Ernest Henry	Bridges	Pearl May	17 Nov. 1905	
Clifford	George Bassett	Teale	Grace Louise	17 May 1912	
Clifford	John	McSherry	Mary	5 Aug. 1912	
Clifton	Thomas K.	Clifton	Ollie E.	12 Dec. 1912	
Clinch	Henry W. R.	Donahue	Minnie C.	4 Feb. 1912	
Cline	Arthur Allen	Gilmore	Minerva Ruth	9 Nov. 1916	
Cline	Henry C.	Stewart	Lillian E.	29 Jan. 1907	
Cline	Joseph V.	Bussman	Annie	3 Mar. 1900	
Cline	Thomas J.	Nauert	Fredda	20 Oct. 1919	
Clinesmith	Fred	Bowman	Mamie Francis	23 Nov. 1905	
Clisbee	Albert	Carr	Maggie	14 Nov. 1877	witness: Nelson Carr
Clokey	Robert	Woods	Elizabeth, Mrs.	6 June 1867	
Close	Frank D.	Athey	Olive M.	29 Dec. 1920	
Close	William A.	Ross	Hazel M.	19 Sept. 1914	
Clutterbuck	Ernest	Hodges	Elizabeth F.	22 Dec. 1915	
Cluver	Harold H.	Evans	Alma M.	21 July 1917	
Cluver	Henry A.	Hinkston	Alice	14 June 1892	

Groom		Bride			
Surname	**Given Name**	**Surname**	**Given Name**	**Date**	**Comments**
Cnopius	Eugene B.	Stone	Gladys C.	13 Nov. 1917	
Cnopius	Lewis C.	Miller	Birdie E.	19 Mar. 1914	
Cnopius	Louis Christian	Holden	Carrie B.	5 Nov. 1894	
Coakley	Daniel John	Crowley	Ceclia Catherine	8 Oct. 1907	
Coates	Norman Frank	Joyce	Theresa Alice	7 Apr. 1917	
Coats	Charles A., Jr.	Williams	Lotta A., Mrs.	19 Nov. 1898	br: widow
Coats	William B.	Kimes	Deeda C.	12 Nov. 1904	
Cobb		Walker	Elizabeth H.	29 Jan. 1872	gr: John Cobb,father; witness John Graunilick (?)
Cobb	Clarence Leroy	Wells	Stella Evlin	21 May 1913	
Cobb	Darwin L.	Johnson	Emma	18 Nov. 1885	br: John F. Johnson, father
Cobb	George G.	Reubburt (?)	May	10 May 1879	
Cobb	George O.	Haskell	Jessie T.	6 Nov. 1907	
Cobb	Omar O.	Lauteran	Antoinette M., Mrs.	31 July 1897	
Cobb	Omar Otto	Torliatt	Marie Blanche	26 Sept. 1908	
Cobb	Tony A.	Osborn	Elrene	25 June 1910	
Cobos	Norberto B.	Lynden	Sylvia Vallejo	30 Aug. 1915	
Coburn	Ernest A.	Hodges	Ethel A.	31 Mar. 1921	gr: Mary Alice Coburn, mother
Coburn	James A.	Donner	Bettie L.	3 Oct. 1888	br: Margaret J. Donner, mother
Coburn	William	Bigham	Lula Jane		br: John Bigham, father
Cochran	A. E.	Marshall	Sarah A.	3 Sept. 1883	
Cochran	Albert Francis	Fairman	Ethel Florence	2 Aug. 1906	
Cochran	Arthur F.	Davis	Ina A.	23 Sept. 1896	not to be published until Sept. 24th
Cochran	Arthur Payne	Coffman	Mary Gertrude	25 Apr. 1912	
Cochran	Claude T.	Hays	Grace E.	4 Sept. 1920	
Cochran	Horace	Campion	Nellie	2 June 1896	
Cochran	L. P.	Herman	Alice B.	7 Apr. 1888	
Cochran	Willis B.	Haynes	Zoe E.	20 May 1916	
Cochrane	John T.	Hanna	Catherine	8 Sept. 1888	
Cochrane	Marcus Edward	Armstrong	Flora A.	14 Jan. 1889	
Cockrill	Obe A.	Pellascio	Vera	7 Nov. 1906	
Cockrill	Robert L.	Vogt	Gertrude G.	2 Oct. 1920	
Cockrill	Theadore L.	Potter	Frankie	19 Oct. 1865	

Groom		Bride			
Surname	Given Name	Surname	Given Name	Date	Comments
Cockrill	Travis Lee	Armstrong	Ella L.	20 Sept. 1908	
Cockrill	William A.	Colburn	Lulu I.	10 Feb. 1903	
Cockrill (?)	John L.	Winzell	Kate A.	1 Nov. 1917	
Cockrill (?)	Thomas Jefferson	Mercer	Simi	15 Apr. 1878	
Codd	David E.	Derick	Lena M.	3 Aug. 1901	
Codding	George C.	Colby	Minnie A.	30 Dec 1892	
Code	Reginald F.	Delfino	Ethel Victorine	16 Jan. 1917	
Codiga	Antonio	Donati	Mary	30 Dec. 1911	
Codner	Frank E.	King	Evelyn Irene	28 Sept. 1917	
Coe	Fred R.	Steller	Rossella A.	26 Feb. 1913	
Coe	Geo. W.	Crawford	Mary, Mrs.	20 Aug. 1883	
Cofer	Clinton Tice	Knolty	Dora Edith	21 Jan. 1910	
Coffee	S. R.	Barham	Luda V.	13 Aug. 1911	
Coffey	J. H.	Lemay	A. Ellen	13 May 1889	
Coffey	Charles	Banty	Clara B.	30 Nov. 1887	
Coffey	Charles H.	Scutt	Maggie	23 Feb. 1894	
Coffey	Maurice J.	Connihan	Julia V.	24 Nov. 1891	
Coffey	Samuel A.	Houx	Nellie	5 Jan. 1888	
Coffey	Wm. M.	Koutmire	Emma Etta	4 Mar. 1887	
Coffman	Charles	Palmer	Georgia M.	5 July 1909	
Coffman	James T.	Luce	Jennie D.	17 July 1893	
Coffman	John Isaac	Stone	Sidney S.	6 Jan. 1875	requested by Henry Light
Coffman	N. B.	Willson	Anna M.	2 Nov. 1885	
Coggin	Clarence A.	Muller	Margaret H.	3 Oct. 1914	
Coggins	Andrew H.	Welch	Grace M.	20 Dec. 1911	
Coggins	Chas. W.	Tripp	Lillian C.	9 July 1900	do not publish
Cohen	Harold J.	Malcolm	Catherine B.	24 Oct. 1914	
Cohen	Joel C.	Johnson	Laura W.	15 May 1894	
Cohen	Maxwell	Gantner	Julia	20 Sept. 1919	
Cohenour	Joseph Herbert	Gossage	Belle, Mrs.	3 July 1906	
Coke	Joseph Homer	Branson	Minnie	30 Dec. 1916	br: Clara Branson, mother
Coker	Charles L.	Hugh	Flossie	18 Dec. 1908	
Coker	Wiley	German	Susan	16 May 1882	br: William W. German, guardian

Groom		Bride		Date	Comments
Surname	Given Name	Surname	Given Name		
Colabella	Carlo	DeMeo	Angelina	25 Apr. 1910	
Colbert	William	Karl	Florence	25 Apr. 1914	
Colbroth	Harry W.	Hornbuckle	Molly B.	21 Dec. 1897	
Colburn	Frank	Schriver	Ida	20 Oct. 1898	don't publish until Tuesday
Colburn	Frank N.	Button	Jessie R.	11 Jan. 1887	
Colburn	Joseph	Thorogood	Esther	15 June 1912	
Colburn	Leroy H.	Barnes	Alice M.	25 May 1910	
Colburn	Lester F.	Devello	Frances Julia	22 Dec. 1919	
Colburn	Orlin F.	Johnson	Nancy L.	14 Nov. 1883	
Colburn	Orlin Merle	Resendes	Annita Mary	14 Sept. 1914	gr: Orlin F. Colburn, parent
Colburn	Orrin E.	Farrer	Etta Rebecca	9 Apr. 1907	gr: O. F. Colburn, parent
Colburn	Rayman C.	Garrison	Laura E.	3 Oct. 1903	
Colburn	Rufus Paul	Hardisty	Cora Ethel	4 Oct. 1890	br: Charles W. Hardisty, father
Colby	Alfred Wright	Schultz	Marion Georgia	10 Mar. 1917	
Colby	Edwin	Nowell	Hattie A.	15 Apr. 1885	
Coldwell	Edrie Sayor	Doyle	Allien Evelyn	3 May 1911	
Cole	Charles B.	Poulson	Addie E.	28 Sept. 1891	
Cole	Clarence Eugene	Porcher	Marion Louise	9 Oct. 1906	
Cole	Francis M.	Luby	Mabel E.	21 Apr. 1921	
Cole	Fred Grant	Shulte	Grace Evelyn	13 Apr. 1907	
Cole	George E.	Johnson	Dora J.	19 Nov. 1875	br: Fannie Johnson, mother
Cole	Harold	Talkington	Gladys	7 July 1915	
Cole	Henry L.	Throop	Emily M.	26 Apr. 1883	
Cole	Lee	Garms	Pauline	16 May 1906	
Cole	Nathaniel J.	Bauder	May	20 Mar. 1917	
Cole	Thomas Hoarse	Gartner	Elsie Louise	8 July 1914	
Cole	Vincent Letton	Hereford	Hattie Elvira	7 July 1906	br: Mrs. Harriet L. Hereford, mother
Cole	W. E.	Proschold	Hazel	30 Nov. 1912	
Cole	W. E.	Isaacs	Lillie	31 May 1893	
Cole	Walter Vernon	Chio	Emma	16 Aug. 1906	
Cole	William Lester	Livingston	Katherine Rock	16 Oct. 1909	
Coleman	Gary	Hayes	Anna	10 Apr. 1885	
Coleman	George E.	Davis	M., Mrs.	9 Aug. 1893	

Groom		Bride		Date	Comments
Surname	Given Name	Surname	Given Name		
Coleman	John E.	Lindsey	Margaret Jane	21 Sept. 1905	
Colen	Lewis H.	Caughey	Corinne Alice	14 Feb. 1917	
Coli	Lorenzo	Dinnucci	Mary	13 Oct. 1910	
Collier	Richard B. H.	Smith	Nellie T.	30 Aug. 1901	
Collier	S. F.	Chadwick	Belle	20 July 1883	
Collings	Walter	Thompson	Lizzie	19 Apr. 1900	
Collins	Charles Albert	Shepherd	Medora Alma	7 Oct. 1905	
Collins	Charles F.	Clark	Lizzie	8 Jan. 1897	
Collins	David R.	Pope	Lillie N.	19 Apr. 1899	
Collins	Eldorado	McCombs	Leanna Jewel	25 Jan. 1908	
Collins	Frederick A.	Kaiser	Charlotte S.	8 Sept. 1917	
Collins	George W.	Alten	Elizabeth	27 July 1897	
Collins	Howard Benfield	Peterson	Etta	23 Feb. 1907	
Collins	Howard J.	McGrew	Ruby L.	22 Nov. 1920	
Collins	James Michael	Comber	Nora	19 Aug 1907	
Collins	William A.	McMinn	Clara J.	4 June 1891	
Collischonn	Otto	Tiedemann	Martha B.	28 Sept. 1901	br: requested license
Collister	Stanley W.	Smith	Fannie A.	9 Apr. 1894	gr: Oscar Collister, father, gives consent and signs
Colombani	Primo	Bertoni	Maria	2 June 1910	gr: F. Lombardi, witness to his mark
Colombo	John Edward	Welling	Susie Mae	22 Sept. 1917	
Colton	Frank B.	Kidd	Mina	10 June 1892	br: Mrs. F. A. Kidd gives consent for marriage
Colton	Maury R.	Rosenblum	Henrietta C.	23 Mar. 1908	
Coltrin	Hugh C.	Litchfield	Laura B.	17 Oct. 1896	
Coltrin	Hugh C.	Cooper	May N.	30 Mar. 1889	
Columbo	Charles H.	Perottini	Mary L.	18 Aug. 1910	
Columbo	Romeo M.	Pozzi	Linda M.	1 June 1918	br: Rosalie Pozzi Campana, mother
Colville	Thomas P.	Conklin	Minnie	18 Dec. 1893	br: Mrs. E. C. Lane, mother, gives consent and signs.
Colvin	Thomas Floyd	Mayer	Emily	21 Nov. 1917	
Colwell	Abner M.	Bagley	Mary L.	8 Dec. 1887	
Coman	George L.	Haddlesten	Annie L.	29 Sept. 1914	

Groom		Bride			
Surname	Given Name	Surname	Given Name	Date	Comments
Coman	Robert Grimes	McMeans	Mary Alice	9 June 1916	
Combs	Alvin Roots	Valandhan	Mary	3 Sept. 1878	
Combs	George	Berry	Ethel	22 Mar. 1913	
Combs	Henry C.	Jacobs	Lorita M.	22 Oct. 1907	
Combs	Henry C.	Grant	Muriel Grace	22 July 1920	
Combs	John F.	Odell	Amanda J.	8 Oct. 1886	
Combs	Monroe	Kolb	Belle	8 June 1897	
Cominos	George N.	Karedis	Helen M.	30 Dec. 1919	
Commary	John A.	Patton	Emma	20 Oct. 1865	
Commers	Robert	Chaffee	Lenna	2 Dec. 1908	
Compton	John Andrew	Clair	Stella Louise	21 Sept. 1908	gr: A. J. Compton, parent
Compton	Theodore J.	Williamson	Emilia L.	28 Sept. 1908	gr: Thomas J. Compton, father
Comstock	George F.	Lindsey	Georgiana	1 Aug. 1913	
Comstock	Harold Earl	Shriver	Evelyn	27 Nov. 1920	
Comstock	Herbert G.	Hoodly	Eppie L.	29 Mar. 1899	no previous marriage
Comstock	Horace William	Brandlein	Alma Theresa	10 Aug. 1916	
Comstock	Leslie F.	McAskill	Margaret J.	8 Aug. 1917	
Concerse	Earl Flower	Studley	Alsy	17 Nov. 1909	
Condeff	Gerry	Walce	Pauline	26 Apr. 1916	
Condeff	Harry P.	Balsley	Edith Evalyn	8 June 1916	
Condict	H. M.	Howell	Ella M.	6 May 1886	
Condrey	Edward Phillip	Herrick	Eva Elizabeth	11 Sept. 1916	
Conemac	Byron Patrick	Young	Agnes	25 Apr. 1914	
Conger	Charles W.	Kemper	Sarah E.	24 July 1900	
Conger	Glenn A.	Hilmer	Alma G.	28 June 1919	
Conger	Harry E., Jr.	Lucas	Leta A.	24 Apr. 1916	
Conger	John I.	Porter	Annie L.	24 July 1880	gr: Jacob M. Gonterman, guardian from Iowa; witness: Loeda T. Porter
Congleton	A. C.	Hoar	Jennie S.	17 Oct. 1903	
Congleton	Geo. W.	Ball	Agnes	6 Sept. 1878	
Congrove	Jonathan	Crow	Lucy A.	14 July 1877	
Conisto	Achille	Clark	Jennie	30 Aug. 1883	

Groom		Bride			
Surname	Given Name	Surname	Given Name	Date	Comments
Conklin	Thomas	Howard	Beulah	8 Dec. 1896	gr: Moses Conklin gives consent and signs; br: Mr. and Mrs. H. A. Howard give consent. Mrs. H. A Howard signs. Beulah Howard, born in Chattanooga, Tenn. on the 17th day of Nov. 1879. Mrs. H. Howard born in Dalton, GA. Mr. H. Howard born in Dublin, Ireland. Mrs. Howard's mother's name is Mrs. Nancy Couch, her father's name Mr. Tom Couch. Mr. H. A. Howard's mother's and father's names are Mr. Francis Howard and Mrs. Betsy Howard.
Conkling	Glenn R.	Whipple	Jennie E.	28 June 1919	
Conley	Philip	O'Rourke	Teresa	9 May 1910	
Conley	William M.	Gray	Daisy	4 June 1900	
Conlin	William George	Stone	Agnes	16 Aug. 1877	
Connell	Chas. H.	Graham	Mary E.	9 Apr. 1887	
Connell	John	Connell	Mary	26 June 1899	no previous marriage; gr: mark witnessed by F. A. Wickersham
Conner	Arch C.	Yates	Amy May, Mrs.	3 June 1907	
Conner	Charles W. G.	Daniels	Jessie Marian	7 Sept. 1920	
Conner	Frank Stanley	Jones	Flora M.	23 Dec. 1910	
Conner	George W.	Gibbin	Theresa I.	1 Mar. 1920	
Conners	Alexander F.	Harmon	Nellie G.	7 Jan. 1896	br: George Conners, guardian, gives consent and signs
Conners	Alexr F.	McCray	Emma E.	17 Nov. 1902	
Conners	Charles F.	Siemer	Minnie	26 Nov. 1902	
Conners	George W.	Valdes	Vincent E.	24 Dec. 1901	
Conness	John, Jr.	Raupach	Caroline, Mrs.	24 Feb. 1900	
Connick	Arthur E.	Robertson	Florence	17 June 1913	
Conniff	Thomas E.	Holland	Josephine	18 Nov. 1903	
Conniff	William Francis	Fowler	Lue Della	15 May 1907	
Connott	William John	Mackie	Mary	22 Sept. 1908	
Connor	Edward H.	McMeans	Helen S.	30 Aug. 1913	
Connor	J.	Emerson	Nellie	19 July 1887	

Groom		Bride			
Surname	Given Name	Surname	Given Name	Date	Comments
Conover	Howard J.	Shannon	Marion F.	26 Aug. 1918	
Conquest	Earl A.	Riehl	Emma S.	21 July 1917	
Conrad	Charles Francis	Meyer	Anna	8 July 1916	
Conrad	E. A.			8 Oct. 1901	gr: E. F. Conrad, parent; note from Middletown; confidential; do not issue license as he is under age for 3 yrs.
Conrad	James	Riffe	Mattie	24 Jan. 1919	
Conrad	Joseph	Hale	Jean	16 Dec. 1919	
Conroy	Edmund C., Jr.	Kast	Amelia N.	29 Mar. 1912	don't publish
Consoli	Peter	Patocchi	Olimpia	31 Dec. 1912	
Consoni	Alfredo	Nicoletti	Listina	28 May 1912	
Constantine	Arthur Philip	Timmons	Eva Ethel	21 Oct. 1905	
Continho	Joseph	Augusta	Clara	13 Apr. 1903	
Contreras	Baltimore Y.	Lillard	Fleet	21 Oct. 1900	br: Mrs. Nancy E. Lillard, mother
Converse	Gervase V.	Monroe	Adalene S.	30 Aug. 1913	gr: Albert E. Converse, father
Conway	Edward P.	Bourke	Mary E.	22 June 1896	
Conway	Thomas James	Conniff	Annie L.	7 Dec. 1901	
Conyers	William E.	Peterson	Lucy L.	1 July 1907	
Cook	Andrew J.	Warren	May	4 Jan. 1902	br: 310 8th St., San Francisco
Cook	Andrew Joseph	Ducker	Minnie May	27 Nov. 1895	gr: Mrs. Eliza Cook gives consent and signs.
Cook	Andrew Joseph	Wheeler	Myrtle	23 June 1904	br: no parental consent; document notes "original defective"
Cook	Archibald	Akers	Willie	28 June 1892	
Cook	Charles Edward	Koch	Mamie	13 Apr. 1895	
Cook	Charles T.	Rex	Hulda I.	19 Apr. 1902	
Cook	De Roy	Lundholm	Lydia	4 Sept. 1902	
Cook	Delbert R.	Cowan	Permilla I.	1 Oct. 1898	
Cook	Edward	Cockrill	Fidella	blank	
Cook	Edward	Pike	Amanda J.	8 Oct. 1904	
Cook	Erle	Hitchcock	Myrtle	22 Apr. 1912	
Cook	Ernest E.	Franklin	Alta M.	29 Jan. 1920	gr: Richard F. Cook, father
Cook	Ernest Ward	Christie	Lizzie, Mrs.	4 Jan. 1908	
Cook	F. R.	Bacon	Iona A.	28 Apr. 1879	br: John S. Bacon, father

Groom		Bride		Date	Comments
Surname	Given Name	Surname	Given Name		
Cook	Frank A.	Black	Villa	13 Oct. 1899	no previous marriage
Cook	Fred B.	Hughes	Pearl M.	1 July 1893	
Cook	George	Mansfield	Maude	27 Sept. 1915	
Cook	George M.	Richards	Josephine	13 May 1881	
Cook	Glenn A.	Guillice	Adeline I.	6 Sept. 1901	
Cook	Grover C.	Woods	Lily B.	18 Dec. 1911	
Cook	Harry L.	Hanson	Minnie E.	6 Feb. 1904	license requested by Louis Beck
Cook	Harvey M.	Reed	Carrie B.	17 Apr. 1888	requested by E. Lerch
Cook	Herbert E.	Wiseman	Susie	18 Oct. 1871	br: David Fulton, guardian
Cook	Isaac N.	Badger	Basha	7 May 1892	
Cook	John Gilbert	Scorille	Katie	16 Oct. 1884	
Cook	John S.	Cox	Emma Elizabeth	26 Apr. 1880	br: Mrs. F. A. Cox, mother; A. Skillman, witness
Cook	Leo Francis	Lentz	Edith	28 Jan. 1904	gr: Mrs. Minnie Cook, mother
Cook	Levi F.	Massa	Clara	17 Sept. 1888	
Cook	Peter	Proctor	Julia M.	25 Apr. 1888	
Cook	Peter	Hunt	Margaret	3 July 1918	
Cook	Ralph W. E.	Kaeintz	Ruby Amanda	12 Aug. 1916	
Cook	Raymond E.	Quigley	Beatrice	17 Mar. 1915	
Cook	Reuben Grant	Haigh	Alice Estella	30 Dec. 1901	
Cook	Roy (?)	Joseph	Mary E.	15 Jan. 1921	
Cook	Shelby Erington	Turner	Ada Marie	14 July 1909	
Cook	Walter D. B.	Brooks	Pauline	10 Oct. 1895	
Cook	William	Kuhm	Louisa	17 Jan. 1898	no previous marriage
Cook	William E.	New	Rose	4 Sept. 1918	
Cook	William E., Jr.	Cambra	Jimella	13 June 1914	
Cook	William H.	de Shiell	Virginia	24 June 1919	
Cook	William H.	Park	Bertha M.	11 May 1901	br: Clara A. Park, mother
Cook	William H.	Lewis	Pearl M.	26 Jan. 1908	
Cook	William Irl	Pharris	Bernice Wilda	12 Feb. 1907	gr: J. W. Cook, father ; letter from Tehama Co. gives birthdate; b: born 5 Mar. 1886
Cook	William M.	Carrillo	Rafelia	28 July 1888	requested by Jesse Cook
Cook	William W.	Minkel	Martha	23 Oct. 1883	

Groom		Bride		Date	Comments
Surname	Given Name	Surname	Given Name		
Cooke	Frank W.	Hendrickson	C. Grace	8 Feb. 1902	
Cooke	James F. R.	LaPlant	Louisa	25 Nov. 1882	
Cooke	James Hew	Rouse	Eda May	7 Nov. 1898	no previous marriage
Cooke	John Blucker	Nagel	Alvina	19 Dec. 1908	
Cooke	Reuben	Cupp	Olga L.	23 Aug. 1919	
Cooley	Charles H.	Hiatt	Myrtle P.	19 Apr. 1902	gr: requested by J. B. Cooley, father
Cooley	Edward A.	Hunziker	Flora	13 June 1888	
Cooley	James F.	Harris	Etta	7 Oct. 1899	
Cooley	John S.	Snodgrass	Ida M., Mrs.	21 Oct. 1896	
Cooley	Mayberry D.	Munro	Emily A.	27 Mar. 1909	
Cooley	Walter S.	Rosen	Lenny	3 Oct. 1916	
Coolidge	George Harry	Wright	Katherine	9 Aug. 1906	
Coolidge	Homer H.	Butler	Grace V.	2 June 1917	
Coomes	Albert M.	Monroe	Mary E.	12 June 1886	
Coon	Edward B.	Graves	Laurie E.	21 May 1901	
Coon	John T.	Varneo	Clara J.	15 May 1889	
Coon	Parmenas C.	Norris	Hannah A., Mrs.	6 May 1895	
Coon	Robt. W.	Torrence	Lydia A	5 July 1865	
Cooper	Alfred B.	Geer	Mamie	17 Dec. 1902	
Cooper	B. F.	Shultz	Mary E.	22 Nov. 1866	
Cooper	C. J.	Davis	Hattie L.	10 June 1893	
Cooper	Charles Alexander	Agnew	Ella V.	7 May 1892	
Cooper	Charles Crawford	Gericke	Agnes Veronica	21 Apr. 1917	
Cooper	Charles H.	Rudd	Emma	22 Dec. 1903	
Cooper	Fred Evart	Razee	Carol Reaha	16 Oct. 1920	
Cooper	Frederick A.	Hyde	Francis G.	9 June 1897	
Cooper	Geo. W.	Tupper	Hattie	25 Apr. 1879	
Cooper	Harry Anderson	Guidotti	Edythe Ida	13 Mar. 1908	
Cooper	J. A.	Davidson	Fannie S.	1 May 1878	
Cooper	James M.	Bouse	Urith	21 Apr. 1871	
Cooper	John H.	Hutsell	Mary E.	12 Oct. 1903	
Cooper	John Harmon	Struter	Ruth Florence	18 Feb. 1914	br: Mrs. E. R. Mitchell, mother
Cooper	John R.	Carmer	Alma Bell	18 Nov. 1896	

Groom		Bride			
Surname	Given Name	Surname	Given Name	Date	Comments
Cooper	Lawrence H.	Buckley	Viola I.	9 May 1914	
Cooper	Morris B.	Poppe	Edna E.	9 Feb. 1915	
Cooper	Peter G.	Earle	Grace L.	15 May 1919	
Cooper	Sarshel Amos	Ray	Lola Catherine	18 Oct. 1915	
Cooper	Sash D.	Atchinson	Lella	17 Jan. 1900	no previous marriage
Cooper	Thomas J.	Bailey	Elizabeth	2 July 1898	no previous marriage
Cooper	Thomas S.	Dunn	Fannie J.	7 Oct. 1889	
Copeland	James	Robbins	Marboy (?) C.	18 Nov. 1881	
Coppedge	Charles O.	Heller	Laura E., Mrs.	3 Jan. 1891	br: widow
Coppedge	Ernest Frank	Johnson	Edna Louise	18 Dec. 1916	br: Syverine Johnson, mother
Coppedge	Robert	Graper	Mabel	15 Dec. 1914	
Copple	William H.	Shearer	Louisa	1 Nov. 1893	
Copps	Willis	Moore	Huldie Jane	12 Feb. 1877	
Copsey	Lumin	Beard	Gertrude V.	16 Jan. 1920	gr: Bertin Copsey, guardian
Corbaley	Frank R.	Cook	Katie (?)	24 June 1879	
Corbin	G. Benjamin	Hardin	Ida Jane	17 Dec. 1902	
Corbin	Warren	Logan	Adelia	6 Oct. 1915	
Corcoran	William D.	Allen	Hattie L.	31 Mar. 1917	
Corda	Joseph	Capello	Delila	16 Jan. 1897	gr: birthdate given as June 5 1866; Mark Fauery, Notary Public, witness
Cordano	Victor V.	Silva	Isabelle C.	7 June 1915	
Cordill	Lewis C.	McHarvey	Sadie	10 Feb. 1900	
Cordoza	Joseph	Silveira	Louise	12 Dec. 1908	
Coreia	Joaquim	Silvia (?)	Maria A.	30 July 1888	
Corfield	Thomas H.	Newman	Bessie E.	30 Dec. 1902	
Corfir	Carlo	Buletti	Elvezia	4 Feb. 1915	
Corippo	Benjamin H.	Gilardi	Edith A.	23 May 1916	
Corippo (?)	Steve	Swanson	Matilda	29 Nov. 1907	
Corliss	Albert	Ray	R. Belle	20 Feb. 1885	
Cormer	Frank F.	Wilson	Sophia	17 Sept. 1894	
Cornagie	Geo. W.	Sheuhart	L. B.	23 Oct. 1880	
Cornalson	Peter	Cooper	Charlotte	22 Jan. 1908	br: her mark witnessed by Harvey R. (?)
Cornelius	Clemens F.	Reechler	Bertha J.	8 Nov. 1919	

Groom		Bride			
Surname	**Given Name**	**Surname**	**Given Name**	**Date**	**Comments**
Cornelius	Emil	Englund	Etta	11 Oct. 1910	
Cornelius	George	Cornelius	Ella M.	24 Dec. 1907	
Cornell	Reynolds T.	Adamson	Mary	20 Jan. 1891	
Cornett	Ernest William	Munday	Verna Adelaide	23 Nov. 1905	
Cornett	N. W.	Frisbie	Mercie E.	18 Mar. 1895	
Cornett	William H.	Freeman	Lillian	28 Aug. 1900	
Cornwell	F. J.	Lynch	Maggie	24 Nov. 1894	
Cornwell	Jesse Roberts	Denton	Itasca Mae	7 Aug. 1905	
Corria	Antone F.	Hart	Myrthena Grace	18 Nov. 1916	witness to signature because of physical disability John T. Young
Corrick	William B.	Beasley	Bessie C.	14 Oct. 1908	
Corrillo	Leo Arthur	Billings	Nellie I.	15 Mar. 1916	
Corry	Julio	Corry	Marie	31 Dec. 1903	license requested by Antone Louis
Corstensen	Henry M.	Andersen	Josie E.	22 Oct. 1900	br: Ida M. Anderson, parent
Corts	Frank James	Cella	Beatrice	25 Sept. 1913	
Corum	Herbert A.	Rice	Mary E.	5 July 1904	
Corville	Richard	Adams	Alice P.	23 May 1901	br: Laura C. & W. D. Jones, mother & step-father
Cossa	Luigi	Ghisletta	Antonia	14 Dec. 1893	
Costa	Joseph W.	Smith	Mae D.	12 Dec. 1917	
Coster	George J.	Mays	Rilla L.	25 Nov. 1890	
Cotrell	Charles William	Wooley	Emma E.	6 Dec. 1905	
Cotter	William	Bates	Lottie	27 Oct. 1890	
Cottini	Erico	Belli	Flora	10 June 1914	
Cottle	Edmund J.	Baruch	Anita	6 Mar. 1905	
Cottle	Harold Bertrand	Meyer	Annie Dora	24 Dec. 1906	
Cottle	William Leonard	Wolcott	Edna Irene	15 July 1909	
Coul	Peter	Coventry (?)	Mary A.	11 Sept. 1880	
Coulter	Charles	Chambers	Elizabeth, Mrs.	13 Aug. 1904	
Coulter	Paul	Kirkpatrick	Grace Cynthia	19 Feb. 1907	
Counihan	Jeremiah	Sullivan	Kate	11 Feb. 1898	no previous marriage
Courtney	John George	Woods	Mary A.	25 Nov. 1903	
Courtney	Willard J.	Miller	Esther A.	20 July 1920	

Groom		Bride			
Surname	Given Name	Surname	Given Name	Date	Comments
Courtright	R.	Jackson	Mary M.	24 Apr. 1911	
Coutts	John	Minick	Viola E.	5 Dec. 1907	
Coutts	Maxwell C.	Block	Mamie M.	14 Oct. 1911	
Covell	R. William	Delany	Sarelda M.	10 Nov. 1919	
Covey	Alphaeus Vincel	Henderson	Alma R.	9 Apr. 1915	
Covey	Daniel	Ross	Laura M.	20 May 1890	
Covey	Geo. W.	Isaacs	Fanny	26 Nov. 1877	br: A. Isaacs, father
Covey	George W.	German	Charlotte	15 Dec. 1890	
Covey	Harmon	Miranda	Lee	26 May 1898	
Covey	James Walter	Ridenhour	Annie May	3 May 1904	
Covey	William	Ross	Hattie G.	21 Feb. 1899	no previous marriage
Covington	J. M.	Gentry	Amanda G., Mrs.	28 Jan. 1865	
Cowan	Edward	McDonald	Martha	15 Nov. 1913	
Cowan	James M.	Small	Agnes M.	26 Oct 1889	
Cowan	John	Orr	Alberta E.	16 Dec. 1911	
Cowan	Kenneth B.	Fuidge (?)	Rhea E.	11 Dec. 1919	
Cowan	Samuel Nelson	Russell	Eveline	28 Feb. 1884	
Cowan	William F.	Braughler	Florence I.	11 Nov. 1891	
Cowen	Frederick S.	Jacobs	Sarah	20 Feb. 1889	br: M. Jacobs, parent
Cowen	Joseph A.	Austin	Rose, Mrs.	13 Oct. 1897	br: widow
Cowger	William H.	Roberts	Ella W.	15 Aug. 1908	
Cowles	Ralph	Irwin	Elizabeth A.	15 Sept. 1915	
Cowley	Arthur S.	Shaw	May L.	16 Jan. 1893	license requested by Levina R. Shaw
Cowper	Charles Wallace	Laughlin	Willa Lee	28 Nov. 1908	
Cox	Alvin Joseph	Barnett	Mary Amelia	20 Mar. 1906	
Cox	Axley C.	Hassett	Ella L., Mrs.	8 Mar. 1898	br: divorced from J. T. Hassett, 16 Dec.1889, Sonoma Co.
Cox	Charles	Lewis	Julia	6 Mar. 1906	
Cox	Charles A.	Hughes	Virgia L.	11 Oct. 1900	
Cox	Clarence J.	Storer	Flossie	11 May 1903	
Cox	E. Morris	Anderson	Mary E.	10 July 1901	requested by Alvin J. Cox, brother of groom
Cox	Earl W.	Gilman	Barbara	19 June 1920	
Cox	George Edwin	Hughes	Alice Viola	6 June 1916	

Groom		Bride			
Surname	Given Name	Surname	Given Name	Date	Comments
Cox	George Mervon	Witherell	Laura Jane	29 Mar.1910	
Cox	Grover C.	Philbert	Rosa M.	14 Aug. 1911	br: Jennie Philbert, mother
Cox	Homer M.	Baine	Lola	4 Sept. 1909	
Cox	Hugh	Howard	Lulu M.	5 Nov. 1896	
Cox	James M.	Odell	Sophrmia	8 Nov. 1884	
Cox	Jessee C.	Wright	Eveline	10 Feb. 1866	
Cox	John	Knox	Edith	15 Sept. 1914	br: John P. Plover, guardian
Cox	John N.	Graves	Mary M.	28 Aug. 1897	npm
Cox	John Walter	Roduner	Alice Evelyn	21 Feb. 1921	
Cox	Leslie	Finley	Louise	21 Jan. 1908	
Cox	Nathan H.	Hopper	Ida Ione	4 Nov. 1876	br: her parents consenting; witness: F. G. Cunningham
Cox	Stacy Verne	Bower	Grace Lillian	5 Nov. 1920	
Cox	Thomas W.	Bell	Sarah Emma	9 Sept. 1876	
Cox	Willard S.	Church	Myrtle E.	26 May 1917	
Cox	William Frederick	Shriver	Loleta	26 Nov. 1909	
Cox	William M.	Beaver	Rosa E.	16 Aug. 1884	
Cox	William Martin	Jamison	Eugenia	1 Apr. 1896	
Cox	William Toliver	Beach	Helen G.	28 Feb. 1901	gr: Mrs. Ann Eliza Cox, aunt; br: Margarite Beach, mother; Sarah R. Moltman, witness
Cox	Winfred R.	Jamison	Mildred M.	7 May 1910	
Coy	Charles S.	Philbrick	Josie R.	15 Dec. 1886	
Coy	Charles S.	Hastings	Sallie E., Mrs.	20 July 1895	
Coy	Wm. B.	Proctor	Effie L.	4 Feb. 1885	
Coyan	Wilson S.	Sullivan	Leatha J.	15 Dec. 1888	
Coykendall	Chauncey B.	McMahon	Margaret	10 July 1896	
Coyne	Lawrence J.	Barman	Clara B.	4 Feb. 1920	
Cozad	Samuel L.	Stone	Ella	3 July 1888	
Cozort	John Gaines	Shuler	Cecil A.	8 June 1896	gr: signs with his mark, F. G. Nagle, witness; br: Mr. and Mrs. George Shuler give consent.
Cozzins	Davenport	Bowmer	Abbie W.	26 Aug. 1882	
Cozzo	Joseph, Jr.	Fry	Mildred M.	18 Apr. 1921	
Crabtree	Albert F.	Taylor	Lena P.	23 July 1910	

Groom		Bride			
Surname	Given Name	Surname	Given Name	Date	Comments
Crabtree	Albert H.	Sullivan	Nancy E.	14 Sept. 1895	
Cragin	Charles Chester	Williams	Laura Emily	23 Oct. 1912	do not publish
Cragun	Wilson H.	Sanborn	Flora L.	5 Dec. 1919	
Craib	William Joseph	Thierkoff	Florence	10 Apr. 1913	
Craig	Albert James	Matthews	Ina Marguite	28 Feb. 1911	
Craig	Bert F.	Palmer	Grace Pearl	13 May 1904	
Craig	Edwin Alfred	Gustafson	Esther E.	27 July 1918	
Craig	Francis A.	Beam	Alice May	17 Jan. 1905	
Craig	George Washington	Banta	Mary Alice	19 Jan. 1906	
Craig	Isaac	O'Connor	Florence M.	3 Nov. 1919	
Craig	Robert Geo.	Herger	Martha F.	17 Feb. 1912	
Craig	Robert John	Cheney	Irene Margaret	18 Sept. 1905	
Cramer	David R.	Gill	Elizabeth	3 Jan. 1866	
Cramer	John F.	Bosworth	Fannie L.	9 Nov. 1885	
Cramer	Walter	Scott	Lou Alice	10 Aug. 1901	gr: 4 Antonio St., San Francisco
Crandall	Charles I.	Tellefson	Dora	16 Oct. 1919	do not publish
Crandall	Edward	Arata	Rose	27 June 1902	
Crandall	Fred C.	Newcom	Lena, Mrs.	28 Jan. 1907	
Crandall	George A.	Stevens	Eva L.	16 Dec. 1912	
Crandall	James	Smith	Leona	15 Jan. 1910	
Crandall	John Calhoun	Snider	Joanna	6 Dec. 1875	gr: Mary J. Witlock, mother; father being dead; br: Mrs. Margaret Jane & John D. Snider, parents
Crandall	Walter W.	Keast	Mary A.	20 Oct. 1913	br: Caroline Keast, mother
Crandell	Clarence F.	Suetta	Elizabeth H.	15 June 1920	
Crandle	Frank	Snider	Naoma	23 Feb. 1881	gr: Mary J. Whitloch, mother; father dead; br: Mrs. Margaret J. Snider, mother; father out of state
Crane	Charles B.	Clay	Effie E.	24 Dec. 1878	
Crane	George S.	Faulconer	Jennie M.	24 Dec. 1878	br: Mr. & Mrs. Faulconer, parents
Crane	Homer W.	Grainger	Gertrude	12 Apr. 1907	
Crane	O. L.	Hinebauch	Allie	21 Sept. 1887	
Crane	Price T.	Savory	Nellie J.	2 Feb. 1895	

Groom		Bride			
Surname	Given Name	Surname	Given Name	Date	Comments
Crane	Richard Henry	Vogt	Anne D.	20 July 1911	
Crane	Tarlslm (?) L.	Wilkes	Mary E.	22 Dec. 1882	
Crane	Wade H.	Hicks	Allie B.	20 Sept. 1895	gr: Robert Crane gives consent and signs.
Crane	Wade Hampton	Himebauch	Lulu May	14 Jan. 1904	
Crane	William P.	Hughes	Edith A.	28 June 1892	
Cranmer	George O.	Rairdin	Virginia C.	9 Nov. 1914	
Cranwford	James A.	Metcalfe	Mary M.	2 Apr. 1883	
Craver	Frank W.	Leggett	Lizzie M.	18 Oct. 1902	
Craver	J. Edward	Hutchins	Mildred G.	19 June 1911	br: Willger H. Hutchins, parent
Crawford	Albert J.	Frisk	Hilda T.	18 Oct. 1915	
Crawford	Andrew Kerr	Alexander	Alice Maria	8 July 1875	
Crawford	Edwin Henry	Pohlmann	Carlotta Gertrude	31 Aug. 1906	
Crawford	Harry F.	Meyer	Francis M.	23 Mar. 1912	
Crawford	Jesse Blacker	Bernier	Frances Ellen, Mrs.	5 Oct. 1905	
Crawford	Roy S.	Walker	Marion E.	25 Mar. 1916	
Crawford	Russel D.	McDonald	Lillian	28 Oct. 1892	br: Gilbert McDonald, father, gives consent
Crawford	Thomas	Graham	Lettie	24 Nov. 1888	
Crawford	William E.	Taylor	Minnie G.	13 Nov. 1899	no previous marriage
Crayne	Stephen D.	Horgan	Julia C.	30 Oct. 1915	
Creagh	Michael	Miller	Jane, Mrs.	3 Nov. 1886	
Creagmile	James Albert	Guirach	Dora Rose	26 Aug. 1915	
Creagmile	John Cowan	Thompson	Catherine Ruth	5 Sept. 1916	
Crease	Henry George	Genochio	Elizabeth R.	20 Nov. 1913	
Creely	James H.	Cerini	Florence M.	19 July 1890	
Creighton	Charles Oscar	Johnson	Julia Lizette	7 Nov. 1895	
Cresante	Sepe	Casey	Bridget	15 Nov. 1910	
Cresap	Daniel	Gann	Martha	3 Apr. 1890	
Cresap	Gallant	Large	Byrtie	20 Aug. 1912	
Crescenzo (?)	Louis	Reynolds	H. T., Mrs.	13 Oct. 1883	
Crews	Artie C.	Green	Lucy M.	4 Aug. 1906	gr: Geo. W. & H. M. Crews, father & mother
Crigler	Albert P.	Bates	Laura E.	20 Dec. 1878	
Crigler	Thomas Millard	Porter	Martha Elizabeth	28 Dec. 1878	
Crigler	W. E.	Williams	Mary C., Mrs.	19 June 1878	

Groom		Bride		Date	Comments
Surname	Given Name	Surname	Given Name		
Crigler	Walter M. D.	Weselsky	Tillie	6 Oct. 1904	
Crimmings	Ernest Fulton	Byrne	Agnes	17 Nov. 1917	
Crips	Melvin T.	Strasser	Lizette C.	14 Nov. 1900	
Crispin	Charles A.	Brown	Esther E.	6 May 1916	
Crist	Henry A.	Locke	Ethel M.	19 Oct. 1912	
Crist	Walter K.	Campion	May	18 May 1893	
Crist	William	Hutter (?)	Rhoda	10 Mar. 1883	
Crist	Wm.	Jackson	Rosa Ann	18 Oct. 1866	
Crist	Wm. H.	Brown	Katie Maybell	10 Oct. 1888	br: Mrs. Louisa A. Brown, mother
Cristofani	Louis	Bartholdy	Ottilie	14 Dec. 1910	
Crivelli	Alexandro	Nonella	Celestine	10 Sept. 1910	
Crocker	Earl F.	Andersen	Anna Margaret	14 Sept. 1920	
Crocker	George S.	Parker	Angie F.	20 July 1892	
Crocker	J. M.	Johnson	Martha	31 July 1865	
Crocker	S. K.	Strait	Marie A.	13 June 1912	
Crocker	William Franklin	Higgins	Gertrude Vivian	24 Aug. 1905	
Crockett	Edmund Bowden	Arvilla	Florence, Mrs.	29 June 1909	
Crockett	George E.	Goddard	Viola M.	30 Dec. 1920	
Crockett	James D.	Isaacs	Retta	18 Dec. 1891	gr: W. F. Wines, witness to his mark
Crofoot	Willard H.	Fitch	Rosalin L.	20 Nov. 1916	
Croll	E. E. W.	Turner	Jennie B.	18 Oct. 1893	
Croman	Edward	Randall	Eliza S.	21 Dec. 1915	
Cromer	A. M.	Smith	Emma	27 Jan. 1881	
Crommett	Clyde Leon	Montgomery	Edwinnie	26 Aug 1907	
Cromwell	Bert G.	Sheehy	Lottie	5 July 1907	
Cromwell	Frederick H.	Jones	Nell A.	24 Dec. 1912	
Cromwell	J. G.	Coyn	Anna E.	4 May 1893	
Cromwell	John T.	Paschal	Ada M.	22 May 1890	
Cromwell	William O.	White	Florence	25 Feb. 1880	
Crone	Edwin	Knight	Mary	9 Nov. 1908	
Cronin	Joseph A.	McClancy	Isabella M.	23 June 1917	
Crooks	Asa S.	Connon	Mildred E.	12 Apr. 1920	
Crooks	Robert Lee	Keogh	Marion	9 July 1891	

Groom		Bride			
Surname	Given Name	Surname	Given Name	Date	Comments
Cropley	R. T.	Turnidge	Martha A.	5 Dec. 1914	
Cross	F. G.	Marshall	Josephine	16 May 1914	
Crossfield	Archa F.	Holmes	Nora M.	4 Oct. 1902	
Crossley	Edwin Hall	Wadsworth	Mildred Jeanette	16 Nov. 1915	
Crosta	Mateo	Gobbi	Rosie M.	9 June 1903	
Crotts	Charles Maxwell	Rose	Annie Gertrude	10 Dec. 1907	
Crotts	Louis U.	Rose	Maggie I.	19 Nov. 1907	
Crotyogini (?)	Battista	Lisignoli	Marie C.	27 Aug. 1919	
Croughin	Thomas	Sherlock	Abbie	5 July 1893	Alex McDonald, witness
Crow	Edward	Manin	Mary Ellen, Mrs.	27 Mar. 1877	gr: signs with his mark
Crowell	Albert	Vaughn	Belle, Mrs.	26 Mar. 1878	
Crowell	Elmer Harlow	Weltz	Katherine	5 May 1917	
Crowford	Thomas	Davidson	Mary Jane	22 Feb. 1865	
Crowley	Cornelius Joseph	Hrusa	Barbara	25 June 1904	
Crowley	David	Orre	Jeanette	4 Oct. 1918	
Crowley	John	Crafoot	Annie	13 Jan. 1894	br: surname could be Crofoot
Crowley	Timothy J.	Coffey	Mary E.	28 Sept. 1911	
Crozier	Alfred B.	Evans	Edith	30 Mar. 1921	
Crull	Frank M.	Brickley	Hattie	28 Apr. 1900	br: Preston B. Brickley, father
Crumley	Francis M.	Parsons	Nellie	9 Jan. 1893	
Cruse	James C.	Scudder	Edith B.	29 Dec. 1920	
Cruz	Joe	Bingham	Margaret	19 Oct. 1914	
Cruzan	Donald E.	Griffitts	Blanche U.	5 Aug. 1914	br: E. S. Griffitts, parent
Crystal	Melvin	Ewing	Sadie, Mrs.	18 May 1895	br: widow
Crystal	Richard Randolph	Silzle	Minnie Augusta	9 Jan. 1907	
Cuicci	Filippo	Alberigi	Amelia	24 Nov. 1890	br: Gioseppe Alberigi, father
Cuicello	Frank Louis	Baum	Pearl J.	10 July 1906	br: Cora E. Miller, mother
Cuicello	Manuel G.	Souza	Rosaline	10 Feb. 1899	no previous marriage
Culberson	Harold	Kelly	Elisabeth	8 May 1911	
Culbertson	John B.	Kennedy	Ida Belle	30 Mar. 1892	license requested by E. C. Bray; signed with X, no witness
Cullen	Edwin Patrick	Hopkins	Lottie	2 July 1903	license requested by Frank J. Cornwell
Cullen	Fred T.	Stephens	Sarah V.	21 June 1898	

Groom		Bride			
Surname	Given Name	Surname	Given Name	Date	Comments
Cullen	William Edward	Driscoll	Rinetta	26 Nov. 1895	
Culler	Albert Roy	Altman	Emma	9 Nov. 1914	
Culligan	Francis J.	Foss	Gertrude	24 May 1912	
Cummings	Frederick Merritt	Wright	Flora Agnes	27 June 1910	
Cummings	George Lawrence	Fulkerson	Ida Helen	28 Sept. 1905	
Cummings	Harry W.	King	Sarah I.	15 Oct. 1894	
Cummings	Harvey W.	Grennert	Carrie	7 July 1908	
Cummings	James M.	Johns	Martha	30 Sept. 1865	
Cummings	Ralph M.	Nielsen	Anna Marie	15 June 1917	
Cummings	William Frank	Parker	Virginia Belle	23 June 1908	
Cummings	William J.	Keiser	Josephine M.	18 Apr. 1902	
Cummins	George Arthur	Taylor	Martha Nina	14 May 1909	
Cummins	George Washington	Schroder	Helene Wilhelmine	20 Mar. 1901	br: 1919 Oak St., San Francisco; requested byAdelbert Sherman, friend
Cummins	J. L.	Lock	Phebe	19 Mar. 1887	
Cummins	W. E.	Lock	Mary F.	22 Nov. 1879	
Cuneo	Antonio	Tiscornia	Caterina	26 Apr. 1917	
Cuneo	G.	Cuneo	Amelia	15 Aug. 1889	
Cuneo	Joseph	Foppiano	Mary	22 Oct. 1908	
Cuneo	William J.	Greeott	Virginia G.	15 Sept. 1920	
Cunihan	John	Walsh	Sarah	17 June 1889	
Cunmmings	Charles E.	Bidwell	Lennie G.	11 Dec. 1919	
Cunningham	Charles John	Fox	Verna May	20 Aug. 1908	
Cunningham	Edmund James	Klein	Grace Lena	1 Dec. 1908	
Cunningham	Frank Michael	McCowen	Mary Louise	15 Feb. 1908	
Cunningham	George B.	Gregson	Nellie	6 Sept. 1919	
Cunningham	Hugh Ronald	Martin	Jennie	10 Oct. 1912	
Cunningham	John G.	McClure	May	4 Nov. 1891	
Cunningham	William Park	Hoffer	Gretchen	1 Aug. 1906	
Cunningham	Wm. N.	McCaughey	Mabel	30 June 1903	do not publish ages
Cunninghamc	Alcxandcr L.	Furlong	Margaret M.	10 Jan. 1903	
Cunninghame	Reuben H.	Colby	Mae L.	5 Dec. 1901	
Curran	Phillip Joseph	King	Blanche Elizabeth	2 June 1917	

Groom		Bride			
Surname	Given Name	Surname	Given Name	Date	Comments
Curran	William H.	Stender	Jeanette	7 Sept. 1920	
Current	Thomas David	Maddux	Martha E.	22 Nov. 1876	br: Wm. L. C. & Sarah B.? Maddux
Currie	Charles W.	Montgomery	Zimmie	12 Aug. 1914	
Currie	Claude Raymond	Parsons	Esther Ruby	5 Apr. 1917	
Currie	Robert Alvin	Church	Deets	18 Sept. 1915	
Curries	Wm. H.	Clark	Allice S.	23 Apr. 1884	
Curry	Sylvester James	Wilson	Alice Charie (?)	29 May 1920	
Curtin	Daniel J.	Breheny	Katie E.	5 Feb. 1918	
Curtis	Benj. A.	Humphrey	Rebecca A.	1 Dec. 1866	
Curtis	Charley C.	Gulland	Muriel	29 Aug. 1917	
Curtis	James H.	Green	Sarah J., Mrs.	28 Aug. 1865	
Curtis	Jos. S.	Brookfield	Marie R.	2 June 1883	
Curtis	L. A.	Williams	M. C., Mrs.	22 Nov. 1865	
Curtis	Robert Ross	Bradley	Mary Ellen	25 July 1905	br: Maggie Elizabeth Bradley, mother, gives consent
Curtis	Thomas J.	Thompson	Vera A.	23 Dec. 1905	br: Eliza J. Thompson, mother
Curtis	William G.	Fitzgerald	Mary	28 Apr. 1890	
Curtiss	Albert Melton	Stewart	Caroline F.	20 Mar. 1911	
Curtiss	George C.	Hormon	Mabel F.	22 Dec. 1897	license requested by J. H. Curtiss
Curtiss	Thomas E.	Martin	Fannie Susie, Mrs.	31 Mar. 1900	
Curtiss	Thomas Edson	Waltham	R. M., Mrs.	10 Oct. 1894	
Curtner	Alan E., Jr.	Burch	Celesta Jane	3 July 1920	
Cushman	Zacheus?	McDonald	Mary R.	12 Aug. 1879	
Cussins	William Edison	Bartlow	Edith Mable	17 Aug. 1912	br: Emma C. Bartlow, mother
Cussins	John E.	Jinks	Harriett M.	27 Mar. 1912	br: Amanda Jinks, mother
Custer	Albert S.	Schaefer	Minnie	6 July 1915	
Cuthill	James Sinclair	Oberfell	Mary	5 Nov. 1906	
Cutter	Charles Samuel	Thompson	Florence L.	2 Feb. 1898	
Cutter	Ephraim M.	Manuel	Florence I.	19 Apr. 1889	
Cutts	Lloyd C.	Anholm	Marie B.	7 Jan. 1905	
Cuvrean	Oscar F.	Gerst	Bertha A.	17 Apr. 1916	
d'Abreu	John Silveira	Tomazio	Maria	9 May 1885	
Da Roza	Antonio Domingo	Josephe	Maria	3 Apr. 1896	

Groom		Bride			
Surname	Given Name	Surname	Given Name	Date	Comments
Dabner	Manuel	Mathews	May	Dec. 1886	gr: Mary Dabner, mother; witness Frank Dabner; br: B. S. Matthews, father
Dabner	Manuel	Kahrs	Marie	31 Dec. 1903	
Dad	R.	Weatherly	Julia	7 Feb. 1919	
Dado	Arnold Walter	Respini	Flaminia L.	8 July 1898	no previous marriage
Dado	Atilio Anthony	Gambonini	Olivia Lettitia	27 Oct. 1906	
Daggett	Mathew H.	Moore	Margaret	13 June 1914	
Dagi	Augostino	Dellavedora	Maria	8 Feb. 1902	
Dahack	Elsia	Frost	Jennie	30 Sept. 1894	
Dahl	Oscar	Hollar	Nora	21 Sept. 1909	
Dahlmann	Otto Hugo	Davis	Mary	4 Nov. 1907	
Dailey	Lawrence L.	Skee	Mary	25 June 1920	
Dailey	Le Roy C.	Svilovivh	Evelyn N.	26 Dec. 1917	
Dake	John A.	Wall	Ada M.	20 Dec. 1913	
Dal Pino	Guiseppe	Dinucci	Mary	30 July 1906	
Dalbalcon	Louis	Dalmaso	Olinpia	15 June 1912	
Dale	J. W.	Boswell	Cora L.	20 Apr. 1894	
Dalessi	Walter	Clausen	Minnie	17 Oct. 1919	
Daley	George	Cooper	Ida May	21 Jan. 1896	
Dallas	John P.	Everhart	Effie	13 Sept. 1915	
Dalpoggetto	Charles	Proletti	Mary	27 Mar. 1890	
Dalton	Edwin P.	Belcher	Ruth A.	3 July 1919	
Dalton	Thomas Benton	Lawrence	Linny Belle	25 June 1883	
Daly	Thomas B.	Smith	Fannie	15 Mar. 1884	br: C. W. Smith, parent; born 15 Mar. 1867
Damaino	Mike	Esaia	Natalina	10 Oct. 1914	
Damario	Damacati	Lucchesi	Pauline	25 Jan. 1907	
Damon	Henry Stuart	Peterson	Pearl	29 Jan. 1908	
Damon	Myron H.	Churchman	Maggie A.	3 Feb. 1883	br: Vernon Downs, guardian
Dana	Alfred H.	Ballard	Mae B.	26 Aug. 1901	
Dana	George Sherman	Fay	Cora	29 Nov. 1893	
Dana	Martin V. B.	Long	Hattie Irene	29 June 1903	
Dana	P. F.	Perz	Dora	27 Jan. 1913	
Dana	Fred C.	Wheeler	Isabella M.	6 May 1907	

Groom		Bride			
Surname	**Given Name**	**Surname**	**Given Name**	**Date**	**Comments**
Daniels	Claude William	Bridges	Katie L.	2 Feb. 1904	br: I. N. Bridges, parent
Daniels	Corel (?) J.	Nally	Jennie M.	2 Sept. 1918	
Daniels	Fred J.	Vassar	Lizzie	11 June 1897	npm
Daniels	George Eaton	Luedke	Mae Florence	24 Dec. 1907	
Daniels	H. A.	Lownes	Mary	10 Sept. 1911	
Daniels	Herbert Mason	Short	Myra Lydia	28 May 1898	not to be published till Monday
Daniels	Leroy E.	Davaz	Rose	2 June 1914	gr: Mrs. Emma Carter, mother
Daniels	William E.	Gardner	Emma	23 Nov. 1892	
Danly	Lloyd Elmer	Hennessy	Rose Mary	2 Feb. 1921	
Dannals	Charles H.	Sheldon	Harriet L.	15 Mar. 1889	
Dannells	Walter Byron	Morton	Georgia Norene	22 Dec. 1905	
Dannhausen	William	Dannhausen	Meta, Mrs.	5 Dec. 1905	
Dapelo	Luigi	Maggio	Maria	28 Oct. 1908	
Dar	David	Young	Flora E.	24 Sept. 1902	gr: witness to mark T. C. Barnes
Darby	Jasper	Truett	Josephine	2 June 1887	
Darby	Jasper B.	Gwin	Jessie	27 July 1908	gr: Jasper N. Darby, father
Darby	Jasper N.	Warner	Augusta, Mrs.	30 Nov. 1900	
Darby	Martin Ernest	Baker	Julia	27 June 1914	please do not publish
Darden	L. T.	Hodgson	May V.	1 Nov. 1883	
Darling	Floyd Willis	Daniels	Edith Edna	10 May 1916	
Darrow	John O.	Maxwell	Mary E.	26 Nov. 1866	
Dart	William E.	Tracy	Hazel J.	29 July 1919	
Dasquith	Sidney W. G.	Drake	Dora Luella	15 June 1916	
Dasso	Dante A.	Field	Edna	15 May 1919	
Dauer	Charles R.	Davis	Ada	6 Aug. 1880	
Davall	Melvin O.	Smith	Ellen E.	25 May 1903	
Daveiro	John	Gonsalves	Rose	17 Feb. 1912	
Daveiro	Manuel J.	Gonsalves	Anna C.	18 Dec. 1912	
Davello	Joseph L.	Wedge	Josephine M.	14 July 1917	
Davello	Tony J.	Wedge	Clara B.	11 Nov. 1916	
Davenport	Harry A.	Greavor	Betrina	17 Sept. 1910	
Davenport	P. C.	Smith	Daisy	6 Mar. 1893	br: consent given by step-father, W. T. Snyder who signs his name

Groom		Bride			
Surname	Given Name	Surname	Given Name	Date	Comments
Davidson	Allen	Archambeau	Mary O.	17 Oct. 1865	
Davidson	Chris	Schilly	Hattie	4 Mar. 1904	
Davidson	Edward	Haehl	Cora	4 Dec. 1906	
Davidson	F. W.	Morey	Florence A.	28 May 1914	
Davidson	Fay L.	Root	Vida D.		gr: letter from Mrs. Z. M. Davidson stating his age 18, 14 Sept. 1917 SF
Davidson	Fred C.	Senecal	Pearl Harrison	21 Dec. 1909	
Davidson	John	Brugge	Loretta R.	1 Oct. 1913	
Davidson	John	Davidson	Martha	8 Feb. 1866	
Davidson	Roy Frederick	Kimes	Mabel Ann	3 Jan. 1908	
Davidson	W. W.	Wright	Nellie J.	14 Aug. 1879	
Davie	Henry A.	Wilson	Alice A.	10 Apr. 1912	
Davila	Antonio S.	Bispo	Mary E.	28 Nov. 1887	
Davini	Joe	Domitille	Carlotina	13 July 1916	br: Mrs. Angellina Domitille, mother
Davis	Adelbert A.	Stine	Syvia C.	20 Nov. 1901	
Davis	Alphonse G. W.	Wilsey	Ida M.	22 Dec. 1877	br: H. Wilsey, parent; A. E. Shattuck, witness
Davis	B. F.	Beebe	Frances J.	10 May 1916	
Davis	Barton J.	Dutton	Loraine K.	11 Oct. 1899	gr: widower; br: formerly Bamber, divorced 28 Sept.1898, Monterey Co.
Davis	Charles Alva	Fine	Mary M.	20 Apr. 1882	
Davis	Charles E.	Coleman	Jennie	10 Feb. 1915	
Davis	Charles E.	Davis	Edith M.	23 Nov. 1895	
Davis	Charles Henry Alexander	Jewell	Sally	24 Aug. 1903	br: requested license
Davis	Charles Louis	Banks	Esther E.	18 July 1919	
Davis	Charles M.	Da Shiell	Annie	5 Feb. 1908	
Davis	Charles Marion	Walton	Ida O.	13 June 1904	
Davis	Charles N.	Hoover	Elizabeth	14 June 1894	
Davis	Christopher C.	Gray	Florence Olive, Mrs.	20 June 1895	br: widow
Davis	Claude H.	Cook	Estella M.	17 Sept. 1914	
Davis	Clyde Leroy	Ford	Mildred Agnes	2 Jan. 1919	
Davis	Daniel O., Jr.	Murch	Jennie S.	29 June 1880	

Groom		Bride			
Surname	**Given Name**	**Surname**	**Given Name**	**Date**	**Comments**
Davis	Edward J.	Wood	Francis A.	4 Sept. 1912	
Davis	Edward W.	Young	Margaret L.	21 Mar. 1891	
Davis	Erastus L.	Davis	Mary L.	30 Dec. 1918	
Davis	Erastus L.	Davis	Mary L., Mrs.	1 Jan. 1919	
Davis	Ernest J.	Robinett	Ida L.	29 Apr. 1915	
Davis	Floyd E.	Huntington	Eva J.	29 Nov. 1916	
Davis	Frank N.	Stine	Joysa R.	20 Nov. 1901	
Davis	Fred William	Rima	Alta L.	6 June 1896	
Davis	G. W.	Warner	Mary E.	20 July 1878	
Davis	George A.	Spurr	Rose R.	22 Sept. 1884	
Davis	George Armstead	Smith	Helen Amanda	19 Nov. 1880	gr: D. O. Davis, parent; Emma R. Hill & H. K. Brown, witnesses
Davis	George B.	Doane	Lulu M.	16 Apr. 1892	
Davis	George W.	Richards	Penelope R.	17 July 1919	
Davis	Gilman Bush	Clark	Mollie	9 Aug. 1879	
Davis	H. H.	Hope	Natalie	15 Nov. 1887	
Davis	H. Ruliff	Churchman	Edith	2 Oct. 1900	
Davis	Harry A.	Rines	Luella	27 July 1910	
Davis	Harry Edward	Stottlemyer	Rena Ada	18 Aug.1909	
Davis	Henry A.	Timme	Millie, Mrs.	16 Nov. 1904	
Davis	J. Harris	Starkey	Josephine P.	3 Aug 1892	
Davis	J. M.	Viestentz	Alma A.	29 Aug. 1912	
Davis	James M.	Smith	Agnes	12 Aug. 1896	br: Albert Smith gives consent; W. J. T. Orr, witness
Davis	John	Drake	Maud	2 Sept. 1894	
Davis	John Elmer	Deal	Mary Catherine	10 Oct. 1885	br: handwritten by her father Amos Deal on second page
Davis	John H.	Montgomery	Ambrosine	17 June 1901	
Davis	John M.	Flesher	Elsie V.	5 Mar. 1915	
Davis	Jonah W.	Huntley	Emma	18 Mar. 1893	
Davis	Joseph Isaac	Smith	Nolia Malinda	15 Nov. 1906	
Davis	Mac A.	Kopp	Frances M.	30 Sept. 1911	
Davis	Mack A.	Neurauter	Agnes	22 Apr. 1901	

Groom		Bride		Date	Comments
Surname	Given Name	Surname	Given Name		
Davis	Manra (?) J.	Case	Susie	12 June 1883	
Davis	Milton M.	Garvin	Nora S.	14 Sept. 1916	
Davis	Monroe	Leek	Mary Jane	14 Nov. 1874	
Davis	Percy E.	Ward	Lalitte I.	26 Nov. 1913	
Davis	Preston R.	Neergaard	Grace Lovell, Mrs.	14 Jan. 1897	not to be published
Davis	Robert E.	Frost	Phoebe A.	21 May 1914	
Davis	Ulysses G.	Flesher	Josephine M.	23 Dec. 1898	br: B. F Flesher, parent
Davis	Walter Allen	Hermann	Ethel Clifford	22 Aug. 1917	
Davis	Walter S.	Perkins	Eva F.	21 Feb. 1894	
Davis	William Henry	Fields	Lucinda	3 July 1879	gr: born 1859, Robt. Thompson & B. J. Davis, parents; br: born 1861
Davis	William L.	Sullivan	Margaret Catherine	6 June 1891	
Davis	Henry D.	Kelsey	Mary H.	2 Oct. 1900	do not give ages
Davison	George W.	Eccles	Grace S.	18 Feb.1901	br: Matilda M. Wentworth, mother
Davison	Henry W.	Thompson	Fannie S.	13 Aug 1907	
Davison	Robert W. S.	Totman	Ruth M.	4 Nov. 1916	
Daw	J. M.	Berger	Anna E.	30 Dec. 1913	
Dawe	George C.	Guirand	Ella	4 May 1914	
Day	Carl F.	Bowersmith	Lottie V.	28 June 1919	
Day	Charles Eugene	Fallon	Edna Brown	6 Mar. 1906	
Day	Denny	Fay	Laura, Mrs.	11 Sept. 1907	
Day	George Frank	Dicke	Lizzie	25 Sept. 1906	
Day	Harmon A.	Gilbert	May E.	23 Aug. 1915	br: Hattie E. Gilbert, mother
Day	John	Swanson	Louisa	5 Oct. 1903	
Day	Louie	Kelly	Stella	19 June 1915	
Day	William B.	Luce	Mary E.	19 Jan. 1899	gr: widower
Day	William T.	Gould	Bessie E.	27 Nov. 1906	
Dayton	John J.	Sharp	Gertie P.	22 July 1916	
Dayton	Wm. L.	Kreamer	Nellie	20 Jan. 1879	br: George Kreamer, father: witness: Alex Caseres
de Avilla	Jose Fereira	Rose	Mary	8 Dec. 1891	br: Frank Rose, guardian
de Betencur	Joao	da Silva	Maria Jozc	16 Aug. 1886	
de Emparon	Ricordo	Vallejo	Lulu E.	21 Aug. 1882	requested by N. P. Vallejo

Groom		Bride			
Surname	**Given Name**	**Surname**	**Given Name**	**Date**	**Comments**
De France	John	Steed	Martha	29 Oct. 1906	
De Groot	Frank	Henningsen	Mary	23 Jan. 1895	
de Klark	Henry	Perry	Minnie	21 Jan. 1912	
De Lappe	Fred R.	Guerne	Edith G.	22 Mar. 1896	
de Lappe	Wisley R.	Sheldon	Dorothy P.	13 Mar. 1915	
De Martini	John	Ariasi	Margaret	28 Aug. 1913	
De Matei	Louis Paul	Bacigalupi	Josephine	30 Aug. 1918	
De Maura	Antonio	Viera	Mary	2 Apr. 1901	
de Neuf	Emil A.	Chamberlain	Georgie	23 Aug. 1920	
De Patta	Joseph Miles	Fisher	Claire G.	24 Feb. 1913	
De Rosa	Roque P.	Aguiar	Maria S.	26 Jan. 1911	
de Silva	Manuel R.	Beteneur	Marianna Teadora	30 Mar. 1885	
de Souza	Jose	Williams	Jennie	29 Sept. 1915	
De Souza	Manuel T.	De Matos	Maria	5 Aug. 1901	
De Souza	Tony	Rose	Mary D.	24 Apr. 1901	
de Violini	Arduino	Garton	Harriet P.	2 Oct. 1915	
Deakin	Henry C.	Moore	Catharine	20 Feb. 1893	
Deal	John L.	Cromwell	Edith M., Mrs.	20 Aug. 1898	br: divorced more than one year
Deal	Oliver Morton	Deal	Minnie Etta	29 Aug. 1899	no previous marriage; br: requested license
Dealy	Charles A.	Ganske	Mabel K.	8 June 1918	
Dean	Carl R.	Heartwell	Jessie B.	23 Nov. 1912	
Dean	Herbert Burroughs	Hanseb	Agnes M.	22 Nov. 1919	
Dean	James Monroe	Gjedberg	Clara	25 Aug. 1915	
Dean	John E.	Preston	Mabel G.	15 Nov. 1917	
Dean	Leslie Chauncy	Harford	Ethel Florence	14 July 1905	
Dean	Lewis F.	Weidman	Emerine	11 Nov. 1865	
Dean	Oliver Franklin	Pember	Ethel Marie	4 June 1917	
Deas	Joseph Vargas, Jr.	Gresham	Gladys Elizabeth	9 Apr. 1917	
Deaueare (?)	John	Binner (?)	Elizabeth	23 May 1876	br: E. Wooldridge, grandmother; Cloverdale; her parents are dead; another letter from mother D. B. Morgan
Debo	Emil C.	Sarzotti	Teresa	4 Feb. 1921	
DeBolt	John H.	Schultz	Leonora	19 May 1899	gr: widower; don't publish until Monday

Groom		Bride			
Surname	Given Name	Surname	Given Name	Date	Comments
DeBolt	Ralph A.	Barnett	Loretta B.	5 Mar. 1912	
Decanini	Giovanni	Proletti	Josephina	11 Mar. 1902	br: Guiseppe Proletti, father; Robert A. Poppe, witness
Decarli	Antonio	Miranda	Mary	21 Apr. 1913	
DeCarli	Bathista	Mascoinini	Lily	22 July 1911	
DeCarli	Victor	Filippini	Elmira Mary	18 Oct. 1906	
Decco	Henry	Mendoco	Laura	6 Oct. 1904	
Decker	Elmer E.	Moran	Florence B.	28 Jan. 1913	
Decker	Frank William	McDonnell	Louise	24 Dec. 1906	
Decker	John T.	Coary	Gusta	1 Sept. 1865	
Decker	Martin Arthur	Isaac	Eva	23 Oct. 1912	
Decker	Nias M.	Poulson	Nettie E.	17 July 1888	
Decoe	T. C.	Barnes	Henrietta A.	21 Sept. 1881	
Decvursoy (?)	John	Beedle	Lena E.	13 July 1878	br: S. Beedle, parent
Dedmond	Edward F.	McHugh	Bertha E.	29 July 1919	
Deeds	William W.	Barnes	Annie	20 Aug. 1915	
Deevy	Daniel J.	Marron	Nellie	30 July 1915	
Defanti	Albert Alphonse	Ferrari	Elva	25 Apr. 1914	
Deffenbaugh	Louis M.	Hopkins	Ruby B.	10 June 1920	
Degn	Jorgen Andersen	Beier	Mette M.	24 Oct. 1888	
DeGoa	Victor G.	Page	Gladys H.	8 Feb. 1921	
DeGregorio	Peter Martin	Davidson	Mable Ann	8 Dec. 1914	
DeGuerre	Harold	Haywood	Ruth A.	19 May 1917	
Dei	Henry	Bennett	Alice H.	7 Aug. 1920	
Dei	John W.	Finley	Annette	24 Jan. 1916	br: J. D. & Mrs. C. A. Finley, parents & John Plover, Probation Officer, guardian
Dei	Peter	Tognacca	Lizzie	22 May 1911	
Deily	James B.	Coventry	Adelle	27 Dec. 1880	br: Peter Caul, guardian
Deini	Leonardo	Sullivan	Andrea, Mrs.	11 May 1905	
Deiss	William F.	Riewerts	Marie Josephine	14 June 1909	
Del Bianco	Attilio	Bisordi	Emma M.	11 Nov. 1912	
Del Piano	Giovanni	Cavallo	Catherina	25 Oct. 1918	
Del Prette	Ferdinando	Stefani	Carrie	11 Jan. 1909	

Groom		Bride			
Surname	Given Name	Surname	Given Name	Date	Comments
Delahunty	Bernard	Cunningham	Mattie	20 Apr. 1885	handwritten
DeLaney	Everett M.	Butin	Elsie Lee	7 June 1913	
Delbary	Marcel	Anglade	Ida	20 July 1905	
DelCarlo	Arcangelo	Puccinelli	Assunta	29 May 1920	
Delehanty	James E.	Armstrong	Alice	24 July 1915	
Delevan	Frederick S.	Carvell	Lucia E. E.	3 Oct. 1896	
Delong	Albert N.	Schuster	Josie	10 Dec. 1895	gr: Harriet L. Hereford gives consent and signs
DeLong	William L.	Gouley	Mollie, Mrs.	20 Nov. 1920	
Deloran	Jefferson	Werick	N. Tewella M.	26 June 1883	br: Erwin Brady, guardian
Deluca	Amadeo	Papear	Louisa, Mrs.	28 Mar. 1901	gr: F. Guido Otti, witness to make; br: widow
Demartini	Albert	Moretti	Irene	11 Oct. 1901	
DeMartini	Benigno	DeMartini	Irene, Mrs.	7 Sept. 1907	
DeMartini	Louis	Moretti	Rose	21 July 1899	no previous marriage
DeMartini	Mansueto	Monghette	Angealina	21 Jan. 1903	
DeMell	Joseph	Kelley	Florence Euyler?	17 Feb. 1904	
Demman	John R.	Parsons	Ella M.	5 Dec. 1888	
Demousset	Armand	Frirot (?)	Fanny	23 Sept. 1879	
Dempsey	Patrick	McKeown	Margaret	6 Jan. 1883	
Denchy	Cornelius	Stone	Alice	16 Dec. 1919	
Denham	Drury	Egner	Martha	12 June 1916	
Denham	Frank P.	Nesbitt	Eva Elizabeth	11 Oct. 1918	
Denicke	H.	Dutton	Emma J.	3 Dec. 1884	
Denis	Foster	Stuart	Isabel	29 Apr. 1887	signed by Charles D. Stuart
Denis	George Edward	Shinn	Anna Helen	22 Dec. 1909	
Denise	Louis H.	Shelley	Mabel	23 June 1897	
Denison	Joseph N.	Davis	Dara A.	17 Sept. 1879	
Denman	F. H.				
Denman	Frank H.	Edwards	Charlotte T.	4 Feb. 1885	
Denner	Russell L. A.	Dreyer	Helena E.	20 Mar. 1915	
Dennes	Edward F.	Ray	Hattie	17 Nov. 1891	
Dennis	William Whan	Clark	Clara Belle	28 Sept. 1908	
Dennison	Ezra D.	Lloyd	Emma	22 June 1892	

Groom		Bride			
Surname	Given Name	Surname	Given Name	Date	Comments
Dennison	Ezra D.	Kinne	Ethel S.	26 Feb. 1916	
Denny	Lloyd L.	Hardin	Lucinda T.	30 July 1910	br: George M. Hardin, father
Dent	Elmer S.	Doyle	Ruth	18 Aug. 1917	
Dent	William	Steer	Marian	1 Dec. 1898	gr: widower
Denton	Paul R.	Ward	E. May	28 Dec. 1912	
Denucci	Angelo	Rossi	Maddalena	30 Apr. 1888	
Depole	Giovanni	Rondinella	Maria	13 May 1908	
Deremer	Fred Richard	MacCaskie	Alice Jane	14 Apr. 1905	
Derham	Christopher	Hall	Nola	29 May 1915	br: Mrs. Ida Hall, mother
Derham	Herbert	McCloskey	Ida	2 June 1906	
Derham	Le Roy	Kaster	Dena	30 Apr. 1904	
DeRoco	Leo U.	Ferrasci	Theresa L.	18 Oct. 1913	
DeRosa	Manuel	Beffa	Lillie	31 Mar. 1917	
DeRose	William	Whitaker	Rena Pearl	14 July 1909	
Derrick	C. A.	Crandal	Annie, Mrs.	5 May 1887	
Derrick	Charles Erwin	Francesco	Mary Lenora	5 Feb. 1921	
Derrick	Geo. W.	Bacon	Lillie T.	30 Nov. 1880	
Derrick	George L.	Clawson	Lucy E.	15 Oct. 1900	
Derrick	Grant	Snyder	Laura	26 Oct. 1888	
Derrick	Herbert D.	Stinchfield	Florence V.	30 Sept. 1913	br: G. E. Stinchfield, parent
Derrick	Jesse W.	Davis	Mary J.	8 Oct. 1883	
Descalso	James R.	Moore	Helen E.	22 July 1914	
Descalso	Luke M.	Kerschner	Juanita Evangeline	11 Feb. 1918	
DeSelle	Howard L.	Shaffer	Fern Rebbeca	8 Nov. 1915	
Desin	John N.	Campbell	Etta M.	28 Nov. 1913	
Despain	Silas M.	Steifel	Matilda L.	24 Aug. 1918	
Deter	Harry R.	Spencer	Emma V.	30 Sept. 1913	
Deter	John	Elburn (?)	Laura	25 June 1902	do not publish until Saturday
Detroit	Philip Adam	Kelley	Lulu Salome	14 Jan. 1908	
DeTurk	William S.	Mooney	Anna J.	13 Nov. 1894	
Deu Vaul	Bert E.	Martin	Violet D.	26 June 1920	
Deuprey	Munson	Swisher	B. Clifton	22 Dec. 1904	
Deutch	Edward	Wood	Mellicent	27 Aug. 1915	

Groom		Bride			
Surname	Given Name	Surname	Given Name	Date	Comments
Devencenzi	Victor	Gipp	Margaret C.	17 June 1912	br: Mrs. Katie Curtis, mother
Devine	Patrick	Meghan	Fannie M.	9 Nov. 1891	
Devlin	Thomas H.	Morris	Elvin B.	27 Mar. 1916	
Devoto	Tonni	Guissi	Mary	4 Apr. 1914	
Devow	George	Drever	Harriet	12 Apr. 1880	
Dewey	Dean	Daniels	Lilly M.	26 Oct. 1908	
Dewey	Gra M.	Nye	Adelaide D.	5 Nov. 1908	
Dewey	Victor R.	Hilgereoh	Helen Mildred	31 Oct. 1916	
DeWitt	Harry Arthur	Jeans	Jessie Lee	4 May 1909	
DeWitt	Henry C.	Dix	Annie M.	7 June 1894	
Dexter	Wm. A.	Sacrey	Mary J.	29 Sept. 1866	
Di Grazia	Giocondo	Passarino	Dalia	8 Jan. 1900	
Dias	Antone	Richi	Sarah E.	25 Nov. 1918	
Dias	I. S.	Rhoades	Alzina	7 Feb. 1883	
Dibble	Lawrence Levinice	Tomblinson	Gertrude Annie	28 Nov. 1905	
Dibble	Leroy Earl	Bohn	Jennie	10 Feb. 1906	
Dibble	Roland C.	Muther	Georgie M.	22 Nov. 1898	
Dibble	Walter	Locke	Veravuche (?)	30 July 1875	br: Morgan & Mary E. Locke, parents
Dibble	William I.	Butler	Bessie	11 May 1883	
Dibblee	William Henry	Lewis	Georgiana	14 Jan. 1904	
Diceare ?	Salvatore	Barsuglia	Josie	12 Nov. 1912	br: John Barsuglia, father; calls her Giovanni
Dicke	George	Baxman	Hattie Laurietta	8 July 1916	
Dickerson	Melvin R.	Liddell	Anna	30 June 1910	
Dickerson	Roy Ernest	Howard	Delle	9 July 1904	
Dickerson	George E.	McInerney	Isabel M.	24 May 1920	
Dickey	Arthur E.	Herman	Bessie	18 Nov. 1910	
Dickey	William James	Phillips	Mabel	18 Aug.1909	br: requested license
Dickmann	Charles H.	Wilson	Jessie E.	11 Aug. 1920	
Dickson	David Simms	Middogh	Myrtle	12 Dec. 1908	gr: Lizzie B. Dickson, mother
Dickson	Frank B.	Winans	Luella M.	30 Dec. 1889	
Dickson	Frank Maurice	McGovern	Annie Lauretta	23 June 1917	
Dickson	J. C.	Caldwell	Jane	17 Oct. 1865	
Dickson	J. M.	Spence	W. O.	3 Nov. 1885	

Groom		Bride			
Surname	Given Name	Surname	Given Name	Date	Comments
Dickson	Joshua B.	Griffiths	Josie E.	19 Feb. 1896	
Dickson	Joshua Bates, Jr.	Gates	Ethel G.	20 Dec. 1920	
Dickson	William H.	Jones	Laura H.	24 Aug. 1881	
Dickson	William M.	Dickson	Lizzie B.	25 Aug. 1904	
Diehl	Henry N.	de Martini	Millie	20 July 1920	
Dietert	Rudolph H.	Wiberg	Betty	2 May 1910	
Dietrich	Gottlieb	Hoffstetter	Albertine	16 Feb. 1886	
Dietrich	Joseph W.	Harrison	Florence	4 Sept. 1912	
Dietz	Henry Werner	Barrows	Edith Ainslie	15 Nov. 1907	
Dietz	Otto Frank	Hooper	Harriet	6 July 1908	
Dightman	W. E.	Gimtley	Emma	6 Feb. 1885	
Dilena	Simon	Guggia	Josephine Mary	27 Oct. 1907	
Dilges	William	Lines	Lulu	25 Jan. 1904	
Dillingham	John L.	Martin	Susie	21 Jan. 1899	gr: divorced more than one year
Dillingham	John Lee	Willis	Lulu	6 July 1896	
Dillman	Charles	Doss	Iva	14 Feb. 1899	no previous marriage
Dillon	Charles	Bailiff	Geraine M.	15 Sept. 1885	
Dillon	Charles E.	Thompson	Francis E.	13 Apr. 1901	
Dillon	David	Peyton	Lillian	20 Mar. 1915	
Dillon	Isaac Parry	St. John	Edith Lenore	29 May 1901	
Dillon	James E.	Bagan	Emma M., Mrs.	24 Nov. 1902	
Dillon	John H.	Bones	Lida M.	8 Oct. 1900	
Dillon	Melville C.	Dillon	Margaret G.	31 Aug. 1893	
Dingle	Chas. Edward	Sims	Nellie	14 Aug. 1880	
Dinmore	Walter Robert	Lewis	Nannie May	5 Jan. 1891	license requested by G. P. Hall
Dinsdale	George D.	Stenrud (?)	Nellie J.	24 Oct. 1913	
Dinucci	Adolph	Moes	Ernestine	7 July 1919	
Dinucci	Antonio	Dinucci	Filomina	4 Aug. 1900	
Dinucci	Fred	Hayes	Grace	26 May 1914	br: Mrs. Harriet Hayes, mother
Dinucci	Richard	Vellutini	Lizzie	26 Sept. 1914	
Dinucci	Romeo	Garetti	Lena	3 Oct. 1916	
Dioke	Joseph	Bush	Lesa	23 Dec. 1886	
Dirvin	Peter	Bugbee	Evalyn	23 Oct. 1909	

Groom		Bride			
Surname	Given Name	Surname	Given Name	Date	Comments
Disbro	Ernest F.	Workover	Edwine C.	23 Apr. 1917	
Disher	George W.	Leigh	Amanda J.	2 Nov. 1878	
Disher	William F.	Maddocks	Erminia	2 Jan. 1891	
Disney	John H.	Callison	Leona E.	26 Dec. 1912	
Ditlersen	Albert	Judd	Mable Florence	31 Dec. 1913	
Dittemon	Loven J.	Fay	Edith	1 Nov. 1898	gr: divorced over 3 years
Dittman	Fred August	Phillips	Katherine Wendell	14 Aug. 1912	
Dittmann	Henry	Drickhammer	Meta	22 May 1891	
Dittmann	Wilhelm E. J.	Hinoch	Katherine Margarette Minna	18 Oct. 1897	
Dittmore	Clarence A.	Teaby (?)	Ora A.	1 Oct. 1898	no previous marriage
Dixon	Harold G.	Heselschwerdt	Inez E.	8 May 1911	
Dixon	James W.	Shaler	Eliza E.	28 Mar. 1867	
Dixon	John T.	Crigler	Lottie	11 Nov. 1896	
Dixon	R. Dawson	Riley	Bessie M.	28 Oct. 1912	
Dixon	Walter C.	Huckabay	Maude Sarah	5 May 1917	
Dixon	William Gordon	Canfield	Gertrude	9 May 1906	
do Rego	Francisco Theodoro	Medeiros	Victoria Gloria	25 May 1883	
Dobel	William L.	McClure	Emma	14 June 1913	
Doble	John Luther	St. John	Hattie B.	28 Mar. 1898	
Dobyne	William H.	Cohenous	Jennie F.	31 Dec. 1889	
Doda	Hobart J.	Fiori	Frances	28 Oct. 1919	
Doda	Victor	Adams	Sadie	13 Dec. 1910	
Dodge	A. C.	Barker	Sophie	31 Jan. 1880	br: H. W. Tyler, father
Dodge	Harold Carew	Woolsey	Louise	20 June 1914	
Dodge	James Arthur	Hopkins	Alma Luella	2 July 1910	
Dodge	Milton	Bossen	Sophia	2 June 1915	
Dodge	Milton	Mann	Lulu	5 Nov. 1908	
Dodge	Neal E.	Simmons	Gladys F.	29 July 1920	
Dodgson	John C.	Oustott (?)	Ruth C.	14 Jan. 1920	not signed by either party
Dodson	William Howard	Merrick	Eleanor Dorothy	26 Aug. 1915	
Doe	Edgar A.	Pallo	Victoria	21 Nov. 1917	
Doelling	Harry J. W.	Bruner	Olive L.	2 Feb. 1918	please don't publish ages

Groom		Bride			
Surname	Given Name	Surname	Given Name	Date	Comments
Doepfner (?)	Robert	Finn	Nellie L.	15 Sept. 1920	please do not publish in local papers
Doering	Julius	Mickle	Clara A.	20 Apr. 1908	
Dogali	Paolo	Gargini	Giulia	2 Oct. 1913	
Dogge	Rudolph S.	Nelson	Alzire	29 Aug. 1914	
Doglio	Frank	Pierucci	Marie	31 Jan. 1913	
Dohn	George Arthur	Trowbridge	Mabel Bertram	3 Dec. 1903	
Doir	Edgar	Dishong	Lucinda L.	3 Jan. 1911	
Doiza	Joseph A.	Joseph	Flora	13 Dec. 1893	br:18 in July of 1893; mother's name is also Flora Joseph.
Dokkedal	Niels Peter	Iverson	Hedda	20 Mar. 1905	
Dolan	J. L.	Hanily	Elizabeth	22 Oct. 1914	
Dolcini	Arnold Tully	Connolly	Katherine Rose	31 Jan. 1916	
Dolcini	Charles E.	Rogers	Elizabeth A.	26 Aug. 1918	gr: Peter Dolcini, father
Dolcini	Joseph Samuel	Wallman	Georgiana	14 June 1906	
Dolph	Peter Joseph	Shaw	Cathryn	15 June 1918	
Dolson	Fred	Skinner	Mary	23 Aug. 1916	
Dombrowski	Johann	Monson	Alvine Mathilde	25 Apr. 1903	
Domenzet	Joseph	Gates	Caroline J.	6 May 1914	
Domine	August F.	Ward	Lillian Belle	15 Apr. 1901	
Dominick	Herbert	Wood	Hazel Bea	3 Mar. 1916	do not publish
Dont	Joseph	Wernecke	Katie	30 Jan. 1894	
Donahue	James M.	Grace	Ella C.	17 Sept. 1901	
Donald	John Hall	Quigley	Flora Lucinda	29 May 1916	
Donaldson	Alexander B.	Gooch	Florence Irene	18 Sept. 1907	
Donaldson	Philip	Graham	Beatrice	9 June 1919	
Donegan	William	McKay	Isabella	12 Feb. 1903	
Donel	P. A.	Notingham	Mary Jane	30 Mar. 1885	
Donley	Charlie E.	Petit	Augusta L.	3 July 1914	
Donlin	Frank L.	Felt	Freda Elizabeth	10 Sept. 1918	
Donmecq	Ben	Laffourguette	Marie	24 Apr. 1911	
Donnelly	Thomas F.	Carter	Ellen	6 Sept. 1890	
Donnely	John Z.	Turman	Margaret S.	17 Nov. 1865	
Donner	George Jacob	Tillman	Margaret	12 May 1904	

Groom		Bride			
Surname	**Given Name**	**Surname**	**Given Name**	**Date**	**Comments**
Donner	John Carter	McReynolds	May Violet	18 Feb. 1903	
Donogh	Andrew	Spotswood	Eliza	7 Apr. 1886	
Donogh	Russell W.	Kulberg	Engre C.	11 Sept. 1917	
Donohoe	Patrick	Brogan	Frances Catherine	25 Jan. 1902	
Donovan	A. H.	Quinn	Mary E.	30 Dec. 1904	
Donovan	Jeremiah C.	Miller	Bertha	17 Feb. 1900	no previous marriage
Donovan	Ney L.	Guerne	Evalyn R.	25 Feb. 1895	
Dont	Clifford W.	Jobson	Verda Mae Belle	24 Sept. 1920	
Dont	John G.	Danz	Rosa	24 Nov. 1890	
Doran	James	O'Connor	Mary	7 Jan. 1888	
Doras	Leicester	Gilbertson	Annie	18 Jan. 1908	
Dorman	Den H.	Smith	Josephine	16 Mar. 1918	
Dorman	Ira	Walters	Catharine	18 Nov. 1896	
Dorman	William E.	Marshall	Lillian B.	3 July 1895	
Dormetta	Georgie	Castellino	Maria	22 Aug. 1912	
Dornbach	Fred	Brown	Ella F.	28 June 1911	
Dornel	Paul A.	Slater	Louise G.	4 Nov. 1891	
Dornin	John C.	Neff	Anna K.	11 Apr. 1896	
Dorris	Fred O.	King	Jessie I.	22 June 1914	
Dorroh	Carleton C.	Oellig	Ruth	25 Jan, 1915	
Dorsen	Isaiah P.	Shields	May E., Mrs.	17 Sept. 1898	br: widow
Dorsett	Fred Edward	Allen	Alice Elizabeth	15 Dec. 1916	
Dorsett	William A.	Allen	Lydia Jane	31 Dec. 1920	
Doss	Earl M.	Nelson	Hazel M.	13 Mar. 1920	
Doss	George W.	Perry	Minnie S.	14 June 1902	
Doss	Joel A.	Potter	Josephine I.	4 Nov. 1889	
Doss	John W.	Leszinsky	Estelle	27 Aug. 1898	no previous marriage
Doss	Seth B.	Simmons	Susan	16 Oct. 1899	no previous marriage
Doty	Albert	Looney	Curvera M.	15 Feb. 1866	
Doty	Archie A.	Standley	Esther Ramiea	2 Mar. 1920	
Dougherty	S. K.	Sippitt	Helen M.	26 Dec. 1888	
Douglas	Alexander S.	Noble	Madge	7 Sept. 1918	don't publish until Tuesday
Douglas	David J.	Douglas	Edith R.	3 Oct. 1911	

Groom		Bride			
Surname	Given Name	Surname	Given Name	Date	Comments
Douglas	David W.	McCutcheon	Hazel Genieveve	16 Jan. 1912	
Douglas	James Herbert	Holmes	Emma Mabel	2 Oct. 1907	
Douglas	Thomas James	Rose	Sylva Clare	27 Dec. 1909	
Douglass	Geo. V.	Brown	Annie I.	10 July 1888	
Douglass	Stephen Chester	Bennett	Susie Edna	24 Dec. 1912	
Douglass	W. A.	Cooper	M. L.	20 Sept. 1865	
Dovo	Joseph	Rocco	Josephine	22 June 1916	
Dow	A. J.	Catlin	Delia Resellen	18 Apr 1875	br: Ellen (?) Catlin, parent, Healdsburg; L. A. Norton, attorney, witness
Dow	Archie	Motroni	Dena	29 Aug. 1918	
Dow	Geo. W.	Button	Jennie	1 Nov. 1879	
Dowd	George William	McLaughlin	Kate Theresa	8 May 1899	no previous marriage
Dowdall	Edward J.	Ferry	Maggie E.	8 Apr. 1896	
Dowdall	John N.	Kearney	Clara T.	11 Nov. 1890	
Dowdall	Leo Edward	Haraszthy	Eleonor Marie	6 June 1902	
Dowdall	Richard J.	Redmond	Ellen	11 May 1891	
Dower	John R.	Leventhal	Gertrude	8 Dec. 1905	
Dowing	Ludwig D.	Hogrelius	Clara A.	4 Aug. 1920	
Dowler	Allen Lewis	Wickersham	Mary Catherine	6 June 1906	
Dowling	Charles W.	Gates	Lulu M.	5 Mar. 1896	license requested by Miss Lulu M. Gates
Downes	Ernest	Gray	Angie	22 June 1901	
Downing	Arthur B.	Benson	Rowena	5 June 1915	
Downs	Vernon, Jr.	LeGro	Bernice	14 June 1911	
Doyle	Charles M.	Chauvet	Adele M.	21 June 1919	
Doyle	Clement A.	Gongenbach	Elsie	23 Dec. 1914	
Doyle	Frank A.	Cummings	Mary	12 Oct. 1907	
Doyle	Frank P.	O'Meara	Mary A. L. (Polly)	25 Nov. 1903	
Doyle	Fred R.	Meldrum	Rachael	1 June 1901	
Doyle	Milton	Nicolaisen	Elizabeth	18 Jan. 1913	
Doyle	Peter J.	Conran	Margaret H.	21 Nov. 1901	
Drago	Frank	Glynn	Agnes M.	18 Feb.1901	
Drake	Albert Eli	Terrel	Flora Mabel	3 July 1905	
Drake	Floyd G.	Gale	Carrie L.	30 Oct. 1909	br: Minnie L. Popenoe, mother

Groom		Bride			
Surname	Given Name	Surname	Given Name	Date	Comments
Drake	George	Curtis	Katie L. D.	25 Mar. 1881	gr: signed with his mark; br: has been married and has obtained a divorce
Drake	George A.	Murray	Lottie J.	26 July 1902	br: Cleveland & Mrs. Belle Murray, parents; Wm. Baker, witness
Drake	Jacob Hopper	Bedwell	Belva	27 Feb. 1908	gr: Mrs. Katie Drake, mother; br: Mattie Bedwell, mother
Drake	Lennard Arthur	Engler	Annie Marie	5 Nov. 1919	
Drake	Lewis	Yerger	Hazel	2 Oct. 1911	
Drapeau	Frank M.	O'Neill	Ella A.	5 Jan. 1911	
Draper	John	Allison	Elizabeth	2 Oct. 1880	
Drees	Ernest E.	Gossage	Emma L.	27 Oct. 1894	
Drees	Gustave A.	Phillips	Matilda A.	2 May 1890	
Drees	Herman A.	Lawler	Lucy H.	8 Dec. 1898	no previous marriage
Dreher	Frank	Rietce	Pauline	3 Mar. 1886	
Dreisback	William E.	Vogt	Margaret	28 May 1904	
Drennon	George	Walls	Grace E.	17 Oct. 1899	requested by David Walls
Dresbach	William	Kahn	Bertha S.	5 Aug. 1908	
Dressler	J. F.	Cockrill	Ida May	5 Feb. 1887	
Drever	Andrew M.	Davis	Medna		filed between 12 May and 15 Oct. 1878
Drever	John ?	Shuster	Margaret A.	19 May 1865	
Drew	Morgan P.	Higgins	Margaret A.	16 July 1902	
Drew	Albert E.	Heatley	Eva E.	25 June 1914	
Drewes	William P.	Schalat	Delia C.	21 Sept. 1909	
Driesbach	F. K.	Swann	Florence	29 Feb. 1888	
Driscol	John	Burk	Mrs.	7 Sept. 1866	by Jas. Halloman
Driver	Clarence A.	Stinchfield	Mary G.	16 Feb. 1921	gr: Esther Driver, mother
Driver	Edward L.	Woodbury	Alice Gertrude	1 June 1911	gr: Mrs. E. Driver, mother
Driver	Maurice Leon	Nay	Abbie M.	10 June 1895	
Driver	Nickolas	Lautenschlager	Amelia M.	3 Oct. 1905	
Driver	William W.	Meyers	Hazel M.	1 June 1911	gr: Sarah E. Driver, mother
Drucks	Edward S.	Williams	Adah	10 June 1912	
Drummond	E. W.	Post	C. E.	20 Nov. 1879	
Drummond	R. S.	Woodworth	Mary	8 Oct. 1887	requested by C. W. Woodworth

Groom		Bride			
Surname	Given Name	Surname	Given Name	Date	Comments
Drury	Eugene Vernon	Eddelbuttel	Henrietta W. M.	23 June 1908	
Dryden	William	Seward	Evalyn I.	25 May 1918	
Dryden	William Robert	Stevens	Carla	30 Oct. 1909	
Dryer	Hiram George	Murphy	Madeline Marion	18 July 1916	
Drysdale	Robert Hugh	Vest	Pearl Maud	20 Mar. 1919	
Du Vander	David H.	Ward	Mabel F.	31 Mar. 1915	
Duane	Edward A.	Mills	Martha Pauline	7 May 1910	br: Pauline Mills, mother
Duarte	Nicholas	Witherell	Catherine, Mrs.	5 Mar.1901	gr: F. G. Nagle, witness to mark
Dublin	Isidore	Maidenbaum	Lillian	9 Apr. 1919	
DuBois	Clarence	Holdworth	Gertrude, Mrs.	2 Oct. 1902	
Dubois	J. C.	Peterson	Albertine	29 May 1885	
DuBose	James Gaillard	Hunt	Vitas C.	10 Sept. 1910	
Ducharm	George	Ducker	Sarah A.	18 May 1901	
Ducharm	Lambert A.	Ivans	Olive Violet	10 June 1905	
Ducharm	Leon	Green	Birdie	24 Dec. 1906	
Ducheneau	Fred	Williams	Iva Selina	7 June 1917	
Ducker	Barton	Hopkins	Grace J.	14 June 1913	
Ducker	John	Underhill	Catherine	30 Nov. 1877	
Ducker	William Laurence	Jensen	Ellen	9 May 1908	
Duckwortth	HenryAlmon	Hesse	Augusta P.	23 June 1899	gr:1312 Grove St., Oakland; no previous marriage
Dudley	Albert Allen	Hembree	Eliza Ellen	20 June 1903	
Dudley	Albert P.	Pearce	Pearl	26 Aug. 1916	
Dudley	W. S.	Mason	Annie E.	29 May 1886	
Dudley	William Seawell	Kennedy	Alice Cary	7 Feb. 1883	
Duerner	William, Jr.	Bateman	Harriett N.	4 Oct. 1915	br: Ada Bassett, mother
Duerson	John T.	Kynoch	Lydia L.	28 Sept. 1912	
Duerson	Richard C.	Horne	Hadie W.	1 Sept. 1909	
Duerson	Wm. H.	Horn	Jessie E.	29 Mar. 1899	no previous marriage
Dufau	Joseph	Lafon	Henriette	5 June 1901	gr: 702 Vallejo St., San Francisco; br: 841 Isabel St., Oakland
Duff	Harry Arnold	Strickert	Alvina Agnes	28 May 1906	
Duffell	George	Smith	Marcia P., Mrs.	22 Apr. 1878	

Groom		Bride			
Surname	Given Name	Surname	Given Name	Date	Comments
Duffield	Fred	Stidum (?)	Etta, Mrs.	6 Nov. 1919	
Dufranc	Isidore	Crohare	Rose	2 Dec. 1911	
Dugan	James Oliver	White	Cora Belle	11 Nov. 1908	
Duggan	Edward Bernard	Barnes	Dora Harlan	25 July 1906	
Dugue	Fernand	Kirk	Elise	30 Sept. 1915	
Dukes	Arthur H.	Dannhausen	Kate	23 Mar. 1911	
Dukes	Elmer Frank	Browne	Ida Lee	3 July 1906	gr: E. Hezekiah Dukes, father
Dukes	William A.	Place	Bertha E.	16 Aug. 1904	br: Mary Corum, mother; requested by her
Dulac	Ernest E.	Overton	Grace V.	7 Apr. 1917	
Dumas	Alphonse	Chanmet	Felectie	7 Oct. 1918	
Dumas	Harry Thos.	Perkenson	Hannah	13 June 1877	
Dunagan	Alva J.	Curry	Charlotte C.	16 Nov. 1917	
Dunbar	Charles O.	Reynolds	Fannie	17 Oct. 1900	
Dunbar	John J.	Agnew	Ida A.	5 Sept. 1896	
Dunbar	Lee A.	Sullivan	Nellie	30 Jan. 1909	
Duncan	C. A.	Cunningham	Minnie	4 Sept. 1885	
Duncan	Charles W.	Fairclo	Serena	4 Apr. 1896	
Duncan	Clarence E.	Myers	Bessie	12 Oct. 1907	
Duncan	Elmer A.	Winton	Edith May	22 Apr. 1905	gr: W. M. Duncan, parent; br: S. C. Winton, parent
Duncan	Geo. B.	Childers	Emma	2 June 1883	
Duncan	George Benjamin	Duncan	Mattie McDonald	10 May 1879	
Duncan	James A.	Boyle	Catherine J.	18 Aug. 1890	
Duncan	James E.	Winkler	Clara A.	29 Oct. 1908	
Duncan	James W.	Gilman	Elba Ellen	8 Oct. 1900	
Duncan	John	Gray	Eleanor	11 Nov. 1892	
Duncan	Mark VanHattren	Gorski	Lizzie May	25 May 1907	br: Charles Gorski, father
Duncan	Richard	Duncan	Ada M.	22 Oct. 1890	license requested by H. M. Taylor
Duncan	Robert A.	Hyde	Mary M.	19 Aug. 1920	
Duncan	Samuel	Coffer	Maggie	19 Nov. 1881	
Duncan	Sebastian	Mallory	Nina Leonna	13 July 1907	
Duncan	William M.	Rima	Minnie A.	10 Nov. 1883	br: Harriet A. Rima, mother
Duncan	William P.	Nowlin	Lillie L.	26 July 1915	br: Ernest Nowlin, father

Groom		Bride			
Surname	Given Name	Surname	Given Name	Date	Comments
Duncon	Wm. T.	Rains	Alice H.	25 Aug. 1888	br: Mrs. C. Rains, mother
Dunlap	J. L.	Brightenstein	Maggie	5 Mar. 1867	
Dunlap	Joseph B.	Paxton	Melinda C.	18 Jan. 1910	
Dunlap	Joseph B.	Millard	Addie F., Mrs.	1 Dec. 1900	
Dunlap	Robert E.	Brown	Florence	15 Dec. 1915	
Dunlap	Wilson	Gowen	M. E.	blank	
Dunn	James	Ehrlich	Miriam D.	24 Aug. 1915	
Dunn	Robert K.	Myer	Priscilla G.	5 Oct. 1907	
Dunn	William A.	Millington (?)	N. M.	23 Dec. 1881	
Dunne	Robert H.	Vincent	Mary C.	10 Aug. 1915	
Dunner ?	Martin P.	Schoffield	Nettie E.	24 Sept. 1866	
Dunsmore	Harry O.	Walker	Florence J.	10 Feb. 1914	
Dunster	Frank J.	O'Brien	Mary E.	20 Aug. 1918	
Dunton	Oscar	Armstrong	Fannie	2 Jan. 1894	
Dunton	Oscar	Morrison	Mary Jane	15 June 1903	
Dunwoody	Seth M.	Gardner	Lizzie	30 July 1883	
Dupon	Julius F.	Kupper	Melaine	27 Nov. 1915	
Dupont	Albert	Meyer	Mary Josephine	13 Oct. 1896	gr: signature witnessed by R. L. Thompson.
Dupont	Joseph	Maccabe	Hilda Susanna, Mrs.	20 Oct. 1903	
Durando	Felice	Canevascini	Ella	27 Nov. 1908	br: Anna Canevanscini, mother
Durant	William	Mull	Ellen	21 Feb. 1896	
Durr	Otto R.	Courtz	Mary E.	4 Oct. 1916	
Durst	David M.	Hair	Ruth Marie	19 July 1916	
Duryea	Stanton Bun	Auger	Annie Irene	6 Apr. 1912	br: Mollie Auger, mother
Dusek	Russell Ray	Russell	Elizabeth	10 June 1914	gr: Albert Dusek, father
Dushane	Frank L.	Henneken	Christina	16 Feb. 1906	
Dusick	Albert H., Jr.	Howard	Mary C.	11 Aug. 1913	
Dusserre	Vincent	Brochier (?)	Eulalie	24 Apr. 1919	
Duston	Byrne A.	Spangler	Annie B.	24 Dec. 1887	
Dutcher	Burt W.	Morrill	Cassie F.	24 Dec. ????	br: Susan M. Morrill, mother; Healdsburg; filed with 1860s and 1870s
Dutcher	Steve Joseph	Miller	Florence Emily	5 Oct. 1920	

Groom		Bride			
Surname	Given Name	Surname	Given Name	Date	Comments
Dutra	John E.	Blazer	Mabel Edna	17 July 1901	requested by C. N. Blazer, mother of bride
Dutra	Manuel F.	Carey	Isabel	25 Nov. 1910	witness his mark J. W. Ford
Dutra	Manuel S.	Raymond	Mary	2 Feb. 1897	
Dutro	James M.	Eten	Olive A.	12 Jan. 1921	
Dutro	Joseph J.	Morris	Mamie	16 Nov. 1899	
Dutton	Arthur L.	Reese	Della	27 Oct. 1915	
Dutton	George W.	Graham	Hallie M. Miss	15 May 1901	do not publish ages
Dutton	N. T.	Kerby	Phoebe P.	29 Mar. 1895	
Dutton	Windslow D.	Perez	Mary A.	20 Feb. 1915	
Duttweiler	Frederick	Bowie	Mae Josephine	25 Nov. 1916	
Dwinelle	C. H.	Woolsey	Marie Louise	9 June 1885	
Dwyer	Harold	Hayes	May Frances	21 Apr. 1919	
Dwyer	James J. B.	Brasher	Irene I.	6 Feb. 1908	
Dwynes	Antone	Salias	Pena	21 July 1906	W. S. Coulter, witness to mark, both signatures
Dyer	Roy C.	Arnold	Josephine L.	28 Sept. 1914	
Dysart	Thomas	Rothford	Violet	14 Sept. 1908	
E?tola	Arnold	Redmond	Zella	5 July 1918	
Eachus	Edgar P.	Phillips	Mabel G.	9 Nov. 1908	
Eager	Marcus K.	O'Celeghan	Frances E.	22 Jan. 1877	
Eagle	Bert	Caughey	Alice	16 Mar. 1912	
Eagle	Edward	Valentine	Christine	17 Aug. 1888	
Eagle	W. F.	Underhill	Mary	25 Mar. 1882	
Eagleson	E. G.	Musselman	Frona	26 June 1886	
Eagleson	Welcome E.	Lucas	Pauline	18 Dec. 1909	
Eaglin	Elmer Harrison	Cleland	Mary Martha	22 Dec. 1916	
Eakle	George H.	Andrews	Mary E.	11 Aug. 1920	
Eakle	Henry P.	Edington	Eliza Francis	28 Oct 1865	
Eardley	William J.	Harden	Jinella	27 Sept. 1887	
Earhart	George Hammond	Lamb	Edna May	24 Dec. 1900	br: & gr: 122 Albion Ave., San Francisco
Earhart	William H.	Martin	Emma R.	23 Nov. 1910	
Earl	John H. P.	Taylor	Brooksie A.	6 Nov. 1920	
Earll	F. A.	Barnes	Ida F.	12 Oct. 1878	

Groom		Bride			
Surname	Given Name	Surname	Given Name	Date	Comments
Early	J. Frank	Butler	Harriette M.	21 Apr. 1903	
Easley	William P.	Kearney	Mary E.	31 May 1890	
Eason	Andrew	Grant	Mary	7 June 1915	
Eason	Joseph A.	Higby	Birdie	29 Dec. 1913	
East	Linzey	Gilson	Myrtle Dora	21 Sept. 1905	
Easter	James Marcellus Thomton	Swanson	Hilda	3 Jan. 1912	
Easterbrook	Thomas	Case	Ellen M.	15 Feb. 1888	
Eastlick	A. D.	Cox	Mattie A.	11 July 1882	
Eastlick	Charles F.	Sheldon	Abbie T., Mrs.	11 Aug. 1892	br: widow
Eastlick	Wellington B.	Jones	Minnie	21 May 1910	
Eastman	Charles Ward	Harrigan	Florence Katherine	22 Sept. 1914	
Eastman	Fred A.	Safford	Adeline	17 June 1919	
Eastman	Tarleton	Downie	Catherine Lilias	18 Oct. 1890	
Eathorne	Alexander	Eddy	Zulpha L.	23 Oct. 1908	
Ebbets	Harry G.	Phillips	Gertrude	15 Apr. 1911	
Ebeigh	Henry	Smith	Carrie B.	30 July 1907	
Eberling	C. W.	Mack	Ida	18 Aug. 1892	br and gr: in both cases Calistoga residence crossed out and replaced with "Sonoma Co."
Ebers	Henry F.	Lenout	Nellie J.	9 Jan. 1890	br: widow
Eby	Edward D.	Peck	Mabel	1 Nov. 1895	
Eby	Edwin Dayton	Maddern	Sophia Elgin	22 Nov. 1913	
Echelmeier	Fred	Adel	Annetta	24 Aug. 1892	
Eck	John W.	Spellacy	Ella J.	25 Jan. 1918	
Eckel	Tobias Lewis	Tartter	Frances	5 Aug. 1903	
Eckert	Julius M.	Rickett	Leah	7 Dec. 1901	do not publish ages
Eckes	Clarence J.	Smith	Grace M.	16 Oct. 1920	
Eckhart	Percy	Hinshaw	Wilma E.	7 Oct. 1918	
Eckman	Albert R.	Foscha	Lenora A.	13 May 1914	
Eckman	John	Stevens	Jennie	21 Aug. 1877	br: Mrs. M. Matson, stepmother; A. E. Shattuck, witness
Eddinger	Charles Winfield	Derrick	Nellie Annie	17 June 1907	
Edgar	Herbert L.	Gorter	Dorothea	31 Dec. 1920	

Groom		Bride			
Surname	**Given Name**	**Surname**	**Given Name**	**Date**	**Comments**
Edmiston	Frank L.	Silva	Julia Lopes	14 Oct. 1916	
Edmonds	Francis J.	Scannell	Grace A.	1 Sept. 1920	
Edmunds	Clarence	Tapscott	Mary Emma	25 June 1908	
Edmunds	Clyde Jordan	Moxley	Gladys Beulah	16 Mar. 1920	
Edmunds	George R.	Farish	May P., Mrs.	28 May 1900	both widowed
Edrington	James B.	Cook	Hattie	17 Mar. 1902	do not publish until Tuesday
Edvardo	Bettelotti	Viviani	Marie	8 Sept. 1910	
Edwards	Alfred Atherton	Turner	Belle	22 Aug. 1911	
Edwards	Arthur S.	Braunton	Blanche	24 June 1907	
Edwards	Clarence A.	Martin	Lola Lee	6 Feb. 1902	br: E. E. Martin, parent
Edwards	Clarence Alvin	Miller	Eva Mabel	29 Mar. 1909	
Edwards	Claude A.	Pritchett	Laura E.	14 Apr. 1913	
Edwards	David	Needham	Grace	12 Mar. 1910	
Edwards	Henry Seymour	Studdert	Susie Estella	27 Jan. 1906	
Edwards	Herbert Hereward	Studdert	Angela Gertrude	17 June 1907	
Edwards	Matthew	Lambert	Mima	24 Feb. 1897	
Edwards	Ralph Walter	Hamilton	Pearl	21 Sept. 1916	
Edwards	Thomas M.	Essner	Joan D.	4 Jan. 1902	gr: 1613 Clay St., San Francisco
Eells	Frank Lorne	Hulbert	Laura Emily	30 Mar. 1895	
Eferly	John	Bauer	Caroline	23 Dec. 1909	
Egan	Daniel F.	Pressey	L. Beatrice	19 Nov. 1904	
Egbert	Warren	Pearce	Martha	4 Sept. 1901	
Egenhoff	Julius A.	Bernauer	Frieda	23 Jan. 1917	
Ehret	Alexander W.	Solomon	Lena	11 Nov. 1903	
Eichbaum	Edwin Treat Betts	Perkins	Margaret Edna	15 May 1908	
Einwalter	Paul	Poe	Rosa B.	26 Apr. 1911	
Elder	Henry Elmer	Lawrence	Kate Amanda	26 May 1906	
Elder	James H.	Hether	Christine	21 Jan. 1913	
Elder	Louis Ely	Pedersen	Mary Magdeline	23 June 1906	
Elder	Newton	Russell	Mattie E.	19 Dec. 1889	br: H. A. Russell, parent
Elder	Ralph D.	Stratton	Susie I.	23 Aug. 1915	
Eldridge	A. C.	Frederick	Hallie	5 Sept. 1893	
Eldridge	George G.	Dornin	Julia	11 Aug. 1896	

Groom		Bride			
Surname	Given Name	Surname	Given Name	Date	Comments
Eldridge	Joseph B.	Burns	Jennie T.	16 Feb. 1883	
Elgin	Ira P.	Blackmon (?)	Emily A.	11 Apr. 1887	
Eliggi	Bartolomeo	Schurba	Celia A.	21 Sept. 1918	br: Peter Schurba, father
Elkington	Thomas	Head	Rosalis	2 July 1891	
Elkins	I. B.	Rickard	Barbara A.	14 Feb. 1887	
Elkins	John C.	Curry	Lillian M.	12 Mar. 1901	
Elkins	Richard L.	Hutchinson	Mary E.	8 Jan. 1897	br: Mrs. Clara D. Hutchinson gives consent and signs; Sarah A. Covey, witness
Elkins	Stephen F.	Smith	Eva M.	14 Aug. 1900	
Ellingen	Casper W.	Dana	May L.	7 Apr. 1916	
Ellinger	Charles	Grosch	Frieda	12 Apr. 1910	
Elliott	Archie E.	Gibson	Lulu E.	8 Apr. 1915	
Elliott	Carter W.	Meyers	Bessie R.	24 Dec. 1914	br: E. E & Grace H. Meyers, parents
Elliott	Charles Milton	Plum	Bessie Irene	10 July 1906	br: Mrs. W. H. Plum, mother
Elliott	Chester L.	Standley	Sadie R.	5 June 1915	
Elliott	Daniel	Nelsen	Josepha	29 Sept. 1915	
Elliott	Edward Cyrus	Pruitt	Nellie Reba	11 Sept. 1909	gr: Mrs. Fannie Elliott, mother; br: B. F. & Ida Pruitt, parents
Elliott	Frank Edward	Ward	Annie May	2 Apr. 1904	
Elliott	Irving R.	Johns	Anna C.	12 Aug. 1918	
Elliott	J. B.	Nicoll	Fannie	22 Mar. 1886	
Elliott	James J.	Donahue	Violet P.	7 Aug. 1918	
Ellis	Arthur	Welling	Rose A.	21 Oct. 1920	
Ellis	Arthur Clarence	Meyers	Lorene Emeline	31 Jan. 1916	
Ellis	Bert Cecil	Groshong	Sue	6 Mar. 1906	
Ellis	Edward	Van Keppel	Mary L.	19 May 1891	
Ellis	James	Smith	Mary A.	23 Nov. 1895	
Ellis	John Arthur	Stiles	Louisa Isobel	23 Feb. 1893	
Ellis	Leander Gilbert, Jr.	Leigh	Delia	15 Jan. 1894	
Ellis	Walter A.	Portlock	Earl	29 Dec. 1903	br: Mrs. S. J. Portlock, mother
Ellis	William	Walker	Alma	14 Aug. 1884	
Ellis	William A.	Hotle	Effie C.	5 Nov. 1892	
Ellis	William C.	Leard	Laura J.	17 Aug. 1865	

Groom		Bride			
Surname	**Given Name**	**Surname**	**Given Name**	**Date**	**Comments**
Ellis	William H.	Knowles	Nanon	28 Dec. 1897	
Ellison	Charles Edwin	Philbee	Rachel N.	17 Jan. 1877	
Ellison	Charles Eugene	Gray	Rosa	28 June 1898	gr: Charles Edwin Ellison, father
Ellison	Ebert R.	Wright	Ella		located between 5 & 6 May 1903 applications; not issued on advice of District Atty Pond
Ellsworth	Henry L.	Shattuck	Aletha S.	30 Sept. 1886	
Ellsworth	Leonard	Jones	Clara	27 July 1886	br: Wm. Jones, father
Ellsworth	Percy Leland	Mathews	Asentha Vera	12 Mar. 1910	
Elphick	Clarence R.	Vallier	Emma M.	15 Jan. 1900	no previous marriage
Elphick	Eugene	Roberts	Hazel	11 Feb. 1909	
Elphick	Henry, Jr.	Briggs	Birdie	23 Jan. 1900	no previous marriage
Elphick	James	Roberts	Edna N.	15 Aug. 1903	
Elphick	Oscar Frank	Orender	Alma May	24 Aug 1907	
Elphick	Roy J.	Horne	Jeanie R.	20 Sept. 1913	
Elphick	Thomas R.	Duerson	Elizabeth C.	22 Aug. 1889	
Elsbree	Charles Dyer	Du Vander	Rebecca L.	19 Dec. 1906	
Elton	Arthur M.	Lowrey	Helen W.	2 Aug. 1918	gr: E. A. Elton, parent
Elwell	Charles E.	Hooper	Lizzie	12 May 1887	
Ely	Albert W.	Buell	Ida M.	28 Oct. 1880	
Ely	Frank G.	Hampton	Ida May	20 Oct. 1900	
Ely	Robert L.	Hollar	Flora Dell	30 Dec. 1893	
Elzey	R. H.	Thompson	M. Ruth	23 Apr. 1914	
Emenegger	Frank	Mason	Centennia	5 Oct. 1903	
Emerson	George Edwin	Lewin	Catherine Ellen	26 Apr. 1906	
Emerson	Harry E.	Cooper	Eva U.	7 Sept. 1907	
Emerson	Harry E.	Graves	Nora B.	31 May 1894	
Emerson	John S.	Rickman	Nancy S.	16 Jan. 1866	
Emerson	Mark Lewis	Folger	Alice	19 Dec. 1905	
Emery	Fred A.	Wilson	Daisy	2 Aug. 1902	
Emery	Vernon V.	Zunnino	Annie K.	12 Jan. 1920	br: Madelina Quartaroli, mother
Emes	Walter H.	Goldman	Ida	11 Aug. 1913	
Emmons	Edward L.	Willis	Lillian A.	17 May 1892	

Groom		Bride			
Surname	Given Name	Surname	Given Name	Date	Comments
Emmrich	Gustav Moritz	Heinze	Bertha Emilie	15 Sept. 1891	license requested by Andrew Price
Empey	William A.	Turner	Lucille C.	1 Aug. 1916	
Emrick	George W.	Miller	Oliva B.	9 Dec. 1899	br: Ed. Miller, father
Enders	Charles R.	Hornbuckle	Harriet	15 Dec. 1899	neither party has been divorced within one year
Endicott	Charles L.	Brayton	Ester Ruth	16 Aug. 1911	
Endicott	Perry A.	Boyer	Margerette A.	2 June 1920	
Enemark	Frank R.	Shelford	Lola L. B.	21 Nov. 1916	
Enfield	Joseph Louis	Marzo	Matilda Clelia	18 Sept. 1907	
Engelberg	Henry W.	Rouch	Josephine	3 June 1915	
Engelhardt	August George	Pomeroy	Irene Byrle	14 June 1909	
Engelhardt	Richard R.	Alexander	Lucille B.	13 May 1919	
Engelland	Detlef	Mockel	Anna	3 Sept. 1901	
Engh	Peter B.	Fish	Lucetta A.	26 June 1919	
Engle	Lewis Joseph	Craig	Cora Allida	8 Oct. 1907	
Englehard	Sam A.	Jewell	Libbie	20 Dec. 1878	br: F. E. Rose, stepfather
Ennis	Frank	Teineira	Rosa	20 May 1912	gr: I. J. Winans, W. W. Felts, Jr., witnesses to his mark
Enos	Manuel Joseph	Moniz	Marion Ursala	27 Jan. 1913	
Enz	Albin	Meyer	Josephine	29 Apr. 1912	
Enz	Joseph	Schaly	Christina	26 Aug 1907	
Enzenauer	Ed.	Campbell	Etta Edith	8 Nov. 1902	
Enzenauer	Joe	Blazer	Ethel Rae	2 Apr. 1907	
Enzenauer	Louis	Burnham	Phebe	30 Apr. 1904	
Epperly	Hiram	Coleman	Amanda	17 Feb. 1872 ?	
Erickson	Albert	Steenberg	Maria	9 Nov. 1908	
Ernest	Albert J.	McElhany	Olive E.	3 Sept. 1891	
Ernst	August M.	Faught	Hazel S.	10 Dec. 1917	
Ernst	John Louis	Schow	Bertha	18 Apr. 1905	
Erntson	Martin	Steinberg	Maude	24 Feb. 1916	
Erskine	Alvin Chester	Evans	Annie B., Mrs.	1 June 1907	
Erving	Richard	Moore	Eva B.	1 July 1920	
Esaia	Bartholomew	Nelson	Clara	25 Oct. 1911	

Groom		Bride			
Surname	Given Name	Surname	Given Name	Date	Comments
Esaia	John B.	Yancey	Minnie M.	23 Aug. 1915	
Escola	Charles A.	Sutherland	Hilda A.	9 July 1919	
Esmond	Frank L.	Bruner	Amanda	1 Oct. 1891	
Espey	George E.	Brown	Lizzie R.	29 Oct. 1904	Edna B. Fallon, witness
Espey	George M.	Mills	Effa	18 Nov. 1895	
Essig	Frank	Owens	Emma F.	5 July 1889	
Esslinger	John A.	Mayshark	Stella N.	30 Nov. 1918	
Estep	Henry S.	Parks	L. F.	20 July 1878	br: O. B. Parks, parent
Esterly	Ward Benjamin	Judy	Emily Virginia	8 July 1910	
Estes	Frank H.	McIntosh	Emma	26 Sept. 1893	
Estes	Geo.	Hennessee	Mary F.	11 Nov. 1865	
Estes	George Henry	Arfsten	Dora Lizzie	30 Sept. 1905	
Estes	John	Bohn	Mary Lena	31 Dec. 1910	
Estes	John E.	Wheeler	Anna	4 Mar. 1918	
Estes	William J., Jr.	Johnson	Nellie I.	30 Aug. 1898	
Estill	Byron Dee	Hartley	Aneita	5 Nov. 1919	
Estinghausen	William	Fairbanks	Clara I.	3 Jan. 1893	
Etherridge	Cecil William	Vinyard	Olive Barr	17 Nov. 1915	
Etz	Arthur Kenyon	Nielson	Emma Marie	13 July 1908	
Eugley	Walter Arthur	Richards	Anna Belle, Mrs.	31 Mar. 1905	
Evans	Alexander	Penny	Olive E.	2 July 1904	
Evans	Arthur B.	Matzen	Dora	9 Sept. 1911	
Evans	C. D.	Haigh	Lena	14 Mar. 1900	no previous marriage
Evans	Charles E.	Bojorques	Elizabeth L.	9 Apr. 1902	
Evans	E. Esley	Koch	Anna E.	20 Mar. 1912	
Evans	E. R.	McClary	Bella	4 Jan. 1916	
Evans	Frank Leslie	Smith	Mollie Rebecca	1 Sept. 1905	
Evans	Harrison H.	Seery	Evelyn	27 Dec. 1919	
Evans	John	Johnson	Agnes L.	5 June 1915	
Evans	John D.	Lawrence	Maggie M.	13 Nov. 1899	gr: E. H. Evans, father; no previous marriage; note dated 1 Nov., Selma, Iowa
Evans	Merle Lester	Batt	Alice May	17 June 1910	gr: Mrs. Edwin Mitchell, mother; br: Alice E. Batt, mother

Groom		Bride			
Surname	Given Name	Surname	Given Name	Date	Comments
Evans	Robert H.	Bryant	Margery	12 Nov. 1919	
Evans	Roy M.	Green	May C.	18 Sept. 1920	
Evans	Samuel C.	Ward	Bertha May	17 Oct. 1898	no previous marriage
Evans	Thomas	Leigh	Mary Ellen	2 Dec. 1865	
Evans	Tipton Edward	Clark	Agnes Emma	20 June 1906	br: Mrs. Jennie Clark, mother
Evans	William	Williams	Nada Roll	3 Nov. 1913	
Evans	William P.	McCoubrey	Nettie	12 Sept. 1914	
Evans	William Henry	Schneider	Alice Laura	30 Mar. 1899	
Evart	Edwin J.	Jacobsen	Frances N.	6 Sept. 1913	
Evart	Frank R.	Keegan	Clara Mae	3 Oct. 1904	
Evart	William P.	Howard	Celia G.	15 May 1911	
Everett	Harry D.	Wilson	Edna M.	13 May 1919	
Everett	Walter H.	Hayden	Anna Valentine	29 Jan. 1917	
Eversole	Abraham	Hubart	Jennie E.	11 July 1878	
Evey	David D.	Lawrence	Alfa N.	21 Dec. 1895	
Ewing	James	Gough	Annie Emily	8 Feb. 1904	
Ewing	James E.	Mazota	Lillie	1 July 1890	br: Louis Mazota, father
Ewing	John Virgil	Hembree	Ivy Olivia	31 Dec. 1906	
Exlay	George	Green	Mary	1 Aug. 1919	br: Nellie M. Green, mother
Exley	William	King	Marie Elizabeth	3 Sept. 1910	
Faber	H. Charles	Millman	Mamie L.	6 June 1902	
Faccini	Giovani	Saitone	Maria	3 June 1910	
Fadeli	Angelo	Tisolin	Louise	6 Aug. 1915	
Fagan	Shuler F.	Grant	Effa	3 June 1919	
Fahrion	George W.	Glenn	Lilly M.	2 Apr. 1887	
Fairbanks	Joseph F.	Wilson	Hattie	24 Sept. 1902	
Fairbanks	Julius T.	Hanson	Emelia J., Mrs.	29 Aug. 1901	
Fairbanks	Percy M.	Erwin	May	1 Dec. 1884	
Fairbanks	William B.	Clark	Alice L.	16 Feb. 1903	
Fairchild	Fred F.	Batten	Mattie H.	16 Dec. 1902	
Fairchild	Leon H.	Thomas	Anna E.	18 Dec. 1912	
Fairchild	Olif G.	Clark	Ruth M.	9 Sept. 1896	do not publish notice
Fairclo	Charles	Cariaga	Refuge	26 Sept. 1905	

Groom		Bride			
Surname	Given Name	Surname	Given Name	Date	Comments
Fairclo	Richard	Weyhe	Dora	31 Dec. 1910	
Faires	James B.	Peck	Mary H.	8 Apr. 1920	
Fairfield	William M.	Morrow	Ethel M.	27 Jan. 1897	
Fairfield	Wm.	Rawson	Ella	12 May 1866	
Fairman (?)	William J.	Butts	Mary E.	26 Apr. 1880	requested by F. J. Butts
Faithful	H. R.	Conlin	Nellie A.	10 June 1893	
Falanery	Charles A.	Elliott	Mary A.	3 Aug. 1920	
Fallmer	Charles Frederick	Cozzens	Pearl Adele	28 June 1916	
Fallon	John D.	Wyckoff	Cora	17 July 1899	
Fallon	John Franklin	Brown	Edna L.	17 Jan. 1901	
Fallon	Martin	Duher	Catherine	27 Apr. 1897	
Faltin	Wilhelm	Kahle	Agnes D. J.	22 June 1915	
Falvey	Dennis	Mangili	Mary, Mrs.	4 Oct. 1913	
Fambrini	Federico	Puccioni	Julia	23 Apr. 1915	br: Angelo Puccioni, father
Fandre	Crockett	Crist	M. Jennie	6 Oct. 1888	br: William Crist, father
Fanucchi	Angelo	Barberie	Rose Lee	4 Dec. 1919	
Fanucchi	Angelo	Barsi	Silvia	19 Nov. 1914	
Farahm	John Henry Adolph, Jr.	Hyatt	Emma Beatrice	3 Aug.1909	
Faraoni	Frank	Rogers	Ottillie C.	6 Sept. 1916	br: Mrs Rebecca Rogers, mother
Faribanks	Joseph Frank	Maynard	Eva E.	27 July 1885	
Farley	Charles	Huffman	Florence	26 Aug. 1904	gr: C. T. Farley, parent; J. W. Ford, witness to his mark
Farley	George F.	Bojorques	Mary A.	1 Apr. 1902	
Farley	Henry	McGowan	Maggie	27 Oct. 1890	
Farley	J. B.	Roberts	Elizabeth G.	10 Oct. 1888	
Farley	James B.	Wilson	Hattie A. ?	10 July 1878	
Farley	James H.	Wilson	Mary	24 Sept. 1888	
Farley	Thomas Bachariah	Cauckwell	Minnie Bell	30 Jan. 1904	
Farley	William James McA.	Fitzgerald	Nora Gertrude	5 May 1920	
Farley	William T.	Barbour	Clementine	14 Feb. 1895	
Farmer	B. F.	Wilson	Martha E.	26 Feb. 1883	
Farmer	Eugene Columbus	Shelton	Grace	27 May 1905	

Groom		Bride			
Surname	Given Name	Surname	Given Name	Date	Comments
Farmer	Geo. L.	Wilson	Marela	1 May 1884	
Farmer	George	Michael	Emma A.	14 Feb. 1882	
Farmer	John H.	Marshall	Mary Alice	23 Dec. 1895	license requested by James W. Farmer
Farner	David Paul	Irwin	Edna H.	14 May 1919	
Farnham	James W.	Sargent	Ella N.	9 May 1883	
Farnham	Leroy T.	Brown	Mildred	28 Jan. 1918	
Farnsworth	Raymond W.	Hunt	Laura Ellen	16 Nov. 1908	
Farquar	Calvin S.	Clark	Mary I.	21 Oct. 1876	
Farquar	Frederic Stewart	Herbert	Hester R.	6 June 1903	
Farrance	Charles Evert	Hillyer	Ethel	9 June 1917	
Farrar	Edmund H.	Roberts	Grace M.	30 Sept. 1902	gr: 310 Santa Rosa Ave., Santa Rosa
Farrell	John T.	Green	Kate	28 Apr. 1890	
Farrell	William F.	Glynn	Sarah A.	30 Dec. 1889	
Farrer	Ernest Eugene	Eten	Ella Agnes	23 Feb. 1918	
Farwell	Marcus Morton	Lambert	Donna E.	27 Aug. 1920	
Farwell	Sidney C.	Haeckl	Elene	29 Jan. 1916	
Fasel	George	Odermatt	Theresia	8 Sept. 1914	
Faudre	Crocket	Young	Louella St John, Mrs.	31 Dec. 1894	
Faudre	Stuart William	Pells	Agnes Nettie	10 Apr. 1893	gr: consent given by father S. W. Faudre who signs.
Faught	A.	Smith	Annie A.	4 Jan. 1888	
Faught	Jabez	Morrison	Violet	21 Nov. 1902	
Faught	John H.	Sanborn	Emma	16 Dec. 1880	
Faught	Lewis Cass	Rodgers	Ruth	11 Oct. 1875	
Faulconer	Joseph C.	Gildersleeve	Elizabeth	25 Mar.1910	
Faulkender	Everett F.	Faulkender	Millie M.	26 July 1920	
Faulkner	M. H.	Donnelly	Amelia A.	27 Oct. 1866	
Fava	Lorenzo	Papero	Angellina	15 Sept. 1913	
Fawcett	S.	Lowery	Mary	27 June 1894	
Fawcett	Thomas	Fowler	Mary Otis	24 Feb. 1865	
Fawver	James Clark	Bales	Della Morton	25 July 1905	
Fay	Frank	Ryley	Mary Agnes	4 Sept. 1900	

Groom		Bride			
Surname	Given Name	Surname	Given Name	Date	Comments
Fay	John	Orr	Mary E.	19 June 1909	
Fay	John F.	Ellis	Leona G.	21 Sept. 1895	
Fay	John P.	Patterson	Stella F.	5 Mar. 1891	
Fay	Wilbert Lee	Corrick	Lucela Catherine	7 Aug. 1906	
Faylor	John F.	Walker	Hazel	17 Nov. 1899	br: L. F. Walker, parent
Faylor	Orson	Grubbe	Minnie	2 Apr. 1890	license requested by Eleanor Plunkett
Faylor	William P.	Wood	Marie E.	30 Apr. 1914	gr: Orson C. Faylor, father
Fearn	John R.	Dimmick	Lillian M.	23 Mar. 1895	
Fearns	Lawrence H.	Stewart	Bertha F.	27 June 1891	br: requested by Mrs. E. J. Stewart, mother
Fechtelkotter	Harry B.	Thomas	Minnie Frances	26 Aug. 1916	
Fechter	David A.	Fulkerson	Alma K.	9 Aug. 1919	gr: Geo. Fechter, father
Feckenscher	Edward R.	Dewey	Ruby	3 Mar. 1903	
Feehan	W. J.	Murbar	Mae	22 Sept. 1894	
Fees	Elmer	Graham	Lilly	13 July 1904	
Fehrensen	Claude William	Jones	Sussie Elizabeth Ellen	2 Oct. 1912	
Fehringer	John	Seifert	Maud	10 Oct. 1903	
Feige	Albert H.	Gibson	Hazel C.	24 Mar. 1914	
Feillers	Daniel	Toppini	Marie V.	7 Dec. 1907	
Felciano	Antone	Soares	Mary	26 Oct. 1912	
Felciano	John	Vier	Flora	1 Feb. 1908	
Felciano	Manuel	Pierucci	Matilda	27 Apr. 1907	br: Mrs. M. Pierucci, mother
Feldman	William	Landgren	Louisa, Mrs.	3 Aug. 1904	
Feldmeyer	Clemens A.	Sutten	Pearl	22 Nov. 1901	br: Mr. & Mrs. A. Sutten, parents
Feldmeyer	Wm. B.	Minto	Ive Pearl	24 Dec. 1904	
Felis	Fred R., Jr.	Albert	Pearl Ione	11 Sept. 1919	
Felix	Gustav H.	Laske	Katherine	26 June 1909	
Feliz	Gumisindo, Jr.	Comte	Blanche	14 Nov. 1898	no previous marriage
Feliz	Sisto J.	Gailer	Ada B.	30 Sept. 1899	gr: Mary J. Feliz, mother; Mrs. Geor. Coll?more, witness to mother's signature; br: Mrs. Herman L. Hankel, mother; no previous marriage
Felldin	John Joseph	Connolly	Mary V.	8 Apr. 1918	

Groom		Bride		Date	Comments
Surname	Given Name	Surname	Given Name		
Fellers	Frank L.	Hillard	Mildred A.	14 Sept. 1915	
Fellers	Lorenzo	Browne	Minnie	22 Aug. 1893	
Fellows	Fred C.	Dovey	Eva	8 Feb. 1894	
Felt	William W., Jr.	Leroux	Nellie T.	26 May 1905	
Felte	William A.	Perry	Pearl E.	10 Sept. 1918	
Felton	Clarence W.	Graff	Lilliebell	20 May 1916	
Fendner	Edward Ludwig	Prestwood	Louella M.	6 May 1907	
Fenkhausen	W. R.	Kopf	Victoria Louise	11 Apr. 1887	
Fenn	Theodore	Hayne	Laura	26 Sept. 1918	
Fennell	James E.	Hamilton	Alice	16/17 Sept. 1919	
Fenner	Henry	Thormann	Martha T. H.	29 Dec. 1896	
Fenton	Claude Merton	Dodenhoff	Ceres Wanda	24 May 1909	
Ferenbach	Charles	Feddersen	Annie	1 Dec. 1899	
Ferguson	Andrew T.	Petrich	Agnes	22 Apr. 1920	
Ferguson	Angus V.	Knox	Lizzie E.	20 Dec. 1892	
Ferguson	Charles P.	Shinn	Ida	5 Aug. 1901	
Ferguson	Charles T.	Woodward	Mattie M.	27 Mar. 1883	
Ferguson	Clarence M.	Patterson	Minnie C.	27 May 1890	
Ferguson	Edward	Beach	Bertha	3 May 1898	gr: R. Ferguson, father
Ferguson	Edward J.	Sullivan	Mary	27 Aug. 1891	
Ferguson	Erwin Emmet	Wagers	Martha Elizabeth	13 Nov. 1906	
Ferguson	Geo. P.	Smith	Dacie R.	13 July 1901	
Ferguson	Henry O.	Miller	Mary E.	2 May 1878	
Ferguson	John N.	Beeson	Eunice Naomi	26 Aug. 1909	
Ferguson	Newton J.	Cober	Jane	24 Apr. 1901	
Ferguson	O. J.	Looney	Ethel	17 Oct. 1904	
Ferguson	W. R.	Perry	Emma R.	20 June 1893	
Ferguson	W. R.	Meyer	Lilly R. S.	11 Nov. 1903	
Ferguson	W. W., Jr.	Watson	Josephine	24 Dec. 1883	
Fernald	Eli V.	Johnson	Francis G.	14 Oct. 1895	
Fernandez	Clemente	Ambrose	Mary	31 Aug. 1918	
Fernando	C. R.	Hammel	Rose M.	20 Oct. 1915	

Groom		Bride			
Surname	Given Name	Surname	Given Name	Date	Comments
Ferrari	Augustino	ReSaglia	Mattie	6 Mar. 1893	
Ferrari	Guiseppe Joseph	Perazzo	Rosie	8 Mar. 1899	no previous marriage
Ferrari	Tealue	Verzasconi	Bessie	26 Aug. 1898	no previous marriage
Ferreiro	Jose Gracia	Freitas	Maria	19 Oct. 1895	gr: signs with x mark witnessed by H. H. Atwater, notary public.
Ferrell	John	Warner	Rebekah	26 Jan. 1885	
Ferretti	John V.	Lagorio	Therese B.	6 June 1917	
Ferroni	Louise	Lozzori	Rosa	1 Mar. 1912	
Ferrori	Enrico	Cenini	Ersilia	30 Oct. 1897	no previous marriage
Fesso	Antonio	Zanoni	Lillie	2 Feb. 1915	br: Maria Zenoni, mother
Fetterly	Charles	Newman	Esther H.	15 Sept. 1911	
Fevrier	George Taylor	Farrell	Angela Helen	26 July 1917	
Fevrier	Harold C.	Farrell	Gertrude M.	15 July 1916	
Fewel	William Cicero	Gober	Elizabeth Tennessee	29 Sept. 1908	
Fick	John Frederick	Fickas	Norrie Elizabeth	25 May 1906	
Fidler	Joseph L.	Nichols	Lois	13 Sept. 1919	br: Minnie P. Nichols, mother
Fiege	Carl William	Brooks	Viola Marie	28 June 1919	
Fiege	Joseph	Lepper	Lena	10 Dec. 1892	
Field	Harry B.	Phair	Helen	24 Nov. 1899	
Field	James	Goddard	Silvia C.	2 Apr. 1866	
Field	John	Singley	Mary	14 May 1879	
Field	John K.	Cooper	Alice L.	6 July 1908	
Field	Sydney L.	Hartly	Birdie M.	18 Apr. 1908	
Field	Walter E.	Hays	Jennie	9 Sept. 1882	
Fielding	Edward Joseph	Swaner	Bulah	8 Oct. 1914	
Fields	Fred S.	Thompson	Laura A.	14 Mar. 1896	
Fields	Seraphin F.	Rose	Inez Margaret	1 Oct. 1907	
Fields	William A.	Kriedell	Amelia, Mrs.	9 May 1896	
Fieux	Constant	Longuet	Louise	22 May 1915	
Figera	Louie	Velazquez	Carmen	5 Nov. 1919	
Figone	August	Batta	Katie	9 Nov. 1903	
Fike	N.	Wallace	Elizabeth J.	11 Dec. 1865	

Groom		Bride			
Surname	Given Name	Surname	Given Name	Date	Comments
Filbert	Major (?)	Windsor	Sarah A.	30 Oct. 1877	
Files	Charles M.	Flesher	Retta M.	2 Nov. 1898	no previous marriage
Filippelli	John	Buzzi	Nora	27 Feb. 1904	
Filippini	Achille	Morelli	Irene	16 Feb. 1903	
Filippini	Basilio	Pifferi	Anita	23 Sept. 1913	
Filippini	Emidio John	Koch	Pauline Josephine	17 Dec. 1907	
Filippini	John Ernest	Bloom	Celia Virginia	2 Apr. 1909	
Fillppini	John	Zamaroni	Egidia	7 Dec. 1914	
Finatti	Guilio	Gambroni	Angiolina	22 Sept. 1913	
Finch	Frank W.	Senn	Lydia E.	15 June 1920	
Finch	Fred F.	de Veuve	Anna M.	15 June 1918	
Finch	Gordon Wilbur	Lindley	Hannah Melba	7 Apr. 1917	
Fine	Alex	Miller	Annie Wickershaw	26 Feb. 1865	
Fink	Monte C.	Hutchinson	Sarah J.	18 July 1917	
Finke	Joseph H.	Andersen	Julia Jane	2 Nov. 1920	
Finlayson	James	Thompson	Anna F.	11 Nov. 1912	
Finley	Allan W.	Abraham	Dorthey E.	1 June 1918	
Finley	Alvin W.	Head	Frances Gertrude	4 Sept. 1901	
Finley	Asa L.	Pascoe	Caroline M.	19 Nov. 1920	
Finley	Ernest L.	Woolsey	Ruth	14 Dec. 1912	
Finley	Jackson	Stemple	Alfaretta	27 Apr. 1887	
Finley	Jefferson	McCready	Carrie	30 July 1892	
Finley	Leon Grover	Kee	Mary Elizabeth	3 Oct. 1918	
Finley	Robert	Malaney	Ella Nora	21 June 1906	
Finley	Wilson E.	Hudson	Alice	26 Nov. 1895	
Finn	Robert B.	Johnston	Grace G.	15 June 1917	
Finney	Clarence	Moore	Belle	2 July 1898	no previous marriage; don't publish
Fiori	Antonio	Parinoli	Annie	15 July 1920	
Fiori	Attilio A.	Sarori	Elizabeth	20 Sept. 1920	
Fiori	Celestino	Rossi	Mary	4 Sept. 1906	br: Sabina Rossi, mother; L. D. Battagia, witness to her mark
Firth	Christopher C.	Mury	Elise	31 May 1890	license requested by W. C. Hill
Fischer	Francis	Nolan	Rose	29 Mar.1893	

Groom		Bride		Date	Comments
Surname	Given Name	Surname	Given Name		
Fischer	Henry F.	Kobler	Rosa	18 Apr. 1910	
Fischer	William R.	Blaine	Lillian M.	5 June 1894	
Fiscus	Fred Irwin	Gould	Maud	20 Nov. 1907	
Fish	Clarence P.	Michalake	Barbara M.	1 June 1911	
Fish	Franklin Janus	Gage	Vivian Ada	6 Oct. 1905	gr: J. G. Fish, father
Fish	George	Lockwood	Mary	7 Dec. 1912	
Fishel	John E.	Mallory	Margaret L.	7 Sept. 1916	
Fisher	Charles	Yob	Rosa	27 June 1891	
Fisher	David	Blakley	Annie	24 Dec. 1895	
Fisher	Eugene	Samuels	Mollie	27 June 1888	
Fisher	Francis	Cole	Celia A.	14 May 1889	
Fisher	Fred W.	Wilztmann	Lulu	2 Sept. 1890	
Fisher	Isaac Willard	Vandeleur	Mayme Alloysious	16 Feb. 1906	
Fisher	Louis Fredk.	Paschal	Rosa Belle	27 Feb. 1896	
Fisher	Theodoric L.	Miller	Cora E.	21 Mar. 1898	gr: J. J. Fisher, parent
Fisk	Arthur M.	Buchan	Marjorie L.	25 Nov. 1914	
Fisk	Charles Grosvenor	Nisson	Gertrude	13 Sept. 1905	
Fisk	Chas. H.	Johnson	J. A.	20 Oct. 1866	
Fisk	Frank F.	Cooper	Lula May	21 June 1911	
Fisk	Geo. S.	Clark	Tillie	21 Nov. 1885	
Fisk	W. C.	Bundy	Edith	29 Mar. 1915	
Fitch	Arthur	Hance	Louise K.	20 Sept. 1916	
Fitch	Charley	Brown	Carrie	6 Nov. 1877	
Fitch	John B.	Graham	Libbie	6 Feb. 1882	br: Augusta L. Graham, parent; Angeline A Pearey, witness
Fitch	John Byron	Ford	Bessie, Mrs.	18 June 1902	
Fitch	Joseph	Moraga	Martena	29 Apr. 1878	
Fitch	Joseph	Filebot ?	Maria C.	20 Oct. 1865	
Fitch	Joseph, Jr.	Freshour	Sarah Jane	14 Jan. 1891	
Fitch	Romualdo A.	Gaspari	Lenora	22 Nov. 1917	
Fites	Charles E.	Brown	Emma G.	28 Feb. 1916	
Fitsimmons	Miron Ray	Baitey	Minnie Elvie	2 July 1904	
Fitz	Anton	Obram	Mary H.	15 June 1918	

Groom		Bride			
Surname	Given Name	Surname	Given Name	Date	Comments
Fitzgerald	Daniel Holland	Heatley	Edna M.	16 Sept. 1905	gr: John J. Fitzgerald, father, gives consent
Fitzgerald	Halcie	Cox	Ruby Marie	16 Dec. 1919	
Fitzgerald	James G. B.	Hiatt	Wanda	6 July 1912	br: J. W. Hiatt, parent
Fitzgerald	James R.	Azevedo	Mary Cecilia	14 Apr. 1917	
Fitzgerald	John A.	Cuneo	Palma	23 June 1914	
Fitzgerald	John Clayton	Ross	Genevieve Loiree	15 Oct. 1913	
Fitzgerald	John F.	Rogers	Maud	22 Dec. 1910	
Fitzgerald	John J., Jr.	Taylor	Ethel	27 Dec. 1920	
Fitzgerald	Thomas	Duffy	Susie	28 Dec. 1889	gr: H. H. Atwater, witness to his mark
Fitzpatrick	James H.	Dempsey	Catherine F.	15 June 1918	
Fitzpatrick	Lawrence F.	McLain	Lavina B.	26 Nov. 1918	br: Catherine M. McLain, parent
Fitzpatrick	Peter D.	Keefe	Maggie A.	27 Aug. 1891	
Fitzpatrick	Wm. E.	Herlihy	Elizabeth	13 July 1912	
Fitzsimmons	Charles S.	Henry	Cassie	1 July 1892	
Fix	J. K.	Shedd	R. J., Mrs.	12 Aug. 1886	
Fix	J. K.	Webster	Mary F., Mrs.		
Flack	John	Field	Rucilla R.	20 Oct. 1866	
Flack	John A.	McClish	Ella N.	23 Mar. 1900	
Flagg	Rollo E.	Lind	Marion E.	7 Sept. 1910	
Flaherty	Albert W.	Cook	Della T.	26 May 1919	
Flaherty	Philip Hyde	Fields	Theresa	22 Sept. 1905	
Flanary	Adam	Joslin	Alma	3 Feb. 1893	
Flechner	Lloyd L.	Buckle	Elsie G.	19 June 1920	
Fleck	G. C.	Scott	Agnes	13 Jan. 1919	
Fleet	Walter Sidney	Howard	Ethel May	9 May 1902	br: John C. Howard, father; gr: Walter Fleet, father
Fleischman	Louis E.	Reed	Ellen F.	30 Nov. 1889	
Fleishmon	Moses	Helbarh	Terria (?)	7 Dec. 1879	
Fleissner	Hugo Herman	Gamage	Lillian Lewis	14 June 1911	
Fleming	Eddie Ellis	Kingwell	Avis B.	25 May 1903	
Fleming	Frank M.	Kingwell	Phebe M.	24 Dec. 1901	
Fleming	Paul X.	Wisecarver	Norma Eugenia	10 July 1914	
Fleming	William	Carson	Mary	2 Nov. 1870	

Groom		Bride			
Surname	Given Name	Surname	Given Name	Date	Comments
Fleming	William	Carson	Mary	2 Nov. 1870	
Flemming	William	Olsen	Thora	30 Dec. 1918	
Flesher	Harry	Thomas	Ora A.	19 Dec. 1893	br: D. W. Thomas gives consent and signs.
Fletcher	Andrew	Kuffel	Gertrude	26 July 1890	
Fletcher	Harry A.	Murphy	Irene R.	5 Nov. 1920	br: Mrs. Laura V. Noland, mother
Fletcher	James A.	Rayner	Polly	8 Sept. 1914	
Fletcher	John H.	Murphy	Kate	12 Apr. 1919	
Fletcher	Lee C.	Nylen	Elivira L.	17 Aug. 1917	
Fletcher	Marion A.	Rohrback	Clara	1 Sept. 1900	
Fletcher	William R.	Dovey	Margaret	25 Apr. 1881	
Fletcher	Wm. F.	Barber	Flora G.	30 Nov. 1900	
Flickinger	Andrew Grant	Muller	Rose Helen	20 Feb. 1906	
Flint	T. B.	Flint	Ella J. (?)	4 May 1881	
Flint	Willard B.	Ross	Belle D.	14 Sept. 1899	
Fliori	Anchise	Prevedel	Aurora	3 July 1918	
Flippi	Toney	Cordano	Rose	7 Mar. 1908	br: requested and signed by her
Flockhart	Joseph J.	Wagner	Annie E.	8 Jan. 1921	
Flockhart	Robert E.	Feltz	Frieda L.	8 Jan. 1921	
Flohr	Charles W.	Michaels	Kate	8 Sept. 1899	
Flohr	Charles William	Zamaroni	Elvira	16 Sept. 1903	
Flohr	Frank G.	Downs	Catherine H.	21 June 1919	
Flohr	Marcus	Boyson	Gertrude E.	25 Nov. 1898	no previous marriage
Florence	Arthur	Manchester	Vieva Florence	16 Dec. 1898	
Flournoy	Alexander H.	Enzenauer	Ethel R.	2 June 1917	
Flournoy (?)	William H.	Throop	Fannie C.	28 Oct. 1878	
Floyd	Fred	Bowers	Elizabeth Clara	20 Dec. 1919	
Floyd	Fred	Pierce	May L.	30 Oct. 1900	
Floyd	James Andrew	Shaffer	Pearl Julia	16 Dec. 1907	
Flynn	John J.	Susoff	Lucile A.	19 Apr. 1920	
Flynn	Patrick	Quinlan	Ellie	22 July 1911	
Fobes	Charles Fitch	Brown	Bernice Luretta	9 Oct. 1906	
Focha	Joseph	Cerini	Dell	2 Sept. 1913	
Fochetti	Julius W.	Quartaroli	Leonora	14 May 1910	

Groom		Bride		Date	Comments
Surname	Given Name	Surname	Given Name		
Focht	Samuel S.	Harmer	Althea L.	12 Oct. 1910	
Foelker	Adam H.	Watson	Elizabeth E.	25 June 1912	
Foelone	Domenico	Nicoletti	Virginia	29 Apr. 1916	br: Carlo Nicoletti, father
Foerstler	William C.	Hershberger	Ruby D.	30 July 1917	
Fogarty	James V.	Beach	Clara M.	21 July 1913	
Folco	Eugenio M.	Graham	Elizabeth M.	3 Apr. 1913	
Foletti	Louis G.	Guizo	Angela C.	20 Apr. 1918	
Foley	Michael	Thistle	Bell	21 Sept. 1886	
Foley	Michael A.	Habinger	Irene E.	15 Feb. 1908	
Foley	Michel J.	Jasperson	Henrietta M.	7 Sept. 1917	
Folk	James	Caughey	Agnes	30 Apr. 1908	
Folks	Charles	Manning	Ella J.	3 June 1885	gr: John Folks, father; br: N. E. Manning, parent
Follini	Louis	Longo	Mary Florence	27 June 1917	
Follows	Jack Apperley	Miramontes	Marie Leanor	3 July 1920	
Folsom	Fred Newton	Kinyon	Bessie M.	21 Oct. 1915	
Foltz	Edward P.	McMinn	Etta	12 June 1895	
Fomasi	Peter	Albini	Mary	4 May 1908	
Fontch	Bert	Spraggins	Florence E.	31 Aug. 1918	
Fontes	Manuel Rodgers, Jr.	Perry	Roseline	20 Sept. 1902	br: Joseph M. Perry, father
Fonts	Fred	Weyl	Clara	8 Aug. 1903	
Fonts	Lee	Wakeland	Maggie E.	21 Oct. 1910	
Foote	Charles M.	Harris	Cecile Vivian	11 Apr. 1916	
Foote	W. D.	Davis	Lena	25 Feb. 1914	
Fopiano	Giuseppe	Rosasco	Rosa	20 July 1877	br: parents reside in Italy, Joseph Rosasco, brother
Forbes	Alfred L.	Black	Myrtle E.	13 Dec. 1913	
Forbes	Cleveland	Vrooman	Mae Baldwin	18 June 1898	
Forcha	Catano Jose	Medeiros	Anna	6 May 1887	br: Lipoldina Madeiros (widow), parent; H. H. Atwater & A. E. Rafael, witnesses
Ford	Barnett	Loury	Mary	16 Aug. 1884	
Ford	C. W. R.	Robinson	Julia S.	12 Mar. 1892	
Ford	Charles	Kennedy	Unice Pearl	21 Dec. 1898	no previous marriage

Groom		Bride			
Surname	**Given Name**	**Surname**	**Given Name**	**Date**	**Comments**
Ford	David	Field	Mary	5 Sept. 1889	
Ford	Earl A.	Singley	Theo. E.	14 July 1915	br: Henry A. Singley, father
Ford	Edward Franklin	Gibbs	Zoie Alva	25 Apr. 1913	
Ford	Fred J.	Lewis	Maretta E.	22 Aug. 1920	br: John F. Lewis, father
Ford	George T.	Crane	Eva Grace	13 Oct. 1907	
Ford	J. A.	Hayes	Hattie	17 Dec. 1913	
Ford	James Russell	Phillbrook	Martha	12 Dec. 1876	
Ford	John	Morris	Anna	25 Sept. 1912	
Ford	Michael	Moore	Amanda	12 Jan. 1888	
Ford	William A.	Campbell	Mollie	18 Dec. 1917	
Fordanse	Henry P.	Scott	Delilah	21 June 1884	
Forde	John M.	Freeman	Dorothy M.	4 June 1919	
Fordemwalt	C. E.	Kise	Ida	29 May 1886	
Fore	Walter Francis	O'Conner	Amy Joan	15 Oct. 1913	
Foreman	Andrew Macpherson	Lee	Annabel	24 Nov. 1915	
Foreman	C.	Fairchild	Gipsy	26 Oct. 1892	
Foreman	Charles	Stemer	Anna	24 Apr. 1911	
Foreman	Edward L.	Flournoy	Emma I.	27 Nov. 1920	
Foreman	Lorin	Brigham	Mamie L.	19 Dec. 1896	
Foreman	Park	Gilmore	Sarah E.	28 May 1892	
Forest	H. A.	Rieffel	Hortense L.	8 Jan. 1887	
Foresti	Giuseppe	Filosi	Lucia	25 May 1904	gr: Louis Filosi, guardian; license requested by Louis Filosi
Forgett	Frank Alma	Parara	Florence	31 Oct. 1891	
Forgett	Fred F.	Schwan	Minnie	4 Aug. 1892	
Forgett	Isadore	Bargagliotti	Louisa	21 Feb. 1903	
Forgett	Joseph Nelson	Eby	Jessie Leone	18 Sept. 1905	
Formschlag	August Elias	Buhl	Josie Mabel	20 Nov. 1906	
Formway	Utah S.	Bronsert	Anita M.	12 July 1920	
Forneris	Albert	Cole	Mary E.	21 Oct. 1920	
Forni	Charles B.	Ghiringhelli	Teressa	9 Aug. 1911	
Forno	Alasandro	Bologna	Lina	12 Mar. 1921	
Forrest	Richard Kenneth	Kelly	Erma Heidel	27 Apr. 1916	

Groom		Bride			
Surname	Given Name	Surname	Given Name	Date	Comments
Forrester	Henry A.	Steele	Viva B.	22 Aug. 1918	
Forsberg	Hans Peter	Tell	Ida Amanda	27 Apr. 1907	
Forsey	Warren F.	French	Francis J.	15 July 1890	
Forsman	William T.	Hilliard	Carrie B.	1 Apr. 1884	
Forsyth	Henry M.	Reid	Mary E.	7 Feb. 1891	
Forsyth	Jess Thomas	Dehay	Louise A.	19 Dec. 1903	
Forsyth	John Hamilton	Clark	Nancy C.	15 May 1890	
Forsyth	W. B.	Crandall	Edna	2 May 1888	
Forsythe	Myrl D.	Hockin	Maude A.	25 Mar. 1911	
Fortado	Jose Jacinto	Silva	Anna Pereira	3 Aug. 1886	
Fortado	Lawrence F.	Thomas	Vivian G.	13 June 1920	
Fortier	Louis	Looson (?)	Ann M.	11 Aug. 1884	gr: signs with his mark
Fortier	Peter	Hart	Hattie L.	10 Dec. 1887	
Fortier	William	Couper	Jennie	1 Nov. 1907	
Fortson	John T.	Howell	Margaret Lent	13 Dec. 1875	letters from L. V. H. Honck; San Francisco
Fortunati	Alfredo	Caselli	Beatrice	3 Aug. 1918	
Fosgett	Jay Dernard	Rudd	Minnie A.	11 Sept. 1905	
Fosgett	Jay Derward	Rhoades	Georgie A.	18 Sept. 1896	gr: Mrs. Caroline Fosgett of Oakland, CA gives consent and signs.
Foss	Charles C.	Proctor	Hattie	19 Feb. 1900	
Foss	Charles C.	Phillfott	Fanny (?) I.	31 Dec. 1881	
Foss	Leonard Rangwell	Noyes	Ruby Thersa	13 Aug. 1915	
Foss	Werner C.	Naselli	Mary E.	30 Nov. 1917	
Foste	Manuel	Nunes	Mary S.	26 July 1915	
Foste	Manuel V.	Victor	Julia C.	3 Mar. 1919	
Foster	Aubrey M.	Elsdon	Winifred J.	31 May 1919	
Foster	Charles L.	Baker	Crystabel K.	10 June 1913	
Foster	Charles Simpson	Benson	Marcia E.	20 June 1908	
Foster	Chas.	Gourley	Sarah A.	29 Apr. 1867	
Foster	Clarence E.	Gordon	Alice M.	18 July 1914	
Foster	Edwin J.	Breaks	Florence F.	21 May 1913	
Foster	Geo. Alonzo	Scott	Mary Ellen	17 Mar. 1883	
Foster	H. G.	Miller	Marion C.	14 Dec. 1915	

Groom		Bride			
Surname	Given Name	Surname	Given Name	Date	Comments
Foster	John Warren	Murphy	Nellie Agnes	24 June 1907	
Foster	Joseph	Morgan	Eva L.	10 June 1901	br: birth date 29 Jan. 1886; Irene Morgan, mother
Foster	Joseph Walter	Mordecai	Frances Elizabeth	25 May 1908	
Foster	Lewis Keyston	Waterbury	Ada Muriel	10 Dec. 1920	
Foster	Robert A.	Gibson	Susan A.	10 May 1894	
Foster	William E.	Addison	Eliza J.	10 Nov. 1870	
Foster	William E.	Addisen	Eliza J.	10 Nov. 1870	
Fouch	Albert	Talbot	Eliza P.	9 Dec. 1865	
Foucrault	Edward Chas.	Caligari	Celestina	4 Oct. 1900	
Fournier	Arthur, Dr.	Brittain	Grace C.	9 Feb. 1904	
Foutch	Albert P.	Dunlap	Melinda	31 Aug. 1911	br: Mildred Mathews, W. E. Saunders, witnesses to her mark
Foutch	Thomas G.	Anderson	Florence	27 Aug. 1910	
Fouts	Alvin Roy	Davis	Amanda	13 June 1914	
Fouts	Edwin Lee	Barnum	Evaline	10 Nov. 1905	br: Lizzie Barnum, mother
Fouts	William V.	Gleason	Mattie	6 Apr. 1906	gr: Jacob G. Fouts, father
Fouts	Clyde E.	Baney	Elsie R.	12 July 1919	
Fowler	Alfred	Deeds	Louisa C.	no date	no father or mother living to her knowledge
Fowler	David	Knolty	May M.	29 July 1912	
Fowler	Dewey	Druck	Elizabeth M.	2 July 1919	
Fowler	Edgar James	Rien	Sarah Cordelia	15 May 1877	
Fowler	Harvey	Rice	Eunice	29 Jan. 1867	
Fowler	J. H.	Connor	Jennie	10 Nov. 1886	
Fowler	Lorenzo Gipson	Peters	Flora	10 Apr. 1903	br: applied for license
Fowler	Nathaniel D.	McTarnahan	Addie, Mrs.	26 Feb. 1900	
Fowler	Nicholas R.	Lowrey	Minnie	25 July 1891	
Fowler	Scott D.	Dixon	Jessie	23 Oct. 1893	
Fowler	William C.	Faught	Ethel A.	1 Mar. 1902	
Fowles	Stephen	Gould	Minnie R.	3 Oct. 1896	license requested by Charles J. Kirsch
Fox	Ancel Elmer	Hixson	Zella Irene	16 Aug. 1917	
Fox	Chas. W.	Farmer	Sarah Angeline	31 Dec. 1879	
Fox	Francis Gordon	Steele	Grace Olney	15 May 1919	

Groom		Bride			
Surname	Given Name	Surname	Given Name	Date	Comments
Fox	Henry	Hall	Lola Jesse	5 Aug. 1880	
Fox	Joseph	Price	Lucy M.	19 June 1913	
Fox	Louis H.	Steitz	Julia C.	17 June 1902	
Frame	R. A.	Davis	Eliza S.	24 Dec. 1881	
Frampton	Charles E.	Miser	Hannah	22 Dec. 1886	
Francard	Ernest	Babbino	Carlotta	14 Sept. 1915	
Francard	John B.	Gallard	Genevive	29 June 1892	
Franceschi	Ceasre	Perinoni	Rose	5 July 1918	
Francesconi	Federico	Albreigi	Madelina	21 Dec. 1909	br: Olinto, parent
Franchi	Nildo	Bacci	Beppa	4 Jan, 1915	
Francis	Edwin Charles	Norris	Henrietta	5 Oct. 1908	
Francis	Joseph Andrew	Peat	Pearle E.	1 July 1918	
Francis	William A.	Bowie	Vera	1 July 1918	
Francis	William S.	Perry	Mary	27 Jan. 1902	
Francisco	Anton	Cardoza	Mary Ann	29 Nov. 1897	Frank Wedge, witness signature
Francisco	Antone	Limes	Annie	11 Sept. 1906	
Francisco	Antone J.	Silva	Mary	28 Mar. 1891	br: Frank Silva, father
Frank	C. E.	Spitzer	Clara S.	13 Apr. 1916	
Frank	Christian	Mangole	Pauline	15 Nov. 1898	no previous marriage; requested by Jud Christian
Frank	Frederick	Feltz	Amelia	18 June 1889	
Frank	James	Eager	Loretta	21 May 1867	
Frank	Samuel	Locsen (?)	Amelia		
Franklin	Alex R.	Partridge	Katherine	6 Dec. 1920	
Franklin	Benjamin	McKinnon	Gertrude E.	24 Mar. 1896	
Fraser	D. Herbert	Roussey	Mildred, Mrs.	10 Aug. 1910	not signed by br: or gr:
Fraser	Dan W.	Cameron	Hazel	18 Nov. 1913	
Fraser	George Willard	Ware	Helen	25 Apr. 1905	
Fraser	James Grant	Walker	Nellena E.	15 Dec. 1902	br: Sarah E. Hassett, guardian
Fraser	John N.	Clark	Lettie A.	23 Dec. 1913	
Frasier	Frank B.	Crimmins	Agnes Marie	22 May 1909	
Frasier	Fred A.	Graeff	Dora	10 Jan. 1911	
Frasier	Malcome J.	Kane	Maggie	23 Oct. 1884	

Groom		Bride			
Surname	Given Name	Surname	Given Name	Date	Comments
Frates	Joseph A.	Ramos	Mary	9 Oct. 1908	
Frates	Joseph V. A.	McChristian	Delphine G.	15 June 1901	gr: 226 Hollis St., Oakland
Frates	Joseph W.	Morris	Mary S.	30 Aug. 1902	
Frates	Manuel Suza	Dabuer	Rosa Emilia	7 Oct. 1886	
Frati	Abramo	Acquistapace	Amelia	2 Nov. 1907	
Frati	Francesco	Gregori	Maria	3 June 1901	
Frati	Giuseppe	Bertoni	Natalina	19 Sept. 1900	
Frawley	Richard Edward	Reed	Mattie Agnes	7 May 1906	
Frazee	Henry Dewitt	Lockwood	Linnie Katherine (?)	8 Apr. 1899	
Frazer	Joe E.	Corey	Mary	2 Oct. 1913	
Frazier	Elisha H.	Dodson	Mary R.	9 Nov. 1892	br: age is four days short of 18; C. H. Dodson gives consent; witness Charles H. Dodson
Frazier	Elisha H.	McNew	Orpah Belle	7 Feb. 1881	br: J. & Emily McNew, parents
Frazier	Isaac B.	Ross	Lizzie E.	27 Dec. 1894	
Freck	Louis P.	Bridges	Minnie	25 June 1917	
Frederick	Leonard B.	Harland	Adeline I.	4 June 1904	
Fredericks	Adolph N.	Campigli	Effie	9 Oct. 1909	
Fredericks	George	Showalter	Belle	29 Mar. 1889	
Fredericks	Martin	Cline	Mary A.	6 July 1920	
Fredericks	Ray Ernest	Hammell	Edna May	18 May 1912	
Frederickson	Frederick C.	Koppen	Emma C.	23 Aug. 1902	
Frederickson	Hans J.	Johnson	Annie C.	17 Aug. 1887	
Frederiksen	Andreas	Mathisen	Ingeburg M.	10 Aug. 1888	
Frediani	Angelo	Freggiro	Christine	3 May 1900	br: Frank Freggiro, father
Fredrichsen	Cornelius	Hansen	Meta	22 June 1900	
Fredson	Chris A.	Eagle	Geneva	22 Dec. 1911	
Fredson	Israel	Thompson	Sophia	17 Apr. 1885	
Freeborn	Francis Maurice	Crepin	Louise Cecelia	16 Nov. 1907	
Freeman	Albert J.	Barnes	Mary E.	3 May 1890	br: widow
Freeman	Albert J.	Hardisty	Emma L.	19 Feb.1901	
Freeman	Carlos J.	Carmichael	Belle	4 May 1897	do not publish until May 5
Freeman	Charles E.	Shelton	Lucy E.	7 July 1886	

Groom		Bride			
Surname	Given Name	Surname	Given Name	Date	Comments
Freeman	Charles Henry	Carter	Alice Blanche	7 May 1910	
Freeman	David	Crawford	Annie	29 Sept. 1888	
Freeman	M. L.	Hurton	E. Estella	5 Feb. 1887	
Freeman	Orin	Lawson	Rosetta	27 Nov. 1886	
Freeman	Wm. H.	Maddux	Martha E.	1 Sept. 1882	
Freenor	Francis Joseph	Gries	Roberta L.	24 Mar. 1919	
Freese	Frederich	Fischer	Mary	26 June 1915	
Frehe	Alfred Louis	Chittenden	Cornelia F.	11 Apr. 1903	
Frei	L. A.	Mooney	Joan E.	15 Apr. 1913	
Frei	Walter C.	Tyler	Leatha Ruth	9 Feb. 1918	
Freidrichsen	Peter	Petersen	Dora	6 Apr. 1903	
Freitas	Anton	Howe	Johanna V.	8 June 1895	
Freitas	Antone	Freels	Julia Louise	21 June 1916	
Freitas	Joao M.	Vieira	Francisca	29 Oct. 1887	
Freitas	Tony	Costa	Bella	31 May 1913	
Freitas (?) on index	Frederick Augustius	Barrett	Linnie Mary	13 Feb. 1912	
Frellson	Hans	Krounest	Emily	5 Mar. 1888	
Frellson	Oscar August	Meeker	Winifred M.	14 Dec. 1908	
Frellson	Walter B.	Wright	Nellie Wilson	22 May 1913	
French	Charles F.	Emery	Eva J.	28 Sept. 1882	date from note; requested by D. B. Morgan
French	George Bonzana	Wulff	Cecile I.	21 Aug. 1911	
French	George Robert	Harmeson	Pearl	26 Dec. 1908	
French	Jno. H.	Folks	Ella	11 Sept. 1880	
French	William	Cook	May M.	9 Oct. 1901	
Frese	Henry	Maack	Lily	16 Dec. 1899	
Freshour	John L.	Cobb	Frances	18 May 1905	
Freshwater	Albert H.	Halligan	Francis B.	30 Apr. 1917	
Frey	Elmer	Sanders	Nadie	2 Dec. 1919	
Frey	Frank J.	Davis	Ida B.	4 May 1897	br: M. S. Davis, father, gives consent and signs.
Frey	Herbert R.	Wilson	Helen A.	29 Nov. 1920	
Frey	Howard L.	Cherne	Mollie F.	26 June 1917	
Frey	John G.	Hoff	Emma H.	17 Dec. 1919	

Groom		Bride			
Surname	**Given Name**	**Surname**	**Given Name**	**Date**	**Comments**
Friar	James N.	Smith	Phena May	26 June 1919	
Fricke	Richard	Huyck	Pearl	14 Sept. 1914	
Fried	Henry W.	Watson	Lola Etta	20 Nov. 1894	
Friel	Patrick	Friel	Mary	6 Jan. 1910	
Friend	Joseph A.	Ivans	Laura Alice	9 July 1883	br: Wm. & Mary Ivans, parents
Fries	Theodore	Witt	Ellen V.	3 Nov. 1919	
Frisch	Finnly W.	Waterman	Gertrude M.	18 June 1912	
Fritsch	J. R.	Hope	Anna M.	18 Feb. 1891	
Fritsch	Walter S.	Mecham	Mary I.	26 Jan. 1887	
Frohmoder	Thomas	Lawson	Catherine	28 Sept. 1914	
Fronk	Edwin B.	Striver	Alice E.	2 June 1917	
Frost	Ervin	Singleton	Jennie	26 Nov. 1907	br: she requested/signed
Frost	G. W.	Myres	Susanna	16 Aug. 1888	
Frost	Harvey Chester	McBride	Elizabeth May	16 Oct. 1907	
Frost	Martin	Warner	Cora E.	3 Apr. 1882	
Frost	Norman Seaver	Thurman	Anastasia	11 Apr. 1914	
Frost	Walter C.	Knight	Jennie	1 Dec. 1877	
Frugoli	Virgilio	Usseglio	Catterina	9 Dec. 1911	gr: W. E. Sauddners, Henty Silvershield, witnesses to his mark
Frugoli	Virgilio	Rose	Mary	3 Nov. 1906	gr & br: Edith Griffith, Herbert Slater, witness to their marks
Fruits	George Alexander	Gregson	Delia	14 Feb. 1877	
Fruitt	Charles E.	Hall	Alice E.	6 Jan. 1899	
Frus	Hans	Johansen	Cecilia	2 Mar. 1894	umlat over the u in Frus or could be Friis
Frutiger	George F.	Parkerson	Jane Edith	14 May 1892	
Fry	Albert S.	Allen	Ione May	28 Feb. 1910	
Fuchs	Ewald A.	Barrows	Olive M.	16 Oct. 1916	
Fujimoto	Togro	Furuta	Tori	26 Aug. 1920	
Fulkerson	Bruce C.	Wheeler	Maude	28 May 1910	
Fulkerson	Bruce C.	Dimick	Viola	24 Dec. 1900	gr: S. T. Fulkerson, father
Fulkerson	Chas. A.	McGill	Minnie	5 June 1897	
Fulkerson	Richard	Wendt	Paulina	2 May 1891	gr: S. T. Fulkerson, father
Fulks	C. E.	Gilkison	Norah F.	22 Aug. 1888	

Groom		Bride		Date	Comments
Surname	Given Name	Surname	Given Name		
Fullan	Thomas	Hall	Jessie	4 June 1918	
Fuller	Charles E.	Smith	India	4 Mar. 1896	
Fuller	Frank Leslie	Armstrong	Ruby Ann	12 Dec. 1905	
Fuller	Harve	Syme	Annie	14 Nov. 1902	
Fuller	Lyman T.	Marshall	Clara	3 Nov. 1898	no previous marriage
Fuller	Percy V.	Scott	Esther	29 Nov. 1913	br: Mrs. Annie Scott, mother
Fuller	Wm. F. H.	Willis	Ruth E.	13 Jan. 1894	
Fulmer	James S.	Milford	Ellen M.	23 July 1920	
Fulton	James E.	Moore	Ella Jane	18 Nov. 1908	
Fulton	Jasper A.	Franklin	Dora	22 Nov. 1911	
Fulwider	Earl N.	VanWormer	Charlotte E.	2 June 1916	
Fumasoli	Giacomo	Domeniconi	Rachel	4 May 1907	
Furber	John Judd	Smith	Jessie Alberta	8 June 1909	
Furber	William W.	Hinds	Marguerite	3 June 1912	
Furia	Alfonzo	Furia	Elvira	26 July 1911	
Furia	Ettore	Santini	Casimira	13 Oct. 1906	gr: E. Furia, parent; br: E. Santini, parent
Furia	Quinto	Bertoni	Amelia	24 Dec. 1913	
Furlong	Charles Edward	Focha	Frances Agnes	14 Jan. 1918	
Furlong	Hugh C.	Gericke	Margaret L.	18 Dec. 1920	
Furlong	Patrick	Gallegher	Sarah	20 Oct. 1877	witness: Nathaniel Keefe
Furlong	Thomas F.	Gleason	Mary Agnes	29 Mar. 1918	
Fuson	Amandus U.	Cavanagh	May Alice	13 Aug. 1910	
Futsch	Walter Mecham	Hodgson	Irene Mae	5 June 1918	

Part II

Groom, Bride, Age, Residence, Place of Birth

Groom					Bride				
Surname	Given Name	Age	Residence	BP	Surname	Given Name	Age	Residence	BP
?hreeve (?)	Levi	34	Freestone	OR	Staggs	Phebe	26	Sebastopol	IA
Aanensen	Peider	57	Petaluma	NRY	Downham	Alma N.	47	Petaluma	NRY
Aaronson	Phillip V.	40	San Francisco	IL	Blattenberger	Zoe N.	27	San Francisco	CA
Abbey	Alfred	23	Oakland	CA	Bailhache	Ruth	22	Healdsburg	CA
Abbey	Alfred B.	22	Guerneville	CA	Bigsby	Macueleta	21	Guerneville	CA
Abbey	Bert	30	Winters	CA	Lewis	Haltie	20	Santa Rosa	IL
Abbey	William Newton	26	Santa Rosa	CA	Allen	Nellie Angeline	18	Mt. Olivet	CA
Abbott	George Henry	26	Healdsburg	CA	Shire	Maude Frances	17	Healdsburg	CA
Abbott	Joel A.	23	San Francisco	NV	Hendricks	Myrtle	18	San Francisco	CA
Abeel	James Martin	30	Sebastopol	MO	Pepper	Ada Elaine	22	Santa Rosa	CA
Abels	Ihuk?	48	Petaluma Twp.	GER	Rubben	Helene	30	Petaluma Twp.	GER
Ables	Horace T.	23	Tomales	Mac	Stephen	Mabel Alice	17	Petaluma	Lon
Abra	Jack W.	27	San Antonio, Los Angeles Co.	CND	Vickery	Nellie G.	21	Santa Rosa	AR
Abraham	Louis F.	23	Petaluma	Pet	Burston	Francis E.	22	Petaluma	Sfo
Abraio	William Franklin	27	Petaluma	CA	Kelton	Alice R.	16	Petaluma	CA
Abrams	J. William	25	Hanford	CA	Florin	Lucile H.	24	Santa Rosa	MO
Abrott	Fred Henry	38	Lytton Springs	CA	Lyons	Henrietta	40	Lytton Springs	CA
Abshire	Alfred C.	23	Windsor	CA	Laughlin	Myrtle	16	Windsor	IA
Abshire	Farley A.	23	Cloverdale	CA	Crow	Susie E.	19	Cloverdale	CA
Abshire	Francis P.	21	Cloverdale	CA	Ross	Vera M.	21	Forestville	CA
Abshire	Alfred Cecil	21	Geyserville	CA	Thompson	Maude Elnora	21	Cloverdale	CA
Achey	Clarence M.	20	Healdsburg	MO	Fogarty	Ida	18	Mendocino Twp.	CA
Acker	James W.	23	Santa Rosa	NY	Pattison	Jean M. O.	19	Santa Rosa	SCT
Ackerman	Charles J.	20	Healdsburg	CA	Petray	Gladys Valentine	19	Healdsburg	CA
Ackerman	Clarence M.	25	Petaluma	CA	Ward	Ada L.	21	Petaluma	CA
Ackerman	Oliver Norton	22	Santa Rosa	CA	Ranarde	Lina Francis	18	Petaluma	CA
Ackermann	Anton	29	San Francisco	GER	Weismann	Alvina	40	San Francisco	MN
Acorne	Melville G.	23	Petaluma	CA	Boman	Marian Beatrice	18	Petaluma	CA

Groom					Bride				
Surname	Given Name	Age	Residence	BP	Surname	Given Name	Age	Residence	BP
Acquistapace	Amadio	27	Greenwood	ITL	Rossotte	Aurellia	18	Greenwood	ITL
Acquistapace	Guiseppe	23	Kenwood	ITL	Piezzi	Sabina	28	Kenwood	ITL
Acquistapace	Pietro	28	Guerneville	ITL	Antonietta	Manne	20	Guerneville	ITL
Acuff	Metcalf				Hunt	Luella A.			
Adair	C. H.	50	Colusa	IN	Burckhalter	Agnes	45	Santa Rosa	SCT
Adams	Alfred F.	23	Sausalito	CA	Thomas	Nettie E.	23	Santa Rosa	CA
Adams	Arthur Joseph	31	San Francisco	CA	Munro	Margaret J.	26	San Francisco	CA
Adams	Arthur Miron	26	Petaluma	CA	Johnson	Ella B.	24	Petaluma	CA
Adams	Claude W.	24	Oakland	CA	Patterson	Bell	24	Santa Rosa	CA
Adams	Clement Scott	21	Eureka	CA	Cartwright	Leta May	18	Eureka	CA
Adams	Darwin C.	26	Stockton	OR	McGowan	Daisy Fedora	28	Stockton	CA
Adams	Frank	23	Bodega		Carlile	Etta	19	Bodega	
Adams	Frank E.	33	Humbolt, IA	NY	Jones	Carrie E.	27	Cloverdale	CA
Adams	Frank T.	26	Santa Rosa	ME	Skaggs	Clara C.	20	Santa Rosa	CA
Adams	George Edward	23	Watsonville	AR	Fogerty	Annie May	22	Healdsburg	NV
Adams	George H.	30	Healdsburg	CA	Green	Una	26	Healdsburg	CA
Adams	George William	28	Warner, NH	NH	Richman	Elizabeth Eleanor	20	Oakland	CA
Adams	J. S.	33	Fulton	IL	Greening	Laura A.	22	Mark West	CA
Adams	John F.	24	San Francisco	CA	Riley	Gertrude E.	21	San Francisco	CA
Adams	John Henry	22	Santa Rosa Twp.	CA	Dunkley	Mattie J.	19	Santa Rosa	MO
Adams	John L.	35	Santa Rosa	CA	Halst	Maggie M.	18	Santa Rosa	MN
Adams	Joseph	33	Cloverdale Twp.	CA	Crawford	Harriet Anna	19	Cloverdale	CA
Adams	Joseph Walker	32	Santa Rosa Twp.	CA	Holst	Annie Mary	17	Santa Rosa Twp.	MN
Adams	Merrit	19	Oakland	Wat	Murphy	Jennie R.	17	Cloverdale	CA
Adams	Robert L.	26	Santa Rosa	CA	Morgan	Nellie W.	23	Occidental	CA
Adams	Robert S.	26	Petaluma	Toron-to	Keys	Amelia	25	Petaluma	Pet
Adams	Ross B.	26	Santa Rosa	MI	Lambert	Lotus L.	20	Santa Rosa	CA
Adams	Wallace A.	21	Petaluma	IL	Brown	Adelaide M.	21	Petaluma	CA

Groom					Bride				
Surname	Given Name	Age	Residence	BP	Surname	Given Name	Age	Residence	BP
Adams	William	49	Fresno	CND	Calder	Mary Jane	35	Petaluma	CND
Adams	William A.	35	Oakland	CA	Hendricks	Mayme E.	31	Healdsburg	CA
Adams	William H.	34	Cloverdale	CA	Hillyer	Daisy B.	29	Cloverdale	CA
Adams	William J.	46	Sebastopol	MO	Russell	Martha Jane	37	Sebastopol	IL
Adamson	Forrest E.	24	Petaluma	SD	Gregg	Myrtle M.	24	Petaluma	CA
Adamson	Isaac N.	33	Petaluma	UT	Willson	Nellie, Mrs.	21	Petaluma	CA
Adamson	Isaac Newton	31	Santa Rosa	UT	Bell	Lucinda	17	Windsor	CA
Adamson	Isaac Newton	47	Sebastopol	Utt	Matthews	Ella, Mrs.	44	Sebastopol	CA
Adamson	John Martin	24	Yorkville	Utt	Adams	Martha	18	Yorkville	CA
Adcock	Abe	35	Cloverdale	CA	Francis	Hattie	21	Healdsburg	CA
Adcock	George	21	Cloverdale	CA	Dodson	Rosa	17	Cloverdale	Lak
Adcock	Joseph C.	37	Cloverdale	CA	Dodson	Mary Jane	47	Cloverdale	CA
Adcock	Samuel W.	33	Cloverdale	CA	Murray	Bertie	18	Cloverdale	CA
Adler	Adam Winkle	27	Sonoma	Son	Quartaroli	Florence M. E.	17	Sonoma	Son
Adler	Hans	24	Santa Rosa	GER	Rohleder	Betti	21	Santa Rosa	GER
Adolphson	Gustav	34	San Francisco	SWD	Fingahl	Nellie	27	Berkeley	SWD
Affonso	Joseph T.	27	Nicasio	AZR	Brazil	Rose Helen	22	Petaluma	AZR
Affranchino	Guiseppe	30	Santa Rosa	ITL	Guglielmini	Rosa	26	Santa Rosa	ITL
Agnew	Asahel Warner	27	Petaluma	CA	Shaver	Bertha Catherine	23	Petaluma	CA
Agnew	Hugh C.	47	Bethel, Contra Costa Co.	IA	Barber	Josephine	47	Stuartsville, NJ	PA
Agnew	James F.	21	San Francisco	CA	Arnold	Alberta L.	24	San Francisco	CA
Agnew	Newton W.	22	Sonoma	Son	Cozini	Lottie May	18	Sonoma	CA
Agren	Arthur L.	30	San Francisco	OR	Pohley	Margaret F.	31	Windsor	CA
Aguiar	Frank	40	Santa Rosa	PRT	Silva	Arnicenda Augusta	35	Santa Rosa	PRT
Aguirre	Amadeo	33	Cotati	SPN	Apodaca	Fermina Saturnina	24	Los Angeles	SPN
Aguirre	Martin	27	Cotati	SPN	Archabal	Julia	22	Cotati	SPN
Ahern	George F.	21	San Francisco	CA	Bones	Hazel Celia	19	Duncans Mills	CA

Groom					Bride				
Surname	**Given Name**	**Age**	**Residence**	**BP**	**Surname**	**Given Name**	**Age**	**Residence**	**BP**
Ahern	James B.	26	Tiburon	CA	Davidson	Sarah E.	23	Petaluma	CA
Ahern	Nicholas	22	Sonoma	IRL	Hardford	Mary	19	Sonoma	CA
Ahl	Harry Jacob	22	Santa Rosa	CO	Hiatt	Kate D.	19	Santa Rosa	OR
Ahl	John	23	Santa Rosa	CO	Mayfield	Maud	23	Santa Rosa	CA
Ahlstedt	Gustave	60	Agua Caliente	SWD	Nelson	Johanna	58	Agua Caliente	SWD
Ahrens	William M.	21	Santa Rosa	CA	Frehe	Annie M.	21	Santa Rosa	CA
Aiken	Henry S.	31	Petaluma	IL	Smith	Dollie A.	28	Petaluma	IL
Aiton	Wensley T.	33	Oakland	CND	Davis	Anna E.	35	Los Angeles	ME
Akers	Austin G.	21	Santa Rosa	CA	Cuda	Rose E.	18	Santa Rosa	GER
Akers	Earl L.	31	Santa Rosa	CA	Strickler	Ida Grace	18	Santa Rosa	CA
Akers	Edward W.	26	Kelseyville	CA	Banks	A. Varde	23	Forestville	OR
Akers	Lawrence	26	Healdsburg	MO	Parker	Pearl	26	Healdsburg	KS
Akers	Stephen	26	Petaluma	Son	Lawler	Grace	23	Shellville	Pet
Alapi	Hans	24	Santa Rosa	AUS	Szalay	Rosa	19	Santa Rosa	AUS
Albera	Michele	31	Santa Rosa	FRN	Cabaup	Maria	24	Santa Rosa	FRN
Alberigi	Americo	26	Healdsburg	CA	Ceraille	Jennie	27	Healdsburg	CA
Alberti	Francisco	23	Santa Rosa	SWT	Voletti	Maria	24	Santa Rosa	ITL
Albertson	Iver Magnus	27	Oakland	NRY	Dahl	Mole Hansen	30	Alameda	NRY
Albini	Abramo	25	Tomales	ITL	Rossi	Elvera	19	Valley Ford	ITL
Albini	Charles	26	Fallon	ITL	Poncia	Maria	35	Fallon	ITL
Albini	Domenico	27	Valley Ford	ITL	Furia	Ersilia	18	Santa Rosa	ITL
Albini	John	25	Bodega	ITL	Pelaccini	Maria	20	Bodega	ITL
Albini	John	28	Occidental	ITL	Albini	Elvira	28	Tomales	ITL
Albini	John	19	Bodega	ITL	Barella	Amellia	19	Bodega	ITL
Albini	Paul	24	Bodega	ITL	Donati	Romilda	24	Bodega	CA
Albini	Paul, Jr.	22	Bodega	SAM	Pozzi	Dora	19	Bodega	ITL
Albini	Peter	23	Bodega	ITL	Barella	Emilia	19	Bodega	ITL
Albini	Pietro	31	Bodega	ITL	Illia	Adele	25	Bodega	ITL
Albrecht	Asmas	28	Green Valley	GER	Hoirneche	Mary	22	Green Valley	IN
Albrecht	Charles	38	San Francisco	Alsace	Marshall	May	23	Santa Rosa	TX

Groom					Bride				
Surname	Given Name	Age	Residence	BP	Surname	Given Name	Age	Residence	BP
Albright	Frederick W. H.	27	Healdsburg	NY	Boyer	Mabel C.	24	San Francisco	PA
Albright	James O.	53	Petaluma	MI	Matthews	Helen	48	Petaluma	AL
Alderson	Earl Ray	22	Graton	IL	Barnum	Inez Mildred	17	Forestville	CA
Alessandrini	Charles	27	Santa Rosa	ITL	Bertoli	Erminia	34	Santa Rosa	ITL
Alessi	Ignazio	35	Petaluma	ITL	Beltrametti	Teodolinda	24	Petaluma	SWT
Alexander	David N.	49	Petaluma	PA	Heald	Sarah E.	35	Petaluma	CA
Alexander	Ernest F.	64	Mendocino City	KY	Garvin	Helen	24	Mendocino	CA
Alexander	George C.	31	Healdsburg	CA	Sarginsson	Nellie Maude	26	Healdsburg	ENG
Alexander	John	37	Tomales	IRL	Morrow	Jennie	25	Bennett Valley	IRL
Alexander	John	30	Sebastopol	CA	Bill	Lucy A.	22	Sebastopol	MO
Alexander	Lawrence	26	Healdsburg		Price	Laura A.	24	Healdsburg	
Alexander	Lemuel H.	23	Healdsburg	IA	Russell	M. A.	20	Healdsburg	CA
Alexander	Rufus	49	Petaluma	NY	Humphres	Allie L.	23	Petaluma	OH
Alexander	Thomas	32	Alexander Valley	CA	Patrick	H. A.	19	Alexander Valley	CA
Alexanderson	Philip E.	23	Petaluma	CA	Cooper	Clara B.	20	Santa Rosa	OR
Alfiere	Joseph	34	Bodega		Beedle	Addie	19	Bodega	
Alford	Charles A., Jr.	22	Guerneville	CA	Hollar	Viola	19	Forestville	IA
Alford	Erastus	50	Santa Rosa	IA	Ward	Elizabeth, Mrs.	42	Santa Rosa	IA
Alford	Frederick	27	Glen Ellen	ENG	Soto	Trinidad	27	San Diemas, MEX	MEX
Alfrey	Harry K.	33	San Francisco	OH	Senner	Mabel E.	29	San Francisco	CA
Algeo	Andrew J.	28	Langell Valley, Klamath Co. OR	CA	Peterson	Nellie I.	25	Santa Rosa	CA
Aliphat	Eugene D.	21	San Francisco	MEX	Rafael	Lydia	18	San Francisco	CA
Alison	Archie	32	Oakland	PA	Ross	Lucy B.	21	Oakland	CA
Allan	Frank Walker	38	Oakland	CA	Morrison	Katie May	26	Healdsburg	CA
Allegrini	Julius	25	Asti	SWT	Peruzzo	Jennie	19	Asti	CA
Allen	Anderson	70	Healdsburg	MO	Rees	Harriet A., Mrs.	65	Healdsburg	KY
Allen	Anthony	25	Cloverdale	Soc	Todd	Mary E.	17	Cloverdale	MO
Allen	Charles P.	33	San Francisco	CA	Smith	Geneva	23	Cloverdale	CA

Groom					Bride				
Surname	Given Name	Age	Residence	BP	Surname	Given Name	Age	Residence	BP
Allen	Chesley M.	26	San Francisco	CA	Dohl (?)	Effa B.	26	San Francisco	MD
Allen	D. B.	26	Ukiah	NV	McPeak	Hattie E.	26	Ukiah	Sar
Allen	Evan R.	22	Glen Ellen	IA	Wright	Olive	21	Glen Ellen	IA
Allen	Frank	29	Petaluma	MA	Sylva	Emelia Emma	23	Petaluma	CA
Allen	Frederick William	31	Sebastopol	IA	Warren	Emma Louise	33	Sebastopol	CA
Allen	George A.	27	College City, CA	CA	McPherson	Hazel	27	Healdsburg	CA
Allen	George Harrison	22	Oakland	CA	Hagan	Mignon C.	18	San Francisco	CA
Allen	George O.	23	Sebastopol	CA	Alten	Anna E.	18	Sebastopol	CA
Allen	George P.	62	St. Helena	ME	Clary	Emma	48	Livermore	CA
Allen	Gerald M.	26	Oakland	CA	Tuttle	Lilla R.	26	Santa Rosa	IA
Allen	Gilbert W.	22	Santa Rosa	CO	Lockman	Ella Ray	20	Santa Rosa	CA
Allen	Harry R.	26	Santa Rosa	CA	Templeman	Agnes M.	24	Santa Rosa	CA
Allen	Henry C.	30	Petaluma		Story	Susan	24	Mendocino Twp.	
Allen	James Edgar	26	Rockville, IN	Rock-ville,IN	Deuman	Carrie Elizabeth	25	Petaluma	Soc
Allen	James Rodney	22	Riverside	CA	Bonham	Rena Lucile	21	Oakland	CA
Allen	James T.	25	Petaluma	MO	Bailey	Elma G.	18	Petaluma	CO
Allen	Jay B.	21	Santa Rosa	ID	Sherwood	Delphia L.	18	Santa Rosa	CA
Allen	John F.	27	Petaluma	CA	Munday	Mabel	24	Petaluma	CA
Allen	John Harvey	25	Geyserville	IL	Painter	Katie Iowa	21	College City, CA	IL
Allen	John T.	28	Healdsburg	OR	Gray	Lotta L.	17	Winters	CA
Allen	John W.	52	Santa Rosa	MO	Wilson	Amy	32	Santa Rosa	ENG
Allen	Leslie Russell	29	Stockton	CA	LeWarne	Anna Jean	26	San Jose	MT
Allen	Maxwell W.	26	Berkeley	CA	Nicholson	Rose K.	28	Santa Rosa	CA
Allen	Merton C.	21	San Francisco	CA	Penrod	Lillie L.	22	Petaluma	CND
Allen	Robert	24	Cloverdale	CA	Graham	Bertha	23	Cloverdale	SWT
Allen	Thomas Edgar	23	Upper Lake	CA	Booher	Mary Luemma	26	Santa Rosa	CA
Allenberg	Ferdinand Arthur	25	Petaluma	CA	Voris	Isabell Alice	22	Petaluma	CA
Allenden	Gerald	-21	Geyserville		Murray	Eva			
Allenden	William H.	31	Alexander Valley	ENG	Young	Myrtle L.	21	Alexander Valley	CA

Groom					Bride				
Surname	**Given Name**	**Age**	**Residence**	**BP**	**Surname**	**Given Name**	**Age**	**Residence**	**BP**
Allenwood	Frank	33	San Francisco	CA	Roehling	Agnes M.	33	San Francisco	CA
Alley	Leonard Samuel	23	Upper Lake	CA	Clark	Ada	22	Santa Rosa	CA
Alley	Omery Elmo	31	Santa Rosa	MO	Dunham	Alta Faye	25	Santa Rosa	IA
Allis	Edmund C.	31	San Francisco	MN	Stevens	Louisa E.	24	San Francisco	CA
Allison	Jay J.	22	Healdsburg	OR	Mead	Jenevieve I.	20	Healdsburg	CA
Allison	Samuel				Walker	Dasey	17	Santa Rosa	CA
Allman	Joe Peter	44	Dry Creek	GER	Minasco	J. Lee, Mrs.	40	San Jose	MO
Almann	John	27	Cloverdale	GER	Patronak	Mamie	19	Dry Creek	IL
Alsbarge	Charles A.	25	San Francisco	IL	Skinner	Mabel A.	27	Santa Rosa	CA
Alten	Henry	32	Sebastopol	CA	Power	Mary E.	26	Green Valley	CA
Alten	John H.	26	Forestville	CA	Clayborne	Florence E.	24	Forestville	CA
Alten	Pete	35	Vine Hill	CA	Miller	Maggie E., Mrs.	32	Vine Hill	CA
Alten	Wendell	21+	Sebastopol	CA	McNeil	Minnie Clara	21+	Windsor	CA
Altenreuther	Leopold C.	36	Lakeville	CO	Masciorini	Erminia Agnes	29	Petaluma	CA
Alvernaz	Manuel Brum	40	Petaluma	PRT	Norouha (?)	Maria	25	Petaluma	PRT
Alves	Frank S.	19	Sebastopol	CA	Clark	Gladys A.	18	Forestville	CA
Amann	Wendalin	30	Healdsburg	GER	Koch	Minnie	20	Healdsburg	CA
Amanso	Antone	23	Oakland	PRT	Perry	Rosie	17	Oakland	Hon
Amaral	Anthony	23	Cotati	CA	Cory	Isabelle L.	20	Sebastopol	CA
Ambler	J. Raymond	28	San Francisco	Phx	Bender	Madeleine L.	32	San Francisco	Phl
Ambler	John	45	Petaluma	ENG	Dolan	Anna	23	Petaluma	CA
Ambler	Lawrence J.	30	Healdsburg	CA	Stanley	Laura	22	Healdsburg	CA
Ambrose	Frank	39	San Francisco	CA	Biagi	Lottie	35	San Francisco	CA
Ambrosini	John	26	Sonoma	ITL	Roe	Kate	28	Sonoma	CA
Ameral	Manuel S.	31	Sebastopol	BER	Olivera	Annie	17	Occidental	BER
Ames	Benjamin J.	21	San Francisco	CA	Sullivan	Nellie	30	Petaluma	CA
Ames	Charles S.	24	Windsor	CA	Jerome	Frances	22	Windsor	CA
Ames	Earl L.	27	Sebastopol	CA	Gericke	Ethel M.	26	Sebastopol	CA
Ames	George Spencer	36	San Francisco	MA	Skelly	Tessie	30	San Francisco	OH
Ames	Irvin E.	21	Sebastopol	CA	Casmore	Adella L.	21	Vacaville	CA

Groom					Bride				
Surname	**Given Name**	**Age**	**Residence**	**BP**	**Surname**	**Given Name**	**Age**	**Residence**	**BP**
Ames	Louis	37	New Castle, CA	CA	Stone	Ada Myrtle	22	Petaluma	CA
Ames	Lynwood Passen	20	Sebastopol	CA	Kelly	Orpah Grace	18	Sebastopol	CA
Ames	Raymond J.	21	Sebastopol	CA	Doyle	Anna	18	Sebastopol	KS
Amesbury	Geo. M.	21	Healdsburg	CA	Snider	Lucy B.	21	Healdsburg	CA
Amrhein	John	44	Mt. Olivet	SWT	Nydeffer	Mary, Mrs.	36	Santa Rosa	SWT
Anbucbon	John E.	29	Bakersfield	MO	Pizzotti	Marie R.	29	Bakersfield	CA
Ancill	Harold J.	34	San Francisco	ENG	Roe	Martha R.	33	Bodega	CA
Andersen	Cyril Harry	20	San Francisco	CA	Beitels	Jewel	18	San Francisco	CA
Andersen	Henry	32	Alameda	CA	Ericksen	Dagmar	22	San Francisco	CA
Andersen	Paul	34	San Francisco	DNK	Barnes	Anna M.	30	San Francisco	CA
Andersen	Peter C.	56	Petaluma	DNK	Gale	Marie F.	42	Petaluma	CA
Andersen	Phillip N.	28	Penngrove	GER	Wessels	Ruth B.	20	Cotati	CA
Andersen	Rasmus Theodore	25	Petaluma	DNK	Nisson	Lena	28	Petaluma	CA
Andersen	Robert	27	Tacoma, WA	WA	Furr	Maud E., Mrs.	33	Napa	ENG
Anderson	A. F.	27	Guerneville	KS	Cramer	Gladys	21	Petaluma	CA
Anderson	Albert Gustav	45	San Francisco	IA	Barrass	Mayme Lowery	36	San Francisco	KY
Anderson	Albert S. J.	24	Sonoma	ID	Martinez	Mollie I.	23	Sonoma	ITL
Anderson	Albert V.	27	Forestville	CA	Bohn	Edna M.	18	Hilton	CA
Anderson	Almer Parker	35	Graton	NE	Peterson	Julia C.	19	Sebastopol	IA
Anderson	Arthur	20	Napa	CA	Chapman	Helen Edith	19	Napa	CA
Anderson	August	32	Guerneville	SWD	Herman	Laura A.	32	Guerneville	IN
Anderson	Caesar William	26	Petaluma	CA	Pometta	Florence G.	21	Petaluma	CA
Anderson	Carl	34	Vallejo	DNK	Perry	Clara M.	19	Santa Rosa	CA
Anderson	Charles F.	30	Sonoma	FIN	Cornelius	Matilda J.	23	Sonoma	Son
Anderson	Chris H.	23	Cotati	GER	Green	Lovina D.	17	Cotati	CA
Anderson	David P.	23	Santa Rosa	SC	Reid	Mattie L.	22	Santa Rosa	CA
Anderson	Ellis R.	21	San Francisco	CA	Walker	Hazel L.	21	Oakland	CO
Anderson	George	22	Healdsburg	KY	Haigh	Ethel	19	Healdsburg	CA
Anderson	George	28	Oakland	CA	Palmsten	Hildur Elvira	23	Oakland	SWD
Anderson	George H.	29	San Francisco	NE	Ritchie	Mary A., Mrs.	32	San Francisco	CA

Groom					Bride				
Surname	**Given Name**	**Age**	**Residence**	**BP**	**Surname**	**Given Name**	**Age**	**Residence**	**BP**
Anderson	Haus	28	Windsor	SWD	Hardt	Mamie	16	Cazadero	GER
Anderson	Herbert A.	30	Santa Rosa	CA	Dohn	Ella	28	Santa Rosa	CA
Anderson	Irvine John	25	Hayward	WI	Turner	Verona Marie	19	Sonoma	CA
Anderson	J. A.	55	Santa Rosa	TX	Leigh	Josephine	44	Santa Rosa	CA
Anderson	James	39	San Francisco	IRL	Gordon	Edith A.	29	San Francisco	CA
Anderson	James G.	23	Modesto	CA	Summerfield	Hattie R.	19	Cotati	CA
Anderson	James H.	32	Santa Rosa	IA	Skaggs	Nellie A.	21	Santa Rosa	CA
Anderson	James H.	22	Healdsburg		Bidwell	Nancy Jane	23	Healdsburg	
Anderson	James Orrin	21	Santa Rosa	CA	Wilson	Jessie Frances	22	Santa Rosa	CA
Anderson	Joe	23	Forestville	CA	Wise	Goldie	19	Forestville	IA
Anderson	John G.	27	Myrtle Creek, OR	SWD	Silva	Julia Mendonca	25	Santa Rosa	CA
Anderson	Joseph A.	31	Petaluma	NY	Perry	Leonora A.	20	Petaluma	Pet
Anderson	Joseph W.	28	Eureka	WA	Kellaway	Birdie	28	Weed	CA
Anderson	Julius J.	28	San Francisco	DNK	Smith	Effa	20	Healdsburg	KS
Anderson	Leroy	22	Geyserville	CA	Pritchett	Jennie	25	Geyserville	CA
Anderson	Mathew	26	Sonoma		Brockmon	Elizabeth J.	18	Sonoma	
Anderson	Mose A.	34	San Francisco	MO	Borba	Margaret Genevieve	24	Hayward	CA
Anderson	Nicols	40	Green Valley		Perry	Catherine	45	Pocket Canyon	
Anderson	Oscar	40	San Francisco	CA	Messerle	Nellie	25	Santa Rosa	CA
Anderson	Oscar E.	44	Mt. Olivet	NRY	Lowrey	Elizabeth F.	57	Mt. Olivet	CA
Anderson	Peter	30	Santa Rosa		Pearson	Lena	26	Santa Rosa	
Anderson	Rex A.	22	Roseville	CA	Griffin	Lucile	23	Santa Rosa	CA
Anderson	Robert Marion	21	Santa Rosa	CA	Webster	Anna	19	Santa Rosa	CA
Anderson	Seymour E.	23	Healdsburg	MN	Perry	Theo M.	21	Oakland	ND
Anderson	Thomas W.	24	San Francisco	PA	Ames	Clementine	26	San Francisco	MO
Anderson	Victor Henry	26	Windsor	CA	Smith	Anna Jessie	27	Sonoma	SD
Anderson	Vinson		Santa Rosa		Tebbs	A. L.	18		
Anderson	William F.	40	Santa Rosa	NJ	Freeman	Clara B.	32	Santa Rosa	CA

Groom					Bride				
Surname	**Given Name**	**Age**	**Residence**	**BP**	**Surname**	**Given Name**	**Age**	**Residence**	**BP**
Anderson	William I.	22	Geyserville	CA	Coombs	Lulu M.	20	Healdsburg	CA
Anderson	William J.	29	Forestville	IL	Robinson	Jennie M.	18	Forestville	CA
Anderson	William P.	27	Santa Rosa	MO	Hawkins	M. L, Mrs.	30	Santa Rosa	PA
Anderton	Harry Thomas	21	Petaluma	CA	Lewis	Alletta C.	18	Petaluma	CA
Andre	Anton	34	Shellville	PRT	Cabral	Emilia	21	Sonoma	PRT
Andreasen	Andrew	32	Santa Rosa	DNK	Huth	Valenteen	26	Santa Rosa	CA
Andreasen	James P.	40	Santa Rosa	DNK	Olstad	Anna	22	Santa Rosa	NRY
Andreini	Pietro	29	San Francisco	ITL	Cardellini	Maria	27	Santa Rosa	ITL
Andreini	Silvio	30	San Francisco	ITL	Balestracci	Adele	20	Santa Rosa	ITL
Andresen	Carl A.	25	Oakland	IA	Peters	Margaret Helen	21	Petaluma	CA
Andrew	Dennis	33	Sebastopol	PRT	Francis	Isabella	18	Sebastopol	MA
Andrews	A. J.	23	Santa Rosa	CA	West	Mary	16	Santa Rosa	CA
Andrews	Admiral Leonadi	27	Eugene, OR	OR	Moore	Jessie Marie	24	Healdsburg	CA
Andrews	Albert	40	Geyserville	CA	Walker	Eva	33	Geyserville	IL
Andrews	Geo. Francis	25	Petaluma	CA	Partington	Lydia H.	21	Petaluma	CND
Andrews	George	48	Middletown	ENG	Gordon	Melissa, Mrs.	28	Middletown	
Andrews	George B.	32	Healdsburg	ENG	Warren	Ollie A.	22	Alexander Valley	ME
Andrews	Howard	30		CA	Freeman	M. E.	27	Two Rock	
Andrews	Leslie Watson	26	Sebastopol	CA	Morris	Louie Eva	25	Sebastopol	CA
Andrews	Robert Shaw	31	San Francisco	MO	Kline	Eletha Alice	26	St Louis	MI
Andrews	Vernon	24	Santa Rosa	CA	Witherell	Minnie E.	20	Santa Rosa	CA
Andrews	Walter J.	23	San Francisco	CA	Archer	Ruth E.	23	San Francisco	CA
Andrews	Walter J.	31	Petaluma	MI	Maggetti	Carrie	29	Petaluma	CA
Angel	Percy	29	Los Angeles	CA	Raulet	Annyta	25	Santa Rosa	CA
Angelo	Antonie	26	Geyserville	CA	Pacini	Ida	18	Cloverdale	CA
Angelo	Wallace P.	48	San Francisco	MO	Welker	Alice	35	San Francisco	CA
Anker	Erik Jessen	57	Cloverdale	DNK	Warner	Alma	35	Santa Rosa	CA
Anker	Neal	34		DNK	Ludwig	Katy	17		DNK
Annis	Wm. O.				Melton	Elizabeth A., Mrs.			

Groom					Bride				
Surname	Given Name	Age	Residence	BP	Surname	Given Name	Age	Residence	BP
Anthony	Edward Augustus	22	Sonoma	Sfo	Dey	Ella Bell	18	Sonoma	TN
Anthony	George Francis	43	Healdsburg	CA	Lilja	Olive, Mrs.	49	Healdsburg	CA
Anthony	John H.	26	St. Helena	NSC	Horman (?)	Lena Harmon	21	Healdsburg	CA
Anthony	M. J.	36	Guerneville		Hitchcock	Lavina K.	17	Guerneville	
Anthony	William Jas.	34	Jamesan, Fresno Co.	CA	Moes	Rosa M.	23	Healdsburg	OH
Antognini	Alfred	34	Petaluma	SWT	Antognini	Gabriella	32	Petaluma	SWT
Antognini	Carlo	42	Petaluma	ARG	Boradori	Nettie	38	Santa Rosa	SWT
Antrim	Joseph A.	23	Pt Arena	CA	Simpson	Ella	21	Wellington, NV	NV
Apiarius	Palmer H.	37	Santa Rosa	CA	Lottritz	Elizabeth B.	33	Santa Rosa	CA
Apostle	Arthur	50	San Francisco	NY	Raymond	Julia M. Ball	33	Penngrove	WA
Appleby	Ray	24	Waterville, WA	NE	Prout	Florence G.	23	Preston	CA
Appleton	Willington	44	Preston	MI	Moody	Jessie Leona	33	Preston	CA
Aquistapace	Louis	23	Santa Rosa	CA	Moore	Marguerite	18	Santa Rosa	MO
Aquisttapace	Giovanni	33	Santa Rosa	ITL	Aquisttapace	Domenica	18+	Guerneville	ITL
Arata	John King	28	Santa Rosa	CA	Norton	Wilma Mae	19	Santa Rosa	CA
Arata	Joseph	30	San Francisco	ITL	Foppiano	Louise	21	Healdsburg	CA
Arbogast	Ernest	31	San Francisco	FRN	Schilling	Valerie	25	Schellville	GER
Arbuckle	Cyrus P.				Stone	Prisila M.	-18		
Archambault	George E.	21	Oakland	CA	Owens	Imelda C.	21	San Francisco	CA
Archer	Arthur S.	27	Santa Rosa Twp.	CA	Gregg	Orbie J.	20	Santa Rosa Twp.	CA
Archer	Claud H.	25	Windsor	CA	McCracken	Edna E.	26	Healdsburg	CA
Archer	Horace E.	34	Healdsburg	CA	McCracken	Emily G.	18	Healdsburg	CA
Archer	James J.	36	Santa Rosa	MO	Kennedy	Ann S.	40	Santa Rosa	CA
Archer	John W.	28	Guerneville	CA	Austin	Jessie M.	19	Guerneville	CA
Archer	Oliver	24	Santa Rosa	CO	Frank	Emilie	23	Santa Rosa	CA
Archer	Walter M.	22	Santa Rosa	CO	Frank	Lydia E.	21	Santa Rosa	CA
Archibald	Edward Joseph	36	San Francisco	IRL	Modeste	Julia Charlotte	35	San Francisco	CA
Ardis	Livy L.	43	Sebastopol	LA	Snyder	Beula V.	25	Sebastopol	NE
Ardoin	Victor	35	Cloverdale	CA	Zurcher	Irma	23	Cloverdale	KS

Groom					Bride				
Surname	**Given Name**	**Age**	**Residence**	**BP**	**Surname**	**Given Name**	**Age**	**Residence**	**BP**
Arfsten	Ben	28	Blucher Valley	CA	Kolb	Ola	19	Blucher Valley	CA
Arfsten	Conrad H.	23	Petaluma	GER	Bohn	Ida E.	20	Petaluma	GER
Arfsten	Martin Theodore	25	Petaluma	GER	Jappen	Lena Gerdina	20	Petaluma	GER
Arfsten	William Arthur	21	Sebastopol	CA	Neel	Jennie	18	Sebastopol	CA
Arfsten	Adolph	31	Petaluma	GER	Avilla	Mary	21	Petaluma	Pet
Argoud	Alfred L.	26	San Francisco	CA	McPike	Edith G.	28	San Francisco	CA
Arguello	Alexander	23	Santa Clara	CA	Mehlhorn	Martha	21	Santa Clara	MO
Arguello	Henry T.	23	Santa Clara	CA	Freebern	Abbe Gail, Mrs.	26	Sonoma	WI
Ariasi	Peter	40	Santa Rosa	ITL	Bertossi	Liberata	28	Santa Rosa	ITL
Arlett	George	21	Santa Rosa	CND	Stoner	Tessa B.	18	Santa Rosa	OH
Armello	Manuel	28	Petaluma Twp,	AZR	Rafael	Mary	19	Petaluma Twp.	CA
Armfield	Tyrus A.				Henry	Amanda B.	16		
Armitage	J. D.	24	Cloverdale	CND	Schultz	Ellen A.	21	Cloverdale	CA
Armos	Ruel Rogers	25	San Francisco	Boston	Johnson	Wilma Regina	21	San Francisco	Sfo
Armstrong	Alfred E.	23	Middletown	CA	Fromm	Martha	21	Santa Rosa	WA
Armstrong	Benjamin	23	Guerneville	MO	Faudre	Lusettie	17	Forestville	CA
Armstrong	Charles Newton	25	Santa Rosa	MO	Dennis	Nellie	19	Santa Rosa	CA
Armstrong	Charley H.	21	Petaluma	PA	Pedrotti	Lucinda E.	21	Petaluma	CA
Armstrong	Edward J.	26	Petaluma	CA	Graham	Lola M.	18+	Petaluma	IL
Armstrong	Frank L.	25	Petaluma	CA	Feliz	Cassie	41	Petaluma	CA
Armstrong	Frederic W.	51	Yreka	NY	Akers	Malinda C.	47	Medford, OR	CA
Armstrong	George R.	34	Santa Rosa	CA	Meador	Nannie	28	Cloverdale	CA
Armstrong	Harry George	17	Sebastopol	CA	Winkler	Florence Estella	16	Green Valley	CA
Armstrong	James C.	20	Petaluma	CA	Ayers	Elise May	20	Petaluma	CA
Armstrong	M. V. B.				Menighan	Mary P.	22		
Armstrong	Oatie M.	24	Brooks, Yolo Co.	CA	Arnold	Rose L.	18	Guinda, Yolo Co.	CA
Armstrong	Roy V.	27	Petaluma	CA	Lipe	Ina	29	Petaluma	IL
Armstrong	Thos. E.	30	Healdsburg	NY	Thompson	Alice M.	25	Hopland	CA
Armstrong	Walter Ernest	39	Oakland	CA	Crowell	Elizabeth	42	Sacramento	KS
Armstrong	William J.	24	Ukiah	CA	Munson	Edith O.	22	Ukiah	CO

Groom					Bride				
Surname	**Given Name**	**Age**	**Residence**	**BP**	**Surname**	**Given Name**	**Age**	**Residence**	**BP**
Arndt	Benjamin F.	32	Petaluma	PA	Haskell	Vera F.	19	Petaluma	NV
Arnett	Floyd F.	21	Sebastopol	CA	Clark	Wilma S.	19	Forestville	CA
Arnett	Vivian O.	18	Sebastopol	CA	Lane	Irene J.	17	Santa Rosa	CA
Arnold	C. W.				Hoit	Matilda			
Arnold	Edward	22	Santa Rosa	OR	Lewis	Addie	22	Santa Rosa	CA
Arnold	Floyd Hilton	19	Petaluma	CT	McCoubrey	Josephine Eva	19	Petaluma	CA
Arnold	Harry P.	40	San Francisco	CA	Holland	Elsie	27	San Francisco	CA
Arnold	Hobart Le G.	22	Santa Rosa	NY	Gauldin	Mattie A.	22	Santa Rosa	CA
Arnold	John W.	30	Sebastopol	MO	Kauffman	Minnie I.	17	Sebastopol	CA
Arnold	Richard	33	Philadelphia	PA	Paulson	Anna L.	23	Salt Lake, UT	UT
Arrighi	Cesare G.	21	Santa Rosa	ITL	Guidotti	Emma Agnes	23	Santa Rosa	CA
Arrowood	Daniel A.	26	Santa Rosa	GA	Williamson	Florence E.	27	Santa Rosa	NE
Arsistide	George	29	San Francisco	CA	Gilmartin	Josie	25	San Francisco	CA
Arthur	George	26	San Rafael	AUT	Frank	Julia L.	36	San Rafael	CA
Artner	Michael	38	Santa Rosa	AUS	Weber	Rosa	24	Santa Rosa	AUS
Arville	Archie B.	21	San Francisco	CO	Mueting	Charlotte Rose	17	Santa Rosa	NE
Arvold	Louis	48	Petaluma	NRY	Waage	Ollie A.	30	Oakland	NRY
Ascherman	Charles F.	29	Petaluma	IN	Petersen	Annie M.	22	Petaluma	CA
Ash	Emerson F.	44	Santa Rosa	RI	Silvia	Mary E.	38	Santa Rosa	RI
Ash	Emerson F.	45	Santa Rosa	RI	Silvia	Mary E.	39	Santa Rosa	RI
Ash	Frank E.	38	Martinez	Wdc	Bourras	Catherine	34	Oakland	FRN
Ash	Isador	24	Petaluma	PLD	Goldstein	Sarah	20	Petaluma	NY
Ash	Leroy	30	Petaluma	CA	Church	Clara Rosa	30	Petaluma	CO
Ashcroft	J. A.				Gregory	M. A., Mrs.			
Ashe	William W.	25	Glen Ellen	CA	Wheeler	Evelyn S.	31	San Francisco	CA
Asher	Charles Lewis	58	San Francisco	CT	Marin	Hermina	49	San Francisco	MEX
Asher	Sidney	22	Oakland	CA	Behrens	Henrietta	18	Oakland	CA
Ashley	David C.	59	San Francisco	NY	Squyer	Ida E.	57	Oakland	CA
Ashley	S. Thomas	25	Santa Rosa	CA	Garrison	Orletta	19	Guerneville	CA
Ashley	William T.	43	Bloomfield	MO	Waldron	Kate	38	Alameda	SEA

Groom					Bride				
Surname	**Given Name**	**Age**	**Residence**	**BP**	**Surname**	**Given Name**	**Age**	**Residence**	**BP**
Ashurst	William R.	25	Azusa	AZ	Patton	Ora Lillian	23	Santa Rosa	TN
Askins	Samuel M.	27	Berkeley	SC	Doyle	Mary K.	21	Berkeley	CA
Asplund	John A.	28	South Los Guilicos	SWD	Nielsen	Christine	28	South Los Guilicos	DNK
Assenti	Louis	28	San Francisco	CA	Hillson	Louisa	38	San Francisco	ENG
Asti	Erminio	25	Santa Rosa	ITL	Albini	Victoria, Mrs.	30	Santa Rosa	ITL
Asti	Joseph	34	Occidental	ITL	Brusa	Julia	18	Occidental	ITL
Asti	Joseph P.	25	Santa Rosa	ITL	Rossi	Christina	19	Santa Rosa	ITL
Astorg	Louie M.	24	San Francisco	CA	Shannon	Clara May	21	San Francisco	CA
Astredo	Anthony Dominick	45	San Francisco	LA	Walsh	Dixie Edith	30	Oakland	IL
Atchinson	Fred R.	35	Santa Rosa	CA	Story	Myrtle J.	24	Santa Rosa	CA
Atherton	Albert W.	22	Healdsburg	IA	Mead	Susie E.	21	Healdsburg	IN
Atkins	L. G. F.	27	Glen Ellen	CA	Willis	Harrietta T.	27	Glen Ellen	AUT
Atkinson	Joseph	55	near Petaluma	ENG	Higgins	Minnie J., Mrs.	30	Petaluma	CA
Atkinson	Joseph	66	Petaluma	ENG	Miller	Sadie L.	47	Petaluma	IL
Atkinson	Robert Kavanaugh	22	Crete, IL	CA	Gale	Eliza Maude	21	Petaluma	CA
Atkinson	William K.	26	Vallejo Twp.	Vts	Moretti	Candeda	26	Petaluma	SWT
Atlon	Theodore F.	44	Kenwood	OR	Wahl	Louisa	36	Santa Rosa	GER
Atwater	Edwin L.	24	San Rafael	NY	Millett	Nettie J.	23	Petaluma	CA
Atwood	George C.	47	Saratoga	CA	Fairchild	Lee	41	Palo Alto	KS
Atwood	Joseph C.	40	San Francisco	CA	DeBow	Sallie	40	San Francisco	CA
Atzeroth	Henry	25	San Francisco	CA	Scott	Mabel F.	22	Healdsburg	CA
Audero	Giovanni	30	Santa Rosa	ITL	Ferrero	Maria	28	Santa Rosa	ITL
Auerbach	Howell Bidwell	23	Oakland	CA	Short	Helen Hutchuis	19	Oakland	CA
Augustus	Martin	34	Santa Rosa	MA	Bonneau	Laura N.	36	Cloverdale	CA
Auld	Royal I.	48	San Francisco	ME	Hoesch	Margaret C.	37	San Francisco	CND
Ausmus	Delbert	28	Arkansas City	KS	Weyman	Cletys	25	San Francisco	KS
Aussresses	Diderot P.	23	Sebastopol	FRN	Herzog	Rosalie	21	San Francisco	FRN

Groom					Bride				
Surname	**Given Name**	**Age**	**Residence**	**BP**	**Surname**	**Given Name**	**Age**	**Residence**	**BP**
Austen	John O.	28	Guerneville	CA	Oberfell	Clara	23	Guerneville	IA
Austin	Ashton E.	26	Santa Rosa	CA	Cummins	Metta H.	20	Santa Rosa	CA
Austin	Chas.	37	San Francisco	NY	Bloch	Rosa	22	Healdsburg	CA
Austin	George	24	San Francisco	Lon	Paulsch	Susie A., Mrs.	27	San Francisco	Alba-ny,NY
Austin	Harry C.	21	Guerneville	CA	Hardisty	Daisy D.	19	Healdsburg	OR
Austin	Louis Cecil	26	San Francisco	CA	Sears	Ethel Matilda	24	San Francisco	CA
Austin	Malcolm O.	25	Santa Rosa	CND	Hotaling	Lillian B.	22	San Francisco	CA
Austin	Mervyn Maison	29	Santa Rosa	CA	Brand	Katie	25	Santa Rosa	IN
Austin	Raymond Thomas	22	Oakland	CA	Ogan	Mabel Dorothy	24	Oakland	CA
Austin	Sewell S.	25	Santa Rosa	CND	Godman	Ida L.	22	Santa Rosa	MO
Austin	William G.	22	Healdsburg	CA	Willsie	Lydia	20	Guerneville	CA
Auten	George M.	45	Seattle	PA	Casky	Alta M.	32	Seattle	IA
Avellar	Jose	27	Sebastopol	AZR	Valentine	Frances	20	Sebastopol	AZR
Avereia	Antonio Silveira	24	Petaluma Twp.	AZR	Galinda	Mary M.	18	Petaluma Twp.	CA
Averill	Herbert O.	48	Goldfield, NV	ME	Ober	Bessie I.	39	Seattle	NV
Avery	Howard	22	Petaluma	CT	Mason	Lenna	22	Petaluma	WV
Avery	W. J.	37	Berkeley	PA	Williams	Margaret	36	Berkeley	CA
Avila	Joao Maria	27	Sebastopol	AZR	Vieira	Maria Joseph	36	Sebastopol	AZR
Avilla	Frank	25	Point Reyes	PRT	Joseph	Mary	17	Petaluma Twp.	CA
Avilla	Manuel	30	Santa Rosa	PRT	Cunha	Anna	19	Santa Rosa	CA
Avilla (?)	A. I.	41	Cotati	PRT	Bettencourt	Belmera	28	Cotati	PRT
Avjona	Daniel J.	31	Santa Rosa	SPN	Velasques	Mary	27	Santa Rosa	SPN
Axley	John R.	25	Los Angeles	KS	Maldonado	Helen	21	Los Angeles	AZ
Axtell	Asher F.	27	Healdsburg	OH	Hanson	Minnie	22	Hurley, SD	DNK
Ayer	John	36	Bodega		Nichols	Vesta	28	Bodega	
Ayers	Andrew M.	22	Timber Cove	CA	Farnsworth	Clara	22	Bloomfield	CA
Ayers	Archie	22	Petaluma	Saj	Stewart	Neva	18	Santa Cruz	KS
Ayers	B. F.	20	Santa Rosa		Hitchcock	Ida	17	Guerneville	

Groom					Bride				
Surname	**Given Name**	**Age**	**Residence**	**BP**	**Surname**	**Given Name**	**Age**	**Residence**	**BP**
Ayers	Frank	23	San Francisco	Sfo	Lawrence	Edith	22	Nevada City	Neva-da Cty
Ayers	George Lemuel	25	Santa Rosa	CA	Talmadge	Hattie May	19	Santa Rosa	CA
Ayers	George Lemuel	36	Santa Rosa	CA	Cromwell	Pearl Gertrude	25	Santa Rosa	CA
Ayers	George W.	25	Guerneville	CA	Arland	Lela D.	21	Guerneville	NY
Ayers	Omar	22	Petaluma	CA	McNabb	Jessie I.	18	Petaluma	CA
Ayers	Robert B.	26	Petaluma	CA	Melehan	Anna E.	25	Petaluma	CA
Ayers	Robert Charles	21	Petaluma	CA	Earley	Olive J.	22	Petaluma	CA
Ayers	William C.	23	Petaluma	IA	Gray	May	22	Petaluma	CA
Ayers	William M.	22	Guerneville	CA	Brown	Maggie	15	Guerneville	CA
Aylsworth	Niles W.	24	Sonoma		Wrottero (?)	Edith	18	Sonoma	
Azevedo	Frank Augusto	24	Santa Rosa	PRT	Lacerda	Mary Augusta	17	Santa Rosa	PRT
Azevedo	Joseph A.	22	Santa Rosa	CA	Brazil	Nellie	22	Petaluma	MA
Azevedo	Manuel Jacinto	45	Petaluma	PRT	D' Noximento	Maria	32	Petaluma	PRT
Azevedo	Tony Thomas	34	Cresent City	PRT	Augusto	Mary	30	Ribeira Secca, AZR	AZR
Azevedo	William J.	22	Half Moon Bay	CA	Ramos	Roselind G.	20	Sebastopol	CA
Azveado	John	28	Tomales	AZR	DeSouza	Katie	18	Bodega	CA
Azzari	Eriglio	25	Glen Ellen	ITL	Petri	Annie	18	Kenwood	CA
Baago	Edmund A.	27	San Francisco	DNK	Mendenhall	Lola I.	26	Santa Rosa	CA
Babbini	Alvise	22	Santa Rosa	ITL	Asti	Lizzie	17	Santa Rosa	ITL
Babbini	Antonio	23	San Francisco	ITL	Forni	Kate	21	Santa Rosa	CA
Babbini	Arthur	28	Santa Rosa	ITL	Babbini	Katherine G.	19	Santa Rosa	ITL
Babbini	Ernesto	32	Santa Rosa	ITL	Ottoboni	Rosa A.	24	Santa Rosa	CA
Babbini	Paul	26	Santa Rosa	ITL	Bologne	Lizzie	18	Santa Rosa	ITL
Babbino	Fred	23	Santa Rosa	CA	Werner	Marie	18	Santa Rosa	DNK
Babbino	Thomas	45	near Santa Rosa	ITL	Lagomarsino	Marie	26	Santa Rosa	CA
Babcock	Albert A.	45	Oakland	QUE	Riedel	Selma E.	30	Oakland	NH
Babcock	Joseph L.	40	Santa Rosa	IL	Nichalson	Agnes Maye	26	Santa Rosa	IL
Babcock	Kilbern J.	21	Santa Rosa	MI	Monroe	Carrie May	19	Santa Rosa	KS

Groom					Bride				
Surname	Given Name	Age	Residence	BP	Surname	Given Name	Age	Residence	BP
Baccala	Antonio	28	Sonoma	SWT	Anselmi	Martini	24	Sonoma	SWT
Baccala	Joseph K.	23	Petaluma	CA	Finnerty	Mary Alice	23	Petaluma	CA
Bacchini	Romeo	25	Asti	ITL	Zanzi	Annie	15	Asti	Asti
Bacci	Amoto	31	Santa Rosa	ITL	Pardini	Emma	25	Santa Rosa	ITL
Bacci	Joseph	31	Trenton	ITL	Pera	Mary	32	Trenton	CA
Bacci	Vincent	30	Korbel	ITL	Dinucci	Katherine	20	Hilton	CA
Bachelder	Horace	27	San Francisco	WA	Titus	Seba	27	Santa Rosa	CA
Bachrach	Arthur E.	25	Berkeley	CA	Donovan	Nadine G.	22	Santa Rosa	CA
Bacigalupi	Albert C.	25	Santa Rosa	CA	Gaddini	Olive	23	Healdsburg	CA
Bacigalupi	Giovanni B.	48	Healdsburg	ITL	Bacigalupi	Maria	39	Healdsburg	ITL
Bacigalupi	John E.	21	Santa Rosa	CA	Guidotti	Jemella	20	Guerneville	CA
Bacigalupi	Louis	23	Healdsburg	NY	Caulfield	Catherine F.	20	Petaluma	CA
Bacon	Arthur D.	27	Peachland	MI	Flesher	L. Maude	18	Forestville	NE
Bacon	Charles E.	26	Petaluma	Clark Co., WI	Perry	Marie Jane	17	Petaluma	Sfo
Bacon	Charles S.	44	San Francisco	OH	Johnson	Alice	32	San Francisco	MO
Bacon	George Dudley	22	Forestville	MI	Davis	Dora J.	19	Forestville	CA
Bacon	Herbert Wm.	40	Santa Rosa	CA	Migliano (?)	Elizabeth	39	Oakland	ITL
Bacon	Jay S.	40	Petaluma	MI	Trautner	Frances	49	Petaluma	GER
Bacon	Mark J.	25	Ione	OH	Walker	Margaret I.	23	Windsor	CA
Badenhop	Chris	25	Petaluma	GER	Person	Emma	36	Petaluma	SWD
Badenhop	John Henry	31	Petaluma	GER	Clausen	Dorothy Helen	33	Petaluma	GER
Badger	Albert Neil	24	Melita	CA	Ricketts	Anice Iva	18	Rincon Valley	CA
Badger	Douglas	23	Santa Rosa	CA	Fulkerson	Laura E.	17	Santa Rosa	CA
Badger	Henry L.	21	Rincon Valley	CA	Peatross	Carrie	17	Rincon Valley	CA
Badger	Joseph J.	66	Santa Rosa	OH	Hewitt	Emma M.	40	Santa Rosa	IA
Badger	Percy	23	Bennett Valley	CA	Staley	Mabel Mae	19	Kenwood	CA
Badgerow	Weston	54	Lakeport	NY	Preston	L.	18	Windsor	MI
Badgley	Ira Walter	33	Healdsburg	IL	Isaacs	Dora	21	Healdsburg	CA
Badgley	Sherman	24	Healdsburg	IL	Covey	Frances	26	Healdsburg	CA

Groom					Bride				
Surname	Given Name	Age	Residence	BP	Surname	Given Name	Age	Residence	BP
Badgley	Sherman	31	Healdsburg	IL	Ingalls	Lillie, Mrs.	32	Healdsburg	CA
Baer	Geo. B.	24	Cloverdale	PA	Markell	Sarah A.	19	Cloverdale	CND
Baer	Reuben E.	29	Cloverdale	Somer-set, PA	Markell	Helen I.	26	Cloverdale	CND
Bagley	Carl Elmer	24	Guerneville	CA	Smaker	Anna Francis	21	Guerneville	CA
Bagley	Donald E.	24	Sebastopol	OR	Shuster	Jessie A.	16	Sebastopol	CA
Bagley	Herbert L.	24	Guerneville	CA	Cole	Edna C.	18	Guerneville	IA
Bagley	Weaver T.	24	Healdsburg	CA	Hughes	Georgia A.	25	Healdsburg	CA
Bagley	Willard D.	32	Oroville	CA	Osborne	Angie L.	29	Healdsburg	CA
Baglietto	Ambrogio	23	San Francisco	ITL	Solaro	Ernestina, Mrs.	33	Concord	SWT
Bahnsen	Daniel	24	San Francisco	GER	Springer	Catherine	20	near Petaluma	Soc
Baier	Clemens Loyal	24	San Francisco	CA	Sillemann	Ruth Augusta	21	San Francisco	CA
Bailey	Allan Leonard	32	Petaluma	CA	Poehlmann	Marie Dorothy	22	Petaluma	CA
Bailey	Charles M.	23	Tiburon	CA	Rowland	Maude	22	Healdsburg	CA
Bailey	Douglas A.	24	Berkely	NY	Kienle	Loretta M.	24	Oakland	IL
Bailey	Eugene B.	25	Santa Rosa	CA	Fischer	Hilda	25	Santa Rosa	MO
Bailey	Frank R.	32	San Francisco	OH	Wittkoff (?)	Mary A.	23	Petaluma	CA
Bailey	J. E.	24	Santa Rosa	SC	Laughlin	Amanda	24	Mark West	CA
Bailey	Jessie William	53	Eldridge	OH	Deardorff	Anna M.	36	Eldridge	OH
Bailey	Johnathan J.	46	Santa Rosa	IL	Happy	Mary	48	Santa Rosa	ALB
Bailey	Percy D.	34	Santa Rosa	ENG	Du Commun	Marcelle M.	26	Santa Rosa	MI
Bailey	T. E. C.	30	Cloverdale	OR	Smyth	Pashie	25	Petaluma	OH
Bailey	Terry Elmer	33	Healdsburg	NM	Weir	Mary Gertrude	28	Healdsburg	CA
Bailey	Wilson Roy	25	San Francisco	IN	Drew	Hester	21	Santa Rosa	KS
Bailhache	Arthur L.	26	Healdsburg	CA	Pickard	Annie H.	18	Healdsburg	IL
Bailhache	Frederick	37	Healdsburg	CA	Williams	Mattie M.	22	Healdsburg	CA
Bailhache	Frederick	31	Healdsburg	Soc	Clark	Addie Louise	21	Healdsburg	ME
Bailhache	George	21	Healdsburg		Hammond	Eva H.	24	Healdsburg	
Bailhache	J. Temple	32	Healdsburg	CA	Waterman	Melvina B.	20	Healdsburg	CA
Bailhache	Nicholas	24	Healdsburg	CA	Gully	Winona	20	Healdsburg	CA

Groom					Bride				
Surname	Given Name	Age	Residence	BP	Surname	Given Name	Age	Residence	BP
Bailhache	Solon William	26	Vallejo	CA	Harbin	Amanda	24	Healdsburg	CA
Bailiff	John D.	29	Santa Rosa	CA	Tuttle	Edith M.	24	Santa Rosa	CA
Baillesderr	Joseph C.	52	Vineburg	FRN	Lescure	Julia	25	San Francisco	FRN
Bainbridge	Clarence E.	36	Anderson, Shasta Co.	CA	White	Amy F.	36	Kenwood	CA
Baine	Lafayette	21	Cloverdale	CA	Kelley	Virginia Ann	19	Cloverdale	IL
Baines	Latin L.	27	San Francisco	CA	Fay	Anna	16	Petaluma	CA
Bains	Gallant	24			Humphrey	Agnes	18+		
Baiocchi	Guido F.	20	Geyserville	ITL	Mazzoni	Lena M.	21	Geyserville	ITL
Baiocchi	Nello	22	San Francisco	ITL	Giorgetti	Nellie	19	San Francisco	ITL
Baird	Fred E.	24	Santa Rosa	CA	Marchant	Ethel	20	Petaluma	CA
Baird	J. G.	44	Riverside	CND	Humphrey	Marion	37	Petaluma	CND
Baitano	Fortunato	26	Santa Rosa	ITL	Matteucci	Florence	19	Santa Rosa	CA
Baker	Albert	29	Duncans Mills	IL	Kellogg	Anna	21	Santa Rosa	CA
Baker	Albert Marion	21	Santa Rosa	CA	Andrews	Bernice V.	22	Santa Rosa	KS
Baker	Asa L.	57	Tacoma, WA	NY	Jewell	Ida	35	Petaluma	NY
Baker	Charles A.	21	Windsor	CA	Peterson	Lillie A.	17	Santa Rosa Twp.	CA
Baker	Cicero H.	39	Portland, OR	OR	Fieldler	Mary D.	24	Perkin, MN	MN
Baker	David	27	San Francisco	WI	Withycombe	Ethel	28	Sacramento	IL
Baker	Fred H.	33	San Francisco	NSC	Flood	Evelyn V.	29	Oakland	IRL
Baker	Fred Lester	22	Oakland	CA	Banta	Evalyn F.	22	Calistoga	CA
Baker	George E.	23	Stony Point		Sharron	Maggie R.	19	Bloomfield	
Baker	Jesse F.	28	Turlock	CA	Martin	Jennette	16	Santa Rosa	OK
Baker	Joel F.	20	Dry Creek	CA	Ball	Sue	20	Healdsburg	CA
Baker	Louis Alexander	19	Healdsburg	CA	Miller	Emma Estella	18	Santa Rosa	CA
Baker	Peter S.	29	[illegible]	FRN ?	Smith (?)	?chn (?)	24 ?	[illegible]	CA
Baker	Ralph Weber	21	Chicago	IL	Spencer	Genovena Nella	22	San Francisco	CA
Baker	Samuel S.	26	Mayhen (?)	CA	McClellan	Mary E., Mrs.	31	Oakland	MD
Baker	Theodore	21	Healdsburg	CA	Farley	Ruby	18	Healdsburg	CA
Baker	William J.	31	San Francisco	CA	Zeiph	Anna Zanona	28	San Francisco	CA

Groom					Bride				
Surname	**Given Name**	**Age**	**Residence**	**BP**	**Surname**	**Given Name**	**Age**	**Residence**	**BP**
Baker	Wm. M.	33	Windsor	MO	Small	Alice	21	Windsor	NZD
Balatti	Peter	29	Valley Ford	ITL	Petiti	Maria	23	Cloverdale	ITL
Baldi	Anselmo	26	Melita	ITL	Gambogi	Eda M.	20	Melita	CA
Baldizzone	Charles Louis	35	Davis	ITL	Fankhausen	Clara	35	San Francisco	CA
Baldocchi	Alfred A.	26	San Francisco	CA	Nighturne	Helen M.	18	San Francisco	CA
Baldocchi	Henry	23	Fulton	CA	Canevari	Clara	22	Santa Rosa	CA
Baldocchi	Lawrence	44	San Francisco	ITL	Brodbeck	Elizabeth	43	San Francisco	ENG
Baldwin	C. A.	29	Tiburon	MI	Alloway	Mary	26	Petaluma	CND
Baldwin	Charles Ellsworth	32	Petaluma	MO	Peck	Ida Viola	25	Petaluma	CA
Baldwin	Clyde R.	26	Turlock	MO	Wheeler	Lela Alpha	20	Hessel	CA
Baldwin	D. A.	30	Fresno	NBW	Carr	Mary A.	18	Guerneville	PA
Baldwin	James M.	28	St. Helena	CND	Howard	Edith V.	15	Petaluma	St. Helena
Baldy	O. Cass	59	Los Angeles	MI	Judd	Pauline, Mrs.	37	San Francisco	TN
Bales	Marion	21	Napa	CA	Versell	Carolyn J.	23	Napa	CA
Balette	Ernest	29	Oakland	CA	Rossi	Mary	25	Santa Rosa	CA
Baley	George Moses	38	Geyserville	CA	Meyers	Rose	32	Geyserville	USA
Baley	Joshua	28	Cloverdale	CA	Bargaglotti	Della	24	Cloverdale	CA
Ball	Leo Raymond	35	San Francisco	Bir	Gates	Jane Isabell	27	San Francisco	Cha
Ball	Raymond Oliver	27	Plymouth	CA	Ahl	Ruby Ada	23	Santa Rosa	CA
Ball	Walter E.	23	Stewarts Point	NH	Herbert	Ina E.	22	Bloomfield	CA
Ball	Wm. P.				Pickle	Mary E.			
Ballagh	Ehrnest Ellsworth	24	Oil Center, CA	CA	Campbell	Minnie Lucile	23	Cloverdale	NM
Ballard	Augustus Seaton	24	San Francisco	CA	Farrell	Carmeleta U.	18	Sebastopol	CA
Ballard	Benjamin F.	21	Santa Rosa	MO	McDaniel	Emma U.	22	Santa Rosa	MO
Ballard	Hooker				Rodgers	Carrie			
Ballard	John Henry	33	Merced	CA	Purrington	Marguerite	34	Peachland	CA
Ballard	Robert L.	25	Healdsburg	CA	Crane	Catherine H.	21	Santa Rosa	CA
Ballard	S. E.	22	Cottonwood, Shasta Co.	CA	Miller	Irena B.	23	Santa Rosa	CA

Groom					Bride				
Surname	Given Name	Age	Residence	BP	Surname	Given Name	Age	Residence	BP
Ballestra	Johnie	25	Healdsburg	ITL	Ravegno	Mary	16	Healdsburg	CA
Ballou	Albert L.	34	Santa Rosa Twp.	IL	McWilliams	Edna Alice	19	Santa Rosa	NE
Ballou	Arthur M.	24	Santa Rosa Twp.	CA	Carlyon	Elizabeh	23	Santa Rosa Twp.	CA
Ballou	Miner (?) H.	61	Chicago	WI	Relyea	Ida May	41	Chicago	NY
Balsley	Iven E.	21	Santa Rosa	NE	Penrice	Lizzie R.	19	Santa Rosa	KS
Baltzell	Alfred	39	Healdsburg	WV	Loucks	Kate Myrick	27	Healdsburg	NY
BalVelde	Antonio	40	Santa Rosa	SPN	Bravo	Meri	40	Santa Rosa	SPN
Balzari	David	35	Nicasio	SWT	Mignimi	Maria	30	Petaluma	SWT
Balzari	J. T.	28	Petaluma	SWT	Nickelsen	Naudine	24	Petaluma	GER
Balzari	James Albino	24	Petaluma	CA	Ramatici	Lily	22	Petaluma	CA
Banchiero	Antone T.	21+	Antioch	ITL	Basaglia	Amelia E.	17	Sonoma	ITL
Bandiera	Emil	23	Elk	ITL	Bertolucci	Liduina	18	Cloverdale	ITL
Bandieu	Alibrando	24	Santa Rosa	ITL	Caselli	Angie A.	24	Santa Rosa	CA
Bane	David A.	23	Healdsburg	CA	Eby	Lucretia	20	Healdsburg	CA
Banfield	Frederic H.	25	Duttons Landing	CA	Christinsen	Martha B.	19	Cotati	CA
Banfield	Isaac Newton	27	Petaluma	CA	Holland	Rosa Ellen	19	Hicks Valley, Marin Co.	CA
Banfield	John T.	28	Forestville	CA	Cheney	Sarah E.	17	Forestville	CA
Banfield	William F.	36	Forestville	CA	Gregory	Bertha E.	20	Forestville	GER
Banks	Ansel W.	29	Sebastopol	WA	Peterson	Gretta M.	29		CA
Banks	Earl Arthur	21	Sebastopol	WA	Van Vicel	Bertha L.	20	Sebastopol	CA
Banks	George	29	Scotia	IL	Masten	Helen	28	Novato	IN
Banks	Herbert John	20	Healdsburg	CA	Sanborn	Etta Leivee (?)	20	Healdsburg	MI
Banks	James A.	26	Guerneville	CND	Wescott	Mamie	15	Guerneville	CA
Banks	Lester D.	24	Santa Rosa	CA	Brians	Ruth E.	18	Sebastopol	CA
Banks	Louis Albert	64	Roseburg, OR	OR	Aiken	Florence	42	Roseburg, OR	OR
Bannon	Peter	36	Penngrove	CA	Short	Mary	26	Petaluma Twp.	IRL
Banta	John H.	33	Alameda		Bennett	Mary A.	23	Geyserville	
Banta	Joseph A.	30	Fulton	MO	Harte	Lydia J.	27	Geyserville	MO
Banton	Belva	21	Santa Rosa	OR	Love	Lou Donie	18	Santa Rosa	CA

Groom					Bride				
Surname	**Given Name**	**Age**	**Residence**	**BP**	**Surname**	**Given Name**	**Age**	**Residence**	**BP**
Banton	James	34	Lakeville	CA	Walsh	Nora	42	Lakeville	IRL
Banton	James	45	Lakeville	CA	Hart	Carrie Esther	35	Lakeville	PA
Barangini	Charlie	24	Petaluma	SWT	Mossi	Annie	24	Petaluma	SWT
Barbee	Elias W.	29	San Francisco	IL	La Blanc	Carrie	19	Penngrove	CA
Barber	Lewis R.	39	Petaluma	NY	Rodd	Dorothy C.	29	Petaluma	CA
Barber	Walter P.	35	Santa Rosa	CA	Eberts	Berwin E.	27	Warrensburg, MO	MO
Barberie	Joseph				Schiapacape	Antonia Flora			
Barbier	Harry A.	30	Camp Meeker	IL	Cochrane	Evelyn E.	26	San Rafael	CA
Barbier	Howard E. W.	28	Camp Meeker	IL	Feige	Mabel A.	19	Camp Meeker	CA
Barbieri	Peter	30	Santa Rosa	ITL	Asti	Ersiglia	15	Santa Rosa	ITL
Barboni	Joseph H.	21	Petaluma	CA	Dolcini	Irene D.	23	Petaluma	CA
Barbreri	Agostino	26	Santa Rosa	ITL	Carli	Giudita	17	Santa Rosa	ITL
Barceloux	Henry J.	26	Willows	CA	Tremblay	Laura M.	20	Santa Rosa	CA
Bardell	Luzius	34	Healdsburg	SWT	Myer	Mary	21	Healdsburg	GER
Bardoni	Charles Costantino	23	Penngrove	CA	Soldati	Effie Olympia	20	Petaluma	CA
Barela	John	22	Tomales	ITL	Poncia	Maria	23	Tomales	ITL
Barella	Fred	24	Bodega	ITL	Crosta	Anna	24	Valley Ford	ITL
Bargoloti	Louis J.	23	Ukiah	CA	Maine	Annie	21	Boonville	CA
Barham	Abwey	24	Santa Rosa	CA	Christianson	Minnie	18	Santa Rosa	CA
Barham	Byrd	30	Santa Rosa	CA	Cunningham	Pearl Gertrude	16	Santa Rosa	IA
Barham	Byrd B.	44	Santa Rosa	CA	Flippi	Rose V.	40	Santa Rosa	CA
Barham	Edwin C.	24	Santa Rosa	CA	Fulkerson	Linda V.	23	Santa Rosa	CA
Barham	Fred	26	Santa Rosa	CA	Hottinger	Gertrude E.	18	Santa Rosa	CA
Barham	J. A.				Cook	Mary			
Barilani	Guglielmo	31	Asti	ITL	Trusendi	Laura	20	Asti	ITL
Barindelli	Charles	28	Petaluma	ITL	DelCarlo	Emma	20	Petaluma	ITL
Barisich	Peter	40	Oakland	AUS	Rodman	Lieuary A.	46	Oakland	IN
Barisione	Baci	29	Colma	ITL	Ponzo	Valentina	19	Healdsburg	ITL

Groom					Bride				
Surname	Given Name	Age	Residence	BP	Surname	Given Name	Age	Residence	BP
Barker	Ambrose B.	38	San Jose	CA	Goodrich	Mamie	26	San Jose	CA
Barker	Frank E.	21	Oakland	CA	Lillard	Dora M.	17+	Santa Rosa	TX
Barker	Henry				Cooper	Rachael			
Barker	Richard, Jr.	21	San Francisco	MD	Lewis	Edna	19	Olema	CA
Barkway	Henry Thomas	25	Santa Rosa	CA	Stevenson	May Frances	25	Santa Rosa	CA
Barkway	Wm M.	33	Fresno	CA	Barnes	Marien E.	30	Santa Rosa	MN
Barlieri	Italo	21	Santa Rosa	ITL	Albini	Rosie	17	Santa Rosa	ITL
Barling	Wm. H.	30	Santa Rosa	NY	Higson	Dora E.	20	Santa Rosa	CA
Barlow	Richard Wright	40	San Francisco	ENG	McDonald	Mary	29	San Francisco	NY
Barlow	Thomas E.	24	Santa Rosa	CA	Miller	Laura E.	21	Santa Rosa	CA
Barndt	Julius	30	Fulton	GER	Hart	Grace P.	18	Fulton	NE
Barnes	Aaron	69	Sebastopol	PA	Burk	Jessie	32	Santa Rosa	MA
Barnes	Aaron H.	20	Sebastopol	CA	Urton	Eunice D.	19	Sebastopol	CA
Barnes	Aaron, Jr.	26	Sebastopol	CA	Ross	Mary E.	18	Sebastopol	OH
Barnes	Allen Percival	34	Albion	CA	Mallory	Hazel Florence	29	Little River	CA
Barnes	Arthur John	28	Geyserville	ENG	Haddock	Marion T.	29	Alhambra	WI
Barnes	Ben H.	31	Healdsburg	MO	Nichols	Cynthia	31	Healdsburg	AR
Barnes	Ben H.	46	Healdsburg	MO	Ferguson	Velma Crawford	32	Petaluma	CA
Barnes	Benjamin Franklin	22	Sebastopol	CA	Robinson	Alice	16	Sebastopol	CA
Barnes	Edward D.	38	San Joaquin		Parks	Tamy (?) H.	28	Santa Rosa	
Barnes	Edwin E.	23	Santa Rosa	IL	Soule	Frances	27	Healdsburg	CND
Barnes	Ellis James	23	Penngrove	CA	Craig	Ina Margaret	28	Penngrove	CA
Barnes	George Otis	34	Santa Rosa	IN	Parrish	Harriet	21	Santa Rosa	IL
Barnes	H. G.	27	Cloverdale	CA	Glatfelder	Lulu	25	Santa Rosa	KS
Barnes	Henry	35	Petaluma	CA	Risk	Jennie	27	Petaluma	IRL
Barnes	Henry L.	57	Santa Rosa	OH	Carrillo	Amelia	27	Santa Rosa	CA
Barnes	Henry L.	64	Santa Rosa	OH	Campion	Margaret M.	18+	Santa Rosa	Mac
Barnes	Henry S.	39	Sebastopol		Siston (?)	Kattie (?) E.	26	Sebastopol	

Groom					Bride				
Surname	**Given Name**	**Age**	**Residence**	**BP**	**Surname**	**Given Name**	**Age**	**Residence**	**BP**
Barnes	Jesse W.	32	Long Beach	AL	Shull	Beulah B.	28	San Jose	CO
Barnes	John B.	27	Santa Rosa	IL	Toney	Ada	21	Santa Rosa	CA
Barnes	L. J.	23	Sebastopol	CA	Fredrichs	Sophia A.	20	Sebastopol	CA
Barnes	Louis G.	30	Healdsburg	CA	Walker	Ella M.	18	Healdsburg	CA
Barnes	Millard L.	26	Forestville	MO	Clover	Leonora	26	Forestville	CA
Barnes	P. D.	24	Princeton, Colusa Co.	CA	Armstrong	Lucy	23	Guerneville	MO
Barnes	Perry S.	18	Fulton	CA	Gauldin	Gennevieve	18	Rincon Valley	CA
Barnes	Thomas P.	52	Santa Rosa	CND	Findley	C. J., Mrs.	32	Santa Rosa	CA
Barnes	Thomas Sturgis	30	San Francisco	MD	Berry	Carrie Ella	26	Santa Rosa	ME
Barnes	Thos. J.	53	Healdsburg	MO	Thing	Sarah J.	44	Healdsburg	NY
Barnes	W. P.				Rader	Elizabeth A.			
Barnes	William A.	24	Fulton	CA	Landis	Hattie	25	Sisson	OR
Barnes	William Julius	27	Edna, TX	IA	Denham	Lena Ethel	27	Santa Rosa	MO
Barnett	Frank W.	24	Sebastopol	CA	Kirlin	Annie E.	21	Sebastopol	CA
Barnett	Garrett C.	40	San Francisco	MO	Schultis	Julia E.	35	Santa Rosa	IA
Barnett	Harry J.	24	Santa Rosa	OH	Lentz	Grace A.	22	Santa Rosa	MN
Barnett	Lester H.	21	Sebastopol	CA	Gibbs	Harriet E.	18	Sebastopol	CA
Barnett	Marion L. R.	21	Petaluma	CA	Kirkbride	Blanche Bernice	19	Sebastopol	IL
Barnett	Montie	23	San Francisco	WLS	Ward	Jessie M.	19	San Francisco	WA
Barnett	Stanley	28	Guerneville	CA	Martin	Mathilde	27	Berkeley	NRY
Barnett	Walter E.	32	Sebastopol	CA	Gibbs	Evangeline C.	20	Sebastopol	CA
Barney	Henry W.	30	Santa Rosa	CA	Gauldin	Minnie L.	21	Santa Rosa	CA
Barnhart	Frank McGowan	19	Los Gatos	Pit	Allen	Nina	20	Cloverdale	Edg
Barnhill	A. F.				Bryan	Susan			
Barnum	Clarence L.	19	Forestville	CA	Fouts	Elsie M.	17	Forestville	NE
Barnum	Samuel	32	Forestville	MS	Covey	Elizabeth	17	Forestville	CA
Barr	Elmere Roy	21	Oakland	OK	De Gassick	Aylene Stewart	18	San Francisco	CA
Barr	John	28	San Francisco	CND	Zehringer	Adel	22	San Francisco	PA
Barr	William Holt	70	Santa Rosa	IN	Van Riper	Catherine	58	Santa Rosa	OH

Groom					Bride				
Surname	Given Name	Age	Residence	BP	Surname	Given Name	Age	Residence	BP
Barre	Charles Munson	47	Oakland	OH	Smith	Mable Turner	37	Oakland	NY
Barre	Lyman C.	33	Petaluma	CA	Tucker	Jessica B.	27	New York City	CA
Barrett	Albert	24	Vacaville	CA	Timme	Ora E.	19	Forestville	CA
Barrett	Francis E.	27	Alexander Valley	CA	Stone	Nora	19	Alexander Valley	IA
Barrett	John	28	Empire City, NV	IRL	Hamilton	Lulu	25	Stony Point	CA
Barrett	John J.	23	San Francisco	CA	Glover	Margaret C.	22	San Francisco	CO
Barricklaw	David George	21	Santa Rosa		Gaby	Emma	18	Santa Rosa	
Barrie	Nelson T.	61	Cloverdale	VA	Barnell	Barbara	59	Cloverdale	USA
Barron	Harold	26	San Francisco	CA	Dollar	Grace E.	20	San Francisco	CA
Barrows	Arthur C.	31	Shant (?), OR	OR	Hepner	Virginia M.	22	Santa Rosa	VA
Barry	Garland	17	Napa	CA	Lockard	Ruby	16	Napa	CA
Barry	John J.	24	St. Helena	CA	Brown	Gertrude E.	22	Petaluma	CA
Barry	Norman J.	25	Janesville, Lassen Co.	MO	Hardin	Etta	21	Lakeville	CA
Barry	William R.	31	Petaluma	CA	Willis	Margaret M.	20	Petaluma	CND
Barsi	Nichol	25	Mt. Olivet	CA	Rovai	Carolina	18	Santa Rosa	CA
Barsi	Nicholas	29	Guerneville	ITL	Dinucci	Clara	18	Green Valley	CA
Barsi	Santi	33	Healdsburg	ITL	Motroni	Filomina	35	Healdsburg	ITL
Barsi	Nichol	33	Olivet	CA	Wehrspon	Carrie	23	Guerneville	CA
Barsot	Robert Eugene	29	San Francisco	CA	Cole	Chrissie V.	22	San Francisco	WI
Barsotti	Antonio	44	Guerneville	ITL	Camiglia	Marssimiglia	42	Guerneville	SWT
Barsotti	Frank	33	San Francisco	ITL	Guidotti	Annette Jane	21	Guerneville	CA
Bartalini	Joseph	32	San Francisco	ITL	Pardi	Venice	26	San Francisco	ITL
Barth	Adolf	27	Petaluma	SWT	Muller	Babetta	30	Petaluma	SWT
Bartlett	Alexander	37	Ukiah	MO	Delzell	Maggie	21	Bennett Valley	
Bartlett	Fred	23	Cloverdale	WI	Moran	Elenor Elizabeth	27	Cloverdale	NY
Bartlett	Frederick D.	28	San Francisco	CA	Robinson	Marjorie C.	23	Sebastopol	CA
Bartoli	Efisio	33	Santa Rosa	ITL	Zopetti	Vittoria	23	Santa Rosa	ITL
Bartolomei	John	22	Santa Rosa	ITL	Frugoli	Lena	19		CA

Groom					Bride				
Surname	Given Name	Age	Residence	BP	Surname	Given Name	Age	Residence	BP
Bartolomei	Salvatore	22	Santa Rosa	ITL	Cassani	Rica	22	Santa Rosa	ITL
Bartolomei	Victor	22	Santa Rosa	ITL	Pauluci	Giulia	18	Petaluma	CA
Barton	John W.				Martin	Elizabeth, Mrs.			
Barton	John W.				Williamson	Cynthia A.			
Bartosh	William	24	San Francisco	NE	Heath	Annie M.	24	Santa Rosa	NH
Bartsch	Charles	62	Petaluma	GER	Wittkowski	Anna	45	Petaluma	GER
Bascom	Elmer	34	Oakland	IA	Martin	Leona	30	Santa Rosa	CA
Basileu	Jordan	23	El Verano	TRK	Forni	Angeline	18	El Verano	CA
Bass	Seymour S.	23	Shasta Co.		Edringlow	Carrie B.	22	Shasta Co.	
Bassett	Henry F.	33	San Francisco	PEI	Grey	Carrie	19	Healdsburg	CA
Bassett	Henry W.	30	Sebastopol	CA	Beattie	Alice M.	24	Santa Rosa	WA
Bassett	William David	32	Petaluma	WLS	Nielsen	Marie	41	Petaluma	DNK
Bassi	Abramo	32	Healdsburg	ITL	Carotta	Catherina	30	Healdsburg	ITL
Bassi	Amando G.	42	Petaluma	ITL	Tunzi	Geneva M.	36	Petaluma	SWT
Bassi	Giatano	30	Bodega		LaFranci	Margaret	35		
Bassignani	Cesare	28	Santa Rosa	ITL	Bellotti	Minnie	19	Santa Rosa	ITL
Bassini	Bernard	31	Sebastopol	CA	Pedrotti	Clara	37	Santa Rosa	AZ
Batchelder	Thaddeus	33	Clinton, Amador Co.	NH	Stewart	Agnes R.	22	Occidental	CA
Batchelor	David William	35	Penngrove	SCT	MacFarlane	Susie W.	23	Penngrove	SCT
Bates	Alphonzo	27	Hercules	AR	Garrett	Phrona E.	26	Sebastopol	KS
Bates	Ezekiel F.	34	Salt Point Twp.		Price	Mary	18+	Salt Point Twp.	
Bates	Frank Earle	26	San Francisco	CA	Wagner	Jessie Adeline	28	San Francisco	CA
Bates	George H.	24	Santa Rosa	MA	Delamater	Mary E.	16	Santa Rosa	MT
Bates	Henry Frederick	21	Sonoma	Son	Clark	Zoe Ruah	22	Sonoma	Iowa City
Bates	Philip				England	Angeline, Mrs.			
Bates	Vernon G.	29	San Francisco	WA	Manion	Edith L.	25	Santa Rosa	
Bateson	Claude William	28	Petaluma	CND	Clarke	Delia	30	Petaluma	ICE
Bath	Thomas	27	Santa Rosa	ENG	Letterman	Hattie F. A.	16	Occidental	Dou

Groom					Bride				
Surname	**Given Name**	**Age**	**Residence**	**BP**	**Surname**	**Given Name**	**Age**	**Residence**	**BP**
Bathurst	Roland L.	28	Santa Rosa	PA	Barker	Bertha B.	28	Santa Rosa	CA
Batsakis	Nicholas	37	Berkeley	GRC	Appiarius	Victoria B.	36	Berkeley	FRN
Batt	Elmer M.	23	Annapolis	CA	Brown	Elsie I.	19	Healdsburg	CA
Batt	Leo F.	22	Annapolis	CA	Crispin	Hazel M.	17	Comfort	CA
Battaglia	Lorance Daniel	19	Santa Rosa	CA	Silvia	Mary	16	Santa Rosa	CA
Batten	Albert	24	Bennett Valley	CA	Fagon	Margaret	20	Bennett Valley	CA
Batten	George	21	Santa Rosa	CA	Simonton	Cora May	19	Santa Rosa	CA
Battero	Vittorio E.	34	Oakland	ITL	Coco	Ugolina	26	Richmond	ITL
Batton	John Wesley	21	Bennett Valley		Hastings	Sarah A.	17	Bennett Valley	
Bauer	Earl F.	24	Santa Rosa	PAN	Hindringer	Louisa B.	20	Santa Rosa	PA
Bauer	Ernest William	28	Petaluma	Pet	Lundholm	Esther Leone	27	Petaluma	WI
Baugh	Clive Evertt	23	Campbell	CA	Lee	Rachel Orlena	23	Fulton	OR
Baugh	Douglas Guy	31	Petaluma	ENG	Potter	Ruby Elizabeth	27	Petaluma	CA
Baugh	Douglas Guy	33	Petaluma	ENG	Doss	Pearl Elizabeth	27	Petaluma	CA
Baugh	Ernest	22	Petaluma	Ceylon, IDA	Phillips	Letitia R.	18	Petaluma	PA
Baughman	Horace Ray	23	Petaluma	CND	King	Ruby E.	22	Petaluma	Wood-land
Baum	Alexander R.	23	San Francisco	Sfo	Scott	Laulu	19	Healdsburg	NY
Baum	John Wesley	25	Santa Rosa	CA	Adams	Nellie May	18	Santa Rosa	IA
Baum	Thomas J.	30	Santa Rosa	CA	Arfsten	Emma D.	19	Sebastopol	CA
Bauman	Charles Henry	19	Santa Rosa	NE	Schmidt	Katherine Francis	19	Santa Rosa	CA
Bauman	Conrad	34	Windsor	SWT	Haubrich	Clara G.	17	Windsor	Sfo
Bauman	Edward	42	San Francisco	WI	Greer	Lizzie A.	46	San Francisco	WI
Baumann	Charles	45	Cloverdale	GER	Rose	Emma	39	Cloverdale	IA
Baumeister	Carl A.	25	Cloverdale	CA	Walker	Hazel E.	17	Cloverdale	CA
Baumgartner	Leonhard	24	Sonoma	SWT	Wasserfallen	Anna	29	Sonoma	SWT
Baumhogger	John C.	23	Valley Springs, Calavaras Co.	CA	Jewell	Mary E.	23	Bloomfield	CA
Bauright	Wilson	38	Ukiah	IN	Odell	Nettie	23	Geyserville	CA

Groom					Bride				
Surname	Given Name	Age	Residence	BP	Surname	Given Name	Age	Residence	BP
Baxman	Charles F.	30	Petaluma	CA	Jensen	Ida H.	20	Petaluma	CA
Baxman	Ernest B.	22	Sea View	CA	Davis	Rebecca Dorothy	19	Guerneville	CA
Baxman	Fred	29	Salt Point	GER	Crusher (?)	Eliza	15	Salt Point	CA
Baxman	Fred				Crocker	Eliza			
Baxmann	Arthur V.	21	Petaluma	CA	Johnson	Elvira	21	Petaluma	CA
Baxter	Arthur W.	30	Camp Vacation, Sonoma Co.	IL	McCoy	Cora	23	Camp Vacation	MO
Bay	Edward L.	42	Petaluma	IA	Howard	Sarah, Mrs.	45	Petaluma	CT
Bayer	Herman Henry	32	Santa Rosa	GER	Fick	Hernine D.	20	Santa Rosa	NY
Bayes	Lou	29	Healdsburg	CA	Dugan	Edith	20	Alexander Valley	Lak
Bayler	John R.	21	Santa Rosa Twp.	CA	Steiger	Hermina A.	18	Santa Rosa	CA
Bayler	Joseph Anthony	25	Santa Rosa	CA	Lewis	Emma Isabella	30	Santa Rosa	CA
Baymiller	Fred C.	29	Hamilton City, CA	IL	Rued	Margaret	30	Santa Rosa	SWT
Bayol	Frank P.	26	El Verano	AL	Clements	Katherine	18	El Verano	CA
Beach	Alva Frank	26	San Rafael	IL	Maniz	Cassie	31	San Rafael	PRT
Beach	Charles Henry	55	Walnut Creek	IL	Smith	Louise Marie	50	Sonoma	PA
Beach	Gordon S.	22	San Rafael	IL	Blair	Gertie	20	San Rafael	CA
Beach	Riley	46	Cazadero	CA	Gibbs	Rosa M.	19	Cazadero	OR
Beagle	William H.	29	Cloverdale	NE	Adams	Emma D.	20	Cloverdale	CA
Beal	S. Pryor	31	Sherwood	IN	Babcock	Edith M.	24	Laytonville	CA
Bealer	George A.	28	Duncans Mills	OH	O'Laughlin	May A.	19	Duncans Mills	CA
Beales	Edmund	43	Honolulu	ENG	Polk	Josephine, Mrs.	40	Petaluma	CA
Beales	George F.	27	Niles	NY	Wilson	Hannah J.	22	Petaluma Twp.	Pett
Beall	Asbury	37	Hopland	OR	Rippey	Clara E.	32	Hopland	CA
Bean	Eben D.	28	Santa Rosa	ME	Abshire	Laura P.	22	Santa Rosa	CA
Bean	Oliver F.	30	San Francisco	CA	Franquelin	Adelaide M.	30	San Francisco	CA
Bean	Ulysses S.	35	Scales	CA	Hodgson	Alice	36	Santa Rosa	CA
Bearden	James M.	25	Duncans Mills		Freeman	Martha E.	18	Duncans Mills	

Groom					Bride				
Surname	Given Name	Age	Residence	BP	Surname	Given Name	Age	Residence	BP
Beardin	Hubert W.	31	Santa Rosa	CA	Delaney	Blanche M.	37	Santa Rosa	MO
Beardslee	John W.	60	Healdsburg	NY	Hyatt	F. G., Mrs.	45	Healdsburg	CA
Beardsley	J. A.	35	Petaluma	NY	Evans	Eva L.	31	Petaluma	NY
Beasley	Jaba	44	Cloverdale	MO	Southern	Lucy, Mrs.	27	Cloverdale	KS
Beasley	Russell L.	23	Geyserville	CA	Yeager	Cynthia Eleanor	21	Geyserville	CA
Beasom	John Frank	26	San Francisco	MN	Finley	Willie Camille	23	Santa Rosa	CA
Beatie	Walter C.	28	Selma	CA	Hite	Eva B.	21	Selma	VA
Beattie	John	28	Santa Rosa	SCT	Barnes	Mary Susannah	27	Santa Rosa	CND
Beatty	Edward Waldron	28	Santa Rosa	KY	Gilbert	Minnie E.	22	Santa Rosa	CA
Beatty	James H.	51	near Calistoga	CND	Borhinger	Margaret, Mrs.	47	near Calistoga	GER
Beaulieu	Charles B.	33	Cloverdale	CA	Hayward	Mary O.	23	Cloverdale	CA
Beaurgard	Harry Julius	26	Sausalito	CA	Pedrotti	Stella Julia	22	Duncans Mills	CA
Beaver	J. S.	22	Guerneville		Bigsby (?)	Bell	18	Guerneville	
Beaver	W. J.	22	Ukiah	CA	Beaver	Sylvia	22	Ukiah	IA
Bebagliati	Eugene	22	Geyserville	ITL	Angeli	Madalain	16	Geyserville	Geyser ville
Beck	Christian Hansen	36	Petaluma	GER	Bahr	Elsie	22	Petaluma	GER
Beck	Edward H.	37	Healdsburg	PA	Hockins	Lee	26	Healdsburg	CA
Beck	Frank Ross	30	San Rafael	CA	Janssen	Elsie	28	San Rafael	CA
Beck	George N.	21	Santa Rosa	CA	Thomas	Vera Jewell	19	Santa Rosa	CA
Beck	Hans Madison	25	Fresno	DNK	Kunzler	Della Adele	18	Point Arena	CA
Beck	John E.	27	Healdsburg	DNK	Jacobson	Dora E.	23	Healdsburg	IA
Beck	Louis	27	Santa Rosa	CA	Hansen	Florence	20	Santa Rosa	MT
Beck	Mads Sorensen	39	Fresno	GER	Olsen	Esther Alena	21	Point Arena	CA
Beck	Niels Anderson	26	Santa Rosa	DNK	Schelling	Elizabetha	29	Santa Rosa	GER
Becker	Burton F.	32	Piedmont	IL	Grassly	Clara H.	34	Oakland	IA
Becker	Myron B.	30	San Francisco	PA	Carroll	Virginia E.	34	San Francisco	CA
Becker	Roy D.	27	Santa Rosa	IL	Munday	Jessie	19	Petaluma	CA
Becker	W. F.	39	Santa Rosa	CND	McNalta	Delia	40	Santa Rosa	IL
Beckett	Frank E.	26	Sacramento	CA	Smith	Rhoda	23	Sacramento	CA

Groom					Bride				
Surname	Given Name	Age	Residence	BP	Surname	Given Name	Age	Residence	BP
Beckman	Albert	30	Sebastopol	MO	Barr	Myrtle	20	Graton	OR
Beckman	Louis Henry	35	Sebastopol	CA	Oehlman	Gertrude Clara	31	Sebastopol	CA
Beckner	W. S.	54	Santa Rosa	KY	Ashcraft	Rebekah, Mrs.	48	Santa Rosa	MO
Beckner	William S.	48	Santa Rosa	KY	Lockwood	Linnie, Mrs.	23	Santa Rosa	CA
Beckwith	Nelson M.	23	Guerneville	CND	Catlin	Kate	18	Guerneville	CA
Bedford	Frederick A.	23	Santa Rosa	ENG	Hammel	Ruth I.	23	Sebastopol	CA
Bedwell	S. J.	20	Windsor	CA	Brooks	Mattie	17	Windsor	CA
Bee	Edward L.	21+	San Jose	CA	Potter	Edna A.	19	Santa Rosa	CA
Bee	Louis	35	Cloverdale	CA	Moes	Anna Mary	26	Healdsburg	MA
Bee	Milliard F.	24	Santa Rosa		Ayers	Alice	22	Guerneville	
Beebe	Edward T.	29	Guerneville	Pt. Arena	German	Kate, Mrs.	23	Guerneville	CA
Beebe	Elbert E.	22	Santa Rosa	CA	Dollar	Alice	18	Mark West	CA
Beebe	Elijah W.	22	Santa Rosa Twp.	CA	Hitchcock	Clara G.	21	Santa Rosa	CA
Beebe	John Franklin	21	Santa Rosa	CA	Barnett	Lillian May	21	Sebastopol	CA
Beebe	Louis W.	25	Guerneville	CA	Gisel	Frieda	24	Guerneville	SWT
Beebe	Thomas E.	24	Cazadero	CA	Pare	Della	24	Napa	CA
Beene	Luther Garnett	22	Sebastopol	TX	Patterson	Alma Vivian	21	Sebastopol	TX
Beeson	Charles Wesley	28	Geyserville	CA	Bartle	Fannie Myrtle	28	Geyserville	WA
Beeson	E. I.	29	Healdsburg	CA	Logan	Emma C.	23	Healdsburg	OH
Beeson	Isaac R.	22	Healdsburg		Mathews	Salina	19	Healdsburg	
Beeson	Jesse R.	26	Redwood City	CA	Nelson	Tekla B.	23	Palo Alto	SWD
Beeson	Orville W.	37	Healdsburg	IL	Flago (?)	Mary A.	39	Healdsburg	IL
Beeson	William I.	24	Healdsburg	CA	Burbank	Emma L.	33	Santa Rosa	MA
Beeson	William S.	60	Alexander Valley		Lafferty	Naoma E., Mrs.	45	Healdsburg	
Beeson	Willis Lewis	22	San Francisco	CA	Russell	Ruth	18	San Francisco	CA
Beevers	Robert L.	26	Santa Rosa	CA	Smith	Harriet E.	19	Santa Rosa	CA
Beffa	Caesar F.	43	Geyserville	SWT	Burris	Nellie, Mrs.	27		CA
Beffa	James	49	Petaluma	SWT	Carroz	Mary	42	Petaluma	SWT
Beffa	James, Jr.	23	Petaluma	CA	Elphick	Clytie	17	Penngrove	CA

Groom					Bride				
Surname	**Given Name**	**Age**	**Residence**	**BP**	**Surname**	**Given Name**	**Age**	**Residence**	**BP**
Beffa	Joseph Edward	22	Petaluma	CA	Pool	Elba	19	Guerneville	CA
Beffa	Quillie W.	25	Petaluma	CA	Paulucci	Marie E.	26	Petaluma	CA
Beffa	Tony	22	Petaluma	CA	Zamaroni	Jessie	24	Petaluma	CA
Beffa	Tony	26	Petaluma	CA	Zamaroni	Lillie	28	Petaluma	CA
Beggs	Thomas G.	22	Petaluma	CA	Burns	Rose A.	21	Petaluma	CA
Beggs	W. H.	25	Cloverdale	IA	Black	Alice	21	Cloverdale	CA
Beggs	William John	20	Petaluma	CND	McCoy	Carrie	18	Petaluma	CA
Beggs	William P.	27	San Francisco	CA	McBrown	Jenevive	25	Petaluma	CA
Behler	Benjamin J.	45	Glen Ellen	CA	Henke	Bertha C.	35	Kenwood	MN
Behler	William	31	Glen Ellen	CA	Kunde	Alice	22	Russian River Twp.	CA
Behmer	John	31	Santa Rosa	OH	Miller	Rosa A.	29	Santa Rosa	IN
Behmer	John	23	Santa Rosa		Harley	Ella	19	Santa Rosa	
Behrens	Albert Percy	27	Petaluma	CA	Cole	May	26	Petaluma	CA
Behrns	Carl Nisson	25	Petaluma	CA	Church	Juanita Sybil	20	Petaluma	CA
Bei	Giulio	28	Molitto (?)	ITL	Rossi	Mary	22	ITL	ITL
Belati	John	28	Santa Rosa	ITL	McCollough	Mary	35	Santa Rosa	IL
Belden	Ralph Austin	23	Santa Rosa	CA	Ungerwitter	M. Gretchen	20	Santa Rosa	CA
Belfils	Ernest	24	Oakland	CA	DeCosta	Annie	25	Oakland	PRT
Belford	Frank G.	28	Fairmead	CA	Radekey	Revia	22	Cloverdale	CA
Bell	Edward H., Jr.	36	St. Louis	MO	Garcia	Margaret M.	30	San Francisco	CA
Bell	Geo. K.				Bice	M. E.			
Bell	Grant	28	Fisk's Mill	WI	McCappen	Jennie	28	Fisk's Mill	CA
Bell	Henry	71	Windsor	NY	Herbert	Retta	25	Windsor	IN
Bell	Henry	72	Windsor	NY	Linebaugh	Kate, Mrs.	32	Santa Rosa	MI
Bell	Holly E.	27	St Helena	CA	Beguhl	Emma	18	Calistoga	CA
Bell	Luther	29	Windsor	CA	Fisher	Ada	22	Windsor	MO
Bell	Noah	30	Windsor	CA	Bamber	Elsie	30	San Francisco	IN
Bell	Raymond C.	38	San Francisco	CA	Patrow	Clara May	23	Durand, WI	WI
Bell	Walter C.	22	Santa Rosa	IA	Adams	Lillie D.	20	Mark West	CA

Groom					Bride				
Surname	**Given Name**	**Age**	**Residence**	**BP**	**Surname**	**Given Name**	**Age**	**Residence**	**BP**
Bell	Walter C.	31	Vacaville	IA	Burt	Blanche A.	27	Santa Rosa	CA
Bell	Warren	24	Windsor	CA	Shular	Ella	18	Windsor	IA
Bell	Wellie Samuel	29	Petaluma	Hld	Fairbanks	Zoe	25	Petaluma	Pet
Bella	Angelo	29	Healdsburg	ITL	Zanderina	Virginia	15	Dry Creek	ITL
Bellah	W. M.	27	Healdsburg	CA	Johnson	Vida	18	Healdsburg	MO
Bellany	Severino R.	25	San Francisco	SWT	Johnson	Jennie N.	26	San Francisco	SWD
Bellazzini	Senio	31	Santa Rosa	ITL	Bondi	Claudina	26	Santa Rosa	ITL
Bellesi	Achelli	21	Santa Rosa	ITL	Bellesi	Domenica	20	Santa Rosa	ITL
Bellesi	Nestore	23	Santa Rosa	ITL	Moretti	Elisa	22	Santa Rosa	ITL
Belli	Albert Joseph	26	Healdsburg	CA	Dogia	Anociata	22	Healdsburg	ITL
Belli	Angelo	22	Santa Rosa	ITL	Gerali	Elvira	22	Santa Rosa	ITL
Belli	Harry Alfred	21	Healdsburg	Hld	Malpiede	Angeline	20	Healdsburg	Sfo
Belli	Luigi	26	Castroville	SWT	Domenighini	Maria	23	Petaluma	CA
Belli	Ostaguio	29	Healdsburg	ITL	Massoni	Laurina	18	Healdsburg	ITL
Belli	Sante	23	Santa Rosa	ITL	Capri	Maria	21	Santa Rosa	ITL
Bello	Frank N.	25	Petaluma	CA	Rudolph	Elizabeth	19	Petaluma	CA
Bello	Joseph G.	27	Petaluma	CA	Finnerty	Gertrude F.	24	Petaluma	CA
Bellon	Walter M.	26	Sebastopol	PA	Pomi	Mabel D.	23	Sebastopol	CA
Belluomini	Matteo	23	San Francisco	ITL	Lituanio	Marie B.	19	Healdsburg	CA
Belluomini	Palmiro	24	Healdsburg	ITL	Benedetti	Edith M. (Tela)	19	Healdsburg	ITL
Beltrami	Lorenzo	32	Petaluma	ITL	Zanoni	Delia	22	Petaluma	CA
Belvail	John H.	29	Petaluma	IA	Daugherty	Maria Theresa	28	Petaluma	CA
Belvail	John H.	56	Petaluma	IA	Bierkle	Emma Christine	44	Petaluma	SWD
Belvail	Lewis	23	Healdsburg	CA	Phillips	Mae E.	26	Healdsburg	CA
Belveal	Otis E.	49	Oakland	IA	Howard	Daisy M.	46	Oakland	IA
Bement	Leighton W.	39	Santa Rosa	WI	Slaten	Eva	31	Yountville, CA	IL
Bemis	Charles G.	26	Petaluma	WA	Johnson	Estelle M.	17	Petaluma	PA
Bendorf	Derby	23	San Francisco	WI	Bartlett	Sibyl	22	San Francisco	CA
Benedetti	Conrad	30	Petaluma	SWT	Zimmerman	Elizabeth	28	San Francisco	SWT
Benedetti	John	28	Occidental	ITL	Dondero	Katie	19	Santa Rosa	NV

Groom					Bride				
Surname	Given Name	Age	Residence	BP	Surname	Given Name	Age	Residence	BP
Benelli	Harry	25	Mt. Olivet	ITL	Albini	Mary	17	Mt. Olivet	ITL
Benelli	Joseph	26	Occidental	ITL	Martinelli	Mary	18	Duncans Mills	CA
Benelli	Lucca	30	Mt. Olivet	ITL	Giannecchini	Serofina	19	Healdsburg	ITL
Benepe	Charles S.	22	Sebastopol	KS	Gilmore	Lizzie E.	21	Santa Rosa	CA
Benepe	Selden C.	30	Sebastopol	KS	Milne	Laura	20	Ukiah	CA
Benepe	W. Weimer	22	Sebastopol	KS	Blazer	Lena A.	21	Sebastopol	CA
Benepe	Wesley L.	25	Sebastopol	KS	Libby	Martha M.	24	Sebastopol	ME
Bengtson	Carl	37	San Francisco	SWD	Hultgren	Emma	39	San Francisco	SWD
Benjamin	Frank E.	20	Healdsburg	CA	Brown	Minnie	22	Healdsburg	IA
Benjamin	William E.	34	Santa Rosa Twp.	IL	Smith	Jennie, Mrs.	19	Santa Rosa Twp.	IL
Benjegerdes	Carl L.	28	Eureka	IA	Rapun	Annie	26	Healdsburg	IA
Benkiser	Fred	29	Oakland	CA	Mosna	Anna	28	Healdsburg	AUS
Bennesen	Peter L.	38	Santa Rosa	CA	Darling	Nora M., Mrs.	46	Santa Rosa	IA
Bennett	Charley	19	Santa Rosa	CA	Cunningham	May	17	Santa Rosa	MO
Bennett	Edwin George	41	Petaluma	NY	Lewis	Grayce Edna	26	Petaluma	WI
Bennett	George H.	34	New York City	VT	Lee	Emmie H.	23	San Francisco	TN
Bennett	Gilbert Louis	25	Oakland	CA	Cullen	Mary Alice	25	Oakland	CA
Bennett	Glover Henry	31	Sebastopol	Cob	Thompson	Fannie Jane	35	Elmira, NY	Bin
Bennett	Grant	23	Santa Rosa	CA	Brown	Laura	22	Santa Rosa	CA
Bennett	James	50	Vallejo	OH	Burns	Sarah, Mrs.	34	Petaluma	IRL
Bennett	John C.	36	Sebastopol	CA	Casey	Katherine	31	Petaluma	CA
Bennett	Joseph	51	Molino	NY	Kane	Catherine	37	Santa Rosa	CA
Bennett	Ralph	21	Santa Rosa	CA	Broback	Naomi	16	Santa Rosa	CA
Bennett	W. J.	32	Petaluma	PA	Bailey	Annie	16	Petaluma	CA
Bennett	Warner	22	Alexander Valley		Danules (?)	Alice	18	Alexander Valley	
Bennett	William C.	30	San Francisco	ENG	Ichtertz	Mary Emily	38	San Francisco	CA
Bennett	William Stephan	30	Geyserville	CA	Northern	Hattie Belle	21	Geyserville	OR
Bennetts	Herbert Franklin	30	Reno, NV	CA	Baker	Jennie Cecelia	30	Tonopoh, NV	WY
Benns	Clarence F.	27	Penngrove	NY	Brake	A. Edith	26	Penngrove	IL
Benson	A. F.	32	Petaluma	UT	Heisen	Lillian	19	Petaluma	CA

Groom					Bride				
Surname	**Given Name**	**Age**	**Residence**	**BP**	**Surname**	**Given Name**	**Age**	**Residence**	**BP**
Benson	August	38	Sausalito	ENG	McDermott	Flora A.	38	Healdsburg	CA
Benson	Benjamin James	38	San Francisco	CA	Mooney	Rachael Bertha	31	Petaluma	CA
Benson	Elwin D.	19	Petaluma	CA	Lewis	Mabel C.	17	Petaluma	MO
Benson	H. Urban	24	Petaluma	CA	Torr	Agnes Leona	18	Petaluma	CA
Benson	Harry	34	Alameda	CA	Leiva	Irene M.	31	Oakland	CA
Benson	Henry	40	Petaluma	IA	Braman	Mary	30	Healdsburg	CA
Benson	Henry	32	Petaluma	IA	Hurd	Charlotte	20	Petaluma	CA
Benson	Josiah H.	42	Petaluma	IA	Hardin	Sarah C.	19	Petaluma	CA
Benson	L. E.	21	Petaluma	CA	Derby	Cora	19	Petaluma	CA
Benson	Nathaniel W.	26	Petaluma	IA	Merritt	Ida J.	17	Petaluma	CA
Benson	Roy	26	Penngrove	CA	Koster	Bertha Josephine	21	Petaluma	CA
Benson	Vernon Henry	36	Oakland	CND	Snyder	Sarah Rebecca	45	Oakland	PA
Benson	William	44	Guerneville	CND	Sartzer	Augusta	43	Mankato, MN	IL
Bent	Edwin M.	22	Santa Rosa	CA	Farrell	Genevieve M.	19	Petaluma	CA
Bentley	Rufus W.	23	Cloverdale	CA	Thompson	Christie D.	22	Cloverdale	CA
Benton	C. C.	21	Geyserville	OK	Bryant	Mary E.	18	Geyserville	CA
Benton	Henry Benjamin	33	Sausalito	MO	Atkinson	Laura M.	37	Petaluma	CA
Benton	Louis J.	20	Petaluma	CA	Snyder	Anna E.	18	Santa Rosa	CA
Bequette	Julian P.	28	San Francisco	CA	Patton	Bertha V.	18	San Francisco	OR
Beretta	Angelo	26	Sonoma	SWT	Modini	Mary	18+	Sonoma	Son
Beretta	Angelo P.	42	Sonoma	SWT	Mazza	Angelina M.	20	Sonoma	CA
Berger	Charles O.	21+	Oakland	Hon	Harris	Maud E.	18+	Santa Rosa	CA
Berger	Emil Julius	44	Oakland	SWT	Haun	Alice Edna	40	Eureka	CA
Berger	Frederick W.	28	Santa Rosa	CA	Pinches	Marie G.	21	Santa Rosa	CA
Berger	Otto William	21	Santa Rosa	Wdc	Pierce	Edna Langley	21	Santa Rosa	CA
Berger	William	32	San Francisco	AUS	Older	Edith M.	27	Alameda	CA
Bergevin	Alexander M.	30	Chicago	CND	Wickersham	Mae S.	23	Petaluma	Pet
Berglund	Harvey M.	23	Santa Rosa	MN	Forsyth	Mary E.	22	Santa Rosa	CA
Bering	Edward A.	29	San Francisco	CA	Farmer	Carrie J.	23	Santa Rosa	CA

Groom					Bride				
Surname	Given Name	Age	Residence	BP	Surname	Given Name	Age	Residence	BP
Berizzi	John	35	Geyserville	ITL	Dominechelli	Luigina	19	Geyserville	ITL
Berka	F.	38	Santa Rosa	BOH	Boettcher	Pollie A.	26	Santa Rosa	MO
Berkman	James H.	43	Cozzens	IN	McFarling	Eva J.	17	Coygens	CA
Berlin	William Herman	25	Santa Cruz	CA	Newell	Flossie Clair	18	Petaluma	CA
Bernard	Gerardus	31	San Francisco	HLD	Fennell	Mary J.	31	San Francisco	CA
Bernard	John Leo	23	Alameda	CA	Equi	Marie	19	Sonoma	CA
Bernard	Robert L.	22	Sand, Mendocino Co.	CND	Weybright	Anna	21	Sand, Mendocino Co.	KS
Berndt	Paul	27	Healdsburg	GER	Moldenhauer	Milea	28	Healdsburg	WI
Bernhard	Rudolph H.	25	Napa	CA	Bruphacher	Elisabeth	30	Napa	ENG
Bernhardt	Chas. F.	26	Santa Rosa	IL	Fitzgibbon	Helen B.	21	San Francisco	IL
Bernnan	Patrick	32	Eldridge	IRL	Buchanan	Anna	29	Eldridge	IRL
Bernstein	David	36	Petaluma	RUS	Greenstein	Mary	35	San Francisco	RUS
Berruti	Emilio	34	San Francisco	ITL	Zappa	Mary M.	19	Santa Rosa	CA
Berry	C. S.	40	Sebastopol	IA	Wilson	Jennie	24	Santa Rosa	SCT
Berry	George H.	23	Healdsburg	CA	England	Susan A.	26	Healdsburg	CA
Berry	George Herod	21	Healdsburg	Solano Co.	England	Martha Isabel	20	Healdsburg	CA
Berry	John E.	21	Boonville	CA	Clow	Crystal M.	18	Philo	CA
Berry	Joseph P.	24	Santa Rosa	MA	Koenig	Lillie F.	22	Healdsburg	CA
Berry	S. B.	33	Sebastopol		Purvince	Lew J.	23	Sebastopol	
Berry	Samuel B.				Miller	Mary J.			
Berry	Samuel C.	29	Sebastopol	CA	Williams	Willmina	21	Sebastopol	MO
Berry	W. P.				Menefee	Emma			
Berryhill	Archie Tanner	34	Fort Bragg	CA	Sawyers	Hazel Marjory	26	Fort Bragg	CA
Berryhill	Joscph F.	22	Geyserville	CA	Burright	Retta	21	Geyserville	CA
Berryman	Samuel	32	Grass Valley	CA	O'Laughlin	Maggie	26	Monte Rio	CA
Bertellotti	Pio	25	Sonoma	ITL	Nina	Florence Dello	22	Sonoma	ITL
Bertholdi	Stephen P.	30	Petaluma	MA	Orozco	Julia V.	32	San Rafael	CA
Bertino	Thomas	22	Santa Rosa	CO	Moore	May T.	20	Santa Rosa	NV

Groom					Bride				
Surname	Given Name	Age	Residence	BP	Surname	Given Name	Age	Residence	BP
Bertolani	Angelo L.	22	Santa Rosa	CA	McCumiskey	Florence	20	Santa Rosa	CA
Bertolani	Martino	29	Healdsburg	ITL	Guirgu	Assunta	18	Healdsburg	ITL
Bertoli	Paul	23	Santa Rosa	ITL	Frati	Sarah	16	Occidental	CA
Bertoli	Paul Pete	21	Sebastopol	ITL	Forrest	Agnes May	15	Sebastopol	CA
Bertoli	Paulo	21	Santa Rosa	ITL	Bernetti	Lizza	25	San Francisco	ITL
Bertoli	Romeo	27	Santa Rosa	ITL	Gainnini	Della	19	Santa Rosa	ITL
Bertolucci	Guido C.	27	Trenton	ITL	Picchi	Frances A.	20	Trenton	CA
Berton	Mars F.	23	Healdsburg	FRN	Laughlin	Irene J.	20	Healdsburg	CA
Bertoni	Guido	25	Healdsburg	ITL	Porta	Mary	23	Hilton	ITL
Bertossi	Carlo	23	Santa Rosa	ITL	Mandarini	Guiseppina	21	Duncans Mills	ITL
Bertossi	Joseph	26	Santa Rosa	ITL	Leonardini	Theresa	18	Santa Rosa	ITL
Bertossi	Louis	24	Santa Rosa	ITL	Cassani	Nora	18	Santa Rosa	CA
Bertram	Arthur H.	48	Oakland	SCT	Spring	Rosenia	47	Oakland	SWT
Bertrand	Paul Emil	25	San Francisco	IL	Huni	Sophe	24	San Francisco	SWT
Bertron	Albert	30	Alexander Valley	OH	Basford	Ida Ellen	17	Alexander Valley	MO
Bertsch	Frank	27	Crescent City	OH	Brown	Elyda, Mrs.	28	Eureka	MA
Bertuccelli	Fabo	24	San Francisco	CA	Proctor	Gladys C.	20	Healdsburg	CA
Bertulucci	Lorenzo	23	Duncans Mills	ITL	Cassini	Giuseppina	17	Duncans Mills	ITL
Besenthal	Adolph	34	San Francisco	GER	Kolasa	Stanislaw	20	Oakland	GER
Bethune	John	28	Guilicos		Fenwick	Juanita	18	Guilicos	
Bettega	Louis	24	Covelo	ITL	Kelley	Hazel C.	18	Santa Rosa	CA
Bettencorte	Manuel Martin	22	Olema	PRT	Souza	Caroline M.	30	Olema	PRT
Bettencourt	John M.	22	Tomales	PRT	Alves	Mary C.	22	Valley Ford	PRT
Bettencourt	Joseph A.	22	Vallejo	CA	Frates	Irene	19	Petaluma	CA
Bettencourt	Manuel	26	Wilfred	AZR	Aveil	Maria	20	Wilfred	AZR
Bettiga	Bruno	57	Kenwood	ITL	Sarzotti	Minnie	18	Healdsburg	ITL
Bettiga	Pietro	30	Kenwood	ITL	Pinoli	Catherina	18	Kenwood	CA
Bettiga	Vincenzo	30	Greenwood	ITL	Deghi	Prima	25	Greenwood	ITL
Bettinelli	Filippo	27	Chileno Valley	SWT	Pedrelli	Margheritta	20	Petaluma	SWT
Bettinelli	Silvio L.	25	Petaluma	CA	Kuhule	Irene Genevieve	19	Petaluma	CA

Groom					Bride				
Surname	**Given Name**	**Age**	**Residence**	**BP**	**Surname**	**Given Name**	**Age**	**Residence**	**BP**
Bettini	Alessio J.	26	Santa Rosa	CA	Wade	Grace E.	23	Santa Rosa	CO
Betts	Ross Everett	27	Laytonville	CA	Dill	Nettie	29	Laytonville	CA
Beukers	Peter Gerard	26	Sacramento	CA	Berka	Regina	26	Santa Rosa	CA
Beutel	Christian	31	Santa Rosa	GER	Scott	Bertha	27	Santa Rosa	GER
Beutel	Gottlieb	45	Santa Rosa	GER	Spieth	Anna	27	Santa Rosa	GER
Bever	Thomas J.	30	Visalia	KS	Renfrew	Anna L.	25	Healdsburg	OH
Bever	Tunis V.	23	Guerneville	IN	Howard	Martha G.	19	Guerneville	TN
Beveridge	James	29	Los Angeles	CA	Horwege	Loretta C.	29	Petaluma	
Beveridge	William, Jr.	28	Oakland	PAN	Hendrickson	Ida	26	Oakland	CA
Bevington	Walter Clark	31	Dunsmuir	IL	Law	Tammy	21	Sonoma	Son
Bewick	William Young	33	Reedley	NV	Torgelson	Anna	21	Santa Rosa	SWD
Beyer	Edward	33	Santa Rosa	GER	Baldrusch	Katie	29	Santa Rosa	RUS
Biagggi	Antony	29	Fallon, CA	SWT	Tunzi	Albina	21	Bloomfield	CA
Biaggi	B.	26	Bodgea Corners	SWT	Nobelli	Philomena	21	Bodega Corners	SWT
Biaggi	John Robert	26	San Francisco	CA	Bree	Eva	26	San Francisco	CA
Bianchi	Antonio	24	Santa Rosa	ITL	Ferrari	Edith Margaret	19	Santa Rosa	CA
Bianchi	Attilio	32	San Francisco	ITL	Lucchesi	Elvira Rosa	16	Santa Rosa	CA
Bianchi	Peter	26	Sebastopol	ITL	Perinoni	Annie	18	Sebastopol	CA
Bianchini	Bernardino	23	Vineburg	ITL	Viviani	Maria	23	Vineburg	ITL
Bianchini	Fred P.	25	Santa Rosa	CA	Rowe	Leona V.	22	Santa Rosa	ME
Bianchini	Giovanni	40	Santa Rosa	ITL	Hasnip	Sarah	24	Santa Rosa	AUT
Bianchini	Giovanni W.	18	Santa Rosa	CA	Bertino	Rose N.	17	Santa Rosa	UT
Bianchini	Mariano	24	Glen Ellen	ITL	Allesandri	Elisa	19	Glen Ellen	ITL
Bianchini	Mario	23	Santa Rosa	ITL	Bianchini	Sarah, Mrs.	26	Santa Rosa	AUT
Bianconi	Mansueto	28	Santa Rosa	ITL	Buzzi	Mary	19	Santa Rosa	CA
Biasotti	Giovanni	45	Emeryville	ITL	Leonardini	Teresa	35	Alameda	ITL
Biasotti	Luigi	28	Healdsburg	ITL	Ghiozzi	Marie	24	San Francisco	NY
Biavaschi	Emil	31	Santa Rosa	ITL	Lemmon	Ethel	25	Santa Rosa	MI
Bice	Fred L.	24	Healdsbug	Soc	Higgins	Adeline	21	Healdsburg	Men
Bickford	Elmer Leonard	28	Napa	Vir	Putnam	Ada	26	Petaluma	Pet

Groom					Bride				
Surname	**Given Name**	**Age**	**Residence**	**BP**	**Surname**	**Given Name**	**Age**	**Residence**	**BP**
Biddings	Henry A.	22	Healdsburg	Arcata	Bel	Ida May	18	Healdsburg	Hld
Bidwell	Albert	23	Alexander Valley	CA	Morrill	Mary Francis	25	Santa Rosa	CA
Bidwell	Charles E.	20	Alexander Valley	CA	Combs	Kittie L.	18	Healdsburg	CA
Bidwell	James	27	Alexander Valley		Martin	Lucy	19	Healdsburg	
Bidwell	James E.	18	Alexander Valley	CA	Peck	Annie	16	Healdsburg	SCT
Bidwell	John W.	20	Alexander Valley	CA	St. Clair	Ellen	18	Alexander Valley	CA
Bierer	David William	34	Guerneville	KS	Sutherlan	Grace Elizabeth, Mrs.	26	Guerneville	CA
Bigelow	Calvin	48	Guerneville	ME	Jones	Louisa	42	Guerneville	VA
Bigelow	Frank L.	31	Occidental	MI	Adgate	Nannie	28	Occidental	AR
Bigelow	George A.	23	San Francisco	Ca	Griffin	Jessie E.	18	San Francisco	CA
Biggs	Frank Leland	36	Petaluma	CA	Fore	Mable Edith	26	Petaluma	IL
Biggs	George C.	31	Petaluma	CND	Veale	Margaret	23	Petaluma	CA
Biggs	George C.	22	Petaluma		Hardin	Alice M.	18+	Petaluma	
Bigham	M.	26	Windsor	CA	Brooks	Emma	18	Windsor	CA
Bigham	Ray E.	24	Windsor	CA	Dollar	Daisy B.	18	Mark West	CA
Bignell	James	52	Petaluma	CND	Blair	Josephine	48	Petaluma	FRN
Bigsby	Milton S.	24		TN	Willis	Mary	20	Sonoma	
Bill	Frank B.	27	Sebastopol	CA	Barry	Margaret M.	20	Santa Rosa	NY
Bill	Henry	31	Sonoma	GER	Gerlach	Elizabetha	19	San Francisco	GER
Bill	Howard	20	Petaluma	AR	Rodgers	Edna Isabelle	22	Petaluma	CA
Bill	Philip C., Jr.	22	Sonoma	CA	Schuhmann	Johanna	21	Sonoma	GER
Billett	Frank E.	28	Occidental	CA	Twitchell	Henrietta Genevia	17	Occidental	CA
Billings	J. F.	60	Santa Rosa	NY	Madden	Elizabeth	45	Santa Rosa	IL
Bills	Lemuel James	26	Santa Rosa Twp.		Chaffee	Carrie	18	Santa Rosa	
Bilstein	Alfred George	30	Los Angeles	IA	Tenter	Elizabeth Mary	16	Santa Rosa	NE
Bindi	Acille	42	Sebastopol	ITL	Battaglia	Luisa	39	Sebastopol	ITL
Bindt	Rudolph	26	Honolulu	Koloa, HWI	Johnson	Clara Belle	17	Petaluma	Koh

Groom					Bride				
Surname	Given Name	Age	Residence	BP	Surname	Given Name	Age	Residence	BP
Bingaman	Joseph Wheeler Dores	28	Oakland	CA	Kimball	Edna Genevieve	24	Healdsburg	MI
Binggeli	George	25	Windsor	SWT	Balozs	Rose M.	18	Windsor	AUS
Bink	Conrad	29	Healdsburg	GER	Holst	Annie M.	18	Healdsburg	CT
Bino	John	24	Petaluma	GER	Pedrotti	Annie Teresa	18	Santa Rosa	CA
Biocca	Louis	26	San Francisco	ITL	Cassina	Margaret	17	Sebastopol	ITL
Birch	James F.	29	Santa Rosa	NY	Wilson	Nellie K.	24	Santa Rosa	CA
Birch	Russell J.	23	Santa Rosa	CA	Schelling	Marie C.	19	Santa Rosa	CA
Bird	Charles A.	35	Davison, MI	MI	Dewey	Beatrix C.	29	Healdsburg	MI
Bird	George Francis	25	San Francisco	ENG	Hale	Mabel	22	Geyserville	CA
Bird	Harry	28	Alameda	ENG	Sawyer	Jennie L.	23	Oakland	CND
Bird	Jesse	26	Guerneville	MA	Thorpe	Louise E.	21	Russian River Twp.	MI
Bird	Seth J.	27	Los Angeles	OH	Jensen	Anna	22	Los Angeles	SD
Bird	James	43	Porter Creek	ENG					
Birkle	Nickolas	49	Petaluma	GER	Berta	Emma Mengere	28		SWD
Birmingham	Winfred W.	34	Los Angeles	NY	Dick	Mayme S.	35	Los Angeles	IL
Bisbee	George Marion	21	Petaluma	MO	Samuels	Pearl Katherine	17	Santa Rosa	CA
Bischof	Martin T.	32	San Francisco	JPN	Pillsbury	Harriet	30	Los Angeles	TX
Bish	Lewis M.	36	Santa Rosa	MO	Norris	Bertha M.	17	Santa Rosa	CA
Bishop	E. L.	54	San Francisco	MA	Burr	Flora I.	42	San Bruno	IL
Bishop	William A.	31	Santa Rosa		Greene	Vilette	21		
Bishop	William Raymond	25	Eureka	ME	Caughey	Elizabeth Annie	20	Cloverdale	CA
Bisinger	Hubert G.	34	San Francisco	GER	Throckmorton	Margaret M.	34	San Francisco	CA
Bisordi	Frank	34	Santa Rosa	ITL	Paulinelli	Emma	22	Santa Rosa	ITL
Bisordi	Angelo	28	Sebastopol	CA	Banks	Bertha	24	Sebastopol	CA
Bisordi (?)	Pasqualc	21	Santa Rosa Twp.	ITL	Gianella	Theresa	17	Santa Rosa	CA
Bitcon	George	32	Vallejo	IRL	Ingalsbe	Luinie	34	Vallejo	IL
Bizzini	Joseph	34	Petaluma	SWT	Bolla	Domenica	25	Petaluma	SWT
Bizzini	Julius	29	Santa Rosa	SWT	Kuhl	Catharina	18	Santa Rosa	CA

Groom					Bride				
Surname	Given Name	Age	Residence	BP	Surname	Given Name	Age	Residence	BP
Bjorman	Henry	27	San Francisco	RUS	Nelson	Christine B.	23	San Francisco	DNK
Black	Charles A.	21	Cloverdale	CA	Groshong	Anna E.	24	Cloverdale	CA
Black	Charles M.	30	San Francisco	MO	Bowman	Jessie Z.	20	San Francisco	Pet
Black	Claude Henry	23	Dry Creek	CA	Phillips	Pauline	20	Dry Creek	CA
Black	George H.	22	Cloverdale	CA	Crew	Minnie M.	17	Cloverdale	CA
Black	George H.				Ward	Sarah A.			
Black	Harry Edward	24	Geyserville	CA	Smith	Maude Alma	21	Geyserville	CA
Black	Homer W.	22	Healdsburg	CA	Leard	Bernice Edna	22	Healdsburg	CA
Black	Martin L.	29	Sacramento	NE	McCready	Laura T.	36	Sacramento	CA
Black	Oscar W.	20	Cloverdale	CA	Read	Hazel G.	18	Cloverdale	CA
Black	Samuel	30	Guerneville	CND	Lowe	Teresa, Mrs.	19	Guerneville	CA
Black	Shirley R.	20	Geyserville	CA	Leroux	Cora F.	18+	Cloverdale	KS
Black	V. D.	34	Salinas	IN	Norris	Dalia	29	Santa Rosa	MO
Black	Walter C.	24	Eureka	CA	Terry	Nora L.	25	Healdsburg	CA
Black	Wilbur C.	24	Geyserville	CA	Smith	Belle Anna	23	Geyserville	CA
Black	William Earl	20	Dry Creek	CA	Cooper	Hazel Marguerite	18	Geyserville	CA
Black	William H.	20	Cloverdale	CA	Hulbert	Eleonora Agnes	18	Cloverdale	CA
Black	Wm. H.	44	Cloverdale		Hall	Ensima	19	Cloverdale	
Black	Wm. H.	22	Dry Creek		Easlie	Nora Emma	21	Cloverdale	
Blackburn	Allen H.	21	San Francisco		Winquist	Annie S.	23	San Francisco	
Blackburn	Charles Walter	24	San Francisco	Sfo	Kyle	Maude	21	Petaluma	Pet
Blackburn	Frank L.	21+	Petaluma	CA	Williams	Caroline T. D.	18+	Petaluma	CA
Blackburn	George	27	Healdsburg	ENG	Thurman	Margaret	22	Healdsburg	CA
Blackford	Clyde R.	25	San Mateo	CA	Schneider	Katherine	22	Santa Rosa	CA
Blackford	Ernest F.	39	Santa Rosa	IA	Lane	Lottie E.	46	Santa Rosa	CA
Blackly	Frank E.	28	San Francisco	WA	McCario	Minnie	20	Melita	CA
Blackman	Samuel	32	Petaluma	CND	Williams	Rebecca	20	Santa Rosa	CA
Blackman	W. S.	23	Santa Rosa	CA	Harrow	Frances S.	21	Santa Rosa	ID
Blackwell	Edward E.	25	Petaluma	MA	Wilkinson	Leonora F.	24	Portland, ME	ME

Groom					Bride				
Surname	**Given Name**	**Age**	**Residence**	**BP**	**Surname**	**Given Name**	**Age**	**Residence**	**BP**
Blair	Duke	33	Skaggs Springs	WA	Otis	Flora		Annapolis	CA
Blair	F. M. D.				Masey	Vesta, Mrs.			
Blair	James K.	21	Vancouver, WA	OR	Monticello	Sylvia C.	17	Guerneville	CA
Blair	John	74	Guerneville	NY	Ushman	Frederika	50	Redwood Twp.	GER
Blair	Thomas N.	60	Alexander Valley	AR	Gober	Sarah J., Mrs.	45	Alexander Valley	
Blair	William E.	27	Santa Rosa	WI	Feltz	Mary S.	17	Santa Rosa	GER
Blaisdell	Harry Lee	27	San Jose	WA	Wiswell	Wyima (?) Florence	21	Preston	CA
Blake	Frank T.	35	Marysville	CA	Askam	Lillian	33	Los Angeles	CA
Blake	James B.	38	San Luis Obispo	CA	Singley	Katherine	30	Petaluma	Pet
Blake	Jeremiah Burton	35	Occidental	CA	Hockin	Grace Mabel	21	Santa Rosa	CA
Blake	John R.	42	Marin Co.	NY	Mays	Mattie H.	32	Forestville	OR
Blake	John R.	33	Bloomfield		Hines	Alice J.	19	Bloomfield	
Blakeley	Leslie A.	29	Healdsburg	NE	Burns	Jessie E.	29	Healdsburg	WA
Blakely	T. M.	25	Oakland	NY	Ayers	Rosalie	24	Petaluma	CA
Blakesley	Claude	21	Forestville	CA	Teel	Ida	23	Hilton	CA
Blakesley	Franklin C.	32	Geyserville	CA	Miller	Hazel	19	Windsor	CA
Blakeway	Horace	24	Sebastopol	IA	Richardson	Emma	19	Sebastopol	CA
Blakley	Albert Edward	22	Healdsburg	CA	Taylor	Junita Eyleen	18	Stites, CA	CA
Blakley	James M.	48	Hilton	MO	Simpson	Rebecca, Mrs.	46	Hilton	IL
Blakley	Jesse E.	32	Kenwood	KS	Leon	Lupe	32	Kenwood	CA
Blakley	Thomas F.	61	Santa Rosa	CA	Woods	Katie	27	Santa Rosa	CA
Blakley	Thos. S.	27	Tyrone	CA	Beardon	Martha E.	21	Redwood Twp.	CA
Blanchard	Bowman	25	San Jose	MO	Purvine	Olive	23	Petaluma	CA
Blanchard	D. N.	34	Stockton	ME	Edwards	Helen R.	31	Healdsburg	CA
Blanchard	Frank	23	New York City		Loyan (?)	Annie	16	OR	
Blanchard	Frank I.	28	Occidental	MI	Glynn	Mamie	26	Occidental	CA
Blaney	John W.	31	Occidental	CA	Zilhart	Ella F.	21	Freestone	CA
Blank	George	23	Stony Point	GER	Huber	Emily A.	21	Petaluma	CA
Blank	John	28	Sebastopol	CA	Baker	Amy T.	24	Stony Point	CA

Groom					Bride				
Surname	**Given Name**	**Age**	**Residence**	**BP**	**Surname**	**Given Name**	**Age**	**Residence**	**BP**
Blank	John	38	San Leandro		Greist	Leah Agnes	19	Healdsburg	
Blank	Louis	25	Stony Point	CA	Baker	Eva M.	21	Stony Point	CA
Blast	Leo A.	21	San Francisco	OH	Edwards	Evelyn Maud	18	San Francisco	CA
Blazer	C. Lloyd	23	Healdsburg	CA	Gardella	Emily I.	18	Honent	CA
Blazer	Charlie	26	Healdsburg	CA	Ottmer	Adelia B.	18	Healdsburg	MO
Blazer	John J.	22	Healdsburg	CA	Harbine	Addie	18	Healdsburg	CA
Bleakley	William	24	Fisk's Mill		Richardsen	Sarah Jane	17+	Fisk's Mill	
Bledsoe	A. J.	28	Santa Rosa	MO	Woodruff	Clara J.	19	Santa Rosa	
Bledsoe	Henry Thornton	25	Healdsburg	CA	Schulz	Matilda Lucille	21	Santa Rosa	NE
Bledsoe	Isaac				Michaid	Mary, Mrs.			
Bledsoe	John H.	33	Healdsburg	CA	Bane	Eleanor, Mrs.	30	Healdsburg	CA
Bledsoe	John Henry	23	Healdsburg	CA	Conger	Cornelia Constance	17	Healdsburg	CA
Bledsoe	Linn	56	Healdsburg	MO	Vaughn	Louisa F., Mrs.	52	Healdsburg	MO
Bledsoe	Robert R.	23	Healdsburg	CA	Thorton	Thusa	21	Healdsburg	CA
Bledsoe	W. O.	26	Healdsburg	CA	Molleston	Catheline	26	Windsor	TN
Blik	Ell Carl Dunda	23	Salinas	AUS	Rassmussen	Hazel M.	26	Salinas	CA
Bliss	Philip P.	34	Santa Cruz	CA	LeBaron	Beryl	25	Santa Rosa	CA
Bloch	Albert	29	Healdsburg	CA	Walker	Carrie Belle	20	Healdsburg	CA
Block	George	20		CA	Ottmer	Lora A.	16	Dry Creek	MO
Block	George Henry	19	El Verano		Baines	Irene		El Verano	
Block	Walter Ottmer	24	Healdsburg	CA	Guerin	Ella	20	Lytton	CA
Blogg	Ernest J.	25	Fairfax	AUT	Philkill (?)	Nell M.	28	Fairfax	CA
Blomme	John	49	Santa Rosa	BLG	Desmue	Ida	49	San Francisco	BLG
Blomquist	John	35	Occidental	FIN	Chapman	Catherine	36	Occidental	CND
Bloom	Americo James	26	Petaluma	CA	Filippini	Vivian Mabel	20	Petaluma	CA
Bloom	Plauso G.	22	Petaluma	CA	Dado	Irene E.	20	Petaluma	CA
Bloom	Valenti J.	28	Olema	CA	Casarotti	Mary O.	24	Nicasio	CA
Blosser	Thomas G.	55	Willits	PA	Hardwick	Mary	27	Willits	CA
Blot	Louis	25	San Francisco	CA	Gaffney	Madeleine	20	San Francisco	CA

Groom					Bride				
Surname	Given Name	Age	Residence	BP	Surname	Given Name	Age	Residence	BP
Blow	James	22	Santa Rosa	CND	Clark	Susie	17	Santa Rosa	CA
Blower	Sumner J.	23	St. Helena	Napa Co.	Leininger	Carrie	19	Healdsburg	CA
Blum	Jacob	30	Butte, MT	GER	Huber	Helena	27	Santa Rosa	GER
Blum	Louis	59	Santa Rosa	GER	Haas	Theresa	48	Santa Rosa	GER
Blumenthal	Albert M.	38	San Francisco	ROM	Blumenthal	Valerie	33	San Francisco	FRN
Blundell	Vance D.	42	Healdsburg		Acker	Eolim (?)	20	Mendocino Twp.	
Bly	Albert R.	45	Glen Ellen	OH	Quinby	Ella	37	Glen Ellen	IA
Blythe	Frank	40	San Francisco	CA	Ashmore	Emily F.	40	San Francisco	Sfc
Board	Horace D.	23	Healdsburg		Ottmer	Ida F.	19	Dry Creek	
Board	William	53	Mendocino Twp.		Oleven (?)	Azora A.	28	Healdsburg	
Boardman	Edward Madison	40	San Francisco	NV	Augeir	Adelia Anna	45	San Francisco	MO
Bobb	H. I.	30	Tomales	IL	Galle	Mary V.	32	Tomales	IA
Bobkiewicz	Louis	38	San Francisco	GER	Einfeldt	Mary Ellen, Mrs.	28	San Francisco	WA
Bobst	George M.	20	Healdsburg	MO	Button	Flossie	18	Santa Rosa	KS
Bobst	John W.	21	Trenton	NE	Harmon	Lilly	18	Trenton	NE
Bobst	Richard M.	20	St. Helena	NE	McFarling	Jessie M.	17	Mt. Olivet	CA
Bock	Walter D.	29	Goshen, Tulare Co.	CA	Parks	Anna M.	20	Bloomfield	MO
Boden	Jack	23	San Jose	ENG	McFarlane	Leonore May	23	Sebastopol	CA
Bodin	Walter B.	31	San Francisco	MN	Wentzy	Bessie F.	30	San Francisco	OR
Boding	Raymond O.	25	San Francisco	NE	Ward	Gertrude Alice	21	Healdsburg	CA
Boerner	Richard F.	27	Cazadero	MO	Parkins	Tamson	20	Cazadero	NE
Bogale	John	35	Sonoma	ITL	Benedetti	Clarinda	22	Sonoma	ITL
Bogard	William J.	34	ID	MO	White	Julia Emma	26	Boise City, ID	ID
Boggiono	Antonio	29	San Francisco	ITL	Grambruna	Mary	20	Santa Rosa	ITL
Boggs	Geo. W.				McMeans	Alabama			
Bogle	Samuel S.	48	San Francisco	TN	Woodward	Bess Van Alst	31	Santa Rosa	CA
Bogni	Enrico	27	Santa Rosa	ITL	Sorio	Annie	17	Santa Rosa	CA

Groom					Bride				
Surname	Given Name	Age	Residence	BP	Surname	Given Name	Age	Residence	BP
Bogusch	Herbert W.	21	San Francisco	TX	Becker	Alice M.	22	Oakland	CA
Bohan	Michael	43	Cazadero	IRL	Miller	Martha E.	18	Cazadero	PA
Bohlin	Bernard	30	Cloverdale	GER	Stagman	Anna C.	16	Cloverdale	CA
Bohlin	Frank Anton	30	Cloverdale	GER	Steigeman	Mary Gertrude	16	Cloverdale	Sierra Co.
Bohmer	Jacob				Kady	Mary	22		
Bohn	Johannes W.	60	El Verano	SWD	Niquet	Katie	56	Fetters Springs	GER
Bohni	Frederick	22	Sonoma	SWT	Steiger	Rosa	19	Agua Caliente	Santa Clara
Boice	John Dudley	44	Santa Rosa		Chambers	California	22	Petaluma	
Boida	G.	48	Asti	ITL	Blandini	Armenia	46	Santa Rosa	ITL
Boida	Lorenzo	25	San Francisco	MEX	Goodrich	Rosa Meador	22	Santa Rosa	TX
Boien	P.	31	San Francisco	GER	Arfsten	Giene	32	Sebastopol	GER
Boitano	Leo	27	Healdsburg	ITL	Rosasco	Anna Maria	29	Healdsburg	CA
Boivin	Emile Peter	25	Petaluma	CA	Burns	Elsie Viola	26	Petaluma	CA
Bojorques	John	70	Santa Rosa	CA	Young	Adeline	64	Santa Rosa	MI
Boldi	Giacomo	31	Kenwood	ITL	Rossi	Luigia	21	Kenwood	ITL
Boldi	Gioseppe	26	Kenwood	ITL	Gufanti	Rosa	19	Kenwood	ITL
Bolla	Olympio G.	28	Petaluma	CA	Soldate	Louisa, Mrs.	39	Petaluma	SWT
Bolla	Pacific J.	27	Petaluma	SWT	Gambonini	Emma A.	27	Petaluma	CA
Bolla	Romelio G.	43	Petaluma	SWT	Tognaldo	Elvizia C.	28	Petaluma	CA
Bolles	Walter A.	27		CT	Greott	Marie (?) F.	21	Healdsburg	CA
Bollinger	David K.	32	Sebastopol	KS	Gregson	Ruth Annie	22	Green Valley	CA
Bollinger	Fred	22	Santa Rosa	CA	Jones	Susie C.	18	Santa Rosa	CA
Bolser	Chester Arthur	25	Geyserville	IA	Campbell	Grace Evelyn	24	Healdsburg	CA
Bolton	John F.	21	Stockton	Tulare Co.	Robinson	Sadie L.	19	Stockton	Soc
Bolton	Walter A.	23	Tempe, Ariz. Ter.	CA	Kline	K. Isabelle	20	Santa Rosa	CA
Bolton	William L.	47	San Francisco	VA	Lewis	Faye B.	39	San Francisco	OR
Bolz	Albert W.	27	San Francisco	UT	Whitlatch	Leila M.	23	Petaluma	CA

Groom					Bride				
Surname	Given Name	Age	Residence	BP	Surname	Given Name	Age	Residence	BP
Bolz	Francis J.	23	Petaluma	NY	Petersen	Marie	19	Sonoma Co.	DNK
Bolz	Phillip C.	24	Petaluma	Wdc	Smith	Mary F.	22	Petaluma	Por
Bomemann	Arthur F.	34	Fort Bragg	CA	Mann	Embie (?)A.	24	Fort Bragg	CA
Bonardi	Guiseppe	38	Santa Rosa	ITL	Pagani	Katie E.	28	Santa Rosa	CA
Bond	Charles Allen	24	Healdsburg	CA	Wilcox	Grace E.	19	Healdsburg	IL
Bondi	Oreste	23	Santa Rosa	ITL	Novelli	Clariee	16	Santa Rosa	
Bondietti	Frank	31	Duncans Mill	SWT	Mazzolini	Clementina	25	Duncans Mills	SWT
Bondietti	W. J. T.	37	Duncans Mill	SWT	Fiori	Francis	28	Duncans Mills	SWT
Bones	Albert E.	24	Occidental	CA	Stewart	Lettie May	19	Cazadero	CA
Bones	Benjamin Marcus	33	Glen Ellen	CA	Bishop	Nellie M.	24	Glen Ellen	IL
Bones	Charles H.	28	Cloverdale	CA	Francisco	Emma	20	Occidental	ITL
Bones	Francis L.	27	Occidental	CA	Peters	Gertrude A.	25	Occidental	CA
Bones	Frank M.	27	Occidental	CA	Leggett	Maud Lillian	19	Occidental	CA
Bones	John F.				Stone	Sardmier ?			
Bones	John Franklin	60	Occidental	MO	Gillett	Kate, Mrs.	36	Occidental	CA
Bones	Lester	23	Sebastopol	CA	Derrickson	Hila	17	Sebastopol	IL
Bones	R. W.	21	Occidental	CA	Duke	Ethel E.	18	Occidental	CA
Bones	Thomas J.	23	Occidental	CA	Foster	Rose S.	21	Graton	OR
Bones	William H.	36	Occidental	MO	Patterson	Martha	24	Occidental	CA
Bonetti	Joseph	23	Santa Rosa Twp.	SWT	Tamba	Annetta	18	Petaluma Twp.	SWT
Bonfigli	Alvise	23	Santa Rosa	ITL	Bathaglia	Lena	21	Santa Rosa	CA
Bonham	James B.	25	Sebastopol		Rima	Rosa M.	16	Sebastopol	
Bonham	John P.	29	Santa Rosa	CA	Johnson	Ada T.	23	Santa Rosa	CA
Bonham	Melvin	28	Santa Rosa	CA	Hulbert	Belle	27	Cloverdale	CA
Bonham	Willard C.	26	Santa Rosa	CA	Green	Gertrude A.	25	Santa Rosa	TX
Bonini	Olivero	25	Willits	ITL	Alessandri	Dina	20	Sonoma	ITL
Bonnard	Constant	26	Petaluma	FRN	Cabaup	Marie G.	22	Petaluma	FRN
Bonnecaze	Joseph	21	Santa Rosa	FRN	Bonnemason	Louise M.	21	Santa Rosa	FRN
Bonner	Chas. D.	28	Santa Rosa	CA	Lumsden	Fannie L.	26	Santa Rosa	CA
Bonnet	Robert A.	34	Petaluma	OH	McConaghy	Annie N.	34	Petaluma	CA

Groom					Bride				
Surname	Given Name	Age	Residence	BP	Surname	Given Name	Age	Residence	BP
Bonney	Alfred T.	29	San Francisco	ENG	Staton	Cora W.	28	Healdsburg	LA
Bonnie	B. F.				Petray	Parthenia			
Bonugli	Peter	49	Santa Rosa	ITL	Tocchini	Julia	27	Santa Rosa	ITL
Bonward	P. N.	32	Red Bluff	FRN	Lund	Annie L.	31	Santa Rosa	CA
Booth	John	21	Graton	CA	Condon	Ruth	15	Graton	CA
Boothe	William N.	33	Sonoma	VT	Norcross	Alice	20	Sonoma	VT
Borba	Emanuel Ignacio	28	Sebastopol	RI	Vier	Angeline Genevieve	20	Sebastopol	CA
Borba	Frank	23	Sebastopol	CA	Kirsch	Frances Margaret	20	Sebastopol	KS
Bordessa	Antonio	23	Tomales	ITL	Bordessa	Juiliana	23	Tomales	ITL
Bordessa	Davide	26	Valley Ford	ITL	Pozzi	Margheritta	26	Bodega Corners	ITL
Bordessa	Dominico	26	Tomales	ITL	Poncio	Carolina	17	Marshall	CA
Bordessa	Martin	27	Occidental	ITL	Maffioli	Catherina	25	ITL	ITL
Bordges	Joseph S.	37	Salinas	CA	Dutro	Josephine	31	Salinas	CA
Bordwell	Fred Albert	27	Alameda	CA	Graves	Georgia	26	Petaluma	CA
Borelli	Matteo	43	Asti	ITL	Benatti	Italia	48	Asti	ITL
Borello	Pietro J.	18	Santa Rosa	ITL	Findley	Ruby F.	17	Santa Rosa	OR
Borges	George Louis	26	Sacramento	CA	Marks	Lena	19	Healdsburg	CA
Borgess	Antone E.	22	Sebastopol	CA	Simoni	Mary	24	Sebastopol	
Borgo	Filippo	30	Melita	ITL	Marmori	Luigia	22	Santa Rosa	ITL
Borgwardt	August	22	Vallejo	CA	Stevenson	Grace	18	Vallejo	CA
Bork	Julius	22	Petaluma Twp.	GER	Kopken	Sophia	22	Petaluma Twp.	GER
Borland	Lee				Dempsey	Maggie M.			
Borlini	Augustine	40	Petaluma	SWT	Pozzi	Valeria	21	San Francisco	SWT
Borman	Noel	29	Presidio, San Francisco	KY	Ullman	Edna	21	San Francisco	CA
Bormolini	Louis	35	Novato	ITL	Pedroli	Antonietta	28	San Rafael	ITL
Borri	Lodovico Vincenzo	23	Healdsburg	ITL	Yancey	Ruby V.	15	Healdsburg	CA
Borserini	Zeno	40	San Francisco	ITL	de Cungi	Lina	20	San Francisco	ITL

Groom					Bride				
Surname	**Given Name**	**Age**	**Residence**	**BP**	**Surname**	**Given Name**	**Age**	**Residence**	**BP**
Bortone	Michel	39	Petaluma	ITL	LeCam	Marie C.	43	San Rafael	FRN
Borziny	Bob	22	San Rafael	ITL	Milano	Teresa	21	San Rafael	CA
Bosch	Arnold	30	Windsor	SWT	Huffman	Myrtle	23	Windsor	CA
Boschetti	Centuria	25	Fulton	ITL	Furia	Cisara	18	Fulton	ITL
Boschke?	George W.	26	Merced	MA	Smith	Carrie M.	23	Santa Rosa	CA
Bose	John Edward	31	San Francisco	CA	McAlpin	Edith S.	35	San Francisco	CA
Boss	George W.	24	Martinez	CA	Hale	Laura I.	18	Healdsburg	CA
Bostwick	N. W.				Looney	Addie			
Boswell	Ernest J.	26	San Francisco	CA	Nelson	Rose B.	19	Healdsburg	CA
Boswell	F. C.	32	Fresno	MI	Kerrn	Ella R.	23	Fresno	KS
Boswell	William L.	22	Sebastopol	CA	Earl	Deta	19	Sebastopol	CA
Bosworth	Bernard P.	39	Chicago	VT	Gabriel	Hazel	32	Seattle	CA
Bosworth	Fred E.	25	Geyserville	CA	Gibson	Margaret E.	22	Healdsburg	CA
Bottomley	Thomas H.	25	Oakland	MN	Shaw	May Francis	28	Oakland	CND
Boudin	Lucien Victor	33	San Francisco	CA	Assenti	Lillian F.	22	San Francisco	CA
Bouhaben	Emil H.	21	Oakland	CA	Frary	Adele M.	18	Oakland	CA
Bouk	Alva Roy	38	Santa Rosa	CND	Kircke	Amelia Anna	29	Santa Rosa	CA
Boulden	Frederick N.	29	Escondido	ENG	Weymouth	Mae Z.	23	Escondido	WA
Bound	Joseph	66	Butte City	OH	Picknell	Catharini M., Mrs.	37	Butte City	CND
Bouneau	Louis	30	Petaluma		Whitaker	Lottie N.	24	Petaluma	
Bourbeau	Joseph	26	Santa Rosa	CND	Bisordi	Emilia	21	Sebastopol	CA
Bousse (?)	Daniel				Burrus	Mary C.			
Bovett	George Harold	22	Healdsburg	CA	Adams	Gladys Eleanor	23	Healdsburg	CO
Bowbeer	Benjamin F.	22	Penngrove	CND	Overton	Mary A.	18	Penngrove	CA
Bowbeer	C. W.	24	Vallejo Twp.	CND	Beeson	Anna	22	Vallejo	AUT
Bowbeer	Earl V.	25	Oakland	CA	Hall	Mabel G.	20	Penngrove	CA
Bowden	Isaac	42	Petaluma		Delaney	Elizabeth A.	32	Petaluma	
Bowden	J. W.	40	Santa Rosa	PA	Peterson	Ellen J.	17	Santa Rosa	CA
Bowden	John Wesley	63	Santa Rosa	PA	Lansdale	Mary Elizabeth	48	Santa Rosa	IL

Groom					Bride				
Surname	**Given Name**	**Age**	**Residence**	**BP**	**Surname**	**Given Name**	**Age**	**Residence**	**BP**
Bowen	Arthur R.	37	Navarro	AUT	Hartley	Nellie Frances	23	Boonville	CA
Bowen	John Thomas	40	Santa Rosa	ENG	Irving	Martha	32	Santa Rosa	SCT
Bowen	Lorenzo H.	38	Ukiah	NJ	King	Getrude	39	Ukiah	CA
Bowen	R. Hunt	32	Ukiah	NJ	Starr	Vera L.	23	Ukiah	MI
Bower	Bertram H.	23	Santa Rosa	CA	McDaniel	Olive L.	23	Santa Rosa	CA
Bower	G. N.	30	Myrtle Point, OR	CA	Lockwood	Beulah M.	25	Santa Rosa	OR
Bower	George A.	22	Sebastopol	IA	Churchman	Hattie L.	20	Cazadero	CA
Bower	J. Elmer	29	Santa Rosa	CA	McCausland	Amy	30	Santa Rosa	CA
Bower	William G.	30	Sebastopol	NY	Meyer	Marguerite	20	Sebastopol	CA
Bower (?)	Daniel	29	Santa Rosa Twp.	PA	Hammett (?)	Martha	18	Vallejo	CA
Bowers	Colon R.	24	Davis	MI	Shreve	Guineviere L.	21	Calistoga	CA
Bowers	Edward B.	21	San Francisco	CA	Rowe	Elizabeth A.	20	Cloverdale	CA
Bowers	George	50	Stockton	NY	Case	Susie A.	45	Santa Rosa	CA
Bowers	Henry P.	25	Fulton	IA	Jacobs	Stella M.	19	Healdsburg	CA
Bowers	Herbert Andrews	18	Preston	Sfo	Green	Hazel	17	Preston	CA
Bowers	Joseph Ellsworth	55	Santa Rosa	IL	Kindler	Amelia L.	45	Santa Rosa	LA
Bowers	Oliver Clyde	24	Butte, Silver Bow Co., MT	NE	DeLong	Nellie Alice	21	Santa Rosa	MT
Bowker	William C.	49	Oakland	IL	Hanley	Sophie E.	46	Oakland	CA
Bowles	Frank Herbert	26	Petaluma	CA	Fowler	Ada Rosella	27	Santa Rosa	CA
Bowman	James C.	36	San Francisco	CA	Aced	Pilar S.	38	San Francisco	FRN
Bowman	Thomas Franklin	33	Santa Rosa	CA	Nunley	Isabelle	29	Oakland	TX
Bowman	Walter	21	Petaluma	ID	Shader	Florence	16	Petaluma	CA
Bowman	William Frederick	64	Petaluma	MA	Miller	Louise Sunderhouse	54	Petaluma	SWT
Bowmer (?)	William	40	Mendocino Twp.	KY	Pool	Abby, Mrs.	29	Russian River Twp.	MO
Boyce	F. O.	25	Santa Rosa	CA	Seawell	Bessie	20	Santa Rosa	CA
Boyd	Alfred Hillis	30	Sebastopol	CA	Powers	Marguerite	24	Sebastopol	CA
Boyd	B. C.	35	Healdsburg	TN	Wilfley	Rhoda A.	31	Healdsburg	TN

Groom					Bride				
Surname	Given Name	Age	Residence	BP	Surname	Given Name	Age	Residence	BP
Boyd	Bennie C.	24	Guerneville	CA	Shoemake	Ella	17	Santa Rosa	CA
Boyd	Dan	33	Santa Rosa	CA	Haas	Bertha M.	32	Santa Rosa	CA
Boyd	Elmer	21	Santa Rosa	Solano Co.	Newbert	Byrdie Geneva	19	Healdsburg	Yuba Co.
Boyd	George	26	Santa Rosa	IRL	Lewis	Lucy	19	Santa Rosa	CA
Boyd	Henry	39	San Francisco	CA	Ryan	Minnie	25	San Francisco	CA
Boyd	Hugh Coleman	23	Santa Rosa	MT	Dunham	Essie	24	Santa Rosa	IA
Boyd	James K., Jr.	23	Santa Rosa	OR	Francisco	Mabel Grace	21	Santa Rosa	WI
Boyd	John	35	Oakland	SCT	Macdonald	Helen Gertrude	20	Petaluma	CA
Boyd	John David	49	Annapolis	CA	Nobles	Adeline May	17	Point Arena	CA
Boyd	Leon G.	24	Santa Rosa	OR	Hinman	Mae	19	Forest Grove, OR	OR
Boyd	Noah M.	37	Oroville	MO	Lubas	Marie J.	26	El Verano	FRN
Boyd	Sloan	30	Kenwood	IRL	Mayfield	Gussie B.	25	Santa Rosa	CA
Boyd	William M.	31	Santa Rosa	GA	Poff	Ella E.	24	Santa Rosa	CA
Boyer	Ernest D.	47	San Francisco	FRN	Lambert	Elise Mary	30	San Francisco	FRN
Boyer	Henry W.	26	Santa Rosa	CA	Harmon	Maggie	17	Santa Rosa	CA
Boyer	Otis J.	24	Vallejo	IL	Storey	Frieda G.	24	Healdsburg	CA
Boyer	Sidney Roswell	51	Geyserville	PA	Eproson	Addie	42	Geyserville	CA
Boyse	Clarence	36	Santa Rosa	OR	Venon	Nora G.	32	Sonoma	OR
Boysen	Charley M.	23	Petaluma	CA	Wells	Grace Eva	20	Petaluma	CA
Boysen	Fred B.	29	San Francisco	CA	Petersen	Annie M.	24	Orland	MI
Boysen	William Henry	20	Petaluma	CA	Wyrick	Blanche Christina	18	Petaluma	CA
Boysen	William Henry	23	San Francisco	CA	Krusick	Eva Angelina	19	San Francisco	CA
Boysen	Clarence Constant	22	Petaluma	CA	Boyes	Lola M.	21	Santa Rosa	CA
Boyson	Simon C.	26	Alameda	GER	Henrickson	Alma I.	19	Petaluma	CA
Brackett	J. B.	21	Mesa Grande	CA	Gedney	Della	22	Mesa Grande	CA
Brackett	Jack H.				Gregory	Joanna			
Brackett	Raymond Gregory	21	Santa Rosa	CA	Gater	Lillian Edith	22	Geyserville	CA
Bradbury	Edward A.	37	Santa Rosa	KS	McMillan	Leonora	35	Santa Rosa	ENG

Groom					Bride				
Surname	Given Name	Age	Residence	BP	Surname	Given Name	Age	Residence	BP
Bradbury	Halta	21	Healdsburg	KS	Piatt	Lela M.	21	Healdsburg	IL
Braden	Charley	33	Geyserville	CA	Pittman	Ada, Mrs.	36	Geyserville	CA
Bradford	Branch Johnson	37	Cloverdale		Badell	Ellen M.	18+	Cloverdale	
Bradford	Christopher W.	26	Sherwood	CA	Fowler	Irene F.	24	Santa Rosa	CA
Bradford	Clifford G.	47	San Rafael	ENG	Kirwan	Nellie E.	38	San Rafael	CA
Bradford	D. J.	27	Healdsburg	IL	Varney	Helen	19	Healdsburg	CA
Bradford	Elbert	29	Healdsburg	IL	Baker	Harriet F.	18	Healdsburg	CA
Bradford	Frank	21	Sacramento	CA	Neil	Francis E.	18	Ukiah	CA
Bradford	George W.	56	Upper Lake	NJ	Adams	Sarah M., Mrs.	52	Upper Lake	MO
Bradford	Robert A.	25	Healdsburg	IL	Robertson	Fannie F.	19	Healdsburg	OR
Bradlee	Adelbert S.	22	Santa Rosa	CA	Ball	Addie L.	18	Santa Rosa	CA
Bradlee	Arthur S.	35	Santa Rosa	CA	Lukas	Emma M.	21	Santa Rosa	CA
Bradlee	Arthur S.	20	Santa Rosa	CA	Wiseman	Edna O.	25	Melita	MO
Bradlee	Arthur Seawell	30	Santa Rosa	CA	Montgomery	Rose Bagley, Mrs.	23	Santa Rosa	CA
Bradley	A. F.	46	Marin Co.		Bradley	Lydia F.	36	Petaluma	
Bradley	Byron B.	29	Salem, OR	NY	Mangis	Lola E.	17	Santa Rosa	KS
Bradley	Henry L.	23	Santa Rosa	PA	Ely	Sarah E.	22	Santa Rosa	MN
Bradley	Hugh	37	Santa Rosa	IRL	Navins	Mary	27	Santa Rosa	IRL
Bradley	William A.	52	Keeler, CA	NY	Smith	Gertrude R.	29	Alameda	CA
Brady	C. H.	30	Santa Rosa	MI	Ross	Mary M.	21	Santa Rosa	CA
Brady	Howard	27	Petaluma	CA	Mason	Violet Belle	23	Petaluma	KS
Brady	Jerry F.	28	Santa Rosa	CA	Thompson	Josie M.	23	Santa Rosa	CA
Brady	Thomas M.	19	Santa Rosa	CA	Streeter	Emma I.	16	Healdsburg	CA
Brady	Thomas M.	28	Santa Rosa	CA	Nobles	Pearl E.	16	Santa Rosa	CA
Brady	William Franklin	25	Petaluma	CA	Mastrup	Anna Sophia	20	Petaluma	CA
Braga	Joe F.	30	Sebastopol	SMI	Dutra	Margarida P.	19	Sebastopol	AZR
Braga	John	28	Petaluma	ITL	Dambrogia	Mary	18	Petaluma	SWT
Braga	Peter	27	Bodega	ITL	Piezzi	Mary	20	Bodega	ITL
Brain	Herbert Roy	24	Oakland	CA	Dillian	Lillian Pearl	19	Oakland	CA

Groom					Bride				
Surname	**Given Name**	**Age**	**Residence**	**BP**	**Surname**	**Given Name**	**Age**	**Residence**	**BP**
Brain	Walter Earl	25	Plantation	CA	O'Loughlin	Leah Hester	24	Duncans Mills	CA
Brain	William H.	31	Green Valley	CA	McFarland	Amelia	24	Fulton	CA
Brain	William H.	25	Green Valley	CA	Burgess	Jennie	18	Forestville	MI
Brainard	W. H.	22	Oakland	PA	Bush	Ella M.	23	Sonoma	IL
Brammer	Jochim F.	34	Santa Rosa	GER	Greens (?)	Florence (?)	19	Santa Rosa Twp.	CA
Brand	Fenton M.	31	Chico	MI	Bingham	Olga R.	26	Glen Ellen	CA
Brand	Philip Edward	26	Glen Ellen	IN	Delahanty	May Frances	23	Santa Rosa	CA
Brand	William H.	32	San Francisco	TX	Lyons	Helen	25	San Francisco	Sfo
Brandis	William G.	34	Forestville	MO	Shortridge	Ethel Mae	22	Pocket Canyon	CA
Brandt	August	30	Healdsburg	GER	Starck	Bertha	35 ?	Healdsburg	GER
Brandt	August J.	27	Healdsburg	WI	Mazzucchi	Theresa E.	17	Healdsburg	ITL
Branelenberg	Heinrich	26	San Francisco	GER	Hasche	Emma M.	30	Los Angeles	IL
Branern	William F.	30	Healdsburg	CA	Nelson	Irine Mae	27	Healdsburg	CA
Branigan	Charles Floyd	27	Plantation	TX	Anderson	Frieda Cecelia	23	Stewarts Point	CA
Brannan	G. Clark	38	Petaluma	IL	Krug	Anna Agnes	28	San Francisco	CA
Brannum	Casswell	54	Healdsburg	TN	Priak	Mary Jane, Mrs.	40	Healdsburg	CA
Brannum	Caswell	58	Healdsburg	TN	Linebarger	Marinda, Mrs.	43	Napa	CA
Brannum	Leonard B.	35	San Jose	CA	Scott	Ethel A.	20	Los Gatos	CA
Branson	John	24	Petaluma	DNK	Jacobsen	Dorthea	21	Petaluma	DNK
Branstetter	Charles H.	21	Loomis, Placer Co.	CA	Crow	Charlie Eveline	18	San Francisco	CA
Brantley	Robert L.	64	Napa	KY	Silva	Martha	56	Napa	ENG
Brassill	James Frederic	22	Cloverdale	WI	Kneller	Emilie Florence	18	Cloverdale	CA
Brattain	Arthur Lane	46	San Francisco	OR	Davis	Edell	29	Oakland	VA
Braugher	Oscar H.	28	Sacramento	PA	Sutherland	Ella C.	28	Santa Rosa	CA
Bray	Elisha Jessie	26			Stevens	Louisa June	14	Santa Rosa Twp.	
Bray	Elyah C.	32	Sonoma	MO	Urhr	Chlara M.	26	Sebastopol	
Bray	Frank Jerome	29	Santa Rosa	CA	Aldridge	Crystal G.	16	Santa Rosa	MN
Bray	Lester F.	27	San Francisco	CA	Jones	Emma M.	25	Alameda	PA
Bray	William	46	Santa Rosa	OH	Hartman	Hattie	37	Santa Rosa	NV

Groom					Bride				
Surname	**Given Name**	**Age**	**Residence**	**BP**	**Surname**	**Given Name**	**Age**	**Residence**	**BP**
Brayer	Geo. H.	32	Petaluma Twp.	NY	Nunes	Mary L.	19	Petaluma Twp.	CA
Brayman	Willard V.	28	San Jose	CA	Horstmann	Ethel B.	21	San Jose	CA
Brayton	Leon Conway	23	Willits	CA	Lewis	Mildred Marie	19	Occidental	CA
Brayton	William H.	30	Santa Rosa	CA	Crane	Grace L.	21	Santa Rosa	CA
Brazil	Anthony	29	Petaluma	AZR	Paula	Maria	17	Petaluma	Soc
Brazil	Manuel M.	43	Santa Rosa	AZR	Matos	Margarete Etelvena	22	Vine Hill	CA
Breaks	Gent D.	24	Sebastopol	NE	Bryan	Iva May	22	Sebastopol	MI
Breeding	Charles	25	Petaluma	KY	Brune	Anna	19	Petaluma	KS
Breen	John M.	49	Cotati	IRL	Bohen	Josie	47	Cotati	GER
Bregal	Manuel S.	21	Petaluma Twp.	AZR	Jason	Julia	18	Petaluma Twp.	CA
Breiling	Alfred F.	28	Healdsburg	CA	Muller	Louise	18	Healdsburg	CA
Breitenbach	Louis	35	Santa Rosa	NY	Fick	Annie S.	25	Santa Rosa	NY
Brendel	Fred W.	28	Santa Rosa		Doran	Mamie J.	19	Santa Rosa	
Brewer	Clyde Clinton	38	Ukiah	OH	Kendall	Thelma	21	Ukiah	CA
Brewer	Frank F.	26	Sacramento	IA	Rossi	Louise	17	Sacramento	Sac
Brians	Benjamin	25	Occidental	CA	Bones	Hattie	21	Occidental	CA
Brians	Daniel Boone	19	Guerneville		Pippin	Josie A.	18	Guerneville	
Brians	James Cameron	25	Guerneville	CA	Smith	Carrie May	17	Guerneville	CA
Brians	John F.	24	Occidental	CA	Craig	Henrietta	21	Penngrove	CA
Briard	George H.	39	Bodega		Gsobo (?)	Elizabeth	36	Bodega	
Brichetto	Edmund J.	22	San Francisco	CA	Cassoni	Josephine B.	20	Santa Rosa	CA
Brick	Joseph V.	19	San Rafael	AUS	Hawkins	Evalyn	16	Sebastopol	CA
Bridges	Ira T.	21	Cloverdale	IL	Haberman	Gertrude	22	Dry Creek	CA
Bridges	Isaac Newton	43	Cloverdale	IL	Wright	Grace Anna	27	Cloverdale	NY
Bridgford	Chester Allen	26	San Francisco	CA	Petray	Laura May	26	Healdsburg	CA
Briganti	Angelo	25	Healdsburg	ITL	Lei/Sei	Norina	19	Healdsburg	ITL
Briggs	Albert D.	29	Winters	CA	Thompson	Ione G.	26	Winters	OH
Briggs	C. A.				Walker	E. L., Mrs.			
Briggs	E. C.	23	Petaluma	RI	Suhling	Sophie	18	Petaluma	CA

Groom					Bride				
Surname	Given Name	Age	Residence	BP	Surname	Given Name	Age	Residence	BP
Briggs	Edgar W.	25	Healdsburg	CA	Jones	Beulah M.	25	Healdsburg	CA
Briggs	Ezra	22	Sebastopol	NY	Hall	Carrie E.	18	Santa Rosa	IA
Briggs	George S.	22	Sebastopol		Thrift	Laura	20	Santa Rosa	
Briggs	Hanley	21	Sebastopol	ENG	Mapes	Leora	19	Santa Rosa	CA
Briggs	James M.	31	Healdsburg	CA	Keller	Annie	21	Healdsburg	CA
Briggs	Lawrence E.	32	Tracy	CA	Haynes	Belle	18	Tracy	CA
Briggs	Paul C.	27	Fulton	CA	McClure	Arabelle	25	Fulton	PA
Briggs	Peter C.				Holler	Elizabeth A.			
Briggs	Stiles Harlan	37	Fulton	CA	Denner	Emily Rose	41	Santa Rosa	CA
Briggs	William Edward	23	Oakland	MI	Denning	California	18	Oakland	NE
Briggs	William H.	21	Santa Rosa		Cooper	Sarah Alice		Santa Rosa	
Briggs	William Henry	25	Santa Rosa		Owen	Jennie Mabell	18	Santa Rosa	
Brigham	Edward S.	22	Healdsburg	CA	Sparks	Emma L.	22	Healdsburg	MO
Brigham	George H., Jr.	24	Healdsburg	Ut	McClish	Florence	20	Healdsburg	CA
Brighouse	Thomas H.	30	Healdsburg	NZD	Heald	Henriette E.	26	Healdsburg	CA
Bright	John Farr	33	Berkeley	IN	Jerome	Theresa	29	Berkeley	CA
Brightenstine	Theodore	32	Dry Creek		Sellers	Annie	16	Dry Creek Valley	CA
Brikenstock	Evert F.	29	Santa Rosa	SAF	Hargreaves	Juanita M.	26	Santa Rosa	CA
Brink	Johannes	26	San Francisco	HLD	Norris	Zona E.	19	Santa Rosa	CA
Briseno	Ruben C.	21	San Francisco	CA	Quintero	Annie	21	Santa Rosa	FL
Brittain	Norris	37	Santa Rosa	CA	Mize	Julia	26	Santa Rosa	CA
Brittian	George McAlpine	24	Sebastopol	CA	Boyd	Viola	24	Sebastopol	CA
Brittisigi?	Leo	29	Bloomfield	SWT	Bihli	Eliza	19	Bloomfield	SWT
Britton	Clyde A.	28	San Rafael	WI	Hulbert	Katherine A.	19	Cloverdale	CA
Britton	Leland M.	34	Santa Rosa	CA	Underhill	Allene R.	27	Santa Rosa	CA
Britton	Norris	23	Santa Rosa Twp.		Catron	Nellie	18	Santa Rosa Twp.	
Broaddus	Andrew S.	33	Leavenworth, KS	KS	Ellis	Eva M.	25	Geyserville	CA
Brocco	Emil	23	Santa Rosa	SWT	Frugoli	Virginia	17	Santa Rosa	CA
Brockelman	Ernest A.	30	Santa Rosa	OR	Moxley	Alta R.	24	Santa Rosa	CA
Brockman	Joseph				Brady	Delia			

Groom					Bride				
Surname	**Given Name**	**Age**	**Residence**	**BP**	**Surname**	**Given Name**	**Age**	**Residence**	**BP**
Brockmann	Henry	28	Glen Ellen	GER	Schicoh (?)	Agnes	18	Glen Ellen	CA
Brockmann	Henry M.	24	Santa Rosa	CA	Menow	Virginia L.	21	Santa Rosa	NJ
Brockowsky	Otto R.	35	San Francisco	TX	Stein	Nora L.	32	San Francisco	CA
Broder	Lee S.	31	Vallejo	IA	Nesbitt	Chetanna M.	24	Santa Rosa	PA
Brodersen	Julius Peter	21	Petaluma	GER	Kochuke	Margaret Martha	18	Petaluma	GER
Brodie	Louis F.	33	San Francisco	CA	Belding	Jessica	31	San Francisco	CA
Brody	Sam	24	San Francisco	RUS	Meyer	Doris	23	Santa Rosa	CA
Bromley	Frank A.	20	Santa Rosa	MI	King	May Louisa	17	Santa Rosa	CA
Bronnais	Victor	22	El Verano	NJ	Lafore	Marie	26	San Francisco	FRN
Bronson	Harry R.	40	Oakland	CA	Wight	Ida M.	48	Oakland	IA
Bronson	William M.	29	Suisuin	CA	Tracey	Olive	27	Santa Rosa	CA
Brooke	Robert	28	Portland, OR	ENG	Farmer	Marie G.	25	Portland, OR	OR
Brooker	Frank Russell	36	Windsor		Gordon	Sarah A.	22	Ukiah	
Brooks	Arthur M.	21	Windsor	CA	Freshour	Louise M.	18	Windsor	CA
Brooks	C. E.	29	Santa Rosa	CA	Stites	Katheryn I.	24	Geyserville	CA
Brooks	Charles	19	Healdsburg	CA	Hillbrant	Nellie	15	Healdsburg	CA
Brooks	Charles W.	25	Windsor	CA	Pallady	Bessie	16	Windsor	CA
Brooks	Charles Wesley	35	Windsor	CA	McDonald	Mary E.	23	Sebastopol	CA
Brooks	Cicero C.	21	Fulton	CA	Young	Jennie N.	16	Fulton	CA
Brooks	Elmer E.	35	San Francisco	IA	Yagemann	Henrietta P.	35	San Francisco	MI
Brooks	George	21	Windsor	CA	Miller	Emma	22	Windsor	MO
Brooks	Henry C.	31	Russian River Twp.	CA	Runyon	Mary J.	23	Russian River Twp.	CA
Brooks	Henry W.	21	Windsor	CA	Bidwell	Antonia P.	16	Windsor	CA
Brooks	James	29	Windsor	CA	Miller	Maud	16	Santa Rosa	KS
Brooks	James Monroe	31	Healdsburg	CA	Schalchli	Leona	24	Healdsburg	CA
Brooks	Joseph F.	21	Santa Rosa	NE	Corbett	Hazel M.	20	Santa Rosa	MI
Brooks	Reginald Charles	26	Napa	CA	Cambra	Mary Roseline	26	Napa	CA
Brooks	Silas	43	Knights Valley		Sensebaugh	Rebecca	36	Knights Valley	

Groom					Bride				
Surname	Given Name	Age	Residence	BP	Surname	Given Name	Age	Residence	BP
Brooks	Thomas J.	32	Windsor		Mordon	Emma S.	23	Windsor	
Brooks	Walter	32	Oakland	CA	Richten	Stella	31	Swanton, CA	CA
Brooks	Walter	32	San Francisco	Sfo	McMahon	Gertrude	24	San Francisco	Sfo
Brooks	William H.	32	Petaluma	CA	Zalud	Annie C.	25	San Francisco	IL
Brookshire	Thos. J.				Harris	Margaret A.			
Broomfield	Byrd	22	Santa Rosa	CA	Terry	Annie	19	Santa Rosa	CA
Brosnahan	Terrance F.	25	Fresno	CA	McMahon	Rose	25	Santa Rosa	CA
Brott	Edward S.	42	Santa Rosa	IL	Hockensmith	Mary L.	44	Santa Rosa	PA
Brovelli	Emilio	25	Healdsburg	ITL	Nangeroni	Lettizia	21	Healdsburg	ITL
Brower	Walter J.	24	Sebastopol	CA	Arfsten	Eva M.	20	Sebastopol	CA
Brown	Alenzo Theodore	22	near Windsor		Drake	Mary Emily	18	Windsor	
Brown	Alfred	60	San Francisco	GER	Page	Georgiana	42	Oakland	CND
Brown	Arthur	30	Whitsinsville, MA	MA	Dalton	Edna M.	23	San Francisco	CA
Brown	Arthur	32	San Francisco	WI	Duenwald	Ethyl E.	27	San Francisco	KS
Brown	Ben C.	37	Santa Rosa	IL	Howard	Mary Emma	38	Geyserville	CA
Brown	Benjamin F.	24	Santa Rosa	MN	Price	Carrie Francis Park	24	Santa Rosa	CA
Brown	Carl J.	21	Stockton	CA	Sherwood	Ivah R.	24	Stockton	OR
Brown	Charles				Scott	Betsy, Mrs.			
Brown	Charles A.	30	Santa Rosa	DNK	Wise	A. F., Mrs.	45	Santa Rosa	IN
Brown	Charles A.	33	Santa Rosa		McCarthy	Maggie	30	Santa Rosa	
Brown	Charles Alfred	24	San Francisco	CA	Souza	Anna Clara	17	Petaluma	CA
Brown	Charles D., Jr.	25	Stockton	CA	Sharpe	Geneva L.	23	Stockton	MI
Brown	Charles F.	24	Calistoga	CA	Sherman	Mary M.	34	Calistoga	CND
Brown	Charles W.	25	San Diego	MN	Walds	Jennie	22	Fort Bragg	CA
Brown	Charley	26	Santa Rosa	WV	Maxwell	Ollie V.	15	Santa Rosa	CA
Brown	Chesney E.	22	San Francisco	CA	Elphick	Blanche	20	Penngrove	CA
Brown	Chester B.	30	Fisk's Mill	CA	Von Arx	Emma	23	Fisk's Mill	CA
Brown	Chester B.	23	Salt Point Twp.	CA	Case	Martha J.	18	Salt Point Twp.	CA

Groom					Bride				
Surname	**Given Name**	**Age**	**Residence**	**BP**	**Surname**	**Given Name**	**Age**	**Residence**	**BP**
Brown	E. W.	24	Vallejo	MA	Cannon	Julia V.	21	Santa Rosa	CA
Brown	Earl D.	26	Oakland	CA	Copeland	H. Edith	26	Santa Rosa	AZ
Brown	Edgar Allen	25	Carson City, NV	CA	Vitonsek	Hazel Peryl	25	Healdsburg	CA
Brown	Edward	45	Concord	IL	Martins	Libania Jason	38	Concord	PRT
Brown	Edward A.	21	Petaluma	CA	Lockwood	Cora B.	21	Petaluma	CA
Brown	Edwin Francis	42	Eureka	WI	Downing	Annette Robie	25	Healdsburg	CA
Brown	Frank Cornelius	49	Petaluma	IL	Sugher	Ida	38	Petaluma	FIN
Brown	Frank G.	30	Selby, CA	CND	Wolf	Anna Marie	20	Sebastopol	Sfo
Brown	Frank J.	35	San Francisco	CA	Bartlett	Ella Lillian	25	Healdsburg	CA
Brown	Frank W.	37	Santa Rosa	CA	Switzer	Avis V.	20	Santa Rosa	MO
Brown	Fred H.	22	Windsor	CA	Grove	Blanche	23	Windsor	CA
Brown	George C.	55	Santa Rosa	PA	Kellogg	F. E.	35	Santa Rosa	
Brown	George F.	34	Petaluma	CA	Jensen	Carrie	28	Petaluma	CA
Brown	George G.	26	Guerneville	CA	Coon	Laura	20	Guerneville	CA
Brown	George L.	64	Santa Rosa	IA	Simpson	Edith M.	52	Santa Rosa	OR
Brown	George W.	34	San Francisco	MI	Case	Mary E.	36	San Francisco	IL
Brown	H. H.	26	Willits	OR	Bailey	Ethyl A.	21	Willits	CA
Brown	Henry B.	28	Santa Rosa	CA	Engelund	Marie C.	22	Sonoma	CA
Brown	Henry W.	51	Petaluma	NY	Teters	Dora G.	32	OR	OR
Brown	Horace E.	38	Santa Rosa	MO	Hunkler	Amie L.	25	Santa Rosa	FRN
Brown	Horace Herman	30	San Francisco	CA	Pons	Bertha	34	San Francisco	LA
Brown	J.				Wright	Angeline			
Brown	James A. R.	21	Healdsburg	CA	Smith	Hazel M.	16	Healdsburg	CA
Brown	James R.	30	Willits	CA	Gallaway	Ella May	18	Tomales	AR
Brown	John	32	Petaluma	AZR	Brown	Francis E.	40	Petaluma	AZR
Brown	John	31	Santa Rosa	NRY	Haltman	Gertrude	30	Santa Rosa	SWD
Brown	John				Whallon	Lielia E.			
Brown	John McA.	21	Petaluma	CA	Bullis/Butler?	Mabel Ella	22	Petaluma	CA
Brown	Lawrence Edward	26	Petaluma	IA	Halverson	Alice Ethelyn, Mrs.	29	Petaluma	CA

Groom					Bride				
Surname	Given Name	Age	Residence	BP	Surname	Given Name	Age	Residence	BP
Brown	Leo Allyn	21	Santa Rosa	KS	Drennan	Hazel Estelle	18	Santa Rosa	CA
Brown	Lynn R.	22	Sebastopol	PA	Van Vicel	Pauline	21	Sebastopol	CA
Brown	M. V.				Butler	Clara L.			
Brown	Manuel J.	25	San Francisco	CA	Lockwood	Alice	24	Petaluma	CA
Brown	Marqus	35	Santa Rosa		Laughlin	Eliza Jane	20	Mark West	
Brown	Orson Dana	34	Oakland	CA	Wilson	Rose Hanhart	33	Oakland	LA
Brown	Ralph				Walker	Olive			
Brown	Raymond E.	24	San Francisco	CA	Scott	Laura E.	19	Fulton	WA
Brown	Richard	19	Santa Rosa		Stump	Mary C.	18	Santa Rosa	
Brown	Richard E.	28	Petaluma	CA	Penn	Caroline L.	23	Petaluma	CA
Brown	Robert	60	San Francisco	CND	Dabel	Ida	25	San Francisco	GER
Brown	Robert Curtis	26	Petaluma	Clo	Brown	Lena May	23	Petaluma	CA
Brown	Robert Henry	30	Petaluma	CA	Mooney	Mary Ellen	30	Petaluma	CA
Brown	Rudolph M.	24	Santa Rosa	CA	Moyer	Carrie S.	24	Santa Rosa	PA
Brown	Samuel	57	Petaluma	OH	Scott	Harriett	33	Petaluma	IN
Brown	Thomas Howard	28	Stockton		Williams	Carrie	23	Santa Rosa	
Brown	Thomas J.	39	Portland, OH	OH	Hallahan	Elizabeth	29	Sonoma	CA
Brown	Thomas P.				Ridenhour	Emily			
Brown	Thos.				Congleton	Augusta			
Brown	W. M.	24	Petaluma	Pet	Cox	May M.	21	Petaluma	SCT
Brown	William	34	Alameda	CA	Bartlett	Clara	24	Healdsburg	CA
Brown	William Carl	22	San Francisco	KS	Farbstein	Anna	20	San Francisco	GER
Brown	William E.	49	Santa Rosa	PA	Kline	Lena E.	30	Santa Rosa	CA
Brown	William Herbert	27	Luisberg ?, ID	CA	Potter	Charlotte Isabell	24	Shellville	CA
Brown	William M., Jr.	37	Oakland	IN	Trowbridge	Leslie A.	24	Glen Ellen	NV
Brown	Wilson J.	23	Willits	MT	Olmsted	Helen M.	22	Petaluma	CA
Brown	Wm. M.				Tann	Catharine A.			
Browne	William Frank	35	Sacramento	ENG	Gaige	Alpha Eunice	29	Glen Ellen	KS
Browning	Edmond	26	Santa Rosa	UT	Beard	Jennie	19	Ukiah	CA
Brownscombe	Travis D.	26	Fresno	IA	Thomas	Hazel B.	21	Sonoma	CA

Groom					Bride				
Surname	**Given Name**	**Age**	**Residence**	**BP**	**Surname**	**Given Name**	**Age**	**Residence**	**BP**
Broyles	Fred H.	36	San Francisco	TN	Anderson	Anna M.	21	San Francisco	CA
Brubeck	L. S.	22	Sonoma	CA	DeSart	Florence J.	24	Sonoma	IA
Bruce	Charles L.	34	Geyserville	OH	Campbell	Jennie L.	29	Healdsburg	CA
Bruce	Fred Clarence	25	Santa Rosa	NE	Kennedy	Rosa Belle	16	Santa Rosa	KS
Bruce	Willis L.	25	Santa Rosa	VT	Harris	Louisa J.	32	Santa Rosa	MO
Bruce	William	39	Santa Rosa	ME	Foster	Caroline	37	Santa Rosa	PA
Bruch	Calvin C.	50	Oakland	IN	Stegmuire	Helen V.	29	Oakland	MI
Bruck	Ernest	43	near Yuba City	ENG	Jenny	Sabilla	29	Santa Rosa	SWT
Brucker	Martin	30	Trenton	GER	Samuels	Louisa	16	Santa Rosa	CA
Bruening	Charles	34	Green Valley	GER	Young	Maggie I., Mrs.	34	Green Valley	MA
Bruer	Fred Matthew	23	Windsor	Little Rock, AR	Philpott	Gertrude	19	Windsor	IA
Brugge	George E.	32	Alameda	CA	Maestretti	Dena M.	30	Napa	CA
Bruggy	George H. W.	25	Santa Rosa	CA	Pool	Mamie	19	Windsor	CA
Bruhn	Andrew Peter	23	Petaluma	GER	Bruhn	Mary	20	Petaluma	GER
Bruhn	Nickels	22	Petaluma	GER	Domenighini	Lettie	21	Petaluma	CA
Brum	Manoel S.	32	Reesefield, Adams Co., WA	PRT	Goulart	Maria E.	23	Sebastopol	AZR
Brumbaugh	Raymond	32	Oakland	OH	Pedrotti	Estella Belle	19	Santa Rosa	CA
Brumfield	Chas. A.	30	Healdsburg	CA	Capell	Minnie O.	18	Healdsburg	CA
Brundige	A. L.	29	Santa Rosa	KS	Daffort	Marie	22	Santa Rosa	PA
Bruner	Clement M.	27	Santa Rosa	IA	McWilliams	Edith T.	21	Santa Rosa	MO
Bruner	Herman D.	23	Santa Rosa	CA	Gates	Leonora V.	24	Santa Rosa	CA
Brunh	Ernest Roy	23	Vallejo	NE	Magnani	Paulina Zita	19	Santa Rosa	KS
Brunings	John H.	22	San Jose	CA	Benson	Mabel E.	19	San Jose	CA
Brunings	John H., Jr.	25	Rio Nido	CA	Barnard	Panchita C.	21	Rio Nido	CA
Brunk	Hezakiah				Stevens	I. A., Mrs.			
Brunk	Hugh Dennis	24	Berkeley	KY	Benson	Velma Lee	21	Petaluma	CA
Brunner	Robert	33	Petaluma	GER	Stocker	Dora	23	Petaluma	IA

Groom					Bride				
Surname	**Given Name**	**Age**	**Residence**	**BP**	**Surname**	**Given Name**	**Age**	**Residence**	**BP**
Brunning	John H.	30	San Francisco	CA	Marshall	Effie L.	29	Cloverdale	CA
Bruns	John Henrich Henry	61	Alameda	GER	Semler	Marie Phillipine	52	Alameda	GER
Bruns	Richard F. C.	30	Alameda	CA	Lucas	Edna W.	23	Santa Rosa	CA
Brunskill	Ralph W.	29	Petaluma	IA	Parson	Sarah Elizabeth	16	Petaluma	CA
Brunson	Frank L.	36	Petaluma	IA	Hall	Florence L.	22	Petaluma	CA
Brusa	Carlos	21	Occidental	ITL	Frati	Celia	18	Occidental	ITL
Brusco	Henry D.	31	San Francisco	CA	Erno	Winifred	23	San Francisco	CA
Brush	Charlie W.	22	Cloverdale	CA	Downing	Annie M.	17	Cloverdale	CA
Brush	Daniel	21	Occidental	CA	Franceski	Nellie	19	Occidental	CA
Brush	Frank A.	22	Santa Rosa	IA	Swain	Lena G.	20	Santa Rosa	CA
Brush	Fred W.	23	Cloverdale	CA	Cheeks	Lena A.	20	Cloverdale	DC
Brush	Samuel	23	Occidental	CND	Gobetti	Kate	20	Occidental	ITL
Brush	Wm. T.				Walker	Lucy			
Bryan	Frederick J.	28	Vallejo Twp.	CA	Freeman	Lulu	20	Vallejo Twp.	CA
Bryan	Joseph	32	Petaluma	CA	Sodergren	Hilda	21	Petaluma	SWD
Bryan	Thomas Welsh	43	Petaluma	Vts	Conniff	Mary Ellen	35	Petaluma	Pet
Bryan	William F.	28	Petaluma	CA	Howells	Jessie	28	Petaluma	ENG
Bryan (?)	John Leo	30	Petaluma	CA	Gustafson	Ellen	29	Petaluma	SWD
Bryant	Abner	57	Santa Rosa	VA	Harrington	Hattie A.	34	Santa Rosa	IN
Bryant	Albert James	22	Cloverdale	OR	Treehan	Catherine R.	20	Cloverdale	CA
Bryant	Allen	50	Santa Rosa	NH	Mynatt	Bettie, Mrs.	52	Santa Rosa	USA
Bryant	George E.	29	Cazadero	AUT	Armeau	Elisabeth Anne	23	Cazadero	AUT
Bryant	George Gilbert	25	San Francisco	Hon	Zuur	Gustine Helen	25	San Francisco	HLD
Bryant	Hubert	26	San Francisco	ENG	Dornin	Alice	26	Fulton	Oak
Bryant	Jay	58	Santa Rosa	OH	Sinclair	Elizabeth M.	58	Sebastopol	CA
Bryant	John I.	34	Mendocino Twp.	CA	Pritchett	Elenor E.	17	[illegible]	CA
Bryant	John Kenneth	23	Santa Rosa	IA	Dexter	Alicc B.	24	San Francisco	CA
Bryant	William Henry	29	Healdsburg		Hendricks	Susan E.	23	Mendocino Twp.	
Buchan	James E.	40		NY	Poppe	Catherine	23	Sonoma	Son

Groom					Bride				
Surname	**Given Name**	**Age**	**Residence**	**BP**	**Surname**	**Given Name**	**Age**	**Residence**	**BP**
Buchanan	Frank T.	33	Guerneville	KY	Tomblinson	Myrtle	21	Guerneville	CA
Buchanan	James A.	35	Petaluma	NE	Loosley	Bonnis	18	Petaluma	OR
Buchanan	John A.	36	San Rafael	CA	Nieman	Laura B.	35	San Rafael	OR
Bucher	Conrad	35	San Francisco	NRY	Brien	Laura	24	San Francisco	CA
Buchi	John Henry	75	Santa Rosa	SWT	Schwarting	Dorothe Magarethe	55	Santa Rosa	GER
Buchignani	Rizieri	27	Healdsburg	ITL	Sbragia	Fanny	18	Healdsburg	ITL
Buchignani	Victor	24	Healdsburg	ITL	Georgi	Eva V.	17	Healdsburg	CA
Buck	Charles	29	Bloomfield		Ashley	Louisa R.	31	Bloomfield	
Buckingham	Edwin B.	21	Oakland	CA	Parriott	Lois I.	18	Oakland	CA
Buckingham	T. H.	22	San Francisco	WI	Holmes	Minnie A.	17	San Francisco	NY
Buckle	John	22	Healdsburg	CND	Owen	Mary	21	Healdsburg	OH
Buckley	Dennis	37	San Francisco	CA	Staeubli	Bertha	39	San Francisco	MN
Buckmaster	Rlando	18	Santa Rosa	CA	Fowler	Gladys M.	18	Santa Rosa	CA
Bucknell	Bert Monroe	43	Ukiah	CA	Levreau	Hattie La Dow	34	Ukiah	CA
Bucknell	Roy	22	Upper Lake	CA	Armstrong	Mabel F.	19	Forestville	CA
Buckner	E. L.	42	San Francisco	IN	O' Brien	Ellen	26	San Francisco	IRL
Buckner	Zachariah E.	38	Santa Rosa	GA	Rector	Zerah	29	Santa Rosa	OR
Budde	Frederic/Fritz	26	Santa Rosa		Kohl	Charlotte	29	Santa Rosa	
Buechler	John	43	San Francisco	PA	Parks	Clara Adele	43	San Francisco	CA
Buechler	Lewis	33	San Francisco	Clv	Denehy	Helen	23	San Francisco	CA
Buegge	Harry	23	San Francisco	IA	Wendte	Felicitas E.	18	San Francisco	CA
Buell	Park A.	19	Sebastopol	CA	Moore	Essie B.	21	Watsonville	IA
Buell	Robert	35	Petaluma	NY Cty	Wyatt	Catherine	24	Petaluma	Pet
Buffett	Chas. C.	37	Oakland	NY	McCray	Amanda	26	Cloverdale	MO
Bufford	Lawrence	26	Glen Ellen	CA	Warboys	Irene	19	Kenwood	CA
Bufton	Harvey M.	22	Oakland	IL	Davis	Marion	19	Berkeley	MA
Bufton	William Arthur	28	Alameda	PA	King	Martha Winifred	21	Santa Rosa	CA
Bugbee	Bert	34	Santa Rosa	MI	Von Grafen	Nellie	31	Santa Rosa	

Groom					Bride				
Surname	**Given Name**	**Age**	**Residence**	**BP**	**Surname**	**Given Name**	**Age**	**Residence**	**BP**
Bugbee	Troby E.	22	Santa Rosa	MO	DeBord	Nevada	17	Santa Rosa	CA
Buger	Henry Antes	28	Glen Ellen	CA	Bruning	Natalie Lucile	25	Glen Ellen	CA
Buher	Florentin	25	Petaluma	SWT	Miller	Emma	21	Petaluma	CA
Buhs	Henry F.	26	Oakland	IL	Hall	Emily H.	23	Oakland	CA
Buisson	Eugene	52	Cloverdale	FRN	Richards	Hannah D.	45	Cloverdale	PA
Buleis	Wesley	31	Santa Rosa	KY	Wassman	Ida	18	Santa Rosa	CA
Bullock	Lewis M.	55	Healdsburg	KY	Lambert	Clara V.	54	Healdsburg	VA
Bulotti	Alexio	22	Sonoma	SWT	Bulotti	Mary	23	San Francisco	SWT
Bulotti	Frederick	25	Sonoma	Son	Small	Catherine Norine	20	Sonoma	Son
Bulotti	Lee	22	Sonoma	SWT	Bulotti	Gina	26	San Rafael	SWT
Bumbaugh	Erle Leroy	25	Santa Rosa	CA	Cofer	Lydia May	23	Santa Rosa	CA
Bunch	John B.	23	Santa Rosa	OR	Abshire	Alice	20	Santa Rosa	IL
Bundesen	Karl	33	Petaluma	GER	Kolkmeyer	Freda C.	25	Petaluma	CA
Bundesen	Martin	37	Petaluma	GER	Riewerts	Blanche L.	21	Petaluma	CA
Bundesen	Martin	34	Petaluma	GER	Peterson	Anna	25	Petaluma	GER
Bundesen	Martin	25	Petaluma	GER	Bahr	Sophie	27	Petaluma	GER
Bundesen	William	31	Petaluma	GER	Johnson	Nan	30	San Francisco	SWD
Bundesen	William Frederick	22	Petaluma	CA	Wittkowski	Christine Janette	22	Petaluma	GER
Bundschu	Ralph M.	27	San Francisco	CA	Geary	Jean L.	26	Santa Rosa	CA
Bundy	Pete D.	32	San Francisco	AUS	Liebscher	Lucy B.	31	San Francisco	CA
Bunker	Frank	42	Windling, CA	ME	Kameyer	Josie A.	25	Colusa	CA
Bunney	Alexander, Jr.	34	Grass Valley	CA	Hyde	Cora Lee	38	Santa Rosa	ME
Burbank	David B.	58	Tomales	MA	Burgess	Ella	21	Forestville	MI
Burch	George Alexander	21	Santa Rosa	IL	McGregor	Loella Rea	19	Santa Rosa	CA
Burch	George M.	23	Healdsburg	IA	Chamley	Charlotte E.	18	Healdsburg	AR
Burchard	Karl Sieden	24	Kings City	CA	Thomsen	Alma Erna (?)	19	Lathrop	Lath-rop
Burden	William D.	26	San Francisco	WI	Grainger	S. Margery	24	Healdsburg	MO

Groom					Bride				
Surname	**Given Name**	**Age**	**Residence**	**BP**	**Surname**	**Given Name**	**Age**	**Residence**	**BP**
Burdette	Charles O.	40	Santa Rosa	MA	Chaffee	Maud E.	22	Santa Rosa	CA
Burdick	O. U.	40	Suisun	KS	Pyle	Anna	40	Fall City, NE	NE
Burdick	Fred E.	35	Oakland	MA	Bailey	Emily E.	34	Oakland	CND
Burger	Calvin	20	Santa Rosa	Sar	Van Buren	Stella	17	Santa Rosa	Sar
Burgess	Alauson T.	22	Santa Rosa	CA	Yeager	Susie	20	Santa Rosa	CA
Burgess	Edward Homer	22	Forestville	CA	Silverthorn	Martha Jane	23	Healdsburg	WI
Burgess	James F.	50	Santa Rosa	MO	Peter	Jesserah	36	Santa Rosa	CA
Burgess	Louis L.	31	Sebastopol	CA	Waldorf	Maude, Mrs.	30	Mark West	CA
Burgett	William	22	Healdsburg		Walker	Elizabeth H.	24	Healdsburg	
Burghard	G. F.	36	Freestone	GER	Valenzuela	Mary	30	Freestone	CA
Burghardt	Frank A.	27	Oakland	MI	Hollenbeck	Nella E.	19	Los Angeles	OH
Burginger	John Frank	26	Santa Rosa	MN	Weeks	Laura Jane	24	Santa Rosa	CA
Burk	John C.	26	Occidental		Osbam	Susan A.	17	Occidental	
Burke	Abner L.	26	Calistoga	IL	Mangis	Nora E.	22	Calistoga	IL
Burke	Benjamin L.	21	Santa Rosa	CA	Cotrell	Minnie E.	21	Santa Rosa	KS
Burke	Claude E.	21	Santa Rosa	CA	McCappin	Ruth Olive	15	Santa Rosa	CA
Burke	Edmund J.	36	Eureka	MA	Drake	Edith Martha	26	Eureka	CA
Burke	James G.	27	Santa Rosa	CA	Stump	Margaret A.	18	Santa Rosa	CA
Burke	John H.	31	Guerneville	NJ	Johnston	Jennie M.	43	Cazadero	CND
Burke	Joseph	62	Guerneville	NJ	Williams	Etta C., Mrs.	34	San Francisco	CA
Burke	Leo A.	30	Los Angeles	PA	Forster	Lulu L.	34	Springfield, IL	IL
Burke	Nevel Ross	68	Richmond	MO	Shriver	Martha Ann	65	Santa Rosa	CA
Burke	Sylvester	25	Burke	CA	Christie	Mabel F.	18	Burke	CA
Burke	Walter A.	41	Guerneville	NJ	Burke	Lillian M.	21	Guerneville	CA
Burke	Walter A.	25	Guerneville	NJ	Burne	Mary A.	25	Guerneville	NJ
Burling	Geo. W.	27	Petaluma	NJ	Holland	Bella	18	Petaluma	CA
Burling	William B.	37	Glen Ellen	CA	Blake	Minerva	26	San Francisco	CA
Burlingam	Raleigh W.	37	San Francisco	SD	Cornelius	Elizabeth L.	26	San Francisco	NY
Burlingame	Claude	22	San Francisco	IA	Appleton	Carrie S.	18	Sonoma	CA
Burmann	Adolf	38	Santa Rosa	GER	Schultz	Marie	30	Santa Rosa	GER

Groom					Bride				
Surname	**Given Name**	**Age**	**Residence**	**BP**	**Surname**	**Given Name**	**Age**	**Residence**	**BP**
Burmeister	Charles H.	21	Santa Rosa	CA	Stevens	Intha May	16	Santa Rosa	CA
Burmester	Charles F. D.	34	Petaluma	GER	Benedetti	Amalia Rosa	30	Petaluma	SWT
Burnett	A. J.	52	Sebastopol	TN	World	Dolley	20	Sebastopol	IA
Burnett	Horace Malcohm	28	Los Angeles	KY	Roessle	Stella W.	28	Santa Rosa	PA
Burnett	Thomas B.	28	Cloverdale	OR	Cook	Jennie	19	Cloverdale	PA
Burnett	William	30	Davisville, Yolo Co.	CA	Reid	Alice	29	Santa Rosa	CA
Burnham	A. E., Jr.	38	Healdsburg	UT	Smith	Annie E.	21	Geyservllie	CA
Burnham	Leslie J.	35	San Francisco	IA	Clayman	Margaret McI.	30		IL
Burns	E. F.	27	Alameda	CA	Donahue	May	23	Shellville	CA
Burns	Eugene	22	Bloomfield	CA	Clairy (?)	Anna	22	Bloomfield	IRL
Burns	Eugene L.	22	Sebastopol	CA	Snow	Edna N.	18	Sebastopol	CA
Burns	Harry David	60	Cloverdale	MO	Gill	Jennie, Mrs.	50	Santa Rosa	MO
Burns	James F.	25	Sebastopol	CA	Cereghino	Nellie D.	19	Sebastopol	CA
Burns	Jas.	28	Tomales	IRL	Hendren	Lizzie	28	Santa Rosa	IRL
Burns	John M.	36	San Jose	OH	Macomber	Pearl A.	22	San Jose	CA
Burns	John T.	23	Alameda	CA	Donahue	Georgia	19	Sonoma	CA
Burns	Robert A.	23	San Francisco	CA	Dollar	Mary E.	20	Trenton	CA
Burns	Robt. W.	26	Freestone	CA	McGah	Mary E.	22	Bodega	CA
Burr	Robert L.	24	Los Angeles	CA	Lawrence	Mabel M.	21	St Louis	PA
Burrel	Wesley Jay	40	Santa Clara	CA	Sparks	Mattie Belle	24	Healdsburg	MO
Burrier	Edgar V.	26	San Francisco	MD	Cambra	Mae A.	23	Santa Rosa	CA
Burris	Luther W.	28	Santa Rosa	CA	Mathews	Laura	21	Santa Rosa	CA
Burris	Shirley David	22	Santa Rosa	CA	Espey	Evelyn Blanche	20	Santa Rosa	CA
Burroughs	David	22	Sebastopol	CA	Solomon	Hattie C.	21	Sebastopol	CA
Burroughs	John	21	Sebastopol	CA	Hayden	Eva	22	Sebastopol	CA
Burrows	Robt. K.				Hubbard	Nancy K.			
Burs	Henry S.	40	Los Angeles	PA	Leland	Maude	30	Los Angeles	CA
Burt	Charles Arthur	45	Santa Rosa	NY	Prince	Helen M.	42	Santa Rosa	CA
Burt	Roy J.	20	Santa Rosa	MN	Badger	Blanche	17	Santa Rosa	CA

Groom					Bride				
Surname	**Given Name**	**Age**	**Residence**	**BP**	**Surname**	**Given Name**	**Age**	**Residence**	**BP**
Burtchaell	George C.	21	Oakland	CA	Ward	Henrietta	19	Oakland	CA
Burtchall	Walter L.	22	Oakland	CA	Marvin	Evalyne Lottie	22	Glen Ellen	CA
Burtner	Jesse H.	33	Petaluma	CA	Armbruster	Marie W.	25	Petaluma	CA
Burtnett	Charles Gordon	25	Lake Co.		Nutter	Josephine Hattie	16	Healdsburg	
Burton	Francis A.	29	Vallejo Twp.	CA	Overton	Martha Jane Mildred	21	Vallejo Twp.	AL
Burton	George M.	48	San Francisco	OH	Ponyferrie	Madeline	30	San Francisco	FRN
Burton	George Walter	24	Petaluma	CA	Marango	Verlie Elden	17	Petaluma	CA
Burton	John C.	26	Oakland	OH	Smith	Elva Sirena	28	Oakland	CA
Burton	Oliver F.	23	Petaluma	CA	Duncan	Susan A.	18	Petaluma	CA
Bury	John F.	36	Sebastopol	WI	Burroughs	Edith A.	28	Portland, OR	CA
Bury	Joseph L.	31	San Francisco	CA	Pasage	Clare	22	San Francisco	FRN
Bury	William G.	37	San Francisco	CA	Goyheneix	Helen M.	31	San Francisco	CA
Bush	Eli F.	25	Healdsburg	IL	Cullum	Alice M.	21	Healdsburg	KY
Bush	Giles H.	22	Healdsburg	IL	Ruffner (?)	Anna	22	Healdsburg	MO
Bush	Joe	29	San Francisco	NE	Calestini	Freida E.	24	San Francisco	CA
Bush	Joe	59	Santa Rosa	GER	Heiss	Henrietta	54	Santa Rosa	GER
Bush	William H.	78	Boyes Springs	NY	Phippen	Mary A.	61	Boyes Springs	WI
Bush	William Herbert	22	Healdsburg	CA	Hunt	Pearl	20	Healdsburg	MO
Bush	William P.	21	Healdsburg	MN	Sholes	Pearl J.	21	Cloverdale	
Busher	Walter H.	21	Dixon	OH	Gage	Iva L.	24	Novato	MI
Bushnell	Edwin R.				Smith	M.			
Bushnell	John D.	50	Vine Hill	NY	Norton	Bessie, Mrs.	50	Vine Hill	MA
Bushnell	John D.	24	Sebastopol		Scales	Anna	18	near Santa Rosa	
Bussman	Frank	26	Santa Rosa	Sar	Edgewood	Margaret	24	Sebastopol	IRL
Bussman	Frederick	30	Santa Rosa	CA	Fehrensen	Susie Elizabeth	23	Santa Rosa	CA
Bussman	Peter William	22	Santa Rosa	CA	Camp	Eva D.	21	Santa Rosa	IA
Bussman	William G.	20	Fulton	CA	Gibson	Nona M.	19	Santa Rosa	IL
Butchen	W. P.	30	Santa Rosa	MO	Small	Nettie V.	25	Santa Rosa	CA
Butcher	Albert W.	30	Vacaville	CA	Morrison	Junietta	23	Santa Rosa	CA

Groom					Bride				
Surname	Given Name	Age	Residence	BP	Surname	Given Name	Age	Residence	BP
Butcher	Charles Walter	21	Windsor	CA	Zweifel	Lulu Rosa	20	Windsor	CA
Butenop	Wilhelm	37	Fitchburg, Alameda Co.	GER	Ehlers	Margaretta	37	Geyserville	GER
Butin	Charles J.	24	Santa Rosa	IA	Schaumberg	Emma J.	20	Santa Rosa Twp.	CA
Butler	A. B.	30	Fresno	AL	Middleton	Tilly	24	Santa Rosa	
Butler	A. M.	40	Santa Rosa	IL	Cox	Anna	abt 40	Santa Rosa	
Butler	Carl Guy	21	Petrified Forest, Sonoma Co.	CA	Remer	Frances Effie	20	Petaluma	KS
Butler	Carl Guy	26	Santa Rosa	CA	Smith	Ruth Evelyn	19	Healdsburg	OR
Butler	Charles H.	23	Healdsburg	WI	Miller	Mary E.	23	Healdsburg	CA
Butler	Clyde A.	21	Placerville	CA	Gregson	Juanita C.	17	Santa Rosa	CA
Butler	Edmund J.	38	San Francisco	CA	O'Sullivan	Josephine	26	San Francisco	CA
Butler	Edward H.	25	Placerville	CA	Burns	Margaret	24	Petaluma	CA
Butler	H. G.	26	Myrtle Point, OR	AUT	Taylor	Vivian	26	Santa Rosa	CA
Butler	Harry Alfred	29	Cazadero	OR	Rodgers	Mary Ann	36	Cazadero	CND
Butler	James T.	24	Santa Rosa	CA	Murphy	Helen E.	22	Santa Rosa	CA
Butler	Jesse L.	21	Santa Rosa	CA	Schultz	Bertha	18	Santa Rosa	UT
Butler	John Samuel	23	Mark West		Durham	Elizabeth	23	Mark West	
Butler	John Walter	22	Bellevue	CA	Tullar	Diadama Helen	22	Bellevue	Olema
Butler	Osmand W.	20	Forestville	CA	Robertson	Myrtle	18	Sebastopol	CA
Butler	Samuel Reed	26	Calistoga	CA	Luebberke	Clara F.	24	Windsor	MO
Butler	Thomas B.	36	Toledo, Benton Co., OR	TN	Wilson	Susan Emily	36	Santa Rosa	IL
Butler	Thomas B.	35	Mark West Creek		Gregsen	Eliza J.	21+	Green Valley	
Butler	Thomas I.	22	San Francisco	CA	Page	Yuma L.	19	San Francisco	AZ
Butler	Vernon Miller	21	Healdsburg	CA	Boyd	Dorothy Juanita	16	Petaluma	CA
Butler	Willie	21	Santa Rosa	IIon	De Bolt	Kate	21	Santa Rosa	IA
Butler	Wm. M.	24	Healdsburg	WI	Hooten	Lillian	18	Healdsburg	CA
Butt	George A.	20	San Jose	ENG	Ball	Mary M.	20	Santa Rosa	CA

Groom					Bride				
Surname	Given Name	Age	Residence	BP	Surname	Given Name	Age	Residence	BP
Butterworth	Thomas C.	40	San Francisco	CA	Davis	Margaret L.	29	San Francisco	CA
Buttler	Wilmer	22	Santa Rosa	CA	Smith	Georgia C.	18	Santa Rosa	CA
Buttner	Joseph F.	30	Guerneville	CA	Pickrell	Cordie M.	18	Cazadero	CA
Button	Eugene R.	48	Santa Rosa	MI	Mendenhall	Florence	36	Santa Rosa	IA
Button	Floyd Walter	22	San Francisco	MI	Kenworthy	Vera	20	Kenwood	CA
Button	H. H.	21	Santa Rosa	CA	Pool	Eva A.	21	Santa Rosa	UT
Button	Horace H.	35	Santa Rosa	CA	Patteson	Adeline G.	32	Alexander Valley	CA
Button	Ray E.	32	Sonoma	OH	Baker	Julia J.	31	Petaluma	NE
Butts	Alfred	22	Healdsburg	CA	Martin	Nellie	19	Healdsburg	CA
Butts	Charles M.	19	Fulton	CA	Greening	Emma R.	19	Fulton	CA
Butts	Claude	22	Santa Rosa	CA	Jackson	Lula	18	Modesto	CA
Butts	Raymond L.	22	Vallejo	CA	Hillhouse	Elsie	19	Sebastopol	IA
Butts	Robert Samuel	28	Santa Rosa	CA	Thompson	Irene Ethel	25	Santa Rosa	CA
Butts	Thomas J.	35	Santa Rosa	MO	Dean	Jeannie	25	Santa Rosa	MD
Butts	Thomas Jefferson	22	Fulton		Robinson	Amoret Malinda	18+	Blucher Valley	
Buxton	Ernest Edward	21	Healdsburg	AR	Derrick	Lulu Maude	22	Healdsburg	CA
Buxton	Natt	26	Peabody, MA	MA	Smith	Camilla G.	23	Santa Rosa	SC
Buzzell	Albert A.	40	Freestone		Philbrooks	Lucinda	27	near Freestone	
Buzzi	Joseph L.	28	Santa Rosa	CA	Bertossi	Josie	28	Santa Rosa	ITL
Byce	Gideon A.	26	Petaluma	CND	Scott	Evaline	21	Petaluma	CA
Byce	L. C.	35	Petaluma	CND	Gray	Lily C.	21	Petaluma	ENG
Byce	Malcolm Lyman	22	Petaluma	CA	Coggeshall	Catherine	23	Petaluma	OR
Byerly	Frank F.	33	Stockton	TN	Warner	Mary E.	26	Petaluma	CA
Byers	Judson A.	48	Santa Rosa	IL	Ryan	Clara A.	36	Santa Rosa	MN
Byers	Thomas Homer	25	Healdsburg	TN	Loe	Dorothy E.	22	Healdsburg	MO
Byers	William A.	30	Healdsburg	IN	Mitchell	Emma E.	29	Healdsburg	CA
Byington	Charles T.	24	Healdsburg	CA	Ryan	Kate C.	24	Healdsburg	CA
Byle	Joseph H.	33	San Francisco	WI	Samuelsen	Elizabeth Marie	20	Petaluma	CA
Byrd	J. L.	22	Eureka	NE	Russ	Dora J.	17	Santa Rosa Twp.	MO

Groom					Bride				
Surname	Given Name	Age	Residence	BP	Surname	Given Name	Age	Residence	BP
Byrn	George M.	21	Windsor	CA	Pohley	Adelaide C.	19	Windsor	CA
Byrne	James	34	Salt Point Twp.		Johnsen	Nellie M.	17	Petaluma	
Byrne	Malachy L.	61	Santa Rosa	IRL	Hibbitts	Amelia Francis	46	Santa Rosa	MA
Byrne	Marshal H.	27	Windsor		Skaggs	Emma L.	16+	Russian River Twp.	
Byrne	William W.	40	San Francisco	CND	Jelinski	Mary	38	Elmhurst	CA
Byron	Chester	25	Cloverdale	CA	Hale	Mabel	25	Cloverdale	CA
Cabarrubia	Frank	21	Redding	CA	Watts	May	20	Vacaville	MO
Cabeceira	Henry J.	21	Petaluma	MA	Schlicker	Ida Bertha	19	Petaluma	CA
Cabeleira	Antonio Silveira	30	Petaluma	PRT	Nunes	Lucy	18	Petaluma	CA
Cabral	Fernando	22	Santa Rosa	PRT	Gomez	Agnes R.	22	Santa Rosa	CA
Cadd	Edwin	25	Healdsburg	CA	Galloway	Charlotte	28	Healdsburg	TN
Cadd	Thomas	21	Santa Rosa	Sab	Enzenauer	Annie	18	Healdsburg	MO
Cade	H. C.	32	San Francisco		Smith	May E., Mrs.	30	San Francisco	
Cader	Israel	30	Petaluma	RUS	Lehman	Lilian H.	20	Petaluma	CA
Cadra (?)	Emil C.	23	Del Monte	SWT	Patten	Mary	19	Dry Creek	CA
Cahill	James Felix	22	Santa Rosa	MI	Wescoatt	Alice Clare	19	Santa Rosa	CA
Cahill	James Morden	36	Santa Rosa	NY	McCann	Eva Theresa	21	Mark West Springs	AUT
Cailleaud	Henry, Jr.	29	San Francisco	FRN	Gaye	Adele	27	Sebastopol	CA
Cain	Walter	22	Santa Rosa	CA	Hahn	Lena	18	Santa Rosa	MO
Cake	Charles M.	22	Healdsburg	MO	Williams	Stella Price	20	Healdsburg	CA
Cake	Luther B.	21	Geyserville	CA	Parrott	Elsie E.	20	Geyserville	CA
Calanchini	Emil Phillip	25	San Francisco	CA	Filippini	Louise Elvezia	23	Petaluma	CA
Calder	Alexander E.	22	Watsonville		Spotswood	Mary Jane	21	Petaluma	
Calderwood	Ambrose	24	Santa Rosa	CA	Waterman	Tempy	24	Santa Rosa	MO
Calderwood	Henry E.	39	Sonoma	ME	Neil	Bell	26	Sonoma	MN
Caldwell	Edward J.	38	San Francisco	MT	Shearer	Rena	26	Santa Rosa	CA
Caldwell	J. G.	28	Santa Susana, CA	CA	Bidwell	Freda M.	19	Healdsburg	CA

Groom					Bride				
Surname	**Given Name**	**Age**	**Residence**	**BP**	**Surname**	**Given Name**	**Age**	**Residence**	**BP**
Caldwell	John Charles	25	Oakland		Seely	Martha	26	Santa Rosa	
Caldwell	Samuel T.	27	Cloverdale	MO	Patteson	Mollie D.	20	Healdsburg	Soc
Caldwell	William Beatty	26	Cloverdale	CA	Oman	Genevieve Ida	26	Cloverdale	CA
Cale (?)	Theodore Webster	23	Oakland	MA	Partridge	Marion	23	Petaluma	CA
Calhoun	J. W.				Henderson	S. M.			
Calkins	Charles F.	34	Oakland	IL	Hawks	Hazel R.	24	Oakland	IL
Call	Clyde C.	27	San Jose	CA	Medland	Florence F.	22	San Francisco	CA
Call	George B.	27	Forestville	CA	Banfield	Ida F.	24	Forestville	CA
Callahan	Walter H.	24	Santa Rosa	CA	Beckner	Lillian E.	21	Santa Rosa	CA
Callahan	William Daniel	22	Sebastopol	NV	Finnell	Lurena Hulse	18	Sebastopol	CA
Callahan	William H.	38	Santa Rosa	CA	Reinhart	Mary J.	27	Santa Rosa	OH
Callen	S. H.	21	Williams	IA	Bell	Carrie V.	20	Cloverdale	IA
Callenberg	Hugo, Jr.	25	San Francisco	HLD	Russell	Cora	23	Santa Rosa	CA
Calliman	William G.	47	San Francisco	CA	Lahne	Gerda H.	33	San Francisco	GER
Calzascia	Emilio	40	Bodega	SWT	Pellascio	Minnie	27	Valley Ford	CA
Camarda	Joe	26	Santa Rosa	ITL	Orlando	Rosa	18	Santa Rosa	ITL
Cambra	Manuel F.	28	Santa Rosa	CA	Foyd	Lucy	24	Santa Rosa	CA
Camenzind	Lewis	31	Mt. Eden, CA	SWT	Yori/Jori	Mary	27	Santa Rosa	SWT
Camerlo	James A.	30	Healdsburg	ITL	Anderson	Myrtle	20	Healdsburg	CA
Camero	Nathan	60	San Francisco	VT	Lovejoy	Mary M.	50	San Francisco	NY
Cameron	Alan F.	27	San Francisco	WI	Mills	Blanche B.	23	Oakland	CA
Cameron	Charles Edwin	40	Oakland	CA	Enlow	Ada	30	Oakland	CA
Cameron	Charles L.	28	Oakland	IL	Lyttaker	Martha M.	24	Santa Rosa	CA
Cameron	Donald B.	26	Santa Rosa	CA	Morris	Marie L.	23	Windsor	IA
Cameron	Donald C.	35	Fulton	SCT	Meacham	Elvira F.	28	Fulton	CA
Cameron	Fred J.	21	Santa Rosa	CA	Barnhardt	Minnie	22	Santa Rosa	IA
Cameron	George H.	30	Fresno	NSC	Watson	Mamie	31	Fresno	PA
Cameron	Henry I.	64	Middletown	OH	Squires	Ella, Mrs.	45	Petaluma	IA
Cameron	John Willard	29	Healdsburg	OH	Cladden	Mary Ella	29	Healdsburg	IL
Cameron	Russell L.	24	Cloverdale	CA	Murphy	Jennie	18	Cloverdale	CA

Groom					Bride				
Surname	Given Name	Age	Residence	BP	Surname	Given Name	Age	Residence	BP
Cameron	Wallace A.	25	Windsor	CA	Welch	Lois L.	23	Windsor	CA
Camotta	Joe	29	Valley Ford	ITL	Donati	Annie	20	Bodega	CA
Camotta	Laurence	32	Valley Ford	ITL	Bartoli	Edith	18	Santa Rosa	Sfo
Camozzi	Walter C.	26	Bodega	CA	Deal	Dorothy May	18	Santa Rosa	CA
Campaglia	Domenick	28	Santa Rosa	ITL	Roux	Anna G.	19	Cloverdale	CA
Campana	Joe	47	Petaluma	ITL	Pozzi	Rosalia	50	Petaluma	SWT
Campbell	Alexander	29	Oakland	SCT	Joachim	Bessie	21	Healdsburg	IL
Campbell	Arthur B.	41	Healdsburg	CA	Tully	Alice J.	39	Healdsburg	CA
Campbell	B. F.	40	Sonoma	IA	Smith	Essie E.	32	Sonoma	CA
Campbell	Boyd	32	Berkeley	PA	Martin	Mabel S.	24	Sacramento	ENG
Campbell	C. I.	25	Altruria	IL	Van Winkle	Lola	22	Altruria	CA
Campbell	David L.	32	Lakeport	NE	Richardson	Mabel A.	24	Petaluma	IA
Campbell	Frank	21+	Sonoma		Smith	Mary	20	Sonoma	
Campbell	Geo. S.	27	Windsor		Adams	Allie	18	Windsor	
Campbell	George	41	Oakland	CND	Campbell	Alice	44	Oakland	CA
Campbell	Harold George	22	Santa Rosa	WI	Orr	Marguerite Ellen	17	Sebastopol	CA
Campbell	Ira Samuel	24	Santa Rosa	CA	Baird	Leona Lovel	18	San Francisco	CA
Campbell	J. Otto	21	Santa Rosa	OR	Denham	Ada B.	21	Santa Rosa	OK
Campbell	James J.	26	San Francisco	CA	Michaels	Mae A.	21	San Francisco	IRL
Campbell	R. E.	24	Healdsburg	IL	Ruffins (?)	Jessie	24	Healdsburg	MO
Campbell	Walter	26	Cloverdale	PEI	Jordan	Amy	18	Cloverdale	KS
Campbell	Walter G.	24	Healdsburg	IL	Barth	Susie A.	21	Healdsburg	CA
Campbell	William A.	52	Petaluma	CND	Eakin	Mary E.	50	Petaluma	CND
Campbell	William A.	24	Petaluma	Sar	Crickett	Lizzie	21	Petaluma	OR
Campbell	William E.	23	Santa Rosa	Lak	Rubly	Clara E.	16	Santa Rosa	PA
Campbell	Wm.				Ayers	Martha J.			
Campi	Lorenzo	28	Duncans Mills	ITL	Roncalli	Annie	21	Duncans Mills	ITL
Campigli	Albert E.	28	Cloverdale	CA	Mack	Florine	24	Petaluma	CT
Campigli	Albert E.	24	Petaluma	CA	Steele	Effie M.	22	Petaluma	MI

Groom					Bride				
Surname	**Given Name**	**Age**	**Residence**	**BP**	**Surname**	**Given Name**	**Age**	**Residence**	**BP**
Campigli	Frank Charles	26	Reclamation, Sonoma Co.	CA	Koster	Anna D.	23	Chileno Valley	CA
Campion	George W.	30	Santa Rosa	CA	Wallis	Lena, Mrs.	26	Santa Rosa	CA
Campion	James	29	Santa Rosa	MA	Cunningham	Lillie A., Mrs.	27	Santa Rosa	IA
Campion	Thomas	28	Santa Rosa	MA	Samuels	Jennie	16	Santa Rosa	CA
Campion	Thomas	65	Santa Rosa	IRL	Harris	Eunice Caroline	49	Santa Rosa	WI
Campodonica	Adolpho P.	27	San Francisco	CA	Pancrazi	Josephine Florence	18	Glen Ellen	CA
Camron	John T.	19	Petaluma	CA	Morton	Carrie	19	Petaluma	Sac
Canada	Alonzo M.	25	Oakland	PUR	Josephs	Emily H.	19	Oakland	MA
Canello	Henry G.	23			Howell	Margaret Lent	15	San Francisco	
Canepa	Ben	31	Petaluma	SWT	Tunzi	Lily B.	24	Petaluma	CA
Canessa	Attilo	31	San Francisco	ITL	Paladini	Amelia	28	San Francisco	ITL
Canevara	Don A.	25	Santa Rosa	CA	Cooper	Minnie L.	25	Santa Rosa	TX
Canevari	Adolph	30	Santa Rosa	ITL	Scaroni	Romilda	28	Santa Rosa	SWT
Canevari	John J.	25	Vallejo	CA	Spooncer	Letha P.	22	Santa Rosa	CA
Canevascini	S. J.	36	Petaluma	SWT	McFarland	Margaret	33	Petaluma	CND
Canfield	Albert				Baker	Matilda			
Cannell	Fletcher	25	Santa Rosa	IOM	Smalley	Jessie	23	Santa Rosa	CA
Canney	Edward Phillip	39	San Francisco	CA	Shane	Mary Gertrude	36	San Francisco	OH
Cannon	Calvin W.	22	Petaluma	CA	Jensen	Mary	17	Petaluma	IA
Cannon	Chester G.	19	Penngrove	CA	Marsh	Dora E.	20	Santa Rosa	CA
Cannon	Earl	20	Penngrove	CA	Cook	Illiene	18	Santa Rosa	CA
Cannon	James P.	30	Bloomfield	OR	Cocknill (?)	Ida J.	30	Bloomfield	MO
Cannon	Jerome				Gist	Meda	17	Petaluma	
Cannon	L. L.	30	Bloomfield	OR	Clark	Nettie	18	Vallejo Twp.	CA
Cannon	Louis	20	Penngrove	CA	Ducker	Mary	26	Petaluma	CA
Cannon	R. D.	23	Santa Rosa	CA	Bishop	May M.	21	Santa Rosa	CA
Canobbio	Ferdinando	30	Sonoma	ITL	Toroni (?)	Edith	19	Sonoma	CA
Canobbio	Serafino	25	Sonoma	ITL	Bacigalupi	Lena	18	Agua Caliente	CA

Groom					Bride				
Surname	**Given Name**	**Age**	**Residence**	**BP**	**Surname**	**Given Name**	**Age**	**Residence**	**BP**
Cantel	Eugene	48	Petaluma	NY	Fritsch	Mary Ealie	38	Petaluma	CA
Cantel	Eugene Jean Baptista	26	Petaluma		Graham	Ida	19	Petaluma	
Cantoni	Romeo	37	Sonoma	SWT	Barbarin	Augustine	22	Sonoma	TX
Cantor	Nathan	49	San Francisco	RUS	Bauer	Jennie	35	San Francisco	AUS
Cantrell	Joe W.	26	Healdsburg	Genesee , ID	Steeter	Floretta N.	18	Santa Rosa	CA
Cantwell	William L.	32	San Francisco	CA	Niblett	Metta B.	25	San Francisco	IN
Capell	Chas. W.	24	Healdsburg	CA	Johnson	Elizabeth E.	19	Healdsburg	MO
Capella	James	33	San Francisco	SWT	Nelson	M. M., Mrs.	30	San Francisco	CA
Capella	James C.	27	Petaluma	SWT	Martignoni	Rosa	22	Petaluma	SWT
Capitani	Antonio	48	Reno, NV	ITL	Pedrini	Clementina	28	Reno, NV	ITL
Capitani	Michele	27	San Francisco	ITL	Maroni	Mary	24	Santa Rosa	CA
Capps	John W.	43	Santa Rosa	TX	Holder	Clara M.	42	Santa Rosa	OH
Capps	Lennie C.	22	Santa Rosa	CA	Rubly	Nettie E.	17	Santa Rosa	PA
Capucetti	L. A.	34	Petaluma	SWT	Gianini	Marie	32	Petaluma	SWT
Capucetti	Frank Charles	22	Petaluma	CA	Pedrotti	Beatrice Margaret	23	Santa Rosa	CA
Carah	J. H.	36	San Francisco	NJ	Bavricklow	Emma Alice	26	Santa Rosa	OR
Carden	Arthur G.	22	Seattle	WA	Waugh	Lenna M.	25	Santa Rosa	WV
Carden	William Joseph	22	San Francisco	CA	Newman	Marguerite F.	17	San Francisco	CA
Cardinet	Edward H.	21	San Francisco	CA	Hegler	Myrtlye	18	Santa Rosa	CA
Cardinet	Ernest H.	23	Alameda	CA	Harris	Elva	21	Santa Rosa	CA
Cardoza	John H.	37	Santa Rosa	FRN	Burnett	Leonora	24	Santa Rosa	CA
Cardoza	Joseph S.	32	Petaluma	CA	Cerini	Nora A.	32	Petaluma	CA
Cardoza	Manuel	22	Valley Ford	AZR	Holtslander	Lizzie	22	San Francisco	Chi
Cardoza	Thomas	24	Sebastopol	PRT	Cardoza	Virginia	23	Sebastopol	CA
Cardozo	Joseph S.	24	Petaluma Twp.	AZR	Pereira	Calara	17	Petaluma Twp.	CT
Caretto	Pete	25	Santa Rosa	ITL	Marcucci	Ida	25	Santa Rosa	ITL
Carey	Albert Brock	39	Burke	CND	Somerville	Margaret Rodgers	38	Burke	Dun

Groom					Bride				
Surname	**Given Name**	**Age**	**Residence**	**BP**	**Surname**	**Given Name**	**Age**	**Residence**	**BP**
Carey	Charles Edward	51	Santa Rosa	ME	Patterson	Mattie A.	42	Santa Rosa	IL
Carey	Edward J.	38	Petaluma	CA	Miller	Hattie E.	40	Petaluma	MN
Carey	John	30	Guerneville	IRL	Sabini	Mary	28	Santa Rosa	SWT
Carey	William F.	29	San Francisco	CA	McCarren	Rita H.	22	San Francisco	CA
Cargile	Charles W.	34	Santa Rosa	CA	Kennedy	Rosa M.	19	Santa Rosa	KS
Cargile	James L.	21	Redwood Twp.	CA	Shuler	Blanche R.	16	Windsor	CA
Carico	John W., Dr.	60	Cloverdale	KY	Hill	Effie	30	Cloverdale	CA
Carillo	Frank				Enright	Margaret	15		
Carillo	Joseph	25	Sonoma	Seb	Olbrich	Lou F.	25	Sonoma	IA
Carithers	David N.	54	Santa Rosa	IL	Carithers	Mary E.	50	Santa Rosa	IL
Carithers	William R.	29	Santa Rosa	CA	Ewing	Ida B.	27	Santa Rosa	MO
Carl	William T.	36	Santa Rosa	IL	Higgins	Carnelia, Mrs.	31	Cotati Ranch	DNK
Carleton	Calvin W.	21	Santa Rosa	NV	Dutton	Ada W.	20	Santa Rosa	CA
Carleton	John M.				Stout	Mary Ellen	17		
Carlisle	Herbert L.	42	Oakland	CA	McLaren	Eugenie	36	Oakland	CA
Carlsen	Thorval T.	26	San Francisco	CA	Harrison	Emma Burlington	26	San Francisco	CA
Carlson	Gust	40	Sonoma	SWD	Belin	Agnes	38	Sonoma	WI
Carlton	Thomas				Smith	Sonora			
Carman	Cecil C.	34	Los Angeles	OH	Lamb	Laura B.	28	Santa Rosa	WI
Carman	Harry Vanoy	30	Tracy	CA	Blessing	Josephine	29	Oakland	IL
Carmana	Frederick A.	21	Berkeley	CA	Johnson	Carinne E.	21	Berkeley	CA
Carmody	Chester Arthur	22	Bloomfield	CA	Kennedy	Ruby Gwendoline	18	Freestone	AZ
Carmody	Fred L.	24	Petaluma	CA	Kennedy	Nellie	23	Santa Rosa	AZ
Carmody	Thos. B.	22	Petaluma	IA	Griffin	Annie	19	Petaluma	CT
Carner	Ohmer E.	23	Sebastopol	CA	Roelle	Anna F.	21	Santa Rosa	NE
Carniglia	Charles A.	25	Santa Rosa	CA	Bertoni	Rose I.	23	Fulton	CA
Carothers	John W.	32	San Francisco	IL	Smith	Lillian C.	35	San Francisco	at sea
Carpenter	Charles Thomas	33	Sebastopol	TN	Amstael	Gina Matildos	29	San Francisco	MN

Groom					Bride				
Surname	**Given Name**	**Age**	**Residence**	**BP**	**Surname**	**Given Name**	**Age**	**Residence**	**BP**
Carpenter	Clair W.	25	Petaluma	CA	Trondsen	Ruth	25	Petaluma	NRY
Carpenter	Jay W.	66	Petaluma	NY	Stump (?)	Susie	65	Petaluma	CA
Carpenter	Laurence	25	Petaluma	CA	Northrop	Lenna May	22	Petaluma	CA
Carpenter	Perl R.	28	Anaheim	NE	Williams	Alice L.	18	Santa Rosa	CA
Carpenter	S. E.	26	Petaluma	CA	Monahan	Mamie L.	21	Petaluma	CA
Carr	Arthur C.	35	San Francisco	IA	Kent	Winifred L.	31	San Francisco	ENG
Carr	Charles F.	27	Santa Rosa	IN	Brain	Alice P.	23	Santa Rosa	CA
Carr	Elgin Otto	22	Healdsburg	KS	Nielson	Helen Ione	20	Healdsburg	CA
Carr	George David	25	Santa Rosa	OK	Davis	Alice	28	Santa Rosa	PA
Carr	Mark, Jr.	24	Petaluma	CA	Johnson	Mamie	19	Petaluma	CA
Carr	T. M.	22	Petaluma		Allaway	Sarah E. (?)	18	Oakland	
Carr	William	68	Guerneville	PA	Cole	Beatrice	41	Guerneville	WI
Carrico	Charles E.	30	Santa Rosa	IN	Anderson	Botella	22	Santa Rosa	PUR?
Carrie	Henry C.	28	Cloverdale	Sfo	Taylor	Jennie E.	30	Cloverdale	Por
Carrier (?)	Fred J.	49	Willits	MI	Partlow	Loella M.	36	Willits	CO
Carriger	I. C.	30	Sonoma		Carriger	Emma	19	Sonoma	
Carriger	William W.	33	Sonoma	CA	O'Brien	Katie C.	21	Sonoma	CA
Carrilla	Cassie	28	Santa Rosa	CA	Salies	Annie	19	Santa Rosa	CA
Carrillo	Abraham	27	Santa Rosa	CA	Cook	Lydia M.	16	Santa Rosa	CA
Carrillo	Albert Frank	24	Calistoga		Enright	Margaret	15	Calistoga	
Carrillo	Frank Joseph	20	Sebastopol		Thompson	Mary E.	19+	Santa Rosa	
Carrillo	Manuel	27	Santa Rosa	CA	Meyer	Elizabeth	26	Green Valley	CA
Carrillo	Paul Abraham	34	Vallejo	CA	Carrillo	Jennie Rose	32	Napa	CA
Carrington	Bartine	33	Santa Rosa	CHN	Abeel	Lola Elizabeth	26	Santa Rosa	MO
Carrington	Charles N.	36	Santa Rosa	NJ	Patterson	Clara	24	Santa Rosa	CA
Carrington	George	22	Oakland	CA	Lamer	Annie, Mrs.	22	Oakland	USA
Carrington	Homer Bennett	23	Santa Rosa	CA	Haynie (?)	Annie	19	Santa Rosa	CA
Carrington	Joseph H.	58	Santa Rosa	NJ	Gardner	Sarah Cornelia, Mrs.	56	Woodland	PA
Carrington	Olo Robert	27	Camp Fremont	CA	Taylor	Lela Marjorie	27	San Francisco	TX

Groom					Bride				
Surname	**Given Name**	**Age**	**Residence**	**BP**	**Surname**	**Given Name**	**Age**	**Residence**	**BP**
Carroll	James P.	28	Bloomfield	CA	Carvey	Mary	21	Bloomfield	CA
Carroll	Wm. F.	28	Petaluma	IL	Woodson	Leona Eleanor	20	Bloomfield	CA
Carson	Fred	22	Trenton	CA	Isaacs	Myrtle	18	Windsor	CA
Carstensen	Charlie R.	23	Petaluma	CA	Geils	Elsie May	22	Petaluma	CA
Carston	Godfrey M.	51	San Francisco	SWD	Jacobs	Flora B.	43	San Francisco	NV
Carter	A. E.	20	Santa Rosa	OR	Hitchcock	Lizzie B.	23	Santa Rosa	CA
Carter	Albert	23	Oakland	PA	Marmori	Katie	23	Sonoma	CA
Carter	Andrew Jackson	40	Windsor	CA	Wilson	Mary Mitchell	25	Windsor	CA
Carter	C. Gilbert	25	San Francisco	PA	Brodie	Mabel Gray	22	San Francisco	CA
Carter	Geo. W.				Switzer	A. E.			
Carter	Grant	27	Sebastopol	MN	Snow	Thelma Fay	17	Sebastopol	CA
Carter	Harvey H.	30	Santa Rosa	CA	Rimmer	Mae	33	Los Angeles	CA
Carter	Herbert Eaton	35	San Francisco	CA	Thorne	Grace G.	30	San Francisco	CA
Carter	Lawrence J.	23	San Francisco	CA	Ogilvie	Mable L.	23	San Anselmo	CA
Carter	Oliver C.	39	Bloomington, IN	IN	Cathcart	Mary	23	Bloomington, IN	IN
Carter	Raymond	21	Petaluma	Pet	Holcomb	Daisy	21	Petaluma	CA
Carter	Robert L.	40	San Francisco	IN	Monroe	Dora B.	36	San Francisco	IN
Carter	William A.	23	Petaluma	CA	Murphy	Florence M.	20	Petaluma	CA
Carter	James W.	39	Healdsburg	IN	Peterson	Hettie	26	Healdsburg	CA
Cartwright	Aubrey Badger	28	San Francisco	ENG	Bjornskob	Nicolina Christina	22	Petaluma	CA
Cartwright	Frank	21	Santa Rosa	IA	Englebright	Eva	19	Santa Rosa	IL
Cartwright	George W.	30	Eureka	CA	Hembree	Mattie L.	26	Windsor	CA
Carvalho	J. P.	52	Sebastopol	PRT	Costa	Maria L.	44	Sebastopol	PRT
Carvalho	Joaquin P.	30	Petaluma	PRT	Green	Filomena	17	Sebastopol	CA
Carvalho	Joseph	28	San Francisco	CA	Gardner	Geneveve	26	San Francisco	CA
Carvey	Dennis	25	Bloomfield	CA	Jones	Mabel	20	Bloomfield	CA
Casaday	Fred W.	24	Watsonville	CA	Renshaw	Myrtle M.	24	Santa Rosa	KS
Casarotti	Americo E.	28	Petaluma	SWT	Garzoli	Clara Irene	20	Petaluma	CA
Casassa	Dominic, Jr.	23	Mt. Olivet	CA	Simoncini	Julia	17	Mt. Olivet	IL

Groom					Bride				
Surname	**Given Name**	**Age**	**Residence**	**BP**	**Surname**	**Given Name**	**Age**	**Residence**	**BP**
Casassa	Frank A. J.	21	Santa Rosa	Sfo	Lyttaker	Lenora	18	Santa Rosa	CA
Casassa	Louis	26	Napa	Napa	Adams	Pearl	26	Napa	KS
Casazza	Ricardo	32	Healdsburg	ITL	Ricci	Ottavia	20	Healdsburg	ITL
Cascardozo	Frank	30	Sonoma Co.	WTS	Silva	Laura	16	Sonoma Co.	SWT
Case	Benjamin B.	78	Healdsburg	NY	Nowlin	Margaret A.	78	Healdsburg	NY
Case	Benjamin Bascom	72	Healdsburg	NY	Norton	Philinda	77	Healdsburg	OH
Case	Drury G.	22	Willits	CA	Thompson	May I.	18	Westminster	CA
Case	J. W.				Lockley	Susie			
Case	John Wyatt	19	Santa Rosa		Lockley	Susie E.	19	Santa Rosa	
Case	Wm. E.	50	Santa Rosa	CA	Page	Sarah Jane	47	Santa Rosa	WA
Caseres	Albert H.	37	Freestone	CA	Kricke	Ernestena	19	Cazadero	GER
Caseres	J. O.	28	San Francisco	CA	Williams	Mary R. M.	20	Occidental	CA
Caseri	Arthur	21	Petaluma	CA	Benedetti	Agnes	22	Petaluma	SWT
Caseri	Robert A.	27	Petaluma	CA	Tunzi	Emma M.	20	Crows Landing	CA
Casey	Edward C.				Hunt	Anna L.			
Casey	John	23	Larkspur	CA	Murray	Mary	20	Santa Rosa	CA
Casey	Thurman G.	27	San Francisco	MO	Bord	Dixie O.	21	San Francisco	TX
Cash	O. P.	65	Petaluma	KY	Hopkins	Mary E., Mrs.	53	Petaluma	WI
Casini	Neibo	22	Duncans Mills	ITL	Foresti	Mollie A.	22	Duncans Mills	CA
Cassab	Elias Kalile	33	Santa Rosa	Bey	Englander	Minnie Diana	18	Santa Rosa	CA
Cassel	Wm. F.				Low	Sarah A., Mrs.			
Cassiday	Samuel D.	26	Petaluma	CA	Holland	Helen C.	24	Petaluma	MA
Cassidy	Albert H.	21	Petaluma	CA	Armstrong	Bessie	18	Petaluma	CA
Cassin	Richard J.	64	San Francisco	NY	Bray	Mae	47	San Francisco	IL
Cassine	Frank	26	Santa Rosa	ITL	Barsi	Abbina	18	Santa Rosa	CA
Cassini	Charley	26	Santa Rosa	ITL	Buzzi	Carrie	18	Santa Rosa	CA
Castagnasso	Enrico A.	29	Sonoma	CA	Chelini	Anita Mary	16	Sonoma	CA
Casteel	J. C.	25	Petaluma	KS	Jardelle	Bertha	18	Petaluma	FRN
Castiglio	Louis	33	So. San Francisco	ITL	Baldocchi	Julia C.	23	Windsor	CA

Groom					Bride				
Surname	**Given Name**	**Age**	**Residence**	**BP**	**Surname**	**Given Name**	**Age**	**Residence**	**BP**
Castiglioni	Peter	22	Santa Rosa	ITL	Stroll	Evelyn	19	San Rafael	CA
Castle	Raymond R.	30	Los Banos	IL	Silvia	Louise A.	24	Healdsburg	CA
Castro	Manuel C.	25	Oakland	PRT	Focha	Isabel	18	Sebastopol	CA
Catarina	Antonio	30	San Francisco	SPN	Ananos	Joaquina	21	Oakland	SPN
Catelani	Leonori	27	Melita	ITL	Maccano	Mary	22	Melita	ITL
Catendo	Albert G.	20	Sebastopol	CA	Wright	Elois	18	Santa Rosa	CA
Cathey	C. L.	25	Anderson Valley	MO	Fletcher	E. J., Mrs.	26	San Francisco	NSC
Catlin	D. Willis	30	Glen Ellen	KY	Lewis	Mabel M.	27	Glen Ellen	CA
Catlin	Lovel D.	22	Guerneville	CA	Quigley	Julia M.	17	Guerneville	CA
Cattanep	Louis P.	27	Camp Meeker	ITL	Mazza	Louisa	18	Camp Meeker	ITL
Cauckwell	Isaac Newton	25	Santa Rosa	CA	Weatherington	Myrtle Alberta	24	Santa Rosa	CA
Caughey	Alexander	21	Cloverdale	CA	McMichael	Eula	21	Cloverdale	CA
Caughey	Chester	29	Point Arena	CA	Baxman	Alice	18	Sea View	CA
Caughey	John	34	Bodega		Watson	Mary, Mrs.	26	Valley Ford	
Caughey	Robert	42	Cloverdale	CA	Martin	Millie M.	42	San Francisco	CA
Caulfeild	W. Stafford	40	Tahama Co.	IRL	Neuman	Maggie	44	San Francisco	CND
Caulfield	Daniel Philip	25	Calistoga	MA	Cruson	Minnie	22	Stockton	MT
Cautel	Louis	32	Petaluma	NY	Keller	Fannie	24	San Francisco	CA
Cavagna	Emile	30	San Francisco	SWT	Balemi	Giacomina	22	Santa Rosa	SWT
Cavagna	Joseph	31	Santa Rosa	SWT	Scaroni	Celestina	25	Santa Rosa	SWT
Cavagnaro	Charles V.	29	Cloverdale	CA	Pope	Elizabeth I.	18	Cloverdale	CA
Cavallero	C. L.	22	Santa Rosa	ITL	Solari	Vittoria	17	Santa Rosa	ITL
Cavalli	Antone	23	Petaluma	SWT	Canevascini	Irene	16	Petaluma	SWT
Cavanagh	John Edward	23	Petaluma	CA	Ingram	Nellie	19	Petaluma	CA
Cavanagh	Stephen Patrick	37	Olema	CA	Sutton	Anna Eliza	27	San Francisco	CA
Cavanagh	William	40	San Francisco	CA	Flinn	Frances	30	San Francisco	CA
Cavanaugh	William M.	30	New York City	CT	Overton	Harriet L.	25	Glen Ellen	CA
Cayla	Raymond Marcellin	21	Petaluma	FRN	Asti	Josephine Lucy	17	Santa Rosa	CA
Caylor	John J.	28	Point Arena	TN	Storenetta	Ida M.	26	Point Arena	CA

Groom					Bride				
Surname	**Given Name**	**Age**	**Residence**	**BP**	**Surname**	**Given Name**	**Age**	**Residence**	**BP**
Cecchi	Pietro	40	Forestville	ITL	Bertozzi	Pascuina	42	Forestville	ITL
Cella	Dominick	43	Petaluma	ITL	Paulucci	Celistina	31	Petaluma	ITL
Cellarius	William	40	Oakland	KS	Henry	Ella Etta	33	Oakland	CA
Cepernich	Maxin J.	32	San Francisco	Sebia	Ferris	Helen M.	28	Los Angeles	IN
Cereghino	Nathaniel	30	Sebastopol	CA	Downer	Mae	30	Sebastopol	CA
Cereghino	Tony	30	Glen Ellen	CA	Frideger	Margaret	23	Glen Ellen	CA
Cerini	Henry	28	Seattle	SWT	Cerini	Olga	18	Olema	SWT
Cerini	Isidaro	30	Tomales	SWT	Pancio	Domenica	18	Tomales	ITL
Cerutti	Paul	38	Covelo	ITL	Bettiga	Anna	28	Covelo	ITL
Ceva	Daniele	49	San Francisco	ITL	Sacchaz	Jennie	38	San Francisco	MEX
Chace	Ernest B.	30	Oakland	NE	Buckley	Margaret J.	20	Sebastopol	CA
Chadd	George H.	38	Santa Rosa	CA	McCombs	Nellie D.	21	Santa Rosa	KS
Chadwick	James W.	30	San Francisco	TX	Stevens	Harriet Ann, Mrs.	29	San Francisco	ME
Chaffee	E. S.	24	Fulton	NY	Adams	Lucy K.	20	Fulton	IL
Chaffee	Jarvis	53	Fulton	NY	Greening	Lenna	22	Fulton	CA
Chaffee	Joseph E.	40	Santa Rosa	IRL	Bryant	Margaret J.	40	Santa Rosa	IL
Chaffer	Chester C.	15	Healdsburg	CA	Osborne	Grace M.	15	Healdsburg	KS
Chaffie	Weaver S.	23	Santa Rosa	CA	Buckbee	Violia	20	Santa Rosa	CA
Chahon	Gustave Cecil	21	Willits	CA	Adams	Clara Violet	19	Santa Rosa	OR
Chaix	Emile Adrien	21	Alameda	CA	DeSoto	Dorthey Christa	18	Alameda	CA
Chamberlain	Albert F.	33	Santa Rosa	CA	Young	Corinthia A.	23	Santa Rosa	MO
Chamberlain	Selah	32	San Francisco	OH	McDonald	Edith M.	27	Santa Rosa	NY
Chamberlain	W. Warren G.	31	San Francisco	MD	Hopper	M. Myrtle	28	Santa Rosa	CA
Chamberlain	William H.	27	Fulton	VT	Chaffee	Nellie	23	Fulton	CA
Chambers	Benjamin H.	53	Boyes Springs	CA	Boehm	Ella L.	44	Boyes Springs	CA
Chambers	David M. C.	33	San Francisco	IRL	Moller	Georgine N.	29	San Francisco	GER
Chambers	E. W.	28	Point Arena	CND	Baker	Bertha H.	24	Point Arena	TX
Chambers	Edward C.	30	Cloverdale	PA	Field	Olive B.	22	Cloverdale	
Chambers	Joseph A.	37	Camp Meeker	IL	Smith	Kate C.	44	Camp Meeker	OH

Groom					Bride				
Surname	**Given Name**	**Age**	**Residence**	**BP**	**Surname**	**Given Name**	**Age**	**Residence**	**BP**
Chambers	King	22	Santa Rosa		English	Dora	18+	Santa Rosa	
Chambers	Peter	30	Petaluma	MO	Jones	Mattie	20	Petaluma	CA
Chambers	William D.	26	Guerneville	CND	Bill	Estelle L.	23	Sonoma	CA
Champion	John E.	38	Oakland	CA	Paul	Theresa M.	26	Oakland	AZ
Champion	Stanley W.	26	Altoona, IA	IA	Seavers	Deborah M.	20	Sebastopol	CA
Champlin	Charles V.	35	Sonoma	IL	Agnew	Lizzie	22	Sonoma	CA
Chance	Glenn I.	30	San Francisco	OR	Davis	Anna E.	34	San Francisco	CA
Chandler	Ernest R.	24	Petaluma	CA	Chamberlin	Carrie	21	Petaluma	CA
Chandler	Haven Burwell	22	Franz Valley	CA	Sweetnam	Evelyn Mae	22	Sebastopol	WI
Chandler	Leo F.	22		NE	Lehn	Marguerite	19	Windsor	CA
Chandler	W. R.	25	Santa Rosa Twp.	LA	Curtis	Mary J.	19	Russian River Twp.	CA
Chandler	Joseph	28	Cloverdale	TN	Barnes	Zella	17	Cloverdale	CA
Chaney	John W.	61	Healdsburg	OH	Reardon	Mary J.	57	Healdsburg	OH
Chaney	Vernon E.	25	Healdsburg	CA	Crain	Hazel M.	21	Healdsburg	CA
Chaney	William Henry, Jr.	22	Healdsburg	CA	Vaughan	Jessie A.	21	Geyserville	CA
Chaney	William Levi	33	Windsor	MO	Elkerton	Ida May	20	Windsor	WI
Chanin	Peter	34	Napa Junction	GRC	Crivelli	Lizzie	22	Napa Junction	SWT
Channel	L. M.	57	Oakland	WV	Farquar	Mary I.	60	Glen Ellen	CA
Chapman	Charles M.	23	Santa Rosa	CA	Simpson	Alice C.	23	Santa Rosa	
Chapman	Edwin A.	27	Oakland	Soc	Lunt	Addie R.	26	Oakland	ME
Chapman	Elliot C.	25	Oakland	CA	Peoples	Cora M.	19	Stony Point	CA
Chapman	Frank H.	47	San Francisco	MA	Nielsen	Violet	28	Brigham, UT	UT
Chapman	Guy Lee	23	Santa Rosa	OR	Huckabay	Ferne Elizabeth	21	Santa Rosa	IL
Chapman	H. E.	26	Vallejo Twp.	CA	Ayers	Edith	27	Petaluma	CA
Chapman	Lawrence L.	21	Santa Rosa	NC	Caldweil	Sarah O.	21	Santa Rosa	CA
Chapman	Rockwell Jerome	21	Sonoma	CA	Bailey	Bania ? Mary	20	Sonoma	OH
Chapman	Thomas A.	43	Bakersfield	IRL	Yates	Alice D.	23	Windsor	Soc
Chappell	Alfred U.	20	Alexander Valley	IA	Knight	Rosetta	18	Alexander Valley	WA
Chappell	Emmet	24	Oakland	NE	Tindall	Frankie	18	Talmadge	CA

Groom					Bride				
Surname	**Given Name**	**Age**	**Residence**	**BP**	**Surname**	**Given Name**	**Age**	**Residence**	**BP**
Charles	Elbert R.				Rowlett	Virginia, Mrs.			
Charles	Everett L.	28	Petaluma	CA	Lewis	Mabel E.	19	Preston	CA
Charles	Geo. W.				Richardson	Vernette			
Charles	Isaiah B.	25	Sonoma Co.		Lowry	Jennie	23	Sonoma Co.	
Chartrand	Louis	79	Santa Rosa	CA	Locke	Alice	48	Santa Rosa	CA
Chase	Charles Edwin	58	Glen Ellen	OH	Mathews	Amanda	48	Glen Ellen	IL
Chase	Frank J.	57	Sebastopol	WI	Bryan	Angie	56	Sebastopol	NY
Chase	Gay Henry	27	San Francisco	OR	Ferguson	Laura Virginia	22	San Francisco	CA
Chase	George M.	45	San Francisco	MA	Seipp	Maria S.	32	Sonoma	CA
Chase	John W.	26	Glen Ellen	OR	Hensley	Vina L.	18	Glen Ellen	OR
Chase	Louis Walter	22	Reno, NV	CA	McLain	Marjorie Lewis	17	Sebastopol	IA
Chase	Ralph Noble	22	Berkeley	NE	Wallace	May Etta	18	Santa Ana	IN
Chatard	Philbert	23	San Francisco	CO	Goyheneix	Marie E.	19	San Francisco	CA
Chatburn	Joseph L.	35	Philadelphia	PA	Ralston	Alta	35	Chicago	IL
Chattman	Beverly B.	50	near Glen Ellen	Algiers, LA	Crosby	Mary	19	near Glen Ellen	CA
Chauvet	Henry J.	28	Glen Ellen	CA	Lounibos	Annie	22	Madrona Station	FRN
Checchi	Luigi	24	Mercury	ITL	Ciabbatini	Serafina	22	Mercury	ITL
Check	Elliott E.	28	Berkeley	NC	Cartwright	Mary M.	25		Hon
Chelini	Americo D.	42	El Verano	ITL	Zampa	Dorotea	23	El Verano	ITL
Cheney	Ansel Colby	30	Alameda	CA	Preston	Winifred Wood	20	Santa Rosa	CA
Cheney	Charles	21	Sonoma	CA	Durant	Ella	20	Agua Caliente	NY
Cheney	Edward L.	26	Healdsburg	IL	Martin	Estella M.	22	Downie	KY
Cheney	John L.	39	Cazadero	MO	Cozad	Dora E.	23	Cazadero	CA
Cheney	Thomas W.	35	Bodega	CA	Wall	Florence V.	28	Valley Ford	OH
Chenoweth	A. Roy	24	Sacramento	IA	Hickman	Minnie E.	25	Santa Rosa	IN
Chenoweth	Frank B.	22	Santa Rosa	IN	Miller	Henrietta	20	Santa Rosa	CA
Chenoweth	Hardin Talman	25	Occidental	CA	Barnes	Harriet Florence	22	Graton	CA
Chenoweth	Warren L.	24	Petaluma	TX	Rudolph	Mae	22	Petaluma	CA

Groom					Bride				
Surname	**Given Name**	**Age**	**Residence**	**BP**	**Surname**	**Given Name**	**Age**	**Residence**	**BP**
Cherry	Edwin E.	30	Wendling, Mendocino Co.	IL	Morgan	Marguerite M.	24	Alameda	CA
Cheyney	Earl H.	21	Sebastopol	CA	Williamson	Camella	23	Sebastopol	IA
Chiappero	Domenico	31	Mt. Olivet	ITL	Mancini	Liduina	26	Trenton	ITL
Chiaroni	Daniel	20	Occidental	CA	French	Meta A.	17	Santa Rosa	CA
Chicca	Americo	23	Santa Rosa	ITL	Bernasconi	Della	24	Santa Rosa	SWT
Chick	D. A.	25	Occidental	CA	Brians	Olive May	16	Occidental	CA
Childers	Arnold, Jr.	24	Santa Rosa		Clark	Linnie P.	18	Santa Rosa	
Childers	Dennis Spencer	26	Petaluma	CA	Melehan	Ella Gertrude	25	Petaluma	CA
Childers	Eugene Lester	24	Sonoma	CA	Williams	May E.	19	Sonoma	OR
Childers	George T.	27	San Francisco	CA	Culligan	Petronilla	22	San Francisco	IL
Childers	J. S.	22	Santa Rosa	CA	Bryant	Ida E.	21	Santa Rosa	CA
Childers	William E.	24	Santa Rosa	CA	Forrest	Annie	23	Santa Rosa	ENG
Childs	George B.	25	Cloverdale	CA	Ellis	Carrie E.	18	San Francisco	CA
Chinn	Joseph M.	29	Santa Rosa		Grohs (?)	Jennie	23	Mark West	
Chiotte	Giovanni	29	Santa Rosa	ITL	Reinero	Catterina	17	Santa Rosa	ITL
Chiotti	James	28	Santa Rosa	CA	Vanina	Tilly	21	Santa Rosa	NV
Chisholm	Donald	45	Cloverdale	NSC	Adam	Catherine M.	40	Cloverdale	NSC
Chisholm	William	37	Windsor		Coul (?)	Annie	36	Windsor	
Chisholm	William C.	32	Irvington	NSC	Barnes	Nettie A.	27	Healdsburg	CA
Chittenden	Justin L.	30	Geyserville	CA	Graham	Violia M.	25	Santa Rosa	MN
Chittenden	Louis F.	46	Lima, OH	PA	Hapkal	Mary A.	42	Lyma, OH	GER
Chitwood	James M., Jr.	21	Windsor	CA	Matthews	Jerenia E.	18	Healdsburg	CA
Chitwood	John F.	25	Windsor	CA	Brooks	Mary	22	Windsor	CA
Chitwood	Joseph Andrew	29	Livermore	MO	Chitwood	Anna Eliza	23	Santa Rosa	Soc
Chitwood	Joseph I.	23	Windsor	CA	Runyan	Sarah E.	21	Windsor	CA
Chodrow	Samuel	29	San Francisco	RUS	Ochsenreiter	Helen L.	27	Richmond	SD
Choney	Lawrence	29	Alameda	ITL	Crutchen	Virginia	29	Ukiah	CA
Choquette	Stephen	21	Santa Rosa	MA	Garrison	Ora M.	17	Santa Rosa	CA
Choquette	Stephen A.	21	Petaluma	MA	Brown	Myrtle M.	21	Petaluma	CA

Groom					Bride				
Surname	Given Name	Age	Residence	BP	Surname	Given Name	Age	Residence	BP
Christansen	John	29	San Francisco	GER	Veasne (?)	Anna	21	San Francisco	Sfo
Christensen	Christian	37	Berkeley	DNK	Nicol	Harriet J.	49	Santa Rosa	ENG
Christensen	Clarence	19	Sebastopol	CA	Barnes	Etta	18	Sebastopol	CA
Christensen	Harry Edward	21	San Francisco	CA	Maritzen	Florence Otilla	18	San Francisco	CA
Christensen	Martin Petersen	32	San Francisco	DNK	Larsen	Laura Christina	23	San Francisco	CA
Christensen	Wm. E.	23	San Jose	NE	Noble	Ada	24	Ukiah	CA
Christenson	James Rasmussen	30	Fisherman's Bay	DNK	Cole	Mary Violet	20	Fisherman's Bay	IA
Christian	Charles E.	26	Santa Rosa	CA	Tracey	Amy M.	18	Santa Rosa	CA
Christian	Harry E.	22	Guerneville		Ragan	Mary C.	17	Guerneville	
Christian	Harry Henry	27	Gualala	CA	Hood	Alzina Rose	20	Gualala	CA
Christian	Herman B.	27	Richmond	KY	Fallon	Ruth	21	Richmond	CA
Christiansen	Christian	57	Santa Rosa	GER	Schienmann	Ida	32	Santa Rosa	GER
Christiansen	Walter	28	Petaluma	CA	Whitehead	Florence Estella	20	Santa Rosa	CT
Christie	Frank B.	21	Scribner, Humboldt Co.	ME	Thompson	Kate	16	Windsor	CA
Christie	Wilfred A.	28	Sebastopol	CND	Wilkie	Grace E.	30	Sebastopol	IL
Christiensen	Ernest	26	Marin Co.	GER	Hinricksen	Mary	18	Petaluma	GER
Christoffel	Jacob	62	Petaluma	GER	Kling	Christine	39	Petaluma	GER
Christopher	Irvine T.	33	San Francisco	KY	Masvik	Hanna	35	San Francisco	NRY
Christopher	Jas. C.				Tully	Catharine			
Christy	Henry Alfred	24	Caspar	CA	Campbell	Leonore Francorce (?)	18	Cloverdale	CA
Chrones	Lebertus	34	Oakland	GRC	Silva	Elizabeth	25	Hayward	CA
Chuny ?	J. M.				McHeary ?	Tammy A.			
Church	Charlie				Hare	Lillie			
Church	Claude Leslie	23	Petaluma	CA	Winn	Rosa Clara	19	Petaluma	CO
Church	Douglas				Fowler	Margaret A.			
Church	Jessie Raymond	21	Fresno	Fresno	Shaw	Maude May	20	Healdsburg	NE
Church	John L.	30	Santa Rosa	CA	Evans	Rose	29	Santa Rosa	IL
Church	Royal Ira	20	Petaluma	CA	Linebaugh	Mae Olivia	20	Sebastopol	CA

Groom					Bride				
Surname	**Given Name**	**Age**	**Residence**	**BP**	**Surname**	**Given Name**	**Age**	**Residence**	**BP**
Church	William Thomas	29	Sonoma	CA	Marcucci	Jennie Mary	18	Sonoma	CA
Churchill	H. Harry	36	Santa Rosa	OR	Wright	Emma A.	33	Santa Rosa	CA
Churchill	Jabez F.	26	Santa Rosa	CA	Howell	Elva C.	22	Sebastopol	CA
Churchill	William F.	31	Denver	MO	Huffman	Bessie J.	23	San Jose	CA
Churchman	George				Wilson	Sarah Maria			
Churchman	John W.	26	Green Valley	CA	Thomas	Rachel A.	23	Green Valley	Soc
Churchman	John William	44	Sebastopol	CA	Poe	Ina Alma	33	Sebastopol	CA
Churchman	Schuyler				Wilson	Eliza Ann			
Cia	Domenico	33	Healdsburg	ITL	Guera	Henrietta	23	Healdsburg	ITL
Cia	Silvio	21	Healdsburg	ITL	Giannecchini	Crotilde	17	Fulton	ITL
Ciancio	Charles	21	Ukiah	CA	Brightenstine	Nettie E.	21	Covello	CA
Ciancio	Giuseppe	28	Santa Rosa	ITL	Guidi	Ida	17	Santa Rosa	ITL
Ciavarelli	Nello	23	Fulton	ITL	Bondi	Mary	18	Santa Rosa	ITL
Ciezere	Lavagino	33	San Francisco	ITL	Lavagnino	Mary	21	Petaluma	ITL
Cills	Rudolph F.	27	Berkeley	AUS	Gann	Gladys G.	21	Berkeley	CA
Cinquini	D.	22	Forestville	ITL	Giusti	Eda	17	Green Valley	CA
Cirimele	Angelo	26	San Francisco	ITL	Arnold	Philippina	18	San Francisco	AUS
Civa (?)	Joseph	26	Analy Twp.	PRT	?atorce (?)	Anna	22	Analy Twp.	PRT
Clanton	George	41	Oakland	AL	Haase	Bertha K.	39	San Francisco	WI
Clanton	Samuel B.	22	Woodland	MO	Davies	Florence C.	19	Santa Rosa	CA
Clanton	Thomas D.	70	Santa Rosa	TN	Millsap	Amanda Jane	42	Santa Rosa	MO
Clare	George A.	64	Petaluma	CND	Clough	Julia M.	67	Petaluma	NY
Clark	A. N.	25	Healdsburg	OH	Black	Harriet Isabel	18	Healdsburg	CA
Clark	Albert Earl	24	Berkeley	NE	Skinner	Goldie B.	18	Hanford	IA
Clark	Alfred Churchill	60	Glen Ellen	NY	Amons	Susannah	47	Glen Ellen	CA
Clark	Benjamin Henderson	20	Soda Rock	MO	Brown	Carrie	21	Soda Rock	CA
Clark	Charles A.	39	San Francisco	CND	Ketcham	Agnes Grace	38	San Francisco	CA
Clark	Charles E.	28	Los Angeles	MO	Millington	Anna E.	22	Santa Rosa	CA
Clark	Charles Preston	31	Santa Rosa	CA	Keller	Nevada	18	Santa Rosa	CA

Groom					Bride				
Surname	**Given Name**	**Age**	**Residence**	**BP**	**Surname**	**Given Name**	**Age**	**Residence**	**BP**
Clark	Charles Raymond	26	Middletown	CA	Andrews	Alice May	19	Middletown	CA
Clark	Charles Raymond	32	Middletown	CA	Doughty	Lula Amelia	22	Forestville	OR
Clark	Doane	28	Santa Rosa	VT	Court	Caroline	32	Santa Rosa	MI
Clark	Duval L.	22	Healdsburg	CA	Skinner	Minnie M.	16	Napa	CA
Clark	Edwin Curtis	31	Los Angeles	IL	Hendrickson	Etta Pearl	29	Santa Rosa	CA
Clark	Frank	21	Sebastopol	CA	Wonacott	Esther B.	19	Santa Rosa	MO
Clark	Frank A.	29	Healdsburg	ME	Brown	Georgia A.	24	Hilton	CA
Clark	Fred L.	34	Sonoma	IA	Judkins	Alice M.	26	Lowell, MA	MA
Clark	Geo. C.	23	Vallejo Twp.	CA	Evans	Catherine J.	20	Stony Point	IRL
Clark	Geo. C.	38	Vallejo Twp.	CA	Guill	Elizabeth	24	Penngrove	KS
Clark	George F.	25	Santa Rosa	ME	Talbot	Allena	21	Santa Rosa	CA
Clark	Grant Guildford	31	Penngrove	ENG	Rilf	Marie	32	London, ENG	ENG
Clark	H. O.	23	San Francisco	CA	West	Nellie G.	19	Santa Rosa	CA
Clark	Harry A.	26	Kellogg	IA	Vier	Clara	25	Sebastopol	CA
Clark	Harry H.	24	Reno, NV	KS	Watt	Chrissie L.	22	Austin, NV	NV
Clark	J. W.				Howe	Catharine, Mrs.			
Clark	James E.	35	Mt. Olivet	CA	Denner	Bessie K. (?)	25	Mt. Olivet	CA
Clark	James H. H.	36	Windsor	IL	Michelsen	Agusta	32	Windsor	NRY
Clark	James H. H.	29	Windsor		Copple	Annie	23	Windsor	
Clark	James M.	22	San Francisco		Hill	Nellie	22	San Francisco	
Clark	James R.	32	Petaluma	AUT	Weinreich	Ann, Mrs.	30	Petaluma	NV
Clark	James Wesley	36	Santa Rosa	ME	Marshall	Jennie S.	26	Santa Rosa	IRL
Clark	John Thomas	29	Santa Rosa Twp.	CA	Mallon	Bridget P.	23	Vallejo Twp.	CA
Clark	Joseph B.	27	San Francisco		Cameron	Maggie	25	San Francisco	
Clark	Joseph H.	27	Lakeville	CA	Spotswood	Hattie B.	27	Reclamation, CA	CA
Clark	Leonard P.	19	Santa Rosa	IL	Freshour	Marie A.	16	Santa Rosa	CA
Clark	Leslie D.	31	Fresno	MO	Overton	Laurene	25	Santa Rosa	CA
Clark	Mathew	29	Tomales	CA	Stemple	Henrietta E.	22	Tomales	CA

Groom					Bride				
Surname	**Given Name**	**Age**	**Residence**	**BP**	**Surname**	**Given Name**	**Age**	**Residence**	**BP**
Clark	Richard L.	30	San Francisco	Pierce City, MO	Cummings	Olive	30	Healdsburg	Geyser ville
Clark	Richard R.	21	San Francisco	CA	Pedranti	Estelle V.	20	Santa Rosa	CA
Clark	Robert F.	21	Sausalito	CA	Rima	Estella	19	Santa Rosa	CA
Clark	Samuel Berry	31	Santa Rosa	IL	Franz	Minnie L.	25	Franz Valley	CA
Clark	Stephen D.	39	Forestville	IL	Clark	Jennie B.	25	Red Bluff	CA
Clark	Terrence	28	Bodega		Fitzpatrick	Mary Ann	20	Bodega	
Clark	William D.	21	Sebastopol	CA	Hudspeth	Alice S.	18	Sebastopol	CA
Clark	Willie L.	25	Forestville	CA	Jewett	Emma L.	21	Forestville	CA
Clark	Winfred P.	26	Healdsburg	CA	Duncan	Gemma E.	26	Healdsburg	CA
Clark	Wm. E.	21	Santa Rosa	ME	Thompkins	Carrie	19	Santa Rosa	IA
Clarke	Leslie Albert	19	Santa Rosa	IL	Wright	Ruth Irene	19	Santa Rosa	CA
Clarke	P. F.	36	San Francisco	CA	Stradling	Julia	21	Petaluma	CA
Clary	Clarence H.	30	Healdsburg	KS	Imbler	Elsie	28	Delano	OR
Clary	Dennis G.	56	Santa Rosa	IRL	Mulvehill	Margaret	38	Santa Rosa	MA
Clary	Paul Dennis	26	Santa Rosa	MN	Temple	Christie	26	Santa Rosa	CA
Clary	Thomas Peter	32	Burke	MN	Temple	Rosamond	30	Santa Rosa	CA
Clasby	Michael M.	30	Sausalito	CA	Brush	Jennie M.	20	Occidental	NY
Clasquin	Emil	34	Sonoma	GER	Cames	Justine	35	Sonoma	FRN
Clattenbury	Alexander	50	Santa Rosa	NSC	Robinson	Mary	36	Santa Rosa	GER
Clausen	Dietrich	21	Petaluma	GER	Geertz	Josephine	18	Petaluma	CA
Clawson	Ardent Benjamin	35	Windsor	CA	Murray	Lola	16	Windsor	CA
Clawson	Charles D.	37	Santa Rosa	CA	Reimer	Jessie	25	Santa Rosa	CA
Clawson	Chas.				Kennedy	Mary Jane			
Clawson	Cyrus R.	22	Santa Rosa	CA	Beatty	Maggie	18	Glen Ellen	CA
Clay	E. W.	21	Santa Rosa	CA	Monroe	Lois	18	Santa Rosa	KS
Claypool	Jerry W.	29	Santa Rosa	CA	Dearborn	Mollie Theresa	21	Santa Rosa	CA
Claypool	Stephen B.	32	Santa Rosa	CA	Riddle	Sue Frances	26	Santa Rosa	CA
Clayton	Capius Henry	24	Santa Rosa		Smith	Ann Elizabeth	18	Santa Rosa	

Groom					Bride				
Surname	**Given Name**	**Age**	**Residence**	**BP**	**Surname**	**Given Name**	**Age**	**Residence**	**BP**
Clayton	Howard B.	23	Sebastopol	IA	Seavers	Ida Ruth	23	Sebastopol	NE
Clayton	S. A.	42	Petaluma	VA	Hennigan	Ida J.	24	Petaluma	
Cleary	Edward	34	Alaska	CND	Riley	Mary	24	Petaluma	CA
Cleaveland	H. J.	23	Bolinas	CA	Cordingly	Lila H.	23	Santa Rosa	IA
Cleaveland	Robert Fuller	21	Santa Rosa	KS	Langhlin	Ida, Mrs.	30	Forestville	CA
Cleek	Samuel P.	24	Sebastopol	CA	Snow	Ruby E.	22	Sebastopol	CA
Clegg	Frances L.	38	Santa Rosa	CA	Egli	Emma	46	Santa Rosa	CA
Clement	Jesse Edward	33	Sherwood	CA	McGimsey	Marie M.	26	Sonoma	CA
Clement	Walter L.	22	San Francisco	CA	Branick	Mary P.	18	San Francisco	CA
Clement	Walter L.	27	San Francisco	CA	Weber	Josephine E.	28	San Francisco	KS
Clements	T. H.	28	San Francisco	CA	Dolan	Mary	18	San Francisco	CA
Clements	Edgar J.	27	Sonoma	Fairmede, CND	Porter	Nell W.	28	Santa Rosa	IL
Clementz	Fred A.	25	San Francisco	CA	Wright	Violet E.	22	San Francisco	CA
Clemo	William H.	25	Petaluma	CA	Dahlmann	Eunice F.	23	Petaluma	CA
Clemons	William L.	47	San Francisco	MD	Mulgew	Josephine	27	Healdsburg	CA
Clerici	August	28	San Francisco	ITL	Castagnasso	Annie	18	Sonoma	Son
Clevenger	Thomas P.				Williams	Ellen, Mrs.			
Clewe	William F.	30	Sonoma	CA	Smith	Harriet Porche	24	Santa Rosa	CA
Cliff	Ernest Henry	35	El Verano	GER	Bridges	Pearl May	18	El Verano	OH
Clifford	George Bassett	40	Calistoga	CA	Teale	Grace Louise	21	Calistoga	CA
Clifford	John	43	Forestville	IRL	McSherry	Mary	28	Forestville	IRL
Clifton	Thomas K.	29	Santa Rosa	CA	Clifton	Ollie E.	28	Sacramento	WA
Clinch	Henry W. R.	58	Fresno	IRL	Donahue	Minnie C.	41	Santa Rosa	CA
Cline	Arthur Allen	25	Sebastopol	IA	Gilmore	Minerva Ruth	18	Sebastopol	MI
Cline	Henry C.	34	Santa Rosa	CA	Stewart	Lillian E.	24	Santa Rosa	CA
Cline	Joseph V.	28	San Francisco	CA	Bussman	Annie	24	Santa Rosa	CA
Cline	Thomas J.	28	Petaluma	WI	Nauert	Fredda	28	Petaluma	CA
Clinesmith	Fred	23	Redding	CA	Bowman	Mamie Francis	20	Santa Rosa	ID
Clisbee	Albert	32	Santa Rosa		Carr	Maggie	18+	Santa Rosa	

Groom					Bride				
Surname	Given Name	Age	Residence	BP	Surname	Given Name	Age	Residence	BP
Clokey	Robert				Woods	Elizabeth, Mrs.			
Close	Frank D.	22	Forestville	NE	Athey	Olive M.	18	Healdsburg	CA
Close	William A.	28	Santa Rosa	NE	Ross	Hazel M.	25	Santa Rosa	CA
Clutterbuck	Ernest	27	Penryn	ENG	Hodges	Elizabeth F.	22	Graton	ID
Cluver	Harold H.	23	Petaluma	CA	Evans	Alma M.	23	Petaluma	CA
Cluver	Henry A.	27	Petaluma	CA	Hinkston	Alice	18	Petaluma	CA
Cnopius	Lewis C.	52	Santa Rosa	HLD	Miller	Birdie E.	45	Santa Rosa	NV
Cnopius	Louis Christian	33	Santa Rosa	NTH	Holden	Carrie B.	35		NY
Coakley	Daniel John	38	Scotia	CA	Crowley	Ceclia Catherine	27	Scotia	CA
Coates	Norman Frank	21	San Francisco	CA	Joyce	Theresa Alice	18	San Francisco	CA
Coats	Charles A., Jr.	24	Sebastopol	CA	Williams	Lotta A., Mrs.	23	Sebastopol	CA
Coats	William B.	24	Sebastopol	CA	Kimes	Deeda C.	18	Sebastopol	CA
Cobb		20	Healdsburg		Walker	Elizabeth H.	19	Healdsburg	
Cobb	Clarence Leroy	21	Sebastopol	CA	Wells	Stella Evlin	19	Sebastopol	CA
Cobb	Darwin L.	24	Windsor	WI	Johnson	Emma	17	Sebastopol	UT
Cobb	George G.	31	Petaluma		Reubburt (?)	May	19	Petaluma	
Cobb	George O.	31	Glen Ellen	CA	Haskell	Jessie T.	33	Glen Ellen	UT
Cobb	Omar O.	45	Guerneville	MI	Lauteran	Antoinette M., Mrs.	39	Guerneville	HLD
Cobb	Omar Otto	21	Petaluma	CA	Torliatt	Marie Blanche	19	Petaluma	CA
Cobb	Tony A.	31	Vallejo	MO	Osborn	Elrene	25	Sebastopol	OR
Cobos	Norberto B.	50	NY	ARG	Lynden	Sylvia Vallejo	28	NY	CA
Coburn	Ernest A.	19	Graton	CA	Hodges	Ethel A.	19	Graton	KS
Coburn	James A.	25	Guerneville	CA	Donner	Bettie L.	17	Sebastopol	CA
Coburn	William	21	Guerneville	CA	Bigham	Lula Jane	17	Forestville	CA
Cochran	A. E.	32	Healdsburg	GA	Marshall	Sarah A.	32	Healdsburg	CND
Cochran	Albert Francis	29	Sausalito	CA	Fairman	Ethel Florence	18	Santa Rosa	OR
Cochran	Arthur F.	29	Santa Rosa	IL	Davis	Ina A.	29	Green Valley	CA
Cochran	Arthur Payne	24	Healdsburg	Soc	Coffman	Mary Gertrude	23	Healdsburg	Soc

Groom					Bride				
Surname	**Given Name**	**Age**	**Residence**	**BP**	**Surname**	**Given Name**	**Age**	**Residence**	**BP**
Cochran	Claude T.	22	San Diego	CA	Hays	Grace E.	19	San Diego	CA
Cochran	Horace	25	Santa Rosa	CA	Campion	Nellie	20	Santa Rosa	CA
Cochran	L. P.	25	Petaluma	MO	Herman	Alice B.	19	Petaluma	PA
Cochran	Willis B.	46	Tacoma, WA	PA	Haynes	Zoe E.	39	Ross	CA
Cochrane	John T.	22	San Rafael	NJ	Hanna	Catherine	19	Alameda	CA
Cochrane	Marcus Edward	21	Eureka	MO	Armstrong	Flora A.	20	Petaluma	CA
Cockrill	Obe A.	25	Bloomfield	CA	Pellascio	Vera	22	Valley Ford	CA
Cockrill	Robert L.	31	Santa Rosa	CA	Vogt	Gertrude G.	18	Healdsburg	
Cockrill	Theadore L.				Potter	Frankie			
Cockrill	Travis Lee	36	Ukiah	KY	Armstrong	Ella L.	22	San Francisco	CND
Cockrill	William A.	24	Bloomfield	CA	Colburn	Lulu I.	21	Bloomfield	CA
Cockrill (?)	John L.	35	Eureka, NV	CA	Winzell	Kate A.	35	Eureka, NV	NV
Cockrill (?)	Thomas Jefferson	37	Santa Rosa		Mercer	Simi	34	Santa Rosa	
Codd	David E.	22	Lambert	CA	Derick	Lena M.	19	Lambert	CA
Codding	George C.	27	Petaluma	Soc	Colby	Minnie A.	25	Petaluma	VT
Code	Reginald F.	21	San Francisco	CA	Delfino	Ethel Victorine	18	Tiburon	CA
Codiga	Antonio	35	Tomales	SWT	Donati	Mary	19	Bodega	CA
Codner	Frank E.	44	Parkersburg, IA	IA	King	Evelyn Irene	32	Kansas City, MO	MO
Coe	Fred R.	21	Santa Rosa	KS	Steller	Rossella A.	19	San Francisco	WA
Coe	Geo. W.	42	Santa Rosa	OH	Crawford	Mary, Mrs.	35	Cloverdale	NY
Cofer	Clinton Tice	31	Santa Rosa	CA	Knolty	Dora Edith	22	Sebastopol	MI
Coffee	S. R.	30	San Francisco	MI	Barham	Luda V.	30	Santa Rosa	CA
Coffey	J. H.	33	Santa Rosa	MI	Lemay	A. Ellen	28	Mark West	MO
Coffey	Charles	24	Santa Rosa	CA	Banty	Clara B.	22	Fulton	IA
Coffey	Charles H.	31	Santa Rosa	CA	Scutt	Maggie	22	Santa Rosa	IL
Coffey	Maurice J.	29	San Francisco	MA	Connihan	Julia V.	19	Petaluma Twp.	NV
Coffey	Samuel A.	21	Santa Rosa	CA	Houx	Nellie	21	Cloverdale	CA
Coffey	Wm. M.	28	Santa Rosa	IA	Koutmire	Emma Etta	19	Windsor	OR
Coffman	Charles	42	Healdsburg	OH	Palmer	Georgia M.	34	Santa Rosa	CA
Coffman	James T.	32	Healdsburg	OH	Luce	Jennie D.	27	Healdsburg	CA

Groom					Bride				
Surname	**Given Name**	**Age**	**Residence**	**BP**	**Surname**	**Given Name**	**Age**	**Residence**	**BP**
Coffman	John Isaac	26	Bodega Corners		Stone	Sidney S.	19	Bodega Corners	
Coffman	N. B.	36	Healdsburg	OH	Willson	Anna M.	26	Healdsburg	Hld
Coggin	Clarence A.	29	San Francisco	CA	Muller	Margaret H.	24	San Francisco	CA
Coggins	Andrew H.	31	Sacramento	CA	Welch	Grace M.	26	Petaluma	NY
Coggins	Chas. W.	26	San Francisco	CA	Tripp	Lillian C.	24	San Francisco	RI
Cohen	Harold J.	23	San Francisco	AK	Malcolm	Catherine B.	19	San Francisco	SCT
Cohen	Joel C.	31	San Francisco	NY	Johnson	Laura W.	21	San Francisco	MS
Cohen	Maxwell	24	Santa Rosa	AK	Gantner	Julia	21	Santa Rosa	CA
Cohenour	Joseph Herbert	29	Santa Rosa	IA	Gossage	Belle, Mrs.	28	Santa Rosa	CA
Coke	Joseph Homer	28	Cloverdale	CA	Branson	Minnie	17	Cloverdale	CO
Coker	Charles L.	25	Ukiah	OR	Hugh	Flossie	18	Petaluma	IA
Coker	Wiley	27	Guerneville	MO	German	Susan	16		
Colabella	Carlo	32	Fulton	ITL	DeMeo	Angelina	23	Santa Rosa	ITL
Colbert	William	42	San Francisco	PA	Karl	Florence	29	San Francisco	CA
Colbroth	Harry W.	27	Santa Rosa	CA	Hornbuckle	Molly B.	22	Healdsburg	MO
Colburn	Frank	25	Maxwell, Colusa Co.	CA	Schriver	Ida	18+	Maxwell, Colusa Co.	CND
Colburn	Frank N.	27	Stockton	CA	Button	Jessie R.	30	Santa Rosa	VT
Colburn	Joseph	21	Santa Rosa	CA	Thorogood	Esther	18	Santa Rosa	UT
Colburn	Leroy H.	21	Caspar	CA	Barnes	Alice M.	22	Caspar	CA
Colburn	Lester F.	29	So. San Francisco	CA	Devello	Frances Julia	30	Santa Rosa	CA
Colburn	Orlin F.	29	Valley Ford	IA	Johnson	Nancy L.	19	Bloomfield	OH
Colburn	Orlin Merle	20	Bloomfield	CA	Resendes	Annita Mary	18	Valley Ford	CA
Colburn	Orrin E.	18	Bloomfield	CA	Farrer	Etta Rebecca	19	Bloomfield	UT
Colburn	Rayman C.	23	Bloomfield	CA	Garrison	Laura E.	23	Sebastopol	TX
Colburn	Rufus Paul	28	Tomales	IL	Hardisty	Cora Ethel	17	Santa Rosa	IL
Colby	Alfred Wright	21	Burlingame	IL	Schultz	Marion Georgia	19	Burlingame	NM
Colby	Edwin	27	Oakland	WI	Nowell	Hattie A.	36	Santa Rosa	IN
Coldwell	Edrie Sayor	22	Berkeley	CA	Doyle	Allien Evelyn	18	Fresno	Fresno

Groom					Bride				
Surname	**Given Name**	**Age**	**Residence**	**BP**	**Surname**	**Given Name**	**Age**	**Residence**	**BP**
Cole	Charles B.	22	Healdsburg	TX	Poulson	Addie E.	25	Healdsburg	CA
Cole	Clarence Eugene	32	Redding	NY	Porcher	Marion Louise	25	Petaluma	CA
Cole	Francis M.	22	Calistoga	CA	Luby	Mabel E.	20	Scranton, KS	KS
Cole	Fred Grant	23	Guerneville	OR	Shulte	Grace Evelyn	18	Guerneville	CA
Cole	George E.				Johnson	Dora J.			
Cole	Harold	21	Healdsburg	CA	Talkington	Gladys	20	Healdsburg	CA
Cole	Henry L.	21	Fisherman's Bay	CA	Throop	Emily M.	19	Fisherman's Bay	IN
Cole	Lee	23	Petaluma	MO	Garms	Pauline	22	Petaluma	CA
Cole	Nathaniel J.	40	Pixley	CA	Bauder	May	38	San Lorenzo	MO
Cole	Thomas Hoarse	22	San Francisco	CA	Gartner	Elsie Louise	20	San Francisco	CA
Cole	Vincent Letton	23	Santa Rosa	MO	Hereford	Hattie Elvira	17	Freestone	CA
Cole	W. E.	21	Santa Rosa	OR	Proschold	Hazel	20	Cazadero	CA
Cole	W. E.	27	Santa Rosa	MI	Isaacs	Lillie	19	Portland, OR	OR
Cole	Walter Vernon	30	Santa Rosa	CA	Chio	Emma	20	Healdsburg	CA
Cole	William Lester	33	Guerneville	IA	Livingston	Katherine Rock	27	Toronto, CND	CND
Coleman	Gary	42	Freestone	IRL	Hayes	Anna	37	Freestone	IRL
Coleman	George E.	45	Santa Rosa	WI	Davis	M., Mrs.	39	Santa Rosa	NY
Coleman	John E.	42	Occidental	CA	Lindsey	Margaret Jane	28	Occidental	CA
Colen	Lewis H.	34	San Francisco	CA	Caughey	Corinne Alice	33	San Francisco	IA
Coli	Lorenzo	23	San Francisco	ITL	Dinnucci	Mary	24	Green Valley	NV
Collier	Richard B. H.	21+	San Francisco	CND	Smith	Nellie T.	18+	Santa Rosa	CA
Collier	S. F.	23	Santa Rosa	CA	Chadwick	Belle	23	Sebastopol	MO
Collings	Walter	33	Petaluma Twp.	ENG	Thompson	Lizzie	30	Petaluma	CND
Collins	Charles Albert	42	Independence, Inyo Co.	IL	Shepherd	Medora Alma	31	Independence, Inyo Co.	CA
Collins	Charles F.	21	Valley Ford	CA	Clark	Lizzie	20	Valley Ford	CA
Collins	David R.	50	San Francisco	CND	Pope	Lillie N.	28	San Francisco	CA
Collins	Eldorado	27	Santa Rosa	CA	McCombs	Leanna Jewel	18	Bellevue	NE
Collins	Frederick A.	27	Oakland	ENG	Kaiser	Charlotte S.	21	Oakland	CA

Groom					Bride				
Surname	**Given Name**	**Age**	**Residence**	**BP**	**Surname**	**Given Name**	**Age**	**Residence**	**BP**
Collins	George W.	28	Berthoud, Larimer Co., CO	KS	Alten	Elizabeth	24	Sebastopol	CA
Collins	Howard Benfield	24	Santa Rosa	CA	Peterson	Etta	19	Santa Rosa	CA
Collins	Howard J.	21	Freestone	CA	McGrew	Ruby L.	20	Freestone	CA
Collins	James Michael	43	San Francisco	IRL	Comber	Nora	35	San Francisco	IRL
Collins	William A.	23	Santa Rosa	MI	McMinn	Clara J.	20	Santa Rosa	CA
Collischonn	Otto	21+	Alameda	CA	Tiedemann	Martha B.	18+	San Francisco	CA
Collister	Stanley W.	19	Cazadero	WY	Smith	Fannie A.	18	Occidental	NV
Colombani	Primo	22	Santa Rosa	ITL	Bertoni	Maria	22	Santa Rosa	ITL
Colombo	John Edward	26	Valley Ford	CA	Welling	Susie Mae	20	Bodega	CA
Colton	Frank B.	22	Santa Rosa	CA	Kidd	Mina	17	Santa Rosa	CA
Colton	Maury R.	21	San Francisco	CA	Rosenblum	Henrietta C.	18	San Francisco	CA
Coltrin	Hugh C.	33	Santa Rosa	UT	Litchfield	Laura B.	30	Sebastopol	IL
Coltrin	Hugh C.	26	San Francisco	Wat	Cooper	May N.	30	Santa Rosa	OR
Columbo	Charles H.	22	Bodega	CA	Perottini	Mary L.	18	Santa Rosa	CA
Columbo	Romeo M.	23	Valley Ford	CA	Pozzi	Linda M.	16	Petaluma	CA
Colville	Thomas P.	35	Santa Rosa Twp.	IRL	Conklin	Minnie	17	Forestville	OH
Colvin	Thomas Floyd	25	Healdsburg	CO	Mayer	Emily	22 ?	San Francisco	PLD
Colwell	Abner M.	28	Guerneville	CND	Bagley	Mary L.	24	Guerneville	CA
Coman	George L.	36	Napa	CA	Haddlesten	Annie L.	38	Ukiah	CA
Coman	Robert Grimes	28	Mare Island	WI	McMeans	Mary Alice	28	Santa Rosa	
Combs	Alvin Roots	45	Healdsburg		Valandhan	Mary	22	Healdsburg	
Combs	George	21	Healdsburg	CA	Berry	Ethel	18	Sebastopol	CA
Combs	Henry C.	23	Healdsburg	CA	Jacobs	Lorita M.	18	Geyserville	CA
Combs	Henry C.	26	Healdsburg	CA	Grant	Muriel Grace	21	Healdsburg	MO
Combs	John F.	26	Healdsburg	CA	Odell	Amanda J.	30	Healdsburg	CA
Combs	Monroe	28	Healdsburg	CA	Kolb	Belle	29	Healdsburg	MO
Cominos	George N.	34	Salinas	GRC	Karedis	Helen M.	21	Sebastopol	GRC
Commary	John A.				Patton	Emma			
Commers	Robert	29	Santa Rosa	CA	Chaffee	Lenna	43	Santa Rosa	CA

Groom					Bride				
Surname	**Given Name**	**Age**	**Residence**	**BP**	**Surname**	**Given Name**	**Age**	**Residence**	**BP**
Compton	John Andrew	20	Santa Rosa	CA	Clair	Stella Louise	18	Oakland	CA
Compton	Theodore J.	20	Graton	CA	Williamson	Emilia L.	20	Graton	NE
Comstock	George F.	25	Richmond	IL	Lindsey	Georgiana	26	Richmond	CA
Comstock	Harold Earl	24	Oakland	CA	Shriver	Evelyn	21	Santa Rosa	CA
Comstock	Herbert G.	35	Santa Rosa	CA	Hoodly	Eppie L.	19	Penngrove	CA
Comstock	Horace William	27	Camp Meeker	CA	Brandlein	Alma Theresa	21	Camp Meeker	CA
Comstock	Leslie F.	26	Oakland	NV	McAskill	Margaret J.	25	Petaluma	CA
Concerse	Earl Flower	22	Sonoma	SD	Studley	Alsy	18	Sonoma	OR
Condeff	Gerry	31	San Francisco	BUL	Walce	Pauline	20	Santa Rosa	CA
Condeff	Harry P.	24	Berkeley	BUL	Balsley	Edith Evalyn	19	Santa Rosa	NE
Condict	H. M.	30	Lakeport	IA	Howell	Ella M.	38	Santa Rosa	CT
Condrey	Edward Phillip	47	Richmond	CA	Herrick	Eva Elizabeth	42	San Francisco	CA
Conemac	Byron Patrick	21	San Francisco	NY	Young	Agnes	19	San Francisco	CA
Conger	Charles W.	47	Garberville	IA	Kemper	Sarah E.	32	Garberville	CA
Conger	Glenn A.	36	Petaluma	CA	Hilmer	Alma G.	26	Petaluma	CA
Conger	Harry E., Jr.	22	San Francisco	MT	Lucas	Leta A.	18	Santa Rosa	CA
Conger	John I.	19	Healdsburg		Porter	Annie L.	19	Healdsburg	
Congleton	A. C.	21	Healdsburg	CA	Hoar	Jennie S.	21	Healdsburg	CA
Congleton	Geo. W.	21	Healdsburg		Ball	Agnes	18	Healdsburg	
Congrove	Jonathan	53	Petaluma		Crow	Lucy A.	38	Santa Rosa	
Conisto	Achille	29	Bodega	SWT	Clark	Jennie	18	Bodega	CA
Conklin	Thomas	17	Sea View	NE	Howard	Beulah	17	Sea View	TN
Conkling	Glenn R.	35	Santa Rosa	OH	Whipple	Jennie E.	29	Santa Rosa	WI
Conley	Philip	31	San Francisco	MO	O'Rourke	Teresa	26	Petaluma	CA
Conley	William M.	31	Petaluma	MA	Gray	Daisy	24	Petaluma	MO
Conlin	William George	22	San Francisco		Stone	Agnes	28	Santa Rosa	
Connell	Chas. H.	38	Petaluma	IRL	Graham	Mary E.	23	Petaluma	CA
Connell	John	37	Petaluma	IRL	Connell	Mary	26	San Francisco	IRL
Conner	Arch C.	55	Santa Rosa	IL	Yates	Amy May, Mrs.	37	Santa Rosa	CA
Conner	Charles W. G.	49	Calistoga	KS	Daniels	Jessie Marian	49	San Francisco	CA

Groom					Bride				
Surname	**Given Name**	**Age**	**Residence**	**BP**	**Surname**	**Given Name**	**Age**	**Residence**	**BP**
Conner	Frank Stanley	32	Petaluma	NV	Jones	Flora M.	34	Petaluma	CA
Conner	George W.	24	San Francisco	KY	Gibbin	Theresa I.	20	San Francisco	CA
Conners	Alexander F.	22	Santa Rosa	CA	Harmon	Nellie G.	17	Santa Rosa	ME
Conners	Alexr F.	29	Angels Camp	CA	McCray	Emma E.	22	Guerneville	MO
Conners	Charles F.	27	Santa Rosa	CA	Siemer	Minnie	22	Santa Rosa	CA
Conners	George W.	30	Eureka	CA	Valdes	Vincent E.	21	near Santa Rosa	CA
Conness	John, Jr.	45	Berkeley	CA	Raupach	Caroline, Mrs.	42	Oakland	CA
Connick	Arthur E.	31	Eureka	CA	Robertson	Florence	27	Santa Rosa	CA
Conniff	Thomas E.	32	Petaluma	CA	Holland	Josephine	24	Petaluma	CA
Conniff	William Francis	24	Petaluma	CA	Fowler	Lue Della	24	Petaluma	MN
Connoff	William John	30	Petaluma	CA	Mackie	Mary	25	Petaluma	GER
Connor	Edward H.	28	Clinton, IA	IA	McMeans	Helen S.	26	Santa Rosa	CA
Connor	J.	41	Healdsburg	IN	Emerson	Nellie	21	Healdsburg	CA
Conover	Howard J.	39	Oakland	NJ	Shannon	Marion F.	27	Los Angeles	CA
Conquest	Earl A.	21	San Francisco	CA	Riehl	Emma S.	18	San Francisco	CA
Conrad	Charles Francis	41	Oakland	CA	Meyer	Anna	35	Oakland	CA
Conrad	E. A.								
Conrad	James	57	Cloverdale	PA	Riffe	Mattie	62	Cloverdale	IL
Conrad	Joseph	24	San Francisco	CA	Hale	Jean	22	Los Angeles	CA
Conroy	Edmund C., Jr.	31	San Francisco	CA	Kast	Amelia N.	31	Yolo	CA
Consoli	Peter	31	Chileno Valley	ITL	Patocchi	Olimpia	21	Chileno Valley	SWT
Consoni	Alfredo	29	Healdsburg	ITL	Nicoletti	Listina	24	Healdsburg	ITL
Constantine	Arthur Philip	24	Santa Rosa	NV	Timmons	Eva Ethel	18	Santa Rosa	OR
Continho	Joseph	32	Sebastopol	AZR	Augusta	Clara	22	Sebastopol	PRT
Contreras	Baltimore Y.	21	Santa Rosa	Sfo	Lillard	Fleet	16	Santa Rosa	CA
Converse	Gervase V.	18	Sonoma	SD	Monroe	Adalene S.	19	Sonoma	CA
Conway	Edward P.	25	Petaluma	CA	Bourke	Mary E.	25	Petaluma	Peoria, IL
Conway	Thomas James	29	Petaluma	Sfo	Conniff	Annie L.	24	Petaluma	Pet
Conyers	William E.	27	Sebastopol	ID	Peterson	Lucy L.	20	Sebastopol	CA

Groom					Bride				
Surname	**Given Name**	**Age**	**Residence**	**BP**	**Surname**	**Given Name**	**Age**	**Residence**	**BP**
Cook	Andrew J.	27	Santa Rosa	CA	Warren	May	18	San Francisco	NE
Cook	Andrew Joseph	20	Santa Rosa	CA	Ducker	Minnie May	20	Santa Rosa	CA
Cook	Andrew Joseph	28	Santa Rosa	CA	Wheeler	Myrtle	16	Santa Rosa	CA
Cook	Archibald	26	San Francisco	CA	Akers	Willie	24	Shellville	CA
Cook	Charles Edward	23	Santa Rosa	CA	Koch	Mamie	20	Santa Rosa	CA
Cook	Charles T.	23	Cincinnati	OH	Rex	Hulda I.	23	Santa Rosa	CA
Cook	De Roy	22	Petaluma	WI	Lundholm	Lydia	20	Petaluma	Chi
Cook	Delbert R.	23	Santa Rosa	CA	Cowan	Permilla I.	26	Santa Rosa	MO
Cook	Edward	21	Guerneville	MO	Cockrill	Fidella	23	Guerneville	East (?)
Cook	Edward	53	Santa Rosa	CND	Pike	Amanda J.	43	Santa Rosa	TX
Cook	Erle	21	Healdsburg	CA	Hitchcock	Myrtle	19	Healdsburg	CA
Cook	Ernest E.	20	Eagleville	CA	Franklin	Alta M.	22	Lake City, CA	CA
Cook	Ernest Ward	28	Oakland	MO	Christie	Lizzie, Mrs.	28	Oakland	IA
Cook	F. R.	31	Mendocino Twp.		Bacon	Iona A.	17	Mendocino Twp.	
Cook	Frank A.	32	Healdsburg	CA	Black	Villa	28	Healdsburg	CA
Cook	Fred B.	22	Bennett Valley	CA	Hughes	Pearl M.	20	Bennett Valley	CA
Cook	George	55	Oakland	IA	Mansfield	Maude	40	Ross Valley	CA
Cook	George M.	23	Healdsburg		Richards	Josephine	22	Healdsburg	
Cook	Glenn A.	21+	Healdsburg	MI	Guillice	Adeline I.	18+	Healdsburg	CA
Cook	Grover C.	23	Santa Rosa	CA	Woods	Lily B.	22	Santa Rosa	CA
Cook	Harry L.	38	San Francisco	IL	Hanson	Minnie E.	43	San Francisco	IL
Cook	Harvey M.	25	Healdsburg	CA	Reed	Carrie B.	22	Healdsburg	WI
Cook	Herbert E.		Mark West		Wiseman	Susie	16	Mark West	
Cook	Isaac N.	21	Santa Rosa	CA	Badger	Basha	19	Santa Rosa	CA
Cook	John Gilbert	23	Santa Rosa	CA	Scorille	Katie	22	Santa Rosa	MO
Cook	John S.	26	Healdsburg		Cox	Emma Elizabeth	16	Healdsburg	
Cook	Leo Francis	19	Santa Rosa	OR	Lentz	Edith	20	Santa Rosa	CA
Cook	Levi F.	19	Santa Rosa	IL	Massa	Clara	18	Santa Rosa	CA

Groom					Bride				
Surname	Given Name	Age	Residence	BP	Surname	Given Name	Age	Residence	BP
Cook	Peter	27	Rio Vista	CND	Proctor	Julia M.	23	Petaluma	MA
Cook	Peter	33	Crockett	RUS	Hunt	Margaret	25	Crockett	PA
Cook	Ralph W. E.	34	San Leandro	IA	Kaeintz	Ruby Amanda	30	San Francisco	CA
Cook	Raymond E.	40	Santa Rosa	IL	Quigley	Beatrice	19	Santa Rosa	CA
Cook	Reuben Grant	32	Healdsburg	CA	Haigh	Alice Estella	27	Healdsburg	CA
Cook	Roy (?)	39	Oakland	VT	Joseph	Mary E.	39	Oakland	CA
Cook	Shelby Erington	39	Healdsburg	CA	Turner	Ada Marie	39	Healdsburg	CA
Cook	Walter D. B.	29	Healdsburg	CA	Brooks	Pauline	19	Santa Rosa	CA
Cook	William	51	Windsor	GER	Kuhm	Louisa	33	San Francisco	CA
Cook	William E.	35	Oakland	CA	New	Rose	37	Oakland	CA
Cook	William E., Jr.	25	Santa Rosa	CA	Cambra	Jimella	27	Santa Rosa	CA
Cook	William H.	28	Santa Rosa	CA	de Shiell	Virginia	21	San Francisco	CA
Cook	William H.	24	Santa Rosa	CA	Park	Bertha M.	15	Santa Rosa	CA
Cook	William H.	48	Merced	CA	Lewis	Pearl M.	32	Merced	IA
Cook	William Irl	20	Santa Rosa	MO	Pharris	Bernice Wilda	20	Bloomfield	CA
Cook	William M.	19	Santa Rosa	OH	Carrillo	Rafelia	19	Santa Rosa	CA
Cook	William W.	29	Healdsburg	CA	Minkel	Martha	19	Healdsburg	TX
Cooke	Frank W.	42	Healdsburg	CA	Hendrickson	C. Grace	30	Santa Rosa	MN
Cooke	James F. R.	30	Santa Rosa	CA	LaPlant	Louisa	19	Cloverdale	CA
Cooke	James Hew	31	Guerneville	VA	Rouse	Eda May	20	Guerneville	IA
Cooke	John Blucker	24	Vallejo	AR	Nagel	Alvina	19	Vallejo	CA
Cooke	Reuben	44	Santa Rosa	CND	Cupp	Olga L.	44	Cotati	CT
Cooley	Charles H.	22	Cloverdale	CA	Hiatt	Myrtle P.	21	Cloverdale	Sutter Co.
Cooley	Edward A.	25	Cloverdale	CA	Hunziker	Flora	21	Cloverdale	MS
Cooley	James F.	25	Santa Rosa	MO	Harris	Etta	22	Santa Rosa	CA
Cooley	John S.	36	Sonoma Co.	CA	Snodgrass	Ida M., Mrs.	23	Sonoma	OR
Cooley	Mayberry D.	33	Santa Rosa	CA	Munro	Emily A.	28	Santa Rosa	CA
Cooley	Walter S.	48	Petaluma	MO	Rosen	Lenny	34	San Francisco	GER
Coolidge	George Harry	23	San Francisco	CA	Wright	Katherine	21	Oakland	CA

Groom					Bride				
Surname	Given Name	Age	Residence	BP	Surname	Given Name	Age	Residence	BP
Coolidge	Homer H.	28	Healdsburg	CA	Butler	Grace V.	26	Healdsburg	CA
Coomes	Albert M.	40	Cloverdale	MA	Monroe	Mary E.	25	Cloverdale	CND
Coon	Edward B.	40	Santa Rosa	NY	Graves	Laurie E.	25	Santa Rosa	MO
Coon	John T.	22	Guerneville	CA	Varneo	Clara J.	19	Guerneville	KS
Coon	Parmenas C.	38	Forestville	Soc	Norris	Hannah A., Mrs.	36	Forestville	OH
Coon	Robt. W.				Torrence	Lydia A			
Cooper	Alfred B.	28	Santa Rosa	CA	Geer	Mamie	28	Santa Rosa	OH
Cooper	B. F.				Shultz	Mary E.			
Cooper	C. J.	40	San Miguel	OH	Davis	Hattie L.	19	Petaluma	CA
Cooper	Charles Alexander	32	Portland, OR	IL	Agnew	Ella V.	21	Sonoma	CA
Cooper	Charles Crawford	21	Bloomfield	CA	Gericke	Agnes Veronica	19	Sebastopol	CA
Cooper	Charles H.	22	Cloverdale	CA	Rudd	Emma	20	Ukiah	CA
Cooper	Fred Evart	25	Sebastopol	KS	Razee	Carol Reaha	18	Sebastopol	IA
Cooper	Frederick A.	25	Santa Rosa	CA	Hyde	Francis G.	24	Santa Rosa	CA
Cooper	Geo. W.	24	Santa Rosa		Tupper	Hattie	19	Santa Rosa	
Cooper	Harry Anderson	24	Guerneville	OR	Guidotti	Edythe Ida	18	Guerneville	CA
Cooper	J. A.	25	Ukiah		Davidson	Fannie S.	19	Petaluma	
Cooper	James M.	22	Cloverdale		Bouse	Urith	16+	Cloverdale	
Cooper	John H.	21	Oakland	CA	Hutsell	Mary E.	20	Oakland	CA
Cooper	John Harmon	23	Santa Rosa	CA	Struter	Ruth Florence	17	Santa Rosa	CA
Cooper	John R.	47	Sonoma	CA	Carmer	Alma Bell	32	Sonoma	
Cooper	Lawrence H.	21	San Francisco	CA	Buckley	Viola I.	20	San Francisco	CA
Cooper	Morris B.	31	Eldridge	MI	Poppe	Edna E.	25	Glen Ellen	CA
Cooper	Peter G.	25	Oakland	CA	Earle	Grace L.	21	San Francisco	CA
Cooper	Sarshel Amos	29	Sacramento	CA	Ray	Lola Catherine	24	San Diego	CA
Cooper	Sash D.	27	Winters	CA	Atchinson	Lella	27	Santa Rosa	NV
Cooper	Thomas J.	38	Mendocino Co.	CA	Bailey	Elizabeth	28	Mendocino Co.	CA
Cooper	Thomas S.	41	Sonoma	CA	Dunn	Fannie J.	24	Sonoma	CA
Copeland	James	61	San Joaquin Co.	TN	Robbins	Marboy (?) C.	58	Guerneville	OH

Groom					Bride				
Surname	Given Name	Age	Residence	BP	Surname	Given Name	Age	Residence	BP
Coppedge	Charles O.	32	Windsor	MO	Heller	Laura E., Mrs.	29	Windsor	CA
Coppedge	Ernest Frank	22	San Francisco	CA	Johnson	Edna Louise	16	Santa Rosa	OR
Coppedge	Robert	23	Windsor	CA	Graper	Mabel	19	Windsor	CA
Copple	William H.	31	Healdsburg	MO	Shearer	Louisa	38	Healdsburg	IA
Copps	Willis	28	Mark West		Moore	Huldie Jane	20	Mark West	
Copsey	Lumin	19	Santa Rosa	CA	Beard	Gertrude V.	22	Santa Rosa	MI
Corbaley	Frank R.	25	Healdsburg		Cook	Katie (?)	21	Healdsburg	
Corbin	G. Benjamin	20	Sebastopol	CT	Hardin	Ida Jane	20	Petaluma	
Corbin	Warren	21	San Francisco	CA	Logan	Adelia	20	San Francisco	OR
Corcoran	William D.	60	San Francisco	ENG	Allen	Hattie L.	50	San Francisco	CA
Corda	Joseph	30	Petaluma Twp,	Can	Capello	Delila	25	Petaluma Twp.	Can
Cordano	Victor V.	24	Windsor	CA	Silva	Isabelle C.	23	Windsor	CA
Cordill	Lewis C.	26	Angel Island	IN	McHarvey	Sadie	25	Sonoma	Son
Cordoza	Joseph	22	Sebastopol	CA	Silveira	Louise	20	Petaluma	CA
Coreia	Joaquim (?)	27	Sebastopol	PRT	Silvia (?)	Maria A.	18	Sebastopol	PRT
Corfield	Thomas H.	32	Milner, MT	ENG	Newman	Bessie E.	34	Lancaster, WI	WI
Corfir	Carlo	26	Petaluma	SWT	Buletti	Elvezia	21	Petaluma	CA
Corippo	Benjamin H.	28	Petaluma	CA	Gilardi	Edith A.	22	Petaluma	CA
Corippo (?)	Steve	23	Petaluma	CA	Swanson	Matilda	18	Eureka	CA
Corliss	Albert	49	Petaluma		Ray	R. Belle	32	Petaluma	
Cormer	Frank F.	28	El Verano	MI	Wilson	Sophia	21	Sonoma	CA
Cornagie	Geo. W.	22	Healdsburg		Sheuhart	L. B.	18+	Healdsburg	
Cornalson	Peter	49	Sears Point	GER	Cooper	Charlotte	39	Sears Point	ENG
Cornelius	Clemens F.	26	Sonoma	CA	Reechler	Bertha J.	20	Sonoma	CA
Cornelius	Emil	24	Sonoma	CA	Englund	Etta	20	Sonoma	CA
Cornelius	George	56	Santa Rosa	PA	Cornelius	Ella M.	37	Santa Rosa	PA
Cornell	Reynolds T.	26	Seattle	NE	Adamson	Mary	19	Healdsburg	PA
Cornett	Ernest William	27	Santa Rosa	CA	Munday	Verna Adelaide	23	Petaluma	CA
Cornett	N. W.	34	Tomales	NY	Frisbie	Mercie E.	27	Tomales	CA

Groom					Bride				
Surname	**Given Name**	**Age**	**Residence**	**BP**	**Surname**	**Given Name**	**Age**	**Residence**	**BP**
Cornett	William H.	32	Fallon, Marin Co.	CND	Freeman	Lillian	36	Fallon	Mac
Cornwell	F. J.	27	Petaluma	CA	Lynch	Maggie	27	Petaluma	CA
Cornwell	Jesse Roberts	31	San Rafael	CA	Denton	Itasca Mae	21	Petaluma	SD
Corria	Antone F.	50	Healdsburg	AZR	Hart	Myrthena Grace	23	Healdsburg	CA
Corrick	William B.	23	Santa Rosa	CA	Beasley	Bessie C.	20	Santa Rosa	CA
Corrillo	Leo Arthur	37	Petaluma	CA	Billings	Nellie I.	37	Petaluma	CA
Corry	Julio	48	Sebastopol	PRT	Corry	Marie	34	Sebastopol	PRT
Corstensen	Henry M.	25	Petaluma	GER	Andersen	Josie E.	17	Petaluma	GER
Corts	Frank James	29	Petaluma	MN	Cella	Beatrice	20	Petaluma	CA
Corum	Herbert A.	27	Guerneville	OR	Rice	Mary E.	34	Guerneville	CA
Corville	Richard	33	Healdsburg	CA	Adams	Alice P.	17	Healdsburg	CA
Cossa	Luigi	29	Hicks Valley, Marin Co.	SWT	Ghisletta	Antonia	24	Hicks Valley, Marin Co.	SWT
Costa	Joseph W.	24	Ross	PRT	Smith	Mae D.	24	Ignacio	CA
Coster	George J.	25	Healdsburg	CA	Mays	Rilla L.	21	Healdsburg	CA
Cotrell	Charles William	24	Santa Rosa	KS	Wooley	Emma E.	18	Santa Rosa	OR
Cotter	William	24	Healdsburg	CA	Bates	Lottie	19	Healdsburg	CA
Cottini	Erico	25	Healdsburg	ITL	Belli	Flora	18	Lytton	CA
Cottle	Edmund J.	22	Geyserville	CA	Baruch	Anita	20	Geyserville	CA
Cottle	Harold Bertrand	21	Oakland	CA	Meyer	Annie Dora	21	Geyserville	CA
Cottle	William Leonard	25	San Francisco	CA	Wolcott	Edna Irene	23	San Francisco	CA
Coul	Peter	30	Windsor		Coventry (?)	Mary A.	29	Windsor	
Coulter	Charles	40	Guerneville	CND	Chambers	Elizabeth, Mrs.	40	Guerneville	CND
Coulter	Paul	31	Tonopah, Nye Co., NV	CA	Kirkpatrick	Grace Cynthia	26	Santa Rosa	IA
Counihan	Jeremiah	32	Petaluma	NV	Sullivan	Kate	30	Petaluma	NY
Courtney	John George	27	Petaluma	CA	Woods	Mary A.	26	Santa Rosa	CA
Courtney	Willard J.	54	Quincy	CA	Miller	Esther A.	56	Oakland	MN
Courtright	R.	52	Nevada	MO	Jackson	Mary M.	47	Redding	CA

Groom					Bride				
Surname	**Given Name**	**Age**	**Residence**	**BP**	**Surname**	**Given Name**	**Age**	**Residence**	**BP**
Coutts	John	29	Kenwood	SCT	Minick	Viola E.	19	Kenwood	CA
Coutts	Maxwell C.	23	Kenwood	SCT	Block	Mamie M.	21	El Verano	UT
Covell	R. William	31	San Francisco	NM	Delany	Sarelda M.	37	Boyes Springs	IL
Covey	Alphaeus Vincel	23	Santa Rosa	CA	Henderson	Alma R.	22	Santa Rosa	CA
Covey	Daniel	26	Forestville	MO	Ross	Laura M.	19	Forestville	CA
Covey	Geo. W.	21	Healdsburg		Isaacs	Fanny	16	Healdsburg	
Covey	George W.	34	Guerneville	CA	German	Charlotte	22	Guerneville	CA
Covey	Harmon	21	Forestville	CA	Miranda	Lee	18	Forestville	MO
Covey	James Walter	23?	Forestville	CA	Ridenhour	Annie May	30	Hilton	CA
Covey	William	24	Forestville	CA	Ross	Hattie G.	19	Forestville	CA
Covington	J. M.				Gentry	Amanda G., Mrs.			
Cowan	Edward	33	Marshall	IRL	McDonald	Martha	20	Petaluma	CA
Cowan	James M.	24	Glen Ellen	MO	Small	Agnes M.	19	San Francisco	CA
Cowan	John	30	Guernwood	IRL	Orr	Alberta E.	23	Santa Rosa	CND
Cowan	Kenneth B.	30	San Francisco	TN	Fuidge (?)	Rhea E.	27	San Francisco	MO
Cowan	Samuel Nelson	21	Bennett Valley	MO	Russell	Eveline	28	Sonoma Co.	CA
Cowan	William F.	23	Santa Rosa	CA	Braughler	Florence I.	21	Santa Rosa	PA
Cowen	Frederick S.	29	Santa Rosa	CA	Jacobs	Sarah	17	Santa Rosa	NY
Cowen	Joseph A.	39	Petaluma	CA	Austin	Rose, Mrs.	32	Healdsburg	CA
Cowger	William H.	27	Kansas City, MO	MO	Roberts	Ella W.	24	Santa Rosa	CA
Cowles	Ralph	79	Mellette, SD	OH	Irwin	Elizabeth A.	55	Santa Rosa	CND
Cowley	Arthur S.	26	San Francisco	NY	Shaw	May L.	25	Healdsburg	IA
Cowper	Charles Wallace	23	Modesto	CA	Laughlin	Willa Lee	18	Healdsburg	CA
Cox	Alvin Joseph	30	Palo Alto	KS	Barnett	Mary Amelia	25	Santa Rosa	WI
Cox	Axley C.	39	Healdsburg	IL	Hassett	Ella L., Mrs.	33	Healdsburg	CA
Cox	Charles	26	Cloverdale	MO	Lewis	Julia	20	Preston	CA
Cox	Charles A.	21	Healdsburg	CA	Hughes	Virgia L.	19	Healdsburg	MO
Cox	Clarence J.	21	Ukiah	CA	Storer	Flossie	18	Sonoma	CA
Cox	E. Morris	35	Santa Rosa	IA	Anderson	Mary E.	20	Santa Rosa	CA

Groom					Bride				
Surname	**Given Name**	**Age**	**Residence**	**BP**	**Surname**	**Given Name**	**Age**	**Residence**	**BP**
Cox	Earl W.	26	Ukiah	CA	Gilman	Barbara	22	Santa Rosa	CA
Cox	George Edwin	23	Roseville	WY	Hughes	Alice Viola	22	Healdsburg	IL
Cox	George Mervon	23	Cloverdale	CA	Witherell	Laura Jane	19	Cloverdale	CA
Cox	Grover C.	22	Fort Bragg	CA	Philbert	Rosa M.	15	Lytton	CA
Cox	Homer M.	31	Yorkville	CA	Baine	Lola	21	Cloverdale	CA
Cox	Hugh	26	Ukiah	CA	Howard	Lulu M.	19	Ukiah	CA
Cox	James M.	21	Ukiah	CA	Odell	Sophrmia	19	Geyserville	CA
Cox	Jessee C.				Wright	Eveline			
Cox	John	26	Healdsburg	CA	Knox	Edith	15	Healdsburg	CA
Cox	John N.	29	Stewarts Point	CA	Graves	Mary M.	18	Stewarts Point	CA
Cox	John Walter	25	Herman (?), CA	MD	Roduner	Alice Evelyn	28	Graton	CA
Cox	Leslie	21	Sacramento	CA	Finley	Louise	22	Santa Rosa	CA
Cox	Nathan H.	23	near Healdsburg		Hopper	Ida Ione	16+	near Healdsburg	
Cox	Stacy Verne	23	Sebastopol	CA	Bower	Grace Lillian	19	Sebastopol	CA
Cox	Thomas W.	21	Ukiah		Bell	Sarah Emma	18	Geyserville	
Cox	Willard S.	27	San Francisco	IA	Church	Myrtle E.	25	San Francisco	CA
Cox	William Frederick	30	Healdsburg	CA	Shriver	Loleta	26	Healdsburg	CA
Cox	William M.	23	Ukiah	CA	Beaver	Rosa E.	22	Guerneville	IA
Cox	William Martin	35	Ukiah	CA	Jamison	Eugenia	30	Ukiah	CA
Cox	William Toliver	20	Columbia, Tuolumne Co.	CA	Beach	Helen G.	16	Santa Rosa	CA
Cox	Winfred R.	21	Ukiah	CA	Jamison	Mildred M.	19	Ukiah	CA
Coy	Charles S.	25	Occidental	WI	Philbrick	Josie R.	19	Occidental	CA
Coy	Charles S.	33	Occidental	WI	Hastings	Sallie E., Mrs.	31	Occidental	NJ
Coy	Wm. B.	26	Occidental	WI	Proctor	Effie L.	18	Occidental	WI
Coyan	Wilson S.	25	Green Valley	CA	Sullivan	Leatha J.	23	Green Valley	CA
Coykendall	Chauncey B.	32	Los Angeles	MI	McMahon	Margaret	27	Santa Rosa	CA
Coyne	Lawrence J.	32	San Francisco	CA	Barman	Clara B.	30	Santa Rosa	WA
Cozad	Samuel L.	25	Santa Rosa	KS	Stone	Ella	23	Santa Rosa	
Cozort	John Gaines	22	Windsor	FRN	Shuler	Cecil A.	16	Windsor	CA

Groom					Bride				
Surname	**Given Name**	**Age**	**Residence**	**BP**	**Surname**	**Given Name**	**Age**	**Residence**	**BP**
Cozzins	Davenport	59	Geyserville	NY	Bowmer	Abbie W.	30	Mark West	MO
Cozzo	Joseph, Jr.	25	San Francisco	ITL	Fry	Mildred M.	19	Santa Rosa	MI
Crabtree	Albert F.	22	Oakland	CA	Taylor	Lena P.	20	Healdsburg	CA
Crabtree	Albert H.	37	Healdsburg	CA	Sullivan	Nancy E.	36	Green Valley	Green Valley
Cragin	Charles Chester	70	San Jose	RI	Williams	Laura Emily	55	Santa Rosa	IL
Cragun	Wilson H.	38	Ogden, UT	UT	Sanborn	Flora L.	26	Lemoore	CA
Craib	William Joseph	22	Glen Ellen	MA	Thierkoff	Florence	21	Glen Ellen	CA
Craig	Albert James	23	Penngrove	CA	Matthews	Ina Marguite	20	Penngrove	CA
Craig	Bert F.	29	Healdsburg	IA	Palmer	Grace Pearl	22	Healdsburg	CO
Craig	Edwin Alfred	21	Healdsburg	CA	Gustafson	Esther E.	18	Healdsburg	WA
Craig	Francis A.	21	Occidental	CA	Beam	Alice May	23	Guerneville	CA
Craig	George Washington	36	Claremont	CA	Banta	Mary Alice	36	Claremont	OH
Craig	Isaac	24	Oakland	TN	O'Connor	Florence M.	19	Oakland	ENG
Craig	Robert Geo.	21	San Francisco	CA	Herger	Martha F.	18	San Francisco	CA
Craig	Robert John	25	Penngrove	CA	Cheney	Irene Margaret	24	Penngrove	CA
Cramer	David R.				Gill	Elizabeth			
Cramer	John F.	23	Petaluma	CA	Bosworth	Fannie L.	19	Petaluma	CA
Cramer	Walter	21+	San Francisco	CA	Scott	Lou Alice	18+	Petaluma	CA
Crandall	Charles I.	36	Healdsburg	WA	Tellefson	Dora	19	Healdsburg	CA
Crandall	Edward	25	Healdsburg	CA	Arata	Rose	24	Windsor	CA
Crandall	Fred C.	27	Healdsburg	CA	Newcom	Lena, Mrs.	35	Healdsburg	GER
Crandall	George A.	40	San Francisco	NY	Stevens	Eva L.	40	San Francisco	CA
Crandall	James	26	Healdsburg	WA	Smith	Leona	18	Healdsburg	OR
Crandall	John Calhoun	20	Dry Creek		Snider	Joanna	17	Dry Creek	
Crandall	Walter W.	22	Petaluma	CA	Keast	Mary A.	17	Petaluma	
Crandell	Clarence F.	35	Healdsburg	WA	Suetta	Elizabeth H.	25	Healdsburg	CA
Crandle	Frank	18			Snider	Naoma	17		
Crane	Charles B.	21	Santa Rosa Twp.		Clay	Effie E.	18	Santa Rosa	

Groom					Bride				
Surname	**Given Name**	**Age**	**Residence**	**BP**	**Surname**	**Given Name**	**Age**	**Residence**	**BP**
Crane	George S.	22	Santa Rosa Twp.		Faulconer	Jennie M.	17	Santa Rosa Twp.	
Crane	Homer W.	26	San Francisco	MN	Grainger	Gertrude	28	Healdsburg	CA
Crane	O. L.	27	Tucson, AZ	CA	Hinebauch	Allie	22	Santa Rosa	CA
Crane	Price T.	29	Santa Rosa	MO	Savory	Nellie J.	21	Santa Rosa	MA
Crane	Richard Henry	22	Santa Rosa	Sar	Vogt	Anne D.	20	Santa Rosa	Soc
Crane	Tarlslm (?) L.	22	Cloverdale	MO	Wilkes	Mary E.	20	Bennett Valley	IL
Crane	Wade H.	20	Santa Rosa Twp.	CA	Hicks	Allie B.	18	Santa Rosa Twp.	CA
Crane	Wade Hampton	28	Santa Rosa	CA	Himebauch	Lulu May	28	Penngrove	CA
Crane	William P.	25	Calpella	CA	Hughes	Edith A.	20	Santa Rosa Twp.	CA
Cranmer	George O.	30	Oakland	MN	Rairdin	Virginia C.	22	Oakland	IA
Cranwford	James A.	46	Cloverdale	SCT	Metcalfe	Mary M.	37	Cloverdale	OH
Craver	Frank W.	30	Santa Rosa	IL	Leggett	Lizzie M.	24	Santa Rosa	CA
Craver	J. Edward	36	Stockton	IL	Hutchins	Mildred G.	17	Santa Rosa	CA
Crawford	Albert J.	38	San Francisco	TX	Frisk	Hilda T.	27	San Francisco	SWD
Crawford	Andrew Kerr	45	Healdsburg		Alexander	Alice Maria	21	near Healdsburg	
Crawford	Edwin Henry	26	Santa Rosa	IL	Pohlmann	Carlotta Gertrude	20	Santa Rosa	NY
Crawford	Harry F.	33	San Francisco	LA	Meyer	Francis M.	20	San Francisco	CA
Crawford	Jesse Blacker	62	Sebastopol	PA	Bernier	Frances Ellen, Mrs.	62	Sebastopol	IL
Crawford	Roy S.	36	Sebastopol	IA	Walker	Marion E.	21	Sebastopol	CA
Crawford	Russel D.	35	Sonoma	Paris, KY	McDonald	Lillian	16	Petaluma	CA
Crawford	Thomas	33	Sebastopol	ENG	Graham	Lettie	19	Sebastopol	IA
Crawford	William E.	34	Knob, Shasta Co.	CA	Taylor	Minnie G.	25	Bodega	CA
Crayne	Stephen D.	32	Freestone	IA	Horgan	Julia C.	20	Freestone	CA
Creagh	Michael	53	Santa Rosa	IRL	Miller	Jane, Mrs.	50	Santa Rosa	HLD
Creagmile	James Albert	25	Berkley	CA	Guirach	Dora Rose	23	Oakland	CA
Creagmile	John Cowan	25	Berkeley	CA	Thompson	Catherine Ruth	20	Cloverdale	CA
Crease	Henry George	42	San Francisco	ENG	Genochio	Elizabeth R.	29	San Francisco	OH

Groom					Bride				
Surname	**Given Name**	**Age**	**Residence**	**BP**	**Surname**	**Given Name**	**Age**	**Residence**	**BP**
Creely	James H.	21	San Francisco	CA	Cerini	Florence M.	20	Alameda	CA
Creighton	Charles Oscar	27	Mojave, CA	MO	Johnson	Julia Lizette	23	Sebastopol	CA
Cresante	Sepe	66	Bodega	CHL	Casey	Bridget	70	Bodega	IRL
Cresap	Daniel	36	Petaluma	OH	Gann	Martha	27	Petaluma	CA
Cresap	Gallant	21	Penngrove	CA	Large	Byrtie	18	Petaluma	CA
Crescenzo (?)	Louis	21	Healdsburg	NV	Reynolds	H. T., Mrs.	23	Healdsburg	IL
Crews	Artie C.	19	San Jose	WA	Green	Lucy M.	19	Santa Rosa	MI
Crigler	Albert P.	24	Lower Lake		Bates	Laura E.	18	Cloverdale	
Crigler	Thomas Millard	22	Cloverdale		Porter	Martha Elizabeth	22	Healdsburg	
Crigler	W. E.	53	Cloverdale		Williams	Mary C., Mrs.	42	Santa Rosa	
Crigler	Walter M. D.	22	Cloverdale	CA	Weselsky	Tillie	21	Ukiah	NE
Crimmings	Ernest Fulton	25	San Francisco	CA	Byrne	Agnes	21	San Francisco	CA
Crips	Melvin T.	28	San Francisco	OH	Strasser	Lizette C.	24	San Francisco	CA
Crispin	Charles A.	31	Yorkville	CA	Brown	Esther E.	22	Philo	CA
Crist	Henry A.	21	Santa Rosa	CA	Locke	Ethel M.	18	Santa Rosa	CA
Crist	Walter K.	22	Santa Rosa	CA	Campion	May	21	Santa Rosa	CA
Crist	William	22	Santa Rosa	PA	Hutter (?)	Rhoda	21	Santa Rosa	CA
Crist	Wm.				Jackson	Rosa Ann			
Crist	Wm. H.		Salt Point Twp.		Brown	Katie Maybell		Salt Point Twp.	
Cristofani	Louis	40	San Francisco	ITL	Bartholdy	Ottilie	30	San Francisco	GER
Crivelli	Alexandro	25	Sonoma	SWT	Nonella	Celestine	18	Sonoma	CA
Crocker	Earl F.	27	Alameda	CA	Andersen	Anna Margaret	31	San Francisco	DNK
Crocker	George S.	21	Alameda	CA	Parker	Angie F.	18	Alameda	CA
Crocker	J. M.				Johnson	Martha			
Crocker	S. K.	29	Tacoma, WA	WA	Strait	Marie A.	26	Monterey	CA
Crocker	William Franklin	30	Santa Rosa	MO	Higgins	Gertrude Vivian	18	Santa Rosa	CA
Crockett	Edmund Bowden	39	San Francisco	ME	Arvilla	Florence, Mrs.	31	Petaluma	CA
Crockett	George E.	21	Healdsburg	ME	Goddard	Viola M.	21	Healdsburg	CA
Crockett	James D.	25	Ukiah	CA	Isaacs	Retta	19	Healdsburg	CA

Groom					Bride				
Surname	Given Name	Age	Residence	BP	Surname	Given Name	Age	Residence	BP
Crofoot	Willard H.	26	San Francisco	OH	Fitch	Rosalin L.	20	Healdsburg	CA
Croll	E. E. W.	31	Great Western Mine, Lake Co.	GER	Turner	Jennie B.	20	Knights Valley	CA
Croman	Edward	81	Santa Rosa	MI	Randall	Eliza S.	53	Santa Rosa	NY
Cromer	A. M.	26	Ukiah		Smith	Emma	20	Healdsburg	
Crommett	Clyde Leon	31	St. Helena	IA	Montgomery	Edwinnie	26	Graton	IA
Cromwell	Bert G.	21	Petaluma	IL	Sheehy	Lottie	20	Petaluma	CA
Cromwell	Frederick H.	28	San Francisco	IL	Jones	Nell A.	22	Healdsburg	CA
Cromwell	J. G.	42	Glen Ellen	NY	Coyn	Anna E.	33	Glen Ellen	OR
Cromwell	John T.	39	Santa Rosa	MO	Paschal	Ada M.	19	Santa Rosa	IL
Cromwell	William O.	26	Sebastopol		White	Florence	18	Bloomfield	
Crone	Edwin	30	Santa Rosa	CA	Knight	Mary	30	Santa Rosa	CA
Cronin	Joseph A.	31	Cotati	IRL	McClancy	Isabella M.	25	Cotati	CA
Crooks	Asa S.	33	San Francisco	CA	Connon	Mildred E.	21	San Francisco	CA
Crooks	Robert Lee	23	Santa Rosa	CA	Keogh	Marion	22	San Francisco	CA
Cropley	R. T.	27	San Francisco	CA	Turnidge	Martha A.	26	San Francisco	CA
Cross	F. G.	50	Corcoran	IL	Marshall	Josephine	24	Santa Rosa	IA
Crossfield	Archa F.	21+	Forestville	NE	Holmes	Nora M.	18+	Forestville	CA
Crossley	Edwin Hall	22	San Jose	CA	Wadsworth	Mildred Jeanette	21	Sebastopol	CA
Crosta	Mateo	26	Valley Ford	ITL	Gobbi	Rosie M.	22	Valley Ford	ITL
Crotts	Charles Maxwell	28	Sebastopol	CA	Rose	Annie Gertrude	24	Sebastopol	CA
Crotts	Louis U.	23	Sebastopol	CA	Rose	Maggie I.	23	Sebastopol	CA
Crotyogini (?)	Battista	32	Valley Ford	ITL	Lisignoli	Marie C.	20	Fallon	ITL
Croughin	Thomas	23	Minneapolis, MN	IA	Sherlock	Abbie	24	Portland, OR	St Louis, MO
Crow	Edward	35	Ranchera, Mendocino Co.		Manin	Mary Ellen, Mrs.	22	Ranchera, Mendocino Co.	
Crowell	Albert	45	Geyserville		Vaughn	Belle, Mrs.	31	Butte Co.	
Crowell	Elmer Harlow	24	Santa Rosa	MO	Weltz	Katherine	21	Santa Rosa	CA

Groom					Bride				
Surname	Given Name	Age	Residence	BP	Surname	Given Name	Age	Residence	BP
Crowford	Thomas				Davidson	Mary Jane			
Crowley	Cornelius Joseph	27	San Francisco	IRL	Hrusa	Barbara	20	Korbel	AUS
Crowley	David	37	San Francisco	Sfo	Orre	Jeanette	24	San Francisco	Chi
Crowley	John	44	Glen Ellen	IRL	Crafoot	Annie	40	Glen Ellen	NY
Crowley	Timothy J.	35	Healdsburg	MA	Coffey	Mary E.	30	Healdsburg	CA
Crozier	Alfred B.	38	Eureka	CA	Evans	Edith	31	Ukiah	ID
Crull	Frank M.	25	Cotati	OR	Brickley	Hattie	16	Cotati	Wat
Crumley	Francis M.	32	Calistoga	TN	Parsons	Nellie	24	Sonoma Co.	IA
Cruse	James C.	31	Sebastopol	NE	Scudder	Edith B.	28	Sebastopol	CA
Cruz	Joe	38	Forestville	GAM	Bingham	Margaret	29	Forestville	IA
Cruzan	Donald E.	29	Santa Rosa	HI	Griffitts	Blanche U.	17	Santa Rosa	CA
Crystal	Melvin	32	Eureka	IA	Ewing	Sadie, Mrs.	38	Eureka	CA
Crystal	Richard Randolph	22	Healdsburg	CA	Silzle	Minnie Augusta	21	Healdsburg	IL
Cuicci	Filippo	28	Healdsburg	ITL	Alberigi	Amelia	17	Healdsburg	ITL
Cuicello	Frank Louis	24	near Sebastopol	CA	Baum	Pearl J.	16	Petaluma	IA
Cuicello	Manuel G.	26	Sebastopol	CA	Souza	Rosaline	21	Two Rock	MO
Culberson	Harold	24	Sebastopol	WI	Kelly	Elisabeth	22	Sebastopol	CA
Culbertson	John B.	21	Santa Rosa	CA	Kennedy	Ida Belle	20	Santa Rosa	CA
Cullen	Edwin Patrick	26	Petaluma	NV	Hopkins	Lottie	20	Petaluma	Pet
Cullen	Fred T.	24	Petaluma	NY	Stephens	Sarah V.	20	Cotati	WI
Cullen	William Edward	27	Santa Rosa	CA	Driscoll	Rinetta	26	Santa Rosa	CA
Culler	Albert Roy	30	San Francisco	OH	Altman	Emma	26	San Francisco	CA
Culligan	Francis J.	21	San Francisco	CA	Foss	Gertrude	19	San Francisco	CA
Cummings	Frederick Merritt	23	Sonoma	CA	Wright	Flora Agnes	22	Healdsburg	CA
Cummings	George Lawrence	23	Santa Rosa	CA	Fulkerson	Ida Helen	19	Santa Rosa	CA
Cummings	Harry W.	26	Healdsburg	CA	King	Sarah I.	20	Healdsburg	NV
Cummings	Harvey W.	39	Healdsburg	CA	Grennert	Carrie	32	Healdsburg	PA
Cummings	James M.				Johns	Martha			
Cummings	Ralph M.	25	San Francisco	CA	Nielsen	Anna Marie	18	San Francisco	CA
Cummings	William Frank	23	Healdsburg	CA	Parker	Virginia Belle	23	Healdsburg	CA

Groom					Bride				
Surname	Given Name	Age	Residence	BP	Surname	Given Name	Age	Residence	BP
Cummings	William J.	25	Santa Rosa	CA	Keiser	Josephine M.	25	Sonoma	CA
Cummins	George Arthur	32	Santa Rosa	KS	Taylor	Martha Nina	29	Santa Rosa	CA
Cummins	George Washington	46	New York	IA	Schroder	Helene Wilhelmine	37	San Francisco	Sfo
Cummins	J. L.	23	Santa Rosa	CA	Lock	Phebe	23	Santa Rosa	CA
Cummins	W. E.	22	Rincon Valley		Lock	Mary F.	18	Rincon Valley	
Cuneo	Antonio	31	Petaluma	ITL	Tiscornia	Caterina	22	Petaluma	ITL
Cuneo	G.	28	Healdsburg	ITL	Cuneo	Amelia	21	Healdsburg	ITL
Cuneo	Joseph	26	San Francisco	CA	Foppiano	Mary	20	Healdsburg	CA
Cuneo	William J.	28	San Francisco	CA	Greeott	Virginia G.	20	Santa Rosa	CA
Cunihan	John	24	Petaluma	NV	Walsh	Sarah	22	Petaluma	Sfo
Cunmmings	Charles E.	23	Healdsburg	CA	Bidwell	Lennie G.	21	Healdsburg	CA
Cunningham	Charles John	30	Two Rock	CA	Fox	Verna May	21	Bloomfield	NE
Cunningham	Edmund James	24	Bodega	CA	Klein	Grace Lena	24	Valley Ford	CA
Cunningham	Frank Michael	26	Ukiah	CA	McCowen	Mary Louise	25	Ukiah	CA
Cunningham	George B.	31	San Francisco	WA	Gregson	Nellie	27	Santa Rosa	CA
Cunningham	Hugh Ronald	29	Fallon, CA	CA	Martin	Jennie	19	Bloomfield	CA
Cunningham	John G.	26	Guerneville	CND	McClure	May	26	Guerneville	CA
Cunningham	William Park	21	Windsor	CA	Hoffer	Gretchen	25	Santa Rosa	CA
Cunningham	Wm. N.	30	Bloomfield	CA	McCaughey	Mabel	30	Bodega	CA
Cunninghame	Alexander L.	26	Healdsburg	CA	Furlong	Margaret M.	24	Bodega	CA
Cunninghame	Reuben H.	30	Bodega	CA	Colby	Mae L.	23	Bodega	NY
Cuopius	Eugene B.	30	Santa Rosa	CA	Stone	Gladys C.	22	Santa Rosa	CA
Curran	Phillip Joseph	24	San Francisco	CA	King	Blanche Elizabeth	29	San Francisco	IA
Curran	William H.	42	San Francisco	CA	Stender	Jeanette	38	San Francisco	CA
Current	Thomas David	23	Guerneville		Maddux	Martha E.	16+	Guerneville	
Currie	Charles W.	31	Chico	IA	Montgomery	Zimmie	29	Chico	CA
Currie	Claude Raymond	21	Ross	IA	Parsons	Esther Ruby	18	San Francisco	CA
Currie	Robert Alvin	22	Salt Lake City	UT	Church	Deets	18	Ashland, OR	OR

Groom					Bride				
Surname	**Given Name**	**Age**	**Residence**	**BP**	**Surname**	**Given Name**	**Age**	**Residence**	**BP**
Curries	Wm. H.	22	Healdsburg	CA	Clark	Allice S.	21	Healdsburg	CA
Curry	Sylvester James	28	San Francisco	CA	Wilson	Alice Charie (?)	22	San Francisco	CA
Curtin	Daniel J.	34	Windsor	IRL	Breheny	Katie E.	27	Windsor	IRL
Curtis	Benj. A.				Humphrey	Rebecca A.			
Curtis	Charley C.	48	Cloverdale	CA	Gulland	Muriel	42	Cloverdale	AUT
Curtis	James H.				Green	Sarah J., Mrs.			
Curtis	Jos. S.	37	San Francisco	MA	Brookfield	Marie R.	24	Santa Rosa	OH
Curtis	L. A.				Williams	M. C., Mrs.			
Curtis	Robert Ross	36	Petaluma	CA	Bradley	Mary Ellen	17	Sebastopol	CA
Curtis	Thomas J.	40	Santa Rosa	VA	Thompson	Vera A.	17	Rincon Valley	NE
Curtis	William G.	21	San Francisco	ENG	Fitzgerald	Mary	26	San Francisco	IRL
Curtiss	Albert Melton	33	Chicago	Clv	Stewart	Caroline F.	26	New York City	NY City
Curtiss	George C.	24	Healdsburg	CA	Hormon	Mabel F.	20	Healdsburg	CA
Curtiss	Thomas E.	30	Healdsburg	CA	Martin	Fannie Susie, Mrs.	28	Healdsburg	CA
Curtiss	Thomas Edson	24	Healdsburg	CA	Waltham	R. M., Mrs.	23	Healdsburg	KS
Curtner	Alan E., Jr.	26	Sunnyvale	CA	Burch	Celesta Jane	28	San Francisco	IL
Cushman	Zacheus?	42	Fort Ross	MA	McDonald	Mary R.	19	Fort Ross	IA
Cussins	William Edison	22	Healdsburg	CA	Bartlow	Edith Mable	17	Healdsburg	CA
Cussins	John E.	21	Trinity Co.	CA	Jinks	Harriett M.	16	Healdsburg	OR
Custer	Albert S.	24	Chicago	IL	Schaefer	Minnie	24	Los Angeles	MN
Cuthill	James Sinclair	42	Guerneville	ENG	Oberfell	Mary	31	Guerneville	IA
Cutter	Charles Samuel	24	Sonoma	CA	Thompson	Florence L.	22	Sonoma	CA
Cutter	Ephraim M.	22	Sonoma	Sfo	Manuel	Florence I.	18	Sonoma	Yuba Co.
Cutts	Lloyd C.	29	San Francisco	NV	Anholm	Marie B.	28	Santa Rosa	GER
Cuvrean	Oscar F.	27	Oakland	CA	Gerst	Bertha A.	34	Gridley	OR
d'Abreu	John Silveira	28	Petaluma		Tomazio	Maria	20	Petaluma	
Da Roza	Antonio Domingo	27	Petaluma	PRT	Josephe	Maria	18	Petaluma Twp.	CA

Groom					Bride				
Surname	Given Name	Age	Residence	BP	Surname	Given Name	Age	Residence	BP
Dabner	Manuel	20	Petaluma	CA	Mathews	May	17	Grasen (?)	CA
Dabner	Manuel	37	Napa	CA	Kahrs	Marie	33	Santa Rosa	OH
Dad	R.	38	Petaluma	AFG	Weatherly	Julia	22	South Bend, WA	WA
Dado	Arnold Walter	26	Tomales	CA	Respini	Flaminia L.	20	Petaluma	CA
Dado	Atilio Anthony	30	Chileno Valley	CA	Gambonini	Olivia Lettitia	25	Marshall	CA
Daggett	Mathew H.	41	Santa Rosa	CA	Moore	Margaret	42	Santa Rosa	MA
Dagi	Augostino	29	Santa Rosa	ITL	Dellavedora	Maria	24	Santa Rosa	ITL
Dahack	Elsia	29	Santa Rosa	IL	Frost	Jennie	20	Santa Rosa	CA
Dahl	Oscar	37	Portland, OR	NRY	Hollar	Nora	25	Windsor	CA
Dahlmann	Otto Hugo	44	Sebastopol	GER	Davis	Mary	30	Sebastopol	CA
Dailey	Lawrence L.	22	Berkeley	MO	Skee	Mary	21	Healdsburg	OR
Dailey	Le Roy C.	22	San Francisco	IL	Svilovivh	Evelyn N.	18	San Francisco	CA
Dake	John A.	24	Eureka	CA	Wall	Ada M.	24	Sebastopol	CA
Dal Pino	Guiseppe	28	Guerneville	ITL	Dinucci	Mary	18	Hilton	CA
Dalbalcon	Louis	24	Santa Rosa	ITL	Dalmaso	Olinpia	21	Santa Rosa	ITL
Dale	J. W.	31	Sebastopol	IL	Boswell	Cora L.	18	Sebastopol	CA
Dalessi	Walter	23	Petaluma	Pet	Clausen	Minnie	20	Petaluma	Pet
Daley	George	28	Sacramento	CA	Cooper	Ida May	28	Santa Rosa	CA
Dallas	John P.	30	Santa Rosa	GRC	Everhart	Effie	24	Santa Rosa	MO
Dalpoggetto	Charles	29	Sonoma	ITL	Proletti	Mary	26	Sonoma	ITL
Dalton	Edwin P.	27	Benicia	CA	Belcher	Ruth A.	24	Benicia	TX
Dalton	Thomas Benton	35	San Francisco	MO	Lawrence	Linny Belle	22	Petaluma	CA
Daly	Thomas B.	21	Lakeport	CA	Smith	Fannie	17	Cloverdale	Ruther ford
Damaino	Mike	25	Santa Rosa	ITL	Esaia	Natalina	18	Healdsburg	ITL
Damario	Damacati	30	Kenwood	ITL	Lucchesi	Pauline	22	Kenwood	CA
Damon	Henry Stuart	24	Santa Rosa	CA	Peterson	Pearl	19	Santa Rosa	CA
Damon	Myron H.	26	Santa Rosa	MA	Churchman	Maggie A.	17	Mark West Creek	CA
Dana	Alfred H.	29	San Francisco	GER	Ballard	Mae B.	26	Sonoma Co.	CA
Dana	George Sherman	31	Geyserville	CA	Fay	Cora	26	Geyserville	CA

Groom					Bride				
Surname	**Given Name**	**Age**	**Residence**	**BP**	**Surname**	**Given Name**	**Age**	**Residence**	**BP**
Dana	Martin V. B.	35	Geyserville	CA	Long	Hattie Irene	18	Geyserville	CA
Dana	P. F.	39	San Francisco	MO	Perz	Dora	29	San Francisco	AUS
Dana	Fred C.	36	Santa Rosa	KS	Wheeler	Isabella M.	32	Santa Rosa	AR
Daniels	Claude William	24	Cloverdale	Lake Co., OR	Bridges	Katie L.	16	Cloverdale	IL
Daniels	Corel (?) J.	36	Ukiah	CA	Nally	Jennie M.	35		NV
Daniels	Fred J.	24	Cloverdale	CA	Vassar	Lizzie	21	Cloverdale	CA
Daniels	George Eaton	38	Healdsburg	IL	Luedke	Mae Florence	31	Healdsburg	CA
Daniels	H. A.	26	San Francisco	KS	Lownes	Mary	19	Santa Rosa	CA
Daniels	Herbert Mason	26	Santa Rosa	MI	Short	Myra Lydia	21	Santa Rosa	Napa
Daniels	Leroy E.	20	Santa Rosa	CA	Davaz	Rose	19	Santa Rosa	CA
Daniels	William E.	22	Santa Rosa	CA	Gardner	Emma	18	Santa Rosa	CA
Danly	Lloyd Elmer	32	San Francisco	CA	Hennessy	Rose Mary	27	San Francisco	CA
Dannals	Charles H.	22	San Francisco	CA	Sheldon	Harriet L.	20	Green Valley	CA
Dannells	Walter Byron	21	Mountain View	CA	Morton	Georgia Norene	21	Santa Rosa	CA
Dannhausen	William	34	Mark West Springs	GER	Dannhausen	Meta, Mrs.	37	Mark West Springs	GER
Dapelo	Luigi	26	Shellville	ITL	Maggio	Maria	18	Sonoma	ITL
Dar	David	30	Rocklin, Placer Co.	KY	Young	Flora E.	30	Cloverdale	ME
Darby	Jasper	27	Healdsburg	MO	Truett	Josephine	18	Healdsburg	CA
Darby	Jasper B.	20	Healdsburg	CA	Gwin	Jessie	20	Healdsburg	CA
Darby	Jasper N.	39	Healdsburg	MO	Warner	Augusta, Mrs.	38	Healdsburg	SWI
Darby	Martin Ernest	32	Petaluma	WY	Baker	Julia	28	Petaluma	NE
Darden	L. T.	25	Santa Rosa	IA	Hodgson	May V.	21	Santa Rosa	OR
Darling	Floyd Willis	22	Santa Rosa	CA	Daniels	Edith Edna	18	Santa Rosa	CA
Darrow	John O.				Maxwell	Mary E.			
Dart	William E.	24	Sebastopol	IL	Tracy	Hazel J.	24	Sebastopol	CND
Dasquith	Sidney W. G.	31	Berkeley	CND	Drake	Dora Luella	22	Berkeley	MN
Dasso	Dante A.	37	Oakland	CA	Field	Edna	39	Oakland	CA

Groom					Bride				
Surname	Given Name	Age	Residence	BP	Surname	Given Name	Age	Residence	BP
Dauer	Charles R.	31	San Francisco		Davis	Ada	26	San Francisco	
Davall	Melvin O.	22	Santa Rosa	PA	Smith	Ellen E.	25	Santa Rosa	ENG
Daveiro	John	21	Sebastopol	Hon	Gonsalves	Rose	22	Sebastopol	BER
Daveiro	Manuel J.	23	Sebastopol	HWI	Gonsalves	Anna C.	20	Sebastopol	BER
Davello	Joseph L.	24	Sebastopol	CA	Wedge	Josephine M.	18	Sebastopol	CA
Davello	Tony J.	26	Santa Rosa	CA	Wedge	Clara B.	24	Sebastopol	CA
Davenport	Harry A.	30	San Francisco	NE	Greavor	Betrina	22	Healdsburg	CA
Davenport	P. C.	26	Santa Rosa	ENG	Smith	Daisy	17	Santa Rosa Twp.	WI
Davidson	Allen				Archambeau	Mary O.			
Davidson	Chris	32	Cotati	NRY	Schilly	Hattie	36	Cotati	ID
Davidson	Edward	35	Ukiah	CA	Haehl	Cora	29	Ukiah	CA
Davidson	F. W.	23	Petaluma	CA	Morey	Florence A.	23	Petaluma	CA
Davidson	Fay L.	18			Root	Vida D.			
Davidson	Fred C.	33	Cloverdale	SCT	Senecal	Pearl Harrison	24	Fruitvale	CA
Davidson	John	29	Oakland	VA	Brugge	Loretta R.	27	Healdsburg	IL
Davidson	John				Davidson	Martha			
Davidson	Roy Frederick	23	San Rafael	CA	Kimes	Mabel Ann	19	Forestville	CA
Davidson	W. W.	22	Santa Rosa		Wright	Nellie J.	24		
Davie	Henry A.	24	San Francisco	BCL	Wilson	Alice A.	19	Oakland	CA
Davila	Antonio S.	22	Petaluma	PRT	Bispo	Mary E.	20	Petaluma	PRT
Davini	Joe	23	Healdsburg	ITL	Domitille	Carlotina	15	Healdsburg	CA
Davis	Adelbert A.	26	Forestville	NE	Stine	Sylvia C.	21	Forestville	IA
Davis	Alphonse G. W.				Wilsey	Ida M.	15		
Davis	B. F.	45	San Francisco	IL	Beebe	Frances J.	45	San Francisco	IL
Davis	Barton J.	63	Geyserville	VA	Dutton	Loraine K.	28	Geyserville	CA
Davis	Charles Alva	27	Chico	MO	Fine	Mary M.	20	Santa Rosa	CA
Davis	Charles E.	33	Eureka	CA	Coleman	Jennie	30	Petaluma	CA
Davis	Charles E.	22	Santa Rosa	CA	Davis	Edith M.	21	Santa Rosa	CA
Davis	Charles Henry Alexander	21+	San Francisco	Toronto	Jewell	Sally	21+	Petaluma	Pet

Groom					Bride				
Surname	**Given Name**	**Age**	**Residence**	**BP**	**Surname**	**Given Name**	**Age**	**Residence**	**BP**
Davis	Charles Louis	29	Santa Rosa	WY	Banks	Esther E.	24	Santa Rosa	CA
Davis	Charles M.	23	Healdsburg	CA	Da Shiell	Annie	31	Healdsburg	CA
Davis	Charles Marion	45	Forestville	IL	Walton	Ida O.	45	Forestville	IA
Davis	Charles N.	38	Forestville	CA	Hoover	Elizabeth	28	Forestville	MO
Davis	Christopher C.	34	Forestville	CA	Gray	Florence Olive, Mrs.	29	Forestville	CA
Davis	Claude H.	24	Petaluma	WV	Cook	Estella M.	24	Petaluma	MO
Davis	Clyde Leroy	38	San Francisco	MI	Ford	Mildred Agnes	34	San Francisco	CA
Davis	Daniel O., Jr.	21	Healdsburg		Murch	Jennie S.	20	Healdsburg	
Davis	Edward J.	24	Santa Rosa	CA	Wood	Francis A.	21	Santa Rosa	CA
Davis	Edward W.	41	Santa Rosa	IA	Young	Margaret L.	31	Santa Rosa	CA
Davis	Erastus L.	52	Freestone	IL	Davis	Mary L.	59	Santa Rosa	GER
Davis	Erastus L.	52	Freestone	IL	Davis	Mary L., Mrs.	59	Santa Rosa	GER
Davis	Ernest J.	26	Santa Rosa	IA	Robinett	Ida L.	21	Santa Rosa	CA
Davis	Floyd E.	21	Sebastopol	NE	Huntington	Eva J.	21	Santa Rosa	CA
Davis	Frank N.	24	Forestville	CA	Stine	Joysa R.	19	Forestville	OR
Davis	Fred William	21	Santa Rosa	CA	Rima	Alta L.	18	Santa Rosa	CA
Davis	G. W.	59	Santa Rosa		Warner	Mary E.	40	Santa Rosa	
Davis	George A.	22	Healdsburg	ME	Spurr	Rose R.	26	Healdsburg	IA
Davis	George Armstead	19	Healdsburg		Smith	Helen Amanda	21	Healdsburg	
Davis	George B.	25	Healdsburg	MI	Doane	Lulu M.	18	Healdsburg	MI
Davis	George W.	39	Potter Valley	GER	Richards	Penelope R.	38	Potter Valley	CA
Davis	Gilman Bush	24	San Francisco		Clark	Mollie	24	Petaluma	
Davis	H. H.	45	Sonoma	PA	Hope	Natalie	26	Sonoma	CA
Davis	H. Ruliff	22	Corralitas	CA	Churchman	Edith	19	Cazadero	CA
Davis	Harry A.	23	Pleasanton	CA	Rines	Luella	22	Santa Rosa	MN
Davis	Harry Edward	21	Petaluma	CA	Stottlemyer	Rena Ada	23	Vacaville	CA
Davis	Henry A.	29	Forestville	CA	Timme	Millie, Mrs.	30	Forestville	IA
Davis	J. Harris	39	New York City	ENG	Starkey	Josephine P.	25	Redwood Valley	CA
Davis	J. M.	26	Marion, IL	IL	Viestentz	Alma A.	25	Shawano, WI	WI

Groom					Bride				
Surname	**Given Name**	**Age**	**Residence**	**BP**	**Surname**	**Given Name**	**Age**	**Residence**	**BP**
Davis	James M.	21	Healdsburg	IA	Smith	Agnes	15	Healdsburg	CA
Davis	John	48	Arcata	SCT	Drake	Maud	20	Sebastopol	MI
Davis	John Elmer	23	Guerneville	PA	Deal	Mary Catherine	15		NRY
Davis	John H.	25	Petaluma	Cambria	Montgomery	Ambrosine	25	Petaluma	Sfo
Davis	John M.	25	Forestville	CA	Flesher	Elsie V.	20	Sebastopol	CA
Davis	Jonah W.	32	Petaluma	IA	Huntley	Emma	27	Guerneville	ME
Davis	Joseph Isaac	25	Forestville	CA	Smith	Nolia Malinda	19	Guerneville	CA
Davis	Mac A.	34	Santa Rosa	CA	Kopp	Frances M.	27?	Santa Rosa	CA
Davis	Mack A.	21	Santa Rosa	CA	Neurauter	Agnes	19	Santa Rosa	MN
Davis	Manra (?) J.	22	Guerneville	CA	Case	Susie	19	Healdsburg	CA
Davis	Milton M.	44	San Francisco	CA	Garvin	Nora S.	35	San Francisco	MI
Davis	Monroe	26	Bennett Valley		Leek	Mary Jane	23	Bennett Valley	
Davis	Percy E.	25	Oakland	CA	Ward	Lalitte I.	20	San Francisco	IL
Davis	Preston R.	52	Santa Rosa	OH	Neergaard	Grace Lovell, Mrs.	26	Santa Rosa	MA
Davis	Robert E.	28	San Francisco	MO	Frost	Phoebe A.	27	San Jose	CA
Davis	Ulysses G.	31	Forestville	NH	Flesher	Josephine M.	17	Forestville	IA
Davis	Walter Allen	22	Santa Rosa	CA	Hermann	Ethel Clifford	30	Santa Rosa	CA
Davis	Walter S.	37	Santa Rosa	OH	Perkins	Eva F.	32	Santa Rosa	CA
Davis	William Henry	20	Cloverdale	MO	Fields	Lucinda	18	Cloverdale	MO
Davis	William L.	33	San Francisco	IA	Sullivan	Margaret Catherine	22	Petaluma	Pet
Davis	Henry D.	40	Penngrove	CA	Kelsey	Mary H.	25	Petaluma	CA
Davison	George W.	31	Healdsburg	CA	Eccles	Grace S.	15+	Healdsburg	OR
Davison	Henry W.	57	Bloomfield	VT	Thompson	Fannie S.	30	Bloomfield	CA
Davison	Robert W. S.	27	San Francisco	PA	Totman	Ruth M.	21	San Francisco	CA
Daw	J. M.	23	Eureka	CA	Berger	Anna E.	22	Santa Rosa	CA
Dawe	George C.	24	Hopland	NY	Guirand	Ella	18	Hopland	CA
Day	Carl F.	25	Oakland	CA	Bowersmith	Lottie V.	22	Oakland	CA

Groom					Bride				
Surname	**Given Name**	**Age**	**Residence**	**BP**	**Surname**	**Given Name**	**Age**	**Residence**	**BP**
Day	Charles Eugene	36	Bridgeport, Mono Co.	CA	Fallon	Edna Brown	28	Fulton	CA
Day	Denny	38	Petaluma	MN	Fay	Laura, Mrs.	41	Petaluma	CA
Day	George Frank	26	Healdsburg	CA	Dicke	Lizzie	18	Healdsburg	CA
Day	Harmon A.	21	San Francisco	KS	Gilbert	May E.	17	Santa Rosa	CA
Day	John	43	Healdsburg	ENG	Swanson	Louisa	40	Healdsburg	SWD
Day	Louie	22	San Francisco	CA	Kelly	Stella	19	San Francisco	CA
Day	William B.	41	Healdsburg	WI	Luce	Mary E.	18	Healdsburg	CA
Day	William T.	29	Santa Cruz	CA	Gould	Bessie E.	19	Penngrove	NE
Dayton	John J.	22	Sebastopol	CA	Sharp	Gertie P.	18	Sebastopol	CA
Dayton	Wm. L.	45	Santa Rosa		Kreamer	Nellie	15	Santa Rosa	
de Avilla	Jose Fereira	24	Petaluma	AZR	Rose	Mary	17	Sebastopol	AZR
de Betencur	Joao	28	Petaluma	AZR	da Silva	Maria Joze	25	Petaluma	AZR
de Emparon	Ricordo	29	San Diego	MEX	Vallejo	Lulu E.	26	Sonoma	CA
De France	John	44	Salt Lake City	KY	Steed	Martha	43	Salt Lake	KY
De Groot	Frank	28	Petaluma	NTH	Henningsen	Mary	29	Petaluma	GER
de Klark	Henry	30	Tomales	HLD	Perry	Minnie	28	Petaluma	CA
De Lappe	Fred R.	22	Santa Rosa	CA	Guerne	Edith G.	20	Santa Rosa	CA
de Lappe	Wisley R.	28	San Francisco	CA	Sheldon	Dorothy P.	25	Santa Rosa	CA
De Martini	John	27	San Francisco	CA	Ariasi	Margaret	21	Santa Rosa	CA
De Matei	Louis Paul	31	San Francisco	CA	Bacigalupi	Josephine	27	Agua Calente	CA
De Maura	Antonio	25	Tomales	AZR	Viera	Mary	18	Petaluma	AZR
de Neuf	Emil A.	24	Petaluma	WA	Chamberlain	Georgie	19	Petaluma	CA
De Patta	Joseph Miles	21	San Francisco	CA	Fisher	Claire G.	18	San Francisco	CA
De Rosa	Roque P.	52	Novato	AZR	Aguiar	Maria S.	42	Novato	AZR
de Silva	Manuel R.	33	Santa Rosa	PRT	Beteneur	Marianna Teadora	34	Santa Rosa	PRT
de Souza	Jose	34	Watsonville	PRT	Williams	Jennie	33	Petaluma	CA
De Souza	Manuel T.	30	Healdsburg	PRT	De Matos	Maria	18+	Healdsburg	PRT
De Souza	Tony	21	Bodega	CA	Rose	Mary D.	19	Sebastopol	CA

Groom					Bride				
Surname	Given Name	Age	Residence	BP	Surname	Given Name	Age	Residence	BP
de Violini	Arduino	24	San Francisco	ITL	Garton	Harriet P.	26	San Francisco	ENG
Deakin	Henry C.	60	Napa	IL	Moore	Catharine	49	Vacaville	CND
Deal	John L.	36	Vine Hill	IN	Cromwell	Edith M., Mrs.	27	Vine Hill	IL
Deal	Oliver Morton	26	Guerneville	IA	Deal	Minnie Etta	24	Guerneville	CA
Dealy	Charles A.	51	Salt Lake, UT	NV	Ganske	Mabel K.	37	Ogden, UT	CA
Dean	Carl R.	25	Sebastopol	KS	Heartwell	Jessie B.	21	Sebastopol	SD
Dean	Herbert Burroughs	25	Stockton	CA	Hanseb	Agnes M.	25	Stockton	IA
Dean	James Monroe	38	Healdsburg	KS	Gjedberg	Clara	47	Humboldt, KS	IA
Dean	John E.	29	Garberville	CA	Preston	Mabel G.	24	Healdsburg	OR
Dean	Leslie Chauncy	27	Petaluma	MI	Harford	Ethel Florence	24	Petaluma	CA
Dean	Lewis F.				Weidman	Emerine			
Dean	Oliver Franklin	22	Healdsburg	KS	Pember	Ethel Marie	23	Healdsburg	IA
Deas	Joseph Vargas, Jr.	24	Oakland	CA	Gresham	Gladys Elizabeth	24	Oakland	CA
Deaueare (?)	John				Binner (?)	Elizabeth			
Debo	Emil C.	35	San Francisco	FRN	Sarzotti	Teresa	20	Healdsburg	CA
DeBolt	John H.	60	Santa Rosa	OH	Schultz	Leonora	26	Cloverdale	CA
DeBolt	Ralph A.	31	Santa Rosa	IA	Barnett	Loretta B.	19	Santa Rosa	CA
Decanini	Giovanni	22	Sonoma	ITL	Proletti	Josephina	15	Sonoma	Son
Decarli	Antonio	22	Penngrove	SWT	Miranda	Mary	37	Santa Rosa	CA
DeCarli	Bathista	30	Petaluma	SWT	Mascoinini	Lily	25	Lakeville	CA
DeCarli	Victor	30	Nicasio	SWT	Filippini	Elmira Mary	24	Petaluma	CA
Decco	Henry	52	Glen Ellen	LA	Mendoco	Laura	28	Glen Ellen	CA
Decker	Elmer E.	23	San Francisco	CA	Moran	Florence B.	29	Sebastopol	CA
Decker	Frank William	25	San Francisco	CA	McDonnell	Louise	28	Knights Valley	CA
Decker	John T.				Coary	Gusta			
Decker	Martin Arthur	24	San Rafael	CA	Isaac	Eva	19	San Rafael	CA
Decker	Nias M.	24	Healdsburg	CA	Poulson	Nettie E.	20	Healdsburg	CA
Decoe	T. C.	30	Santa Rosa	CND	Barnes	Henrietta A.	21	Petaluma	CA

Groom					Bride				
Surname	**Given Name**	**Age**	**Residence**	**BP**	**Surname**	**Given Name**	**Age**	**Residence**	**BP**
Decvursoy (?)	John	30	Bodega Twp.		Beedle	Lena E.	17	Bodega Twp.	
Dedmond	Edward F.	29	San Francisco	CA	McHugh	Bertha E.	25	San Francisco	IRL
Deeds	William W.	53	Windsor	CA	Barnes	Annie	59	Windsor	MO
Deevy	Daniel J.	30	Petaluma	IRL	Marron	Nellie	30	Petaluma	CA
Defanti	Albert Alphonse	21	Santa Rosa	SWT	Ferrari	Elva	20	Santa Rosa	ARG
Deffenbaugh	Louis M.	27	Santa Rosa	PA	Hopkins	Ruby B.	28	Santa Rosa	CA
Degn	Jorgen Andersen	54	Santa Rosa	DNK	Beier	Mette M.	35	Santa Rosa	DNK
DeGoa	Victor G.	27	Willows	CA	Page	Gladys H.	25	Petaluma	SD
DeGregorio	Peter Martin	26	Forestville	CA	Davidson	Mable Ann	25	Forestville	CA
DeGuerre	Harold	24	San Francisco	CA	Haywood	Ruth A.	19	San Francisco	PA
Dei	Henry	28	Bodega	CA	Bennett	Alice H.	25	Santa Rosa	IL
Dei	John W.	31	Bodega	CA	Finley	Annette	16	Bodega	CA
Dei	Peter	23	Freestone	CA	Tognacca	Lizzie	19	Bodega	CA
Deily	James B.	26	San Francisco		Coventry	Adelle	16	Windsor	
Deini	Leonardo	39	Petaluma	ITL	Sullivan	Andrea, Mrs.	35	Petaluma	CA
Deiss	William F.	31	Petaluma	PA	Riewerts	Marie Josephine	26	Petaluma	GER
Del Bianco	Attilio	25	Olivet	ITL	Bisordi	Emma M.	18	Fulton	ITL
Del Piano	Giovanni	38	Healdsburg	ITL	Cavallo	Catherina	46	Healdsburg	ITL
Del Prette	Ferdinando	28	Duncans Mills	ITL	Stefani	Carrie	18	Cazadero	CA
Delahunty	Bernard		Bodega		Cunningham	Mattie		Bodega	
DeLaney	Everett M.	29	San Francisco	CA	Butin	Elsie Lee	19	Penngrove	OR
Delbary	Marcel	35	Sonoma	FRN	Anglade	Ida	23	San Francisco	FRN
DelCarlo	Arcangelo	42	Healdsburg	ITL	Puccinelli	Assunta	29	Healdsburg	ITL
Delehanty	James E.	22	Sonoma	RI	Armstrong	Alice	19	Sonoma	CA
Delevan	Frederick S.	31	San Francisco	ME	Carvell	Lucia E. E.	32	Santa Rosa	ME
Delong	Albert N.	20	Freestone	MI	Schuster	Josie	28	Freestone	CA
DeLong	William L.	62	Occidental	NY	Gouley	Mollie, Mrs.	58	Occidental	LA
Deloran	Jefferson	26	Two Rock	CA	Werick	N. Tewella M.	17	Two Rock	OH
Deluca	Amadeo	28	Healdsburg	ITL	Papear	Louisa, Mrs.	19	Healdsburg	CA
Demartini	Albert	29	Petaluma	SWT	Moretti	Irene	22	Tomales	SWT

Groom					Bride				
Surname	Given Name	Age	Residence	BP	Surname	Given Name	Age	Residence	BP
DeMartini	Benigno	29	Petaluma	SWT	DeMartini	Irene, Mrs.	28	Petaluma	SWT
DeMartini	Louis	33	Petaluma	ITL	Moretti	Rose	22	Petaluma	SWT
DeMartini	Mansueto	30	Petaluma	SWT	Monghette	Angealina	23	Petaluma	SWT
DeMell	Joseph	22	Mill Creek	PRT	Kelley	Florence Euyler?	20	Dry Creek	Hayward
Demman	John R.	23	Petaluma	CA	Parsons	Ella M.	21	Petaluma	CA
Demousset	Armand	31	Healdsburg		Frirot (?)	Fanny	29	Healdsburg	
Dempsey	Patrick	36		IRL	McKeown	Margaret	30	Healdsburg	IRL
Denchy	Cornelius	21	San Francisco	CA	Stone	Alice	20	Alameda	CA
Denham	Drury	74	Santa Rosa	MO	Egner	Martha	74	Santa Rosa	OH
Denham	Frank P.	24	Penngrove	CA	Nesbitt	Eva Elizabeth	22	Penngrove	CA
Denicke	H.	26	Sebastopol	GER	Dutton	Emma J.	20	Santa Rosa	CA
Denis	Foster	32	Kingman, AZ		Stuart	Isabel	24	Glen Ellen	CA
Denis	George Edward	22	Petaluma	NY	Shinn	Anna Helen	19	Petaluma	KS
Denise	Louis H.	21	Healdsburg	CA	Shelley	Mabel	19	Healdsburg	CA
Denison	Joseph N.	24	Napa Co.		Davis	Dara A.	19	Vacaville	
Denman	F. H.								
Denman	Frank H.	28	Santa Rosa	CA	Edwards	Charlotte T.	23	Santa Rosa	NJ
Denner	Russell L. A.	34	Mt. Olivet	CA	Dreyer	Helena E.	28	Sebastopol	CA
Dennes	Edward F.	27	Healdsburg	ENG	Ray	Hattie	33	Healdsburg	CA
Dennis	William Whan	23	San Francisco	CA	Clark	Clara Belle	26	Healdsburg	ME
Dennison	Ezra D.	26	Alameda	CA	Lloyd	Emma	20	Alameda	IL
Dennison	Ezra D.	48	Stockton	CA	Kinne	Ethel S.	28	Sonoma	NE
Denny	Lloyd L.	24	Petaluma	CA	Hardin	Lucinda T.	15	Petaluma	CA
Dent	Elmer S.	28	Berkeley	MT	Doyle	Ruth	24	Oakland	CA
Dent	William	63	Petaluma Twp.	ENG	Steer	Marian	58	Petaluma Twp.	ENG
Denton	Paul R.	29	Big Pine, CA	IA	Ward	E. May	28	Berkeley	CA
Denucci	Angelo	30	Forestville	ITL	Rossi	Maddalena	18	Guerneville	ITL
Depole	Giovanni	42	Santa Rosa	ITL	Rondinella	Maria	36	Santa Rosa	ITL
Deremer	Fred Richard	35	San Francisco	NY	MacCaskie	Alice Jane	25	San Francisco	CA

Groom					Bride				
Surname	**Given Name**	**Age**	**Residence**	**BP**	**Surname**	**Given Name**	**Age**	**Residence**	**BP**
Derham	Christopher	21	Santa Rosa	MA	Hall	Nola	17	Santa Rosa	CND
Derham	Herbert	24	Oakland	CA	McCloskey	Ida	22	Oakland	CA
Derham	Le Roy	24	San Francisco	CA	Kaster	Dena	24	San Francisco	CA
DeRoco	Leo U.	29	Richmond	CA	Ferrasci	Theresa L.	30	Richmond	SWT
DeRosa	Manuel	24	Petaluma	CA	Beffa	Lillie	18	Petaluma	CA
DeRose	William	24	Santa Rosa	CA	Whitaker	Rena Pearl	22	Santa Rosa	CA
Derrick	C. A.	25	Healdsburg	CA	Crandal	Annie, Mrs.	27	Healdsburg	Wat
Derrick	Charles Erwin	25	Healdsburg	CA	Francesco	Mary Lenora	19	Sebastopol	CA
Derrick	Geo. W.	34	Healdsburg		Bacon	Lillie T.	19	Healdsburg	
Derrick	George L.	22	Healdsburg	CA	Clawson	Lucy E.	18	Santa Rosa	CA
Derrick	Grant	22	Dry Creek	IN	Snyder	Laura	18	Dry Creek	CA
Derrick	Herbert D.	23	Healdsburg	CA	Stinchfield	Florence V.	17	Healdsburg	CA
Derrick	Jesse W.	33	Guerneville	CA	Davis	Mary J.	18	Guerneville	CA
Descalso	James R.	46	Santa Rosa	CA	Moore	Helen E.	36	Santa Rosa	CA
Descalso	Luke M.	50	San Francisco	CA	Kerschner	Juanita Evangeline	40	San Jose	CA
DeSelle	Howard L.	25	Santa Rosa	MA	Shaffer	Fern Rebbeca	18	Santa Rosa	NE
Desin	John N.	43	San Francisco	AUS	Campbell	Etta M.	28	San Francisco	CA
Despain	Silas M.	42	San Francisco	IA	Steifel	Matilda L.	36	San Francisco	CA
Deter	Harry R.	21	Santa Rosa	IN	Spencer	Emma V.	19	Santa Rosa	PA
Deter	John	36	Sebastopol	IN	Elburn (?)	Laura	23	Sebastopol	IN
Detroit	Philip Adam	31	The Geysers	NY	Kelley	Lulu Salome	21	The Geysers	IL
DeTurk	William S.	26	Petaluma	Soc	Mooney	Anna J.	26	Petaluma	Soc
Deu Vaul	Bert E.	34	Albion	OR	Martin	Violet D.	23	Albion	ENG
Deuprey	Munson	21	Sausalito	CA	Swisher	B. Clifton	22	Healdsburg	CA
Deutch	Edward	22	San Francisco	CA	Wood	Mellicent	19	San Francisco	CA
Devencenzi	Victor	21	Oakland	CA	Gipp	Margaret C.	17	Oakland	NJ
Devine	Patrick	39	Santa Rosa	IRL	Meghan	Fannie M.	26	Santa Rosa	IRL
Devlin	Thomas H.	42	Howard Station	NJ	Morris	Elvin B.	21	Howard	CA
Devoto	Tonni	35	Santa Rosa	ITL	Guissi	Mary	24	Santa Rosa	ITL

Groom					Bride				
Surname	**Given Name**	**Age**	**Residence**	**BP**	**Surname**	**Given Name**	**Age**	**Residence**	**BP**
Devow	George	38	Santa Rosa		Drever	Harriet	41	Santa Rosa	
Dewey	Dean	30	Healdsburg	IA	Daniels	Lilly M.	26	Cloverdale	OR
Dewey	Gra M.	37	Healdsburg	IA	Nye	Adelaide D.	34	Healdsburg	MI
Dewey	Victor R.	26	Healdsburg	IA	Hilgereoh	Helen Mildred	21	Healdsburg	CA
DeWitt	Harry Arthur	26	San Francisco	MI	Jeans	Jessie Lee	22	Santa Rosa	CA
DeWitt	Henry C.	30	Santa Rosa	MD	Dix	Annie M.	25	Santa Rosa	IL
Dexter	Wm. A.				Sacrey	Mary J.			
Di Grazia	Giocondo	32	San Francisco	ITL	Passarino	Dalia	20	Healdsburg	ITL
Dias	Antone	51	Oakland	PRT	Richi	Sarah E.	50	Oakland	BRA
Dias	I. S.	27	Petaluma	LA	Rhoades	Alzina	30	Petaluma	MN
Dibble	Lawrence Levinice	22	Forestville	NV	Tomblinson	Gertrude Annie	18	Guerneville	CA
Dibble	Leroy Earl	21	Forestville	CA	Bohn	Jennie	19	Forestville	CA
Dibble	Roland C.	21	Santa Rosa	MO	Muther	Georgie M.	20	Santa Rosa	CA
Dibble	Walter	27	Salt Point	ME	Locke	Veravuche (?)	15	Salt Point	IL
Dibble	William I.	23	Santa Rosa	MO	Butler	Bessie	19	Santa Rosa	OR
Dibblee	William Henry	30	San Francisco	CA	Lewis	Georgiana	20	Brandon, OR	OR
Diceare ?	Salvatore	28	Santa Rosa	ITL	Barsuglia	Josie	16	Santa Rosa	ITL
Dicke	George	23	Healdsburg	CA	Baxman	Hattie Laurietta	18	Cazadero	CA
Dickerson	Melvin R.	37	Santa Rosa	MO	Liddell	Anna	34	Los Angeles	MI
Dickerson	Roy Ernest	27	Cloverdale	IL	Howard	Delle	28	Cloverdale	CA
Dickerson	George E.	40	Bisbee, AZ	CA	McInerney	Isabel M.	38	Oakland	CA
Dickey	Arthur E.	26	Santa Rosa	ME	Herman	Bessie	22	Santa Rosa	CA
Dickey	William James	52	Santa Rosa	ME	Phillips	Mabel	36	Santa Rosa	LA
Dickmann	Charles H.	44	San Francisco	GER	Wilson	Jessie E.	37	Denver	IA
Dickson	David Simms	20	Petaluma	CA	Middogh	Myrtle	18	Petaluma	CA
Dickson	Frank B.	24	San Fernando, Los Angeles Co.	CA	Winans	Luella M.	25	Petaluma	OH
Dickson	Frank Maurice	33	Petaluma	CA	McGovern	Annie Lauretta	30	Petaluma	Pet
Dickson	J. C.				Caldwell	Jane			

Groom					Bride				
Surname	Given Name	Age	Residence	BP	Surname	Given Name	Age	Residence	BP
Dickson	J. M.	32	Santa Rosa	CND	Spence	W. O.	21	Santa Rosa	CA
Dickson	Joshua B.	21	Petaluma	SWI	Griffiths	Josie E.	26	Grass Valley	CA
Dickson	Joshua Bates, Jr.	23	Petaluma	CA	Gates	Ethel G.	24	Geyserville	CA
Dickson	William H.	23	Sacramento	CND	Jones	Laura H.	19	Santa Rosa	MA
Dickson	William M.	43	Petaluma	CA	Dickson	Lizzie B.	40	Petaluma	VT
Diehl	Henry N.	35	Camp Meeker	GER	de Martini	Millie	28	Camp Meeker	CA
Dietert	Rudolph H.	45	San Francisco	TX	Wiberg	Betty	29	San Francisco	SWD
Dietrich	Gottlieb	56	Sebastopol	GER	Hoffstetter	Albertine	35	Santa Rosa	FRN
Dietrich	Joseph W.	25	Point Richmond	IA	Harrison	Florence	23	Oakland	NY
Dietz	Henry Werner	28	Mitchell, NE	CA	Barrows	Edith Ainslie	27	Santa Rosa	NE
Dietz	Otto Frank	23	San Jose	GER	Hooper	Harriet	23	Petaluma	NY
Dightman	W. E.	22	Anderson Valley	CND	Gimtley	Emma	19	Anderson Valley	CA
Dilena	Simon	31	Petaluma	SWT	Guggia	Josephine Mary	31	Petaluma	SWT
Dilges	William	34	Oakland	GER	Lines	Lulu	34	Oakland	IL
Dillingham	John L.	42	Healdsburg	CA	Martin	Susie	24	Healdsburg	CA
Dillingham	John Lee	40	Healdsburg	CA	Willis	Lulu	18	San Bernardino	CA
Dillman	Charles	30	Petaluma	IL	Doss	Iva	19	Petaluma	CA
Dillon	Charles	24	Santa Rosa	CND	Bailiff	Geraine M.	18	Santa Rosa	CA
Dillon	Charles E.	37	Petaluma	CA	Thompson	Francis E.	30	Petaluma	CA
Dillon	David	24	Santa Rosa	IRL	Peyton	Lillian	26	Santa Rosa	CA
Dillon	Isaac Parry	30	Sacramento	CA	St. John	Edith Lenore	22	Healdsburg	OH
Dillon	James E.	31	San Francisco	CA	Bagan	Emma M., Mrs.	30	Vallejo	CA
Dillon	John H.	24	Dillons Beach	CA	Bones	Lida M.	20	Occidental	CA
Dillon	Melville C.	30	Napa	CND	Dillon	Margaret G.	26	Santa Rosa	CA
Dingle	Chas. Edward	28	Yolo Co.		Sims	Nellie	28	Sonoma Co.	
Dinmore	Walter Robert	30	Petaluma	Phl	Lewis	Nannie May	20	Petaluma	CA
Dinsdale	George D.	24	Woodland	CA	Stenrud (?)	Nellie J.	24	Petaluma	MN
Dinucci	Adolph	32	Healdsburg	ITL	Moes	Ernestine	29	Healdsburg	MN
Dinucci	Antonio	39	Forestville	ITL	Dinucci	Filomina	35	Forestville	ITL
Dinucci	Fred	25	Healdsburg	CA	Hayes	Grace	15	Healdsburg	CA

Groom					Bride				
Surname	**Given Name**	**Age**	**Residence**	**BP**	**Surname**	**Given Name**	**Age**	**Residence**	**BP**
Dinucci	Richard	27	San Francisco	ITL	Vellutini	Lizzie	20	Forestville	ITL
Dinucci	Romeo	24	Forestville	CA	Garetti	Lena	18	Forestville	CA
Dioke	Joseph	26	Healdsburg	GER	Bush	Lesa	22	Healdsburg	GER
Dirvin	Peter	42	Healdsburg	PA	Bugbee	Evalyn	32	Elmhurst	CA
Disbro	Ernest F.	22	Freestone	CA	Workover	Edwine C.	19	Sebastopol	CA
Disher	George W.	25	Sherwood		Leigh	Amanda J.	24	Geyserville	
Disher	William F.	34	Coquille City, Coos Co., OR	IN	Maddocks	Erminia	31	Forestville	CA
Disney	John H.	29	Santa Rosa	PA	Callison	Leona E.	27	Santa Rosa	CA
Ditlersen	Albert	23	Santa Rosa	MN	Judd	Mable Florence	20	Santa Rosa	NE
Dittemon	Loven J.	36	San Francisco	CA	Fay	Edith	21	Geyserville	CA
Dittman	Fred August	27	Santa Rosa	WI	Phillips	Katherine Wendell	24	Santa Rosa	WI
Dittmann	Henry	24	Petaluma	GER	Drickhammer	Meta	23	Petaluma	GER
Dittmann	Wilhelm E. J.	33	Petaluma	GER	Hinoch	Katherine Margarette Minna	24	Petaluma	GER
Dittmore	Clarence A.	22	San Francisco	CA	Teaby (?)	Ora A.	18	Geyserville	CA
Dixon	Harold G.	24	Santa Rosa	CA	Heselschwerdt	Inez E.	22	Santa Rosa	
Dixon	James W.				Shaler	Eliza E.			
Dixon	John T.	41	Cloverdale	MO	Crigler	Lottie	36	Cloverdale	CA
Dixon	R. Dawson	39	Santa Rosa	CA	Riley	Bessie M.	36	Santa Rosa	CA
Dixon	Walter C.	23	Skaggs Springs	CA	Huckabay	Maude Sarah	25	Santa Rosa	IL
Dixon	William Gordon	26	Santa Rosa	NE	Canfield	Gertrude	28	Santa Rosa	IA
do Rego	Francisco Theodoro	35	Sebastopol	PRT	Medeiros	Victoria Gloria	19	Sebastopol	PRT
Dobel	William L.	33	San Francisco	IN	McClure	Emma	20	Kansas City	Kansa s City
Doble	John Luther	22	San Francisco	MN	St. John	Hattie B.	22	Healdsburg	CA
Dobyne	William H.	46	Santa Rosa	OH	Cohenous	Jennie F.	20	Santa Rosa	KS
Doda	Hobart J.	21	Duncans Mills	CA	Fiori	Frances	18	Duncans Mills	ITL

Groom					Bride				
Surname	**Given Name**	**Age**	**Residence**	**BP**	**Surname**	**Given Name**	**Age**	**Residence**	**BP**
Doda	Victor	21	Sebastopol	CA	Adams	Sadie	18	Bay	NY
Dodge	A. C.	45	Healdsburg		Barker	Sophie	17	Healdsburg	
Dodge	Harold Carew	28	NY	IL	Woolsey	Louise	24	Santa Rosa	OR
Dodge	James Arthur	25	Mendocino	CA	Hopkins	Alma Luella	20	Santa Rosa	CA
Dodge	Milton	39	San Francisco	CND	Bossen	Sophia	29	San Francisco	CA
Dodge	Milton	23	Kansas City, MO	CA	Mann	Lulu	20	Kenwood	MN
Dodge	Neal E.	25	Sonoma	NE	Simmons	Gladys F.	24	Sonoma	CA
Dodgson	John C.	23	Glen Ellen	CA	Oustott (?)	Ruth C.	18	Glen Ellen	CA
Dodson	William Howard	25	San Francisco	IL	Merrick	Eleanor Dorothy	18		OH
Doe	Edgar A.	34	Petaluma	CA	Pallo	Victoria	20	Petaluma	CA
Doelling	Harry J. W.	29	Petaluma	IL	Bruner	Olive L.	22	Petaluma	CA
Doepfner (?)	Robert	48	San Francisco	CO	Finn	Nellie L.	45	San Francisco	CA
Doering	Julius	25	Algona, IA	IA	Mickle	Clara A.	33	Fulton	WI
Dogali	Paolo	26	Cloverdale	ITL	Gargini	Giulia	23	Cloverdale	ITL
Dogge	Rudolph S.	21	San Francisco	UT	Nelson	Alzire	22	San Francisco	CA
Doglio	Frank	30	Santa Rosa	ITL	Pierucci	Marie	22	Santa Rosa	CA
Dohn	George Arthur	22	Santa Rosa	CA	Trowbridge	Mabel Bertram	22	Santa Rosa	CA
Doir	Edgar	31	Vallejo	OH	Dishong	Lucinda L.	23	Claremont, IL	IL
Doiza	Joseph A.	26	Petaluma Twp.	PRT	Joseph	Flora	18	Petaluma Twp.	CA
Dokkedal	Niels Peter	48	Petaluma	DNK	Iverson	Hedda	33	Petaluma	GER
Dolan	J. L.	41	San Francisco	MI	Hanily	Elizabeth	30	Healdsburg	IRL
Dolcini	Arnold Tully	28	Nicasio	CA	Connolly	Katherine Rose	25	Petaluma	CA
Dolcini	Charles E.	20	Nicasio	CA	Rogers	Elizabeth A.	20	Nicasio	CA
Dolcini	Joseph Samuel	34	Petaluma	SWT	Wallman	Georgiana	19	Sonoma	CA
Dolph	Peter Joseph	35	Oakland	OH	Shaw	Cathryn	39	New York City	NY
Dolson	Fred	25	Santa Barbara	MI	Skinner	Mary	21	Santa Barbara	CA
Dombrowski	Johann	33	Petaluma	GER	Monson	Alvine Mathilde	50	Petaluma	GER
Domenzet	Joseph	33	Valdez, AK	FRN	Gates	Caroline J.	22	Graton	CA
Domine	August F.	29	Cloverdale	IL	Ward	Lillian Belle	26	Hermitage	CA

Groom					Bride				
Surname	Given Name	Age	Residence	BP	Surname	Given Name	Age	Residence	BP
Dominick	Herbert	27	Richmond	MS	Wood	Hazel Bea	25	Oakland	CA
Dont	Joseph	24	Santa Rosa	IL	Wernecke	Katie	26	San Francisco	GER
Donahue	James M.	21+	Santa Rosa	NY	Grace	Ella C.	18+	Santa Rosa	NY
Donald	John Hall	34	San Francisco	SCT	Quigley	Flora Lucinda	28	San Francisco	MI
Donaldson	Alexander B.	22	Pasadena	CA	Gooch	Florence Irene	18	Santa Rosa	MO
Donaldson	Philip	28	Douglas, AZ	CA	Graham	Beatrice	28	Los Angeles	CA
Donegan	William	31	San Mateo	Cork Co., IRL	McKay	Isabella	31	Freestone	IRL
Donel	P. A.	33	Santa Rosa	Paris, FRN	Notingham	Mary Jane	21	Santa Rosa	Sfo
Donley	Charlie E.	37	Redding	CA	Petit	Augusta L.	40	Redding	PA
Donlin	Frank L.	35	Worcester, MA	MA	Felt	Freda Elizabeth	32	Chicago	SWD
Donmecq	Ben	46	San Francisco	FRN	Laffourguette	Marie	35	San Francisco	FRN
Donnelly	Thomas F.	59	Petaluma	IRL	Carter	Ellen	50	Petaluma	IRL
Donnely	John Z.				Turman	Margaret S.	18		
Donner	George Jacob	36	Sebastopol	CA	Tillman	Margaret	33	Santa Rosa	PA
Donner	John Carter	33	Sebastopol	CA	McReynolds	May Violet	26	Sebastopol	CA
Donogh	Andrew	31	Vallejo Twp.	CND	Spotswood	Eliza	25	Petaluma	CND
Donogh	Russell W.	22	Lakeville	CA	Kulberg	Engre C.	20	Petaluma	CA
Donohoe	Patrick	32	San Francisco	IRL	Brogan	Frances Catherine	21	Schellville	Susuin
Donovan	A. H.	34	Santa Rosa	CA	Quinn	Mary E.	26	Santa Rosa	CA
Donovan	Jeremiah C.	30	Santa Rosa	IRL	Miller	Bertha	24	Santa Rosa	CA
Donovan	Ney L.	29	Santa Rosa	MA	Guerne	Evalyn R.	23	Santa Rosa	CA
Dont	Clifford W.	21	Santa Rosa	CA	Jobson	Verda Mae Belle	19	Santa Rosa	CA
Dont	John G.	32	Santa Rosa	NY	Danz	Rosa	18	Freestone	CT
Doran	James	45	San Francisco	IRL	O'Connor	Mary	27	Healdsburg	CA
Doras	Leicester	48	Stony Point	IOJ	Gilbertson	Annie	44	Santa Rosa	ENG
Dorman	Den H.	33	Covelo	CA	Smith	Josephine	20	Santa Rosa	CA

Groom					Bride				
Surname	**Given Name**	**Age**	**Residence**	**BP**	**Surname**	**Given Name**	**Age**	**Residence**	**BP**
Dorman	Ira	36	Healdsburg	CA	Walters	Catharine	35	Healdsburg	CA
Dorman	William E.	24	Santa Rosa	MO	Marshall	Lillian B.	24	Santa Rosa	CA
Dormetta	Georgie	25	Petaluma	ITL	Castellino	Maria	19	Petaluma	PAR
Dornbach	Fred	24	San Francisco	MA	Brown	Ella F.	21	San Francisco	CA
Dornel	Paul A.	38	Santa Rosa	FRN	Slater	Louise G.	22	Santa Rosa	CA
Dornin	John C.	31	Oakland	CA	Neff	Anna K.	24	Oakland	PA
Dorris	Fred O.	24	San Diego	TN	King	Jessie I.	26	Healdsburg	CA
Dorroh	Carleton C.	21	Petaluma	CA	Oellig	Ruth	21	Petaluma	CA
Dorsen	Isaiah P.	23	Santa Rosa	IL	Shields	May E., Mrs.	28	Santa Rosa	IL
Dorsett	Fred Edward	22	Petaluma	MN	Allen	Alice Elizabeth	20	Petaluma	IL
Dorsett	William A.	29	Petaluma	ND	Allen	Lydia Jane	28	Petaluma	IL
Doss	Earl M.	22	Petaluma	CA	Nelson	Hazel M.	20	Petaluma	OH
Doss	George W.	28	Petaluma	CA	Perry	Minnie S.	22	Petaluma	CA
Doss	Joel A.	29	Vallejo Twp.	CA	Potter	Josephine I.	21	Vallejo Twp.	CA
Doss	John W.	27	Petaluma	CA	Leszinsky	Estelle	20	Petaluma	CA
Doss	Seth B.	34	Healdsburg	CA	Simmons	Susan	23	Healdsburg	CA
Doty	Albert				Looney	Curvera M.			
Doty	Archie A.	23	Sebastopol	OR	Standley	Esther Ramiea	20	Sebastopol	CA
Dougherty	S. K.	37	Santa Rosa	MI	Sippitt	Helen M.	26	Petaluma	OH
Douglas	Alexander S.	36	Santa Rosa	IA	Noble	Madge	21	Santa Rosa	OR
Douglas	David J.	32	Tomales	IRL	Douglas	Edith R.	18	Petaluma	NY
Douglas	David W.	21	Santa Rosa	CA	McCutcheon	Hazel Genieveve	18	Santa Rosa	CA
Douglas	James Herbert	43	Eldridge	CA	Holmes	Emma Mabel	41	Eldridge	IL
Douglas	Thomas James	22	Santa Margarita	IA	Rose	Sylva Clare	18	Forestville	CA
Douglass	Geo. V.	28	Freestone	CA	Brown	Annie I.	26	Santa Rosa	CND
Douglass	Stephen Chester	26	Graton	KS	Bennett	Susie Edna	23	Sebastopol	CA
Douglass	W. A.				Cooper	M. L.			
Dovo	Joseph	30	San Francisco	ITL	Rocco	Josephine	20	Cloverdale	ITL
Dow	A. J.				Catlin	Delia Resellen	15		

Groom					Bride				
Surname	Given Name	Age	Residence	BP	Surname	Given Name	Age	Residence	BP
Dow	Archie	21	Napa	NE	Motroni	Dena	25	Healdsburg	CA
Dow	Geo. W.	27	Healdsburg		Button	Jennie	23	Santa Rosa	
Dowd	George William	30	Sausalito	Sausa-lito	McLaghlin	Kate Theresa	36	Petaluma	Soc
Dowdall	Edward J.	25	Sonoma	CA	Ferry	Maggie E.	22	Sonoma	CA
Dowdall	John N.	28	Sonoma	CA	Kearney	Clara T.	22	Sonoma	CA
Dowdall	Leo Edward	25	Eureka	CA	Haraszthy	Eleonor Marie	27	Sonoma	CA
Dowdall	Richard J.	33	Sonoma	CA	Redmond	Ellen	23	El Verano	
Dower	John R.	24	San Francisco	CA	Leventhal	Gertrude	27	San Francisco	NV
Dowing	Ludwig D.	45	San Francisco	NRY	Hogrelius	Clara A.	43	San Francisco	SWD
Dowler	Allen Lewis	40	San Francisco	OH	Wickersham	Mary Catherine	35	Petaluma	CA
Dowling	Charles W.	33	San Francisco	CND	Gates	Lulu M.	28	San Francisco	IL
Downes	Ernest	34	Santa Rosa	CA	Gray	Angie	32	Santa Rosa	CA
Downing	Arthur B.	23	Stratford	MO	Benson	Rowena	24	Petaluma	CA
Downs	Vernon, Jr.	40	Santa Rosa	CA	LeGro	Bernice	26	Santa Rosa	CA
Doyle	Charles M.	24	Oakland	CA	Chauvet	Adele M.	22	Glen Ellen	CA
Doyle	Clement A.	26	San Francisco	CA	Gongenbach	Elsie	20	San Francisco	NY
Doyle	Frank A.	32	San Francisco	CA	Cummings	Mary	27	San Francisco	CA
Doyle	Frank P.	40	Santa Rosa	CA	O'Meara	Mary A. L. (Polly)	35	Santa Rosa	ID
Doyle	Fred R.	23	Santa Rosa	CA	Meldrum	Rachael	22	Santa Rosa	CA
Doyle	Milton	23	Antioch	CA	Nicolaisen	Elizabeth	21	Petaluma	CA
Doyle	Peter J.	25	San Francisco	CA	Conran	Margaret H.	22	Healdsburg	CA
Drago	Frank	29	San Francisco	CA	Glynn	Agnes M.	24	Occidental	CA
Drake	Albert Eli	21	Petaluma	MN	Terrel	Flora Mabel	19	Petaluma	KS
Drake	Floyd G.	24	Petaluma	MN	Gale	Carrie L.	17	Petaluma	CA
Drake	George	23	Windsor		Curtis	Katie L. D.	18	Mark West	
Drake	George A.	21	Windsor	CA	Murray	Lottie J.	17	Windsor	CA
Drake	Jacob Hopper	19	Windsor	CA	Bedwell	Belva	17	Windsor	CA
Drake	Lennard Arthur	31	Calistoga	CA	Engler	Annie Marie	31	Sonoma	CA

Groom					Bride				
Surname	**Given Name**	**Age**	**Residence**	**BP**	**Surname**	**Given Name**	**Age**	**Residence**	**BP**
Drake	Lewis	23	Guerneville	CA	Yerger	Hazel	22	Guerneville	CA
Drapeau	Frank M.	27	Vallejo	MI	O'Neill	Ella A.	26	Vallejo	CA
Draper	John	55	San Francisco		Allison	Elizabeth	57	Healdsburg	
Drees	Ernest E.	32	Petaluma	CA	Gossage	Emma L.	26	Petaluma	CA
Drees	Gustave A.	29	Petaluma	CA	Phillips	Matilda A.	29	Petaluma	CA
Drees	Herman A.	25	Petaluma	Soc	Lawler	Lucy H.	22	Petaluma	Soc
Dreher	Frank	37	Santa Rosa	GER	Rietce	Pauline	48	Santa Rosa	GER
Dreisback	William E.	30	Cloverdale	TN	Vogt	Margaret	18	Cloverdale	CA
Drennon	George	36	Oakland	CA	Walls	Grace E.	24	Petaluma	Soc
Dresbach	William	28	Petaluma	CA	Kahn	Bertha S.	27	Petaluma	CA
Dressler	J. F.	23	Santa Rosa	CA	Cockrill	Ida May	19	Santa Rosa	CA
Drever	Andrew M.	21	Mark West		Davis	Medna	19	Mark West	
Drever	John ?				Shuster	Margaret A.			
Drew	Morgan P.	23	San Francisco	CA	Higgins	Margaret A.	19	San Francisco	CA
Drew	Albert E.	24	San Francisco	NY	Heatley	Eva E.	19	Santa Rosa	CA
Drewes	William P.	21	San Francisco	CA	Schalat	Delia C.	19	San Francisco	CA
Driesbach	F. K.	27	Sacramento	IN	Swann	Florence	25	Sebastopol	IN
Driscol	John				Burk	Mrs.			
Driver	Clarence A.	20	Healdsburg	CA	Stinchfield	Mary G.	20	Healdsburg	CA
Driver	Edward L.	20	Sebastopol	CA	Woodbury	Alice Gertrude	18	Sebastopol	NE
Driver	Maurice Leon	25	San Jose	NZD	Nay	Abbie M.	18	Petaluma	CA
Driver	Nickolas	43	San Gregorio, San Mateo Co.	CND	Lautenschlager	Amelia M.	43	San Gregorio	CA
Driver	William W.	20	Sebastopol	Pet	Meyers	Hazel M.	15	Sebastopol	Sfo
Drucks	Edward S.	31	Susanville	OR	Williams	Adah	31	Cloverdale	CA
Drummond	E. W.	27	Santa Rosa Twp.		Post	C. E.	25	S. A. Twp.	
Drummond	R. S.	53	San Francisco	VA	Woodworth	Mary	33	Stony Point	CA
Drury	Eugene Vernon	32	Green Valley	IL	Eddelbuttel	Henrietta W. M.	23	San Francisco	CA
Dryden	William	28	Geyserville	OK	Seward	Evalyn I.	29	Great Falls, MT	OR
Dryden	William Robert	31	Santa Rosa	CA	Stevens	Carla	24	Santa Rosa	CA

Groom					Bride				
Surname	Given Name	Age	Residence	BP	Surname	Given Name	Age	Residence	BP
Dryer	Hiram George	22	Santa Rosa	NE	Murphy	Madeline Marion	18	Cloverdale	CA
Drysdale	Robert Hugh	21	Santa Rosa	MO	Vest	Pearl Maud	20	Santa Rosa	Sar
Du Vander	David H.	38	Windsor	ID	Ward	Mabel F.	37	Healdsburg	MN
Duane	Edward A.	28	Kenwood	OR	Mills	Martha Pauline	16	Santa Rosa	CA
Duarte	Nicholas	40	Hopland	CA	Witherell	Catherine, Mrs.	44	Hopland	IL
Dublin	Isidore	29	Petaluma	RUS	Maidenbaum	Lillian	25	Petaluma	RUS
DuBois	Clarence	27	Santa Rosa	CA	Holdworth	Gertrude, Mrs.	30	Santa Rosa	IL
Dubois	J. C.	23	Blacks, Yolo Co.	CA	Peterson	Albertine	22	Windsor	OH
DuBose	James Gaillard	32	Santa Rosa	SC	Hunt	Vitas C.	22	Two Rock	CA
Ducharm	George	26	Santa Rosa	CA	Ducker	Sarah A.	24	Santa Rosa	CA
Ducharm	Lambert A.	32	Santa Rosa	CA	Ivans	Olive Violet	20	Ukiah	CA
Ducharm	Leon	29	Santa Rosa	CA	Green	Birdie	27	Santa Rosa	CA
Ducheneau	Fred	28	San Francisco	RI	Williams	Iva Selina	38	San Francisco	ENG
Ducker	Barton	34	Sebastopol	CA	Hopkins	Grace J.	19	Santa Rosa	CA
Ducker	John	28	Santa Rosa		Underhill	Catherine	19	Santa Rosa	
Ducker	William Laurence	28	Petaluma	CA	Jensen	Ellen	20	Two Rock	AR
Duckwortth	HenryAlmon	26	Oakland	IL	Hesse	Augusta P.	20	Santa Rosa	CA
Dudley	Albert Allen	22	Arcata	Humbo-ldt Co.	Hembree	Eliza Ellen	20	Windsor	Wind-sor
Dudley	Albert P.	21	San Francisco	CND	Pearce	Pearl	19	San Francisco	CA
Dudley	W. S.	27	Healdsburg	CA	Mason	Annie E.	24	Healdsburg	CA
Dudley	William Seawell	23	Healdsburg	CA	Kennedy	Alice Cary	19	Healdsburg	CA
Duerner	William, Jr.	22	San Francisco	IA	Bateman	Harriett N.	17	San Francisco	CA
Duerson	John T.	34	Penngrove	CA	Kynoch	Lydia L.	21	Penngrove	Pet
Duerson	Richard C.	28	Santa Rosa	CA	Horne	Hadie W.	24	Penngrove	CA
Duerson	Wm. H.	28	Santa Rosa	CA	Horn	Jessie E.	19	Penngrove	CA
Dufau	Joseph	30	San Francisco	FRN	Lafon	Henriette	29	Oakland	FRN
Duff	Harry Arnold	27	Monte Rio	CA	Strickert	Alvina Agnes	21	Monte Rio	IL
Duffell	George	65	Sebastopol		Smith	Marcia P., Mrs.	59	Healdsburg	

Groom					Bride				
Surname	**Given Name**	**Age**	**Residence**	**BP**	**Surname**	**Given Name**	**Age**	**Residence**	**BP**
Duffield	Fred	44	Philo	OR	Stidum (?)	Etta, Mrs.	45	San Jose	CA
Dufranc	Isidore	24	Sebastopol	CA	Crohare	Rose	18	Sebastopol	FRN
Dugan	James Oliver	25	San Francisco	MO	White	Cora Belle	19	San Francisco	CA
Duggan	Edward Bernard	24	Santa Rosa	CA	Barnes	Dora Harlan	21	Santa Rosa	CA
Dugue	Fernand	35	San Francisco	FRN	Kirk	Elise	30	San Francisco	FRN
Dukes	Arthur H.	26	Santa Rosa	OR	Dannhausen	Kate	18	Santa Rosa	Hon
Dukes	Elmer Frank	20	Guerneville	OR	Browne	Ida Lee	18	Santa Rosa	CA
Dukes	William A.	26	Guerneville	OR	Place	Bertha E.	17	Guerneville	CA
Dulac	Enest E.	23	Petaluma	CA	Overton	Grace V.	21	Petaluma	CA
Dumas	Alphonse	52	Sonoma	FRN	Chanmet	Felectie	42	Sonoma	FRN
Dumas	Harry Thos.	23	Santa Rosa		Perkenson	Hannah	21	Santa Rosa	
Dunagan	Alva J.	28	Fort Baker	TN	Curry	Charlotte C.	25	San Francisco	CA
Dunbar	Charles O.	29	Santa Rosa	CA	Reynolds	Fannie	27	Santa Rosa	CA
Dunbar	John J.	31	Sonoma	CND	Agnew	Ida A.	29	Sonoma	CA
Dunbar	Lee A.	27	Sonoma	IA	Sullivan	Nellie	23	Sonoma	CA
Duncan	C. A.	24	Healdsburg	MO	Cunningham	Minnie	20	Healdsburg	CA
Duncan	Charles W.	22	Santa Rosa	CA	Fairclo	Serena	19	Sebastopol	CA
Duncan	Clarence E.	23	Hopland	CA	Myers	Bessie	19	Hopland	CA
Duncan	Elmer A.	20	Santa Rosa	OR	Winton	Edith May	16	Santa Rosa	CA
Duncan	Geo. B.	29	Santa Rosa	CA	Childers	Emma	25	Santa Rosa	IA
Duncan	George Benjamin	25	Santa Rosa		Duncan	Mattie McDonald	19	Santa Rosa	
Duncan	James A.	27	San Francisco	SCT	Boyle	Catherine J.	20	Glen Ellen	PA
Duncan	James E.	40	Vallejo	CA	Winkler	Clara A.	30	Oakland	CA
Duncan	James W.	38	Santa Rosa	NV	Gilman	Elba Ellen	27	Santa Rosa	CA
Duncan	John	29	Petaluma	IRL	Gray	Eleanor	19	Petaluma	IRL
Duncan	Mark VanHattren	21	Santa Rosa	CA	Gorski	Lizzie May	17	Santa Rosa	CA
Duncan	Richard	25	Santa Rosa	CA	Duncan	Ada M.	24	Santa Rosa	CA
Duncan	Robert A.	27	San Francisco	CA	Hyde	Mary M.	32	San Francisco	IRL
Duncan	Samuel	25	Mendocino Co.	CA	Coffer	Maggie	20	Cloverdale	MO

Groom					Bride				
Surname	**Given Name**	**Age**	**Residence**	**BP**	**Surname**	**Given Name**	**Age**	**Residence**	**BP**
Duncan	Sebastian	26	Stockton	CA	Mallory	Nina Leonna	22	Santa Rosa	MO
Duncan	William M.	25	Santa Rosa	CA	Rima	Minnie A.	17	Santa Rosa	KS
Duncan	William P.	38	Graton	KY	Nowlin	Lillie L.	17	Santa Rosa	KS
Duncon	Wm. T.	23	Woodland	MO	Rains	Alice H.	17	Petaluma	CA
Dunlap	J. L.				Brightenstein	Maggie			
Dunlap	Joseph B.	58	Santa Rosa	IN	Paxton	Melinda C.	56	Santa Rosa	AL
Dunlap	Joseph B.	50	Santa Rosa	IN	Millard	Addie F., Mrs.	49	Mt. Olivet	VT
Dunlap	Robert E.	27	San Francisco	CA	Brown	Florence	19	Healdsburg	CA
Dunlap	Wilson	38	San Francisco	NY	Gowen	M. E.	36	San Francisco	ME
Dunn	James	27	San Francisco	CA	Ehrlich	Miriam D.	24	San Francisco	CA
Dunn	Robert K.	48	San Francisco	ME	Myer	Priscilla G.	43	Oakland	IL
Dunn	William A.	62	Analy Twp.	VA	Millington (?)	N. M.	52	Bennett Valley	VA
Dunne	Robert H.	55	San Francisco	NY	Vincent	Mary C.	48	San Francisco	CA
Dunner ?	Martin P.				Schoffield	Nettie E.			
Dunsmore	Harry O.	28	Redding	IA	Walker	Florence J.	18	Red Bluff	CA
Dunster	Frank J.	36	Richmond	CA	O'Brien	Mary E.	26	Richmond	CA
Dunton	Oscar	37	Petaluma	MI	Armstrong	Fannie	27	Petaluma	CA
Dunton	Oscar	49	Petaluma	MI	Morrison	Mary Jane	39	Detroit	CND
Dunwoody	Seth M.	33	Santa Rosa	IA	Gardner	Lizzie	17	Santa Rosa	
Dupon	Julius F.	27	Petaluma	BLG	Kupper	Melaine	30	Petaluma	SWT
Dupont	Albert	40	Santa Rosa	CA	Meyer	Mary Josephine	30	Santa Rosa	CA
Dupont	Joseph	59	Occidental	CND	Maccabe	Hilda Susanna, Mrs.	39	Occidental	SWD
Durando	Felice	24	Petaluma	ITL	Canevascini	Ella	17	Petaluma	CA
Durant	William	43	Agua Caliente	CND	Mull	Ellen	42	Sonoma	OH
Durr	Otto R.	31	San Francisco	GER	Courtz	Mary E.	40	San Francisco	OH
Durst	David M.	29	Susanville	CA	Hair	Ruth Marie	22	Sebastopol	CA
Duryea	Stanton Bun	29	Graton	NY City	Auger	Annie Irene	17	Graton	
Dusek	Russell Ray	20	Petaluma	OK	Russell	Elizabeth	18	Petaluma	Sfo

Groom					Bride				
Surname	**Given Name**	**Age**	**Residence**	**BP**	**Surname**	**Given Name**	**Age**	**Residence**	**BP**
Dushane	Frank L.	36	San Francisco	PA	Henneken	Christina	24	Oakland	CA
Dusick	Albert H., Jr.	21	Petaluma	IA	Howard	Mary C.	18	Petaluma	CA
Dusserre	Vincent	33	San Francisco	FRN	Brochier (?)	Eulalie	25	San Francisco	FRN
Duston	Byrne A.	39	Boston	NY	Spangler	Annie B.	36	Albany, NY	NY
Dutcher	Burt W.				Morrill	Carrie/Cassie F.			
Dutcher	Steve Joseph	42	Santa Rosa	OH	Miller	Florence Emily	36	CA	CA
Dutra	John E.	22	Healdsburg	CA	Blazer	Mabel Edna	17	Healdsburg	CA
Dutra	Manuel F.	52	Sebastopol	AZR	Carey	Isabel	39	Sebastopol	AZR
Dutra	Manuel S.	36	Novato	AZR	Raymond	Mary	19	Petaluma Twp.	CA
Dutro	James M.	47	Philo	IL	Eten	Olive A.	31	Philo	CA
Dutro	Joseph J.	21+	Petaluma	AZR	Morris	Mamie	22	Petaluma	CA
Dutton	Arthur L.	49	San Luis Obispo	ME	Reese	Della	42	Berkeley	ENG
Dutton	George W.	26	Santa Rosa	CA	Graham	Hallie M. Miss	25	Santa Rosa	CA
Dutton	N. T.	42	Petaluma	VT	Kerby	Phoebe P.	23	Petaluma	CA
Dutton	Windslow D.	30	San Francisco	CA	Perez	Mary A.	34	San Francisco	CA
Duttweiler	Frederick	28	San Francisco	KS	Bowie	Mae Josephine	23	Oakland	CA
Dwinelle	C. H.	38	Berkeley	NY	Woolsey	Marie Louise	33	Fulton	NY
Dwyer	Harold	22	San Francisco	CA	Hayes	May Frances	22	San Francisco	CA
Dwyer	James J. B.	45	Santa Rosa	IRL	Brasher	Irene I.	37	Oakland	IA
Dwynes	Antone	22	Jenner	GAM	Salias	Pena	19	Jenner	CA
Dyer	Roy C.	21	TX	KS	Arnold	Josephine L.	18	CA	CA
Dysart	Thomas	30	Vallejo	NE	Rothford	Violet	22	San Jose	NE
E?tola	Arnold	21	San Francisco	CA	Redmond	Zella	20	San Francisco	CA
Eachus	Edgar P.	24	Newman	CA	Phillips	Mabel G.	24	Healdsburg	CA
Eager	Marcus K.	28	Sonoma Co.		O'Celeghan	Frances E.	19	Sonoma Co.	
Eagle	Bert	28	Healdsburg	CA	Caughey	Alice	22	Healdsburg	CA
Eagle	Edward	22	Santa Rosa	IA	Valentine	Christine	19	Santa Rosa	CA
Eagle	W. F.	26	Santa Rosa	IL	Underhill	Mary	22	Rincon Valley	CA
Eagleson	E. G.	22	Santa Rosa	CA	Musselman	Frona	19	Santa Rosa	CA
Eagleson	Welcome E.	22	Santa Rosa	CA	Lucas	Pauline	20	Santa Rosa	SD

Groom					Bride				
Surname	Given Name	Age	Residence	BP	Surname	Given Name	Age	Residence	BP
Eaglin	Elmer Harrison	21	Petaluma	CA	Cleland	Mary Martha	19	Petaluma	CA
Eakle	George H.	35	Healdsburg	CA	Andrews	Mary E.	25	Healdsburg	CA
Eakle	Henry P.				Edington	Eliza Francis			
Eardley	William J.	24	Santa Rosa	UT	Harden	Jinella	22	Santa Rosa	CA
Earhart	George Hammond	38	San Francisco	VA	Lamb	Edna May	25	San Francisco	Sfo
Earhart	William H.	28	Petaluma	CA	Martin	Emma R.	22	Petaluma	CA
Earl	John H. P.	25	San Francisco	NJ	Taylor	Brooksie A.	18	San Francisco	CO
Earll	F. A.	22	Alameda		Barnes	Ida F.	22	Petaluma	
Early	J. Frank	24	Petaluma	CA	Butler	Harriette M.	21	Petaluma	CA
Easley	William P.	35	Ventura	CA	Kearney	Mary E.	30	Santa Rosa	MO
Eason	Andrew	30	San Francisco	AL	Grant	Mary	30	San Francisco	GA
Eason	Joseph A.	38	Fallon, NV	NV	Higby	Birdie	38	Santa Rosa	NV
East	Linzey	27	Gamaliel, Monroe Co., KY	KY	Gilson	Myrtle Dora	23	Bogne, Graham Co., KS	KS
Easter	James Marcellus Thomton	28	Los Angeles	KS	Swanson	Hilda	31	San Francisco	SWD
Easterbrook	Thomas	34	San Diego	ENG	Case	Ellen M.	30	Sonoma	CT
Eastlick	A. D.	29	Cloverdale	IL	Cox	Mattie A.	18	Cloverdale	MO
Eastlick	Charles F.	32	Cloverdale	IL	Sheldon	Abbie T., Mrs.	22	Cloverdale	CA
Eastlick	Wellington B.	59	Geyserville	IL	Jones	Minnie	42	Santa Rosa	IL
Eastman	Charles Ward	30	Petaluma	CA	Harrigan	Florence Katherine	20	Petaluma	CA
Eastman	Fred A.	26	Willits	OR	Safford	Adeline	22	Crescent City	CA
Eastman	Tarleton	23	Petaluma Twp.	CA	Downie	Catherine Lilias	20	Petaluma	SCT
Eathorne	Alexander	35	Petaluma	ENG	Eddy	Zulpha L.	31	Penngrove	CA
Ebbets	Harry G.	23	Chicago	WI	Phillips	Gertrude	18	Spokane	WA
Ebeigh	Henry	27	Santa Rosa	KS	Smith	Carrie B.	21	Santa Rosa	CA
Eberling	C. W.	23	Sonoma Co.	IL	Mack	Ida	18	Sonoma Co.	CA
Ebers	Henry F.	50	near Cazadero	GER	Lenout	Nellie J.	50	Northfield, MN	ENG
Eby	Edward D.	23	Healdsburg	IL	Peck	Mabel	19	Healdsburg	CA

Groom					Bride				
Surname	**Given Name**	**Age**	**Residence**	**BP**	**Surname**	**Given Name**	**Age**	**Residence**	**BP**
Eby	Edwin Dayton	41	Healdsburg	IL	Maddern	Sophia Elgin	27	San Francisco	OR
Echelmeier	Fred	27	Analy Twp.	MO	Adel	Annetta	38	Analy Twp.	WI
Eck	John W.	50	Santa Rosa	PA	Spellacy	Ella J.	49	Santa Rosa	CA
Eckel	Tobias Lewis	28	Fulton	CA	Tartter	Frances	22	Fulton	CA
Eckert	Julius M.	32	Sea View	CA	Rickett	Leah	29	Forestville	MO
Eckes	Clarence J.	22	San Francisco	CA	Smith	Grace M.	18	Sebastopol	CA
Eckhart	Percy	36	Ukiah	OR	Hinshaw	Wilma E.	22	Bloomfield	CA
Eckman	Albert R.	21	Guerneville	CA	Foscha	Lenora A.	19	Petaluma	CA
Eckman	John				Stevens	Jennie			
Eddinger	Charles Winfield	27	Skaggs	NC	Derrick	Nellie Annie	18	Healdsburg	CA
Edgar	Herbert L.	24	Berkeley	CA	Gorter	Dorothea	21	Berkeley	CA
Edmiston	Frank L.	24	San Rafael	WA	Silva	Julia Lopes	22	San Rafael	CA
Edmonds	Francis J.	30	San Francisco	CA	Scannell	Grace A.	25	San Francisco	CA
Edmunds	Clarence	37	Santa Rosa	IA	Tapscott	Mary Emma	33	Santa Rosa	IL
Edmunds	Clyde Jordan	23	Santa Rosa	CO	Moxley	Gladys Beulah	18	Santa Rosa	CA
Edmunds	George R.	74	Santa Rosa	NY	Farish	May P., Mrs.	68	Santa Rosa	TN
Edrington	James B.	45	Windsor	KY	Cook	Hattie	25	Healdsburg	KY
Edvardo	Bettelotti	29	Sonoma	ITL	Viviani	Marie	28	Sonoma	ITL
Edwards	Alfred Atherton	30	San Francisco	Fredericton, CND	Turner	Belle	28	San Francisco	Gage Co., NE
Edwards	Arthur S.	34	San Francisco	CA	Braunton	Blanche	28	San Francisco	IA
Edwards	Clarence A.	22	Alexander Valley	IA	Martin	Lola Lee	17	Alexander Valley	CA
Edwards	Clarence Alvin	30	Healdsburg	IA	Miller	Eva Mabel	30	Healdsburg	CA
Edwards	Claude A.	23	Santa Rosa	CA	Pritchett	Laura E.	19	Healdsburg	CA
Edwards	David	25	San Francisco	CA	Needham	Grace	25	Los Angeles	IA
Edwards	Henry Seymour	35	San Antone, Marin Co.	NZD	Studdert	Susie Estella	36	Petaluma	CA
Edwards	Herbert Hereward	33	Petaluma	NZD	Studdert	Angela Gertrude	25	Petaluma	CA
Edwards	Matthew	34	Cloverdale	CA	Lambert	Mima	38	San Francisco	

Groom					Bride				
Surname	Given Name	Age	Residence	BP	Surname	Given Name	Age	Residence	BP
Edwards	Ralph Walter	26	Oakland	CA	Hamilton	Pearl	19	Sebastopol	HI
Edwards	Thomas M.	28	San Mateo	CA	Essner	Joan D.	19	San Francisco	CA
Eells	Frank Lorne	27	Santa Rosa	IA	Hulbert	Laura Emily	26	Santa Rosa	Occidental
Eferly	John	46	Santa Rosa	GER	Bauer	Caroline	37	Oakland	GER
Egan	Daniel F.	32	Petaluma	CA	Pressey	L. Beatrice	22	Petaluma	CA
Egbert	Warren	21+	San Francisco	CA	Pearce	Martha	18+	Santa Rosa	CA
Egenhoff	Julius A.	29	San Jose	OR	Bernauer	Frieda	23	San Jose	CA
Ehret	Alexander W.	27	Sebastopol	CA	Solomon	Lena	20	Sebastopol	CA
Eichbaum	Edwin Treat Betts	26	Kenwood	FL	Perkins	Margaret Edna	21	Kenwood	CA
Einwalter	Paul	42	Sebastopol	IA	Poe	Rosa B.	26	Sebastopol	NY
Elder	Henry Elmer	25	Forestville	WA	Lawrence	Kate Amanda	18	Forestville	OR
Elder	James H.	53	Santa Rosa	MO	Hether	Christine	51	Santa Rosa	RUS
Elder	Louis Ely	26	Santa Rosa	MO	Pedersen	Mary Magdeline	19	Santa Rosa	SD
Elder	Newton	26	Selma	MO	Russell	Mattie E.	17	Santa Rosa	CA
Elder	Ralph D.	27	Forestville	OR	Stratton	Susie I.	34	Forestville	IA
Eldridge	A. C.	31	Elko, NV	MA	Frederick	Hallie	24	Santa Rosa	MI
Eldridge	George G.	26	Fulton	IA	Dornin	Julia	29	Fulton	N. San Juan, CA
Eldridge	Joseph B.	26	Healdsburg	SWI	Burns	Jennie T.	18	Healdsburg	CA
Elgin	Ira P.	32	St. Helena	CA	Blackmon (?)	Emily A.	23	St. Helena	IA
Eliggi	Bartolomeo	26	Cloverdale	ITL	Schurba	Celia A.	16	Cloverdale	ITL
Elkington	Thomas	25	Napa	CA	Head	Rosalis	22	Santa Rosa	CA
Elkins	I. B.	31	Cloverdale	CA	Rickard	Barbara A.	26	Cloverdale	CA
Elkins	John C.	24	Forestville	CA	Curry	Lillian M.	24	Santa Rosa	NE
Elkins	Richard L.	32	Yorkville	CA	Hutchinson	Mary E.	17	Forcstville	CA
Elkins	Stephen F.	21	Forestville	CA	Smith	Eva M.	19	Guerneville	CA
Ellingen	Casper W.	43	Mineral Point, WI	WI	Dana	May L.	35	Sacramento	PA

Groom					Bride				
Surname	Given Name	Age	Residence	BP	Surname	Given Name	Age	Residence	BP
Ellinger	Charles	46	Fulton	DNK	Grosch	Frieda	28	San Francisco	GER
Elliott	Archie E.	26	Occidental	ENG	Gibson	Lulu E.	26	Occidental	CA
Elliott	Carter W.	21	Healdsburg	MO	Meyers	Bessie R.	16	Healdsburg	OH
Elliott	Charles Milton	22	Santa Rosa	IA	Plum	Bessie Irene	16	Santa Rosa	CA
Elliott	Chester L.	21	Sebastopol	CA	Standley	Sadie R.	18	Sebastopol	CA
Elliott	Daniel	30	Fresno	IL	Nelsen	Josepha	29	Seattle	NRY
Elliott	Edward Cyrus	20	Cloverdale	CA	Pruitt	Nellie Reba	17	Cloverdale	MEX
Elliott	Frank Edward	29	Santa Rosa	Boston	Ward	Annie May	28	Santa Rosa	CA
Elliott	Irving R.	36	Los Angeles	CA	Johns	Anna C.	29	Los Angeles	CA
Elliott	J. B.	30	Cloverdale	CA	Nicoll	Fannie	30	Cloverdale	CA
Elliott	James J.	26	Sacramento	WV	Donahue	Violet P.	18	San Francisco	CA
Ellis	Arthur	35	Bodega	OH	Welling	Rose A.	27	Bodega	CA
Ellis	Arthur Clarence	32	Petaluma	TX	Meyers	Lorene Emeline	22	Petaluma	CA
Ellis	Bert Cecil	28	Petaluma	CA	Groshong	Sue	28	Santa Rosa	CA
Ellis	Edward	31	Santa Rosa	ME	Van Keppel	Mary L.	21	Santa Rosa	CA
Ellis	James	26	Santa Rosa	CND	Smith	Mary A.	23	Santa Rosa	IA
Ellis	John Arthur	29	Geyserville	CA	Stiles	Louisa Isobel	23	Geyserville	CA
Ellis	Leander Gilbert, Jr.	21	Geyserville	CA	Leigh	Delia	18	Geyserville	CA
Ellis	Walter A.	22	Petaluma	KS	Portlock	Earl	16	Petaluma	TX
Ellis	William	24	Guerneville	CDN	Walker	Alma	22	Santa Rosa	MO
Ellis	William A.	26	Sebastopol	TX	Hotle	Effie C.	23	Sebastopol	IA
Ellis	William C.				Leard	Laura J.			
Ellis	William H.	23	Geyserville	CA	Knowles	Nanon	22	Geyserville	IA
Ellison	Charles Edwin	22	Fulton		Philbee	Rachel N.	18+	Fulton	
Ellison	Charles Eugene	20	Santa Rosa	Fulton	Gray	Rosa	21	Chico	Chico
Ellison	Ebert R.	21	Corona	NE	Wright	Ella	21	Healdsburg	NE
Ellsworth	Henry L.	22	Petaluma	CA	Shattuck	Aletha S.	21	Petaluma	CA
Ellsworth	Leonard	21	Petaluma	CA	Jones	Clara	17	Petaluma	CA
Ellsworth	Percy Leland	25	San Francisco	CA	Mathews	Asentha Vera	19	San Francisco	CA

Groom					Bride				
Surname	Given Name	Age	Residence	BP	Surname	Given Name	Age	Residence	BP
Elphick	Clarence R.	21	Penngrove	CA	Vallier	Emma M.	19	Penngrove	CA
Elphick	Eugene	22	Sebastopol	CA	Roberts	Hazel	21	Sebastopol	CA
Elphick	Henry, Jr.	25	Sebastopol	CA	Briggs	Birdie	24	Sebastopol	CA
Elphick	James	24	Sebastopol	CA	Roberts	Edna N.	21	Sebastopol	CA
Elphick	Oscar Frank	22	Petaluma	CA	Orender	Alma May	18	Ukiah	CA
Elphick	Roy J.	23	Penngrove	CA	Horne	Jeanie R.	23	Penngrove	CA
Elphick	Thomas R.	32	Vallejo Twp.	OH	Duerson	Elizabeth C.	21	Vallejo Twp.	CA
Elsbree	Charles Dyer	32	Sonora	CA	Du Vander	Rebecca L.	27	Santa Rosa	ID
Elton	Arthur M.	18	Freestone	CA	Lowrey	Helen W.	18	Freestone	CA
Elwell	Charles E.	23	Santa Rosa	CA	Hooper	Lizzie	23	Healdsburg	KS
Ely	Albert W.	36	Santa Rosa		Buell	Ida M.	22	Santa Rosa	
Ely	Frank G.	32	Santa Rosa	IL	Hampton	Ida May	28	Santa Rosa	CA
Ely	Robert L.	33	Winters	CA	Hollar	Flora Dell	18	Sebastopol	NE
Elzey	R. H.	24	Sacramento	MO	Thompson	M. Ruth	20	Santa Rosa	CA
Emenegger	Frank	29	Petaluma	SWT	Mason	Centennia	27	Petaluma	MO
Emerson	George Edwin	36	Petaluma	ENG	Lewin	Catherine Ellen	33	Petaluma	ENG
Emerson	Harry E.	36	Healdsburg	CA	Cooper	Eva U.	20	Geyserville	CA
Emerson	Harry E.	24	Healdsburg	CA	Graves	Nora B.	20	Healdsburg	IA
Emerson	John S.				Rickman	Nancy S.			
Emerson	Mark Lewis	33	Oakland	CA	Folger	Alice	27	Oakland	CA
Emery	Fred A.	35	Windsor	WI	Wilson	Daisy	26	Kenwood	CA
Emery	Vernon V.	30	Santa Rosa	NE	Zunnino	Annie K.	17	Santa Rosa	ID
Emes	Walter H.	31	San Francisco	NY	Goldman	Ida	21	San Francisco	CA
Emmons	Edward L.	25	Petaluma	OH	Willis	Lillian A.	19	Petaluma	CND
Emmrich	Gustav Moritz	31	Healdsburg	GER	Heinze	Bertha Emilie	26	Healdsburg	GER
Empey	William A.	21	San Francisco	CA	Turner	Lucille C.	18	San Francisco	CA
Emrick	George W.	22	Healdsburg	CA	Miller	Oliva B.	17	Healdsburg	CA
Enders	Charles R.	25	Santa Rosa	MI	Hornbuckle	Harriet	21	Santa Rosa	MO
Endicott	Charles L.	22	Petaluma	Winters CA	Brayton	Ester Ruth	22	Oakland	CA

Groom					Bride				
Surname	Given Name	Age	Residence	BP	Surname	Given Name	Age	Residence	BP
Endicott	Perry A.	52	Oroville	MO	Boyer	Margerette A.	45	Oroville	IN
Enemark	Frank R.	25	Campbell	IA	Shelford	Lola L. B.	22	Cloverdale	CA
Enfield	Joseph Louis	22	Sonoma	CA	Marzo	Matilda Clelia	22	Sonoma	CA
Engelberg	Henry W.	25	San Francisco	NY	Rouch	Josephine	25	San Francisco	IA
Engelhardt	August George	26	San Francisco	CA	Pomeroy	Irene Byrle	18	Santa Rosa	CA
Engelhardt	Richard R.	33	San Francisco	CA	Alexander	Lucille B.	20	Petaluma	CA
Engelland	Detlef	21+	Petaluma	GER	Mockel	Anna	21+	Petaluma	GER
Engh	Peter B.	36	Los Angeles	NRY	Fish	Lucetta A.	21	San Francisco	CA
Engle	Lewis Joseph	23	Healdsburg	SD	Craig	Cora Allida	18	Healdsburg	CA
Englehard	Sam A.	26	Healdsburg		Jewell	Libbie	17	Healdsburg	
Ennis	Frank	30	Healdsburg	PRT	Teineira	Rosa	21	Healdsburg	PRT
Enos	Manuel Joseph	28	Sebastopol	St. George Island, AZR	Moniz	Marion Ursala	20	Sebastopol	CA
Enz	Albin	31	Shellville	SWT	Meyer	Josephine	18	Shellville	CA
Enz	Joseph	46	Oakland	SWT	Schaly	Christina	38	Sonoma	SWT
Enzenauer	Ed.	25	Lambert	MO	Campbell	Etta Edith	20	Lambert	CA
Enzenauer	Joe	21	Healdsburg	MO	Blazer	Ethel Rae	18	Healdsburg	CA
Enzenauer	Louis	22	Lambert	MO	Burnham	Phebe	20	Lambert	CA
Epperly	Hiram	32	Santa Cruz		Coleman	Amanda	20	near Santa Rosa	
Erickson	Albert	54	Petaluma	NRY	Steenberg	Maria	50	San Francisco	NRY
Ernest	Albert J.	26	Bradley, Monterey Co.	MA	McElhany	Olive E.	19	Healdsburg	CA
Ernst	August M.	37	San Francisco	DNK	Faught	Hazel S.	30	Fulton	CA
Ernst	John Louis	63	Santa Rosa	DNK	Schow	Bertha	45	San Francisco	DNK
Erntson	Martin	41	Oakland	NE	Steinberg	Maude	30	Healdsburg	CA
Erskine	Alvin Chester	26	Sebastopol	CA	Evans	Annie B., Mrs.	30	Sebastopol	KS
Erving	Richard	21	Santa Rosa	HWI	Moore	Eva B.	19	Sebastopol	KS
Esaia	Bartholomew	21	Healdsburg	ITL	Nelson	Clara	18	Healdsburg	CA
Esaia	John B.	23	Healdsburg	ITL	Yancey	Minnie M.	20	Healdsburg	CA

Groom					Bride				
Surname	Given Name	Age	Residence	BP	Surname	Given Name	Age	Residence	BP
Escola	Charles A.	33	Mendocino	CA	Sutherland	Hilda A.	27	Albion	CA
Esmond	Frank L.	24	Berkeley	CA	Bruner	Amanda	24	Windsor	CA
Espey	George E.	23	Fulton	CA	Brown	Lizzie R.	18	Fulton	CA
Espey	George M.	27	Sebastopol	CA	Mills	Effa	19	Sebastopol	CND
Essig	Frank	27	Guerneville	IN	Owens	Emma F.	34	Guerneville	CA
Esslinger	John A.	48	San Francisco	OH	Mayshark	Stella N.	35	San Francisco	PLD
Estep	Henry S.	27	Analy Twp.		Parks	L. F.	17	Bloomfield	
Esterly	Ward Benjamin	26	Berkeley	KS	Judy	Emily Virginia	28	Healdsburg	OR
Estes	Frank H.	21	Trenton	CA	McIntosh	Emma	22	Forestville	CA
Estes	Geo.				Hennessee	Mary F.			
Estes	George Henry	31	Sebastopol	CA	Arfsten	Dora Lizzie	26	Sebastopol	CA
Estes	John	34	Sebastopol	CA	Bohn	Mary Lena	34	Healdsburg	CA
Estes	John E.	32	Denver	CO	Wheeler	Anna	32	Salem, OR	KS
Estes	William J., Jr.	22	Brentwood	CA	Johnson	Nellie I.	18	Santa Rosa	CA
Estill	Byron Dee	27	Boonville	CA	Hartley	Aneita	20	Boonville	UT
Estinghausen	William	32	Fulton	IA	Fairbanks	Clara I.	27	Fulton	CA
Etherridge	Cecil William	23	Santa Rosa	IA	Vinyard	Olive Barr	18	Santa Rosa	CA
Etz	Arthur Kenyon	34	San Francisco	NY	Nielson	Emma Marie	29	Oakland	GER
Eugley	Walter Arthur	25	Cloverdale	OR	Richards	Anna Belle, Mrs.	27	Cloverdale	CA
Evans	Alexander	25	Petaluma	CA	Penny	Olive E.	21	Petaluma	CA
Evans	Arthur B.	24	Petaluma	CA	Matzen	Dora	20	Petaluma	CA
Evans	C. D.	24	Healdsburg	Colusa Co., CA	Haigh	Lena	22	Healdsburg	Son
Evans	Charles E.	32	Olema	CA	Bojorques	Elizabeth L.	23	Marshall	CA
Evans	E. Esley	26	Rust, CA	CA	Koch	Anna E.	19	Petaluma	CA
Evans	E. R.	59	Forestville	IA	McClary	Bella	51	Riverside	PA
Evans	Frank Leslie	23	Forestville	NE	Smith	Mollie Rebecca	22	Guerneville	CA
Evans	Harrison H.	31	San Francisco	IA	Seery	Evelyn	22	San Francisco	CA
Evans	John	60	San Francisco	CA	Johnson	Agnes L.	45	San Francisco	CA

Groom					Bride				
Surname	Given Name	Age	Residence	BP	Surname	Given Name	Age	Residence	BP
Evans	John D.	19	Duncans Mill	IA	Lawrence	Maggie M.	19	Forestville	CO
Evans	Merle Lester	18	Annapolis	OH	Batt	Alice May	17	Annapolis	CA
Evans	Robert H.	25	Oakland	CA	Bryant	Margery	22	Omaha, NE	NE
Evans	Roy M.	31	Petaluma	CA	Green	May C.	26	Petaluma	CA
Evans	Samuel C.	22	San Andreas	NE	Ward	Bertha May	19	Petaluma	Soc
Evans	Thomas				Leigh	Mary Ellen			
Evans	Tipton Edward	21	Forestville	NE	Clark	Agnes Emma	17	Forestville	CA
Evans	William	25	Santa Rosa	CA	Williams	Nada Roll	18	Santa Rosa	CA
Evans	William P.	66	San Rafael	PA	McCoubrey	Nettie	53	San Rafael	MO
Evans	William Henry	29	Santa Rosa	IL	Schneider	Alice Laura	19	Santa Rosa	IL
Evart	Edwin J.	25	Penngrove	CA	Jacobsen	Frances N.	24	Petaluma	CA
Evart	Frank R.	24	Penngrove	CA	Keegan	Clara Mae	22	Stony Point	CA
Evart	William P.	27	Penngrove	CA	Howard	Celia G.	23	Petaluma	MI
Everett	Harry D.	25	Guinda	CA	Wilson	Edna M.	22	Healdsburg	CA
Everett	Walter H.	32	Berkeley	IL	Hayden	Anna Valentine	30	Berkeley	MA
Eversole	Abraham	28			Hubart	Jennie E.	38	Salt Point	
Evey	David D.	31	Santa Rosa	CA	Lawrence	Alfa N.	25	Santa Rosa	CA
Ewing	James	35	San Francisco	IRL	Gough	Annie Emily	19	Sonoma	CA
Ewing	James E.	25	Healdsburg	NY	Mazota	Lillie	17	Healdsburg	CA
Ewing	John Virgil	23	Forestville	NE	Hembree	Ivy Olivia	20	Windsor	CA
Exlay	George	36	Santa Rosa	CA	Green	Mary	16	Santa Rosa	MO
Exley	William	32	Vallejo	ENG	King	Marie Elizabeth	36	Santa Rosa	MI
Faber	H. Charles	23	New York	NY	Millman	Mamie L.	24	San Francisco	IL
Faccini	Giovani	28	Mt Olivet	ITL	Saitone	Maria	34		ITL
Fadeli	Angelo	27	Petaluma	ITL	Tisolin	Louise	22	Petaluma	ITL
Fagan	Shuler F.	24	Sanitarium, CA	NM	Grant	Effa	26	Healdsburg	CA
Fahrion	George W.	24	Santa Rosa	OH	Glenn	Lilly M.	20	Santa Rosa	TN
Fairbanks	Joseph F.	25	Tomales	CA	Wilson	Hattie	25	Tomales	CA
Fairbanks	Julius T.	49	Stony Point	MI	Hanson	Emelia J., Mrs.	30	Stony Point	PA
Fairbanks	Percy M.	22	Freestone	CA	Erwin	May	18	Mendocino Co.	CA

Groom					Bride				
Surname	**Given Name**	**Age**	**Residence**	**BP**	**Surname**	**Given Name**	**Age**	**Residence**	**BP**
Fairbanks	William B.	28	Tomales	CA	Clark	Alice L.	21	Tomales	CA
Fairchild	Fred F.	26	Santa Rosa	VA	Batten	Mattie H.	19	Santa Rosa	CA
Fairchild	Leon H.	23	San Francisco	CA	Thomas	Anna E.	23	San Francisco	CA
Fairchild	Olif G.	46	Geyserville	NY	Clark	Ruth M.	35	Healdsburg	MA
Fairclo	Charles	29	Sebastopol	CA	Cariaga	Refuge	18	San Jose	CA
Fairclo	Richard	27	Sebastopol	CA	Weyhe	Dora	26	Forestville	CA
Faires	James B.	50	Cloverdale	TX	Peck	Mary H.	61	Cloverdale	CA
Fairfield	William M.	25	Arlington, OR	OH	Morrow	Ethel M.	18	Healdsburg	CA
Fairfield	Wm.				Rawson	Ella			
Fairman (?)	William J.	25			Butts	Mary E.	19	Fulton	
Faithful	H. R.	21	Sonoma	CA	Conlin	Nellie A.	24	Sonoma	CA
Falanery	Charles A.	33	Healdsburg	MO	Elliott	Mary A.	27	Healdsburg	MO
Fallmer	Charles Frederick	36	Oakland	CA	Cozzens	Pearl Adele	19	Oakland	CA
Fallon	John D.	23	Napa	NY	Wyckoff	Cora	22	Ukiah	CA
Fallon	John Franklin	24	Nevada	Seb	Brown	Edna L.	23	Fulton	USA
Fallon	Martin	49	Santa Rosa	IRL	Duher	Catherine	35	San Francisco	IRL
Faltin	Wilhelm	24	Modesto	GER	Kahle	Agnes D. J.	25	Hollywood	GER
Falvey	Dennis	57	Petaluma	ENG	Mangili	Mary, Mrs.	43	Petaluma	CA
Fambrini	Federico	23	Willits	ITL	Puccioni	Julia	16	Healdsburg	CA
Fandre	Crockett	21	Forestville	CA	Crist	M. Jennie	16	Santa Rosa	CA
Fanucchi	Angelo	33	Fulton	ITL	Barberie	Rose Lee	24	Fulton	ITL
Fanucchi	Angelo	29	Santa Rosa	ITL	Barsi	Silvia	30	Santa Rosa	ITL
Farahm	John Henry Adolph, Jr.	23	Petaluma	IL	Hyatt	Emma Beatrice	23	Petaluma	CND
Faraoni	Frank	25	San Francisco	ITL	Rogers	Ottillie C.	16	Petaluma	CA
Faribanks	Joseph Frank	26	Petaluma	Augusta IA	Maynard	Eva E.	21	Petaluma	Pet
Farley	Charles	20	Windsor	CA	Huffman	Florence	18	Windsor	CA
Farley	George F.	25	Marshall	CA	Bojorques	Mary A.	22	Marshall	CA
Farley	Henry	29	Napa	CA	McGowan	Maggie	25	Sonoma	CA

Groom					Bride				
Surname	Given Name	Age	Residence	BP	Surname	Given Name	Age	Residence	BP
Farley	J. B.	28	Marin Co.	CA	Roberts	Elizabeth G.	24	Petaluma	CA
Farley	James B.	21	Healdsburg		Wilson	Hattie A. ?	19	Windsor	
Farley	James H.	30	Marshall	IRL	Wilson	Mary	25	Santa Rosa	IRL
Farley	Thomas Bachariah	28	Santa Rosa	CA	Cauckwell	Minnie Bell	25	Santa Rosa	CA
Farley	William James McA.	41	Nicasio	CA	Fitzgerald	Nora Gertrude	25	Petaluma	KS
Farley	William T.	58	Santa Rosa	TN	Barbour	Clementine	42	Santa Rosa	PA
Farmer	B. F.	25	Santa Rosa	MO	Wilson	Martha E.	20	Santa Rosa	Soc
Farmer	Eugene Columbus	27	Santa Rosa	CA	Shelton	Grace	23	Santa Rosa	CA
Farmer	Geo. L.	21	San Francisco	CA	Wilson	Marela	20	Santa Rosa	CA
Farmer	George	36	Healdsburg	MI	Michael	Emma A.	33	Healdsburg	OH
Farmer	John H.	23	Santa Rosa	CA	Marshall	Mary Alice	20	Santa Rosa	CA
Farner	David Paul	24	Santa Rosa	FRN	Irwin	Edna H.	19	Santa Rosa	CA
Farnham	James W.	26	Santa Rosa	ME	Sargent	Ella N.	26	Santa Rosa	CA
Farnham	Leroy T.	23	Fort Winfield Scott	CA	Brown	Mildred	27	San Francisco	MA
Farnsworth	Raymond W.	24	Petaluma	CA	Hunt	Laura Ellen	21	Petaluma	CA
Farquar	Calvin S.	27	Santa Rosa		Clark	Mary I.	18+	Santa Rosa	
Farquar	Frederic Stewart	23	Penngrove	CA	Herbert	Hester R.	18	Bloomfield	CA
Farrance	Charles Evert	28	San Francisco	CA	Hillyer	Ethel	30	San Francisco	CA
Farrar	Edmund H.	46	Santa Rosa	ME	Roberts	Grace M.	18	Santa Rosa	IA
Farrell	John T.	39	San Francisco	NY	Green	Kate	38	San Francisco	NY
Farrell	William F.	26	Freestone	CA	Glynn	Sarah A.	26	Occidental	CA
Farrer	Ernest Eugene	28	Boonville	UT	Eten	Ella Agnes	20	Philo	CA
Farwell	Marcus Morton	22	Fresno	CO	Lambert	Donna E.	23	Santa Rosa	CA
Farwell	Sidney C.	32	San Francisco	IA	Haeckl	Elene	32	San Francisco	CA
Fasel	George	40	Sacramento	GER	Odermatt	Theresia	45	Sacramento	SWT
Faudre	Crocket	27	Forestville	CA	Young	Louella St John, Mrs.	31	Guerneville	CA
Faudre	Stuart William	19	Forestville	CA	Pells	Agnes Nettie	22	Guerneville	CA

Groom					Bride				
Surname	**Given Name**	**Age**	**Residence**	**BP**	**Surname**	**Given Name**	**Age**	**Residence**	**BP**
Faught	A.	49	Mark West	IN	Smith	Annie A.	34	Mark West	ME
Faught	Jabez	26	Windsor	CA	Morrison	Violet	19	Geyserville	CA
Faught	John H.	25	Mark West		Sanborn	Emma	22	Mark West	
Faught	Lewis Cass	27	Russian River Twp.		Rodgers	Ruth	19	Mendocino Twp.	
Faulconer	Joseph C.	70	Santa Rosa	KY	Gildersleeve	Elizabeth	71	Santa Rosa	CT
Faulkender	Everett F.	32	San Francisco	AZ	Faulkender	Millie M.	25	San Francisco	RUS
Faulkner	M. H.				Donnelly	Amelia A.			
Fava	Lorenzo	51	Trenton	ITL	Papero	Angelllina	32	Forestville	ITL
Fawcett	S.	49	Santa Rosa	OH	Lowery	Mary	35	Santa Rosa	OH
Fawcett	Thomas				Fowler	Mary Otis			
Fawver	James Clark	40	Napa	MO	Bales	Della Morton	28	Napa	IA
Fay	Frank	37	Glen Ellen	NY	Ryley	Mary Agnes	28	Glen Ellen	IRL
Fay	John	48	San Francisco	MA	Orr	Mary E.	30	Auburn	CA
Fay	John F.	23	Geyserville	CA	Ellis	Leona G.	23	Geyserville	CA
Fay	John P.	35	San Jose	MA	Patterson	Stella F.	31	Santa Rosa	WI
Fay	Wilbert Lee	31	Santa Rosa	MO	Corrick	Lucela Catherine	31	Santa Rosa	CA
Faylor	John F.	32	Guerneville	CA	Walker	Hazel	17	Guerneville	CA
Faylor	Orson	24	Guerneville	CA	Grubbe	Minnie	21	Sebastopol	GER
Faylor	William P.	20	Santa Rosa	CA	Wood	Marie E.	18	Santa Rosa	CA
Fearn	John R.	23	Oakland	ENG	Dimmick	Lillian M.	23	Oakland	Wind-sor
Fearns	Lawrence H.	24	Petaluma	ENG	Stewart	Bertha F.	16	Petaluma	IN
Fechtelkotter	Harry B.	23	Santa Rosa	CA	Thomas	Minnie Frances	20	Santa Rosa	CA
Fechter	David A.	19	Santa Rosa	CA	Fulkerson	Alma K.	23	Santa Rosa	CA
Feckenscher	Edward R.	26	Redding	Omaha, NE	Dewey	Ruby	29	Healdsburg	Correctionville, IA
Feehan	W. J.	21	Santa Rosa	CA	Murbar	Mae	19	Santa Rosa	CA
Fees	Elmer	22	Santa Rosa	CA	Graham	Lilly	24	Occidental	CA

Groom					Bride				
Surname	**Given Name**	**Age**	**Residence**	**BP**	**Surname**	**Given Name**	**Age**	**Residence**	**BP**
Fehrensen	Claude William	28	Lompoc	IL	Jones	Sussie Elizabeth Ellen	20	Santa Rosa	CA
Fehringer	John	45	Trenton	GER	Seifert	Maud	20	Napa	CA
Feige	Albert H.	25	Occidental	CA	Gibson	Hazel C.	22	Occidental	CA
Feillers	Daniel	21	Oakland	ITL	Toppini	Marie V.	22	Santa Rosa	SWT
Felciano	Antone	25	Sebastopol	HWI	Soares	Mary	24	Sebastopol	HWI
Felciano	John	25	Santa Rosa	PRT	Vier	Flora	25	Sebastopol	CA
Felciano	Manuel	28	Santa Rosa	PRT	Pierucci	Matilda	17	Santa Rosa	CA
Feldman	William	79	Petaluma	GER	Landgren	Louisa, Mrs.	58	Petaluma	SWD
Feldmeyer	Clemens A.	26	Geyserville	CA	Sutten	Pearl	17	Cloverdale	CA
Feldmeyer	Wm. B.	26	Geyserville	CA	Minto	Ive Pearl	22	Geyserville	IL
Felis	Fred R., Jr.	22	San Francisco	CA	Albert	Pearl Ione	24	San Francisco	OR
Felix	Gustav H.	22	San Jose	GER	Laske	Katherine	22	Santa Rosa	HWI
Feliz	Gumisindo, Jr.	24	Petaluma	CA	Comte	Blanche	19	Petaluma	CA
Feliz	Sisto J.	20+	Santa Rosa	CA	Gailer	Ada B.	16	Santa Rosa	
Felldin	John Joseph	33	San Francisco	CA	Connolly	Mary V.	28	San Francisco	CA
Fellers	Frank L.	21	Sebastopol	CA	Hillard	Mildred A.	18	Sebastopol	PA
Fellers	Lorenzo	32	Byron	IA	Browne	Minnie	22	Kenwood	MD
Fellows	Fred C.	22	Santa Rosa	NV	Dovey	Eva	19	Santa Rosa	CA
Felt	William W., Jr.	27	Santa Rosa	KS	Leroux	Nellie T.	27	Cloverdale	IA
Felte	William A.	32	San Diego	CA	Perry	Pearl E.	32	Chico	CA
Felton	Clarence W.	22	Petaluma	IL	Graff	Lilliebell	22	Petaluma	MN
Fendner	Edward Ludwig	27	Dixon	CA	Prestwood	Louella M.	28	Berkeley	CA
Fenkhausen	W. R.	23	San Francisco	CA	Kopf	Victoria Louise	20	Santa Rosa	MN
Fenn	Theodore	57	Sebastopol	GA	Hayne	Laura	50	Sebastopol	MO
Fennell	James E.	29	San Francisco	CA	Hamilton	Alice	27	San Francisco	CA
Fenner	Henry	32	Soda Rock	SWT	Thormann	Martha T. H.	24	Soda Rock	GER
Fenton	Claude Merton	29	Sebastopol	IA	Dodenhoff	Ceres Wanda	18	Sebastopol	CA
Ferenbach	Charles	28	Petaluma	GER	Feddersen	Annie	20	Petaluma	Pett
Ferguson	Andrew T.	34	San Francisco	MA	Petrich	Agnes	34	San Francisco	TX

Groom					Bride				
Surname	Given Name	Age	Residence	BP	Surname	Given Name	Age	Residence	BP
Ferguson	Angus V.	24	Tiburon	IN	Knox	Lizzie E.	25	Tiburon	CA
Ferguson	Charles P.	24	Healdsburg	Sfo	Shinn	Ida	22	Healdsburg	NY
Ferguson	Charles T.	23	Santa Cruz	CA	Woodward	Mattie M.	23	Santa Rosa	IA
Ferguson	Clarence M.	23	Alexander Valley	CA	Patterson	Minnie C.	22	Alexander Valley	CA
Ferguson	Edward	20	Geyserville	CA	Beach	Bertha	19	Geyserville	CA
Ferguson	Edward J.	27	Glen Ellen	IRL	Sullivan	Mary	19	Glen Ellen	CA
Ferguson	Erwin Emmet	41	Alexander Valley	CA	Wagers	Martha Elizabeth	28	Healdsburg	MO
Ferguson	Geo. P.	22	Healdsburg	CA	Smith	Dacie R.	20	Healdsburg	CA
Ferguson	Henry O.	40	Healdsburg		Miller	Mary E.	23	Healdsburg	
Ferguson	John N.	73	Alexander Valley	IN	Beeson	Eunice Naomi	69	Healdsburg	OH
Ferguson	Newton J.	72	Alexander Valley	OH	Cober	Jane	51	Alexander Valley	CA
Ferguson	O. J.	29	Geyserville	CA	Looney	Ethel	21	Fulton	CA
Ferguson	W. R.	21	Geyserville	CA	Perry	Emma R.	19	Geyserville	BCL
Ferguson	W. R.	31	Geyserville	CA	Meyer	Lilly R. S.	21	Geyserville	CA
Ferguson	W. W., Jr.	28	Healdsburg	CA	Watson	Josephine	26	Green Valley	CA
Fernald	Eli V.	29	Petaluma	ME	Johnson	Francis G.	30	Petaluma	CA
Fernandez	Clemente	36	Sebastopol	SWI	Ambrose	Mary	38	Sebastopol	PRT
Fernando	C. R.	21	Honolulu	CA	Hammel	Rose M.	22	Sebastopol	CA
Ferrari	Augustino	35	Santa Rosa	ITL	ReSaglia	Mattie	35	Santa Rosa	SWT
Ferrari	Guiseppe Joseph	27	Asti	SWT	Perazzo	Rosie	19	Asti	CA
Ferrari	Tealue	24	Santa Rosa	SWT	Verzasconi	Bessie	24	Santa Rosa	SWT
Ferreiro	Jose Gracia	24	Petaluma Twp,	PRT	Freitas	Maria	25	Petaluma Twp.	PRT
Ferrell	John	35	Cloverdale		Warner	Rebekah	22	Cloverdale	
Ferretti	John V.	48	Alameda	ITL	Lagorio	Therese B.	26	Alameda	ITL
Ferroni	Louise	51	Healdsburg	ITL	Lozzori	Rosa	38	Healdsburg	ITL
Ferrori	Enrico	28	Santa Rosa Twp.	ITL	Cenini	Ersilia	19	Santa Rosa	ITL
Fesso	Antonio	31	Petaluma	ITL	Zanoni	Lillie	17	Petaluma	CA
Fetterly	Charles	27	Los Angeles	OH	Newman	Esther H.	18	Santa Rosa	CA
Fevrier	George Taylor	28	Oakland	CA	Farrell	Angela Helen	22	Freestone	CA

Groom					Bride				
Surname	Given Name	Age	Residence	BP	Surname	Given Name	Age	Residence	BP
Fevrier	Harold C.	24	San Francisco	CA	Farrell	Gertrude M.	20	Freestone	CA
Fewel	William Cicero	24	Healdsburg	CA	Gober	Elizabeth Tennessee	20	Healdsburg	MO
Fick	John Frederick	32	Santa Rosa	NY	Fickas	Norrie Elizabeth	29	Redding	CA
Fidler	Joseph L.	24	Modesto	CA	Nichols	Lois	16	Madera	CA
Fiege	Carl William	24	Healdsburg	CA	Brooks	Viola Marie	18	Santa Rosa	CA
Fiege	Joseph	36	Healdsburg	GER	Lepper	Lena	35	Healdsburg	IL
Field	Harry B.	27	Ross Station	CA	Phair	Helen	28	San Francisco	ENG
Field	James				Goddard	Silvia C.	22		
Field	John	47	Cloverdale		Singley	Mary	28	Petaluma	CA
Field	John K.	31	San Francisco	ENG	Cooper	Alice L.	33	San Francisco	ENG
Field	Sydney L.	30	Harris, CA	CA	Hartly	Birdie M.	21	Boonville	CA
Field	Walter E.	36	Healdsburg	ME	Hays	Jennie	24	Healdsburg	MO
Fielding	Edward Joseph	32	Eureka	CA	Swaner	Bulah	30	Eureka	OK
Fields	Fred S.	26	Cloverdale	OH	Thompson	Laura A.	18	Santa Rosa	CA
Fields	Seraphin F.	26	Petaluma	AZR	Rose	Inez Margaret	26	Sebastopol	CA
Fields	William A.	30	Santa Rosa	TX	Kriedell	Amelia, Mrs.	24	Santa Rosa	OH
Fieux	Constant	48	San Francisco	FRN	Longuet	Louise	47	San Francisco	FRN
Figera	Louie	22	Santa Rosa	SPN	Velazquez	Carmen	19	Santa Rosa	SPN
Figone	August	21	San Francisco	ITL	Batta	Katie	19	Sonoma	CA
Fike	N.				Wallace	Elizabeth J.			
Filbert	Major (?)	25	Point Arena		Windsor	Sarah A.	23	Healdsburg	
Files	Charles M.	31	Loomis, Placer Co.	CO	Flesher	Retta M.	24	Peachland	IA
Filippelli	John	36	Santa Rosa	SWT	Buzzi	Nora	35	Santa Rosa	ITL
Filippini	Achille	34	Petaluma	SWT	Morelli	Irene	23	Santa Rosa	SWT
Filippini	Basilio	30	Ignacio	SWT	Pifferi	Anita	30	Petaluma	CA
Filippini	Emidio John	27	Napa	CA	Koch	Pauline Josephine	25	Santa Rosa	CA
Filippini	John Ernest	21	Nicasio	CA	Bloom	Celia Virginia	26	Petaluma	CA

Groom					Bride				
Surname	**Given Name**	**Age**	**Residence**	**BP**	**Surname**	**Given Name**	**Age**	**Residence**	**BP**
Fillppini	John	29	Petaluma	SWT	Zamaroni	Egidia	28	Petaluma	CA
Finatti	Guilio	27	Nicasio	SWT	Gambroni	Angiolina	21	Petaluma	SWT
Finch	Frank W.	36	Vallejo	MO	Senn	Lydia E.	19	Oakland	GER
Finch	Fred F.	28	Irvington, NE	NE	de Veuve	Anna M.	29	Petaluma	AUT
Finch	Gordon Wilbur	23	San Francisco	CA	Lindley	Hannah Melba	19	San Francisco	CND
Fine	Alex				Miller	Annie Wickershaw			
Fink	Monte C.	33	San Francisco	CA	Hutchinson	Sarah J.	29	San Francisco	CA
Finke	Joseph H.	26	San Francisco	IL	Andersen	Julia Jane	20	San Francisco	CA
Finlayson	James	38	San Francisco	SCT	Thompson	Anna F.	33	San Francisco	CA
Finley	Allan W.	21	San Francisco	CA	Abraham	Dorthey E.	18	San Francisco	CA
Finley	Alvin W.	21+	Sebastopol	CA	Head	Frances Gertrude	18+	Santa Rosa	CA
Finley	Asa L.	33	Richmond	CA	Pascoe	Caroline M.	24	Oakland	CA
Finley	Ernest L.	39	Santa Rosa	OR	Woolsey	Ruth	25	Santa Rosa	OR
Finley	Jackson	23	Bodega	CA	Stemple	Alfaretta	18	Santa Rosa	CA
Finley	Jefferson	30	Bodega Twp.	CA	McCready	Carrie	18	Bodega Twp.	CA
Finley	Leon Grover	30	Occidental	Bodega	Kee	Mary Elizabeth	21	Bodega	Bod-ega
Finley	Robert	56	Santa Rosa	CND	Malaney	Ella Nora	42	Santa Rosa	CA
Finley	Wilson E.	24	Santa Rosa	CA	Hudson	Alice	20	America P. C.	CA
Finn	Robert B.	33	Mill Valley	CA	Johnston	Grace G.	27	Mill Valley	CA
Finney	Clarence	23	Ukiah	CA	Moore	Belle	22	Ukiah	CA
Fiori	Antonio	28	Sebastopol	ITL	Parinoli	Annie	28	Valley Ford	ITL
Fiori	Attilio A.	34	Petaluma	CA	Sarori	Elizabeth	32	Petaluma	CA
Fiori	Celestino	21	Santa Rosa	ITL	Rossi	Mary	17	Occidental	ITL
Firth	Christopher C.	34	San Francisco	KY	Mury	Elise	32	San Francisco	NJ
Fischer	Francis	34	San Rafael	MA	Nolan	Rose	24	San Rafael	CA
Fischer	Henry F.	24	Santa Rosa	MO	Kobler	Rosa	22	Mt. Olivet	NJ
Fischer	William R.	29	San Francisco	Ontario, CND	Blaine	Lillian M.	29	San Francisco	IN

Groom					Bride				
Surname	**Given Name**	**Age**	**Residence**	**BP**	**Surname**	**Given Name**	**Age**	**Residence**	**BP**
Fiscus	Fred Irwin	21	Sebastopol	CA	Gould	Maud	18	Sebastopol	CA
Fish	Clarence P.	31	San Francisco	CT	Michalake	Barbara M.	28	San Francisco	Wi
Fish	Franklin Janus	20	Bancroft, Coos Co., OR	OR	Gage	Vivian Ada	19	Santa Rosa	OR
Fish	George	48	Santa Rosa	ENG	Lockwood	Mary	49	San Francisco	ENG
Fishel	John E.	39	San Francisco	PA	Mallory	Margaret L.	48	San Francisco	DC
Fisher	Charles	25	Santa Rosa	BOH	Yob	Rosa	19	Santa Rosa	AUT
Fisher	David	24	Forestville	NE	Blakley	Annie	18	Forestville	CA
Fisher	Eugene	29	Santa Rosa	CA	Samuels	Mollie	18	Santa Rosa	CA
Fisher	Francis	45	Gridley, Butte Co.	NH	Cole	Celia A.	39	Santa Rosa	MI
Fisher	Fred W.	27	Fresno	MO	Wilztmann	Lulu	24	Santa Rosa	GER
Fisher	Isaac Willard	30	Napa	MO	Vandeleur	Mayme Alloysious	20	Napa	CA
Fisher	Louis Fredk.	31	Mt. Olivet	NE	Paschal	Rosa Belle	20	Santa Rosa	NE
Fisher	Theodoric L.	20	Forestville	NE	Miller	Cora E.	18+	Forestville	CA
Fisk	Arthur M.	23	San Francisco	WA	Buchan	Marjorie L.	22	Sonoma	IA
Fisk	Charles Grosvenor	31	San Rafael	CA	Nisson	Gertrude	26	Petaluma	CA
Fisk	Chas. H.				Johnson	J. A.			
Fisk	Frank F.	38	Davis	CA	Cooper	Lula May	28	Santa Rosa	CA
Fisk	Geo. S.	26	Fisherman's Bay	CA	Clark	Tillie	18	Fisherman's Bay	CA
Fisk	W. C.	26	Modesto	PA	Bundy	Edith	26	Modesto	IA
Fitch	Arthur	36	Santa Rosa	WI	Hance	Louise K.	29	Santa Rosa	NJ
Fitch	Charley	34	Healdsburg		Brown	Carrie	21	Healdsburg	
Fitch	John B.		Petaluma		Graham	Libbie	17	Petaluma	
Fitch	John Byron	21	Healdsburg	CA	Ford	Bessie, Mrs.	21	Santa Rosa	USA
Fitch	Joseph	42	Healdsburg		Moraga	Martena	26	Santa Rosa	
Fitch	Joseph				Filebot ?	Maria C.			
Fitch	Joseph, Jr.	24	Healdsburg	CA	Freshour	Sarah Jane	20	Healdsburg	CA
Fitch	Romualdo A.	25	Santa Rosa	MEX	Gaspari	Lenora	18	Healdsburg	CA

Groom					Bride				
Surname	Given Name	Age	Residence	BP	Surname	Given Name	Age	Residence	BP
Fites	Charles E.	30	Oakland	IN	Brown	Emma G.	24	Petaluma	CA
Fitsimmons	Miron Ray	24	Sebastopol	KS	Baitey	Minnie Elvie	22	Sebastopol	NE
Fitz	Anton	41	San Francisco	AUS	Obram	Mary H.	40	Sebastopol	AUS
Fitzgerald	Daniel Holland	18	Santa Rosa	CA	Heatley	Edna M.	18	Santa Rosa	CND
Fitzgerald	Halcie	34	Oleum	CA	Cox	Ruby Marie	18	Oakland	CA
Fitzgerald	James G. B.	21	Santa Rosa	CA	Hiatt	Wanda	17	Santa Rosa	CA
Fitzgerald	James R.	23	San Francisco	CA	Azevedo	Mary Cecilia	22	San Francisco	CA
Fitzgerald	John A.	49	San Francisco	CA	Cuneo	Palma	33	San Francisco	CA
Fitzgerald	John Clayton	27	Bakersfield	MA	Ross	Genevieve Loiree	27	Vineburg	CA
Fitzgerald	John F.	27	Los Angeles	MA	Rogers	Maud	20	Fresno	CA
Fitzgerald	John J., Jr.	22	Santa Rosa	CA	Taylor	Ethel	19	Santa Rosa	CA
Fitzgerald	Thomas	38	Petaluma	PEI	Duffy	Susie	28	Petaluma	CA
Fitzpatrick	James H.	36	Vallejo	WI	Dempsey	Catherine F.	35	Healdsburg	CA
Fitzpatrick	Lawrence F.	26	Bodega	Bodega	McLain	Lavina B.	16	Freestone	Free-stone
Fitzpatrick	Peter D.	26	Bodega	CA	Keefe	Maggie A.	22	Bodega	CA
Fitzpatrick	Wm. E.	22	San Francisco	CA	Herlihy	Elizabeth	19	San Francisco	CA
Fitzsimmons	Charles S.	30	San Francisco	MN	Henry	Cassie	23	Healdsburg	TN
Fix	J. K.	66	Sebastopol	IN	Shedd	R. J., Mrs.	54	Petaluma	
Fix	J. K.	61	Green Valley	IN	Webster	Mary F., Mrs.	33	Green Valley	
Flack	John				Field	Rucilla R.			
Flack	John A.	26	Healdsburg	CA	McClish	Ella N.	23	Healdsburg	CA
Flagg	Rollo E.	25	Oakland	WI	Lind	Marion E.	24	Santa Rosa	NE
Flaherty	Albert W.	22	Willows	CA	Cook	Della T.	24	Petaluma	CA
Flaherty	Philip Hyde	32	Santa Rosa	CA	Fields	Theresa	31	Santa Rosa	CA
Flanary	Adam	28	Santa Rosa Twp.	VA	Joslin	Alma	19	Santa Rosa Twp.	MI
Flechner	Lloyd L.	21	Vallejo	CA	Buckle	Elsie G.	21	Ukiah	CA
Fleck	G. C.	35	Vallejo	GER	Scott	Agnes	28	Santa Rosa	Sfo

Groom					Bride				
Surname	**Given Name**	**Age**	**Residence**	**BP**	**Surname**	**Given Name**	**Age**	**Residence**	**BP**
Fleet	Walter Sidney	20	Petaluma	ENG	Howard	Ethel May	16	Petaluma	CA
Fleischman	Louis E.	23	Tulare	CA	Reed	Ellen F.	23	Petaluma	CA
Fleishmon	Moses	32	San Francisco		Helbarh	Terria (?)	26	Sebastopol	
Fleissner	Hugo Herman	39	Petaluma	OH	Gamage	Lillian Lewis	34	Petaluma	CA
Fleming	Eddie Ellis	26	Occidental	IA	Kingwell	Avis B.	18	Occidental	CA
Fleming	Frank M.	22	Cazadero	IA	Kingwell	Phebe M.	24	Occidental	ENG
Fleming	Paul X.	24	San Diego	CA	Wisecarver	Norma Eugenia	21	Geyserville	OR
Fleming	William		Bodega		Carson	Mary	20+	Bodega	
Fleming	William		Bodega		Carson	Mary	20+	Bodega	
Flemming	William	40	Mendocino	CND	Olsen	Thora	37	Petaluma	NRY
Flesher	Harry	28	Peachland	IA	Thomas	Ora A.	17	Peachland	IA
Fletcher	Andrew	36	Fisherman's Bay	SCT	Kuffel	Gertrude	21	Petaluma	CA
Fletcher	Harry A.	30	San Francisco	CA	Murphy	Irene R.	16	San Francisco	CA
Fletcher	James A.	26	Graton	CA	Rayner	Polly	21	Graton	CA
Fletcher	John H.	60	Cloverdale	CND	Murphy	Kate	59	Cloverdale	CA
Fletcher	Lee C.	21	San Francisco	CA	Nylen	Elivira L.	22	San Francisco	CA
Fletcher	Marion A.	25	Green Valley	CA	Rohrback	Clara	24	Green Valley	CA
Fletcher	William R.	45	Analy Twp.		Dovey	Margaret	35	Analy Twp.	
Fletcher	Wm. F.	30	San Francisco	ENG	Barber	Flora G.	23	Cloverdale	CA
Flickinger	Andrew Grant	36	Vallejo	KY	Muller	Rose Helen	20	Petaluma	CA
Flint	T. B.	33	Sacramento		Flint	Ella J. (?)	33	Petaluma	
Flint	Willard B.	28	Santa Rosa	KS	Ross	Belle D.	26	Santa Rosa	CA
Fliori	Anchise	39	Asti	ITL	Prevedel	Aurora	28	Asti	ITL
Flippi	Toney	27	Windsor	ITL	Cordano	Rose	28	Windsor	CA
Flockhart	Joseph J.	27	Santa Rosa	CA	Wagner	Annie E.	19	Santa Rosa	CA
Flockhart	Robert E.	30	Santa Rosa	GA	Feltz	Frieda L.	25	Santa Rosa	CA
Flohr	Charles W.	27	Petaluma	Mac	Michaels	Kate	23	Petaluma	Marys ville, CA
Flohr	Charles William	31	Petaluma	CA	Zamaroni	Elvira	22	Petaluma	SWT

Groom					Bride				
Surname	**Given Name**	**Age**	**Residence**	**BP**	**Surname**	**Given Name**	**Age**	**Residence**	**BP**
Flohr	Frank G.	21	San Francisco	CA	Downs	Catherine H.	20	San Francisco	CA
Flohr	Marcus	24	Petaluma	Pet	Boyson	Gertrude E.	22	Petaluma	MA
Florence	Arthur	23	Guerneville	Forest-ville	Manchester	Vieva Florence	19	Guerneville	USA
Flournoy	Alexander H.	42	Healdsburg	OR	Enzenauer	Ethel R.	29	Healdsburg	CA
Flournoy (?)	William H.	27	Fisherman's Bay		Throop	Fannie C.	23	Fisherman's Bay	
Floyd	Fred	46	Healdsburg	ENG	Bowers	Elizabeth Clara	42	Healdsburg	IA
Floyd	Fred	27	Healdsburg	ENG	Pierce	May L.	24	Healdsburg	IL
Floyd	James Andrew	29	Santa Rosa	AR	Shaffer	Pearl Julia	21	Santa Rosa	NE
Flynn	John J.	21	San Francisco	CA	Susoff	Lucile A.	20	San Francisco	RUS
Flynn	Patrick	33	Graton	IRL	Quinlan	Ellie	22	Graton	IRL
Fobes	Charles Fitch	25	Petaluma	CA	Brown	Bernice Luretta	24	Petaluma	NY
Focha	Joseph	31	Petaluma	CA	Cerini	Dell	31	Petaluma	CA
Fochetti	Julius W.	25	Sonoma	CA	Quartaroli	Leonora	22	Sonoma	CA
Focht	Samuel S.	39	Sebastopol	MO	Harmer	Althea L.	26	Sebastopol	KS
Foelker	Adam H.	21	Kenwood	NY	Watson	Elizabeth E.	20	Kenwood	NY
Foelone	Domenico	27	Healdsburg	ITL	Nicoletti	Virginia	17	Healdsburg	CA
Foerstler	William C.	21	Santa Rosa	CA	Hershberger	Ruby D.	18	Santa Rosa	CA
Fogarty	James V.	31	Los Angeles	CA	Beach	Clara M.	25	Eureka	CA
Folco	Eugenio M.	31	Nice, FRN	FRN	Graham	Elizabeth M.	26	San Francisco	CA
Foletti	Louis G.	30	Sonora	SWT	Guizo	Angela C.	21	Sonora	
Foley	Michael	30	Healdsburg	IA	Thistle	Bell	18	Healdsburg	CA
Foley	Michael A.	21	San Francisco	CA	Habinger	Irene E.	19	San Francisco	IN
Foley	Michel J.	27	Cotati	IRL	Jasperson	Henrietta M.	20	Sebastopol	CA
Folk	James	31	Eureka	CA	Caughey	Agnes	28	Cloverdale	CA
Folks	Charles	19	Guerneville	CA	Manning	Ella J.	17	Guerneville	CA
Follini	Louis	22	San Francisco	BUA	Longo	Mary Florence	19	San Francisco	MA
Follows	Jack Apperley	21	Oakland	CA	Miramontes	Marie Leanor	20	San Francisco	CA
Folsom	Fred Newton	44	Sebastopol	CA	Kinyon	Bessie M.	26	Sebastopol	MO

Groom					Bride				
Surname	Given Name	Age	Residence	BP	Surname	Given Name	Age	Residence	BP
Foltz	Edward P.	25	Linden, San Joaquin Co., CA	CA	McMinn	Etta	25	Santa Rosa	CA
Fomasi	Peter	35	Bodega	ITL	Albini	Mary	20	Bodega	ITL
Fontch	Bert	30	Stockton	CA	Spraggins	Florence E.	26	Stockton	CA
Fontes	Manuel Rodgers, Jr.	26	Corte Madera, Marin Co.	Boston	Perry	Roseline	17	Petaluma	Pet
Fonts	Fred	28	Sonoma	CA	Weyl	Clara	22	Sonoma	CA
Fonts	Lee	27	Forestville	NE	Wakeland	Maggie E.	30	Sebastopol	IA
Foote	Charles M.	35	San Francisco	OH	Harris	Cecile Vivian	27	San Francisco	CA
Foote	W. D.	28	Tahoe	CA	Davis	Lena	21	San Francisco	CA
Fopiano	Giuseppe	30	Healdsburg		Rosasco	Rosa	16	Healdsburg	
Forbes	Alfred L.	24	Oakland	PA	Black	Myrtle E.	21	Oakland	CA
Forbes	Cleveland	40	San Francisco	Sfo	Vrooman	Mae Baldwin	22	Santa Rosa	CA
Forcha	Catano Jose	25	Petaluma Twp.	AZR	Medeiros	Anna	17	Petaluma Twp.	AZR
Ford	Barnett	30	Freestone	TN	Loury	Mary	20	Freestone	CA
Ford	C. W. R.	44	San Francisco	MA	Robinson	Julia S.	42	Los Angeles	MA
Ford	Charles	25	Santa Rosa	CA	Kennedy	Unice Pearl	18	Santa Rosa	KS
Ford	David	23	San Francisco	CA	Field	Mary	22	Healdsburg	CA
Ford	Earl A.	21	Ukiah	CA	Singley	Theo. E.	17	Ukiah	CA
Ford	Edward Franklin	30	Suisun	TX	Gibbs	Zoie Alva	18	Petaluma	CA
Ford	Fred J.	22	Willits	CA	Lewis	Maretta E.	15	Cloverdale	CA
Ford	George T.	28	Santa Rosa	IA	Crane	Eva Grace	37	Santa Rosa	CA
Ford	J. A.	56	Calpella	CA	Hayes	Hattie	26	Calpella	CA
Ford	James Russell	21	Freestone		Phillbrook	Martha	18	Freestone	
Ford	John	52	San Francisco	IRL	Morris	Anna	42	San Francisco	ENG
Ford	Michael	31	Santa Rosa	NY	Moore	Amanda	37	Santa Rosa	IA
Ford	William A.	55	Ukiah	CA	Campbell	Mollie	52	Healdsburg	MO
Fordanse	Henry P.	31	Cloverdale	WI	Scott	Delilah	20	Cloverdale	CA
Forde	John M.	33	San Francisco	CA	Freeman	Dorothy M.	30	San Francisco	ENG
Fordemwalt	C. E.	26	Sacramento	IA	Kise	Ida	26	Windsor	CA

Groom					Bride				
Surname	**Given Name**	**Age**	**Residence**	**BP**	**Surname**	**Given Name**	**Age**	**Residence**	**BP**
Fore	Walter Francis	28	Sebastopol	IL	O'Conner	Amy Joan	25	Santa Rosa	CA
Foreman	Andrew Macpherson	33	Berkeley	CA	Lee	Annabel	23	Santa Rosa	CA
Foreman	C.	23	Healdsburg	CA	Fairchild	Gipsy	23	Healdsburg	OH
Foreman	Charles	38	Stockton	CA	Stemer	Anna	24	Stockton	GER
Foreman	Edward L.	21	Healdsburg	CA	Flournoy	Emma I.	19	Oakland	CA
Foreman	Lorin	24	Healdsburg	CA	Brigham	Mamie L.	21	Healdsburg	UT
Foreman	Park	23	Healdsburg	CA	Gilmore	Sarah E.	23	Healdsburg	OH
Forest	H. A.	28	Santa Rosa	ENG	Rieffel	Hortense L.	20	San Francisco	CA
Foresti	Giuseppe	20	Cloverdale	AUS	Filosi	Lucia	28	Cloverdale	SWT
Forgett	Frank Alma	23	Santa Rosa	CA	Parara	Florence	23	San Francisco	CA
Forgett	Fred F.	21	Santa Rosa	CA	Schwan	Minnie	21	Santa Rosa	CA
Forgett	Isadore	37	Petaluma	CA	Bargagliotti	Louisa	21	Petaluma	CA
Forgett	Joseph Nelson	33	Santa Rosa	CA	Eby	Jessie Leone	21	Santa Rosa	CA
Formschlag	August Elias	27	Penngrove	CA	Buhl	Josie Mabel	19	Penngrove	CA
Formway	Utah S.	26	Stockton	MO	Bronsert	Anita M.	20	Guerneville	CA
Forneris	Albert	40	Sonoma	ITL	Cole	Mary E.	40	Sonoma	CA
Forni	Charles B.	24	St. Helena	ITL	Ghiringhelli	Teressa	18	Cloverdale	ITL
Forno	Alasandro	27	Petaluma	ITL	Bologna	Lina	19	Asti	ITL
Forrest	Richard Kenneth	32	Sacramento	MA	Kelly	Erma Heidel	30	Sacramento	MO
Forrester	Henry A.	48	Ceries	MO	Steele	Viva B.	33	Vallejo	MO
Forsberg	Hans Peter	34	San Francisco	SWD	Tell	Ida Amanda	23	San Francisco	SWD
Forsey	Warren F.	23	Fresno	MO	French	Francis J.	22	Santa Rosa	CND
Forsman	William T.	31	Santa Rosa	KY	Hilliard	Carrie B.	28	Santa Rosa	MI
Forsyth	Henry M.	24	Santa Rosa	CA	Reid	Mary E.	24	Santa Rosa	CA
Forsyth	Jess Thomas	21	San Francisco	CA	Dehay	Louise A.	18	Cloverdale	CA
Forsyth	John Hamilton	40	Fulton	MO	Clark	Nancy C.	26	Forestville	CA
Forsyth	W. B.	24	Reno, NV	CA	Crandall	Edna	29	Cloverdale	WI
Forsythe	Myrl D.	28	Santa Rosa	CA	Hockin	Maude A.	26	Santa Rosa	CA
Fortado	Jose Jacinto	34	Petaluma Twp.	WTS	Silva	Anna Pereira	37	Vallejo Twp.	WTS

Groom					Bride				
Surname	**Given Name**	**Age**	**Residence**	**BP**	**Surname**	**Given Name**	**Age**	**Residence**	**BP**
Fortado	Lawrence F.	42	Berkeley	CA	Thomas	Vivian G.	33	Berkeley	CA
Fortier	Louis	72	Healdsburg	GER	Looson (?)	Ann M.	54	Healdsburg	GER
Fortier	Peter	30	Healdsburg	MO	Hart	Hattie L.	24	Healdsburg	IA
Fortier	William	26	Healdsburg	NE	Couper	Jennie	19	Healdsburg	CA
Fortson	John T.				Howell	Margaret Lent	15		
Fortunati	Alfredo	24	Santa Rosa	ITL	Caselli	Beatrice	21	Santa Rosa	CA
Fosgett	Jay Dernard	24	Oakland	MN	Rudd	Minnie A.	18	Ukiah	CA
Fosgett	Jay Derward	20	Hopland	MN	Rhoades	Georgie A.	20	Hopland	CA
Foss	Charles C.	43	Calistoga	NY	Proctor	Hattie	26	Healdsburg	CA
Foss	Charles C.	25	Knights Valley	NY	Phillfott	Fanny (?) I.	21	Napa Co.	CA
Foss	Leonard Rangwell	26	Oakland	CA	Noyes	Ruby Thersa	21	Oakland	CA
Foss	Werner C.	25	San Francisco	GER	Naselli	Mary E.	24	San Francisco	IL
Foste	Manuel	29	Santa Rosa	PRT	Nunes	Mary S.	28	Sebastopol	CA
Foste	Manuel V.	24	Cotati	PRT	Victor	Julia C.	19	Sebastopol	SWI
Foster	Aubrey M.	21	San Francisco	CO	Elsdon	Winifred J.	20	San Francisco	WA
Foster	Charles L.	34	St. Helena	MO	Baker	Crystabel K.	27	Hluag (?)	CA
Foster	Charles Simpson	24	Petaluma	CA	Benson	Marcia E.	20	Petaluma	CA
Foster	Chas.				Gourley	Sarah A.	20		
Foster	Clarence E.	27	San Francisco	NSC	Gordon	Alice M.	25	San Francisco	CA
Foster	Edwin J.	23	Sebastopol	IL	Breaks	Florence F.	22	Sebastopol	NE
Foster	Geo. Alonzo	22	Santa Rosa Twp.	OR	Scott	Mary Ellen	19	Santa Rosa Twp.	CA
Foster	H. G.	42	San Francisco	NY	Miller	Marion C.	33	San Francisco	CA
Foster	John Warren	25	Petaluma	MO	Murphy	Nellie Agnes	23	Petaluma	CA
Foster	Joseph	21	Santa Rosa	CA	Morgan	Eva L.	15+	Santa Rosa	IA
Foster	Joseph Walter	24	Petaluma	CA	Mordecai	Frances Elizabeth	22	Petaluma	CA
Foster	Lewis Keyston	21	Santa Rosa	NY	Waterbury	Ada Muriel	19	Santa Rosa	CA
Foster	Robert A.	50	Healdsburg	MO	Gibson	Susan A.	23	Healdsburg	CA
Foster	William E.	24	Bodega		Addison	Eliza J.	23	Bodega	
Foster	William E.	24	Bodega		Addisen	Eliza J.	23	Bodega	

Groom					Bride				
Surname	Given Name	Age	Residence	BP	Surname	Given Name	Age	Residence	BP
Fouch	Albert				Talbot	Eliza P.			
Foucrault	Edward Chas.	25	Tomales	CA	Caligari	Celestina	21	Tomales	CA
Fournier	Arthur, Dr.	25	Garnerville, Nev.	CND	Brittain	Grace C.	21	Santa Rosa	CA
Foutch	Albert P.	52	Santa Rosa	IA	Dunlap	Melinda	56	Santa Rosa	AL
Foutch	Thomas G.	28	Santa Rosa	CA	Anderson	Florence	20	Santa Rosa	CA
Fouts	Alvin Roy	29	Forestville	NE	Davis	Amanda	28	Forestville	CA
Fouts	Edwin Lee	22	Forestville	NE	Barnum	Evaline	16	Forestville	CA
Fouts	William V.	19	Forestville	IA	Gleason	Mattie	19	Forestville	KS
Fouts	Clyde E.	22	Forestville	NE	Baney	Elsie R.	24	Santa Rosa	MT
Fowler	Alfred				Deeds	Louisa C.	17		
Fowler	David	21	Santa Rosa	CA	Knolty	May M.	18	Santa Rosa	MI
Fowler	Dewey	22	Freestone	CA	Druck	Elizabeth M.	18	Freestone	WI
Fowler	Edgar James	21	Valley Ford		Rien	Sarah Cordelia	20	Valley Ford	
Fowler	Harvey				Rice	Eunice			
Fowler	J. H.	21	Valley Ford	CA	Connor	Jennie	18	Valley Ford	CA
Fowler	Lorenzo Gipson	28	San Francisco	CA	Peters	Flora	22	Petaluma	CA
Fowler	Nathaniel D.	55	Redding	NY	McTarnahan	Addie, Mrs.	54	Santa Rosa	MS
Fowler	Nicholas R.	24	Occidental	CA	Lowrey	Minnie	18	Freestone	CA
Fowler	Scott D.	30	Cloverdale	WI	Dixon	Jessie	24	Cloverdale	CA
Fowler	William C.	21	Santa Rosa	CA	Faught	Ethel A.	18	Fulton	CA
Fowles	Stephen	30	San Francisco	UT	Gould	Minnie R.	27	San Francisco	NSC
Fox	Ancel Elmer	29	San Jose	CA	Hixson	Zella Irene	22	Cloverdale	CA
Fox	Chas. W.	29	Santa Rosa		Farmer	Sarah Angeline	20	Santa Rosa	
Fox	Francis Gordon	28	Yolanda	MO	Steele	Grace Olney	28	Yolanda	IL
Fox	Henry	32	Healdsburg		Hall	Lola Jesse	21	Healdsburg	
Fox	Joseph	53	Healdsburg	OH	Price	Lucy M.	48	Healdsburg	CA
Fox	Louis H.	31	Petaluma	CA	Steitz	Julia C.	29	Petaluma	CA
Frame	R. A.	39	Santa Rosa	IL	Davis	Eliza S.	25	San Francisco	ENG
Frampton	Charles E.	32	Healdsburg	IL	Miser	Hannah	33	Healdsburg	SWD
Francard	Ernest	45	Santa Rosa	BLG	Babbino	Carlotta	47	Santa Rosa	ITL

Groom					Bride				
Surname	**Given Name**	**Age**	**Residence**	**BP**	**Surname**	**Given Name**	**Age**	**Residence**	**BP**
Francard	John B.	31	Santa Rosa Twp.	BLG	Gallard	Genevive	29	Santa Rosa Twp.	FRN
Franceschi	Ceasre	36	San Francisco	ITL	Perinoni	Rose	41	San Francisco	ITL
Francesconi	Federico	31	Occidental	ITL	Albreigi	Madelina	17	Occidental	CA
Franchi	Nildo	28	Wendling, Medocino Co	ITL	Bacci	Beppa	35	Wendling	ITL
Francis	Edwin Charles	30	Petaluma	ENG	Norris	Henrietta	29	Petaluma	TN
Francis	Joseph Andrew	23	Oakland	Oak	Peat	Pearle E.	24	Sebastopol	Berk-eley
Francis	William A.	41	Friutvale	WA	Bowie	Vera	36	Oakland	OR
Francis	William S.	28	San Francisco	Pet	Perry	Mary	18	Petaluma	Pet
Francisco	Anton	53	Sebastopol	AZR	Cardoza	Mary Ann	28	Sebastopol	AZR
Francisco	Antone	27	Petaluma	PRT	Limes	Annie	22	Petaluma	PRT
Francisco	Antone J.	28	San Francisco	WTS	Silva	Mary	18	Petaluma Twp.	CA
Frank	C. E.	38	Pittsburg, PA	PA	Spitzer	Clara S.	26	San Francisco	NY
Frank	Christian	23	Santa Rosa	GER	Mangole	Pauline	23	Santa Rosa	GER
Frank	Frederick	36	Forestville	GER	Feltz	Amelia	26	Fulton	GER
Frank	James				Eager	Loretta			
Frank	Samuel	29	Alameda Co.	NY	Locsen (?)	Amelia	20	Healdsburg	CA
Franklin	Alex R.	34	San Francisco	CA	Partridge	Katherine	22	Sausalito	CA
Franklin	Benjamin	21	Petaluma	OH	McKinnon	Gertrude E.	26	Petaluma	CA
Fraser	D. Herbert	37	San Francisco	CND	Roussey	Mildred, Mrs.	26	San Francisco	CA
Fraser	Dan W.	26	Eureka	CA	Cameron	Hazel	20	Santa Rosa	CA
Fraser	George Willard	49	Santa Rosa	OH	Ware	Helen	30	Santa Rosa	MN
Fraser	James Grant	34	Healdsburg	NY	Walker	Nellena E.	17	Healdsburg	CA
Fraser	John N.	28	Swanton	IL	Clark	Lettie A.	28	Calistoga	CA
Frasier	Frank B.	24	Petaluma	CA	Crimmins	Agnes Marie	22	Petaluma	CA
Frasier	Fred A.	28	Petaluma	Fresno	Graeff	Dora	20	Sebastopol	Son
Frasier	Malcome J.	23	Petaluma	NY	Kane	Maggie	23	Petaluma	CA
Frates	Joseph A.	30	Two Rock	CA	Ramos	Mary	20	Petaluma	CA
Frates	Joseph V. A.	32	Oakland	NV	McChristian	Delphine G.	26	San Francisco	CA

Groom					Bride				
Surname	**Given Name**	**Age**	**Residence**	**BP**	**Surname**	**Given Name**	**Age**	**Residence**	**BP**
Frates	Joseph W.	25	Petaluma	CA	Morris	Mary S.	19	Petaluma	CA
Frates	Manuel Suza	37	Petaluma Twp.	WTS	Dabuer	Rosa Emilia	27	Petaluma Twp.	WTS
Frati	Abramo	25	Guerneville	ITL	Acquistapace	Amelia	24	Guerneville	ITL
Frati	Francesco	29	Santa Rosa	ITL	Gregori	Maria	21	Santa Rosa	ITL
Frati	Giuseppe	25	Healdsburg	ITL	Bertoni	Natalina	18+	Healdsburg	ITL
Frawley	Richard Edward	26	San Francisco	CA	Reed	Mattie Agnes	24	San Francisco	Pet
Frazee	Henry Dewitt	21	Santa Rosa	CA	Lockwood	Linnie Katherine (?)	20	Santa Rosa	CA
Frazer	Joe E.	24	Sebastopol	AZR	Corey	Mary	22	Sebastopol	CA
Frazier	Elisha H.	37	Cloverdale	CA	Dodson	Mary R.	17	Cloverdale	CA
Frazier	Elisha H.				McNew	Orpah Belle	19		
Frazier	Isaac B.	26	Forestville	CA	Ross	Lizzie E.	21	Forestville	CA
Freck	Louis P.	55	Cincinnati, OH	OH	Bridges	Minnie	53	Sonoma	IN
Frederick	Leonard B.	22	Boulder, CO	CO	Harland	Adeline I.	23	Nevada City	CA
Fredericks	Adolph N.	29	Petaluma	GER	Campigli	Effie	29	Petaluma	MI
Fredericks	George	21	Sebastopol	CA	Showalter	Belle	20	Sebastopol	CA
Fredericks	Martin	27	Petaluma	CA	Cline	Mary A.	27	Petaluma	Minne apolis
Fredericks	Ray Ernest	21	Sebastopol	CA	Hammell	Edna May	20	Sebastopol	CA
Frederickson	Frederick C.	55	San Francisco	DNK	Koppen	Emma C.	45	San Francisco	NY
Frederickson	Hans J.	33	Sonoma	DNK	Johnson	Annie C.	21	Sonoma	DNK
Frederiksen	Andreas	27	Los Guillicos	GER	Mathisen	Ingeburg M.	23	Santa Rosa	GER
Frediani	Angelo	27	El Verano	ITL	Freggiro	Christine	17	El Verano	San Juan, CA
Fredrichsen	Cornelius	25	Petaluma	GER	Hansen	Meta	20	Petaluma	GER
Fredson	Chris A.	21	Healdsburg	CA	Eagle	Geneva	20	Healdsburg	CA
Fredson	Israel	35	Healdsburg	SWD	Thompson	Sophia	23	Healdsburg	GER
Freeborn	Francis Maurice	26	Guanacevi, MEX	ENG	Crepin	Louise Cecelia	24	Glen Ellen	CA
Freeman	Albert J.	32	Santa Rosa	CA	Barnes	Mary E.	25	Santa Rosa	CA
Freeman	Albert J.	43	Santa Maria	CA	Hardisty	Emma L.	29	Santa Rosa	IL

Groom					Bride				
Surname	**Given Name**	**Age**	**Residence**	**BP**	**Surname**	**Given Name**	**Age**	**Residence**	**BP**
Freeman	Carlos J.	30	Petaluma	CA	Carmichael	Belle	19	Petaluma	CND
Freeman	Charles E.	24	San Francisco	PA	Shelton	Lucy E.	18	San Francisco	CA
Freeman	Charles Henry	21	Laughlin	CA	Carter	Alice Blanche	18	Laughlin	CA
Freeman	David	23	Petaluma	CA	Crawford	Annie	26	Petaluma	
Freeman	M. L.	31	Petaluma	CA	Hurton	E. Estella	20	Two Rock	CA
Freeman	Orin	24	Petaluma	CA	Lawson	Rosetta	22	Santa Rosa	MO
Freeman	Wm. H.	26	Moscow, Sonoma Co.	CA	Maddux	Martha E.	21	Guerneville	CA
Freenor	Francis Joseph	40	Seattle	WI	Gries	Roberta L.	34	Portland, OR	TX
Freese	Frederich	29	San Francisco	CA	Fischer	Mary	25	Santa Rosa	MO
Frehe	Alfred Louis	26	Ukiah	Sar	Chittenden	Cornelia F.	25	Petaluma	MI
Frei	L. A.	29	Santa Rosa	CA	Mooney	Joan E.	24	Petaluma	CA
Frei	Walter C.	36	Santa Rosa	CA	Tyler	Leatha Ruth	30	San Francisco	IA
Freidrichsen	Peter	27	Petaluma	GER	Petersen	Dora	23	Petaluma	GER
Freitas	Anton	22	Petaluma	PRT	Howe	Johanna V.	37	Petaluma	CA
Freitas	Antone	23	Oakland	PRT	Freels	Julia Louise	28	Oakland	CA
Freitas	Joao M.	42	Petaluma Twp.	AZR	Vieira	Francisca	42	Petaluma Twp.	AZR
Freitas	Tony	21	Sebastopol	Hon	Costa	Bella	28	Sebastopol	Hon
Freitas (?) on index	Frederick Augustius	30	San Francisco	CA	Barrett	Linnie Mary	30	San Francisco	WA
Frellson	Hans	21	St. Helena	GER	Krounest	Emily	18	Napa	Sfo
Frellson	Oscar August	22	Geyserville	CA	Meeker	Winifred M.	20	Geyserville	WA
Frellson	Walter B.	28	Healdsburg	Napa	Wright	Nellie Wilson	28	Healdsburg	Reno, NV
French	Charles F.	33	Cloverdale		Emery	Eva J.	25	Cloverdale	
French	George Bonzana	29	San Francisco	New Orleans	Wulff	Cecile I.	20	San Francisco	Sfo
French	George Robert	30	Healdsburg	CA	Harmeson	Pearl	21	Healdsburg	IL
French	Jno. H.	29	Guerneville		Folks	Ella	19	Guerneville	
French	William	29	Healdsburg	CA	Cook	May M.	28	Healdsburg	IA
Frese	Henry	32	Petaluma	GER	Maack	Lily	32	Marin Co.	CA

Groom					Bride				
Surname	Given Name	Age	Residence	BP	Surname	Given Name	Age	Residence	BP
Freshour	John L.	26	Windsor	CA	Cobb	Frances	20	Dry Creek Valley	AR
Freshwater	Albert H.	38	San Francisco	PA	Halligan	Francis B.	24	San Francisco	CO
Frey	Elmer	22	Kenwood	CA	Sanders	Nadie	19	Healdsburg	CA
Frey	Frank J.	34	Santa Rosa	OH	Davis	Ida B.	17	Middletown	CA
Frey	Herbert R.	21	Healdsburg	OK	Wilson	Helen A.	18	Healdsburg	CA
Frey	Howard L.	25	Alameda	MO	Cherne	Mollie F.	21	Oakland	SWT
Frey	John G.	31	Kenwood	KS	Hoff	Emma H.	21	Kenwood	CA
Friar	James N.	21	Oakland	CA	Smith	Phena May	20	Oakland	OR
Fricke	Richard	56	Oakland	GER	Huyck	Pearl	39	Butler, IN	IN
Fried	Henry W.	34	Healdsburg	CA	Watson	Lola Etta	24	Healdsburg	CA
Friel	Patrick	55	San Francisco	IRL	Friel	Mary	50	Petaluma	VA
Friend	Joseph A.	25	Santa Rosa	IA	Ivans	Laura Alice	16	Forestville	MO
Fries	Theodore	22	Penngrove	CA	Witt	Ellen V.	22	Two Rock	CA
Frisch	Finnly W.	23	Seattle	WA	Waterman	Gertrude M.	22	Healdsburg	CA
Fritsch	J. R.	36	Petaluma	CA	Hope	Anna M.	33	Petaluma	CND
Fritsch	Walter S.	28	Petaluma	CA	Mecham	Mary I.	25	Petaluma	CA
Frohmoder	Thomas	24	Salem, OR	OR	Lawson	Catherine	35	San Francisco	SCT
Fronk	Edwin B.	48	Richmond	CA	Striver	Alice E.	44	Richmond	IN
Frost	Ervin	57	Windsor	WI	Singleton	Jennie	37	Santa Rosa	OH
Frost	G. W.	38	Cloverdale	WI	Myres	Susanna	29	Cloverdale	MN
Frost	Harvey Chester	23	Healdsburg	CA	McBride	Elizabeth May	22	Healdsburg	NY
Frost	Martin	24	Healdsburg	CA	Warner	Cora E.	20	Healdsburg	IL
Frost	Norman Seaver	65	Petaluma	CND	Thurman	Anastasia	58	Petaluma	MA
Frost	Walter C.	27	Washoe House, Sonoma Co.		Knight	Jennie	22	San Francisco	
Frugoli	Virgilio	58	Santa Rosa	ITL	Usseglio	Catterina	40	Santa Rosa	ITL
Frugoli	Virgilio	54	Santa Rosa	ITL	Rose	Mary	38	Santa Rosa	PRT
Fruits	George Alexander	32	Sebastopol		Gregson	Delia	18	Green Valley	
Fruitt	Charles E.	22	Healdsburg	CA	Hall	Alice E.	22	near Healdsburg	MA
Frus	Hans	28	Petaluma	GER	Johansen	Cecilia	26	Petaluma	GER

Groom					Bride				
Surname	**Given Name**	**Age**	**Residence**	**BP**	**Surname**	**Given Name**	**Age**	**Residence**	**BP**
Frutiger	George F.	23	Fulton	NV	Parkerson	Jane Edith	23	Santa Rosa	CA
Fry	Albert S.	22	Santa Rosa	CA	Allen	Ione May	21	Santa Rosa	CA
Fuchs	Ewald A.	30	Tracy	CA	Barrows	Olive M.	18	Santa Rosa	OR
Fujimoto	Togro	46	Santa Rosa	JPN	Furuta	Tori	36	Santa Rosa	JPN
Fulkerson	Bruce C.	28	Santa Rosa	CA	Wheeler	Maude	25	Santa Rosa	CA
Fulkerson	Bruce C.	19	Santa Rosa	CA	Dimick	Viola	21	Santa Rosa	WA
Fulkerson	Chas. A.	21	Santa Rosa	CA	McGill	Minnie	22	Santa Rosa	CA
Fulkerson	Richard	20	Santa Rosa Twp.	CA	Wendt	Paulina	19	Santa Rosa Twp.	CA
Fulks	C. E.	32	Forestville	OH	Gilkison	Norah F.	24	Forestville	OH
Fullan	Thomas	21	San Francisco	WI	Hall	Jessie	18	San Francisco	CA
Fuller	Charles E.	58	Freestone	MA	Smith	India	38	Petaluma	MI
Fuller	Frank Leslie	22	Petaluma	CA	Armstrong	Ruby Ann	18	Petaluma	CA
Fuller	Harve	27	Petaluma	CA	Syme	Annie	26	Petaluma	CA
Fuller	Lyman T.	21	Healdsburg	CA	Marshall	Clara	23	Healdsburg	CA
Fuller	Percy V.	19	Petaluma	CA	Scott	Esther	17	Petaluma	CA
Fuller	Wm. F. H.	37	Greenwood	NSC	Willis	Ruth E.	18	Peachland	CA
Fulmer	James S.	30	Santa Rosa	UT	Milford	Ellen M.	25	Santa Rosa	CND
Fulton	James E.	70	Lakeport	NY	Moore	Ella Jane	48	Lakeport	IL
Fulton	Jasper A.	21	Geyserville	AL	Franklin	Dora	19	Geyserville	MO
Fulwider	Earl N.	23	Santa Rosa	CA	VanWormer	Charlotte E.	23	Santa Rosa	WI
Fumasoli	Giacomo	36	Santa Rosa	SWT	Domeniconi	Rachel	36	Santa Rosa	SWT
Furber	John Judd	25	Klamath Falls, OR	MN	Smith	Jessie Alberta	21	Healdsburg	CA
Furber	William W.	33	Cloverdale	CA	Hinds	Marguerite	24	Cloverdale	CA
Furia	Alfonzo	23	Santa Rosa	ITL	Furia	Elvira	19	Santa Rosa	ITL
Furia	Ettore	20	Santa Rosa	ITL	Santini	Casimira	16	Fulton	ITL
Furia	Quinto	21	IL	ITL	Bertoni	Amelia	18	Fulton	CA
Furlong	Charles Edward	26	San Francisco	CA	Focha	Frances Agnes	21	Petaluma	CA
Furlong	Hugh C.	24	Sebastopol	CA	Gericke	Margaret L.	24	Sebastopol	CA
Furlong	Patrick	29	Bodega		Gallegher	Sarah	23	Green Valley	

Groom					Bride				
Surname	**Given Name**	**Age**	**Residence**	**BP**	**Surname**	**Given Name**	**Age**	**Residence**	**BP**
Furlong	Thomas F.	32	Bodega	CA	Gleason	Mary Agnes	24	Bodega	CA
Fuson	Amandus U.	41	San Francisco	KS	Cavanagh	May Alice	28	San Francisco	CA
Futsch	Walter Mecham	22	Petaluma	CA	Hodgson	Irene Mae	22	Santa Rosa	CA

Other Heritage Books by the Sonoma County Genealogical Society, Inc.:

CD: *Sonoma County [California] Records, Volume 1*

Early School Attendance Records of Sonoma County, California, Beginning 1858

Early School Attendance Records of Sonoma County, California, Volume II: 1874–1932

Index and Abstracts of Wills, Sonoma County, California: 1850–1900

Index to Naturalization Records in Sonoma County, California, Volume 1: 1841–1906

Naturalization Records in Sonoma County, California, Volume II: 1906–1930

Index to The Sonoma Searcher*: Volume 16, No. 1 to Volume 28, No. 3*
(Including Index to The Sonoma Searcher*: Volume 1, No. 1 to Volume 15, No. 4, SCGS, August 1993)*

Index to Vital Data in Local Newspapers of Sonoma County, California, Volume 1: 1855–1875

Index to Vital Data in Local Newspapers of Sonoma County, California, Volume 2: 1876–1880

Index to Vital Data in Local Newspapers of Sonoma County, California, Volume 3: 1881–1885

Index to Vital Data in Local Newspapers of Sonoma County, California, Volume 4: 1886–1890

Index to Vital Data in Local Newspapers of Sonoma County, California, Volume 5: 1891–1899

Index to Vital Data in Local Newspapers of Sonoma County, California, Volume 6: 1900–1903

Index to Vital Data in Local Newspapers of Sonoma County, California, Volume 7: 1904–1906

Index to Vital Data in Local Newspapers of Sonoma County, California, Volume 8: 1907–1909

Index to Vital Data in Local Newspapers of Sonoma County, California, Volume 9: 1910–1912

Indigent Records in Sonoma County, California 1878 to 1926, Volume 1: The Indigents

Indigent Records in Sonoma County, California 1878 to 1926, Volume 2: Taxpayers Who Certified Indigent Need

Marriage License Affidavits, 1861–1921, Sonoma County, California, Volume I: A–F

Marriage License Affidavits, 1861–1921, Sonoma County, California, Volume II: G–M

Marriage License Affidavits, 1861–1921, Sonoma County, California, Volume III: N–Z

Marriage License Affidavits, 1861–1921, Sonoma County, California, Volume IV: Index to Bride's Surname

Militia Lists of Sonoma County, California, 1846 to 1900

Santa Rosa Rural Cemetery, 1853–1997

Sonoma County, California Cemetery Records, 1846–1921, Third Edition

Sonoma County, California Death Records, 1873–1905, Second Edition

Sonoma County California Reconstructed 1890 Census

The 1930 School Census of Sonoma County, California

HERAUSGEGEBEN VON GERHARD BAUER,
KATJA PROTTE, ARMIN WAGNER
MILITÄRHISTORISCHES MUSEUM DER BUNDESWEHR

SANDSTEIN VERLAG

KRIEG MACHT NATION

Wie das deutsche Kaiserreich entstand

Eva Langhals, die sich mit der freiwilligen Krankenpflege im Krieg beschäftigt, und von Heidi Mehrkens zu den Anfängen des humanitären Völkerrechts. Gerade die Idee, dass Krieg Sache der ganzen Nation sei, warf über Ländergrenzen hinweg Fragen auf, die das humanitäre Völkerrecht bis heute im Kern berühren: Wie sind Verletzte und Kriegsgefangene zu behandeln? Wie sollen Besatzungssoldaten der einheimischen Bevölkerung begegnen, wie mit dem Kulturgut der Gegner umgehen? Wer gilt als regulärer Kämpfer und wer nicht? Vielleicht liegt hier eine der bis heute nachhaltigsten Wirkungen der Kriege in der zweiten Hälfte des 19. Jahrhunderts. Das Leid auf den Schlachtfeldern, bei der betroffenen Zivilbevölkerung oder die Zerstörungen von Kulturgut wurden von vielen Menschen nicht mehr als unvermeidliches Übel hingenommen, sondern sollten durch internationale Vereinbarungen begrenzt werden – eine Entwicklung, die 1864 mit der ersten Genfer Konvention »betreffend die Linderung des Loses der im Felddienst verwundeten Militärpersonen« begann.

Der letzte Teil des Begleitbuchs greift wie die Ausstellung das Bild des Panoramas auf, als Symbol einer Nation, die das Wieder- und Nacherleben vergangener Schlachten einte und all die Bruchlinien, die die Gesellschaft des neu gegründeten Kaiserreichs durchzogen, vergessen ließ. Spektakel und nationale Erbauung zugleich, erfreuten sich monumentale Rundgemälde der Schlachten des Deutsch-Französischen Krieges in den 1880er und 1890er Jahren enormer Beliebtheit. Abschließend zieht Andreas Platthaus Parallelen zwischen dem Militarismus des Kaiserreichs und dem Verhältnis von Militär und Gesellschaft in den heutigen USA, um für ein Verständnis von Nation zu plädieren, das keines militärischen Auftrumpfens mehr bedarf, um zu sich selbst zu finden.

Die Möglichkeit der Realisierung dieser Ausstellung ist der glücklichen Situation zuzuschreiben, dass internationale Kooperationen in der Museumswelt die Regel sind und von nationalen Egoismen nicht beeinträchtigt werden. Allen Kolleginnen und Kollegen in ausländischen und deutschen Museen, Sammlungen und Archiven, die in der anliegenden Leihgeberliste genannt sind, fühlen sich das durch die freien Mitarbeiterinnen Eva Langhals und Alma Hannig kompetent verstärkte Kuratorenteam und der Direktor verpflichtet. Wir danken für Ideen, Hinweise und konstruktive Kritik ebenso wie für die Unterstützung bei Restaurierungsvorhaben, bei der Abwicklung der Leihformalitäten und der Transporte.

Weiterhin gilt unser Dank Sylvie Le Ray-Burimi, die in bewährter Weise am Pariser Musée de l'Armée als Ansprechpartnerin in unterschiedlichen Belangen fungierte und als Autorin an diesem Band mitwirkte. Monique Fuchs unterstützte mit Recherchen in und Leihgaben aus ihrem Haus, dem Musée Historique de la Ville de Strasbourg. Sie stellte sich auch als Interviewpartnerin zur Verfügung. In Metz öffnete uns der Archäologe Michaël Landolt die Augen für Relikte und die Rezeption der deutschen Herrschaft in seiner Heimat. Er stellte darüber hinaus Kontakte her zu Philippe Brunella, dem Leiter des Musée de la Cour d'Or in Metz, und seiner Kustodin Claire Meunier. Laurent Thurnherr organisierte den Besuch des von ihm geleiteten Musée de la Guerre de 1870 et de l'Annexion in Gravelotte. Ebenso herzlich war die Aufnahme in den Museen und Gedenkstätten im Umfeld von Sedan. Die Teilnahme an der Eröffnung des neu gestalteten Musée Guerre et Paix en Ardennes wurde vermittelt durch die beiden deutschen Mitarbeiter Alfred Umhey und dessen (mittlerweile verstorbenen) Bruder Roland. Im Musée Maison de la Dernière Cartouche in Bazeilles führte Laurent Clement durch die Ausstellung und ermöglichte den Besuch im

Beinhaus des Friedhofs von Bazeilles. Hubert Walther, der frühere Direktor des Musée la Bataille du 6 août 1870, erwies sich als exzellenter Führer über das Schlachtfeld von Woerth. Ihm und der Association des Amis du Musée du 6 août 1870 ist auch eine Einladung anlässlich der »retour de la tête«, der Rückkehr des Denkmalskopfes von Kaiser Friedrich III. nach Woerth, zu verdanken. Der Leiter des Danewerkmuseums Nis Hardt scheute keine Mühen, unsere Vorort-Recherchen zum Deutsch-Dänischen Krieg zu unterstützen, Kontakte zu vermitteln und Informationen zusammenzustellen, obwohl er gerade zum ersten Mal Großvater geworden war und das Danewerk kurz zuvor den UNESCO-Welterbetitel erhalten hatte. Bjørn Østergaard, der Leiter des Historiecenter Dybbøl Banke, hat unermüdlich in allen militärfachlichen Fragen beraten. Unsere freie Mitarbeiterin Alma Hannig hat von zahlreichen österreichischen Institutionen und privaten Leihgebern wertvolle Hinweise und Unterstützung erhalten.

Ebenso hervorzuheben ist das Engagement deutscher Fachkollegen und -kolleginnen, von denen hier nur einige genannt werden können. Dieter Storz vom Bayerischen Armeemuseum hatte stets ein offenes Ohr für waffenkundliche Fragen des Kuratorenteams. Alexander Jordan, Direktor des Wehrgeschichtlichen Museums in Rastatt, Wolfgang Schrader vom Vogtland-Museum in Plauen, André Uebe am Sächsischen Rotkreuz-Museum Beierfeld, Thomas Weißbrich und Rainer Wiehagen am Deutschen Historischen Museum in Berlin waren inspirierende und pragmatische Partner. Mario Kramp und Stefan Lewejohann vom Kölnischen Stadtmuseum ermöglichten es, die sogenannte Batterie Leo des Rheinischen Feldartillerie-Regiments mitsamt zweier C/67-Feldkanonen der Vergessenheit zu entreißen und ihre Feldzugs- und Nachkriegsgeschichte für die Ausstellung aufzubereiten.

Wertvolle fachliche Anregungen und Hinweise auf potenzielle Exponate kamen von den französischen Heeres- und Uniformkundlern Louis Delperier und Laurent Mirouze. Immer in Fachfragen ansprechbar waren Ute Scherb, Sibylle Kußmaul, Heiner Bröckermann, Roland Gräfe, Wolfgang Hamann, Ulrich Herr, Thomas Eberle und die Mitglieder der KLIO Dresden, Thomas Pechmann, Markus Stein, Bernhard Wenning und Martin Wos. Ernst Aichner brachte in einer denkwürdigen Nachtsitzung nahe, wie einfache Soldaten den Krieg von 1870/71 erlebten. Lars Zacharias und Thorsten Loch setzten gemeinsam mit dem MAT-Autorenteam der Offizierschule des Heeres eine Medienstation zur Schlacht von Königgrätz um. Daniel Finke programmierte in bewährter Weise weitere Medienstationen und schuf das Screendesign. Elmar Heinz brillierte bei der Auswertung von Kriegstagebüchern und als waffenkundlicher Berater. Thomas Pasche war ein fachkundiger Rechercheur und Lektor. Peter Palm erarbeitete die Karten, die in Ausstellung und Katalog die geografische Orientierung ermöglichen.

In der Ausstellung zu sehen und zu hören sind Historikerinnen und Historiker aus Dänemark, Frankreich, Österreich und Tschechien, die sich freundlicherweise bereiterklärt hatten, auf Fragen über die kurz- und langfristigen Auswirkungen der Siege und Niederlagen 1864, 1866 und 1870/71 in ihren Heimatländern zu antworten. Wir danken Birgit Aschmann, Monique Fuchs, Manfried Rauchensteiner, Miloš Řezník und Uffe Østergård.

Für die Gestaltung der Ausstellung konnte die Firma Exposition Ebersbach aus Leipzig gewonnen werden. Thomas Ebersbach sei gedankt für eine in schwierig zu bespielenden Räumen attraktive und dem Thema entsprechende

Szenografie und ebenso für seine Geduld mit einem text- und objektverliebten Kuratorenteam. Annette Wunschel und Sina Volk begleiteten mit Klugheit und Strenge die Textarbeiten.

Vor allem aber ist den Mitarbeiterinnen und Mitarbeitern aller Abteilungen und Sachgebiete des Militärhistorischen Museums und des Bundeswehrdienstleistungszentrums Dresden zu danken, die sich für das Ausstellungsprojekt begeistern ließen und in ihrem Zuständigkeitsbereich zum Gelingen beitrugen. In diesem Zusammenhang gilt, frei nach einem Diktum Napoleons I. über die Bedeutung der Kampfunterstützungstruppen, dass für die Fertigstellung einer Ausstellung Mitarbeiterinnen und Mitarbeiter von Ausstellungsmanagement, Verwaltung, Objektdisposition, Restaurierung, Fuhrwesen und in den Werkstätten ebenso wichtig sind wie Wissenschaftlerinnen und Wissenschaftler. Großer Dank gilt insbesondere Steffen Jungmann, ohne dessen akribische und weitsichtige Bildredaktion dieser Katalog nicht möglich gewesen wäre. Im Museum repräsentiert durch Mareike Sedlmeier, trug das Bundessprachenamt dazu bei, die Ausstellungstexte auch für Gäste zur erschließen, die des Deutschen nicht mächtig sind.

Die Ausstellung und der vorliegende Katalog nähern sich diesem Thema, das ein deutsches und ein europäisches zugleich ist, mit einer möglichst vielschichtigen Herangehensweise und verschiedenen nationalen Perspektiven, wie schon an dem umfangreichen Dank an die zahlreichen Leihgeberinnen und Leihgeber deutlich geworden ist. Vor vielen Jahren hat Golo Mann eingangs seiner »Deutschen Geschichte des 19. und 20. Jahrhunderts« festgehalten, dass man »die Geschichte einer europäischen Nation zu irgendeiner Zeit nicht erzählen [kann], ohne zugleich das ganze Europa im Auge zu haben; man kann die Geschichte Europas nicht erzählen, ohne die Einheit des Gegenstandes in nationale Vielheit zerfallen zu lassen und aus ihr wieder zur Einheit zu sammeln.«[2] So sehr die historische wie jede andere Wissenschaft geprägt wird von der Revisionsfähigkeit und -bedürftigkeit ihrer zeitgebundenen Erkenntnisse, so sehr scheint es doch – mit Golo Mann gesprochen – so etwas wie »Grundtatsachen« zu geben. Zumindest in der Verbindung der deutschen Geschichte mit den anderen Geschichten Europas mag eine solche liegen. Dieser Sicht fühlt sich die Ausstellung »KRIEG MACHT NATION« verpflichtet und versucht, ihr einen angemessenen Ausdruck zu verleihen.

1 Der Begriff »Reichseinigungskriege« wird in der Forschung mit Vorsicht verwendet, da er suggeriert, diese Konflikte hätten von Anfang an auf die Gründung eines deutschen Nationalstaats abgezielt. Aus Gründen der Lesbarkeit wird in diesem Band jedoch auf eine durchgehende Verwendung von Anführungszeichen verzichtet. **2** Golo Mann: Deutsche Geschichte des 19. und 20. Jahrhunderts, Neuaufl., Frankfurt am Main 1992 [zuerst ebenda 1958], S. 14.

Leihgeberinnen und Leihgeber

Archiv der Otto-von-Bismarck-Stiftung, Friedrichsruh

Bismarck-Museum, Friedrichsruh

Bayerisches Armeemuseum, Ingolstadt

Berliner Medizinhistorisches Museum der Charité

Bundesarchiv, Bibliothek

Bundesmobilienverwaltung, Hofmobiliendepot – Möbel Museum Wien

Comité national des traditions des Troupes de marine

Danevirke Museum

Deutsche Bundesbank, Frankfurt am Main

Deutsches Medizinhistorisches Museum, Ingolstadt

Deutsches Museum Nordschleswig, Sonderburg

Deutsches Zollmuseum, Hamburg

Eigentum des Hauses Hohenzollern, SKH Georg Friedrich Prinz von Preußen

Erstes Nussknackermuseum Europas, Inhaber Uwe Löschner

Familienarchiv von Rosen

Bibliothek der Friedrich-Ebert-Stiftung, Bonn

Historiecenter Dybbøl Banke

Historisches Museum Hannover

Institut für Stadtgeschichte, Frankfurt am Main

Kölnisches Stadtmuseum

Kunsthalle zu Kiel

Landesarchiv Berlin

Landessammlungen Niederösterreich

Mährisches Landesarchiv in Brünn (Moravský zemský archiv v Brně)

Militärhistorisches Museum der Bundeswehr, Flugplatz Berlin-Gatow

Musée d'art et d'histoire Paul Eluard de Saint-Denis

Musée Bouilhet Christofle, en dépôt au musée d'art et d'histoire Paul Eluard de Saint-Denis

Musée de l'air et de l'Espace – Le Bourget

Musée de l'Armée, Paris

Musée d'Orsay, Paris

Musée historique de la ville de Strasbourg

Museum für Archäologie Schloss Gottorf, Landesmuseen Schleswig-Holstein

Museum für Stadtgeschichte Templin

Nachrichtentechnische Sammlung Aachen, Institut für Nachrichtentechnik, RWTH Aachen

Dr. Rudolf Novak

Österreichische Nationalbibliothek, Sammlung von Handschriften und alten Drucken

Österreichische Nationalbibliothek, Bildarchiv und Grafiksammlung

Österreichisches Staatsarchiv, Abteilung Haus-, Hof- und Staatsarchiv

Österreichisches Staatsarchiv, Abteilung Kriegsarchiv

Stefan Rest

Sächsisches Rot-Kreuz-Museum Beierfeld

Sächsisches Staatsarchiv – Staatsarchiv Leipzig

Salzburger Wehrgeschichtliches Museum

Sammlung Ronnie Strauch, Sindelsdorf

Sanitätsakademie der Bundeswehr

Schleswig-Holsteinische Landesbibliothek

Schloß Schönbrunn Kultur- und Betriebsges. M.b.H.

Museum Sønderjylland – Sønderborg Slot

Stadt Zwiesel

Städtische Galerie Dresden – Kunstsammlung / Museen der Stadt Dresden

Stiftung Deutsches Historisches Museum, Berlin

Stiftung Deutsches Technikmuseum Berlin

Stiftung Preußische Schlösser und Gärten Berlin-Brandenburg

Theodor-Fontane-Archiv Potsdam

Vogtlandmuseum Plauen

Wehrgeschichtliches Museum Rastatt

Zentrum für Informationsarbeit der Bundeswehr

Zentrum für Militärgeschichte und Sozialwissenschaften der Bundeswehr

und weitere private Leihgeber

Auf dem Weg zur Nation

Die Französische Revolution 1789 verhalf der Idee der Nation in Europa erstmals zum Durchbruch. Sie stellte althergebrachte Herrschaftsansprüche infrage und forderte unveräußerliche Menschenrechte wie Freiheit und Gleichheit. Als sich das Heilige Römische Reich Deutscher Nation 1806 unter dem Druck der französischen Expansionspolitik auflöste, wuchs mit dem Widerstand gegen Napoleon I. bei deutschen Studenten und Professoren, bei Künstlern und Schriftstellern die Idee einer Nation, die Menschen deutscher Sprache, Kultur und Herkunft unter neuen Vorzeichen vereinen sollte. Einen ersten Höhepunkt erlebte diese frühe Nationalbewegung in den Befreiungskriegen zwischen 1813 und 1815. Doch nach dem Sieg über Napoleon erneuerten Fürsten und Diplomaten 1814/15 auf dem Wiener Kongress ihre Macht.

Statt eines deutschen Nationalstaats gründeten sie den Deutschen Bund als lose Vereinigung souveräner Staaten. Die deutsche Nation schien bloße Idee zu bleiben. Die französische Julirevolution 1830 und vor allem die europäischen Revolutionen 1848/49 gaben überall Nationalbewegungen neuen Auftrieb. Doch während in Parlamenten und auf der Straße die unterschiedlichen politischen und sozialen Vorstellungen der Beteiligten immer klarer zutage traten, erlangten die Gegner der Revolution, gestützt auf das Militär, die Oberhand. Langfristig hielt dies die nationalen Bewegungen in Deutschland und auch in Italien nicht auf. Doch nahm die Machtfrage gegenüber idealistischen Vorstellungen von Freiheit und Gleichheit an Bedeutung zu.

»Kämpft, blutet, siegt für das einige Deutschland!«

Bürgerlich-liberale Positionen zu Nation und Krieg vor 1871

CHRISTIAN JANSEN

Für Kant und andere Vordenker der bürgerlichen Gesellschaft waren Liberalisierung und Demokratisierung die Mittel zur fortschreitenden Zivilisierung des Menschen und Einhegung sowohl der innerstaatlichen Gewalt als auch des Krieges. Gleichwohl vertrat die bürgerliche Opposition gegen Feudalismus und Absolutismus von Anfang an ein kriegerisches Männlichkeitsideal. Sie übernahm die Verherrlichung des Soldatentums und die Ästhetisierung des Militärischen und leistete so einem spezifisch bürgerlichen Militarismus Vorschub, der den Heldentod fürs Vaterland idealisierte und popularisierte. Im Lauf des 19. Jahrhunderts avancierte die freiwillige militärische Ertüchtigung in Schützen- und Turnvereinen sowie in den Studentenverbindungen zur bürgerlichen Norm.

Die historische Forschung sieht die bürgerlichen Ideen zunächst meist als friedlich und kosmopolitisch an. Erst im späten 19. Jahrhundert hätten sie sich radikalisiert zu einem »integralen Nationalismus«. In diesem Kontext sei auch die deutsche Gesellschaft militarisiert worden. Durch die Schulen (nationalistischer Geschichtsunterricht durch ehemalige Offiziere), Sedanfeiern, kriegsverherrlichende Jugendliteratur, die allgemeine Wehrpflicht in der kaiserlichen Armee und den Reserveoffizier als bürgerliches Leitbild sei ein ursprünglich von der Aristokratie getragener »preußischer« Militarismus verbreitet worden.[1] Dass sich daneben ein teilweise von anderen Werten getragener, spezifisch bürgerlicher, liberaler und sogar demokratischer Militarismus durch das gesamte 19. Jahrhundert zieht, wurde oft übersehen.

Das Ideal dieses bürgerlichen Militarismus war der Kriegsfreiwillige. Die aus Bürgern bestehende Miliz oder Wehrpflichtigenarmee sollte sich prinzipiell von den stehenden Heeren absolutistischer Fürsten mit ihren Söldnern oder Berufssoldaten unterscheiden: Militärische Verhaltensweisen und Maximen sollten von Jugend auf eingeübt werden und allen männlichen Mitgliedern der Nation in Fleisch und Blut übergehen. Das Bürgertum war zwar misstrauisch gegen die stehenden Fürstenheere, aber in seiner Mehrheit nie prinzipiell militärskeptisch. Nach Anfängen im Kontext der antinapoleonischen Kriege bekam der bürgerliche Militarismus durch das Scheitern der europäischen Revolutionen von 1848/49 neuen Auftrieb. Der zunehmend antagonistische Charakter

»Lützow's wilde Jagd«
Letzte Strophe des Gedichts aus Theodor Körners »Leier und Schwert« (erstmals 1813)
Farblithografie von W. Becker nach einem Aquarell von Carl Grünwedel (1815–1895)
London und München 1850
Abb. 1

In den »Freiheitskriegen« 1813 bis 1815 wurden bürgerliche Kriegsfreiwillige zum Mythos, insbesondere die Jäger des Lützowschen Freikorps. Obwohl militärisch unbedeutend, gewannen sie durch Körners Gedichte Kultstatus. Das Blatt zeigt den sterbenden Dichter (1791–1813), der selbst dem Lützowschen Freikorps angehörte.

→
Barrikadenkampf im Mai 1849 in Dresden

Julius Scholtz (1825–1893), 1849
Öl auf Leinwand, 23 × 34 cm
Kat. 22

Als die Gegenrevolution 1849 erstarkte, versuchten Aufständische gewaltsam die neue gesamtdeutsche Verfassung durchzusetzen. Preußische und königstreue sächsische Truppen schlugen den Dresdner Maiaufstand jedoch nieder. Als zweiter von links unter den Barrikadenkämpfern ist ein Kommunalgardist zu erkennen. Neben den sich 1848/49 spontan bildenden Bürgerwehren bestanden in manchen Städten bürgerliche National- oder Kommunalgarden, deren Wurzeln bis ins Mittelalter zurückreichten. Mal mehr, mal weniger militärisch organisiert, oft eng mit Schützengesellschaften verbunden, sollte solches Bürgermilitär dem Schutz der eigenen Stadt dienen. 1849 kämpften Kommunalgardisten teils mit und teils gegen die Revolutionäre. Offiziell aufgelöst wurde das Bürgermilitär erst 1870.

des Nationalismus in ganz Europa trug ein Übriges zur Ausbreitung militärischer Denk- und Verhaltensweisen und zur Entstehung von Organisationen bei, die bürgerlich-soldatische Normen propagierten.[2]

Vielfach beschrieben und analysiert sind der Kult und die Ästhetisierung des Militärischen bei namhaften bürgerlichen Autoren und Politikern des späten 19. Jahrhunderts wie Heinrich von Treitschke, Maurice Barrés, Charles Maurras oder Rudyard Kipling. Dass im Liberalismus soldatische Tugenden jedoch von Anfang an verherrlicht, dass der Bürger also ein mannhafter Kämpfer und, wenn es um die Vaterlandsverteidigung ging, ein freiwilliger Soldat sein sollte, ist erst seit der Jahrtausendwende breiter thematisiert worden.[3] Die Militarisierung der europäischen Gesellschaften während des 19. Jahrhunderts, an deren Ende nicht nur ein zunehmend aggressiver Nationalismus, sondern auch die Einübung der Massen in militärische Sekundärtugenden wie Disziplin, Gehorsam, Unterordnung stand, erfolgte – so kann man diesen neueren Studien entnehmen – nicht nur »von oben«, sondern kam zu einem erheblichen Teil auch aus der Gesellschaft selbst, vor allem aus der aufsteigenden bürgerlichen Mittelschicht.

In seiner Schrift »Über stehende Heere und Nationalmiliz« von 1816 lehnte der badische Liberale Karl von Rotteck stehende Heere ab und plädierte für eine Wehrpflichtigenarmee oder »Nationalmiliz«. Sie sei volksnäher als ein stehendes Heer und lasse sich nicht »gegen das Volk« einsetzen, sondern nur zur Landesverteidigung. Rottecks Argumentation hat den bürgerlichen militärpolitischen Diskurs im Deutschen Bund geprägt. Nach diesen egalitären und demokratischen Ideen sollte das Kriegführen nicht mehr das Handwerk einer abgesonderten Kriegerkaste sein, sondern Aufgabe aller Bürger. Der Militärhistoriker und Friedensforscher Wolfram Wette hat die dahinter stehende Hoffnung der liberalen und demokratischen Opposition im absolutistischen Staat in die Formel »Kriegsverhinderung durch allgemeine Volksbewaffnung« gefasst.[4] Zugleich war aber mit der Einbeziehung jedes Einzelnen in die Kriegführung jene schiefe Ebene betreten, die den Krieg schließlich zum gemeinsamen Anliegen aller Staatsbürger, zum Nationalkrieg machte und so den Militärs zu einer schier unerschöpflichen Reserve, einem beispiellosen »Menschenmaterial« verhalf.

Rechtlich und symbolisch stand die allgemeine Wehrpflicht am Anfang des Weges aus der ständischen in die bürgerliche Gesellschaft. Zum ersten Mal in der preußischen Geschichte wurden in den Militärgesetzen von 1813 die Untertanen »ohne Unterschied der Geburt« angesprochen, war von »Untertanen des Staates« und nicht mehr »des Königs« die Rede. Bürgerliche Meisterdenker – etwa Johann Gottlieb Fichte und Ernst Moritz Arndt – griffen die Idee einer preußischen »Nationalarmee« begeistert auf und (er)fanden Traditionen, die die moderne Idee der allgemeinen Wehrpflicht historisch stützten. Die folgenreichste war die Rede von einer spezifisch germanischen Tradition der allgemeinen Beteiligung an Kriegszügen: Die aus Frankreich importierte Levée en masse wurde so zu einer germanisch-deutschen Eigenheit stilisiert. In großer Zahl meldeten sich zwischen 1813 und 1815 Freiwillige. Wenn Bürger, die bis dahin Distanz zu den absolutistischen Staaten gewahrt hatten, sich nun in deren Dienst stellten, spielte neben nationalistischer Begeisterung die Hoffnung eine Rolle, ihre Bewährung als Soldaten werde ihre politische Emanzipation und die Durchsetzung bürgerlicher Werte erleichtern.

Obwohl das Bürgertum auch nach dem Sieg über Napoleon politisch kaum Rechte hatte, entwickelte sich unter den absolutistischen Oberflächen die bürgerliche Gesellschaft weiter. In den Familien, in der Literatur, in Vereinen, kulturellen und wohltätigen Gesellschaften wurden die neuen bürgerlichen Tugenden und Ehrbegriffe verbreitet und eingeübt. In besonders ausgeprägter Form verkörperte seit 1815 die »Burschenschaft« die neue bürgerliche Männlichkeit. Hier übten Studenten, die in den folgenden Jahrzehnten in gesellschaftliche und ökonomische Führungspositionen einrückten, den komplexen bürgerlich-nationalistischen Wertekanon ein: Opposition gegen den Obrigkeitsstaat, teilweise demokratische innere Strukturen, Duelle als Ausweis von Männlichkeit und zur Verteidigung der »Ehre«, Kult der antinapoleonischen »Befreiungskriege«, Germanenkult und ein ethnisch-christlich fundierter Nationalismus. Nachdem die Burschenschaftsbewegung zunächst großen Zulauf unter den Studenten hatte, konnte sie nach ihrem Verbot durch die Karlsbader Beschlüsse 1819 nur noch klandestin wirken, was ihre politischen Möglichkeiten stark einschränkte, ihren Nimbus aber nicht minderte.

Als 1848 die neoabsolutistischen Regime (vorübergehend) stürzten, übernahm die großenteils in der Burschenschaft sozialisierte bürgerliche Elite die politische Führung, teils in liberalen Regierungen, teils in der Deutschen Nationalversammlung, in der etwa 150 Abgeordnete der Burschenschafter saßen. Allerorten bildeten sich Bürgerwehren, die die Zeughäuser der Landwehr stürmten und plünderten. Während die Bürgerwehren in der Lage waren, Krawalle und Übergriffe von Angehörigen der Unterschichten in Schach zu halten,

Sebastopol und seine Befestigungen aus der Vogelschau

Beilage zur Sächsischen Dorfzeitung
Neustadt-Dresden, 29. September 1854
Holzstich
Abb. 2

Der Krimkrieg war auch ein Medienereignis, an dem Menschen in nicht direkt beteiligten Staaten regen Anteil nahmen.

waren sie als Machtfaktor gleichwohl unbedeutend. Da die regulären (Linien-) Truppen loyal blieben, hatten die Bürgerwehren keine Chance, den inneren Machtkampf für sich zu entscheiden. Im Gefängnis, im Exil oder als Geschlagene zurück in der Heimat, mussten sich die 48er eingestehen, dass sie im Duell mit der Staatsmacht versagt hatten. Die meisten von ihnen litten am Trauma dieser Niederlage und empfanden sie als Infragestellung ihrer Männlichkeit.

Gerade National*demokraten*, die besonders häufig durch Burschen- und Turnerschaften sozialisiert waren, setzten nach der Revolution auf eine Militarisierung der bürgerlichen Gesellschaft, weil sie das Scheitern der Revolution auf militärische Schwäche zurückführten. Im Rahmen der populären Schützen- und Turnvereine wurden allerorten paramilitärische Übungen durchgeführt. Diese »Wehrpolitik« der bürgerlichen Vereine verfolgte zwei Ziele: Einerseits sollten die Regierungen bewegt werden, die stehenden Heere durch Volksmilizen zu ersetzen; andererseits sollte die paramilitärische Ausbildung die Bürger auf den erwarteten Einigungskrieg vorbereiten. Die meisten bürgerlichen Strömungen waren sich einig, dass es ohne Krieg gegen Frankreich keinen deutschen Nationalstaat geben werde. Die Militarisierung der deutschen Einigungsbewegung war nicht nur eine Konsequenz aus der Niederlage von 1848/49, sondern reagierte auch auf jüngste Entwicklungen in Europa. Denn der Krimkrieg (1853–1856) bedeutete einen tiefen Einschnitt. Dieser erste europäische Krieg seit 1815 begann im Oktober 1853 mit der Kriegserklärung des Osmanischen Reichs an Russland und weitete sich 1854/55 durch das Eingreifen von Großbritannien, Frankreich und Piemont-Sardinien auf der Seite des Sultans zu einem Konflikt aus, der Bewegung in das europäische Machtgefüge brachte.

Österreich hatte sich gegen das Expansionsstreben seines traditionellen Verbündeten Russland gestellt. Die seit den Kriegen gegen Napoleon bestehende »Heilige Allianz« (Russland – Österreich – Preußen) war damit geschwächt, während Piemont-Sardinien internationale Unterstützung für eine Einigung der italienischen Staaten unter seiner Führung gewann. Es ist ein Indiz für die Verbreitung realpolitischen Denkens seit Mitte der 1850er Jahre,[5] dass der Umschwung hin zu einer hoffnungsvollen Stimmung in der deutschen Opposition von einem außenpolitischen Ereignis – und zumal einem blutigen Krieg – ausging und nicht von einer revolutionären Erhebung oder innenpolitischen Reformen in einem deutschen oder mitteleuropäischen Staat. Ein weiterer Krieg, den Piemont-Sardinien 1859 zusammen mit Frankreich gegen Österreich führte, verdeutlichte, dass nach dem Ende der Pentarchie in Europa wieder territoriale Veränderungen und die Bildung neuer Nationalstaaten möglich waren – durch Krieg!

Diese Erfahrung entfachte eine heftige Debatte, zumal bei der Einigung Italiens bürgerliche Freiwillige eine große, in der deutschen Öffentlichkeit freilich überschätzte Rolle spielten. Außerdem setzte die Expansion Frankreichs unter der populistischen Militärdiktatur Napoleons III. massive Ängste vor einer Wiederholung der Niederlage von 1805/06 frei. Der linksliberale 48er Jacob Venedey rief 1859 voller religiösem Pathos zu einem neuen antinapoleonischen Krieg auf, der die deutsche Einheit ermöglichen werde:

»Um Frieden wieder auf Menschenalter möglich zu machen und zu sichern, rufe ich das ganze Deutschland zu den Waffen. Deutschland ist das Land und Volk des Friedens. Und wenn es einig, mächtig ist, in den Dingen Europas mitspricht, wird der Friede gesichert sein. [...] Herr Gott, sollte mich zu diesem Kriegsrufe ein Wahn beirren, so laß den Samen, den ich auswerfen will, auf kalte Felsen fallen. Ist es aber Dein Ruf, dem ich folge, so laß ihn Wurzeln schlagen in allen tapferen Herzen des ganzen deutschen Volkes, sie zum Kampfe begeisternd [...]. Als der Baier, der Sachse, der Schwabe, der Franke, Alle im Zorn aufspringen und dem Preußen zurufen: ›Hierher, hilf, dort hetzt der Napoleonide seine afrikanischen Hunde gegen den Österreicher [...] – heraus mit deinem stolzen Schwerte, hilf uns den Franzosen heimtreiben‹ – da darf in deiner Mitte, in deiner Hauptstadt die geistreiche Thatlosigkeit, wenn nicht bezahlter Verrath, sich spreizen und dem Bruder [...] kalten Hohn und Verachtung entgegenwerfen! [...] Kämpft, blutet, siegt für das einige Deutschland und ihr werdet das einige deutsche Parlament von den Schlachtfeldern [...] heimbringen! [...] Wenn erst das Blut aller deutschen Stämme im bewussten Kampfe für das Eine Deutschland auf den Schlachtfeldern des kommenden Krieges zusammengeflossen, gemeinsam die deutsche Erde getränkt, gemeinsam das deutsche Banner geweiht hat; – dann könnt ihr ruhig ein zweites Parlament berufen [...].«[6]

Die Begeisterung für Nationalmilizen heizte auch den Konflikt um die preußische Heeresreform an, den Liberale und Demokraten gemeinsam mit großer Härte austrugen. Der seit Oktober 1858 regierende Wilhelm I. wollte die Landwehr schwächen, deren vielfach bürgerlich geführte Regimenter sich 1848 als unzuverlässig erwiesen hatten. Außerdem sollte der Wehrdienst von zwei Jahren auf drei verlängert werden, da die Militärführung glaubte, die immer selbstbewussteren bürgerlichen Rekruten nur durch ein drittes Jahr zu einer gefügigen Truppe »schleifen« zu können. Diese Heeresreform wollte das Gegenteil der liberalen Vorstellungen: statt dem Ausbau der Milizkomponente den Abbau

Jacob Venedey (1805–1871)
Daguerreotypie von Hermann Biow, 1848
Abb. 3

der Landwehr; statt mehr Wehrgerechtigkeit die Verlängerung der Dienstzeit bei Aufrechterhaltung der ständischen Privilegien, aufgrund deren sich viele Adelssöhne der Wehrpflicht entzogen.

Die erste grundlegende Kritik an diesen Plänen aus Sicht des bürgerlichen Nationalismus stammte von dem Burschenschafter und 48er Heinrich Simon. Er war mit dem Ziel der Heeresreform, die preußische Wehrkraft zu stärken, ausdrücklich einverstanden, kritisierte jedoch, dass die Reform mit Schulden und Steuererhöhungen finanziert und das stehende Heer vergrößert werden sollte. Um eine schlagkräftigere Armee und gleichzeitig höhere Wehrgerechtigkeit – und dies beides ohne zusätzliche Kosten – zu erreichen, schlug er vor, die zweijährige Dienstzeit beizubehalten, dafür aber entsprechend mehr junge Männer einzuziehen. Auch andere Liberale wiesen darauf hin, dass freiheitlich-republikanischen Staaten wie den USA und der Schweiz eine Milizarmee ausreiche, um sich gegen äußere Feinde zu schützen. Wenn man in Preußen wie in der Schweiz militärische Jugenderziehung als Teil des Schulunterrichts einführte, sei die Grundausbildung bei der Armee binnen eines Jahres möglich; dadurch könnten die jungen Männer schneller wieder erwerbstätig sein und seien der Indoktrinierung und den Schikanen der Offiziere weniger lange ausgesetzt. Die Stoßrichtung der bürgerlichen Opposition im preußischen Heereskonflikt zielte auf eine Schwächung der Armee als Disziplinierungsinstanz und innenpolitisches Machtinstrument. Gleichzeitig befürwortete die Opposition die Stärkung der Armee für den erwarteten Krieg um die deutsche Einheit: »Nur wenn das *ganze* preußische Volk militairisch durchgebildet ist, wenn es *wirklich* ein Volk in Waffen ist«, so der demokratische Politiker Heinrich Simon, könne Preußen »die Hoffnungen, die Deutschland auf Preußen setzt, verwirklichen.«[7] Mit dieser Formel verknüpfte Simon zwei Hauptanliegen der bürgerlichen Opposition: die Nationalstaatsgründung und die Erziehung aller Männer zu einsatzbereiten Soldaten.

Ein neues, bürgerliches Männlichkeitskonzept setzte sich also *vor* der Reichsgründung zusammen mit dem Ideal des Nationalstaats in mehreren Etappen durch: von den antinapoleonischen Kriegen der 1810er Jahre über die Burschenschaft und die bürgerlichen Vereine des Vormärz, die Revolutionen von 1848/49 bis zum Wiederaufleben der Einigungsbewegung seit den späten 1850er Jahren. Vorstellungen wie die, dass der freie Mann bereit sein müsse, fürs Vaterland zu sterben, dass der künftige Nationalstaat nicht nur freiheitlich, sondern auch mächtig sein solle und dass die nationale Einigung nur über einen Krieg möglich sei, bedeuteten keine Unterwerfung des liberalen Bürgertums unter den »preußischen Militarismus«. Diese Ideen setzten sich vielmehr in einem langen Prozess der bürgerlichen Selbstorganisation und Selbstmobilisierung durch. Das bürgerliche Männlichkeitsideal des 19. Jahrhunderts verstand Wehrhaftigkeit als konstitutiv für den freien Bürger, und die Forderung nach Schaffung einer Nationalmiliz leitete sich unter anderem vom demokratischen Gleichheitspostulat her. Sie sollte mehr Wehrgerechtigkeit und im Gegenzug kürzere Dienstzeiten bringen.

Auch die Differenz zwischen Bismarck, der im Herbst 1862 preußischer Ministerpräsident wurde, und der liberal-nationalistischen Mehrheit im Abgeordnetenhaus lag keineswegs darin, dass Bismarck meinte, ein deutscher Nationalstaat sei nur mit »Eisen und Blut« zu gründen. Hierin lag sogar einer der wenigen Berührungspunkte zwischen dem Ministerpräsidenten und der Opposition. Deren Sprecher Friedrich Wilhelm Löwe, ebenfalls ein 48er, betonte:

Flügelmütze für Mannschaften der Landwehrhusaren

Königreich Preußen, eingeführt 1842
Kat. 38

Das Landwehrkreuz an dieser Kopfbedeckung hat die gleiche Form wie das 1813 gestiftete Eiserne Kreuz. Es erinnert an die Volksbewaffnung in den Kriegen gegen Napoleon 1813–1815.

»Die Deutsche Race ist eine kriegslustige Race, nichts ist von dem feigen Geiste in diesem Volke, der den Frieden um jeden Preis will.« Das deutsche Volk werde freudig Krieg führen, aber »nur für die Interessen des Deutschen Volkes, nur für die Herstellung des Deutschen Einheitsstaates«. Wenn jedoch Bismarck von einer Nationalstaatsgründung durch »Eisen und Blut« rede, sei dies nur eine »Redensart«, denn er sei ein partikularistischer preußischer Feudalist und somit ein Gegner der deutschen Einheit.[8] In puncto Kriegsbereitschaft wollten sich die liberalen Bürger von niemandem übertreffen lassen.

Nur eine bis 1871 immer kleiner werdende Minderheit, die demokratischen Föderalisten, plädierte für eine Nationalstaatsgründung ohne Krieg, durch schrittweisen Zusammenschluss der deutschen Staaten. Dagegen wollten der Deutsche Nationalverein, die Organisation des liberalen Nationalismus und sein parlamentarischer Arm, die Fortschrittspartei, dass ein liberales Preußen die 1848/49 gescheiterte kleindeutsche Lösung realisiere. In einem hierfür zu entfachenden »Nationalkrieg« sollte Preußen die Reichsverfassung von 1849 in Kraft setzen. Für diese Ziele wollte der Nationalverein möglichst breite bürgerliche Kreise mobilisieren.

Den Austritt Preußens aus dem Deutschen Bund und den Krieg von 1866 deuteten Zeitgenossen vielfach als Fortsetzung der 1848/49 gescheiterten Einigung. Johann Caspar Bluntschli fand für die Lösung der deutschen Fragen durch Bismarck und die preußische Armee die immer wieder zitierte Formel »deutsche Revolution in Kriegsform, geleitet von oben statt von unten«.[9] Wichtige Ziele der Einigungsbewegung – die »Befreiung« Schleswigs, der Ausschluss Österreichs, der Sturz der verhassten Dynastien in Hannover und Kurhessen, die Schaffung eines Parlaments und einer Regierung über den Einzelstaaten – wurden in den Kriegen von 1864 und 1866 erreicht. Doch nicht »nach einem großen Kriege mit dem Auslande und nach einer großen Volksbewegung«, sondern, wie der Oppositionelle Löwe schrieb, »die Sache *hat sich* in einer ganz anderen Weise *gemacht*, als wir vorher geglaubt haben«. Schon diese Formulierung zeigt, dass Löwe jene Erfolge nicht allein der Regierung zugestehen wollte. Er kritisierte Bismarcks Halbherzigkeit, da dieser den Krieg nicht bis zum Zusammenbruch der süddeutschen Monarchien fortsetzen wolle, und unterstrich die »geistige Vorarbeit« der Nationalisten für das Projekt der deutschen Einigung, das die Regierung nun ausführe.[10]

Die Kriegsbereitschaft in den nationalistischen Bewegungen sowie bei den führenden Militärs beider Länder gehörte zu den Gründen, warum Bismarck so kurz nach den anderen beiden einen dritten Einigungskrieg riskierte. Bereits die Luxemburg-Krise (1867) hatte gezeigt, wie explosiv die Situation war. Hatte sich die liberale Öffentlichkeit 1867 überwiegend gegen Krieg ausgesprochen, so war die Stimmung 1870 umgeschlagen. Aus Unzufriedenheit über den seit der Gründung des Norddeutschen Bundes herrschenden Stillstand bei der deutschen Einigung, aber auch als Reaktion auf die regelmäßig vorgebrachten französischen Forderungen nach der Rheingrenze als Kompensation für die erhebliche Vergrößerung Preußens war in Deutschland wieder häufiger die Rede davon, dass die deutsche Einheit ohne Nationalkrieg nicht zu haben sei. Und in Frankreich war eine Politik populär, die Preußen in die Schranken weisen und möglichst die linksrheinischen Gebiete erobern sollte. Außerdem unterschätzten große Teile der französischen Öffentlichkeit die preußische Wehrpflichtigenarmee. Die französische Armee galt in den 1860er Jahren als die beste der Welt. Sie hatte sich im Krimkrieg und an der Seite Italiens gegen Österreich bewährt und würde mit den Postboten, bebrillten Referendaren und anderen Dilettanten in den Reihen der preußischen Streitkräfte leichtes Spiel haben, meinten viele Franzosen.[11] Diese selbstgefällige nationalistische Agitation mischte sich mit zunehmender Kritik am Regime Napoleons III., der deshalb einen außenpolitischen Erfolg zur Stabilisierung seiner Herrschaft benötigte.

Die Kriegsbereitschaft und die geschickte Inszenierung durch Bismarck (Emser Depesche) überwanden die antipreußischen Ressentiments in Süddeutschland, sodass die Gegner von 1866 vereint gegen den »Erbfeind« kämpften. Die Zeitungen und nationalistische Professoren, Publizisten, Poeten und Pfarrer erinnerten unablässig an die antinapoleonischen Kriege (1813–1815), um Napoleon III. und Frankreich zu verteufeln. Zahllose junge Männer rückten freiwillig ein und kämpften 1870 den »Nationalkrieg«, in dem das zweite französische Kaiserreich unterging und der zur Gründung des zweiten deutschen Kaiserreichs führte. Italien, der andere nach 1848/49 entstandene Nationalstaat, nutzte die französische Schwäche, um seine territoriale Einigung zu einem vorläufigen Abschluss zu bringen. Als Frankreich seine Truppen, die seit 1849 den Kirchenstaat beschützt hatten, nach Kriegsbeginn abzog und eine Niederlage nach der anderen erlitt, eroberten italienische Truppen fast kampflos Rom. 1871 wurde es zur Hauptstadt des Königreichs Italien.

Das Trauma der Niederlage führte zu einer zweiten französischen Nationsbildung, in deren Verlauf viele Intellektuelle und Politiker dazu rieten, man solle von den Deutschen lernen. Durch klassische Instrumente der Modernisierung wie allgemeine Schulpflicht (1882) und allgemeine Wehrpflicht (1887) gelang in der Dritten Republik die Integration der Bauern, des ländlich-provinziellen Frankreich, das bis dahin antizentralistisch und antirepublikanisch war, in die Nation; flächendeckende Postzustellung und der Ausbau des Eisenbahnnetzes brachten Zeitungen und andere Informationen in die Dörfer, und auch neue Nationalsymbole förderten die Integration: 1881 machte die Regierung den 14. Juli zum Nationalfeiertag und die »Marseillaise« zur Nationalhymne; an allen Rathäusern mussten die Symbole der Republik (Trikolore, Marianne, die Parole »Freiheit – Gleichheit – Brüderlichkeit«) gezeigt werden. Auf deutscher Seite trugen Kulturkampf (1871–1887), Antisozialistengesetze (1878–1890), die Eroberung von Kolonien (seit 1879) sowie wachsender Antisemitismus (seit 1878) zu einer zweiten, inneren Nationsbildung bei, an deren Ende – ebenso wie in Frankreich – fast alle jungen Männer bereit waren, für das Vaterland in den Krieg zu ziehen.

So kehrte zwischen 1848 und 1871 in Europa der »große«, viele Opfer insbesondere in der Zivilbevölkerung fordernde Krieg in die europäische Politik zurück. Zwar war das 19. Jahrhundert das friedlichste der gesamten Neuzeit. Nach 1848/49 brach jedoch die (nach innen repressive) Friedensordnung von 1815 zusammen. Verlustreiche Kriege, der Krimkrieg, der Italienische Krieg, der Deutsche Krieg unter italienischer Beteiligung und der Nationalkrieg gegen Frankreich wurden als Mittel der Politik wieder bejaht. Am Ende dieses Entwicklungspfads stand die Eskalation der europäischen Konflikte in den beiden Weltkriegen des 20. Jahrhunderts.

1 Der Begriff »integraler Nationalismus« geht auf Carlton Hayes: The Historical Evolution of Modern Nationalism (1928) zurück. Die geschilderte Entwicklung findet sich in vielen wissenschaftlichen Darstellungen des 20. Jahrhunderts (z. B. von Otto Dann, Hans-Ulrich Wehler, Peter Alter), aber auch in Schulbüchern, auf den Seiten der Bundeszentrale für politische Bildung usw. Vgl. exemplarisch www.bpb.de/geschichte/deutsche-geschichte/kaiserreich/138915/nation-und-nationalismus/ (letzter Zugriff 13. 8. 2019). **2** Vgl. Christian Jansen (Hg.): Der Bürger als Soldat. Die Militarisierung europäischer Gesellschaften im langen 19. Jahrhundert: ein internationaler Vergleich, Essen 2004, insb. S. 11 f. zum Militarismusbegriff. **3** Nicholas Stargard: The German Idea of Militarism, Cambridge 1994; Ralf Pröve: Stadtgemeindlicher Republikanismus und die »Macht des Volkes«, Göttingen 2000; ders.: Militär, Staat und Gesellschaft im 19. Jahrhundert, München 2004; Ute Frevert: Die kasernierte Nation. Militärdienst und Zivilgesellschaft in Deutschland, München 2001; dies. (Hg.): Militär und Gesellschaft im 19. und 20. Jahrhundert, Stuttgart 1997; Frank Becker: Bilder von Krieg und Nation. Die Einigungskriege in der bürgerlichen Öffentlichkeit Deutschlands 1864–1913, München 2001; Karen Hagemann: »Mannlicher Muth und Teutsche Ehre«. Nation, Militär und Geschlecht zur Zeit der Antinapoleonischen Kriege Preußens, Paderborn 2002; Christian Jansen: Einheit, Macht und Freiheit. Die Paulskirchenlinke und die deutsche Politik in der nachrevolutionären Epoche (1849–1867), Düsseldorf [2]2004. Vgl. zu Frankreich als Ursprungsland des modernen Militarismus: Wolfgang Kruse: Die Erfindung des modernen Militarismus. Krieg, Militär und bürgerliche Gesellschaft im politischen Diskurs der Französischen Revolution 1789–1799, München 2003. **4** Wolfram Wette: Militarismus und Pazifismus. Auseinandersetzung mit den deutschen Kriegen, Bremen 1991, S. 1–11. **5** Grundlegend für dieses Umdenken war: Ludwig August von Rochau: Grundsätze der Realpolitik, angewendet auf die staatlichen Zustände Deutschlands, Stuttgart 1853, Reprint Berlin 1972; vgl. Christian Jansen: »Revolution« – »Realismus« – »Realpolitik«. Der nachrevolutionäre Paradigmawechsel in den 1850er Jahren im deutschen oppositionellen Diskurs und sein historischer Kontext, in: Kurt Bayertz/Myriam Gerhard/Walter Jaeschke (Hg.): Weltanschauung, Philosophie und Naturwissenschaft im 19. Jahrhundert, Bd. 1: Der Materialismusstreit, Hamburg 2007, S. 223–259. **6** Jacob Venedey: Der italienische Krieg und die deutsche Volkspolitik, Hannover 1859, insb. S. 5 f., 11 und 25. **7** Heinrich Simon: Soll die Militairlast in Preußen erhöht werden?, Berlin 1860, S. 16. **8** Stenographische Berichte über die Verhandlungen des preußischen Hauses der Abgeordneten, 1.12.1863, S. 231; 22.1.1864, S. 861; 18.12.1863, S. 490. **9** Johann Caspar Bluntschli: Denkwürdigkeiten aus meinem Leben, Nördlingen 1884, Bd. 3, S. 160. **10** Stenographische Berichte, 7. 9. 1866, S. 262 f.; Volks-Zeitung, Berlin, 3.11.1866. **11** Jansen (Hg.): Der Bürger als Soldat, 2004, S. 163.

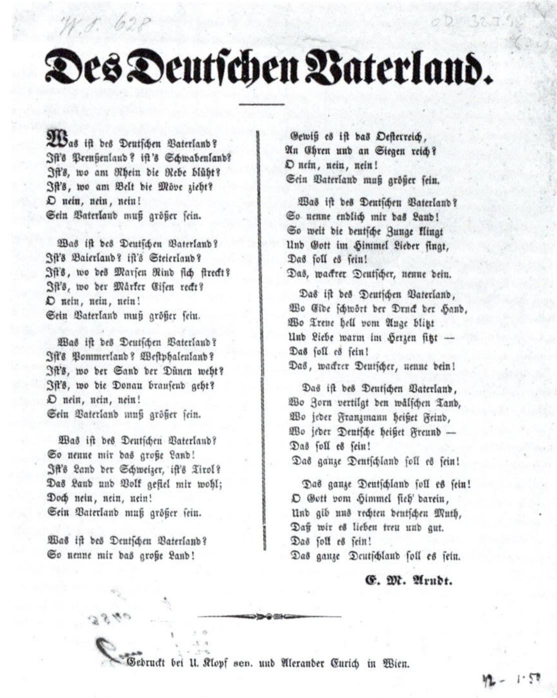

Des Deutschen Vaterland.

Was ist des Deutschen Vaterland?
Ist's Preußenland? ist's Schwabenland?
Ist's, wo am Rhein die Rebe blüht?
Ist's, wo am Belt die Möve zieht?
O nein, nein, nein!
Sein Vaterland muß größer sein.

Was ist des Deutschen Vaterland?
Ist's Baierland? ist's Steierland?
Ist's, wo des Marsen Rind sich streckt?
Ist's, wo der Märker Eisen reckt?
O nein, nein, nein!
Sein Vaterland muß größer sein.

Was ist des Deutschen Vaterland?
Ist's Pommerland? Westphalenland?
Ist's, wo der Sand der Dünen weht?
Ist's, wo die Donau brausend geht?
O nein, nein, nein!
Sein Vaterland muß größer sein.

Was ist des Deutschen Vaterland?
So nenne mir das große Land!
Ist's Land der Schweizer, ist's Tirol?
Das Land und Volk gefiel mir wohl;
Doch nein, nein, nein!
Sein Vaterland muß größer sein.

Was ist des Deutschen Vaterland?
So nenne mir das große Land!
Gewiß es ist das Oesterreich,
An Ehren und an Siegen reich?
O nein, nein, nein!
Sein Vaterland muß größer sein.

Was ist des Deutschen Vaterland?
So nenne endlich mir das Land!
So weit die deutsche Zunge klingt
Und Gott im Himmel Lieder singt,
Das soll es sein!
Das, wackrer Deutscher, nenne dein.

Das ist des Deutschen Vaterland,
Wo Eide schwört der Druck der Hand,
Wo Treue hell vom Auge blitzt
Und Liebe warm im Herzen sitzt —
Das soll es sein!
Das, wackrer Deutscher, nenne dein!

Das ist des Deutschen Vaterland,
Wo Zorn vertilgt den wälschen Tand,
Wo jeder Franzmann heißet Feind,
Wo jeder Deutsche heißet Freund —
Das soll es sein!
Das ganze Deutschland soll es sein!

Das ganze Deutschland soll es sein!
O Gott vom Himmel sieh' darein,
Und gib uns rechten deutschen Muth,
Daß wir es lieben treu und gut.
Das soll es sein!
Das ganze Deutschland soll es sein.

E. M. Arndt.

Gedruckt bei U. Klopf sen. und Alexander Eurich in Wien.

Kat. 2

Kat. 6

Nation und Revolution

Freiheit und politische Teilhabe forderten 1848/49 Revolutionäre in weiten Teilen Europas. Jedes Volk sollte sein Schicksal selbst in die Hand nehmen dürfen. Viele glaubten, dies sei am besten in einem Nationalstaat möglich. Menschen in Frankreich besannen sich auf die Revolution von 1789, die der Idee der Nation in Europa erstmals zum Durchbruch verholfen hatte. Deutsche, Italiener und Italienerinnen, Polen und Polinnen hofften auf nationale Einigung und Unabhängigkeit. Gekämpft wurde nicht nur auf den Barrikaden. In der Habsburger Monarchie entwickelten sich Aufstände in Ungarn und Oberitalien zu Unabhängigkeitskriegen. Im ersten Deutsch-Dänischen Krieg (1848–1851) prallten in Schleswig-Holstein die Interessen der deutschen und der dänischen Nationalbewegung aufeinander. Gleichzeitig schrieben Karl Marx und Friedrich Engels ihr »Kommunistisches Manifest«. Dem bürgerlichen Ideal der Nation begegneten sie mit dem Schlachtruf »Proletarier aller Länder, vereinigt Euch!« Einige wenige begannen, auf Friedenskongressen über eine Welt ohne Krieg nachzudenken.

Flugblatt mit Ernst Moritz Arndts Gedicht »Des Deutschen Vaterland«
Wien 1848
Kat. 2

»Das ganze Deutschland soll es sein!«, forderte der Schriftsteller Ernst Moritz Arndt (1769–1860) Anfang 1813, als Preußen in den sogenannten Freiheitskriegen gegen Napoleon kämpfte. Aber was war das? Arndt bestimmte kein Territorium, sondern feierte deutsche Sprache und »deutsches Wesen«. Die französische und italienische Kultur galten ihm als minderwertig, als »wälscher Tand«. Gegen Napoleon I. setzte er nicht nur auf Nationalstolz, sondern beschwor Abgrenzung und Völkerhass. Mehrfach vertont, diente der Text als inoffizielle Hymne der deutschen Nationalbewegung. Als während der Revolutionen 1848/49 Flugblätter mit dem Gedichttext gedruckt wurden, schien der Traum vom Vaterland zum Greifen nah. Über die konkrete Umsetzung wurde heftig gestritten: ein Nationalstaat mit Österreich? Oder ohne Österreich unter preußischer Führung? Oder ein Bund, dem das gesamte Habsburger Reich angehörte, auch ungarische, italienische und weitere Landesteile? Oder ein Deutscher Bund, in dem das »Dritte Deutschland«, die Klein- und Mittelstaaten, eine gleichberechtigte Rolle würden spielen können? Monarchie oder Republik?

»Zur Erinnerung an das Jahr 1848«
Prämienblatt als Jahresendbeilage der Zeitschrift »Der Familienfreund«
Neusalza, um 1848/49
Lithografie
Kat. 6

Das Blatt zeigt revolutionäre Ereignisse in bunter Mischung. Im Zentrum steht Reichsverweser Erzherzog Johann von Österreich, das Oberhaupt der provisorischen ersten gesamtdeutschen Regierung. Aus dem Hochadel stammend, galt der volksnahe Gegner des österreichischen Staatskanzlers Clemens Wenzel von Metternich als Kompromisskandidat. Eine Szene links oben zeigt die »Ausrufung Friedrich Wilhelm IV. zum Deutschen Kaiser«. Am 21. März 1848 machte der preußische König in seiner Proklamation »An mein Volk und an die Deutsche Nation« weitgehende Zugeständnisse an die Revolutionäre und ritt mit einer schwarz-rot-goldenen Armbinde durch Berlin. Stimmen aus der Menge ließen ihn als »Kaiser von Deutschland« hochleben.

»Die Deutsche Nationalversammlung in der Paulskirche zu Frankfurt a/M«
Stahlstich nach Heinrich Hasselhorst (1825–1904) von J. M. Kolb und F. Giersch, Darmstadt, um 1850
Kat. 7

In der Frankfurter Paulskirche trat am 18. Mai 1848 das erste gesamtdeutsche Parlament zusammen, gewählt nach weitgehend allgemeinem, gleichem Männerwahlrecht. Nach französischem Vorbild saßen links die Anhänger einer Republik und rechts die Befürworter einer mehr oder weniger reformierten Monarchie. Die Abgeordneten mussten sich über Verfassung, Staatsaufbau und Ausdehnung des künftigen Reiches einigen, während besonders die Großmächte Preußen und Österreich sich immer stärker gegen die Volksvertreter wandten. Im März 1849 fiel die Entscheidung zugunsten einer konstitutionellen, kleindeutschen Monarchie ohne Österreich. Doch der preußische König Friedrich Wilhelm IV. lehnte die ihm angetragene Kaiserwürde ab. Am 18. Juni wurde das nach Stuttgart geflohene Rumpfparlament von württembergischem Militär aufgelöst.

Kat. 7

Grundrechte des Deutschen Volkes.

Dem deutschen Volke sollen die nachstehenden Grundrechte gewährleistet sein. Sie sollen den Verfassungen der deutschen Einzelstaaten zur Norm dienen, und keine Verfassung oder Gesetzgebung eines deutschen Einzelstaates soll dieselben je aufheben oder beschränken können.

Artikel I.

§. 1. Das deutsche Volk besteht aus den Angehörigen der Staaten, welche das deutsche Reich bilden.

§. 2. Jeder Deutsche hat das deutsche Reichsbürgerrecht. Die ihm kraft dessen zustehenden Rechte kann er in jedem deutschen Lande ausüben. Ueber das Recht, zur deutschen Reichsversammlung zu wählen, verfügt das Reichswahlgesetz.

§. 3. Jeder Deutsche hat das Recht, an jedem Orte des Reichsgebietes seinen Aufenthalt und Wohnsitz zu nehmen, Liegenschaften jeder Art zu erwerben und darüber zu verfügen, jeden Nahrungszweig zu betreiben, das Gemeindebürgerrecht zu gewinnen.

Die Bedingungen für den Aufenthalt und Wohnsitz werden durch ein Heimathgesetz, jene für den Gewerbebetrieb durch eine Gewerbeordnung für ganz Deutschland von der Reichsgewalt festgesetzt.

§. 4. Kein deutscher Staat darf zwischen seinen Angehörigen und andern Deutschen einen Unterschied im bürgerlichen, peinlichen und Prozeßrechte machen, welcher die letzteren als Ausländer zurücksetzt.

§. 5. Die Strafe des bürgerlichen Todes soll nicht stattfinden, und da, wo sie bereits ausgesprochen ist, in ihren Wirkungen aufhören, soweit nicht hierdurch erworbene Privatrechte verletzt werden.

§. 6. Die Auswanderungsfreiheit ist von Staatswegen nicht beschränkt; Abzugsgelder dürfen nicht erhoben werden.

Die Auswanderungsangelegenheit steht unter dem Schutze und der Fürsorge des Reichs.

Artikel II.

§. 7. Vor dem Gesetze gilt kein Unterschied der Stände.

Der Adel als Stand ist aufgehoben.

Alle Standesvorrechte sind abgeschafft.

Die Deutschen sind vor dem Gesetze gleich.

Alle Titel, insoweit sie nicht mit einem Amte verbunden sind, sind aufgehoben und [illegible] eingeführt werden.

Kein Staatsangehöriger darf von einem auswärtigen Staate einen Orden annehmen.

Die öffentlichen Aemter sind für alle Befähigten gleich zugänglich.

Die Wehrpflicht ist für Alle gleich; Stellvertretung bei derselben findet nicht statt.

Artikel III.

§. 8. Die Freiheit der Person ist unverletzlich.

Die Verhaftung einer Person soll, außer im Falle der Ergreifung auf frischer That, nur geschehen in Kraft eines richterlichen, mit Gründen versehenen Befehls. Dieser Befehl muß im Augenblicke der Verhaftung oder innerhalb der nächsten vier und zwanzig Stunden dem Verhafteten zugestellt werden.

Die Polizeibehörde muß Jeden, den sie in Verwahrung genommen hat, im Laufe des folgenden Tages entweder frei lassen oder der richterlichen Behörde übergeben.

Jeder Angeschuldigte soll gegen Stellung einer vom Gerichte zu bestimmenden Caution oder Bürgschaft der Haft entlassen werden, sofern nicht dringende Anzeigen eines schweren peinlichen Verbrechens gegen denselben vorliegen.

Im Falle einer widerrechtlich verfügten oder verlängerten Gefangenschaft ist der Schuldige und nöthigenfalls der Staat dem Verletzten zur Genugthuung und Entschädigung verpflichtet.

Die für das Heer- und Seewesen erforderlichen Modificationen dieser Bestimmung werden besondern Gesetzen vorbehalten.

§. 9. Die Todesstrafe, ausgenommen, wo das Kriegsrecht sie vorschreibt, oder das Seerecht im Falle von Meutereien sie zuläßt, so wie die Strafen des Prangers, der Brandmarkung und der körperlichen Züchtigung sind abgeschafft.

§. 10. Die Wohnung ist unverletzlich.

Eine Haussuchung ist nur zulässig:

1) In Kraft eines richterlichen, mit Gründen versehenen Befehls, welcher sofort oder innerhalb der nächsten vier und zwanzig Stunden dem Betheiligten zugestellt werden soll,
2) im Fall der Verfolgung auf frischer That durch den gesetzlich berechtigten Beamten,
3) in den Fällen und Formen, in welchen das Gesetz ausnahmsweise bestimmten Beamten auch ohne richterlichen Befehl dieselbe gestattet.

Die Haussuchung muß, wenn thunlich, mit Zuziehung von Hausgenossen erfolgen.

Die Unverletzlichkeit der Wohnung ist kein Hinderniß der Verhaftung eines gerichtlich Verfolgten.

§. 11. Die Beschlagnahme von Briefen und Papieren darf, außer bei einer Verhaftung oder Haussuchung, nur in Kraft eines richterlichen, mit Gründen versehenen Befehls vorgenommen werden, welcher sofort oder innerhalb der nächsten vier und zwanzig Stunden dem Betheiligten zugestellt werden soll.

§. 12. Das Briefgeheimniß ist gewährleistet.

Die bei strafgerichtlichen Untersuchungen und in Kriegsfällen nothwendigen Beschränkungen sind durch die Gesetzgebung festzustellen.

Artikel IV.

§. 13. Jeder Deutsche hat das Recht, durch Wort, Schrift, Druck und bildliche Darstellung seine Meinung frei zu äußern.

Die Preßfreiheit darf unter keinen Umständen und in keiner Weise durch vorbeugende Maßregeln, namentlich Censur, Concessionen, Sicherheitsbestellungen, Staatsauflagen, Beschränkungen der Druckereien oder des Buchhandels, Postverbote oder andere Hemmungen des freien Verkehrs beschränkt, suspendirt oder aufgehoben werden.

Ueber Preßvergehen, welche von Amtswegen verfolgt werden, wird durch Schwurgerichte geurtheilt. [illegible]

Artikel V.

§. 14. Jeder Deutsche hat volle Glaubens- und Gewissensfreiheit.

Niemand ist verpflichtet, seine religiöse Ueberzeugung zu offenbaren.

§. 15. Jeder Deutsche ist unbeschränkt in der gemeinsamen häuslichen und öffentlichen Uebung seiner Religion.

Verbrechen und Vergehen, welche bei Ausübung dieser Freiheit begangen werden, sind nach dem Gesetze zu bestrafen.

§. 16. Durch das religiöse Bekenntniß wird der Genuß der bürgerlichen und staatsbürgerlichen Rechte weder bedingt noch beschränkt. Den staatsbürgerlichen Pflichten darf dasselbe keinen Abbruch thun.

§. 17. Jede Religionsgesellschaft ordnet und verwaltet ihre Angelegenheiten selbstständig, bleibt aber den allgemeinen Staatsgesetzen unterworfen.

Keine Religionsgesellschaft genießt vor andern Vorrechte durch den Staat; es besteht fernerhin keine Staatskirche.

Neue Religionsgesellschaften dürfen sich bilden; einer Anerkennung ihres Bekenntnisses durch den Staat bedarf es nicht.

§. 18. Niemand soll zu einer kirchlichen Handlung oder Feierlichkeit gezwungen werden.

§. 19. Die Formel des Eides soll künftig lauten: „So wahr mir Gott helfe.“

§. 20. Die bürgerliche Gültigkeit der Ehe ist nur von der Vollziehung des Civilactes abhängig; die kirchliche Trauung kann nur nach der Vollziehung des Civilactes stattfinden.

Die Religionsverschiedenheit ist kein bürgerliches Ehehinderniß.

§. 21. Die Standesbücher werden von den bürgerlichen Behörden geführt.

Artikel VI.

§. 22. Die Wissenschaft und ihre Lehre ist frei.

§. 23. Das Unterrichts- und Erziehungswesen steht unter der Oberaufsicht des Staats, und ist, abgesehen vom Religionsunterricht, der Beaufsichtigung der Geistlichkeit als solcher enthoben.

§. 24. Unterrichts- und Erziehungsanstalten zu gründen, zu leiten und an solchen Unterricht zu ertheilen, steht jedem Deutschen frei, wenn er seine Befähigung der betreffenden Staatsbehörde nachgewiesen hat.

Der häusliche Unterricht unterliegt keiner Beschränkung.

§. 25. Für die Bildung der deutschen Jugend soll durch öffentliche Schulen überall genügend gesorgt werden.

Eltern oder deren Stellvertreter dürfen ihre Kinder oder Pflegebefohlenen nicht ohne den Unterricht lassen, welcher für die unteren Volksschulen vorgeschrieben ist.

§. 26. Die öffentlichen Lehrer haben die Rechte der Staatsdiener.

Der Staat stellt unter gesetzlich geordneter Betheiligung der Gemeinden aus der Zahl der Geprüften die Lehrer der Volksschulen an.

§. 27. Für den Unterricht in Volksschulen und niederen Gewerbschulen wird kein Schulgeld bezahlt.

Unbemittelten soll auf allen öffentlichen Unterrichtsanstalten freier Unterricht gewährt werden.

§. 28. Es steht einem Jeden frei, seinen Beruf zu wählen und sich für denselben auszubilden, wie und wo er will.

Artikel VII.

§. 29. Die Deutschen haben das Recht, sich friedlich und ohne Waffen zu versammeln; einer besondern Erlaubniß dazu bedarf es nicht.

Volksversammlungen unter freiem Himmel können bei dringender Gefahr für die öffentliche Ordnung und Sicherheit verboten werden.

§. 30. Die Deutschen haben das Recht, Vereine zu bilden. Dieses [illegible] soll durch keine vorbeugende [illegible]

§. 31. Die in den §§. 29 und 30 enthaltenen Bestimmungen finden auf das Heer und die Kriegsflotte Anwendung, insoweit die militärischen Disciplinarvorschriften nicht entgegenstehen.

Artikel VIII.

§. 32. Das Eigenthum ist unverletzlich.

Eine Enteignung kann nur aus Rücksichten des gemeinen Besten, nur auf Grund eines Gesetzes und gegen gerechte Entschädigung vorgenommen werden.

Das geistige Eigenthum soll durch die Reichsgesetzgebung geschützt werden.

§. 33. Jeder Grundeigenthümer kann seinen Grundbesitz unter Lebenden und von Todes wegen ganz oder theilweise veräußern. Den Einzelstaaten bleibt überlassen, die Durchführung des Grundsatzes der Theilbarkeit alles Grundeigenthums durch Uebergangsgesetze zu vermitteln.

Für die todte Hand sind Beschränkungen des Rechts, Liegenschaften zu erwerben und über sie zu verfügen, im Wege der Gesetzgebung und aus Gründen des öffentlichen Wohls zulässig.

§. 34. Jeder Unterthänigkeits- und Hörigkeitsverband hört für immer auf.

§. 35. Ohne Entschädigung sind aufgehoben:

1) Die Patrimonialgerichtsbarkeit und die grundherrliche Polizei, sammt den aus diesen Rechten fließenden Befugnissen, Exemtionen und Abgaben.
2) Die aus dem guts- und schutzherrlichen Verbande fließenden persönlichen Abgaben und Leistungen.

Mit diesen Rechten fallen auch die Gegenleistungen und Lasten weg, welche dem bisher Berechtigten dafür oblagen.

§. 36. Alle auf Grund und Boden haftenden Abgaben und Leistungen, insbesondere die Zehnten, sind ablösbar: ob nur auf Antrag des Belasteten oder auch des Berechtigten, und in welcher Weise, bleibt der Gesetzgebung der einzelnen Staaten überlassen.

Es soll fortan kein Grundstück mit einer unablösbaren Abgabe oder Leistung belastet werden.

§. 37. Im Grundeigenthum liegt die Berechtigung zur Jagd auf eignem Grund und Boden.

Die Jagdgerechtigkeit auf fremdem Grund und Boden, Jagddienste, Jagdfrohnden und andere Leistungen für Jagdzwecke sind ohne Entschädigung aufgehoben.

Nur ablösbar jedoch ist die Jagdgerechtigkeit, welche erweislich durch einen lästigen mit dem Eigenthümer des belasteten Grundstücks abgeschlossenen Vertrag erworben ist; über die Art und Weise der Ablösung haben die Landesgesetzgebungen das Weitere zu bestimmen.

Die Ausübung des Jagdrechts aus Gründen der öffentlichen Sicherheit und des gemeinen Wohls zu ordnen, bleibt der Landesgesetzgebung vorbehalten.

Die Jagdgerechtigkeit auf fremdem Grund und Boden darf in Zukunft nicht wieder als Grundgerechtigkeit bestellt werden.

§. 38. Die Familienfideicommisse sind aufgehoben. Die Art und Bedingungen der Aufhebung bestimmt die Gesetzgebung der einzelnen Staaten.

Ueber die Familienfideicommisse der regierenden fürstlichen Häuser bleiben die Bestimmungen den Landesgesetzgebungen vorbehalten.

§. 39. Aller Lehnsverband ist aufzuheben. Das Nähere über die Art und Weise der Ausführung haben die Gesetzgebungen der Einzelstaaten anzuordnen.

§. 40. Die Strafe der Vermögenseinziehung soll nicht stattfinden.

Artikel IX.

§. 41. Alle Gerichtsbarkeit geht vom Staate aus. Es sollen keine Patrimonialgerichte bestehen.

§. 42. Die richterliche Gewalt wird selbstständig von den Gerichten geübt. Cabinets- und Ministerialjustiz ist unstatthaft. Niemand darf seinem gesetzlichen Richter entzogen werden. Ausnahmegerichte sollen [illegible]

§. 43. Es soll keinen privilegirten Gerichtsstand der Personen oder Güter geben.

Die Militärgerichtsbarkeit ist auf [illegible] Aburtheilung militärischer Verbrechen und Vergehen, so[illegible] der Militärdisciplinarvergehen beschränkt, vorbehaltlich [illegible] Bestimmungen für den Kriegsstand.

§. 44. Kein Richter darf, außer durch Urtheil und Recht, von seinem Amte entfernt oder an Rang und Gehalt beeinträchtigt werden.

Suspension darf nicht ohne gerichtlichen Beschluß erfolgen.

Kein Richter darf wider seinen Willen, außer durch gerichtlichen Beschluß in den durch das Gesetz bestimmten Fällen und Formen, zu einer andern Stelle versetzt oder in Ruhestand gesetzt werden.

§. 45. Das Gerichtsverfahren soll öffentlich und mündlich sein.

Ausnahmen von der Oeffentlichkeit bestimmt im Interesse der Sittlichkeit das Gesetz.

§. 46. In Strafsachen gilt der Anklageprozeß.

Schwurgerichte sollen jedenfalls in schwereren Strafsachen und bei allen politischen Vergehen urtheilen.

§. 47. Die bürgerliche Rechtspflege soll in Sachen besonderer Berufserfahrung durch sachkundige, von den Berufsgenossen frei gewählte Richter geübt oder mitgeübt werden.

§. 48. Rechtspflege und Verwaltung sollen getrennt und von einander unabhängig sein.

Ueber Competenzconflikte zwischen den Verwaltungs- und Gerichtsbehörden in den Einzelstaaten entscheidet ein durch das Gesetz zu bestimmender Gerichtshof.

§. 49. Die Verwaltungsrechtspflege hört auf; über alle Rechtsverletzungen entscheiden die Gerichte.

Der Polizei steht keine Strafgerichtsbarkeit zu.

§. 50. Rechtskräftige Urtheile deutscher Gerichte sind in allen deutschen Landen gleich wirksam und vollziehbar.

Ein Reichsgesetz wird das Nähere bestimmen.

Einführungsgesetz.

Die Grundrechte des deutschen Volks werden im ganzen Umfange des deutschen Reichs unter nachfolgenden Bestimmungen hiermit eingeführt:

I. Mit diesem Reichsgesetze treten in Kraft die Bestimmungen:

1) der §§. 1 und 2.
2) des §. 3, jedoch in Beziehung auf Aufenthalt, Wohnsitz und Gewerbebetrieb unter Vorbehalt [illegible]
3) der §§. 4, 5 und 6.
4) des §. 7, unter Vorbehalt der in III. und VIII. dieses Gesetzes enthaltenen Beschränkungen.
5) des §. 8, und zwar rücksichtlich des letzten, Heer- und Seewesen betreffenden, Absatzes unter Verweisung auf III. dieses Gesetzes.
6) des §. 10, unter Vorbehalt der unter III. und VII. enthaltenen Bestimmungen.
7) der §§. 11 und 12.
8) des §. 13, mit der Maßgabe, daß, wo Schwurgerichte noch nicht eingeführt sind, bis zu deren Einführung über Preßvergehen die bestehenden Gerichte entscheiden.
9) der §§. 14, 15, 16, so wie des zweiten und dritten Absatzes im §. 17 und des §. 18.
10) der §§. 22, 24, 25 und 28.
11) der §§. 29, 30 und 31.
12) des §. 32, des zweiten Absatzes im §. 33, der §§. 34, 35, mit Ausnahme des ersten Absatzes (III. 8), des zweiten Absatzes im §. 36, dann 37, unter Vorbehalt der über die Ablösung der betreffenden Jagdgerechtigkeiten und über die Ausübung des Jagdrechts zu erlassenden Gesetze (IV).
13) des §. 42 und des ersten Absatzes im §. 44.

Alle Bestimmungen einzelner Landesrechte, welche hiermit in Widerspruch stehen, treten außer Kraft.

II. In Beziehung auf den im §. 17 ausgesprochenen Grundsatz der Selbstständigkeit der Religionsgesellschaften sollen die organischen Einrichtungen und Gesetze, welche für die bestehenden Kirchen zur Durchführung dieses Princips erforderlich sind, in den Einzelstaaten möglichst bald getroffen und erlassen werden.

III. Abänderungen oder Ergänzungen der Landesgesetzgebungen, so weit dieselben durch die folgenden Bestimmungen der Grundrechte geboten sind, sollen ungesäumt auf verfassungsmäßigem Wege getroffen werden, und zwar

1) statt der im §. 9 und §. 40 abgeschafften Strafen des Todes, des Prangers, der Brandmarkung, der körperlichen Züchtigung und der Vermögenseinziehung durch gesetzliche Feststellung einer anderweiten Bestrafung der betreffenden Verbrechen;
2) durch Ausfüllung der Lücken, welche in Folge der im §. 7 ausgesprochenen Aufhebung der Standesunterschiede im Privatrecht eintreten;
3) durch Regelung der Wehrpflicht auf Grund der im §. 7 enthaltenen Vorschrift;
4) durch Feststellung der beim Heer- und Seewesen vorbehaltenen Modificationen des §. 8;
5) durch Erlassung der Gesetze, welche den dritten im §. 10 erwähnten Fall der Haussuchung ordnen;
6) durch Erlassung der nach §. 19, 20 und 21 erforderlichen Vorschriften über Eid, Ehe und Standesbücher;
7) durch Einrichtung des Schulwesens auf Grund der §§. 23, 26 und 27;
8) durch Aenderungen im Gerichts- und Verwaltungswesen gemäß den Bestimmungen des §. 35 im ersten Absatz, der §§. 41, 43, 44 im zweiten und dritten Absatze, sowie der §§. 45 bis einschließlich 49.

IV. Ebenso ist ungesäumt die weitere Feststellung der in den §§. 33, 36 bis einschließlich 39 geordneten Eigenthumsverhältnisse in den einzelnen Staaten vorzunehmen.

V. Die Erlassung und Ausführung der vorstehend gedachten neuen Gesetze sollen von Reichswegen überwacht werden.

VI. Bis zu Erlassung der in den §§. 3, 13, 32 und 50 erwähnten Reichsgesetze sind die betreffenden Verhältnisse der Landesgesetzgebung unterworfen.

VII. In den Fällen, in welchen nach dem Vorstehenden neue Gesetze erforderlich oder in Aussicht gestellt sind, bleiben bis zur Erlassung derselben für die betreffenden Verhältnisse die bisherigen Gesetze in Kraft. Rücksichtlich der Haussuchung bleibt denjenigen öffentlichen Beamten, welche zum Schutz der Abgabenerhebung und des Waldeigenthums zur Haussuchung befugt sind, vorläufig diese Befugniß.

VIII. Abänderungen der Grundverfassung einzelner deutscher Staaten, welche durch die Abschaffung der Standesvorrechte nothwendig werden, sollen innerhalb sechs Monaten durch die gegenwärtigen Organe der Landesgesetzgebung nach folgenden Bestimmungen herbeigeführt werden:

1) die durch die Verfassungsurkunden für den Fall der Verfassungsänderungen vorgeschriebenen Erschwerungen der Beschlußnahme finden keine Anwendung, vielmehr ist in den Formen der gewöhnlichen Gesetzgebung zu verfahren;
2) wenn in Staaten, wo zwei Kammern bestehen, dieser Weg keine Vereinigung herbeiführen sollte, so treten diese zusammen, um in einer Versammlung durch einfache Stimmenmehrheit die erforderlichen Beschlüsse zu fassen.

Uebrigens bleibt es den gegenwärtigen Organen der Landesgesetzgebung unbenommen, sich darüber, daß die gedachten Abänderungen durch eine neuzuwählende Landesversammlung vorgenommen werden, zu vereinbaren, für welche Vereinbarung die Bestimmungen unter 1 und 2 gleichfalls maßgebend sind.

Sind in der bezeichneten Frist die betreffenden Gesetze nicht erlassen, so hat die Reichsgewalt die Regierung des einzelnen Staates aufzufordern, ungesäumt auf Grundlage des Reichswahlgesetzes eine aus einer einzigen Kammer bestehende Landesversammlung zur Revision der Landesverfassung und übrigen Gesetzgebung in Uebereinstimmung mit den Beschlüssen der Nationalversammlung zu berufen.

Frankfurt, den 27. December 1848.

Der Reichsverweser: **Erzherzog Johann.**

Die Reichsminister: H. v. Gagern. v. Peucker. v. Beckerath. Duckwitz. R. Mohl.

In Hannover bei den Gebr. Jänecke.

In Bremen bei J. G. Heyse.

Kat. 8

Manifest

der

Kommunistischen Partei.

Veröffentlicht im Februar 1848.

Proletarier aller Länder vereinigt Euch!

London.

Gedruckt in der Office der „Bildungs-Gesellschaft für Arbeiter"
von J. E. Burghard.

46, Liverpool Street, Bishopsgate.

Kat. 9

»Grundrechte des Deutschen Volkes«

Frankfurt, 27. Dezember 1848
Kat. 8

Ein wegweisender Erfolg der Frankfurter Paulskirche war die Verabschiedung der »Grundrechte des Deutschen Volkes«. Sie schrieben nicht nur Gleichheit vor dem Gesetz sowie Freiheit der Person fest, sondern auch Volksvertretungen in den Mitgliedstaaten und Ministerverantwortlichkeit. Die soziale Frage spielte eine untergeordnete Rolle. Viele Abgeordnete meinten, Freiheit und Gleichheit würden von selbst zu weniger Armut und Verelendung führen. Sie setzten auf kostenfreie Schulbildung für »Nichtbemittelte«.

Manifest der Kommunistischen Partei

Karl Marx (1818–1883) und Friedrich Engels (1820–1895)
Druck: Office der Bildungs-Gesellschaft für Arbeiter
London, Februar 1848
Exemplar, das Walter Ulbricht wohl 1958 als Geschenk zum 65. Geburtstag erhielt
Kat. 9

Das »Kommunistische Manifest« begegnet der bürgerlichen Idee der Nation mit dem Aufruf »Proletarier aller Länder, vereinigt Euch!«. Es beschreibt den Gegensatz zwischen Lohnarbeitern und Bürgertum, der 1848/49 immer mehr hervortrat. Missernten, soziale Not, rebellierende Bauern, Lohnarbeiter und Handwerksgesellen beförderten die Dynamik der Revolution. Die meisten Abgeordneten der Paulskirche waren jedoch bürgerlich und fürchteten ein wachsendes Selbstbewusstsein und eine Radikalisierung der Unterschichten.

Umgearbeiteter dänischer Dragonerhelm

Herzogtümer Schleswig und Holstein, 1848
Kat. 191

Die Herzogtümer Schleswig und Holstein wurden vom dänischen König in Personalunion regiert. Anders als Holstein gehörte Schleswig nicht zum Deutschen Bund, sondern war ein altes dänisches Lehen. Die deutsche Nationalbewegung forderte eine Aufnahme Schleswigs in den Deutschen Bund, die dänische seine engere Anbindung an das Königreich. Während in Kiel am 24. März 1848 eine provisorische Regierung ausgerufen wurde, vertrieben Bürgerwehr, Studenten und Turner die dänische Besatzung der Festung Rendsburg. Aus dänischen Diensten übergelaufene Truppen, Freiwillige und später auch Wehrpflichtige bildeten die neue Schleswig-Holsteinische Armee. Freikorps waren ebenso im Einsatz. Die Ausrüstung war improvisiert. Dieser ursprünglich dänische Dragonerhelm aus der Zeit um 1820/1830 wurde 1848 mit einem schleswig-holsteinischen Doppeladler versehen. (Zur Schleswig-Holsteinischen Erhebung siehe auch den Beitrag von Uffe Østergård und Bjørn Østergaard in diesem Band, S. 72–87.)

Kat. 19

Segelfregatte »Eckernförde«,

1844 in Dänemark als »Gefion« in Dienst gestellt
Modell 1:100, wahrscheinlich 1960er Jahre
Kat. 21

Am 14. Juni 1848 beschloss die Frankfurter Nationalversammlung die Aufstellung einer Flotte. Sie war, anders als die Heere

Kat. 21

Kat. 22

der Einzelstaaten, eine nationale Streitkraft und fuhr unter schwarz-rot-goldener Flagge. Am 5. April 1849 verhinderten die Küstenbatterien bei Eckernförde eine dänische Landung. Die Segelfregatte »Gefion« wurde gekapert und als »Eckernförde« übernommen. Als einziges Schiff der kleinen Flotte war sie von Anfang an für den Kriegseinsatz gebaut worden. Doch beim ersten und einzigen Seegefecht der Reichsflotte bei Helgoland am 4. Juni 1849 war sie nicht dabei. 1852 gab der Deutsche Bund das kostspielige Projekt auf und ließ die Schiffe der Flotte versteigern.

Stofffetzen vom Dannebrog des dänischen Linienschiffs »Christian VIII.«

Kat. 22

Herzog Gustav Wilhelm zu Mecklenburg verwahrte in seiner Reliquiensammlung einen »Fetzen von der Dannebrog [Flagge Dänemarks] vom Christian VIII bei Eckernförde zum Himmel gefahren«. Nach dem überraschenden deutschen Sieg bei Eckernförde 1849 wurde die Flagge des explodierten Linienschiffs geborgen und feierlich dem Reichsverweser übergeben. Ob der Fetzen wirklich vom Original stammte oder ob die Flagge wie viele Reliquien eine wundersame Vermehrung erfuhr, ist nicht bekannt.

»Die Reaction am Baum der Freiheit«

Holzstich nach Wilhelm Scholz (1824–1893) aus dem humoristisch-satirischen Wochenblatt »Kladderadatsch«, 19. Januar 1850

Kat. 12

Diese Karikatur aus dem 1848 gegründeten »Kladderadatsch« kritisierte, dass Kirche und Adel demokratische Errungenschaften rückgängig machten. Über allem schwebt hier wie eine große Krähe Albrecht von Roon (1803–1879). Er hatte als Generalstabschef eines der beiden Armeekorps geführt, die im Sommer 1849 die letzten Aufstände in der Pfalz und in Baden niederschlugen. Seitdem gehörte er zum engeren Kreis um Wilhelm, Prinz von Preußen und damaliger Oberkommandierender. Zehn Jahre später wurde er dessen Kriegsminister.

Kat. 12

»Die Völkerschlacht bei Bronzell«

Holzstich aus dem humoristisch-satirischen Wochenblatt »Kladderadatsch«, 17. November 1850

Kat. 25

Nach den Revolutionen von 1848/49 strebte Preußen eine Union deutscher Staaten ohne Österreich an. Die Habsburger Monarchie hingegen wollte den Deutschen Bund und damit die eigene Führungsrolle erneuern. Kurz vor einer militärischen Eskalation lenkte Preußen auf russischen Druck hin ein. Am 8. November 1850 waren österreichische und bayerische Bundestruppen bei Bronnzell nahe Fulda auf eine preußische Vorhut getroffen. Nach kurzem Scharmützel zogen sich die Preußen zurück. Verletzt wurde nur ein Schimmel, der sprichwörtlich wurde für das klägliche Scheitern großer Pläne. Als Preußen am 29. November 1850 in Olmütz einer Erneuerung des Deutschen Bundes zustimmte, waren viele Anhänger einer kleindeutschen Lösung enttäuscht. Der Abgeordnete Otto von Bismarck (1815–1898) verteidigte am 3. Dezember vor der Zweiten Kammer des Preußischen Landtags wortgewaltig die Entscheidung gegen den Krieg: »Es ist leicht für einen Staatsmann [...] von dieser Tribüne donnernde Reden zu halten, und es dem Musketier, der auf dem Schnee verblutet, zu überlassen, ob sein System Sieg und Ruhm erwirbt oder nicht. Es ist nichts leichter als das, aber wehe dem Staatsmann, der sich in dieser Zeit nicht nach einem Grunde zum Kriege umsieht, der auch *nach* dem Kriege noch stichhaltig ist.«

Einladung und Programm zum »Congress der Friedensfreunde«, 22.–24. August 1850

Frankfurt am Main 1850

Kat. 24

Die Erfahrungen der Napoleonischen Kriege waren Ausgangspunkt für die Friedensbewegung in Europa. Ein erster Friedenskongress tagte 1843 in London. Nach Zusammenkünften in Brüssel und Paris trafen sich Friedensfreunde 1850 in der Frankfurter Paulskirche. Als oberstes Ziel hatte sich der Kongress die Abschaffung von Kriegen gesetzt. Unter den 550 Teilnehmenden waren nur 40 Deutsche, die meisten kamen aus Großbritannien oder den USA. Größeres Interesse fand die Friedensbewegung in Deutschland erst in den 1880er/1890er Jahren.

Kat. 25

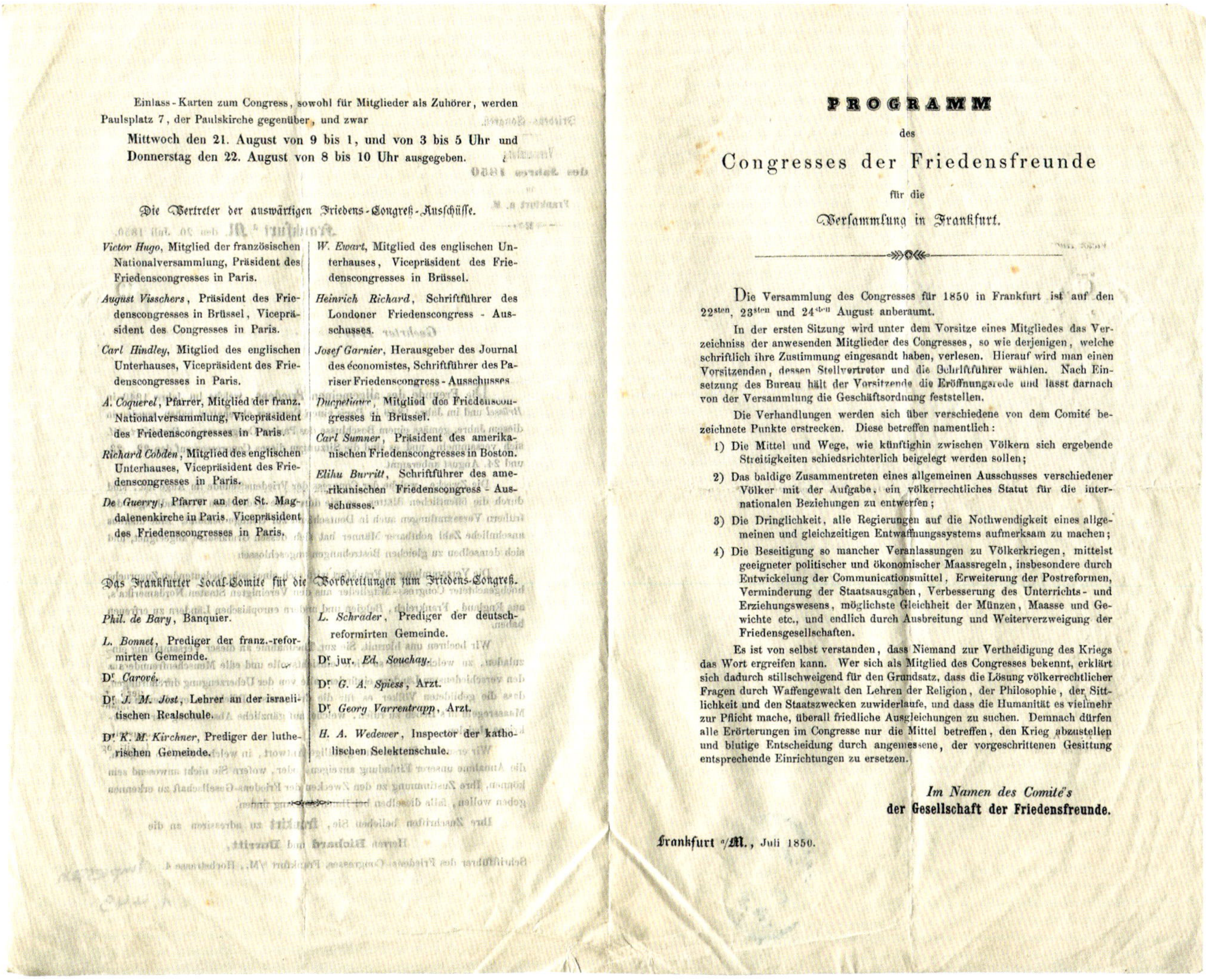

Einlass-Karten zum Congress, sowohl für Mitglieder als Zuhörer, werden Paulsplatz 7, der Paulskirche gegenüber, und zwar

Mittwoch den 21. August von 9 bis 1, und von 3 bis 5 Uhr und **Donnerstag den 22. August von 8 bis 10 Uhr** ausgegeben.

Die Vertreter der auswärtigen Friedens-Congreß-Ausschüsse.

Victor Hugo, Mitglied der französischen Nationalversammlung, Präsident des Friedenscongresses in Paris.

August Visschers, Präsident des Friedenscongresses in Brüssel, Vicepräsident des Congresses in Paris.

Carl Hindley, Mitglied des englischen Unterhauses, Vicepräsident des Friedenscongresses in Paris.

A. Coquerel, Pfarrer, Mitglied der franz. Nationalversammlung, Vicepräsident des Friedenscongresses in Paris.

Richard Cobden, Mitglied des englischen Unterhauses, Vicepräsident des Friedenscongresses in Paris.

De Guerry, Pfarrer an der St. Magdalenenkirche in Paris, Vicepräsident des Friedenscongresses in Paris.

W. Ewart, Mitglied des englischen Unterhauses, Vicepräsident des Friedenscongresses in Brüssel.

Heinrich Richard, Schriftführer des Londoner Friedenscongress-Ausschusses.

Josef Garnier, Herausgeber des Journal des économistes, Schriftführer des Pariser Friedenscongress-Ausschusses.

Ducpetiaux, Mitglied des Friedenscongresses in Brüssel.

Carl Sumner, Präsident des amerikanischen Friedenscongresses in Boston.

Elihu Burritt, Schriftführer des amerikanischen Friedenscongress-Ausschusses.

Das Frankfurter Local-Comite für die Vorbereitungen zum Friedens-Congreß.

Phil. de Bary, Banquier.

L. Bonnet, Prediger der franz.-reformirten Gemeinde.

Dr. *Carové*.

Dr. *J. M. Jost*, Lehrer an der israelitischen Realschule.

Dr. *K. M. Kirchner*, Prediger der lutherischen Gemeinde.

L. Schrader, Prediger der deutsch-reformirten Gemeinde.

Dr. jur. *Ed. Souchay*.

Dr. *G. A. Spiess*, Arzt.

Dr. *Georg Varrentrapp*, Arzt.

H. A. Wedewer, Inspector der katholischen Selektenschule.

PROGRAMM

des

Congresses der Friedensfreunde

für die

Versammlung in Frankfurt.

Die Versammlung des Congresses für 1850 in Frankfurt ist auf den 22sten, 23sten und 24sten August anberaumt.

In der ersten Sitzung wird unter dem Vorsitze eines Mitgliedes das Verzeichniss der anwesenden Mitglieder des Congresses, so wie derjenigen, welche schriftlich ihre Zustimmung eingesandt haben, verlesen. Hierauf wird man einen Vorsitzenden, dessen Stellvertreter und die Schriftführer wählen. Nach Einsetzung des Bureau hält der Vorsitzende die Eröffnungsrede und lässt darnach von der Versammlung die Geschäftsordnung feststellen.

Die Verhandlungen werden sich über verschiedene von dem Comité bezeichnete Punkte erstrecken. Diese betreffen namentlich:

1) Die Mittel und Wege, wie künftighin zwischen Völkern sich ergebende Streitigkeiten schiedsrichterlich beigelegt werden sollen;

2) Das baldige Zusammentreten eines allgemeinen Ausschusses verschiedener Völker mit der Aufgabe, ein völkerrechtliches Statut für die internationalen Beziehungen zu entwerfen;

3) Die Dringlichkeit, alle Regierungen auf die Nothwendigkeit eines allgemeinen und gleichzeitigen Entwaffnungssystems aufmerksam zu machen;

4) Die Beseitigung so mancher Veranlassungen zu Völkerkriegen, mittelst geeigneter politischer und ökonomischer Maassregeln, insbesondere durch Entwickelung der Communicationsmittel, Erweiterung der Postreformen, Verminderung der Staatsausgaben, Verbesserung des Unterrichts- und Erziehungswesens, möglichste Gleichheit der Münzen, Maasse und Gewichte etc., und endlich durch Ausbreitung und Weiterverzweigung der Friedensgesellschaften.

Es ist von selbst verstanden, dass Niemand zur Vertheidigung des Kriegs das Wort ergreifen kann. Wer sich als Mitglied des Congresses bekennt, erklärt sich dadurch stillschweigend für den Grundsatz, dass die Lösung völkerrechtlicher Fragen durch Waffengewalt den Lehren der Religion, der Philosophie, der Sittlichkeit und den Staatszwecken zuwiderlaufe, und dass die Humanität es vielmehr zur Pflicht mache, überall friedliche Ausgleichungen zu suchen. Demnach dürfen alle Erörterungen im Congresse nur die Mittel betreffen, den Krieg abzustellen und blutige Entscheidung durch angemessene, der vorgeschrittenen Gesittung entsprechende Einrichtungen zu ersetzen.

Im Namen des Comité's
der Gesellschaft der Friedensfreunde.

Frankfurt a/M., Juli 1850.

Kat. 24

Der »Kartätschenprinz«

Prinz Wilhelm von Preußen, der Thronfolger und Bruder von König Friedrich Wilhelm IV., war als »Kartätschenprinz« verschrien. Während der Märzrevolution 1848 in Berlin hatte er für eine militärische Niederschlagung der Aufstände plädiert und galt als treibende Kraft der Gegenrevolution. Um die Lage zu entschärfen, floh er auf Druck des Königs inkognito nach London. Ein Jahr später erhielt er den Oberbefehl über die 55 000 Mann starken Truppen, die die Aufstände in der Pfalz und Baden niederschlugen und damit die Revolution in den deutschen Staaten beendeten. Der spätere König von Preußen und Kaiser fühlte sich zeitlebens als Soldat.

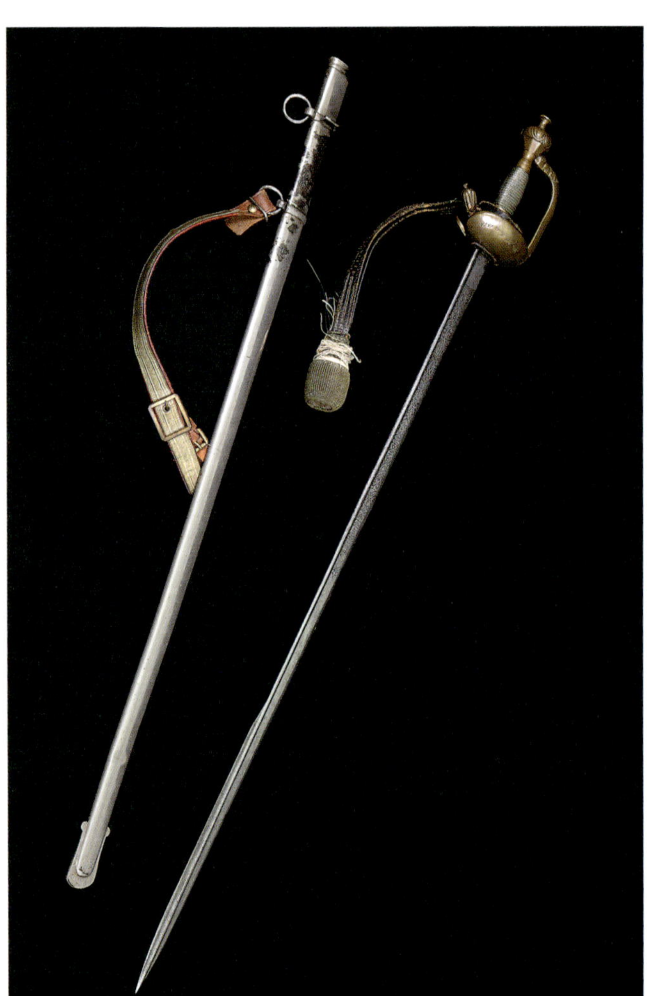

Kat. 15

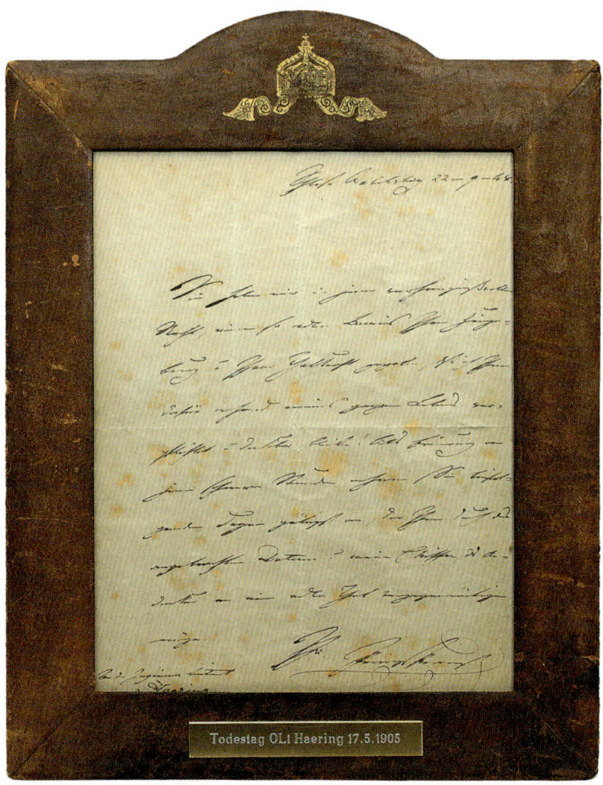

Kat. 16

Infanterieoffizier-Degen
Geschenk Wilhelms, Prinz von Preußen, an Premierleutnant Heinrich Haering
Überreicht am 22. September 1848
Kat. 15

Dankschreiben Wilhelms, Prinz von Preußen
Babelsberg, 22. September 1848
Kat. 16

Premierleutnant Heinrich Haering führte das Ruderboot über die Havel, mit dem Wilhelm in der Nacht vom 20. auf den 21. April heimlich die Festung Spandau verließ, um nach London zu fliehen. Später erhielt Haering einen Degen nebst Dankschreiben des Prinzen: »Sie haben mir in jener verhängnisvollen Nacht einen so edlen Beweis Ihrer Hingebung und Ihrer Thatkraft gegeben, daß ich Ihnen dafür während meines ganzen Lebens verpflichtet und dankbar bleibe. Als Erinnerung an jene schweren Stunden nehmen Sie beifolgenden Degen gütigst an, der Ihnen durch das angebrachte Datum und meine Chiffre das Andenken an eine edle That vergegenwärtigen möge.«

Kat. 18

Kat. 17

Kartätschkugel
Erinnerungsstück des Messerschmieds David Reuschle an die Märzrevolution 1848
Kat. 17

Eine Kartätsche ist ein Artilleriegeschoss mit einer Schrotladung. In eine Menschenmenge geschossen, wirkten Kartätschen verheerend. Unter den Revolutionären verbreiteten sie besonderen Schrecken. Der junge badische Messerschmied Reuschle nahm wohl am 18. März an den Berliner Barrikadenkämpfen teil. Über 300 Menschen wurden dabei getötet, darunter viele Handwerksgesellen. Reuschle überlebte und ließ sich in den 1850er Jahren in Templin nieder.

Hinrichtung Johann Ludwig Maximilian Dortus (1826–1849) am 31. Juli 1849
Tusche auf Papier, Berlin 1849
Kat. 18

Der angehende Jurist und Radikaldemokrat soll in einer Rede am 12. Mai 1848 den Schmähnamen »Kartätschenprinz« für Wilhelm geprägt haben, wohl in der Annahme, dieser habe am 18. März die Truppen geführt und mit Kartätschen auf die Bevölkerung schießen lassen. Dortu saß dafür mehrere Monate in Haft. 1849 beteiligte er sich an der Badischen Revolution und wurde deshalb zum Tod verurteilt. Seine Hinrichtung löste landesweit Empörung gegen die preußische Militärjustiz aus.

Kat. 43

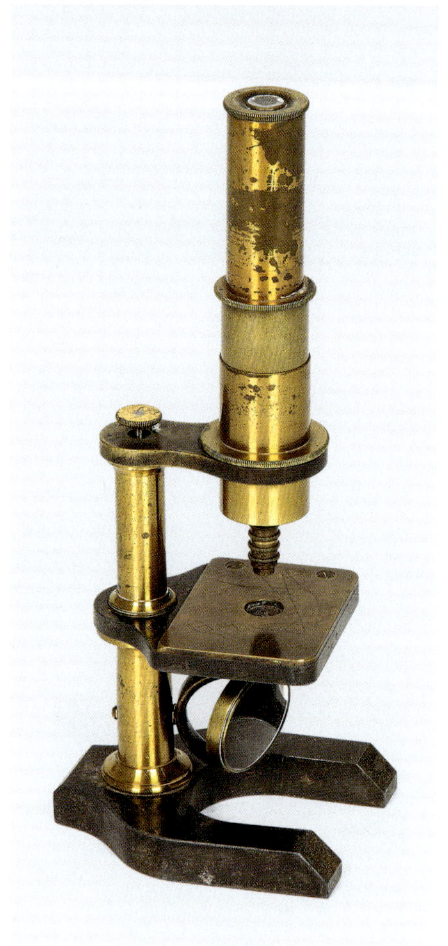

Kat. 44

Deutsche Fortschrittspartei

Fortschritt war das Schlagwort der Zeit. In Preußen hatte Wilhelm Ende 1858 die Regierungsgeschäfte seines erkrankten Bruders übernommen und zunächst ein liberal-konservatives Kabinett berufen. 1848 noch als Kartätschenprinz geschmäht, weckte sein Eintreten für ein starkes, modernes Preußen Hoffnungen auf eine »Neue Ära«. Doch es kam zum Bruch mit den Liberalen, als die Mehrheit im Abgeordnetenhaus Anfang der 1860er Jahre versuchte, durch das Haushaltsbewilligungsrecht Änderungen an einer geplanten Heeresreform durchzusetzen. Wilhelm lehnte dies als Einmischung in seine Kommandogewalt entschieden ab. Linksliberale, Demokraten und Mitglieder des Deutschen Nationalvereins schlossen sich daraufhin im Juni 1861 zur Deutschen Fortschrittspartei zusammen. Sie gilt als erste deutsche Partei mit verbindlichem Parteiprogramm. Dieses forderte »die konsequente Verwirklichung des verfassungsmäßigen Rechtsstaates« und »Einheit und Freiheit Deutschlands unter Preußens Führung«. Viele Mitglieder der Fortschrittspartei sind heute nicht als Politiker bekannt, sondern für ihre innovativen Ansätze in Wissenschaft, Bildungswesen, Wirtschaft und Technik.

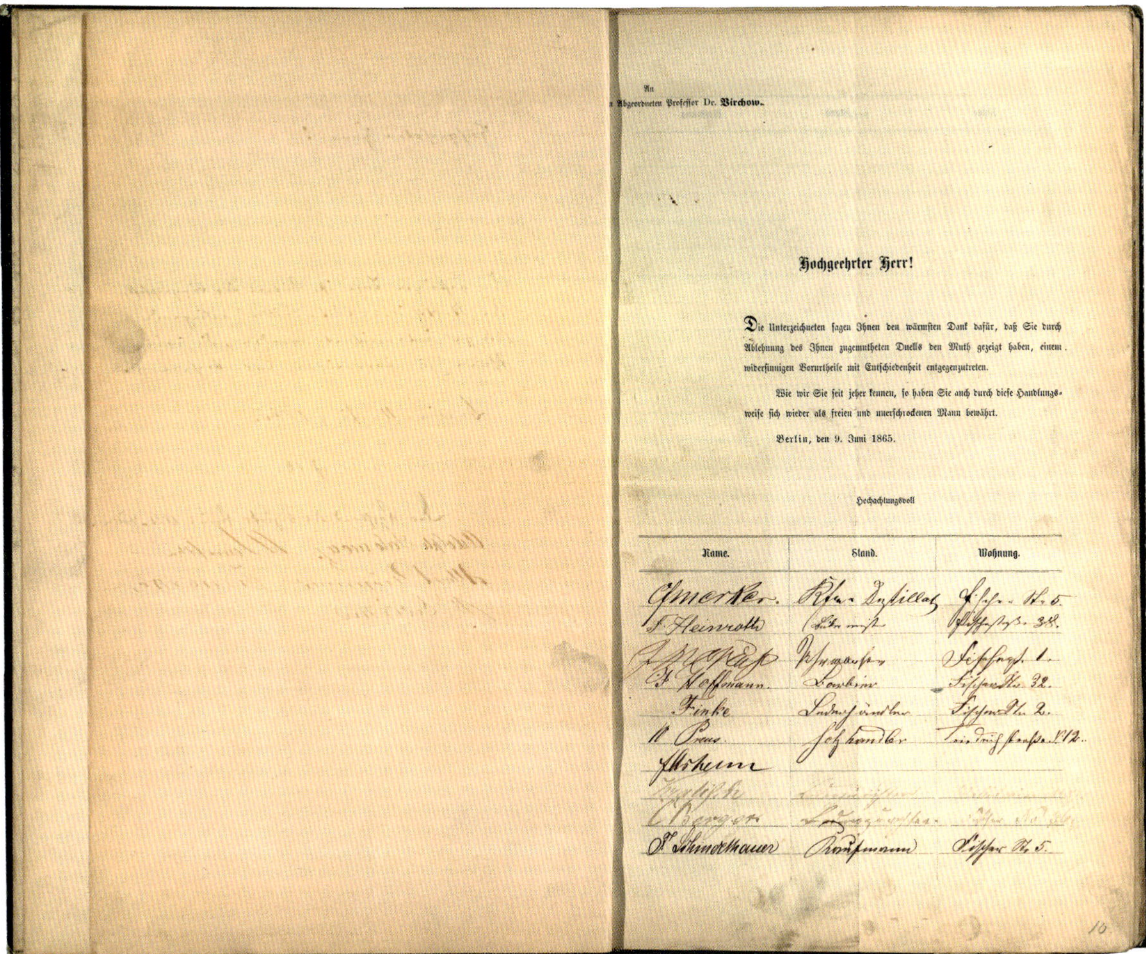

An
[de]n Abgeordneten Professor Dr. Virchow.

Hochgeehrter Herr!

Die Unterzeichneten sagen Ihnen den wärmsten Dank dafür, daß Sie durch Ablehnung des Ihnen zugemutheten Duells den Muth gezeigt haben, einem widersinnigen Vorurtheile mit Entschiedenheit entgegenzutreten.

Wie wir Sie seit jeher kennen, so haben Sie auch durch diese Handlungsweise sich wieder als freien und unerschrockenen Mann bewährt.

Berlin, den 9. Juni 1865.

Hochachtungsvoll

Name.	Stand.	Wohnung.

Kat. 45

Rudolf Virchow (1821–1902)
Carte-de-Visite-Fotografie
Kat. 43

Der bekannte Pathologe und Revolutionär von 1848 war Gründungsmitglied der Fortschrittspartei. Als der preußische Ministerpräsident Otto von Bismarck ohne genehmigten Haushalt agierte, warf er ihm 1863 offen Verfassungsbruch vor. Später trat Virchow für die Beschränkung von Militärausgaben und eine allgemeine Abrüstung ein.

Messingmikroskop, wie es zur Trichinenschau genutzt wurde
Firma Wasserlein, nach 1860
Kat. 44

Virchow begründete die moderne Zellularpathologie, förderte aber auch eine professionelle Krankenpflege und bessere hygienische Verhältnisse. Unter anderem sorgte er für die Einführung der »Trichinenschau« in Preußen: Zum Verzehr bestimmtes Fleisch musste dort ab 1866 verbindlich auf Parasiten wie Fadenwürmer untersucht werden.

Dankadresse des Bezirksvereins Alt-Cölln an Rudolf Virchow wegen der Ablehnung eines Duells mit Bismarck
Berlin, 11. Juni 1865
Kat. 45

Am 2. Juni 1865 forderte Bismarck Virchow zum Duell, als er sich in einer Landtagsdebatte über Anleihen für die Marine beleidigt fühlte. Virchow lehnte diese antiquierte Ehrauffassung und gewaltsame Form der Konfliktlösung ab. Über mehrere Tage hinweg hielt Bismarcks wiederholte Forderung die Berliner Öffentlichkeit in Atem. Über 700 Bürger des Stadtteils »Alt-Cölln« beglückwünschten Virchow am 11. Juni zu der Entschiedenheit, mit der er »einem widersinnigen Vorurtheile« entgegengetreten sei.

Kat. 46

Kat. 47

Werner von Siemens (1816–1892)
Carte-de-Visite-Fotografie
Kat. 46

In seinen Lebenserinnerungen schildert der Erfinder und Industrielle, dass er selbst 1861 den Namen »Fortschrittspartei« vorgeschlagen habe, bevor man sich auf »Deutsche Fortschrittspartei« einigte.

Zeigertelegraf
Telegraphen-Bauanstalt von Siemens & Halske, Berlin 1847
Kat. 47

Noch als Artillerieoffizier gründete Siemens 1847 mit dem Mechaniker Johann Georg Halske (1814–1890) ein Unternehmen zur Herstellung von Zeigertelegrafen. Identische Sender und Empfänger übermittelten per Zeiger die Buchstabenfolge, sodass keine Kenntnis des Morsealphabets mehr nötig war. 1848 stattete das Unternehmen die Telegrafenlinie von Berlin nach Frankfurt aus. Dass die Frankfurter Nationalversammlung 1849 dem preußischen König die Kaiserwürde antragen wollte, wusste Siemens in Berlin schon eine Stunde nach der Abstimmung.

Adolph Diesterweg (1790–1866)
Carte-de-Visite-Fotografie
Kat. 51

Diesterweg kämpfte als Pädagoge gegen die »traurige Herrschaft der Authorität« und für eine freie, auf die Individualität der Lernenden abgestimmte Erziehung, für »Selbstthätigkeit« und »Selbstdenken«. 1859 wurde er Abgeordneter für Berlin und unterstützte später die Fortschrittspartei. Sein jüngster Sohn gründete den Moritz Diesterweg Verlag mit den Schwerpunkten Schulbuch und Pädagogik.

Graf Albrecht von Roon (1803–1879)
General und preußischer Kriegsminister
Carte-de-Visite-Fotografie, vor 1879
Kat. 40

Roon verfasste im Juli 1858 eine Denkschrift zur Heeresverfassung und wurde im Dezember 1859 Kriegsminister. Er sah im Verhalten der Abgeordneten einen unzumutbaren Angriff auf die königliche Machtvollkommenheit, wollte ihnen aber in der Frage der Dienstzeit entgegenkommen. Als der König dies ablehnte und an Abdankung dachte, setzte Roon die Berufung Bismarcks zum Ministerpräsidenten durch. Dieser regierte ohne parlamentarisch genehmigten Etat, suchte aber auch einen Ausgleich mit den Liberalen. Nach dem Sieg über Österreich 1866 billigte das Abgeordnetenhaus Bismarcks Vorgehen nachträglich. Roon und der König hatten ihre Reform durchgesetzt.

Kat. 51

Kat. 40

Kat. 39

Wilhelm I. (1797–1888)

Carte-de-Visite-Fotografie, 1860er Jahre
Kat. 39

Ein zentraler Streitpunkt im Heereskonflikt war die Länge der Dienstzeit. Alle Kompromissvorschläge scheiterten an Wilhelms Beharren auf einer Dauer von drei Jahren. Er fürchtete, die von den Liberalen geforderte Dienstzeitverkürzung auf zwei Jahre werde die Zuverlässigkeit der Truppen untergraben. Zwei Jahre mochten für die militärische Ausbildung genügen, nicht aber, um dem König treu ergebene, soldatisch denkende Untertanen heranzuziehen.

»Der General Grolman rühmte sich einst, er wolle einen Rekruten in einem Jahre ausexerzieren. Ich antwortete ihm, dies sei viel zu lange, drei Monate genügten dazu vollkommen; aber einen Soldaten auszubilden getraute ich mir kaum innerhalb dreier Jahre. Zwei Jahre hindurch würde er durch Dressur und Instruktion vollständig übermannt, erst im dritten Jahre lerne er sich fühlen, bekäme er Sinn für die Würde des Rocks, für den Ernst des Berufes und zöge der Standesgeist bei ihm ein, ohne welchen eine Armee nicht bestehen könne.«

Wilhelm I. in einem Vortrag über die Reorganisation der Armee, gehalten im Staatsministerium am 3. Dezember 1859

Carte-de-Visite-Fotografie

Mit Porträtaufnahmen im Format von Visitenkarten fanden Fotografien erstmals weitere Verbreitung. Konnten mit den ersten, ab 1839 praktisch nutzbaren fotografischen Verfahren nur Unikate hergestellt werden, so setzte sich nach 1854 die kostengünstigere Carte de Visite im Porträtbereich durch. Mehrere Bilder konnten mit einer Spezialkamera gleichzeitig aufgenommen und Abzüge in beliebiger Zahl hergestellt werden. Als 1859 Napoleon III. und nach ihm andere europäische Herrscherhäuser anfingen, ihre Porträts in dieser modernen Form unters Volk zu bringen, entwickelten sich die kleinen »Visitformate« zu beliebten Sammelobjekten. Jeder konnte sich nun seine eigene Heldengalerie zusammenstellen.

Kaiser Wilhelm und Kaiserin Augusta
die Mitglieder der Königlichen Familie
dem Reichskanzler Fürsten Bismarck
zum 1. April 1885.

Bismarck

und

Bebel

Der preußische Ministerpräsident und spätere Reichskanzler Otto von Bismarck (1815–1898) steht wie kein anderer für eine deutsche Reichseinigung »von oben« und durch »Eisen und Blut«. Generationen von Historikerinnen und Historikern haben sich an ihm und der Frage abgearbeitet, wie seine Rolle bei der Schaffung eines deutschen Nationalstaats zu gewichten sei. Unbestritten ist, dass sein Ziel nicht die Gründung eines deutschen Nationalstaats um seiner selbst willen war. Vielmehr sah er die Reichsgründung als beste Möglichkeit, Preußens Vormachtstellung auszubauen und die auf Einheit und politische Teilhabe zielenden Strömungen der deutschen Nationalbewegung einzuhegen. Bismarck setzte auch nicht allein auf Krieg, sondern reagierte flexibel auf die verschiedenen Möglichkeiten, die sich ihm zum Erreichen seiner Ziele boten. Eine »Verpreußung« fürchtete dagegen ein bedeutender Widersacher Bismarcks: August Bebel (1840–1913), der gemeinsam mit Wilhelm Liebknecht 1866 die Sächsische Volkspartei und 1869 die Sozialdemokratische Arbeiterpartei Deutschlands (SDAP) gegründet hatte. Denn für ihn war ein Deutschland unter Preußens Führung gleichbedeutend mit einem Obrigkeitsstaat, der die Arbeiterschaft an der Durchsetzung ihrer Rechte hindere. Gleichzeitig lehnte er das »Nationalitätsprinzip« ab, da es nur dazu führe, dass sich die Völker gegenseitig zerfleischten.

Bismarcks Reichseinigung

ULRICH LAPPENKÜPER

Wir schreiben den 18. Januar 1871. Während im belagerten Paris französische Truppen einen letzten Ausbruchsversuch vorbereiten, setzt sich im nahen Versailles ein illustrer Zug mit dem preußischen Kronprinzen Friedrich Wilhelm in Richtung Schloss in Bewegung. Beim Eintritt in den Vorhof intoniert ein Musikkorps Ernst Moritz Arndts Lied »Was ist des Deutschen Vaterland«. Wenig später trifft Preußens König ein und lässt sich von seinem Sohn in den Spiegelsaal geleiten. In seiner Ansprache an die erlauchte Schar deutscher Fürsten rühmt Wilhelm I. die »Wiederherstellung des Deutschen Reiches« und erklärt sich bereit, die »Kaiserwürde« anzunehmen. Unter lautem Jubel empfängt er die Glückwünsche der Festgemeinde. Nur seinen Kanzler, den Grafen Otto von Bismarck, würdigt er keines Blickes ...

Wie das? War Bismarck, in dem viele Zeitgenossen die Verkörperung des nationalen Gedankens schlechthin erblickten, nicht der »Bauherr« des Kaiserreichs, und zwar unter Einsatz militärischer Mittel? Um diese Frage zu beantworten, wird der folgende Essay den Stationen der Einigung Deutschlands nachgehen und erörtern, welchen Anteil Bismarck an ihr besaß. Zugleich soll seine höchst ambivalente Haltung zu allem Militärischen beleuchtet werden. Der Verlauf der Ereignisse wird dazu wie ein Drama in einem Vorspiel und drei Akten in Szene gesetzt.

VORSPIEL

Die Vorstellung von der Nation als Leitbegriff der politischen Selbstorganisation einer Gesellschaft entstand im Frankreich der Großen Revolution. Auch in Deutschland kam damals ein Nationalgefühl auf, doch es richtete sich nicht auf die Idee einer der Souveränität des Volkes verpflichteten Gemeinschaft von Staatsbürgern, sondern auf die gemeinsame Sprache und Kultur. Wie Deutschland staatlich organisiert werden sollte, ließen die Nationalbewegten meist offen. Fest stand für sie nur, dass die Einheit mit Freiheit zu buchstabieren sei und von Preußen ausgehen sollte.

Die Proklamierung des deutschen Kaiserreichs am 18. Januar 1871

Friedrichsruher Fassung

Anton von Werner (1843–1915), 1885

Öl auf Leinwand, 167 × 202 cm

Kat. 360

Die Friedensordnung des Wiener Kongresses 1814/15 resultierte für Deutschland weder in Einheit noch in Freiheit. Auch die Revolution von 1848 vermochte nicht, beide Größen auf einen Nenner zu bringen. Wenn im Deutschen Bund fortan von der »deutschen Frage« die Rede war, konkurrierten im Wesentlichen drei Modelle miteinander: die in Preußen propagierte Idee zweier loser Einheiten aus dem Habsburgerreich und eines deutschen Bundesstaats mit Preußen als Vormacht; der von Österreich favorisierte großösterreichische Bund mit dem Kaiserstaat an der Spitze; und der von deutschen Mittel- und Kleinstaaten verfochtene »Trias«-Gedanke an eine zwischen den Großmächten Preußen und Österreich gebildete unabhängige dritte Kraft.

AKT 1

Am 1. April 1815 als Spross eines brandenburgischen Adelsgeschlechts in Schönhausen an der Elbe geboren, war Bismarck im März 1838 als Einjährig Freiwilliger ins Königliche Gardejäger-Bataillon Potsdam eingetreten;[1] dies geschah eher nolens volens, nachdem seine Hoffnung, den Militärdienst durch eine vorgeschobene Muskelschwäche zu umgehen, zerplatzt war. Ende August zum 2. Pommerschen Jäger-Bataillon in Greifswald versetzt, wurde ihm das Privileg eines Sonderurlaubs zuteil, da sich seine Einheit im Manöver befand. Sieben Monate später endete Bismarcks Dienstzeit mit einigem Aplomb. Bei einem Zechgelage mit Studenten einer nahen Akademie hatte der Einjährig Freiwillige ein solches Spektakel gemacht, dass die Polizei Anzeige erstattete. Nur dank der Aussage der Militärwachhabenden verlief die Sache glimpflich für ihn. Ende März 1839 wurde Bismarck im Rang eines Unteroffiziers in den Reservistenstand entlassen, gut zwei Jahre später zum Seconde-Lieutnant im 1. Infanterie-Bataillon des 9. Landwehr-Regiments befördert. 1842 erhielt er die Versetzung zur Kavallerie.

Nach seinem Eintritt in die Politik 1847 erwarb sich Bismarck den Ruf eines erzkonservativen Verteidigers der monarchischen Ordnung. Preußen dürfe nicht dem »Schwindel der Paulskirche« verfallen, mahnte er im Revolutionsjahr 1848/49.[2] Nachdem König Friedrich Wilhelm IV. den Junker 1851 als Bevollmächtigten zum Bundestag nach Frankfurt entsandt hatte, verfolgte Bismarck vor allem ein Ziel: die Juniorrolle der Hohenzollern gegenüber Habsburg abzustreifen. Preußen solle keinen deutschen Träumen nachhängen, sondern Österreich den Rang auf dem »Exercierplatz Deutschland« streitig machen, forderte der mittlerweile zum 26. Landwehr-Regiment versetzte Diplomat 1853.

Ende der 1850er Jahre gewann die »deutsche Frage« für Bismarck neue Bedeutung. Ohne den Ruf nach Freiheit und Einheit der Nationalbewegung zu teilen, machte er sich deren Herzenswunsch insofern zu eigen, als er im Zeichen der »Realpolitik«, die ab Mitte der 1850er Jahre die internationalen Beziehungen grundlegend veränderte, die Überzeugung gewann, dass Preußens Monarchie zwecks Machtsteigerung zu fast jedem Bündnis bereit sein müsse. Die »gegenwärtige Lage«, so schrieb der 1859 mit dem Charakter des Rittmeisters ausgestattete Premier-Lieutnant nach Ausbruch des italienischen Einigungskriegs, habe »wieder einmal das große Loos für uns im Topf«. Preußen müsse den Kampf »sich scharf einfressen lassen« und dann mit seinen Armeen »nach Süden aufbrechen, die Gränzpfähle im Tornister mitnehmen und sie entweder am Bodensee oder da, wo das protestantische Bekenntniß aufhört vorzuwiegen, wieder einschlagen«.

Otto von Bismarck (1815–1898)
G. Linde, Putbus (Insel Rügen), um 1862
Carte-de-Visite-Fotografie
Kat. 41

Vor der Hand ähnelten Bismarcks Gedanken dem Programm des Deutschen Nationalvereins, der Preußen die Rolle eines »deutschen Piemont« zuwies.[3] Prinzregent Wilhelm, der seit 1858 die Regierungsgeschäfte für seinen kranken Bruder führte, mochte indes weder von den Plänen des Nationalvereins noch von jenen Bismarcks etwas wissen – und versetzte Letzteren deshalb nach St. Petersburg. Diese Kaltstellung hielt den Gesandten freilich nicht davon ab, das Bündnis mit der bürgerlich-liberalen Nationalbewegung weiter zu schmieden. Es gebe für Preußen nur eine verlässliche Stütze, »die nationale Kraft des deutschen Volkes«, beteuerte Bismarck 1860. Einen festen Plan zur Realisierung der deutschen Einheit besaß auch er nicht. »Man kann nicht selber etwas schaffen«, bemerkte er einmal vielsagend; »man kann nur abwarten, bis man den Schritt Gottes durch die Ereignisse hallen hört; dann vorspringen und den Zipfel seines Mantels zu fassen – das ist Alles«.

Den »Mantel Gottes« bekam Bismarck erstmals 1862 zu fassen, als König Wilhelm I. dem zum Landwehr-Major avancierten Diplomaten vor dem Hintergrund des damaligen schweren Heeres- und Verfassungskonflikts die Regierungsgeschäfte übertrug. Ein erster Versuch, seiner Zielvorstellung von der Machtsteigerung Preußens näherzukommen, endete jedoch mit einer empfindlichen Schlappe. Nach seiner »Blut-und-Eisen«-Rede vom 30. September in der Budget-Kommission des Preußischen Landtags stand der Ministerpräsident im Ruf eines skrupellosen Gewaltpolitikers.

» **Nicht auf Preußens Liberalismus sieht Deutschland, sondern auf seine Macht; [...] nicht durch Reden und Majoritätsbeschlüsse werden die großen Fragen der Zeit entschieden – das ist der große Fehler von 1848 und 1849 gewesen – sondern durch Eisen und Blut.** «

Bismarck am 30. September 1862 vor der Budgetkommission

Da sich die beiden deutschen Großmächte mit ihren Reformprojekten gegenseitig blockierten und Wien auch nicht auf Berlins Vorschlag eingehen mochte, seinen Interessenschwerpunkt nach Südosteuropa zu verlagern, blieb die nationale Frage in der Schwebe. Zwar drohte Bismarck Österreich mit »Katastrophen«, wenn es Preußens »Aktion und Lebensluft« einenge; den Janustempel öffnen wollte er aber nicht. Es sei sehr leicht, die Interessen eines Staates mit militärischen Mitteln durchzusetzen, hatte er bereits 1850 beteuert. Doch »wehe dem Staatsmann, der sich in dieser Zeit nicht nach einem Grunde zum Kriege umsieht, der auch nach dem Kriege noch stichhaltig ist«.

Dass Bismarck vor einem Krieg keineswegs zurückschreckte, bewies er 1864, als er dem preußisch-österreichischen Dualismus eine kurzzeitige Wendung gab. Seite an Seite erzwangen beide Mächte im Krieg gegen Dänemark die Abtretung von Schleswig und Holstein. Für die Lösung der »deutschen Frage« besaß die Zession weitreichende Konsequenzen. Denn mit dem in den

Herzogtümern nun eingerichteten Kondominium bekam Bismarck ein Zündholz in die Hand, mit dem er den Dualismus nach Belieben am Köcheln halten konnte. Zur Bereinigung des Konflikts hielt er zwei Optionen für denkbar: eine Aufteilung Großdeutschlands in zwei Interessensphären oder ein Hinausdrängen Österreichs aus Deutschland. Auch zur Realisierung gab es seines Erachtens zwei Wege: Diplomatie oder Krieg.

Dass die Würfel letztlich für den Kampf fielen, hing mit Ereignissen zusammen, die sich fernab des europäischen Kontinents abspielten, in Mexiko. Dort hatte der Kaiser der Franzosen ein von ihm abhängiges Kaisertum unter dem habsburgischen Erzherzog Maximilian errichtet. Als die USA das Second Empire 1866 zwangen, seine Truppen aus Mexiko abzuziehen, und das Reich Maximilians allmählich kollabierte, sah sich Napoleon III. genötigt, die Scharte in Europa auszuwetzen. Seit seinem Machtantritt 1852 hatte der Kaiser der Franzosen eine durchaus preußenfreundliche Politik betrieben, die allerdings eine Grundbedingung besaß: den Erhalt des Deutschen Bundes. Doch je deutlicher sich die Hohenzollernmonarchie von diesem Fundament der bilateralen Partnerschaft entfernte, desto energischer meinte Napoleon ihr Einhalt gebieten zu müssen. Vor diesem Hintergrund begaben sich Wien und Berlin immer deutlicher auf einen militärischen Konfrontationskurs. Preußen müsse »deutsche Politik« betreiben, ermunterte Bismarck den zögerlichen Wilhelm I. Um auch die Nationalbewegten für sich einzunehmen, legte er einen Bundesreformplan vor, der die Bildung eines auf allgemeinen, direkten Wahlen beruhenden Parlaments vorsah. Eigentlich glaubte er nicht mehr an einen Ausgleich mit Österreich, setzte vielmehr auf eine »›chirurgische‹ Operation«.

Krieg war für das 19. Jahrhundert gemäß dem bekannten Diktum des preußischen Heeresreformers Carl von Clausewitz die Fortsetzung der Politik mit anderen Mitteln,[4] also legitim zur Durchsetzung staatlicher Interessen. Der Deutsche Krieg aber war im Bund höchst unpopulär. Ferdinand Cohen-Blind, Sohn eines führenden 48er-Revolutionärs, glaubte den Waffengang gar durch ein Attentat auf den »Verräter an Deutschland«[5] Otto von Bismarck vereiteln zu können. Nachdem Preußen Österreich am 3. Juli in der Schlacht bei Königgrätz besiegt hatte, verrauchte die Wut der Liberalen freilich rasch. Weit weniger wohlwollend fielen die Reaktionen in Wien, Paris und St. Petersburg aus.

Fotoalbum mit Offiziersporträts des mobilen 7. schweren Landwehr-Reiter-Regiments
Kat. 42

1852 gehörte Bismarck dem 7. schweren Landwehr-Reiter-Regiment an. Nach dem Sieg über Österreich 1866 schenkten die Offiziere seines Regiments ihrem berühmtesten Major dieses Album. Kurz darauf wurde er direkt zum Generalmajor befördert.

Extra-Beilage

zu Nr. 106 der

Deutschen Allgemeinen Zeitung

vom 9. Mai 1866.

Leipzig, 8. Mai, früh 7 Uhr.

Wir erhielten noch gestern Abend folgende telegraphische Depesche über ein versuchtes, aber misglücktes Attentat auf Bismarck, mit deren Veröffentlichung wir nicht bis heute Nachmittag warten zu dürfen glauben:

* **Berlin**, 7. Mai, 7 Uhr 15 Min. abends. Ein elegant gekleideter Mensch schoß heute Nachmittag gegen 6 Uhr auf der Straße Unter den Linden aus einem Revolver mehrere Schüsse auf den Ministerpräsidenten Grafen von Bismarck ab. Letzterer ist nicht verwundet. Der Thatbestand wird noch festgestellt werden. Bismarck ergriff den Thäter selbst.

Den Leipziger Nachrichten ging folgende Depesche zu:

Berlin, 7. Mai. Der Attentäter gegen Bismarck ist der zweiundzwanzigjährige Sohn Karl Blind's, des bekannten republikanischen Flüchtlings.

Wir schließen hieran die seit gestern Nachmittag eingelaufenen Depeschen und sonstigen wichtigern Nachrichten, von denen nur einige noch in einer Anzahl Exemplaren unsers gestrigen Blattes Aufnahme fanden:

†† **Berlin**, 7. Mai nachmittags. Soeben, 5 1/2 Uhr, ist auf den Grafen Bismarck, als er aus dem königlichen Palais zu Fuße nach dem Ministerium der auswärtigen Angelegenheiten zurückkehrte, in der Straße Unter den Linden, gerade vor dem russischen Gesandtschaftshotel, ein Attentat begangen worden. Ein junger Mensch von etwa 26–28 Jahren folgte ihm und schoß auf etwa zehn Schritt Entfernung aus einem Revolver drei Schüsse auf ihn ab, ohne ihn zu treffen. Graf Bismarck wandte sich schnell um und packte ihn am linken Arm, was der Mensch benutzte, um noch zwei Schüsse auf den Ministerpräsidenten abzufeuern. Das 2. Garderegiment zu Fuß kam inzwischen gerade von einem Marsch zurück, und Mannschaften von demselben nahmen den Menschen in ihre Mitte und führten ihn weg. Es herrscht eine ungewöhnliche Aufregung wegen dieses Vorfalls, und in dem Augenblick, wo wir dies schreiben, sind große Menschenmassen in der Straße Unter den Linden versammelt. Graf Bismarck scheint auch von den beiden letzten Schüssen nicht verwundet worden zu sein, sondern nur eine Contusion auf der Brust erhalten zu haben. Der Thäter war anständig gekleidet. Es wird behauptet, derselbe sei ein Oesterreicher. Hierüber liegt uns jedoch in diesem Augenblick noch nichts Näheres vor.

* **Frankfurt a. M.**, 7. Mai. Der preußische Bundestagsgesandte Hr. v. Savigny ist heute nach Berlin abgereist. Es ist kaum anzunehmen, daß derselbe bis zur nächsten Bundestagssitzung zurückgekehrt sein wird.

Frankfurt a. M., 7. Mai mittags. Die für heute beabsichtigte Sitzung des Ausschusses für die Bundesreformangelegenheit unterblieb abermals, weil der königlich preußische Bundestagsgesandte heute Morgen infolge einer Berufung nach Berlin abgereist ist. Derselbe hat Oesterreich substituirt, und es ist noch ungewiß, ob Hr. v. Savigny bis zu der auf Mittwoch anberaumten Bundestagssitzung zurück sein wird. (Dr. J.)

* **Frankfurt a. M.**, 7. Mai. Veranlaßt durch den Antrag Sachsens an den Bund, ersuchte Baiern das preußische Cabinet dringendst um eine Erklärung bezüglich der Bedrohung Sachsens. Preußen gab die Zusicherung ab, in Sachsen nicht einzurücken, wenn Oesterreich nicht dort einrücke.

* **Berlin**, 7. Mai. Es wird versichert, die zweite Gardedevision habe beschleunigte Marschbereitschaftsordre nach Görlitz erhalten. — Fürst Hohenzollern ist, nachdem er viel mit Bismarck conferirte, nach Düsseldorf zurückgereist.

Berlin, 6. Mai. Seit gestern sind hier die Einberufungsordres für Reservisten und Landwehrmänner des 3. Armeecorps ausgetragen worden. Die Beorderten haben sich zum 9. d. M., also zum künftigen Mittwoch, bei ihren Regimentern zu gestellen. Nur die Infanterie der in Preußen, Pommern und Westfalen stehenden Armeecorps bleibt auf dem Friedensetat, die gesammte übrige Armee wird auf den Kriegsfuß gesetzt. Hinsichtlich der Führung der mobilisirten Truppen scheint dem Prinzen Friedrich Karl, den Generalen Vogel v. Falckenstein und Herwarth v. Bittenfeld eine hervorragende Rolle zugedacht zu sein. Die Offiziere, welche bei den hiesigen kriegswissenschaftlichen Anstalten, der Kriegsakademie, Artillerie- und Ingenieurschulen, ihren Studien obliegen, sind abberufen und die Anstalten geschlossen worden. Dem Generalstabsarzt der Armee Dr. Grimm ist der Auftrag ertheilt, 800 Militärärzte disponibel zu halten. In den Militärwerkstätten wird mit verstärkten Kräften gearbeitet und die Munitionsfabrikation auf neue Weisung des Kriegsministers so lebhaft gefördert, daß die Arbeiter Tag und Nacht beschäftigt sind. Morgen erwartet man die Veröffentlichung der Mobilmachungsordre, welche vom 5. Mai datirt ist. (Dr. J.)

* **München**, 7. Mai. Durch Rescript des Kriegsministeriums sind sofortige Ankäufe einer weitern größern Anzahl von Pferden für die Cavalerie und Artillerie angeordnet worden.

* **Stuttgart**, 7. Mai. Der Kriegsminister Wiederhold ist zurückgetreten. General Hardegg übernimmt das Portefeuille des Kriegs. Ein Theil der Armee wird mobilisirt.

* **Hannover**, 7. Mai. Der Präsenzstand sämmtlicher 20 Infanteriebataillone wird durch Einberufung der Beurlaubten auf je 560 Mann erhöht; als officieller Grund dafür ist angegeben: die Vermeidung der üblichen Herbstübungen aus Ernterücksichten.

* **Darmstadt**, 6. Mai. Prinz Alexander von Hessen ist zum Commandeur des 8. deutschen Armeecorps (Würtemberg, Baden und Hessen-Darmstadt) designirt. Die Mobilmachung wird in den nächsten Tagen erwartet.

* **Darmstadt**, 7. Mai. Man erwartet noch heute ein großherzogliches Decret wegen Mobilmachung des diesseitigen Bundescontingents. Prinz Alexander von Hessen ist zum Commandanten des 8 Bundesarmeecorps designirt.

Attentat auf Bismarck am 7. Mai 1866

Extra-Beilage zu Nr. 106 der Deutschen Allgemeinen Zeitung
Leipzig, 9. Mai 1866
Kat. 130

Das Attentat verübte der 22-jährige Ferdinand Cohen-Blind, Stiefsohn des nach London emigrierten badischen Revolutionärs Karl Blind. Cohen-Blind glaubte, dass »die einzige Lösung der jetzigen verwickelten Lage in Deutschland die Beseitigung Bismarcks« sei (Brief an Mathilde Weber vom 6. Mai 1866). Nach seiner Festnahme schnitt er sich die Halsschlagader auf.

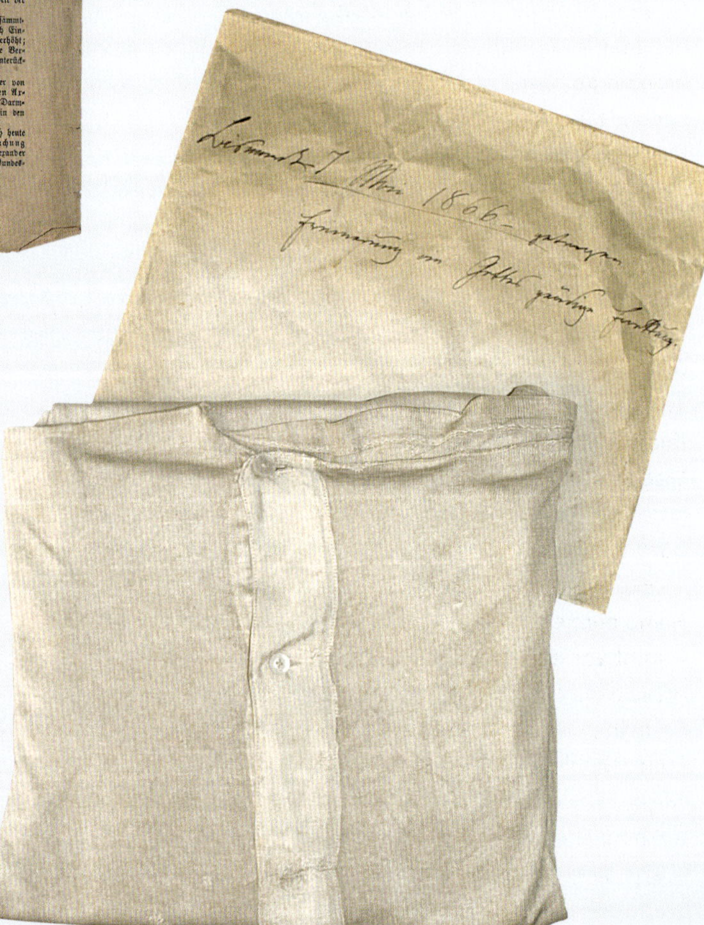

Seidenhemd Bismarcks mit geflickten Einschusslöchern

Kat. 131

Seine Ehefrau Johanna vermerkte zu dem Hemd: »Bismarck – 7 Mai 1866 – getragen / Erinnerung an Gottes gnädige Errettung.«

Waffe des Attentäters, die Bismarck in seinem Schreibtisch aufbewahrte

Sechsschüssiger Bündelrevolver, Kaliber 7 mm, mit Elfenbeingriff
Kat. 132

Der kleine Revolver ließ sich gut verbergen, war aber mehr zur Abschreckung als für ein Attentat geeignet. Die fünf abgegebenen Schüsse hatten nicht genug Durchschlagskraft, um Bismarck durch seine mehrlagige Kleidung hindurch ernsthaft zu verletzen.

»Casca il Mondo!« (Die Welt stürzt ein), entsetzte sich Kardinalstaatssekretär Giacomo Antonelli im fernen Vatikan, als er vom Ausgang der Schlacht erfuhr. Eine epochenwendende Bedeutung kam dem böhmischen Krieg tatsächlich zu, zumindest für Deutschland. Noch ehe der Waffengang im Prager Frieden vom 23. August beigelegt war, schloss Preußen mit den deutschen Staaten nördlich des Mains ein Bündnis, dem früher oder später auch die süddeutschen Monarchien beitreten sollten. Bismarck vollzog den impliziten Wechsel zur deutschen Nationalpolitik nur zögerlich. Altpreußisch, macht- und staatszentriert, wie er war, leitete ihn, wie Thomas Nipperdey betont hat, kein »›Wille zu Deutschland‹«.[6] Wenn er sich der Aufgabe der staatlichen Einheit nicht verweigerte, gab es dafür vor allem drei Gründe: erstens das relative Machtvakuum in Süddeutschland; zweitens die Existenz des Deutschen Zollvereins und die vom Norddeutschen Bund mit den süddeutschen Staaten geschlossenen Schutz- und Trutzbündnisse; und drittens seine Wahrnehmung, dass der Zeitgeist eine Lösung der deutschen Frage verlange. Die »Mauer« der Mainlinie entspreche durchaus Preußens »Bedürfniß«, schrieb Bismarck im März 1867; doch sei sie eigentlich ein »Gitter«, durch das »der nationale Strom [...] seinen Weg findet«. »Setzen wir Deutschland, sozusagen, in den Sattel! Reiten wird es schon können«, rief er den Abgeordneten des Norddeutschen Reichstags kurz darauf zu.

Eile legte der neue Bundeskanzler damit nicht an den Tag, im Gegenteil. Seine doppelte Überzeugung, der Süden Deutschlands müsse angesichts der Furcht vor einer »Verpreußung« besonders von der Einigung überzeugt und diese dann auch europaverträglich gestaltet werden, gemahnte zur Zurückhaltung. Insbesondere Frankreich meldete Bedenken an. Um die Ansprüche Napoleons III. abzuwehren, boten sich zwei Möglichkeiten an: ein diplomatischer Ausgleich oder Krieg. Bismarck präferierte zunächst die erste Alternative, was auch mit dem Sterben der »Blüte unsrer Jugend« 1866 auf den Schlachtfeldern und in den Lazaretten zusammenhing, wie er gesprächsweise im Frühjahr 1867 betonte. Da sein Versuch, den Ausbreitungsdrang Frankreichs nach Luxemburg

Extrablatt.

Kölnische Zeitung.

Telegraphische Depeschen.

Ems, 13. Juli. 1870

Nachdem die Nachricht von der Entsagung des Erbprinzen von Hohenzollern der französischen Regierung amtlich mitgetheilt war, stellte der französische Botschafter in Ems an den König die Forderung, ihn zu autorisiren, daß er nach Paris telegraphire, der König verpflichte sich für alle Zukunft, niemals wieder zuzustimmen, wenn die Hohenzollern auf die Candidatur zurückkämen. Se. Majestät der König lehnte ab, den französischen Botschafter nochmals zu empfangen, und ließ demselben durch den Adjutanten vom Dienst sagen, Se. Majestät habe dem Botschafter nichts weiter mitzutheilen.

Paris, 13. Juli.

Im gesetzgebenden Körper verliest der Herzog von Gramont nachstehende Erklärung: Olozaga theilte uns gestern officiel die Verzichtleistung des Prinzen von Hohenzollern auf die Throncandidatur Spaniens mit. Die Verhandlungen, welche wir mit Preußen fortsetzen und welche keiner Zeit einen anderen Gegenstand berührten, sind noch unbeendet, daher es uns unmöglich ist, über dieselben zu sprechen und schon heute der Kammer und dem Lande einen allgemeinen Bericht zu unterbreiten.

Jerome David bringt darauf eine Interpellation folgenden Inhalts ein: „In Erwägung der festen, bestimmten Erklärungen des Ministeriums auf die Interpellation Cochery, die günstig durch das Land aufgenommen wurden, ferner in Erwägung der heutigen Erklärung, welche in starkem Widerspruche stehen mit der Langsamkeit der Verhandlungen, wünsche ich das Ministerium über seine Haltung zu interpelliren, welche die nationale Würde verletzt."

Der Minister des Aeußern, Gramont, schlägt vor, die Interpellation Duvernois' und David's am Freitag zu beantworten.

Keratry verlangt sofortige Berathung, die Kammer beschließt jedoch, am Freitag in die Berathung einzutreten.

Berlin, 13. Juli.

Es heißt, daß die französische Regierung sich durch die Entsagung des Erbprinzen Leopold von Hohenzollern nicht für befriedigt hält; es wird daher die Berufung des norddeutschen Reichstages für die nächste Woche erwartet.

Verantwortlicher Redacteur: Heinrich Kruse in Köln.
Druck und Verlag von M. DuMont-Schauberg in Köln, Breitstraße 76, 78.

»Emser Depesche« vom 13. Juli 1870

Extrablatt. Kölnische Zeitung.
Telegraphische Depesche
Kat. 217

oder Belgien abzulenken, am Widerstand der Großmächte scheiterte, verengten sich seine Handlungsspielräume. Obwohl Napoleon III. zu einer Strategie der Eindämmung überging, hielt Bismarck zunächst daran fest, dass Preußen einen Krieg »nur für die Ehre seines Landes – nicht zu verwechseln mit dem sogenannten Prestige« beginnen dürfe. »Daß die deutsche Einheit durch gewaltsame Ereignisse gefördert werden würde«, hielt er durchaus für wahrscheinlich. »Aber eine ganz andere Frage ist der Beruf, eine gewaltsame Katastrophe herbeizuführen.« Dann jedoch trug Bismarck mit dazu bei, die »gewaltsame Katastrophe« nicht zu verhindern.

Der Deutsch-Französische Krieg entzündete sich schließlich an der spanischen Thronkandidatur des Prinzen Leopold von Hohenzollern-Sigmaringen. Als die streng geheime Offerte am 3. Juli 1870 öffentlich wurde, wirkte sie wie eine Bombe. Frankreich drohte postwendend mit Krieg und erreichte so, dass der Chef des Hauses Sigmaringen, Fürst Karl Anton, in Absprache mit dem Oberhaupt der Hohenzollern, König Wilhelm, den Verzicht auf die Thronkandidatur verkündete. Frankreichs Regierung hätte sich mit diesem Erfolg begnügen können, tat es aber nicht. Unter dem Druck einer aufgeputschten Öffentlichkeit beauftragte sie ihren Botschafter Vincent Graf Benedetti, dem in Bad Ems kurenden preußischen König die Zusicherung abzuringen, dass er der Thronkandidatur eines Hohenzollern-Prinzen in Spanien auch in Zukunft nicht zustimmen werde. Wilhelm I. konnte sich einer solchen Forderung nicht unterwerfen und ließ dem Diplomaten ausrichten, dass die Angelegenheit für ihn erledigt sei. Nachdem Bismarck in Berlin am 13. Juli Nachricht von den Ereig-

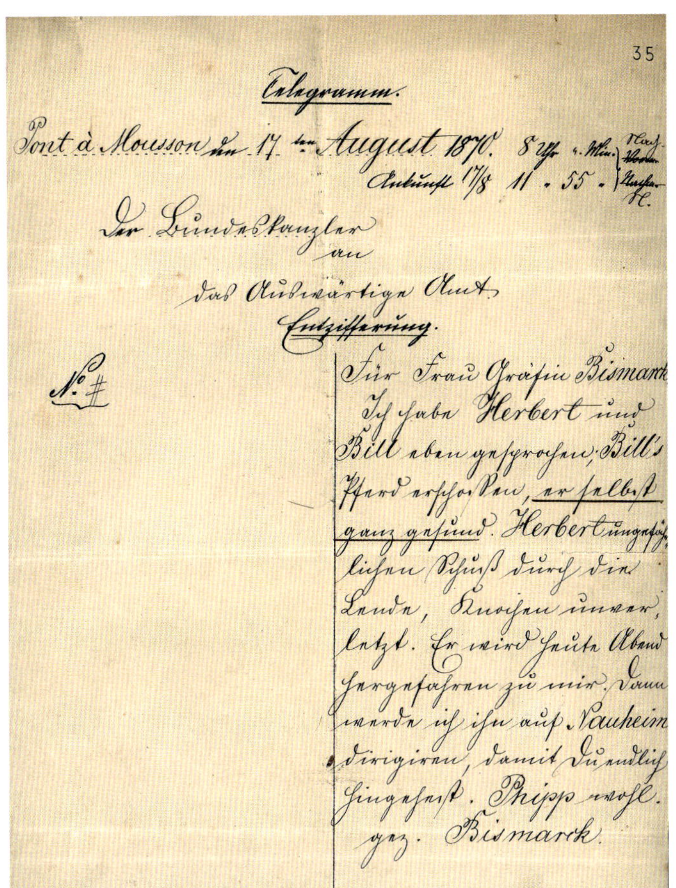
35

Telegramm.

Pont à Mousson den 17ten August 1870. 8 Uhr

Ankunft 17/8 11 . 55 .

Der Bundeskanzler an das Auswärtige Amt.

Entzifferung.

Für Frau Gräfin Bismarck
Ich habe Herbert und Bill eben gesprochen; Bill's Pferd erschossen, er selbst ganz gesund. Herbert ungefährlichen Schuß durch die Lende, Knochen unverletzt. Er wird heute Abend hergefahren zu mir, dann werde ich ihn auf Nauheim dirigieren, damit Du endlich hingehst. Phipps wohl.
gez. Bismarck

Telegramm Bismarcks an seine Ehefrau Johanna

Pont-à-Mousson, 17. August 1870, 8 Uhr
Kat. 257

Bismarck telegrafierte seiner Ehefrau am Tag nach der Schlacht von Mars-la-Tour, an der beide Söhne beteiligt waren: »Ich habe Herbert und Bill [Wilhelm] eben gesprochen; Bill's Pferd erschossen; *er selbst ganz gesund*. Herbert ungefährlicher Schuß durch die Lende, Knochen unverletzt. Er wird heute Abend hergefahren zu mir. Dann werde ich ihn auf Nauheim dirigieren, damit Du endlich hingehst [sic].«

nissen an der Lahn erhalten hatte, lancierte er diese von ihm bearbeitete »Emser Depesche« in der Presse und hielt dem »gallischen Stier« damit nach seinem eigenen Urteil ein »rotes Tuch« vor. Wenngleich nicht davon geredet werden kann, Bismarck habe Frankreichs Kriegserklärung vom 19. Juli von langer Hand vorbereitet, besteht doch kein Zweifel, dass er die von Napoleon III. aus Prestigegründen zugespitzte Frage der Thronkandidatur eskalieren ließ, um der Einigung Deutschlands den nötigen Kitt zu liefern.

Nicht wie 1866 ein preußisches, sondern ein deutsches Heer zog jetzt in den Kampf und entschied ihn am 1. September in der Schlacht von Sedan für sich. Drei Tage später fiel das Second Empire einem republikanischen Staatsstreich zum Opfer. Eigentlich hätte damit der Weg für einen raschen Friedensschluss frei sein können. Doch die in der deutschen Presse aufgekommene, vom preußischen Generalstab unterstützte Forderung nach einer Abtretung Elsass-Lothringens zerstörte die Gunst der Stunde. Auch Bismarck machte sich die Idee zu eigen, denn zum einen hielt er das Verhältnis zu Frankreich für dauerhaft vergiftet und glaubte, schon jetzt die Ausgangslage für den nächsten Krieg verbessern zu müssen. Zum anderen hoffte er, so ein Bindeglied zur nationalen Bewegung herzustellen, um die Verhandlungen über die deutsche Einigung zu erleichtern. Aus Furcht vor einer Einmischung der neutralen Mächte wie aus Sorge um seine beiden im Feld stehenden Söhne drängte er jedoch zu einem baldigen Waffenstillstand. Höchst ungelegen kam ihm daher ein im Versailler Hauptquartier ausbrechender Streit mit den »Halbgöttern« im Generalstab, wie Bismarck die hohen Offiziere noch in seinen Memoiren verächtlich nennen sollte.

Brief Bismarcks über die Kaiserproklamation an seine Ehefrau Johanna
Versailles, 21. Januar 1871
Kat. 361

»Mein Liebling / ich habe Dir schrecklich lange nicht geschrieben, verzeih, aber diese Kaisergeburt war eine schwere, und Könige haben in solchen Zeiten ihre wunderlichen Gelüste, wie Frauen bevor sie der Welt hergeben was sie doch nicht behalten können. Ich hatte, als Accoucheur [Hebamme], mehrmals das dringende Bedürfnis eine Bombe zu sein und zu platzen, daß der ganze Bau in Trümmer gegangen wäre. *Nöthige* Geschäfte greifen mich wenig an, aber die unnöthigen verbittern.«

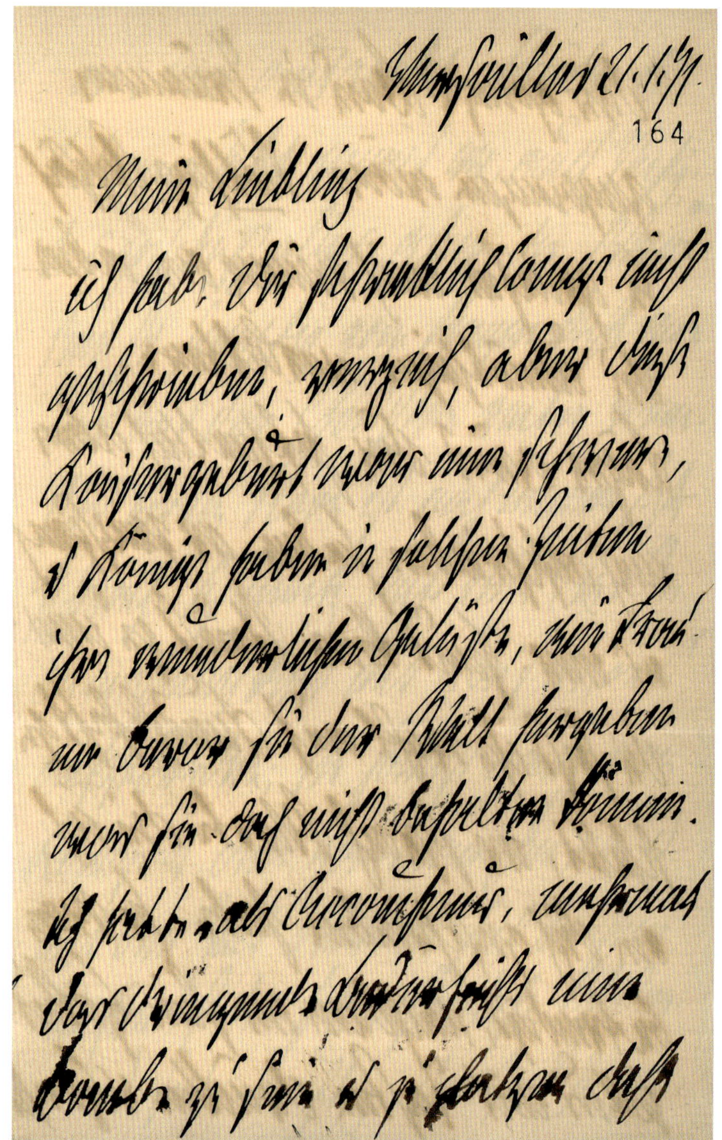

Versailles 21.1.71
164

Mein Liebling
ich habe Dir schrecklich lange nicht
geschrieben, verzeih, aber diese
Kaisergeburt war eine schwere,
u Könige haben in solchen Zeiten
ihre wunderlichen Gelüste, wie Frau-
en bevor sie der Welt hergeben
was sie doch nicht behalten können.
Ich hatte, als Accoucheur, mehrmals
das dringende Bedürfniß eine
Bombe zu sein u zu platzen daß

Während der Kanzler, seit 1866 Generalmajor und seit 1868 Chef des 1. Magdeburger Landwehr-Regiments Nr. 26, die französische Hauptstadt durch Artilleriebeschuss zur Aufgabe zwingen wollte, dachte der Chef des Generalstabs Helmuth von Moltke an einen Exterminationskrieg mittels Aushungerung. Überhaupt sollten die Politiker seines Erachtens erst dann zu Wort kommen, wenn das Kriegswerk vollendet sei. Bismarck wähnte sich einem »Complott« gegenüber und musste sich bestätigt fühlen, als Moltke den Generalgouverneur von Paris, General Louis Jules Trochu, ohne Rücksprache mit ihm zur Inspizierung der Lage einlud. Immerhin fasste die militärische Führung bald darauf den Beschluss, Paris unter Beschuss zu nehmen und zu bestürmen, erfüllte also Bismarcks Forderung. Für den Bundeskanzler ein unbezweifelbarer militärischer Erfolg, den er durch einen nicht minder wichtigen politischen Durchbruch zu ergänzen wusste: die nationale Einigung Deutschlands.

Anfang September hatte Bismarck den von nationalliberaler Seite angeregten Beratungen über die Bildung eines »1000-jährigen« Deutschen Reichs zugestimmt. Die Widerstände Bayerns und Württembergs waren nicht unbeträchtlich, konnten aber bis Ende November durch zugestandene Sonderrechte und diskrete Geldzahlungen an König Ludwig II. überwunden werden. Weit euphorischer als der Monarch in München wirkte eine Reichstagsdeputation aus Berlin, die den preußischen König Mitte Dezember in Versailles um die Annahme der Kaiserwürde bat. Der Proklamation selbst wohnten die Abgeordneten indes nicht bei, weil dieser Akt nach Meinung des Bundeskanzlers nur »von oben«, von den Fürsten, vollzogen werden sollte. Eine ähnlich hohe Bedeutung wie die Entscheidung über die Teilnehmer besaß für ihn die Frage von Ort und Zeitpunkt der historischen Feier. Indem sie auf den Tag genau 170 Jahre nach der ersten Krönung eines preußischen Königs und im Spiegelsaal des Schlosses von Versailles stattfand, symbolisierte sie sowohl die preußische Fundamentierung des Reiches als auch den Triumph Deutschlands über die Politik des Sonnenkönigs Ludwig XIV.

Fast bis zur letzten Minute feilten die Zeremonienmeister am Programm. Vor allem ein Punkt bereitete ihnen Kopfzerbrechen: das Hoch auf den Kaiser, für das dessen Schwiegersohn Großherzog Friedrich von Baden auserkoren war. Wilhelm I. war nur bereit, die preußische Krone gegen den »Charakter-Major« einzutauschen, wenn er sich »Kaiser von Deutschland« nennen durfte.[7] Diese Titulatur implizierte jedoch einen landesherrlichen Anspruch auf nichtpreußische Gebiete und war von Bayern in den November-Verhandlungen abgelehnt worden. Bismarck riet daher zur Formel »Deutscher Kaiser«, die Wilhelm I. aber nicht passte. Friedrich von Baden umging die heikle Frage schließlich sehr geschickt, indem er sein Hoch auf »Kaiser Wilhelm« ausbrachte; für Wilhelm I. Grund genug, Bismarck beim Ausmarsch aus dem Spiegelsaal zu ignorieren. Sein Ärger hielt nicht lange an. Noch am selben Tag beförderte er den Bundeskanzler zum Generalleutnant, wenige Wochen später erhob er ihn in den erblichen Fürstenstand und zum Reichskanzler.

Unterstützt von nationalliberalen und monarchischen Kräften, hatte Bismarck den Weg zum kleindeutschen Nationalstaat nicht alleine geebnet, aber auch nicht bloß als dessen »Hebamme«[8] gewirkt. Bis zuletzt war dem preußischen Royalisten die Verschmelzung der Staaten Deutschlands zu einer einheitlichen Nation suspekt geblieben. Deshalb führte er die Deutschen auch nicht in eine unitarische Nation, sondern in ein »Bündnis der Fürsten und Freien Städte«. In diesem Sinne war die Reichsgründung für Bismarck Akt einer konservativen Politik. Im Gegensatz zu manch Nationalbewegten dürfte es ihn daher keineswegs gegrämt haben, dass über die gewonnene Einheit die Freiheit aus dem Auge verloren worden war.

1 Die Informationen zu Bismarcks Militärlaufbahn sind sowohl dem Karton A 32 im Bismarck-Archiv Friedrichsruh als auch dem Band von Victor Köhler: Das Kürassier-Regiment von Seydlitz (Magdeburgisches) Nr. 7, seine Geschichte. Nach amtlichen Unterlagen und Berichten von Kriegsteilnehmern, Hannover 1935, entnommen. **2** Wenn nicht anders vermerkt, handelt es sich bei den Zitaten um Aussagen Bismarcks, die in den im Anhang zu diesem Band aufgelisteten einschlägigen Editionen abgedruckt vorliegen. Zur weiteren Orientierung sei auf die dort ebenfalls genannte Literatur sowie auf die ausführliche Studie des Autors verwiesen: Bismarck und Frankreich 1815–1898. Chancen zur Bildung einer »ganz unwiderstehlichen Macht?«, Paderborn 2019. **3** Wie das Königreich Piemont die Einigung Italiens herbeigeführt hatte, sollte Preußen jene Deutschlands umsetzen. Vgl. Shlomo Na'aman: Der Deutsche Nationalverein. Die politische Konstituierung des deutschen Bürgertums 1859–1867, Düsseldorf 1987. **4** Carl von Clausewitz: Vom Kriege [1832], (Ost-)Berlin 1957, S. 34. **5** Zitiert nach: Volker Ullrich: Fünf Schüsse auf Bismarck. Historische Reportagen 1789–1945, München 2002, S. 45. **6** Thomas Nipperdey: Deutsche Geschichte 1866–1918, Bd. 2, München 1992, S. 26. **7** Zitiert nach: Otto von Bismarck, Gedanken und Erinnerungen: Neue Friedrichsruher Ausgabe, Abt. IV., bearb. von Michael Epkenhans und Eberhard Kolb, Paderborn 2012, S. 285. **8** So bei Christoph Nonn: Bismarck. Ein Preuße und sein Jahrhundert, München 2015, S. 356.

August Bebel

Ein Sozialdemokrat gegen Eroberungskrieg und »Verpreußung«

JAMES RETALLACK

Am 26. November 1870 ergriff August Bebel im Reichstag des Norddeutschen Bundes das Wort, um sich gegen den Deutsch-Französischen Krieg von 1870/71 und die Annexion der französischen Departements Elsass und Lothringen auszusprechen.[1] Bebel war Mitbegründer der radikaldemokratischen Sächsischen Volkspartei (1866) und der Sozialdemokratischen Arbeiterpartei (1869). Seit Februar 1867 saß er im Reichstag als Vertreter des XVII. sächsischen Wahlkreises Glauchau-Meerane. In seiner Rede begründete er die Weigerung seiner Partei, die für eine Fortführung des Feldzugs gegen Frankreich erforderlichen Finanzmittel zu bewilligen, und hob die Gefahr eines französischen Revanchismus hervor, sollte der in der deutschen Bevölkerung laut werdenden Forderung nach einer Annexion nachgegeben werden.

»Also, meine Herren, man hat ja die verschiedensten Gründe für die Annexion geltend gemacht. Man sagt, Elsaß und Lothringen müsse aus *strategischen* Gründen deutsch werden, es müsse aus *nationalen* Gesichtspunkten deutsch werden, weil es seinerzeit zu Deutschland gehört habe, es müsse aus *politischen* Gründen deutsch werden, es müsse womöglich noch aus *volkswirtschaftlichen* Gründen deutsch werden.«

Keiner dieser Gründe, so Bebel, rechtfertige es, Elsass und Lothringen als Kriegsbeute zu nehmen. Der Präsident des Reichstags unterbrach die Rede mehrfach, um den Sprecher, der sich an der Grenze der parlamentarischen Schicklichkeit bewegte, zum Schweigen zu bringen. Bebel aber fuhr unbeirrt in seinem Plädoyer für einen Frieden ohne Eroberung fort. »Das *Nationalitätsprinzip* ist meiner Ansicht nach ein durchaus *reaktionäres* Prinzip. [...] Es würden die Völker sich gegenseitig zerfleischen bis an das Ende aller Dinge.« Bebel ist von diesem Prinzipienstandpunkt nie abgewichen. In seiner Reichstagsrede

August Bebel (1840–1913), um 1865
Kat. 201

vom 25. Mai 1871, in der er auch gegen die neue Reichsverfassung polemisierte und die tapferen Mitglieder der Pariser Kommune lobte, bezeichnet er die Annexionen als »Verbrechen gegen das Völkerrecht« und als »Schandfleck in der deutschen Geschichte«.[2]

Sowohl die Vorgeschichte als auch die Folgen dieser beiden Reden erhellen die ungeheure Bedeutung des historischen Dreiklangs von Krieg, Macht und Nation in der Entstehungsgeschichte der deutschen Arbeiterbewegung. Nirgends wird dies deutlicher als im Zeitraum zwischen 1866 und 1872.

Es war zwar Ferdinand Lassalles »Offenes Antwortschreiben« vom 1. März 1863 an die Vertreter der Arbeiterschaft in Leipzig, das zur Gründung des Allgemeinen Deutschen Arbeitervereins (ADAV) führte.[3] Doch Bebel und sein enger Mitstreiter Wilhelm Liebknecht verfolgten eine ganz eigene politische Linie. Im August 1866, just als der Deutsche Krieg seinem Ende zuging, gründeten Bebel und Liebknecht zusammen mit anderen Demokraten die Sächsische Volkspartei (1866–1869). Eines der Parteiziele war es, einer Hegemonialstellung Preußens im entstehenden Deutschland entgegenzuwirken, verkörperte Preußen doch ein politisches System, in dem es für die Arbeiter mit größter Wahrscheinlichkeit unmöglich sein würde, ihre angestrebten Rechte und Freiheiten zu erlangen. In seiner ersten Rede im Reichstag am 10. April 1867 erklärte Bebel, dass Preußen nicht daran interessiert sei, die Führung auf dem Weg zu einem vereinigten Deutschland zu übernehmen. Vielmehr verfolge es »ein spezifisch *Preußisches* Interesse [...], die Stärkung der Hohenzollernschen Hausmacht«.[4] 1869, auf einem Kongress in Eisenach, war Bebel einer der Mitbegründer der Sozialdemokratischen Arbeiterpartei (SDAP, 1869–1875).[5] Im Gegensatz zum ADAV war die neue Partei demokratisch aufgebaut. Die Parteiziele der »Eisenacher« waren in der Broschüre »Unsere Ziele« (1870) zusammengefasst; Bebel hatte sie im sächsischen Gefängnis verfasst, wo er wegen Verbreitung staatsgefährdender Schriften einsaß. Um diese Zeit reisten Bebel und Liebknecht fast ununterbrochen, um ihre Botschaft der wachsenden Zahl Parteigetreuer näherzubringen. Das gesprochene Wort ergänzten sie durch eine expansive Pressearbeit und weitreichende Bemühungen, der Bewegung eine solide Organisationsbasis in Form örtlicher Arbeitervereine zu verschaffen. Besonders Liebknecht prangerte den Norddeutschen Reichstag unnachgiebig an und bezeichnete ihn als das »Feigenblatt des Absolutismus«.[6]

Einige Tage, nachdem der Krieg gegen Frankreich Preußen und die süddeutschen Staaten in gemeinsamer Sache vereint hatte, gingen Bebel und Liebknecht das größte Wagnis in der frühen Geschichte der deutschen Arbeiterbewegung ein. Sie weigerten sich, für die 120 Millionen Reichstaler umfassende Kriegsanleihe zu stimmen, die Bismarck vom Reichstag gefordert hatte. Der Krieg gegen Frankreich, so ihr Vorwurf, sei ein dynastisch geführter Eroberungskrieg. In einer Stellungnahme vom 21. Juli 1870 begründeten sie ihre Position wie folgt: »Die [...] abverlangten Geldmittel können wir *nicht bewilligen*, weil dies ein Vertrauensvotum für die preußische Regierung wäre, die durch ihr Vorgehen im Jahre 1866 den gegenwärtigen Krieg vorbereitet hat. Ebensowenig können wir die geforderten Geldmittel *verweigern*, denn es könnte dies als Billigung der frevelheften und verbrecherischen Politik Bonapartes [Kaiser Napoleon III.] aufgefaßt werden.«[7] Der ADAV und das Zentralkomitee der SDAP in Braunschweig kritisierten Bebel und Liebknecht für diese Haltung: Sie erlagen der durch Bismarck erzeugten Suggestion, dass es einen deutschen Verteidigungskrieg gegen den Erbfeind zu führen gelte. Aus Norddeutschland reisten Anhänger Lassalles nach Sachsen, um sich gegen Bebels und Liebknechts Antikriegskurs zu positionieren und Stimmung gegen sie zu machen. Unter anderem warfen sie Steine durch die Fenster von Liebknechts Haus, in dem sich seine Ehefrau Natalie mit ihrem kleinen Sohn aufhielt.[8] Doch als Bismarck den Krieg gegen Frankreich nach dem entscheidenden Sieg über die französischen Truppen bei der Schlacht von Sedan (1./2. September 1870) fortsetzte und die Mitglieder des Braunschweiger Zentralkomitees in Ketten auf die Festung Boyen in Lötzen (Ostpreußen) gebracht worden waren, urteilten Bebel, Marx und andere Sozialdemokraten wieder übereinstimmend: Ein Eroberungskrieg und Preußens Aufstieg konnten keinesfalls im Interesse der Arbeiter sein.[9] Ab dem 21. September enthielt jede Ausgabe der Parteizeitung Der Volksstaat die Forderung: »*Ein billiger Friede mit der französischen Republik! Keine Annexionen, Bestrafung Bonaparte's und seiner Mitschuldigen!*«[10]

Bebel und Liebknecht griffen auch die verfassungsrechtlichen Verträge an, die in den letzten Monaten des Jahres 1870 ausgearbeitet worden waren und zur Proklamierung des Deutschen Reiches und Krönung des preußischen Königs Wilhelm I. zum Deutschen Kaiser (am 18. Januar 1871 im Spiegelsaal von Versailles) führten. Am 6. Dezember 1870 lehnte Bebel den von Bismarck vorgelegten Verfassungsentwurf ab. Dabei bediente er sich bewusst einer provokanten Ausdrucksweise, verurteilte scharf den geringen Einfluss des Reichstags und stellte fest, dass die Einigungskriege die erbrachten Opfer keinesfalls wert gewesen seien:

»Erst wenn das Volk einsieht, daß es von seinen Regierungen, von seinen Fürsten nichts zu hoffen hat, daß jeder Krieg, der geführt wird, immer nur gegen sein Interesse geführt wird, erst wenn es eingesehen [sic], daß die

3 Kriege, die seit 10 Jahren in Deutschland geführt worden sind, nur uns jedesmal in freiheitlicher Beziehung zurückgebracht haben, dann wird es besser werden; das Volk wird zur Selbsterkenntnis kommen, das Volk wird anfangen, denken zu lernen – und, meine Herren, das Resultat wird sein, daß das Volk begreift und einsieht, daß es von seinen Fürsten, von seinen Regierungen nichts zu erwarten hat, daß es nur gestützt auf seine eigene Macht, auf sein eigenes Selbstbestimmungsrecht, eine neue Verfassung sich schaffen muß [...].«[11]

Drei Tage darauf erklärte Liebknecht vor dem Reichstag, der passendste Ort für die Krönung des modernen Kaisers sei der Berliner Gendarmenmarkt, »denn dieses Kaiserthum kann in der That nur durch den Gensdarmen aufrecht erhalten werden«.[12] Diese mutigen Reden wurden von Arbeitervertretern inner- und außerhalb Deutschlands gefeiert. Auch Friedrich Engels war beindruckt: »die Opposition, die unsere Freunde Bebel und Liebknecht [im Reichstag] gegen den Eroberungskrieg organisieren konnten, hat im Interesse unserer internationalen Propaganda mächtiger gewirkt, als jahrelange Propaganda durch die Presse und Versammlungen es vermocht haben«.[13]

Unterdessen waren Bismarck und andere hochrangige deutsche Politiker mit ihrer Geduld am Ende. Mit der einseitigen Erklärung, dass der Schutz der parlamentarischen Immunität als Mitglied des Reichstags für Bebel nur bis zum Abschluss der jeweiligen Session gelte, wurde ihrer »Galgenfrist« (Liebknecht) ein jähes Ende bereitet.[14] In seinen Memoiren schildert Bebel, was

August Bebels Gesellenstück, ein Miniatursteckspiel, um 1857, und sein Siegelring, 1864
Kat. 199, 200

Bebel, geboren in Deutz bei Köln, kam aus ärmlichen Verhältnissen. Der Vater, ein Unteroffizier, starb früh. Bebel lernte das Drechslerhandwerk und ging nach seiner Gesellenprüfung auf Wanderschaft. 1860 ließ sich der bildungshungrige Drechslergeselle in Leipzig nieder, das damals ein Zentrum des Vereinswesens von Arbeitern und Handwerkern war. 1864 eröffnete er eine eigene kleine Werkstatt.

Liebknecht.
Marx.
Lassalle.
Kühn.
Bebel.
Hepner.
Geib.
Ehlers.
Proletarier aller Länder vereinigt Euch
J. Ph. Becker.
Joh. Jacoby.
Bracke.
Bonhorst.
Spier.

weiter geschah: »Am 17. Dezember morgens arbeitete ich in meiner Werkstatt, als plötzlich meine Frau totenbleich hereinstürzte und mir mitteilte, daß oben in unserer Wohnung ein Polizeibeamter sei«, der von »einem Soldaten in kriegsmäßiger Ausrüstung« begleitet werde. Ins Bezirksgerichtsgefängnis überführt, sah er einer noch unsichereren Zukunft entgegen. Es war damit zu rechnen, dass seine Untersuchungshaft – sowie die seiner Mitangeklagten Liebknecht und Adolf Hepner, dem zweiten Redakteur des »Volksstaats« neben Liebknecht – bis zum Sommer 1871 andauern würde, weil die Behörden für eine Verurteilung wegen Landesverrats Beweismaterial aus Braunschweig sicherstellen mussten. »Der Winter 1870/71 war wohl der strengste, den wir in vielen Jahrzehnten hatten«, berichtete Bebel. »Ich fror hundemäßig.« Und seine Zelle »wimmelte von Ungeziefer«.[15]

Am 21. März 1871 wurde die erste Parlamentssitzung des frisch geeinten Deutschen Reichs abgehalten. Da ein Antrag auf Freilassung Bebels als Reichstagsabgeordneter eingereicht worden war, entließ die Regierung zur Vermeidung eines Eklats Bebel am 28. März – einen Tag, bevor der Antrag diskutiert werden sollte – aus dem Gefängnis. Bebel eilte nach Berlin und sprach am 3. April während einer Debatte über die Reichsverfassung für seine Partei. Er wiederholte im Wesentlichen seine Kritikpunkte vom 6. Dezember 1870, die auf die starke Machtkonzentration im Reich und das Fehlen von in der Verfassung verankerten Freiheitsrechten zielten. Am 14. April war Bebel einer von nur 14 Reichstagsabgeordneten, die gegen die Verfassung stimmten.

In den vorausgegangenen Monaten hatte sich die politische Situation dramatisch verändert. Ein vorläufiger Frieden mit Frankreich war unterzeichnet, Reichstagswahlen waren am 3. April 1871 abgehalten worden – wobei Bebel als einziger Sozialdemokrat ins Nationalparlament gewählt wurde –, und die Pariser Kommune hatte in der französischen Hauptstadt die Kontrolle übernommen. Am 25. Mai sprach Bebel erneut vor dem Reichstag. Der konterrevolutionäre Terror gegen die Kommunarden war mittlerweile in vollem Gang, von der französischen Regierung entfesselt, die sowohl eigene Truppen als auch die von Bismarck zur Rückeroberung der Hauptstadt zurückgesandten Kriegsgefangenen einsetzte. Soeben war ein Telegramm aus Paris eingetroffen, in dem es hieß, antikommunardische Truppen seien ins Stadtzentrum vorgestoßen. Diese Nachricht bewog Bebel zu einer leidenschaftlichen Rede gegen die verhasste Paarung von Krieg und Nation:

»Meine Herren, mögen die Bestrebungen der Kommune in Ihren Augen auch noch so verwerfliche oder [...] verrückte sein, seien Sie fest überzeugt, das ganze europäische Proletariat und alles, was noch ein Gefühl für Freiheit und Unabhängigkeit in der Brust trägt, sieht auf Paris. (Große Heiterkeit.) Meine Herren, und wenn auch im Augenblick Paris unterdrückt ist, dann erinnere ich Sie daran, daß der Kampf in Paris nur ein kleines Vorpostengefecht ist, daß die Hauptsache in Europa uns noch bevorsteht und daß ehe wenige Jahrzehnte vergehen, der Schlachtenruf des Pariser Proletariats ›Krieg den Palästen, Friede den Hütten, Tod der Not und dem Müßiggange!‹ der Schlachtruf des gesamten europäischen Proletariats werden wird. (Heiterkeit.)«[16]

Diese Rede wurde später als Beweis dafür zitiert, dass die Sozialdemokraten fest entschlossen gewesen seien, die bestehende Ordnung mit Gewalt zu stürzen. Sieben Jahre später, während einer im Jahr 1878 stattfindenden Debatte über das Sozialistengesetz, behauptete Bismarck, Bebels Rede vom 25. Mai 1871 habe ihm die Augen geöffnet: »jener Anruf der Kommune war ein Licht-

←
»Kettenbild«

Kat. 281

Wilhelm Bracke illustrierte sein Buch »Der Braunschweiger Ausschuß der socialdemokratischen Arbeiter-Partei in Lötzen und vor dem Gericht« (1872) mit einer Fotocollage, die Porträts führender Sozialisten von Schlössern und Ketten eingerahmt zeigt. Als die SDAP die Annexion des Elsasses und Lothringens im September 1870 ablehnte und einen Friedensschluss mit der neuen republikanischen Regierung in Frankreich forderte, folgten Verhaftungen. Bracke selbst und weitere Parteiführer wurden teils in Ketten wie Schwerverbrecher abgeführt.

strahl [...], und von diesem Augenblick an habe ich in den sozialdemokratischen Elementen einen Feind erkannt, gegen den der Staat, die Gesellschaft sich im Stande der Nothwehr befindet«.[17]

In den vorausgegangenen Jahren hatte Bebel mehrfach erneut einige Zeit im Gefängnis verbracht, teils wegen seiner Haltung gegen den Krieg im Jahr 1870, teils wegen anderer angeblich begangener Vergehen gegen die Nation (oder gegen Bismarck persönlich). Der Fall Bebels, Liebknechts und Hepners wurde vom 11. bis zum 26. März 1872 vor dem Leipziger Bezirksschwurgericht verhandelt. Die offizielle Anklage lautete »Vorbereitung zum Hochverrat«.[18] Das dem Trio zur Last gelegte Verbrechen bestand darin, den Widerstand gegen Deutschlands Annexion von Elsass und Lothringen mit dem Kampf der Kommunarden in Paris verquickt zu haben. Der zweiwöchige Prozess war für damalige Verhältnisse recht lang, und die Staatsanwaltschaft war genötigt, ihre Anklage hauptsächlich auf angeblich verräterische Passagen in den Schriften der beiden Hauptangeklagten zu stützen. Letzterer Umstand spielte Bebel und Liebknecht in die Hände, denn er sorgte dafür, dass Schriften mit sozialdemokratischem Gedankengut in großer Zahl Eingang in die Gerichtsakten fanden und damit ohne jede Beschränkung in die Öffentlichkeit gelangen konnten. Am 26. März 1872 wurden Bebel und Liebknecht zu jeweils zwei Jahren Festungshaft in Schloss Hubertusburg in Sachsen verurteilt. Das Urteil schloss die beiden profiliertesten Sprecher der SDAP aus der aktiven Politik des neuen Reiches aus – ein Ergebnis, für das der Präsident des Schwurgerichts Alexander Eduard von Mücke mit dem Königlich Preußischen Kronenorden 3. Klasse geehrt wurde.[19]

Am 8. Juli 1872 trat Bebel seine Festungshaft in Hubertusburg an, wo Liebknecht bereits einsaß. Da Bebel aber unterdessen wegen Majestätsbeleidigung bei Versammlungsreden zu weiteren neun Monaten Gefängnis verurteilt und ihm sein Reichstagsmandat aberkannt worden war, folgten auf seine Haftzeit in der Hubertusburg in kurzem Abstand weitere Monate hinter Gittern auf der Festung Königstein und im Landesgefängnis Zwickau. Endgültig entlassen wurde er am 1. April 1875, Bismarcks 60. Geburtstag. Somit hatte er etwa drei Jahre vom ersten halben Jahrzehnt des Kaiserreichs in Haft verbracht.

Bebel hatte seit 1866 alles darangesetzt, sichtbar zu machen, dass der historische Prozess, der zur deutschen Einigung führte, durch Gewaltausübung geprägt war. Gewalt gegen die Feinde Preußens, gegen »echten« Föderalismus, gegen die Rechte und die Freiheiten des deutschen Volkes und gegen die aufkeimende Arbeiterbewegung in und außerhalb von Deutschland. Aus seiner Sicht war Deutschlands blutige Geburt eine Tragödie – und im Übrigen, ob auf den Schlachtfeldern von Königgrätz und Sedan oder im Plenarsaal des Reichstags, das Gegenteil eines Befreiungskriegs. Wie von Bebel vorhergesehen, sollte die Bejahung von Krieg und Gewalt als Mittel zum Zweck nicht nur weitreichende Auswirkungen auf die politischen und militärischen Verstrickungen des Kaiserreichs haben, sondern auch auf seine politische Kultur. Die Jahre zwischen 1866 und 1872 hinterließen ein verhängnisvolles Erbe.

1 Stenographische Berichte über die Verhandlungen des Reichstags des Norddeutschen Bundes (im Folgenden SBRNB), I. Legislatur-Periode, II. Außerordentliche Session 1870, Bd. XV, Berlin 1870, S. 9–13, 16 (26. Nov. 1870). **2** August Bebel: Ausgewählte Reden und Schriften (im Folgenden BARS), Bd. 1, Berlin 1970, S. 150. **3** Ferdinand Lassalle: Gesammelte Reden und Schriften, hg. von Eduard Bernstein, Bd. 3, Berlin 1919, S. 39–92. **4** SBRNB 1867, Bd. 1, Berlin 1867, S. 678 (10. Apr. 1867). **5** Vgl. Eisenacher Programm der Sozialdemokratischen Arbeiterpartei (8. August 1869), in: James Retallack (Hg.): Deutsche Geschichte in Dokumenten und Bildern, Bd. 4, Reichsgründung: Bismarcks Deutschland (1866–1890), Sektion 7, Politik II: http://germanhistorydocs.ghi-dc.org/sub_document.cfm?document_id=688&language=german (letzter Zugriff 06.12.2019). **6** SBRNB, I. Leg.-Per., Session 1867, Bd. 1, Berlin 1867, S. 452 (17. Okt. 1867). **7** Motiviertes Votum der Reichstagsabgeordneten Liebknecht und Bebel in Sachen der 120-Millionen-Kriegsanleihe (21. Juli 1870), in: Der Volksstaat (Leipzig), Nr. 59, 23. Juli 1870, S. 4. **8** Vgl. August Bebel: Alte Erinnerungen, in: Vorwärts (Berlin), Nr. 114, 1. Beilage, 19. Mai 1910, S. 1. **9** Zum Braunschweiger Manifest (5. Sept. 1870) vgl. Wilhelm Bracke jr.: Der Braunschweiger Ausschuß der socialdemokratischen Arbeiter-Partei in Lötzen und vor dem Gericht, Braunschweig 1872, S. 7–9. **10** Wilhelm Liebknecht: Einleitung, in: Der Hochverrats-Prozeß wider Liebknecht, Bebel, Hepner vor dem Schwurgericht zu Leipzig vom 11. bis 26. März 1872, mit einer Einleitung von W. Liebknecht und einem Anhang, 2. Auflage, Berlin 1911, S. 7. **11** SBRNB, I. Leg.-Per., II. Außero. Session 1870, Bd. XV, Berlin 1870, S. 91. **12** Ebd., S. 152–154 (9. Dez. 1870). **13** Briefe Engels an den Spanischen Föderalrat der Internationalen Arbeiterassoziation, 13. Feb. 1871, in: Karl Marx/Friedrich Engels: Werke, Bd. 17, Berlin 1962, S. 288. **14** Liebknecht: Einleitung, Hochverrats-Prozeß, S. 13. **15** Bebel: Aus meinem Leben (= BARS, Bd. 6), Berlin 1983, S. 328, 330. **16** Stenographische Berichte über die Verhandlungen des Deutschen Reichstags (SBDR), I. Leg.-Per., I. Session 1871, Bd. 2, Berlin 1871, S. 921 (25. Mai 1871). **17** SBDR, 4. Leg.-Per., I. Session 1878, Bd. 1, Berlin 1878, S. 70 (17. Sept. 1878). **18** Die Verhandlungen des Schwurgerichts zu Leipzig (11.–26. März 1872) sind vollständig dokumentiert in Hochverrats-Prozeß, S. 61–638; über Mücke vgl. auch Bebel: Aus meinem Leben, S. 359 f. **19** Vgl. Königlich Sächsisches Justizministerial-Blatt, 6. Jg., Nr. 6 (26. Juni 1872), S. 71.

4

Kriege
und
Nationen

1864
Deutsch-Dänischer Krieg

Um die Zugehörigkeit des vom dänischen König in Personalunion regierten Herzogtums Schleswig war bereits während der Schleswig-Holsteinischen Erhebung von 1848 bis 1851 gekämpft worden. Die dänische Nationalbewegung strebte eine engere Bindung an das Königreich an, die deutsche eine Loslösung von Dänemark und die Aufnahme in den Deutschen Bund. Doch eine internationale Konferenz in London garantierte 1852 lediglich den Status quo. Ein erneuter Versuch Dänemarks, das Herzogtum Schleswig enger an sich zu binden, bot dem 1862 zum preußischen Ministerpräsidenten ernannten Otto von Bismarck die Gelegenheit, Stärke nach außen zu demonstrieren, während im Inneren ein Machtkampf mit Liberalen und Demokraten um die geplante Heeresreform das politische Leben lähmte. Anders als Anhänger der deutschen Nationalbewegung forderte Bismarck nur die Einhaltung des Londoner Protokolls von 1852. So konnte er Österreich davon überzeugen, am 1. Februar 1864 gemeinsam in Schleswig einzurücken. Trotz der verheerenden Niederlage bei den Düppeler Schanzen am 18. April zeigte sich Dänemark auf der Londoner Konferenz zur Beilegung des Konflikts kompromisslos. Am 29. Juni gelang preußischen Truppen der Übergang auf die Insel Alsen, am 20. Juli gab Dänemark auf. Es verlor die Herzogtümer Schleswig, Holstein und Lauenburg, die Preußen und Österreich zunächst gemeinsam verwalteten. Die Niederlage wurde für Dänemark zum nationalen Trauma; sie bewirkte den Abschied von der offensiven Außenpolitik und eine Konzentration auf den inneren Ausbau des Landes.

Deutsch-Dänischer Krieg 1864
Jütland
Omme Å
Varde Å
Horsens
Samsø
Vejle
8.3.
KGR. DÄNEMARK
8.3.
Fredericia
Esbjerg
Kolding
Fanø
(Königsau)
Kongeåen
Odense
Ribe
Ribeå
NORDSEE
Assens
Fünen
Haderslev/
Hadersleben
Rømø
Åbenrå/
Apenrade
Fåborg
Svendborg
29.6.
Alsen
Tønder/
Tondern
Graven-
stein
18.4.
Düppel
Ærø
bis 1864 zu Schleswig
HZM.
SCHLESWIG
Flensburg
Langeland
6.2.
Oversee
Kappeln
Arnis
OSTSEE
Schleswig
Missunde
Husum
2.2.
3.2.
Friedrichstadt
Rendsburg
Kiel
Eider
Überquerung der
Eider am 1.2.1864
Plön
Eutin
Neumünster
HZM. HOLSTEIN
Helgoland (brit.)
9.5.1864 Seeschlacht
0 10 20 30 km
Grenze des Deutschen Bundes
Nordgrenze Schleswigs bis 1864
Nordgrenze nach 1864
heutige deutsch-dänische Grenze
1. (Preußisches) Korps
2. (Österreichisches) Korps
3. (Preußische Garde) Korps
Dänische Truppen
Dänische Verteidigungsstellungen
Danewerk
Schlacht
A Allgemeiner dänischer Rückzug Richtung Flensburg in der Nacht zum 6.2.
B Rückzug über See in Richtung Fünen am 29.6.
C Seetransport der 3. Division über Alsen nach Fredericia am 9.2.
D Rückzug der 3. dänischen Division nach Fünen am 29.4.
E Dänische Kav. Division erreicht zunächst über Randers und Aalborg, Frederikshavn und zieht sich von dort über See am 12.7. in Richtung Fünen zurück

1848 – 1851

Schleswig-Holsteinische Erhebung
(1. Deutsch-Dänischer Krieg)

1852

8. Mai Londoner Protokoll zur völkerrechtlichen Regelung des Status der Herzogtümer Schleswig, Holstein und Lauenburg

1863

13. November Beschluss der dänischen Novemberverfassung, die Schleswig enger an das dänische Königreich bindet

23. Dezember Bundesexekution gegen die Herzogtümer Holstein und Lauenburg, die formal bis zum 5. Dezember 1864 andauert

1864

1. Februar Ohne Zustimmung des deutschen Bundestags marschieren preußische und österreichische Truppen in Schleswig ein

5. Februar Räumung der Danewerk-Stellung durch dänische Truppen und im weiteren Verlauf Rückzug auf die Düppeler Schanzen, Sonderburg und Fredericia

6. Februar Gefecht von Oeversee

8. März Österreichische und preußische Truppen rücken in Jütland ein

15. März Dänische Seeblockade der preußischen Küste beginnt

18. April
Erstürmung der Düppeler Schanzen durch preußische Truppen

25. April – 25. Juni Londoner Konferenz: vergeblicher Versuch zur diplomatischen Beilegung des Konflikts

29. April Besetzung der Festung Fredericia durch österreichische Truppen

9. Mai Seegefecht bei Helgoland

12. Mai – 25. Juni Erster Waffenstillstand

29. Juni Preußische Truppen erobern die Insel Alsen

10. Juli Österreichische und preußische Heere überschreiten den Limfjord in Nordjütland

18. Juli Zweiter Waffenstillstand

1. August Vorfrieden von Wien

22. August Beschluss der Genfer Konvention durch zwölf europäische Staaten

30. Oktober Frieden von Wien. Der dänische König muss die Herzogtümer Schleswig, Holstein und Lauenburg abtreten, die vorläufig von Preußen und Österreich gemeinsam verwaltet werden

Der Krieg 1864

Dänemarks Trauma und Chance

UFFE ØSTERGÅRD
UND BJØRN ØSTERGAARD

Das heutige Dänemark resultiert aus der Niederlage im Deutsch-Dänischen Krieg von 1864, die seitdem die politische Kultur in Deutschlands nördlichen Nachbarland prägt. Dies zeigte das Gedenkjahr 2014, und es wird auch 2020 das Thema der Feierlichkeiten sein, die in Dänemark an die »Wiedervereinigung« mit dem nördlichen, dänischsprachigen Teil Schleswigs im Jahr 1920 erinnern sollen. Im Gedächtnis der Deutschen nimmt der Konflikt weniger Raum ein. Kaum jemand, der heute in Berlin an der 1873 errichteten Siegessäule vorbeigeht, denkt noch daran, dass der preußische Sieg von 1864 den Anlass zum Bau dieses Nationaldenkmals gegeben hat.[1]

Rückblickend erscheint der Krieg als Konflikt zwischen einem übermächtigen Deutschland auf der einen Seite und einem schwachen dänischen Kleinstaat auf der anderen – eine Vorstellung, die vor allem in Dänemark Anklang findet. Sie entspricht jedoch eher dem Ergebnis des Krieges als der Ausgangslage Mitte des 19. Jahrhunderts, als die deutschen Staaten nur lose im Deutschen Bund zusammengefasst waren. Der dänische Gesamtstaat (helstaten) war bis 1814 eine mittelgroße europäische Macht, die aus den Königreichen Dänemark und Norwegen, den Herzogtümern Holstein und Schleswig sowie Island, den Färöer Inseln und Grönland bestand. Hinzu kamen Kolonien in der Karibik (»Dänisch-Westindien«), Afrika und Asien (»Dänisch Ostindien«). Dieses mehrsprachige Reich hätte eigentlich nach der regierenden Dynastie die »Oldenburgische Monarchie« heißen müssen. Es war ein multinationales Konglomerat ähnlich der Habsburger Monarchie, nur kleiner. Das Königshaus war in erster Linie deutschsprachig. Einen schweren Schlag erlitt der dänische Gesamtstaat, als der König nach der Niederlage Napoleons 1814 Norwegen an Schweden abtreten musste. Zunehmend stellte aber auch das Aufkommen konkurrierender Nationalbewegungen unter Deutsch- bzw. Dänischgesinnten den Gesamtstaat infrage. Das Herzogtum Schleswig wurde zum Zankapfel. Während das vom dänischen König in Personalunion regierte Holstein und das ihm seit 1815 ebenfalls unterstehende kleine Herzogtum Lauenburg zum Deutschen Bund gehörten, war Schleswig ein altes dänisches Lehen. Wo im mehrsprachigen Schleswig der deutsche Sprachraum endete und der dänische anfing, war heftig umstritten. Dänische Historiker versuchten zu beweisen, dass die Grenze im Süden an der Eider verlaufen müsse; deutsche Historiker zogen sie an der Königsau im Norden und beriefen sich auf den Rippener Vertrag von 1460, um die Unteilbarkeit von Schleswig und Holstein zu belegen (»Up ewig ungedeelt«). Während die »Eiderdänen« eine engere Anbindung ganz Schleswigs an das Königreich Dänemark forderten, strebten viele Deutschgesinnte die Aufnahme des Herzogtums in den Deutschen Bund an, zusammen mit Holstein als eigenständigem Staat. Die nationale Radikalisierung führte zweimal zum Krieg und endete nach der Niederlage 1864 für Dänemark mit dem Verlust Schleswigs, Holsteins und Lauenburgs.[2]

Der Erste Schleswigsche Krieg von 1848 bis 1851 wurde auf dänischer Seite lange als dänisch-deutscher Konflikt erinnert. Erst in letzter Zeit ist es üblich geworden, von einem Bürgerkrieg zwischen dänisch- und deutschgesinnten Nationalisten zu sprechen, in den von außen durch Truppen des Deutschen Bundes eingegriffen wurde. Die dänische Partei errang in der blutigen Schlacht bei Idstedt am 24./25. Juli 1850 einen Sieg über die verbliebenen Schleswig-Holsteiner Truppen. Über den Ausgang des Krieges entschieden aber letztlich die Großmächte, vor allem Russland und Großbritannien, die nicht nur Preußen zu einem vorzeitigen Waffenstillstand gedrängt hatten, sondern auch auf der Londoner Konferenz 1852 eine Wiederherstellung der Vorkriegslage durchsetzen konnten. Das Londoner Protokoll hielt am Gesamtstaat fest, schrieb jedoch auch vor, Schleswig nicht stärker an Dänemark zu binden als Holstein.

»Fra forposterne i 1864« / Auf Vorposten 1864

Vilhelm Rosenstand (1838–1915)
Kopenhagen 1896
Öl auf Leinwand, 126,5 × 189,5 cm
Kat. 468

Der in Kopenhagen geborene Maler nahm als Sekondeleutnant im 20. Regiment am Deutsch-Dänischen Krieg 1864 teil. Auch unter dem Titel »Vort forsvar« (Unsere Verteidigung) bekannt, zeigt das Gemälde wahrscheinlich eine Szene Anfang Februar. Unter den unerschrockenen Verteidigern hat sich Rosenstand selbst dargestellt: Er verbindet sich die Hand, ohne die Gegner aus den Augen zu lassen. Gemälde wie diese prägten die Kriegserinnerung in Dänemark. Als im Gedenkjahr 2014 mit »1864« die bislang teuerste dänische TV-Serie entstand, bildete Rosenstands Gemälde den Vorspann.

»Nationalitäten- und Sprachenkarte des Herzogthums Schleswig. Der Deutschen Nationalversammlung gewidmet«

Hermann Biernatzki (1818–1895), 1849

Kat. 61

Eine gemeinsame Sprache gilt oft als Grundlage einer Nation. Wie in vielen Grenzregionen war es aber im Herzogtum Schleswig Mitte des 19. Jahrhunderts kaum möglich, klare Sprachgrenzen zu ziehen.

Erst die Danisierungspolitik nach dem Krieg 1848 bis 1851 und die Germanisierungsversuche nach 1864 machten die Mehrheit der Bevölkerung zu Deutschen oder Dänen im nationalen Sinne. Die Unterdrückung einer Sprache erzielte oft genau das Gegenteil der gewünschten Vereinheitlichung: Die jeweilige Minderheit identifizierte sich umso mehr mit der eigenen Sprache und Kultur.

Somit war weder die von Deutschgesinnten noch die von Dänischgesinnten gewünschte nationalstaatliche Lösung realisierbar.

Der Glaube, den Bürgerkrieg aus eigener Kraft gewonnen zu haben, trug entscheidend zu der dänisch-nationalen Selbstüberschätzung der 1850er und 1860er Jahre bei. Kann man die harten Maßnahmen gegen deutschgesinnte Schleswiger und Holsteiner, von denen viele in die USA emigrierten, vielleicht noch in Grenzen nachvollziehen, so erscheint etwa der Verkauf der Innenausstattung von Schloss Gottorf und seine Umwidmung zur Kaserne als ein Racheakt, der schlecht zum dänischen Selbstbild passt – und von der dänischen Geschichtsschreibung wenig beachtet worden ist. 1851 wurde Dänisch durch zwei Spracherlasse in Nordschleswig als Regierungs-, Rechts-, Schul- und Kirchensprache festgelegt und in Mittelschleswig in 49 Gemeinden anstelle des Deutschen als Schulsprache vorgeschrieben. Diese Dänisierungspolitik hinterließ bei den Deutschgesinnten im Herzogtum Schleswig Wut und Hass.

Seit 1848/49 war das Königreich Dänemark eine liberal regierte, konstitutionelle Monarchie, während es in Schleswig und Holstein althergebrachte Ständeversammlungen gab. Die sogenannte zweisprachige Gesamtstaatsverfassung aus dem Jahr 1855 sollte eine verfassungsrechtliche Klammer für Königreich und Herzogtümer bilden – mit wenig Erfolg. Vor allem die deutsche Oberschicht in Holstein und mit ihr der Deutsche Bund boykottierten gleichermaßen liberale Bestrebungen wie die engere Einbeziehung der Herzogtümer in den Gesamtstaat. Zunehmend verzweifelt schlug die dänische nationalliberale

»Der Dänische Spion Blaunfeldt. Wie man ›Dänisches Ungeziefer‹ fängt, von dem Schleswig-Holstein geplagt wurde«
Hamburg 1864
Lithografie
Kat. 67

Nach der Schleswig-Holsteinischen Erhebung 1848 bis 1851 wurden oft deutschgesinnte durch dänischgesinnte Beamte ersetzt. Der »Hardesvogt« Maximilian Franciscus Blaunfeldt (1799–1880) in Fleckeby war als Vertreter dieser Danisierungspolitik und wegen seiner despotischen Amtsführung verhasst. Als Spion denunziert, wurde er am 2. Februar 1864 von preußischem Militär verhaftet, kam aber am 1. Juni 1864 mit der Auflage wieder frei, die Herzogtümer zu verlassen.

Büste Christians IX. (1818–1906), König von Dänemark
Höhe 33 cm
Kat. 69

Nach dem Aussterben der älteren, dänischen Königslinie des Hauses Oldenburg bestieg am 15. November 1863 Christian IX. den Thron. Er entstammte dem Glücksburger Zweig einer Nebenlinie des Gesamthauses Oldenburg, der bis heute die dänischen Könige und Königinnen stellt.

Regierung schließlich einen hochriskanten Kurs ein: Im Alleingang und gegen die internationalen Vereinbarungen erließ sie die Novemberverfassung von 1863, die den Verbund mit Holstein zugunsten einer engeren Eingliederung Schleswigs auflöste. König Christian IX. aus dem Haus Glücksburg, eigentlich ein Anhänger der Gesamtstaatsidee, hatte gerade erst den Thron bestiegen. Er fürchtete, mit seiner Zustimmung zur neuen Verfassung einen Krieg zu provozieren; doch mehr noch sah er die Gefahr, im Fall einer Weigerung zu deutschfreundlich und zu konservativ zu erscheinen und von der nationalliberalen Regierung und einer aufgebrachten Bevölkerung gestürzt zu werden.

Dies gab Preußens geschicktem Machtpolitiker Otto von Bismarck die gewünschte Gelegenheit, Österreich für ein gemeinsames Eingreifen gegen das unvorbereitete Dänemark zu gewinnen. Die erhoffte Unterstützung der anderen europäischen Großmächte oder Schwedens, das mit Norwegen eine Union bildete, blieb allerdings aus, obwohl auf dänischer Seite zahlreiche schwedische Freiwillige teilnahmen, darunter über 100 Offiziere. Diese konnten

Ditlev Gothard Monrad (1811–1887), königlich dänischer Ministerpräsident
Holzstich aus der »Illustrirten Zeitung«, Leipzig
Kat. 70

Seit 1848 war Dänemark eine konstitutionelle Monarchie. Der Nationalliberale Monrad entwarf 1849 ihr erstes Grundgesetz. In der Krise Ende 1863 wurde er zum Ministerpräsidenten ernannt. Im April 1864 lehnte er einen Rückzug von den Düppeler Schanzen ab. Nach der Niederlage ging Monrad für einige Jahre als Farmer nach Neuseeland. Ab 1871 bekleidete er, wie bereits von 1849 bis 1854, das Amt des Bischofs von Lolland-Falster.

Dänischer Soldat 1864

Abb. 4

Dänemark war schlecht auf einen Krieg gegen zwei deutsche Großmächte vorbereitet. Die Mobilisierung verlief chaotisch. Vor Anfang März hatte man nicht mit Kampfhandlungen gerechnet. Es fehlte an Uniformen und Unterkünften für die Einberufenen, die ihre Anreise teils selbst bezahlen mussten.

aber kaum ausgleichen, dass viele Deutschgesinnte in Schleswig ihren Gestellungsbefehlen ebenso wenig nachkamen wie Männer aus Holstein und Lauenburg. So stand das dänische Heer den Armeen der beiden deutschen Großmächte allein gegenüber. Das Stärkeverhältnis betrug 38 000 zu 57 000 Mann. Binnen eines knappen halben Jahres wurde es vollständig geschlagen – mit dem Sturm auf Düppel am 18. April und der Eroberung von Alsen am 29. Juni als den tragisch-heroischen Höhepunkten.

Preußische und österreichische Truppen überschritten am 2. Februar die Eider, um das dänische Heer anzugreifen. Es hatte bei dem sagenumwobenen »Danewerk« zwischen der Schlei und den Sumpfgebieten vor Husum Stellung bezogen. In Parolen wie »ein Danewerk in der Brust eines jeden Dänen« drückten sich die hohen Erwartungen an diese Verteidigungsanlage aus, bei der es sich letztlich nur um eine 15 Kilometer lange Feldbefestigung aus dem Sommer 1861 ohne feste Unterkünfte für die Verteidiger handelte. Im strengen Winter

1864 froren die Sumpfgebiete im Westen zu, sodass die deutschen Truppen das viel kleinere dänische Heer durch einen gleichzeitigen Angriff über die schmale Förde der Schlei hätten umringen können. In dieser hoffnungslosen Situation entschied der Oberkommandierende des dänischen Heeres, General Christian Julius de Meza, sich zu den Flankenstellungen bei Düppel gegenüber von Sonderburg und Fredericia zurückzuziehen. Diese Strategie gründete auf der Überlegenheit der dänischen Flotte gegenüber den Angreifern und war 1848 recht erfolgreich gewesen. Kriegsminister Carl Christian Lundbye versuchte vergeblich, die Aufgabe des Danewerks noch zu stoppen; de Meza hatte die Telegrafenleitung nach Kopenhagen kappen lassen. In der Hauptstadt drohte die aufgewühlte Volksstimmung in einen Aufruhr umzuschlagen. De Meza wurde abgelöst, obwohl er militärisch richtig gehandelt hatte und von seinen Gegnern

SUPPLEMENT, JAN. 23, 1864 — THE ILLUSTRATED LONDON NEWS — 85

THE SCHLESWIG-HOLSTEIN DIFFICULTY.

THE COMMANDER-IN-CHIEF OF THE DANISH FORCES.

Christian Julius De Meza, who now occupies the important post of Commander-in-Chief of the Danish forces, was born, on Jan. 14, 1792, in Elsineur (or, as the Danes call it, Helsingör), spoken of by Shakspeare in his tragedy of "The Prince of Denmark." By-the-by, it may be here mentioned, as a curious fact, that Hamlet (pronounced Amlet) was a native of Jutland, and that his name in the land of the Jutes signifies "madman."

At the siege of Copenhagen by the English, in 1807, De Meza was made "Stylk-junker" (First Artillery Cadet) in the citadel of Frederickshafen; and later he became teacher in the Artillery Institution and Military High School of Denmark. This post he quitted, in 1842, in order to become Major in one of the artillery corps. At the breaking out of the Revolution, in 1848, De Meza was appointed Commander of the Artillery, in which capacity he distinguished himself at the attacks upon Schleswig, Bau, and other places. In December, 1848, De Meza was made Colonel, and on April 16, 1849, he was nominated Chief of the Artillery as well as of the brigade, consisting of 15,000 men, which the Danish Commander-in-Chief had left in the Isle of Alsen. At the head of this force De Meza took an active part in the battle of Fredericia. On the 1st of January, 1850, he was promoted to the rank of Major-General; but, on account of illness, he was unable to take command at the third fight in Schleswig. Still, being too restive to remain idly at home, he followed the Staff of General Kroghs, with whom he was associated on the 24th and 25th of July, when the news of the misfortune in the fight by Stolk (Isded) arrived. By desire, De Meza at once took the command of the fallen General Schleppegrell's troops, reorganised the scattered divisions, and for the second time led the artillery and columns to the attack of the enemy, and at length completely routed the opposing troops. After the war, De Meza was appointed Inspector of the United Artillery Corps. This post, however, he gave up, and was made commanding General of the forces in Flensburg (Schleswig), Jutland, and Fynen. On the 21st of April, 1860, De Meza became Lieutenant-General.

GENERAL DE MEZA, COMMANDER-IN-CHIEF OF THE DANISH ARMY AT THE DANNEWERK POSITION.

Many of our readers will doubtlessly feel surprised at the oddity of the Portrait of the General here given. This, however, is from a photograph taken in Copenhagen, in which his Excellency appears dressed in the negligé of morning attire rather than decked out in all the splendour of a Commander-in-Chief's uniform. But De Meza, like many a great man, has his peculiarities, and, instead of dazzling the world with the bright shoulder-knots and decorations of military paraphernalia, prefers rather to let himself be recognised in the unostentatious dress of morning civilian life.

Whilst staying in Flensburg our Correspondent happened to put up at the same hotel that General De Meza had previously occupied when officiating as Commander of that city; and during his residence there he heard of many of the peculiarities of the good-natured but eccentric officer. His Excellency occupied the whole of the first floor, consisting of a suite of six rooms, one leading into another; nevertheless, he was accustomed to live in the two end apartments, for he had an especial horror of draughts, so that any-one wishing to see him had to pass through four rooms which were kept duly heated, before being admitted to an audience. How the gallant Commander manages to exclude the cold air in field life it is impossible to explain; but it is said that he insists upon having a series of tents in connection with his own. Despite his oddities, however, every one agrees that De Meza is a right good fellow, and one of the finest Generals that Denmark has seen for many a year.

THE DANNEWERK.

The great fortification of Schleswig which bears the above name, signifying literally the work par excellence of the Danes, consists of an enormous series of earth-banks stretching right across the long narrow peninsula of Schleswig, Holstein, and Jutland. This peninsula is 300 miles long (which is nearly the length of the southern base line of our own triangular island), and in some parts as much as 100 miles in breadth. The extensive fastness itself is situated within a few miles of the southern boundary of the duchy of Schleswig, and stretches close up to the capital from which the duchy derives its

THE SEMICIRCULAR RAMPART AT THE DANNEWERK, NEAR BUSTRUP.

Generalleutnant Christian Julius de Meza (1792–1865), Oberkommandierender der dänischen Truppen am Danewerk

Holzstich aus der »Illustrated London News«, 23. Januar 1864

Kat. 79

De Meza kannte die Schwächen der Danewerk-Stellung, der ersten wichtigen Verteidigungslinie. Der 1861 begonnene Ausbau der alten Befestigungsanlagen war längst nicht abgeschlossen.

Dänische Soldaten retten eine Kanone während des Rückzugs vom Danewerk am 5./6. Februar 1864
Holzstich nach einem Gemälde von Niels Simonsen (1807–1885), 1865
Kat. 81

Anerkennung erntete, die gehofft hatten, das dänische Heer in offener Feldschlacht vernichten zu können. Der von den Angreifern zunächst unbemerkte Rückzug gelang über alle Erwartungen gut, mit Ausnahme eines Rückzugsgefechts gegen österreichische Truppen bei Sankelmark südlich von Flensburg am 6. Februar 1864, das als Schlacht von Oeversee in die österreichische Erinnerung einging.

Die Stellung bei Düppel, die der größte Teil des dänischen Heeres am 7. Februar erreichte, bestand aus zehn nicht fertiggestellten Erdschanzen, verteilt über einen drei Kilometer langen Halbkreis vom Alsensund bis zum Wenningbund. Die Soldaten versuchten unter Hochdruck, die Schanzen weiter auszubauen, zu armieren und Laufgräben anzulegen. Die Anlagen entsprachen jedoch bei Weitem nicht der verbreiteten Vorstellung einer Befestigung vergleichbar dem russischen Sewastopol, das Franzosen und Briten während des Krimkriegs 1854/55 nur unter großen Schwierigkeiten hatten erobern können. Die preußische Führung, die der Propaganda über die Uneinnehmbarkeit der Düppeler Schanzen glaubte, schlug vor, den Krieg auf Jütland auszudehnen, also über die Herzogtümer hinaus aus das Territorium des Königreichs Dänemark. Ein preußischer Regimentschef allerdings handelte wohl noch eigenmächtig, als er am 18. Februar entdeckte, dass die dänischen Truppen das nördlich der Grenze zu Schleswig gelegene Kolding verlassen hatten, und daraufhin die Stadt besetzte. Nach heftiger diplomatischer Aktivität und Protesten der neutralen Großmächte England, Frankreich und Russland gelang es Bismarck am 6. März, Österreich von einer Besetzung ganz Jütlands zu überzeugen, um dadurch die Dänen zu Verhandlungen zu zwingen. Die Österreicher rückten erfolgreich vor, gewannen eine Schlacht bei Vejle und belagerten die Festung von Fredericia.

**»Düppel 18. April 1864.
Schanze VIII. Innere Ansicht«**
Charles Junod (1828–1877), Hamburg
Nach dem 18. April 1864 aufgenommen auf Befehl des Prinzen Friedrich Karl von Preußen
Kat. 100

Dennoch wünschten Österreich und auch Bismarck einen preußischen Angriff auf Düppel, während die dänische Regierung unter Ditlev Gothard Monrad von ihren Truppen forderte, die Stellung bis zum Äußersten zu verteidigen. Beide Seiten wollten mit einem militärischen Erfolg ihre Position auf der bevorstehenden Konferenz in London verbessern; zu dieser sollten sich auf britische Initiative hin am 20. April die Unterzeichnermächte des Londoner Protokolls von 1852 versammeln. Am 18. April griffen die preußischen Truppen nach sechsstündigem schwerem Bombardement schließlich an. Die Schlacht nimmt seither aufgrund des tapferen, doch aussichtslosen dänischen Gegenangriffs einen zentralen Platz in der dänischen Erinnerungskultur ein. Es wäre vernünftiger gewesen, das Heer durch einen Rückzug auf die Insel Alsen intakt zu halten, doch die Regierung hatte dem nicht zugestimmt. Fast die Hälfte der Verteidiger verlor ihr Leben, wurde verletzt oder kam in Kriegsgefangenschaft, insgesamt fast 5 000 Mann, während die preußischen Verluste 1 201 Mann zählten, darunter 938 Verletzte und 263 Gefallene. Obwohl Dänemark zur gleichen Zeit die stärkere Festung in Fredericia räumen musste, zeigten sich die dänischen Vertreter auf der Londoner Konferenz kompromisslos. Aus Angst vor dem Volkszorn und im Glauben an das eigene historische Recht auf ganz Schleswig gingen sie nicht auf einen preußischen Vorschlag ein, der eine Teilung unweit des heutigen Grenzverlaufs in Aussicht stellte.

Sprengung des verschanzten Lagers von Fredericia durch österreichische Einheiten im Mai 1864
August Beck (1823–1872), 1864
Bleistift auf Papier
Kat. 83

Der in Dresden lebende Zeichner August Beck berichtete als »Specialartist« der Leipziger Illustrirten Zeitung über den Krieg.

Übergang nach Alsen am 29. Juni 1864
Ulrich von Salpius (1828–1867), 1864
Aquarell, weiß gehöht, auf blaugetöntem Papier
Kat. 111

Der preußische Gardeoffizier und Kunstsammler Salpius, selbst Kriegsteilnehmer, zeichnete den nächtlichen Übergang. Diese Operation galt neben der Erstürmung der Düppeler Schanzen als zweiter großer preußischer Sieg.

Kostenlose Ausgabe von Pflanzen zur Kultivierung von Heideflächen in Jütland, 1889
Kat. 121

Vortragssaal der Volkshochschule Testrup in Mårslet südlich von Aarhus, ca. 1890er Jahre
Kat. 122

Nach der Niederlage 1864 konzentrierte sich Dänemark auf den inneren Ausbau des Landes. Heidegebiete Jütlands wurden urbar gemacht, flache Fjorde entwässert, die Landwirtschaft genossenschaftlich organisiert. Die Mitte des 19. Jahrhunderts entstandene Volkshochschulbewegung erlebte einen enormen Aufschwung.

Fredrik Bajer (1837–1922) in Uniform
Vor 1865
Kat. 123

Als Berufsoffizier kämpfte Bajer 1864 in Nordjütland. Nach seinem Ausscheiden aus der dänischen Armee 1865 wandte er sich der Friedenspolitik zu. 1872 ins Parlament gewählt, setzte er sich gemeinsam mit seiner Frau Mathilde für Frieden und Frauenrechte ein. Entschieden forderte er die Neutralität Dänemarks nach Schweizer Vorbild. Für sein Engagement als erster Präsident des 1891 gegründeten Internationalen Ständigen Friedensbüros erhielt er 1908 den Friedensnobelpreis.

So wurden die Kampfhandlungen wieder aufgenommen und österreichisch-preußische Truppen rückten bis ins nördliche Jütland vor. Das geschwächte dänische Heer war auf den Inseln Alsen, Fünen und Vendsyssel nördlich des Limfjordes verteilt. Am 29. Juni morgens setzten preußische Truppen auf Alsen über. Der dänische Versuch, den Alsensund mit dem Panzerschiff Rolf Krake zu verteidigen, misslang. Viele Soldaten konnten über See evakuiert werden, aber das Heer war geschlagen. Die Verlustzahlen sprechen für sich: 3 092 Dänen gegenüber 378 Preußen.[3]

Nun gab die nationalliberale Regierung auf und überließ den Friedensschluss ihren konservativen Gegnern. Die Niederlage, die der Frieden von Wien am 30. Oktober 1864 besiegelte, war nicht nur eine militärische, sondern auch ein politische und moralische. Die dänische Monarchie musste die Herzogtümer Schleswig, Holstein und Lauenburg abtreten: Damit verlor sie zwei Fünftel ihres Territoriums und fast ein Drittel ihrer Bevölkerung. Dänemark wurde zu einem national homogenen Kleinstaat im Schatten der aufstrebenden deutschen Großmacht. Es behielt seine Selbstständigkeit nicht aus eigener Kraft, sondern vielmehr, weil die anderen europäischen Großmächte, vor allem Großbritannien und Russland, einen neutralen, nicht zu dominanten Staat am Ostseezugang wünschten. Sonst wäre Dänemark wohl deutsch geworden, oder es wäre als Teil einer »Skandinavischen Union« an Schweden gefallen.

Milchkännchen mit dänischen Flaggen und der Aufschrift »Vergiss mich nicht«
Nach 1864
Kat. 120

Der Danebrog, die dänische Flagge, wurde unter preußischer Verwaltung in Schleswig verboten. Dänischgesinnte Schleswiger fanden trotzdem Wege, ihre Verbundenheit mit Dänemark auszudrücken.

Eine Zeit lang hofften viele Dänen auf Revanche. Doch König Christian IX. und die Regierung beteiligten sich 1870 klugerweise nicht auf französischer Seite am Krieg gegen die deutschen Staaten, sodass Dänemark der Katastrophe entging, die Frankreich Elsass und Lothringen kostete. Der zurückhaltend und vorsichtig agierende König wurde zum »Schwiegervater Europas«, dessen Kinder in regierende europäische Königshäuser einheirateten – ein wichtiger, oft übersehener Faktor für das Überleben des dänischen Staates in der gefährlichen Zeit vor 1914. Außenpolitisch defensiv handelnd, setzte Dänemark ganz auf den inneren Ausbau des Landes. Etwa durch neue Anbauflächen und Verbesserung der Bildung im ländlichen Raum wollte man nach innen gewinnen, was nach außen verloren worden war (vinde indad, hvad udad var tabt). Während sich Dänemark wirtschaftlich am britischen Markt orientierte und gleichzeitig erfolgreich in anderen Teilen der Welt zu investieren begann, blieb der deutsche Einfluss im kulturellen Leben trotz aller Abgrenzung groß.

Der auf französischen Druck hin aufgenommene Artikel 5 des Prager Friedensvertrags vom August 1866 zwischen Preußen und Österreich sah eine Volksabstimmung innerhalb der nächsten sechs Jahre vor, die über eine Vereinigung des überwiegend dänischsprachigen Nordschleswig mit Dänemark entscheiden sollte. Doch Bismarck einigte sich 1878 mit Österreich auf eine Streichung dieses Passus. Dänemark schwenkte – ohne es für die Bevölkerung deutlich zu machen – auf einen Anpassungskurs gegenüber dem deutschen Nachbarn ein, der abfällig auch »deutscher Kurs« (tyskerlinjen) genannt wurde. Das ist der Hintergrund jener »Kleinstaat-Haltung«, die später als Ausdruck des dänischen Nationalcharakters aufgefasst worden ist.

Die Wunde von 1864 saß tief. Die deutschsprachige holsteinische Elite, die im ehemaligen dänischen Gesamtstaat großen Einfluss ausgeübt hatte, war gezwungen, entweder die Verbindung zu Dänemark abzubrechen oder dänisch zu werden. Gleichzeitig waren dänischsprachige Menschen in Schleswig zu einer nationalen Minderheit im Deutschen Reich geworden. Letzteres führte in den abgetretenen Gebieten, anders als im Königreich, zunächst nicht zu einer nationalen Mobilisierung. Die preußische Verwaltung in den Herzogtümern interessierte sich vorerst kaum für nationale Fragen. Oberpräsident Carl von Scheel-Plessen – ein Holsteiner, der zuvor in dänischen Diensten gestanden hatte – war zufrieden, solange die dänischen Bauern es hinnahmen, unter preußischem Gesetz zu leben, und ausreichend Deutsch verstanden, um das Alltagsleben zu meistern. Folglich riet er davon ab, Deutsch verpflichtend als einzige Schulsprache einzuführen. Dazu kam es erst 1888. Wie die polnische galt auch die dänische Minderheit zunehmend als ein Fremdkörper im neuen deutschen Staat, den es »einzudeutschen« galt. Als Reaktion darauf begann die dänische Minderheit in Nordschleswig um 1890, sich politisch zu organisieren.

Ein Großteil der Bevölkerung in Schleswig war vor den Kriegen 1848 bis 1851 und 1864 zwar im sprachlichen, jedoch nicht im modernen nationalpolitischen Verständnis dänisch oder deutsch gewesen. Ein Sprachwechsel erfolgte meist unauffällig über einen längeren Zeitraum, wie etwa bei den ursprünglich Südjütisch, einen dänischen Dialekt, sprechenden Grundbesitzern in Nordschleswig, die später den Kern der deutschen Minderheit bilden sollten. Erst die Abgrenzung gegenüber den Germanisierungsversuchen durch eine verschärfte Sprachenpolitik Ende des 19. Jahrhunderts machte die Mehrheit der Nordschleswiger (Sønderjyder) zu Dänen im politischen Sinn. Mit dem allmählichen Sieg des nationalstaatlichen Prinzips wurde es unmöglich, die Sprache zu wechseln, ohne dabei die eigene Identität aufzugeben. Die berühmte »südjütländische Kaffeetafel«, zu der sich Dänischgesinnte trafen, da sie ihre Versammlungen nicht öffentlich in Gasthäusern abhalten durften, hat hier ihren Ursprung.[4]

Die Volksabstimmungen von 1920 machten einen Teil der Gebietsverluste von 1864 rückgängig und legten den bis heute gültigen Grenzverlauf fest, der ungefähr der Sprachgrenze entspricht. Schleswig oder Sønderjylland – beide Namen stammen aus dem Mittelalter – wurde geteilt, in das deutsche Südschleswig und jenes dänische Gebiet, das bis zur Schaffung von »Sønderjyllands Amt« 1970 die »südjütländischen Landesteile« (sønderjyske landsdele) genannt wurde. Dänemark feierte die Volksabstimmungen als große Wiedervereinigung. Erst jetzt war der Krieg von 1864 aus Sicht vieler Dänen und Däninnen wirklich beendet.

»Stem Dig Hjem« / Stimm Dich heim!
Plakat, 1920
Kat. 124

Im Ersten Weltkrieg war Dänemark neutral geblieben. Infolge des Versailler Friedensvertrags kam es jedoch 1920 zu den lange geforderten Volksabstimmungen über die staatliche Zugehörigkeit Schleswigs. Die neue, noch heute gültige Grenze trennte überwiegend deutschsprachige von überwiegend dänischsprachigen Gebieten.

Rückzug dänischer Streitkräfte aus Afghanistan

Karikatur von Roald Als (geb. 1948)
für die dänische Tageszeitung »Politiken«
vom 21. Juli 2013
Signierter Computerausdruck, 2020
Kat. 125

Nach der Erfahrung der deutschen Besatzung im Zweiten Weltkrieg gab Dänemark seine Neutralität auf. Es trat der NATO bei und unterstützte UN-Missionen. Als letzter herkömmlicher Krieg, den das Land führte, ist der Konflikt 1864 bis heute ein wichtiger Bezugspunkt. Die Karikatur zitiert das Gemälde »Rückzug vom Danewerk« des dänischen Malers Niels Simonsen aus dem Jahr 1865 (siehe zum Vergleich den Holzstich S. 79, Kat. 81). Die Soldaten haben die Gesichter von Politikern, die für den Einsatz dänischer Truppen in Afghanistan stimmten.

Langfristig gesehen, begann mit 1864 ein Weg, der Dänemarks Selbstverständnis als kleines, friedliches Land mit einem dauerhaften Misstrauen gegen Heroismus und große Worte ebenso begründete wie eine Skepsis gegenüber Minderheiten und das distanzierte Verhältnis zu Deutschland und zu Europa. Unterdessen wurde Deutschland groß, verlor zwei Weltkriege und hatte die nationalsozialistische Barbarei zu verantworten. Vielsagend ist, dass dem ersten sozialdemokratischen Premierminister Dänemarks, Thorvald Stauning, am 30. Januar 1933, dem Tag, als Hitler an die Macht kam, ein bahnbrechender Kompromiss mit der Opposition gelang. Dieser Kompromiss begründete den demokratischen Wohlfahrtsstaat, der die deutsche Besatzung von 1940 bis 1945 überlebte. 1955 bestätigten die Bonn-Kopenhagener Erklärungen die Grenze von 1920 und erlangten Modellcharakter für die friedliche Lösung von Minderheitenfragen. Obwohl Deutschland nach der Wiedervereinigung im Jahr 1990 erneut einen dominanten Platz in der Mitte Europas einnimmt, scheint in Dänemark wohlwollende Unkenntnis an die Stelle der traditionellen Abneigung gegen Deutschland getreten zu sein. Die packend-realistische Darstellung »Schlachtbank Düppel«,[5] die der dänische Autor Tom Buk-Swienty 2008 veröffentlichte, wurde trotzdem ein Bestseller und zur Vorlage der umstrittenen achtteiligen TV-Serie »1864«[6] – Dänemarks bisher teuerster Fernsehproduktion. 2014, im Jahr der 150. Wiederkehr des Krieges, schlug sie einen Bogen von 1864 bis zum NATO-Einsatz dänischer Truppen in Afghanistan und brachte den Deutsch-Dänischen Krieg zurück ins kollektive Gedächtnis. Wie immer man die Bedeutung dieses Krieges für die Gegenwart in beiden Ländern beurteilen mag: Es ist wichtig, die gemeinsame Geschichte zu kennen.

1 Von Uffe Østergård liegen zahlreiche Publikationen über das dänische Selbstverständnis und die deutsch-dänischen Beziehungen vor. Vgl. bes.: Den Slesvigske lære (interview ved Arne Hardis), in: Weekendavisen 1. 2. 2019, S. 5; Hvem er tyskerne? De tyske og de nordiske lande i Europa, in: Rasmus Mariager/Niklas Olsen (Hg.): Venskab og fjendskab. Danmark og Tyskland i det 19. og 20. århundrede. Festschrift für Karl Christian Lammers, Kopenhagen 2018, S. 30–57; Danmark – småstat, imperium og kolonimagt, in: Danmark og kolonierne. Danmark en Kolonimagt, Bd. 1, hg. von Mikkel Vedborg Pedersen, Kopenhagen 2017, S. 13–57; Nation-Building and Nationalism in the Oldenburg Empire, in: Stefan Berger/Alexei Miller (Hg.): Nationalizing Empires, Budapest/New York 2015, S. 461–510; Nederlaget i 1864 i dansk og europæisk erindring, in: Lars Bangert Struwe/Mikkel Vedby Rasmussen (Hg.): Læren af 1864. Krig, politik og stat i Danmark i 150 år, Odense 2014, 129–147; Schleswig and Holstein in Danish and German Historiography, in: Disputed Territories and Shared Pasts. Overlapping National Histories in Modern Europe. Writing the Nation. National Historiographies and the Making of Nation States in 19th and 20th Century Europe, Bd. 6, hg. von Tibor Frank/Frank Hadler, Houndsmill 2011, S. 200–223; 1864 i dansk og tysk historie, in: Carsten Jahnke/Jes Fabricius Møller (Hg.): 1864 og historiens lange skygger. Den dansk-østrigsk-preussiske krig og dens betydning i dag / 1864 und der lange Schatten der Geschichte. Der österreichisch-dänisch-preußische Krieg und seine Gegenwartsbedeutung, Husum 2011, S. 27–42; En røvet datter dybt begrædt. 1864 i perspektiv, in: Jakob Kidde Sauntved/Jakob Eberhardt (Hg.): 1864, Århus 2007, S. 10–23; Feindbilder und Vorurteile in der dänischen Öffentlichkeit, in: Günter Trautmann (Hg.): Die hässlichen Deutschen?, Darmstadt 1991, S. 145–166. Zu dieser Thematik vgl. auch Steen Bo Frandsen: Danmark og Tyskland. Et naboskab i Europa (erscheint 2020); Rasmus Glenthøj: 1864. Sønner af de slagne, Kopenhagen 2016; Inge Adriansen: Dansk og tysk spejlet i hinanden, in: Uffe Østergård (Hg.): Dansk identitet?, Århus 1992. **2** Vgl. Michael Bregnsbo/Kurt Villads Jensen: Det danske imperium – storhed og fald, Kopenhagen 2004; Steen Bo Frandsen: Holsten i helstaten. Holsten inden og uden for det danske monarki i første halvdel af 1800-tallet, Kopenhagen 2008. **3** Vgl. u. a. Johs. Nielsen: Den dansk-tyske krig 1864, Ausst.-Kat. Tøjhusmuseet, Kopenhagen 1991; ders.: 1864 – Da Europa gik af lave, Odense 1987. **4** Vgl. bes. Gottlieb Japsen: Statspatriotisme og nationalfølelse i Sønderjylland før 1848, in: Historie 1979, S. 107–122; ders.: Den fejlslagne germanisering: Den tyske forening for det nordlige Slesvig. Bidrag til det tyske mindretals historie efter 1864, Åbenrå 1983. **5** Tom Buk-Swienty: Slagtebænk Dybbøl, Kopenhagen 2008 (dt.: Schlachtbank Düppel, 18. April 1864. Die Geschichte einer Schlacht, Osburg, Berlin 2011). **6** Drehbuch und Regie: Ole Bornedal. Deutsche Erstausstrahlung am 11. 6. 2015 auf Arte.

Kampf um die Vorzeit

Mit einem wachsenden Nationalbewusstsein ging in vielen europäischen Staaten am 19. Jahrhundert auch ein besonderes Interesse an Geschichte einher. Je weiter sich die Entwicklung des eigenen Volkes in eine geheimnisvolle, sagenumwobene Vorzeit zurückverfolgen ließ, desto berechtigter erschienen die Ansprüche und Selbstbilder der jeweiligen Nationalbewegungen. Gefördert vom dänischen König Frederik VII. gelangen dem in Kopenhagen geborenen und in Flensburg als Lehrer tätigem Archäologen Conrad Engelhardt (1825–1881) zwischen 1852 und 1864 spektakuläre Funde im Thorsberger und im Nydam-Moor. Letzteres lag nur wenige Kilometer nördlich der Düppeler Schanzen. Während des Krieges 1864 schaffte Engelhardt den beweglichen Teil dieser archäologischen Sammlung nach Seeland. Preußische Offiziere und Museumsleute unternahmen teils noch in Kriegszeiten eigene Grabungen im Nydam-Moor, selbst Prinz Friedrich Karl, Oberkommandierender der alliierten Truppen, widmete sich archäologischen Studien. Im Wiener Friedensvertrag von 1864 war eigens die Rückführung der zerstreuten »Antikensammlung« nach Schleswig gefordert (Artikel XIV), was allerdings nur zögerlich und nie vollständig geschah. (Angelika Abegg-Wigg: Das Nydamboot – versenkt – entdeckt – erforscht, Schleswig 2014; Stine Wiell: Thorsberg und Nydam: Zwei berühmte Moorfunde aus forschungsgeschichtlicher Perspektive, in: Archäologische Nachrichten aus Schleswig-Holstein, 1998/99, H. 9/10, S. 139–158; Stine Wiell: Der Kampf um die Vorgeschichte – nationale Altertümer seit 1864, Abenraa 2000)

Kat. 62

»Aufgefundenes Schiff aus dem Nydammer Moor in Schleswig«

Das sogenannte Nydamboot auf dem Dachboden des Flensburger Gerichtsgebäudes
Holzstich von Ludwig Burger aus einer illustrierten Zeitung
Kat. 62

Unter Engelhardts Funden wurde vor allem ein über 20 Meter langes Eichenboot aus der Zeit um 320 n. Chr. bekannt. Es war 1863 im Nydam-Moor ausgegraben und nach Flensburg gebracht worden. Schon aufgrund seiner Größe blieb das Nydamboot 1864 im Herzogtum Schleswig, aber Dänemark forderte noch 1945 seine Auslieferung. Heute ist es im Archäologischen Landesmuseum in Schleswig ausgestellt, war aber 2003/04 während einer Sonderausstellung im Kopenhagener Nationalmuseum zu sehen.

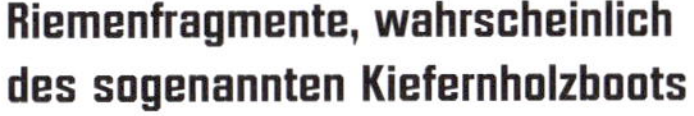

Riemenfragmente, wahrscheinlich des sogenannten Kiefernholzboots

Nydam-Moor, um 300 n. Chr.
Ahornholz, ca. 5 × 20 cm
Kat. 63

1863 wurde im Nydan-Moor auch ein Kiefernholzboot freigelegt, das jedoch aufgrund der Kriegswirren 1864 nicht sachgemäß geborgen werden konnte. Daher sind nur Fragmente erhalten.

Kat. 63

Schwertriemenhalter, gefunden in Grube 21

2. Hälfte 4. Jahrhundert n. Chr.
Kupferlegierung, 12,6 × 11 cm
Kat. 64

Kat. 64

Lanzenspitze

Mitte 3. Jahrhundert n. Chr.
Eisen, 3,1 × 26,5 cm
Kat. 65

Kat. 65

Von der Bundesexekution zu Bismarcks Krieg

Unter Sachsens Oberbefehl besetzten neben sächsischen Truppen auch Hannoveraner, Preußen und Österreicher ab dem 23. Dezember 1863 kampflos die zum Deutschen Bund gehörigen Herzogtümer Holstein und Lauenburg. Diese »Bundesexekution« war eine Reaktion auf die neue dänische Verfassung, die als Verstoß eines Bundesmitglieds, des dänischen Königs, gegen Bundesrecht betrachtet wurde. Als preußische und österreichische Truppen am 1. Februar 1864 in Schleswig einrückten, dauerte die Bundesexekution zwar an, doch für den Kriegsverlauf spielten sächsische und hannoversche Truppen keine Rolle. Gegen den Willen vieler deutscher Klein- und Mittelstaaten führten Preußen und Österreich den Krieg gegen Dänemark allein – ohne den Deutschen Bund. Der preußische Ministerpräsident Otto von Bismarck berief sich auf das Londoner Protokoll und erhob zunächst keine weiteren Ansprüche. Auf diese Weise konnte er Österreich zu einer gemeinsamen Intervention bewegen und das Eingreifen der anderen europäischen Großmächte verhindern. Gleichzeitig gewann er gegenüber der deutschen Nationalbewegung die Initiative zurück.

Kat. 68

Kat. 71

»Mein Recht ist Eure Rettung!«
Gedenkblatt auf die Proklamation Herzog Friedrichs VIII. von Schleswig-Holstein
P. Grosenich, Hamburg 1863
Lithografie
Kat. 68

Der letzte dänische Monarch der älteren Oldenburger Königslinie war ohne Nachkommen gestorben. Das Londoner Protokoll von 1852 sah vor, dass ein Zweig der Glücksburger Nebenlinie das Herzogtum Schleswig weiter in Personalunion regieren sollte. Doch auch Friedrich von Schleswig-Holstein-Sonderburg-Augustenburg (1829–1880) erhob Ansprüche darauf. Die deutsche Nationalbewegung unterstützte ihn begeistert, da dies die Trennung Schleswigs von Dänemark bedeutet hätte. Ende 1863 zog er in Kiel ein und ließ sich als Herzog huldigen, konnte seine Forderungen aber letztlich nicht durchsetzen.

Einzug sächsischer Exekutionstruppen in Altona unter dem Jubel der Bevölkerung am 24. Dezember 1863
August Beck (1823–1872), 1864
Bleistift auf Papier
Kat. 71

Der in Dresden lebende Zeichner August Beck folgte im Auftrag der Leipziger »Illustrirten Zeitung« den sächsischen Truppen nach Holstein.

Bataillonswagen des Königlich Sächsischen 4. Jäger-Bataillons mit Bataillonsarzt Dr. Reichel und Oberleutnant Lehmann, Wirtschaftsoffizier, nebst Trainsoldat und Offiziersdienern, 1864
Kat. 72

Strandbatterie in Neustadt/Holstein, 7. Batterie des Königlich Sächsischen Fußartillerie-Regiments, 1864
Kat. 73

Batterien wie diese schützten die Küste vor Angriffen dänischer Schiffe.

Kat. 72

Kat. 73

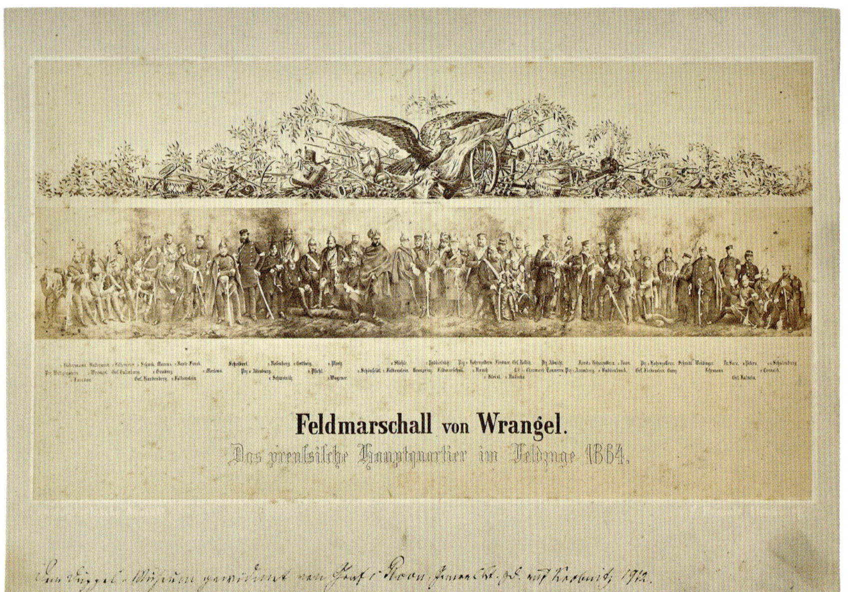

Kat. 74

Kat. 75

Generalfeldmarschall Friedrich von Wrangel (1784–1877) und das preußische Hauptquartier

Photographische Anstalt von Friedrich Brandt, Flensburg 1864
Fotomontage
Kat. 74

Feldmarschallleutnant Ludwig von Gablenz (1814–1874) und das österreichische Hauptquartier

Photographische Anstalt von Friedrich Brandt, Flensburg 1864
Kat. 75

»In Gottes Namen – drauf!«, befahl der preußische Generalfeldmarschall von Wrangel. Preußische und österreichische Truppen rückten unter seinem Oberbefehl ab dem 1. Februar 1864 im Herzogtum Schleswig ein. Das gemeinsame Erkennungszeichen war eine weiße Armbinde. Nach der Einnahme des Danewerks am 6. Februar wandten sich die Österreicher und zunächst auch die preußischen Garden nach Norden. Das Gros der Preußen marschierte nordostwärts zur stark befestigten Düppel-Stellung.

Generalleutnant Helmuth von Moltke (1800–1891)

Carte-de-Visite-Fotografie, 1864
Kat. 76

Moltke war in Dänemark aufgewachsen und hatte dort seine militärische Karriere begonnen. 1822 zur preußischen Armee gewechselt, wurde er 1857 Generalstabschef. 1864 kam er zunächst kaum zum Zug. Die Vorbereitungen lagen weitgehend beim Kriegsministerium; der 80-jährige Wrangel konnte mit Moltkes Planungen wenig anfangen. Erst am 30. April wurde Moltke mit den Geschäften des Stabschefs der verbündeten Armeen beauftragt.

Kat. 76

Prinz Friedrich Karl von Preußen (1828–1885) als Oberstinhaber des österreichischen Husarenregiments Nr. 7

Carte-de-Visite-Fotografie, 1864
Kat. 77

Der Neffe Wilhelms I. führte im Krieg gegen Dänemark zunächst nur die preußischen Truppen. Als Wrangel Mitte Mai als Oberkommandierender der alliierten Truppen abgelöst wurde, weil er politische Anweisungen ignorierte und der Lage nur noch bedingt gewachsen war, wurde der Prinz sein Nachfolger.

Kat. 77

»Die Schleswig-Holsteinische Volksversammlung zu Rendsburg am 8. Mai 1864«

Johann Friedrich Fritz (1798–1870)
Lithografie
Kat. 110

»Up ewig ungedeelt« – dieser Passus aus dem Rippener Vertrag von 1460 war das Motto der Schleswig-Holsteiner. Schützen-, Turn- und andere Vereine kämpften für ein selbstständiges, von Dänemark unabhängiges Land. Während der Londoner Konferenz forderten sie die Loslösung von Dänemark. Gleichzeitig wuchs die Sorge, der Krieg werde nicht für, sondern um Schleswig-Holstein geführt. Kein Vertreter der Herzogtümer war zur Konferenz eingeladen, der französische Vorschlag einer Volksabstimmung konnte sich nicht durchsetzen.

Kat. 110

»Schlachtbank Düppel«

Am 18. April 1864 erstürmten preußische Truppen die Befestigungsanlagen auf der Halbinsel Sundewitt, die einen Übergang zur strategisch wichtigen Insel Alsen sicherten. Vorausgegangen war ein fünfwöchiger Stellungskrieg mit Anlage eines Grabensystems und massivem Beschuss, bei dem erstmals Geschütze mit gezogenen Stahlrohren der Firma Krupp zum Einsatz kamen. Die dänische Armee erlitt bei der Verteidigung der Düppeler Schanzen eine blutige Niederlage. Ihre Verluste waren mit 4 894 Mann, darunter 898 Toten, fast viermal so hoch wie die der Angreifer (1 201, darunter 263 Tote). Kurz vor Beginn einer internationalen Konferenz in London, die den Konflikt mit diplomatischen Mitteln beenden sollte, war dieser Sieg für Preußen besonders wichtig.

Kat. 85

Belagerungsplan der Düppeler Schanzen
Pietsch, Feuerwerker in der preußischen 4. Artilleriebrigade und Zeichner bei der kombinierten Artilleriebrigade des 1. preußisch kombinierten Armeekorps für Schleswig-Holstein
Berlin, um 1864
Kat. 84

In den Laufgräben vor Düppel
Adolf Northen (1828–1876), 1867
Öl auf Leinwand, 59 × 95,5 cm
Kat. 85

Northen bereiste 1864 die Schlachtfelder. Das Gemälde zeigt eine Szene aus dem Grabenkampf vor der Erstürmung der Düppeler Schanzen. Soldaten hatten Tausende Schanzkörbe geflochten. Beim Anlegen der Gräben wurden die Körbe mit dem ausgehobenen Sand gefüllt. So sollten sie die Soldaten bereits beim Graben vor gegnerischem Feuer schützen.

Belagerungs Plan der
DÜPPELER SCHANZEN
mit zu Grundelegung der Dänischen Generalstabskarte
aufgenommen und gezeichnet
von
PIETZSCH
Armirungs-Tabelle
Zeichen-Erklärung.
Die Grundrisse der Düppeler Schanzen vor ihrer Belagerung.
Maassstab = 1 : 10,000.
Wenningbund
SONDERBURG
Düppel
Wester Düppel
Oster Düppel
Rackebüll
Sandberg
Kjärwig
Alsen Sund
Sottrup
Surlücke
Mölle
Stengaard
Lille Mölle
Batterup
Ravenskoppel
Staugaard
Kandsad
Fiskebaekgaard
Frydendal
Mölleskovgaard
Ringbaek
Lindegaard
Engeshoj
Baadsager
Lysmosegaard
Ladegaard
Langbro
Düppelstein
Schmiede
Düppel Mühle
Hörlyk
Sucy
Wilhoj
Wenningwedt
Düppellund
Steenbeck
Spitz Berg
Frydendal Kr.
Frydendal Schlucht
Kirche
Pfarre
Schule
Potsdam
Krug
von Flensburg
Büffel Koppel
Stendeuper
Holz
Sallingshoved
Ziegelei
Willersholm
Gammelmark
Wenning
Schloss
I.
II.
III.
IV.
V.
VI.
VII.
VIII.
IX.
X.

Kat. 84

Spatenblatt
Bodenfund an den Düppeler Schanzen
Kat. 88

Faschinenmesser M 1855 mit Sägerücken, wie es preußische Pioniere 1864 bei Düppel verwendeten
Kat. 89

Sprenggranate mit Bleimantel für 12-Pfünder-Feldgeschütze
Kat. 86

Sprengstücke von Granaten für 6-, 12- und 24-Pfünder-Feldgeschütze
Bodenfunde an den Düppeler Schanzen
Kat. 87

Bei der Belagerung von Düppel setzte Preußen moderne Hinterladergeschütze mit gezogenen Rohren ein. Sie besaßen eine höhere Reichweite und Treffgenauigkeit als ältere Rohre. So konnten preußische Batterien die Schanzen nicht nur frontal unter Beschuss nehmen, sondern von der Halbinsel Broacker über den Wenningbund hinweg auch ihre Südflanke erreichen. Die Strandbatterien bedrohten vor allem den Schiffsverkehr im Alsensund und selbst die auf Alsen liegende Stadt Sonderburg.

Kat. 89

Kat. 88

Feldflasche eines dänischen Soldaten
Kat. 90

In ruhigen Phasen des Grabenkriegs herrschte zwischen deutschen und dänischen Soldaten reger Austausch. Dänische Feldflaschen sollen bei Preußen besonders beliebt gewesen sein. Denn im preußischen Heer wurden diese elementaren Ausrüstungsstücke erst 1867 eingeführt. Nur Krankenträger führten schon vorher regulär »Labeflaschen« mit sich.

Kat. 86

Kat. 87

»Prost, Danske!«
Ein preußischer und ein dänischer Soldat trinken zusammen

Wilhelm Camphausen (1818–1885), 1864
Bleistift auf Transparentpapier, 12 × 10 cm
Kat. 93

Camphausen schrieb in seinem Erlebnisbericht »Ein Maler auf dem Kriegsfelde«: »Bis zu den letzten Tagen vor dem Sturm galt [...] unter den gegenseitigen Vorposten das stillschweigende Abkommen der Menschlichkeit, nicht einzeln aufeinander zu schießen, ja es kam vor, daß Offiziere und Gemeine zueinander hinüber und herüber kamen und einen Trunk aus der Feldflasche miteinander wechselten.«

Kat. 90

Kat. 93

»Gade i Sönderborg under Bombardementet« / Eine Straße in Sonderburg unter Bombardement

Carl Frederik Aagaard (1833–1895)
Lithografie
Kat. 96

Am 15. März 1864 beschossen preußische Batterien erstmals Sonderburg. Trotz des geringen materiellen Schadens löste der Beschuss Entsetzen aus, da die Einwohner und Einwohnerinnen nicht damit gerechnet hatten, dass ihre Stadt in Reichweite der gegnerischen Artillerie lag. Vom 2. April an wurde Sonderburg gezielt in Brand geschossen, viele Menschen flohen. Nach zeitgenössischen Berichten wurden zwei Menschen getötet und 20 verwundet.

Kat. 96

Kat. 104

Prinz Friedrich Karl und sein Stab vor der Düppeler Mühle

Heinrich Graf (1835–1906) oder sein Mitarbeiter Adolf Halwas, beide Berlin, nach dem 18. April 1864
Kat. 104

Vierter von rechts ist Prinz Friedrich Karl von Preußen. Die Mühle war einige Tage vor dem Sturmangriff unter dem Beschuss der preußischen Artillerie zusammengestürzt. Sie war einer der wenigen markanten Orientierungspunkte in der Gegend und diente den Dänen als Beobachtungs- und Telegrafenstation. Sowohl während der Schleswig-Holsteinischen Erhebung 1849 wie auch 1864 zerstört und wieder aufgebaut, wurde die Mühle zum dänischen Nationalsymbol.

DÜPPEL

18. APRIL 1864

SCHANZE IV EINGANG

Kat. 98

Kat. 99

»Düppel 18. April 1864. Schanze IV. Eingang«

Charles Junod (1828–1877), Hamburg, nach dem 18. April 1864

Kat. 98

Der gebürtige Schweizer Junod fotografierte die Düppeler Schanzen im Auftrag des preußischen Prinzen Friedrich Karl. Die Leichname der Gefallenen waren zu diesem Zeitpunkt bereits weggeschafft worden. Die auf Karton aufgezogenen Fotos wurden zwar mit »Düppel 18. April 1864« betitelt, sind aber erst in den Tagen nach der Schlacht entstanden.

»Düppel 18. April 1864. Schanze IV. Innere Ansicht mit dem Blockhaus«

Charles Junod, Hamburg, nach dem 18. April 1864

Kat. 99

Kat. 105

Betontrümmer des zersprengten Pulvermagazins auf Schanze VI

Heinrich Graf oder sein Mitarbeiter Adolf Halwas, beide Berlin, nach dem 18. April 1864

Kat. 105

Kriegshospital des Johanniterordens in Wester Schnabek bei Ulderup

Kat. 106

1864 waren erstmals internationale Beobachter und freiwillige Helferinnen und Helfer im Sinne der Rotkreuzbewegung im Einsatz. Das Kriegshospital des Johanniterordens lag etwa zehn Kilometer nordwestlich der Düppeler Schanzen.

Kat. 106

Rathaus und Apotheke in Sonderburg

Charles Junod, Hamburg, nach dem Übergang nach Alsen am 29. Juni 1864
Kat. 103

Kat. 103/1

Kat. 103/2

Die Überlegenheit der dänischen Flotte hatte auf den Kriegsverlauf keinen wesentlichen Einfluss. Kapitän zur See Eduard von Jachmann führte die preußischen Marineeinheiten in der Ostsee, Linienschiffskapitän Tegetthoff ein österreichisches und ein kleines preußisches Geschwader in der Nordsee. Dort fand am 9. Mai bei Helgoland das einzige größere Seegefecht statt, das beide Seiten als Sieg für sich reklamierten. Tegetthoff, aber auch Jachmann wurden noch im Krieg zum Konteradmiral befördert. Bleibenden Eindruck hinterließ das damals hochmoderne dänische Turmschiff »Rolf Krake«, obwohl es kaum wirksam zum Einsatz kam. Noch Theodor Fontane lässt in seinem Roman »Der Stechlin« (1898) mit Schulze Kluckhuhn einen Veteranen von 1864 auftreten, für den die »Rolf Krake« Synonym für alles Unheilvolle, Bedrohliche ist, insbesondere für die Sozialdemokratie.

Turmschiff »Rolf Krake«
Modell 1:50, angefertigt von der Marinestation Sonderburg für die Düppel-Gedächtnisausstellung in der Exerzierhalle bei Schloss Sonderburg 1914
Kat. 107

Die »Rolf Krake« war das modernste Kriegsschiff der dänischen Marine – gepanzert und mit Geschützen in drehbaren Pivottürmen, 56 Meter lang, 12 Meter breit und mit etwa 3,5 Meter Tiefgang. Gebaut von der Glasgower Werft Robert Napier & Sons, lief sie 1863 vom Stapel. Wegen ihres geringen Tiefgangs eignete sie sich besonders für küstennahe Operationen. Der Auftrag für dieses Schiff war auch eine Folge des Gefechts bei Eckernförde 1849, das die Verwundbarkeit der Flotte durch Beschuss von Land aus gezeigt hatte. Allein der ungewohnte Anblick und der legendäre Ruf der »Rolf Krake« verbreiteten Angst und Schrecken unter den Preußen. Doch obwohl das Schiff dem massiven Beschuss weitgehend standhielt, konnte es weder wirksam in die Kämpfe bei Düppel eingreifen noch den Übergang preußischer Truppen nach Alsen verhindern.

Kat. 107

Kat. 108

Kat. 109

Das für die große deutsche Gedächtnisausstellung zum 50. Jahrestag Düppels angefertigte Modell zeigt abweichend vom Original nur ein Geschütz pro Turm. 1864 war das Schiff pro Turm mit je zwei 60-Pfünder-Vorderladergeschützen mit glatten Rohren ausgerüstet.

Die Mannschaft des preußischen Flaggschiffs SMS Arcona, 1864
Kat. 108

Der österreichische Konteradmiral Wilhelm von Tegetthoff (1827–1871) auf dem Flaggschiff SMS Schwarzenberg, 1864
Kat. 109

Helden, Löwen, Siegeshymnen

»[...] der Tag von Düppel bleibt ein unverlöschliches Ruhmesblatt in der Geschichte Preußens und Deutschlands; wir wagen jetzt auch zu hoffen, daß er die ersehnten Früchte tragen, daß die Tausende und Abertausende von Opfern, die ihm fallen mußten, der gerechten Sache, der Freiheit und dem Vaterlande, nicht einem volksfeindlichen Systeme und exclusiven Militär- und Junkertendenzen, zu Gute kommen werden«.

(Der Tag von Düppel. Nach den Mittheilungen eines preußischen Officiers, in: Die Gartenlaube, 1864, Nr. 24, S. 383)

Am Abend nach der Erstürmung der Düppeler Schanzen notierte der preußische Unteroffizier Gustav Schade im preußischen Hauptquartier Schloss Gravenstein: »Der 18e Ap. 1864 ist ein Tag, wie die preußische Armee seit dem 18e Juni 1815 nicht erlebt hat« (siehe S. 390, Kat. 91). Indem er das Ereignis mit dem Sieg über Napoleon I. in der Schlacht bei Waterloo verglich, betonte er die große Bedeutung für das preußische Selbstbewusstsein. Kinder lernten später im Kaiserreich den Merkspruch: »Ohne Düppel kein Königgrätz, ohne Königgrätz kein Sedan, ohne Sedan kein deutsches Kaiserreich!« Nach der Niederlage Dänemarks 1864 stimmte selbst das liberal gesinnte illustrierte Familienblatt »Die Gartenlaube« vorsichtig in die allgemeine Siegesbegeisterung ein. Eine vielfältige Erinnerungskultur entwickelte sich, blieb jedoch nicht ohne Kritik.

Kat. 112

Zum Gedächtniss
der am 18. April 1864
gefallenen
Königlich Preussischen
Pioniere.
Hier fiel der Pionier
KLINKE.

Kat. 113

Kat. 115

»Pionier Klinke öffnet der Sturmkolonne den Weg zur Schanze II, am 18. April 1864«
Postkarte, Sonderburg
Kat. 112

Tafel für Carl Klinke (1840–1864) vom Gedenkstein für die bei Düppel gefallenen preußischen Pioniere
Kat. 113

Klinke starb, als eine Öffnung in den Palisadenzaun von Schanze II gesprengt wurde. Dass er selbst die Sprengung vornahm und sich bewusst opferte, um für die stürmenden Preußen den Weg frei zu machen, ist zweifelhaft. Dem Aufstieg des einfachen Soldaten zum Kriegshelden tat dies aber keinen Abbruch. Im Mai 1945 fand ein Angehöriger der deutschen Minderheit in Nordschleswig die zerschlagene Tafel und verwahrte sie zu Hause.

Offizierdegen, graviert zur Erinnerung an die Aufpflanzung der ersten preußischen Sturmfahne auf den Düppeler Schanzen
Königreich Preußen
Kat. 115

»Aufgefundener Degen«
Suchanzeige im »Militair-Wochenblatt« vom 25. April 1871, Nr. 62, S. 407
Kat. 114

In der militärischen Fachzeitschrift »Militair-Wochenblatt« wurde 1871 der Fund eines Degens auf dem Schlachtfeld von Wörth inseriert. Es könnte sich um diesen oder einen ähnlichen Degen gehandelt haben.

Nr. 62. Militair-Wochenblatt. 407

Aufgefundener Degen.

Auf dem Schlachtfelde von Wörth hat ein Unteroffizier des unten genannten Bataillons, welcher später geblieben ist, einen Degen gefunden, auf dessen Klinge die Worte eingravirt sind:

„Für das Aufpflanzen der ersten Preußischen Fahne auf den erstürmten Düppeler Schanzen am 18. April 1864."

Da sich vermuthen läßt, daß dieser Degen einem bei Wörth gefallenen Preußischen Offizier gehört hat, so werden die Angehörigen desselben, welche in den Besitz des Degens zu gelangen wünschen, ersucht, sich an das unterzeichnete Kommando zu wenden.

K.-Q. Montbéliard, den 25. April 1871.

Königliches Kommando des Füsilier-Bataillons 3. Niederschlesischen Infanterie-Regiments Nr. 50.
v. Sperling,
Oberstlieutenant und Bataillons-Kommandeur.

Kat. 114

Erinnerung
an die
Einzugsfeier in Berlin
am 7. December 1864.

Wer kommt? wer? —
Fünf Regimenter von Düppel her.
Fünf Regimenter vom dritten Corps
Rücken durch's Brandenburger Thor;
Prinz Friedrich Carl, Wrangel, Manstein,
General Roeder, General Canstein,
Fünf Regimenter, — vom Sundewitt
Rücken sie an in Schritt und Tritt.

Wer kommt? wer? —
Zuerst die Achter. A la bonne heure!
Die Achter; Hut ab, Sapperment,
Hut ab vor dem Leibregiment;
Was sich Vater York nicht scheute,
Können wir auch, müssen wir heute.
Schanze Neun und Schanze Drei
Waren keine Spielerei.
Hut ab und Hurrah ohne End',
Allemal hoch das Leibregiment! —

Wer kommt? wer? —
Hurrah, die Vierundzwanziger.
Guten Tag, guten Tag, ganz gehorsamst Ihr Diener!
Hurrah, das sind ja meine Ruppiner;
Flinke Kerle, ohne Flattusen,
Grüß Gott Dich, Görschen und Brockhusen!
Möchte Manchen von Euch umhalsen,
Düppel war gut, besser war Alsen, —
's war keine Kunst, Euch half ja die Fee,
Die Wasserfee vom Ruppiner See.

Wer kommt? wer? —
Hurrah, die Vierundsechsziger.
Hurrah, die sind wieder breiter und stärker,
Das macht, es sind richtige Uckermärker,
Die sind schon mehr für Kolbe und Knüppel,
Conferatur Wester- und Oster-Düppel,
Verstehn sich übrigens auch auf Gewehre,
Siehe Fohlenkoppel und Arnkiel-Oere, —
Funfzig Dänische Feuerschlünde
Können nichts gegen Prenzlau und Angermünde.

Wer kommt? wer? —
Füsiliere, Fünfunddreißiger.
Hurrah, das wirbelt und schreitet geschwinder,
Hurrah, das sind Berliner Kinder!
Jeder, als ob er ein Gärtner wäre,
Trägt drei Sträußer auf seinem Gewehre.
Gärtner freilich, — gegraben, geschanzt,
Dann sich selber eingepflanzt,
Eingepflanzt auf Schanze zwei —
Die flinken Berliner sind vorbei.

Wer kommt? wer? —
Hurrah, unsre Sechsziger.
Oberst von Hartmann, fest im Sitze,
Grüßt mit seiner Säbelspitze.
Hut ab und heraus die Tücher!
Das sind unsere Oderbrücher.
Keine Knattrer und bloße Verschluser,
Lauter Barnimer und Lebuser;
Fest ihr Tritt, frank und frei —
Major von Jena ist nicht mehr dabei.

Wer kommt? wer? —
Artillerie und Ingenieur;
Elfte Ulanen, Zieten-Husaren,
Paukenwirbel und Fanfaren.
Halt! — Der ganze Waffenblitz
Präsentirt vor König Fritz.
Alles still, kein Pferdegeschnauf,
Zehntausend blicken zu ihm auf,
Der neigt sich leise und lüpft den Hut:
„Concedire, es war jut."

Th. Fontane.

Den lieben Vierundsechszigern gewidmet von Fr. Wassermann in Templin.

Schnellpressendruck von Fr. Wassermann in Templin.

Kat. 118

»Erinnerung an die Einzugsfeier in Berlin am 7. December 1864«
Gedicht von Theodor Fontane (1819–1898)
Druck: Fr. Wassermann, Templin 1864
Kat. 118

Fontane feiert in seinem Gedicht die Regimenter, die die Düppeler Schanzen erstürmt haben, und lässt Friedrich den Großen wohlgefällig von seinem Denkmal auf sie herabnicken. Der Journalist und Schriftsteller reiste im Mai und September 1864 an die Kriegsschauplätze, berichtete für die regierungstreue »Kreuzzeitung« und erhielt von der Kgl. Geheimen Oberhof-Druckerei Rudolf von Decker den Auftrag für ein Buch über den Krieg. Werke über die Kriege 1866 und 1870/71 folgten.

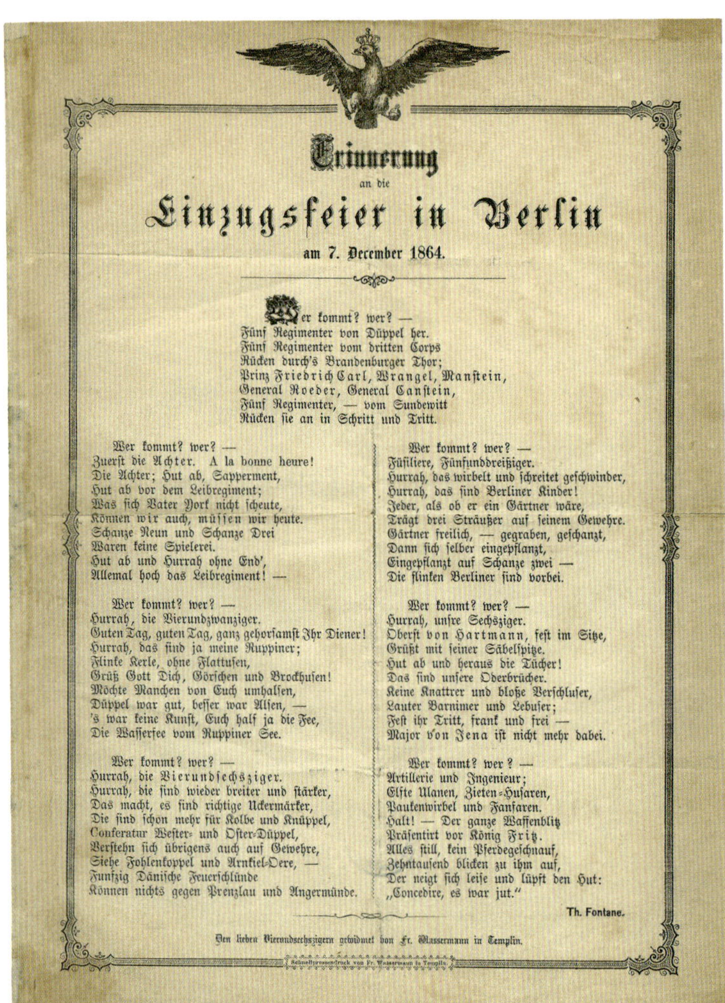

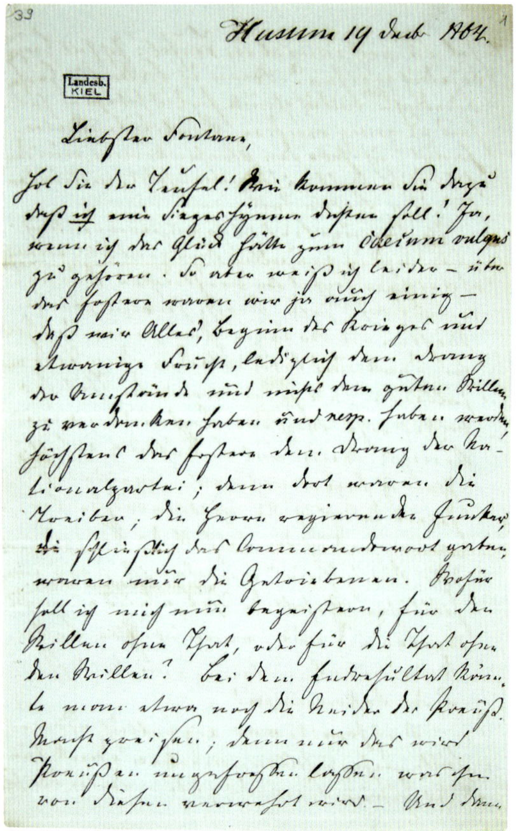

Husum 19 Decb 1864.

Landesb. KIEL

Liebster Fontane,

Hol Sie der Teufel! Wie kommen Sie dazu daß ich eine Siegeshymne dichten soll!

Kat. 119

Schreiben Theodor Storms an Theodor Fontane
Husum, 19. Dezember 1864
Kat. 119

»Hol Sie der Teufel! Wie kommen Sie dazu daß ich eine Siegeshymne dichten soll!«, beginnt der Husumer Schriftsteller Storm (1817–1888) seinen Brief an Fontane. Auf der folgenden Seite kritisiert er an dessen »Einzugslied«, dass »der Zipfel der verfluchten Kreuzzeitung aus jeder Strophe« heraushänge: »Möchten Sie der letzte Poet jener, doch Gott sei Dank und trotz alledem dem Tode verfallenen Zeit sein, worin die That des Volkes erst durch das Kopfnicken eines Königs Weihe und Bedeutung erhält.«

Kat. 116

»Uebermuth thut selten gut!‹ Beseitigung des Idstedter Löwen durch schleswig-holsteinische Patrioten am 28. Februar 1864«

S. Hamburger, 1864
Lithografie
Kat. 116

Nationalliberale Dänen hatten 1862 in Flensburg ein sieben Meter hohes Denkmal der Schlacht von Idstedt errichtet. Doch anders als auf der Grafik dargestellt, gelang es 1864 »schleswig-holsteinischen Patrioten« nicht, den Löwen vom Sockel zu stürzen – nur der Schwanz und ein Bein brachen bei dem Versuch ab. Die Demontage geschah auf Veranlassung der preußischen Verwaltung. 1867 folgte der Abtransport nach Berlin, wo der Löwe erst im Zeughaus und später in der Hauptkadettenanstalt in Groß-Lichterfelde stand.

Idstedt-Löwe

Gipskopie des Flensburger Denkmals
von Herman Wilhelm Bissen (1798–1868)
Höhe 48,5 cm
Kat. 117

Souvenirs hielten die Erinnerung an das Denkmal in dänischen Haushalten wach. 1945 überzeugte ein dänischer Journalist die US-Militärbehörden, den Löwen nach Kopenhagen überführen zu lassen. Immer wieder wurde über eine erneute Aufstellung in Flensburg gestritten. Sie erfolgte 2012 »als Zeichen von Freundschaft und Vertrauen zwischen Deutschen und Dänen«.

Kat. 117

Österreich und Preußen stritten im Deutschen Bund weiter um die Vorherrschaft. Konflikte um die zunächst gemeinsam verwalteten Herzogtümer Schleswig und Holstein boten 1866 Anlass für den endgültigen Bruch. Im April schloss Preußen ein geheimes Bündnis mit Italien. Der drohende Krieg zwischen deutschen Staaten war anders als der Kampf gegen Dänemark anfangs sehr unpopulär. Im Bündnis mit kleineren, vor allem norddeutschen Staaten marschierten preußische Truppen am 15./16. Juni in Hannover, Sachsen und Kurhessen ein, am 21. Juni überschritten sie die Grenze nach Österreich. Die Schlacht bei Königgrätz am 3. Juli 1866 entschied den

Krieg für Preußen. Trotz Erfolgen gegen Italien musste Österreich kapitulieren und Venetien abtreten. Preußen annektierte Schleswig-Holstein, Hannover, Kurhessen, Nassau und Frankfurt. Die Staaten nördlich der Mainlinie vereinigten sich unter preußischer Führung zum Norddeutschen Bund. Österreich hatte auf die weitere Einigung Deutschlands keinen Einfluss mehr und musste um seine Führungsrolle im Habsburger Vielvölkerstaat bangen: Ungarn setzte nun seine Forderung nach mehr Gleichberechtigung durch. Aus dem österreichischen Kaiserreich wurde die österreichisch-ungarische Doppelmonarchie, auch k. u. k. (kaiserliche und königliche) Monarchie genannt.

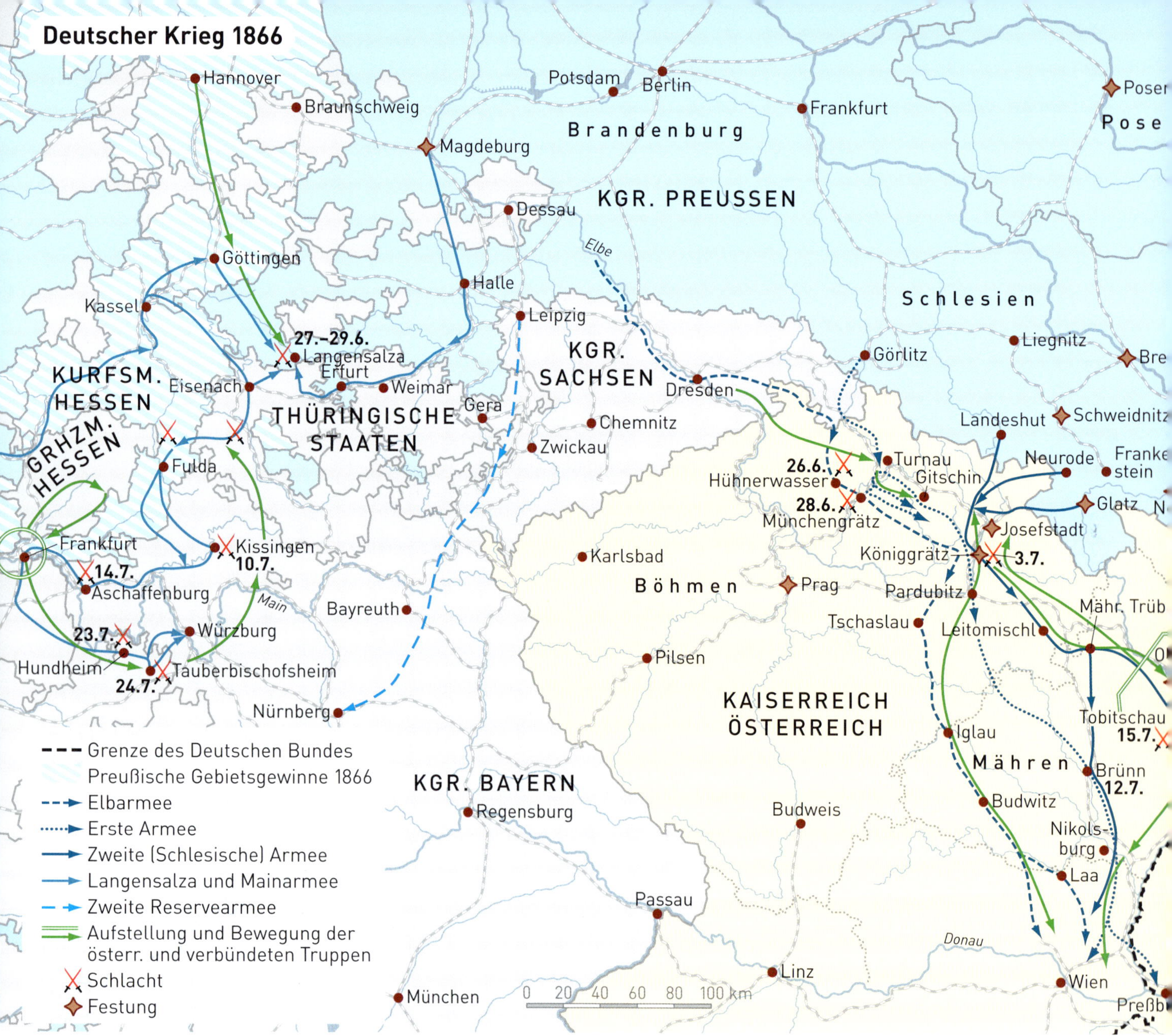
Deutscher Krieg 1866
Hannover
Braunschweig
Potsdam
Berlin
Frankfurt
Posen
Magdeburg
Brandenburg
KGR. PREUSSEN
Dessau
Elbe
Göttingen
Halle
Schlesien
Kassel
Leipzig
27.–29.6.
Langensalza
KGR. SACHSEN
Görlitz
Liegnitz
KURFSM. HESSEN
Erfurt
Eisenach
Weimar
Dresden
THÜRINGISCHE STAATEN
Gera
Chemnitz
Landeshut
Schweidnitz
GRHZM. HESSEN
Fulda
Zwickau
26.6.
Hühnerwasser
Turnau
Gitschin
Neurode
Glatz
28.6.
Münchengrätz
Josefstadt
Frankfurt
Kissingen
10.7.
Karlsbad
Königgrätz
3.7.
14.7.
Aschaffenburg
Main
Böhmen
Prag
Pardubitz
Bayreuth
Tschaslau
Leitomischl
Mähr. Trüb
23.7.
Würzburg
Hundheim
24.7.
Tauberbischofsheim
Pilsen
KAISERREICH ÖSTERREICH
Tobitschau
15.7.
Nürnberg
Iglau
Mähren
Brünn
12.7.
KGR. BAYERN
Regensburg
Budweis
Budwitz
Nikolsburg
Laa
Passau
Donau
Linz
Wien
München
0 20 40 60 80 100 km
Preßb
Grenze des Deutschen Bundes
Preußische Gebietsgewinne 1866
Elbarmee
Erste Armee
Zweite (Schlesische) Armee
Langensalza und Mainarmee
Zweite Reservearmee
Aufstellung und Bewegung der österr. und verbündeten Truppen
Schlacht
Festung

1863

14. August Gasteiner Konvention zwischen Österreich und Preußen. Letzter Versuch einer einvernehmlichen Lösung der Schleswig-Holstein-Frage: Österreich verwaltet Holstein und tritt seine Rechte an Lauenburg gegen eine finanzielle Entschädigung an Preußen ab. Preußen verwaltet Schleswig

1866

8. April Geheimes Bündnis Preußens und Italiens gegen Österreich

9. April Preußen beantragt beim Bundestag die Wahl eines Nationalparlaments

1. Juni Österreich will den Deutschen Bund über Holsteins Zukunft entscheiden lassen

9. Juni Preußische Truppen marschieren in Holstein ein

10. Juni Vorschlag Bismarcks an die Bundesstaaten mit einer neuen Bundesverfassung für eine kleindeutsche Lösung ohne Österreich

12. Juni Österreichs Truppen räumen Holstein
Geheimvertrag zwischen Österreich und Frankreich: Abtretung Venetiens an Frankreich im Fall eines österreichischen Sieges im Gegenzug für die Neutralität Frankreichs

14. Juni Beschluss einer Bundesexekution gegen Preußen. Preußen betrachtet den Bund deswegen als aufgelöst

15./16. Juni Preußische Truppen marschieren in Hannover, Sachsen und Kurhessen ein

20. Juni Kriegserklärung Italiens an Österreich

24. Juni Schlacht bei Custozza

27. Juni Die hannoversche Armee siegt in der Schlacht bei Langensalza, muss aber zwei Tage später trotzdem kapitulieren

1. – 27. Juli Mainfeldzug

3. Juli Schlacht bei Königgrätz

20. Juli Seeschlacht bei Lissa

26. Juli Vorfrieden von Nikolsburg

August Geheime Schutz- und Trutzbündnisse zwischen Preußen und Baden, Bayern sowie Württemberg

23. August Prager Frieden zwischen Preußen und Österreich: offizielle Auflösung des Deutschen Bundes und Gründung der Norddeutschen Bundes

3. Oktober Frieden von Wien zwischen Italien und Österreich: Abtretung Venetiens an Italien

1867

11. April Schutz- und Trutzbündnis zwischen Preußen und Hessen-Darmstadt

1. Juli Die Verfassung des Norddeutschen Bundes tritt in Kraft

Beide deutsche Monarchen schreckten lange vor einem »Bruderkrieg« zurück. Ihre Aufrufe vom 17. bzw. 18. Juni 1866 zeigen allein durch ihre Länge, wie groß das Bedürfnis war, sich gegenüber der Bevölkerung zu rechtfertigen. Anders als König Wilhelm I. wendete sich Kaiser Franz Joseph I. in seiner Proklamation nicht an sein »Volk«, sondern an seine »Völker«. Denn die Habsburger Monarchie war ein Vielvölkerstaat, in dem elf unterschiedliche Sprachen amtlich anerkannt waren. Nationale Bewegungen sah Franz Joseph als große Gefahr für den Zusammenhalt seines Reiches.

An Mein Volk!

In dem Augenblicke, wo Preußens Heer zu einem entscheidenden Kampfe auszieht, drängt es Mich, zu Meinem Volke, zu den Söhnen und Enkeln der tapferen Väter zu reden, zu denen vor einem halben Jahrhundert Mein in Gott ruhender Vater unvergessene Worte sprach: „das Vaterland ist in Gefahr!“

Oesterreich und ein großer Theil Deutschlands steht gegen dasselbe in Waffen! Nur wenige Jahre sind es her, seit Ich aus seinem Entschlusse und ohne früherer Unbill zu gedenken, dem Kaiser von Oesterreich die Bundeshand reichte, als es galt, ein Deutsches Land von fremder Herrschaft zu befreien. Aus dem gemeinschaftlich vergossenen Blute, hoffte Ich, würde eine Waffenbrüderschaft erblühen, die zu fester, auf gegenseitige Achtung und Anerkennung beruhender Bundesgenossenschaft und mit ihr zu all dem gemeinsamen Wirken führen würde, aus welchem Deutschlands innere Wohlfahrt und äußere Bedeutung als Frucht hervorgehen sollte. Aber meine Hoffnung ist getäuscht worden. Oesterreich will nicht vergessen, daß seine Fürsten einst Deutschland beherrschten, in dem jüngeren, aber kräftig sich entwickelnden Preußen will es keinen natürlichen Bundesgenossen, sondern nur einen feindlichen Nebenbuhler erkennen. Preußen, so meint es, muß in allen seinen Bestrebungen bekämpft werden, weil, was Preußen frommt, Oesterreich schade. Die alte unselige Eifersucht ist in hellen Flammen wieder aufgelodert. Preußen soll geschwächt, vernichtet, entehrt werden. Ihm gegenüber gelten keine Verträge mehr, gegen Preußen werden deutsche Bundesfürsten nicht blos aufgerufen, sondern zum Bundesbruch verleitet. Wohin wir in Deutschland schauen, sind wir von Feinden umgeben, deren Kampfgeschrei ist: „Erniedrigung Preußens!“ Aber in Meinem Volke lebt der Geist von 1813. Wer wird uns einen Fuß breit Preußischen Bodens rauben, wenn wir ernstlich entschlossen sind, die Errungenschaften unserer Väter zu wahren, wenn König und Volk, durch die Gefahren des Vaterlandes fester als je geeint, an die Ehre desselben Gut und Blut zu setzen, für ihre höchste und heiligste Aufgabe halten. In sorglicher Voraussicht dessen, was nun eingetreten ist, habe Ich seit Jahren es für die erste Pflicht Meines Königlichen Amtes erkennen müssen, Preußens streitbares Volk für eine starke Machtentwickelung vorzubereiten. Befriedigt und zuversichtlich wird mit Mir jeder Preuße auf die Waffenmacht blicken, die unsere Grenzen deckt. Mit seinem König an der Spitze wird sich Preußens Volk ein wahres Volk in Waffen fühlen! Unsere Gegner täuschen sich, wenn sie wähnen, Preußen sei durch innere Streitigkeiten gelähmt. Dem Feinde gegenüber ist es einig und stark, dem Feinde gegenüber gleicht sich aus, was sich entgegen stand, um demnächst im Glück und Unglück vereint zu bleiben. Ich habe Alles gethan, um Preußen die Lasten und Opfer eines Krieges zu ersparen; das weiß Mein Volk, das weiß Gott, der die Herzen prüft. Bis zum letzten Augenblicke habe ich in Gemeinschaft mit England, Frankreich und Rußland die Wege für eine gütliche Ausgleichung gesucht und offen erhalten. Oesterreich hat nicht gewollt, und andere deutsche Staaten haben sich offen auf seine Seite gestellt. So sei es denn.

Nicht Mein ist die Schuld, wenn Mein Volk schweren Kampf kämpfen und vielleicht harte Bedrängniß wird erdulden müssen. Aber es ist uns keine Wahl mehr geblieben! wir müssen fechten um unsere Existenz, wir müssen in einen Kampf auf Leben und Tod gehen gegen Diejenigen, die das Preußen des großen Churfürsten, des Großen Friederich, das Preußen, wie es aus den Freiheitskriegen hervorgegangen ist, von der Stufe herabstoßen wollen, auf die es seiner Fürsten Geist und Kraft, seines Volkes Tapferkeit, Hingebung, Gesittung emporgehoben haben. Flehen wir den Allmächtigen Lenker der Geschicke der Völker, den Lenker der Schlachten an, daß er unsere Waffen segne! Verleiht uns Gott den Sieg, dann werden wir auch stark genug sein, das lose Band, welches die deutschen Lande mehr dem Namen als der That nach zusammenhielt, und welches jetzt durch Diejenigen zerrissen ist, die das Recht und die Macht des nationalen Geistes fürchten, in anderer Gestalt fester und heilvoller zu erneuen. Gott sei mit uns!

Berlin, den 18. Juni 1866.

(gezeichnet) **Wilhelm.**

H. Bär, vormals Rosenkranz und Bär in Neisse.

Kat. 134

Kat. 135

Kat. 136

»An mein Volk!« – Aufruf Wilhelms I.
Berlin, 18. Juni 1866
Kat. 134

Büste Wilhelms I., König von Preußen, ab 1871 deutscher Kaiser
Carl Keil (1838–1889), Ems, nach 1871
Metallguss von H. Gladenbeck, Berlin
Höhe 35,5 cm
Kat. 135

Büste Franz Josephs I., Kaiser von Österreich
Um 1860
Höhe 30 cm
Kat. 136

»An meine Völker!« – Aufruf Franz Josephs I.
Wien, 17. Juni 1866
Kat. 137

An Meine Völker!

Mitten in dem Werke des Friedens, das Ich unternommen, um die Grundlagen zu einer Verfassungsform zu legen, welche die Einheit und Machtstellung des Gesammtreiches festigen, den einzelnen Ländern und Völkern aber ihre freie innere Entwicklung sichern soll, hat Meine Regentenpflicht Mir geboten, Mein ganzes Heer unter die Waffen zu rufen.

An den Gränzen des Reiches, im Süden und Norden, stehen die Armeen zweier verbündeter Feinde, in der Absicht, Oesterreich in seinem europäischen Machtbestande zu erschüttern.

Keinem derselben ist von Meiner Seite ein Anlaß zum Kriege gegeben worden. Die Segnungen des Friedens Meinen Völkern zu erhalten, habe Ich, dessen ist Gott der Allwissende Mein Zeuge, immer für eine Meiner ersten und heiligsten Regentenpflichten angesehen, und getreu sie zu erfüllen getrachtet.

Allein, die eine der beiden feindlichen Mächte bedarf keines Vorwandes; lüstern auf den Raub von Theilen Meines Reiches, ist der günstige Zeitpunct für sie der Anlaß zum Kriege.

Verbündet mit den preußischen Truppen, die uns als Feinde nunmehr entgegenstehen, zog vor zwei Jahren ein Theil Meines treuen und tapferen Heeres an die Gestade der Nordsee.

Ich bin diese Waffengenossenschaft mit Preußen eingegangen, um vertragsmäßige Rechte zu wahren, einen bedrohten deutschen Volksstamm zu schützen, das Unheil eines unvermeidlichen Krieges auf seine engsten Gränzen einzuschränken, und in der innigen Verbindung der zwei mitteleuropäischen Großmächte — denen vorzugsweise die Aufgabe der Erhaltung des europäischen Friedens zu Theil geworden — zum Wohle Meines Reiches, Deutschlands und Europa's eine solche dauernde Friedensgarantie zu gewinnen.

Eroberungen habe Ich nicht gesucht; uneigennützig beim Abschlusse des Bündnisses mit Preußen habe Ich auch im Wiener Friedensvertrage keine Vortheile für Mich angestrebt. Oesterreich trägt keine Schuld an der trüben Reihe unseliger Verwicklungen, welche bei gleicher uneigennütziger Absicht Preußens nie hätten entstehen können, bei gleicher bundestreuer Gesinnung augenblicklich zu begleichen waren.

Sie wurden zur Verwirklichung selbstsüchtiger Zwecke hervorgerufen, und waren deßhalb für Meine Regierung auf friedlichem Wege unlösbar.

So steigerte sich immer mehr der Ernst der Lage.

Selbst dann aber noch, als offenkundig in den beiden feindlichen Staaten kriegerische Vorbereitungen getroffen wurden, und ein Einverständniß unter ihnen, dem nur die Absicht eines gemeinsamen feindlichen Angriffes auf Mein Reich zu Grunde liegen konnte, immer klarer zu Tage trat, verharrte Ich im Bewußtsein Meiner Regentenpflicht, bereit zu jedem mit der Ehre und Wohlfahrt Meiner Völker vereinbaren Zugeständnisse, im tiefsten Frieden.

Als Ich jedoch wahrnahm, daß ein weiteres Zögern die wirksame Abwehr feindlicher Angriffe und hiedurch die Sicherheit der Monarchie gefährde, mußte Ich Mich zu den schweren Opfern entschließen, die mit Kriegsrüstungen unzertrennlich verbunden sind.

Die durch Meine Regierung gegebenen Versicherungen Meiner Friedensliebe, die wiederholt abgegebenen Erklärungen Meiner Bereitwilligkeit zu gleichzeitiger gegenseitiger Abrüstung, erwiederte Preußen mit Gegenansinnen, deren Annahme eine Preisgebung der Ehre und Sicherheit Meines Reiches gewesen wäre.

Preußen verlangte die volle vorausgehende Abrüstung nicht nur gegen sich, sondern auch gegen die an der Gränze Meines Reiches in Italien stehende feindliche Macht, für deren Friedensliebe keine Bürgschaft geboten wurde und keine geboten werden konnte.

Alle Verhandlungen mit Preußen in der Herzogthümerfrage haben immer mehr Belege zu der Thatsache geliefert, daß eine Lösung dieser Frage, wie sie der Würde Oesterreichs, dem Rechte und den Interessen Deutschlands und der Herzogthümer entspricht, durch ein Einverständniß mit Preußen bei seiner offen zu Tag liegenden Gewalts- und Eroberungspolitik nicht zu erzielen ist. —

Die Verhandlungen wurden abgebrochen, die ganze Angelegenheit den Entschließungen des Bundes anheimgestellt, und zugleich die legalen Vertreter Holsteins einberufen.

Die drohenden Kriegsaussichten veranlaßten die drei Mächte Frankreich, England und Rußland auch an Meine Regierung die Einladung zur Theilnahme an gemeinsamen Berathungen ergehen zu lassen, deren Zweck die Erhaltung des Friedens sein sollte. Meine Regierung, entsprechend Meiner Absicht, wenn immer möglich den Frieden für Meine Völker zu erhalten, hat die Theilnahme nicht abgelehnt, wohl aber ihre Zusage an die bestimmte Voraussetzung geknüpft, daß das öffentliche europäische Recht und die bestehenden Verträge den Ausgangspunct dieser Vermittlungsversuche zu bilden haben, und die theilnehmenden Mächte kein Sonderinteresse zum Nachtheile des europäischen Gleichgewichtes und der Rechte Oesterreichs verfolgen.

Wenn schon der Versuch von Friedensberathungen an diesen natürlichen Voraussetzungen scheiterte, so liegt darin der Beweis, daß die Berathungen selbst nie zur Erhaltung und Festigung des Friedens hätten führen können.

Die neuesten Ereignisse beweisen es unwiderleglich, **daß Preußen nun offen Gewalt an die Stelle des Rechtes setzt.**

In dem Rechte und der Ehre Oesterreichs, in dem Rechte und der Ehre der gesammten deutschen Nation erblickte Preußen nicht länger eine Schranke für seinen verhängnißvoll gesteigerten Ehrgeiz. Preußische Truppen rückten in Holstein ein, die von dem kaiserlichen Statthalter einberufene Ständeversammlung wurde gewaltsam gesprengt, die Regierungsgewalt in Holstein, welche der Wiener Friedensvertrag gemeinschaftlich auf Oesterreich und Preußen übertragen hatte, ausschließlich für Preußen in Anspruch genommen, und die österreichische Besatzung genöthigt zehnfacher Uebermacht zu weichen.

Als der deutsche Bund, vertragswidrige Eigenmacht hierin erkennend, auf Antrag Oesterreichs die Mobilmachung der Bundestruppen beschloß, da vollendete Preußen, das sich so gerne als Träger deutscher Interessen rühmen läßt, den eingeschlagenen verderblichen Weg. Das Nationalband der Deutschen zerreißend, erklärte es seinen Austritt aus dem Bunde, verlangte von den deutschen Regierungen die Annahme eines sogenannten Reformplanes, welcher die Theilung Deutschlands verwirklicht, und schritt mit militärischer Gewalt gegen die bundesgetreuen Souveräne vor.

So ist der unheilvollste, ein Krieg Deutscher gegen Deutsche unvermeidlich geworden!

Zur Verantwortung all' des Unglücks, das er über Einzelne, Familien, Gegenden und Länder bringen wird, rufe Ich diejenigen, die ihn herbeigeführt, vor den Richterstuhl der Geschichte und des ewigen allmächtigen Gottes.

Ich schreite zum Kampf mit dem Vertrauen, das die gerechte Sache gibt, im Gefühle der Macht, die in einem großen Reiche liegt, wo Fürst und Volk nur von Einem Gedanken — dem guten Rechte Oesterreichs — durchdrungen sind, mit frischem vollem Muthe beim Anblicke Meines tapferen kampfgerüsteten Heeres, das den Wall bildet, an welchem die Kraft der Feinde Oesterreichs sich brechen wird, im Hinblick auf Meine treuen Völker, die einig entschlossen opferwillig zu Mir emporschauen.

Die reine Flamme patriotischer Begeisterung lodert gleichmäßig in den weiten Gebieten Meines Reiches empor; freudig eilten die einberufenen Krieger in die Reihen des Heeres; Freiwillige drängen sich zum Kriegsdienste; die ganze waffenfähige Bevölkerung einiger zumeist bedrohter Länder rüstet sich zum Kampfe und die edelste Opferwilligkeit eilt zur Linderung des Unglücks und zur Unterstützung der Bedürfnisse des Heeres herbei.

Nur Ein Gefühl durchdringt die Bewohner Meiner Königreiche und Länder, das Gefühl der Zusammengehörigkeit, das Gefühl der Macht in ihrer Einigkeit, das Gefühl des Unmuthes über eine so unerhörte Rechtsverletzung.

Doppelt schmerzt es Mich, daß das Werk der Verständigung über die inneren Verfassungsfragen noch nicht so weit gediehen ist, um in diesem ernsten, zugleich aber erhebenden Augenblicke, die Vertreter aller Meiner Völker um Meinen Thron versammeln zu können.

Dieser Stütze für jetzt entbehrend, ist Mir jedoch Meine Regentenpflicht um so klarer, Mein Entschluß um so fester, dieselbe Meinem Reiche für alle Zukunft zu sichern.

Wir werden in diesem Kampfe nicht allein stehen.

Deutschlands Fürsten und Völker kennen die Gefahr, die ihrer Freiheit und Unabhängigkeit von einer Macht droht, deren Handlungsweise durch selbstsüchtige Pläne einer rücksichtslosen Vergrößerungssucht allein geleitet wird; sie wissen, welchen Hort für diese ihre höchsten Güter, welche Stütze für die Macht und Integrität des gesammten deutschen Vaterlandes sie an Oesterreich finden.

Wie wir für die heiligsten Güter, welche Völker zu vertheidigen haben, in Waffen stehen, so auch unsere deutschen Bundesbrüder.

Man hat die Waffen uns in die Hand gezwungen. Wohlan! jetzt, wo wir sie ergriffen, dürfen und wollen wir sie nicht früher niederlegen, als bis Meinem Reiche sowie den verbündeten deutschen Staaten die freie innere Entwicklung gesichert und deren Machtstellung in Europa neuerdings befestiget ist.

Auf unserer Einigkeit, unserer Kraft ruhe aber nicht allein unser Vertrauen, unsere Hoffnung; Ich setze sie zugleich noch auf einen Höheren, den allmächtigen gerechten Gott, Dem Mein Haus von seinem Ursprunge an gedient, Der die nicht verläßt, die in Gerechtigkeit auf Ihn vertrauen.

Zu Ihm will Ich um Beistand und Sieg flehen, und fordere Meine Völker auf, es mit Mir zu thun.

Gegeben in Meiner Residenz- und Reichs-Hauptstadt Wien am siebenzehnten Juni Eintausend achthundert sechsundsechzig.

Franz Joseph m. p.

Aus der k. k. Hof- und Staatsdruckerei.

Kat. 137

Kat. 141

Kat. 140

Die verlorene Krone

Das Ende des Königreichs Hannover 1866

Auf dem Höhepunkt des Konflikts um die Herzogtümer Schleswig und Holstein marschierten preußische Truppen am 9. Juni 1866 im von Österreich verwalteten Holstein ein. Österreich räumte Holstein kampflos, erreichte aber am 14. Juni die Mobilisierung von Bundestruppen – eine »Bundesexekution« – gegen Preußen, das seinerseits den Deutschen Bund für erledigt erklärte. Ziel des am 15. Juni beginnenden preußischen Feldzugs in West- und Mitteldeutschland war zunächst, die Vereinigung der hannoverschen und kurhessischen Truppen mit der bayerischen Armee zu verhindern. Obwohl Preußen in der Schlacht bei Langensalza am 27. Juni unterlag, musste die erschöpfte hannoversche Armee zwei Tage später mangels Munition und Verpflegung kapitulieren.

König Georg V. floh zunächst nach Wien und ging dann nach Paris. Seinen Anspruch auf die Krone gab er nie auf und initiierte sogar eine »Welfenlegion«, die im Falle eines Krieges auf französischer Seite gegen Preußen kämpfen und die nun preußische Provinz Hannover zurückerobern sollte. Deshalb verweigerte ihm Preußen eine Abfindung und beschlagnahmte sein Privatvermögen.

Kat. 142

Kat. 143

Tschako (Käppi) für Mannschaften von Linieninfanterieregimentern
Königreich Hannover, 1859/1867
Kat. 141

Helm (»Pickelhaube«) für Mannschaften der Garde du Corps
Königreich Hannover, 1846/1866
Kat. 140

Die Einführung von Pickelhauben ab 1846/1850 und einreihigen Waffenröcken ab 1849 orientierte sich am Vorbild Preußens, das auf dem Gebiet zeitgemäßer Uniformierung führend war. Als Zeichen seiner politischen Abgrenzung von Preußen befahl König Georg V. jedoch 1859, bei der Infanterie die Pickelhauben durch »Käppis« nach österreichischem Vorbild zu ersetzen. Nur Garde du Corps und Gardekürassiere waren 1866 noch mit Pickelhauben ausgestattet. Um Verwechslungen zu vermeiden, trugen sie im Feld oft blaue Feldmützen.

Waffenrock eines Sergeants des 1. Infanterie-(Leib-)Regiments
Königreich Hannover, 1858/1867
Kat. 142

Feldflasche (»Kantine«) der 7. Kompanie des 1. Infanterie-(Leib-)Regiments
Königreich Hannover, 1858/1867
Kat. 143

Das Königreich Hannover wurde bis 1837 in Personalunion mit Großbritannien regiert. Daran erinnern zur Verpflegungsausrüstung gehörende hellblau gestrichene, runde Feldflaschen aus zwei Holz-

Kat. 145

böden und -dauben, zusammengehalten von eisernen Reifen. In Anlehnung an das englische Wort »canteen« wurden sie »Kantine« genannt. Dieses Exemplar wurde unbrauchbar durch ein Projektil, das beide Böden durchschlug.

Schlacht bei Langensalza am 27. Juni 1866

Johann Bernhard Schmelzer (1833–1909)
Lithografie
Kat. 145

Am Nachmittag der Schlacht griff hannoversche Kavallerie – die der Zeichner hier zum Teil noch mit Pickelhauben dargestellt hat – preußische Truppen auf dem Rückzug an. Reste des Landwehrbataillons Potsdam bildeten mit anderen versprengten preußischen Einheiten ein Karree und konnten die Attacke abwehren.

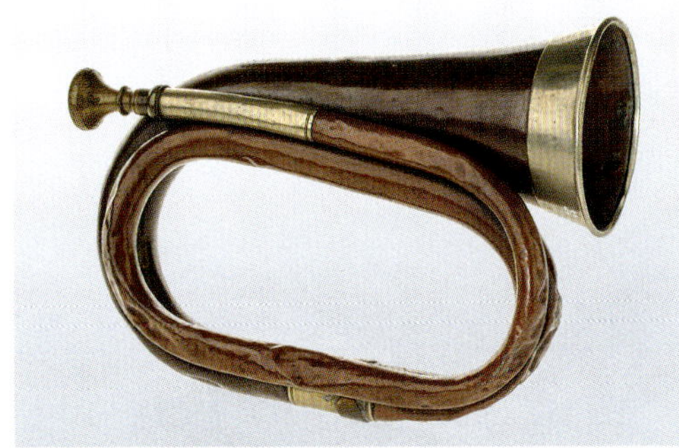

Kat. 146

Kat. 193

Kat. 194

Signalhorn des 2. Jäger-Bataillons, mit dem bei Langensalza 1866 das letzte Signal gegeben wurde
Königreich Hannover
Kat. 146

Hannoversche Offiziere der Welfenlegion 1868 in Paris
Kat. 194

Hannoveraner, die sich nicht mit der Annexion ihres Landes durch Preußen abfinden konnten, sammelten sich erst in den Niederlanden, nach der Ausweisung dort in der Schweiz und 1868 schließlich in Paris, um im Falle eines Krieges Frankreich gegen Preußen zu unterstützen.

Nachbildung der hannoverschen Königskrone von 1843
Metallblech, Glas
Kat. 193

Diese Nachbildung wurde wahrscheinlich bei der Aufbahrung König Georgs V. verwendet, der 1878 im Pariser Exil starb. Seinen Leichnam ließ Queen Victoria in die Kapelle des Schlosses Windsor überführen.

Unfreiwillige Annäherungen und eine auswärts gefeierte Massenhochzeit

Sachsen und das »Dritte Deutschland« in den Jahren vor der Reichsgründung

ULF MORGENSTERN

1815 trat der Deutsche Bund ins Leben, als Zusammenschluss der »souveränen Fürsten und freien Städte Deutschlands« einschließlich vierer Monarchen, die auch nicht-deutsche Territorien regierten (der österreichische Kaiser sowie der dänische, der niederländische und der preußische König).[1] Ein halbes Jahrhundert später endete diese Union der deutschen Staaten durch den Austritt ihres zweitgrößten Mitgliedslands, Preußen, das nach langer Zermürbung einen »harten Prexit«[2] vollzog.

Das deutschsprachige Mitteleuropa wurde nicht länger von einer föderalen Klammer umspannt, die ungefähr das alte Heilige Römische Reich deutscher Nation umfasste. Vielmehr gliederte sich dieser Großraum nun in drei Teile: den Norddeutschen Bund aus dem großen Brandenburg-Preußen und seinen Zwangsverbündeten, die sogenannten süddeutschen Staaten zwischen Mainlinie und Alpen und die österreichischen Kronländer im Südosten. Die Machtposition Letzterer war nach dem Ausscheiden Österreichs aus Deutschland und nach den Gebietsverlusten in Italien geschrumpft; dem trugen sie nach dem

Lederhelm mit Spitze (»Pickelhaube«) für das Infanteriebataillon
Fürstentum Reuß jüngere Linie, um 1845
Kat. 151

Die Infanterie des Fürstentums Reuß der jüngeren Linie war nur durch ihre Pickelhauben von dem mit Feldmützen ausgestatteten Kontingent des Fürstentums Reuß ältere Linie zu unterscheiden. Die 1866 getragenen Helme waren etwas niedriger als das hier gezeigte erste Modell. Im Krieg 1866 blieb die jüngere Linie der Fürsten von Reuß zunächst neutral, stellte sich dann aber auf die Seite Preußens.

Waffenrock eines Hornisten der 2. Kompanie der Jägerabteilung
Fürstentum Reuß ältere Linie, 1865
Kat. 152

Der kleinste deutsche Staat stand traditionell auf der Seite Österreichs. 1866 lag seine Jägerabteilung in der Festung Rastatt. Am 11. August 1866 marschierte preußische Landwehr im Fürstentum ein und entwaffnete die dort verbliebenen 17 reußischen Soldaten. Nach Kriegsende musste das antipreußisch gesinnte Fürstenhaus dem Norddeutschen Bund beitreten, stimmte aber noch nach der Reichsgründung gegen jede Form von Vereinheitlichung und fühlte sich dem Kaiser in Wien enger verbunden als dem in Berlin.

Krieg von 1866 gegenüber den zur Habsburgermonarchie gehörenden mittelosteuropäischen Ländern Rechnung durch die Aufwertung Ungarns innerhalb der neuen Doppelmonarchie Österreich-Ungarn.

Als traditionelle Schutzmacht der kleinen, nicht-preußischen Staaten hatte Wien mithin ausgedient. Das hatte direkte Auswirkungen, wie sich 1870 zeigte. Ohne österreichische Optionen zogen Bayern, Württemberg und Baden, die nicht zum Norddeutschen Bund gehörten, in der Frage eines plötzlichen Krieges gegen Frankreich ungewollt mit am Berliner Strang – und fanden sich umgehend als Bundesstaaten in einem von Bismarck entworfenen zweiten deutschen Kaiserreich wieder.

So oder so ähnlich könnte die verknappte Erzählung jener gravierenden Ereignisse ab der Mitte der 1860er Jahre lauten. Aber ergeben diese groben Linien ein adäquates Bild der Wirklichkeiten im »Dritten Deutschland«? Kann es ein solches überhaupt geben, blickt man auf das Mosaik aus mehr als 30 Klein- und Mittelstaaten mit ihren unterschiedlichen politischen und wirtschaftlichen Identitäten und Zielrichtungen? Erfuhren hansische Kaufleute den mit Gewalt und Lockung vollzogenen Einigungsprozess ähnlich wie thüringische Landarbeiter im Fürstentum Reuß älterer Linie, wo man sich vom wettinischen Nachbarn gelegentlich im gleichen Maß genötigt fühlte wie von den annexionslüsternen Hohenzollern? Und bestanden nicht selbst innerhalb eines Königreichs wie Sachsen fundamentale Gegensätze zwischen liberalen Wirtschaftseliten im Einflussbereich der Messe- und Verlagsstadt Leipzig und den auf den Hof und die fast 800-jährige Dynastie fixierten politischen, militärischen und kulturbürgerlichen Kreisen Dresdens?

Solche rhetorischen Fragen machen deutlich, dass es innerhalb der Klein- und Mittelstaaten keine einheitliche Zeiterfahrung gab. Regionale Eigenheiten wurden zwar von deutschlandweiten Großtrends wie der Nationalbewegung oder der aufkommenden Arbeiterfrage überlagert. Aber die überkommenen Eigeninteressen der Eliten und Bevölkerungen der Staatenlandschaft zwischen Rhein, Main, Elbe und Donau auf der einen Seite und die Herausforderungen der aufziehenden Moderne auf der anderen ergeben ein überaus uneinheitliches Bild.

Diese – nicht zuletzt auch konfessionelle – Verschiedenheit der nicht-habsburgischen und nicht-hohenzollernschen Deutschen erklärt, warum es in den 1850er und 1860er Jahren kein einziges Mal gelungen ist, in den drängenden Fragen der Zeit einen annähernd gemeinsamen Verhandlungsstandpunkt zu erreichen. Am ehesten geeignet, auf einen solchen zumindest hinzuwirken, waren die Großen unter den Kleinen, sprich die verantwortlichen Minister in München, Dresden, Stuttgart und Karlsruhe.

Eine selbsternannte Führungsrolle im Kreis der Mittelmächte hatte der langjährige Kopf der sächsischen Außenpolitik inne, Friedrich Ferdinand von Beust, der von 1849 bis 1866 sächsischer Außenminister und seit 1858 auch Vorsitzender des Gesamtministeriums war. Beust und Bismarck gehörten der gleichen Generation an und verkörperten die Rivalität zwischen Sachsen und Preußen. Seit dem 17. Jahrhundert hatte es ein Kräftemessen zwischen den mitteldeutschen Nachbarn gegeben, die in Polen und im ostpreußischen Ordensstaat auch osteuropäische Konkurrenten gewesen waren. Mit der sächsischen Niederlage im Siebenjährigen Krieg war seit 1763 unmissverständlich klar, dass Sachsen auf den »nach den Wittelsbachern vierten Platz [...], jedoch mit weitem Abstand hinter Österreich und Preußen«[3] abgerutscht war. In der

Napoleonzeit kehrten sich diese Machtverhältnisse noch einmal kurzzeitig um. Doch nach dem Wiener Kongress wurde Sachsen empfindlich verkleinert, wenn es auch die Königswürde behalten durfte.

Das Königreich Sachsen erlebte im Deutschen Bund seit der Verfassungsgebung des Jahres 1831 eine Blütezeit. Reformen in Verwaltung, Landwirtschaft, Justiz, Militär und Bildungswesen ebneten den Weg für neue wirtschaftliche Chancen, die der Beitritt Sachsens zum Deutschen Zollverein im März 1833 eröffnete. Das kurz- und mittelfristige Regierungsziel in der Außenpolitik war es dabei, Sachsen neben oder vor Bayern als Sprecher der Mittelmächte zu installieren, also die Führungsposition bei den Verhandlungen zwischen Habsburg und Preußen zu übernehmen. Spiritus Rector dieser ambitionierten Bestrebungen war Beust, der den Deutschen Bund als einen reformfähigen Staatenbund, nicht als einen Bundesstaat interpretierte.[4] Der französische Gesandte in Dresden, Henri Mercier, brachte es in den 1850er Jahren auf den Punkt, als er nach Paris schrieb, Beust ordne der Wiederherstellung der Heiligen Allianz »alle anderen Interessen unter«.[5] Rückendeckung bekam Beust von den Königen, denen er diente, Friedrich August II. und Johann, und alle drei konnten sich auf die erfreuliche wirtschaftliche Stabilität Sachsens stützen.

Beust versuchte in enger Anlehnung an Wien, jedoch ohne zu deutliche Distanzierung gegenüber Berlin, Sachsen bei der Bundesreform zum Zünglein an der Waage zu machen. Die Verve, mit der er noch auf der Londoner Konferenz im Juli 1864 die Mittelstaaten im Deutschen Bund zu exponieren suchte, ist nicht zu verstehen ohne die eben nicht nur von Rückschlägen, sondern immer wieder auch durch Fortschritte und Hoffnungsschimmer geprägten Entwicklungen der späten 1850er und frühen 1860er Jahre. Nur vor diesem Hintergrund erhalten die sächsischen Reformbemühungen Beusts und König Johanns einen Sinn. Sie waren Teil einer komplexen politischen Großwetterlage, in der sich deutsche »Innen«-Politik mit allgemeinen nationalstaatlichen Bestrebungen und hegemonialen Konkurrenzen der Großmächte mischte. An der Lösung dieser Probleme hatten die Klein- und Mittelstaaten kaum noch teil. Im Dezember 1863 waren hannoversche und sächsische Truppen für den Deutschen Bund (gegen die Stimmen der Großmächte) in Holstein einmarschiert. Sie sahen einen deutschen Mittelstaat bedroht, als der Streit um die in Personalunion vom dänischen König regierten Herzogtümer Holstein, Schleswig und Lauenburg durch die Einführung einer neuen Verfassung eskalierte, die diese Länder enger an Dänemark binden sollte. Aber die Berliner und Wiener Politik einigte sich taktisch und übernahm im Winter 1864 auch die militärische Initiative: Auf die »Pfandbesetzung« des Herzogtums Holstein durch Preußen im Januar folgte im Februar auch formal ein von Preußen und Österreich geführter Krieg gegen Dänemark, in dem Sachsen und Hannoveraner nur noch eine marginale Rolle spielten. Vor diesem Hintergrund konnte der sächsische Minister Beust auf der Londoner Konferenz im Frühsommer 1864 mit aller diplomatischen Kunst versuchen, die Positionen der deutschen Klein- und Mittelstaaten im europäischen Konzert zum Klingen zu bringen. Den Ton gaben dennoch die preußischen und österreichischen Kapellmeister an, so wenig Harmonie zwischen beiden Großmächten auch herrschte.

Die Misstöne sollten durch eine bilaterale Vereinbarung aus der Welt geschafft werden, was die übrigen Staaten des Deutschen Bundes empörte: Das Schlagwort »Länderschacher« brachte das Unverständnis über die hemdsärmelige Art zum Ausdruck, mit der Preußen und Österreich in der Gasteiner

Friedrich Ferdinand von Beust (1809–1886)

Holzstich aus der »Illustrirten Zeitung«, Leipzig, 8. Dezember 1866
Kat. 138

Der sächsische Staatsmann Beust sah sich als Gegenspieler Bismarcks. Er versuchte, mit anderen deutschen Mittelstaaten ein »Drittes Deutschland« zu bilden, das gegenüber Preußen und Österreich Gewicht haben sollte. 1866 führte er Sachsen an Österreichs Seite in den Krieg. Nach der Niederlage wurde Sachsens starker Mann österreichischer Außenminister; ab 1867 bis zu seiner Ablösung 1871 trug er den Titel »Reichskanzler«.

Die Meißner Elbbrücke nach der Sprengung vom 15./16. Juni 1866
Lith. Anstalt v. E. Müller
Lithografie
Kat. 153

Preußische Truppen zogen kampflos in Sachsen ein, während die sächsische Armee die Elbbrücken bei Riesa und Meißen sprengte, Eisenbahnlinien zerstörte und über das Erzgebirge Richtung Böhmen auswich. Sachsen wurde nicht Kriegsschauplatz und blieb von weiteren Zerstörungen verschont.

Einmarsch preußischer Truppen in Löbau am 16. Juni 1866
Adolph Göhde, Löbau
Lithografie
Kat. 154

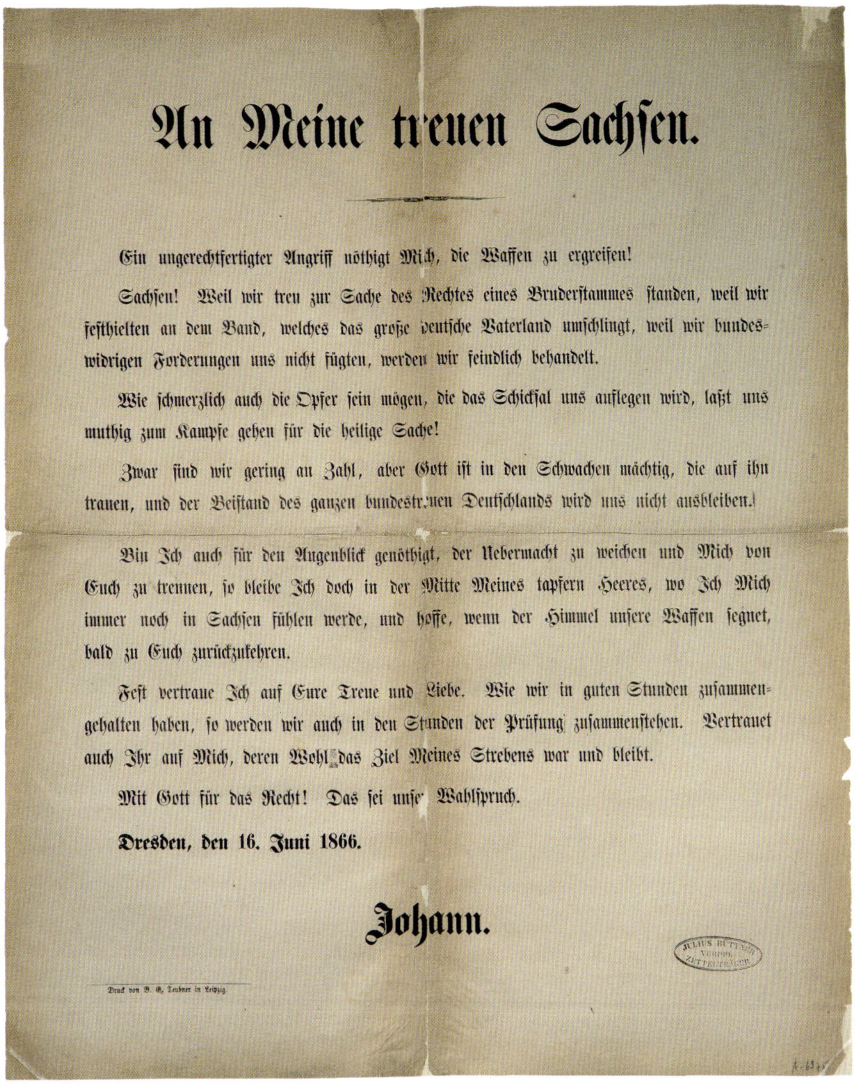

An Meine treuen Sachsen.

Ein ungerechtfertigter Angriff nöthigt Mich, die Waffen zu ergreifen!

Sachsen! Weil wir treu zur Sache des Rechtes eines Bruderstammes standen, weil wir festhielten an dem Band, welches das große deutsche Vaterland umschlingt, weil wir bundeswidrigen Forderungen uns nicht fügten, werden wir feindlich behandelt.

Wie schmerzlich auch die Opfer sein mögen, die das Schicksal uns auflegen wird, laßt uns muthig zum Kampfe gehen für die heilige Sache!

Zwar sind wir gering an Zahl, aber Gott ist in den Schwachen mächtig, die auf ihn trauen, und der Beistand des ganzen bundestreuen Deutschlands wird uns nicht ausbleiben.

Bin Ich auch für den Augenblick genöthigt, der Uebermacht zu weichen und Mich von Euch zu trennen, so bleibe Ich doch in der Mitte Meines tapfern Heeres, wo Ich Mich immer noch in Sachsen fühlen werde, und hoffe, wenn der Himmel unsere Waffen segnet, bald zu Euch zurückzukehren.

Fest vertraue Ich auf Eure Treue und Liebe. Wie wir in guten Stunden zusammengehalten haben, so werden wir auch in den Stunden der Prüfung zusammenstehen. Vertrauet auch Ihr auf Mich, deren Wohl das Ziel Meines Strebens war und bleibt.

Mit Gott für das Recht! Das sei unser Wahlspruch.

Dresden, den 16. Juni 1866.

Johann.

Druck von B. G. Teubner in Leipzig.

»An Meine treuen Sachsen«
Erklärung König Johanns
Dresden, 16. Juni 1866
Abb. 5

Konvention vom August 1865 die drei norddeutschen Herzogtümer Schleswig, Holstein und Lauenburg unter sich aufteilten. Dieser Vorgang stellte jedoch »nur eine Zwischenstation dar in der großen Auseinandersetzung der beiden deutschen Mächte im Kampfe um die Führung in Deutschland«.[6]

Die letzte souveräne Entscheidung der Staaten des »Dritten Deutschlands« lag darin, sich zwischen Wien und Berlin zu positionieren. Sachsen stellte sich traditionell an die Seite Wiens, als die Österreicher im Frühjahr 1866 wieder den mittelstaatlichen Reformplänen zuneigten. Das bedeutete, Abstand vom preußischen Antrag auf Reform des Bundes zu nehmen und nicht auf die Forderungen Berlins nach Beendigung der sächsischen Rüstungen einzugehen. Diese Parteinahme war gleichbedeutend mit der Teilnahme an einer antipreußischen Bundesexekution, als trotz des Gasteiner Abkommens der Streit um die Verwaltung der Herzogtümer Schleswig und Holstein nicht beigelegt werden konnte und preußische Truppen in Holstein einmarschierten. Mithin handelte es sich um eine Entscheidung von einer Tragweite, wie sie zuletzt im napoleonischen Zeitalter getroffen werden musste.

Der sächsische Kronprinz Albert in der Schlacht bei Königgrätz
Theodor von Götz (1826–1892), 1868, Öl auf Leinwand, 85 × 113,5 cm
Kat. 471

Das Bild ist die kleinere Version eines im Auftrag der sächsischen Kronprinzessin entstandenen Gemäldes. Es zeigt die sächsische Stellung bei Problus am Mittag der Schlacht, als die Lage für die mit Österreich verbündeten Sachsen noch günstig zu sein schien. Die Leibbrigade führte gerade einen Offensivstoß auf Hradek durch, um eine Umgehung durch die preußische Elbarmee zu verhindern. Dass inzwischen auch die preußische II. Armee eingetroffen war, wussten die Sachsen noch nicht. Zentral im Bildmittelgrund ist der Kronprinz zu Pferd mit seinem Stab zu sehen. Der Künstler kämpfte als Hauptmann mit der 3. Kompanie des 3. Jägerbataillons selbst bei Königgrätz. Vorne ganz rechts zeigt er sich im Gespräch mit dem kommandierenden Offizier der 1. Kompanie. (Ruhmesthaten Deutscher Krieger in Bild und Wort, Oberstlieutenant von Götz, Dresden 1894, S. 7–9)

Seine Majestät König Johann von Sachsen überschreiten in Begleitung Sr. Königl. Hoheit des Kronprinzen Albert von Sachsen und beiderseitigem Gefolge am 18. Juni 1866 früh 8 Uhr die Landesgrenze unweit Hellendorf.

1. Seine Majestät König Johann von Sachsen.
2. Seine Königliche Hoheit Kronprinz Albert von Sachsen, [illegible]
3. Schmalz, Albert; [illegible]
4. von Rabenhorst; [illegible]
5. Funcke, [illegible]
6. von Stammer I. [illegible]
7. Senfft von Pilsach, [illegible]
8. Graf Vitzthum von Eckstädt, [illegible]
9. Garten, [illegible]
10. von Thielau a. Kitzing, [illegible]
11. Prinz Georg von Schönburg-Waldenburg; [illegible]
12. von Witzleben, [illegible]
13. von Thielau, [illegible]
14. Freiherr von Welck, [illegible]
15. von Fabrice, Alfred; [illegible]
16. Schubert, [illegible]
17. Winkler, [illegible]

Legende
zum Bild oben

Für diejenigen deutschen Klein- und Mittelstaaten, die wie Sachsen im Frühsommer 1866 an der Seite Österreichs als Bundestruppen gegen Preußen in den Krieg zogen, ging es bald um nichts Geringeres als den Erhalt der eigenständigen Staatlichkeit. Spätestens nach der Niederlage von Königgrätz lautete für die Mittelstaaten an der Seite Österreichs die Frage: »To be or not to be.« So zitierte der seinerzeitige sächsische Gesandte in London Karl Friedrich Vitzthum von Eckstädt auf dem Titelblatt seiner 1889 erschienenen Erinnerungen jener Jahre Shakespeares Hamlet.[7]

König Johann verlegte Anfang Mai wie üblich sein »Hoflager« nach Pillnitz vor die Tore Dresdens, gleichzeitig begann die Mobilmachung der Truppen auf Kriegsstärke. Als Preußen am 15. Juni 1866 Sachsen den Krieg erklärte, ver-

←
König Johann und Kronprinz Albert von Sachsen überschreiten am 18. Juni 1866 bei Hellendorf die Landesgrenze nach Böhmen
Fotografie nach einem Gemälde von Theodor von Götz (1826–1892)
Kat. 155

Am 16. Juni verließ der sächsische König Dresden und erreichte am 18. Juni die böhmische Grenze. Der Kronprinz führte das sächsische Armeekorps Richtung Iser, um gemeinsam mit den österreichischen Truppen gegen die preußischen Armeen zu kämpfen.

Tschako eines Offiziers des 6. Infanteriebataillons der 2. Infanteriebrigade »Prinz Friedrich August«
Königreich Sachsen, 1862–1867
Kat. 161

ließen der König, Teile des Ministerkollegiums, der Bürokratie und Kronprinz Albert mit der Armee das Land. Sächsische Truppen kämpften an der Seite Österreichs, maßgeblich im Gefecht bei Gitschin und in der Schlacht von Königgrätz. Ihr Oberbefehlshaber, Kronprinz Albert, erwarb sich durch sein Geschick höchstes Ansehen bei allen Kriegsparteien. Unterdessen wurde das kleine Königreich besetzt. Die Leitung der Zivilverwaltung übernahm der Landrat von Weißenfels, Lothar von Wurmb, dessen Karriere – er wurde später Polizeipräsident von Berlin und anschließend Regierungspräsident von Wiesbaden – die Ambivalenz der mittelstaatlichen Territorialzugehörigkeiten im 19. Jahrhundert widerspiegelt: Der 1824 geborene Wurmb stammte aus einem thüringisch-sächsischen Adelsgeschlecht, wurde aber ohne Annäherungsprobleme Beamter in der neu gegründeten preußischen Provinz Sachsen. Er blieb somit im engeren Umkreis seiner Heimat, allerdings auf der Seite der preußischen Okkupanten. Und als solcher hielt er 1866 auch seinen Einzug in Dresden.

Eine der ersten Amtshandlungen Wurmbs galt Bismarcks Intimfeind Beust: Er ließ nach dessen in Berlin bekannter Geliebter fahnden. Frau von Uckermann tauchte jedoch unter und sollte Beust später nach Wien folgen. Auch Beusts Ehefrau entging nur durch den Schutz des französischen Gesandten in Dresden einem preußischen Verhör. In Mitleidenschaft gezogen wurden das Interieur und die Weinvorräte der Beustschen Villa am Stadtrand,[8] da ein unvorsichtiger Dienstbote den vorbeimarschierenden preußischen Truppen auf Nachfrage den Besitzer des Anwesens genannt hatte.[9]

»Einzug der 3. Schwadron des sächs. Gardereiterregiments in Dresden am 31. Oktober 1866«
Adolph Göhde, Löbau
Nach Abschluss des Berliner Friedensvertrags zwischen Preußen und Sachsen am 21. Oktober 1866 konnten die sächsischen Truppen in ihre Heimat zurückkehren.
Abb. 6

Mit dem Friedensvertrag von Prag wurde am 23. August 1866 der Deutsche Bund aufgelöst, Österreich schied ganz aus der deutschen Staatenwelt aus, und Preußen wurde durch die Annexion von Hannover, Hessen-Kassel, Nassau und Frankfurt zu dem Deutschland dominierenden Flächenstaat, der es bis 1947 bleiben würde. Sachsen konnte zwar seinen Status als Königreich retten, musste aber wie die mit Preußen verbündeten Klein- und Mittelstaaten dem Norddeutschen Bund beitreten. Schlimmeres, das heißt die Annexion durch Preußen, blieb Sachsen nur aufgrund der Interessen Frankreichs und auch Österreichs erspart. Außerhalb des Norddeutschen Bundes verblieben nur die Königreiche Bayern und Württemberg sowie die Großherzogtümer Baden und Hessen-Darmstadt ohne seine nördlich des Mains gelegenen Landesteile. Mit Ausnahme dieser vier Mittelstaaten verlor das gesamte »Dritte Deutschland« einschließlich Sachsens seine Wehrhoheit. Die Armeen der zum Norddeutschen Bund gehörenden Staaten wurden als Korps in das neue Bundesheer aufgenommen. Verloren gingen zudem die Souveränität des Zoll-, Post-, Telegrafie- und Eisenbahnwesens und jegliche außenpolitische Beweglichkeit.

Ins Positive gewendet, bedeuteten die Beschneidungen jedoch eine Vereinheitlichung, die neben dem neuen, nach allgemeinem Wahlrecht gewählten Norddeutschen Reichstag maßgeblich zur rasch voranschreitenden Integration des geeinten Nord-, Mittel- und Westdeutschland beitrug.

Einen Verlust ganz eigener Art verzeichnete die sächsische Politik durch den Weggang ihres langjährigen Leiters Beust, der auf Druck Bismarcks seine Entlassung einreichen musste. Er trat noch im Herbst 1866 als Außenminister und Ministerpräsident in österreichische Dienste und behauptete später, er habe sich nie »in einen solchen Wechsel meines Geschickes hineingeträumt«.[10] Um dem nunmehr auch als Bundeskanzler des Norddeutschen Bundes amtierenden preußischen Ministerpräsidenten Bismarck ebenbürtig zu sein, führte Beust ab 1867 auch den Titel Reichskanzler. Diese Bezeichnung erlosch auf ungarischen Wunsch nach Beusts Entlassung 1871. Sie ist seitdem synonymisch mit Bismarck verbunden, der ohne nennenswerten Beitrag Beusts die deutschen Geschicke in die Hand genommen hatte.

Als Mitglied des Norddeutschen Bundes folgte Sachsen Preußen 1870 in den Krieg; Bayern, Baden und Württemberg, die 1866 Schutz- und Trutzbündnisse mit Preußen unterzeichnet hatten, schlossen sich an. Im Januar 1871 fand in Versailles eine staatliche Massenhochzeit statt, bei der mit dem Beitritt auch der drei süddeutschen Mittelstaaten zu dem zum Deutschen Kaiserreich aufgewachsenen Norddeutschen Bund der deutsche Nationalstaat entstand.

Die »Integrationsprozesse ins Bismarckreich«,[11] das heißt der Wandel der Mentalitäten von überkommener Eigenstaatlichkeit mit zuletzt klein- und mittelstaatlichem Selbstbewusstsein zu einer bundesstaatlichen Reichsnationalität von jeweils dynastisch loyaler, konfessionell-landsmannschaftlicher Couleur, vollzog sich unterschiedlich schnell und unterschiedlich tief.[12] Nachdem man sich, zunächst vielerorts nur zähneknirschend, in das Notwendige gefügt hatte, wurden Prosperitätszuwächse und Reichszugehörigkeit nicht selten in eins gesetzt. Aber es blieben stets auch kritische Stimmen hörbar, beileibe nicht nur in den ländlichen, traditionelleren Regionen. Genährt durch die verbreitete Anhänglichkeit an die Dynastien, wurden die einstigen »unfreiwilligen Annäherungen« über Generationen tradiert und bildeten bis zum Ende des Kaiserreichs eine Gegenerzählung zum Reichsmythos, wie ihn besonders Wilhelm II. pflegte. Dass das Deutsche Reich letztlich den Zusammenschluss der Monarchien als Republik überlebte, spricht hingegen unzweifelhaft für den Erfolg der Einigung auch in den Klein- und Mittelstaaten.

1 Dieser Text nimmt Anleihen bei einem umfangreicheren Aufsatz des Verfassers, vgl. Ulf Morgenstern: »Whether 'tis nobler in the mind to suffer [...]. Or to take arms against a sea of troubles.« Das Jahr 1866 in der sächsischen Geschichte, in: Winfried Heinemann/Lothar Höbelt/Ulrich Lappenküper (Hg.): Der preußisch-österreichische Krieg 1866, Paderborn 2018, S. 209–239. **2** Jürgen Müller: Harter Prexit. Der Austritt Preußens aus dem Deutschen Bund 1866, in: Historische Mitteilungen der Ranke-Gesellschaft 30 (2018), S. 99–118. **3** Volker Press: Wettiner und Wittelsbacher – die Verlierer im dynastischen Wettlauf des Alten Reiches. Ein Vergleich, in: Reiner Groß (Hg.): Sachsen und die Wettiner. Chancen und Realitäten, Dresden 1989, S. 63–71, hier S. 71. **4** Vgl. Jonas Flöter: Beust und die Reform des deutschen Bundes 1850–1866. Sächsisch-mittelstaatliche Koalitionspolitik im Kontext der deutschen Frage, Köln/Weimar/Wien 2001, S. 18. Neben Beust sahen das auch die Regierungen in München und Stuttgart so. Die Ausnahme war das an Preußen angelehnte Baden. **5** Mercier an den französischen Außenminister Édouard Drouyn de Lhuys am 30. September 1854, in: Französische Akten zur Geschichte des Krimkrieges. Bd. 2: 28. März 1854 bis 2. März 1855, bearb. von Martin Senner, München 1999, S. 562. **6** Richard Dietrich: Das Jahr 1866 und das »Dritte Deutschland«, in: ders. (Hg.): Europa und der Norddeutsche Bund, Berlin 1968, S. 85–108, hier S. 102. **7** Karl Friedrich Graf Vitzthum von Eckstädt: London, Gastein und Sadowa 1864–1866. Denkwürdigkeiten, Stuttgart 1889. **8** Vgl. Sächsisches Hauptstaatsarchiv Dresden, Best. 10696, Landeskommission, C. Besetzung der Villa von Staatsminister Beust in Laubegast bei Dresden durch preußische Truppen. **9** Vgl. Friedrich Ferdinand von Beust: Aus drei Viertel Jahrhunderten. Bd. 1, Stuttgart 1887, S. 444. **10** Ebd., Bd. 2, S. 3. **11** Siegfried Weichlein: Nation und Region. Integrationsprozesse im Bismarckreich, Düsseldorf 2004. **12** Vgl. dazu grundlegend Stefan Gerber (Hg.): Das Ende der Monarchie in den deutschen Kleinstaaten. Vorgeschichte, Ereignis und Nachwirkungen in Politik und Staatsrecht 1914–1939, Köln 2018, bes. die Einleitung des Herausgebers, S. 7–37.

Königgrätz 1866

Zwischen politischem Konstrukt und militärischer Entscheidung

THORSTEN LOCH UND
LARS ZACHARIAS

Am Abend des 3. Juli 1866 war den Beteiligten auf beiden Seiten noch nicht klar, welche Auswirkungen die soeben beendete Schlacht haben würde. Fest stand nur, dass die preußischen Armeen der österreichischen Nordarmee eine weitere Niederlage beigebracht und sie zum Ausweichen über die Elbe gezwungen hatten. Eine militärische Entscheidungsschlacht – die mit der Vernichtung des Gegners geendet hätte – war es indes eindeutig nicht. Erst nach weiteren mühsamen Wochen der Verfolgung der Österreicher durch die Preußen und durch die Einleitung eines Friedensanbahnungsprozesses, der am 23. August im Frieden von Prag mündete, wurde die politische Dimension des Deutschen Krieges von 1866 deutlich. Österreich hatte das in der europäischen Nachkriegsordnung des Wiener Kongresses angelegte – unterdessen aber seit den Schlesischen Kriegen des 18. Jahrhunderts virulente – innerdeutsche Ringen um die Vorherrschaft des deutschsprachigen Raums gegen seinen preußischen Rivalen verloren. In dem Maß, in dem Preußen nun nach Deutschland hineinwuchs, schied Österreich aus Deutschland aus und orientierte sich seinerseits nach Südosten. Diese gegenläufigen Bewegungen begünstigten die 1871 realisierte sogenannte kleindeutsche Reichsgründung unter preußischer Führung. Von mindestens ähnlicher Bedeutung wie sein Ausscheiden aus Deutschland war für Österreich zudem der 1867 vollzogene Wandel von der k.k.-Monarchie zur k.u.k.-Monarchie mit einem nun gleichberechtigten ungarischen Reichsteil. Im Norden entstand in der Folge dieses Krieges der Norddeutsche Bund, der mit dem Königreich Sachsen und dem von Preußen annektierten Königreich Hannover ein Gebiet umfasste, das nun erstmals über eine ununterbrochene West-Ost-Verbindung verfügte und im Norden und Süden durch Küsten und den Main begrenzt war.

Oberstleutnant Luitbert von Friesen wird verwundet vom Schlachtfeld bei Königgrätz getragen

G. v. Bauck, um 1866 / Aquarell, 20 × 28,5 cm

Kat. 166

Luitbert von Friesens blutiges Schnupftuch

Kat. 167

»Schnupftuch am 3. Juli in der Schlacht bei Königgrätz in der Tasche meines Vaters an diesem Tag geblieben!«, schrieb sein Sohn Alexander später auf dieses Andenken. Oberstleutnant Luitbert von Friesen (1816–1866), Kommandeur des Königlich Sächsischen 16. Infanterie-Bataillons, erlag am 8. Juli seinen im Kampf erlittenen Verletzungen.

S.K.H. Kronprinz
Anmarsch der II. (Schlesischen) Armee
am Morgen der Schlacht von Königgrätz
den 3ten Juli 1866.

Anmarsch der preußischen 2. Armee unter Kronprinz Friedrich Wilhelm am Morgen der Schlacht von Königgrätz, 3. Juli 1866

Otto Heyden (1820–1897), 1870,
Öl auf Leinwand, 163 × 283,5 cm,
219 × 343 cm (mit Rahmen)
Kat. 470

Das Gemälde zeigt einen entscheidenden Moment der Schlacht: das gerade noch rechtzeitige Eintreffen der 2. Armee zur Entlastung der 1. Armee und der Elbarmee. Doch nicht das Kampfgeschehen steht im Mittelpunkt, sondern der preußische Kronprinz mit seinem Stab, umgeben von der Avantgarde der heraneilenden Armeen. Selbst ein britischer Militärbeobachter namens Walker ist mit Fernglas abgebildet. Der spätere Kaiser Friedrich III. hatte den Maler Otto Heyden eingeladen, sich seinem Armeehauptquartier anzuschließen. Er erkannte, wie wichtig diese Form von Öffentlichkeitsarbeit für den Fortbestand der Monarchie in Zeiten war, in denen der Ruf nach nationaler Teilhabe jedes Einzelnen immer lauter wurde.

Waren schon die politischen Ereignisse längst nicht für alle Zeitgenossen offenkundig, so registrierte ein noch kleinerer Personenkreis die höchst bedeutsamen militärischen Weichenstellungen. Auf Seiten Preußens hatte deren militärischer Kopf, der spätere Generalfeldmarschall Helmuth von Moltke, die älteren Gedanken zu einer dezentralen Kampfweise und einer dezentralen Führungsstruktur der preußischen Heeresreformer Gerhard von Scharnhorst und Carl von Clausewitz weiterentwickelt und erstmals konsequent in die Praxis militärischen Handelns überführt. Während Österreichs operative Ansätze auf den Napoleon-nahen Überzeugungen Erzherzog Karls basierten und einer mechanistischen und zentral gesteuerten Anlage folgten, setzten die Preußen erstmals ihre im Geist der Preußischen Reformen als Organismus zusammenwirkende Armee ein. Hierin liegt das entscheidende Momentum des um 1800 entwickelten »operativen Denkens«, das noch bis weit in die zweite Hälfte des 20. Jahrhunderts wirken sollte. Erstmals fand es im Deutschen Krieg Anwendung, aber nicht erst gegen Österreich bei Königgrätz, sondern bereits zuvor gegen die Hannoveraner bei Langensalza.

Unmittelbare Auswirkungen hatten die Ereignisse des 3. Juli 1866 auf die insgesamt etwa 450 000 kämpfenden Soldaten. Von ihnen waren am Abend des Schlachttags rund 7 700 tot und 22 300 verwundet, was etwa acht Prozent aller beteiligten Soldaten entspricht. Daneben wurden 22 000 Österreicher gefangen genommen.

In den zeitgenössischen Darstellungen und Analysen setzte sich bald das Narrativ durch, das die Wiener Regierung infolge der Schlacht von Königgrätz entwarf. Eine schnelle und erfolgreiche Kommunikation war aus Wiener Sicht

Feldzeugmeister Ludwig von Benedek (1804–1881), Oberbefehlshaber der österreichischen Nordarmee

Holzstich von Charles Maurand nach einer Fotografie von M. Angerer, Wien, aus einer französischen Illustrierten, 1866
Kat. 165

Der in Ungarn geborene Arztsohn Benedek hatte im Italienischen Unabhängigkeitskrieg 1859 als einer der wenigen österreichischen Generale erfolgreich gekämpft. 1866 übernahm er das Kommando über die Nordarmee nur widerstrebend, da er weder mit dem Terrain noch dem Gegner vertraut war. Der ebenfalls für den Oberbefehl in Erwägung gezogene Erzherzog Albrecht erhielt das Kommando über den italienischen Kriegsschauplatz. Gegen Benedek wurde nach der Niederlage kriegsgerichtlich ermittelt. Der Kaiser ließ das Verfahren einstellen, distanzierte sich aber gleichzeitig von ihm. In den Ruhestand versetzt, musste Benedek zusichern, nie über die Umstände der Niederlage zu sprechen.

Le Feld-Zeugmeister Benedek, commandant en chef de l'armée autrichienne du Nord.
(Photographie de M. Angerer, de Vienne, communiquée par M. K. Félix.)

Helmuth von Moltke (1800–1891)
Carl Schuler, 1881, Gusseisen,
Höhe: 23,5 cm
Kat. 164

von immenser innenpolitischer Bedeutung, stand doch die Fortexistenz der Donaumonarchie auf dem Spiel. Österreich litt seit der Französischen Revolution und dem Aufkommen der Idee der Nation an den zentrifugalen Kräften der verschiedenen Ethnien des Vielvölkerreichs. Während dies in der vornationalen Zeit der reinen Dynastien kein Problem darstellte, kristallisierte es jetzt zu einem sozialen Phänomen von staatsgefährdender Sprengkraft. Hierin lag auch die Krux der an sich für Wien realistischen Möglichkeit, die militärischen Kämpfe nach Königgrätz wiederaufzunehmen. Das unkalkulierbare Risiko eines kompletten staatlichen Zerfalls ebnete drei Wochen später den Weg zu notwendigen Friedensgesprächen. Mit dieser – politischen – Entscheidung aber konstruierte die Wiener Hofburg ihre militärische Niederlage neu, und Königgrätz wurde mit dreiwöchiger Verspätung das, wofür es lange stehen sollte: die militärische Entscheidungsschlacht im Deutschen Krieg von 1866. Um diese innenpolitisch befriedend erklären zu können, erschuf man das Bild des unfähigen eigenen Oberkommandierenden (Ludwig von Benedek), des genialen preußischen Heerführers (Helmuth von Moltke) sowie der technischen Überlegenheit des preußischen Zündnadelgewehrs. Die offiziöse Berliner Sicht setzte dem wenig entgegen, zumal der folgende Deutsch-Französische Krieg dort Königgrätz schon wenige Jahre später in den Schatten stellte. Das »Genie« Moltkes wurde dadurch scheinbar bestätigt, ebenso wie die Leistungsfähigkeit der preußischen Truppen, ihrer Führer und ihrer Waffen.

Der Krieg von 1866 war in mehrerlei Hinsicht ein moderner Krieg, den das Element der Bewegung kennzeichnet. Beide Kontrahenten waren in einen Mehrfrontenkrieg gezwungen. Österreich war mit einem Drittel seiner Kräfte an seiner Italienfront gebunden (Südarmee), Preußen musste etwa ein Viertel seiner Kräfte gegen das Königreich Hannover und später gegen Österreichs süddeutsche Bundesgenossen aufbieten. Während Wien keine Anstalten machte, seine beiden Fronten zu koordinieren, beobachten wir in Berlin den Versuch, die strategische Leitung über beide Kriegstheater zu behalten. Moltke und der König verließen Berlin auch erst, nachdem der westliche Kriegsschauplatz durch die Entscheidung bei Langensalza einigermaßen bereinigt war. Auf dem böhmischen Kriegsschauplatz entwickelte Moltke die preußische Armee in einem strategischen Aufmarsch in drei Marschkolonnen, der jedoch entgegen der landläufigen Meinung nicht per Eisenbahn, sondern ab Erreichen der sächsischen und böhmischen Grenzregion zu Fuß vollzogen wurde. Die Ratio dieses getrennten Aufmarschs ist weniger spektakulär, als durch die Zeitgenossen und später durch die Historiker angenommen. Seine Form war durch das vorhandene Wegenetz und die Geografie determiniert, und übrigens bereits 100 Jahre vorher ein wohlexerzierter Ansatz in den Kriegen Friedrichs II. mit Österreich. Erst das Gelände südlich der Grenzregion im Raum Gitschin ermöglichte eine lose Zusammenziehung der drei preußischen Armeen auf Schlagdistanz, um eine Entscheidung im Kampf herbeizuführen. Benedek, der, gestützt auf die mährische Festung Olmütz, den preußischen Stoß ursprünglich ins Leere laufen lassen wollte, wurde von Wien zu einem offensiveren Vorgehen nach Norden genötigt. So beurteilte auch Benedek den Raum Gitschin aufgrund derselben geografischen Rahmenbedingungen als geeignet, um die durch ihren Marsch noch voneinander getrennten preußischen Armeen einzeln und nacheinander zu schlagen. Doch schon die ersten Gefechte in Nordböhmen zeigten die Überlegenheit der preußischen Truppen und ihrer Führung. Als es der Nordarmee nicht gelang, die in ihrem strategischen Aufmarsch unverändert getrennten Preußen einzeln zu schlagen, drohte aufgrund des fortgesetzten konzentrischen preußischen Vormarschs vielmehr die Umfassung der Österreicher in Nordböhmen. Benedek entzog sich dieser Gefahr durch ein Ausweichen aller Teile auf die südlich gelegene Festungsstadt Königgrätz. Wenige Kilometer nördlich der Stadt bezog er im Abschnitt der Bistritz mit ihren festungsähnlichen Höhenzügen um die Ortschaft Chlum erstmals in diesem Krieg eine Defensivstellung, von der aus er eine Entscheidung herbeiführen wollte. Die Preußen gingen hierauf ein. Sie hatten nach dem Gefecht bei Gitschin die Fühlung zur Nordarmee verloren und vermuteten bei Königgrätz einen nach Süden über die Elbe ausweichenden Feind, der das nördliche Flussufer lediglich mit einer kampfstarken Nachhut besetzt hatte. Moltke hatte indes seine drei Armeen in der räumlichen Trennung belassen und in Königgrätz – auch durch das Wegesystem bestimmt – den neuen Fluchtpunkt des strategischen Aufmarschs festgelegt. Aus der Bewegung heraus befahl er nun den Angriff bei der kleinen Ortschaft Sadowa nördlich von Königgrätz. Daraus entwickelte sich die Schlacht, die vom frühen Morgen bis zum späten Nachmittag dauern sollte. Moltke beabsichtigte, die stehengebliebenen Teile des feindlichen Heeres frontal zu binden und sie in der Tiefe zu umfassen; dies scheiterte nicht nur an der Entschlossenheit, die Benedek und der Kommandeur des österreichischen linken Flügels, der sächsische Kronprinz Albert, an den Tag legten, sondern auch an den fachlichen Fehlern der preußischen Generale, die die operative Absicht Moltkes in ihrem taktischen Handeln nicht konsequent umsetzten. Aber auch Benedeks Plan ging nicht auf. Zwar konnte die Nordarmee den Gegner anfangs frontal binden, und ein Gegenangriff lag im Bereich des Möglichen, doch durchkreuzte die Insubordination der Kommandeure des rechten Flügels seine Absichten. Ihr Angriff auf den außerhalb der österreichischen Hauptkampflinie liegenden Swiepwald kostete Tausende Soldaten das Leben und entblößte

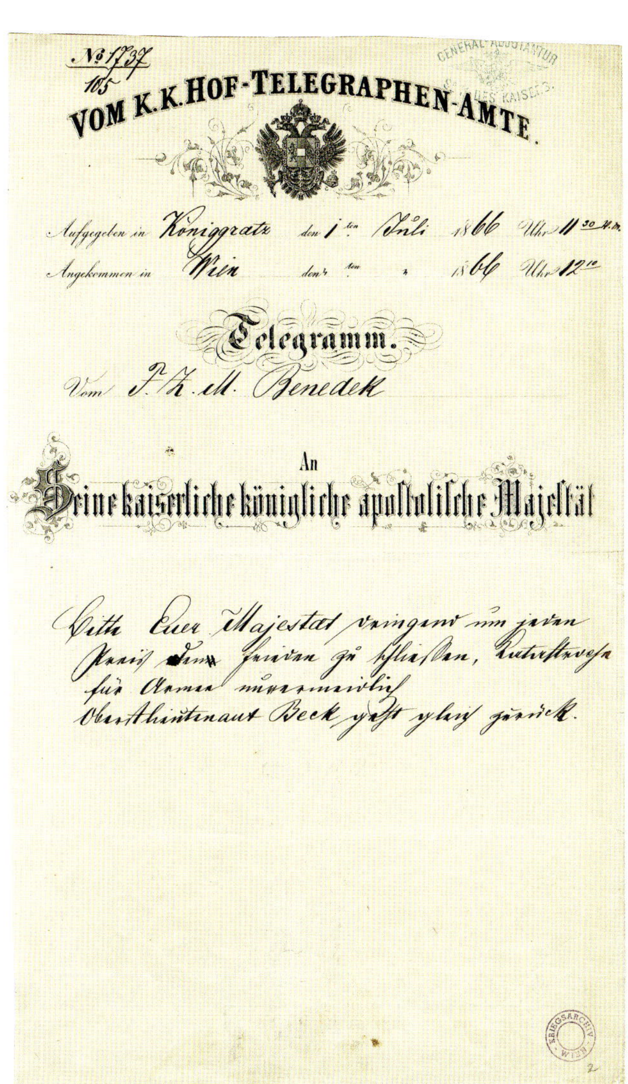

№ 1737
105

VOM K.K. HOF-TELEGRAPHEN-AMTE.

Aufgegeben in Königgrätz den 1ten Juli 1866 Uhr 11 30 V.M.

Angekommen in Wien den " ten " 1866 Uhr 12

Telegramm.

Vom F.Z.M. Benedek

An

Seine kaiserliche königliche apostolische Majestät

Bitte Euer Majestät dringend um jeden Preis den Frieden zu schließen, Katastrophe für Armee unausweichlich Oberstlieutenant Beck geht gleich zurück.

Telegramm von Feldzeugmeister Benedek an Kaiser Franz Joseph, Königgrätz, 1. Juli 1866, 11 Uhr 30

Kat. 158

»Bitte Euer Majestat dringend um jeden Preis den Frieden zu schließen, Katastrophe für Armee unausweichlich / Oberstlieutenant Beck geht gleich zurück.« Benedek konnte den preußischen Vormarsch in Böhmen nicht stoppen. Als seine Nachrichten immer bedrohlicher klangen, schickte der Kaiser einen Vertrauten, Oberstleutnant Friedrich von Beck-Rzikowsky. Benedek sandte diese ultimative Aufforderung an den Kaiser jedoch ohne Becks Wissen ab.

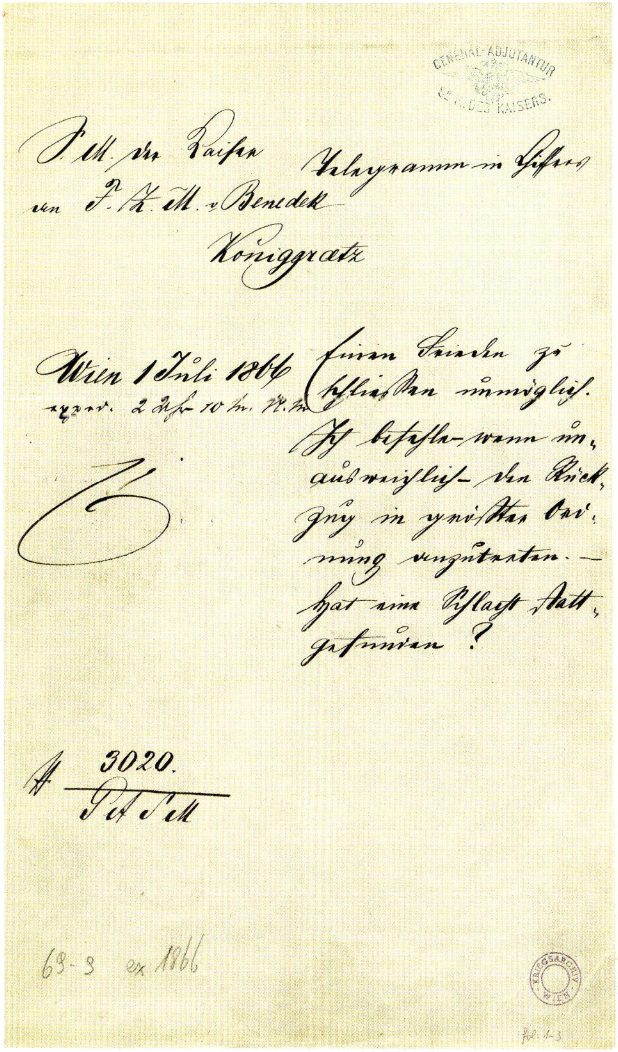

Telegramm von Kaiser Franz Joseph an Feldzeugmeister Benedek, Wien, 1. Juli 1866, 14 Uhr 30

Kat. 159

»Einen Frieden zu schließen unmöglich. Ich befehle – wenn unausweichlich – den Rückzug in größter Ordnung anzutreten. – Hat eine Schlacht stattgefunden?«

Treffen am 29. Juni 1866 (Schlacht bei Gitschin)

Ansicht von Dilec und Eisenstadtl mit den Burgen Těšín, Kumburg und Bradlec
Hugo Tichý, Jičín
Kat. 157

Bewegte Szenen ließen sich wegen der langen Belichtungszeiten noch nicht fotografieren. Auch war es für Fotografen mit ihren empfindlichen Glasplattenkameras und Dunkelkammerzelten oder -wagen viel aufwendiger als für Zeichner, schnellen Truppenbewegungen zu folgen.

zugleich die österreichische tiefe rechte Flanke: In sie konnte die noch in der Nacht von Moltke herbeibeorderte preußische 2. Armee gegen Mittag nahezu ungehindert stoßen, wodurch sie das österreichische Zentrum zu umfassen drohte. Nachdem der Gegenstoß der österreichischen Reserve gescheitert war, befahl Benedek das Ausweichen über die Elbe.

Österreich hatte die größeren Verluste erlitten, aber eine militärische Entscheidung war nicht gefallen. Nach wenigen Tagen der Ruhe und Reorganisation standen sich auf beiden Seiten der Elbe wieder kampfbereite Armeen gegenüber.

Der Kern der preußischen Überlegenheit auf dem Schlachtfeld lässt sich indes weder an der Person Moltkes noch an der technischen Überlegenheit seiner Armee festmachen, wie es das österreichische Generalstabswerk im Sinne österreichischer Staatsräson kommunizierte. Vielmehr sind hier strukturelle Gründe anzuführen, die im Wesentlichen auf die dezentral angelegte Kampf- und Führungsweise hindeuten. Sie verschaffte Moltke trotz aller preußischen Unzulänglichkeiten die notwendige Überlegenheit an entscheidender Stelle, auf die die mechanistisch agierenden Österreicher keine Antwort fanden. Weniger die berechenbaren Größen als die organisch angelegte Führungsstruktur ermöglichte den preußischen Sieg, der freilich erst durch seine politisch motivierte Affirmation durch Wien zu einer Kriegsentscheidung wurde. Auch war sich das Haus Hohenzollern in Berlin im Gegensatz zum Haus Habsburg in Wien wohl darüber im Klaren, dass es auf dem Weg zur Nation in dieser aufgehen musste, um politisch zu überleben. Königgrätz aber wurde von beiden Protagonisten als Scheidepunkt dieser Entwicklung interpretiert und anerkannt.[1]

1 Von den Autoren liegt in ausführlicher Darstellung vor: Mythos Königgrätz: Zum politischen Konstrukt der Schlacht von 1866. Eine operationsgeschichtliche Analyse, in: Winfried Heinemann/Lothar Höbelt/Ulrich Lappenküper (Hg.): Der preußisch-österreichische Krieg 1866, Paderborn 2018 (= Otto-von-Bismarckstiftung. Wissenschaftliche Reihe, 26), S. 161–188. Abgewandelt in englischer Übersetzung erschienen als The Königgrätz Myth: On the Political Construct of the Battle of 1866 (An operations history analysis). In: Mlhy na Chlumu. Prusko-Rakouská válka v optice moderní historiografie. Ed by Museum východních Čech v Hradci Králové and Filozofická fakulta Univerzity Hradec Králové, Hradec Králové 2018, S. 86–103.

Die Festungsstadt Königgrätz von Westen 1866

Druck Ed. Grégr, Prag 1866; Verlag Josef Lorenz, Fotograf in Josefstadt

Abb. 7

Die preußischen Lazarette in Nechanitz 1866

J. F. Stiehm, Berlin

Abb. 8

Nechanitz liegt im Westen des Schlachtfelds von Königgrätz. Zwischen dem 3. und 6. Juli trafen hier 754 Verwundete ein, durchziehende Krankentransporte nicht eingerechnet. In fast jedem der Häuser wurden Verwundete einquartiert. Nur in der Kirche konnte eine größere Anzahl gemeinsam untergebracht werden, um die Erstversorgung zu erleichtern. (Loeffler: Das Preussische Militär-Sanitätswesen und seine Reform nach der Kriegserfahrung von 1866, Berlin 1869, Bd. 2, S. 84–86, 124–126)

Dorf Problus 1866

J. F. Stiehm, Berlin

Abb. 9

Die sächsischen Truppen unter Kronprinz Albert bezogen in der Schlacht von Königgrätz ihre Hauptstellung bei Problus.

Kat. 148

Mainfeldzug
1. bis 27. Juli 1866

Nachdem Hannover am 29. Juni 1866 kapituliert hatte, wandten sich die preußischen Truppen und ihre Verbündeten unter der Bezeichnung »Mainarmee« gegen die bundestreuen süddeutschen Staaten. Vor allem das Königreich Bayern erfüllte seine Bündnisverpflichtungen eher widerwillig, die Koordination unter den Bundestruppen funktionierte schlecht. Nach der österreichischen Niederlage bei Königgrätz am 3. Juli zählten oft nur noch der Schutz des eigenen Territoriums und das eigene militärische Ansehen. Nach dem Vorfrieden von Nikolsburg, den Preußen und Österreich am 26. Juli 1866 abschlossen, endete auch der Mainfeldzug.

Preußische Soldaten in Felduniform

Ph. Hoff, Frankfurt am Main, 1866

Kat. 148

Diese Atelieraufnahme entstand wahrscheinlich während der Besetzung Frankfurts durch die preußische Mainarmee. Sie zeigt von links nach rechts: einen Kürassier im weißen Koller ohne Kürass, zwei Linieninfanteristen, einen weiteren Kürassier, einen Ulanen und einen Gardejäger, dessen Tschako vorn rechts auf dem Marschgepäck liegt.

Porträts bayerischer Soldaten und Offiziere, 1866

Kat. 149

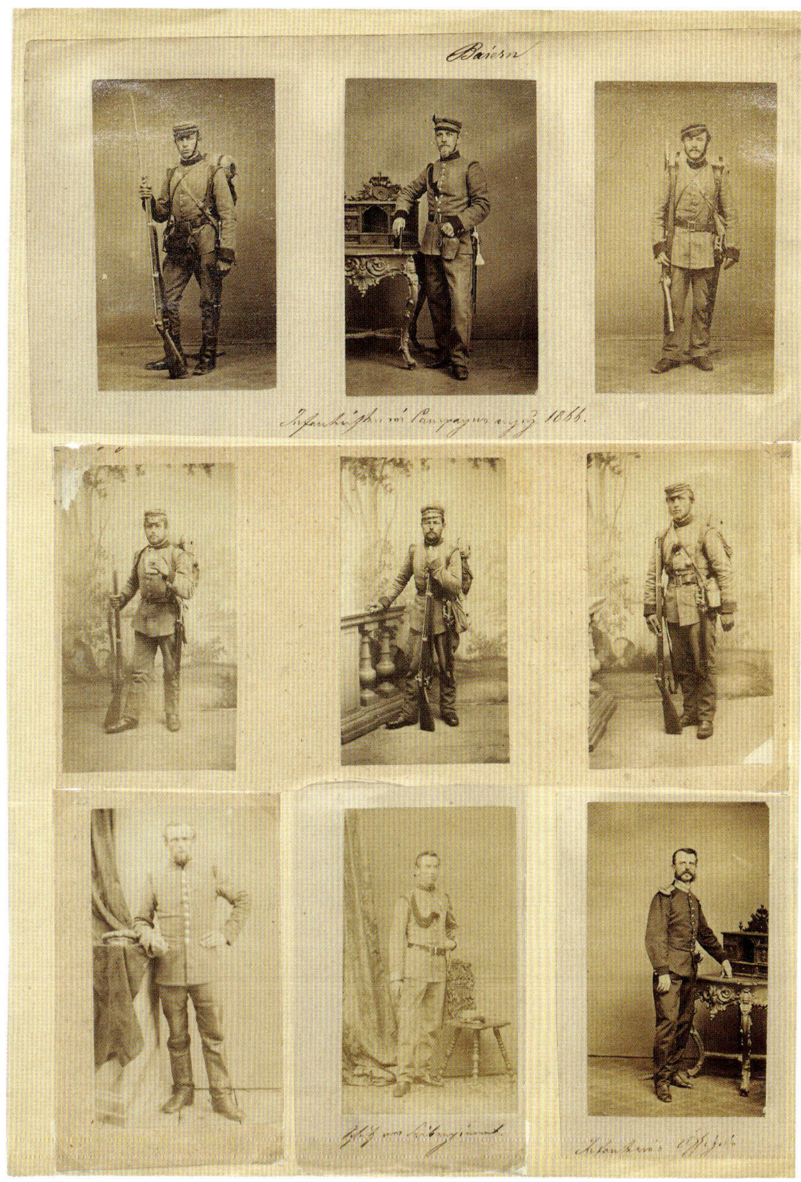

Kat. 149

Schwarz-rot-goldene Armbinde

Großherzogtum Baden, 1866

Kat. 150

Solche Armbinden waren als Erkennungszeichen der mit Österreich verbündeten süddeutschen Staaten vorgesehen, wurden aber nicht allgemein getragen. Die Truppen der preußischen Mainarmee waren an weißen Armbinden zu erkennen.

Kat. 150

Norddeutscher Bund

Im Frieden von Prag stimmte das unterlegene Österreich am 23. August 1866 der Auflösung des Deutschen Bundes zu und erklärte sich mit dem Zusammenschluss der nord- und mitteldeutschen Staaten unter preußischer Führung einverstanden. Preußen annektierte Schleswig-Holstein, Hannover, Kurhessen, Nassau und Frankfurt, nicht jedoch Sachsen, für dessen Fortbestand als Königreich sich Österreich einsetzte. Sachsens Beitritt zum Norddeutschen Bund bedeutete aber den Verzicht auf eine eigenständige Außen- und Militärpolitik, ebenso wie die Abtretung weitgehender Befugnisse in Steuer-, Wirtschafts- und Rechtsfragen. Die Verfassung des Norddeutschen Bundes von 1867 nahm viele Elemente der späteren deutschen Reichsverfassung vorweg.

Die Verfassung des Norddeutschen Bundes.

Mit Hinweisung auf die Stenographischen Protokolle der darüber im Reichstage des Norddeutschen Bundes stattgefundenen Berathungen und mit alphabetischem Sachregister.

Herausgegeben von Dr. Metzel,
Geh. Reg.-Rath und Büreaudirektor des Preuß. Herrenhauses, sowie des zur Berathung der Bundesverfassung berufenen Reichstages.

Berlin 1867.
Verlag der Königlichen Geheimen Ober-Hofbuchdruckerei (R. v. Decker).

Kat. 195

Die Verfassung des Norddeutschen Bundes
Berlin 1867
Kat. 195

Der Reichstag des Bundes wurde nach allgemeinem, gleichem, direktem und geheimem Männerwahlrecht gewählt, was für damalige Verhältnisse sehr fortschrittlich war. Seine Rechte waren jedoch beschränkt. Er konnte den Bundeskanzler weder wählen noch umfassend kontrollieren. An der Gesetzgebung wirkte auch der Bundesrat mit. Er setzte sich aus Regierungsvertretern der einzelnen Mitgliedstaaten zusammen und wurde von Preußen dominiert.

Helm für Mannschaften der Infanterie
Königreich Sachsen, 1867/1871
Kat. 196

Die Streitkräfte der Mitgliedstaaten standen unter dem Oberbefehl des Königs von Preußen, des »Bundesfeldherrn«. Die allgemeine Wehrpflicht galt nun im gesamten Gebiet des Norddeutschen Bundes. Die sächsische Armee wurde als XII. Armeekorps in das Bundesheer eingegliedert. Zu ihrer Reorganisation gehörte für einen Großteil der Truppen auch die Einführung von Pickelhauben und blauen Waffenröcken nach preußischem Vorbild.

Kat. 196

Kat. 197/1

Kat. 197/2

»Der Militarismus als Ursache der Massenverarmung in Europa und die europäische Union als Mittel zur Überflüssigmachung der stehenden Heere«

Eduard Loewenthal (1836–1917)
Potschappel, Februar 1870
Kat. 202

Der Schriftsteller Loewenthal wollte weder den Norddeutschen Bund abschaffen noch in der Staatsform der Republik eine zwingende Voraussetzung für dauerhaften Frieden erkennen, um keine Gegengewalt der Herrschenden zu provozieren. Er hoffte auf den Sieg der Vernunft, als er 1866 in Dresden den Europäischen Unionsverein gründete, der für das Ideal eines pazifistischen europäischen Staatenbunds eintrat. »Warum sollten auch wir ›gebildeten Europäer‹ nicht Dasselbe erlangen können, was die Bürger der ›neuen Welt‹ [...] längst haben, d. h. eben eine Union, einen Staatenbund, der sich über den ganzen Continent erstreckt?«

Kat. 198

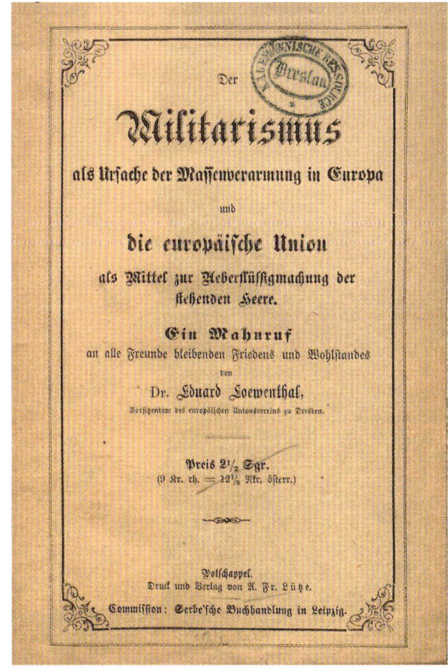

Der
Militarismus
als Ursache der Massenverarmung in Europa
und
die europäische Union
als Mittel zur Ueberflüssigmachung der
stehenden Heere.
Ein Mahnruf
an alle Freunde bleibenden Friedens und Wohlstandes
von
Dr. Eduard Loewenthal,
Vorsitzendem des europäischen Unionsvereins zu Dresden.

Preis 2½ Sgr.
(9 Kr. rh. = 12½ Nkr. österr.)

Potschappel.
Druck und Verlag von A. Fr. Lütze.
Commission: Serbe'sche Buchhandlung in Leipzig.

Kat. 202

Uniformierung der Königlich Sächsischen Armee vor der Reorganisation, März 1867

Hanns Hanfstaengl (1820–1885)
Kat. 197

Anlässlich der Neuuniformierung ab 1. April 1867 schenkte Kronprinzessin Carola von Sachsen ihrem Gemahl Albert zur Erinnerung eine Fotodokumentation der alten sächsischen Uniformen. Diese Monturen waren eher österreichisch als preußisch beeinflusst. Anders als die im Militärhistorischen Museum überlieferten Abzüge aus der Sammlung Wurmb waren die Albert überreichten Fotografien koloriert.

Besichtigung des sächsischen Lehrbataillons durch König Wilhelm von Preußen und König Johann von Sachsen in der Neustädter Reiterkaserne, Dresden, 20. Februar 1867

August Beck (1823–1872)
Radierung, 25,7 × 31,6 cm
Kat. 198

Vom 16. Februar bis zum 2. März 1867 vermittelte Preußen sächsischen Offizieren und Unteroffizieren die Schwerpunkte der Ausbildung preußischer Truppen, darunter die Handhabung von Zündnadelgewehren. Die Angehörigen des Lehrbataillons wirkten anschließend als Instrukteure in ihren Stammeinheiten.

»Wenn man alle Welt gegen sich und gar keinen Freund hat…«

Österreich und der Krieg 1866

ALMA HANNIG

Die Regierungszeit Kaiser Franz Josephs I. von 1848 bis 1916 war sowohl zu Anfang als auch am Ende durch Konflikte und Umbrüche gekennzeichnet, die Europa nachhaltig verändern und prägen sollten.[1] Nach der Niederschlagung der Revolution von 1848 standen für den jungen Monarchen die finanzielle und wirtschaftliche Konsolidierung sowie der Wiederaufbau des absolutistischen Staates im Vordergrund. Da Österreich über ein kompaktes Territorium und die Vorherrschaft in Italien und Deutschland verfügte, war er an Expansionen oder Veränderungen in Europa nicht interessiert. Er bemühte sich vielmehr um den Erhalt des Status quo und des Gleichgewichts der Großmächte. Frankreich, Preußen und Italien hingegen drängten auf eine Umgestaltung Europas zu ihren Gunsten. In den meisten internationalen Krisen, allen voran im Krimkrieg, verhielt sich der Habsburger zurückhaltend, was für Verstimmungen sorgte und ihn außenpolitisch isolierte. Das Zarenreich fühlte sich verraten, als Franz Josephs Unterstützung ausblieb, war doch die Revolution in Ungarn mit russischer Hilfe niedergeschlagen worden.

1859 ließ sich der österreichische Kaiser zu einem Krieg gegen die von Napoleon III. unterstützte italienische Nationalbewegung hinreißen. Der Kriegsverlauf und die schnelle Niederlage führten zu einer übereilten Beendigung des Krieges im Vorfrieden von Villafranca. Österreich erlitt durch die Abtretung der Lombardei nicht nur einen territorialen Verlust, es büßte auch Prestige ein. Kaiser Franz Joseph empfand die verlorene Schlacht von Solferino, bei der er den Oberbefehl übernommen hatte, als persönliche Niederlage. Seither zweifelte er an seiner eigenen militärischen Kompetenz, doch erst die Niederlage von 1866 sollte ihn derart erschüttern, dass ihm Kriege künftig gefährlich erschienen und er sie zu vermeiden suchte. Am meisten befürchtete der österreichische Monarch eine Kombination aus internationalen Verwicklungen und nationalen Bewegungen, welche die Stabilität des Vielvölkerstaats gefährdeten. Existenzielle Bedeutung erlangte dabei die »deutsche Frage«. Während die Habsburgermonarchie auf ihrer Hegemonialstellung im Deutschen Bund bestand, forderte Preußen erst die Gleichrangigkeit und später die Führung, was Österreich entweder zum Juniorpartner degradiert oder ganz ausgeschlossen hätte. Wien konnte lange Zeit auf die Unterstützung konservativer Kreise in den deutschen Staaten zählen. Die deutschen Nationalliberalen hingegen stellten zunehmend Österreichs Berechtigung infrage, als multinationaler Staat die Führung in Deutschland zu beanspruchen. Forderungen nach

Kaminuhr anlässlich der österreichischen Märzverfassung 1849

Kat. 13

Diese Kaminuhr zeigt den jungen österreichischen Kaiser Franz Joseph (1830–1916) als Verfassungsgeber. »Austria« hält einen Lorbeerkranz. Klio, die Muse der Geschichte, schreibt »Constitution« (Verfassung) in ihr Buch. Der 18-jährige Herrscher hatte – den Plänen seines Ministerpräsidenten Felix zu Schwarzenberg gehorchend – am 7. März 1849 den österreichischen Reichstag aufgelöst und ohne Rücksprache mit der Frankfurter Nationalversammlung eine Verfassung für das gesamte Habsburger Reich erlassen. Doch setzte er sie nie ganz um. 1851 zog er sie zurück, um wieder zentralistisch »von Gottes Gnaden« zu regieren. Die Niederlage im Zweiten Italienischen Unabhängigkeitskrieg 1859 schwächte seine Stellung, sodass er mit dem Oktoberdiplom 1860 und dem Februarpatent 1861 erneut versuchte, die Verhältnisse in seinem Vielvölkerstaat verfassungsmäßig zu regeln.

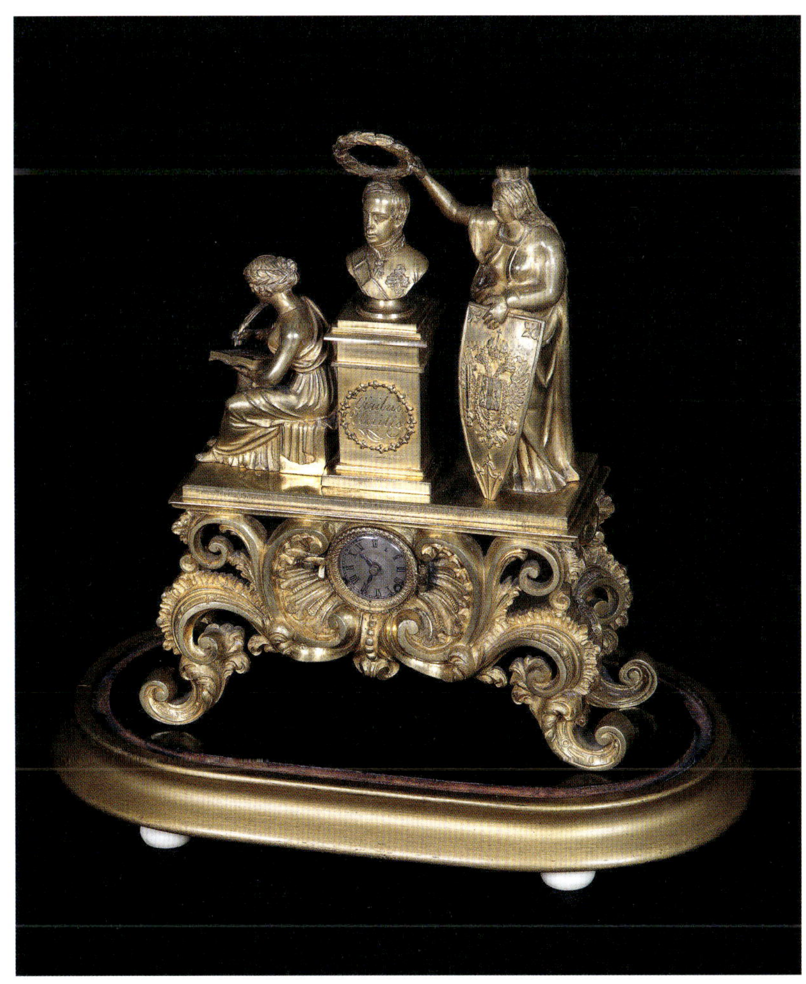

liberalen Reformen und einer Umwandlung des Habsburgerreichs in eine konstitutionelle Monarchie beantwortete Franz Joseph mit zwei Verfassungsentwürfen (dem sogenannten Oktoberdiplom von 1860 und dem Februarpatent von 1861). Diese leiteten eine Entwicklung ein, die zwar erst in der Dezemberverfassung von 1867 ihre Vollendung fand; sie ließ aber zu Zeiten des preußischen Verfassungskonflikts Österreich fortschrittlicher erscheinen.[2]

Franz Josephs Plan, durch eine Reform des Deutschen Bundes die österreichische Position zu stärken, scheiterte an der politischen Raffinesse Bismarcks. Dieser trat seit seiner Ernennung zum preußischen Ministerpräsidenten 1862 in der »deutschen Frage« offensiv auf, sodass die meisten Zeitgenossen eine friedliche Lösung für immer unwahrscheinlicher hielten. Trotz Versuchen der anderen deutschen Souveräne, den preußischen König zur Teilnahme am Fürstentag in Frankfurt im August 1863 zu bewegen, blieb dieser der Zusammenkunft auf Bismarcks Anraten fern, womit Franz Josephs Vorstoß in der »deutschen Frage« ins Leere lief.

Das Zusammenspiel der genannten Probleme, aber vor allem der desolate Zustand der Staatsfinanzen schränkte Wiens Handlungsradius ein. Als 1863 der polnische Aufstand in Russland ausbrach, sorgte Franz Josephs Bekenntnis zum Status quo und zur Neutralität für Enttäuschung auf allen Seiten, denn sowohl Russland als auch Frankreich und Großbritannien erwarteten eine klare Positionierung, jeweils zu ihren Gunsten. Doch der österreichische Kaiser wollte weder das Zarenreich bei der Niederschlagung des Aufstands unterstützen noch sich dem propolnischen Kurs der Westmächte anschließen. Ein Jahr später ließ sich der Habsburger in der Schleswig-Holstein-Krise von Bismarck in einen Konflikt hineinziehen, der die österreichischen Interessen eher am Rande berührte. Ohne vorherige Absprachen mit den anderen deutschen Staaten und den Großmächten beschlossen Wien und Berlin, militärisch gegen Dänemark vorzugehen, das in seiner neuen Verfassung Schleswig enger in den Gesamtstaat einbinden wollte und damit gegen das Londoner Protokoll von 1852

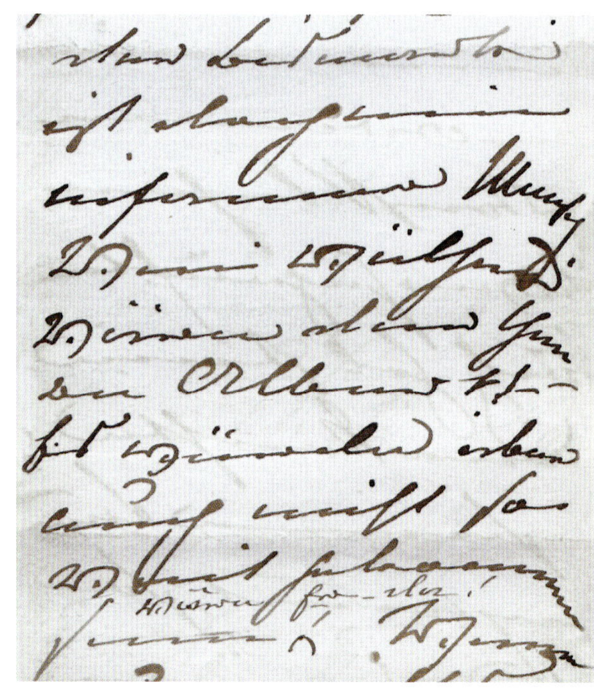

Brief Queen Victorias an ihren Cousin, den österreichischen Außenminister Alexander Graf von Mensdorff-Pouilly
Osborne, 4. August 1865
Kat. 128

Victoria äußerte ihre Sorge wegen »der jetzigen fatalen Spannung zwischen Oestreich und Preußen« und verurteilte Preußens Ansprüche auf Schleswig: »Der Bismarck ist doch ein infamer Mensch. Wie wüthend wäre der theure Albert!! Es würde aber auch nicht so weit gekommen sein wäre er da!«

verstieß.[3] Trotz des schnellen Sieges ist die Kriegsteilnahme Österreichs als verheerend zu bezeichnen. Die deutschen Mittelstaaten zeigten sich über mangelnde Konsultationen und eigenwilliges Handeln der beiden großen Mächte verärgert. Der Konflikt um den Status der beiden Herzogtümer verschärfte zudem den Gegensatz mit Preußen. Die Einigung über die Herrschaftsteilung in Schleswig und Holstein im Vertrag von Bad Gastein vom August 1865 hatte nur wenige Monate Bestand. Der einzige Gewinn für Österreich war, dass es sich als aktionsfähige Großmacht mit einer schlagkräftigen Armee erwiesen hatte.

Franz Josephs Politik wird meist als passiv und fantasielos bewertet, vor allem, weil er am Status quo festhielt und Alternativen ausschlug, die zumindest eine temporäre Beilegung der Konflikte versprachen. Trotz seiner Finanzschwäche lehnte er die von Preußen und Italien angebotenen finanziellen Entschädigungen für das Abtreten Holsteins beziehungsweise Venetiens ab. Dies erschien ihm unehrenhaft – ebenso wie es ihm unehrenhaft erschien, unangemessene territoriale Tauschangebote wie die rumänischen Donaufürstentümer oder Bosnien-Herzegowina zu akzeptieren. Dass Franz Joseph wenig später beide Territorien, Venetien und Holstein, verlieren würde, war bis zum Kriegsausbruch 1866 nicht abzusehen, da die Mehrheit der deutschen Staaten auf Seiten Österreichs stand. Außerdem ließen Signale aus Großbritannien und Frankreich erwarten, beide Großmächte würden eine derartige Ausdehnung und einen Machtzuwachs Preußens nicht hinnehmen.

Spielkarten von einer gemeinsamen Eisenbahnfahrt Kaiser Franz Josephs I. und König Wilhelms I. im August 1865

Französisches Blatt, Hersteller unbekannt
Kat. 127

In exklusiven Salonwagen lagen zur Unterhaltung Kartenspiele aus. Ein Adjutant Franz Josephs behielt dieses Exemplar zum Andenken an die gemeinsame Fahrt der beiden Monarchen nach Abschluss des Gasteiner Vertrags vom 14. August 1865. Von Salzburg ging es nach Ischl zu Kaiserin Elisabeth (»Sisi«) und deren Tante, der preußischen Königinwitwe Elisabeth Ludovika. Der Vertrag war ein letzter Versuch, den Konflikt um Schleswig-Holstein durch eine vorläufige Aufteilung der Einflusssphären friedlich zu regeln.

Waffenrock eines Oberleutnants der Infanterie
Kaisertum Österreich, 1859–1868
Kat. 160

Seit dem 18. Jahrhundert trugen die meisten österreichischen Infanterie- und Kavallerieregimenter weiße Röcke. In ganz Europa galten sie als Markenzeichen der »Kaiserlichen«. Der Krieg 1866 war der letzte Konflikt, in dem österreichische Infanterie, Dragoner und Kürassiere in Weiß kämpften. Die Knöpfe an diesem Rock wurden kürzlich aus der Sammlung Stefan Rest ergänzt.

Der Erfolg lässt Bismarcks Strategie im Rückblick geradezu brillant erscheinen, obwohl seine Ausgangslage ähnlich schlecht war: Er konnte zwar auf Russland und Italien als potenzielle Partner verweisen, der Widerstand gegen seine Politik und Vorgehensweise war jedoch sowohl in Preußen als auch in den meisten deutschen Staaten enorm. Bismarcks Verhalten war hochriskant, zumal unklar war, wie Großbritannien und Frankreich handeln würden. Napoleon III. gelang es, die beiden deutschen Großmächte gegeneinander auszuspielen und Italien zu einem Bündnis mit Preußen zu überreden. Von einer Niederlage Preußens ausgehend, sah er sich selbst bereits in der Rolle des Vermittlers. Er versprach beiden Seiten Neutralität, wofür ihm jeweils territoriale Kompensationen in Aussicht gestellt wurden. Ein Ergebnis des Krieges stand deshalb für Österreich bereits im Vorfeld fest: der Verlust Venetiens. Sogar im Fall eines österreichischen Sieges sollte Napoleon III. für seine Neutralität mit Venetien belohnt werden. Preußen versprach Italien für seine Kriegsteilnahme ebenfalls die nordostitalienische Region. Zu den von Franz Joseph verpassten Chancen gehört auch, die italienische Neutralität durch die Abtretung Venetiens nicht selbst erkauft zu haben. Dies erschien ihm »unter der Würde des alten Kaiserreichs«.[4] Später beklagte er, Frankreich, Preußen und Italien hätten von langer Hand alles geplant und ihn betrogen. Doch das war ebenso falsch wie seine Annahme, er habe »alle Welt gegen sich und gar keinen Freund«[5] gehabt. Damit unterstellte er einerseits Paris, Berlin und Florenz

ein einiges und planvolles Vorgehen, das es in dieser Form nicht gab. Andererseits scheint er die deutschen Souveräne, die mit ihren Armeen auf seiner Seite gekämpft hatten, vergessen beziehungsweise ihre Unterstützung als unzureichend bewertet zu haben.

Anfang Juni 1866 spitzte sich die Lage zu, als Bismarck dem Deutschen Bund seine Pläne zur Schaffung einer Volksvertretung unter Ausschluss Österreichs präsentierte und die preußische Armee in Holstein einmarschieren ließ. Zuvor hatte Wien die Schleswig-Holstein-Frage dem Bundestag zur Entscheidung vorgelegt. Kurz darauf ließ Franz Joseph eine Großmächte-Konferenz absagen, die für eine Beilegung des Konflikts sorgen sollte, weil Zusagen zur Anerkennung des Status quo als Voraussetzung für Verhandlungen ausblieben. Der österreichische Kaiser erkannte, dass er den Krieg gegen Preußen nur durch Verzicht auf die Hegemonie und den Großmachtstatus Österreichs würde verhindern können. Dies kampflos zu tun, war mit seinen Ehrvorstellungen unvereinbar.[6] Trotz unzureichender Vorbereitung, finanzieller Engpässe und nicht zuletzt des schlechteren Bahnnetzes hoffte Franz Joseph, den Krieg gegen Preußen mit Unterstützung der deutschen Mittelstaaten gewinnen zu können.

Dass er den Krieg riskierte, lag vermutlich auch an mehreren Fehleinschätzungen hinsichtlich Großbritanniens und Frankreichs. Wahrscheinlich wurde in Wien der Einfluss des »Coburger Kreises« überschätzt, zu dem neben Queen Victoria, ihrer Tochter Victoria und ihrem Schwiegersohn, dem preußischen

Österreichische Kavallerie im Kampf gegen preußische Truppen bei Nachod am 27. Juni 1866

Johann Baptist Heincfetter (1815–1902), 1877, Öl auf Leinwand, 64,5 × 91 cm
Kat. 156

Bei Nachod trafen das V. Korps der preußischen 2. Armee und das österreichische VI. Korps aufeinander.
Bis zur Ankunft preußischer Verstärkung behielten die österreichische Artillerie und Kavallerie die Oberhand, unterlagen aber letztlich. Die Schlacht bei Trautenau, die gleichzeitig weiter nordwestlich stattfand, sollte der einzige Sieg der Österreicher in Böhmen bleiben.

Kronprinz Friedrich Wilhelm, auch Herzog Ernst II. von Sachsen-Coburg und Gotha, König Leopold von Belgien und der österreichische Außenminister Alexander Graf von Mensdorff-Pouilly gehörten, um nur die wichtigsten zu nennen. Sie alle waren überzeugt, dass allein Bismarck für die Spannungen zwischen Österreich und Preußen verantwortlich und seine Absetzung unabdingbar sei, um den von ihm geplanten, unmittelbar bevorstehenden Krieg zu verhindern. Unterstützt wurden sie vom Großteil der preußischen Konservativen sowie von Königin Augusta, der Königinwitwe Elisabeth und Wilhelms Schwester Alexandrine.[7] Trotz dieser eindrucksvollen Front gegen Bismarck hielt Wilhelm I. an seinem Ministerpräsidenten fest. Denkbar ist, dass Ernst II. mit einem Brief an Außenminister Mensdorff vom 10. März 1866 in Wien falsche Erwartungen geweckt hatte. Darin behauptete der Herzog, dass in England die »Stimmung gegen Preußen immer im Wachsen« sei; Queen Victoria habe »unverhohlen« die Meinung geäußert, »daß es für die Ruhe und Zukunft Europas bald eine Nothwendigkeit sein würde, Preußen in die Schranken zurückzudrängen, die es für die Wohlfahrt der übrigen Staaten niemals hätte überschreiten sollen«.[8]

←

Einzug der preußischen Truppen in Berlin am 20. September 1866: Am Brandenburger Tor

Friedrich Jamrath & Sohn, Berlin
Kat. 174

Die Heimkehr der siegreichen Regimenter wurde aufwendig inszeniert. Mit der Festdekoration war unter anderen der Architekt Martin Gropius beauftragt. Einen Einmarsch der Truppen in Wien, wie er König Wilhelm und Moltke vorschwebte, hatte Bismarck verhindert, um durch einen schnellen Friedensschluss einer befürchteten französischen oder russischen Intervention zuvorzukommen. Gleichzeitig wollte er Österreich nicht unnötig demütigen, um es langfristig nicht als Bündnispartner zu verlieren.

Unter den Linden

Friedrich Jamrath & Sohn, Berlin
Abb. 10

Zu einem gewissen Optimismus mögen auch die Berichte des österreichischen Botschafters in Paris, Fürst Richard Metternich, Sohn des ehemaligen Staatskanzlers, beigetragen haben. Wiederholt behauptete dieser, Paris werde aller Voraussicht nach in den Krieg gegen Preußen eintreten oder zumindest neutral bleiben.[9] Aufgrund seiner freundschaftlichen Beziehung zum französischen Kaiserpaar wurde Metternichs Worten große Bedeutung zugemessen. Zu spät erkannte der Diplomat und mit ihm das Außenministerium am Wiener Ballhausplatz, dass man sich die französische Neutralität durch die Abtretung Venetiens würde erkaufen müssen und ein militärisches Eingreifen Napoleons unwahrscheinlich war.

In seinem Kriegsmanifest vom 17. Juni 1866 machte Franz Joseph Preußens »Gewalt- und Eroberungspolitik« für den Krieg verantwortlich und warnte »Deutschlands Fürsten und Völker« vor der Bedrohung ihrer Freiheit und Unabhängigkeit durch Berlin.[10] Österreich hingegen werde allen ihre freie Entwicklung garantieren, an der Verfassungsreform arbeiten und die Festigung des »Gesamtreiches« anstreben. Obwohl eine Woche später Italien eine zweite Front gegen Österreich eröffnete, überwog in Europa die Überzeugung, Wien werde den Krieg mit der Unterstützung der anderen deutschen Staaten für sich entscheiden. Der Erfolg Österreichs gegen Italien, vor allem bei Custoza, schien dies zu bestätigen.[11] Die Niederlage in der Schlacht von Königgrätz vom 3. Juli veränderte jedoch die Lage. Ob die preußische Armee besser aufgestellt war, ihre Soldaten über eine höhere Bildung und größere Disziplin verfügten oder Bismarck den Krieg diplomatisch besser vorbereitet hatte, wurde vom ersten Tag an diskutiert und ist hinsichtlich der Bedeutung der einzelnen Faktoren bis heute umstritten. Nicht zuletzt hing Preußens Erfolg auch mit Fehlern der österreichischen militärischen Führung und eigenwilligem Handeln einiger Kommandeure sowie mit fehlender Koordination der verbündeten Heere zusammen.

Uns vorgelegt und von Uns geprüft, und in allen Stücken Unseren Intentionen und der von Uns Unseren Bevollmächtigten ertheilten Instruction gemäß befunden worden sind, so erklären Wir, daß Wir diesen Vertrag und seinen Anhang, in allen darin enthaltenen Bestimmungen hierdurch genehmigen und ratificiren, auch versprechen denselben genau zu erfüllen und zu beobachten.

Deß zu Urkund haben Wir die gegenwärtige Ratifications-Urkunde vollzogen und mit Unserem Königlichen Insiegel bedrucken lassen.

Gegeben Berlin, den 28ten August 1866.

Ratifications-Urkunde
des zwischen Preußen und Oesterreich am 23ten August dieses Jahres zu Prag abgeschlossenen Friedensvertrages.

Unzweifelhaft ist, dass die erwartete Vernichtung Österreichs dank Bismarck ausblieb, der dadurch auch einer Intervention anderer Großmächte vorbeugte. Entgegen den Wünschen seines Königs und des Militärs verzichtete der preußische Ministerpräsident auf eine Siegesparade in Wien und österreichische Gebietsabtretungen. Sein Verständigungsfrieden sah lediglich die Zahlung von relativ geringen Kriegsentschädigungen sowie die bereits erwähnte Abtretung Venetiens an Italien vor. Hinzu kamen die Anerkennung der italienischen Grenzen sowie der komplette Rückzug Österreichs aus Deutschland.

Rückblickend wurde der Kriegsausgang von vielen Zeitgenossen und später von der Geschichtsschreibung als Beleg für den unaufhaltsamen Erfolg Preußens und der Nationalbewegungen beziehungsweise für die Schwäche und Unfähigkeit der Habsburgermonarchie interpretiert. Danach erschien es folgerichtig, dass sich die »kleindeutsche« Lösung durchgesetzt und der preußische Ministerpräsident mit seinem aggressiven, in gewissem Sinne revolutionären Vorgehen den Machtkampf für sich entschieden hatte. Lothar Gall hat das Bild zurechtgerückt, als er in seiner Bismarck-Biografie auf die ebenfalls schlechte Vorbereitung und das Fehlen einer stringenten Strategie beim preußischen Ministerpräsidenten hinwies. Laut Gall entschieden vielmehr Zufall und Glück über den Ausgang des Krieges.[12] Wenn beispielsweise die Zweite Armee am 3. Juli 1866 nicht rechtzeitig das Schlachtfeld bei Königgrätz erreicht oder die anderen Großmächte sich in den Konflikt eingemischt hätten, hätte alles mit einer Niederlage Preußens enden oder sogar in einen großen europäischen Krieg münden können. Wäre der österreichische Kaiser dem Rat von Herzog Ernst II. im März 1866 gefolgt und in direkten Austausch sowohl mit dem preußischen König als auch mit der englischen Königin getreten, hätte dies möglicherweise den Krieg verhindern und zu einer Absetzung des unbeliebten Ministerpräsidenten Bismarck führen können, dessen Rolle für die Auslösung des Krieges nicht hoch genug eingeschätzt werden kann.[13] Schließlich schlug Franz Joseph auch das letzte Vermittlungsangebot des sächsisch-preußischen Adligen Anton von Gablenz aus, die Macht- und Interessensphären in Deutschland entlang der Mainlinie zu teilen. Seiner Meinung nach bestand die einzige friedliche Lösung unter Bismarck in Österreichs kampflosem Verzicht auf die Führungsrolle. Darum zog er die Ultima Ratio vor.

Der negative Ausgang des Krieges hatte innenpolitische Veränderungen und Reformen zur Folge: Aus dem Kaiserreich Österreich wurde 1867 eine Doppelmonarchie, in der die beiden Reichshälften – Österreich und Ungarn – eigene Staaten waren und allein durch den Monarchen und die gemeinsame Außen-, Finanz- und Kriegspolitik miteinander verbunden waren. Als Bismarck den Krieg gegen Frankreich 1870 provozierte, hoffte die Mehrheit in der österreichischen Regierung, allen voran Reichskanzler Beust, auf die Niederlage Deutschlands und ein erneutes Aufrollen der »deutschen Frage«. Ein Kriegseintritt zugunsten Frankreichs wurde vor allem wegen der Rückendeckung Russlands für Preußen ausgeschlossen. Nur wenige Jahre später sollten das 1871 gegründete Deutsche Reich und die Doppelmonarchie enge Partner werden. Ihr Zweibund von 1879 hielt bis zum Untergang der beiden Kaiserreiche im Ersten Weltkrieg.

Die Kriege von 1859, 1864, 1866 und 1870/71 werden in den meisten historischen Darstellungen der Vorgeschichte der deutschen Einheit von 1871 zugerechnet. Während Theodor Fontanes Werke über die »Einigungskriege« bis heute zum Kanon gehören, ist das bekannteste Werk der pazifistischen Litera-

←
Ratifikationsurkunde zum Prager Friedensvertrag zwischen Preußen und Österreich vom 23. August 1866
Unterzeichnet von König Wilhelm und Bismarck am 28. August 1866
Kat. 173

Österreich musste Venetien an Italien abtreten, Preußen Holstein überlassen und der Gründung eines Norddeutschen Bundes zustimmen. Weitere Gebietsforderungen erhob Preußen nicht an die Habsburger Monarchie. Die Kriegsentschädigungen fielen mit 20 Millionen preußischen Talern moderat aus.
Der Vertrag schrieb auch fest, dass das Königreich Sachsen erhalten bleiben müsse.

tur aus der Feder Bertha von Suttners, »Die Waffen nieder!«, fast vergessen. Die 1843 geborene Österreicherin hat am Beispiel einer Frauengeschichte beschrieben, welches Leid diese Kriege über die Familien brachten. Zusammen mit den politischen und militärischen Ereignissen evoziert der Roman die Stimmung in der damaligen Öffentlichkeit. »Die Waffen nieder!« (1889) wurde ein Beststeller und verhalf Suttner zu Weltruhm. Leo Tolstoi schrieb an die Baronin: »Ich schätze Ihr Werk sehr und denke, daß die Publikation Ihres Romans ein glückliches Vorzeichen ist. Die Abschaffung der Sklaverei wurde durch das berühmte Buch einer Frau, Mme. Beecher-Stowe, vorbereitet; Gott gebe es, daß die Abschaffung des Krieges durch das Ihre bewirkt wird!«[14] Auch wenn dieser Wunsch nicht in Erfüllung ging, steht Suttners literarische Verarbeitung der »Einigungskriege« am Anfang der organisierten Friedensbewegung, denn die Bekanntheit und Anerkennung, die sie erhielt, ermöglichten ihr die Gründung der Friedensgesellschaften in Österreich (1891) und Deutschland (1892). Im Dezember 1905 wurde ihr als erster Frau der Friedensnobelpreis verliehen. Die Ziele, für die sie zeitlebens gekämpft hatte – Abrüstung, Schiedsgerichtsbarkeit, die Abschaffung des Krieges durch mehr Bildung – wurden nicht erreicht. Suttner starb im Juni 1914, nur eine Woche vor dem Attentat von Sarajevo. Ihre letzten Worte: »Die Waffen nieder!«,[15] sind bis heute Utopie geblieben.

←
Kaiser Franz Joseph I. (1830–1916) in ungarischer Generalsuniform
Franz Russ d. J. (1844–1906)
Öl auf Leinwand, 79,5 × 63,5 cm
Abb. 11

1 Vgl. Alma Hannig: Entscheidung zum Krieg, in: Winfried Heinemann/Lothar Höbelt/Ulrich Lappenküper (Hg.): Der preußisch-österreichische Krieg 1866, Paderborn 2018 (= Otto-von-Bismarckstiftung. Wissenschaftliche Reihe, 26), S. 39–62. **2** Vgl. Heinrich Lutz: Zwischen Habsburg und Preußen. Deutschland 1815–1866, Berlin 1985, S. 385–474. **3** Siehe näher zum Deutsch-Dänischen Krieg den Beitrag von Uffe Østergård und Bjørn Østergaard in diesem Band, S. 72–87. **4** Walter Rauscher: Die fragile Großmacht. Die Donaumonarchie und die europäische Staatenwelt 1866–1914, Bd. 1, Frankfurt am Main 2014, S. 20. **5** Franz Joseph an seine Mutter, 22. 8. 1866, in: Franz Schnürer (Hg.): Briefe Kaiser Franz Josephs I. an seine Mutter, München 1930, S. 357. **6** Vgl. ebd. **7** Vgl. Heinrich von Srbik: Deutsche Einheit. Idee und Wirklichkeit vom Heiligen Reich bis Königgrätz, Bd. 4, München 1941, S. 335 f.; Heinrich Friedjung: Der Kampf um die Vorherrschaft in Deutschland 1859 bis 1866, Bd. 1, Stuttgart 1900, S. 121 f.; Rolf Brütting: Fürstlicher Liberalismus und deutscher Nationalstaat. Herzog Ernst II. von Sachsen-Coburg und Gotha und der »Coburger Kreis« im letzten Jahrzehnt des Deutschen Bundes 1857–1866, Coburg 1991, S. 147–165. **8** Ernst II. an Mensdorff, 10. 3. 1866, in: SOA Brno, G 140, NL Mensdorff, K. 610. **9** Vgl. Metternich an Mensdorff, 14. 4. 1866, 19. 4. 1866, Haus-, Hof- und Staatsarchiv Wien (im Folgenden HHStA) PA IX 82; Heinrich von Srbik (Hg.): Quellen zur deutschen Politik Österreichs 1859–1866, Bd. V/2, Berlin 1938, 5. 5. 1866, S. 600. Vgl. Metternich an Mensdorff, 22., 23., 29. 5. 1866, HHStA PA IX 82. **10** Siehe in diesem Band, S. 113, Kat. 137. **11** Vgl. Friedjung: Kampf um die Vorherrschaft, S. 376–438. **12** Vgl. Lothar Gall: Bismarck. Der weiße Revolutionär, Berlin 1997, S. 396, 405, 416. Vgl. in jüngerer Zeit auch Hans-Christof Kraus: Bismarck. Größe – Grenzen – Leistungen, Stuttgart 2015, S. 96–110. **13** Vgl. Ernst II. an Mensdorff, 10. 3. 1866. **14** Tolstoi an Suttner, 22. 10. 1891, in: United Nations Archives Geneva, NL Bertha von Suttner, K. 28, 377-2/1. Von Harriet Beecher Stowe war 1852 »Uncle Tom's cabin« (deutsch »Onkel Toms Hütte«) erschienen. **15** Neue Freie Presse, 22. 6. 1914, S. 3.

Rudolf – ein Kind erlebt den Krieg

Der österreichische Kaiser Franz Joseph I. verfügte 1858, dass der »Mir geschenkte Sohn von seinem Eintritte in die Welt an Meiner braven Armee angehöre«. Er ernannte den Säugling zum »Oberst-Inhaber« des 19. Infanterie- und später auch des 2. Artillerieregiments. Als Kleinkind wurde Rudolf militärisch gedrillt. Als er sieben Jahre alt war, konnte seine Mutter, Kaiserin Elisabeth, genannt »Sisi«, eine weniger harsche Erziehung durchsetzen. Doch das Militär gehörte weiter zu seinem Alltag. Am 1866er-Krieg zeigte der Achtjährige reges Interesse und wurde detailliert auf dem Laufenden gehalten. Bis zuletzt glaubte er an den Erfolg der österreichischen Truppen, für den er eifrig betete.

Kronprinz Rudolf (1858–1889), 1865
Abb. 12

Kinderuniform eines Obersts der k. k. Artillerie, getragen 1865 von Kronprinz Rudolf
Kat. 169

Abb. 12

Brief von Rudolf an seinen Vater Kaiser Franz Joseph, Ischl, 17. Juni 1866 (Kopialbuch)
Kat. 170

»Lieber Papa!
Wann kommst Du denn einmal nach Ischl? Du hast ja heute kommen sollen. Ich weiß wohl, daß Du jetzt sehr viel zu thun hast. Wo ist jetzt der Onkel Ernst? Ist es wirklich, daß die Preußen in Sachsen sind? Wo sind jetzt die Sachsen? Wie viele Brigaden hat jetzt der Benedek unter sich? Und der Onkel Albrecht, wie viele hat der? Papa, ist es wahr, daß beim Benedek die Musikbanden auch beim Sturm spielen müssen? Wann wird denn der Krieg losgehen? Heute speise ich bei der Mama. Gestern war ich in Wolfgang. Ich umarme Dich, und küsse Dir die Hand. Behalte mich recht lieb.
Dein Rudolf«

Brief von Kaiserin Elisabeth an ihren Sohn Rudolf, Wien, 29. Juni 1866
Kat. 171

»Mein lieber Rudolf!
Ich schreibe Dir von Wien aus, da ich den Papa, dem es in der Stadt, wo er allen Nachrichten näher ist, heimlicher ist, sicher begleitete. Er dankt Dir und Gisela [Rudolfs Schwester] für Eure Briefe, die ihn sehr freuten, ich erzählte ihm viel von Euch und unserem Leben in Ischl. Trotz der traurigen Zeit und den vielen Geschäften sieht der liebe Papa Gott lob gut aus, hat eine bewundernswerthe Ruhe und Vertrauen in die Zukunft, obwohl die preußischen Truppen furchtbar stark sind und ihre Zündnadelgewehre einen ungeheuren Erfolg haben. Tante Maria [Königin von Sachsen] schrieb aus Dresden an die Großmama, daß die ganze Stadt wie eine preußische Kaserne ist, in einem fort ziehen Truppen unter ihren Fenstern vorüber, oft stundenlang, ohne Unterbrechung, eine Truppe schöner wie die andere. Vom Kriegsschauplatz ist heute nichts besonderes gekommen [...]; gestern war das Corps vom Onkel Leopold im Feuer, er soll es mit großer Ruhe und Besonnenheit geführt haben, leider wurde er krank, u. ist nun im Pardubitz. Von den letzten großen Treffen bekam Papa heute Nachmittag ausführliche Berichte,

Kat. 169

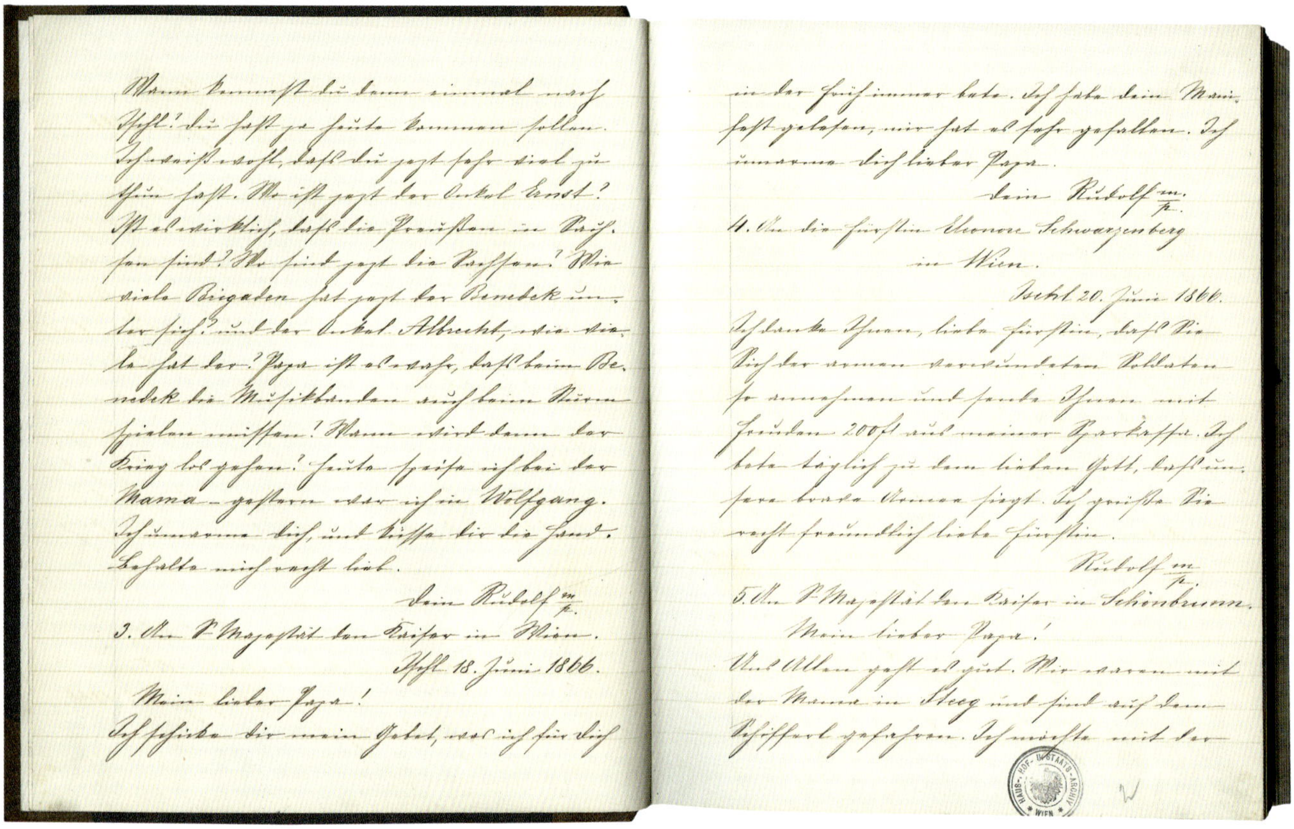

Kat. 170

die beßer sind, als er dachte, nur der Verlust ist furchtbar, da die Truppen zu tapfer und hitzig sind, so daß der Feldzeugmeister einen Armeebefehl erließ, sie sollen mit dem Bajonette Angriff warten bis die Artillerie mehr gewirkt habe. Von Italien hat der Papa auch ausführliche Berichte bekommen, lange Briefe von Onkel Albert und Rainer, Dein Regiment hat sich sehr ausgezeichnet, hat aber auch leider sehr viel Verlust gehabt. [...]

Die Piemontesen benehmen sich ganz unmenschlich gegen die Gefangenen, sie bringen die Verwundeten, Gemeine wie Offizire um, ja sie erhängen sogar einige Jäger, zwei konnte man noch retten, einer wurde aber verrückt. Onkel Albrecht drohte ihnen auch mit Repreßalien. [...]

Schreibe bald Deiner
Dich innig liebenden Mama
Die Corecturen in meinem Brief nimmt Papa vor.«

Kopie eines Briefes von Rudolf an seine Mutter Kaiserin Elisabeth, Wien, 9. Juli 1866

Kat. 172

»Meine liebe Mama!
Ich danke Dir für das Telegramm. Es wird die armen Soldaten sehr freuen, daß Du in die Spitäler gehst. Hat sich der arme Soldat den Arm abschneiden lassen, dem Du so oft zugeredet hast? Sind viele Verwundete in Ofen? Wie viele Spitäler sind dort? Sind Nonnen in den Spitälern? Sind noch Truppen in Ofen? Zupfst du auch Charpier? Ist Gisela auch gesund? Dir lieber Mama, ich küsse Dir die Hände. Dein Rudolf«

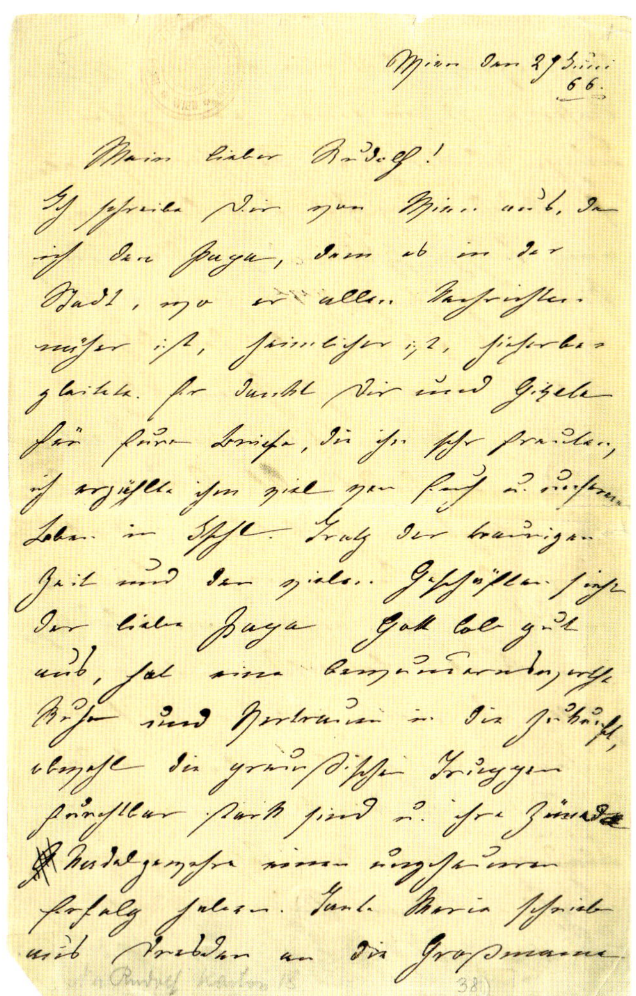

Kat. 171

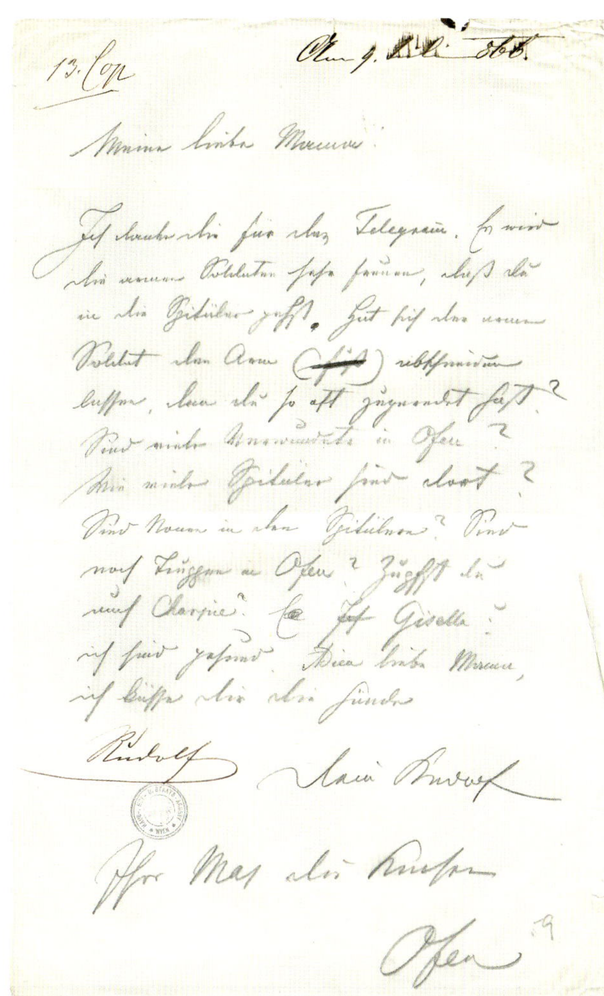

Kat. 172

Briefbeschwerer zum Andenken an Königgrätz mit Fragment eines Granatkopfes und zwei Granatsplittern

Kronprinz Rudolf
gewidmet von Erzherzog Friedrich,
Neu Joachimsthal 1875
Kat. 178

Kat. 178/1

Kat. 178/2

Von Königgrätz zur k. u. k. Monarchie

»Wir waren vor Österreich da, wir werden es auch nach ihm sein.«

František Palacký, »Österreichs Staatsidee«, Prag 1866, S. 77

Im Herbst 1866 fuhr Kaiser Franz Joseph I. durch Mähren, Schlesien und Böhmen, um der Bevölkerung für ihren Einsatz im Krieg zu danken und sich selbst ein Bild von den Kriegsschäden zu machen. Kaiserin Elisabeth, »Sisi«, begleitete ihn trotz seiner dringenden Bitten nicht. Später wurde ihr dies im Vergleich zu ihrem Engagement für Ungarn als mangelndes Interesse an Böhmen ausgelegt. Die Niederlage gefährdete Österreichs Führungsrolle im Vielvölkerstaat. Ungarn konnte durchsetzen, dass 1867 aus dem Kaiserreich Österreich eine Doppelmonarchie wurde, auch k. u. k. (kaiserliche und königliche) Monarchie genannt, die nur noch durch den Monarchen und das gemeinsame Außen-, Finanz- und Kriegsministerium verbunden war. Gleichzeitig führte die Beschäftigung mit den Ursachen der Niederlage nicht nur im Militärwesen zu Reformen, sondern etwa auch im Bildungsbereich. Die Interessen der tschechischen Nationalbewegung und anderer slawischer Bevölkerungsgruppen wurden bei der Neuordnung der Habsburger Monarchie allerdings wenig berücksichtigt. Dies sorgte dauerhaft für Konfliktstoff. So hatte der in Mähren geborene Historiker František Palacký (1798–1876) die Existenz des Habsburger Reiches noch 1848 als Segen für die kleinen Völker Mitteleuropas bezeichnet; nach 1867 aber sah er den Vielvölkerstaat dem Untergang geweiht.

Kaiserin Elisabeth von Österreich (1837–1898), genannt »Sisi«
Wiederholung des Gemäldes der Kaiserin in Hofgala mit Diamantsternen im Haar als Brustbild
Werkstatt Franz Xaver Winterhalter, um 1865
Öl auf Leinwand, 106 × 91 cm
Kat. 168

Im 19. Jahrhundert mussten sich Monarchien neu erfinden. Gottesgnadentum verlor als Begründung ihres Herrschaftsanspruchs an Gewicht. Mehr denn je kam es darauf an, die Herzen und Köpfe der Untertanen zu gewinnen, wofür zunehmend auch moderne Medien genutzt wurden. Porträts der Kaiserin Elisabeth fanden als Kunstdrucke weite Verbreitung. »Sisi« trieb exzessiv Sport und investierte viel Zeit in Haar- und Körperpflege. Ihre Schönheit und ihr Liebreiz halfen, den Kaiser und seine Politik populärer zu machen. Gleichzeitig fiel ihr das Hofleben schwer. Sie zog sich, auch krankheitsbedingt, immer wieder über längere Phasen ganz zurück und war sozial weniger stark engagiert als andere Monarchinnen.

Kat. 168

Kat. 176/1

Kat. 176/2

Tischplatte aus einem Gasthaus in Königgrätz, in das Kaiser Franz Joseph am 4. November 1866 einkehrte
Kat. 176

Am 4. November 1866 besuchte Franz Joseph das Schlachtfeld von Königgrätz. Am gleichen Tag speiste er beim »Restaurater A. Rosenfeld«. Die Platte des Tisches, an dem der Kaiser seine Mahlzeit einnahm, wurde zur Erinnerung an den Besuch aufbewahrt und mit einer gravierten Messingplakette versehen. Der Ablauf der Reise des Kaisers nach Mähren, Schlesien und Böhmen vom 18. Oktober bis zum 9. November 1866 ist in einem Diarium festgehalten, das im Wiener Haus-, Hof- und Staatsarchiv verwahrt wird (siehe S. 394, Kat. 177).

Souvenir mit geweihter ungarischer Krönungserde und Scharnierdeckel in Form der Stephanskrone
Szendrik (Hersteller), Ungarn, um 1867
Messing, vergoldet, graviertes Monogramm »FJI«
Höhe: 6,2 cm
Kat. 179

Die Krönung Franz Josephs und Elisabeths in Buda und Pest wurde – getragen von »Sisis« Ausstrahlung – als große Versöh-

Kat. 179

Kat. 181

nungsfeier inszeniert. Erde aus allen ungarischen Komitaten wurde zum Krönungshügel aufgeschüttet, auf dem Franz Joseph durch symbolische Schwertstreiche in alle Himmelsrichtungen den Schutz des Landes gelobte.

Georg Klapka (1820–1892)
Banater Schwabe mit tschechischen Vorfahren und ungarischer General

Holzstich nach einer Fotografie von Disdéri & Co., Paris, aus einer italienischen Zeitschrift, um 1861/1865
Kat. 180

1848/49 kämpfte Klapka bis zur Niederschlagung der Unabhängigkeitsbewegung für die revolutionäre ungarische Regierung. 1866 bildete er auf Bismarcks Initiative hin eine ungarische Legion, die zur Destabilisierung des Vielvölkerstaates beitragen sollte. Von Oberschlesien her anrückend, spielte die Legion militärisch keine Rolle. Nach dem Ausgleich zwischen Österreich und Ungarn 1867 konnte Klapka dank einer Amnestie trotzdem Abgeordneter des ungarischen Reichstags werden.

Kat. 182

Attila eines Unterführers der Honvéd-Husarenregimenter

Königreich Ungarn, um 1900
Kat. 181

Mit dem Ausgleich von 1867 erhielt Ungarn eine eigene, »Honvéd« (»Vaterlandsverteidiger«) genannte k. u. Landwehr, deren Name an die Tradition der Unabhängigkeitskämpfer von 1848/49 anknüpfte. Daneben bestanden weiterhin ungarische Regimenter als Teil der »Gemeinsamen Armee« (erst k. k., dann k. u. k. Armee genannt), die den größten Teil der Streitkräfte in der Doppelmonarchie ausmachte. Die Kommandosprache war überall Deutsch. Zwischen Dienststellen war in der Gemeinsamen Armee sowie der k. k. Landwehr Deutsch Verkehrssprache, in der Honvéd Ungarisch. Die Regimentssprache richtete sich nach der Mehrheit der Mannschaften. Waren annähernd gleich viele Sprachgruppen vertreten, konnte es mehrere Regimentssprachen geben, die Offiziere innerhalb von drei Jahren zu lernen hatten. Insgesamt waren in der Habsburger Monarchie elf Sprachen anerkannt.

Szene in einer Dorfschule – der Schulmeister

Johann Peter Hasenclever (1810–1853)
Düsseldorf, nach 1840
Öl auf Leinwand, 38 × 51 cm
Kat. 182

Die preußische Volksschule galt als vorbildlich. Um 1850 waren in Preußen nur noch etwa 10 Prozent der Bevölkerung echte Analphabeten, in der Habsburger Monarchie waren es 40 bis 50 Prozent. Ein Artikel über die »Lehren der jüngsten Kriegsgeschichte« in der Zeitschrift »Das Ausland« vom 17. Juli 1866 sah in der »Beweglichkeit und der guten Führung der preußischen Truppen« den Hauptgrund für

Kat. 183

ihren Erfolg. Diese »militärische Intelligenz« sei letztlich ein Sieg der preußischen über die österreichischen »Schulmeister«. Nach der Niederlage wurde im Habsburger Reich 1868/69 neben der allgemeinen Wehrpflicht auch die achtjährige Schulpflicht eingeführt.

Die Einquartierung
Lithografie aus dem Sammelwerk »Erinnerungs-Blätter aus dem Feldzuge in Böhmen und Mähren im Sommer 1866« von Calixt Prinz Biron von Curland (1817–1882) und Alfred Hindorf (1824–1892), Berlin, um 1867
Kat. 183

Neben der Bildung seiner Offiziere rühmte sich Preußen seiner allgemeinen Wehrpflicht, dank deren auch hochgebildete Männer unter den Unteroffizieren und Mannschaften seien. Das Blatt zeigt Geistliche, die auf Latein über die Preußen klagen, die alles zerstören und nichts aufbauen würden. Der preußische Unteroffizier am Nebentisch mischt sich zur Überraschung aller ebenfalls auf Latein in ihr Gespräch: Die Preußen würden doch gerade das große Deutschland errichten.

Die deutschen Staaten und die italienische Einigung

Im 19. Jahrhundert strebten nicht nur Menschen in den deutschen, sondern auch in den italienischen Staaten nach nationaler Einigung. Der Kampf für einen Nationalstaat war hier gleichzeitig ein Unabhängigkeitskampf gegen die Vorherrschaft der spanischen Bourbonen im Königreich beider Sizilien, der österreichischen Habsburger in großen Teilen Mittel- und Oberitaliens und gegen die weltliche Herrschaft des Papstes im Kirchenstaat. Das unabhängige Sardinien-Piemont, in dem das Haus Savoyen regierte, setzte sich in drei Unabhängigkeitskriegen gegen Österreich an die Spitze der sehr heterogenen italienischen Nationalbewegung. Nachdem 1848/49 keine längerfristigen Erfolge erzielt wurden, konnte 1859 gemeinsam mit Frankreich Österreich geschlagen und seine Vorherrschaft in der Lombardei beendet werden. Dies ebnete den Weg für die Gründung eines italienischen Nationalstaats im Jahr 1861. 1866 hoffte das junge Königreich, im Bündnis mit Preußen auch Venetien und das Trentino zu gewinnen. Militärisch misslang dieser Versuch. Doch nach Preußens Sieg über Österreich erhielt Italien trotzdem, wie vorab vereinbart, Venetien. Die italienischen Erfolge gaben der deutschen Nationalbewegung neuen Schwung.

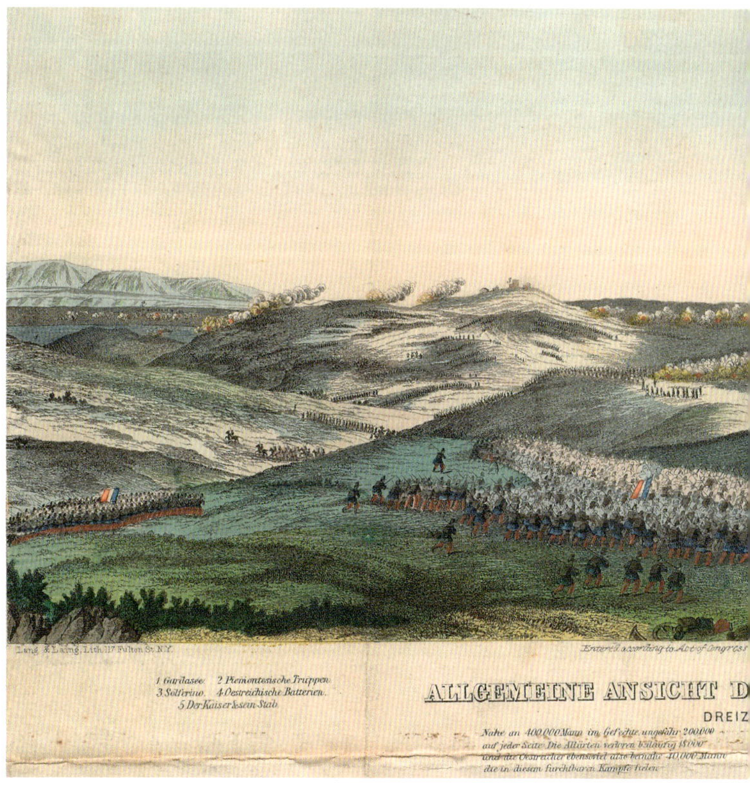

Kat. 29

»Allgemeine Ansicht der grossen Schlacht bei Solferino«
Kolorierte Lithografie nach Hector Giacomelli (1822–1904), New York
Kat. 29

Der Krieg 1859 gipfelte am 24. Juni in der Schlacht von Solferino. Von besonderem Interesse für die Öffentlichkeit waren die ungeheuren Ausmaße der Schlacht.

Kat. 33

Das Treffen von General Garibaldi und König Viktor Emanuel II. von Sardinien am 16. Oktober 1860 bei Teano
Holzstich aus der »Illustrated London News«, 29. Dezember 1860, S. 622–623
Kat. 33

Der als Nationalheld verehrte Giuseppe Garibaldi (1807–1882) setzte auf Guerillakampf. Nachdem der Krieg gegen Österreich 1859 nur mit einem Teilerfolg geendet hatte, zog Garibaldi 1860 mit Freischaren nach Sizilien. Getragen von einem Volksaufstand, stürzte er das dortige Herrscherhaus. Nach Volksabstimmungen zugunsten eines Anschlusses an Sardinien erkannte er mit dem »Handschlag von Teano« den sardischen König Viktor Emanuel II. als »König von Italien« an.

Camillo Benso Graf von Cavour (1810–1861)
Präsident des Ministerrats des Königreichs Sardinien
Lithografie, Paris, London, Berlin, New York
Kat. 32

1847 gründete Cavour die Turiner Zeitung »Il Risorgimento« (Wiedergeburt), die für ein geeintes, liberales Italien eintrat und der italienischen Nationalbewegung später ihren Namen gab. Ab 1852 Ministerpräsident des Königreichs Sardinien, setzt er auf Machtpolitik. 1855 trat er auf Seiten Frankreichs und Englands in den Krimkrieg ein. So gewann er deren Unterstützung für die Einigung Italiens auf Kosten Österreichs. Cavour starb 1861, zwei Monate nach der Ausrufung des italienischen Königreichs. Nach dem Sieg über Österreich 1866 wurde Bismarck von preußischen Liberalen als »deutscher Cavour« gefeiert.

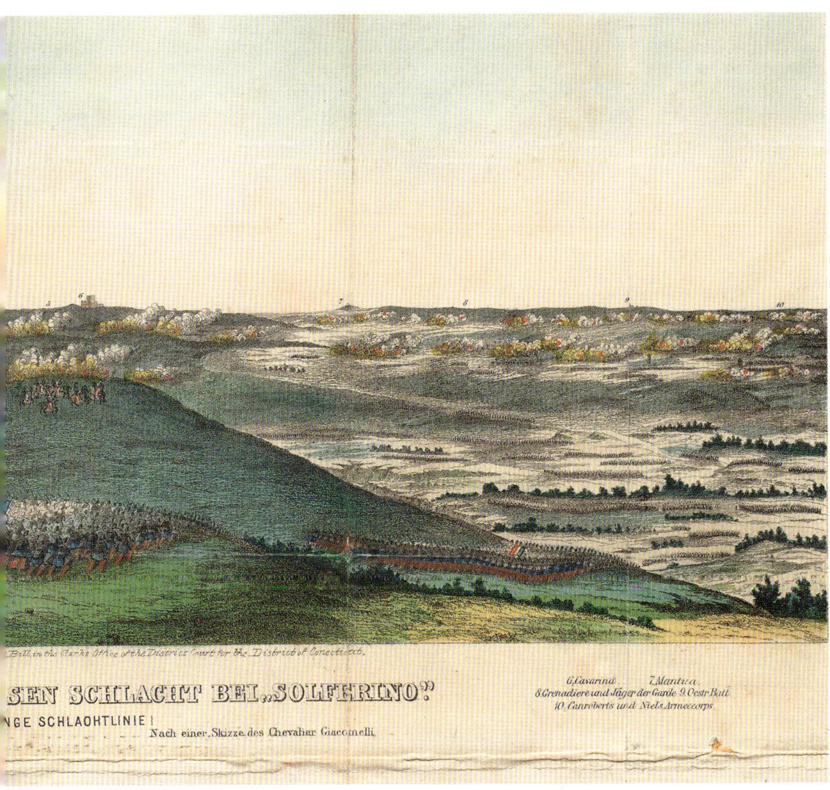

Kat. 32

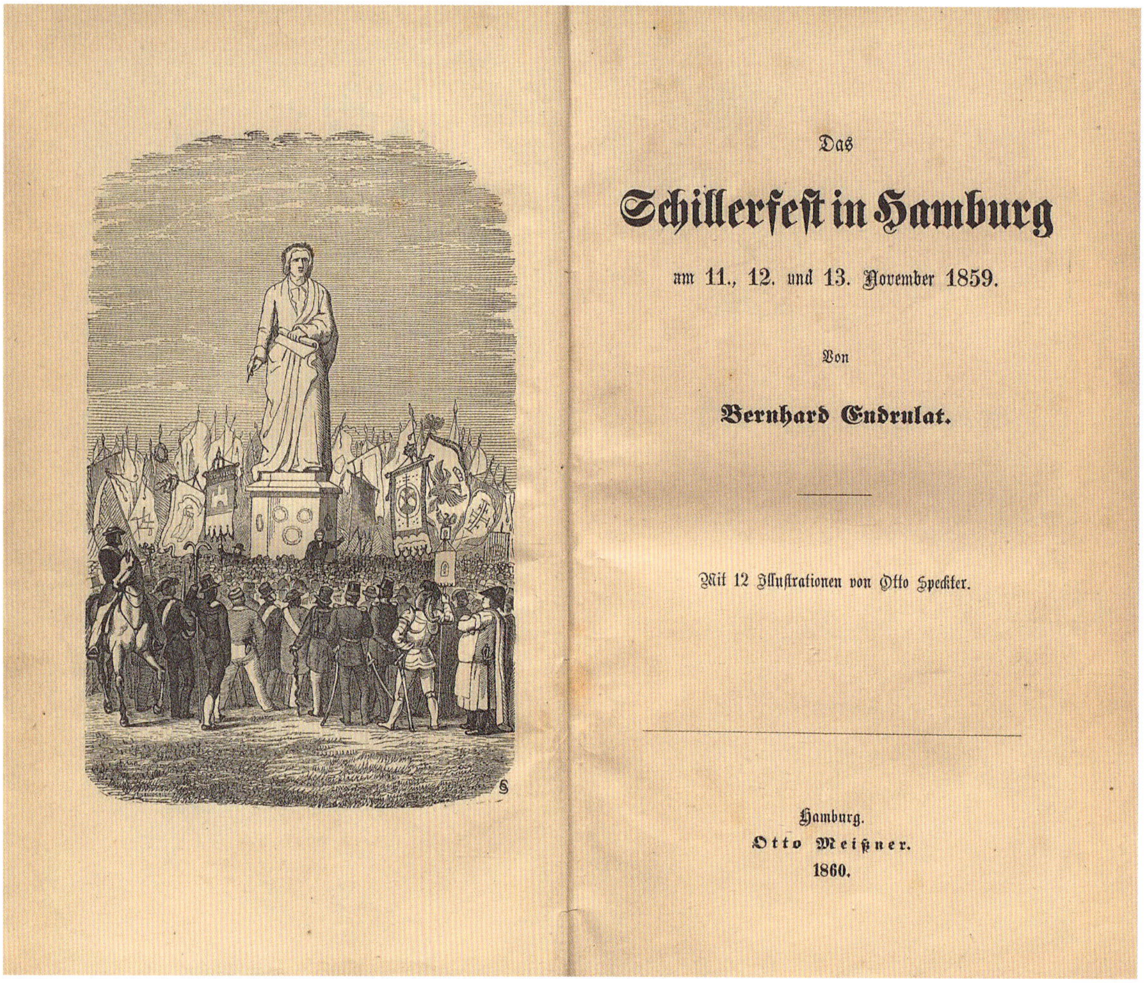

Das

Schillerfest in Hamburg

am 11., 12. und 13. November 1859.

Von

Bernhard Endrulat.

Mit 12 Illustrationen von Otto Speckter.

Hamburg.
Otto Meißner.
1860.

Kat. 35

Kat. 186

Erinnerungsbild an Mathäus Berner, gestorben bei Custoza am 24. Juni 1866
Öl auf Leinwand, 29,3 × 25,7 cm
Kat. 185

Kat. 185

»Das Schillerfest in Hamburg am 11., 12. und 13. November 1859«
Bernhard Endrulat (1828–1886),
mit zwölf Illustrationen
von Otto Speckter, Hamburg 1860
Kat. 35

In den deutschen Staaten war die Stimmung während des Krieges 1859 aufgewühlt. Viele sympathisierten mit der italienischen Einigungsbewegung. Aber auch die Idee, mit Österreich gegen das auf italienischer Seite kämpfende Frankreich zu ziehen, weckte nationale Leidenschaften. Der Überschwang des Jahres 1859 gipfelte in den Feiern zu Schillers 100. Geburtstag. Neben Studenten, bürgerlichen Vereinen, Berufsverbänden und Kaufleuten beteiligten sich auch Handwerker- und Arbeitervereine.

Schärpe, getragen von einem österreichischen Offizier in der Schlacht bei Custoza
Erinnerungsstück der österreichischen Offiziersfamilie Marinelli
Kat. 186

Während die österreichische Nordarmee in Böhmen versuchte, die preußischen Truppen aufzuhalten, kämpfte die Südarmee unter Erzherzog Albrecht in Italien. Bereits vier Tage nach der italienischen Kriegserklärung gelang den österreichischen Truppen am 24. Juni bei Custoza ein wichtiger Sieg.

Roth-Weiss-Roth.
Erinnerung an den 20. Juli 1866.
Von
Hermann Stricker
„Roth-Weiss-Roth"! Euch schönen Farben,
Oestreichs Stolz, Euch: „Ein Hurrah!"
Leuchtend glänzt des Seemanns Auge,
Das Euch siegend flattern sah. —
Gruss! dir Insel, still im Meere,
Aller Welt bist du bekannt,
Preist man Kühnheit, muthig Wagen,
Dann wirst du voran genannt.
Lauter schlagen Oestreichs Herzen,
Nennt man „Lissa", es erwacht
Dankbar Fühlen all' den Mannen,
Die gekämpft die blut'ge Schlacht.
Brausend zieht heran die Woge,
Sie erzählt, was sie geschaut:
Von den Helden, die der Kaiser
Mit der Wehr zur See betraut.
Von dem Siege, den errungen
Tapferkeit mit kleiner Macht,
Von der Lieb' zum Vaterlande,
Die nie schlummert, immer wacht.
Taue, Ketten wurden Panzer,
Als kein Retten mehr sich bot,
Gegen Stahl- und Eisen-Schiffe
Dennoch siegte „Roth-Weiss-Roth".
Und soll wieder je das Zeichen
Flattern auf: „Klar zum Gefecht!"
Höret Todte uns're Eide,
Herzen schwör'n sie, recht und echt.
„Roth-Weiss-Roth", o theure Farben,
Wieder führ'n zum Sieg wir Euch,
Tapfer kämpfend — wie Ihr Brüder,
Sterben wir für „Oesterreich!"
Nach Angabe des Dichters gez. v. G. Weiss.
Druck und Verlag von „Leykam" in Graz.
K. 847.

Kat. 187

»Roth – Weiss – Roth. Erinnerung an den 20. Juli 1866«
Gedicht von Hermann Stricker über die Seeschlacht bei Lissa
Lithografie nach Angabe des Dichters gezeichnet von Georg Weineiss, Graz, um 1890
Kat. 187

Am 20. Juli verhinderte die österreichische Flotte unter Konteradmiral Wilhelm von Tegetthoff die Eroberung der Insel Lissa (heute Vis, Kroatien) durch die italienische Marine. Tegetthoff konnte die technischen Mängel der veralteten Flotte ausgleichen, indem er Schiffe mit Ankerketten und Tauen behelfsmäßig panzern ließ und auf Rammtaktik setzte. Das Gedicht feiert jedoch nicht den als Seehelden verehrten Admiral, sondern die beteiligten Seeleute und mit ihnen allen zukünftigen österreichischen Opfermut.

Kat. 188

»La rivincita di Lissa« / Rache für Lissa
Science-Fiction-Roman von Yambo (d.i. Enrico de' Conti Novelli da Bertinoro)
Rom 1909
Kat. 188

Italiens Stolz war die nach modernsten Maßstäben mit Panzerschiffen ausgebaute Flotte. Ihre Niederlage bei Lissa trotz technischer und zahlenmäßiger Überlegenheit galt als nationale Schmach. Über 40 Jahre später träumte Yambo (1874–1943) von einem glorreichen Seesieg über Österreich, der bei Triest errungen würde.

Verdienstmedaille in Bronze für die Befreier der Stadt Rom
Königreich Italien, 1870
Buntmetall, Durchmesser 32,5 mm
Sammlung Major Rübke
Kat. 191

Als Frankreich seine Truppen, die seit 1849 den Kirchenstaat beschützt hatten, nach Kriegsbeginn 1870 abzog und eine Niederlage nach der anderen erlitt, eroberten italienische Truppen fast kampflos Rom. Damit endete die weltlich-politische Herrschaft des Vatikans über einen Territorialstaat und Rom wurde zur Hauptstadt des Königreichs Italien.

Kat. 191

1870/71

Deutsch-Französischer Krieg

Für die einen, wie den Dachauer Bauern Xaver Stegmeir, kam im Juli 1870 der Krieg »wie eine Bombe in den schönsten Friedens-Traum«. Andere, wie der preußische Ministerpräsident Otto von Bismarck, hatten ihn als Option zur Vollendung einer deutschen Einigung mit einkalkuliert, und viele Deutsche und Franzosen forderten ihn lautstark, um vermeintliche Kränkungen durch die Gegenseite zu rächen. In dem folgenden Konflikt, der fast ausschließlich auf französischem Boden ausgefochten wurde, setzten beide Seiten alle ihnen zur Verfügung stehenden Waffen und technischen Möglichkeiten ein. Besetzungen und Belagerungen trafen auch Hunderttausende unter der

Zivilbevölkerung. Bismarcks Ziel einer deutschen Nationalstaatsgründung unter preußischer Führung wurde erreicht, bevor der Krieg endete. Die deutsche Kaiserproklamation in Versailles und die auf Waffenstillstand und Friedensschluss folgenden Annexionen des Elsass und von Teilen Lothringens demütigten das unterlegene Frankreich. Nicht weniger traumatisch wurde der Aufstand der Pariser Kommune gegen die Regierung der Republik und dessen brutale Niederschlagung empfunden. Das Deutsche Reich, die neue Großmacht in der Mitte Europas, sah sich mit dem Misstrauen seiner Nachbarn konfrontiert. Frankreich sann auf Revanche für die bitteren Niederlagen von 1870/71.

1867

Frühjahr Luxemburgkrise um den beabsichtigen Kauf des Landes durch Napoleon III.

1870

Juli Streit um die Kandidatur des Erbprinzen Leopold von Hohenzollern-Sigmaringen für den spanischen Thron

13. Juli Veröffentlichung der von Bismarck redigierten »Emser Depesche«

14. Juli Mobilmachung in Frankreich

16. Juli Mobilmachung in Preußen und den süddeutschen Staaten

19. Juli Französische Kriegserklärung an Preußen

28. Juli Napoleon III. übernimmt den Oberbefehl über das französische Feldheer

2. – 6. August Gefechte und Schlachten bei Saarbrücken, Weissenburg, Spichern und Wörth

18. August Schlacht bei Gravelotte/St. Privat

15. August – 27. September Belagerung von Straßburg

20. August – 27. Oktober Belagerung von Metz

1./2. September Französische Niederlage bei Sedan. Napoleon III. begibt sich in deutsche Kriegsgefangenschaft

4. September
Proklamation der Dritten Republik in Paris unter Louis Trochu und Kriegsminister Léon Gambetta

19. September 1870 – 28. Januar 1871
Belagerung von Paris

7. Oktober Léon Gambetta verlässt Paris mit einem Ballon, um von Tours aus den Krieg in der französischen Provinz zu organisieren

11. Oktober Bayerische Truppen besetzen erstmals Orléans, das am 9. November wieder geräumt werden muss

November Bismarck verhandelt mit den süddeutschen Staaten über einen Zusammenschluss mit dem Norddeutschen Bund

4. Dezember
Neuerliche Einnahme von Orléans durch deutsche Truppen

27. Dezember Deutsche Truppen beschießen Paris. Das Bombardement endet am 26. Januar 1871

1871

1. Januar Gründungstag des Deutschen Reiches mit Inkrafttreten seiner Verfassung

18. Januar Proklamation Wilhelms I. zum deutschen Kaiser in Versailles

19. Januar Schlacht von Buzenval, letzter Ausfall französischer Truppen aus Paris

28. Januar Ein auf 21 Tage befristeter Waffenstillstand tritt in Kraft

1. Februar Die Konvention von Verrières ermöglicht den Übertritt der französischen Ostarmee des Generals Bourbaki in die Schweiz

8. Februar Wahl der neuen französischen Nationalversammlung

17. Februar Adolphe Thiers wird Ministerpräsident

26. Februar Vorfrieden von Versailles

1. – 3. März Deutsche Besetzung des Zentrums von Paris

3. März Wahlen zum ersten deutschen Reichstag

18. März – 28. Mai Aufstand der Pariser Kommune. Belagerung und blutige Eroberung der Stadt durch französische Regierungstruppen

10. Mai Frieden von Frankfurt

16. Juni Siegesparade in Berlin

28. Juni Elsass-Lothringen wird deutsches »Reichsland«

Deutsch-Französischer Krieg 1870/71
DER KANAL
BELGIEN
LUXEMBURG
PREUSSEN
BIRKENFELD
HESSEN
PFALZ
BADEN
SCHWEIZ
FRANKREICH
Lothringen
Elsass
Mosel
Saar
Somme
Oise
Aisne
Seine
Maas
Meurthe
Saône
Doubs
Loire
Abbeville
Cambrai
Avesnes
3.1.1871
Bapaume
Péronne
Amiens
19.1.1871
St. Quentin
Hirson
Rocroi
Charleville
1.9.1870
Sedan
Mouzon
Montmédy
Dur
La Fère
Laon
Noyon
Rethel
Le Havre
Honfleur
Rouen
Elboeuf
Beauvais
Compiègne
Soissons
16.10.1870
Reims
Evreux
St. Leu
St. Brice
Paris
19.9.1870–28.1.1871
Versailles
Château-Th erry
Epernay
Châlons-sur-Marne
Varennes
Clermont-en-Argonne
8.11.1870
Verdun
18.8.1870
St. Privat
Mars-la-Tour
16.8.1870
Kapitulation
Metz 27.10.1870
Metz
Pont-à-Mousson
Trier
Birken-feld
Kaiserslautern
Saarbrücken
Spichern
6.8.1870
Speyer
Germersheim
Weißenburg
Bitsch
Karls-ruhe
Mainz
4.8.1870
Wörth
Rastatt
Saargemünd
Lützel-stein
Pfalzburg
Straßburg
Kehl
27.9.1870
Marsal
Luxemburg
Longwy
Thionville
Bar-le-Duc
Toul
23.9.1870
Nancy
Lunéville
St. Dizier
Bayon
Neuchâteau
Epinal
Schlettstadt
Colmar
Neu-Breisach
Freiburg
Mülhausen
Basel
Chartres
Fontainebleau
Nogent
Troyes
Sens
Joigny
Chaumont-en-Bassigny
Langres
2.12.1870 Loigny
Toury
Le Mans
Coulmiers
Beaune-la-Rolande
28.11.1870
Montargis
Ladon
3./4.12.1870
Orléans
Vendôme
Beaugency
Sully
Gien
Briare
Blois
26.11.1870 Offensive der franz. Loirearmee
Auxerre
Châtillon-sur-Seine
Noyers
Lure
Belfort
Vesoul
Montbéliard
Dijon
21.–23.1.1871
Gray
Auxonne
Besançon
Dôle
Quingey
Internierung der franz. Ostarmee in der Schweiz 1.2.1871
Neuchâtel
Salins
Pontarlier
Vierzon
Bourges
Nevers
Autun
Chalon-sur-Saône
Preußische Operationer
Preußische Stellungen
Französische Operationen
Französische Stellungen
Wichtige Schlachten
Festung
0 10 20 30 40 50 km

1867 – Glanz und Krise des Zweiten Kaiserreichs

Louis Napoleon Bonaparte (1808–1873), ein Neffe Napoleons I., wurde 1848 zum französischen Staatspräsidenten gewählt. 1851 sicherte er sich durch einen Staatsstreich und eine darauffolgende Volksabstimmung diktatorische Vollmachten. 1852 stimmten die Franzosen für die Wiedererrichtung des Kaiserreichs am symbolträchtigen 2. Dezember, dem Krönungstag Napoleons I. und Jahrestag seines Sieges von Austerlitz.

Napoleon III. profitierte vom Mythos seines Onkels, wurde aber auch an dessen Erfolgen gemessen. Dabei war er weder ein Feldherrntalent noch dem Krieg zugeneigt. Doch es waren nicht zuletzt die Beteiligungen am Krimkrieg von 1853 bis 1856 und am Zweiten Italienischen Unabhängigkeitskrieg 1859, die Frankreich wieder in die Reihe der europäischen Großmächte aufrücken ließen. In den Augen Bismarcks war Frankreich die Macht, die eine deutsche Einigung verhindern konnte. 1867 wurde zu dem Jahr, in dem der sprichwörtliche Glanz des »Second Empire« auf der Pariser Weltausstellung noch einmal hell erstrahlte, während militärische und diplomatische Misserfolge bereits den Ruhm Napoleons III. eintrübten.

Kat. 208

Napoleon I., Napoleon II. und Napoleon III.

Druck Th. Görnert, Dresden nach 1852

Lithografie

Kat. 208

Die bonapartistische Propaganda stellte Napoleon III. in eine Reihe mit dem Begründer der Dynastie, Napoleon I., und dessen in Österreich jung verstorbenem Sohn, der nie die Nachfolge seines Vaters als »Napoleon II.« hatte antreten können.

Kat. 206

Kat. 203

Kat. 207

Spenzer für Reitknechte des Kaiserlichen Marstalls

Kaiserreich Frankreich, 1852–1870

Kat. 206

Die Angehörigen des »Service des Ecuries de l'Empereur« trugen, wie zurzeit des ersten Napoleon, Uniformen in den kaiserlichen Farben Grün und Gold, kombiniert mit einem kräftigen Rot. Ins Rückenfutter dieser Jacke ist eine heute verblasste Jahreszahl, »1870«, gestempelt.

Büste Napoleons III. während des Zweiten Italienischen Unabhängigkeitskriegs 1859

Albert-Ernest Carrier-Belleuse (1824–1887), um 1859

Bronze, Höhe 41,2 cm

Kat. 203

Napoleon III. als Nussknacker

Um 1860

Kat. 207

Gegner Napoleons III. sahen in ihm einen erfolglosen Nacheiferer seines Onkels Napoleon I. Der Schriftsteller Victor Hugo nannte ihn 1852 in einer Streitschrift »Napoléon Le Petit« (Napoleon der Kleine). Eine deutsche Variante dieser Abwertung war die Darstellung Napoleons III. als Nussknacker.

EXPOSITION UNIVERSELLE DE 1867 A PARIS

9

M le Cte de Bismark.

Signature du Porteur

LE CONSEILLER D'ÉTAT
COMMISSAIRE GÉNÉRAL
F Le Play

Cette Carte est essentiellement personnelle et ne peut être prêtée.

Kat. 212

Ansicht des Geländes der Pariser Weltausstellung von 1867

Numa Fils (i. e. Christophe Emile Haering)
Paris 1867
Fotoreproduktion einer Grafik im Carte-de-Visite-Format
Kat. 211

Napoleon III. sah sich in erster Linie als Modernisierer und Förderer von Industrie, Wissenschaften und Künsten. Paris, radikal umgestaltet durch den von Napoleon III. ernannten Präfekten Georges-Eugène Haussmann, wurde zur »Hauptstadt der Welt«. Mit der am 1. April 1867 eröffneten Weltausstellung erlebte das Zweite Kaiserreich seinen letzten glanzvollen Höhepunkt. 26 000 Arbeiter errichteten am Marsfeld ein riesiges ovales Ausstellungsgebäude, 32 Nationen mit 33 000 Ausstellern waren vertreten.

Eintrittskarte Bismarcks für die Pariser Weltausstellung 1867

Kat. 212

Bismarck begleitete König Wilhelm I. von Preußen zur Weltausstellung nach Paris. Das Interesse an Preußens starkem Mann war groß. Pariser Damenschneider benannten sogar die Modefarbe der Saison, »Havanna-Braun«, nach ihm um: »couleur Bismarck« versprach mehr Aufmerksamkeit.

Festungsplan von Luxemburg

H. Baumann, 1854
Kat. 214

Das Großherzogtum Luxemburg wurde in Personalunion vom König der Niederlande, Wilhelm III. (1817–1890), regiert. Seine Hauptstadt hatte bis zur Auflösung des Deutschen Bundes den Status einer Bundesfestung, in der Soldaten aus verschiedenen Mitgliedsstaaten – hier vor allem Preußen – gemeinsam die Westgrenze des Bundes sichern sollten.

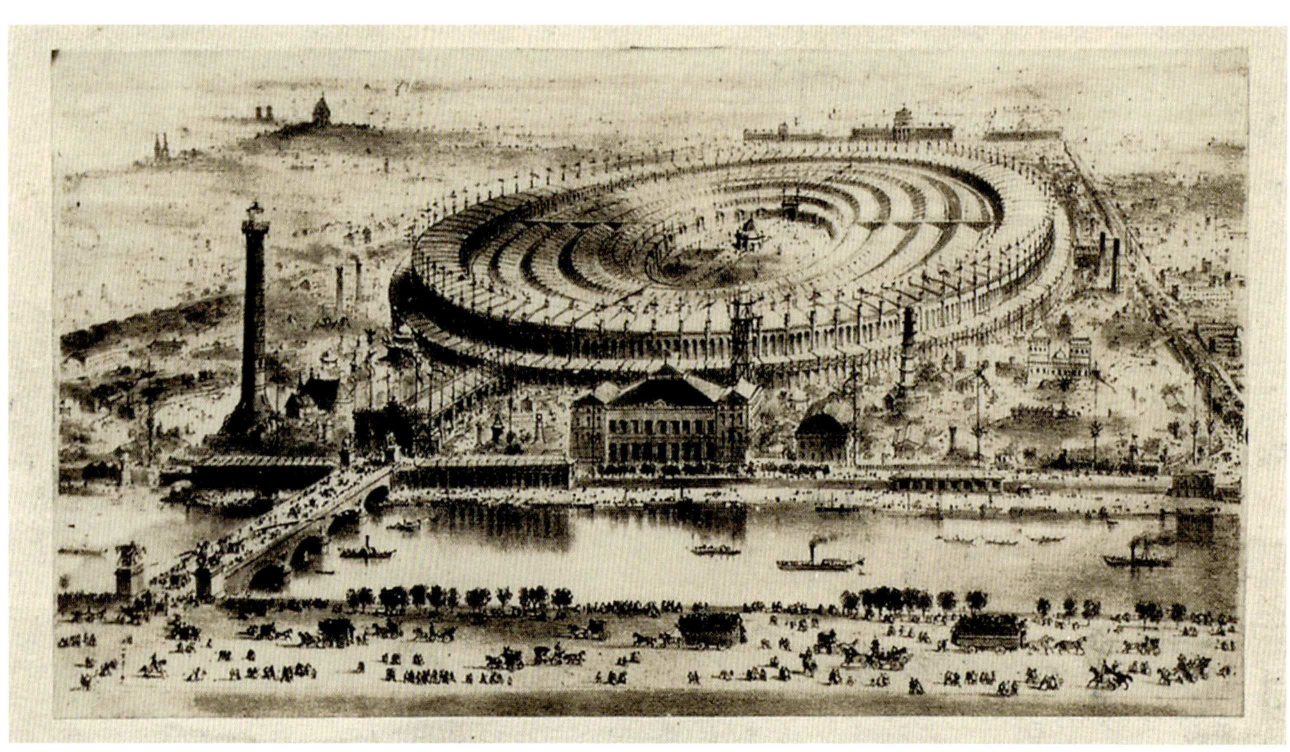

Kat. 211

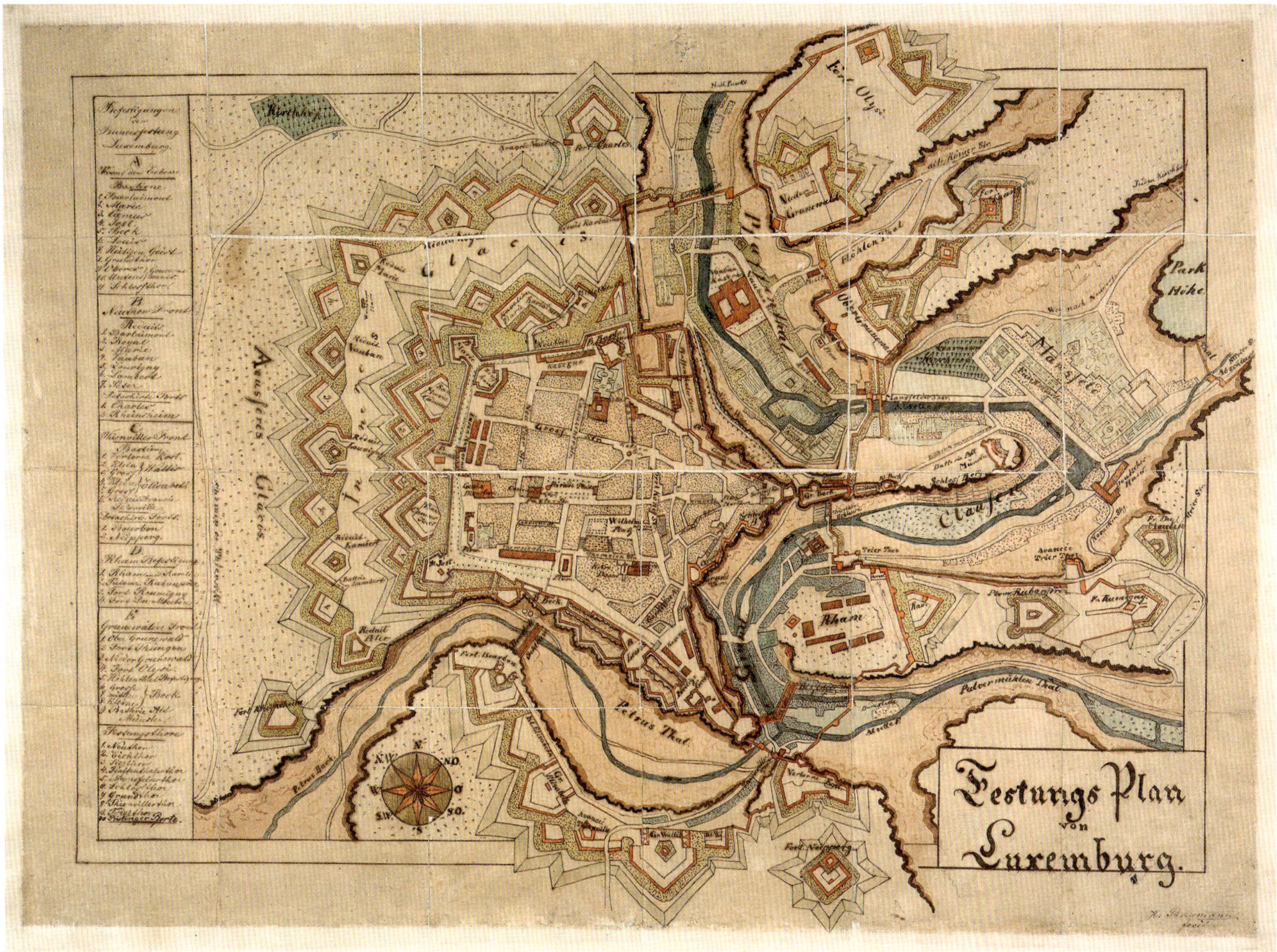

Kat. 214

»To be sold« / Zu verkaufen. Karikatur zur Luxemburg-Krise, 4. Mai 1867

Aus der Beilage »Punch and the Prussian Bully 1857–1914« zu »Punch«, London, 14. Oktober 1914, S. 8
Kat. 215

Napoleon III. verfolgte eine imperiale, auf Gebietserweiterung angelegte Politik. Während des Krieges 1866 signalisierte Bismarck Zustimmung zu einem Anschluss Luxemburgs an Frankreich. Doch als der niederländische König 1867 bereit war, das Großherzogtum zu verkaufen, machte Bismarck einen Rückzieher. Denn der geplante Handel wurde bekannt und löste nationale Empörung aus. Auf einer internationalen Konferenz in London wurde die Neutralität Luxemburgs beschlossen.

SUPPLEMENT TO "PUNCH, OR THE LONDON CHARIVARI."—OCTOBER 14, 1914.

8 "Punch" and the Prussian Bully.

"TO BE SOLD."

Emperor Napoleon: "I-A-HAVE MADE AN OFFER TO MY FRIEND HERE, AND . . ."
The Man in Possession: "NO, HAVE YOU, THOUGH? I RATHER THINK I WAS THE PARTY TO APPLY TO."
Emperor Napoleon: "OH, INDEED! AH! THEN IN THAT CASE I'LL—BUT IT'S OF NO CONSEQUENCE!"

May 4, 1867.

*** The Prussian Bully objects to being turned out of Luxemburg.

Kat. 215

Krieg um die nationale Ehre

Preußens Sieg über Österreich im Krieg von 1866 gefährdete Frankreichs Stellung als mitteleuropäische Ordnungsmacht. Seit der Luxemburgkrise 1867 war das Verhältnis Frankreichs zu Preußen angespannt. Im Juli 1870 heizten Pläne für die Nachfolge eines Hohenzollern auf dem spanischen Thron die Stimmung weiter an. Aus einer Erbfolgefrage wurde rasch ein Streit um die jeweilige Ehre der Nation. Am 19. Juli erklärte Frankreich Preußen den Krieg. Daraufhin richteten die Monarchen Napoleon III. und Wilhelm I. Aufrufe an ihre Völker. Napoleon sprach davon, dass allein ein Krieg die nationale Ehre wiederherstellen könne. Frankreich, betonte er, führe den Kampf jedoch gegen Preußen und nicht gegen Deutschland. Wilhelm hingegen versprach, für »Deutschlands Ehre« einzutreten und beschwor die »einmüthige Erhebung« seines Volkes.

Kat. 210

Napoleon III., Kaiser der Franzosen
Stahlstich von William Holl (1807–1871) nach einer Fotografie, 1870
Kat. 210

Napoleon III. war 1870 gesundheitlich und politisch angeschlagen, als die Spannungen zwischen Frankreich und Preußen eskalierten. Eine Intervention in Mexiko hatte 1867 mit der Hinrichtung des durch ihn als Kaiser eingesetzten Habsburgers Maximilian I. geendet, und in der Luxemburgkrise hatte er eine Niederlage erlitten. Er brauchte dringend einen außenpolitischen Erfolg.

Prinz Leopold von Hohenzollern-Sigmaringen (1835–1905)
Holzstich, 1875
Kat. 216

Von Bismarck ermutigt, kandidierte Leopold am 21. Juni 1870 für den spanischen Königsthron. Nach Protesten aus Frankreich erklärte er am 12. Juli seinen Verzicht.

Kat. 216

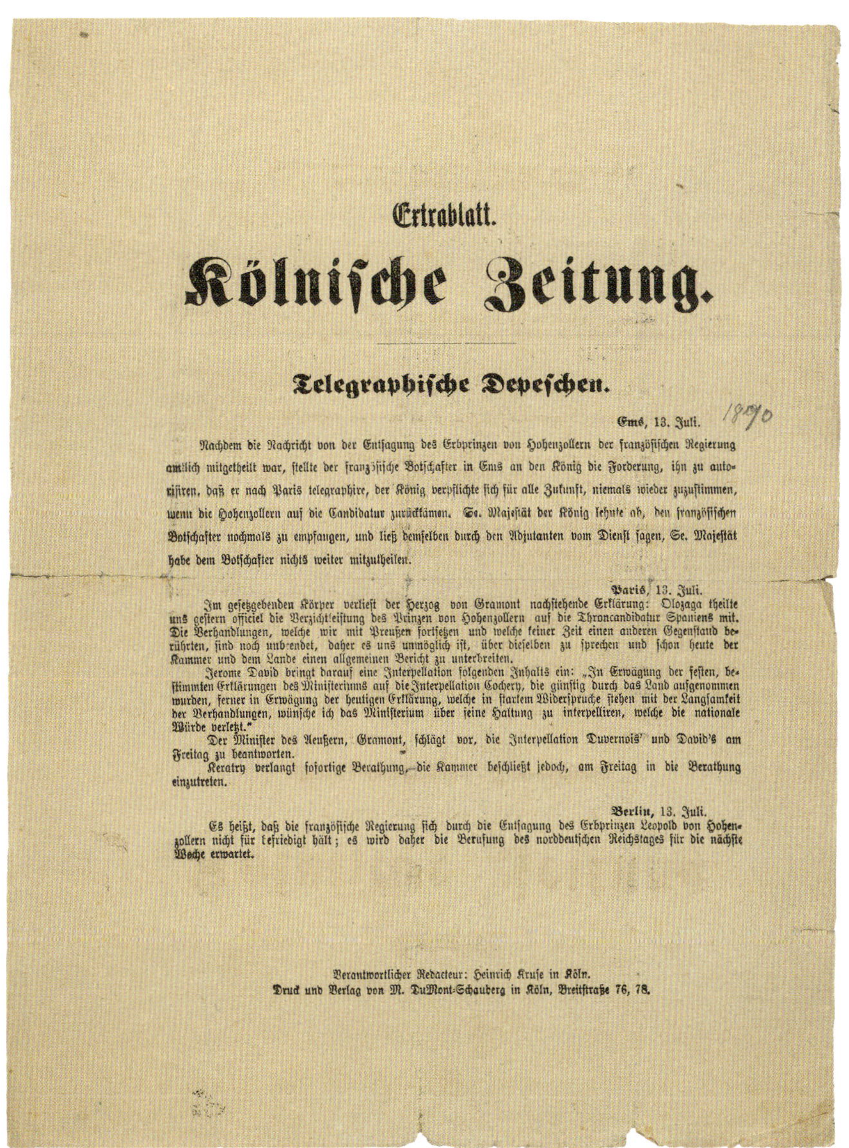

Extrablatt.

Kölnische Zeitung.

Telegraphische Depeschen.

Ems, 13. Juli.

Nachdem die Nachricht von der Entsagung des Erbprinzen von Hohenzollern der französischen Regierung amtlich mitgetheilt war, stellte der französische Botschafter in Ems an den König die Forderung, ihn zu autorisiren, daß er nach Paris telegraphire, der König verpflichte sich für alle Zukunft, niemals wieder zuzustimmen, wenn die Hohenzollern auf die Candidatur zurückkämen. Se. Majestät der König lehnte ab, den französischen Botschafter nochmals zu empfangen, und ließ demselben durch den Adjutanten vom Dienst sagen, Se. Majestät habe dem Botschafter nichts weiter mitzutheilen.

Paris, 13. Juli.

Im gesetzgebenden Körper verliest der Herzog von Gramont nachstehende Erklärung: Olozaga theilte uns gestern officiel die Verzichtleistung des Prinzen von Hohenzollern auf die Throncandidatur Spaniens mit. Die Verhandlungen, welche wir mit Preußen fortsetzen und welche keiner Zeit einen anderen Gegenstand berührten, sind noch unbeendet, daher es uns unmöglich ist, über dieselben zu sprechen und schon heute der Kammer und dem Lande einen allgemeinen Bericht zu unterbreiten.

Jerome David bringt darauf eine Interpellation folgenden Inhalts ein: „In Erwägung der festen, bestimmten Erklärungen des Ministeriums auf die Interpellation Cochery, die günstig durch das Land aufgenommen wurden, ferner in Erwägung der heutigen Erklärung, welche in starkem Widerspruche stehen mit der Langsamkeit der Verhandlungen, wünsche ich das Ministerium über seine Haltung zu interpelliren, welche die nationale Würde verletzt."

Der Minister des Aeußern, Gramont, schlägt vor, die Interpellation Duvernois' und David's am Freitag zu beantworten.

Keratry verlangt sofortige Berathung, die Kammer beschließt jedoch, am Freitag in die Berathung einzutreten.

Berlin, 13. Juli.

Es heißt, daß die französische Regierung sich durch die Entsagung des Erbprinzen Leopold von Hohenzollern nicht für befriedigt hält; es wird daher die Berufung des norddeutschen Reichstages für die nächste Woche erwartet.

Verantwortlicher Redacteur: Heinrich Kruse in Köln.
Druck und Verlag von M. DuMont-Schauberg in Köln, Breitstraße 76, 78.

Kat. 217

»Emser Depesche« vom 13. Juli 1870
Extrablatt. Kölnische Zeitung.
Telegraphische Depesche
Kat. 217

Als die preußisch-französische Krise durch die Verzichtserklärung Leopolds von Hohenzollern am 12. Juli 1870 schon beigelegt schien, eskalierte die Situation neuerlich. Der französische Gesandte Benedetti verärgerte den in Bad Ems weilenden Wilhelm I. von Preußen mit der Forderung nach einer förmlichen Entschuldigung und einer Garantie, niemals wieder eine hohenzollersche Thronkandidatur in Spanien zu unterstützen. Von seinem Kurort aus informierte der König seinen Ministerpräsidenten Otto von Bismarck. Bismarck kürzte und verschärfte den Ton der Nachricht. Die sogenannte Emser Depesche wurde umgehend publiziert.

№ 161.

Erscheint täglich, Sonn- und Festtage ausgenommen.

Expedition: Universitätsstraße 16 (Goldner Bär).

Leipzig, Sonnabend, den 16. Juli.

Sächsische Zeitung.

1870.

Abonnementspreis: vierteljährlich 1 Thlr. monatlich 10 Ngr.

Inserate: die Spaltezeile 1 Ngr.

Müssen denn die Sachsen sich auch todtschießen lassen?

Für heute können wir uns einen Leitartikel ersparen; Prof. Biedermann führt für uns die Feder, in seiner Weise freilich, aber „wir haben unsere Freude daran," an seinem Heldenmuthe nämlich gegen den „Erbfeind", denn einmal muß die Sache zwischen Frankreich und Preußen doch zum Austrag gebracht werden, die jetzigen Zustände sind unhaltbar, sie ruiniren Land und Volk und führen zu keiner Entscheidung; wenn es also sein muß, lieber heut als morgen. Nur über Eines möchten wir aber hierbei Auskunft erhalten, ob denn, wenn Frankreich und Preußen wegen der spanischen Krone in Streit gerathen, die Sachsen sich deshalb todt schießen lassen müssen. Darüber eine tröstliche Antwort von Dresden zu bekommen, würde uns von Herzen erfreuen, und thut uns ein Offiziöser gewiß den Gefallen, uns hierüber ein paar beruhigende Worte zukommen zu lassen.

Der Herr Prof. frohlockt in seiner „Deutschen Allgem. Ztg." über das — „zur Thür-Hinauswerfen" — des französischen Gesandten in Ems in folgender Weise:

„Daß die Franzosen den Krieg mit uns suchen, und daß die Candidatur des Prinzen Leopold nur ein Vorwand, nicht die wirkliche Ursache ihrer plötzlichen leidenschaftlichen Erregung gegen Deutschland war, liegt nun sonnenklar aller Welt vor Augen. Man war geneigt, die Gerüchte von „weiteren Forderungen", welche die französische Regierung bei dieser Gelegenheit an den Nordbund oder Preußen stellen, von „andern Garantien", die sie verlangen wolle, für bloßes Geschwätz zu halten; nun aber ward eine solche weitere Forderung wirklich gestellt, und zwar eine Forderung von solcher „Unverschämtheit", daß sie alle Begriffe übersteigt (folgt nun die bekannte Depesche au[…] […]ten Königs

Dieser höchst w[…]
von Preußen, des […]
herrn Deutschlands, […]
wird die ganze Nati[…]
loses" Ansinnen ge[…]
Hinauswerfen […]
unterfing. Vielleic[…]
mit welchem der […]
Leopold als einen […]
Blut gekostet". […]
etwa König Wilhe[…]
irgendwie zur […]
lichen Stimmen, […]
über die „Demi[…]
wollen geneigt […]
haben — wieder[…]

Allem A[…]
den Krieg zu[…]
soll ihn ha[…]
um den Friede[…]
heuere Verant[…]
sammenstoß […]
selbst, für […]
welche er übe[…]

Also de[…]
so sagen w[…]
das Ende […]

Möge […]
treuen, […]
werden w[…]
es uns […]

[…]sische Volk sich soll todtschießen lassen, für eine Sache, die es von Haut und Haar nichts angeht, das ist uns absolut unerfindlich; um so weniger, als 1866 es gerade Frankreich war, durch dessen Einsprache die Existenz des sächsischen Thrones gerettet wurde.

Es würde sich in der That gut ausnehmen, und gäbe ein interessantes Blatt in der Weltgeschichte, wenn dasselbe Sachsen jetzt gegen seine Retter zu Felde zöge. Der Streit ist ein rein preußisch-französischer und berührt, wie gesagt, Sachsen auch nicht im allerentferntesten, ebensowenig den Nordbund.

Deutschland.

△ **Berlin**, 14. Juli. [Immer mehr Oel in's Feuer.] Die „Nordd. Allg. Ztg." schreibt, der französische Botschafter habe die Regeln des diplomatischen Verkehrs soweit außer Augen gesetzt, daß er den König in der „Badekur stören", ihn auf der Promenade über die Angelegenheit interpelliren und ihm Erklärungen abdringen wollte, und meldet dann, in den Häfen Cherbourg, Brest und L'Orient seien 14 schwere Panzerschiffe in der Ausrüstung begriffen. Es dürfe daher nicht verwundern, wenn man darauf Bedacht nehme, die norddeutschen Häfen gegen Bedrohung durch diese Fahrzeuge zu sichern. Das Blatt druckt sodann eine Reihe preußenfreundlicher Artikel aus dem nur zu gut bekannten Pariser „Siecle", dem Organ der verschiedenen Joëls, ab, dergl. aus den eben so rühmlich bekannten „Wiener Blättern" und will damit die öffentliche Meinung constatiren.

Berlin, 14. Juli. [Frankreich und Süddeutschland.] Zum Beweise einerseits, wie Frankreich einen Krieg mit Norddeutschland seit länger schon ins Auge […] andererseits, wie es bei einem solchen auf die […] Süddeutschlands rechne, veröffentlicht […] Actenstück, das […]heit zu- […] einiger […]schaft in […]n:

[…] vor dem […] Ereignisse […] die demo- […] oder Ein- […] Weise suchen […] ihre Führer […] am meisten […] Aussicht auf […]n der Gesell- […]artei? Würt- […]en? 8) Welche […]ürttemberg seit […]lichsten Gesetze, […] stehen sich seit […]mmer? in der […] hervorgerufen: […]steuer? die An- […] und vom allge- […] auf die Zukunft […] die Armeeorgani- […]elches ist die Lage […] seines Handels? 16) Welchen Einfluß haben die letzten Ereignisse auf Handel und Industrie geübt? 17) Ist seitdem der allgemeine Wohlstand gestiegen? 18) Wie hoch beziffert sich gegenwärtig in Württemberg der Export? der Import? 19) Wie haben sich die Ereignisse von 1866 auf den Geldmarkt geäußert? 20) Das Zollparlament ist das wichtigste Ereigniß dieser zwei Jahre. Was denkt man darüber? Was ist seine Zukunft? 21) Was ist die Ursache der Niederlage der preußischen Partei bei den Zollparlamentswahlen? 22) Warum konnte der Südbund nicht gebildet werden? 23) Woher kommt die Eifersucht, welche die Südstaaten spaltet? 24) Stehen die materiellen Interessen im Süden der Gründung eines Südbundes entgegen? 25) Sind die Interessen des Südens mit denen des Nordens verknüpft? Können sie davon getrennt werden? Welches sind dieselben? 26) Gibt es nicht auch Bande gemeinschaftlichen Interesses zwischen den Südstaaten und Oesterreich? 27) Könnte nicht eine große Handelsbewegung hergestellt werden zwischen dem Osten und dem Westen, zwischen Süddeutschland und dem Adriatischen Meere? 28) Welche Politik verfolgt Preußen gegenüber den Südstaaten? 29) Hat es auf die Einigung Deutschlands verzichtet? 30) Warum sucht Oesterreich seinen alten Einfluß im Süden Deutschlands nicht wiederzugewinnen? 31) Welches ist die jetzige Politik der württembergischen Regierung? Ihre Haltung den verschiedenen Parteien gegenüber? Preußen gegenüber? Oesterreich gegenüber? 32) Bedauert sie das mit Preußen abgeschlossene Schutz- und Trutzbündniß? 33) Würde sie im Kriegsfall mit Preußen gehen? 34) Im Falle eines Krieges mit Preußen, würde Frankreich Bundesgenossen im Süden finden? 35) Wie ist der Geist der württembergischen Armee? 36) Warum sucht die württembergische Regierung ihre Armee immer mehr zu verpreußen? (prussianiser!) 37) Will die Regierung den Eintritt in den Nordbund? 38) Welches sind die politischen Ansichten und die Tendenzen der hauptsächlichsten Mitglieder des Cabinets? 39) Welchen Einfluß hat die Königin Olga auf die Politik? 40) Unterstützt Rußland Württemberg? 41) Kann die gegenwärtige Lage von Dauer sein, und welche Vermuthungen kann man für die Zukunft anstellen?

Die „National-Zeitung" bemerkt dazu: Es ist wohl eine sehr nahe liegende Vermuthung, daß die französischen Gesandtschaften in München, Karlsruhe und Darmstadt sich mit ganz ähnlichen Fragebogen zu beschäftigen gehabt haben.

Berlin, 14. Juli. [Persönlicher Angriff.] Man mußte erstaunt sein, in der neuesten Nummer der „Nordd. Allg. Ztg." gegen den französischen Minister des Auswärtigen einen Angriff so persönlicher Natur zu finden, wie er eigentlich erst nach dem Abbruche der diplomatischen Beziehungen erklärlich wäre. Das Organ des Grafen Bismarck theilt an erster Stelle folgende, wie es sagt, „hübsche" Characteristik des Herzogs von Gramont mit, welche es von einem in Paris lebenden Diplomaten erhalten haben will:

„Tout le monde sait, que M. le Duc de Gramont est doué d'une force physi[…] Napoléon. Pour sa force diplomatique, elle a été moins connue jusqu'à présent, mais après ses derniers discours personne ne doutera plus, que par sa langue il viendrait facilement à bout de faire s'écrouler un empire."

Man bemerke wohl, daß das preußisch-officiöse Organ diese Characteristik, gegen allen Gebrauch, in französischer Sprache mittheilt, natürlich nur, damit dieselbe in Paris ja nicht mißverstanden werde. Wir fügen hier die deutsche Uebersetzung jenes Angriffs auf die Person des französischen Ministers bei:

„Alle Welt weiß, daß der Herzog v. Gramont mit einer außergewöhnlichen Körperstärke begabt ist, und daß er mit seiner Hand einen Napoleon (s. h. Napoleonsd'or) biegen kann. Was seine diplomatische Stärke betrifft, so ist sie bis jetzt weniger bekannt gewesen, aber nach seinen letzten Reden wird Niemand mehr bezweifeln, daß er durch seine Zunge leicht dahin kommen könnte, ein Kaiserreich über den Haufen zu werfen." (D. B. Z.)

[…]ole. Er entwaff- | hinzu und drängten die neugierigen Gaffer vom Rande des

Rep. I^a № 2200

Untersuchungsacten des Kgl. Sächs. Bezirksgerichts Leipzig gegen Wilhelm Obermüller.

Staats Verrath

Verweisungserkenntniss Bll.

Enderkenntniss Bll.

1870

Rep. I^a № 2200.

Steckbrief.

Der wegen versuchten Staatsverrathes bei dem Bezirksgericht in Untersuchung befindliche Redacteur der bis vor Kurzem hier erschienenen „Sächsischen Zeitung"

Wilhelm Obermüller aus Karlsruhe

hat sich unter Verletzung des geleisteten Handgelöbnisses von seinem Wohnorte Neudnitz entfernt und ist sein dermaliger Aufenthalt bisher nicht zu ermitteln gewesen.

Es werden daher alle Criminal- und Polizeibehörden hierdurch ersucht, Obermüller'n im Betretungsfalle sofort zu inhaftiren und Nachricht davon anher zu ertheilen.

Leipzig, am 15. September 1870.

Königliches Bezirksgericht.
Der Untersuchungsrichter:
Holke.

Obermüller ist 61 Jahre alt, 72½ Zoll lang, von übermittlerer Figur, hat blonde mit grauen vermischte Haare und Bart, längliches Gesicht, mangelhafte Zähne und trägt eine Brille.

Extra-Beilage

zu № 164 der Magdeburgischen Zeitung, Montag, den 18. Juli 1870.

Frankfurt, Sonntag, den 17. Juli. Die Französische Regierung hat an die Süddeutschen Regierungen die drohende Aufforderung gerichtet, sich in 24 Stunden darüber zu erklären, ob sie neutral bleiben wollen.

München, Sonntag, den 17. Juli. Eine unzählbare Menschenmenge zog heute Nachmittags, trotz des herrschenden Regenwetters gegen 4½ Uhr vor die Residenz des Königs und brachte daselbst dem Könige für seine Deutschnationale und bundestreue Entschließung ein nicht endenwollendes Hoch aus. Die Volksmenge sang entblößten Hauptes die Volkshymne und das Deutsche Vaterlandslied. Der König verneigte sich wiederholt zum Danke sichtlich bewegt am geöffneten Fenster. – Die Cooperation der Baierschen Armee mit der Preußischen wird sofort beginnen. Auf allen Straßen herrscht die größte Bewegung. Eine höchst erregte Volksmenge erschien vor dem Redactionslocal des ultramontanen Journals „Das Vaterland", um gegen den Redacteur des genannten Blattes zu demonstriren. Derselbe wurde auf sein eigenes Ansuchen zum Schutz seiner Person in das Polizeigewahrsam abgeführt.

Verantwortlicher Redacteur: G. Wandel in Magdeburg. Druck und Verlag von G. C. F. Faber in Magdeburg.

Kat. 218

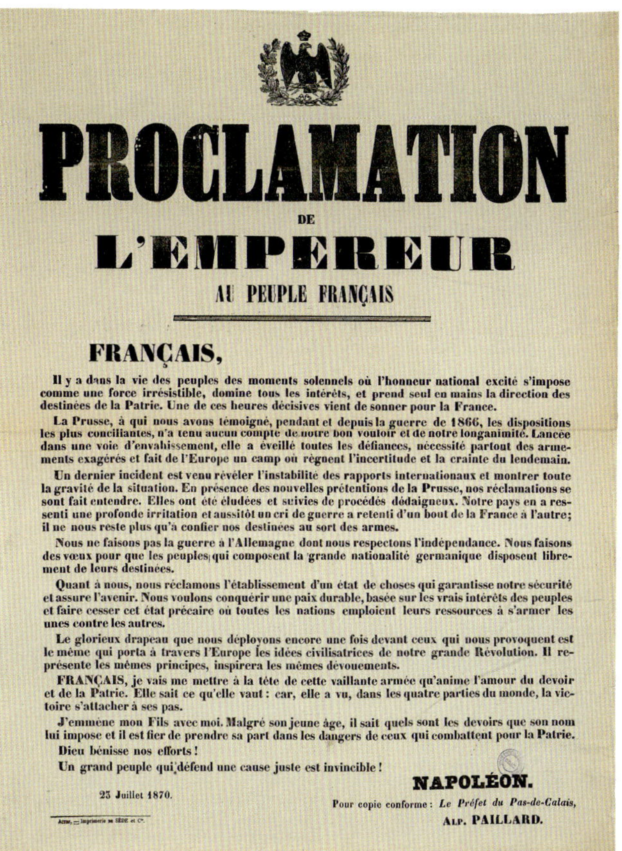

PROCLAMATION

DE

L'EMPEREUR

AU PEUPLE FRANÇAIS

FRANÇAIS,

Il y a dans la vie des peuples des moments solennels où l'honneur national excité s'impose comme une force irrésistible, domine tous les intérêts, et prend seul en mains la direction des destinées de la Patrie. Une de ces heures décisives vient de sonner pour la France.

La Prusse, à qui nous avons témoigné, pendant et depuis la guerre de 1866, les dispositions les plus conciliantes, n'a tenu aucun compte de notre bon vouloir et de notre longanimité. Lancée dans une voie d'envahissement, elle a éveillé toutes les défiances, nécessité partout des armements exagérés et fait de l'Europe un camp où règnent l'incertitude et la crainte du lendemain.

Un dernier incident est venu révéler l'instabilité des rapports internationaux et montrer toute la gravité de la situation. En présence des nouvelles prétentions de la Prusse, nos réclamations se sont fait entendre. Elles ont été éludées et suivies de procédés dédaigneux. Notre pays en a ressenti une profonde irritation et aussitôt un cri de guerre a retenti d'un bout de la France à l'autre; il ne nous reste plus qu'à confier nos destinées au sort des armes.

Nous ne faisons pas la guerre à l'Allemagne dont nous respectons l'indépendance. Nous faisons des vœux pour que les peuples qui composent la grande nationalité germanique disposent librement de leurs destinées.

Quant à nous, nous réclamons l'établissement d'un état de choses qui garantisse notre sécurité et assure l'avenir. Nous voulons conquérir une paix durable, basée sur les vrais intérêts des peuples et faire cesser cet état précaire où toutes les nations emploient leurs ressources à s'armer les unes contre les autres.

Le glorieux drapeau que nous déployons encore une fois devant ceux qui nous provoquent est le même qui porta à travers l'Europe les idées civilisatrices de notre grande Révolution. Il représente les mêmes principes, inspirera les mêmes dévouements.

FRANÇAIS, je vais me mettre à la tête de cette vaillante armée qu'anime l'amour du devoir et de la Patrie. Elle sait ce qu'elle vaut : car, elle a vu, dans les quatre parties du monde, la victoire s'attacher à ses pas.

J'emmène mon Fils avec moi. Malgré son jeune âge, il sait quels sont les devoirs que son nom lui impose et il est fier de prendre sa part dans les dangers de ceux qui combattent pour la Patrie.

Dieu bénisse nos efforts !

Un grand peuple qui défend une cause juste est invincible !

NAPOLÉON.

23 Juillet 1870.

Pour copie conforme : *Le Préfet du Pas-de-Calais,*

ALP. PAILLARD.

Arras, — Imprimerie de SÈDE et Cie.

Kat. 220

»Untersuchungsacten des Kgl. Sächs. Bezirksgerichts Leipzig gegen Wilhelm Obermueller Staatsverrath etc. 1870«

Kat. 223

Artikel »Müssen denn die Sachsen sich auch todtschießen lassen?«

Sächsische Zeitung, Leipzig, 16. Juli 1870, Titelseite
Aus den Untersuchungsakten
Kat. 224

Steckbrief Wilhelm Obermüller

Leipziger Tageblatt, 17. September 1870, S. 8290
Aus den Untersuchungsakten
Kat. 225

Wilhelm Obermüller (1808–1888) war einer der Wenigen, die 1870 dazu aufriefen, Preußen allein in den Krieg ziehen zu lassen. Der aus Karlsruhe stammende Redakteur und Inhaber der »Sächsischen Zeitung« hatte 1832 als Burschenschafter am Hambacher Fest und 1833 an der versuchten Erstürmung der Frankfurter Polizeiwachen teilgenommen. Nach Jahren in Untersuchungshaft 1836 wegen Hochverrats verurteilt, floh er 1837 nach Frankreich und wurde 1848 begnadigt. Als am 16. Juli 1870 die Ausgabe mit der provokanten Schlagzeile erschien, verbrannten Studenten öffentlich Zeitungsexemplare und bedrohten Obermüller in seiner Wohnung.
Am 20. Juli wurde er wegen versuchten »Staatsverrathes« und »der versuchten Anstiftung zu Militärverbrechen« festgenommen. Gegen Kaution am 2. August freigelassen, floh Obermüller nach Wien, wo er fortan zu Themen der Vorgeschichte veröffentlichte.

Nachricht über die Aufforderung Frankreichs an die süddeutschen Staaten, neutral zu bleiben

Sonderbeilage zur Magdeburgischen Zeitung, 18. Juli 1870
Kat. 218

Aufruf Kaiser Napoleons III. an das französische Volk

Paris, 23. Juli 1870
Kat. 220

»An mein Volk!« – Aufruf König Wilhelms I. von Preußen

Berlin, 31. Juli 1870
Kat. 219

An mein Volk!

Indem Ich heute zur Armee gehe, um mit ihr für Deutschlands Ehre und für Erhaltung unserer höchsten Güter zu kämpfen, will Ich, im Hinblicke auf die einmüthige Erhebung Meines Volkes, eine Amnestie für politische Verbrechen und Vergehen ertheilen. Ich habe das Staats-Ministerium beauftragt, Mir einen Erlaß in diesem Sinne zu unterbreiten.

Mein Volk weiß mit Mir, daß Friedensbruch und Feindschaft wahrhaftig nicht auf unserer Seite war.

Aber herausgefordert, sind wir entschlossen, gleich unseren Vätern und in fester Zuversicht auf Gott den Kampf zu bestehen, zur Errettung des Vaterlandes.

Berlin, den 31. Juli 1870.

gez. Wilhelm.

Kat. 219

»Rothosen« und Pickelhauben

Die Uniformierung der Heere 1870/71

GERHARD BAUER

Am Beginn des Deutsch-Französischen Krieges standen sich nicht zwei Heere gegenüber, sondern die Streitkräfte des kaiserlichen Frankreich auf der einen Seite und die Armeen des Königreichs Preußen und der mit ihm verbündeten deutschen Staaten auf der anderen Seite.[1] Die Truppen Napoleons III., vereint unter dem goldenen Adler des Kaisertums und der französischen Trikolore, sahen sich mit Soldaten aus vier Königreichen, sechs Großherzogtümern, fünf Herzogtümern, sieben Fürstentümern und drei Freien und Hansestädten konfrontiert. Jedes der Kontingente führte eigene Feldzeichen.

Das kaiserlich französische Heer erschien im Vergleich zu seinen preußisch-deutschen Gegnern auf den ersten Blick monolithisch. Kannte man die strukturellen und Ausbildungsmängel nicht, die ihre Effizienz zunehmend beeinträchtigten, wirkte die französische Armee 1870 eindrucksvoll. Im Krimkrieg von 1853 bis 1856 und im Italienfeldzug 1859 hatte sie sich bewährt. Das gescheiterte mexikanische Abenteuer war mehr ein politisches als ein militärisches Desaster.

In seinen Traditionen knüpfte das französische Heer an die Grande Armée des Ersten Kaiserreichs unter Napoleon I. an, und in seinem Aussehen spiegelte es den sprichwörtlichen Glanz des Zweiten Kaiserreichs. Zusätzlich zur Aufstellung der Kaiserlichen Garde hatte Napoleon III. nach der Wiedererrichtung des Empire mit den Cent-Gardes eine verschwenderisch ausgestattete Leibtruppe nach der Art der Palastgarden der Alten Monarchie errichten lassen. Garde Impériale und Linientruppen bildeten zusammen die in Frankreich rekrutierte Armée Métropolitaine, die Mutterlandsarmee. Das Gros der Kolonialtruppen in französischen Diensten stellte die Armée d'Afrique. Sie bestand aus den in der Kolonie Algerien, aber auch in angrenzenden Staaten geworbenen Mannschaften und Unteroffizieren, aus europäischen Offizieren und Feldwebeln. An der Seite dieser Truppenteile mit hohem Anteil an autochthonen

Quartiermeister Jules-César Dürr in Felduniform, 1870
Abb. 13

1870 wurden drei Regimenter sogenannter »Turcos« der Afrikaarmee nach Frankreich entsandt. Der Straßburger Jules-César Dürr (1846–1930) war 1866 als Freiwilliger in das 2. Algerische Schützen-Regiment eingetreten.
Die Mannschaften der »Turcos« waren afrikanischer Herkunft, während in ihrem Unteroffizierskorps auch Europäer dienten.

Helm für Mannschaften der Escadron des Cent-Gardes
Kaiserreich Frankreich, 1854–1870
Kat. 204

Die 190 Mann starke Escadron des Cent-Gardes bildete die Leibgarde Napoleons III. Sie begleitete ihn bei allen öffentlichen Auftritten ebenso wie ins Feld. Er knüpfte damit an einen Brauch der bourbonischen Monarchie an, in der man zwischen den Garden unterschied, die zum königlichen Haushalt zählten, und Gardeformationen, die in der Hierarchie des Heeres an der Spitze der Kampftruppen standen.

Soldaten und Unteroffizieren standen die unter Europäern rekrutierten Afrikanischen Jäger und Zuaven sowie die französisch geführte Fremdenlegion, die sich aus Freiwilligen aus aller Herren Länder zusammensetzte.

Die Paradeuniformen französischer Soldaten, zumal der Offiziere, waren das militärische Abbild des Pariser Chics mit breitschultrigen, stark taillierten Jacken und Röcken, weiten Hosen und spitzem Schuhwerk. Eine exotische Note kam mit den orientalisch inspirierten Monturen der Afrikaarmee, den Uniformen der »Turcos« genannten algerischen Schützen, der Zuaven und der nach Art der Berber gewandeten Kavallerieregimenter, der »Spahis«, ins Spiel.

Die Felddienstuniformen der französischen und afrikanischen Regimenter waren etwas schlichter gehalten. Die Silhouetten und die Farbigkeit der Soldaten des Zweiten Kaiserreichs blieben dennoch unverwechselbar. Kürassiere und Dragoner prunkten auch im Einsatz mit eleganten, klassizistischen Helmen à la Minerve aus Eisen oder Messing, mit Fellturbanen und langen Rosshaarschweifen. Die Masse der Infanteristen trug zu blauen Mänteln krapprote Hosen und weiße Gamaschen über ihren Schnürstiefeln. Auf dem Kopf saß ein blau-rotes Képi. Den deutschen Soldaten stach jedoch besonders die auffällige Farbe der Beinkleider ins Auge, weswegen sie ihre Gegner oft als »Rothosen« verspotteten.

Eine Besonderheit der Armee Napoleons III. waren uniformierte Marketenderinnen, die jedes Regiment begleiteten. Diese Cantinières waren vollwertige Angehörige ihres Truppenteils mit vorschriftsmäßigen Monturen. Bei Paraden stand ihnen ein Platz in der Marschordnung ihres Regiments zu.

Die deutschen Armeen unterstanden 1870 der gemeinsamen Führung des Königs von Preußen als Bundesfeldherrn und Helmuth von Moltke als Chef des Generalstabs. Das Feldheer gliederte sich bei Kriegsbeginn in drei Armeen. Gerade die 3. Armee, befehligt vom preußischen Kronprinzen Friedrich Wilhelm,

Hauptfeldwebel des 28. Linien-infanterieregiments

Kaiserreich Frankreich, 1867–1870
Kat. 230

Kennzeichnend für die französische Infanterie waren die »Képis« genannten Feldmützen und die krapproten Hosen, die wie hier zum Waffenrock oder zum Mantel getragen wurden.

führte aber vor, dass nicht ganz Deutschland unter die Pickelhaube gekommen war. Als »multinationaler« Großverband umfasste sie neben anfangs zwei, ab September drei preußischen und den zwei bayerischen Korps die in einem weiteren Armeekorps zusammengefassten württembergischen und badischen Divisionen. Preußische und badische Fußtruppen waren mit ihren dunkelblauen Waffenröcken und Pickelhauben nur unterscheidbar, wenn man ihnen nahe genug kam, um die Helmbeschläge mit den Wappentieren, dem preußischen Adler oder dem badischen Greifen, erkennen zu können. Die Württemberger konnten hingegen mit Franzosen verwechselt werden, denn wie diese trugen sie weite Hosen und Käppis. Auf deutscher Seite stachen aber vor allem die Bayern hervor. Seit dem Beginn des 19. Jahrhunderts war ihre nationale Uniformfarbe ein helles Blau, das irreführenderweise offiziell als Kornblumenblau bezeichnet wurde. Ebenso typisch waren die bayerischen »Raupenhelme«. Die Kalotte mit Vorder- und Hinterschirm war aus Leder.

Helm für Mannschaften der Infanterieregimenter
Königreich Bayern, 1868–1886
Kat. 260

Ihre »Raupenhelme« und kornblumenblauen Uniformen machten 1870/71 bayerische Truppen unverwechselbar. Erst ab 1886 trugen auch bayerische Soldaten Pickelhauben.

Helm und Waffenrock für Musketiere des 2. Thüringischen Infanterie-Regiments Nr. 32
Königreich Preußen, um 1870/71
Kat. 233

Die Uniform der preußischen Infanterie veränderte sich während der Einigungskriege nur in Details. Garde- und Grenadierregimenter unterschieden sich von den Linienregimentern lediglich durch ihre Helmbeschläge und ihren Litzenschmuck. 1870 hatten bereits weitere deutsche Armeen diese Kombinationen aus blauen Waffenröcken und Pickelhauben übernommen, wenn sie auch eigene Embleme beibehielten.

Feldmütze für Mannschaften der Infanterieregimenter

Königreich Württemberg, 1864–1871
Kat. 341

Im Deutsch-Französischen Krieg trugen die württembergischen Truppen nach wie vor Uniformen, die eher österreichisch als preußisch inspiriert waren. Ihre Silhouette war durch ein Käppi gekennzeichnet, was aus der Distanz und bei schlechter Sicht zu Verwechslungen mit französischen Truppen führen konnte.

Tschako eines Fähnrichs des Schützen-Regiments Nr. 108

Königreich Sachsen, 1867–1897
Kat. 342

Die Masse der sächsischen Infanterie tauschte ihre österreichisch anmutenden Tschakos 1867 gegen Helme nach preußischem Vorbild. Von den Kampftruppen zu Fuß behielten nur die Jägerbataillone und das Schützen-(Füsilier-)Regiment Tschakos, wenn auch eines neuen Modells.

Darauf befestigt war eine Raupe aus Wolle oder, für Offiziere, aus Bärenfell. Nur die Kürassiere trugen eiserne Helme mit Bügeln, auf denen ebenfalls Raupen aus Rosshaar oder Fell saßen.

Die bunte Pracht der Uniformen der französischen und deutschen Soldaten im Frieden verblasste unter den Bedingungen des Krieges nur zu bald. Das Lederzeug, die Textilien, Ausrüstungsgegenstände und viele aus verschiedenen Materialien gefertigte Kopfbedeckungen nahmen unter den oft harschen Witterungsbedingungen auf Märschen und im Feldlager Schaden, hinzu kamen die Beschädigungen im Gefecht. Auch lange Märsche setzten dem Schuhwerk zu, und Feuchtigkeit ruinierte die Bekleidung, zumal wenn sie nicht getrocknet werden konnte. Unannehmlichkeiten wie diese wirkten sich unmittelbar auf die Moral der kämpfenden Truppen aus. Die nach dem Krieg gemalten Schlachtengemälde lassen selten erahnen, wie ramponiert die Kombattanten von Sedan, die Belagerer und Verteidiger von Paris oder die Truppen beider Seiten im Loire-Feldzug tatsächlich aussahen. Spätestens zu Beginn des Winters 1870/71 glichen die Verbände, die seit dem Sommer im Einsatz gewesen waren, Vogelscheuchen. Den authentischsten Eindruck vermitteln Grafiken, die auf Skizzen von Augenzeugen basieren. Seltener hatten Fotografen Gelegenheit, den überaus legeren Aufzug vieler Frontsoldaten einzufangen. Langfristig jedoch wurde das »feldmäßige« Erscheinungsbild der Soldaten von 1870/71 in ihren Heimatländern ikonisch. Der junge französische »Pioupiou« mit seinem

verschossenen blauen Mantel, den weiten roten Hosen, die am Knöchel von verrutschten weißen Gamaschen zusammengehalten wurden, und dem zerknautschten Képi auf dem Kopf wurde ebenso zum Sinnbild der »Nation in Waffen« wie der vollbärtige preußische Musketier mit Pickelhaube, abgewetztem Waffenrock und Halbstiefeln, aus denen hochgezogene, derbe Strümpfe sahen. Analoge nationale Stereotypen wurden übrigens in allen deutschen Staaten geprägt.

St. Privat, das 24. Regiment auf Vorposten
Ernst Lucke & Co., Berlin, 1870
Abb. 14

Soldaten des 4. Brandenburgischen Infanterie-Regiments Nr. 24 (Großherzog von Mecklenburg-Schwerin) rasten gemeinsam mit einigen preußischen Gardisten in den Ruinen des am 18. August 1870 erstürmten Dorfes St. Privat. In der Sommerhitze haben sie ihre Helme gegen Feldmützen (sogenannte Krätzchen) vertauscht. Die Offiziere tragen Schirmmützen.

1 Zur Ausstellung wird der Verlag Militaria zwei Bildbände vorlegen, die erstmals eine Gesamtdarstellung der Uniformierung der 1870/71 kriegführenden Staaten bieten werden. Laurent Mirouze/Louis Delperier/Christophe Pommier (Einführung zum französischen Teil), Markus Stein/Gerhard Bauer (Einführung zum deutschen Teil): Der Deutsch-Französische Krieg 1870/71. Uniformierung und Ausrüstung der deutschen und französischen Armeen, 2 Bde., Wien 2020.Bisher verfügbar und empfehlenswert: Martin Lezius: Das Ehrenkleid des Soldaten – Eine Kulturgeschichte der Uniform von ihren Anfängen bis zur Gegenwart. Berlin 1936; Richard Knötel/Herbert Knötel/Herbert Sieg: Farbiges Handbuch der Uniformkunde, 2 Bde., Augsburg 1996; Paul Willing: L'Armée de Napoléon III (1852–1870), Arcueil 1983; Paul Willing: L'Expedition du Mexique (1861–1867) et la Guerre Franco-Allemande (1870–1871), Arcueil 1984, Dérangère Blentait: Cantinières et Vivandières du Second Empire. Tradition Nr. 260, 2012; Louis Delperier: L'armée de Napolèon III, Saint-Cloud 2011; Karl Müller/Louis Braun: Die Organisation, Bekleidung, Ausrüstung und Bewaffnung der Königlich Bayerischen Armee von 1806 bis 1906, Nürnberg 1907; Herbert Knötel/Martin Lezius: Deutsche Uniformen. Das Zeitalter der deutschen Einigung, Bd. 1: Die Kriege von 1864 und 1866, Dresden 1933; Herbert Knötel/Martin Lezius: Deutsche Uniformen. Das Zeitalter der deutschen Einigung, Bd. 2: Die Zeit von 1870 bis 1888; Dresden 1933; Georg Ortenburg/Ingo Prömper: Preußisch-Deutsche Uniformen von 1640–1918, München 1991.

Krieg gegen das französische Zweite Kaiserreich

Das französische Feldheer mit seinen acht Armeekorps war aufgeteilt in Truppen unter Marschall Mac Mahon im Unterelsass und unter Marschall Bazaine, die den Raum zwischen Saarlouis und Saarbrücken bedrohten. Ihnen gegenüber stand die 1. Armee unter General von Steinmetz. Die 2. Armee des Prinzen Friedrich Karl stand in der bayerischen Pfalz und dazu aufschließend die 3. Armee unter seinem Cousin, dem Kronprinzen von Preußen, in der südlichen Pfalz und Baden. Am 19. Juli 1870 eröffnete das II. Korps der Armee Bazaines unter General Frossard im Beisein des Kaisers und seines Sohnes die Kampfhandlungen mit einem Vorstoß auf preußisches Gebiet bei Saarbrücken. In rasch aufeinander folgenden, für beide Seiten verlustreichen Schlachten gelang es den drei deutschen Armeen ab dem 6. August, sowohl Mac Mahons als auch Bazaines Truppen zum Rückzug nach Frankreich hinein zu zwingen und ihre Vereinigung zu verhindern. Bazaines »Rheinarmee« wurde nach der Niederlage von Gravelotte – Saint Privat am 18. August in Metz eingeschlossen; Mac Mahons »Armee von Chalons« am 1./2. September bei Sedan eingekesselt und geschlagen. Der Kaiser der Franzosen Napoleon III. begab sich in deutsche Kriegsgefangenschaft. Die französische Zivilbevölkerung war ab der ersten Augustwoche 1870 stark vom Kriegsgeschehen betroffen, sowohl von Kampfhandlungen und Belagerungen als auch vom Besatzungsregime in den Territorien, aus denen sich die französischen Armeen zurückgezogen hatten.

Kat. 226

Kat. 229

»Siegesbulletin des Mitrailleur an seine Mitrailleuse«, Flugblatt 3 einer Folge zum Deutsch-Französischen Krieg

Kat. 229

Anders als das deutsche Spottblatt vermittelt, war der französische Thronfolger Napoléon Eugène Louis Bonaparte (1856–1879), genannt »Lulu«, bereits 14 Jahre alt, als sein Vater ihn auf den Feldzug gegen Deutschland mitnahm, um ihn auf seine Herrscherrolle vorzubereiten. An die Stelle, wo der »Prince Imperial« angeblich erstmals selbst eine Mitrailleuse abfeuerte, erinnert in Saarbrücken noch heute der sogenannte »Lulustein«.

Fernglas, Geschenk von Captain J. L. Seton an Julius von Rosen, Hauptmann im I. Bataillon des Hohenzollernschen Füsilierregiments Nr. 40

Kat. 240

Den Truppen schloss sich eine wachsende Zahl von »Schlachtenbummlern« an, darunter Reporter und militärische Beobachter. Der Brite Seton stieß zu Rosens Kompanie, als diese bei Saarbrücken ab dem 21. Juli 1870 in Gefechte mit französischen Spähtrupps verwickelt wurde. Da er sich munter an den Kämpfen beteiligte, kam Seton wegen dieser Neutralitätsverletzung für sechs Wochen in Haft. Danach nahm er seinen Abschied und gesellte sich in Frankreich wieder zu Rosen und seinen Soldaten. Zum Abschied bei Saint Quentin schenkte er Rosen dieses Fernglas.

Rohr einer Mitrailleuse, System Reffye

Frankreich 1869/1871
Kat. 226

1870 besaß das französische Heer über 190 Reffye-Mitrailleusen, die der Feldartillerie zugewiesen waren. Deutsche Soldaten fürchteten diese neuen Salvengeschütze zuerst, verloren aber bald den Respekt davor. Die Bedienungsmannschaften der Mitrailleusen wurden in den meisten Schlachten von der weiter schießenden deutschen Artillerie getötet, bevor sie angreifender Infanterie gefährlich werden konnten. Konnten Mitrailleusen allerdings auf kurze Distanz eingesetzt werden, wirkten sie verheerend, wie Karl Tanera, Leutnant des 1. königlich bayerischen Jägerbataillons, berichtete:
»Sie brauchten ja gar nicht zu zielen, nur auf den Platz zu halten und dann loszudrehen. [...] Im Ganzen lagen etwa zehn Mann auf dem Platze. Sie waren freilich tot, denn keiner war nur von einem, manche aber von 15–20 Geschossen getroffen und vollständig durchlöchert.« (Karl Tanera: Ernste und heitere Erinnerungen eines Ordonnanzoffiziers im Jahre 1870/71, 11. Auflage, München 1911, S. 66–67)

Kat. 240

Preußischer Dragoner im Kampf mit französischen Zuaven

Wilhelm Alexander Meyerheim
(1815–1882), 1871
Öl auf Leinwand, 47 × 57 cm
Kat. 243

Wie die »Turcos« gehörten die ähnlich uniformierten Zuaven zur französischen Afrika-Armee, rekrutierten aber nur Europäer. Seit den Schlachten vom August 1870 als Kämpfer gefürchtet, waren »Turcos« und Zuaven wegen ihrer exotischen Uniformierung ein geschätztes Motiv deutscher Kriegsmaler. Das Gemälde zeigt eine Kampfszene bei Weißenburg oder Wörth.

Kat. 243

Kat. 244

»Die erste Kriegsbeute. Ein toll und voll getrunkener Zuave wird in einem auf deutschen Grund und Boden gelegenen Wirthshause von einer deutschen Patrouille gefangen genommen u. nach Saarbrücken abgeliefert«

Zeichnung von Edmund Harburger
(1846–1906) für »Die Gartenlaube«,
1870, Nr. 33, S. 521 (in der Zeitschrift wohl fälschlicherweise als »Eduard Harburger« bezeichnet)
Bleistift und Tusche auf Papier,
18,2 × 12,9 cm
Kat. 244

Diese Zeichnung des Feldmalers Harburger erschien 1870 in der Familienzeitschrift »Die Gartenlaube«. Die Bildunterschrift »Ein Bannerträger der Civilisation« ist bezeichnend für den verächtlichen Ton der deutschen Kriegspropaganda, die den Einsatz von Kolonialtruppen gegen Europäer als besondere Kulturlosigkeit und Barbarei geißelte. Gleichzeitig waren deutsche Soldaten, von denen viele vor dem Krieg noch kaum über ihr eigenes Heimatdorf hinausgekommen waren, fasziniert von Afrikanern wie »Turcos« oder »Spahis«.

Marketenderin des 92. Linieninfanterieregiments
Französische Republik, 1885
Kat. 246

Deutsche Soldaten staunten 1870 über die Marketenderinnen, die den Feldzug der französischen Regimenter begleiteten. Anders als in den deutschen Armeen handelte es sich um reguläre und vorschriftsmäßig uniformierte Militärangehörige. Die gezeigte Kombination aus Hose, Rock, Schürze, Dolman oder Jacke wurde schon im Zweiten Kaiserreich eingeführt. Die Marketenderin Marie Certain-Tester trug sie während der Dritten Republik.

Schnapsfässchen einer Marketenderin des 16. Bataillons, Chasseurs à Pied
Kaiserreich Frankreich, 1863
Kat. 247

Das als »tonnelet« bekannte Fässchen war das Standeszeichen der Marketenderinnen. Es war gewöhnlich mit patriotischen Motiven bemalt und mit Name und Nummer der Einheit der Marketenderin beschriftet. Das 16. Bataillon der Jäger zu Fuß kämpfte 1870 bei Weißenburg, Fröschweiler und Sedan.

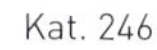

Kat. 246

Kat. 248

Kat. 247

Quartiermeister des 3. Kürassierregiments
Kaiserreich Frankreich, 1870
Kat. 248

Schon in den ersten großen Schlachten des Krieges erwies sich, dass die Feuerkraft der Infanterie und Artillerie beider Seiten Kavallerieattacken nahezu wirkungslos machte. Die massierten Angriffe Tausender französischer Kürassiere bei Wörth wurden blutig abgewiesen. Dennoch ritten Kavallerieregimenter, oft in verzweifelter Lage, Attacken in tödliches Abwehrfeuer. Meist wurden Pferde und Reiter getroffen, bevor sie den Gegner überhaupt erreichten. Diese Uniform gehörte Quartiermeister Rodolphe Edouard Sengenwald (1849–1897). Er kämpfte in der Schlacht von Wörth. Sein Regiment war Teil der Kavalleriedivision von General Charles-Frédéric de Bonnemains (1814–1885), die bei Reichshoffen eine vergebliche Attacke ritt. Sengenwald wurde verwundet und geriet in Gefangenschaft. Nach dem Krieg wurde er Kreisdirektor von Weißenburg.

Kat. 250

Kavalleriepistole M/1850, geführt bei Mars-la-Tour von einem Angehörigen des Altmärkischen Ulanen-Regiments Nr. 16
Kaliber 15,2 mm
Königreich Preußen, 1870
Kat. 250

Helm für Unteroffiziere und Mannschaften der Linienkürassier-regimenter, mit Hiebspuren
Königreich Preußen, 1867/1889
Kat. 252

Koller für Mannschaften des Magdeburgischen Kürassier-regiments Nr. 7
Königreich Preußen, 1870/71
Kat. 251

Kat. 251

Kat. 252

Am 16. August 1870 trafen unweit der Ortschaften Mars-la-Tour und Vionville zwei preußische Korps auf die französische Rheinarmee. Um einer Bedrohung des linken preußischen Flügels zu begegnen, befahl General von Alvensleben, Kommandeur des III. Korps, der 12. Kavalleriebrigade unter Generalmajor Adalbert von Bredow (1814–1890) einen Entlastungsangriff. Die folgende Attacke der Magdeburger Kürassiere und Altmärkischen Ulanen bannte die unmittelbare Gefahr. Allerdings verlor die Brigade durch französische Gegenangriffe fast die Hälfte ihrer 800 Mann. Der »Todesritt« von Mars-la-Tour wurde zum Mythos.

Telegramm Bismarcks an seine Ehefrau Johanna
Pont-a-Mousson, 17. August 1870, 8 Uhr
Kat. 257

Bismarcks ältester Sohn Herbert (1849–1904) war unter den verwundeten Kürassieren. Der preußische Ministerpräsident telegrafierte seiner Frau: »Ich habe Herbert und Bill [Wilhelm] eben gesprochen; Bill's Pferd erschossen; *er selbst ganz gesund*. Herbert ungefährlicher Schuß durch die Lende, Knochen unverletzt. Er wird heute Abend hergefahren zu mir. Dann werde ich ihn auf Nauheim dirigieren, damit Du endlich hingehst [sic].«

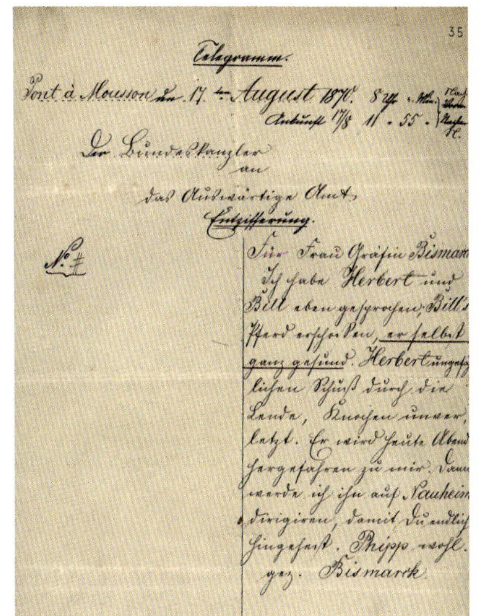

35

Telegramm.

Pont à Mousson den 17. August 1870. 8 Uhr . Min.
Ankunft 17/8 11 . 55 .

Der Bundeskanzler
an
das Auswärtige Amt.
Entzifferung.

No. 7

Für Frau Gräfin Bismarck
Ich habe Herbert und Bill eben gesprochen, Bill's Pferd erschossen, er selbst ganz gesund. Herbert ungefährlichen Schuß durch die Lende, Knochen unverletzt. Er wird heute Abend hergefahren zu mir. Dann werde ich ihn auf Nauheim dirigiren, damit Du endlich hingehst. Phipps wohl.
gez. Bismarck

Kat. 257

Kat. 254

Kat. 255

Nach der Schlacht von Mars-la-Tour bezog die französische Rheinarmee Stellungen bei Gravelotte und St. Privat. Dort boten ummauerte Vorgärten gute Deckung. Am 18. August griffen preußische Truppen und schließlich das sächsische Armeekorps die französischen Positionen frontal an. Das preußische Gardekorps wurde nahezu ausgelöscht. Beim Sturm auf St. Privat erlitten das I. und II. Bataillon der sächsischen 107er schwere Verluste. Mit der Leibfahne in der Hand fielen fünf Träger, ein sechster wurde verwundet. Als das Regiment St. Privat einnahm, war es ein Gefreiter, der die Fahne trug (siehe auch S. 352–353, Kat. 487/4).

Leibfahne des 8. Königlich Sächsischen Infanterieregiments Nr. 107
Königreich Sachsen, 1867–1918
Kat. 254

Versilberter Fahnenring der Leibfahne des 8. Königlich Sächsischen Infanterieregiments Nr. 107, graviert mit den Namen der Träger bei St. Privat und Sedan
Königreich Sachsen
Kat. 255

Kat. 256

»Hundemüde!« Ruhende Soldaten nach der Schlacht von Gravelotte bzw. St. Privat

Zeichnung von Kaspar Kögler (1838–1923)
für »Die Gartenlaube«, 1870, Nr. 45, S. 752
Bleistift auf Papier, 20,4 × 28,8 cm
Kat. 256

»Königliche Hoheit Kronprinz Albert, der Sieger von Beaumont«

Theodor von Götz (1826–1892)
Dresden 1881
Aquarell, 29,4 × 50,1 cm
Kat. 259

Als ihm bei Kriegsbeginn 1870 die Führung des XII. (Königlich Sächsischen) Armeekorps anvertraut wurde, blickte der sächsische Kronprinz Albert (1828–1902) bereits auf eine lange militärische Karriere zurück. Nach der Schlacht von Gravelotte, in der seine Truppen maßgeblich zum Sieg beigetragen hatten, wurde am 19. August als 4. deutsche Armee die Maasarmee gebildet, deren Oberbefehl ihm übertragen wurde. Zusammen mit Teilen der 3. Armee erfocht sie am 30. August bei Beaumont einen weiteren Sieg, der die Einkesselung der Truppen von Marschall Mac Mahon bei Sedan einleitete.

Kat. 259

Kat. 261

Abgetrennter Ärmel vom Uniformrock eines Quartiermeisters der Marine-infanterie

Kaiserreich Frankreich, 1870
Kat. 261

Mit dem Angriff von Truppen des I. Bayerischen Armeekorps auf die Ortschaft Bazeilles begann am frühen Morgen des 1. September die Schlacht von Sedan. Französische Marineinfanterie verteidigte Bazeilles fast acht Stunden lang. Sie verlor dabei 2 655 Mann, während sich die bayerischen Verluste auf 4 089 Gefallene und Verwundete beliefen. Dieser vom Rock eines Marinesoldaten abgetrennte Ärmel wurde in den Ruinen des niedergebrannten Ortes gefunden. In Bazeilles befindet sich heute die wichtigste Gedenkstätte der französischen Marinetruppen.

»A Bazeille[s] 1er Septembre 1870 soir« / Gefallene in den Ruinen von Bazeilles Abend des 1. September 1870

Auguste Lançon (1836–1885), 1871/1876
Radierung, 39,7 × 56,5 cm
Kat. 262

Bazeilles brannte während der Kämpfe fast vollständig nieder, nicht zuletzt, weil bayerische Soldaten versuchten, die in den Häusern verschanzten Gegner »auszuräuchern«. Michael Hechtl, genannt »Schaufimomichl«, 1870/71 Soldat in der 11. Kompanie des 2. Königlich Bayerischen Infanterieregiments »Kronprinz«, notierte seine Erinnerungen an Bazeilles für den Schriftsteller Ludwig Thoma: »die Franzosen in den Häusern schießen auf uns so rauß / das mir uns nicht halten könen und auch die Einwohner haben sich beteihlicht / mir müßen zurük und müßen auf den lingen Fliegel vor gehen / die Franzosen / welche das Dorf drine waren / fochten mit Standhaftigkeit /derselbe wuchs so / daß selbst Frauen die größten Scheußlichkeit verübten / sobalt der Rükzug komantirt wurde und die Bewohner die verwundeten in die breneden Häuser warfen/ da kamm der befehl / das ganze Dorf zusamen schießen und ohne Pardon vorzugehen.«

Kat. 262

Kat. 264

(Aus: Richard Lemp (Hg.): Der Glasl und der Schaufimomichl schreiben für Ludwig Thoma. Die Geschichte vom bayrischen Soldaten anno 1870/71, München 1971, S. 51–52)

Einwohner von Bazeilles werden von bayerischen Truppen zur Hinrichtung abgeführt

Postkarte nach einem Holzschnitt von A. Lanson [Auguste Lançon?], 1912
Kat. 264

Beide Seiten warfen sich nach dem Krieg Gräueltaten vor. Bayerische Soldaten berichteten von Heckenschützen und Gewaltakten gegen Verwundete. Laut französischen Berichten hatten die Bayern Hunderte von Männern und Frauen hingerichtet. Eine Erhebung des Bürgermeisters von Bazeilles im April 1871 ergab, dass 43 Zivilpersonen bei den Kampfhandlungen umkamen und weitere 150 ihren Verwundungen später erlagen.

Kat. 475

Kat. 265

Sächsische Artillerie in der Schlacht bei Sedan 1870, Höhen ostwärts von La Moncelle

Georg von Boddien (1850–1926), 1896
Öl auf Leinwand, 164 × 303 cm
Kat. 475

Das Feuer der massierten deutschen Artillerie trug maßgeblich zum deutschen Sieg bei Sedan bei. Französische Soldaten berichteten, dass sie dem Beschuss hilflos ausgeliefert waren. Der britische Korrespondent William Howard Russell entsetzte sich über die Massen schrecklich zugerichteter Gefallener. Auf dem Gemälde des sächsischen Offiziers und Malers Boddien ist die IV. Abteilung des sächsischen Feldartillerieregiments Nr. 12 zu sehen, die im Galopp zu den Stellungen der III. Abteilung vorgeht. Das Augenmerk des Künstlers galt dem zuvor verwundeten Kommandeur, Oberst Funke, der sich geweigert hatte, aus der Kampfzone weggebracht zu werden und seine vorbeipreschenden Soldaten von der Krankentrage aus grüßt. Das Gemälde hing im Kasino des Regiments in der Dresdner Albertstadt, bis dieses nach dem Ersten Weltkrieg aufgelöst wurde.

Ansicht des Zimmers in Donchery, in dem am 2. September 1870 Otto von Bismarcks Unterredung mit Napoleon III. stattfand

Gereon Pape (1842–1907)
Tusche auf Papier, 41 × 54,2 cm
Kat. 265

Napoleon III., krank und erschöpft, nahm bei Sedan keinen Einfluss auf die Operationsführung, fällte am Abend des 1. September aber die Entscheidung zur Kapitulation, nachdem seine Armee nahezu eingekesselt war. Nach der Meldung, dass Napoleon III. auf dem Weg von Sedan nach Donchery sei, wo er sich Wilhelm I. ergeben wolle, traf Bismarck den Kaiser am Ortseingang, um ihm zu vermitteln, dass die Kapitulationsbedingungen nicht gemildert werden könnten. Die Unterredung fand in dem hier abgebildeten Zimmer in einem ärmlichen Weberhaus statt. Die eigentlichen Verhandlungen erfolgten später ohne die Beteiligung des Kaisers im nahegelegenen Schloss Bellevue. Napoleon reiste anschließend von Sedan aus als Kriegsgefangener nach Kassel, wo er auf Schloss Wilhelmshöhe bis März 1871 interniert blieb.

Nation und Religion

Gottes Schutz und Führung erflehten alle Herrscher und Heere, die 1870 ins Feld zogen. Feldgeistliche begleiteten die Armeen beider Seiten. Ordensleute dienten als Freiwillige in der Verwundeten- und Krankenpflege. Zugleich mit den militärischen Auseinandersetzungen begann ein propagandistischer Kampf zwischen »preußischem« Protestantismus und »französischem« Katholizismus. Katholische Priester waren aus preußischer Sicht gefährliche Fanatiker. Nach französischer Auffassung waren hingegen Protestanten jedes Verbrechens fähig. Der während des Krieges oft beschworene protestantisch-katholische Gegensatz war besonders für Deutschland als nationsbildender Faktor zwiespältig, gehörten doch die Menschen in den süddeutschen Staaten mehrheitlich dem Katholizismus an. In Streitkräften beider Seiten dienten Christen aller Konfessionen, Juden und, in französischen Kolonialregimentern, auch Muslime.

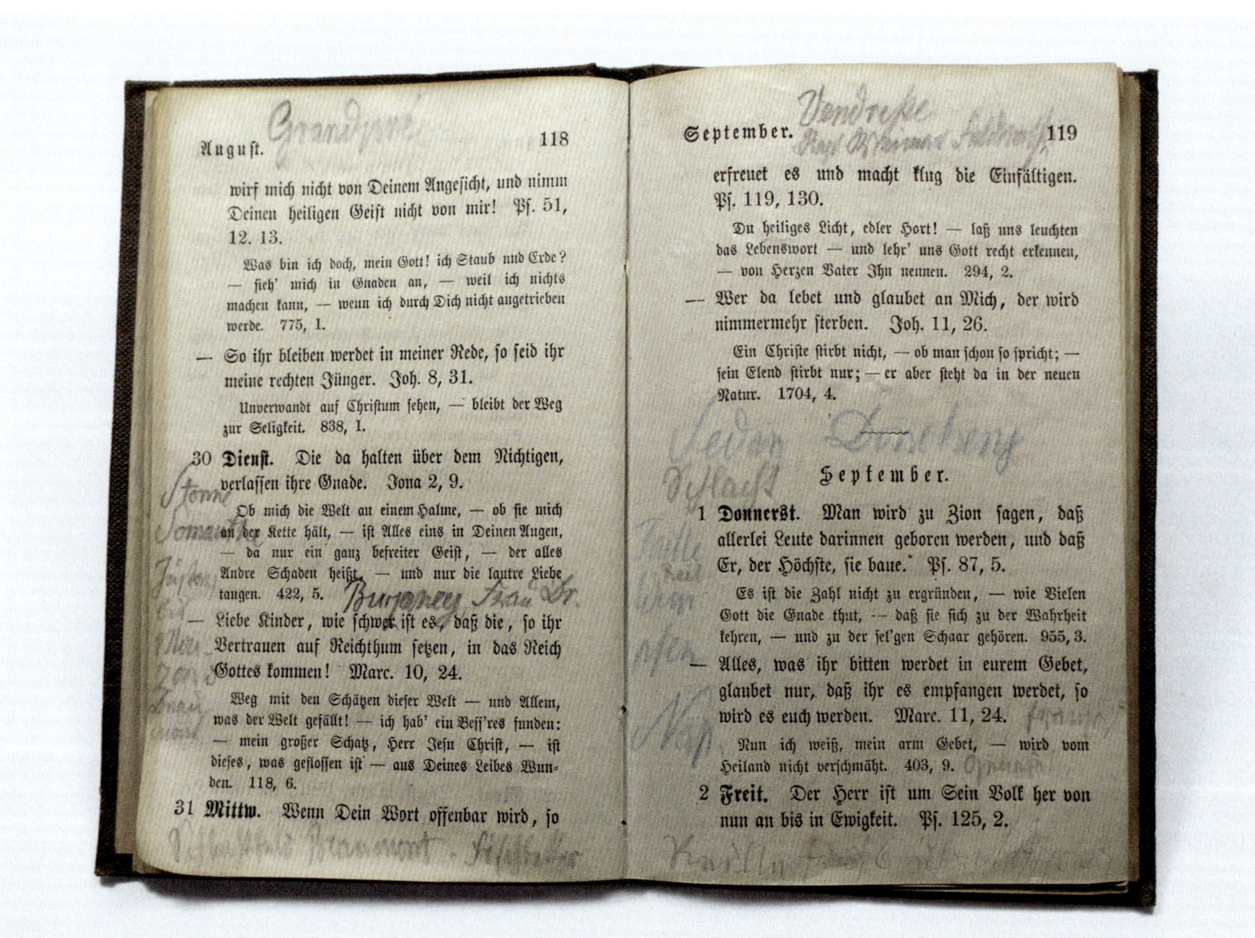

August. 118

wirf mich nicht von Deinem Angesicht, und nimm Deinen heiligen Geist nicht von mir! Ps. 51, 12. 13.

Was bin ich doch, mein Gott! ich Staub und Erde? — sieh' mich in Gnaden an, — weil ich nichts machen kann, — wenn ich durch Dich nicht angetrieben werde. 775, 1.

— So ihr bleiben werdet in meiner Rede, so seid ihr meine rechten Jünger. Joh. 8, 31.

Unverwandt auf Christum sehen, — bleibt der Weg zur Seligkeit. 838, 1.

30 **Dienst.** Die da halten über dem Nichtigen, verlassen ihre Gnade. Jona 2, 9.

Ob mich die Welt an einem Halme, — ob sie mich an der Kette hält, — ist Alles eins in Deinen Augen, — da nur ein ganz befreiter Geist, — der alles Andre Schaden heißt, — und nur die lautre Liebe taugen. 422, 5.

— Liebe Kinder, wie schwer ist es, daß die, so ihr Vertrauen auf Reichthum setzen, in das Reich Gottes kommen! Marc. 10, 24.

Weg mit den Schätzen dieser Welt — und Allem, was der Welt gefällt! — ich hab' ein Bess'res funden: — mein großer Schatz, Herr Jesu Christ, — ist dieses, was geflossen ist — aus Deines Leibes Wunden. 118, 6.

31 **Mittw.** Wenn Dein Wort offenbar wird, so

September. 119

erfreuet es und macht klug die Einfältigen. Ps. 119, 130.

Du heiliges Licht, edler Hort! — laß uns leuchten das Lebenswort — und lehr' uns Gott recht erkennen, — von Herzen Vater Ihn nennen. 294, 2.

— Wer da lebet und glaubet an Mich, der wird nimmermehr sterben. Joh. 11, 26.

Ein Christe stirbt nicht, — ob man schon so spricht; — sein Elend stirbt nur; — er aber steht da in der neuen Natur. 1704, 4.

September.

1 **Donnerst.** Man wird zu Zion sagen, daß allerlei Leute darinnen geboren werden, und daß Er, der Höchste, sie baue. Ps. 87, 5.

Es ist die Zahl nicht zu ergründen, — wie Vielen Gott die Gnade thut, — daß sie sich zu der Wahrheit kehren, — und zu der sel'gen Schaar gehören. 955, 3.

— Alles, was ihr bitten werdet in eurem Gebet, glaubet nur, daß ihr es empfangen werdet, so wird es euch werden. Marc. 11, 24.

Nun ich weiß, mein arm Gebet, — wird vom Heiland nicht verschmäht. 403, 9.

2 **Freit.** Der Herr ist um Sein Volk her von nun an bis in Ewigkeit. Ps. 125, 2.

Kat. 266

Losungsbuch, in dem Bismarck die Schlacht von Sedan und das Treffen mit Napoleon III. vermerkt hat
Kat. 266

In dieser Sammlung von Bibelzitaten für das Jahr 1870 notierte Bismarck die für ihn bedeutsamen Ereignisse, darunter auch den Sieg bei Sedan am 1./2. September. Der Lutheraner Bismarck glaubte an Gottes Allmacht und die Vorsehung. Überzeugt, dass er sich vor Gott zu bewähren hatte, fühlte er sich zu rigorosem Handeln ermutigt.

»Pax Morientibus!« / Friede den Sterbenden!
Wilfrid-Constant Beauquesne (1847–1913)
Nach 1871
Öl auf Leinwand, 46 × 32,5 cm
Kat. 267

Eine Nonne stellt sich schützend vor einen sterbenden französischen Verwundeten, als preußische Soldaten in das Gebäude eindringen. Abwehrend hält sie ihnen ein Kreuz entgegen. So suggeriert der Künstler Barbarei und Gottlosigkeit auf Seiten des Gegners. Kaum besser sahen die preußischen Feindbilder aus, die französischen Katholiken Fanatismus und Rückständigkeit unterstellten.

Jacke und Weste eines Offiziers der Légion des Volontaires de l'Ouest
Republik Frankreich, 1870/71
Kat. 269

Zur französischen Loirearmee zählten unter dem Namen »Volontaires de l'Ouest« die ehemaligen Päpstlichen Zuaven. Bestehend aus französischen und belgischen Katholiken, hatten sie bis zur Einnahme des Kirchenstaats durch Italien 1870 im päpstlichen Heer gedient.

Kat. 267

Kat. 269

Kat. 270

Kat. 271

Einnäher mit dem Herzen Jesu im Futter der Weste zur Uniform eines Offiziers der Légion des Volontaires de l'Ouest

Republik Frankreich, 1870/71
Kat. 270

Das rote Herz Jesu, umschlossen von einer Dornenkrone, wählte der Träger der Uniform als Talisman, der ihn vor Tod oder Verwundung bewahren sollte. Unter dem Schutzzeichen liest man »Arrête! Le cœur de Jésus est avec moi« (Halt' ein! Das Herz Jesu ist mit mir). Auch das Feldzeichen der Volontaires de l'Ouest zeigte das Herz Jesu. Seit der Französischen Revolution war es nicht nur ein katholisches Symbol, sondern stand auch für eine royalistische Gesinnung. Vom Jesuitenorden verbreitet, fand die Herz-Jesu-Verehrung zahlreiche Anhänger. In Frankreich wie in Deutschland war sie nach 1871 gleichermaßen Ausdruck für konfessionelle wie politische Überzeugungen. Franzosen verdeutlichten damit, dass nur eine im katholischen Glauben und seinen Werten verankerte Nation Anfeindungen widerstehen könne. Deutsche Katholiken drückten im Kulturkampf ihre Glaubenstreue und ihren Widerstand gegen staatliche Einflussnahme auf die Kirche aus.

Chechia für Mannschaften der Zuaven- und algerischen Schützenregimenter

Republik Frankreich, um 1900
Kat. 271

13 900 Muslime wurden 1870/71 mit Regimentern der Afrikaarmee auf den Kriegsschauplatz nach Frankreich entsandt. Die algerischen Schützenregimenter waren als »Turcos« bekannt und die nordafrikanische Kavallerie als »Spahis«. Sie wurden begleitet von islamischen Geistlichen und sorgten selbst für die Einhaltung der Speisegesetze. Zur Bekleidung der ab 1830 in Algerien für den französischen Dienst rekrutierten Truppenteile zählten schirmlose Kopfbedeckungen wie diese »Chechia« genannte Mütze. Die in Nordafrika verbreitete Kopfbedeckung wies ihren Träger als Muslim aus.

Kat. 272

Gottesdienst am Versöhnungstag des Jahres 1870 im Lager vor Metz

Instruktionstuch, signiert »GM«
Nach 1870
Kat. 272

14 000 jüdische Soldaten dienten 1870/71 in den deutschen Feldarmeen. In den deutsch-jüdischen Gemeinden diskutierte man allerdings, ob es rechtens sei, auf französische Glaubensbrüder zu schießen oder überhaupt Krieg gegen die Nation zu führen, die als erste Juden das volle Bürgerrecht zuerkannt hatte. Viele deutsche Juden hofften aber, dass ihr Einsatz zu einer vollständigen Emanzipation der jüdischen Bevölkerung in allen deutschen Staaten beitragen würde. Das Bild auf diesem Tuch zeigt eine Jom-Kippur-Feier jüdischer Angehöriger der deutschen Belagerungstruppen am 4./5. Oktober 1870 vor Metz und ist als Sinnbild des Patriotismus deutscher Juden zu verstehen. Tatsächlich fand keine Feldmesse mit über 1 000 Teilnehmern statt. Den Gottesdienst feierte Rabbiner Dr. Isaak Blumenstein in einem Bauernhaus mit 60 bis 70 Soldaten.

Krieg gegen die französische Dritte Republik

Der deutsche Sieg bei Sedan am 1./2. September kostete Napoleon III. den Thron, brachte aber nicht das erhoffte Kriegsende. Die politische und militärische Führung in Preußen war sich mit einem großen Teil der Öffentlichkeit einig, dass die Abtretung von den als deutsch angesehenen Gebieten Elsass und Lothringen Grundvoraussetzung für einen Friedensschluss sei – auch, um Frankreich dauerhaft zu schwächen. In Paris formierte sich jedoch nach der Ausrufung der Republik am 4. September 1870 eine Regierung der Nationalen Verteidigung, die eine Abtretung ablehnte und entschlossen war, den Krieg fortzuführen, bis der letzte Eindringling aus Frankreich verjagt wäre. Die Propaganda beschwor den Geist der Französischen Revolution und warb für die »Nation in Waffen«. Zu den Resten des kaiserlichen Heeres traten Zehntausende von Mobilgardisten, bewaffneten Staatsbediensteten und Freiwilligen.

Léon Gambetta (1838–1882), von September 1870 bis Januar 1871 Innenminister der Regierung der Nationalen Verteidigung
Bronze, 1885
Höhe 38 cm
Kat. 275

Der Jurist und Politiker Gambetta hatte sich im Juli 1870 zuerst gegen den Krieg ausgesprochen, dann aber für die Bewilligung von Kriegskrediten gestimmt. Am 4. September rief er vor dem Pariser Rathaus die Republik aus. Energisch ging er daran, neue Truppen auszuheben.
Um den Widerstand in den Provinzen und den Entsatz der Hauptstadt zu organisieren, verließ er mit einem Ballon das belagerte Paris am 7. Oktober in Richtung Tours. Verfechter einer Kriegführung bis zum Äußersten (»guerre à outrance«), trat er am 6. Februar 1871 zurück, da er den Waffenstillstand mit dem Deutschen Reich ablehnte.

Kat. 275

Kat. 274

Kat. 273

Spottmünzen auf Napoleon III.
Republik Frankreich, 1870
Kat. 276–279

Mit der Ausrufung der Dritten Republik ging ein Bildersturm einher, dem die Symbole des untergegangenen Kaisertums zum Opfer fielen. Napoleon III. wurde zum Alleinverantwortlichen für den unglücklichen Verlauf des Krieges erklärt. In Paris kamen umgestaltete Zehn-Centimes-Münzen in Umlauf, die den entthronten Kaiser verunglimpften.

Fahne der Nationalgarde
Frankreich, um 1850
Kat. 274

Statt der Symbole des napoleonischen Kaisertums wurden bei Nationalfesten die republikanischen Traditionen Frankreichs beschworen. Die Nationalgarde, die in allen drei Revolutionen 1789, 1830 und 1848 eine wichtige Rolle gespielt hatte, trat wieder in den Vordergrund. Ihre mobilen Truppenteile bildeten nach dem Untergang des kaiserlichen Heeres die letzte militärische Reserve Frankreichs.

Leutnant des 4. Bataillons der Mobilgarde des Niederrhein-Departements
Kaiserreich Frankreich, 1870/71
Kat. 273

Die Nationalgarde bestand aus mobilen Einheiten zur Verstärkung der Linientruppen an der Front und stationären Formationen (»gardes sédentaires«). Die Mobilgarden, im Volksmund »les moblots«, bildeten ab September 1870 ein wichtiges Reservoir für die Aufstellung der neuen republikanischen Armeen. Baron Hugues Zorn de Bulach d'Osthouse (1851–1921), der 1870 in Sélestat stationiert war, trug diese Uniform als Offizier der Mobilgarde des Niederrhein-Departements.

Kat. 276–279

Kat. 282

Kat. 285

Kat. 286

Kat. 287

Amerikanisches Spencer-Gewehr, von badischen Truppen bei Nuits am 18. Dezember 1870 erbeutet
USA 1860
Kat. 343

Die französische Regierung kaufte Waffen unter anderem in den USA, um die neu aufgestellten Armeen damit auszurüsten. Dieses Gewehr wurde in Boston hergestellt.

Kat. 343

»Capt. E Hilbot, sa femme et son chien« / »Hauptmann E Hilbot, seine Frau und sein Hund«
L. Pierson, Paris
Carte-de-Visite-Fotografie
Kat. 282

Sapeur und Marketenderin eines unbekannten Truppenteils
Antonin, Paris
Carte-de-Visite-Fotografie
Kat. 285

Ein Freiwilliger oder Nationalgardist und eine Marketenderin, an einem Fass lehnend
Dolivet, Paris
Carte-de-Visite-Fotografie
Kat. 286

Ein Mann und eine Frau in Uniform, vermutlich Angehörige eines Freiwilligenverbands
Carte-de-Visite-Fotografie
Kat. 287

»Hamon père« / »Vater Hamon« in der Uniform der Nationalgarde
L. Pierson, Paris
Carte-de-Visite-Fotografie
Kat. 291

»Hamon fils« / »Sohn Hamon« in der Uniform der Nationalgarde
L. Pierson, Paris
Carte-de-Visite-Fotografie
Kat. 292

Nationalgardist mit Mädchen
Carte-de-Visite-Fotografie
Kat. 293

Junger Trommler der Nationalgarde
Lefèvre, Paris
Carte-de-Visite-Fotografie
Kat. 296

Die Fotografien porträtieren die französische »Nation in Waffen«. Da die Angehörigen der »neuen Armeen« (»armées nouvelles«) der Republik oft unkonventionell bekleidet waren, können nicht alle hier dargestellten Männer und Frauen bestimmten Truppengattungen zugeordnet werden. Die Bilder entstanden während der

Kat. 291

Kat. 292

Kat. 293

Kat. 296

Belagerung von Paris. Sie zeigen einen Querschnitt der Bevölkerung, alle Altersgruppen, Männer, Frauen und Kinder. In den belagerten Städten, aber auch in den Kampfzonen teilten sie Erfahrungen von Beschuss und Besatzung, von Lebensgefahr und Hunger. (Auguste Raffet: Costumes militaires sous les deux Sièges de Paris, 2 Bände mit kolorierten Federzeichnungen und handschriftlichen Kommentaren des Künstlers, Bibliothèque Nationale de France, Paris, https://gallica.bnf.fr/ark:/12148/btv1b52506568c.item, 27.1.2020)

Leutnant Faure, ein weiblicher Offizier der Nationalgarde
Carte-de-Visite-Fotografie
Kat. 288

Marie-Antoinette Lix (1839–1909) in Leutnantsuniform, vermutlich eines Freiwilligenverbands
Carte-de-Visite-Fotografie
Kat. 289

Die Mobilisierung der gesamten Nation durch die Dritte Republik ermöglichte es Frauen, denen der Militärdienst bis dahin nur als Marketenderinnen möglich gewesen war, auch Waffen zu tragen und Truppen zu führen, allerdings nur in subalternen Positionen und nicht im Verband der Linientruppen. Bekannt wurde Marie-Antoinette Lix. Französische Gouvernante einer polnischen Adelsfamilie, schloss sie sich 1863 in Männerkleidung Aufständischen an, die gegen die russische Herrschaft kämpften. Nach Verwundung, Gefangennahme und Ausweisung nach Frankreich zurückgekehrt, war sie 1870 als Lehrerin in den Vogesen tätig. Sie wurde Leutnant bei einem Franktireurverband. Nach einem Zusammentreffen mit Garibaldi-Truppen, die auf französischer Seite kämpften, wurde sie dort Krankenhelferin. (Raymond Caire: La Femme Militaire des Origines à nos Jours, Paris – Limoges 1981, S. 34–35)

Kat. 288

Kat. 289

Kat. 298

Franktireure und Ulanen

Der »Kleine Krieg« in der Provinz

Deutsche Truppen rechneten bereits im Sommer 1870 mit Angriffen von Freischärlern. Schon vor Kriegsbeginn gab es Planungen in Frankreich, im Fall einer Invasion in verschiedenen Departements und zur Unterstützung der Linientruppen und Nationalgarden Verbände von »Franctireurs« (»Freischützen«) zu mobilisieren. Sie sollten nach Partisanenart den Nachschub des Gegners stören und isolierte Posten angreifen. Während deutsche Truppen nicht zwischen bewaffneten Zivilisten und Franktireuren unterschieden, waren Letztere – militärisch organisiert und uniformiert – aus französischer Sicht reguläre Kombattanten. Wurden Franktireure zu einem besonders verhassten Feindbild auf deutscher Seite, so galten Ulanen als Schrecken der französischen Zivilbevölkerung. »Les Uhlans« waren als Späher oft die ersten, die eine Ortschaft erreichten. Mit ihren mehr als drei Meter langen Lanzen und aus französischer Sicht ungewöhnlich großen Pferden wirkten sie besonders furchteinflößend. Sie waren auch häufig bei der Sicherung der deutschen Nachschubwege durch Frankreich in Kämpfe mit Franktireuren verwickelt. In der deutschen bzw. französischen Propaganda wurden Franktireure und Ulanen jeweils zu wahren Bestien stilisiert, die vor keiner Grausamkeit zurückschreckten. Diese Feindbilder wurden bis weit über das Kriegende hinaus gepflegt. (Siehe auch den Beitrag von Heidi Mehrkens in diesem Band. Mündliche Erläuterungen zum Feindbild »Uhlan« verdanken wir Hubert Walther, Woerth.)

»Enfants déguisés« / Verkleidete Kinder Zwei Jungen in der 1867 vorgestellten Uniform der Franctireurs des Vosges
Carte-de-Visite-Fotografie
Kat. 298

Uniform eines Franctireur des Vosges
Republik Frankreich, 1870/71
Kat. 300

Für die »Franctireurs des Vosges« war ursprünglich eine weiße Uniform vorgesehen. Diese Montur, zu der ein verwegener Hut gehörte, wurde 1867 im Umfeld der Pariser Weltausstellung vorgestellt. 1870/71 waren Franktireure jedoch viel schlichter gekleidet, wie diese Uniform zeigt, die dem Pariser Armeemuseum noch von ihrem ursprünglichen Träger geschenkt wurde.

Kat. 300

Kat. 306

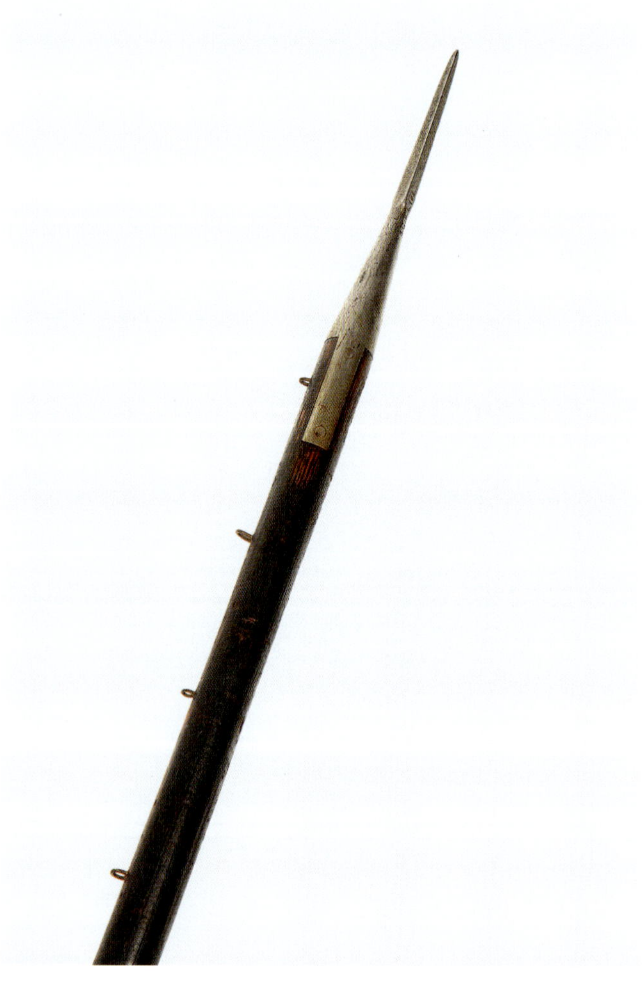

Kat. 308

Tschapka für Mannschaften der Linien-Ulanenregimenter
Königreich Preußen, 1867/1889
Kat. 306

Kavallerielanze, Modell 1856
Königreich Preußen
Kat. 308

»Franc-tireur brûlé vif par les Prussiens«/»Von preußischen Soldaten lebendig verbrannter Franctireur«, Pouilly-lès-Dijon, 23. Januar 1871
Guipet, Dijon 1871
Fotoglyptie
Kat. 310

Beide Seiten bezichtigten sich, Grausamkeiten gegen Wehrlose zu verüben. Fotografien wie diese wurden als Belege für solche Anschuldigungen veröffentlicht. Laut dem Auszug aus einem offiziellen französischen Protokoll, der auf der Bildrückseite abgedruckt ist, wurde die hier abgebildete verkohlte Leiche von französischen Truppen gefunden, als sie das Schloss von Pouilly von den Deutschen zurückeroberten. Es soll sich um eine Vergeltungsmaßnahme für die Erschießung eines preußischen Offiziers durch einen Bauern gehandelt haben.

»La Charge des Uhlans«/ Ulanenangriff, 1870/71
Alphonse de Neuville (1836–1885)
Federzeichnung, Vorlage für eine Abbildung in Quatrelles (d. i. Ernest-Louis-Victor-Jules L'Épine): »À coups de fusil«, mit Illustrationen von Alphonse Neuville, Paris 1877
Kat. 309

Kat. 310

Kat. 309

Deutsche Stellung mit vier 12-cm-Kanonen vor Straßburg, 1870
Ernst Lucke & Co., Berlin
Kat. 314

Kat. 314

Belagerungen

Feldschlachten wurden bis Kriegsende weiterhin geschlagen, um Paris herum, an der Lisaine, an der Loire oder im Norden Frankreichs. Dennoch waren es Belagerungen, die den Krieg nach der französischen Niederlage bei Sedan prägten. Beim Vormarsch der deutschen Armeen nach Frankreich hinein waren eine ganze Reihe bemannter französischer Festungen umgangen worden. Waren sie schwach besetzt, wurden sie lediglich beobachtet. Fehlte auf der deutschen Seite die Feuerkraft, um einen befestigten Ort zu beschießen, dann wurde er »zerniert«, also durch einen Kordon aus Infanterie und Kavallerie abgeriegelt. Um eine Übergabe zu erzwingen, versuchten die Belagerer, wie bei Metz, die Garnison und die verbliebene Einwohnerschaft auszuhungern. Versagte diese Methode und war schwere Artillerie verfügbar, entschieden sich die Belagerer letztlich für ein Bombardement. Davon waren nicht nur militärische Anlagen betroffen, sondern in Straßburg und später in Paris auch Wohnviertel, Kirchen und andere Kulturdenkmäler. Die Festung Belfort (siehe S. 367, Kat. 484) ergab sich erst am 16. Februar 1871 auf Weisung des Regierungschefs Adolphe Thiers, als dies von deutscher Seite zur Vorbedingung für eine Verlängerung des Waffenstillstands gemacht wurde. Die Zitadelle von Bitsch in Lothringen kapitulierte erst am 26. März 1871 nach einer 230 Tage langen Belagerung.

Kat. 316

Straßburg wurde am 12. August 1870 von 40 000 Mann badischer und württembergischer Truppen eingeschlossen, die ab dem 15. August von dem preußischen General August von Werder (1808–1887) befehligt wurden. In der befestigten Stadt lag eine 17 000 Mann starke Besatzung, die von General Jean-Jacques Uhrich (1802–1886), einem Elsässer, befehligt wurde. Um eine schnelle Übergabe zu erzwingen, ließ Werder die Stadt beschießen. Dabei wurden nicht nur Wallanlagen getroffen, sondern auch Wohnviertel und Kulturstätten wie die unersetzliche städtische Bibliothek im Temple Neuf, das Kunstmuseum der Aubette und das gotische Münster. Als die Stadt am 28. September kapitulierte, war ein Drittel der Innenstadt zerstört, 1 400 Soldaten, Bewohner und Bewohnerinnen verwundet oder tot und 10 000 Menschen obdachlos. Werder war schon während der Belagerung heftig für das Bombardement kritisiert worden. Im Elsass wurde sein Name zum Schimpfwort: »Werder – Merder!«. (Monique Fuchs und Sylviane Hatterer: Le Musée Historique de la Ville des Strasbourg- Promenade entre Ville et Musée, Strasbourg 2015, S. 75; mündliche Hinweise auf die elsässische Rezeption der Belagerung von Hubert Walther, Woerth)

Zerstörte Brauerei hinter der I. Parallele in Bischheim, 1870

Ernst Lucke & Co., Berlin

Kat. 316

Im Krieg 1870/71 entstanden eindrucksvolle Aufnahmen von Zerstörungen. Dabei hielten deutsche Fotografen besonders solche fest, die durch das Abwehrfeuer französischer Artillerie gegen deutsche Stellungen verursacht worden waren, wie hier in dem nördlich Straßburgs gelegenen Bischheim.

Kat. 315

Die Hauptstraße in Kehl nach französischem Beschuss, 1870

Paul Sinner (1838–1925)
Kat. 315

Deutsche Belagerungsbatterien feuerten ab dem 19. August aus dem Südfort der rechtsrheinischen badischen Garnisonstadt Kehl auf Straßburg. Französische Geschütze erwiderten den Beschuss und zerstörten 13 Gebäude in Kehl. Solange das deutsche Bombardement der französischen Nachbarstadt andauerte, wurde auch Kehl immer wieder getroffen. Am 26. August brannten der Bahnhof und alle Gebäude entlang der Kehler Hauptstraße nieder. Werder und Uhrich bezichtigten sich im Verlauf der Kämpfe gegenseitig, unmenschlich zu handeln und absichtlich zivile Wohnstätten zu beschießen. (Ute Scherb: Die Grenze als Schicksal, in: Stadt Kehl (Hg.): Kehl am Rhein. Jahresschrift 2010, S. 76)

»The Porte Blanche Strasburg. 30th Sep. 1870«

Aus dem Skizzenbuch des Kriegskorrespondenten William Simpson (1823–1899) mit Bleistift- und Aquarellskizzen, 1870, geöffnet 8,9 × 29,8 cm
Kat. 317

Der schottische Journalist und Künstler Simpson, der bereits im Krimkrieg dabei war, nutzte dieses kleine Notizbuch, als er 1870 aus Straßburg berichtete. Wie andere Korrespondenten musste auch Simpson damit rechnen, als Spion verdächtigt zu werden. Manchmal zeichnete er sogar auf Zigarettenpapier, um die Skizzen im Notfall aufrauchen zu können.

Angesengte Buchseiten aus der von deutscher Artillerie in Brand geschossenen städtischen Bibliothek im Temple Neuf

Straßburg, geborgen 1870
Kat. 321 (siehe S. 266–267)

Die in städtischem Besitz befindliche Bibliothèque du Temple Neuf beherbergte wertvollste Handschriften und Drucke. Am 23./24. August 1870 zerstörte ein durch die deutsche Beschießung ausgelöster Brand einen großen Teil der Sammlung.

Kat. 317

Kat. 322

Handschriftlicher Bericht der Kapitulation von Straßburg und zwei der Unterschriftsfedern
Kat. 322

Die Besatzung von Straßburg kapitulierte, bevor Werder eine Einnahme im Sturm befehlen konnte. Die Übergabe der Stadt wurde am 28. September 1870 in einem Eisenbahnwaggon bei Königshofen vollzogen.

Trümmerstück einer Fiale des Straßburger Münsters
Straßburg, geborgen 1870
Kat. 319 (siehe S. 265)

Das Historische Museum in Straßburg wurde nach der Rückgabe des Elsasses an Frankreich 1919 auch gegründet, um Zeugnisse der Belagerung von 1870 zu sammeln.

Verschmolzene eiserne »Krähenfüsse« aus der Zitadelle von Straßburg
Straßburg, geborgen 1870
Kat. 320

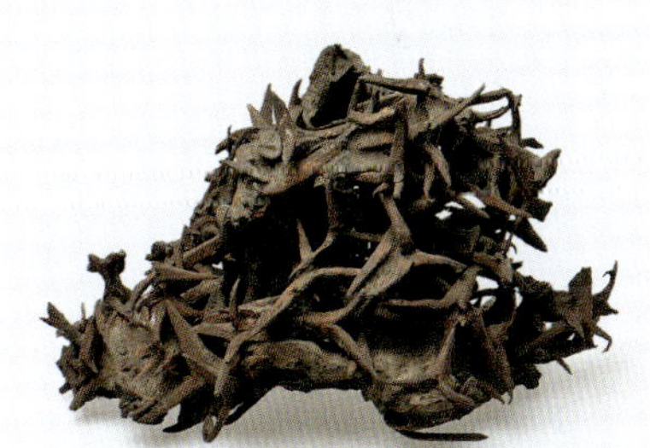

Kat. 320

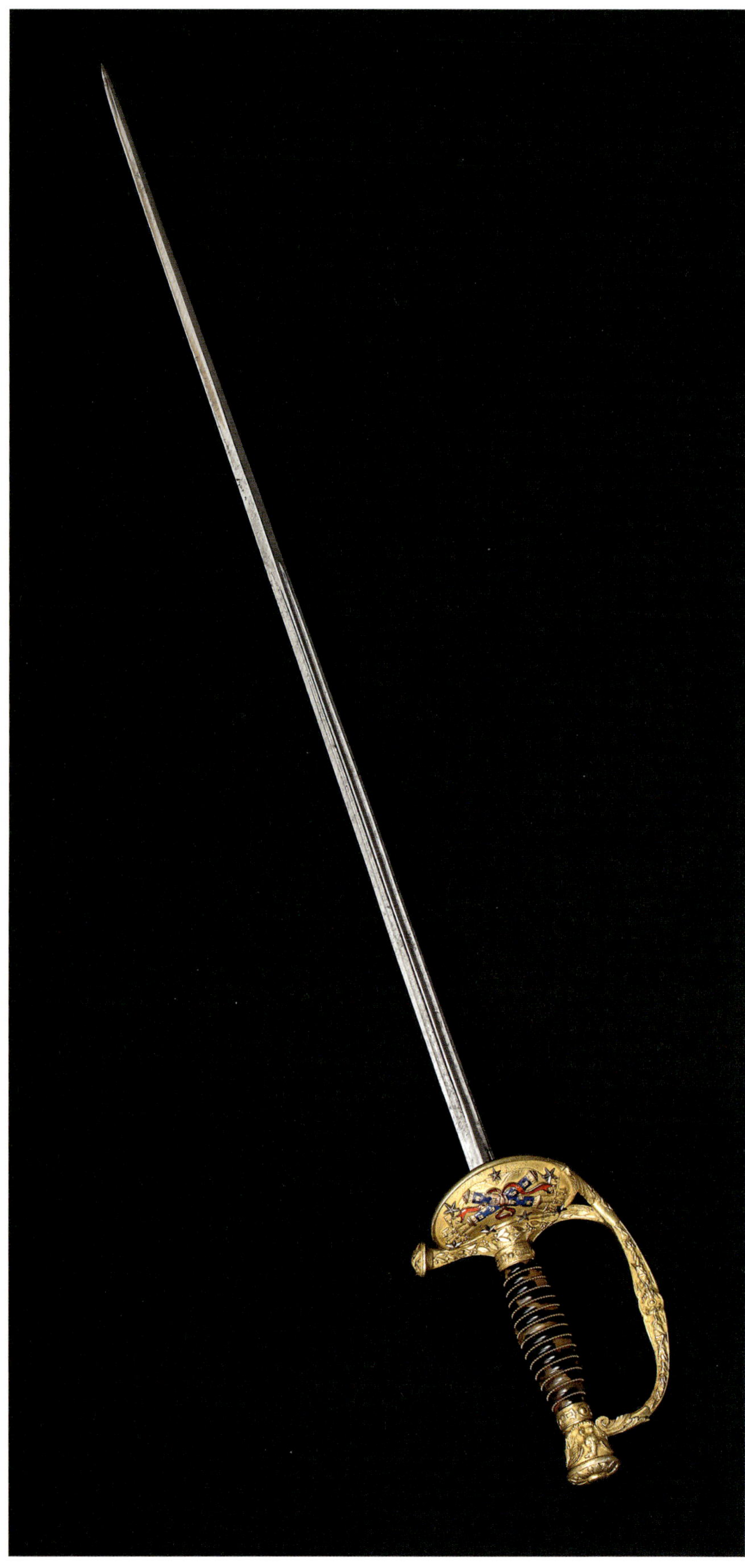

Kat. 323

Degen eines Marschalls von Frankreich François-Achille Bazaine (1811–1888) zugeschrieben

Französisches Kaiserreich, 1864
Kat. 323

Nach der Schlacht von Gravelotte/Saint-Privat am 18. August 1870 zog Marschall Bazaine die französische Rheinarmee in den Schutz der Festung Metz zurück. Die Stadt wurde ab dem 20. August unter dem Oberbefehl des preußischen Prinzen Friedrich Karl von der deutschen 1. und Teilen der 2. Armee eingeschlossen. Man wusste, dass die Stadt vollkommen überbelegt war und hoffte, dass eine bloße Blockade die Besatzung zur Übergabe zwingen würde. Sämtliche Ausbruchsversuche aus Metz scheiterten.
Die Belagerer beschossen die Stadt nicht, aber die Zustände dort wurden aufgrund von Lebensmittelknappheit und eines Ausbruchs der Ruhr für die Verteidiger unerträglich. Die Kapitulation Bazaines am 28. Oktober 1870 wurde von seinen Soldaten dennoch als schändlich empfunden. Die gezeigte Waffe wird in einem alten Bestandskatalog des Militärhistorischen Museums Bazaine zugeschrieben. Für die Zuschreibung fehlen jedoch bislang Belege.

Kat. 325

»Au Maréchal Bazaine, la France reconnaissante« / Marschall Bazaine gewidmet, das dankbare Frankreich
Faustin Betbeder (1847–1914), genannt Faustin
Farblithografie
Kat. 325

Die Garnison von Metz marschierte Regiment für Regiment aus der Stadt, um sich den Siegern zu ergeben. Bazaine nahm an dieser Zeremonie nicht teil, sondern begab sich in einer Kutsche in Gefangenschaft. Seine Übergabe von Metz zerstörte den Ruf des militärischen Hoffnungsträgers und machte ihn des Verrats verdächtig. Der Karikaturist Betbeder hat Bazaine hier im Büßergewand dargestellt. Anstelle eines Ordensbandes trägt er einen Strick um den Hals. Tatsächlich wurde Bazaine nach kurzer Kriegsgefangenschaft in Kassel 1873 von einem französischen Gericht zum Tode verurteilt. Patrice de Mac-Mahon, 1870/71 Marschall und ab dem 24. Mai 1873 Präsident der Republik, begnadigte ihn zu einer 20-jährigen Haftstrafe. Bazaine entwich daraufhin nach Spanien und starb 1888 in Madrid.

Der bei Metz erbeutete Fahnenadler des französischen 4. Linieninfanterieregiments
Kaiserreich Frankreich, 1870
Kat. 324

Goldene Adler zierten als Symbole des Kaisertums die Fahnenspitzen des französischen Heeres. Napoleon III. belebte am 10. Mai 1852 durch eine Verleihung von Adlern an Regimenter aller Garnisonen in Frankreich und Algerien eine Tradition des Ersten Kaiserreichs wieder. Jedes Regiment führte nur einen »aigle«. Als Metz kapitulierte, sollte die Besatzung ihre Feldzeichen an die Sieger ausliefern. 22 der Adler wurden daraufhin binnen Stunden zerstört. 56 gelangten schließlich in deutsche Hände. Die Trophäen von Metz, die reichste Beute dieser Art im ganzen Krieg, wurden nach Berlin geschickt.

Kat. 324

Der Kampf um Paris

Nach dem Sieg von Sedan wurde Paris zum Hauptziel der deutschen Operationen. Am 19. September 1870 war die stark befestigte Stadt eingeschlossen. 17 Forts bildeten den äußeren Verteidigungsring. Die Zahl der Verteidiger war mit rund 350 000 Mann eindrucksvoll. Doch verfügten davon lediglich zwei Linieninfanterieregimenter und die mit Schiffsgeschützen nach Paris verlegten Marinesoldaten über Kampferfahrung. Moltke plante, die mit rund zwei Millionen Einwohnern und Einwohnerinnen damals größte Stadt Europas zunächst auszuhungern. Bismarck forderte hingegen eine möglichst rasche Bombardierung, da er mit zunehmender Kriegsdauer das Eingreifen anderer europäischer Mächte fürchtete. Moltke lehnte dies als Einmischung in militärische Angelegenheiten ab und bereitete den Beschuss der französischen Hauptstadt erst vor, als ausreichend Geschütze zur Verfügung standen. Am 27. Dezember begann die Beschießung der Befestigungsanlagen und am 5. Januar 1871 von Stadtvierteln im Süden und Westen. Bis zum 27. Januar fielen ihr 375 Menschen zum Opfer. Am 28. Januar beendete ein Waffenstillstand die Belagerung.

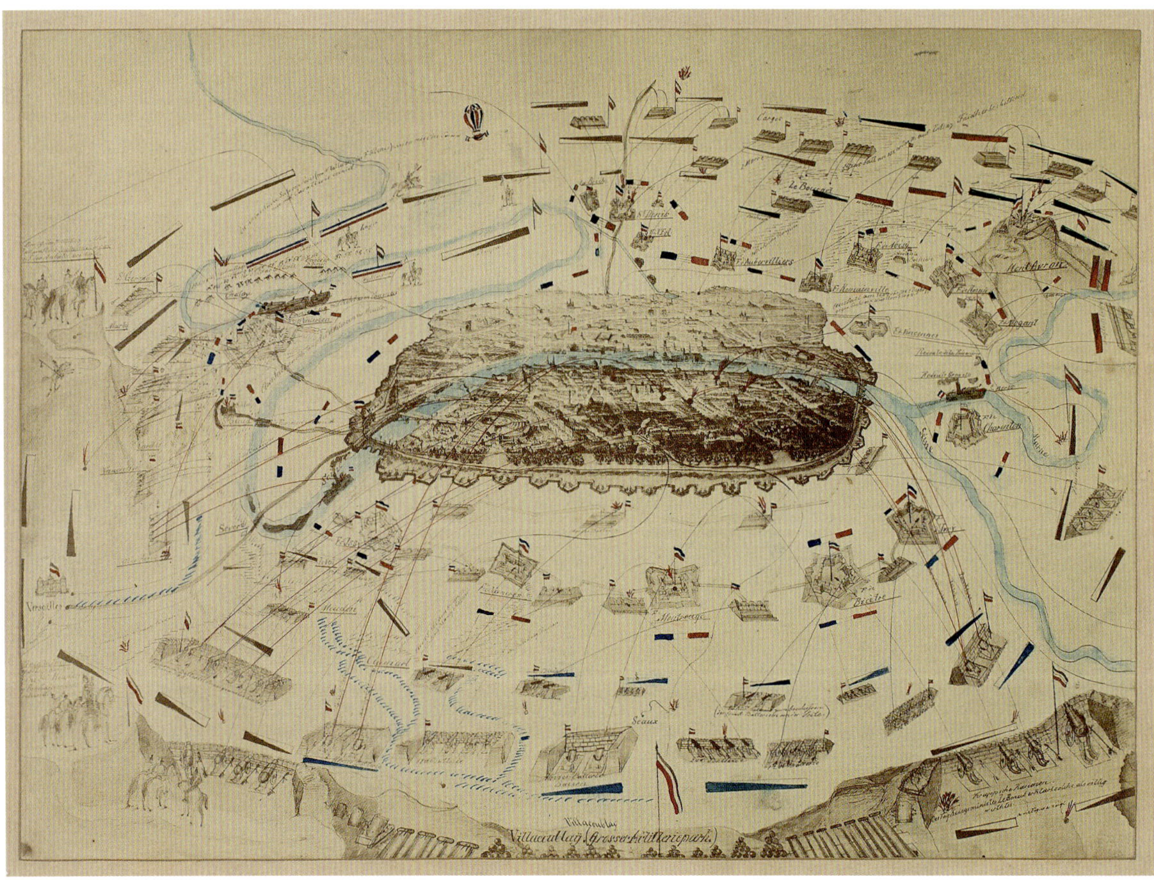

Kat. 327

Kat. 344

Das belagerte Paris aus der Vogelperspektive 1870/71 mit eingezeichneten deutschen und französischen Stellungen
J. [oder F.] Stiel, Karlsruhe, unter Verwendung einer reproduzierten Grafik
»Aus dem Besitz von Major Enderlein, zuletzt im Jahre 1882 als Garnisonsverwaltungsdirektor in Mhm. tätig«
Kat. 327

Blick auf die Befestigungen von Paris während der Belagerung
Entwurf von Félix Philippoteaux (1815–1884), 1872, für das Panorama »Die Belagerung von Paris«
Öl auf Leinwand, 85 × 88 cm
Kat. 344

Kat. 329

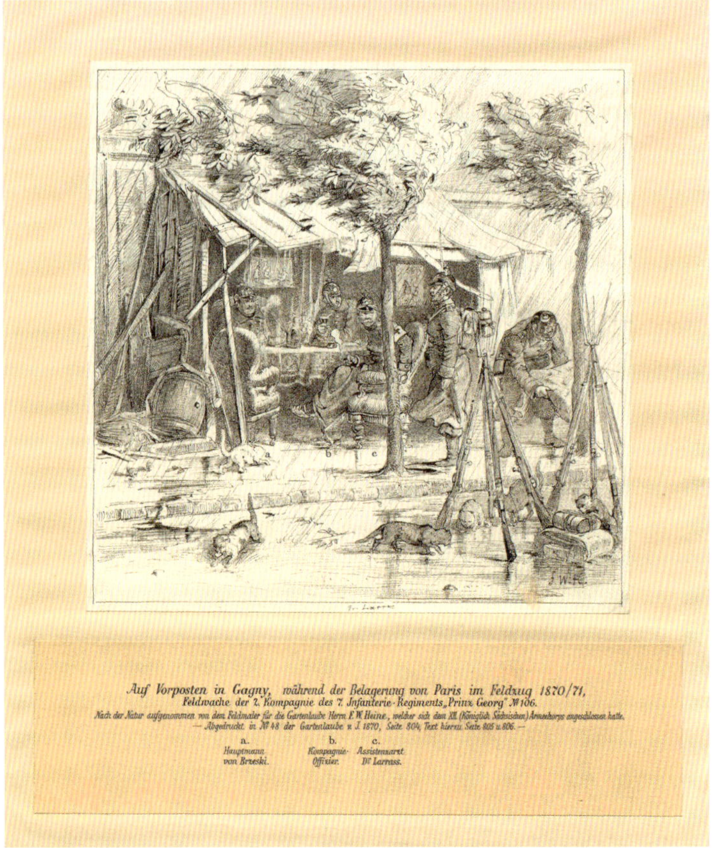

Kat. 330

»Auf Vorposten in Maison-Rouge, dem Schlosse des Herzogs von Orleans, während der Belagerung von Paris im Feldzug 1870/71«

Friedrich Wilhelm Heine (1845–1921), 1870
Aquarellierte Federzeichnung,
19,1 × 19,8 cm
Kat. 329

Heine hatte sich dem XII. (Königlich Sächsischen) Armeekorps bzw. der Maasarmee angeschlossen und berichtete für die illustrierte Zeitschrift »Die Gartenlaube«. Seine beiden Zeichnungen aus der Vorpostenzeit erschienen 1870 in Heftnummer 48, S. 804–806.

»Auf Vorposten in Gagny, während der Belagerung von Paris im Feldzug 1870/71, Feldwache der 2. Kompagnie des 7. Infanterie-Regiments ›Prinz Georg‹ Nr. 106«

Friedrich Wilhelm Heine, 1870
Federzeichnung, 18,7 × 19,3 cm
Kat. 330

Holzholen in Choisy le Roi

Lithografie nach Salzmann von A. Pettinger aus dem Mappenwerk »Erinnerungsblätter aus der Vorpostenzeit der Königl. Preuss. XI. Division gesammelt vor Paris«, Breslau, um 1875
Kat. 332

Als die Einschließung von Paris vollzogen war, prägte Vorpostendienst den Alltag vieler deutscher Soldaten. Gemeinden im Umfeld von Paris erlitten schwere Schäden durch Kampfhandlungen, aber auch durch Einquartierungen und Plünderungen. Schützengräben und Unterstände wurden teilweise mit Mobiliar aus verlassenen Häusern ausgestattet.

Feldwache II – Choisy le Roi

Lithografie nach Höber von Haun aus dem Mappenwerk »Erinnerungsblätter aus der Vorpostenzeit der Königl. Preuss. XI. Division gesammelt vor Paris«, Breslau, um 1875
Kat. 334

Kat. 332

Kat. 334

Gefechtsgelände mit aufgereihten Leichnamen französischer Soldaten vor dem Fort la haute Bruyere des VI. Armeekorps, aufgenommen von Chevilly aus, 30. September 1870
Calixt Prinz Biron von Curland (1817–1882)
Aquarell, 26,9 × 47,7 cm
Kat. 339

Kat. 339

»Straßenkampf in Le Bourget bei der Erstürmung dieses Dorfes während der Belagerung von Paris am 30. October 1870 durch Truppen des Königlich Preußischen Garde-Korps«
Friedrich Wilhelm Heine
Bleistiftzeichnung, 25,1 × 19,3 cm
Entwurf für »Die Gartenlaube«, 1870, Nr. 51, S. 863-866
Kat. 340

Wenn die Pariser Garnison versuchte, mit Ausfällen den Belagerungsring zu durchbrechen, wurden Ortschaften wie Le Bourget, Champigny und weitere in der Stoßrichtung von Angriffen und Gegenangriffen liegende Kommunen zu Schauplätzen heftiger Straßenkämpfe.

Straßenkampf in Le Bourget bei der Erstürmung dieses Dorfes
während der Belagerung von Paris, am 30. October 1870 durch Truppen des Königl. Preußischen Garde-Korps.
Originalzeichnung von Herrn F. Wilhelm Heine, Feldmaler des XII. (Königl. Sächsischen) Armeekorps, bezw. der IV. oder Maas-Armee für die Gartenlaube. Abgedruckt in №51 der Gartenlaube v. J. 1870, Seite 865. – Text hierzu Seite 863 bis mit 866. – Ferner vergleiche „Der Deutsch-Französische Krieg 1870/71, redigirt vom Generalstabe." III. Theil, Seite 197 u.f. –

Kat. 340

Kat. 345

Protokollbuch der Freiwilligen Feuerwehr Zwiesel mit Eintrag zur Bergung des Pariser Ballons »Général Chanzy« vom 20. Dezember 1870

Kat. 347

Der nach dem Befehlshaber der in Paris ungeduldig erwarteten Entsatzarmee benannte Ballon stieg als der 45. oder 46. von Paris auf. Er wurde abgetrieben und schlug unweit von Rothenburg ob der Tauber auf, wobei die Besatzung und ein Teil der Ladung aus dem Korb fielen. Der Ballon riss sich jedoch los und ging am 20. Dezember 1870 bei Zwiesel im Bayerischen Wald nieder, wo seine Bergung für eine Sensation sorgte: »Das war heute ein Rennen! Und was gab es? Ein Pariser Luftballon von kolossaler Größe wird gegen 3 Uhr Nachmittags [...] zuerst gefangengenommen und [...] fest gehalten, bis Richard Schaffner eine große Anzahl von Leuten geholt hat und diese sich versammelten ca. 200 Personen denselben vollends zur Erde ziehen. Ca. 68 Personen haben dieses Ungeheuer von der Pauli-Säge in den

Korb eines aus Paris aufgestiegenen Ballons

Republik Frankreich, 1870

Kat. 345

Nach der Einschließung von Paris begannen die Verteidiger der Stadt mit anfänglich nur drei Ballonen, eine Verbindung zu unbesetzten Gebieten Frankreichs herzustellen. Am 23. September 1870 gelang eine erste erfolgreiche Fahrt. Der Ballonfahrer landete 80 Kilometer westlich von Paris und fuhr von dort mit dem Zug nach Tours weiter. Rasch wurden in zwei Pariser Bahnhöfen Werkstätten eingerichtet, wo man neue Ballone herstellen ließ. Nur acht der 66 Ballone, die bis zur Kapitulation von Paris die Stadt verließen, gingen verloren. Ein Ballon verirrte sich bis nach Mittelnorwegen.

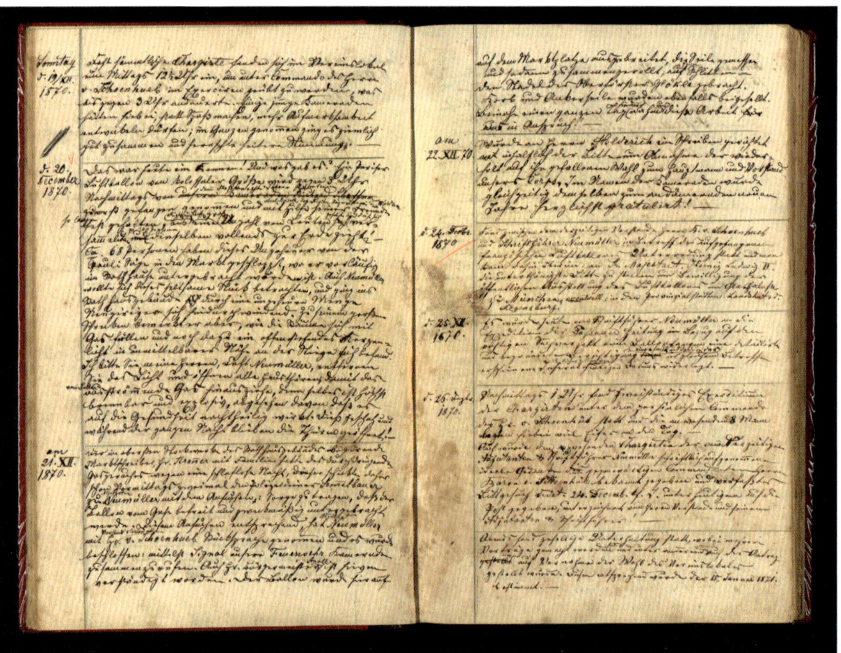

Kat. 347

Markt geschleppt, wo er vorläufig im Rathause untergebracht worden ist.« Später wurde dem Ereignis ein Denkmal gewidmet, das irrtümlich einen Ballon namens »Monté« verzeichnet. Der Irrtum ergab sich aus der Beschriftung der im »Général Chanzy« verbliebenen Postsendungen, die den französischen Vermerk »par ballon monté« (»per Ballonpost«) trugen.

3,7-cm-Ballonabwehrkanone der Firma Krupp

Essen, Königreich Preußen, 1870
Kat. 349

Der Unternehmer Alfred Krupp ließ ein Ballonabwehrgeschütz entwickeln und schenkte es der preußischen Armee zur Erprobung vor Paris. Aus der damals unausgereiften Waffe gingen später die ersten Luftabwehrgeschütze hervor.

Kat. 348

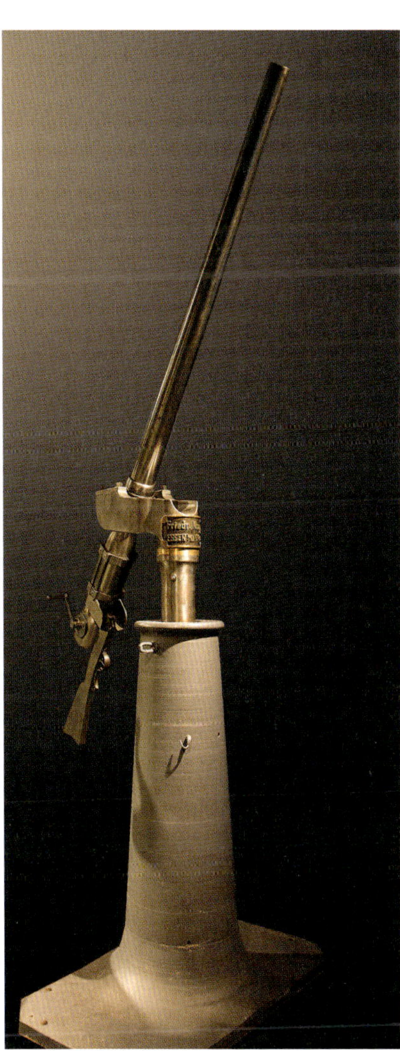

Kat. 349

Preußische Zietenhusaren bei der Verfolgung eines französischen Ballons

Wilhelm Alexander Meyerheim (1815–1882), 1871
Öl auf Leinwand, 57,5 × 47 cm
Kat. 348

Zeitgenössische Schlachtenmaler faszinierte der Zusammenprall von Tradition und Moderne. Oft bildeten sie Kavallerie ab, die Ballone verfolgte und versuchte, sie mit Karabinern abzuschießen.

Kat. 356

Kat. 357

Kat. 358

Einschlag eines deutschen Geschosses auf der Place de l'Observatoire, Januar 1871

Auguste Lançon (1836–1885)
Radierung, 39 × 55,6 cm
Kat. 356

Auguste Lançon, schon vor 1870 als Künstler tätig, hatte sich bei Kriegsbeginn freiwillig zu einer von der Pariser Presse organisierten Ambulanz gemeldet. Während der Belagerung und der Pariser Kommune war er Sergeant eines Bataillons der Pariser Nationalgarde. Er schuf zahlreiche Darstellungen des Krieges, die ungeschönt Leid, Elend und Not von Soldaten und Zivilbevölkerung in den Schlachten und Belagerungen des Krieges wiedergeben. Seine Grafiken mit auf einer Straße detonierenden Granaten, vor einem Laden anstehenden Hungernden oder in einem Keller vor dem Bombardement Schutz suchenden Menschen erinnern heutige Betrachter und Betrachterinnen an Szenen aus den beiden Weltkriegen. (Paul Lidsky: Auguste Lançon un artiste non reconnu à sa juste, veröffentlicht am 10.12.2016, in: www.deartibussequanis.fr/xix/lancon.php, Aufruf am 3.2.2020)

Warteschlange vor einem Laden auf dem Boulevard Montparnasse, Januar 1871

Auguste Lançon
Radierung, 39,5 × 56,8 cm
Kat. 357

Nachtlager in einem Keller, Gonesse, Februar 1871

Auguste Lançon
Radierung, 39,5 × 56,8 cm
Kat. 358

Kat. 350

»Historisches Andenken« an die Belagerung von Paris und die Kommune

E.J.F.S., Lithografische Werkstatt J. Bigal & Cie., Paris 1871
Kat. 350

Solche Erinnerungsstücke wurden in Paris für den heimischen Markt oder wie dieses Exemplar – eher schlecht als recht übersetzt – für die deutschen Besatzer hergestellt. Beide Varianten waren sehr ähnlich gestaltet. Die Texte verwiesen auf die wichtigsten Daten des Krieges, der Belagerung von Paris und der Kommune. Außerdem wurde ihnen eine Liste der Lebensmittelpreise während der Belagerung beigegeben. Das Brotstückchen sollte 300 Gramm »Notbrot« symbolisieren, für das Menschen fünf Stunden bei minus zwölf Grad anstehen mussten. Der Hunger traf besonders die Armen, die die rasant steigenden Lebensmittelpreise nicht bezahlen konnten.

Die Hörner des letzten während der Belagerung von Paris geschlachteten Rindes

Kat. 354

Wann dieses Tier geschlachtet wurde, ist nicht überliefert. In den 135 Tagen der deutschen Belagerung von Paris schrumpften die ursprünglich beträchtlichen Bestände an Schlachtvieh rasch zusammen. Erst die Kapitulation von Paris am 28. Januar setzte der Not ein Ende, und die Hörner des letzten Rindes wurden zu einem kuriosen Andenken.

»Un de siege (!!!) Excuare aliquis nostris ex ossibus ultor!« / Eines aus der Zeit der Belagerung (!!!) Aus unseren Knochen wird ein Rächer erstehen

Carte-de-Visite-Fotografie
Kat. 299

Der Wunsch nach einer Revanche für die Niederlage und die damit verbundenen Demütigungen äußerte sich auf unterschiedlichste Weise, so auch in der Beschriftung zu diesem Bild eines während der Belagerung von Paris geborenen Kindes.

Kat. 299

Kat. 354

Der vergessene Seekrieg

Die Reichseinigungskriege wurden in Schlachten an Land gewonnen oder verloren. Sie waren von Operationen zur See begleitet, die aber in keinem Fall eine Wende in dem betreffenden Konflikt herbeiführten oder ihn auf andere Weise nachhaltig beeinflussten. 1870/71 »lagen die Verhältnisse [...] für die [norddeutsche] Flotte hervorragend ungünstig«, da die französische Marine den Seestreitkräften des Norddeutschen Bundes weit überlegen war und Befestigungsanlagen an den deutschen Küsten noch im Bau oder Umbau begriffen waren. Wilhelmshaven, der 1869 eingeweihte, einzige Kriegshafen, war noch nicht nutzbar. Doch französische Geschwader beschränkten sich auf Blockadeaktionen in Nord- und Ostsee, während die französischen Marinetruppen einen bedeutenden Anteil an den Kämpfen zu Land hatten. Für die Bewaffnung der Festungen stellte die Marine 1000 schwere Geschütze und 176 Feldbatterien sowie 57000 Marineinfanteristen und -artilleristen, darunter die gefürchtete »Division Bleue«, die bei Bazeilles kämpfte. (Alfred Stenzel: Flotte und Küste, in: Julius von Pflugk-Harttung (Hg.): Krieg und Sieg. Ein Gedenkbuch, Berlin 1895, S. 585–611)

Abb. 15

December 3, 1870.] FRANK LESLIE'S ILLUSTRATED NEWSPAPER. 185

CUBA.—THE NAVAL DUEL BETWEEN THE FRENCH DISPATCH BOAT BOUVET, FIVE GUNS, AND THE PRUSSIAN GUNBOAT METEOR, THREE GUNS, FOUGHT OFF THE HARBOR OF HAVANA, NOVEMBER 9, 1870.

Kat. 326

SMS »Natter«, Kanonenboot II. Klasse der Königlich Preußischen Marine

Fotografie nach einer Zeichnung aus der Reichsmarinesammlung
Abb. 15

Frankreich verfügte 1870 über 29 Panzerschiffe verschiedener Klassen, die norddeutsche Flotte über drei Panzerfregatten und zwei Panzerfahrzeuge. Und auch bei den ungepanzerten Schiffen besaß Frankreich eine fünf- bis sechsfache Überlegenheit. »Natter« war eines von 22 deutschen Kanonenbooten. 1860 vom Stapel gelaufen, war sie erstmals 1864 im Einsatz, ohne jedoch in ein Gefecht mit dänischen Einheiten verwickelt zu werden. Das änderte sich auch im Deutsch-Französischen Krieg nicht. »Natter« wurde von der Ost- in die Nordsee verlegt und sicherte die Emsmündung. Im April 1871 wurde sie außer Dienst gestellt.

Seegefecht bei Havanna am 9. November 1870

Holzstich aus Frank Leslies's Illustrated Newspaper, 3. Dezember 1870, S. 185
Kat. 326

In Ermangelung von Seeschlachten zwischen Flottenverbänden berichtete die internationale Presse über das Duell eines deutschen und eines französischen Kriegsschiffs in der Karibik. Der französische Aviso »Bouvet«, ein kleines, schnelles Boot zur Nachrichtenübermittlung, und das preußische Kanonenboot »Meteor« ankerten beide gleichzeitig im Hafen von Havanna. Sie verließen nacheinander ihre Ankerplätze, um am 9. November 1870 in internationalen Gewässern einige Kanonenschüsse, Gewehrfeuer und sogar Handgranatenwürfe auszutauschen. Beide Besatzungen hatten jeweils zwei Tote zu beklagen. Nach einem Treffer in den Kessel des »Bouvet« beanspruchte die Besatzung des »Meteor« den Sieg. Dennoch vermochten es beide Schiffe, wieder in den Hafen von Havanna einzulaufen.

Die Internierung der französischen Bourbaki-Armee in der Schweiz

Ausgehungert, halb erfroren und erschöpft entging die französische Ostarmee unter General Bourbaki einer deutschen Einkesselung durch den Abschluss einer Konvention am 1. Februar 1871 mit dem Schweizer General Hans Herzog bei Les Verrières. Über 87 000 Soldaten überschritten die Schweizer Grenze und wurden dort interniert. Die nachfolgende Verteilung der »Bourbakis« auf das ganze Land und ihre Versorgung begründete das Ansehen der Schweiz als neutraler Staat mit außerordentlichem humanitären Engagement. An dieses Ereignis erinnert in Luzern das große Bourbaki-Panorama, 1881 geschaffen von Édouard Castres.

Kat. 434

Übertritt der Bourbaki'schen Armee in die Schweiz

Bilderbogen Nr. 1568, Verlag C. Burckhardt's Nachf., Weißenburg (Elsass)
Kat. 434

Bunte Bilderbögen waren noch bis in den Ersten Weltkrieg hinein ein populäres Medium, das Ansichten vom Kriegsgeschehen verbreitete. Für wenig Geld waren sie in Läden, von fliegenden Händlern oder auf Jahrmärkten zu erwerben. Nicht nur Schlachten hatten Nachrichtenwert, sondern auch ungewöhnliche Ereignisse wie die Internierung der Bourbaki-Armee in der Schweiz. Wirklichkeitstreue und genaue Fakten spielten oft eine untergeordnete Rolle.

Uebertritt der Bourbaki'schen Armee in die Schweiz.

No. 1568.

Deponirt. Druck u. Verlag v. C. Burckardt's Nachf. in Weissenburg (Elsass.)

armee unter Bourbaki bei Meudon und les Verrières in die Schweiz über, nachdem sie von den 2. und 7. preußischen Korps, die in des General von Werder, der Schweizer Grenze zugedrängt worden waren. Der Oberbefehl lag in den Händen des General von Man- allem Kriegsmaterial dem Schweizer General Herzog. General Bourbaki machte am 27. Januar aus Verzweiflung einen Selbstmordversuch.

Kat. 364

Reichsgründung im Krieg

»Wir stehen unter dem Eindruck, dass eine ungeheure Macht, die sich zum Guten oder zum Bösen entwickeln kann, einigermaßen plötzlich in unserer Mitte aufgetaucht ist, und wir bemühen uns mit interessierter Aufmerksamkeit darum, ihren Charakter und ihre Absichten auszumachen.«

The Times, London, 7. September 1876

Die gemeinsam erfochtenen militärischen Erfolge im Krieg gegen Frankreich vermittelten den deutschen Fürsten und der Bevölkerung, dass Einigkeit stark mache. Bismarck hatte dennoch Mühe, die deutschen Souveräne zu überzeugen, dass eine politische, nationale Einigung längerfristig allen nützen würde. Während den designierten Kaiser die Sorge umtrieb, Preußen werde in Deutschland aufgehen, fürchtete Ludwig II. von Bayern preußische Bevormundung. Als der ranghöchste deutsche Souverän nach dem König von Preußen unterzeichnete Ludwig schließlich doch am 30. November 1870 den von Bismarck formulierten »Kaiserbrief«, der Wilhelm die Kaiserwürde des Reiches antrug. Durch den Beitritt der süddeutschen Staaten wurde im November 1870 aus dem Norddeutschen Bund ein »Deutscher Bund«, der noch vor Jahresende in »Deutsches Reich« umbenannt wurde. Dessen Verfassung basierte wesentlich auf der des Norddeutschen Bundes von 1867. Als eigentliche Reichsgründung ging der Festakt im Versailler Spiegelsaal am 18. Januar 1871 in die Geschichte ein. Aus französischer Sicht stellte die Wahl des Königsschlosses von Versailles als Schauplatz der deutschen Kaiserproklamation eine schwere Demütigung dar. Bewusst entschieden sich 1919 die Sieger des Ersten Weltkriegs, allen voran der französische Ministerpräsident Georges Clemenceau, der 1870/71 die Belagerung von Paris erlebt hatte, für den Spiegelsaal des Schlosses als Ort der Unterzeichnung des Friedens von Versailles.

Über Land und Meer.

Nº 34.

Ausgabe für Oesterreich-Ungarn.

Sand.

Roman von Friedrich Jacobsen.

Eduard von Simson †.

Kat. 363

Gedenk-Tafel

an den 21. Jan. 1871.

Verzeichniß der 48 Abgeordneten,
welche gegen die Verträge stimmten.
(Nach den Wahlbezirken zusammengestellt.)

Dr. Jörg.

Dr. Ant. Schmid, Domkapitular, Bamberg.
Matth. Hilgenrainer, Bürgermeister, Warngau.
F. X. Schmid, geistlicher Rath, Traunstein.
Andr. Freytag, Advokat in Wasserburg.
M. Graf Seinsheim, k. Kämmerer und Reichsrath.
Gg. Mayer, Oeconom in Weiding.
Mart. Leiseder, Bürgermeister in Mühldorf.
K. v. Ow, k. Regierungs-Rath, Landshut.
Dr. Jos. Neumayer, Domkapitular, Regensburg.
A. v. Hafenbrädl, k. Bez.-Ger.-Rath, Regensburg.
Dr. Jos. Pfahler, Pfarrer, Deggendorf.
Joh. Röckl, Bauer, Heindlinberg.
Gg. Haering, Privatier, Deggendorf.
Andr. Sedlmayer, k. Appell.-Ger-Dir., Eichstädt.
Caj. Hofstetter, Gastwirth, Massing.
Ben. Gerauer, Bauer, Hartham.
Aug. Wiesnet, k. Advokat, Passau.
F. X. v. Hafenbrädl, Gutsbesitzer, Schedlhof.
B. Winklhofer, Bauer, Munzing.
W. Schieferer, Eisenhändler, Waldkirchen.
Xav. Greil, Lycealprofessor, Passau.
Dr. Ad. Krätzer, k. Appell.-Ger.-Rath, Passau.
Jos. Söllner, geistlicher Rath, Rottenburg.
Joh. Brückl, Bierbrauer, Mintraching.
Joh. Höchstätter, Mühlbesitzer, Pielmühle.
Franz Mich. Benz, Handelsmann, Heideck.
Joh. Lerzer, Oeconom, Thannhausen.
Mich. Triller, k. Pfarrer, Meckenhausen.
Ant. Russwurm, k. Pfarrer, Theuern.
Mich. Lauerer, Kaufmann, Ar[illegible]g.
Dr. Jos. Lindner, k. Stadtpfarrer, Erbendorf.
Al. Frank, k. Bezirks-Gerichts-Rath, Weiden.
Gg. Schmidbauer, k. Pfarrer, Schwarzenfeld.
Joh. Nep. Schmidkonz, k. Rentbeamter, Naabburg.
Franz Henning, Domkapitular Bamberg.
Dr. Jak. Schüttinger, k. Advokat, Bamberg.
Franz Lothar Weber, Kaufmann, Höchstadt.
Franz Mahr, k. Pfarrer, Ebermannstadt.
Dr. Karl Kurz, k. App.-Ger.-Rath, Aschaffenburg.
Th. Hauck, k. Bezirks-Amtmann, Marktscheinfeld.
Andr. Welmer, Oeconom, Neukirchen.
Dr. Ant. Ruland, Oberbibliothekar, Würzburg.
Gg. Frdr. Kolb, Liter., München.
Joh. Burger, Oeconom, Oberthulba.
Otto Frhr. v. Fuchs, k. Bez.-Ger.-Assessor, Neustadt.
Ludw. Frhr. v. Zu-Rhein, k. Kämmerer, Würzburg.
Franz Burger, Oeconom, Zeil.
Dr. Jos. Edm. Jörg, Archivsconserv., Landshut.

Preis 3 Kreuzer.

Kat. 365

Reliefbild von Schloss Neuschwanstein

Vermutlich Ende 19. Jahrhundert, Rahmen 1. Hälfte 19. Jahrhundert
Keramik und Messing
Kat. 364

Ludwig II. war durch seine Schlossbauten verschuldet. Die Zahlungen, die ihm Bismarck aus dem konfiszierten Vermögen der hannoverschen Welfen (»Welfenfonds«) zusicherte, waren hochwillkommen. Aber ob diese oder vielmehr die Annahme, dass die Reichsgründung sowieso unvermeidlich sei, den Ausschlag für die Unterzeichnung des Kaiserbriefs gab, ist umstritten.

Eduard von Simson (1810–1899) mit zwei deutschen Kaiserkronen

Titelblatt des illustrierten Unterhaltungsblattes »Über Land und Meer«, Ausgabe für Österreich-Ungarn, 1899, Nr. 34
Kat. 363

1849 hatte Simson – damals Präsident der Frankfurter Nationalversammlung – Friedrich Wilhelm IV. von Preußen die deutsche Kaiserkrone angetragen und war abgewiesen worden. Als Präsident des Norddeutschen Reichstags (seit 1867) und des Deutschen Zollparlaments (seit 1868) führte er auch die Kaiserdeputation an, die sie im Dezember 1870 Friedrich Wilhelms jüngerem Bruder Wilhelm I. antrug. Für diesen spielten die Parlamentarier jedoch eine untergeordnete Rolle. Wenn er schon Kaiser werden sollte, dann berufen von den deutschen Fürsten und Freien Städten.

Gedenktafel mit den Namen der 48 Abgeordneten, die am 21. Januar 1871 gegen die Verträge stimmten

Aus einem Erinnerungsalbum, angelegt von Moritz Ratzinger, 1870/71 Leutnant im 1. Königlich Bayerischen Feldartillerie-Regiment
Kat. 365

In Bayern war der Widerstand gegen eine Reichseinigung am größten. Die Zustimmung des bayerischen Landtags erfolgte erst am 21. Januar 1871, drei Tage nach der Kaiserproklamation in Versailles.

»Salon de la Paix« und der Eingang zum Spiegelsaal im Schloss von Versailles

Zwei Fotografien aus Heinrich Schnaebelis »Album der Proclamirung des deutschen Kaiserreiches im Schlosse zu Versailles, 18. Januar 1871«
Abb. 16

Der Berliner Hoffotograf Heinrich Schnaebeli bot eine Schmuckmappe mit großformatigen Fotografien und Fotomontagen an, die den Kaiser, die Angehörigen seines Hauptquartiers, die Armeeführer mit ihren Hauptquartieren usw. vor der Kulisse des Versailler Schlosses sowie Innenansichten aus dem Schloss zeigten. Mit diesen beiden Aufnahmen kam er dem Ereignis der Kaiserproklamation am nächsten. Doch es war nicht das relativ junge Medium Fotografie, sondern Anton von Werners Gemälde »Die Proklamierung des Deutschen Kaiserreichs am 18. Januar 1871«,

Abb. 16/1

Abb. 16/2

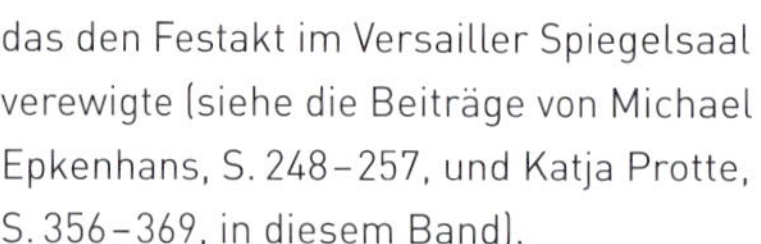

das den Festakt im Versailler Spiegelsaal verewigte (siehe die Beiträge von Michael Epkenhans, S. 248–257, und Katja Protte, S. 356–369, in diesem Band).

1870 1871. — Comment un trône s'écroule, — comment un trône s'élève.

Kat. 362

»Comment un trône s'écroule! – Comment un trône s'élève!« / Der eine Thron stürzt! – Der andere wird errichtet!

Holzstich von Smeeton aus der Zeitschrift »L'Illustration. Journal Universel«, 1871, Nr. 1454

Kat. 362

Die bittere Karikatur zeigt den Sturz Napoleons III. und die Errichtung eines deutschen Kaisertums inmitten von Leichenbergen.

»Das ganze Deutschland soll es sein! 1870. Ein Gedenk-Album in 50 Photographien«

Weissensee/Leipzig/Berlin, 3. Auflage

Kat. 366

Ernst Moritz Arndts Gedicht »Des Deutschen Vaterland« begleitete seit 1813 verschiedene Strömungen der deutschen Nationalbewegung. Wie sehr sich die Vorstellungen davon, was das ganze Deutschland sei, gewandelt hatten, zeigt dieses verbreitete Album, das sich abgesehen von Fotografien Bismarcks und des für die Koordination der freiwilligen Krankenhilfe verantwortlichen Johanniters Fürst von Pless auf deutsche Fürsten und die Generalität beschränkt.

Kat. 366

Triumph und Trauer

Der Deutsch-Französische Krieg endete mit dem Friedensschluss von Frankfurt am 10. Mai 1871. In Deutschland erlebte man das Kriegsende mit Gefühlen zwischen Triumph, Erleichterung und Trauer. Die Repatriierung der Kriegsgefangenen beider Seiten hatte schon mit dem Vorfrieden von Versailles vom 26. Februar 1871 begonnen. Die deutschen Feldarmeen kehrten heim. Ihre Gefallenen wurden nur in seltenen Fällen in die Heimat überführt. Viele Soldatenschicksale blieben ungeklärt.

Kat. 478

Kat. 479

Überlebensgroße Porträts von Bismarck und Moltke Festdekoration für die Siegesparade in Berlin

Adolph Menzel (1815–1905), 1871
Öl auf Leinwand, 395 × 158,5 cm
bzw. 383,5 × 158,5 cm
Kat. 478 und 479

Am 16. Juni 1871 fand in Berlin die Siegesfeier statt: 40 000 Soldaten zogen durch das Brandenburger Tor in Richtung des königlichen Schlosses. Die Paradestrecke war prächtig geschmückt. In den Fenstern der Akademie der Künste standen überlebensgroß diese beiden Porträts, geschaffen von dem Berliner Maler Adolph Menzel. Seit der Reichsgründung und dem Sieg über Frankreich galten Reichskanzler Otto von Bismarck und Generalstabschef Helmuth von Moltke neben Wilhelm I. als Helden der deutschen Geschichte, die die Geschicke der Nation mit sicherer Hand lenkten.

Velarium auf der Prager Straße in Dresden, 11. Juli 1871

Hoffmann & Römler
Kat. 378

Ehrenpforte am Albertplatz in der Dresdner Neustadt, 11. Juli 1871

Hoffmann & Römler
Kat. 379

Die Rückkehr der Truppen des XII. (Königlich Sächsischen) Armeekorps aus Frankreich sollte mit einer Siegesparade am 11. Juli 1871 begangen werden. Straßen und Plätze an der hier gezeigten »Via Triumphalis« wurden aus diesem Anlass mit Allegorien, Porträts und Ortsnamen geschmückt. Gefeiert wurden die Siege, an denen sächsische Truppen beteiligt waren. Der bisherige Bautzner Platz wurde zu Ehren des sächsischen Kronprinzen und Oberbefehlshabers der 4. Armee in »Albertplatz« umbenannt.

Kat. 378

Kat. 379

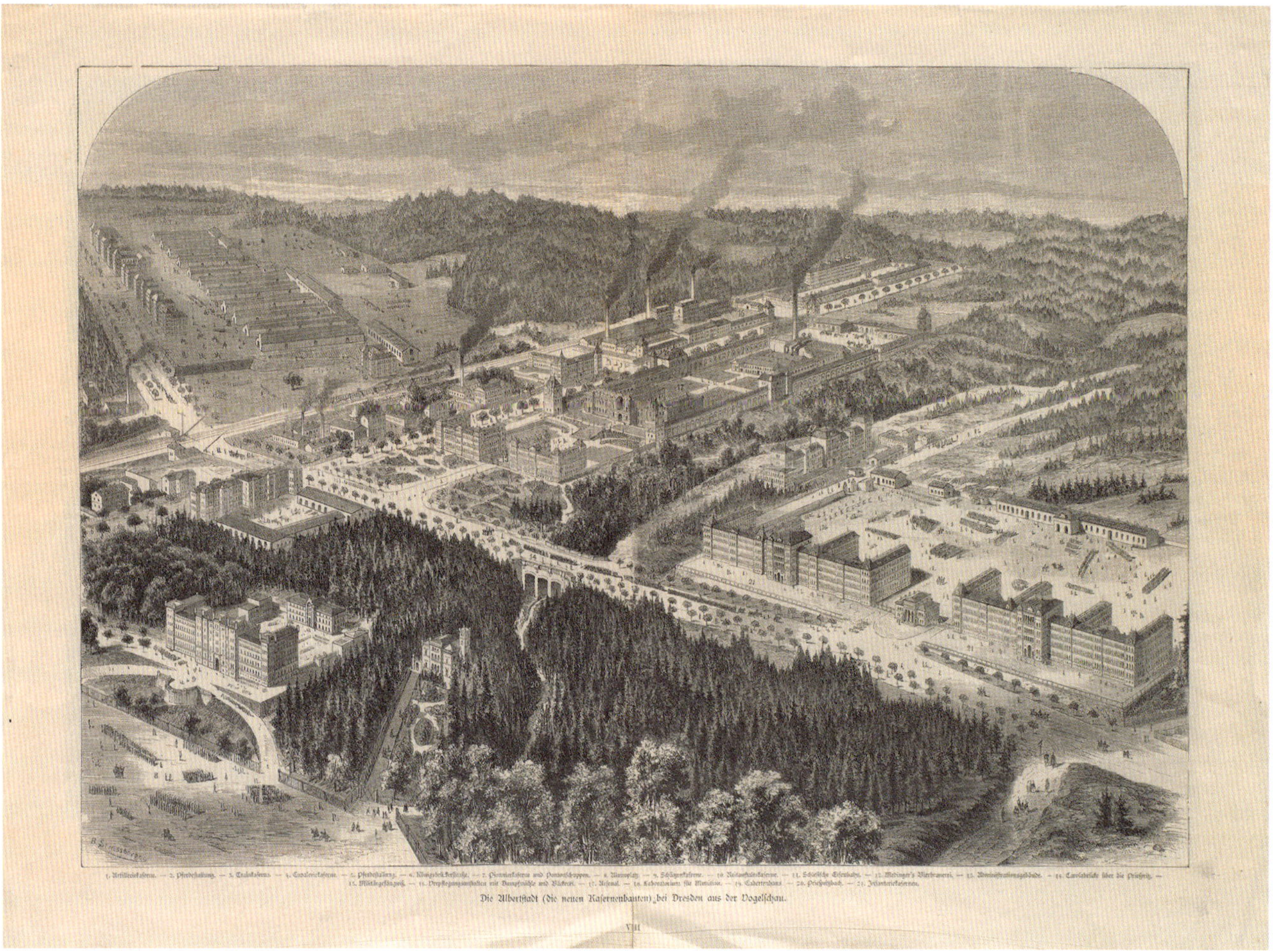

Kat. 377

Die Albertstadt (die neuen Kasernenbauten) bei Dresden aus der Vogelschau

Holzstich nach Adolf Eltzner (1816–1891) von Bruno Strassberger (1832–1910) aus der Leipziger »Illustrirten Zeitung«, 21. April 1877, S. 328 f.
Kat. 377

Die Reparationen, die Frankreich im Frankfurter Frieden auferlegt worden waren, wurden in den Bundesstaaten des Deutschen Reiches auch für Militärbauten verwendet. Unter der Leitung des sächsischen Kriegsministers Alfred von Fabrice (1818–1891), dem die deutschen Besatzungstruppen in Frankreich unterstanden hatten, wurde mit dem Bau einer weitläufigen Kasernenstadt am Nordrand Dresdens begonnen. Der nach König Albert von Sachsen benannte Stadtteil wuchs bis zum Ersten Weltkrieg zu einer der stärksten deutschen Garnisonen an.

Kat. 381

Eisernes Kreuz I. Klasse aus dem Besitz von Hermann von Wichmann (1820–1886)

Königreich Preußen, gestiftet am 19. Juli 1870
Kat. 381

Zu Beginn des Krieges hatte Wilhelm I. von Preußen erstmals seit den Befreiungskriegen gegen Napoleon I. das Eiserne Kreuz neu gestiftet. Die Laufbahn des Empfängers dieses Exemplars erstreckte sich von den Revolutionsjahren 1848/49 bis in die Frühzeit des deutschen Kaiserreichs. Im Deutsch-Französischen Krieg war er als Oberst Chef des Stabes beim II. Armeekorps unter General Fransecky, erlebte die Schlacht von Gravelotte, die Belagerungen von Metz und Paris und schließlich die Operationen der deutschen Südarmee bis zur Abdrängung der Truppen von General Bourbaki in die Schweiz.

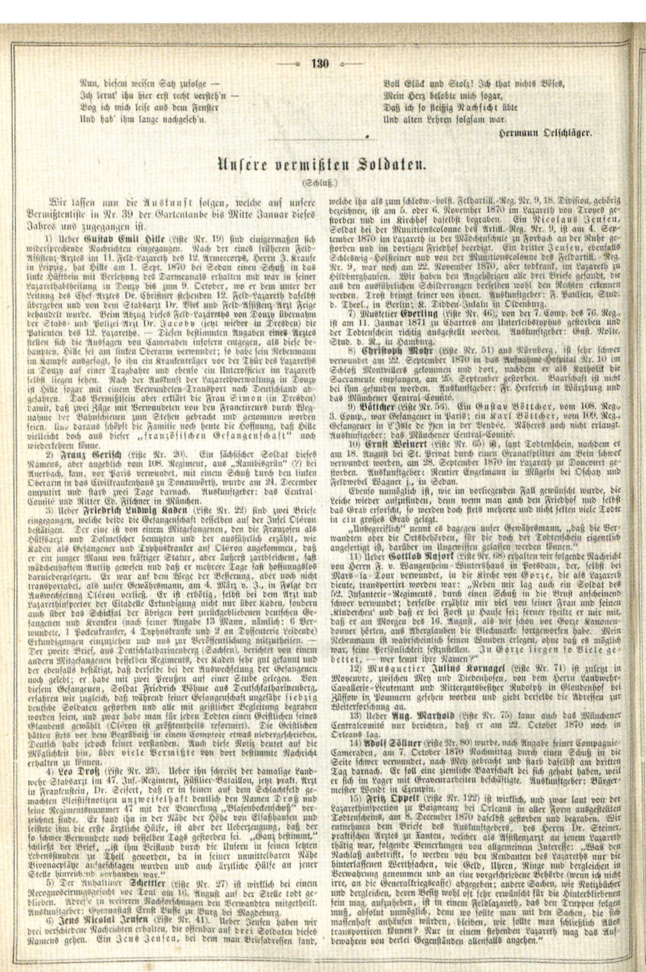

— 130 —

Nun, diesem weisen Satz zufolge —
Ich lernt' ihn hier erst recht versteh'n —
Bog ich mich leise aus dem Fenster
Und hab' ihm lange nachgeseh'n.

Voll Glück und Stolz! Ich that nichts Böses,
Mein Herz belobte mich sogar,
Daß ich so fleißig Nachsicht übte
Und alten Lehren folgsam war.

Hermann Oelschläger.

Unsere vermißten Soldaten.

(Schluß.)

Wir lassen nun die Auskunft folgen, welche auf unsere Vermißtenliste in Nr. 39 der Gartenlaube bis Mitte Januar dieses Jahres uns zugegangen ist.

1) Ueber **Gustav Emil Hille** (Liste Nr. 19) sind einigermaßen sich widersprechende Nachrichten eingegangen. Nach der eines früheren Feld-Assistenz-Arztes im 11. Feld-Lazareth des 12. Armeecorps, Herrn J. Krause in Leipzig, hat Hille am 1. Sept. 1870 bei Sedan einen Schuß in das linke Hüftbein mit Verletzung des Darmcanals erhalten und war in seiner Lazarethabtheilung in Douzy bis zum 9. October, wo er dem unter der Leitung des Chef-Arztes Dr. Christner stehenden 12. Feld-Lazareth daselbst übergeben und von dem Stabsarzt Dr. Biel und Feld-Assistenz-Arzt Feige behandelt wurde. Beim Abzug dieses Feld-Lazareths von Douzy übernahm der Stabs- und Polizei-Arzt Dr. Jacoby (jetzt wieder in Dresden) die Patienten des 12. Lazareths. — Diesen bestimmten Angaben eines Arztes stellen sich die Aussagen von Cameraden insofern entgegen, als diese behaupten, Hille sei am linken Oberarm verwundet; so habe sein Nebenmann im Kampfe ausgesagt, so ihn ein Krankenträger vor der Thür des Lazareths in Douzy auf einer Tragbahre und ebenso ein Unterofficier im Lazareth selbst liegen sehen. Nach der Auskunft der Lazarethverwaltung in Douzy ist Hille sogar mit einem Verwundeten-Transport nach Deutschland abgefahren. Das Vermißtsein aber erklärt die Frau Simon (in Dresden) damit, daß zwei Züge mit Verwundeten von den Franctireurs durch Wegnahme der Bahnschienen zum Stehen gebracht und genommen worden seien. Und daraus schöpft die Familie noch heute die Hoffnung, daß Hille vielleicht doch aus dieser „französischen Gefangenschaft“ noch wiederkehren könne.

2) **Franz Gerisch** (Liste Nr. 20). Ein sächsischer Soldat dieses Namens, aber angeblich vom 108. Regiment, aus „Ranibisgrün“ (?) bei Auerbach, kam, vor Paris verwundet, mit einem Schuß durch den linken Oberarm in das Civilkrankenhaus zu Donauwörth, wurde am 24. December amputirt und starb zwei Tage darnach. Auskunftgeber: das Central-Comité und Ritter Ed. Filchner in München.

3) Ueber **Friedrich Ludwig Kaden** (Liste Nr. 22) sind zwei Briefe eingegangen, welche beide die Gefangenschaft desselben auf der Insel Oléron bestätigen. Der eine ist von einem Mitgefangenen, den die Franzosen als Hülfsarzt und Dolmetscher benutzten und der ausführlich erzählt, wie Kaden als Gefangener und Typhuskranker auf Oléron angekommen, daß er ein junger Mann von kräftiger Statur, aber äußerst zartbleichem, fast mädchenhaftem Antlitz gewesen und daß er mehrere Tage fast hoffnungslos darniedergelegen. Er war auf dem Wege der Besserung, aber noch nicht transportabel, als unser Gewährsmann, am 4. März v. J., in Folge der Auswechselung Oléron verließ. Er ist erbötig, selbst bei dem Arzt und Lazarethinspector der Citadelle Erkundigung nicht nur über Kaden, sondern auch über das Schicksal der übrigen dort zurückgebliebenen deutschen Gefangenen und Kranken (nach seiner Angabe 13 Mann, nämlich: 6 Verwundete, 1 Pockenkranker, 4 Typhuskranke und 2 an Dyssenterie Leidende) Erkundigungen einzuziehen und uns zur Veröffentlichung mitzutheilen. — Der zweite Brief, aus Deutschkatharinenberg (Sachsen), berichtet von einem andern Mitgefangenen desselben Regiments, der Kaden sehr gut gekannt und der ebenfalls bestätigt, daß derselbe bei der Auswechselung der Gefangenen noch gelebt; er habe mit zwei Preußen auf einer Stube gelegen. Von diesem Gefangenen, Soldat Friedrich Böhme aus Deutschkatharinenberg, erfahren wir zugleich, daß während seiner Gefangenschaft ungefähr siebzig deutsche Soldaten gestorben und alle mit geistlicher Begleitung begraben worden seien, und zwar habe man für jeden Todten einen Geistlichen seines Glaubens gewählt (Oléron ist größtentheils reformirt). Die Geistlichen hätten stets vor dem Begräbniß in einem Comptoir etwas niedergeschrieben, Deutsch habe jedoch keiner verstanden. Auch diese Notiz deutet auf die Möglichkeit hin, über viele Vermißte von dort bestimmte Nachricht erhalten zu können.

4) **Leo Droß** (Liste Nr. 23). Ueber ihn schreibt der damalige Landwehr-Stabsarzt im 47. Inf.-Regiment, Füsilier-Bataillon, jetzt prakt. Arzt in Frankenstein, Dr. Seifert, daß er in seinen auf dem Schlachtfeld gemachten Bleistiftnotizen unzweifelhaft deutlich den Namen Droß und seine Regimentsnummer 47 mit der Bemerkung „Blasenbeckenschuß“ verzeichnet finde. Er fand ihn in der Nähe der Höhe von Elsaßhausen und leistete ihm die erste ärztliche Hülfe, ist aber der Ueberzeugung, daß der so schwer Verwundete noch desselben Tags gestorben sei. „Ganz bestimmt,“ schließt der Brief, „ist ihm Beistand durch die Unsern in seinen letzten Lebensstunden zu Theil geworden, da in seiner unmittelbaren Nähe Bivouacplätze aufgeschlagen wurden und auch ärztliche Hülfe an jener Stelle hinreichend vorhanden war.“

5) Der Anhaltiner **Schettler** (Liste Nr. 27) ist wirklich bei einem Recognoscirungsgefecht vor Toul am 16. August auf der Stelle todt geblieben. Adresse zu weiteren Nachforschungen den Verwandten mitgetheilt. Auskunftgeber: Gymnasiast Ernst Busse zu Burg bei Magdeburg.

6) **Jens Nicolai Jensen** (Liste Nr. 41). Ueber Jensen haben wir drei verschiedene Nachrichten erhalten, die offenbar auf drei Soldaten dieses Namens gehen. Ein Jens Jensen, bei dem man Briefadressen fand, welche ihn als zum schlesw.-holst. Feldartill.-Reg. Nr. 9, 18. Division, gehörig bezeichnen, ist am 5. oder 6. November 1870 im Lazareth von Troyes gestorben und im Kirchhof daselbst begraben. Ein Nicolaus Jensen, Soldat bei der Munitionscolonne des Artill.-Reg. Nr. 9, ist am 4. September 1870 im Lazareth in der Mädchenschule zu Forbach an der Ruhr gestorben und im dortigen Friedhof beerdigt. Ein dritter Jensen, ebenfalls Schleswig-Holsteiner und von der Munitionscolonne des Feldartill.-Reg. Nr. 9, war noch am 22. November 1870, aber todkrank, im Lazareth zu Hildburghausen. Wir haben den Angehörigen alle drei Briefe gesandt, die aus den ausführlichen Schilderungen derselben wohl den Rechten erkennen werden. Trost bringt keiner von ihnen. Auskunftgeber: F. Paulsen, Stud. d. Theol., in Berlin; K. Didden-Inlain in Oldenburg.

7) Musketier **Everling** (Liste Nr. 46), von der 7. Comp. des 76. Reg., ist am 11. Januar 1871 zu Chartres am Unterleibstyphus gestorben und der Todtenschein richtig ausgestellt worden. Auskunftgeber: Gust. Nolte, Stud. d. R., in Hamburg.

8) **Christoph Mohr** (Liste Nr. 51) aus Nürnberg, ist sehr schwer verwundet am 22. September 1870 in das Aufnahme-Hospital Nr. 10 im Schloß Montvillers gekommen und dort, nachdem er als Katholik die Sacramente empfangen, am 25. September gestorben. Baarschaft ist nicht bei ihm gefunden worden. Auskunftgeber: Fr. Herterich in Würzburg und das Münchener Central-Comité.

9) **Böttcher** (Liste Nr. 56). Ein Gustav Böttcher, vom 108. Reg., 3. Comp., war Gefangener in Paris; ein Karl Böttcher, vom 109. Reg., Gefangener in L'Isle de Yeu in der Vendée. Näheres noch nicht erlangt. Auskunftgeber: das Münchener Central-Comité.

10) **Ernst Weinert** (Liste Nr. 65) ist, laut Todtenschein, nachdem er am 18. August bei St. Privat durch einen Granatsplitter am Bein schwer verwundet worden, am 28. September 1870 im Lazareth zu Doncourt gestorben. Auskunftgeber: Rentier Engelmann in Mügeln bei Oschatz und Feldwebel Wagner j., in Sedan.

Ebenso unmöglich ist, wie im vorliegenden Fall gewünscht wurde, die Leiche wieder aufzufinden, denn wenn man auch den Friedhof und selbst das Grab erforscht, so werden doch stets mehrere und nicht selten viele Todte in ein großes Grab gelegt.

„Unbegreiflich“ nennt es dagegen unser Gewährsmann, „daß die Verwandten oder die Ortsbehörden, für die doch der Todtenschein eigentlich angefertigt ist, darüber im Ungewissen gelassen werden können.“

11) Ueber **Gottlob Rajork** (Liste Nr. 68) erhalten wir folgende Nachricht von Herrn F. v. Wangenheim-Wintershaus in Potsdam, der, selbst bei Mars-la-Tour verwundet, in die Kirche von Gorze, die als Lazareth diente, transportirt worden war: „Neben mir lag auch ein Soldat des 52. Infanterie-Regiments, durch einen Schuß in die Brust anscheinend schwer verwundet; derselbe erzählte mir viel von seiner Frau und seinen ‚Kinderchen‘ und daß er bei Forst zu Hause sei; ferner theilte er mir mit, daß er am Morgen des 16. August, als wir schon vor Gorze Kanonendonner hörten, aus Aberglauben die Blechmarke fortgeworfen habe. Mein Nebenmann ist wahrscheinlich seinen Wunden erlegen, ohne daß es möglich war, seine Persönlichkeit festzustellen. In Gorze liegen so Viele gebettet, — wer kennt ihre Namen?“

12) Musquetier **Julius Kornagel** (Liste Nr. 71) ist zuletzt in Moyeuvre, zwischen Metz und Diedenhofen, von dem Herrn Landwehr-Cavallerie-Lieutenant und Rittergutsbesitzer Rudolph in Glondenhof bei Züssow in Pommern gesehen worden und giebt derselbe die Adressen zur Weiterforschung an.

13) Ueber **Aug. Marhold** (Liste Nr. 75) kann auch das Münchener Centralcomité nur berichten, daß er am 22. October 1870 noch in Orleans lag.

14) **Adolf Söllner** (Liste Nr. 80) wurde, nach Angabe seiner Compagnie-Cameraden, am 7. October 1870 Nachmittag durch einen Schuß in die Seite schwer verwundet, nach Metz gebracht und starb daselbst am dritten Tag darnach. Er soll eine ziemliche Baarschaft bei sich gehabt haben, weil er sich im Lager mit Graveurarbeiten beschäftigte. Auskunftgeber: Bürgermeister Wendt in Czempin.

15) **Fritz Oppelt** (Liste Nr. 122) ist wirklich, und zwar laut von der Lazarethinspection zu Baigneaux bei Orleans in aller Form ausgestellten Todtenscheins, am 8. December 1870 daselbst gestorben und begraben. Wir entnehmen dem Briefe des Auskunftgebers, des Herrn Dr. Steiner, praktischen Arztes zu Xanten, welcher als Assistenzarzt an jenem Lazareth thätig war, folgende Bemerkungen von allgemeinem Interesse: „Was den Nachlaß anbetrifft, so werden von den Rendanten des Lazareths nur die hinterlassenen Werthsachen, wie Geld, Uhren, Ringe und dergleichen in Verwahrung genommen und an eine vorgeschriebene Behörde (wenn ich nicht irre, an die Generalkriegscasse) abgegeben; andere Sachen, wie Notizbücher und dergleichen, deren Besitz wohl oft sehr erwünscht für die Hinterbliebenen sein mag, aufzuheben, ist in einem Feldlazareth, das den Truppen folgen muß, absolut unmöglich, denn wo sollte man mit den Sachen, die sich massenhaft anhäufen würden, bleiben, wie sollte man schließlich Alles transportiren können? Nur in einem stehenden Lazareth mag das Aufbewahren von derlei Gegenständen allenfalls angehen.“

Kat. 376

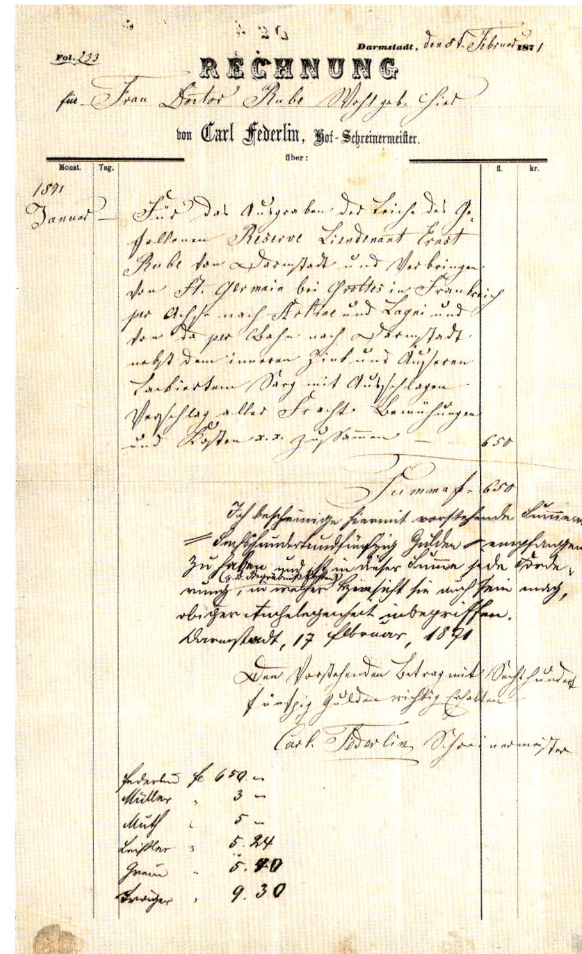

Fol. 233

Darmstadt, den 8t. Februar 1871

RECHNUNG

für Frau Doctor Rube Wohlgeb. [illegible]

von Carl Federlin, Hof-Schreinermeister.

über:

Monat.	Tag.		fl.	kr.
1871 Januar		Für das Ausgraben der Leiche des gefallenen Reserve Lieutenant Ernst Rube von Darmstadt und Verbringen von St. Germain bei [illegible] in Frankreich per Achse nach [illegible] und Lagni und von da per Bahn nach Darmstadt nebst dem inneren Zink und äusseren [illegible] Sarg mit [illegible] [illegible] aller Fracht Bemühungen und Kosten x. x. zusammen —	650	
		Summa fl.	650	

[illegible]

Darmstadt, 17 Februar, 1871

[illegible]

Carl Federlin Schreinermeister

Federlin	fl.	650 –
Müller	„	3 –
Muth	„	5 –
[illegible]	„	5.24
[illegible]	„	5.40
[illegible]	„	9.30

Kat. 374

Kat. 383

Kriegsdenkmünze für die Feldzüge 1870/71, Ausführung für Nichtkombattanten

Deutsches Reich, gestiftet am 20. Mai 1871

Sammlung Major Rübke

Kat. 383

Neben Orden und Tapferkeitsauszeichnungen wurden in allen Bundesstaaten des Deutschen Reiches Denkmünzen und Medaillen an Teilnehmer des Krieges verliehen, die als Soldaten oder in zivilen Funktionen Dienst getan hatten.

»Unsere vermißten Soldaten«

Die Gartenlaube, 1872, Nr. 8, S. 130

Kat. 376

1872 waren die Schicksale von etwa 4 000 im Krieg 1870/71 vermissten deutschen Soldaten noch immer ungeklärt. Neben der andauernden Ungewissheit bedeutete das für die Angehörigen, dass sie keinen Anspruch auf Pensionen oder andere Unterstützung erheben konnten, bis die Vermissten amtlich für tot erklärt wurden.

Rechnung für die Überführung der Leiche des Leutnants d. R. Ernst Rube in die Heimat

Darmstadt, 8. Februar 1871

Kat. 374

Kat. 154

Unter den Augen der Sieger

Die Pariser Kommune

Am 17. Februar 1871 wurde der liberal-konservative Adolphe Thiers von der am 8. Februar gewählten Nationalversammlung zum »chef du pouvoir exécutif« (»Chef der Exekutive«) bestimmt; am 26. Februar 1871 einigten er und Außenminister Jules Favre sich mit Bismarck auf eine Beendigung des Krieges. Die neue französische Regierung gewann damit Handlungsfreiheit, auch gegenüber ihren innenpolitischen Gegnern, die sich während der zermürbenden Zeit der Belagerung radikalisiert hatten. Große Teile der noch in Paris verbliebenen Nationalgarde lehnten Thiers' Politik ab und eigneten sich 400 Geschütze aus Armeebeständen an, mit dem Argument, sie vor den Deutschen in Sicherheit bringen zu wollen. Als Thiers ihnen diese wieder abnehmen lassen wollte, löste er damit am 18. März den Aufstand der Pariser Kommune aus, des sich spontan gebildeten revolutionären, linksliberal bis sozialistisch gesinnten Pariser Stadtrats. Themen wie Frauenrechte, die während der Revolution 1848/49 nur ansatzweise öffentlich wahrgenommen wurden, fanden hier ein breites Forum. Die deutschen Besatzer griffen nicht ein, unterstützten die Regierungstruppen aber zum Beispiel durch die beschleunigte Freilassung von Kriegsgefangenen. Zwischen dem 21. und dem 28. Mai drangen die Truppen der von Versailles aus agierenden Regierung in die Stadt ein und beendeten den Aufstand gewaltsam.

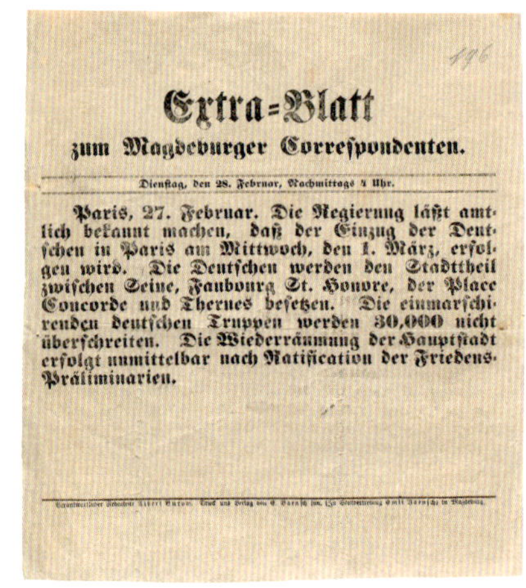

Extra-Blatt

zum Magdeburger Correspondenten.

Dienstag, den 28. Februar, Nachmittags 4 Uhr.

Paris, 27. Februar. Die Regierung läßt amtlich bekannt machen, daß der Einzug der Deutschen in Paris am Mittwoch, den 1. März, erfolgen wird. Die Deutschen werden den Stadttheil zwischen Seine, Faubourg St. Honore, der Place Concorde und Thernes besetzen. Die einmarschirenden deutschen Truppen werden 30,000 nicht überschreiten. Die Wiederräumung der Hauptstadt erfolgt unmittelbar nach Ratification der Friedens-Präliminarien.

Kat. 367

Kat. 368

Kat. 371

Kat. 372

Extrablatt des Magdeburger Correspondenten mit der Ankündigung des deutschen Einmarschs in Paris
Magdeburg, 28. Februar 1871
Kat. 367

Einzug deutscher Truppen in Paris am 1. März 1871
Adolph Göhde, Löbau
Lithografie
Kat. 154

In Paris gaben sich die Sieger mit einer zeitlich und räumlich beschränkten Besatzung der Stadt zufrieden, die am 1. März mit einer Parade über die Champs-Élysées begann.

Barrikade am Eingang zum Fauborg du Temple, Paris, 18. März 1871
Kat. 368

Denkmünze auf die Wahl von Adolphe Thiers (1797– 1877) zum französischen Regierungschef
Republik Frankreich, 8. Februar 1871
Kat. 371

Denkmünze zur Erinnerung an die Verteidigung von Paris
Republik Frankreich, Pariser Kommune, 18. März 1871
Kat. 372

Die französische Regierung unter Adolphe Thiers und die Kommune von Paris präsentierten sich beide als die rechtmäßigen Vertreter der französischen Nation. Adolphe Thiers, von 1834 bis 1836 Minister unter der Julimonarchie Louis-Philippes und danach Gegner des napoleonischen Kaisertums, bezog seine Legitimation daraus, dass er mit der Beendigung des Krieges die Existenz Frankreichs als Staat gerettet habe. Die Kommune wollte durch den Widerstand gegen die Deutschen Frankreichs Ehre bewahren, Profiteure der nationalen Katastrophe vernichten und einen Staat auf Grundlage neuer sozialistisch-republikanischer Ideen gründen. (Bernard Noël: Dictionnaire de la Commune, Paris 1971, S. 94)

Kat. 369

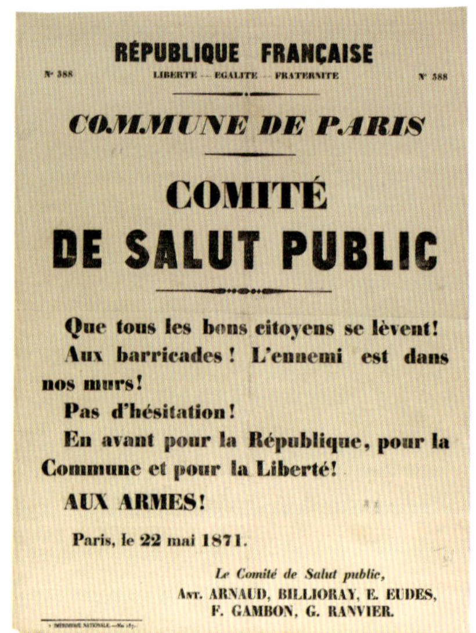

N° 388 RÉPUBLIQUE FRANÇAISE N° 388

LIBERTE — EGALITE — FRATERNITE

COMMUNE DE PARIS

COMITÉ
DE SALUT PUBLIC

Que tous les bons citoyens se lèvent!

Aux barricades! L'ennemi est dans nos murs!

Pas d'hésitation!

En avant pour la République, pour la Commune et pour la Liberté!

AUX ARMES!

Paris, le 22 mai 1871.

Le Comité de Salut public,
ANT. ARNAUD, BILLIORAY, E. EUDES,
F. GAMBON, G. RANVIER.

Kat. 370

Aufruf des »Wohlfahrtsausschusses« der Kommune von Paris

Paris, 22. Mai 1871

Kat. 370

Am 1. Mai beschloss der Rat der Kommune die Wahl eines fünfköpfigen »Wohlfahrtsausschusses« als Führungsgremium. Militärisch stützte er sich auf die »Republikanische Föderation der Nationalgarde«. Mit diesem Plakat rief der »Wohlfahrtsausschuss« alle »guten Bürger« zu den Waffen und auf die Barrikaden, um den in die Stadt eingedrungenen Feind im Namen der Republik und der Freiheit zu bekämpfen. Mit dem »Feind« waren nicht mehr die Deutschen, sondern die Truppen der französischen Regierung gemeint.

In Gefangenschaft gestickte Tasche von Louise Michel

Kat. 373

Louise Michel schenkte dieses vierseitig bestickte Täschchen ihrer Concierge. Wahrscheinlich hat es Michel selbst während ihrer Gefangenschaft gestickt oder erhielt es als Geschenk von einer Mitgefangenen.

Kat. 373

Selbstgefertigte Waffe

Paris, 1871
Kat. 369

Die aus einem Gewehrlauf und einer Pistole bestehende Waffe wurde in der Rue Pelleport in Paris in 50 Zentimetern Tiefe gefunden – in einer Gegend, in der es in der »Blutwoche« im Mai 1871 zu heftigen Kämpfen gekommen war. Vermutlich wurde sie dort von Kommunarden auf der Flucht vergraben.

Louise Michel (1830–1905)

Abb. 17

Louise Michel war als Lehrerin nach Paris gekommen und rasch politisch aktiv geworden. Ihr soziales Engagement machte sie zu einer Heldin der Armen. 1871 gehörte sie zu den militanten Anhängern und Anhängerinnen der Pariser Kommune. In der Uniform der Nationalgarde beteiligte sie sich an den Kämpfen gegen die Regierungstruppen. Im Dezember 1871 zu Festungshaft verurteilt, wurde sie 1873 auf die Pazifikinsel Neukaledonien deportiert. 1880 kehrte sie nach Paris zurück. Bis zu ihrem Tod 1905 setzte sie sich für die gesellschaftlich Benachteiligten ein. Mehr als 100 000 Menschen gaben ihr das letzte Geleit.

Abb. 17

Besatzung und Annexion

Im Frankfurter Frieden vom 10. Mai 1871 verpflichtete sich Frankreich, das Elsass und Teile Lothringens an das Deutsche Reich abzutreten. Außerdem musste es innerhalb von drei Jahren Reparationen von fünf Milliarden Francs entrichten. Um die Forderungen durchzusetzen, sollten deutsche Truppen bis zu ihrer Erfüllung in Frankreich stationiert bleiben. Da Frankreich schneller als festgelegt die Reparationen bezahlte, zogen die Besatzer bereits 1873 ab. Schmerzlicher als die hohen Kontributionen waren für Frankreich die Gebietsverluste an der Ostgrenze. Diese Territorien unterstanden als »Reichsland Elsass-Lothringen« direkt dem Kaiser. Nicht zuletzt aus strategischen Erwägungen wurde die militärische und zivile Infrastruktur dort modernisiert und ausgebaut. Zusätzlich zur Stationierung von Truppen aus den Bundesstaaten des Reiches wurden elsässische und lothringische Verbände aufgestellt. Die Menschen im »Reichsland« mussten sich entscheiden, ob sie unter Verzicht auf die französische Staatsbürgerschaft in der Heimat bleiben oder nach Frankreich ausreisen wollten. Elsässer und »Deutsch-Lothringer« freundeten sich mit der deutschen Herrschaft nur schwer an. Mehr als Sympathiebekundungen für Frankreich standen jedoch Forderungen nach politischer Mitbestimmung und größerer Autonomie im Vordergrund.

Kat. 386

Preußische Paroleausgabe auf dem Marktplatz von Belfort während der deutschen Besetzung 1873
Kat. 386

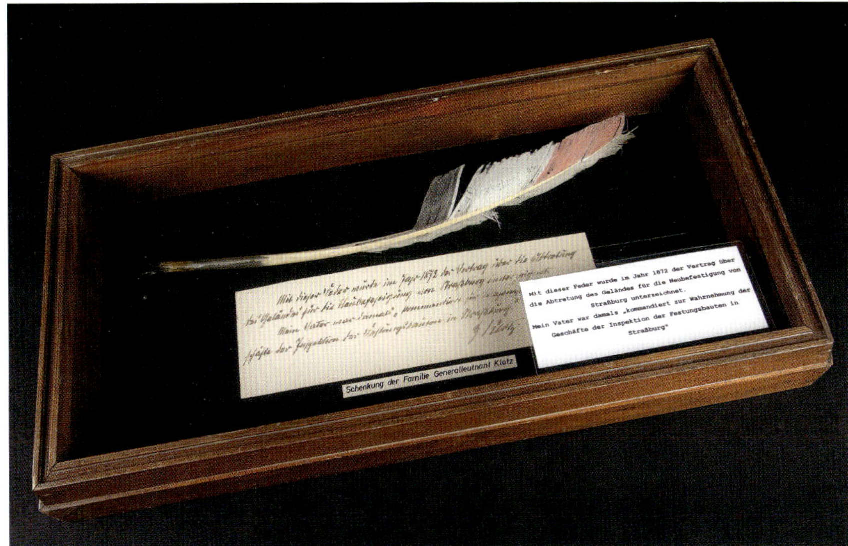

Kat. 387

Feder, mit der 1872 ein Vertrag zur Abtretung des Geländes für die Neubefestigung von Straßburg unterzeichnet wurde

Kat. 387

In Elsass-Lothringen setzte nach der deutschen Annexion eine rege Bautätigkeit ein. Sie begleitete augenfällig die Inbesitznahme der vormals französischen Territorien, brachte aber auch – besonders in den größeren Städten Straßburg und Metz – einen Modernisierungsschub mit sich. Die Bauvorhaben veränderten das Erscheinungsbild beider Städte, die jeweils eine »deutsche« Neustadt erhielten. Parallel dazu wurden sie zu modernen Festungen und starken Garnisonen ausgebaut.

Kat. 388

Ein Paar Epauletten eines Hauptmanns im Königs-Infanterie-Regiment (6. Lothringisches) Nr. 145

Königreich Preußen, 1893–1915

Kat. 388

Das zur Metzer Garnison gehörige Regiment wurde 1890 aufgestellt. Wie alle lothringischen und elsässischen Formationen wurde es in den Verband des preußischen Heeres eingegliedert. Wilhelm II. übernahm nach einer Besichtigung 1893 die Chefstelle des Truppenteils und verlieh ihm seinen Namenszug, der fortan Schulterklappen und Epauletten zierte.

Kat. 389

»Notre drapeau quand même! Épisode historique – Strasbourg 1871« / Trotz allem unsere Fahne! Historische Episode – Straßburg 1871

Lithografie

Kat. 389

Die Grafik zeigt Frauen, die Kleider in Blau, Weiß und Rot tragen, um zusammen die in Elsass-Lothringen verbotene französische Trikolore zu bilden.

Nationale Einigung, nationale Standards

Bis zur Reichsgründung 1871 und darüber hinaus existierte in den deutschen Staaten eine Vielzahl verschiedener Währungen, Maße, Gewichte und selbst unterschiedliche Ortszeiten. Dies beeinträchtigte den Handel und die wirtschaftliche Entwicklung in den deutschen Staaten ebenso wie den Betrieb des neuen Verkehrsmittels, der Eisenbahn. Mit der geplanten Aufhebung der Zölle zwischen Mitgliedsstaaten und der Vereinheitlichung der Währungen und Maße war der 1815 geschaffene Deutsche Bund zunächst kaum vorangekommen. Der Deutsche Zollverein, 1833/34 unter preußischer Führung ohne Österreich gegründet, setzte sich verstärkt für die Schaffung eines deutschen Binnenmarktes ein. Aber erst im Norddeutschen Bund und im deutschen Kaiserreich wurden weitgehende Maßnahmen zur Standardisierung durchgesetzt. Zur Vereinheitlichung der am Sonnenstand orientierten einzelnen Ortszeiten kam es allerdings erst 1893 beim Anschluss an die mitteleuropäische Zeitzone.

Kat. 390

Gewicht zu 20 Zollpfund
1839–1856 abgekürzt »ZP«,
danach nur noch »P«
Kat. 390

1854 legte der Deutsche Zollverein das Pfund auf 500 Gramm für den zwischenstaatlichen Handel fest. Ab 1858 übernahmen einzelne Staaten das Zollpfund auch als Einheit für den Binnenhandel. In Bayern wog das Pfund noch bis 1871 560 Gramm. Eine weitere Standardisierung von Maßeinheiten hatte der Deutsche Bund noch vorbereitet. Festgeschrieben wurde sie 1868 in der »Maß- und Gewichtsordnung« des Norddeutschen Bundes. Ab 1872 wurde sie im gesamten Gebiet des 1871 gegründeten Deutschen Reiches wirksam.

Kat. 391

Münzhumpen zur Reichsgründung 1871
Firma Sy & Wagner, Berlin 1873
Silber (800/1000)
Kat. 391

Dieser mit 33 Talermünzen geschmückte Humpen erinnert an die vielen unterschiedlichen Währungen vor der Reichsgründung und feiert die Einführung der Mark, die hier in die Daumenrast des Deckels eingearbeitet ist. Den oberen Rand des Kruges ziert die Inschrift: »Thalers Abschied * Deutsche Einheit * Mark nun einzieht * seis für allezeit«. Mit dem Münzgesetz von 1873 wurde die gemeinsame Währung »Mark« auf alle deutschen Landeswährungen angewendet. Schrittweise ersetzte sie diese. Die in den Humpen eingebundenen Vereinstaler oder diesen im Wert gleichgestellte ältere Taler blieben noch bis 1907 gesetzliche Zahlungsmittel im Wert von drei Mark. (www.bundesbank.de/resource/blob/607302/60fb3843f36b7648ff7cbd6e4a5ba0b7/mL/glanzstuecke-2015-data.pdf, S. 4–7, Aufruf am 30.1.2020)

Der Deutsch-Französische Krieg in der Erinnerung

Denkmäler, Feiertage und Ansprachen

MICHAEL EPKENHANS

Der Krieg zwischen Deutschland und Frankreich 1870/71 hat lange Zeit tiefe Spuren im jeweiligen kollektiven Gedächtnis hinterlassen. Zu groß waren die Emotionen vor und während des Krieges gewesen, zu hoch die Zahl der Opfer, zu weitreichend seine politischen und gesellschaftlichen Folgen. Wie wurde damals daran erinnert, und was, und warum gerade dies und nicht etwas anderes?

Angesichts der Vielzahl der Formen der Erinnerung – neben privaten Briefen und Tagebüchern selbst »kleiner Leute« sind es Hunderte Prachtbände und offiziöse Werke sowie zahllose Postkarten, Historiengemälde, Panoramen und Fotosammlungen, Sedan-, Wörth-, Weißenburg- und Moltkestraßen, Wilhelm- und Bismarckplätze bzw. -denkmäler – sei hier ausschnitthaft nach dem Ursprung, der Bedeutung und der Rezeption von Denkmälern, nationalen Feiertagen und Reden aus Anlass von Jahrestagen gefragt.

Das im Deutschen Reich mit Abstand sichtbarste und größte Denkmal zur Erinnerung war das Niederwald-Denkmal bei Rüdesheim, das seit 1883 die im Krieg gegen Frankreich gemeinsam erkämpfte Einheit, vor allem aber auch die »Wacht am Rhein« repräsentiert. Im Gegensatz zur »Trauernden Germania« im Kurgarten von Bad Kissingen, die seit 1867 an die gefallenen Bayern und

Preußen des Deutsch-Deutschen Krieges von 1866 erinnerte, demonstrierte die Germania des Niederwald-Denkmals Macht und Stärke über den Einzelerfolg hinaus.

Das Niederwald-Denkmal ist eines von Hunderten, die an die Reichsgründung im Krieg erinnern sollten. Die Bedeutung dieser Monumente war schon für Zeitgenossen höchst unterschiedlich und blieb es auch für deren Nachkommen. Für die einen waren sie Zeichen der Trauer um die gefallenen Kameraden, für andere solche des Heldenkampfs und -tods. Für wieder andere drückten sie nationalen Stolz – manchmal Überheblichkeit – und eine nationale Identität aus. Zugleich dienten sie der Legitimation der zwei Nationen und Gesellschaften, die sich im Krieg neu konstituiert hatten: das Kaiserreich als von oben gegründeter kleindeutscher nationaler Einheitsstaat auf der einen Rheinseite und die nunmehr Dritte Republik als politischer und gesellschaftlicher Neubeginn nach Jahrzehnten royalistischer und monarchistischer Irrwege und innerer Wirren auf der anderen.

Politische Sinnstiftung und Trauer sind bei vielen Denkmälern schwer voneinander zu trennen. Insbesondere die großen Denkmäler auf den Schlachtfeldern versuchten, durch ihre Ikonografie – Löwen, Adler und Germania, gefallene Krieger und griechische Göttinnen – zusammen mit Schlachtfeldüberbleibseln wie Mitrailleusen oder Geschützen die Toten zu ehren, aber auch einen Heldenmythos zu erzeugen.

Doch nicht nur dort, wo die Gefallenen lagen, erinnerten Denkmäler an den Krieg. In fast allen Städten, ja in kleinsten Dörfern wie Stolzenhain an der Röder in Südbrandenburg, das nur zwei Opfer beklagen musste, gab es welche. Das Beispiel der Inschrift des 1879 mithilfe von Spenden errichteten Denkmals, dessen Spitze die griechische Siegesgöttin Nike krönt, kann hier für Hunderte stehen, die reichsweit zu finden waren:

Die Enthüllungsfeier des Niederwald-Denkmals am 28. September 1883
Abb. 18

Das Niederwald-Denkmal bei Rüdesheim am Rhein, 1883 eingeweiht
Postkarte
Abb. 19/1

Die Siegessäule in Berlin, 1873 eingeweiht
Postkarte
Abb. 19/2

Der Bismarckturm bei Halberstadt, 1907 eingeweiht
Postkarte
Abb. 19/3

Das Kaiser-Wilhelm-Denkmal in Metz, 1892 eingeweiht
Postkarte
Abb. 19/4

Das am 18. November 1918 umgestürzte Kaiser-Wilhelm-Denkmal in Metz
Postkarte
Abb. 19/5

»Dem Andenken
Der im Kampfe gegen
Frankreich
1870–1871
Ruhmvoll gefallenen
Krieger
Unsern Toden wir geboten
Gruß und Dank von unserer
Hand
Die im Kampfe tapfer stritten
Und den Heldentod erlitten.
Für uns und das Vaterland.«

Das Bismarck-Denkmal in Hamburg, 1906 eingeweiht
Postkarte
Abb. 19/6

Wie dicht die Denkmäler beieinanderlagen und wie groß neben dem Stolz auf die Einheit offenbar das Bedürfnis nach Erinnerung und Trauer war, zeigt ein Blick auf Karlsruhe: In der Stadt selbst sind es vier, darunter eines für das dort stationierte Leibgrenadierregiment, in den eingemeindeten Ortsteilen elf, im dazugehörigen Landkreis 16. Ein weiteres Denkmal, das man für die im Karlsruher Lazarett gestorbenen französischen Verwundeten errichtet hatte, wurde 1971 zum 100. Jahrestag der Reichsgründung von Unbekannten zerstört. In Orten ohne Denkmal erinnerten schlichte Holztafeln in den Kirchen oder Findlinge an beliebten oder markanten Stellen an die gefallenen Söhne.

Auch in Frankreich waren Denkmäler die sichtbarsten Zeichen der Erinnerung an den Krieg. Sie waren auch hier höchst unterschiedlich lesbar. »Kampfdenkmale« erinnerten an die »Mobilisierung des nationalen Idealismus angesichts der existenziellen Bedrohung des Landes«[1] und sollten die »kathartische Wirkung« der Kriegserfahrung für die Republik betonen: Der Krieg sei ein »patriotisch-moralisches Urereignis«, von dem die »Regeneration des Landes« ausgehen sollte.[2] Sie alle erinnerten an heldenhafte Verteidigung und Sieg, nicht an die Niederlage. »Gloria victis« lautete denn auch die Inschrift mancher Denkmale; trotzig stolz war ihre Symbolik wie in Paris, Sedan, Belfort oder Dijon.

Wie schwierig die Erinnerung an 1870 in einer im Inneren lange zerstrittenen Nation war, zeigt das Dijoner Denkmal, das eine eindeutige Botschaft zu vermitteln versuchte. Seine erste Fassung, eine weibliche »Resistance«-Figur mit der Jakobinermütze der Revolutionäre von 1789, erinnerte viele zu sehr an den Commune-Aufstand. Wenige Tage vor der geplanten Enthüllung des Denkmals am fünften Jahrestag der erfolgreichen Kämpfe der Dijoner Bevölkerung gegen die deutschen Truppen am 30. Oktober 1870 holten Soldaten eines ehemaligen bonapartistischen Generals, der 1871 an der blutigen Niederschlagung der Commune beteiligt gewesen war, diese vom Sockel. Erst als sich die Republik 1879 endgültig durchsetzte, konnte das Denkmal in dieser Arbeiterstadt wiedererrichtet werden. Die Einweihung fand demonstrativ am 14. Juli 1880 statt, dem neuen Nationalfeiertag, der in dem Jahr erstmals begangen wurde.

Neben den Kampfdenkmälern wurden über 900 Monumente errichtet, die überall in Frankreich an die Gefallenen erinnerten. Die staatlichen Monumente formulierten dabei ihre Botschaften relativ zurückhaltend. Dies galt besonders für jene Orte, an denen französische und deutsche Soldaten nebeneinander bestattet waren. »A la mémoire des soldats morts pendant la guerre de 1870–

Gedenktafel für 1870/71 in Frankreich gestorbene Beierfelder
Kat. 375

Das nach 1945 zerstörte Denkmal, von dem nur diese Tafel überliefert ist, erinnerte an aus der Erzgebirgsgemeinde Beierfeld gebürtige Soldaten der sächsischen Infanterieregimenter Nr. 104 und 105, die in Frankreich den Tod gefunden hatten.

Das Kriegerdenkmal auf der Place d'Alsace-Lorraine in Sedan, 2018
Abb. 20

Das 1897 eingeweihte Denkmal des Architekten Ulysse Gravigny und des Gießers A. Durenne erinnert an die Schlacht bei Sedan. Die Skulpturengruppe auf der Spitze zeigt eine Ruhmesgöttin, die einen sterbenden französischen Infanteristen mit Lorbeer bekränzt. Die lateinische Inschrift »Impavidus numero victus« (Ohne Furcht wurde er von der Übermacht besiegt) glorifiziert den Kampfgeist des französischen Heeres im Angesicht der Niederlage.

71« (Zum Gedächtnis der während des Krieges von 1870/71 gefallenen Soldaten), hieß es dort schlicht. Nur wenige versuchten, dem Sterben Sinn zu geben, wie etwa in Sedan und Bazeilles durch die Inschrift »Honneur et Patrie. 31 août – 1er septembre 1870« (Für Ehre und Vaterland). Die auf private Initiative in Städten und Dörfern errichteten Denkmäler waren weniger zurückhaltend, wie diese Inschrift zeigt: »A la mémoire des soldats français tombés glorieusement pour la défense de la patrie à la bataille de Bapaume le 3 janvier 1871« (Den bei der heldenhaften Verteidigung des Vaterlands in der Schlacht von Bapaume am 3. Januar 1871 gefallenen französischen Soldaten zum Gedenken). Manche, wie das Mahnmal in Mars-la-Tour, enthielten sogar eine offen revanchistische Botschaft: Eine weibliche Frankreichgestalt, nach Osten blickend, hält einen sterbenden Soldaten in den Armen, den sie mit Lorbeer bekränzt. Zwei sitzende

Kinder zu Füßen des Soldaten symbolisieren die verlorenen Provinzen Elsass und Lothringen; indem eines seine Waffen übernimmt, verpflichtet es sich zugleich, sie eines Tages zurückzuerobern.

Sinngebung war auch das Ziel nationaler Feiertage – im Deutschen Reich ebenso wie in Frankreich. In Deutschland bot sich der Sedantag regelrecht an. Der Sieg bei Sedan hatte überall in Deutschland Anlass zu spontanem Jubel gegeben. Gemeinsam hatten die deutschen »Stämme«, wie es häufig hieß, gesiegt. Tatsächlich war an jenem 2. September die Nation zusammengewachsen. Kein Tag schien vielen passender als dieser, um die Einheit fortan in jedem Jahr zu feiern. Anfangs galt der Sedantag allerdings nur als die zweitbeste Lösung, nach dem 18. Januar als dem Tag der Kaiserproklamation. Für Wilhelm I. wiederum war der 18. Januar der Tag der preußischen Königskrönung. Und im Sedantag sah er einen Tag der preußischen Armee, die seit Aufstellung der Siegessäule in Berlin alljährlich am 2. September mit großem Pomp paradierte. Inoffiziellen Feiern stimmte er jedoch zu. Städte und Gemeinden sollten selbst darüber entscheiden, wie sie dieses Ereignis feierten.

Und das taten sie. In vielen, jedoch nicht in allen Bundesstaaten wurde der Sedantag Feiertag. Militärparaden etwaiger lokaler Garnisonen, von den Veteranen angeführte Umzüge der Kriegervereine, Feldgottesdienste, Kranzniederlegungen an den örtlichen Denkmälern zu Ehren der Gefallenen und bald auch Wilhelms I., Festreden von Honoratioren, patriotische Darbietungen von Schulklassen, Tanzveranstaltungen, Festessen und Feuerwerke gaben dem Tag einen sowohl militärischen als auch zivilen Charakter. Ein »echter« Nationalfeiertag wurde der Sedantag indes nie. So missfiel der preußische Charakter vielen Bayern. Sie erinnerten lieber an die Schlacht bei Wörth am 6. August, die maßgeblich durch hohe Opfer der bayerischen Truppen gewonnen worden war. Auch die Ausgrenzung von Katholiken und Sozialisten nach der Reichsgründung stand einer reichsweiten Zustimmung zum Sedantag im Weg: Sie boykottierten die Feiern weitgehend. Nach dem Höhepunkt der Sedanfeiern am 25. Jahrestag der Schlacht 1895 sank ihre Bedeutung.

Und der 18. Januar? Anlässlich des 25. Jahrestags der Kaiserproklamation 1896 kam ihm ein letztes Mal große symbolische Bedeutung zu. Reichsweit fanden Feiern und Paraden statt. Besonders groß war der Pomp in Berlin. Dort feierte Wilhelm II. einmal mehr die eigene Dynastie der Hohenzollern. Zugleich nutzte er den Anlass, um sich politisch vom außenpolitischen Grundkonsens der Reichsgründer loszusagen. »Aus dem Deutschen Reich ist ein Weltreich geworden«, verkündete er und machte damit deutlich, dass Bismarcks Politik der »Saturiertheit« an ihr Ende gekommen sei. Die Rechnung für die Abkehr von einer Außenpolitik des Augenmaßes und der Mäßigung erhielt das Reich 1918/19.

Was für die Deutschen der Sedantag, war für die Franzosen der 14. Juli. Und auch diesem Nationalfeiertag ging ein schmerzhafter innenpolitischer Konsolidierungsprozess voraus. Lange Zeit hatte die Erinnerung an die Revolution von 1789 das Land eher gespalten. »La Terreur« hatte ihr das Image einer Katastrophe, nicht des Beginns einer neuen Zeit verpasst. Dies änderte sich erst, als alle Restaurationspläne mit dem Rücktritt des Staatspräsidenten und Marschalls von Frankreich Patrice Mac-Mahon, des Verlierers von Sedan, sich zerschlagen hatten. Wie der Sedantag zum Gründungsmythos des Kaiserreichs wurde, so wurde nun die Gründung der Republik am 4. September 1870 nach

Erinnerungsabzeichen der Sedanfeier des Jahres 1895 in Leipzig
Abb. 21

Le Rêve – Der Traum

Édouard Detaille (1848–1912), 1888
Öl auf Leinwand, 400×300 cm
Abb. 22

Detaille schuf mit diesem Gemälde die bekannteste Allegorie des französischen Wunsches nach Revanche für die Niederlage von 1870/71. Über den auf freiem Feld schlafenden französischen Infanteristen der Dritten Republik stürmen ihre Ahnen, die erste »Nation in Waffen«, über den Nachthimmel: Soldaten der Revolutionskriege und des Ersten Kaiserreichs.

der vom Kaiserreich Napoleons III. verursachten militärischen Katastrophe zum Gründungsmythos des republikanischen Frankreichs. Und so wie die Gründerväter der Republik im Jahr 1870 griffen auch die Initiatoren dieses Mythos auf die Revolution zurück. Der Sturm auf die Bastille 1789 und die *levée en masse* boten sich hierbei als Leitmotive an.

Der 14. Juli wurde nationaler Feiertag. Dessen tragende Elemente waren die reformierte Armee als »Volk in Waffen«, das seither auf den Champs Élysées paradierte, und die »Marseillaise« mit ihren Gemeinschaft und Kampfgeist stiftenden Botschaften als Nationalhymne. Die Parallelen zu den jährlichen Paraden am Sedantag in Berlin sind unübersehbar.

Die Veranstaltungen aus Anlass des 25. Jahrestags waren aus französischer Sicht daher auch Demonstrationen moralischer Überlegenheit. In einem offenen Brief warf der Historiker Ernest Lavisse Wilhelm II. vor, nicht nur die damaligen Kämpfe, sondern den Krieg an sich zu verherrlichen: »Et maintenant l'Allemagne va célébrer des fêtes qui seront des ›commémorations de batailles‹ sur le sol conquis. Ne pouvait-on célébrer autrement la fondation de l'empire? Sire, ces fêtes sont inquiétantes pour l'Europe et pour le monde, parce qu'au fond et en vérité Votre Majesté et l'Allemagne vont célébrer non seulement la guerre d'il y a vingt-cinq ans, mais la guerre.« (Nun wird Deutschland also Feiern zelebrieren, die ›dem Gedenken an die Schlachten‹ auf dem eroberten

Boden dienen sollen. Lässt sich die Reichsgründung nicht anders feiern? Majestät, diese Feste beunruhigen Europa und die Welt, denn innerlich und in Wahrheit werden Eure Majestät und Deutschland nicht nur den Krieg von vor 25 Jahren feiern, sondern den Krieg.) Doch auch der Gedanke an Vergeltung wurde häufig offen ausgesprochen: »Dormez en paix, chers camarades de 1870! Le jour de l'inéluctable revanche, dont il faut bien parler un peu pour y penser toujours, nos enfants auront à coeur de venger nos défaites. Ils s'inspireront de votre valeur et de votre abnégation, et c'est le front haut qu'ils entreront dans la carrière quand leurs aînés n'y seront plus. Vive la France! Vive la République franchement démocratique!« (Ruht in Frieden, liebe Kameraden von 1870! Am Tag der unvermeidlichen Vergeltung, über die wir ein wenig werden reden müssen, um immer daran zu denken, werden unsere Kinder leidenschaftlich danach streben, unsere Niederlagen zu rächen. Eure Größe und eure Selbstaufopferung wird sie begeistern, und mit erhobenen Häuptern werden sie auf diesem Weg fortschreiten, wenn die Älteren nicht mehr sind. Es lebe Frankreich! Es lebe die wahrhaft demokratische Republik!), hieß es in der Rede eines Kriegervereinsvorsitzenden an die Jugend.[3]

Die angekündigte Revanche war dann das Ergebnis des Ersten Weltkriegs. Um den Sieg und damit die Einlösung des Vergeltungsversprechens von 1871 zu unterstreichen, besuchten Staatspräsident Raymond Poincaré und Ministerpräsident Georges Clemenceau noch im November 1918 das wiedergewonnene Elsass und Lothringen. Beide Provinzen sollten, so die Absprache der Alliierten, noch vor einem Vertrag ohne weitere Verhandlungen an Frankreich zurückfallen, um erlittenes Unrecht zu sühnen. Dort wurden die Staatsmänner begeistert empfangen. Stolz wehte vom Straßburger Münster wieder die Trikolore. Am symbolträchtigen 18. Januar 1919, dem 48. Jahrestag der Kaiserproklamation, rief Poincaré die Erinnerung an diesen Tag wach: »Im Unrecht geboren, endete [das Deutsche Reich] in Schande«, erklärte er zu Beginn der Verhandlungen unter den Alliierten. Und am 28. Juni, dem Jahrestag des Attentats von Sarajevo, musste die deutsche Delegation auf ihrem Weg in den Spiegelsaal erst durch ein Spalier von französischen Veteranen des Krieges von 1870/71 gehen, die eigens ihre alten Uniformen angelegt hatten, bevor sie schließlich, an gesichtsversehrten Opfern des Weltkriegs, »Gueules cassées«, vorbei, den Tisch erreichte, an dem die Unterzeichnung stattfinden sollte. Deutlicher ließ sich der Zusammenhang von 1870/71 und 1918/19 kaum herstellen.

Die Sedanfeiern, die trotz fehlender Genehmigung weiterhin stattfanden – nun aber als Parteiveranstaltungen der rechtsnationalen DNVP – sowie auch die Feiern anlässlich der Reichsgründung am 18. Januar, die vor allem Studenten veranstalteten, stellen vor diesem Hintergrund Versuche dar, dem Protest gegen die ungeliebte Weimarer Republik Ausdruck zu verleihen, zugleich aber die Hoffnung auf Wiedererlangung alter Größe und Macht wachzuhalten.

Nach 1933 sollten sich diese Hoffnungen erfüllen, um sich nach einem zweiten totalen Krieg endgültig zu zerschlagen.

Der 100. Jahrestag des Deutsch-Französischen Krieges war noch einmal Anlass zum Gedenken. Den Anfang machten die Franzosen. Sie gedachten allerdings nicht des Kriegs, sondern der Gründung der inzwischen Fünften Republik am 4. September 1970. Am Jahrestag nahm Präsident Georges Pompidou zusammen mit dem Militärkommandanten von Paris, General Metz, vor dem Pariser Rathaus eine Parade ab. In seiner Rede betonte Ministerpräsident Jean Chaban-Delmas zugleich noch einmal die Bedeutung der »Republik«. Sie sei der Inbegriff von »Demokratie«, »wirtschaftlichem Fortschritt« und »sozialen Rechten«. Die Farben eines daran anschließenden Feuerwerks am helllichten Tag symbolisierten die Trikolore, 600 freigelassene Tauben erinnerten an jene, die einst neben den Ballons die einzige Verbindung der eingeschlossenen Hauptstadt zur Außenwelt gebildet hatten.

In der Bundesrepublik Deutschland stand der Jahrestag unter ganz anderen Vorzeichen. Am Vorabend des 18. Januar 1971 erinnerte Bundespräsident Gustav Heinemann in einer Fernsehansprache an die Nation an die Irrwege der deutschen Geschichte seit 1871, die Zerklüftung der Gesellschaft und den Größenwahn.[4] »Für Generationen ist dieser Tag ein Höhepunkt ihres Geschichtsbewusstseins gewesen. Uns ist aber heute nicht nach einer Hundertjahrfeier zumute«, erklärte er gleich zu Beginn. Allen Nationalisten, die im Zuge der schmerzhaften Debatten über die Ostverträge von der Revision von Grenzen, der Wiederherstellung eines Reiches in den Grenzen von 1937 träumten, schrieb er ins Stammbuch: »Hundert Jahre Deutsches Reich – dies heißt eben nicht einmal Versailles, sondern zweimal Versailles, 1871 und 1919, und dies heißt auch Auschwitz, Stalingrad und bedingungslose Kapitulation 1945.« Auch wenn der Bundespräsident die Idee der Wiedergewinnung nationalstaatlicher Einheit betonte, sah er die Zukunft doch eher in einer »gesamteuropäische[n] Grundordnung, in der Staaten und Völker auch bei unterschiedlicher innerer Gestaltung nicht nur nebeneinander bestehen, sondern Krieg und Gewalt gegeneinander ausschließen und sich miteinander zur Erfüllung gemeinsamer Sachaufgaben verbinden – wie etwa Verkehr, Umweltgestaltung, Forschung, Entwicklungshilfe«. Viel wichtiger war ihm jedoch eine andere Lehre aus 1871: »Das sind die im Grundgesetz festgelegten Freiheitsrechte aller Bürger. Im Grundgesetz haben wir uns entschieden für Grundrechte wie Gewissensfreiheit, Redefreiheit, Versammlungsfreiheit, Freizügigkeit. Um all dieses ist in unserer Geschichte gekämpft und gelitten worden. All dieses zu bewahren, immer besser zu verwirklichen und mit sozialer Gerechtigkeit zu verbinden, muß unsere gemeinsame Aufgabe bleiben.«

Und der andere Teil Deutschlands? Dort nahm die DDR-Führung den Jahrestag zum Anlass, sich im Rahmen einer großen Parade von 150 000 Werktätigen, die an den 52. Jahrestag der Ermordung von Karl Liebknecht und Rosa Luxemburg am 15. Januar 1919 erinnerte, am 17. Januar in eine andere Tradition zu stellen. Mit Inbrunst prangerte der Chefideologe der SED, Albert Norden, die Übel und Verbrechen von Neofaschisten, Imperialisten und rechten SPD-Führern in Vergangenheit und Gegenwart an, um sodann den Bruch der DDR mit der Vergangenheit herauszustellen: »Das im Blut seiner eigenen Verbrechen erstickte Reich wird nie mehr auferstehen. Aber hier in Berlin, wo der deutsche Imperialismus seine Untaten gegen das eigene Volk und die Völker der Welt ausbrütete, hier hat die Arbeiterklasse den sozialistischen deutschen Staat errichtet und sich zur sozialistischen Nation konstituiert«,[5] hieß es programmatisch.

Nordens Hoffnungen sollten sich nicht erfüllen. Anders als von ihm behauptet, sahen die Bürger und Bürgerinnen der DDR ihre Zukunft nicht in dem von ihm gepriesenen Arbeiter- und Bauernstaat. Sie fegten ihn in einer friedlichen Revolution keine 20 Jahre später hinweg. Vor allem Frankreich unter François Mitterand sollte sich lange schwertun mit der Wiedervereinigung, rief diese doch alte Ängste vor einer neuen starken Macht in der Mitte Europas hervor. Einen Ausweg bot die entschlossene Integration Europas, so wie von Bundespräsident Heinemann vorgezeichnet, auf der einen Seite. Auf der anderen Seite galt es, die besonderen deutsch-französischen Beziehungen zu stärken. Den 50. Jahrestag des Elysée-Abkommens 2013 feierten Deutsche und Franzosen daher nicht zuletzt in dem Bewusstsein, die Gräben von 1870/71 endgültig überwunden zu haben.

1 Andreas Metzing: Kriegsgedenken in Frankreich (1871–1914). Studien zur kollektiven Erinnerung an den Deutsch-Französischen Krieg von 1870/71, Freiburg 2002, S. 38 (https://freidok.uni-freiburg.de/fedora/objects/freidok:418/datastreams/FILE1/content1/, letzter Zugriff 22. 8. 2019). **2** Ebd., S. 36. **3** Zitiert nach Metzing: Kriegsgedenken, S. 125, 131. **4** Gustav W. Heinemann: Reden und Interviews, 5 Bde., II (1. Juni 1970 – 30. Juli 1971), hg. vom Presse- und Informationsamt der Bundesregierung, Bergisch-Gladbach 1971, S. 67 – 74. **5** Rede Albert Nordens auf der Kampfdemonstration: »Schwert und Flamme der Revolution«, in: Neues Deutschland, 18. 1. 1971, S. 1 f. (http://zefys.staatsbibliothek-berlin.de/ddr-presse/ergebnisanzeige/?id=148&purl=SNP2532889X-19710118-0-2-150-0/, letzter Zugriff 23. 8. 2019).

1870/71 – Krieg, Pariser Kommune und kulturelles Erbe

SYLVIE LE RAY-BURIMI

Am 9. Juli 2017 nahm die UNESCO die »Neustadt« von Straßburg in die Weltkulturerbeliste auf. Dieses von elsässischen und deutschen Architekten auf den Trümmern des Krieges von 1870/71 errichtete Viertel sei »für Straßburg und das Elsass ein wichtiges Symbol der Aussöhnung mit [einer] reichen und vielfältigen Geschichte«.[1] Die Würdigung entsprach dem Wunsch, deutsch-französische Antagonismen zu überwinden, die seit 1871 bestanden.[2] Zwei Weltkriege mit ungeheuren Opferzahlen und Zerstörungen haben die Erinnerung an den Krieg von 1870/71 weitgehend verdrängt. Doch in Frankreich setzte der Erinnerungsverlust bereits kurz nach dem Konflikt ein, zuerst mit einer Ästhetisierung und später mit der Beräumung der Ruinen. Aus französischer Sicht war die Erinnerung an den Krieg mit Schuld belastet: Man hatte den Deutschen den Krieg erklärt und damit unfreiwillig deren Einigung vollendet. Nach der Niederlage bei Sedan stürzte das Zweite Kaiserreich. Die Dritte Republik wurde ausgerufen und ein Volkskrieg gegen die weit auf französisches Gebiet vorgerückten deutschen Armeen proklamiert, ohne dass dies verhindert hätte, dass Paris belagert wurde und schließlich kapitulieren musste. Nach dem Vorfrieden von Versailles sah sich die republikanische Regierung durch den Aufstand der sozialistisch gesinnten Pariser Kommune vom 18. März bis zum 28. Mai 1871 selbst bedroht und ließ ihn blutig niederschlagen. Während Berlin durch die Gründung des deutschen Kaiserreichs enorm an Macht gewann, verlor Paris nach diesen Ereignissen von 1871 bis 1879 seinen Hauptstadtstatus an Versailles.

Straßburg vom Steintor aus gesehen am Tag nach der Kapitulation der belagerten Stadt
Charles Winter (1821–1904)/
Paul Sinner (1838–1925)
Kat. 313

Das Viertel entlang der Steinstraße wurde bei dem schließlich erfolgreichen Versuch der deutschen Artillerie, eine Bresche in die Befestigungsanlagen am Steintor zu schießen, stark zerstört. Die Zerstörungen waren von zentraler Bedeutung für die öffentliche Kontroverse über die Verhältnismäßigkeit der militärischen Mittel während der Belagerung Straßburgs vom 13. August bis zum 28. September 1870. Die Aufnahme stammt höchstwahrscheinlich von Charles Winter, einem bekannten Straßburger Fotografen. Der Tübinger Fotograf Paul Sinner veröffentlichte neben eigenen Aufnahmen, die er vor Ort in Straßburg und an anderen Kriegsschauplätzen anfertigte, auch Kopien von Winters Bildern unter seinem Namen. (Wolfgang Hesse: Ansichten aus Schwaben, Tübingen 1989, S. 77–78.)

Die Trümmer der Vendôme-Säule in Paris 1871
Holzstich aus einer illustrierten Zeitschrift
Abb. 23

Der Brand des Tuilerien-Palasts am 24. Mai 1871
Lithografie von Léon Sabatier und Albert Adam aus »Paris et ses ruines«, 1873
Abb. 24

Die Belagerung und Eroberung von Paris durch französische Regierungstruppen im Kampf gegen die aufständische Kommune richtete größere Verheerungen an als die vorangegangene deutsche Beschießung. Erinnert wurden jedoch vor allem Zerstörungen durch Anhänger und Anhängerinnen der Kommune: erst das Niederreißen von Symbolen des napoleonischen Kaisertums wie der Siegessäule der »Grande Armée« auf der Place Vendôme, dann der Versuch, Pariser Repräsentationsbauten niederzubrennen, als der Sieg der Regierungstruppen unabwendbar war. Das alte Rathaus ging ebenso in Flammen auf wie der Tuilerien-Palast des Louvre-Komplexes.

VERWOBENE ERINNERUNGEN: PREUSSEN UND KOMMUNARDEN

In der Wahrmehmung der Bevölkerung spielte es oft keine Rolle, welche Kriegspartei aus welchen Gründen Gewalt ausgeübt und Verwüstungen verursacht hatte: ob Deutsche oder Franzosen, ob Truppen der Versailler Nationalversammlung oder Anhänger der Pariser Kommune, ob gezielt oder als Kollateralschaden. Während des Krieges waren Straßburg,[3] Châteaudun, Mézières (heute Charleville-Mézières), Brücken über die Loire, Seine und Marne, Gemeinden im Großraum Paris, Teile des Pariser Südens und Belforts von Zerstörungen betroffen gewesen. Im Mai 1871 beschossen französische Regierungstruppen den Pariser Westen, um den Angriff auf die Aufständischen vorzubereiten. Zu den Verwüstungen der Barrikadenkämpfe kam in der »Blutigen Maiwoche« das Inbrandsetzen öffentlicher Gebäude, meist durch die militärisch unterlegene Kommune. In vielen Berichten wurden die preußische »Barbarei« und die den Kommunarden angelastete »orgie rouge« miteinander verquickt. Die »Fédérés« – Nationalgardisten auf Seiten der Kommune – wurden beschuldigt, als Trojanisches Pferd der Preußen gedient und unter der Hand die Zerstörungen finanziert zu haben.

Die Empörung über die Verheerungen zur Zeit der Kommune half vielen Franzosen und Französinnen, sogar über die Spuren der vorangegangenen, demütigenden deutschen Invasion hinwegzusehen.

Am 16. Mai 1871 gab Marschall Mac-Mahon, Befehlshaber der Regierungstruppen, folgenden Tagesbefehl an die Armee aus:

»Soldaten, soeben ist die Säule auf der Place Vendôme gefallen. Die Ausländer hatten sie respektiert. Die Pariser Kommune hat sie gestürzt. Männer, die sich Franzosen nennen, haben es gewagt, unter den Augen der Deutschen dieses Zeugnis der Siege Eurer Väter über die europäischen Koalitionsheere zu zerstören.«[4]

Als die Versailler Regierung zum Ende des Kommune-Aufstands erst den Orientalisten Ernest Renan[5] und später den Architekten und Kunsthistoriker Eugène Viollet-le-Duc entsandte, um die Schäden an mehreren Denkmälern aufzunehmen, darunter die Kirche Notre-Dame, trat das ganze Ausmaß der Zerstörungen durch beide Belagerungen zutage. Es entwickelte sich ein regelrechter Ruinentourismus. Von Überresten wie dem niedergebrannten Pariser Rathaus ging eine morbide Faszination aus:

»Beim Anblick dieses Schauspiels, dessen malerisches Erscheinungsbild dramatische Züge trägt, ertappt man sich bei einer Bewunderung, deren man sich wie einer Untat schämt. An jedem anderen Ort, in Baalbek, Palmyra, Luxor oder Karnak, gäbe man sich seiner Bewunderung ohne Reue oder weiteres Nachdenken hin.«[6]

Doch im Verlauf des zügigen Wiederaufbaus mithilfe von Spenden und staatlicher Unterstützung verschwanden die Ruinen schnell wieder aus dem Stadtbild und aus dem Gedächtnis.[7] 1879 erlangte Paris, besonders auf Betreiben der dortigen Geschäftswelt, seinen Hauptstadtstatus zurück.[8] Die wenigen Vorschläge, Zerstörungen zum Gedenken oder aus ästhetischen Gründen zu erhalten, waren vom Tisch gefegt worden. Dies steigerte natürlich den Wert von Überresten oder Fotografien der Ruinen als Zeugnisse der Katastrophe für die Franzosen und des Sieges für die Deutschen.

→
Empfangszimmer mit der Statue »Tod« im Schloss St. Cloud
Aus: »Bilder aus dem Kriegsleben vor Paris und Strassburg während des Feldzuges 1870/71«, Lieferung V, Bl. 4
Lichtdruck nach einer Aufnahme des Königlich-Preußischen Feld-Photographie-Detachements von J. B. Obernetter, 1870
Abb. 25

Das im Krieg 1870 geschaffene »Feld-Photographie-Detachement« hatte vor allem den Auftrag, durch fotogrammetrische Verfahren Lage und Beschaffenheit feindlicher Stellungen genauer zu erkunden, was wenig erfolgreich war. Es entstanden aber auch Aufnahmen von allgemeinerem Interesse zu Kriegführung und Kriegsfolgen.

Während des Krieges 1870/71 wuchs die Bedeutung der Französischen Revolution und der »Nation in Waffen« als Bezugspunkt für die Gegenwart. Die Vereinnahmung dieses revolutionären Erbes bildete den ideologischen Hintergrund für das »Schreckensjahr« 1870/71, indem sie die Wiedergeburt der Republik in eine kriegerische und opferreiche Traditionslinie einschrieb.[9]

Nach der Ausrufung der Republik am 4. September 1870 ging man überall daran, die Symbole des Kaisertums zu beseitigen.[10] Drei Wochen später machte der Schriftsteller Arsène Houssaye den Minister für öffentliche Bildung Jules Simon auf die bedrohte Lage einer Statue Kaiserin Joséphines in der Nähe des Arc de Triomphe aufmerksam: »Unterstehen Kunstwerke nicht ebenso wie Ambulanzen dem Schutz aller Parteien?«[11] Damit nahm er spätere Vereinbarungen zum Schutz von Kulturgütern vorweg. Zeitungen, die der Regierung der nationalen Verteidigung nahestanden, schwiegen zum republikanischen Bildersturm. Konservativere Zeitungen erkannten darin Vorboten eines Bürgerkriegs:

»Am 4. September gegen zwei Uhr am Nachmittag drang eine tobende Menschenmenge [...] gegen das Pariser Rathaus vor [...]. Die Revolution ist kaum zwei Stunden alt, und schon zeigen sich Anzeichen eines Bürgerkriegs [...]. Unterdessen strömt die Menge von Saal zu Saal, sie [...] reißt [...] ein großes Gemälde von der Wand, das den Titel trägt ›M. Haussmann übergibt dem Kaiser die Urkunde zur Eingemeindung der Vororte nach Paris‹.«[12]

Der Maler Gustave Courbet äußerte am 14. September 1870 den Wunsch, »dass die Regierung der nationalen Verteidigung ihm gestatten möge, die Säule [auf der Place Vendôme] zu entfernen oder dass sie selbst tätig werde und die Verwaltung des Artilleriemuseums hiermit beauftrage und die einzelnen Teile ins Hôtel de la Monnaie überbringen lasse.«[13] Als die Vendôme-Säule während der Pariser Kommune tatsächlich gestürzt wurde, brachte dies Courbet ins Gefängnis und zwang ihn später ins Exil. Vor einem Kriegsgericht erklärte Courbet, er habe die Säule durch ihre Überführung ins Hôtel des Invalides erhalten wollen, ebenso wie die Statue Napoleons I. des Bildhauers Seurre – bekannt als »Le Petit Corporal« mit Gehrock und Dreispitz, hatte diese von 1833 bis 1863 die Säule bekrönt, bevor sie auf Anordnung Napoleons III. gegen eine Napoleon-Statue im Stil eines römischen Imperators ausgetauscht und am Kreisel von Courbevoie aufgestellt worden war. Die Statue von Seurre wurde dort auf Ministerialbeschluss am 23. September 1870 entfernt: Nach ihrer (versehentlichen oder beabsichtigten) Enthauptung wurde sie in der Seine versenkt.[14] Der Schriftsteller Victor Fournel schildert den Fall polemisch:

»Nach dem 4. September verschwand die Bronzestatue von Courbevoie von ihrem Sockel. Arbeiter, von denen bis heute nicht sicher bekannt ist, wer sie geschickt hat, schraubten sie von ihrem Granitsockel ab. Dann wurde sie in die Seine geworfen. Das Bulletin municipal [...] hat dies lauthals verkündet, man schien dafür der Regierung die Ehre zu geben. Die hatte vielleicht in der Versenkung eine Möglichkeit gesehen, das einstige Idol vor dem Volkszorn zu retten, der es wohl zermalmt hätte, hätte man versucht, ihm offenes Geleit nach Paris zu geben.«[15]

Als die Statue bei Niedrigwasser wieder auftauchte, veranlasste der Minister für öffentlichen Unterricht Jules Simon Anfang 1871 ihre diskrete Bergung durch den Architekten Hector Lefuel.[16] Bei der Aufstellung der restaurierten Statue im Ehrenhof des Hôtel des Invalides 1911 schob die Presse den früheren Abriss gleichwohl den Aufständischen des 18. März 1871 in die Schuhe.

Die am 22. Mai 1871 in der Nationalversammlung vorgeschlagene Wiedererrichtung der Vendôme-Säule erfolgte im Mai 1873 – nur wenige Monate, bevor in Berlin anlässlich des ersten Sedan-Gedenktages am 2. September 1873 die Siegessäule zur Erinnerung an die drei Einigungskriege eingeweiht wurde.[17]

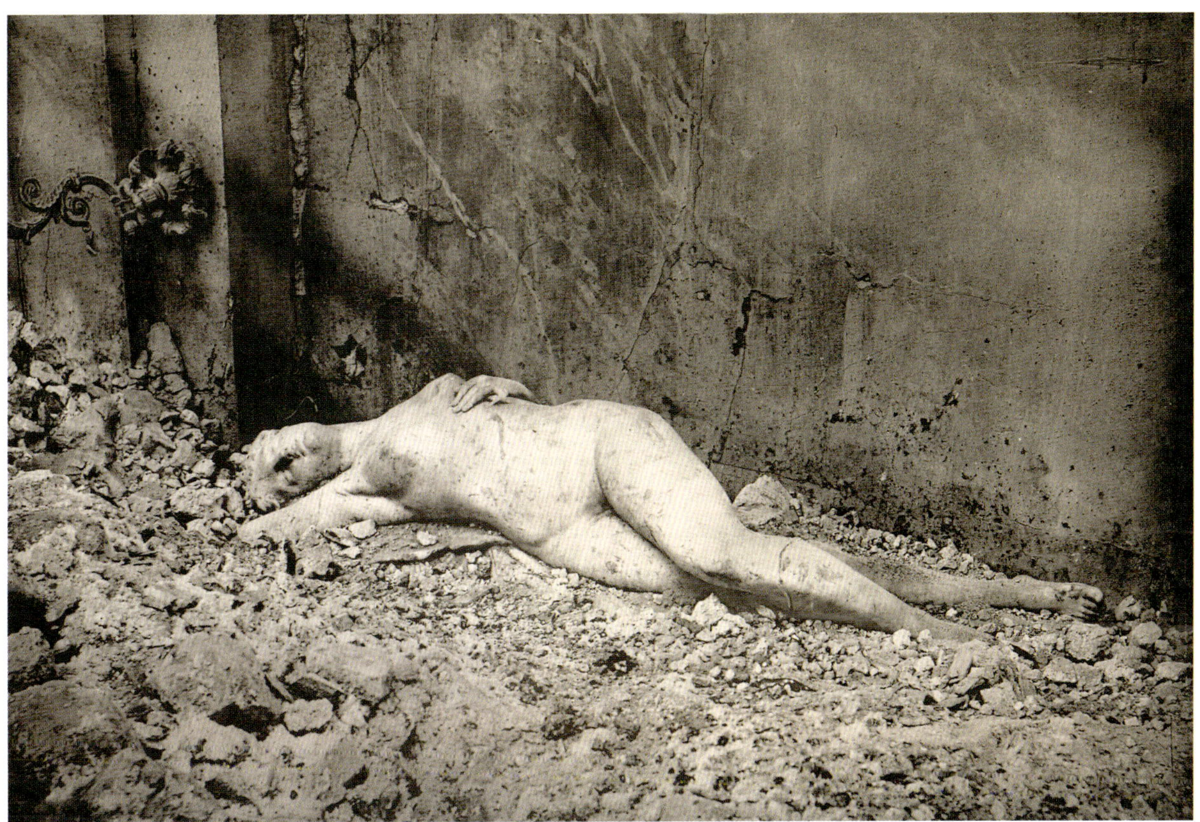

DIE »VERWUNDETE« STATUE

Noch bevor deutsche Truppen die Stadt St. Cloud im Januar 1871 im Zuge von Strafmaßnahmen zerstörten, war das vom 5. Preußischen Armeekorps besetzte Schloss am 13. Oktober 1870 durch französischen Artilleriebeschuss in Brand gesetzt worden; hinzu kamen Vandalismus und Plünderei. Ein Mitglied des »Feldphotographie-Detachements« der Königlich Preußischen Armee fotografierte die unter Trümmern begrabene Statue einer schlafenden Nymphe. Betitelt als »Empfangszimmer mit der Statue ›Tod‹ im Schloss St. Cloud«,[18] zeigt das Bild eine Figurine, die in eine Reihe mit zahlreichen anderen weiblichen Marmorbildnissen gehörte wie der »Sappho«[19] von James Pradier oder der »Nacht« von Joseph Pollet.[20] Wahrscheinlich handelt es sich um eines der Werke, die Marius Vachon, Chronist der Zerstörungen durch Krieg und Bürgerkrieg, beschrieben hat:

»Wenn wir uns recht erinnern, standen im Vorzimmer auf zwei Heizöfen zwei Figurinen unbekannter Schöpfer, ›Der Schlaf‹ und ›Die Ruhe‹. Der Kronprinz hatte ihre Mitnahme angeordnet. Sie sind vollständig verbrannt.«[21]

Das Foto der »verwundeten« Statue wurde als Allegorie auf das geschändete Frankreich verstanden, als Symbol für Tod und Leid, ein Motiv,[22] das während des Ersten Weltkriegs und darüber hinaus wiederkehren sollte.[23]

Vachon, der sich in den 1880er und 1890er Jahren im Auftrag der französischen Kulturadministration mit dem Kunstgewerbe in Europa beschäftigte, entwickelte ab 1914 die Vorstellung eines deutsch-französischen »Krieges der Künste«[24], der die Konkurrenz beider Staaten in Wirtschaft und Handel noch verschärfen würde. In einem acht Mal neu aufgelegten Führer widmete er sich ab 1915 den »Märtyrerstädten« Nordfrankreichs und Belgiens und ging dabei auch auf den Kunstraub der Deutschen in Frankreich ein, der einer Schändung der Werke gleichkomme. Unter der Devise »Patria non immemor« (Das Vaterland wird es nicht vergessen) klagt das mit Ruinenaufnahmen aus der Wochenzeitung L'Illustration ausgestattete Buch an:

»Im 19. Jahrhundert bezeugen Straßburg, St. Cloud, Bazeilles und Châteaudun die Geschichte des deutschen Vandalismus, die sich leider im 20. Jahrhundert in vielen tragischen Akten fortsetzen sollte.«[25]

STATISTIKEN UND ANKLAGEN

Nach dem Krieg von 1870/71 wurden die Folgen der Beschießungen französischer Städte und Festungen erstmals statistisch ausgewertet. So sollte vor allem die Waffenwirkung beurteilt werden. Die Zahlen konnten aber auch zur Begründung für staatliche Wiederaufbauhilfen dienen. Die Folgen des Deutsch-Französischen Krieges wurden so als Kurven oder Balkendiagramme lesbar.

Ernst Engel, Vorstand des Königlich Sächsischen Statistischen Bureaus, später Direktor des Königlich Preußischen Statistischen Bureaus sowie Mitbegründer des internationalen statistischen Congresses, gilt als leidenschaftlicher Wegbereiter für diesen quantifizierenden Ansatz:

»Der unverfälschten Darlegung der Thatsachen gegenüber müssen sich nothwendig Meinungsverschiedenheiten, die nur auf objectiver Anschauung beruhen, ausgleichen und versöhnen; und deshalb ist die wahrheitsvolle Statistik nicht blos die Waage in der Hand der Gerechtigkeit, sondern auch das Schwert, worauf sie sich stützt, denn Kenntniß ist Macht.«[26]

Als Abgeordneter des Reichstags des Norddeutschen Bundes begab sich Engel in den letzten Tagen der Belagerung nach Straßburg, um im Namen des »Berliner Hülfsvereins« Unterstützung anzubieten. Vom Leid der Bevölkerung erschüttert, veröffentlichte er 1870 seinen Bericht,[27] in dem er den Wiederaufbau der Stadt forderte und zugleich hervorhob, dass die Zerstörungen nicht absichtlich herbeigeführt worden seien. Mit dem Nachweis, dass Kinder und ältere Menschen den Großteil der Opfer bildeten, und mit der festgestellten hohen Zahl der zerstörten öffentlichen Gebäude, darunter die Bibliothek, dokumentierte Engel, dass die Kriegswirkungen sowohl die Zivilbevölkerung als auch die Denkmäler der Stadt trafen.

Der französische Oberstleutnant Eugène Hennebert wiederum stellte den preußischen Beschuss von Paris kartografisch dar. Seine Folgerung, dieser habe nur geringe Auswirkungen auf militärische Anlagen gehabt, trug mit zur Verbreitung der französischen Vorstellung eines »psychologischen Bombenhagels« (grêle psychologique) bei, der darauf abziele, die Bevölkerung durch den Beschuss von Arealen mit vielen Kulturdenkmälern einzuschüchtern. Den Preußen warf Hennebert vor, sie würden mit archaischen Methoden einer neuen Form der Kriegführung den Weg bereiten: »Dadurch, dass sie am Ende des 19. Jahrhunderts die vor zwei- oder dreitausend Jahren gebräuchlichen Kampfweisen wieder aufleben ließen, haben unsere Feinde das Völkerrecht schamlos verletzt.«[28] Er verurteilte die Beschießung von Städten scharf:

»1870 haben die Preußen 19 unserer Städte bis zum bitteren Ende bombardiert. Durch ihre Beschießung der wehrlosen Bevölkerung mit *über* einer Million Granaten töteten sie 2000 am Kampf unbeteiligte Frauen, Kinder und Greise. Dieses unschuldige Blut schreit nach Rache, und wir müssen uns dieser Opfer erinnern, die sterbend sprachen: Exoriare aliquis nostris ex ossibus ultor!«

Nach 1919 drohte die aus Vergils »Aeneas« entlehnte Warnung der Dido dann in deutscher Sprache von den Grabsteinen der Besiegten: »Aus unseren Knochen wird ein Rächer erstehen ...«.[29]

SCHUTZ VON KULTURGÜTERN IM KRIEG

Zu den ersten Amtshandlungen des neuen »Gouvernement de Défense Nationale« (Regierung der nationalen Verteidigung) gehörten Verfügungen zum Schutz der Museen, Bibliotheken und Archive, die mit Blick auf die bevorstehende Belagerung von Paris getroffen wurden. Im September 1870 empfahl Paul Lacroix, Kurator der Bibliothèque de l'Arsenal, Minister Simon, ganze Bibliotheken in die Krypten der Pariser Kirchen schaffen zu lassen. Dabei erinnerte er an die Zerstörungen, die Franzosen während der Kriege Ludwigs XIV. und der Revolution in der Pfalz und in den Niederlanden verursacht hatten.[30] Bereits Ende August, noch unter Napoleon III., waren die Sammlungen des Louvre und weiterer kaiserlicher Museen in das Arsenal von Brest gebracht worden. Den Ausschlag für diese Entscheidung gaben zum einen die Vernichtung der Sammlungen des Museums und der Bibliothek von Straßburg in der Nacht zum 24. August, zum anderen die Erinnerung an die Beschießung von Rom durch das französische Expeditionskorps im Juni 1849. Am 18. September 1870 wandten sich die Mitglieder der fünf Akademien des Institut de France mit folgender Erklärung an die internationale Presse:

Trümmerstück einer Fiale des Straßburger Münsters
Straßburg, geborgen 1870
Kat. 319

»Als 1849 französische Truppen Rom belagerten, achteten sie darauf, die Bauwerke und Kunstwerke, die diese Stadt zieren, zu verschonen. [...] Zerstörungen über das im Rahmen des Angriffs oder der Verteidigung notwendige Maß hinaus werden nicht mehr als rechtmäßig hingenommen. Und noch weniger ist es zu dulden, wenn in dieses Zerstörungswerk jene vom Genius der Menschheit geprägten Denkmäler einbezogen werden, die der ganzen Menschheit gehören

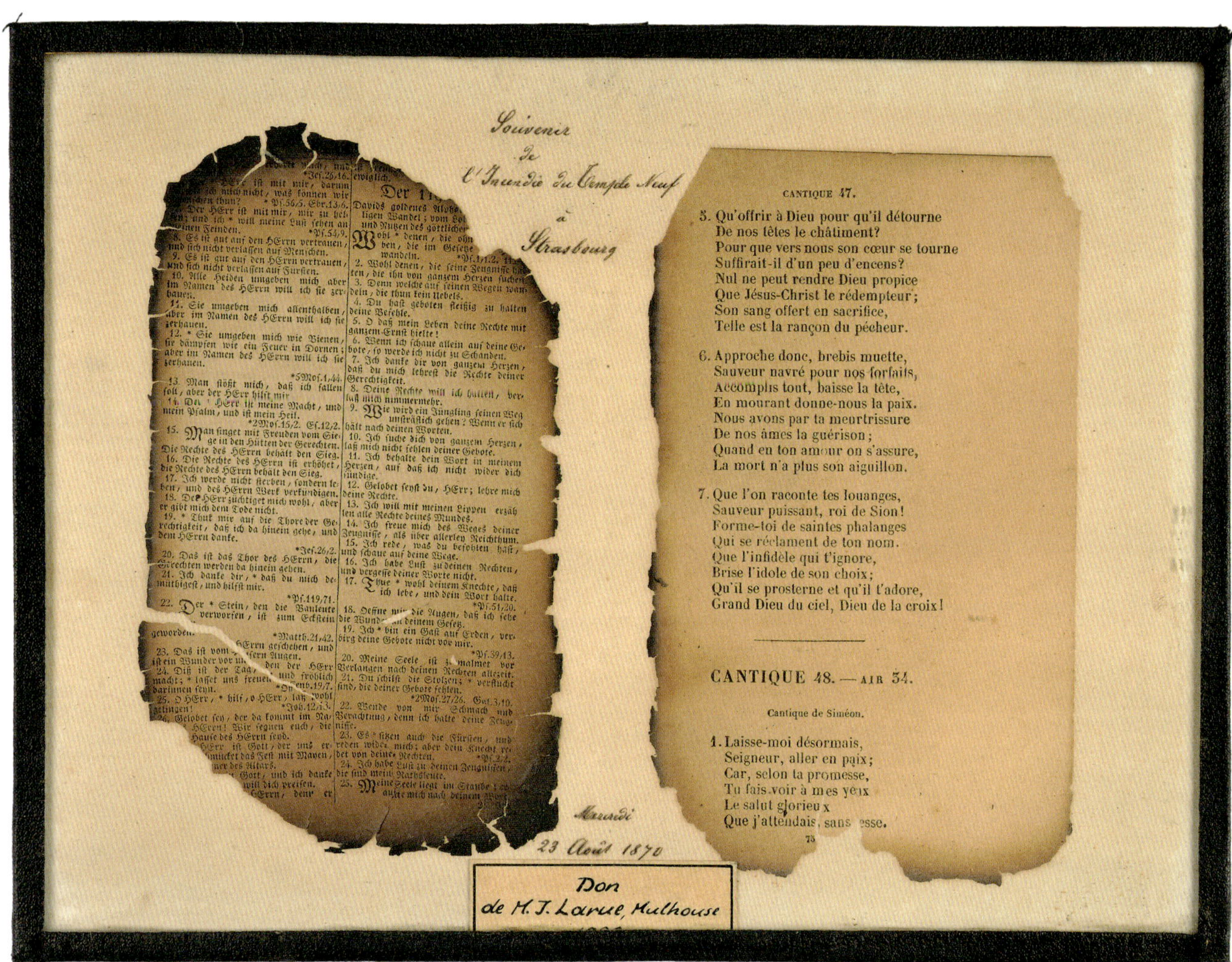

CANTIQUE 47.

5. Qu'offrir à Dieu pour qu'il détourne
De nos têtes le châtiment?
Pour que vers nous son cœur se tourne
Suffirait-il d'un peu d'encens?
Nul ne peut rendre Dieu propice
Que Jésus-Christ le rédempteur;
Son sang offert en sacrifice,
Telle est la rançon du pécheur.

6. Approche donc, brebis muette,
Sauveur navré pour nos forfaits,
Accomplis tout, baisse la tête,
En mourant donne-nous la paix.
Nous avons par ta meurtrissure
De nos âmes la guérison;
Quand en ton amour on s'assure,
La mort n'a plus son aiguillon.

7. Que l'on raconte tes louanges,
Sauveur puissant, roi de Sion!
Forme-toi de saintes phalanges
Qui se réclament de ton nom.
Que l'infidèle qui t'ignore,
Brise l'idole de son choix;
Qu'il se prosterne et qu'il t'adore,
Grand Dieu du ciel, Dieu de la croix!

CANTIQUE 48. — AIR 34.

Cantique de Siméon.

1. Laisse-moi désormais,
Seigneur, aller en paix;
Car, selon ta promesse,
Tu fais voir à mes yeux
Le salut glorieux
Que j'attendais sans cesse.

73

und die gleichsam Gemeingut aller kultivierten Nationen und ihr heiliges Erbe sind [...]. Wir prangern eine solche Zielsetzung vor der zivilisierten Welt als Attentat gegen die Zivilisation selbst an; wir überlassen es der Gerechtigkeit der Geschichte, und wir überlassen es im Voraus der Missbilligung und Rache der Nachwelt.«[31]

Die Belagerungen von Rom 1849[32] und die späteren von Straßburg und Paris 1870/71 markierten eine Wende in der öffentlichen Wahrnehmung von Kriegszerstörungen: durch die neue Verknüpfung des Leids der Zivilbevölkerung mit den Schäden am Kulturerbe, durch Veröffentlichungen persönlicher Berichte und Erlebnisse und durch den zunehmenden Einsatz der Fotografie zur Schadensaufnahme. Die erste Genfer Konvention von 1864 enthielt noch keine Bestimmungen zum Denkmalschutz. Der Gedanke, dass Kunstwerke und Denkmäler genauso geschützt werden sollten wie Ambulanzen, gewann 1870/71 an Bedeutung. Bald nach dem Krieg wurde auf internationalen Kongressen erstmals über den Kunstschutz in Kriegszeiten diskutiert.[33] In der Brüsseler Erklärung »über die Gesetze und Gebräuche des Krieges« (1874) wurden die Zerstörungen von Kunstwerken als rechtswidrig eingestuft. Sie nahm damit die erste Haager Konvention[34] von 1907 vorweg, die von zahlreichen

Staaten ratifiziert wurde, darunter auch Deutschland und Frankreich. Obschon nur in begrenztem Umfang angewandt, legte sie die Grundprinzipien des Denkmalschutzes in Kriegszeiten fest.

Paradoxerweise ging der Gedanke eines universellen Kulturerbes und seines notwendigen Schutzes gestärkt aus dem Deutsch-Französischen Krieg hervor. Er kann noch heute als eine der nachhaltigsten Errungenschaften jener »deutschen Krise des französischen Denkens« gelten, die durch die Ereignisse der Jahre 1870/71 ausgelöst worden war.[35]

Erinnerung an den Brand des Temple Neuf

Angesengte Buchseiten aus der 1870 von deutscher Artillerie in Brand geschossenen Bibliothek Straßburg, geborgen 1870
Kat. 321

Die in städtischem Besitz befindliche Bibliothèque du Temple Neuf beherbergte wertvollste Handschriften und Drucke. Am 23./24. August 1870 zerstörte ein durch die deutsche Beschießung ausgelöster Brand einen großen Teil der Sammlung. Auch das gotische Münster wurde getroffen. Ein Drittel der in der Stadt verbliebenen Einwohner und Einwohnerinnen wurde durch die Zerstörung der dem Rhein zugewandten Wohnviertel obdachlos.

1 L'exception Strasbourgeoise inscrite au patrimoine mondial de l'UNESCO. Mitteilung von Roland Ries, Bürgermeister von Straßburg (https://unesco.strasbourg.eu/lexception-strasbourgeoise-inscrite-au-patrimoine-mondial-de-lunesco/, letzter Zugriff 7.1.2020). **2** Vgl. Sylvie Le Ray-Burimi: Comme un rêve de pierre. Ruines et oubli de la guerre de 1870–1871, in: France-Allemagne(s). 1870–1871: la guerre, la Commune, les mémoires, Ausst.-Kat., Paris 2017, S. 90–97. **3** Vgl. Rachel Chrastil: The Siege of Strasbourg, Cambridge/London 2014. **4** Ordre du jour du 16 mai 1871, in: Lorédan Larchey: Mémorial illustré des deux sièges de Paris, 1870–1871, Paris 1872, S. 306. **5** Vgl. Ernest Renan u. a.: Rapport au Ministre du 24 mai 187 sur les musées et les bibliothèques suite à une mission dans Paris; Eugène Viollet-le-Duc: *État des dégradations causées tant à l'extérieur qu'à l'intérieur de la cathédrale de Paris par suite du commencement d'incendie allumé le 24 mai 1871* (NA, 21 496 B). **6** Victor Fournel: Paris et ses ruines en mai 1871, précédé d'un coup d'*œil sur Paris de 1860 à 1870*, 1872, S. 2. **7** Vgl. Hélène Lewandowski: Les Incendies de la Commune, Paris 2018. **8** Vgl. Alfred de Villefort: Recueil des traités, conventions, lois et décrets et autres actes relatifs à la paix avec l'Allemagne, Paris 1879, Bd. V, S. XII. **9** Vgl. Olivier Le Troquer: Des rites de l'événement à l'événement ritualisé. L'effacement interprétatif d'une révolution: le 4 septembre 1870, in: Hypothèses 1997, Paris 1998, S. 31–40. **10** Vgl. Alain Chevalier: Le temps de la statuaire, 1860–1930, in: Un Empereur de bronze et de papier, Vizille, Musée de la Révolution française – Domaine de Vizille 2015, S. 34–67. **11** Schreiben Houssayes an Simon, 27.9.1870 (NA, 87AP/9). **12** Fournel: Paris et ses ruines, 1872, S. 4. **13** Au gouvernement de la Défense nationale, von Courbet gezeichnetes Schreiben (BnF, Est. Yb3 1739,4°, b7), und Petra Ten-Doesschate Chu (Hg.): Correspondance de Courbet, Paris 1996, S. 342. **14** Vgl. NA, F 21/1566, Dok. 66. **15** Fournel: Paris et ses ruines, 1872, S. 45. **16** Vgl. Schreiben Lefuels an Simon, 25.1.1871 (NA, F 21/1566, Dok. 67). **17** Vgl. Laure Ducos: La restauration de la colonne Vendôme in Laure-Ducos: Alfred-Nicolas Normand (1822–1909) ou les leçons de Rome. Thèse dirigée par Jean-Baptiste Minnaert et soutenue le 24 septembre 2013. Tours, Université François Rabelais de Tours, 2013, S. 591–601 (www.applis.univ-tours.fr/theses/2014/laure.ducos_3312.pdf, letzter Zugriff 6.1.2020). **18** Vgl. France-Allemagne(s). 1870–1871, Ausst.-Kat. 2017, S. 96 und 270. **19** Für diese Information danke ich Stéphanie Deschamps-Tan, Kuratorin für Skulpturen des 19. Jahrhunderts im Louvre. **20** Vgl. Catherine Granger: Le palais de Saint-Cloud sous le second Empire: décor intérieur, in: Livraisons d'histoire de l'architecture, 1, 1. Halbjahr 2001, S. 55. **21** Marius Vachon: Le château de Saint-Cloud. Son incendie en 1870. Inventaire des œuvres d'art détruites ou sauvées, Paris 1880, S. 22 und 58. **22** Vgl. Jean-Marc Hofman (Hg.): 1914–1918. Le patrimoine s'en va-t'en guerre, Ausst.-Kat., Paris 2016. **23** Vgl. Henry La Farge: L'Europe blessée. Inventaire photographique des monuments détruits, New York 1946. **24** Marius Vachon: La Guerre artistique avec l'Allemagne. L'organisation de la victoire, Paris 1916. **25** Marius Vachon: Les Villes martyres de France et de Belgique. Statistique des villes et villages détruits par les Allemands dans les deux pays, Paris 1920, S. 187 f. **26** Ernst Engel: Ueber die Bedeutung der Bevölkerungs-Statistik, in: Zeitschrift des Statistischen Bureaus des Königlich Sächsischen Ministeriums des Innern, 1. Jg., 1855, S. 150. **27** Ernst Engel: Erlebnisse und Wahrnehmungen bei Ueberbringung einer Sendung von Liebesgaben des Berliner Hülfsvereins für die deutschen Armeen im Felde an die Belagerungstruppen von Strassburg, Berlin 1870, S. 18–24. **28** H. de Sarrepont (Ps. von E. Hennebert): Le Bombardement de Paris par les Prussiens en janvier 1871, Paris 1872, S. 202. **29** Vergil: Aeneis, IV, fünfter Gesang. **30** Vgl. Schreiben Lacroix' an Simon, 7.9.1870 (NA, 87AP/9). **31** Protokoll der Erklärung des Institut de France, gez. Victor Baltard (Präsident der Académie des Beaux-arts et des Instituts) und Ernest Renan (Präsident der Académie des Inscriptions et des Belles Lettres), in: Le Temps, 20.9.1870 (NA, 87 AP/9). **32** Vgl. Sylvie Le Ray-Burimi: Rome, année 1849: regards croisés sur un patrimoine monumental menace, in: Napoléon III et l'Italie. Naissance d'une Nation, 1848–1870, Ausst.-Kat. Musée de l'Armée, 19.10.2011–15.1.2012, Paris 2011, S. 143–152. **33** Vgl. Charles-Nicolas Normand (Generalsekretär): Congrès international pour la protection des œuvres d'art et des monuments, tenu à Paris, du 24 au 29 juin 1889. Procès-verbaux et sommaires, Paris 1889; vgl. Pierre Leveau: Le souvenir de la Grande Guerre dans les réseaux de conservation de l'Entre-Deux-Guerres. Une préhistoire du Bouclier bleu, in: In Situ, 23 (2014) (http://insitu.revues.org/10903, letzter Zugriff 7.7.2017). **34** Vgl. Convention (IV) concernant les lois et coutumes de la guerre sur terre et son Annexe. La Haye, 18 octobre 1907, in: Deuxième Conférence internationale de la Paix, Actes et Documents, La Haye 1907, Bd. 1, S. 626–637. **35** Claude Digeon: La crise allemande de la pensée française (1870–1914), Paris 1959.

Gr.
Chloroform
0 20 40 60 80
100 80 60 40 20

An der Schwelle zum modernen Krieg

Offene Feldschlachten, Reiterattacken und bunte Uniformen lassen häufig vergessen, wie viele Elemente der Kriege von 1864, 1866 und 1870/71 dem Ersten Weltkrieg näher waren als den Kabinettskriegen des 18. Jahrhunderts. In den Kriegen der Französischen Revolution und Napoleons waren erstmals Massenheere aufgeboten worden, die mehrheitlich aus eingezogenen Bürgern oder Untertanen bestanden. Die Operationsführung wurde dynamischer, aggressiver und verlustreicher. Die gleichzeitig einsetzende industrielle Revolution zeigte indes erst ab der Mitte des 19. Jahrhunderts Auswirkungen. Rüstungsfabriken ersetzten Manufakturen. Die Produktion von Waffen, militärischer Bekleidung und Ausrüstung wurde standardisiert, konzentriert und mechanisiert. Die Entwicklung gezogener Rohre bzw. Läufe und von Hinterladesystemen steigerte die Wirkung von Artillerie und Handwaffen enorm, doch die Gefechtstaktik mit Truppenbewegungen in dichten Formationen trug dem kaum Rechnung. Dampfkraft revolutionierte das Verkehrs- und Transportwesen und die Telegrafie die Kommunikation. Korrespondentenberichte in der Presse schärften das öffentliche Bewusstsein für das Leid, das Kriege verursachen. Zunehmend wurden Kriege als Sache der ganzen Nation betrachtet. Bürgerinnen und Bürger organisierten sich, um das Leid auf den Schlachtfeldern zu lindern. Unter dem Zeichen des Roten Kreuzes forderte die erste Genfer Konvention 1864, unterschiedslos Verwundete und Kranke aller Kriegsparteien zu pflegen, und stellte sie genauso wie Ärzte und Pflegepersonal unter den Schutz der Neutralität.

Moltke

Kriegsbild und Führungsdenken

FRANK HAGEMANN

Die industrielle Revolution prägte im 19. Jahrhundert zunehmend den Wandel des Kriegsbildes und der Kriegführung. Ausgehend von Großbritannien, brachte sie später auch in Kontinentaleuropa und Nordamerika eine stark beschleunigte Entwicklung von Wissenschaft, Technik und Produktivität mit sich. Der Übergang von der Agrar- zur Industriegesellschaft war in den betreffenden Ländern zugleich mit einem hohen Bevölkerungswachstum verbunden. Bis heute gilt die Dampfmaschine als wichtigste Erfindung und zugleich Symbol der industriellen Revolution. Dieser Vorstellung folgend, wird die Bedeutung der Industrialisierung für das Militär häufig auf die Verfügbarkeit einzelner technischer Innovationen in dieser Zeit verengt: Eisenbahn, Telegrafie und Zündnadelgewehr können hierfür als Beispiele dienen.

Die Erfindung neuer Maschinen zog allerdings nicht zwangsläufig einen militärischen Vorteil im Krieg nach sich. Bester Beleg hierfür ist das Mutterland der industriellen Revolution, Großbritannien. Es verfügte im 19. Jahrhundert viele Jahrzehnte lang über einen gewaltigen wirtschaftlichen und technischen Vorsprung vor seinen kontinentaleuropäischen Konkurrenten, ohne dass dies in einer überlegenen Modernität seiner Armee mündete. Viel entscheidender als die bloße Verfügbarkeit technischer Innovationen war der Grad der militärischen Nutzbarmachung, wie man am Beispiel Preußens erkennen kann.[1] Die Industrialisierung begann dort Jahrzehnte später als in Großbritannien. Dies hing auch damit zusammen, dass Preußen über kein zusammenhängendes Staatsgebiet verfügte und dass die vielen Einzelstaaten im Deutschen Bund den Handel erschwerten. Unter preußischer Führung entstand 1834 der Deutsche Zollverein, der einen einheitlichen Wirtschaftsraum herstellte. Es gelang, ein umfassendes Transport-, Verkehrs- und Fernmeldesystem (Eisenbahn, Schifffahrt, Telegrafie) zu schaffen. Vor allem im Ruhrgebiet und in Oberschlesien entwickelte sich zudem eine leistungsfähige Großindustrie.

Darüber hinaus entwickelte sich in Preußen schon sehr früh ein politisches Bewusstsein für die militärische Nutzbarmachung all dieser industriellen Kapazitäten. Wichtigster militärischer Vordenker der letzteren Entwicklung war Generalfeldmarschall Helmuth Graf von Moltke (1800–1891), seit 1857 Chef des Generalstabs der preußischen Armee. Während viele Soldaten die damaligen technischen Innovationen zunächst lediglich als neue militärische Hilfsmittel begriffen, erkannte Moltke, dass Eisenbahn und Telegrafie den Charakter der

Helmuth von Moltke und Angehörige seines Stabs in Versailles
Aus Heinrich Schnaebelis »Album der Proclamirung des deutschen Kaiserreiches im Schlosse zu Versailles, 18. Januar 1871«, Berlin
Abb. 26

Kriegführung grundsätzlich verändern würden. Die Entscheidung in einem künftigen Krieg könne schneller fallen, wenn man die neuen technischen Möglichkeiten zielgerichtet für Mobilmachung, Aufmarsch und Operationsführung nutzte. Der Sieg im Feldzug von 1866 gegen Österreich und dessen Verbündete bestätigte erstmals Moltkes militärische Ansichten und begründete seinen Ruhm als Feldherr.[2]

VOLKSKRIEG UND VERNICHTUNGSSCHLACHT

Moltke verengte seinen Blick nicht auf die rein technologische Seite der Kriegführung. Anknüpfend an Clausewitz, berücksichtigte er auch die politischen und gesellschaftlichen Veränderungen infolge der Französischen Revolution. Im Zeitalter der Volkskriege sei es nicht mehr ausreichend, das Land des Gegners zu besetzen, vielmehr bedürfe es eines psychologisch überwältigenden Sieges, der den Willen des Feindes und seiner Volksmassen breche. Daher könne in der Regel allein die Zerstörung der feindlichen Hauptmacht in einer Vernichtungsschlacht die Entscheidung möglichst schnell herbeiführen. Moltke ging es dabei nicht um die physische Vernichtung des Feindes, sondern um die Vernichtung seiner Kampfkraft, das heißt seiner Fähigkeit und seines Willens, den Kampf fortzusetzen.

→
»Übersichtskarte über die im Kriege 1870/71 durch die Deutschen in Betrieb genommenen französischen Eisenbahnen«
Aus Hermann Buddes Buch »Die Französischen Eisenbahnen im deutschen Kriegsbetriebe 1870/71«, Berlin 1904
Kat. 399

Wiederum anknüpfend an Clausewitz, hielt Moltke aufgrund der Unberechenbarkeit des Krieges nur den Beginn eines Feldzugs für planbar: »Kein Operationsplan reicht mit einiger Sicherheit über das erste Zusammentreffen mit der feindlichen Hauptmacht hinaus.«[3] Dementsprechend bezeichnete er die Strategie als »System von Aushilfen«. Den untergeordneten Führungsebenen gewährte er weitgehende Handlungsfreiheit bei der Durchführung ihrer Aufträge. Starre Doktrinen lehnte er ab; von seinen Truppenführern forderte er vielmehr hohe Flexibilität und selbstständiges Handeln im Sinne der übergeordneten Absicht. Eine weitere Folge dieser Überlegungen war die Einführung einer neuen »operativen« Ebene zwischen Strategie und Taktik. Moltke wurde damit zum Begründer des operativen Denkens. Dieses ist bis heute ein wesentliches Element der militärischen Führungskultur im deutschen Heer.[4]

MOBILMACHUNG, AUFMARSCH UND UMFASSUNG

Das mit der Industrialisierung verbundene Bevölkerungswachstum machte eine weitere Vergrößerung der Heere möglich. Bereits im Frieden verfügten damals die großen europäischen Mächte über mehrere Hunderttausend Mann unter Waffen. Die Kriegsheere wuchsen durch die Mobilmachung von Reservisten, Pferden und Fuhrwerken weiter auf. Zudem mussten riesige Mengen an Lebensmitteln und militärischen Versorgungsgütern beschafft, bevorratet und verteilt werden. Die Herstellung der Einsatzbereitschaft im Kriegsfall wurde dadurch auf allen Seiten zu einem Wettlauf mit der Zeit. In diesem Zusammenhang gewannen Eisenbahn und Dampfschiff, Telegrafie und Kartografie ihre militärische Bedeutung.

Der Ausbau eines leistungsfähigen Schienennetzes mit strategisch gewählten Bahnendpunkten erlaubte nicht nur eine schnellere Mobilmachung der eigenen Kräfte im Kriegsfall. Der entscheidende Vorteil der Eisenbahn lag im Zeitgewinn beim Aufmarsch: Während ein Infanterieregiment eine Tagesstre-

Von deutschen Pionieren repariertes Eisenbahnviadukt bei Cartigny
Frankreich 1870/71
Kat. 400

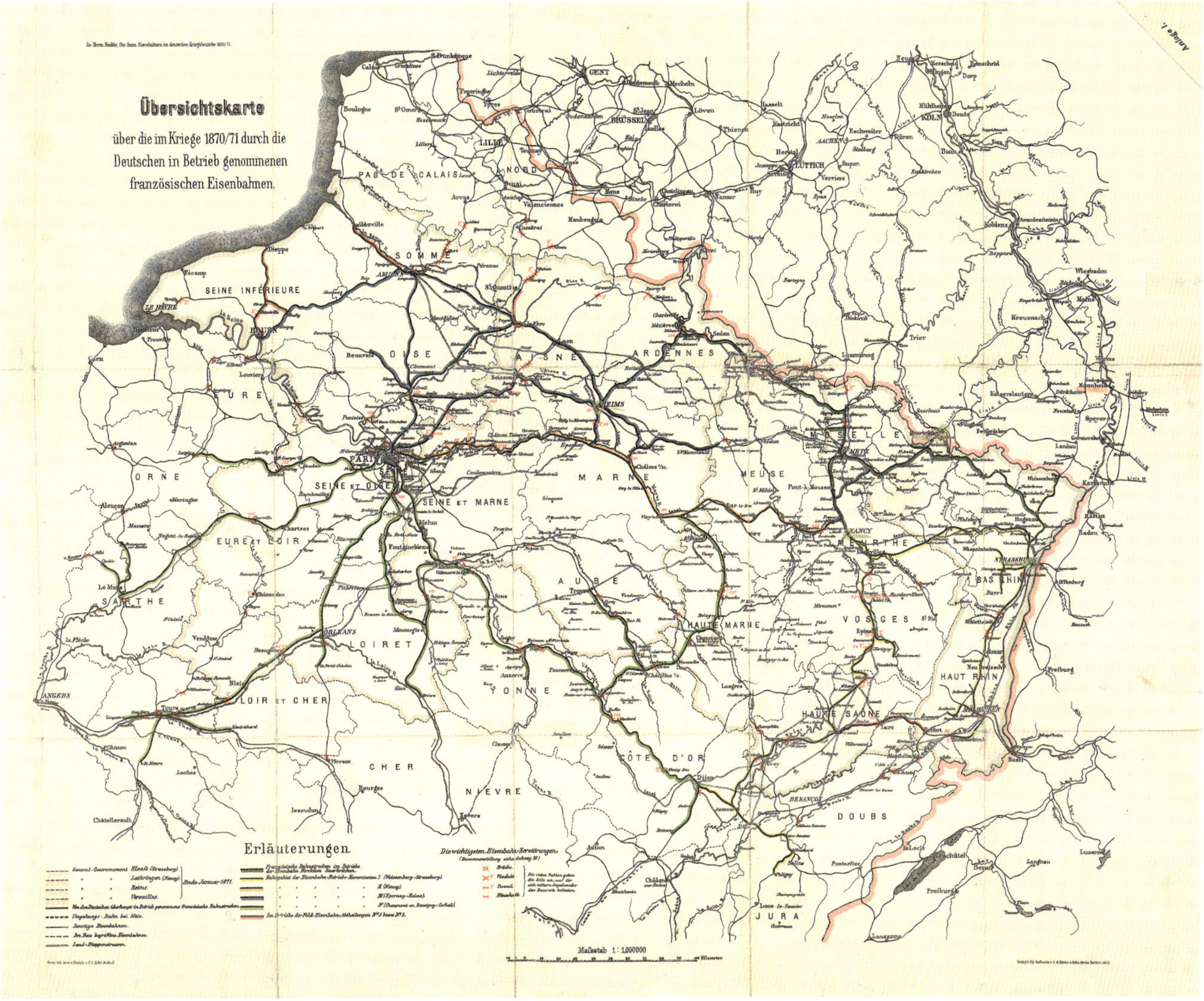
Übersichtskarte
über die im Kriege 1870/71 durch die
Deutschen in Betrieb genommenen
französischen Eisenbahnen.
Erläuterungen
Maßstab 1:1.000000

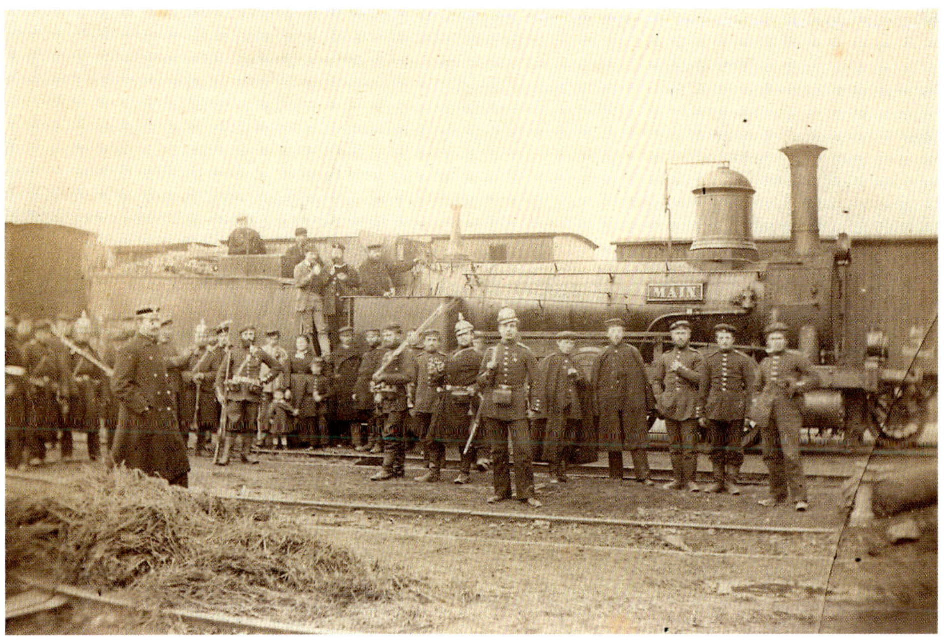

Die Dampflokomotive »Main« auf einem französischen Bahnhof, 1870/71
Kat. 402

MAIN

cke von rund 20 Kilometern, einschließlich erforderlicher Ruhezeiten, marschierte, fuhr die gleiche Truppe mit der Eisenbahn durchschnittlich 25 Kilometer in der Stunde und erreichte ausgeruht den Versammlungsraum der Armee. Außerdem konnten große Mengen an Nachschub bis zu den Bahnendpunkten transportiert werden, um die eigenen Truppen auch über längere Zeit zu versorgen. Sechs bis sieben Güterzüge reichten aus, um den täglichen Bedarf einer 100 000 Mann starken Armee zu decken.[5]

Der elektrische Telegraf wurde gleichzeitig als neues Führungsmittel ins Militär eingeführt. Mit diesem konnten selbst über große Entfernungen sekundenschnell Nachrichten zur Lagebeurteilung nach oben weitergegeben und Weisungen an unterstellte Truppen erteilt werden. Damit war es erstmals möglich, weit »getrennte Heeresabteilungen nach einheitlichem Willen zu gemeinsamen Zielen zu leiten«.[6] Galt bis zu dieser Zeit der Grundsatz, die eigenen Kräfte bereits vor der Schlacht zu vereinigen, ließ Moltke nun seine Truppen von verschiedenen Seiten anrücken, um nach einem letzten kurzen Marsch gleichzeitig gegen Front und Flanke des Feindes vorzugehen. Der getrennte Aufmarsch mehrerer Armeen unter einheitlichem Kommando diente dazu, eine Umfassungsschlacht vorzubereiten, um die feindliche Hauptmacht darin zu vernichten und die Kriegsentscheidung herbeizuführen.

Der Gebrauch der neuen technischen Mittel veränderte auch den Charakter der Truppenführung. Während früher der Oberbefehlshaber vom Feldherrnhügel aus das gesamte Schlachtgeschehen überblickt und seinen Truppen durch Ordonnanzoffiziere mündliche Weisungen erteilt hatte, lag der Schwerpunkt der höheren Führungstätigkeit ab jetzt am »grünen Tisch«. Trotz mancher Vorbehalte setzte sich diese neue Führungsmethode sehr schnell durch, war sie doch eine unmittelbare Folge der vergrößerten Heere, die über weite Räume hinweg eingesetzt wurden. Auf der Lagekarte wurden die Truppenbewegungen beider Seiten während des Vormarsches eingezeichnet. Am Vorabend der

»Die neuen Bahnwärter in Frankreich«

Illustration in Egmont Fehleisens Buch »Der Deutsch-Französische Krieg 1870–71 in Wort und Bild«, Zweiter Band, Reutlingen 1897, S. 539
Abb. 27

In den von deutschen Truppen in Besitz genommenen französischen Bahnanlagen mussten Soldaten, oft abkommandierte Landwehrmänner, Bahnwärterdienste und den Schutz der Strecken übernehmen. Stand der »Bahnwärter« beim Nahen eines Zuges stramm, wusste der Lokführer, dass keine Gefahr drohte.

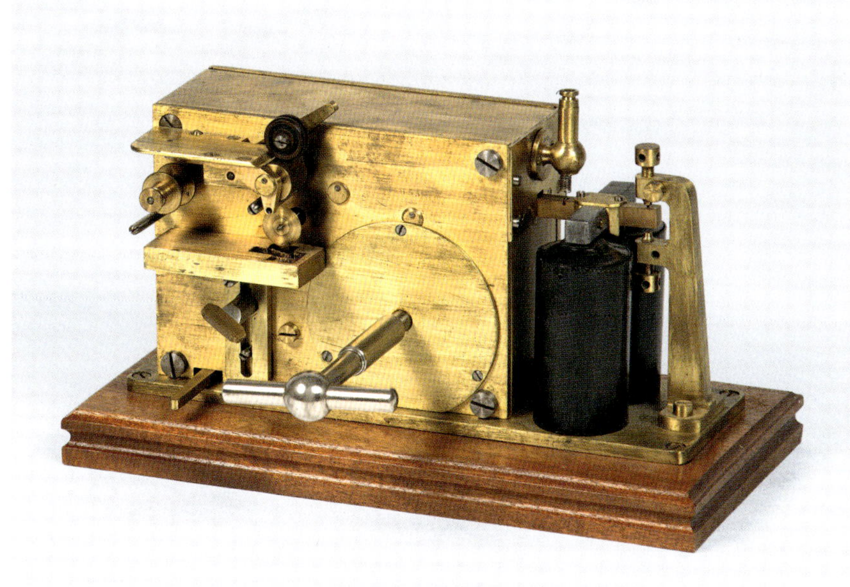

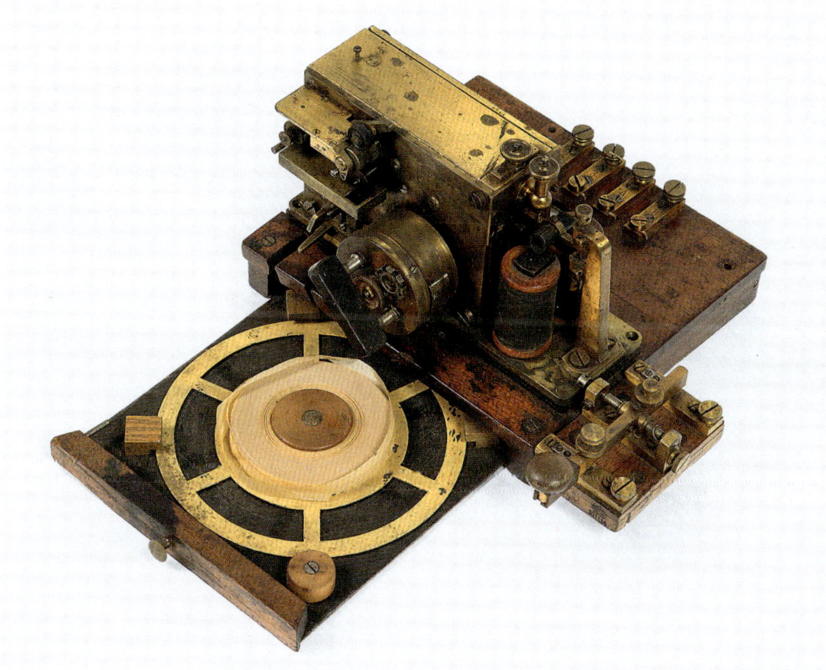

Schreibtelegraf

C.F. Lewert Telegraphen-Bauanstalt Berlin, 1860

Kat. 416

Schreibtelegraf

Königreich Preußen, 1870

Kat. 417

1870/71 war die technische Ausstattung der elektrischen Feldtelegrafie weder in Deutschland noch in Frankreich standardisiert. Es kamen daher alle gebräuchlichen Geräte zum Einsatz, die zum Kriegsdienst abgestellte Angehörige der Staatstelegrafie bedienten. Nachrichten wurden mit Hilfe von Morseapparaten in elektrische Impulse »übersetzt«. Je nachdem, wie lange der Absender mit der Morsetaste den Stromkreis schloss, steuerte ein Elektromagnet im Empfangsgerät ein Farbrädchen, das auf einem Papierstreifen Punkte und Striche von verschiedener Länge erzeugte. Jedes dieser Morsezeichen stand für bestimmte Buchstaben und Zahlen.

Schlacht war über den richtigen Ansatz der eigenen Kräfte gegen den Feind zu entscheiden. In knappen Telegrammen erhielten die Armeeführer anschließend ihre Direktiven. In der Schlacht selbst gab es für Moltke dann nicht mehr viel zu befehlen. Die unterstellten Armeeführer hatten dafür Sorge zu tragen, dass ihre Truppen weisungsgemäß am Ort der Entscheidung eintrafen und dort im Sinne der übergeordneten Führung zusammenwirkten. Aus dem von Moltke praktizierten »Führen mit Direktiven« entwickelte sich in den nächsten Jahrzehnten im preußisch-deutschen Heer die Auftragstaktik.[7]

AvW 1873.

← Abb. S. 278–279
»Moltke mit seinem Stabe vor Paris (19. September 1870)«
Anton von Werner (1843–1915), 1873
Öl auf Leinwand, 190×316 cm
Kat. 476

Die französische Hauptstadt wurde zwischen dem 17. und 19. September durch die 3. und die Maasarmee eingeschlossen. Ungeachtet der Datierung zeigt dieses Gemälde keine Episode, die nachweislich am 19. September 1870 im Beisein Moltkes stattgefunden hätte. Werner nutzte die Symbolkraft des Moments, in dem die Deutschen Paris erblicken, um ein repräsentatives Feldherrenporträt des Generalstabschefs zu schaffen. Am rechten Bildrand sieht man Soldaten eine Telegrafenleitung errichten. Moltke wird so als moderner Feldherr charakterisiert, dessen Einsatzräume zu groß sind, um sie noch überblicken zu können, und der die Geschicke seiner Truppen nicht zuletzt dank moderner Technik souverän lenkt.

Die technischen Entwicklungen im Zuge der Industrialisierung hatten auch erhebliche Auswirkungen auf der taktischen Ebene. Zunächst betraf dies die Infanterie: Mit der Einführung des Zündnadelgewehrs erhielt die preußische Armee ab 1841 die erste Konstruktion einer zuverlässigen Hinterladerwaffe. Während ein geübter Schütze mit dem herkömmlichen Vorderlader stehend etwa zwei bis drei Schuss in der Minute abgeben konnte, war die Feuergeschwindigkeit der neuen Waffe etwa doppelt so hoch. Mehr noch: Das Zündnadelgewehr ließ sich in jeder Lage, auch liegend aus der Deckung heraus, abfeuern und nachladen. Es würde also künftig eine völlig neue Kampfweise der Infanterie ermöglichen.[8] Sein doppelter Vorteil ließ sich insbesondere in der Verteidigung sehr effektiv nutzen. Selbst ein in geschlossener Ordnung schnell vorgetragener Bajonettstoß, wie er zur Zeit Napoleons üblich war, versprach gegen die neuen Infanteriewaffen keinen Erfolg mehr. Das Schnellfeuer der verteidigenden Infanterie erzwang jetzt regelrecht eine weitere Auflockerung der angreifenden Truppen.

Moltke hatte deshalb bereits 1858 eine Änderung der Taktik durch Angriff in Kompaniekolonnen gefordert. Der Übergang von der napoleonischen Bataillonskolonne zur Kompaniekolonne vollzog sich jedoch eher zögerlich über unterschiedliche Zwischenformationen. Bei den Preußen kam es 1866 sowohl zum Angriff in Kompaniekolonnen als auch zum Einsatz von Halbbataillonen. Teilweise wurden sogar schon ganze Kompanien in Schützenschwärmen aufgelöst.[9] Bemerkenswert dabei ist, dass die Änderungen der taktischen Einsatzgrundsätze in praktisch allen Armeen der europäischen Großmächte nicht in weiser Voraussicht der gesteigerten Feuerwirkung vorgenommen wurden, sondern dies erst nach den blutigen Erfahrungen auf den Schlachtfeldern der Einigungskriege geschah. Auffällig ist auch, dass die Erfahrungen im Amerikanischen Bürgerkrieg (1861–1865) in Europa kaum zur Kenntnis genommen wurden.

Bei der Artillerie führte die technische Entwicklung zu einem schnellen Wechsel der Systeme mit einer erheblichen Steigerung der Feuerwirkung. Die älteren glatten Rohre der Feldgeschütze mit einer wirksamen Schussentfernung von weniger als 1000 Metern wurden durch gezogene Rohre ersetzt; die Vorderlader nach und nach von Hinterladern abgelöst. Die nun höhere Reichweite von 1500 Metern und mehr erlaubte eine größere Freiheit bei der Wahl der Feuerstellung. Die im Feldzug von 1866 gewonnenen Erfahrungen führten zu einer verstärkten einheitlichen Leitung der Artillerie auf Divisions- und Korpsebene. Neben der unmittelbaren Feuerunterstützung für die eigenen Truppen trat nun als zweite Hauptaufgabe die Bekämpfung der feindlichen Artillerie hinzu.[10] Angesichts der gesteigerten Feuerwirkung von Infanterie und Artillerie verlor die Kavallerie an Bedeutung auf dem Schlachtfeld. Reiterattacken, wie sie in der napoleonischen Zeit üblich waren, wurden in den Einigungskriegen zwar noch als Heldentaten gefeiert, versprachen aber letztlich keinen Erfolg mehr. Eine wichtige Rolle erfüllte die Kavallerie nur noch bei der Aufklärung.

Trotz der weiteren Auflockerung gaben die neuen Waffen der taktischen Defensive einen Vorteil. Frontale Angriffe führten immer zu hohen Verlusten und meist nicht zum Erfolg. Im Rahmen einer offensiven Operationsführung kam es deshalb darauf an, den Feind mit einem Teil der eigenen Kräfte frontal im (defensiven) Feuerkampf zu binden und ihn mit weiteren Kräften so lange zu umfassen, bis es gelang, einen Angriff gegen seine Flanke zu führen.

Der Wandel des Kriegsbildes und der Kriegführung im Zuge des 19. Jahrhunderts war untrennbar mit den Folgen von zwei unterschiedlichen Revolutionen verbunden: der Französischen und der industriellen Revolution. Der technische Fortschritt erlaubte eine immense Steigerung der Feuerkraft und der Führungsfähigkeit über weite Räume. Zur optimalen Nutzung der neuen Waffen und Geräte bedurfte es allerdings der Entwicklung neuer Einsatzverfahren und entsprechender Anpassungen in der Truppengliederung. Auf diesen Feldern – und nicht in einer insgesamt überlegenen Bewaffnung – lag der entscheidende Vorteil der preußischen Armee in der Zeit der Einigungskriege. Moltke und seine Mitstreiter verstanden es besser als alle Konkurrenten, die technischen Entwicklungen der Zeit für das Militär und die Kriegführung nutzbar zu machen und dabei gleichzeitig den politischen und gesellschaftlichen Wandel infolge der Französischen Revolution zu berücksichtigen. Je stärker alle Potenziale einer Nation für die Kriegführung mobilisiert wurden, desto größer erschien Moltke die Gefahr eines langen Krieges. Sein Streben nach einer Vernichtungsschlacht gegen die feindliche Hauptmacht war der Versuch, auch unter diesen veränderten Bedingungen noch einen schnellen Sieg erlangen zu können.

Moltkes Operationsführung in den Kriegen von 1866 gegen Österreich und 1870/71 gegen Frankreich macht dies deutlich: Sowohl in der Schlacht von Königgrätz am 3. Juli 1866 als auch in der Schlacht von Sedan am 1./2. September 1870 versuchten die Preußen, ihre Gegner in einer Umfassungsschlacht zu vernichten. Weil den verbündeten Österreichern und Sachsen bei Königgrätz der Rückzug aus der preußischen Umklammerung gelungen war, galt vielen der preußische Sieg lediglich als halber operativer Erfolg. Strategisch betrachtet führte die Schlacht von Königgrätz allerdings zur Kriegsentscheidung. Demgegenüber war es in Sedan tatsächlich gelungen, die französische Hauptmacht zur Kapitulation zu zwingen und Kaiser Napoleon III. gefangen zu nehmen. Die Schlacht von Sedan gilt dementsprechend als Moltkes größter operativer Erfolg. Die neue französische Regierung entschloss sich dessen ungeachtet, den »Volkskrieg« (la guerre du peuple) auszurufen und den Kampf fortzusetzen. Erst als Ende Januar 1871 alle Versuche gescheitert waren, die eingeschlossene Hauptstadt Paris zu entsetzen, war der französische Widerstandswille gebrochen. Moltke musste daher 1870/71 erkennen, dass selbst die erfolgreichste Vernichtungsschlacht nicht zwingend eine schnelle strategische Entscheidung herbeiführt.

1 Vgl. Handbuch zur deutschen Militärgeschichte 1648–1939, hg. vom Militärgeschichtlichen Forschungsamt, Bd. 2/1, S. 347–351. **2** Vgl. Agilolf Keßelring: Moltkes strategisches Denken, in: Thorsten Loch/Lars Zacharias (Hg.): Wie die Siegessäule nach Berlin kam. Eine kleine Geschichte der Reichseinigungskriege 1864 bis 1871, Freiburg im Breisgau/Berlin/Wien 2011, S. 102–107. **3** Helmut von Moltke: »Über Strategie« (1871), zitiert nach: Moltkes Militärische Werke, Bd. 2/2: Die Tätigkeit als Chef des Generalstabs der Armee im Frieden, Berlin 1900, S. 291. **4** Vgl. Gerhard Groß: Mythos und Wirklichkeit. Operatives Denken im preußisch-deutschen Heer von Moltke d. Ä. bis Heusinger, Paderborn 2012. **5** Vgl. Klaus-Jürgen Bremm: Die Eisenbahnen 1864–1871, in: Loch/Zacharias (Hg.): Siegessäule, 2011, S. 64–71; Siegfried Fiedler: Taktik und Strategie der Einigungskriege 1848–1871, Bonn 1991, S. 139–142. **6** Moltkes Militärische Werke, Bd. 4/1: Kriegslehren. Die operativen Vorbereitungen zur Schlacht, Berlin 1911, S. 259. **7** Marco Sigg: Der Unterführer als Feldherr im Taschenformat. Theorie und Praxis der Auftragstaktik im deutschen Heer 1869–1945, Paderborn 2014. **8** Vgl. Eugen Lisewski: Der Mythos der Zündnadelwaffe als Gipfel der Handwaffenentwicklung, in: Loch/Zacharias (Hg.): Siegessäule, 2011, S. 58–63. **9** Vgl. Georg Ortenburg: Waffen der Einigungskriege 1848–1871, Bonn 1990, S. 135–149. **10** Vgl. ebd., S. 158–165.

Blick über den großen Teich

Der Amerikanische Bürgerkrieg 1861–1865

Der Bürgerkrieg zwischen den Nord- und Südstaaten der USA setzte Maßstäbe – etwa beim Einsatz von modernen Geschützen, Eisenbahnen, Telegrafen, bei der Entwicklung des Sanitätswesens und nicht zuletzt der fotografischen Berichterstattung über den Krieg. In Europa wurden die Ereignisse mit Interesse verfolgt, eine konkrete militärische Auswertung geschah jedoch in sehr unterschiedlichem Maß. Mitte März 1863 reiste der Ingenieuroffizier Justus Scheibert (1831–1903) im Auftrag des preußischen Kriegsministeriums für sieben Monate an Schauplätze des Amerikanischen Bürgerkriegs. Er schloss sich, anders als geplant, vor allem den Truppen der Südstaaten an. Bei seiner Rückkehr nahm er am Deutsch-Dänischen Krieg teil und später auch an den Kriegen von 1866 und 1870/71. Scheibert publizierte bis in die 1890er Jahre hinein immer wieder zu seinen Erlebnissen und Erkenntnissen. An der Kriegsakademie in Berlin hingegen wurde der Amerikanische Bürgerkrieg kaum wahrgenommen.

Schreiben vom Chef des Ingenieurkorps, General Wilhelm von Radziwill, an Kriegsminister Albrecht von Roon wegen Entsendung eines Beobachters in die USA
Briefentwurf, Berlin, 16. Januar 1863, und Transkript
Kat. 58

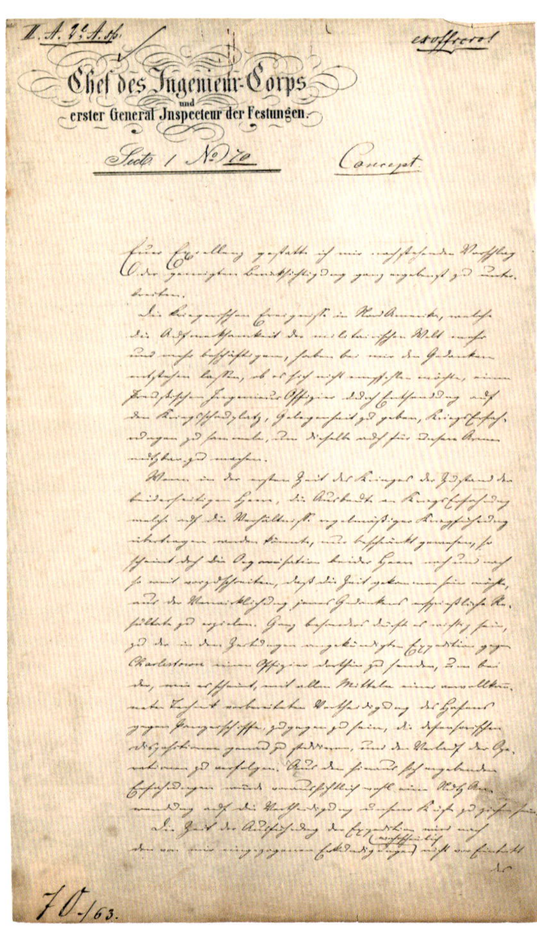
Chef des Ingenieur-Corps und erster General Inspecteur der Festungen.

Concept

Kat. 58

N - 12 880

Chef des Ingenieur-Corps
und erster General Inspecteur der Festungen

Concept

Euer Excellenz gestatte ich mir nachstehenden Vorschlag der geneigten Berücksichtigung ganz ergebenst zu unterbreiten.

Die kriegerischen Ereignisse in NordAmerika, welche die Aufmerksamkeit der militairischen Welt mehr und mehr beschäftigen, haben bei mir den Gedanken entstehen lassen, ob es sich nicht empfehlen möchte, einen Preußischen Ingenieur Offizier durch Entsendung auf den Kriegsschauplatz, Gelegenheit zu geben, KriegsErfahrungen zu sammeln, um dieselbe auch für unsere Armee nutzbar zu machen.

Wenn in der ersten Zeit des Krieges der Zustand der beiderseitigen Heere, die Ausbeute an KriegsErfahrungen, welche auf die Verhältnisse regelmäßiger Kriegführung übertragen werden könnte, nur beschränkt gewesen, so scheint doch die Organisation beider Heere nach und nach so weit vorzuschreiten, daß die Zeit gekommen sein möchte, aus der Verwirklichung jenes Gedankens ersprießliche Resultate zu erzielen. Ganz besonders dürfte es wichtig sein, zu der in den Zeitungen angekündigten Expedition gegen Charlestown einen Offizier dorthin zu senden, um bei der, wie es scheint, mit allen Mitteln einer vervollkommneten Technik vorbereiteten Vertheidigung des Hafens gegen Panzuerschiffe, zugegen zu sein, die defensivischen Dispositionen genauer zu studieren, und den Verlauf der Operationen zu verfolgen. Aus den hieraus sich ergebenden Erfahrungen würde voraussichtlich wohl eine NutzAnwendung auf die Vertheidigung unserer Küste zu ziehen sein.

Die Zeit der Ausführung der Expedition wird nach den von mir eingezogenen Erkundigungen wahrscheinlich nicht vor Eintritt des

Kat. 58

Kat. 59

Unfall auf der Eisenbahnlinie Alexandria & Orange, ausgelöst von Rebellen, 1862

Andrew Joseph Russell (1830–1902)
Kat. 59

Diese Lokomotive entgleiste durch einen Sabotageakt der Südstaaten-Kavallerie. Eisenbahnen wurden im Amerikanischen Bürgerkrieg erstmals im großen Maßstab für Truppen-, Verwundeten- und Materialtransporte eingesetzt. Truppen auf dem Rückzug zerstörten deshalb gezielt Bahngleise.

»A Harvest of Death« / Wenn der Tod Ernte hält Das Schlachtfeld von Gettysburg am 4. Juli 1863

Timothy H. O'Sullivan (ca. 1840–1882)
Aus »Alexander Gardner's Photographic Sketch Book of the Civil War«
Kat. 60

Kat. 60

Reisten im Krimkrieg nur eine Handvoll Fotografen an die Kriegsschauplätze, so waren im Amerikanischen Bürgerkrieg bereits Hunderte Fotografen mit ihren Dunkelkammerwagen unterwegs. Wie in keinem anderen Krieg des 19. Jahrhunderts wurden Tote zum Fotomotiv.

Entwicklung der Bewaffnung zwischen 1850 und 1870

DIETER STORZ

Bis in den Ersten Weltkrieg hinein unterschied das Militärwesen »Feldkrieg« und »Festungskrieg«. In diesem Text wird es um die konkrete Bewaffnung der Feldarmeen gehen, mit der die großen militärischen Entscheidungen der Jahre 1866 und 1870/71 erfochten wurden.

Der Kriegsphilosoph Carl von Clausewitz gelangte bei seinem Nachdenken über den Krieg nicht zuletzt deshalb zu zeitlosen Einsichten, weil er vom Einfluss der Kriegstechnik abstrahieren konnte: Da sie sich seit Generationen nicht wesentlich geändert hatte, war sie für Clausewitz gewissermaßen neutralisiert. Bei der »Einfachheit und inneren Notwendigkeit, zu der alles gediehen ist«, bezweifelte er, dass »irgendein neues großes Hilfsmittel« technischer Art zu erwarten sei.[1] Zwischen dem ausgehenden 17. Jahrhundert und der Mitte des 19. Jahrhunderts hatte im Bereich der Heeresbewaffnung keine wesentliche Wirkungssteigerung stattgefunden. Alle Militärwaffen wurden von der Mündung her geladen, und fast alle hatten »glatte« Läufe, in die Rundkugeln mit Spiel geladen wurden: Ihr Durchmesser war etwas kleiner als jener der Rohre, damit unvermeidliche Verschmutzungen bei längerem Schießen den Ladevorgang nicht behindern konnten. Das ging natürlich auf Kosten der Präzision. Die Wirkung von Infanteriegewehren reichte äußerstenfalls bis 200 Meter, und das nur, wenn sich kompakte Formationen als Ziel boten. Soldaten mussten in dichter Linie stehen, einerseits, um selbst möglichst viele Gewehre einsetzen zu können, andererseits, um sich gegen rasch vorgetragene Massenangriffe der Kavallerie zu schützen. Mannshohe, breite Bretterwände bildeten die »Zielscheiben«, mit denen man damals die Treffwahrscheinlichkeit empirisch untersuchte. Die »wirksamen« Entfernungen der Artillerie lagen, je nach Kaliber und Geschossart, zwischen 300 und 600 Metern. Mit steigender Entfernung sank die Treffwahrscheinlichkeit rasch, sodass ein Schießen über mehr als 1 000 Meter Distanz gewissermaßen unwirtschaftlich wurde. Nur durch den Reichweitenvorteil konnte die Artillerie ihre überlegene Feuerkraft entfalten.[2]

Spezialisten wie »Jäger« und »Schützen«, die für das zerstreute Gefecht und das genaue Schießen besonders ausgebildet wurden, gebrauchten bereits »Büchsen« mit gezogenen Läufen. In deren Inneres waren spiralig den Lauf durchziehende Rillen eingeschnitten, die »Züge«. Die zwischen diesen Zügen stehen gebliebenen »Felder« versetzten das Geschoss bei der Laufpassage in eine Rotation um die eigene Achse, was für eine stabile Flugbahn und somit eine verminderte Streuung sorgte. Für die nötige Reibung zwischen Bleikugel und Laufwand sorgte eine Umwicklung – die »Pflasterung« – aus Leder oder Gewebe, weshalb man solche Waffen auch »Pflasterbüchsen« nannte. Das mochte die wirksame Reichweite gegenüber glatten Gewehren etwa um 100 Meter erhöhen.[3] Weil das Laden solcher Büchsen ein langwieriger Vorgang war und die Schützen sorgfältig, also kostspielig geschult werden mussten, kamen sie für die allgemeine Bewaffnung des Fußvolks nicht infrage.

Schnittmodell des Zündnadelsystems eines Dreyse'schen Infanteriegewehrs M 1841
Königreich Preußen, 1841
Kat. 407

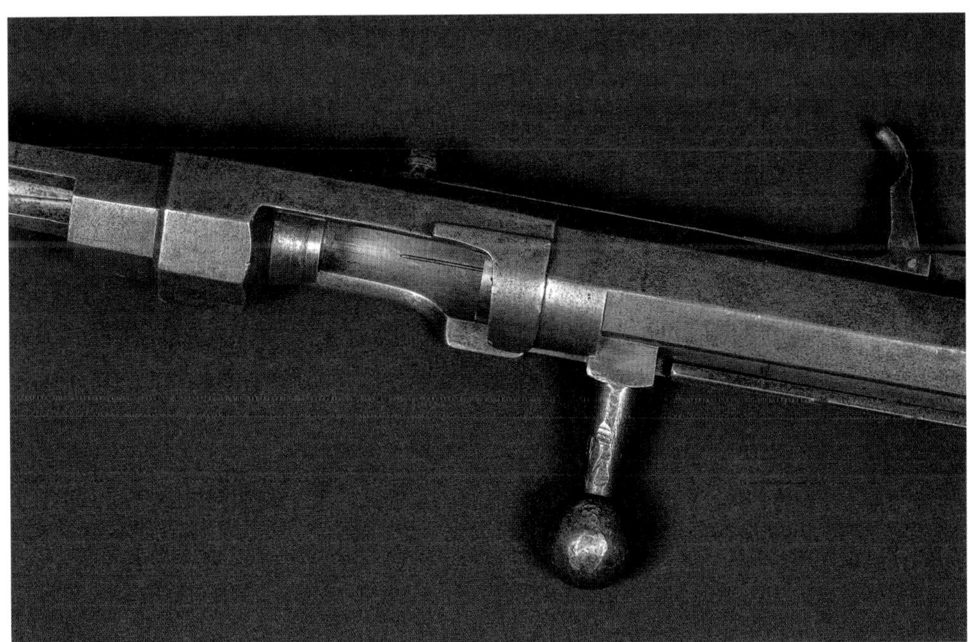

DAS INFANTERIEGEWEHR WIRD ZUR PRÄZISIONSWAFFE

Wenn es nun gelang, diesen Ladevorgang zu vereinfachen, konnte man die Vorteile des »glatten« Infanteriegewehrs – relativ rasche Schussfolge – mit denen der Büchse – Treffgenauigkeit – vereinen. In den 1850er Jahren wurde diese Aufgabe gelöst, jedenfalls für die Waffen der Infanterie. Die Geschosse verloren ihre traditionelle Kugelgestalt. Sie erhielten längliche, leidlich aerodynamische Formen. Vor allem aber presste oder goss man sie mit einem Hohlboden.

Johann Nikolaus von Dreyse (1787–1867), Entwickler des Zündnadelgewehrs
Carte-de-Visite-Fotografie, um 1860
Kat. 403

Ihr Durchmesser war immer noch um ein Geringes kleiner als jener der jetzt allgemein gezogenen Läufe, weshalb sie rasch zu laden waren. Beim Schuss drangen aber die Pulvergase in den hohlen Geschossboden ein, wo sie das aus Blei gefertigte und daher relativ weiche Projektil aufweiteten, sodass es sich in die Züge einformte und dadurch in Rotation geriet. Neue Gewehre dieser Art hatten kleinere Rohrweiten als die alten Musketen. Aber auch ein großer Teil des vorhandenen Gewehrmaterials wurde, wie es damals in der Fachsprache hieß, durch Einschneiden von Zügen für die neue Munition »umgeändert«.

Preußen ging ab 1841 eigene Wege. Der Thüringer Büchsenmacher Nicolaus von Dreyse arbeitete an einem Vorderlader, bei dem das Zündmittel, also das Zündhütchen, nicht mehr von außen aufgesteckt werden musste, sondern in die neuartige Patrone integriert war. Die Zündung erfolgte durch eine axial hinter dem Lauf angebrachte, federgetriebene Zündnadel. Dieses Gewehr war immer noch ein Vorderlader. Hier bestand die Gefahr, dass die Patrone beim Ladevorgang zur Entzündung kommen konnte, wenn die Nadel vom vorhergehenden Schuss noch vorstand. Dreyse beseitigte diese Gefahr, indem er diese Waffe zu einem Hinterlader mit einem Zylinderverschluss umbaute, der nur bei zurückgezogener Zündnadel geöffnet werden konnte.[4] Damit waren weitere Vorteile verbunden: Das Geschoss konnte von vornherein etwas größer als der Laufdurchmesser gehalten werden, weil es von hinten durch die Treibladungsgase zuverlässig durch den Lauf gepresst wurde. Immens aber waren die taktischen Vorteile: Um mit dieser Waffe zu schießen, musste der Soldat nicht mehr stehen – er konnte dabei auch knien, gar liegen –, und er konnte sehr viel rascher feuern, als es mit einem Vorderlader möglich war. In einer Audienz bei Kronprinz Friedrich Wilhelm soll der preußische Major Georg Heinrich Priem,

Georg Heinrich Priem (1794–1870) als Oberstleutnant
Um 1844/1847
Öl auf Leinwand, 36,5 × 31,5 cm
Kat. 404

Der preußische Hauptmann Georg Heinrich Priem wurde erstmals 1830 durch eine Jagdwaffe, damals noch ein Vorderlader, auf Dreyse und sein Zündnadelsystem aufmerksam. Er ermutigte den Unternehmer aus Sömmerda, seine Konstruktion weiterzuentwickeln, unterstützte ihn fachlich und durch Fürsprache bei seinen Vorgesetzten. Ab 1842 wurde Priem, inzwischen Major, dem Kriegsministerium zugeordnet und hatte wesentlichen Anteil an der Einführung des Zündnadelgewehrs im preußischen Heer. Bei seinem Abschied 1852 erhielt er den Charakter eines Generalmajors, 1857 wurde er in den erblichen Adelsstand erhoben. Nach dem Erfolg, den preußische Truppen mit ihren Zündnadelgewehren im Krieg 1866 erzielt hatten, wurde er ebenso wie Dreyse mit dem Roten Adlerorden II. Klasse mit Eichenlaub ausgezeichnet.

← Abb. S. 287
Drei Standardgewehre der Kriege 1864, 1866 und 1870/71: das österreichische Lorenz-Gewehr, das preußische Zündnadelgewehr, das französische Chassepotgewehr
Kat. 162, 163, 231

Das preußische Heer nutzte das ab 1841 eingeführte Dreyse-Gewehr in allen drei Reichseinigungskriegen. In Österreich setzte man aufgrund seiner Treffsicherheit noch 1866 auf das Lorenz-Gewehr des Modells 1854, einen Vorderlader mit Perkussionsschloss. Französische Truppen verfügten ab 1869 mit dem Chassepotgewehr über die modernste Variante eines Zündnadelgewehrs.

einer der Förderer Dreyses, gesagt haben: »Königliche Hoheit, 60.000 mit diesem Gewehre bewaffnete Mann unter Führung eines talentvollen Generals und Se. Majestät der König werden bestimmen können, wo Preußens Grenze gehen soll.«[5] Solche Absichten lagen der Armeeführung indes fern. Die geheim gehaltene neue Waffe wurde seit 1841 für Preußen produziert, und zwar zunächst nur in kleiner Stückzahl für die Zeughäuser. Erst 1858 kam die Bewaffnung der preußischen Linieninfanterie mit dem Zündnadelgewehr zum Abschluss, und ab 1859 wurde die Landwehrinfanterie armeekorpsweise damit ausgestattet.[6] Zwischen dem Produktionsbeginn und der vollständigen Ausrüstung mit dem Zündnadelgewehr vergingen in Preußen also etwa zwei Jahrzehnte.

Eigenartigerweise folgte zunächst niemand dem preußischen Beispiel, obwohl das Geheimnis des Zündnadelgewehrs durch den Berliner Zeughaussturm im Jahr 1848 gelüftet worden war. Verbreitet war die Furcht, die Soldaten würden die rund 60 Patronen ihrer Taschenmunition im sprichwörtlichen Eifer des Gefechts mit einem Hinterlader in wenigen Minuten verbrauchen. So konzentrierten sich alle anderen Länder auf die Verbesserung des Vorderladers. In den 1850er Jahren führten fast alle Armeen neue Gewehre dieser Art ein: Großbritannien 1853, Russland 1857, USA 1861. Als besonders modern galten die neuen süddeutschen Gewehre, deren Laufweiten auf 13,9 Millimeter verringert wurden. Österreich (1854), Württemberg, Baden, Hessen-Darmstadt (1856/57) und Bayern (1858) bewaffneten ihre Infanterie mit solchen Gewehren. 1862 meinte ein damals viel beachteter Autor, »daß das süddeutsche Kleingewehrkaliber schon jetzt die Bedeutung eines deutschen hat«.[7] Das Zündnadelgewehr dagegen werde »niemals eine eigentlich deutsche Waffe werden«.[8]

DIE ARTILLERIE ZIEHT NACH

Die wirksame Reichweite der neuen Infanteriegewehre übertraf die der alten »glatten« Bewaffnung um mehrere Hundert Meter. Dadurch geriet die Artillerie innerhalb ihrer »wirksamen« Kampfentfernungen bereits in den Bereich des Infanteriefeuers. Um auf dem Schlachtfeld überleben zu können, musste sie den Abstand wieder vergrößern, was nur möglich war, wenn auch sie zu gezogenen Rohren überging. Das Verfahren der plastischen Verformung der Geschosse, analog zum Infanteriegewehr, war bei der Eisenmunition der Artillerie nicht anwendbar. Die Lösung fand man in Geschossen, die an ihrer Außenfläche Warzen oder Führungsleisten für die Züge der Rohre besaßen. Das Geschützmaterial ließ sich zu relativ geringen Kosten gewinnen, indem man in vorhandene Bronzerohre solche Züge einschnitt oder die alten Rohre einschmolz und neu goss. So erneuerten Frankreich (1856) und Österreich (1863) das Material ihrer Feldartillerie.[9]

Auch hier wählte Preußen eine andere Lösung, die es einem Zufall zu verdanken hatte: Der Essener Stahlfabrikant Alfred Krupp experimentierte seit den 1850er Jahren mit Kanonenrohren aus Gussstahl, dem Edelstahl jener Epoche. Bei gleicher Widerstandskraft wie Bronzerohre konnten Stahlrohre leichter sein als solche aus Bronze, bei gleichem Gewicht konnten sie länger sein, vertrugen stärkere Ladungen und erzielten so eine höhere ballistische Leistung. Da die Geschütze von Pferden gezogen werden mussten, spielte die Gewichtsfrage eine zentrale Rolle bei der Konstruktion des Feldartilleriematerials. Krupp kombinierte das Stahlrohr mit dem Kolbenverschluss des

Schweden Baron Martin von Wahrendorff. Das 1861 in Preußen neu eingeführte Feldgeschütz war von hinten zu laden und besaß ein gezogenes Rohrinneres. Die Eisengeschosse pressten sich mit einem Bleimantel in diese Züge.[10] Ein Vorbeistreichen der Treibgase, beim gezogenen Vorderlader der Artillerie unvermeidlich, war hier ausgeschlossen. Der Hinterlader verwertete also systembedingt das Treibladungspulver besser als der Vorderlader. Rascher zu laden war er allerdings nicht, da der Ladevorgang beim Rückladungsgeschütz komplex war und dieses wie die Vorderlader beim Schuss nach hinten rollte, was vor dem nächsten Schuss ein erneutes Einrichten verlangte.

Kanonen wurden damals noch nach dem Gewicht einer kalibergroßen Eisenkugel benannt. Die neuen preußischen Rohre waren »6-Pfünder«, was einer Rohrweite von 9 Zentimetern entsprach. Tatsächlich wogen die Granaten 6,9 Kilogramm. Diese Rohre wurden im ganzen Deutschen Bund eingeführt, mit Ausnahme Österreichs, das sich nicht von einer preußischen Lieferfirma abhängig machen wollte, denn zur Herstellung von Gussstahl war die Industrie im Donaureich noch nicht in der Lage. Außerdem kosteten Stahlrohre annähernd fünfmal (!) so viel wie bronzene, deren Material bereits vorhanden war.[11] Die Erzeugung von Gussstahl war teuer, und das Material ließ sich später nicht durch Umguss wiederverwerten. Und wenn Preußen sein Produkt auch den Süddeutschen zur Verfügung stellte, versuchte es natürlich, seinen Einfluss im Bund zu verstärken.

Bronzerohr einer Vorderladerkanone, die auf Hinterladesystem umgerüstet wurde
Königreich Preußen, 1842, aptiert 1868
Kaliber 120 mm
Kat. 409

Die Qualität von Gussstahl variierte im 19. Jahrhundert noch stark. Das wirkte sich auf die Stabilität von Geschützrohren aus. Viele Artilleristen bevorzugten deswegen Waffen mit Bronzerohren. Auch als Fabrikanten wie Alfred Krupp Stahl in guter Qualität herstellten, wurden Bronzerohre weiter genutzt. Dieses ursprünglich als Vorderlader gegossene Rohr wurde unmittelbar vor dem Deutsch-Französischen Krieg mit Zügen versehen und zu einem Hinterlader umgerüstet. Dazu wurde der Stoßboden abgeschnitten und durch einen Verschluss ersetzt, der hier allerdings fehlt.

Zwei Vier-Pfünder-Feldkanonen C/67 der 2. Leichten Feld-Batterie des Rheinischen Feldartillerie-Regiments Nr. 8, genannt »Batterie Leo«
Königreich Preußen, 1867–1872
Hersteller: Krupp, Essen
Kat. 501–502
(siehe auch S. 370–375)

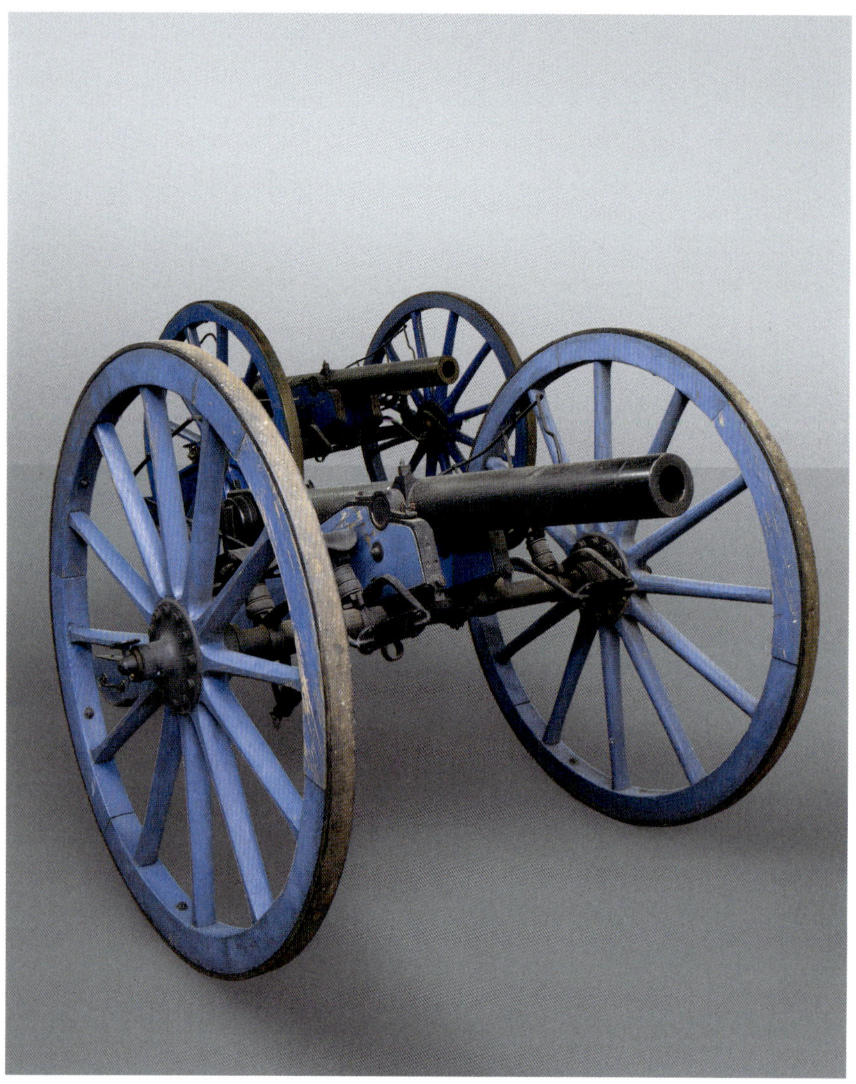

Massivgeschosse, wie sie in der Zeit der glatten Artillerie dominiert hatten, schieden bei der Einführung gezogener Rohre aus der Artilleriebewaffnung aus und wurden durch pulvergefüllte Granaten ersetzt. Die französische Granate hatte einen Brennzünder (Zeitzünder), der sich nur auf zwei Entfernungen einstellen ließ. Die preußische besaß schon einen Aufschlagzünder, was wesentlich zur Überlegenheit der deutschen Artillerie im Krieg von 1870/71 beitragen sollte.

FRANZÖSISCHE VERLEGENHEIT

Zunächst zeigte nun der böhmische Feldzug des Jahres 1866 der ganzen Welt die dramatische Überlegenheit des von hinten zu ladenden Gewehrs über den Vorderlader, mit dem die Österreicher noch ins Feld gerückt waren. Ein Land mit solchen Waffen würde in einem Konflikt mit Preußen militärisch chancenlos sein. Das verhieß vor allem für Frankreich, das doch ein Wort in den deutschen Dingen mitreden wollte, nichts Gutes. Napoleon III. hatte 1857 die einheitliche Bewaffnung seiner Infanterie mit einem gezogenen Vorderlader vom

Kaliber 17,8 Millimeter verfügt.[12] Mit einem so ausgerüsteten Fußvolk erschien ein Feldzug gegen Zündnadeltruppen von vornherein aussichtslos und eine Politik der Stärke somit unmöglich. Es musste also schleunigst ein von hinten zu ladendes Infanteriegewehr her!

Versuche mit einem Hinterlader fanden in Frankreich seit 1860 statt. In nur wenigen Jahren wurden 80 Modelle untersucht, von denen drei in die engere Auswahl des Militärs kamen, darunter das von Antoine-Alphonse Chassepot, das 1866 zur Einführung gelangte.[13] Sein »Modell 1866« bildete Höhepunkt und Abschluss der ballistischen Entwicklung in der Schwarzpulverzeit. Als das Deutsche Reich 1871 ein neues Infanteriegewehr einführte, kopierte es dafür einfach den französischen Lauf vom Kaliber 11 Millimeter. Allerdings verwendete das Chassepot noch das bereits veraltende Zündnadelprinzip. Die Zukunft galt der Patrone mit Metallhülse, die das Problem des gasdichten Abschlusses löste, das dem Hinterlader eigentümlich war. Die Massenanfertigung dieses unscheinbaren Teils warf 1866 für starke Gewehrpatronen noch zahlreiche Fragen auf, und Zeit, sie zu lösen, blieb Paris nicht. Bayern, das zunächst keine militärischen Kraftproben in sein politisches Kalkül einbeziehen musste, konnte wenige Jahre später, 1869, ein Infanteriegewehr mit Metallpatronen einführen. Preußen war noch an sein inzwischen überholtes Zündnadelgewehr gebunden. Die übrigen deutschen Staaten bauten ihre Vorderlader in Zündnadelgewehre des preußischen Kalibers um, soweit sie diese Waffe nicht bereits besaßen. 1870 war die französische Infanteriebewaffnung der deutschen weit überlegen. Der damalige Krieg sollte der letzte Großkonflikt sein, in dem qualitativen Unterschieden auf dieser Ebene eine erhebliche militärische Bedeutung zukam.

ORGANISATION DER RÜSTUNGSPRODUKTION

In den europäischen Großstaaten herrschte das Bestreben vor, Rüstungsgüter in staatseigenen Betrieben zu fertigen. Die Heeresverwaltungen glaubten, dass Beschaffungen auf diesem Weg zu geringeren Kosten als bei der Privatindustrie möglich seien. Außerdem hielt man Eigenbetriebe für zuverlässiger als Privatunternehmen. Viele Kleinaufträge, die wirtschaftlich wenig attraktiv waren, ließen sich bei staatlichen Betrieben auf dem Befehlsweg unterbringen. Indes war es unwirtschaftlich, große Produktionskapazitäten vorzuhalten, die nur für relativ kurze Zeiten ausgelastet werden konnten, sonst aber brachliegen mussten. Bei Umbewaffnungen, die unter Zeitdruck erfolgen mussten, wurden Höchstleistungen verlangt, für welche die vorhandenen Anlagen meist nicht ausreichten. In solchen Fällen wurden die Aufträge auf staatliche und private Fabriken verteilt. Schon damals war es allerdings so, dass private Rüstungsunternehmen wirtschaftlich nur dann bestehen konnten, wenn sie nicht nur für den eigenen Staat arbeiteten, sondern ihre Waffen auch exportierten.

Nicolaus von Dreyse konnte seine Erfindung wirtschaftlich erfolgreich nutzen. Seine Privatfabrik soll insgesamt rund 500.000 Zündnadelgewehre produziert haben, deren weitaus größter Teil von Preußen abgenommen wurde.[14] Beim Ausspruch der Mobilmachung besaß die preußische Armee allein fast 1,1 Millionen Zündnadelgewehre und -karabiner.[15] Die Differenz war von preußischen Staatsbetrieben erzeugt worden. Für die Militärverwaltung bedeutete

Fonderie et Ateliers de Construction H. Gruson

Werbebroschüre des Grusonwerks Magdeburg-Buckau, 1879
Kat. 414

Das Magdeburger Grusonwerk exportierte Rüstungsgüter in alle Welt. Französisch war damals eine internationale Verkehrssprache. 1893 übernahm das Essener Konkurrenzunternehmen, die Friedrich Krupp AG, das Werk.

die Vergebung lukrativer Aufträge an die Privatindustrie auch eine Möglichkeit, das Recht zur Selbsterzeugung von Produkten zu erwerben, an denen die Privaten das geistige Eigentum besaßen.

In Frankreich war die Praxis, Kriegsmaterial in Staatsbetrieben fertigen zu lassen, noch verbreiteter als in Deutschland. 90 Prozent der bei Kriegsbeginn vorhandenen 1 020 000 Chassepotgewehre waren in den vier kaiserlichen Gewehrfabriken hergestellt worden.[16]

Die staatlichen Fertigungsstätten waren zwar leistungsfähige Lieferanten, doch sie waren kaum innovativ. Das machte sich zuerst beim Artilleriematerial bemerkbar. Den Umguss alter Bronzerohre in neue, gezogene konnten die staatlichen Artilleriewerkstätten noch bewältigen. Den modernen Gussstahl vermochten sie aber zunächst weder zu erzeugen noch zu bearbeiten, sodass solche Rohre von Krupp bezogen werden mussten. Konventionelle Teile der Geschütze wie die Lafetten entstanden weiterhin in staatlichen Betrieben.

In dem Maß, in dem moderne Waffen leistungsfähiger und komplexer wurden, stiegen auch die Anforderungen an die Fabrikausrüstungen zu ihrer Anfertigung. Das verlangte teure Investitionen, die sich nur bei größeren Stückzahlen lohnten, das heißt bei Großstaaten. So verzichtete das Königreich Württemberg nach 1871 auf die Modernisierung seiner Gewehrfabrik in Oberndorf und verkaufte die Anlage 1873 an die Brüder Mauser.[17] Das Königreich Bayern, annähernd dreimal so groß wie Württemberg, konnte seine Gewehrfabrik in Amberg dagegen aufrechterhalten.[18] Wirtschaftlich war das gerade noch vertretbar. Der tiefere Grund war aber zweifellos der Wunsch, im neuen Deutschen Reich einen eigenen Betrieb dieser Art zu besitzen und insofern von Preußen »unabhängig« zu sein. Technisch war das Werk natürlich nur eine verlängerte Werkbank für Produkte, die in Berlin definiert wurden.

FAZIT

Die Armeen der sogenannten Einigungskriege kämpften mit einer Bewaffnung, die in den Parametern Treffgenauigkeit und Reichweite den Standard des Jahres 1850 weit hinter sich gelassen hatte. Damit war jedoch kein neues, stabiles Niveau erreicht. Jeder neuen Ausrüstung war es fortan bestimmt, wenige Jahre später von einer neuen Generation abgelöst zu werden. Insofern war der Deutsch-Französische Krieg »modern«. Das französische Chassepotgewehr wurde 1874 für Patronen mit Metallhülsen »aptiert«, und Deutschland ersetzte ab 1871 das veraltete Zündnadelgewehr durch ein Modell von der Leistungsfähigkeit des Chassepot. Schon während des Krieges war der französischen Armee ein neues Geschützmaterial zugegangen, und selbst die deutschen Geschütze, die sich 1870/71 so überlegen gezeigt hatten, gehörten bald buchstäblich zum alten Eisen: Seit 1873 erhielt die Feldartillerie neue Kanonen.

1 Carl von Clausewitz: Vom Kriege, hg. von Werner Hahlweg, Bonn [19]1980, S. 621. **2** Zu den Wirkungsreichweiten der Feldartillerie vgl. Hermann von Müller: Die Entwickelung der Feldartillerie von 1815 bis 1870, Berlin 1893, S. 64. **3** Die praktischen Schussweiten sind natürlich immer niedriger als die physikalisch möglichen Tragweiten. Angaben dazu findet man in zeitgenössischen Waffenlehren, z. B. Joseph von Xylander: Lehrbuch der Taktik. 1. Teil: Waffenlehre, München[2] 1833, S. 104f. **4** Vgl. Heinrich von Löbell: Des Zündnadelgewehrs Geschichte und Konkurrenten, Berlin 1867. **5** Ebd., S. 30. **6** Vgl. Rolf Wirtgen (Bearb.) u.a.: Das Zündnadelgewehr. Eine militärtechnische Revolution im 19. Jahrhundert, Herford/Bonn 1991, S. 146. **7** Woldemar Streubel: Die Kalibereinheit im Bundesheer, in: Deutsche Vierteljahrs-Schrift (1862), Heft 1, S. 173–193, hier S. 175. **8** Ebd., S. 181. **9** Vgl. Anton Dolleczek: Geschichte der österreichischen Artillerie, Wien 1887, Neudruck Graz 1973, S. 550f. **10** Vgl. Müller: Entwicklung der Feldartillerie, 1893, S. 174–177. **11** Vgl. Otto Maresch: Die gezogenen und glatten Feldgeschütze. Vergleichende Untersuchung ihrer Wirksamkeit und taktischen Bedeutung, Wien 1870, S. 230. **12** Vgl. Claude Lombard: La manufacture nationale d'armes de Châtellerault (1819–1968), Poitiers 1987, S. 128. **13** Vgl. Ebd., S. 135f. **14** Vgl. Wirtgen (Bearb.) u.a.: Zündnadelgewehr, 1991, S. 78. **15** Vgl. Gustav Lehmann: Die Mobilmachung von 1870/71, Berlin 1905, Beilage 8, S. 235. **16** Vgl. Jean-Louis Legens/Christian Méry/Pierre Renoix: La guerre franco-allemande 1870–1871. L'armement français, Paris 2001, S. 16. **17** Vgl. Conrad Matschoß/Friedrich Haßler/Adolf Bihl (Hg.): Geschichte der Mauser-Werke, Berlin 1938, S. 35f. **18** Vgl. dazu Thomas Janssens: Die Geschichte der Königlich Bayerischen Gewehrfabrik in Amberg (1871–1918). Ein Beitrag zur Wirtschafts- und Sozialgeschichte Bayerns (= Militärhistorische Untersuchungen, Bd. 4), Frankfurt am Main u. a. 2009.

Alfred Krupp
Schienen und Kanonen

Der Essener Unternehmer Alfred Krupp verbot seinen Arbeitern 1848, sich an revolutionären Aktionen zu beteiligen. Gleichzeitig versprach er, dass jeder seinen Lohn erhalten sollte, egal ob Arbeit da sei oder nicht. Sein bis 1865 auf eine Belegschaft von über 8.000 angewachsenes Unternehmen verstand er als Familie, die er als Patriarch beherrschte und versorgte. Krupps Stärke war die Eisenbahn- und Waffenproduktion. 1853 ließ er sich den nahtlosen Radreifen patentieren, der nicht mehr so schnell brach. Schon ab 1847 begann er, Kanonenrohre aus Gussstahl herzustellen, und ließ sie ständig weiterentwickeln. Während die preußische Militärverwaltung zögerte, zeigte sich Prinz Wilhelm, der spätere preußische König, begeistert. Kurz nach Übernahme der Regierungsgeschäfte erhöhte er 1859 einen Auftrag an Krupp von 72 Kanonenrohr-Rohlingen auf 300 Stück. Nach der Reichsgründung 1871 stieg Krupp zu einem der größten Industrieunternehmen Europas auf.

Krupp-Stand mit Eisenbahnradreifen auf der Londoner Weltausstellung 1862
Kat. 55

Kat. 55

Kat. 54

Kat. 53

Alfred Krupp (1812–1887)
Daguerreotypie, 1849
Kat. 53

Kat. 57

Kleinbahn-Schiene, Breitfuß
Fried. Krupp A. G., Essen 1879
Kat. 57

Mittelteile des Panoramas der Krupp'schen Gussstahlfabrik
Hugo van Werden (1836–1911)
Oktober 1864
Kat. 54

Seit den frühen 1860er Jahren nutzte Krupp das Medium Fotografie für die Selbstdarstellung seines Unternehmens. Mit Hugo van Werden beschäftigte er als einer der ersten Industriellen einen eigenen Werksfotografen. Werbung und repräsentativen Auftritten auf Industrieausstellungen maß der »Kanonenkönig« großes Gewicht bei.

Kat. 56

Bilder von der Internationalen Ausstellung in Paris: Die Krupp'sche Riesenkanone.

Kat. 213

Kat. 412

Ausstellungsstand der Gussstahlfabrik Friedrich Krupp auf der Internationalen Ausstellung in Dublin 1865
London Stereoscopic & Photographic Company
Kat. 56

»Bilder von der Internationalen Ausstellung in Paris: Die Krupp'sche Riesenkanone«
Holzstich aus der »Illustrirten Zeitung«, Leipzig, 25. Mai 1867
Kat. 213

Nach den verlustreichen Kriegen 1864 und 1866 stand die Weltausstellung 1867 im Zeichen des Friedens. Ein Wettstreit der Nationen sollte auf den Gebieten der Wirtschaft, der Wissenschaft und der Künste stattfinden, nicht auf dem Schlachtfeld. Militärtechnische Neuheiten und große Leistungsschauen von Rüstungsunternehmen waren gleichwohl Teil der Ausstellung. »Kanonenkönig« Alfred Krupp erregte Aufsehen mit einem 1000-pfündigen gezogenen Hinterlader-Küstengeschütz aus Gussstahl, dessen Rohr allein 50 Tonnen wog.

21-cm-Belagerungskanone in Lafette, 1871
Fotodruck aus der dreisprachigen, in Leder gebundenen Mappe »Friedrich Krupp Essen A/R.« mit einer Produktschau zu Rüstungsgütern des Unternehmens, nach 1877
Kat. 412

Mitrailleuse und Ballonkanone

Im Deutsch-Französischen Krieg kamen neue Waffen zum Einsatz, die sich nicht unmittelbar bewährten, aber auf künftige Entwicklungen in der Kriegführung vorauswiesen. Die französische Armee nutzte 1870/71 unterschiedliche Modelle von manuell zu bedienenden Salvengeschützen. Diese sogenannten Mitrailleusen wurden 1870/71 oft wie Artillerie und damit zu weit entfernt vom Gegner eingesetzt, sodass sie wenig Wirkung entfalteten. Dennoch waren sie ein Schritt auf dem Weg zu den Maschinenwaffen, die den Ersten Weltkrieg beherrschen sollten. Im Französischen heißt das Maschinengewehr noch heute »la mitrailleuse«. Der Essener Unternehmer Alfred Krupp entwickelte sogar ein erstes speziell für den Kampf gegen Luftziele ausgerüstetes Geschütz – zu einer Zeit, als ein Luftkrieg in der Art des 20. Jahrhunderts noch Science-Fiction war. Die Ballonkanonen, die er der preußischen Armee schenkte, als das belagerte Paris zur Kommunikation mit nicht besetzten Landesteilen Ballone nutzte, kamen allerdings über die Erprobungsphase nicht hinaus.

Kat. 493

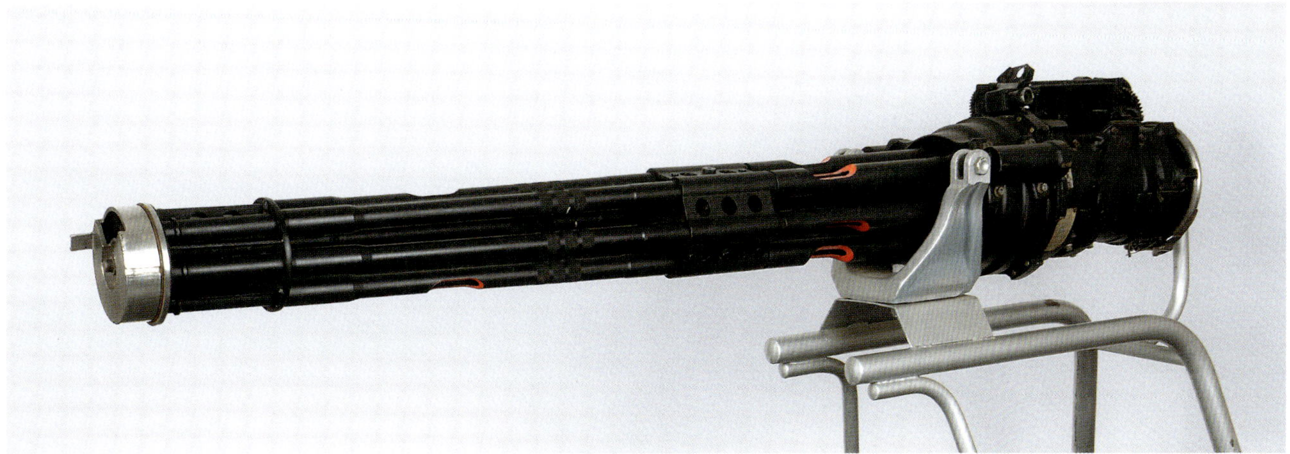

Kat. 498

Mitrailleuse des Systems Christophe-Montigny
Österreich-Ungarn, 1867
Kat. 493

1851 konstruierte ein belgischer Hauptmann namens Toussaint-Henry-Joseph Fafschamps ein Salvengeschütz, das von dem belgischen Waffenfabrikanten Joseph Montigny weiterentwickelt, produziert und 1863 von der belgischen Armee in Dienst gestellt wurde. Die Montigny-Mitrailleuse wurde auch in andere Staaten verkauft, unter anderem nach Österreich und nach Frankreich. Dieses Exemplar wurde in den Werkstätten des Wiener Arsenals oder in Steyr umgerüstet. Aus 37 Rohren konnte es 11-mm-Werndl-Gewehrpatronen verschießen. Die von Jean-Baptiste Verchère de Reffye, General und Leiter der Versuchswerkstätten der französischen Artillerie, entwickelte und 1866 auf Befehl Napoleons III. eingeführte Mitrailleuse mit 25 Läufen basierte auf dem System Montigny (siehe auch S. 190–191, Kat. 226, S. 362, Abb. 41).

Bordkanone M61 Vulcan 20 mm
USA, 1963–1990
Gestell dient der musealen Aufbewahrung und gehört nicht zur Waffe
Kat. 498

Der amerikanische Erfinder Richard Jordan Gatling entwickelte 1861 das im Folgejahr patentierte, erste funktionstüchtige Repetiergeschütz mit acht drehbar um eine Achse angeordneten Läufen. Gatling-Geschütze wurden erstmals von Unionstruppen im Amerikanischen Bürgerkrieg eingesetzt. Anders als Salvengeschütze wie die Montigny- und Reffye-Mitrailleusen wurde das System Gatling stetig weiterentwickelt. Bordkanonen wie diese M61 Vulcan basieren darauf.

4-cm-Ballongeschütz der Firma Krupp von 1870, vorgeführt von einem Angehörigen der Werksfeuerwehr
Fotodruck aus der dreisprachigen, in Leder gebundenen Mappe »Friedrich Krupp Essen A/R.« mit einer Produktschau zu Rüstungsgütern des Unternehmens, nach 1877
Kat. 411

Die Angaben zum Kaliber schwanken zwischen 3,7 und 4 Zentimetern (siehe auch S. 190–191, Kat. 226).

Kat. 413

Kat. 411

Modell im Maßstab 1:10 einer 6,5-cm-Ballonabwehrkanone der Firma Krupp von 1909
Um 1970
Kat. 413

Erst 1909 präsentierte die Firma Krupp erneut ein Luftabwehrgeschütz: eine 6,5-cm-BAK (Ballonabwehrkanone) auf der ersten Internationalen Luftschifffahrt-Ausstellung in Frankfurt am Main. Das Modell zeigt sie in eine Feldlafette eingebaut. Die Waffe wurde zügig weiterentwickelt und im Ersten Weltkrieg eingesetzt.

Nachrichten vom Kriegsschauplatz

FRANK BECKER

Im deutschen Kaiserreich war Clara Viebig eine bekannte Schriftstellerin. Geboren 1860 in Trier, war sie nach eigenem Bekunden durch die Lektüre Emile Zolas zum literarischen Naturalismus gekommen, dem sie sich seither zurechnete. 1902 erschien von ihr »Die Wacht am Rhein« in Buchform. Der Erfolg beim Publikum war so groß, dass der Roman noch im Erscheinungsjahr in die fünfte Auflage ging. Das Buch behandelt die Zeit vom Vormärz bis zur Gründung des deutschen Nationalstaats 1871, doch nicht auf der Ebene der Haupt- und Staatsaktionen, sondern aus der Sicht gewöhnlicher Bürger der Stadt Düsseldorf. Schon der Titel »Die Wacht am Rhein« stellt die Romanhandlung eindeutig in den Kontext der nationalen Frage und des nationalen Einheitsstrebens von der Rheinkrise des Jahres 1840 über die scheiternde Revolution von 1848/49 bis zu den Einigungskriegen von 1864, 1866 und 1870/71.

Die Figuren des Romans sind, wenn auch nur auf unterster Ebene, Teil dieses Ereigniszusammenhangs, sie werden handelnd und erleidend in das Geschehen einbezogen.

So geht bereits die Julikrise im Jahr 1870, diplomatisches Vorspiel des Deutsch-Französischen Krieges, nicht spurlos an der Düsseldorfer Bevölkerung vorbei. Als die Emser Depesche,[1] von Bismarck redigiert und in die Norddeutsche Allgemeine Zeitung gesetzt, beiden rivalisierenden Staaten den Eindruck vermittelt, ihre Repräsentanten seien beleidigt worden, teilt sich dieses Gefühl auch der Zeitung lesenden Öffentlichkeit in Düsseldorf mit. »Soldat oder Bürger«, heißt es in Viebigs Roman, »da war jetzt kein Unterschied, jeder fühlte sich gekränkt, angegriffen in dem, was ihm teuer war: König, Vaterland, Rhein.«[2] Anfang August beginnen die Kampfhandlungen, und wieder sind die Düsseldorfer Bürger und Bürgerinnen kommunikativ einbezogen: Mal sind es Depeschen, mal Extrablätter, mal die »Feldpostkarte« eines Sohnes der Stadt, der bei den Streitkräften steht, die von den militärischen Ereignissen berichten.

Orientierung bietet zudem eine »Spezialkarte« vom Kriegsschauplatz im Schaufenster der lokalen Zeitung; die Maler aus der Schlachtenklasse der ortsansässigen Kunstakademie greifen zu ihren Pinseln und Zeichenstiften, um das Gelesene überdies anschaulich zu machen; schon Anfang 1871 halten die Buchhandlungen die ersten Gesamtdarstellungen des Krieges bereit.[3]

Wie der Roman realistisch schildert, gewährleisteten also zahlreiche Medien, dass die Bürgerschaft der Rheinmetropole über den Kriegsverlauf stets gut informiert war. Dies war keine Besonderheit der Jahre 1870/71, und es war kein Spezifikum Düsseldorfs im Vergleich zu anderen Städten – hatte doch im Lauf des 19. Jahrhunderts in allen Staaten der Welt, die sich industrialisierten, eine dynamische Entwicklung der Medien dafür gesorgt, dass auch in größerer Entfernung stattfindende Ereignisse mit vergleichsweise geringer zeitlicher Verzögerung mitverfolgt werden konnten. Kriege gehörten zu den Geschehnissen, die besonderes Interesse auf sich zogen, sodass für ihre Darstellung in Schrift und Bild besondere Mühen nicht gescheut wurden.

No. 1. Preis 2½ Sgr.

Wacht am Rhein!

Illustrirte Zeitchronik.

Illustrirte Berichte vom Kriegsschauplatz in Deutschland und Frankreich.

Die Wacht am Rhein.

Fort braust ein Ruf wie Donnerhall,
Wie Schwertgeklirr und Wogenprall:
Zum Rhein, zum Rhein, zum deutschen Rhein!
Wer will des Stromes Hüter sein?
Lieb' Vaterland, magst ruhig sein:
Fest steht und treu die Wacht am Rhein!

Durch Hunderttausend zuckt es schnell,
Und Aller Augen blitzen hell:
Der Deutsche, bieder, fromm und stark,
Beschützt die heil'ge Landesmark!
Lieb' Vaterland, magst ruhig sein:
Fest steht und treu die Wacht am Rhein!

Er blickt hinauf in Himmelsau'n,
Da Heldenväter niederschau'n,
Und schwört mit stolzer Kampfeslust:
Du, Rhein, bleibst deutsch wie meine Brust!
Lieb' Vaterland, magst ruhig sein:
Fest steht und treu die Wacht am Rhein!

So lang ein Tropfen Blut noch glüht,
Noch eine Faust den Degen zieht,
Und noch ein Arm die Büchse spannt,
Betritt kein Feind hier deinen Strand!
Lieb' Vaterland, magst ruhig sein:
Fest steht und treu die Wacht am Rhein!

Der Schwur erschallt, die Woge rinnt,
Die Fahnen flattern hoch im Wind
Am Rhein, am Rhein, am deutschen Rhein —
Wir Alle wollen Hüter sein!
Lieb' Vaterland, magst ruhig sein:
Fest steht und treu die Wacht am Rhein!

Müller von Königswinter.

Sie sollen ihn nicht haben,
Den freien deutschen Rhein,
Ob sie wie gier'ge Raben
Sich heiser danach schrein.

So lang' er ruhig wallend
Sein grünes Kleid noch trägt,
So lang' ein Ruder schallend
In seine Wogen schlägt.

Sie sollen ihn nicht haben,
Den freien deutschen Rhein,
So lang' sich Herzen laben
An seinem Feuerwein;

So lang' in seinem Strome
Noch fest die Felsen stehn,
So lang' sich hohe Dome
In seinem Spiegel sehn.

Sie sollen ihn nicht haben,
Den freien deutschen Rhein,
So lang' dort kühne Knaben
Um schlanke Dirnen frei'n;

So lang' die Flosse hebet
Ein Fisch auf seinem Grund,
So lang' ein Lied noch lebet
In seiner Sänger Mund.

Sie sollen ihn nicht haben,
Den freien deutschen Rhein,
Bis seine Flut begraben
Des letzten Mann's Gebein.

Niklas Becker.

»Wacht am Rhein! Illustrirte Zeitchronik. Illustrirte Berichte vom Kriegsschauplatz in Deutschland und Frankreich«
Titelseite der ersten Nummer, 1870
Abb. 28

Die Aufmachung der zahlreichen Kriegsillustrierten, die ab Sommer 1870 das Publikum in Deutschland über das Geschehen informierten, ähnelte sich. Für die noch nicht geeinte Nation stand allegorisch meist eine wehrhafte Germania, wie hier nach dem Vorbild eines Gemäldes von Lorenz Clasen aus dem Jahr 1860. Verwendung fanden auch die Texte der »Wacht am Rhein« von Max Schneckenburger oder das sogenannte Rheinlied von Nikolaus Becker, »Sie sollen ihn nicht haben, den freien deutschen Rhein«.

Generalquartiermeister Theophil von Podbielski (1814–1879)

Aus dem Gedenk-Fotoalbum »Das ganze Deutschland soll es sein. 1870«
Kat. 422

Podbielski verfasste und bearbeitete im Großen Hauptquartier amtliche Depeschen vom Kriegsschauplatz. Diese sollten die Stimmung hochhalten, besonders als trotz des Sieges bei Sedan der Krieg weiterging. Das sozialdemokratische Arbeiter-Wochenblatt »Der Proletarier« vom 17. Dezember 1870 schmähte Podbielski als »telegraphischen Spaßmacher«. Die Ausgabe wurde daraufhin beschlagnahmt.

4 Vom Kriegsschauplatz. Illustrirte Zeitung für Volk und Heer. № 23

Aus Berlin. Eine Depesche vom Kriegsschauplatz. Originalzeichnung von K. Dielitz. (S. 7.)

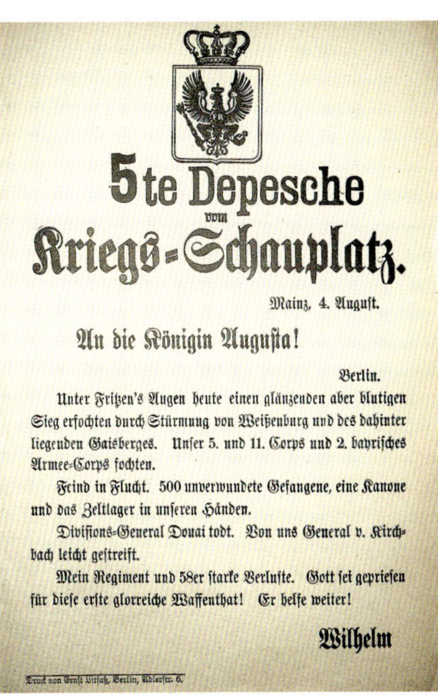

5te Depesche
vom
Kriegs-Schauplatz.

Mainz, 4. August.

An die Königin Augusta!

Berlin.

Unter Fritzen's Augen heute einen glänzenden aber blutigen Sieg erfochten durch Stürmung von Weißenburg und des dahinter liegenden Gaisberges. Unser 5. und 11. Corps und 2. bayrisches Armee-Corps fochten.

Feind in Flucht. 500 unverwundete Gefangene, eine Kanone und das Zeltlager in unseren Händen.

Divisions-General Douai todt. Von uns General v. Kirchbach leicht gestreift.

Mein Regiment und 58er starke Verluste. Gott sei gepriesen für diese erste glorreiche Waffenthat! Er helfe weiter!

Wilhelm

Druck von Ernst Litfaß, Berlin, Adlerstr. 6.

Hurrah!

Am 18. August

Großer Sieg bei Metz!

unter Führung Sr. Majestät des Königs!

Details fehlen noch.

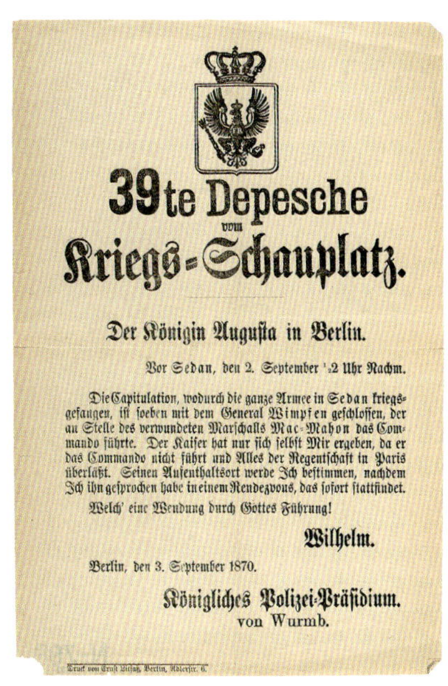

39te Depesche
vom
Kriegs-Schauplatz.

Der Königin Augusta in Berlin.

Vor Sedan, den 2. September ½2 Uhr Nachm.

Die Capitulation, wodurch die ganze Armee in Sedan kriegsgefangen, ist soeben mit dem General Wimpfen geschlossen, der an Stelle des verwundeten Marschalls Mac-Mahon das Commando führte. Der Kaiser hat nur sich selbst Mir ergeben, da er das Commando nicht führt und Alles der Regentschaft in Paris überläßt. Seinen Aufenthaltsort werde Ich bestimmen, nachdem Ich ihn gesprochen habe in einem Rendezvous, das sofort stattfindet.

Welch' eine Wendung durch Gottes Führung!

Wilhelm.

Berlin, den 3. September 1870.

Königliches Polizei-Präsidium.
von Wurmb.

Druck von Ernst Litfaß, Berlin, Adlerstr. 6.

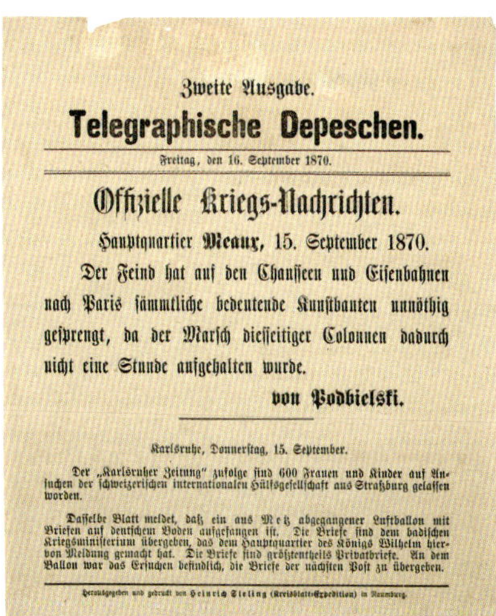

Zweite Ausgabe.

Telegraphische Depeschen.

Freitag, den 16. September 1870.

Offizielle Kriegs-Nachrichten.

Hauptquartier Meaux, 15. September 1870.

Der Feind hat auf den Chausseen und Eisenbahnen nach Paris sämmtliche bedeutende Kunstbauten unnöthig gesprengt, da der Marsch diesseitiger Colonnen dadurch nicht eine Stunde aufgehalten wurde.

von Podbielski.

Karlsruhe, Donnerstag, 15. September.

Der „Karlsruher Zeitung" zufolge sind 600 Frauen und Kinder auf Ansuchen der schweizerischen internationalen Hülfsgesellschaft aus Straßburg gelassen worden.

Dasselbe Blatt meldet, daß ein aus Metz abgegangener Luftballon mit Briefen auf deutschem Boden aufgefangen ist. Die Briefe sind dem badischen Kriegsministerium übergeben, das dem Hauptquartier des Königs Wilhelm hiervon Meldung gemacht hat. Die Briefe sind größtentheils Privatbriefe. An dem Ballon war das Ersuchen befindlich, die Briefe der nächsten Post zu übergeben.

Herausgegeben und gedruckt von Heinrich Sieling (Kreisblatt-Expedition) in Naumburg.

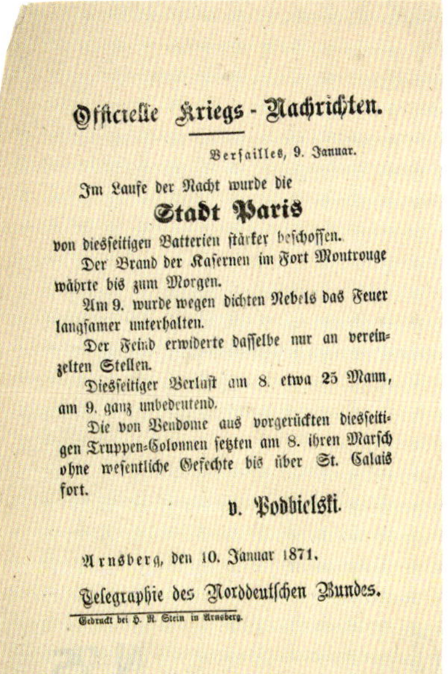

Officielle Kriegs-Nachrichten.

Versailles, 9. Januar.

Im Laufe der Nacht wurde die
Stadt Paris
von diesseitigen Batterien stärker beschossen.

Der Brand der Kasernen im Fort Montrouge währte bis zum Morgen.

Am 9. wurde wegen dichten Nebels das Feuer langsamer unterhalten.

Der Feind erwiderte dasselbe nur an vereinzelten Stellen.

Diesseitiger Verlust am 8. etwa 25 Mann, am 9. ganz unbedeutend.

Die von Vendome aus vorgerückten diesseitigen Truppen-Colonnen setzten am 8. ihren Marsch ohne wesentliche Gefechte bis über St. Calais fort.

v. Podbielski.

Arnsberg, den 10. Januar 1871.

Telegraphie des Norddeutschen Bundes.

Gedruckt bei H. R. Stein in Arnsberg.

Gotha. 29. Jan. 1871, Nachm. 2¾ Uhr. № 170.

Officielle
Kriegs-Nachrichten.

Dem Königlichen Ministerium der Auswärtigen Angelegenheiten ist den 28. d. Mts. Abends spät nachstehende Mittheilung zugegangen:

Versailles, den 28. Januar:

Es ist von dem Reichskanzler Grafen Bismarck und Herrn Jules Favre die Kapitulation aller Pariser Forts und ein 3wöchentlicher Waffenstillstand zu Lande und zu Wasser unterzeichnet worden. Die Pariser Armee bleibt in der Stadt kriegsgefangen.

Berlin, 29. Jan. 1871.

Telegraphie des Norddeutschen Bundes.

Mitgetheilt durch Perthes' Buchdruckerei in Gotha.

←

»Aus Berlin. Eine Depesche vom Kriegsschauplatz«

Holzstich von Konrad Dielitz (1845–1933) aus »Vom Kriegsschauplatz. Illustrirte Zeitung für Volk und Heer«, Nr. 23
Abb. 29

Berliner und Berlinerinnen scharen sich um die 5. Depesche mit der Nachricht vom »glänzenden aber blutigen Sieg« bei Weißenburg am 4. August 1870. Das ganze Volk konnte mitlesen, als der preußische König Wilhelm der Königin telegrafisch über diesen Erfolg unter Führung des Kronprinzen Friedrich Wilhelm (»Fritz«) berichtete.

Depeschen vom Kriegsschauplatz

Unterschiedliche Druckorte
Abb. 30

Die 39. Depesche über den Sieg bei Sedan am 2. September 1870 ist die bekannteste des Krieges. Der letzte Satz: »Welch' eine Wendung durch Gottes Führung!«, wurde immer wieder zitiert und prangte am 25. Jahrestag der Schlacht 1895 in riesigen Lettern am Brandenburger Tor. Die 191 Depeschen aus dem Krieg 1870/71 waren als Büchlein nachgedruckt oder als kleinformatige Fotoreproduktionen in Schmuckalben begehrte Erinnerungsstücke.

»Am Wachtfeuer vor Rézonville nach der Schlacht von Gravelotte bezw. St. Privat am 18. August 1870, abends 10 Uhr. Seine Majestät König Wilhelm I. von Preußen dictirt dem Grafen Bismarck die Siegesdepeche«
Friedrich Schulz (1823–1875), 1870
Bleistift und Tusche auf Papier,
18,9 × 25,3 cm
Abb. 31

Aber auch das militärische Handeln selbst wurde zunehmend durch Medien beeinflusst, die zum Beispiel Befehlswege verkürzten und relevante Informationen schneller zu den Entscheidern gelangen ließen. Napoleon I. setzte den optischen Telegrafen ein, um Nachrichten von A nach B zu senden; selbst noch in der Extremsituation des Russlandfeldzugs von 1812 gelang es ihm, eine Stafette von Kurieren aufzubauen, die für die Strecke Paris – Moskau nur 14 Tage brauchte, während die Briefe seiner Soldaten die französische Heimat erst nach 40 Tagen erreichten.[4]

Große Veränderungen brachten in den folgenden Jahrzehnten die Eisenbahn und der elektrische Telegraf. Die Bahn beschleunigte den Transport von Personen und Gütern, aber auch von Kommunikationsmitteln wie Briefen; der elektrische Telegraf erlaubte Kommunikation in unerhörter Geschwindigkeit, wenn die benötigten Kabel existierten. Für deren Verlegung, sogar quer durch Ozeane, wurden seit der Mitte des 19. Jahrhunderts ungeheure Anstrengungen unternommen. Im Krieg ging es fortan auch darum, die eigenen Truppen an Telegrafenleitungen anzubinden – und die Leitungen des Feindes zu kappen. Im Krimkrieg (1853–1856), in dem England und Frankreich das Osmanische Reich gegen Russland unterstützten, arbeiteten zum Teil sogar schon die Kriegsberichterstatter der Zeitungen mit dem neuen Medium; dies allerdings nur, wenn die Militärs ihnen Kapazitäten einräumten – statt sie allein zu nutzen, was der Regelfall war. Die Reporter sahen sich weiterhin vorrangig an das Medium des Briefes verwiesen. Der bekannteste Sonderkorrespondent aus dem Krimkrieg, der Ire William Howard Russell, löste mit seinen postalisch an die Londoner Times verschickten Darstellungen des Winterelends der britischen Truppen 1854/55 sogar eine Staatskrise in England aus.[5]

»Am Wachtfeuer vor Rézonville nach der Schlacht vom 18. August«
Holzstich nach Friedrich Schulz
aus »Die Gartenlaube«, Nr. 45, 1870, S. 753
Abb. 32

Friedrich Schulz begleitete den Stab der 2. Armee des Prinzen Friedrich Karl ins Feld. Er schickte seine Skizze an »Die Gartenlaube« und schrieb dazu: »Ich stand nur wenige Schritte von der interessanten Gruppe und sah und hörte wie der König dictirte. […] Schließlich wird Sie noch die Mittheilung interessiren, daß die mit Bleistift geschriebenen Notizen, welche sich unter der heutigen Skizze befinden, von der Hand des Königs selbst herrühren […]« (Nr. 45, S. 756)

Neben die schriftlichen traten zahlreiche visuelle Darstellungen des Kriegsgeschehens. Illustrierte Zeitungen wie die London Illustrated News in England oder L'Illustration in Frankreich veröffentlichten regelmäßig die Arbeiten von Grafikern, die ebenfalls auf die Kriegsschauplätze entsandt wurden, sich bei ihren Darstellungen also auf Augenzeugenschaft berufen konnten. Die Zeichnungen gelangten per Brief in die Heimatredaktionen, wo sie in druckfähige Holzstiche übertragen wurden. Zwischen der Anfertigung der Zeichnung und dem Erscheinen des Bildes vergingen im günstigsten Fall nur noch zwei bis drei Wochen.[6] Das neue Bildmedium Fotografie, das im Krimkrieg noch kaum eine Rolle spielte, hatte seinen »Durchbruch« in der Kriegsberichterstattung hingegen erst wenige Jahre später im Amerikanischen Bürgerkrieg (1861–1865), aus dem etwa eine Million Aufnahmen überliefert sind.[7]

Als 1864, 1866 und 1870/71 die deutschen Einigungskriege ausgefochten wurden, stand also bereits ein breites Spektrum an Text- und Bildmedien zur Verfügung. Der zeitliche Abstand zwischen der Produktion und der Rezeption von Kriegsnachrichten hatte sich so stark verkürzt, dass das Publikum in der Heimat den Eindruck gewann, das militärische Geschehen buchstäblich »mitzuerleben«. Das galt zumindest für jene sozialen Schichten, deren Kaufkraft ausreichte, um sich die verfügbaren Medien anzueignen: das Bürgertum, selbstverständlich der Adel, teilweise auch die wohlhabende Landbevölkerung. Arbeiterschaft und ärmere Landbevölkerung konnten die nötigen Mittel meist nur vereinzelt aufbringen. Einige Informationsquellen, die primär in den Städten kursierten, waren aber gratis zugänglich: Zeitungshäuser hängten Blätter mit Sondermeldungen an ihren Fassaden aus, im Druck vervielfältigte Depeschen wurden an Litfaßsäulen angeschlagen, Zeitungen und illustrierte Zeit-

Vor der Litfas-Säule in Berlin während des Kriegs. Originalzeichnung von Ludwig Löffler.

Versammlung gewählt, einer der Führer
und später der Hauptredner des Berges.
e ihn für sechs Jahre vom Schauplatz
rst 1858 kam er wieder durch die pariser
den Körper. Von 1864 an Deputirter
i allen wichtigen Fragen auf der Redner-
Feuer und Leben große Macht ausübte,
stets die Feinheit und Eleganz an-
e er durch seine gewandte Dialektik stets
im Mitglied der Generalräthe des Loire-
ewählt, verweigerte Favre den Eid auf
ber 1857 eine Wendung und gehörte
r „Fünf" an. Als die Kriegsfrage gegen
te v. J. im gesetzgebenden Körper zur
gegen denselben, wurde aber nach der
Minister des Auswärtigen in die Re-
heidigung gewählt und hat als solcher
Bismarck am 19. und 20. September
ührt, welche denn zur Kapitulation von

Mann, der den Krieg bis auf's Aeu-
geführt wissen wollte und über der

sein Amt niederzulegen, wohl nur um in der Konstituante mit neuen ehrgeizigen Plänen aufzutauchen.

Die neusten Depeschen.

Dieses Zauberwort, das in dem an Ueberraschungen so reichen Kriege einen unwiderstehlichen Klang hatte, lockte in Berlin, wo man die Depeschen sogar zur Erinnerung in handlichem Format photographiren ließ, alle Welt vor die Litfas-Säulen, welche die Linden entlang stehen, über und über mit Anschlägen in allen Farben beklebt, und sonst die Vergnügungswegweiser bilden, jetzt aber die Kunde von den Siegen unserer deutschen Heere der Bevölkerung der Hauptstadt brachten. Tag und Nacht — so darf man wohl sagen — waren sie von Neugierigen umstanden, welche diese billige Zeitung lasen und dann die „geflügelten Worte" ihres Königs bis in die entferntesten Ausläufer der riesigen Stadt trugen.

Hrn. A. W. in O. Zurückgesa
in der Intention der Kriegsleitung.
Frln. F. A. in N. Hoffentlich
Sie können den Kriegsschauplatz mi
blättern. F. haben wir an die ange
Hrn. Karl L. in P. Die Lis
Wir senden sie Ihnen unter Kreuzba
Hrn. Maj. v. S. in M. Du
von Mecklenburg. Sie werden die A
des Krieges unseres Blattes finden.
Hrn. K. in H. Wir wollen
Nachbarn jenseit der Berge und kön
aufnehmen.
Hrn. Archit. P. in W. Ger
nung senden.
Hrn. B. in A. Wir acceptire
men Artikel und dieser hat keinen w
Blut zu machen.
Hrn. W. v. R. in R. Wir w
lich ist. Das erfordert mehr Zeit,
wöhnlich glauben.
Hrn. K. in W. Neue Korresp

schriften wanderten von Hand zu Hand etc. Hier genügte bloße Lesefähigkeit für die Rezeption, und in Deutschland hatte die Durchsetzung der allgemeinen Schulpflicht im 19. Jahrhundert dafür gesorgt, dass es kaum noch Analphabeten gab.

Die ersten Nachrichten von bedeutsamen militärischen Ereignissen gelangten in Gestalt von Depeschen in die Heimat. Diese stammten oft aus dem Hauptquartier der preußisch-deutschen Truppen, wo man die Kriegslage am besten überblickte. Die Depeschen wurden öffentlich ausgehängt und ausgerufen, aber auch in den Zeitungen abgedruckt, die bei wichtigen Vorfällen Extrablätter auf den Markt warfen – in Viebigs Roman sind solche Szenen anschaulich beschrieben. Wer genauere Informationen haben wollte, musste auf die Schilderungen der Kriegsberichterstatter warten, die in den Zeitungen erschienen, sobald die entsprechenden Briefe aus Frankreich eingetroffen waren. Bekannte Kriegsreporter auf deutscher Seite waren Reiseschriftsteller wie Friedrich Wilhelm Hackländer, der für die Augsburger Allgemeine Zeitung schrieb, und Hans Wachenhusen, der schon 1864 im Auftrag der Kölnischen Zeitung vom Sturm auf die Düppeler Schanzen berichtet hatte.[8] Wenig Glück hatte Theodor Fontane, damals Theaterkritiker der Vossischen Zeitung und im Auftrag der Kgl. Geheimen Oberhof-Druckerei Rudolf von Decker mit einer umfangreichen Darstellung des Kriegsgeschehens befasst. Er wurde von den

Reporter am Telegrafen, Feldlager St. Avold, Lothringen 1870
Holzstich nach M. Laurédan Larchey aus »Le Monde Illustré«
Abb. 34

←
Vor der Litfaßsäule in Berlin während des Krieges 1870/71
Holzstich nach Ludwig Löffler aus einer illustrierten Zeitschrift
Abb. 33

Der Druckereibesitzer und Buchhändler Ernst Litfaß (1816–1874) errichtete 1855 in Berlin die ersten »Annoncier-Säulen«, die nach ihm »Litfaßsäulen« genannt wurden. Seine Druckerei war die bekannteste unter denen, welche die Kriegsdepeschen meist noch am Tag ihres Eintreffens druckten und verbreiteten.

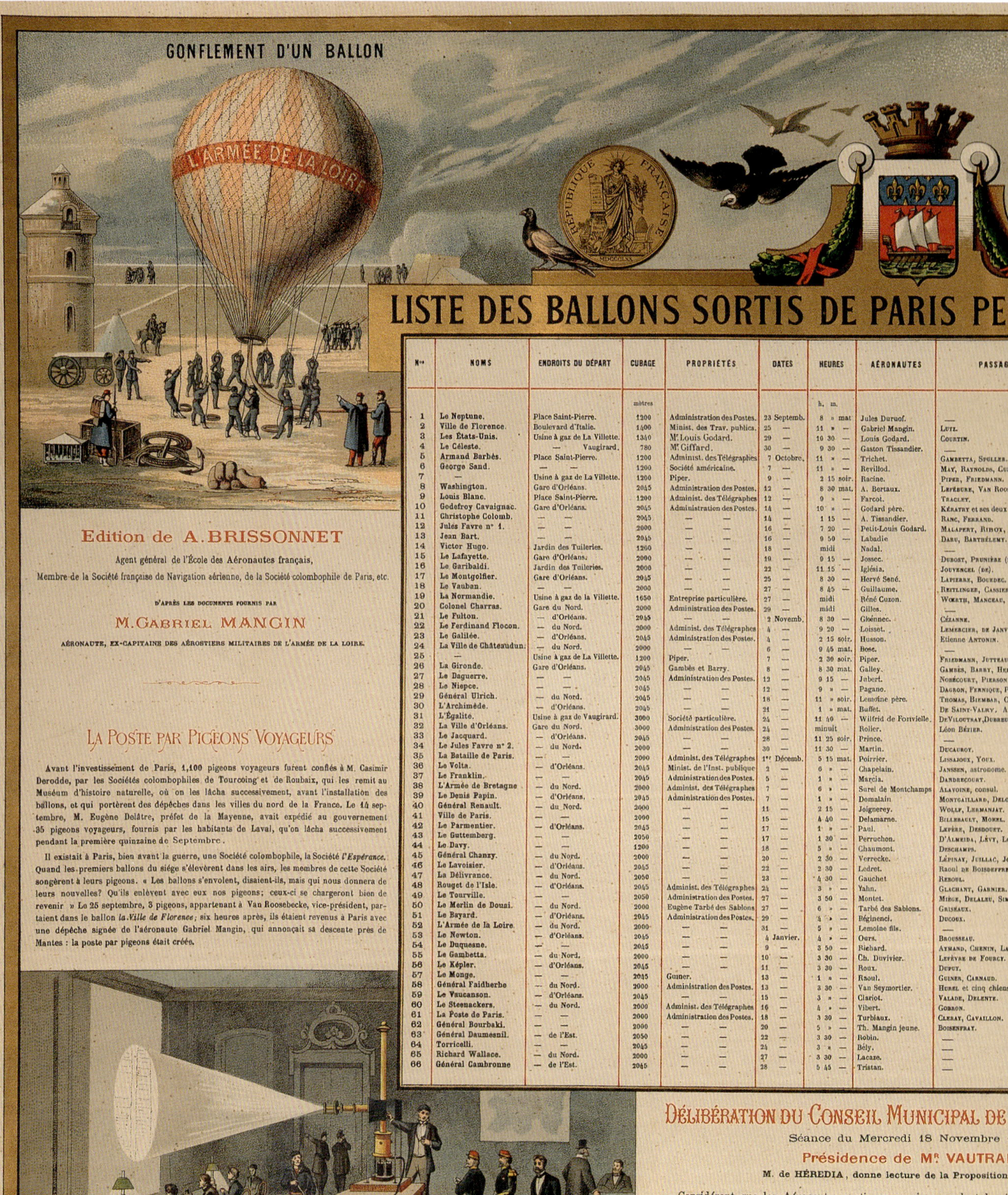

LISTE DES BALLONS SORTIS DE PARIS PE

N°s	NOMS	ENDROITS DU DÉPART	CUBAGE	PROPRIÉTÉS	DATES	HEURES	AÉRONAUTES	PASSAGE
			mètres			h. m.		
1	Le Neptune.	Place Saint-Pierre.	1200	Administration des Postes.	23 Septemb.	8 » mat	Jules Duruof.	—
2	Ville de Florence.	Boulevard d'Italie.	1400	Minist. des Trav. publics.	25 —	11 » —	Gabriel Mangin.	Lutz.
3	Les États-Unis.	Usine à gaz de La Villette.	1340	Mr Louis Godard.	29 —	10 30 —	Louis Godard.	Courtin.
4	Le Céleste.	— Vaugirard.	780	Mr Giffard.	30 —	9 30 —	Gaston Tissandier.	—
5	Armand Barbès.	Place Saint-Pierre.	1200	Administ. des Télégraphes	7 Octobre.	11 » —	Trichet.	Gambetta, Spuller.
6	George Sand.	— —	1200	Société américaine.	7 —	11 » —	Revillod.	May, Raynolds, Cuzo
7	—	Usine à gaz de La Villette.	1200	Piper.	9 —	2 15 soir.	Racine.	Piper, Friedmann.
8	Washington.	Gare d'Orléans.	2045	Administration des Postes.	12 —	8 30 mat.	A. Bertaux.	Lefébure, Van Roose
9	Louis Blanc.	Place Saint-Pierre.	1200	Administ. des Télégraphes	12 —	9 » —	Farcot.	Traclet.
10	Godefroy Cavaignac.	Gare d'Orléans.	2045	Administration des Postes.	14 —	10 » —	Godard père.	Kératry et ses deux se
11	Christophe Colomb.	— —	2045	— —	14 —	1 15 —	A. Tissandier.	Ranc, Ferrand.
12	Jules Favre n° 1.	— —	2000	— —	16 —	7 20 —	Petit-Louis Godard.	Malapert, Ribot, B
13	Jean Bart.	— —	2045	— —	16 —	9 50 —	Labadie	Daru, Barthélemy.
14	Victor Hugo.	Jardin des Tuileries.	1200	— —	18 —	midi	Nadal.	—
15	Le Lafayette.	Gare d'Orléans.	2000	— —	19 —	9 15 —	Jossec.	Dubost, Prunière (de
16	Le Garibaldi.	Jardin des Tuileries.	2000	— —	22 —	11 15 —	Iglésia.	Jouvencel (de).
17	Le Montgolfier.	Gare d'Orléans.	2045	— —	25 —	8 30 —	Hervé Sené.	Lapierre, Bouedec.
18	Le Vauban.	— —	2000	— —	27 —	8 45 —	Guillaume.	Reitlinger, Cassiers.
19	La Normandie.	Usine à gaz de la Villette.	1650	Entreprise particulière.	27 —	midi	Réné Cuzon.	Wœrth, Manceau, H
20	Colonel Charras.	Gare du Nord.	2000	Administration des Postes.	29 —	midi	Gilles.	—
21	Le Fulton.	— d'Orléans.	2045	— —	2 Novemb.	8 30 —	Gloënnec.	Cézanne.
22	Le Ferdinand Flocon.	— du Nord.	2000	Administ. des Télégraphes	4 —	9 20 —	Loisset.	Lemercier, de Janvel
23	Le Galilée.	— d'Orléans.	2045	Administration des Postes.	4 —	2 15 soir.	Husson.	Etienne Antonin.
24	La Ville de Châteaudun.	— du Nord.	2000	— —	6 —	9 45 mat.	Bose.	—
25	—	Usine à gaz de La Villette.	1200	Piper.	7 —	2 30 soir.	Piper.	Friedmann, Jutteau.
26	La Gironde.	Gare d'Orléans.	2045	Gambès et Barry.	8 —	8 30 mat.	Galley.	Gambès, Barry, Herba
27	Le Daguerre.	— —	2045	Administration des Postes.	12 —	9 15 —	Jubert.	Nobécourt, Pierson.
28	Le Niepce.	— —	2045	— —	12 —	9 » —	Pagano.	Dagron, Fernique, Poi
29	Général Ulrich.	— du Nord.	2045	— —	18 —	11 » soir.	Lemoine père.	Thomas, Biembar, Cha
30	L'Archimède.	— d'Orléans.	2045	— —	21 —	1 » mat.	Buffet.	De Saint-Valry, A.
31	L'Égalité.	Usine à gaz de Vaugirard.	3000	Société particulière.	24 —	11 40 —	Wilfrid de Fonvielle.	DeViloutray, Dubreuil,
32	La Ville d'Orléans.	Gare du Nord.	3000	Administration des Postes.	24 —	minuit	Rolier.	Léon Bézier.
33	Le Jacquard.	— d'Orléans.	2045	— —	28 —	11 25 soir.	Prince.	—
34	Le Jules Favre n° 2.	— du Nord.	2000	— —	30 —	11 30 —	Martin.	Ducauroy.
35	La Bataille de Paris.	— —	2000	Administ. des Télégraphes	1er Décemb.	5 15 mat.	Poirrier.	Lissajoux, Youx.
36	Le Volta.	— d'Orléans.	2045	Minist. de l'Inst. publique	2 —	6 » —	Chapelain.	Janssen, astronome.
37	Le Franklin.	— —	2045	Administration des Postes.	5 —	1 » —	Marcia.	Dandrecourt.
38	L'Armée de Bretagne	— du Nord.	2000	Administ. des Télégraphes	7 —	6 » —	Surel de Montchamps	Alavoine, consul.
39	Le Denis Papin.	— d'Orléans.	2045	Administration des Postes.	7 —	1 » —	Domalain	Montgaillard, Delor
40	Général Renault.	— du Nord.	2000	— —	11 —	2 15 —	Joignerey.	Wolff, Lermanjat.
41	Ville de Paris.	— —	2000	— —	15 —	4 40 —	Delamarne.	Billebault, Morel.
42	Le Parmentier.	— d'Orléans.	2045	— —	17 —	1 » —	Paul.	Lepère, Desdouet.
43	Le Guttemberg.	— —	2050	— —	17 —	1 30 —	Perruchon.	D'Almeida, Lévy, Lou
44	Le Davy.	— —	1200	— —	18 —	5 » —	Chaumont.	Deschamps.
45	Général Chanzy.	— du Nord.	2000	— —	20 —	2 30 —	Verrecke.	Lépinay, Juillac, Jou
46	Le Lavoisier.	— d'Orléans.	2045	— —	22 —	2 30 —	Ledret.	Raoul de Boisdeffre.
47	La Délivrance.	— du Nord.	2050	— —	23 —	4 30 —	Gauchet	Reboul.
48	Rouget de l'Isle.	— d'Orléans.	2045	Administ. des Télégraphes	24 —	3 » —	Yahn.	Glachant, Garnier.
49	Le Tourville.	— —	2050	Administration des Postes.	27 —	3 50 —	Montet.	Miège, Delaleu, Simo
50	Le Merlin de Douai.	— du Nord.	2000	Eugène Tarbé des Sablons	27 —	6 » —	Tarbé des Sablons.	Griseaux.
51	Le Bayard.	— d'Orléans.	2045	Administration des Postes.	29 —	4 » —	Réginenci.	Ducoux.
52	L'Armée de la Loire	— du Nord.	2000	— —	31 —	5 » —	Lemoine fils.	—
53	Le Newton.	— d'Orléans.	2045	— —	4 Janvier.	4 » —	Ours.	Brousseau.
54	Le Duquesne.	— —	2045	— —	9 —	3 50 —	Richard.	Aymand, Chenin, Lal
55	Le Gambetta.	— du Nord.	2000	— —	10 —	3 30 —	Ch. Duvivier.	Lefèvre de Fourcy.
56	Le Képler.	— d'Orléans.	2045	— —	11 —	3 30 —	Roux.	Dupuy.
57	Le Monge.	— —	2045	Guiner.	13 —	1 » —	Raoul.	Guiner, Carnaud.
58	Général Faidherbe	— du Nord.	2000	Administration des Postes.	13 —	3 30 —	Van Seymortier.	Hurel et cinq chiens.
59	Le Vaucanson.	— d'Orléans.	2045	— —	15 —	3 » —	Clariot.	Valade, Delente.
60	Le Steenackers.	— du Nord.	2000	Administ. des Télégraphes	16 —	4 » —	Vibert.	Gobron.
61	La Poste de Paris.	— —	2000	Administration des Postes.	18 —	3 30 —	Turbiaux.	Cleray, Cavaillon.
62	Général Bourbaki.	— —	2000	— —	20 —	5 » —	Th. Mangin jeune.	Boisenfray.
63	Général Daumesnil.	— de l'Est.	2050	— —	22 —	3 30 —	Robin.	—
64	Torricelli.	— —	2045	— —	24 —	3 » —	Bély.	—
65	Richard Wallace.	— du Nord.	2000	— —	27 —	3 30 —	Lacaze.	—
66	Général Cambronne	— de l'Est.	2045	— —	28 —	5 45 —	Tristan.	—

Edition de A. BRISSONNET

Agent général de l'École des Aéronautes français,

Membre de la Société française de Navigation aérienne, de la Société colombophile de Paris, etc.

D'APRÈS LES DOCUMENTS FOURNIS PAR

M. GABRIEL MANGIN

AÉRONAUTE, EX-CAPITAINE DES AÉROSTIERS MILITAIRES DE L'ARMÉE DE LA LOIRE.

LA POSTE PAR PIGEONS VOYAGEURS

Avant l'investissement de Paris, 1,100 pigeons voyageurs furent confiés à M. Casimir Derodde, par les Sociétés colombophiles de Tourcoing et de Roubaix, qui les remit au Muséum d'histoire naturelle, où on les lâcha successivement, avant l'installation des ballons, et qui portèrent des dépêches dans les villes du nord de la France. Le 14 septembre, M. Eugène Delâtre, préfet de la Mayenne, avait expédié au gouvernement 35 pigeons voyageurs, fournis par les habitants de Laval, qu'on lâcha successivement pendant la première quinzaine de Septembre.

Il existait à Paris, bien avant la guerre, une Société colombophile, la Société *l'Espérance.* Quand les premiers ballons du siége s'élevèrent dans les airs, les membres de cette Société songèrent à leurs pigeons. « Les ballons s'envolent, disaient-ils, mais qui nous donnera de leurs nouvelles? Qu'ils enlèvent avec eux nos pigeons; ceux-ci se chargeront bien de revenir » Le 25 septembre, 3 pigeons, appartenant à Van Roosebecke, vice-président, partaient dans le ballon *la Ville de Florence;* six heures après, ils étaient revenus à Paris avec une dépêche signée de l'aéronaute Gabriel Mangin, qui annonçait sa descente près de Mantes : la poste par pigeons était créée.

AGRANDISSEMENT DES DÉPÊCHES MICROSCOPIQUES A TOURS & A BORDEAUX PAR DAGRON & SES COLLÈGUES

DÉLIBÉRATION DU CONSEIL MUNICIPAL DE

Séance du Mercredi 18 Novembre 1

Présidence de Mr VAUTRAI

M. de HÉREDIA, donne lecture de la Proposition

Considérant que les Aéronautes partis en province pendant le siég officielles, ont rendu à la patrie et à la ville assiégée les services les plus Ville de Paris ne peut que s'honorer elle-même en honorant des dévoue donnant un témoignage public de sa reconnaissance à des hommes qui ont, risqué leur vie au service de leurs concitoyens;— Par ces motifs : le Consei commémorative, qui sera remise à chacun des Aéronautes du siége de P

Chez A. BRISSONNET, inventeur du *Ballon-Réclame*, boulevard de Sébast

E. PICHOT, IMPRIMEUR

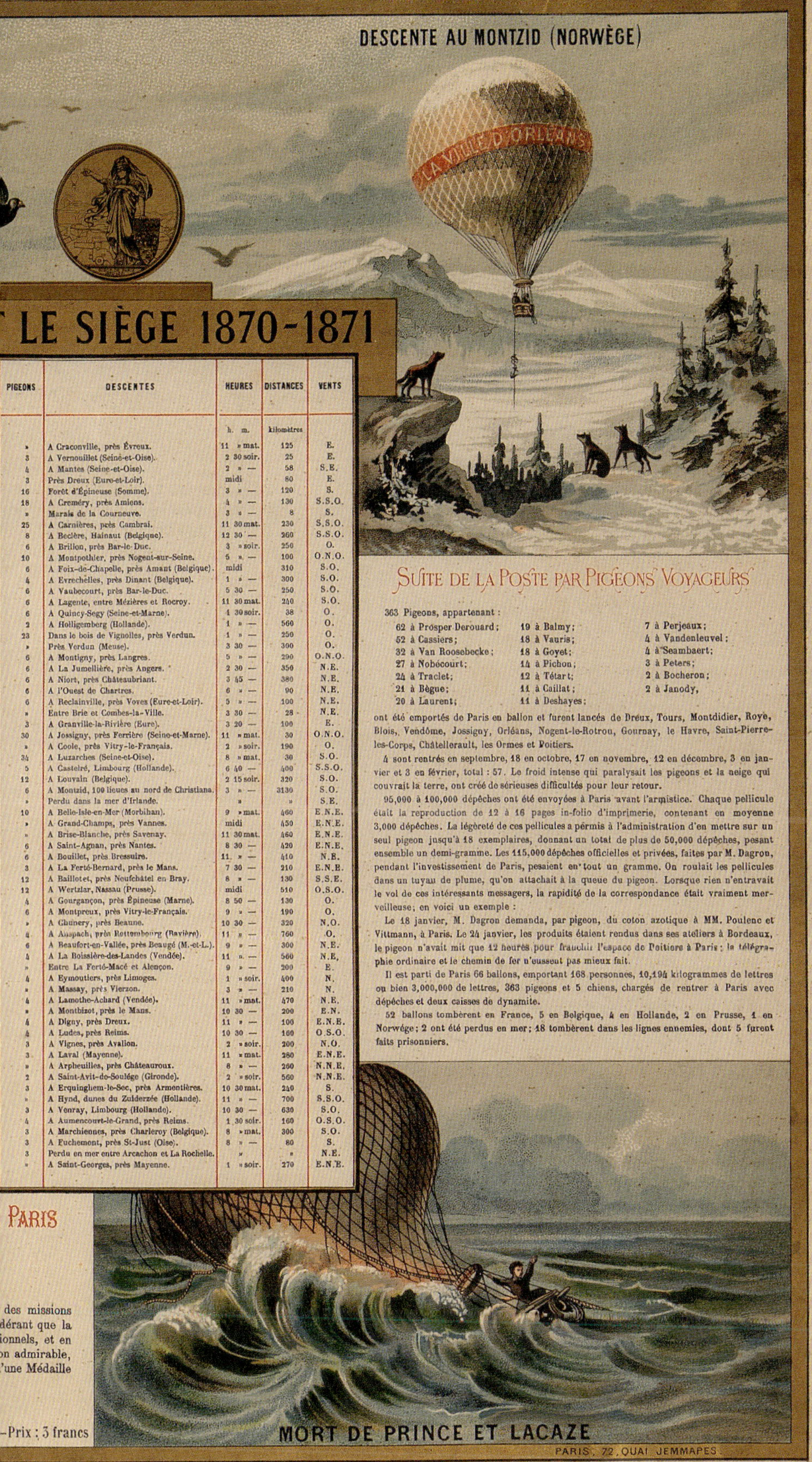

PIGEONS	DESCENTES	HEURES	DISTANCES	VENTS
		h. m.	kilomètres	
»	A Craconville, près Évreux.	11 » mat.	125	E.
3	A Vernouillet (Seine-et-Oise).	2 30 soir.	25	E.
4	A Mantes (Seine-et-Oise).	2 » —	58	S.E.
3	Près Dreux (Eure-et-Loir).	midi	80	E.
16	Forêt d'Épineuse (Somme).	3 » —	120	S.
18	A Cremery, près Amiens.	4 » —	130	S.S.O.
»	Marais de la Courneuve.	3 » —	8	S.
25	A Carnières, près Cambrai.	11 30 mat.	230	S.S.O.
8	A Beclère, Hainaut (Belgique).	12 30 —	260	S.S.O.
6	A Brillon, près Bar-le-Duc.	3 » soir.	250	O.
10	A Montpothier, près Nogent-sur-Seine.	5 » —	100	O.N.O.
6	A Foix-de-Chapelle, près Amant (Belgique).	midi	310	S.O.
4	A Evrechelles, près Dinant (Belgique).	1 » —	300	S.O.
6	A Vaubecourt, près Bar-le-Duc.	5 30 —	250	S.O.
6	A Lagente, entre Mézières et Rocroy.	11 30 mat.	240	S.O.
6	A Quincy-Segy (Seine-et-Marne).	1 30 soir.	38	O.
2	A Holligemberg (Hollande).	1 » —	560	O.
23	Dans le bois de Vignolles, près Verdun.	1 » —	250	O.
»	Près Verdun (Meuse).	3 30 —	300	O.
6	A Montigny, près Langres.	5 » —	290	O.N.O.
6	A La Jumellière, près Angers.	2 30 —	350	N.E.
6	A Niort, près Châteaubriant.	3 45 —	380	N.E.
6	A l'Ouest de Chartres.	6 » —	90	N.E.
6	A Reclainville, près Voves (Eure-et-Loir).	5 » —	100	N.E.
»	Entre Brie et Combes-la-Ville.	3 30 —	28	N.E.
3	A Granville-la-Rivière (Eure).	3 20 —	100	E.
30	A Jossigny, près Ferrière (Seine-et-Marne).	11 » mat.	30	O.N.O.
»	A Coole, près Vitry-le-Français.	2 » soir.	190	O.
34	A Luzarches (Seine-et-Oise).	8 » mat.	30	S.O.
5	A Castelré, Limbourg (Hollande).	6 40 —	400	S.S.O.
12	A Louvain (Belgique).	2 15 soir.	320	S.O.
6	A Montzid, 100 lieues au nord de Christiana.	3 » —	3130	S.O.
»	Perdu dans la mer d'Irlande.	»	»	S.E.
10	A Belle-Isle-en-Mer (Morbihan).	9 » mat.	460	E.N.E.
»	A Grand-Champs, près Vannes.	midi	450	E.N.E.
»	A Brise-Blanche, près Savenay.	11 30 mat.	460	E.N.E.
6	A Saint-Agnan, près Nantes.	8 30 —	420	E.N.E.
6	A Bouillet, près Bressuire.	11 » —	410	N.E.
3	A La Ferté-Bernard, près le Mans.	7 30 —	210	E.N.E.
12	A Baillotet, près Neufchâtel en Bray.	8 » —	130	S.S.E.
12	A Wertzlar, Nassau (Prusse).	midi	510	O.S.O.
4	A Gourgançon, près Épineuse (Marne).	8 50 —	130	O.
6	A Montpreux, près Vitry-le-Français.	9 » —	190	O.
»	A Chunery, près Beaune.	10 30 —	320	N.O.
4	A Anspach, près Rottembourg (Bavière).	11 » —	760	O.
6	A Beaufort-en-Vallée, près Beaugé (M.-et-L.).	9 » —	300	N.E.
4	A La Boissière-des-Landes (Vendée).	11 » —	560	N.E.
»	Entre La Ferté-Macé et Alençon.	9 » —	200	E.
4	A Eymoutiers, près Limoges.	1 » soir.	400	N.
»	A Massay, près Vierzon.	3 » —	210	N.
4	A Lamothe-Achard (Vendée).	11 » mat.	470	N.E.
»	A Montbizot, près le Mans.	10 30 —	200	E.N.
4	A Digny, près Dreux.	11 » —	100	E.N.E.
4	A Ludes, près Reims.	10 30 —	160	O.S.O.
3	A Vignes, près Avalion.	2 » soir.	200	N.O.
3	A Laval (Mayenne).	11 » mat.	280	E.N.E.
»	A Arpheuilles, près Châteauroux.	8 » —	260	N.N.E.
2	A Saint-Avit-de-Soulége (Gironde).	2 » soir.	560	N.N.E.
3	A Erquinghem-le-Sec, près Armentières.	10 30 mat.	240	S.
»	A Hynd, dunes du Zuiderzée (Hollande).	11 » —	700	S.S.O.
3	A Venray, Limbourg (Hollande).	10 30 —	630	S.O.
4	A Aumencourt-le-Grand, près Reims.	1 30 soir.	160	O.S.O.
3	A Marchiennes, près Charleroy (Belgique).	8 » mat.	300	S.O.
3	A Fuchemont, près St-Just (Oise).	8 » —	80	S.
3	Perdu en mer entre Arcachon et La Rochelle.	»	»	N.E.
»	A Saint-Georges, près Mayenne.	1 » soir.	270	E.N.E.

SUITE DE LA POSTE PAR PIGEONS VOYAGEURS

363 Pigeons, appartenant :

62 à Prosper Derouard;	19 à Balmy;	7 à Perjeaux;
52 à Cassiers;	18 à Vauris;	4 à Vandenleuvel;
32 à Van Roosebecke;	18 à Goyet;	4 à Seambaert;
27 à Nobécourt;	14 à Pichon;	3 à Peters;
24 à Traclet;	12 à Tétart;	2 à Bocheron;
21 à Bègue;	11 à Caillat;	2 à Janody,
20 à Laurent;	11 à Deshayes;	

ont été emportés de Paris en ballon et furent lancés de Dreux, Tours, Montdidier, Roye, Blois, Vendôme, Jossigny, Orléans, Nogent-le-Rotrou, Gournay, le Havre, Saint-Pierre-les-Corps, Châtellerault, les Ormes et Poitiers.

4 sont rentrés en septembre, 18 en octobre, 17 en novembre, 12 en décembre, 3 en janvier et 3 en février, total : 57. Le froid intense qui paralysait les pigeons et la neige qui couvrait la terre, ont créé de sérieuses difficultés pour leur retour.

95,000 à 100,000 dépêches ont été envoyées à Paris avant l'armistice. Chaque pellicule était la reproduction de 12 à 16 pages in-folio d'imprimerie, contenant en moyenne 3,000 dépêches. La légèreté de ces pellicules a permis à l'administration d'en mettre sur un seul pigeon jusqu'à 18 exemplaires, donnant un total de plus de 50,000 dépêches, pesant ensemble un demi-gramme. Les 115,000 dépêches officielles et privées, faites par M. Dagron, pendant l'investissement de Paris, pesaient en tout un gramme. On roulait les pellicules dans un tuyau de plume, qu'on attachait à la queue du pigeon. Lorsque rien n'entravait le vol de ces intéressants messagers, la rapidité de la correspondance était vraiment merveilleuse; en voici un exemple :

Le 18 janvier, M. Dagron demanda, par pigeon, du coton azotique à MM. Poulenc et Vittmann, à Paris. Le 24 janvier, les produits étaient rendus dans ses ateliers à Bordeaux, le pigeon n'avait mit que 12 heures pour franchir l'espace de Poitiers à Paris; la télégraphie ordinaire et le chemin de fer n'eussent pas mieux fait.

Il est parti de Paris 66 ballons, emportant 168 personnes, 10,194 kilogrammes de lettres ou bien 3,000,000 de lettres, 363 pigeons et 5 chiens, chargés de rentrer à Paris avec dépêches et deux caisses de dynamite.

52 ballons tombèrent en France, 5 en Belgique, 4 en Hollande, 2 en Prusse, 1 en Norwége; 2 ont été perdus en mer; 18 tombèrent dans les lignes ennemies, dont 5 furent faits prisonniers.

Liste der aus dem belagerten Paris aufgestiegenen Ballons
Verlag E. Pichot, Paris 1874
Farblithografie
Kat. 346

Brieftauben wurden nach Paris gebracht, um während der drohenden Belagerung Nachrichten in nicht besetzte Landesteile zu schaffen. Umgekehrt brachte man auch Brieftauben in Ballons aus dem belagerten Paris hinter die deutschen Linien. Die Tauben flogen mit auf Mikrofilm fotografierten Nachrichten über die feindlichen Linien zurück zu ihrem jeweiligen Ausgangspunkt. Dort wurden die Nachrichten durch Projektion lesbar gemacht.

Franzosen vorübergehend als vermeintlicher Spion festgesetzt.[9] Da das Lesepublikum in Ländern, die nicht an diesem Konflikt beteiligt waren, ebenfalls über den Deutsch-Französischen Krieg informiert werden wollte, war beispielsweise auch Russell auf dem Kriegsschauplatz anwesend und kabelte regelmäßig Berichte an die Londoner Times.[10] Vor allem über London gelangten Nachrichten auch nach Nordamerika. Dafür bediente man sich des Telegrafenkabels, das 1866 durch den Atlantik verlegt worden war.[11]

Neben den Zeitungen berichteten noch weitere Printmedien vom Krieg. Illustrierte Zeitschriften, wie sie für England und Frankreich schon erwähnt wurden, gab es auch in Deutschland. Am wichtigsten war die Leipziger Illustrierte Zeitung; an ihre Seite traten während des Krieges noch spezielle Feldzugspublikationen wie die Blätter »Vom Kriegsschauplatz«, »Deutsche Kriegs-Zeitung 1870/1871« oder »Der Deutsche Volkskrieg«. Reich an Grafiken waren auch die sogenannten Familienzeitschriften, die in der Ära der Einigungskriege unter allen Druckwerken die höchsten Auflagen erreichten. Familienzeitschriften wollten Lesestoff für beide Geschlechter und alle Generationen bieten; Literarisches verband sich hier mit Informationen, und auch eine – wenngleich eher unausgesprochene – politische Agenda war darin wirksam. So verfolgte die »Gartenlaube«, das Flaggschiff unter diesen Zeitschriften, einen nationalliberalen Kurs, wohingegen die fast ebenso bekannte »Daheim« zwar ebenfalls bürgerlich, aber stärker konservativ als liberal ausgerichtet war. In den Kriegsjahren 1870/71 erreichte die »Gartenlaube« eine Auflage von fast 300 000 Exemplaren, was – die Hefte wurden weitergereicht – einem tatsächlichen Rezipientenkreis von rund drei Millionen Menschen entspricht.

Während die Kriegsgrafik, die von solchen Zeitschriften verbreitet wurde, also einen regelrechten Boom erlebte, hatte die Fotografie nach wie vor mit dem Problem langer Belichtungszeiten zu kämpfen. Diese machten Aufnahmen von handelnden Menschen, von bewegten Szenen aller Art unmöglich. Nur das Porträt und das Stillleben, die Abbildung unbewegter Personen und Gegenstände, kamen in Betracht. Der durchaus rege Gebrauch, der hiervon im privaten Bereich gemacht wurde – Soldaten ließen sich auf dem Kriegsschauplatz fotografieren und schickten die Bilder nach Hause –, kann nicht über die marginale Rolle dieses Mediums in der öffentlichen Kommunikation hinwegtäuschen. Hilfreich war die Fotografie indes im Rahmen einer ebenso ungewöhnlichen wie mediengeschichtlich bemerkenswerten Episode, die sich bei der Belagerung von Paris zutrug. Die Franzosen ließen Ballons mit Brieftauben an Bord aus der Hauptstadt aufsteigen und hinter die preußischen Linien fliegen. Dort wurden den Tauben durch Mikrofotografie verkleinerte Briefe beigegeben, die man in Kapseln an ihren Füßen oder ihrem Rücken befestigte. Damit flogen sie nach Paris zurück, was den Nachrichtenfluss zwischen der Seine-Metropole und den Provinzen aufrechterhielt.[12]

Dem großen Informationsangebot zu den militärischen Ereignissen, das in der Öffentlichkeit besonders der kriegführenden Länder vorgehalten wurde, musste eine entsprechende Nachfrage gegenüberstehen. Der Aufwand wäre sonst wirtschaftlich nicht zu rechtfertigen gewesen. Die Nachfrage war jedoch nicht nur deshalb so groß, weil Neugierde, ja Sensationslust befriedigt wurde. Die Ursachen lagen tiefer. Im Lauf des 19. Jahrhunderts hatte der Nationalismus immer größere Teile der Bevölkerung erfasst; ausgehend vom gebildeten Bürgertum, strahlte er auf Teile der Aristokratie, auch und vor allem aber auf die kleinbürgerlichen Massen ab. Aus der Warte des Nationalismus war Politik nicht nur Sache der Regierung, sondern des ganzen Volkes; Kriege, die über die Einheit der Nation entscheiden würden, mussten für jedermann Höchstrelevanz besitzen. Im vornationalen Zeitalter waren Nachrichten von Kriegen fast nur für Politiker und Kaufleute von Interesse gewesen, die ihr Handeln der Kriegslage und ihren politischen und wirtschaftlichen Implikationen anpassen wollten. In der Ära des Nationalismus begehrte jedes bürgerliche Individuum, das sich mit dem Geschick seines Landes identifizierte, solche Informationen.[13]

Das enorme Aufkommen von Nachrichten aus dem Krieg war also eine Folge des wachsenden Nationalismus. Das beschreibt jedoch erst eine Seite des Verhältnisses von Kriegsberichterstattung und Nationalismus. Die Medien profitierten vom Nationalismus, aber trugen auch ihrerseits dazu bei, ihn anzufachen. Kriegsberichterstattung und Nationalismus schaukelten sich gleichsam wechselseitig hoch. Wer sich dicht und anschaulich über die Kriegsereignisse informieren ließ, konnte unmittelbar erleben, wie sehr das Geschehen auch das Wohl und Wehe der eigenen Person berührte. Was der Nationalismus abstrakt postulierte: die politischen Handlungen und Geschicke der Nation gehen jedes Mitglied der Nation direkt und persönlich an, wurde im Mitvollzug der Siege und Niederlagen auf den Schlachtfeldern zur unmittelbaren Erfahrung.[14] Die preußisch-deutsche Armee trat als Sachwalterin des Nationalinteresses auf, und die Übernahme der Perspektive ihrer Soldaten, die durch intensive Kommunikation zwischen Front und Heimat möglich wurde, machte auch den Medienkonsumenten und die Medienkonsumentin daheim zu einem Teil dieses Projekts. Die qualitative und quantitative Steigerung des Nachrichtenflusses zwischen Streitkräften und Zivilbevölkerung im Lauf des 19. Jahrhunderts war also viel mehr als nur ein Effekt verbesserter Kommunikationstechnologie; sie war auch Folge und Faktor eines rasant an Bedeutung gewinnenden Nationalbewusstseins.

1 Zur Emser Depesche vgl. etwa die Studie von Birgit Aschmann: Preußens Ruhm und Deutschlands Ehre. Zum nationalen Ehrdiskurs im Vorfeld der preußisch-französischen Kriege des 19. Jahrhunderts, München 2013. **2** Clara Viebig: Die Wacht am Rhein. Roman, Berlin [5]1902 [1902], S. 397 f. **3** Ebd., S. 414–419, 436–444 und 469 f. **4** Adam Zamoyski: 1812. Napoleons Feldzug gegen Russland, München 2014, S. 382. **5** Ute Daniel: Der Krimkrieg 1853–1856 und die Entstehungsgeschichte medialer Kriegsberichterstattung, in: dies. (Hg.): Augenzeugen. Kriegsberichterstattung vom 18. zum 21. Jahrhundert, Göttingen 2006, S. 40–67, bes. 53–55. **6** Vgl. grundlegend Ulrich Keller: The Ultimate Spectacle. A Visual History of the Crimean War, Amsterdam 2001. **7** Ken Burns: The Civil War – Der Amerikanische Bürgerkrieg, München 1992, S. 208. **8** Frank Becker: Bilder von Krieg und Nation. Die Einigungskriege in der bürgerlichen Öffentlichkeit Deutschlands 1864–1913, München 2001, S. 44. **9** Ebd., S. 43. **10** Tobias Arand: 1870/71. Die Geschichte des Deutsch-Französischen Krieges erzählt in Einzelschicksalen, Hamburg 2018, bes. S. 356–359 und 387–390. **11** Roland Wenzlhümer: Connecting the Nineteenth-Century World. The Telegraph and Globalization, Cambridge 2015, S. 108. **12** Hannah Zindel: Belagerung von Paris. 69 Freiballons, 381 Tauben und fast elf Tonnen Post, in: Lars Nowak (Hg.): Medien – Krieg – Raum, München 2018, S. 141–160. **13** Zum Zusammenspiel von Nationalismus und Krieg vgl. zuletzt auch Dieter Langewiesche: Der gewaltsame Lehrer. Europas Kriege in der Moderne, München 2019. **14** Zu dieser Argumentation auch Frank Becker: Deutschland im Krieg von 1870/71 oder die mediale Inszenierung der nationalen Einheit, in: Daniel (Hg.): Augenzeugen, 2006, S. 68–86, bes. S. 76–81.

Briefe an die Front

Weibliche Perspektiven

Nach dem Krieg gegen Österreich 1866 begann die Modernisierung des Feldpostwesens im Norddeutschen Bund. Im Deutsch-Französischen Krieg 1870/71 beförderte allein die Norddeutsche Feldpost fast 90 Millionen Briefe und Postkarten sowie zwei Millionen Pakete. Die gerade erst eingeführten Postkarten, damals noch »Correspondenz-Karten« genannt, wurden gezielt an Soldaten verteilt und konnten ebenso wie Briefe kostenfrei verschickt werden. Kriegserfahrungen, das Gefühl, Teil einer großen nationalen Anstrengung zu sein, und die Trennung von Angehörigen bewogen auch viele Menschen zum Schreiben, die sonst kaum zu Feder oder Bleistift gegriffen hätten. Die überlieferten Briefwechsel der Offiziersgattin Benedikte von Rosen und der Ehefrau des als Unteroffizier dienenden Friedrich Weidners gewähren Einblicke in weibliche Lebenswelten während des Krieges 1870/71. Im Gegensatz zu dem umfangreichen Nachlass Benedikte von Rosens sind von Karoline Weidner nur wenige Schreiben überliefert.

Benedikte Freifrau von Rosen, geb. Freiin von Rosen (1838–1905)
Kolorierte Fotografie, um 1860/1870
Abb. 35

Benedikte gehörte zum livländischen Zweig des Adelsgeschlechts von Rosen. 1860 lernte sie ihren Cousin Julius kennen. Er hielt um ihre Hand an, aber ihr Vater, ein russischer General, betrachtete den preußischen Hauptmann ohne eigenes Vermögen als keine gute Partie. Erst 1867, als Julius in eine höhere Gehaltsstufe aufgerückt war, konnten er und Benedikte heiraten.

Medaillon mit Porträt und Haaren von Julius von Rosen (1827–1891), als Hauptmann
4,5 × 3 × 0,4 cm
Kat. 428

Der in Mülheim am Rhein geborene Julius von Rosen war sein Leben lang Soldat. 1840, mit 13 Jahren, trat er ins Kadettenhaus Bensberg ein. 1889, zwei Jahre vor seinem Tod, nahm er als Generalleutnant und Inspekteur der 2. Landwehr-Inspektion Potsdam in Bromberg seinen Abschied.

Kat. 428

Brief von Benedikte von Rosen an ihren Ehemann Julius, Trier, 26. August 1870
Kat. 426

Während des Krieges 1870/71 schrieben die Eheleute einander mehrmals in der Woche, oft seitenlange Briefe, allein von Benedikte sind 174 Briefe überliefert. Sie schilderte ihren Alltag in allen Einzelheiten und nahm regen Anteil an den Kriegserlebnissen ihres Mannes. Inzwischen war sie Mutter des zweijährigen Fabians und wieder schwanger. Selbst nachdem die Wehen eingesetzt hatten, schrieb sie noch an Julius. Der Arzt versah den Brief mit einem beruhigenden Zusatz; die Details der schwierigen Zangengeburt wollte er dem Vater nicht zumuten. Das Mädchen wurde auf den Namen Alexandrine Benedikte Johanna Gravelotte getauft und liebevoll »das Gravelottchen« genannt – nach der siegreichen und blutigen Schlacht bei Gravelotte am 18. August, in der ihr Vater gekämpft hatte:

»Trier 26. August 1870 abends 11 Uhr

Mein herzens herzens D a d d y!

Vor paar Stunden schrieb ich Dir noch ganz gesund und jetzt befinde ich mich schon in einem kläglichen Zustande, schreckliche Schmerzen. Ich schickte gleich nach der Schmidt, die eben kam und meinte es könne nicht mehr lange dauern. Da will ich Dir auch einige Worte sagen, ehe ich mich zu Bette lege. Gott gebe das alles gut geht! Ich hoffe es, die Wehen sind stark, es muß rasch gehen. Vor zwei Stunden aß ich noch mein Abendessen ganz ruhig und jetzt bin ich ganz herunter. Fabian wurde eben mit seinem Bett in den Salon transportirt, dort verbringt er die heutige Nacht. Morgen kömmt er mit der Kamnitz ins Hauszimmer. Schmerzlich vermisse ich Dich jetzt, Du mein eigen Mann, aber ich will nicht klagen, sondern dem lieben Gott danken, daß Du gesund bist, der Doktor wird noch einige Worte hinzusetzen, wenn alles vorüber ist. Die Schmidt meinte es wäre noch zu früh, nach ihm zu schicken, die Blan laß ich aber gleich kommen. Heute hatte ich einen so angenehmen Tag, durch die guten Nachrichten die ich von Dir erhielt, gut daß es heute und nicht erst morgen alles kam. Da hätte ich es nicht so erfahren können. Mehr kann ich nicht schreiben, mögst Du das hier, da fange ich wieder an, es ist aber auch so natürlich, daß Du mir in diesem Augenblick ganz besonders fehlst, wann wirst Du unser zweites Kindchen kennen lernen Gott schenke uns allen Leben und Gesundheit und ein glückliches Wiedersehen. Lebe wohl mein heißgeliebter Mann ich küsse und umarme Dich von ganzer Seele. Wie werde ich froh sein, wenn ich Dich wiedersehen kann. Deine Benedicte

[Rückseite, von anderer Hand:] Die Geburt ist ganz glücklich vorüber; Mutter und neugeborenes Mädchen sind gesund. Dr. Ender.«

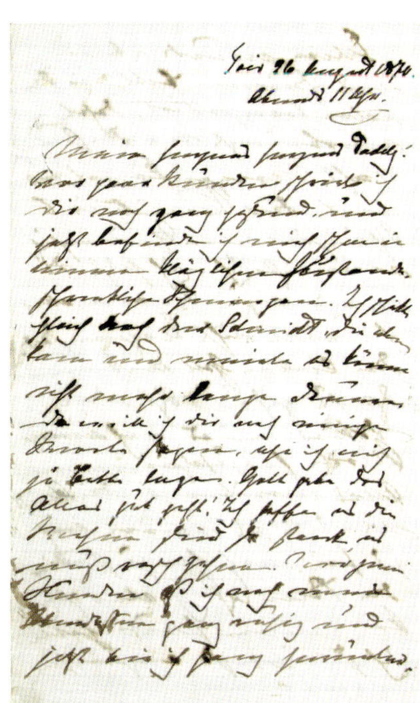

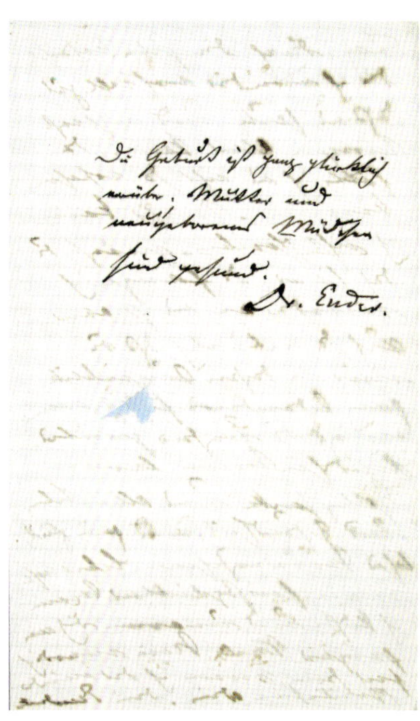

Die Geburt ist ganz glücklich vorüber. Mutter und neugeborenes Mädchen sind gesund. Dr. Ender.

Kat. 426

Brief von Julius von Rosen an seine Ehefrau Benedikte, K.Q. Coin les Cuvry, Frankreich, 15. September 1870

»Mein theuer gutes Herz! Seit vorgestern Morgen pflegen wir hier im Hause eines Notars der gehörigen Ruhe. [...] Der Wirth ist mit allen Leuthen nach Metz geflohen. Und so spielen die Soldaten hier die Herren. [...] Papas Brief gelesen zu haben, hat mir auch Freude gemacht. Wie haben sich die guten Eltern gefreut, als sie die Nachricht von der glücklich abgelaufenen Entbindung erhielten. Merkwürdig bleibt doch, daß die Bewohner Roop's [Benediktes Eltern] dieselbe Idee gehabt als meine Kameraden, als die Nachricht von der Entbindung anlangte, das Kind Gravelotte zu nennen. Der Eine wollte Gravelotte, der andere Victoria sie genannt wissen, doch blieb es nachher auf Gravelotte! Ich glaube, daß Ady ihr Leblang den Zunamen Gravelotte behalten wird. Schadet nichts, braucht sich nicht dieses ehrenvollen Namens zu schämen! [...] Wie lange wir hier noch vor Metz liegen werden, weiß ich nicht, oder jedenfalls bis Bazaine die Festung übergeben haben wird. Möglich, daß unser 8. Corps als danach gen Paris rückt. Wer weiß überhaupt noch wie lange sich der Krieg noch mit der Republik hinziehen wird, denn selbst ich glaube, daß die größte Blutarbeit geschehen ist. Hier schließe ich mein Herzens Schatz. Lebe wohl, der liebe Gott erhalte Dich gesund, Dich und die Kinder.

Küsse von Herzensgrund unsere kleine Ady. Grüße Dr. Enders [...]. Dein dir wahr getreuer Mann Julius«

(Kat. 427)

»Correspondenz-Karte« des Unteroffiziers Friedrich Weidner an seine Ehefrau Karoline, Biwak Billigheim, 3. August 1870

Kat. 424/1

Friedrich Weidner diente im 2. Niederschlesischen Infanterie-Regiment Nr. 47. In der Schlacht bei Weißenburg am 4. August 1870 starb er durch einen Schuss in die Brust. Am Abend vor der Schlacht hatte er diese »Correspondenz-Karte« an seine Frau geschrieben:

Norddeutsches Postgebiet.

Correspondenz-Karte.

Zum Aufkleben der Freimarke.

An

Bestimmungsort:

Wohnung des Empfängers, wenn sie mit Sicherheit angegeben werden kann.

Zur gefälligen Beachtung beim Gebrauch der Correspondenz-Karte.

1) Formulare, welche mit der Freimarke bereits beklebt sind, können bei allen Postaufgabestellen, Briefträgern und Landbriefträgern bezogen werden; für das Formular selbst wird nichts berechnet.
2) Der obige Vordruck für die Adresse ist deutlich und vollständig auszufüllen.
3) Die Rückseite des Formulars kann in ihrer ganzen Ausdehnung zu brieflichen Mittheilungen jeder Art benutzt werden, welche, sowie die Adresse, mit Tinte, Bleifeder oder farbigem Stifte geschrieben sein können.
4) Die Entnahme von Postvorschuß ist bei Correspondenz-Karten nicht zulässig dagegen ist das Verfahren der Recommandation, sowie der Expreßbestellung gestattet.
5) Die Correspondenz-Karte kann zu schriftlichen Mittheilungen sowohl innerhalb des Norddeutschen Postgebiets, als auch für den Verkehr nach den Süddeutschen Staaten, nach Oesterreich und Luxemburg benutzt werden.
6) Der Absender ist nicht verpflichtet, sich namhaft zu machen.

Kat. 424/1

»Liebe Karoline so eben muß ich ein paar Worte an Dich schreiben wir liegen hir im Biwoack zirka 50 000 Mann und befinden uns so zimlich gut so eben ist Sr. Kl. H. der Kronprinz bei uns eingetroffen und sehr jubelnd empfangen worden wir werden womöglich diese Nacht noch vor kommen – wir sind an der [unleserlich] und werden die französischn Kugeln zuerst schmecken

Lebe herzlich wohl und sei herzlich gegrüst von Deinem F. Weidner Die Adresse wie vorige.«

Brief von Karoline Weidner an ihren Ehemann Friedrich, Berlin, 5. August 1870

»Lieber Fridrich!

Soeben erhielt ich Dein schon längst ersehnter Brief, es ist kein Wunder wenn die Briefe so lange unterwegs sind, daß einem da die Zeit recht lange wird Deine Sachen sind bis jetzt noch nicht angekomen, wie ich augenbliklich erfahren hat ein sehr großer bluticher Kampf stattgefunden wozu auch Deine Armee gezählt wird hoffentlich wirst Du noch zu den Lebente gezählt werden jedenfals mögte ich bitten mich alsbald zu benachrichten wenn auch nur einige Zeilen, Vater Zumpe habe ich dieser Tage begegnet wo wir auch von Dir sprachen und Ema Mietz hatte ich auch sobald ich Nachricht hatte davon in Kenntniß gesetzt, von Herrn Jöhl habe ich bis jetzt noch kein Geld bekomen er scheint nicht lußt zu haben damit herraus zurüken wie wohl ich mich schon darum bemüht habe am Gericht habe ich auch noch nichts ausgerichtet weil noch nicht alle Actten zusamen waren nächsten Montag habe ich nochmals Termin, und dann wird Dir die Sache zur Unterschrift zu geschikt werden. Vom Magistrathaus werde ich auch was bekomen ich habe meine Babiere eingereicht, ist aber bis jetzt noch nichts ausgezahlt, einstweilen nähe ich Komißhemden das Stück 2 ½ Sg [Silbergroschen] später gibt es auch von den Vereine noch zu nähen Dies wird auch Alles gehen wenn Dich der liebe Gott mir glüklich läßt zurükkomen in der Hofnung recht bald Antwort zu erhalten

seie herzlich gegrüßt und geküßt von Deiner

Dich treu liebende Karoline Weidner«

(siehe S. 406, Kat. 424/2)

Schreiben von Karoline Weidner an das Regiment ihres Ehemanns Friedrich, Berlin, 18. Oktober 1870 (Rückseite)

Kat. 425

Karoline Weidner erhielt den Brief an ihren Ehemann mit dem Zusatz »Im Gefechte bei Weißenberg getötet« auf dem Umschlag zurück. Als sie zweieinhalb Monate später noch keine offizielle Benachrichtigung über das Schicksal ihres Ehemanns erhalten hatte, schrieb sie an sein Regiment. Ihr Brief kam mit dem Vermerk wieder, dass ihr Mann bei Weißenburg »den schönen Todt für König und Vaterland« gestorben sei. Wie einem weiteren Brief vom 11. Dezember zu entnehmen ist, wartete sie zwei Monate später immer noch auf die Zusendung des Totenscheins, den sie dringend benötigte, um staatliche Unterstützung zu beantragen. Was mit dem Bargeld geschehen war, das ihr Mann mit ins Feld genommen hatte, ließ sich nicht klären:

»Da ich schon seid August keine Nachricht von meinem Mann, dem Unteroficir Fridrich Weidner bei der 3ten Compani des 47ten Regement erhalten habe, und mir anfangs geschrieben falls er, fallen, würde ich von Regement aus Nachricht erhalten, deßhalb wende ich mich mit der Bitte an benanntes Regement mir doch güttigst Aufschluß zu ertheilen, falls mein Mann gefallen mir dies mitzutheilen, und ersuche zu gleich, alsdann mir sein Geld da er bis zwanzig Thaler bei sich führte mehrtheils in Pabier worunter ein zehn Thalerschein, in seinem Notitzbuch bei sich führte, dann noch ein ziemlich neues Portmane mit mehrere Thaler in Silbergeld ferner eine Uhr mit Haarkette sammt Mettalion und ein Ring. Sollte diese Sachen nach seiner Mutter in Altschau Kreis Freistatt geschickt worden sein, so bitte ich nohmals mich davon in Kentniß zu setzen, indem meine La[g]e eine sehr bedränkte ist w[ü]rde ich oben genante Sa[c]hen beanspru[c]hen. In der Hoffnung eine rechtbaldige Aufklärung hieriber zu erhalten schließt achtungsvoll Frau Weidner

Amalienstraße No 8 2Tpp. Berlin

[...] Ville d'Avray, den 27.10.70.

[...] dem I. Bataillon zur directen Erledigung

v. Flotow

Ihr Mann ist im Gefecht bei Weissenburg, den schönen Todt für König und Vaterland gestorben

Ville neuve 30/10 70.

Nachricht über hinterlassene Sachen, wird noch zugehen«

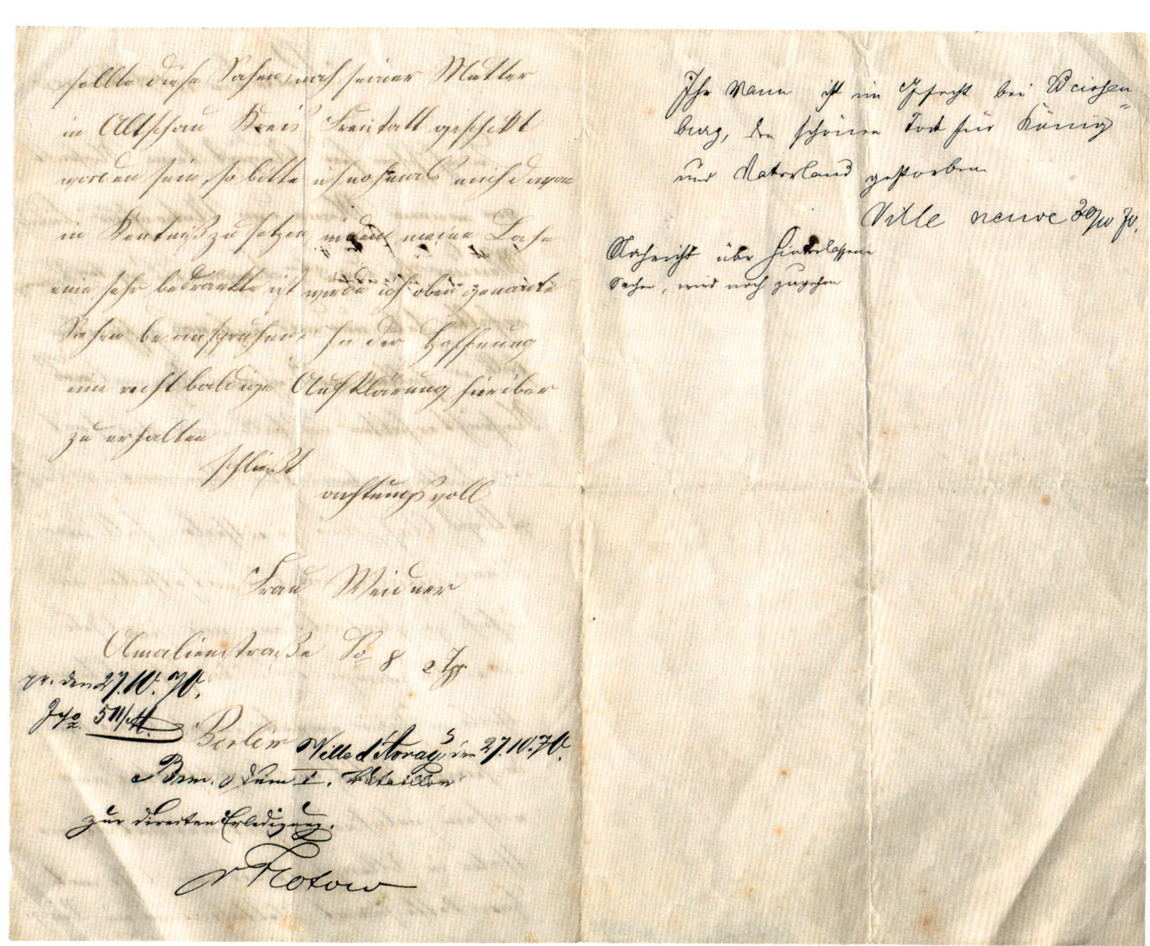

Kat. 425

Freiwillige Krankenpflege

zur Zeit der Reichseinigungskriege

EVA LANGHALS

Verletzte und schwer verwundete Soldaten von den Schlachtfeldern abtransportieren, sie medizinisch versorgen, ihnen Trost zusprechen, Liebesgaben und Spenden sammeln und verteilen, die Angehörigen über ihr Schicksal informieren und die Verwundeten in der Heimat pflegen: All das gehörte zum Aufgabenfeld der freiwilligen Krankenpflege seit ihrer Entstehung Mitte des 19. Jahrhunderts. In der freiwilligen Krankenpflege war es Frauen erstmals möglich, sich aktiv am Sanitätsdienst zu beteiligen und mit Hilfsbereitschaft und Fürsorge, Mut und Organisationsgeschick das Leid der Soldaten zu lindern. Die chirurgische Massenbehandlung von Kriegsverletzungen konnte damals noch auf wenig Erfahrung zurückblicken, und die Nutzung der antibiotischen Wirkung des Penizillins lag noch in weiter Ferne, sodass einer umsichtigen Pflege eine umso wichtigere Rolle zukam.

Augusta (1811–1890), preußische Königin und deutsche Kaiserin
Holzstich, um 1870/71
Abb. 36

Die Geburtsstunde des freiwilligen Sanitätswesens in den europäischen Staaten war der Krimkrieg von 1853 bis 1856. Auf den Schlachtfeldern herrschten katastrophale Zustände, die auch der zivilen Bevölkerung in Frankreich und England nicht verborgen blieben. Eine der Verantwortlichen, die den Umschwung im Sanitätswesen bei den britischen Truppen auf dem Kriegsschauplatz herbeiführte, war die Krankenpflegerin Florence Nightingale. Dank guter Kontakte zum Kriegs-Staatssekretär (Secretary at War) Sidney Herbert, der ihr Fürsprecher in der Politik wurde, mit reichlich Geldmitteln und der nötigen Courage ausgestattet, reiste sie in die Lazarette am Bosporus und vermittelte dort erstmals in der Militär- und Sanitätsgeschichte weibliches Hilfspersonal.[1] Nightingale kämpfte gegen zeittypische Vorurteile, die unter anderem forderten, Frauen sollten sich ausschließlich um die Familie kümmern. Um ihren eigenen Angehörigen Schwierigkeiten zu ersparen, begab sie sich bereits 1851 für einige Zeit nach Düsseldorf, wo sie in der Kaiserwerther Diakonie eine Ausbildung zur Krankenschwester absolvierte.[2]

Drei Jahre nach dem Ende des Krimkriegs, 1859, wurde der Schweizer Geschäftsmann Henry Dunant Zeuge der Schlacht von Solferino im Sardinischen Krieg zwischen Österreich und dem Königreich Sardinien und Frankreich: 40 000 getötete und verwundete Soldaten wurden nach Abschluss der Kämpfe auf den Schlachtfeldern gezählt. Die Gemetzel und die Schrecken danach, die hilflose Lage der Verwundeten, schilderte er in seinem Buch »Eine Erinnerung an Solferino«, von dem er auf eigene Kosten 1 600 Exemplare drucken und an politische und militärische Machthaber in Europa verschicken ließ. In der Folge der darin geäußerten Ideen traten die Schweizer Gustave Moynier, Louis Appia, Guillaume-Henri Dufour und Théodor Maunoir mit Dunant zu einem Fünfergremium mit der Bezeichnung Ständiges Internationales Komitee zusammen, das »die kriegsführenden Armeen durch Korps freiwilliger Krankenpfleger [...] unterstützen«[3] sollte. Mit diesem Comité international de

MISS NIGHTINGALE, IN THE HOSPITAL, AT SCUTARI.—(SEE PRECEDING PAGE.)

Florence Nightingale (1820–1910) in einem Lazarett in Scutari
Holzstich, The Illustrated London News, 24. März 1855, S. 176
Kat. 27

Oft wird Florence Nightingale als »Lady with the Lamp« dargestellt, die spät noch Patienten besucht. Ihr Hauptverdienst lag jedoch in der effizienteren Organisation des britischen Sanitätswesens. Ihre Schriften zu Krankenhausstatistik und -management begründeten die moderne Krankenpflege.

→
Henri Dunant (1828–1910), um 1855
Kat. 31

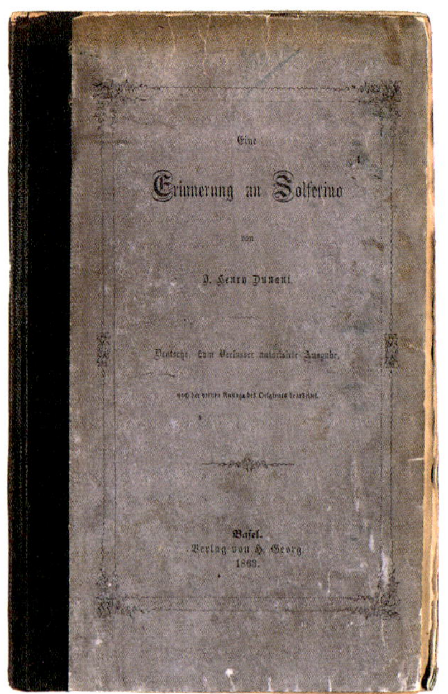

Eine Erinnerung an Solferino
J. Henry Dunant, Basel 1863
Kat. 429

Dunants Bericht über das Leid der Verwundeten auf dem Schlachtfeld von Solferino erschien erstmals 1862. Die Schrift wird bis heute immer wieder aufgelegt. Hier handelt es sich um ein Exemplar der deutschsprachigen Erstausgabe. Bis dahin war das Werk auf Französisch bereits in dritter Auflage verfügbar.

secours aux militaires blessés wurde am 17. Februar 1863 der Grundstein für das spätere Internationale Komitee für das Rote Kreuz gelegt. Die Kernforderungen des Komitees waren die Unantastbarkeit verwundeter und erkrankter Soldaten, der Ärzte, des Pflegepersonals sowie der Lazarette und die unterschiedslose Pflege der Soldaten aller Kriegsparteien. Eine weitere Forderung war die Gründung privater Hilfsgesellschaften in den europäischen Staaten. Diese sollten die professionelle Pflege der Kriegsopfer leisten, um die militärischen Sanitätsdienste zu unterstützen, die ohne Mitwirkung der Bevölkerung nicht in der Lage seien, ihre Aufgabe zu erfüllen.[4]

Acht Monate später, im Oktober 1863, tagte in Genf eine internationale Konferenz, an der Vertreter aus 16 Staaten teilnahmen, die eine Resolution zur besseren Versorgung und Pflege der Verwundeten verabschiedeten. Als einer der ersten Staaten setzte Preußen diese Erklärung in die Tat um: Im Februar 1864 wurde dort eine nationale Hilfsgesellschaft, das »Central-Comité des Preußischen Vereins zur Pflege im Felde verwundeter und erkrankter Krieger« aus der Taufe gehoben.[5]

Bereits im Sommer 1859 entstand im Großherzogtum Baden unter der Leitung und Förderung von Luise von Baden, einer Tochter der preußischen Königin Augusta, der erste Frauenverein. Luise initiierte diesen Verein gemeinsam mit 18 Karlsruher Bürgerinnen nicht ohne Grund: Sie fürchtete, dass sich der Österreichisch-Italienische Krieg durch Bündnisverpflichtungen mit Österreich auf das Großherzogtum Baden ausweiten könnte. Vereinszweck war die »Unter-

»Unter dem rothen Kreuz. Fremde und eigene Erfahrungen auf Böhmischer Erde und den Schlachtfeldern der Neuzeit, gesammelt von Dr. Julius Naundorff, Hauptmann und gewesenem Feldhospitalcommandanten«
Leipzig 1867
Kat. 432

Julius Naundorff (1820–1907), ein sächsischer Offizier, Schriftsteller und Mitbegründer des sächsischen Albertvereins vom Roten Kreuz, warb mit seinem Buch, das auch Erkenntnisse aus dem Krieg von 1866 verarbeitete, für die freiwillige Krankenpflege.

stützung der in Folge der Kriegsbedrohung oder eines Krieges in Not geratenen sowie die Vorsorge für verwundete und erkrankte Militärpersonen«.[6] Der Verein erklärte sich bereit, auf eigene Kosten Frauen und Mädchen in geeigneten Krankenanstalten für die Krankenpflege ausbilden zu lassen.

Im ersten der drei Einigungskriege, dem Deutsch-Dänischen Krieg von 1864, waren erstmals internationale Beobachter und freiwillige Helfer und Helferinnen im Sinne der Rotkreuzbewegung im Einsatz. Da die Bewegung noch ganz am Anfang stand, spielten vor allem religiöse Gemeinschaften und Organisationen wie etwa der Johanniter-Orden eine entscheidende Rolle, da sie die meiste Erfahrung in der Krankenpflege hatten.[7] Ein Novum war 1864 noch der Einsatz freiwilliger weiblicher Pflegekräfte, Diakonissinnen und Ordensschwestern. Elise von Mellenthin war eine der ersten Frauen, die nach Schleswig fuhren, um dort in der freiwilligen Krankenpflege zu helfen. In ihren Briefen beschreibt sie ihre Eindrücke unumwunden:

»Wenn ich starke Anlage zum Trinken hätte, so könnte ich es mir hier angewöhnen. Oft wird einem beim Zusehen all der Leiden, beim Verbinden usw., was nichts weniger als appetitlich ist, ganz schlimm, da wird dann schnell ein Glas Sherry oder Malagageist heruntergestürzt, ein verzweifeltes Mittel, aber es hilft.«[8]

Unmittelbar nach dem Krieg wurde die erste Genfer Konvention unterschrieben, für Preußen zeichnete der Militärarzt im preußischen Heer Friedrich Loeffler. Der 1866 folgende sogenannte Deutsche Krieg stellte Preußens unvol-

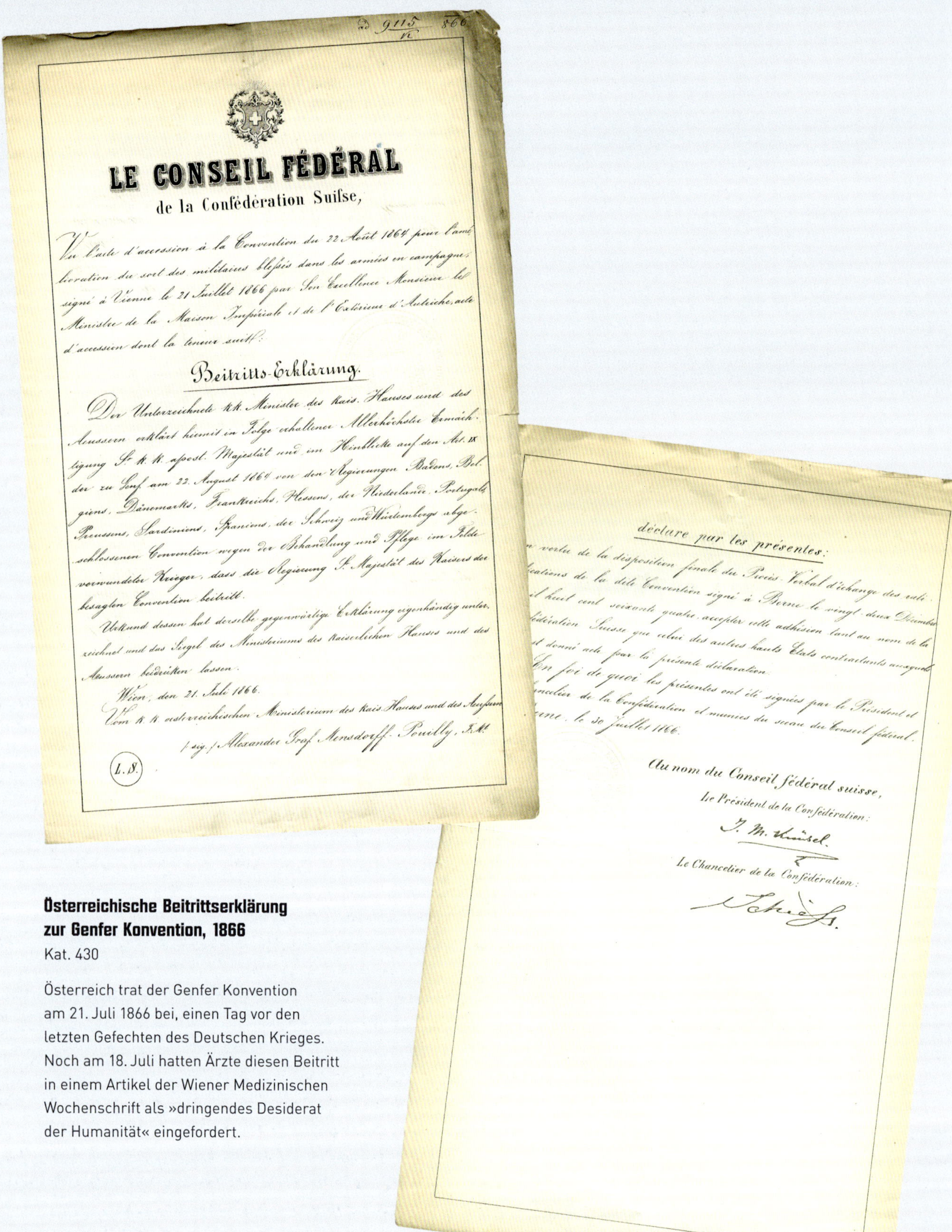

LE CONSEIL FÉDÉRAL
de la Confédération Suiſse,

Vu l'acte d'accession à la Convention du 22 Août 1864 pour l'amé
lioration du sort des militaires blessés dans les armées en campagne,
signé à Vienne le 21 Juillet 1866 par Son Excellence Monsieur le
Ministre de la Maison Impériale et de l'Extérieur d'Autriche, acte
d'accession dont la teneur suit:

Beitritts-Erklärung.

Der Unterzeichnete k.k. Minister des kais. Hauses und des
Aeussern erklärt hiemit in Folge erhaltener Allerhöchster Ermächtigung Sr. k. k. apost. Majestät und im Hinblicke auf den Art. IX
der zu Genf am 22. August 1864 von den Regierungen Badens, Belgiens, Dänemarks, Frankreichs, Hessens, der Niederlande, Portugals,
Preussens, Sardiniens, Spaniens, der Schweiz und Würtembergs abgeschlossenen Convention wegen der Behandlung und Pflege im Felde
verwundeter Krieger, dass die Regierung Sr. Majestät des Kaisers der
besagten Convention beitritt.

Urkund dessen hat derselbe gegenwärtige Erklärung eigenhändig unterzeichnet und das Siegel des Ministeriums des kaiserlichen Hauses und des
Aeussern beidrücken lassen.

Wien, den 21. Juli 1866.
Vom k. k. oesterreichischen Ministerium des kais. Hauses und des Aeußern
(sig.) Alexander Graf Mensdorff-Pouilly, F.M.

(L.S.)

déclare par les présentes:

…n vertu de la disposition finale du Procès-Verbal d'échange des rati-
…fications de la dite Convention signé à Berne le vingt-deux Décembre
…il huit cent soixante quatre, accepter cette adhésion tant au nom de la
…fédération Suisse que celui des autres hauts États contractants auxquels
…st donné acte par la présente déclaration.
En foi de quoi les présentes ont été signées par le Président et
…ancelier de la Confédération et munies du sceau du Conseil fédéral.
…rne, le 30 Juillet 1866.

Au nom du Conseil fédéral suisse,
Le Président de la Confédération:
J. M. Knüsel.
Le Chancelier de la Confédération:
Schieß.

Österreichische Beitrittserklärung zur Genfer Konvention, 1866
Kat. 430

Österreich trat der Genfer Konvention am 21. Juli 1866 bei, einen Tag vor den letzten Gefechten des Deutschen Krieges. Noch am 18. Juli hatten Ärzte diesen Beitritt in einem Artikel der Wiener Medizinischen Wochenschrift als »dringendes Desiderat der Humanität« eingefordert.

Rotkreuzarmbinde für einen Angehörigen der freiwilligen Krankenpflege
Königreich Preußen, 1870/71
Kat. 431

Diese Armbinde, versehen mit dem Stempel des Königlichen Kommissars und Militärinspekteurs der freiwilligen Krankenpflege, trug Carl Rube (geb. 1852 in Darmstadt, Großherzogtum Hessen). Ab dem 18. August 1870 leistete der junge Mann Dienst beim »Hülfsverein im Grossherzogthum Hessen für die Krankenpflege und Unterstützung der Soldaten im Felde«.

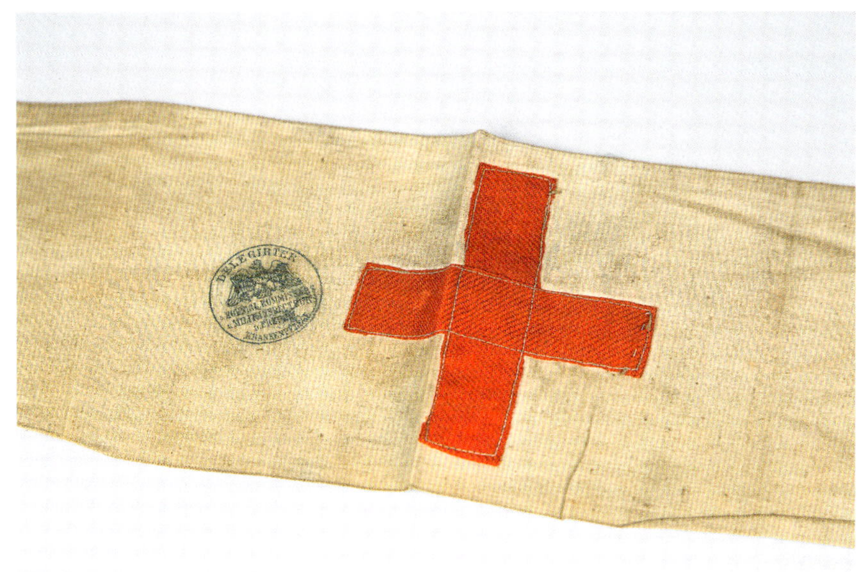

lendetes Militärsanitätswesen auf eine harte Probe, da eine einheitliche Feldführung desselben fehlte.[9] Loeffler, der als Feldarzt der Preußischen Armee am Krieg teilnahm, veröffentlichte zwei Jahre später einen kritischen Bericht, in dem er besonders die Unterstützung der freiwilligen Krankenpflege hervorhob.[10]

Gemäß der Allerhöchsten Kabinettsorder vom 2. Juni 1869 wurde das »Central-Comité der deutschen Vereine zur Pflege verwundeter und erkrankter Krieger« geschaffen und ein »Königlicher Kommissar und Militär-Inspekteur der freiwilligen Krankenpflege« ernannt.[11] Ab Juli 1870 übernahm diese Funktion der General der Kavallerie Hans Heinrich Fürst von Pleß. Unterzeichnet von Wilhelm I. und Kriegsminister Albrecht von Roon, wurden in der Instruktion erstmals auch die Aufgaben der freiwilligen Krankenpflege definiert. Der offizielle Charakter des Dokuments und die neue Institution eines Königlichen Kommissars, der für die Kontrolle und Organisation der freiwilligen Krankenpflege verantwortlich war, zeigen deutlich, wie sehr die private Krankenpflege staatlich-militärischem Einfluss unterstand.[12] Für die militärische und politische Führung war die Aussicht von höchstem Interesse, dass in den nationalen Hilfsgesellschaften auch in Friedenszeiten große Teile der Bevölkerung auf den Krieg vorbereitet werden konnten.[13] Tatsächlich bot der Einsatz Freiwilliger handfeste Vorteile für die militärische Führung: Verwundete Soldaten konnten so schneller wiederhergestellt und erneut auf den Schlachtfeldern eingesetzt werden.

Ein wichtiger Schritt in der Entwicklung der weiblichen Krankenpflege war die Gründung des Vaterländischen Frauenvereins unter der Schirmherrschaft der preußischen Königin Augusta, die anlässlich der Friedensfeiern in Berlin im November 1866 stattfand. Beim Volk war die überzeugte Pazifistin und Bismarck-Gegnerin Augusta nicht besonders beliebt – anders ihr Gemahl Wilhelm, der sein Image als »Kartätschenprinz«[14] abgestreift hatte. Nur auf einem Gebiet genoss sie unbegrenzten Respekt: in ihrem Engagement für verwundete und verletzte Soldaten.[15] Nach der Vereinsgründung nutzte sie jede ihrer Reisen nach England, um Florence Nightingale zu treffen; wenn sie »Bismarcks

Damen aus Adel und Bürgertum verpacken Lebensmittel und Wäsche für die preußischen Armeen in Böhmen und die Mainarmee, Gardes-du-Corps-Kaserne, Berlin 1866
Friedrich Jamrath & Sohn, Berlin
Kat. 450

Das Verpacken und der Versand von »Liebesgaben« genannten Geschenken für Soldaten im Feld wurde in den Reichseinigungskriegen für Frauen geradezu zur patriotischen Pflicht. Dank der Eisenbahn und eines effizienten Feldpostwesens war es möglich, große Mengen solcher Sendungen zu befördern.

Kriege« schon nicht verhindern konnte, wollte sie den Menschen helfen, die ihm zum Opfer gefallen waren. Als Vorsitzende des Vereins amtierte fast ein halbes Jahrhundert lang Charlotte Clementine von Itzenplitz, eine Tochter des preußischen Handelsministers.[16] Dem Verein konnten Frauenn aller Stände und Konfessionen beitreten. Den vormaligen Hilfsarbeiterinnen des Preußischen Vereins zur Pflege im Felde verwundeter und verletzter Krieger bot er in Friedens- wie in Kriegszeiten die Möglichkeit, sich in einer ausschließlich weiblichen Organisation zu betätigen. Zu den bekanntesten Mitgliedern zählten Anna von Roon, die Ehefrau des Kriegsministers, und Anna Borsig, die Ehefrau des Unternehmers Albert Borsig.[17]

In Sachsen gründete unterdessen Kronprinzessin Carola von Wasa-Holstein-Gottorp 1867 gemeinsam mit der sorbischen Krankenpflegerin Marie Simon den Albertverein. Er war ein Frauenverein vom Roten Kreuz, der sich der professionellen Ausbildung von Krankenschwestern widmete, die im Kriegsfall den militärischen Sanitätstruppen zur Seite stehen konnten. Am 1. Januar 1869 wurde in Dresden-Neustadt die erste Albertverein-Poliklinik für die Ausbildung der Albertinerinnen eröffnet. Seine Feuerprobe bestand der Verein im Deutsch-Französischen Krieg 1870/71. Dabei prägten jedoch ein erheblicher Widerstand seitens der geistlichen Pfleger sowie die ständige Suche nach geeigneten Verbandsstationen, schlechte Verpflegungsbedingungen, eigene Erkrankungen der Freiwilligen und anhaltende Erschöpfung zeitweise die freiwillige Arbeit der weltlichen Krankenpflegerinnen.[18]

Nach Kriegsausbruch wurden zahlreiche Appelle verfasst, die eine Aktivierung des weiblichen Engagements zum Ziel hatten. So forderte Charlotte von Itzenplitz, noch weitere Untergliederungen des Vaterländischen Frauenvereins zu gründen, und Königin Augusta ließ am 17. Juli 1870, noch vor der offiziellen Kriegserklärung, einen Aufruf veröffentlichen, in dem sie alle Frauen beschwor, ihre Pflicht zu tun und das Vaterland zu unterstützen. Von Anfang an versuchten die deutschen Staaten, die private Hilfe zu fördern, da offensichtlich war, dass sich die von den Regierungen bewilligten Summen zum Unterhalt der vom Krieg Betroffenen als völlig unzureichend erweisen würden.[19] Von mehr als einer Million Kriegsteilnehmern wurden 1870/71 auf deutscher Seite 92 000 und auf französischer Seite 89 000 Soldaten verwundet. Zu Beginn des Krieges hatte das Preußische Central-Comité satzungsgemäß die Koordination der deutschen Hilfsvereine und deren Interessenvertretung gegenüber der militärischen Führung übernommen.[20] Einem halbwegs geordneten Militärsanitätswesen im Verbund mit der freiwilligen Krankenpflege war es zu verdanken, dass danach erstmals in der Kriegsgeschichte weniger Soldaten an Krankheiten starben als durch Verletzungen im direkten Kampf.[21]

Sechs Monate nach der Reichseinigung schlossen sich unter maßgeblicher Führung Kaiserin Augustas auch die Frauenvereine der deutschen Einzelstaaten zum Verband der Deutschen Frauenvereine vom Roten Kreuz zusammen, um ihre Arbeit im Ernstfall besser koordinieren zu können. Augusta behielt zeitlebens das Protektorat für den Verband, welches sie später an die neue Kaiserin Auguste Viktoria weitergab.[22] Bei aller gesellschaftlichen Anerkennung wurde das Engagement von Frauen mitunter als sentimental belächelt. Kaiser Wilhelm I. kommentierte die wohltätige Arbeit seiner Gattin einmal mit den Worten: »Die Kaiserin möchte jeden verwundeten Soldaten in ein Himmel-

Ehren- oder Mitgliedsabzeichen des Königlich Sächsischen Albertvereins für Krankenpflege
Silber, vergoldet, 41 × 33 mm
Kat. 449

Kronprinzessin Carola von Sachsen wählte den Namen des 1867 gegründeten Frauenvereins zu Ehren ihres Gemahls, des Kronprinzen Albert.

Madame Marie Simon – »The Friend of the Wounded«
Holzstich aus »Cassell's History of the War between France and Germany, 1870 to 1871«, 1874
Kat. 447

Die gebürtige Sorbin Marie Simon (1824–1877), Geschäftsfrau in Dresden, hatte bereits in ihrer Jugend im Selbststudium und an Krankenhäusern Kenntnisse in der Krankenpflege erworben. 1866 pflegte sie Verwundete und Kranke der Kämpfe in Böhmen. Nach der Gründung des von Kronprinzessin Carola geleiteten Albertvereins führte sie in dessen Direktorium die Aufsicht über die Krankenpflegerinnen und die Armenkrankenpflege. Dem ersten Etappen-Delegierten des XII. (sächsischen) Armeekorps zugeteilt, rückte sie zu Beginn des Deutsch-Französischen Krieges mit zunächst sechs Albertinerinnen, einem Jurastudenten und einem Depotdiener zum Einsatz im Feld aus.

Loos-No. 14268

Deutsche National-Lotterie.

Preis 1 Thaler.

Unter der Allerhöchsten Protection

Ihrer Majestät der Kaiserin und Königin.

Zum Besten der kranken u. verwundeten deutschen Krieger, der Invaliden des jetzigen Krieges, und der Hinterbliebenen der Gefallenen.

DEUTSCHE NATIONAL-LOTTERIE

Berlin, am 20. Februar 1871.

Das Central-Comité
der deutschen Vereine zur Pflege verwundeter und erkrankter Krieger.

Der Vorstand
des vaterländischen Frauen-Vereins.

Los der Deutschen National-Lotterie, 20. Februar 1871
Kat. 452

bett legen.«[23] Geschlechterstereotypen zeigten sich auch darin, dass die Frauenvereine in Friedenszeiten Aufgaben wie die allgemeine Verbesserung der Krankenpflege oder die Armen- und Waisenfürsorge wahrnahmen. Die Männervereine vom Roten Kreuz lehnten hingegen zunächst jede Art von Friedenstätigkeit mit dem Argument ab, dies könne zur Vernachlässigung ihrer auf den Kriegsfall ausgerichteten Aufgaben führen.[24] Unbestritten war jedoch, dass zur Zeit der Reichseinigungskriege nicht nur die freiwillige Krankenpflege für die medizinische Versorgung im Krieg unentbehrlich und die Rotkreuzbewegung zu einem wichtigen gesellschaftlichen Faktor geworden war, sondern auch, dass die Einbeziehung und das Engagement von Frauen zunehmend als Teil der nationalen Kriegsanstrengung betrachtet wurden.

1 Vgl. Peter Kolmsee: Unter dem Zeichen des Äskulap: Eine Einführung in die Geschichte des Militärsanitätswesens von den frühen Anfängen bis zum Ende des Ersten Weltkrieges, Bonn 1997, S. 107 f. **2** Vgl. Rainer Emig: Die Domestizierung des Krieges: Florence Nightingales »Public Relations«-Strategien während des Krimkrieges, in: Martina Thiele/Tanja Thomas/Fabian Virchow (Hg.): Medien – Krieg – Geschlecht. Affirmationen und Irritationen sozialer Ordnungen, Wiesbaden 2010, S. 283 f. **3** E. R. Wagner (Hg.): Die Barmherzigkeit auf dem Schlachtfelde: eine Erinnerung an Solferino von Henry Dunant nach der vierten französischen Ausgabe mit Ermächtigung des Verfassers neu übersetzt, Stuttgart 1864, S. 155. **4** Vgl. Dieter Riesenberger: Das Deutsche Rote Kreuz: Eine Geschichte 1864–1990, München 2002, S. 28. **5** Vgl. Gerd Stolz: Louis Appia und Charles van de Velde. Die beiden ersten Rotkreuz-Delegierten der Weltgeschichte 1864 in Schleswig-Holstein und Dänemark, S. 28. **6** Geschichte des Badischen Frauenvereins, Festschrift, hg. vom Centralcomité des Badischen Frauenvereins, Karlsruhe 1881, S. 493. **7** Vgl. Annett Büttner: Die konfessionelle Kriegskrankenpflege im 19. Jahrhundert, Stuttgart 2013, S. 83–85; Gerd Stolz: Die freiwillige Kranken- und Verwundetenpflege im Deutsch-Dänischen Krieg von 1864, in: Jens Ahlers/Inge Adriansen (Hg.): Menschen im Krieg – mennesker i krigen (1864), Kiel 2014, S. 185–231, hier S. 185–187. **8** Elise von Mellenthin: Briefe einer freiwilligen Krankenpflegerin aus den Kriegen von 1864, 1866 und 1870/71 und Aufzeichnungen aus ihrem Leben, Potsdam 1911, S. 29. **9** Vgl. Rüdiger Döhler/Peter Kolmsee: Preußens Sanitätsdienst in den Einigungskriegen, in: Wehrmedizinische Monatsschrift 8/2016, S. 254–258, hier S. 255. **10** Gottfried Loeffler: Das Preußische Militär-Sanitätswesen und seine Reform nach der Kriegserfahrung von 1866, Berlin 1868, S. VIII. **11** Kolmsee: Äskulap, 1997, S. 120. **12** Vgl. Instruktion über das Sanitätswesen der Armee im Felde vom 29. April 1869, § 63, Berlin 1870. **13** Vgl. Daniel Erasmus Khan: Das Rote Kreuz, München 2013, S. 29. **14** Den Spottnamen »Kartätschenprinz« für Wilhelm I. hatte die Bevölkerung nach der militärischen Niederschlagung der Märzunruhen 1848 in Berlin geprägt. Wilhelm hatte zu einem harten Vorgehen gegen die Aufständischen aufgerufen. Siehe in diesem Band, S. 36–37. **15** Vgl. Karin Feuerstein-Praßer: Die deutschen Kaiserinnen, Regensburg 2008, S. 82 **16** In diversen Publikationen wurde fälschlich angenommen, sie sei die Ehefrau von Heinrich Friedrich von Itzenplitz. **17** Vgl. Carl Misch: Geschichte des Vaterländischen Frauenvereins. 1866–1916, Berlin 1917. **18** Vgl. Gustav Emil Enzmann: Die Geschichte des Albert-Vereins (1867–1917), Dresden 1917, und Marie Simon: Meine Erfahrungen auf dem Gebiete der freiwilligen Krankenpflege im Deutsch-Französischen Kriege 1870/71. Briefe und Tagebuchblätter, Leipzig 1872. **19** Vgl. Alexander Seyferth: Kollekten für den Krieg. Unterstützungsvereine im Deutsch-Französischen Krieg 1870/71, in: Militärgeschichtliche Zeitschrift 64 (2005), S. 34–35. **20** Vgl. Riesenberger: Rotes Kreuz, 2002, S. 54. **21** Vgl. Heidi Mehrkens: Statuswechsel. Kriegserfahrung und nationale Wahrnehmung im Deutsch-Französischen Krieg 1870/71, Essen 2008, S. 43. **22** Vgl. Christine von Brühl: Anmut im märkischen Sand. Die Frauen der Hohenzollern, Berlin 2015, S. 349. **23** Feuerstein-Praßer: Kaiserinnen, 2008, S. 82. **24** Vgl. Riesenberger: Rotes Kreuz, 2002, S. 65.

Sidonien-Orden, Großkreuz, verliehen an Großherzogin Luise von Baden am 24. Juli 1881
Königreich Sachsen, gestiftet am 30. Dezember 1870
Gold, emailliert, 83,33 × 61,31 mm
Kat. 453

Olga-Orden
Königreich Württemberg, gestiftet am 27. Juni 1871
Silber, emailliert, 39,81 × 35,35 mm
Kat. 454

Verdienstkreuz für Frauen und Jungfrauen
Königreich Preußen, gestiftet am 22. März 1871
Silber, emailliert, 37,56 × 33,64 mm
Kat. 457

Verdienste von Nichtkombattanten wurden schon vor den Einigungskriegen mit speziellen Auszeichnungen gewürdigt. 1866 und vor allem 1870/71 wuchs im Zusammenhang mit der Ausbreitung der Rotkreuzbewegung der Anteil von Frauen, die solche Auszeichnungen erhielten. Im und nach dem Deutsch-Französischen Krieg wurden zur Anerkennung dieser Einsätze zusätzlich zu Medaillen und Erinnerungskreuzen auch Orden gestiftet. Der Olga-Orden trug den Namen der karitativ stark engagierten Königin von Württemberg. Der sächsische Sidonien-Orden war benannt nach der als fromm und tugendhaft geltenden Gemahlin Herzog Albrechts des Beherzten von Sachsen, Sidonie von Böhmen (1449–1510). Großherzogin Luise von Baden erhielt als eine der Vorkämpferinnen der Rotkreuzbewegung das Großkreuz dieses Ordens.

Kat. 30

»Bersaglieri Kugel aus der Schlacht bei Solferino 24. Juni 1859«
Königreich Sardinien
Deformierte Bleifragmente
Kat. 30

Die in einer kleinen Schachtel aufbewahrten Bleifragmente sollen aus dem Körper eines Verletzten entfernt worden sein. Ein beigelegter Zettel spricht von einer »Bersaglieri Kugel«. Die Bersaglieri genannten Schützenbataillone waren die Elitetruppe des Königreichs Sardinien.

Sanitätswesen

Auf den Schlachtfeldern blieben unzählige Tote und Verwundete zurück. Die Verletzten mussten häufig Stunden, wenn nicht Tage auf Hilfe warten. Im Lazarett erlagen viele von ihnen einer Wundinfektion. Seuchen wie Typhus, Cholera und Pocken breiteten sich aus. Die katastrophale medizinische Versorgung im Krimkrieg (1853–1856) und im Zweiten Italienischen Unabhängigkeitskrieg (1859) führte nicht nur zur Gründung einer in Vereinen organisierten freiwilligen Krankenpflege, sondern in vielen Staaten auch zur Reform des militärischen Sanitätswesens. Fortschritte in der medizinischen Forschung und Lehre verbesserten die Heilungschancen ebenso wie effizientere Erstversorgung und Lazarettorganisation.

Kat. 435

Bayerischer Feldverbandsplatz 1870/71

Louis Braun (1836–1916)
Öl auf Leinwand, 115 × 104 cm
Kat. 435

Der Maler bildete hier exemplarisch die Personen ab, die im Feld mit der Bergung und der Versorgung von Verwundeten betraut waren: Krankenträger, Sanitätssoldaten und eine Ordensschwester. Alle tragen Rotkreuzarmbinden. 1870/71 war die freiwillige Krankenpflege bereits fest in die militärische Organisation des Sanitätsdienstes eingebunden.

Dreiecktuch nach Friedrich von Esmarch (1823–1908)

Nach einer Zeichnung von Johann Heinrich Wittmaack (1822–1878) gestochen von Karl Becker (1820–1900), Kiel 1868
Kat. 436

Friedrich von Esmarch nahm als Chirurg an den Einigungskriegen teil und wurde 1870 Generalarzt der preußischen Armee. Die Einführung des Verbandpäckchens und des Dreiecktuchs zur Erstversorgung – heutzutage in jedem Erste-Hilfe-Kasten zu finden – gehen auf seine Initiative zurück. Dieses Tuch, auch als »Erster Verband auf dem Schlachtfelde nach Dr. F. Esmarck [sic!]« beworben, entspricht dem zuerst eingeführten Modell.

Kat. 436

Kat. 438

Kat. 440

Maske, Tropfflasche und Zungenzange, verwendet im preußischen Militärsanitätswesen

Königreich Preußen, 1869
Kat. 438

Seit dem Ende der 1840er Jahre nutzten Ärzte Äther oder Chloroform, um Patienten und Patientinnen vor Operationen zu narkotisieren. Für die Verabreichung gab es verschiedene Verfahren. Diese Narkosemaske, über die das Chloroform inhaliert wurde, ging ebenfalls auf eine Erfindung des Militärchirurgen Friedrich von Esmarch zurück. Das Besteck war auch nach der Form der zugehörigen Tragetasche als »Narkosebirne« bekannt.

Pockenwarnschild, 1871

Kat. 440

Während des Deutsch-Französischen Krieges wurden weite Teile Westeuropas von einer Pockenepidemie heimgesucht. Allein in Preußen starben in den Jahren 1871 und 1872 rund 125 000 Menschen. Die Feldheere in Frankreich waren unterschiedlich stark betroffen. Französische Soldaten waren nicht geimpft, die meisten deutschen dagegen schon. Dementsprechend hoch waren die Todesraten unter französischen Pockenkranken. Die Zivilbevölkerung in den deutschen Staaten war weitaus stärker als das Militär betroffen, da viele Menschen der bestehenden Impfpflicht nicht nachgekommen waren. Wo die Krankheit ausgebrochen war, wurden solche Warnschilder angebracht.

Lazarett »Amtshaus« in Flensburg, 1864

Kat. 441

Deutsche Verwundete und Sanitätspersonal in einem Gang des Schlosses von Versailles

Aus der Serie »Ansichten des Kriegsschauplatzes«, München/Berlin 1870
Kat. 443

Die Überlebenschancen von Verwundeten hingen auch davon ab, wie gut sie nach ihrer Erstversorgung untergebracht wurden. Im Hinterland der Front nutzten Militärärzte bevorzugt großräumige Gebäude, die gut zu belüften waren, wie Amtsge-

Kat. 441

Kat. 443

B. 220.

7.

Küchen-Personal des Reserve-Lazareths № I zu Dresden-Neustadt, 1870/71.—

8.

1. 2. 3. 4. 5. 6. 7. 8. 9. 10. 11. 12. 13. 14. 15. 16.

Personal des Reserve-Lazareths № I zu Dresden-Neustadt, 1870/71.

Station für innere Krankheiten: Flügel **D.**

1, 2, 4 und 5. Schwestern aus der evangel. luther. Diakonissen-Anstalt zu Dresden-Neustadt, welche als Krankenpflegerinnen bei obengedachter Station thätig waren.—

3. Pommsdorf, Minna, Oberschwester, eine von Ihrer Königl. Hoheit der Frau Kronprinzeßin Carola von Sachsen hochgeschätzte Pflegerin, welche gleichzeitig auch Verwalterin der Verband-, Labe- und Pflege-Materialien bei der obengedachten Station war.

6. Dr. med. Bille, Ernst Richard Maximilian; AR! StnRum 0.RSt³ SCM. u.s.w. Geboren 1839 am 21. Novbr. zu Dresden. 1870/71 Assistenz-, später ordinirender Arzt bei obengedachter Station. Sodann prakticirender Arzt, Wundarzt und Geburtshelfer in Dresden, auch Arzt an der Poliklinik des Albert-Vereins zu Dresden-Neustadt. Verzog 1898 nach Baden-Baden und 1901 nach Oberhof in Thüringen, woselbst er noch — 1901 — als prakticirender Arzt thätig war.

7. Dr. med. Haeußler, ... Geboren 18 am zu . . . . . . 1870/71 Assistenzarzt bei obengedachter Station. War Oesterreicher von Geburt, ging in sein Vaterland zurück und lebte 1901 als prakticirender Arzt zu Aicha bei Aussig in Böhmen.—

8. Dr. med. Schurig, Edmund; AR! OeFJR PK³ Geboren 1830 am 26. Mai zu Dresden; gestorben 1891 am 9. Janr. zu Dresden. Hofrath und Königl. Hofarzt. 1870/71 ordinirender Arzt für obengedachte Station. Prakticirte sodann in Dresden und war Specialist für Gehörleiden. Beerdigt auf dem alten Annen-Friedhof an der Chemnitzer Straße zu Dresden-Westend.—

9. Starke, Gustav Adolph. Geboren 1835 am 13. Decbr. zu Hundshübel bei Schneeberg; . . . . . . 1870/71 als Assistenzarzt bei obengedachter Station thätig. Verblieb in Dresden wohnhaft, Pieschen, Concordien-Straße 72.1, und prakticirte daselbst seit 1872 als approbirter Arzt, Wundarzt, Armen- und Impfarzt, welche Thätigkeit derselbe noch 1901 ausübte.—

10. Oberlazareth-Gehilfe, ...
11, 12, 13, 14, 15 und 16. Lazareth-Gehilfen, } als solche bei obengedachter Station thätig.

bäude, Schulen oder Adelssitze. Viele Räume des Schlosses von Versailles wurden 1870/71 von den deutschen Besatzern mit Verwundeten belegt. Baracken und Zelte waren ein Notbehelf, sollten aber nach dem Prinzip der Zerstreuung auch helfen, zu große Ansammlungen von Kranken zu vermeiden. Insgesamt rund 250 000 Soldaten wurden zur weiteren Behandlung per Eisenbahn in die Heimat geschafft.

Personal des Reservelazaretts N° 1 in Dresden-Neustadt, 1870/71
Kat. 444

Transportkiste des französischen Militärsanitätsdienstes
Kaiserreich Frankreich, 1870
Kat. 439

Zusammen mit Fahrzeugen für das Militärsanitätswesen wurden passende Transportkisten für Instrumente, Verbandszeug und Lebensmittel in verschiedenen Größen gefertigt, wie diese »Cantine Médicale des Corps de Troupe N° 2«.

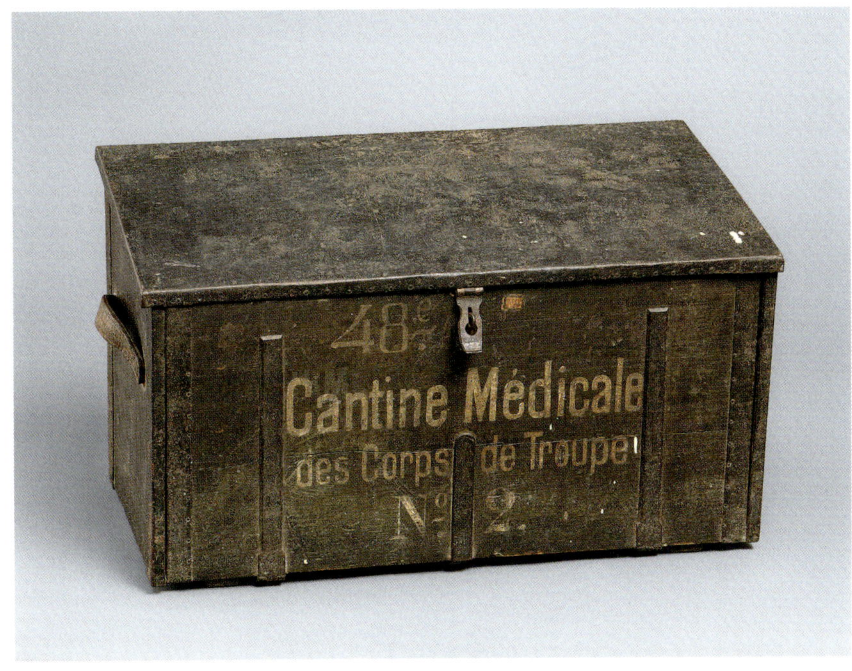

Kat. 439

Verbandmittelwagen mit Feldapotheke
1868–1917
Kat. 492

In den Napoleonischen Kriegen gab es erstmals für die Belange des Sanitätswesens konstruierte Fahrzeuge. Vor der Anerkennung des Roten Kreuzes als Schutzzeichen 1864 waren sie jedoch nicht gekennzeichnet. Dieses Sanitätsfahrzeug, dessen älteste Teile aus dem Jahr 1868 stammen, entspricht Modellen, die von deutschen Armeen 1870/71 im Feld eingesetzt wurden. Es diente zum Transport von Verbandszeug, aber auch als Feldapotheke. Die »Dienstzeit« dieses Wagens endete erst während des Ersten Weltkriegs. 1916 noch immer in Gebrauch, wurde er an der Somme von französischen Truppen erbeutet und einige Monate beim 87. Territorial-Infanterie-Regiment genutzt. Aus dieser Zeit stammt die heutige Beschriftung. 1917 nach Großbritannien geschickt, gelangte der Wagen in die Sammlung des Imperial War Museum in London, das ihn 1958 unbefristet an die Royal Military Academy Sandhurst verlieh. Diese übergab ihn schließlich an die Sanitätsakademie der Bundeswehr in München.

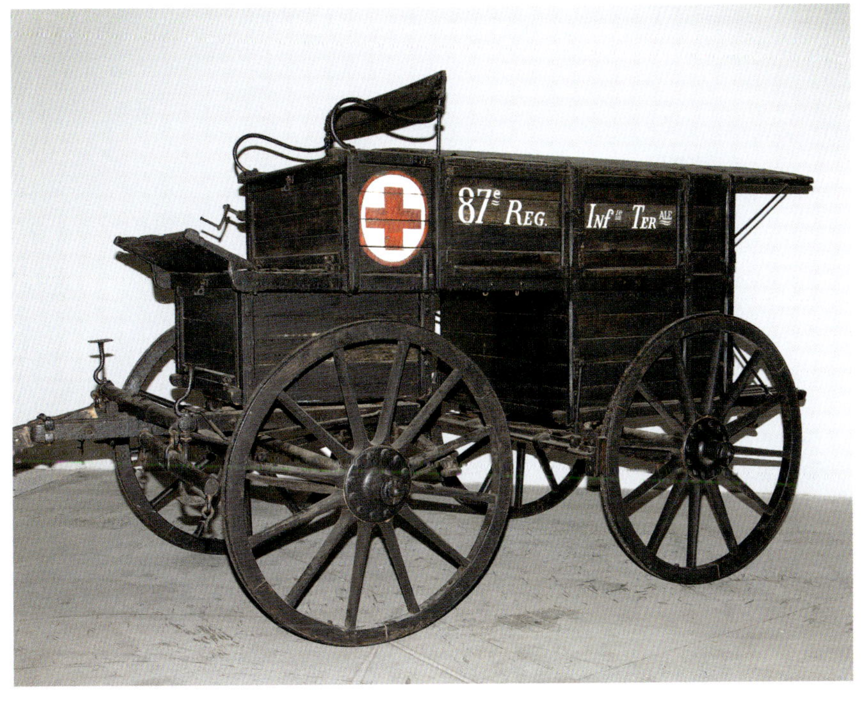

Kat. 492

Kriegsgefangenschaft

1870/71 überstieg die Zahl der Kriegsgefangenen alle Erwartungen. 8 000 deutschen standen bis Februar 1871 rund 383 000 französische Kriegsgefangene gegenüber. Mit der Eisenbahn wurden Letztere in den deutschen Staaten verteilt – auf Festungen, Kasernen und eilig errichtete Barackenlager. Offiziere durften sich oft privat einquartieren und am gesellschaftlichen Leben teilnehmen. Kriegsgefangene, Unteroffiziere und Mannschaften wurden in Massenunterkünften einquartiert und konnten zu nicht kriegsrelevanten Arbeiten herangezogen werden. Die Unterbringung und Versorgung stellte deutsche wie französische Militärbehörden vor erhebliche Probleme, aber beide Seiten bemühten sich um eine Grundversorgung. Mangel und die schnelle Ausbreitung von Infektionskrankheiten gehörten trotzdem zu den Erfahrungen vieler Kriegsgefangener. War die Verwundetenfürsorge im Krieg bereits durch die Genfer Konvention von 1864 international geregelt worden, so fehlten für den Umgang mit Kriegsgefangenen vergleichbare völkerrechtliche Vereinbarungen noch bis zu den Haager Konventionen von 1899/1907. Bei der einheimischen Bevölkerung erregten die Kriegsgefangenen Neugier, und vor allem Angehörige der französischen Afrikaarmee wurden unverhohlen bestaunt.

»Barakenlager auf dem Alaunplatz in Dresden. Erinnerung an 1870/71«
Lithografie, 1872
Kat. 461

Über 6 000 Gefangene lebten zeitweise im Barackenlager auf dem Alaunplatz, der damals noch ein Exerzier- und Paradeplatz war.

Aus dem französischen Lager in Mainz, 1870/71
Philipp Hoff, Frankfurt am Main
Kat. 462

Kat. 462

Kat. 461

Sammelrahmen mit Uniformknöpfen französischer Kriegsgefangener

1870/71

Kat. 459

Die Knöpfe stammen von unterschiedlichen Truppenteilen. Manche zeigen den Kaiseradler. Dieses Symbol war den Regimentern der Kaiserlichen Garde vorbehalten. Obwohl die Garde mit dem Dritten Kaiserreich bei Sedan unterging, dienten ehemalige Gardisten weiter in der ab September 1870 republikanischen Armee.

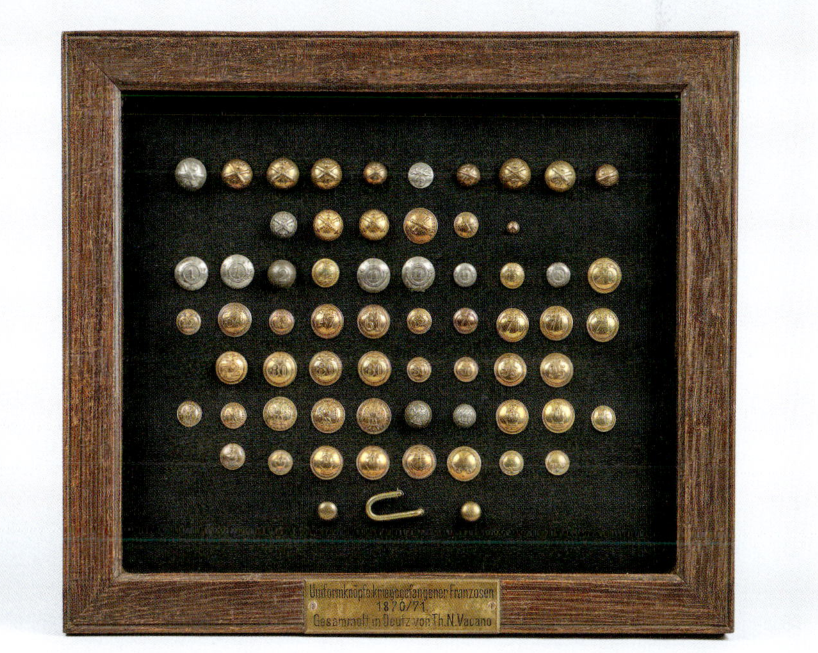

Kat. 459

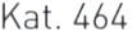

Kat. 464

Kat. 460

Algerische Schützen oder »Turkos« als Kriegsgefangene in Ingolstadt, 1870

Lichtdruck nach Originalaufnahme von Fr. Sölch, Ingolstadt
Kat. 464

Die Namen der aus Afrika stammenden Soldaten sind auf der Rückseite notiert:

1. Tschelul ben Harráth [ben Hareth]
2. Mohammed ben Tombetschi
3. Mesud ben Belél
4. Mussa ben Retep [Reteb]
5. Feratsehi ben Labés [el Abés]

Drei kriegsgefangene französische Unteroffiziere in der bayerischen Landesfestung Ingolstadt, 1870

Photographische Anstalt Fr. Sölch, Ingolstadt
Kat. 465

Der Tod des Sergeanten Gombault

George Moreau de Tours (1848–1901), 1892
Öl auf Leinwand
Kat. 466

Sergeant Gombault, auf der Fotografie ganz rechts, trägt die Uniform der Volontaires de l'Ouest, der früheren Päpstlichen Zuaven. Auf der Rückseite ist auf Französisch vermerkt, dass Gombault am 9. Januar 1871 füsiliert wurde. Der 22-Jährige wurde zum Tod verurteilt, weil er mehrere Ausbruchsversuche unternommen hatte. Seinen Kameraden Leoni und Petragnani gelang die Flucht. Das Gemälde der Hinrichtung Gombaults vor den Wällen von Ingolstadt hängt im Rathaus seiner bretonischen Heimatstadt Dinan, wo er während der Dritten Republik als Held verehrt wurde. Dort erinnert auch eine nach ihm benannte Straße bis heute an den Sergeant.

Kat. 465

Ansicht des Kriegsgefangenenlagers am Brückenkopf in Ingolstadt und Typen französischer Kriegsgefangener
Zwei Lithografien aus einem Erinnerungsalbum, angelegt von Moritz Ratzinger, 1870/71 Leutnant im 1. Königlich Bayerischen Feldartillerie-Regiment
Kat. 460

Kat. 466

»Diese armen Geißeln machen immer ein jämmerliches Gesicht«

Über Anfänge des humanitären Völkerrechts

HEIDI MEHRKENS

Krieg wurde im 19. Jahrhundert nicht als rechtsfreier Raum ohne Regeln aufgefasst. Die internationalen völkerrechtlichen Abkommen zur Ratifizierung des Rechts im Krieg (ius in bello) in den 1860er Jahren beruhten zum einen auf lange tradierten Kriegsgebräuchen, dem sogenannten Völkergewohnheitsrecht, zum anderen auch auf rechtsphilosophischen Überlegungen. Frühneuzeitliche Autoren wie Hugo Grotius oder Emerich de Vattel hatten bedeutende Schriften darüber hinterlassen, wie die Auswirkungen bewaffneter Konflikte auf Unbeteiligte, aber auch auf die Kämpfenden selbst eingehegt werden sollten. Als leitende Grundsätze des ius in bello galten die Unterscheidung von Zivilpersonen und Kämpfenden im Kriegsfall, die Schonung der Zivilbevölkerung sowie eine Verhältnismäßigkeit der im Krieg angewandten Mittel. Wohlgemerkt, der Krieg als politisches Instrument wurde von diesen frühneuzeitlichen Autoren nicht infrage gestellt: Es ging ihnen nicht darum, Kriege pauschal abzuschaffen, sondern sie plädierten lediglich dafür, die Konsequenzen der Kriegführung zu regulieren. Dies sollte sich auch im 19. Jahrhundert nicht ändern.

Die rechtsphilosophischen älteren Vorstellungen des ius in bello stellten keine verbindlichen Rechtsnormen dar. Doch sie waren ein Fundament, auf dem in der zweiten Hälfte des 19. Jahrhunderts internationales Recht gedacht und normative Regelungen verabschiedet wurden. Die ernüchternden Erfahrungen des Krimkriegs und des Italienisch-Österreichischen Krieges von 1859/60, vor allem die katastrophalen Bedingungen bei der Versorgung kranker und verwundeter Soldaten, hatten in der Öffentlichkeit und unter Völkerrechtsgelehrten Diskussionen darüber entfacht, wie das Recht im Krieg auf die modernen internationalen Konflikte des 19. Jahrhunderts anzuwenden sei.

Was hatte sich im Vergleich zu den »Kabinettskriegen« früherer Jahrhunderte verändert? Zum einen sah das 19. Jahrhundert mit seinen Nationalstaatsbewegungen größere Armeen als die frühneuzeitlichen Konflikte. 1870 prallten in den gewaltigen Augustschlachten des Deutsch-Französischen Krieges Heere in der Größenordnung von 70 000 und mehr Soldaten aufeinander.[1] Durch die Einführung der allgemeinen Wehrpflicht in einer Reihe von Staaten kämpften

Reiter des Brandenburgischen Husaren-Regiments (Zietensche Husaren) Nr. 3 im Kampf gegen »Franktireure«
Vermutlich um 1870/71, Öl auf Leinwand, 28,5 × 41 cm
Abb. 37

Das Bild eines namentlich nicht bekannten Malers zeigt preußische Soldaten, die bewaffnete französische Zivilisten überwältigen. Mit Misstrauen wurden im Feindesland nicht nur Bauern und Arbeiter in ihren typischen blauen Kitteln betrachtet, sondern auch katholische Geistliche, denen besonderer Fanatismus nachgesagt wurde.

Als Franktireur (Freischütze) galt bald jeder französische Zivilist, der zur Waffe griff oder kriegswichtige Anlagen zerstörte – ob als Angehöriger einer militärisch organisierten, teils uniformierten Freischar oder auf eigene Faust.

neben Berufssoldaten jetzt oft Männer, die eingezogen worden waren oder die sich freiwillig für einen Kriegseinsatz gemeldet hatten, um einen Beitrag für ihre Nation zu leisten. Und auch wenn sich in den Konflikten des 19. Jahrhunderts noch nicht die Schrecken des Stellungskriegs der Jahre 1914 bis 1918 zeigten, wurde mit modernen Granaten und Maschinenwaffen gleichwohl Technik eingesetzt, die den Weg zum industrialisierten Krieg wies. Hinzu kam, dass die sich entwickelnde Massenpresse und die fortschreitende Alphabetisierung der Bevölkerung Kriege mehr auf einer internationalen öffentlichen Bühne stattfinden ließen: Das Zeitung lesende Publikum in Berlin oder Paris konnte – unter Berücksichtigung der üblichen Zensur in Kriegszeiten – aus der Presseberichterstattung Rückschlüsse darauf ziehen, wie es den eigenen Ehemännern und Söhnen an der Front ging, ob die Truppen gut versorgt wurden oder in schwerem Feuer standen.[2] Die völkerrechtlichen Regelungen können als ein Zugeständnis interpretiert werden: Staaten und Regierungen demonstrierten ihr Verantwortungsbewusstsein dafür, die bestmögliche Versorgung und den Schutz der Bürger und Bürgerinnen ihrer Nation im Feld zu gewährleisten. Dies diente der Aufrechterhaltung des Kriegswillens der Bevölkerung und sollte die Akzeptanz der allgemeinen Wehrpflicht fördern.

Ein Lösungsansatz war die vertragliche Selbstverpflichtung potenzieller Kriegsgegner, im Fall eines Konflikts Regeln der Menschlichkeit zu achten: 1864 wurde die erste Genfer Konvention verabschiedet. Zwölf Staaten unterzeichneten das Abkommen, das in zehn Artikeln Regelungen zur Unterstützung verwundeter und kranker Soldaten und zum Schutz von Sanitätspersonal festlegte. Das Rote Kreuz auf weißem Grund, Symbol des Internationalen Komitees der Hilfsgesellschaften für die Verwundetenpflege (seit 1876 Internationales Komitee vom Roten Kreuz), wurde als Schutzzeichen eingeführt. 1868 folgte die Petersburger Erklärung, ein völkerrechtlicher Vertrag über die Nichtanwendung kleiner Sprenggeschosse im Krieg.[3] Das durch die Petersburger Erklärung erstmals vertraglich formulierte Prinzip, den Einsatz solcher Waffen zu verbieten, die unnötiges Leid verursachen, wurde in späteren völkerrechtlichen Verträgen ausgeweitet und präzisiert, vor allem in der Haager Landkriegsordnung (1899/1907).

Zwei Jahre später standen sich Preußen mit deutschen alliierten Staaten und das Zweite Kaiserreich als Kriegsgegner gegenüber. Der Deutsch-Französische Krieg 1870/71 gibt einen interessanten Einblick in die Rechtspraxis dieser frühen völkerrechtlichen Verträge und des Völkergewohnheitsrechts, denn was auf dem Papier der vertraglichen Vereinbarung stand, war in der Kriegsrealität nicht immer eins zu eins umzusetzen. Mehr noch, der Konflikt offenbarte weiteren Regelungsbedarf. Lücken im System wurden vor allem dort sichtbar, wo moderne Kriegführung die Leitprinzipien des ius in bello auszuhebeln schien: die Unterscheidung von Kämpfenden und Zivilbevölkerung – beiden Gruppen wurden jeweils besondere Verpflichtungen und Schutzansprüche zugestanden –, die Schonung der Zivilbevölkerung und die Verhältnismäßigkeit in der Anwendung von Kriegsmitteln.

Das Völkerrecht des 19. Jahrhunderts unterschied zwischen Kombattanten, also den Angehörigen der Streitkräfte und ihren Hilfskräften (etwa Versorgungseinheiten), und Nichtkombattanten wie Zivilpersonen und Sanitätspersonal. Nur Kombattanten hatten das Recht, bewaffnete Kampfhandlungen durchzuführen. Der asymmetrische Verlauf des Deutsch-Französischen Krieges führte allerdings zu Verunsicherung und auch zu öffentlichen Debatten darüber, welche Personengruppen als Kombattanten anerkannt werden konnten. Der Konflikt spielte sich fast ausschließlich auf französischem Territorium ab. Soldaten der preußischen und verbündeten deutschen Armeen rückten im August 1870 immer weiter auf feindliches Territorium vor. Durch die verheerende Niederlage der kaiserlichen Armeen bei Sedan wurden die französischen regulären Truppen stark dezimiert.[4]

Die »Entscheidungsschlacht« Sedan brachte allerdings nicht die erwartete Entscheidung des Krieges. Der Herbst 1870 sah die Aushebung zahlreicher Ersatzmannschaften, mit denen Innenminister Léon Gambetta, von der französischen Regierung mit der nationalen Verteidigung beauftragt, den Konflikt nach dem Ende des Kaiserreichs fortsetzte. Der Kombattantenstatus der *Armée auxiliaire*, vor allem der mobilen Nationalgarden und der Franktireure, war umstritten. Was bis zur Schlacht von Sedan weitgehend ein traditioneller Konflikt zwischen regulären Armeen gewesen war, ging nach der Einschätzung des preußischen Armeekommandos nun in einen »Volkskrieg« über, in dem Zivilisten sich bewaffneten, um die deutschen Soldaten aus ihrem Land zu vertreiben.[5]

Der Unterscheidungsgrundsatz sieht vor, Kombattanten und Nichtkombattanten im Konfliktfall als getrennte Gruppen wahrzunehmen. Viele preußische Soldaten fanden es schwierig, ihr Gegenüber eindeutig zuzuordnen. Theoretische Kriterien für die Unterscheidung waren durchaus formuliert worden: Kombattanten hatten Uniform zu tragen und unter dem Kommando eines führenden Offiziers zu operieren. Aus Quellen geht aber hervor, dass die oft hastig ausgehobenen französischen Ersatztruppen nicht immer voll uniformiert und insbesondere aus größerer Entfernung oftmals nicht als Kombattanten identifizierbar waren.[6] Die französische Armeeführung bestand darauf, die *Armée auxiliaire* als reguläre Einheiten zu definieren, aber in der Sprache der deutschen Quellen werden diese Soldaten häufig verallgemeinernd als »bewaffnete Zivilisten« bezeichnet. Das hat auch mit der Kampfweise der Hilfstruppen zu tun, die mit »Kleinem Krieg« die verbündeten Truppen zwangen, mit großen Kräften ihre Nachschublinien und rückwärtigen Verbindungen zu sichern.[7] Der Kriegsberichterstatter der Kölnischen Zeitung Georg Horn beschrieb die wachsende Verunsicherung innerhalb der deutschen Truppen:

»Überfälle von einzelnen Ordonnanzen, von kleineren Truppendetachements, von Proviantkolonnen und Postwagen waren an der Tagesordnung, jeder Baum, kann man sagen, wurde jetzt zu einem belebten Wesen, aber nicht durch eine liebliche Dryade, sondern durch einen blaukitteligen Franctireur, der dahinter stand und auf jeden *Prussien* die meuchlerische Kugel abschoß.«[8]

Horns Wortwahl lässt Rückschlüsse darauf zu, wie die Hilfstruppen wahrgenommen wurden: »Blaukittelig« verwies auf die Nationaltracht der französischen Bauern und Arbeiter und deutete somit an, dass die Franktireure zivile Kleidung trugen. Und die »meuchlerische Kugel« widersprach dem militärisch regulären Aufeinandertreffen im offenen Kampf. Eine weitere Frage war, wie mit gefangenen Franktireuren umzugehen sei. Das Recht der Kriegsgefangenschaft wurde ausschließlich Kombattanten zugestanden. Kämpfende, die aufgegriffen und als bewaffnete Zivilisten eingestuft wurden, liefen Gefahr, standrechtlich erschossen zu werden.

DIE SCHONUNG DER ZIVILBEVÖLKERUNG

Auch der Grundsatz, die Zivilbevölkerung möglichst schonend zu behandeln, ließ sich in diesem Konflikt nicht immer umsetzen. Die preußischen und ihre verbündeten Truppen versorgten sich auf ihrem Vormarsch aus dem Land. Es kam zu Einquartierungen deutscher Offiziere in französischen Häusern und zur Beschlagnahmung von Eigentum. Einwohner und Einwohnerinnen flohen vor den herannahenden Truppen und suchten Schutz in den Festungsstädten Metz oder Paris. Hier waren sie dann feindlichem Artilleriebeschuss ausgesetzt. Es war für Zivilpersonen also grundsätzlich sehr schwierig, von dem Konflikt im eigenen Land unbehelligt zu bleiben.

Im Sinne des internationalen Völkerrechts waren die Einquartierungen nicht umstritten, sondern wurden als zu erwartende Folge von Kriegführung toleriert. Problematisch waren indes Situationen, in denen Zivilpersonen beschuldigt wurden, in das Kriegsgeschehen einzugreifen, etwa durch Spionage. Ein berühmter Fall ist der Schriftsteller Theodor Fontane, der auf der Suche nach Material für sein drittes Kriegsbuch (nach 1864 und 1866) nach Frankreich gereist war. Anfang Oktober 1870 wurde er in Domrémy bei der Besichtigung einer Statue der Jeanne d'Arc von einer Patrouille französischer Nationalgardisten festgenommen. Er trug eine Pistole bei sich, eine Karte der Befestigungsanlagen der Stadt Metz, und, obwohl er kein Sanitäter war, eine Armbinde mit dem Schutzzeichen des Roten Kreuzes.[9] Der Verdacht der Spionage wurde schließlich aus Mangel an Beweisen fallen gelassen, und Fontane konnte nach mehrmonatiger Festungshaft nach Berlin zurückkehren. Dies geschah nicht zuletzt aufgrund der Intervention Bismarcks, der sich am 29. Oktober 1870 für die Freilassung des Schriftstellers einsetzte.[10] Im Allgemeinen hatten zivile ebenso wie militärische Spione mit harten kriegsrechtlichen Konsequenzen bis hin zur Todesstrafe zu rechnen. Das hohe Strafmaß erklärt sich daraus, dass die Offenlegung militärischer Geheimnisse für eine Kriegspartei schwerwiegende Folgen haben konnte. Die Schonung der Zivilbevölkerung wurde in solchen Fällen also durchaus den militärischen Notwendigkeiten untergeordnet.

Die Nähe von Soldaten und Zivilpersonen auf und neben dem Kriegsschauplatz ließ auch die Furcht des Militärs vor hasserfüllten Übergriffen und Racheakten wachsen. Das Bild des katholischen französischen Geistlichen, der vom Kirchturm aus auf preußische Soldaten feuert und von der Kanzel zum Kampf aufruft, wurde zu einem starken Motiv des französischen Widerstands, wenngleich diesen Vorwürfen oft die faktische Grundlage fehlte.[11] Der Krieg 1870/71 kennt außerdem viele Erzählungen von Französinnen, oft »alten Mütterchen«, die verwundeten, daher wehrlosen deutschen Soldaten Verletzungen zufügten, ihnen auf dem Schlachtfeld die Augen ausstachen und persönliche Wertgegenstände raubten. Diese Geschichten führen oft aus, wie die Frauen, wurden sie aufgegriffen, von den Soldaten keine Gnade zu erwarten hatten.[12] Der Schutzanspruch der Zivilpersonen, so ließe sich interpretieren, endete dort, wo diese die Grenzen ihrer Rechte überschritten und in den Krieg eingriffen. Häufig erfolgte die Bestrafung allerdings aufgrund einer unübersichtlichen Beweislage und befeuert von der Angst und Panik der deutschen Soldaten, die sich im Feindesland ständiger Bedrohung ausgesetzt sahen.

Eine wichtige Rolle für den Transport von Kriegsgerät, Soldaten und Vorräten spielten die französischen Eisenbahnlinien. Aus Furcht vor Anschlägen auf ihre Transportstrecken gingen die deutschen Soldaten im Herbst 1870 dazu über, Zivilpersonen als Geiseln auf den Lokomotiven mitzuführen. Der Journalist der Kölnischen Zeitung Hans Wachenhusen schreibt:

»Diese armen Geißeln [sic!] machen immer ein jämmerliches Gesicht, wenn sie so auf der Maschine dastehen, und sie sind zu bedauern, diese Bauern-Maires und sonstigen Würde-Personen, die man sich zu diesem Zwecke aufgreift: Oft, ja täglich liegt ein Eisenbahnzug acht und zwölf Stunden unbeweglich an einer Station, ohne vorwärts zu können, und der gute Bauer muss aushalten ohne eine Miene zu verziehen mit der Besorgniß, daß die Herren Franctireurs auf die Rettung des Vaterlandes viel mehr Gewicht legen, als auf die armselige Person eines blaukitteligen Maire's [...].«[13]

Der militärische Nutzen der Gefährdung von Bürgern und Bürgerinnen, die als lebende Zielscheiben stundenlang auf diesen Transporten ausharren mussten, war Gegenstand heftiger Diskussionen in der zeitgenössischen deutschen, französischen und neutralen Presse. Die preußisch-deutsche Armeeführung führte an, es sei unmöglich, die Eisenbahnlinien ausreichend bewachen zu lassen; daher sei die Mitnahme von Geiseln militärisch notwendig. Diese Form der Geiselhaft gehört jedoch zu den Erfahrungen des Krieges, die erheblich zur Verstärkung der Feindschaft zwischen Deutschland und Frankreich beigetragen haben. Die Sorglosigkeit, mit der hier über das Leben von Zivilpersonen verfügt wurde, ging dauerhaft ins Gedächtnis der französischen Bevölkerung ein, und sie beeinflusste auch die künftigen Debatten um den völkerrechtlichen Schutz von Zivilisten und Zivilistinnen.

DIE VERHÄLTNISMÄSSIGKEIT DER KRIEGSMITTEL

Die preußisch-deutsche Truppenführung stand nicht nur wegen Geiselnahmen unter Druck, ihre militärischen Maßnahmen zu rechtfertigen. Ihre über viermonatige Belagerung von Paris entfachte eine öffentliche Kontroverse über die Verhältnismäßigkeit gleich zweier Kriegsmittel: Im September 1870 schloss sich der Belagerungsring um die französische Hauptstadt, und die Einschließungsarmee blockierte die Zufuhr von Vorräten nach Paris. Die erschwerten Lebensbedingungen und die Nahrungsmittelknappheit kosteten im Winter 1870/71 Zehntausende Männer, Frauen und Kinder das Leben. Trotz ihrer hohen Opferzahlen galten Hungerblockaden traditionell als reguläres Mittel in einem Belagerungskrieg und waren zumindest aus völkerrechtlicher Perspektive nicht umstritten.[14]

Der Krieg Deutschlands gegen

Explosion des Pulver-Magazins zu Laon am

Bald nach der Capitulation von Sedan, zu deren Ausführung eine entsprechende Abtheilung unserer Truppen zurückblieb, nahmen die beiden Armeen des Kronprinzen von Preußen und des Kronprinzen von Sachsen den Marsch auf Paris wieder auf, indem sie sich theilweise wieder auf die früher innegehabten Linien der Aisne und der Marne begaben, theilweise vom Nordosten her vorrückten. Der rechte Flügel ging auf der Straße, welche von Belgien her über Laon und Soissons nach Paris führt.

Die kleine Festung Laon war vor einigen Tagen von den wirklichen Besatzungstruppen verlassen worden und nur noch von Mobilgarden besetzt. Als größere deutsche Truppenmassen heranrückten, baten die Bürger der Stadt dem Commandanten, die Citadelle zu übergeben, da sie doch nicht zu halten sei. In der That übergab der Commandant die Festung am 9. September dem Commandeur der 6. Cavallerie-Division Herzog Wilhelm von Mecklenburg. Nachdem die Capitulation abgeschlossen war, besetzte eine Jäger-Compagnie vom 4. (sächsischen) Bataillon die Citadelle. In dem Augenblick aber, wo der letzte Mann der französischen Mobilgarden die Citadelle verlassen hatte, wurde das Pulver-Magazin in die Luft gesprengt. Durch diese allem Völkerrecht Hohn sprechende That wurden 95 Jäger getödtet

oder verwundet, der H
furchtbare Zerstörungen
Diese Schandt
ter Zeit nach allen Rich
indem die pariser Blät
dienstliche Handlung fei
Der traurige
Führer dadurch hinweis
versehen haben, und h
nahme dem Feinde gege
nen Sicherheit vereinba

Original u. Eigenthum №5362.

kreich. Bilderzeitung der Gegenwart. No. 28.

ptember 1870.

von Mecklenburg gleichfalls verwundet. In der Citadelle und Stadt waren
auch 300 der französischen Mobilgarden fanden dabei den Tod oder Verwundung.
er Beleg der nichtswürdigen Gesinnung, von welcher das französische Volk in letz=
hlreiche Beweise gegeben hat. Die Verworfenheit tritt noch schmählicher hervor,
rnt, die völkerrechtswidrige, ehrlose That zu beklagen, dieselbe als eine ver-

doch unfehlbar auch seine guten Folgen haben, indem er unsere Armeen und
Art von Kriegführung sie sich von der hochcivilisirten französischen Nation zu
die dringende Mahnung giebt, die bisherige hochherzige Milde und Rücksicht-
er daßjenige Maaß hinaus walten zu lassen, welches mit der Wahrung der eige-

Verlag von Otto Kraffert & C. in Dresden

»Explosion des Pulver-Magazins zu Laon am 9. September 1870«

Der Krieg Deutschlands gegen Frankreich.
Bilderzeitung der Gegenwart, Nr. 28
Verlag Otto Kraffert & Co., Dresden
Abb. 38

Immer wieder warfen sich Deutsche und Franzosen gegenseitig völkerrechtswidriges Verhalten vor, während gleichzeitig der hohe Stand der eigenen Zivilisation hervorgehoben wurde. Dies gehörte zur Feindbildpropaganda, zeugt aber auch davon, wie sehr Fragen des Völkerrechts Teil des öffentlichen Diskurses waren.

»Nemesis«
Gereon Pape (1842–1907) nach Skizze, 1. Oktober 1870
Tusche auf Papier, 42 × 58 cm
Bezeichnet unten links: »Nemesis« / verso: »[unleserlicher Satz] 1.10.70. (Nach Skizze.)«
Kat. 305

Der in Köln geborene Zeichenlehrer Pape schrieb »Nemesis« auf sein Bild eines Erhängten, ein Begriff aus der griechischen Mythologie für ausgleichende Gerechtigkeit oder Rache. Über den genauen Entstehungszusammenhang dieser Darstellung ist nichts bekannt.

Nachdem die Blockade von Paris nicht den gewünschten Effekt zeigte, eröffnete das preußisch-deutsche Heereskommando am 5. Januar 1871 das Bombardement der Stadt. Die Beschießung dauerte drei Wochen an und entzündete eine weitere Diskussion über die völkerrechtliche Rechtmäßigkeit dieser Maßnahme. Das Heereskommando musste sich zum Beispiel gegen den Vorwurf wehren, man würde gezielt Krankenhäuser und Pflegeeinrichtungen beschießen, um die belagerte Stadt in die Knie zu zwingen. Vom juristischen Standpunkt war auch die Maßnahme des Bombardements gerechtfertigt. In den zeitgenössischen völkerrechtlichen Texten findet sich übereinstimmend die Aussage, dass die Beschießung befestigter und verteidigter Plätze ein legitimes Mittel sei, um den Widerstand des Gegners zu brechen. Dass der »Krieg gegen Paris« dennoch Schlagzeilen machte, lag auch an der besonderen Stellung von Paris als kulturellem und politischem Zentrum Frankreichs: Die Belagerung wurde zum Symbol für das Leid, aber auch für die Widerstandsfähigkeit einer ganzen Nation, die sich erbittert gegen die militärische Eroberung stemmte.

Die jungen völkerrechtlichen Bestimmungen der 1860er Jahre wurden 1870/71 zum ersten Mal von allen kriegführenden Parteien in einem internationalen Konflikt angewendet. Dabei zeigte sich, dass die Abkommen der Belastungsprobe zwar grundsätzlich standhielten, aber auch, dass ihre Regelwerke nicht alle Entwicklungen moderner Kriegführung abdecken konnten, wie zum Beispiel die verschwimmende Grenze zwischen Zivilpersonen und Kombattanten. Im und nach dem Krieg 1870/71 führte dies zu einer umfassenden Diskussion der militärischen Praxis. Sie fand nicht nur innerhalb des Militärs statt, sondern wurde in der deutschen, französischen und neutralen Presse öffentlich ausgetragen. Dass Fragen des Völkerrechts ein großer Stellenwert zugesprochen wurde, zeigen zum Ende des 19. und Anfang des 20. Jahrhunderts weitere Versuche, aus den Erfahrungen internationaler Konflikte zu lernen und die Bestimmungen des Völkerrechts auszuweiten und zu konkretisieren: Zu nennen sind vor allem die Brüsseler Konferenz von 1874 und die Haager Konferenzen in den Jahren 1899 und 1907.

Das heutige humanitäre Völkerrecht ruht auf den Säulen des Völkergewohnheitsrechts und auch auf den Erfahrungen mit diesen frühen internationalen rechtlichen Übereinkünften des 19. Jahrhunderts. Die Sorge um die Sicherheit von Armeeangehörigen und den Schutz der Zivilbevölkerung prägt nach wie vor das moderne Bild vom Krieg. Dennoch gilt es zu verstehen, dass die Vertreter des frühen Völkerrechts ebenso wie viele Regierungen oder vom Konflikt Betroffene Krieg als politisches Mittel und als soziale Realität akzeptierten. Diese Haltung sollte erst durch die katastrophalen Konflikte des 20. Jahrhunderts infrage gestellt werden.

Das als Lazarett genutzte Gehöft Mogador, das während der Schlacht bei Gravelotte abbrannte
Gereon Pape nach Skizze, 2. Oktober 1870
Tusche auf Papier, 33,5 × 51,1 cm
Bezeichnet verso: »Bei Gravelotte. Lazarett wo die Verwundeten verbrandt sind. 2.10.70. (Nach Skizze.)«
Kat. 304

Beide Kriegsparteien hielten sich gewöhnlich an die Genfer Konvention von 1864, die Verwundeten sowie Sanitätspersonal im Zeichen des Roten Kreuzes Schutz und Neutralität zusicherte. Dennoch gerieten immer wieder Verbandsplätze und Lazarette in das Feuer der eigenen oder gegnerischen Artillerie. In dem zwischen Malmaison und Gravelotte gelegenen Gehöft Mogador war am 16. August 1870 ein französisches Lazarett eingerichtet und mit einer großen Rotkreuzflagge gekennzeichnet worden. Am 18. August wurde es unbeabsichtigt – wohl durch französische Granateinschläge – in Brand gesetzt. Laut einer Veröffentlichung des Großen Generalstabs über die Schlacht aus dem Jahr 1874 konnten die Verwundeten nicht gerettet werden.

1 Vgl. François Roth: La Guerre de 1870, Paris 1990, S. 128. **2** Siehe zur sich verändernden medialen Präsenz des Krieges auch den Beitrag von Frank Becker in diesem Band, S. 300–311. **3** Vgl. Dieter Riesenberger: Für Humanität in Krieg und Frieden. Das Internationale Rote Kreuz 1863–1977, Göttingen 1992. **4** Vgl. Dennis E. Showalter: Das Gesicht des modernen Krieges. Sedan, 1. und 2. September 1870, in: Stig Förster/Markus Pöhlmann/Dierk Walter (Hg.): Schlachten der Weltgeschichte. Von Salamis bis Sinai, München 2001, S. 230–247. **5** Vgl. Gerd Krumeich: The myth of Gambetta and the »People's War« in Germany and France, 1871–1914, in: Stig Förster/Jörg Nagler (Hg.): On the Road to Total War. The American Civil War and the German Wars of Unification, 1861–1871, Cambridge/New York 1997, S. 641–656. **6** Vgl. Wolfgang Etschmann: Guerillas und Franctireurs, 1866 und 1870/71, in: Erwin A. Schmidl (Hg.): Freund oder Feind? Kombattanten, Nichtkombattanten und Bürgerkrieg seit dem 18. Jahrhundert, Frankfurt am Main 1995, S. 31–43. **7** Die Bezeichnung »Kleiner Krieg« fasste verschiedene Kampfhandlungen zusammen, z. B. Überfälle aus dem Hinterhalt oder Sabotage von Eisenbahngleisen. Das Ziel konnte militärische Aufklärung sein, aber auch Schädigung des Feindes. Vgl. Martin Rink: Der Kleine Krieg. Entwicklungen und Trends asymmetrischer Gewalt 1740 bis 1815, in: Militärgeschichtliche Zeitschrift 65/2 (2006), S. 355–388. **8** Zitiert nach: Bei Friedrich Karl: Bilder und Skizzen aus dem Feldzuge der zweiten Armee von Georg Horn, zur Zeit Berichterstatter im Hauptquartier S. K. H. des General-Feldmarschalls Prinzen Friedrich Karl von Preußen, Bd. 2, Leipzig 1872, S. 95. **9** Zur näheren Darstellung vgl. Theodor Fontane: Kriegsgefangen. Erlebtes 1870, Berlin 1870, hg. von Adolf Busse, Bielefeld/Leipzig 1916. Fontane räumt ein, dass das Tragen der Waffe und des Zeichens des Roten Kreuzes als Anklagepunkte gegen ihn verwendet werden konnten (ebd., S. 21). **10** Vgl. Günther Jäckel: Fontane und der Deutsch-Französische Krieg 1870/71, in: Fontane-Blätter 2,2 (1970), S. 93–115, hier S. 99 f. **11** Vgl. Heidi Mehrkens: Ein Opfer des Krieges und der Kriegsgesetze? Die Beschießung von Bazeilles im Deutsch-Französischen Krieg 1870, in: Thomas Kolnberger/Benoît Majerus/M. Christian Ortner (Hg.): Krieg in der industrialisierten Welt. Krieg und Gesellschaft Bd. 4, Wien 2017, S. 3–24, hier S. 15. Zu Bazeilles siehe in diesem Band, S. 197–198 und pass. **12** »Eine alte Frau wurde von Soldaten erschlagen, weil sie den Verwundeten die Augen sollte ausgestochen haben.« Tagebuch des Kgl. Sächs. 12. Feldlazaretts, Eintrag vom 20. 8. 1870, Militärhistorisches Museum, Inv.-Nr. BBAL4643. Vgl. auch Christian Brunnenberg: »Es lässt sich nicht leugnen, daß auch Roheiten und unnötige Härten vorkamen.« Gewalterfahrungen im Deutsch-Französischen Krieg von 1870/71, in: Frank Becker (Hg.): Zivilisten und Soldaten. Entgrenzte Gewalt in der Geschichte, Essen 2015, S. 79–102. **13** Hans Wachenhusen: Tagebuch vom französischen Kriegsschauplatz, Berlin 1871, S. 241: Artikel vom 28. Oktober 1870, Nanteuil. Das Tagebuch versammelt Wachenhusens Berichte vom Kriegsschauplatz, die während des Krieges fortlaufend in der Kölnischen Zeitung gedruckt worden waren. **14** Vgl. Robert Tombs: The War against Paris, in: Förster/Nagler (Hg.): On the Road to Total War, 1997, S. 541–564, bes. S. 550.

DER RATH ZU DRESDEN.

Schlachten-Panorama

Aufgenommen, Dresden, am 11. Januar

Panorama

Yadegar Asisis monumentale 360-Grad-Panoramen zum zerstörten Dresden 1945 oder zu Dresden im Barock sind heute ein Besuchermagnet. Weitgehend vergessen ist dagegen das erste Panorama, das 1883 in Dresden für Furore sorgte. Louis Brauns »Die Erstürmung von St. Privat am 18. August 1870« ließ eine Schlacht des Deutsch-Französischen Krieges 1870/71 lebendig werden, an der sächsische Truppen entscheidenden Anteil hatten. Solche Schlachtenpanoramen waren damals in den meisten deutschen Großstädten zu finden. Das aufwendigste von ihnen war Anton von Werners 15 Meter hohes und 115 Meter langes Panorama der Schlacht von Sedan, das im selben Jahr wie Brauns St.-Privat-Rundbild am Berliner

Alexanderplatz in Berlin eröffnete. Eine motorgetriebene Plattform bewegte die Besucher und Besucherinnen entlang des Schlachtgeschehens. Marschmusik erklang. Pappfiguren und reale Gegenstände im Vordergrund erzeugten die perfekte Illusion. Die Ausstellung »KRIEG MACHT NATION« mündet in einer verfremdeten Nachinszenierung von Louis Brauns Panorama – eines Massenmediums, das als eine Extremform der Schlachtenmalerei die Gesellschaft des Kaiserreichs im Wieder- und Nacherleben vergangener Schlachten einte. Durchlässe in dieser Inszenierung gewähren auch Ausblicke auf Konflikte jenseits der geschlossenen Welt der Schlachtenpanoramen.

»Die Erstürmung von St. Privat«

Louis Brauns Schlachtenpanorama für Dresden

1883 schuf Braun innerhalb von sechs Monaten das 360-Grad-Panorama »Die Erstürmung von St. Privat am 18. August 1870«, das am Jahrestag der Schlacht in Dresden eröffnet werden sollte. Mit Malerkollegen und Gehilfen bereitete Braun in seinem Münchner Atelier eine monumentale Leinwand vor, deren genaue Maße nicht überliefert sind. Vor Ort in Dresden porträtierte er militärische Führer sowie weitere Schlachtteilnehmer und befragte sie zu Details des Kampfgeschehens. 92 der dargestellten Figuren waren wiedererkennbare Personen. Panoramen zielten auf ein Massenpublikum. Sie waren keine Staatsaufträge, sondern privatwirtschaftlich finanziert, meist durch deutsche Tochtergesellschaften belgischer oder französischer Panoramaunternehmen. Trotz begeisterter Presseberichte war das Dresdner St.-Privat-Panorama mit 80 000 Besuchern und Besucherinnen in den ersten sechs Monaten kommerziell kein großer Erfolg, erwartet wurden mindestens 20 000 Besuche pro Monat.
Viele der großen Schlachtenpanoramen zum Deutsch-Französischen Krieg sind nicht oder nur in Fragmenten überliefert. Von Louis Brauns »Die Erstürmung von St. Privat« ließen sich bisher nur eine Mappe mit Fotodrucken des ausgeführten Panoramas und Skizzen finden.

Kat. 489

Louis Braun (1836–1916) im Atelier, um 1900

Kat. 489

Der in Schwäbisch Hall geborene Schlachtenmaler fertigte 1880 das erste deutsche 360-Grad-Gemälde zum Krieg von 1870/71, das Sedan-Panorama in Frankfurt am Main. Zwischen 1880 und 1894 schuf er insgesamt acht monumentale Panoramen: fünf zum Deutsch-Französischen Krieg (1880 Sedan, 1883 Weissenburg, 1883 St. Privat, 1885 Mars-la-Tour, 1890 Champigny-Villiers), eines zu den deutschen Kolonien (1885) und zwei zu Schlachten früherer Zeiten (1893 Lützen, 1894 Murten). Als das Interesse an den Panoramen um die Jahrhundertwende nachließ, hatte er es zu Wohlstand gebracht, Burg Wernfels bei Spalt erworben und eine große Militariasammlung zusammengetragen.

»Die Erstürmung von St. Privat am 18. August 1870«

Gemalt vom Schlachtenmaler
Prof. Louis Braun
Aufnahme und Druck Johann Baptist Obernetter in München, deponiert 1883
Schmuckmappe »Panorama Dresden« mit 10 Lichtdrucken
Kat. 487

Das Panorama zeigte die Situation am 18. August 1870, als der preußische Angriff ins Stocken geriet und das XII. (königlich sächsische) Armeekorps in die Schlacht geworfen wurde. Die Dörfer Gravelotte und St.-Privat-la-Montagne bildeten Schlüsselstellungen. Die französischen Truppen nutzten ummauerte Vorgärten an den Ortsrändern zur Deckung.

Solche Mauern sind im Vordergrund der Aufnahmen zu erkennen. Sie waren jedoch zum größten Teil nicht gemalt, sondern gehörten genauso wie das Dach auf Bild 9 zum »Faux-terrain«, dem mit dreidimensionalen Elementen ausgestatteten Raum zwischen der zentralen Besucherplattform des Panoramas und dem Rundbild selbst (siehe zur Schlacht von St. Privat auch S. 189 und 195).

Kat. 487/1

Kat. 487/2

1. Stab Sr. Majestät

Gemeint ist König Albert von Sachsen, der 1870 als Kronprinz das XII. Armeekorps in die Schlacht bei St. Privat führte und dann die neu gebildete Maasarmee übernahm.

2. Auboué

Erstürmung von St. Privat am 18. August 1870. III.

Louis Braun pinx. Reprod. von J. B. Obernetter.

Tod des General Kraußhaar — Stab des Prinzen Georg.

Deponirt 1883.

Kat. 487/3

Erstürmung von St. Privat am 18. August 1870. IV.

Louis Braun pinx. Reprod. von J. B. Obernetter.

Roncourt.

Deponirt 1883.

Kat. 487/4

3. Tod des General Kraußhaar – Stab des Prinzen Georg

»Ergreifend ist die Scene, welche sich dem Auge nach der Seite zwischen Montois und Roncourt mitten auf dem nach dem Dorfeingang führenden Wege darbietet. Auch hier ist der Kampf ein sehr blutiger gewesen, denn überall sieht man erschossene Franzosen, Preussen und Sachsen am Wege liegen und Verwundete ihren letzten Seufzer unter Flüchen oder stillen Gebeten aushauchen. Den Hauptmoment der Scene bildet der Tod des tapferen Führers der Avantgarde Generals von Craushaar, dem beim Vormarsch bereits das Pferd unterm Leibe erschossen war, und welcher etwa 200 Schritt von der Umfassungsmauer schwer verwundet in die Arme seines Adjutanten Lieutenant Schmalz gesunken und in wenigen Minuten darauf verschieden ist.« ([Theodor Seemann]: Panorama. Der Sturm auf St. Privat am 18. August 1870. Gemalt vom Schlachtenmaler Professor Louis Braun, Begleitheft, Dresden [1883])

4. Roncourt

Die Leibfahne des 8. Königlich Sächsischen Infanterieregiments Nr. 107, die rechts auf dieser Aufnahme zu sehen ist, gehört heute zur Sammlung des Militärhistorischen Museums. Traurige Berühmtheit erlangte sie, weil am 18. August fünf ihrer Träger hintereinander starben und ein sechster schwer verwundet wurde (siehe S. 195, Kat. 254 und 255).

5. Wald von Jaumont

6. St. Privat

7. Straßenkampf in St. Privat

Kat. 487/5

Kat. 487/6

Kat. 487/7

Kat. 487/8

Kat. 487/9

Kat. 487/10

8. Ferme Jerusalem

9. Nach Metz – St. Marie aux Chênes

10. Sturm

Fragment aus dem Panorama der Schlacht von Rezonville

Éduard Detaille (1848–1912), um 1883
Öl auf Leinwand, 143 × 169 cm
Kat. 474

Detaille hatte bereits 1882 gemeinsam mit Alphonse de Neuville (1836–1885) ein Rundgemälde zur Schlacht von Champigny am 30. November 1870 geschaffen, das große Erfolge feierte. Im selben Jahr begannen sie ein weiteres Monumentalbild zur Schlacht bei Rezonville am 16. August 1870, die in Deutschland als Schlacht von Mars-la-Tour bekannt wurde. Die Leinwände beider Panoramen wurden nach ihrem Abbau zerschnitten und 1892 bzw. 1896 als Einzelteile verkauft. Das Militärhistorische Museum konnte 2016 eines dieser Fragmente auf einer Auktion erwerben. Das Panorama von Rezonville zeigt keine Kampfhandlungen, sondern die Situation nach der Schlacht. Auf diesem Fragment sind Ambulanzen und Soldaten zu erkennen, die sich in langer Kolonne vom Schlachtfeld entfernen. Nicht nur Siege konnten der nationalen Erbauung dienen: Noch ehe im Deutschen Reich die ersten Schlachtenpanoramen zum Krieg von 1870/71 entstanden, schuf Félix Philippoteaux ein monumentales Rundbild der Verteidigung von Paris, das 1873 eröffnet und auch auf der Weltausstellung 1878 gezeigt wurde. Dort hatte es Louis Braun gesehen (siehe auch S. 219, Kat. 344).

Kat. 474

Risse im Panorama

Die Kriege von 1864, 1866 und 1870/71 in der deutschen Schlachten- und Ereignismalerei

KATJA PROTTE

» Es schweift der Blick zurück in jene Zeiten, / Wo kampfbereit, in heil'ger Gluth entbrannt / Die deutschen Heldensöhne muthig streiten / Für deutsches Recht, für's deutsche Vaterland.

[...]

Dem Meister Dank, der solch' ein Werk geschaffen, / Und Allen, die sich seinem Dienst geweiht, / Der altbewährte Ruhm von Sachsens Waffen, / Er leuchte fort in alle Ewigkeit. / Das Panorama aber mög' für Groß und Klein / Ein bleibend Denkmal der Erhebung sein.[1] 

Am 18. August 1883 eröffneten der sächsische König Albert und seine Gemahlin Carola in Dresden das von dem Schlachtenmaler Louis Braun geschaffene Panorama »Die Erstürmung von St. Privat am 18. August 1870«, an der Albert als Kronprinz mit seinem XII. Armeekorps entscheidenden Anteil gehabt hatte. Für viele Besucher und Besucherinnen war der Eindruck des monumentalen 360-Grad-Gemäldes überwältigend. Von einer erhöhten Plattform im Zentrum des Raumes aus konnten sie die Schlacht überblicken und sich gleichzeitig mitten im Geschehen fühlen. Dreidimensionale Gegenstände wie Trümmerteile, herumliegende Ausrüstungsgegenstände oder eine Mauer ließen den Übergang vom Gemälde zum Raum verschwimmen.

Schlachtenpanoramen verbanden Massenspektakel und Volksbelustigung mit patriotischer Erbauung und Teilhabe. Deutscher Nationalstolz und sächsisches Selbstbewusstsein fanden hier scheinbar zwanglos zusammen.[2] Die vor allem in den 1880er Jahren populären Monumentalgemälde waren die Extremform einer patriotisch ausgerichteten Ereignis- und Schlachtenmalerei, die einen besonderen Anspruch auf Realismus erhob: »[D]ie ›zünftige‹, die professionelle Schlachtenmalerei [...] verlangt daher vom Künstler genaues Studium der Örtlichkeiten, das oft weite Reisen und große Zeitopfer erfordert, sie ver-

Das Schlachtenpanorama in Dresden

Aufnahme für den Dresdner Rat, Tiefbauamt, 11. Januar 1911
Abb. 39

Von 1883 bis 1901 stand an der Prager Straße 20/21 in Dresden ein Panoramagebäude, in dem zunächst Louis Brauns »Sturm auf St. Privat« und später auch ein Panorama der Schlacht bei Wörth gezeigt wurde.

langt eine profunde Kenntnis des Waffen- und Ausrüstungswesens und, im Idealfalle, Begleitung der kämpfenden Heere durch alle Entbehrungen des Feldzuges.«[3] Dieses Verständnis einer berufsmäßigen Schlachtenmalerei entwickelte sich im 19. Jahrhundert, besonders von Frankreich ausgehend. Louis Braun, der an der Stuttgarter Kunstschule studiert hatte, vervollständigte seine Ausbildung 1859 nicht zufällig in Paris, wo er von dem bekannten französischen Schlachtenmaler Horace Vernet gefördert wurde. An den Einigungskriegen nahm Braun als Künstler und Berichterstatter teil und bereiste die Schlachtfelder erneut, wenn es galt, ein Panoramagemälde vorzubereiten.[4]

Beginnend mit dem Deutsch-Dänischen Krieg 1864 war die Gegenwart auch für deutsche Schlachtenmaler geschichtswürdig geworden. Idealtypisch schilderte der Düsseldorfer Historienmaler Wilhelm Camphausen, wie er am 18. April 1864 den Sturm auf die Düppeler Schanzen aus sicherer Entfernung verfolgte: »Wir aber machten es uns bequem und richteten uns für das bevorstehende Schauspiel ein. [...] Es war 9 Uhr morgens, und wir harrten, mit einem guten Fernrohre versehen, des entscheidenden Augenblicks.«[5] Später besuchte er das Schlachtfeld und sprach mit Teilnehmern des Kampfgeschehens. Im Herbst 1864 veröffentlichte er Skizzen und Erlebnisberichte in dem illustrierten Familienblatt »Daheim«, die 1865 unter dem Titel »Ein Maler auf dem Kriegsfelde« als Buch erschienen. Gleichzeitig schuf Camphausen sein erstes Großgemälde zum Deutsch-Dänischen Krieg. Die »Erstürmung der Schanze II durch das Brandenburgische Füsilier-Regiment Nr. 35« zeigt eine Vielzahl von Szenen, die sich im Inneren der Schanze abspielten. So ist zum Beispiel rechts im Bildmittelgrund der Kampf um eine dänische Fahne zu erkennen. Im Zentrum steht die machtvoll vorwärtsstürmende Gruppe um Premierleutnant von Saß-Jaworski, der mit ausgestrecktem Arm auf die Gegner weist. Links davon triumphiert ein Preuße auf einer erbeuteten Kanone, während um die am Schanzenrand aufgepflanzte preußische Fahne herum Tote, Verwundete oder

»3 Schlachtenmaler 1870/71«

Schulz & Buck, Karlsruhe
Kat. 488

Diese Aufnahme zeigt Louis Braun (1836–1916) mit seinen Künstlerkollegen Wilhelm Emelé (Mitte) und Heinrich Lang (links) in Frankreich.

Die Erstürmung der Düppeler Schanze Nr. II durch das Brandenburgische Füsilier-Regiment Nr. 35 am 18. April 1864

Wilhelm Camphausen (1818–1885), 1864/65
Öl auf Leinwand, 158 × 252 cm
Kat. 467

Links im Bildvordergrund sieht man, wie der für die zähe Verteidigung der Schanze II bekannt gewordene dänische Artillerieleutnant Ancker seinen Degen dem preußischen Leutnant Schneider übergibt. Neben ihm liegt ein toter Däne am Boden, weiter rechts ist auch ein toter Preuße zu erkennen, der die weiße Allianzarmbinde der verbündeten preußischen und österreichischen Truppen trägt. Die zurückweichenden Dänen wirken in diesem Gemälde nicht weniger eindrucksvoll als die vorwärtsstürmenden Preußen.

Übergang nach Alsen
Wilhelm Camphausen, 1866
Öl auf Leinwand, 165 × 284 cm
Abb. 40

Noch im Dunkeln setzten preußische Truppen am 29. Juli 1864 nach Alsen über und begannen mit der Eroberung der Insel. Diese Operation beendete den Deutsch-Dänischen Krieg.

auch nur Erschöpfte liegen. Dieses vom preußischen König erworbene Bild nahm schon viel von der Wirkung späterer Panoramagemälde vorweg, sah sich aber auch einer ähnlichen Kritik wie diese ausgesetzt: Es handle sich nicht um ein »geistig bedeutendes, künstlerisch einheitliches Ensemble«.[6] Camphausens 1866 entstandenes Werk »Übergang nach Alsen« kam dem Anspruch nach Geschlossenheit weit mehr entgegen. Verdichtet strebt hier das Kampfgeschehen auf einen klaren Höhepunkt zu. Unmissverständlich stehen die am Boden liegende dänische und die mit Verve aufgepflanzte preußische Fahne für einen glorreichen Sieg über Dänemark. Dieses Schlachtengemälde symbolisierte ungebrochen die Kampfkraft und Dynamik einer ganzen Nation.

Von der wachsenden Bedeutung, die der Schlachtenmalerei von offizieller Seite beigemessen wurde, zeugt ein Artikel in der Zeitschrift »Die Grenzboten« vom 21. September 1866, der freudig vermerkte, dass das preußische Militär seine sonstige Zugeknöpftheit gegenüber »Civilmenschen« abgelegt habe. Der preußische Kronprinz Friedrich Wilhelm und andere militärische Führer hätten im Deutschen Krieg 1866 eigens Maler wie Wilhelm Camphausen, Georg Bleibtreu und Otto Heyden eingeladen, sich den Armeehauptquartieren anzuschließen.[7] Der Kronprinz erkannte sehr genau, wie wichtig diese Form von Öffentlichkeitsarbeit für den Fortbestand der Monarchie in Zeiten war, in denen der Ruf nach nationaler Teilhabe jedes Einzelnen immer lauter wurde. Auf vielen Schlach-

Das Königlich Sächsische 2. Jäger-Bataillon Nr. 13 in der Schlacht bei Sedan am 1. September 1870
Theodor von Götz (1826–1892), 1878, Öl auf Leinwand, 126×190,5 cm
Abb. 41

ten- und Ereignisgemälden sind Monarchen und militärische Führer zwar mehr oder weniger deutlich hervorgehoben, erscheinen aber gleichzeitig als integraler Teil eines Ganzen. Otto Heydens Gemälde »Anmarsch der preußischen 2. Armee unter Kronprinz Friedrich Wilhelm am Morgen der Schlacht von Königgrätz, 3. Juli 1866« zeigt den preußischen Kronprinzen mit seinem Stab und weiterem Gefolge auf leicht erhöhter Position als ruhenden Pol, um den herum seine Truppen in den Kampf ziehen (siehe S. 132–133, Kat. 470). Der sächsische Offizier und Militärmaler Theodor von Götz ließ auf seinem Königgrätz-Gemälde den Kronprinzen Albert lediglich durch die zentrale Positionierung im Bildmittelgrund hervortreten (siehe S. 124–125, Kat. 471). Ein anderes Gemälde von Götz verweist ebenso wie Camphausens Bilder der Schanze II und des Übergangs nach Alsen darauf, dass Truppenoffiziere und ihre Mannschaften auch ohne die Anwesenheit eines hochrangigen militärischen Führers als abbildungswürdig betrachtet wurden. Beim Angriff des 2. Jäger-Bataillons Nr. 13 in der Schlacht bei Sedan auf eine mit Zuaven und Turkos besetzte Mitrailleusenstellung ist lediglich auf französischer Seite ein General erkennbar. Links im Bildmittelgrund hat sich der Künstler – damals Major und Kommandeur des Jäger-Bataillons – selbst dargestellt. Er steht, den Degen ruhig in der Hand haltend, neben dem Adjutanten, der an einer silbernen, über die Schulter geschlungenen Schärpe zu erkennen ist. Die Hauptleute von Sichart und Walde, die ihre Männer mit erhobenem Degen zum Sturm führen, sind genauso wiedererkennbar wie Jäger Ludwig, der am Kopf verwundet zusammenbricht.[8] Solche oft für Offizierskasinos geschaffenen Bilder vergegenwärtigten glorrei-

»Die Proklamierung des Deutschen Kaiserreiches« (18. Januar 1871)
Nach einer Schwarz-Weiß-Fotografie von Anton von Werners (1843–1915) erster Fassung von 1877 (Schlossfassung, Öl auf Leinwand, ca. 430 × 800 cm, Kriegsverlust)
Abb. 42

che Momente der Regiments- oder Bataillonsgeschichte und dienten der Traditionsstiftung. Doch ihre Wirkung ging über den engeren militärischen Bereich hinaus. Die kriegerische Reichsgründung als Gemeinschaftsleistung, die traditionelle monarchische Herrschaftsansprüche und bürgerliche Forderungen nach nationaler Teilhabe versöhnte, war ein Narrativ, das durch zahllose Schlachtenbilder und -panoramen lebendig gehalten wurde und Vorbildcharakter für das Zusammenleben im Kaiserreich erlangte.[9]

Spannungsfrei war dieses Narrativ nicht, es ließ sich jedoch je nach Zielgruppe variieren, wie sich besonders gut am bekanntesten Motiv der Einigungskriege zeigen lässt – der Kaiserproklamation am 18. Januar 1871 im Spiegelsaal des Versailler Schlosses, gemalt von Anton von Werner. Der Künstler, der auf Einladung des preußischen Kronprinzen der Zeremonie beigewohnt hatte, schuf drei verschiedene Fassungen. Die erste war für das Berliner Schloss konzipiert und wurde Kaiser Wilhelm I. von den Fürsten und Freien Städten des Reiches 1877 zu seinem 80. Geburtstag überreicht. Keiner der Protagonisten ragt besonders hervor, es ist die Masse der Offiziere aus den verschiedenen deutschen Staaten, die den größten Teil des Bildraums einnimmt. So erscheint die Reichsgründung als Höhepunkt eines gemeinsamen Kampfes des Norddeutschen Bundes und der süddeutschen Staaten. 1882 vollendete Werner eine zweite Fassung, ein Wandbild für die Ruhmeshalle des Berliner Zeughauses, und 1885 eine dritte, sehr ähnliche, anlässlich Bismarcks 70. Geburtstags (siehe S. 47, Kat. 360). Dabei wurden nicht nur – der räumlichen Situation im Zeughaus geschuldet – das Format verändert und eine Vielzahl der Offiziere weggelassen, sondern gleichzeitig auch Wilhelm I., Moltke und Bismarck so angeordnet, dass diese Trias das Bild vollkommen beherrscht. Bismarck sticht besonders heraus, da er statt mit blauem Rock nun im weißen Koller des Magdeburgischen Kürassier-Regiments Nr. 7 dargestellt ist, den er in Frankreich gar nicht bei sich hatte. So zeigt diese Fassung eine »Reichsgründung von oben« und demonstriert unmissverständlich den Führungsanspruch Preußens.[10] Das, was als Realismus geboten und akzeptiert wurde, war ein ständiger Aushandlungsprozess zwischen Künstlern, Auftraggebern, Augenzeugen und Publikum.

1877 malte der in München ansässige Württemberger Louis Braun ein »Wimmelbild«, wie man es heute nennen würde, das fast wie ein Gegenentwurf zu einer preußisch dominierten Geschichte großer Männer wirkt. »Die Deut-

»Die Deutschen in Versailles«

Louis Braun, 1877

Öl auf Leinwand, 88,5 × 177 cm

Kat. 477

Nur wer genau hinschaut, entdeckt auf Brauns »Wimmelbild« König Wilhelm I., Bismarck und Moltke.

»Kriegsgefangen (Oktober 1870)«
Kunstdruck nach Anton von Werners Gemälde von 1886
106 × 157 cm (Maße des Originals)
Kat. 485

schen in Versailles« zeigt nicht den Tag der Kaiserproklamation, sondern eine Situation im Herbst 1870, nachdem Wilhelm I., Bismarck und Moltke mit dem Großen Hauptquartier am 5. Oktober in Versailles eingetroffen waren.[11] Im Hintergrund ist das Versailler Schloss – Symbol französischer Machtpolitik – zu sehen, auf dem eine schwarz-weiß-rote Fahne weht. Vorder- und Mittelgrund beherrscht das bunte Treiben preußischer, bayerischer, württembergischer, sächsischer und Braunschweiger Soldaten. Eher beiläufig erkennt man rechts hinter einem Soldaten mit Strohbündel Bismarck und Moltke im Gespräch mit General von Blumenthal. Der preußische König Wilhelm ist, mit bloßem Auge kaum zu erkennen, weit hinter der Dreiergruppe in einer Kutsche sitzend dargestellt. Mehr Aufmerksamkeit erregen die rührend bis heiteren Szenen im Vordergrund, wie etwa ein preußischer Artilleriesergeant, der rechts einen verwundeten bayerischen Kameraden untergehakt hat und mit der freien linken Hand einem französischen Invaliden ein Almosen gibt.

Braun verwob nicht nur die politische und militärische Führung mit den Soldaten verschiedener deutscher Staaten zu einem harmonischen Ganzen, sondern bezog darüber hinaus die einheimische französische Bevölkerung mit ein, wie etwa die junge Bürgerin mit ihrem kleinen Sohn an der Hand oder den Mann im Blaukittel mit seiner Familie. Dieses Selbstverständnis als freundlich-kultivierte Besatzer spiegelt auch das bekannte Genregemälde »Kriegsgefangen« wider, das Anton von Werner 1886 schuf. Als ein französischer Kriegsgefangener durch sein Heimatdorf geführt wird, eilt seine Frau herbei und umarmt ihn stürmisch. Ein preußischer Wachsoldat hat sich beherzt ihres schreienden Säuglings angenommen, während die Offiziere verständnisvoll bis belustigt

»Entrée des parlementaires allemands dans Belfort, le 16 février 1871« / Deutsche Verhandlungsführer kommen nach Belfort, 16. Februar 1871
Alphonse de Neuville (1836 – 1885), 1884, Öl auf Leinwand, 82,5 × 119 cm
Kat. 484

zusehen. Die Szene gewinnt eine weitergehende Bedeutung, wenn man sie etwa dem im Bildaufbau ähnlichen Gemälde »Entrée des parlementaires allemands dans Belfort, le 16 février 1871« des französischen Malers Alphonse de Neuville von 1884 gegenüberstellt. Auch hier kommen deutsche Soldaten in einen französischen Ort, diesmal als Unterhändler mit verbundenen Augen, um das belagerte Belfort zur Aufgabe zu bewegen; auch hier erscheint am Straßenrand eine Frau mit einem Säugling. Doch sie ist in Witwentracht und reckt den Deutschen zornig die Faust entgegen. Diese Frauenfigur verkörperte die ganze Wut und die Rachegefühle einer gedemütigten Nation. Während Frankreich, das sein eigenes Land verteidigte, international viel Sympathie erntete, sahen sich die Deutschen zunehmend in die Rolle der grausamen Invasoren gedrängt. So gesehen, waren Werners und Brauns Genrebilder eine Rückversicherung gegenüber einer sehr zwiespältigen, verunsichernden Kriegswirklichkeit, eine Verteidigung des deutschen Gemüts und Anstands gegen den Vorwurf der Barbarei.[12]

Die Darstellung von Verwundung und Tod beschränkte sich meist auf malerisch hingestreckte, intakt wirkende Körper. Ungewöhnlich weit ging Adolph Menzel, als er 1866 am böhmischen Kriegsschauplatz Leichenhäuser und Lazarette besuchte. Eines seiner kleinen Aquarelle zeigt einen sterbenden Soldaten mit entblößtem Unterleib und durchgeblutetem Bauchverband, ein anderes drei ausgezehrte Tote, die verkrümmt und halb nackt auf einem notdürftig mit Stroh bedeckten Boden abgelegt wurden. Doch in Menzels große, repräsentative Gemälde fanden diese Eindrücke keinen Eingang. 1878 von dem Kunstkritiker Friedrich Pecht befragt, warum er keine Schlachten der Kriege

Ein Gefangenentransport des Königlich Sächsischen 1. Ulanen-Regiments Nr. 17 wird von französischen Franktireuren überfallen
Georg von Boddien (1850–1926), 1897
Öl auf Leinwand, 164 × 303 cm
Abb. 43

Links zu Pferd ist – mit dem Rücken zum Betrachter – Vizewachtmeister Engert dargestellt. Obwohl verletzt, führte er den Transport sicher nach St. Quentin. Dass zu seinen Verletzungen auch ein Schrotschuss ins Gesicht gehörte, kann man in der Regimentsgeschichte nachlesen, das Gemälde zeigt es nicht. (Aufzeichnungen über das 1. Königlich Sächsische Ulanen-Regiment Nr. 17, Berlin 1891, S. 134)

1866 und 1870/71 gemalt habe, erklärte er zunächst, als kurzsichtiger, unmilitärischer Mensch kaum zum Maler auf dem Schlachtfeld geschaffen zu sein, endete aber seine Ausführungen mit dem Ausruf: »[…] muß denn der Gräuel gemalt werden?!?«[13] Vor der Realität des Krieges kapitulierte letztlich auch Camphausen. Die bereits erwähnte Zeitschrift »Die Grenzboten« berichtete 1866 über ihn, »daß sein preußisches und auch sein menschliches Herz nicht die Fähigkeit fand«, sich von den »Thaten und den entsetzlichen Leiden derer, die er begleitete«, zu distanzieren: »Er fühlte sich außer Stande zu zeichnen, und verließ Böhmen nach den ersten Gefechten.«[14] Camphausen schuf zwar auch Gemälde zum Krieg 1870/71, zog aber nicht mehr mit ins Feld.

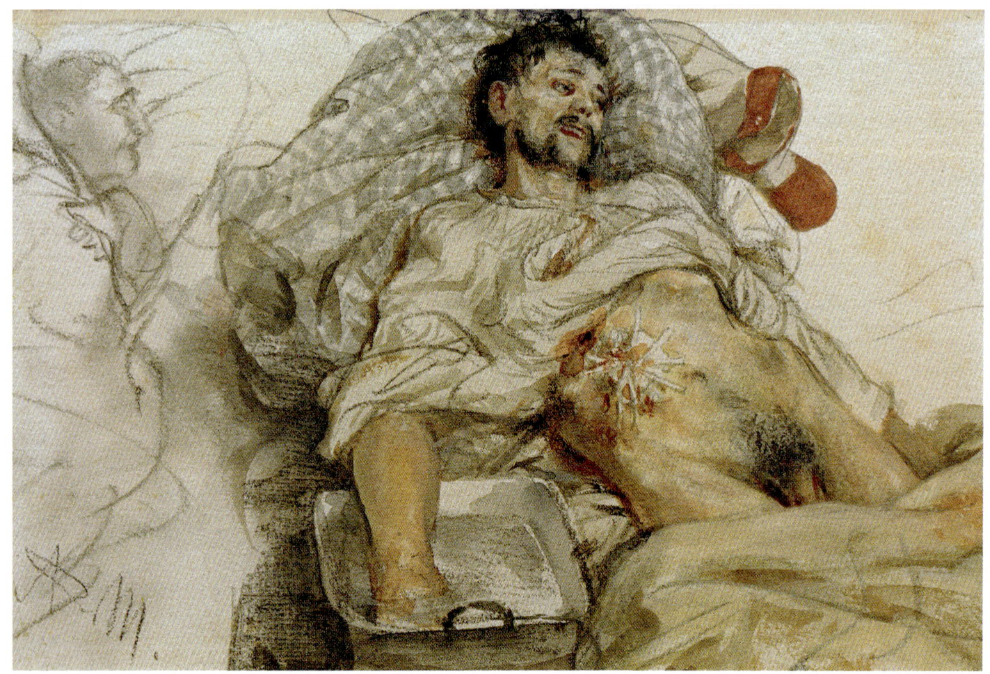

»Der sterbende Soldat«
Adolph Menzel (1815–1905), 1866, Aquarell über Bleistiftzeichnung, 10,2 × 12,8 cm
Kat. 469

Schlachten- und Ereignismalern im Deutschen Reich gelang es anders als ihren französischen Kollegen kaum, langfristig als Künstler ernst genommen zu werden. Anselm Feuerbach etwa verspottete Anton von Werner als »patriotischen Hanswurst«.[15] Doch als Geschichtsbilder waren die Gemälde der Kriege von 1864, 1866 und 1870/71 wirkmächtig. Sie prägten nachhaltig die Vorstellung vom frisch-fröhlichen Krieg, beanspruchten eine wichtige Vorbildfunktion für die jüngere Generation und trugen so zur Militarisierung des deutschen Kaiserreichs bei. 1926 erklärte Reichsarchivrat und Major a. D. George Soldan in seinem Geleitwort zu dem Fotoband »Der Weltkrieg im Bild«: »Wir alle sind, die Prachtgemälde deutscher Künstler aus vergangenen Kriegszeiten im Geiste vor uns tragend, in das Völkerringen hinausgezogen, um nur allzubald zu erfahren, daß der Krieg anders war, als wir ihn uns gedacht hatten.«[16]

1 Dresdner Anzeiger, 20.8.1883. Zu diesem Beitrag vgl. weitere Veröffentlichungen der Autorin: Krieg in Farbe: Die Reichseinigungskriege in der deutschen Malerei, in: Thorsten Loch/Lars Zacharias (Hg.): Wie die Siegessäule nach Berlin kam, Freiburg im Breisgau u. a. 2011, S. 211–222; Guerres et nation dans la peinture allemande, 1864–1871, in: Mathilde Benoistel u. a. (Leitung): France-Allemagne(s). 1870–1871: la guerre, la Commune, les mémoires, Ausst.-Kat., Paris 2017, S. 104–113; Was die Bilder sagen: Kriegsleid eher beim Feind, in: Damals Galerie. Geschichte im Bild, Bildband 2020 in Zusammenarbeit mit dem Militärhistorischen Museum der Bundeswehr, S. 48–53. **2** Vgl. Dresdner Anzeiger, 26. 7.1883; Theodor Seemann: Die Eröffnung des hiesigen Panoramas mit dem Schlachtenbilde des Prof. Louis Braun, Dresdner Anzeiger, 18. 8.1883; Dresdner Journal, 19. 8.1883; Vergessene Dresdner Sehenswürdigkeiten. Das große Schlachtenpanorama an der Prager Straße, in: Dresdner Nachrichten, 24.10.1937, S. 8; Herta Beutter u. a. (Hg.): Der Panoramamaler Louis Braun (1836–1916), Ausst.-Kat., Schwäbisch Hall 2012, bes. S. 15–27, 47–53, S. 83–101, S. 114–127. **3** Wilhelm Michel: Kriegsbilder in Kunst und Dichtung, in: ders./Alfred Steinitzer: Der Krieg in Bildern, München 1912, S. 97–124, hier S. 118. **4** Vgl. Beutter u. a. (Hg.): Panoramamaler, S. 17–18, 25, 86. **5** Wilhelm Camphausen: Ein Maler auf dem Kriegsfelde, Leipzig 1865, S. 22. **6** Bruno Meyer: Wilhelm Camphausen, der Sturm auf die Düppeler Schanze Nr. II (Spener'sche Zeitung, 15. 6.1865), in: ders.: Studien und Kritiken, Stuttgart 1877, S. 1–6, hier S. 2; Theodor Fontane: Der Schleswig-Holsteinische Krieg im Jahre 1864, Berlin 1866, S. 200–204; Jürgen Luh: Wilhelm Camphausens »Kampf im Innern der Schanze 2«, in: BildGeschichte #19, 21. 2. 2018 (https://recs.hypotheses.org/2320, letzter Zugriff 10.2.2020). **7** Kunst und Künstler im Gefolge des Kriegs, in: Die Grenzboten, 21. 9.1866, S. 492. **8** Vgl. Ruhmesthaten deutscher Krieger in Bild und Wort von Oberstlieutenant von Götz, Dresden 1894, S. 3–5, 14–16 (Militärhistorisches Museum, Inv.-Nr. BBAQ9557 und BBAQ9558). **9** Vgl. Frank Becker: Bilder von Krieg und Nation, München 2001, bes. S. 377–482, 495–498; Susanne Parth: Zwischen Bildbericht und Bildpropaganda, Paderborn u. a. 2010, bes. S. 148–241, 350–367; Matthias Eberle: Im Spiegel der Geschichte. Realistische Historienmalerei in Westeuropa 1830–1900, München 2017, S. 222–224. **10** Vgl. Dominik Bartmann: Anton von Werner. Geschichte in Bildern, Ausst.-Kat. Berlin, München 1993, S. 270–289, S. 332–369; Thomas W. Gaethgens: Anton von Werner. Die Proklamierung des Deutschen Kaiserreiches, Frankfurt a. M. 1990. **11** Vgl. Kunstausstellung, in: Hamburger Nachrichten, 8.12.1887. **12** Vgl. Gerhard Paul: Bilder des Krieges. Krieg der Bilder, Paderborn 2004, S. 42–44; Christian Bunnenberg: »Es lässt sich nicht leugnen, daß auch Rohheiten und unnötige Härten vorkamen.«, in: Frank Becker (Hg.): Zivilisten und Soldaten. Entgrenzte Gewalt in der Geschichte, Essen 2015, S. 79–102; Mark Hewitson: The People's Wars. Histories of Violence in German Lands, 1820–1888, Oxford 2017, S. 410–472; siehe auch den Beitrag von Heidi Mehrkens in diesem Band, S. 336–345. **13** Adolph Menzel an Friedrich Pecht, Berlin, 9.12.1878, zit. nach: Claude Keisch/Marie Ursula Riemann-Reyher (Hg.): Adolph Menzel. Briefe, Bd. 2, Berlin u. a. 2009, S. 758; vgl. Jens Christian Jensen: Adolph Menzel im Museum Georg Schäfer. Bestandskatalog, Schweinfurt 2000, S. 174–175; Drei gefallene Soldaten in einer Scheune/Leichen-Kammer zu Königinhof, 21. 7.1866, Kupferstichkabinett Berlin, Ident.-Nr. SZ Menzel N 1741 (www.smb-digital.de/eMuseumPlus?service=ExternalInterface&module=collection&objectId=753420&viewType=detailView, letzter Zugriff 10. 2. 2020). **14** Kunst und Künstler im Gefolge des Kriegs, S. 493–494. **15** Otto Fischer: Anselm Feuerbach. Briefe und Bilder, o. O. 1922, S. 65, zit. nach: Sybille Bock: Bildliche Darstellungen zum Krieg von 1870/71, Diss., Freiburg im Breisgau 1982, S. 8. **16** George Soldan (Bearb.): Der Weltkrieg im Bild. Originalaufnahmen des Kriegs-, Bild- und Filmamtes aus der modernen Materialschlacht, Berlin/Oldenburg, 1927, Geleitwort, unpag.

»Die stolz des Königs Rock in Ehr' getragen«

Die »Feldzugsbatterie Leo 1870/71«

Kriegervereine bildeten sich bereits seit dem späten 18. Jahrhundert, oft als »Kriegerbegräbnisvereine«. Zu einem Massenphänomen und einem wichtigen integrativen Faktor der Nation wurden sie jedoch erst nach der Reichsgründung 1870/71. Die Vereinsmitglieder gehörten mit ihren Fahnen und den Auszeichnungen an ihren Fräcken zu jeder vaterländischen Feier in den Bundesstaaten des Deutschen Reiches, ob es sich um Kaisers Geburtstag, den Sedantag oder ein Regimentsjubiläum handelte. Im Laufe der Zeit bildeten sich Dachorganisationen, die versuchten, die Vereine stärker politisch, besonders gegen die Sozialdemokratie auszurichten, und vermehrt für den Eintritt von Reservisten warben, die noch nicht über Kriegserfahrung verfügten. Für viele Veteranen hatte ihr Verein jedoch vor allem eine soziale Funktion. Sie trafen dort Menschen, die ihre Kriegserfahrungen teilten. Auch die Angehörigen der 1879 gegründeten Vereinigung »Feldzugsbatterie Leo 1870/71« fühlten sich als eine Schicksals- und Solidargemeinschaft. Sie hatten in Frankreich unter dem Befehl des damaligen Hauptmanns Eugen Leo (1833–1904) in der 2. Leichten Batterie der I. Abteilung des Rheinischen Feldartillerie-Regiments Nr. 8 gedient. Ihr Chronist Max Droz schrieb: »Wir hatten gemeinsam schwere Tage im Feldzuge erlebt und ist dies wohl der Grund, weshalb wir alte Soldaten heute noch nach 30 Jahren fast wie eine Familie ein Gefühl der Zusammengehörigkeit haben. Erhöht wird dies durch das Gedenken an unseren Hauptmann Leo mit seinen Offizieren.« (Max Droz: Kurzer Abriss der Geschichte der ehemaligen Feldzugs-Batterie »Leo« 2. leichte Batterie des Rheinischen Feld-Art.-Regts. No. 8, 1870/71, Berlin 1901, S. 101; Zitat im Titel, S. 114)

»Batterie Leo auf dem Marsche im Feldzuge 1870–1871« / »Hauptmann Leo 1871« / »Die Angehörigen der Batterie Leo bei einer Zusammenkunft i. J. 1880«
Kat. 511

Kat. 511

Kartuschhülse einer von der Batterie Leo des Rheinischen Feldartillerie-Regiments Nr. 8 am 2. Januar 1871 verschossenen Granate

Königreich Preußen, 1871

Kat. 503

Im Winter 1870/71 gehörte die Batterie Leo zur Artillerie der 30. Infanterie-Brigade, die im Verband der 1. Armee in Nordfrankreich eingesetzt war. Am 2. Januar 1871 verteidigte die Batterie einen Abschnitt südwestlich von Sapignies, entlang der Chaussee nach Arras, gegen angreifende französische Infanterie. Als Andenken behielten die Kanoniere diese Kartuschhülse einer in jenem Kampf verschossenen Granate.

Kat. 503

Der 3. Zug der Batterie Leo in Bovelles, Nordfrankreich, Anfang April 1871

Kat. 505

Die Batterie Leo mit Feldwebel Otto und Sergeant König in Bovelles, Nordfrankreich, Anfang April 1871

Kat. 506

Die beiden nach Ende der Kampfhandlungen entstandenen Aufnahmen zeigen Angehörige der Batterie in feldmäßiger Ausrüstung und Bekleidung ebenso wie Waffen und Fahrzeuge. Zu sehen sind neben den Feldkanonen und ihren Protzwagen auch solche mit Ersatzrädern. Sergeant König gehörte später zu den Mitbegründern der Vereinigung »Feldzugsbatterie Leo 1870/71«. Zwei der Vier-Pfünder-Feldkanonen C/67 der Batterie wurden als Erinnerungsstücke in der Kölner Eigelsteintorburg aufgestellt, die von 1898 bis 1958 dem Historischen Museum der Stadt Köln als Ausstellungsort diente (siehe S. 290, Kat. 501 und 502).

Kat. 505

Kat. 506

Kat. 504

Gedenkplatte für die Angehörigen der Batterie Leo (2. Leichte Feldbatterie) des Rheinischen Feldartillerie-Regiments Nr. 8

Kat. 504

Der besondere Bezug der Batterie Leo zu Köln ergab sich aus der Zugehörigkeit zur I. Abteilung des Rheinischen Feldartillerie-Regiments Nr. 8, die in der Domstadt stationiert war.

Max Droz, 1870/71

Kat. 510

Droz sammelte alle Beute- und Erinnerungsstücke, Zeichnungen und Fotografien zur Batterie Leo und übergab sie später dem Historischen Museum der Stadt Köln.

Kat. 510

Kat. 512

Aufnahme der Batterie am 5. April 1900

Kat. 512

Oberst a. D. Leo war zuletzt Kommandeur des 2. Hannoverschen Feldartillerie-Regiments Nr. 26 gewesen. Das Treffen der Vereinigung »Feldzugsbatterie Leo 1870/71« wurde durch die Teilnahme des ehemaligen Batteriechefs zu einem besonderen Ereignis: »Der in weiten Kreisen von früher bestens bekannte und in der Bürgerschaft geschätzte Oberst Leo war mit seiner Gattin eigens nach Cöln gekommen, um nach fast 30 Jahren noch einmal seine alten Mitkämpfer wiederzusehen. Hierzu hatten sich 40 Kameraden der Batterie, die theilweise weit hergereist waren, mit ihren Frauen im Hotel zur ewigen Lampe eingefunden.« (Kölnische Zeitung, 6. April 1900)

»Die Grabstätte unseres unvergesslichen Hauptmanns Leo in Florenz«

Fotodruck

Kat. 513

Am 31. Januar 1904 starb Oberst a. D. Leo mit 71 Jahren während einer Italienreise nach kurzer Krankheit in Florenz, wo er auch bestattet wurde. Die Vereinigung »Feldzugsbatterie Leo 1870/71« stiftete eine Grabplatte mit der Inschrift: »Was er seinem Kaiser und seinem Vaterlande gewesen, gehört der Geschichte an. Was er uns gewesen, das kann nur der voll fühlen, der die Ehre und das Glück hatte, unter seinem glorreichen Kommando im Feuer zu stehen.«

Die Grabstätte unseres unvergesslichen

Hauptmanns Leo

in Florenz. Die dankbaren Mitkämpfer der Feldzugsbatterie
1870/71

Breuer, Compes, Dannhauer, Droz, Erben, Feuser, Goedecke, Haas I, Hilgers, Dr. **Huth,**
Kleefuss, Landwehr, Metzger, Otto, Rahm.

Kat. 513

Drei Kriege, drei Siege, eine Nation?

Mit der Reichsgründung 1871 war die staatliche Einigung unter preußischer Führung vollzogen, doch um eine gemeinsame Identität der deutschen Staaten wurde weiter gerungen. Gleichzeitig war die »innere Reichsgründung« von Konflikten geprägt, die in ihrer Schärfe weit über die Gegensätze zwischen den verschiedenen deutschen Staaten hinausreichten. Bei vielen dieser Streitfragen, die in unterschiedlichem Ausmaß auch andere europäische Nationalstaaten bewegten, ging es letztlich darum, zu bestimmen, wer zur deutschen Nation gehörte und wer nicht. Wer sollte welche Möglichkeiten haben, auf die Entwicklung des neuen Reiches Einfluss zu nehmen? Kulturkampf, Sozialistengesetze, Antisemitismus, nationale Minderheiten, die zunächst vergebliche Forderung nach Frauenwahlrecht – in ganz unterschiedlichen Zusammenhängen erlebten Menschen Ausgrenzung. Das Gefühl, Bürger bzw. Bürgerin zweiter Klasse zu sein, hielt häufig auch dann noch an, wenn der Höhepunkt eines Konflikts bereits überschritten war.

Kat. 561

»Zwischen Berlin und Rom«

Karikatur aus dem humoristisch-satirischen Wochenblatt »Kladderadatsch«, 16. Mai 1875

Kat. 561

Der Autoritätsanspruch der katholischen Kirche und ihre übernationale Ausrichtung auf Rom kollidierten oftmals mit den Ordnungsvorstellungen von Nationalstaaten. Nach der Reichsgründung versuchte Bismarck gemeinsam mit Liberalen, durch eine Vielzahl von Gesetzen den Einfluss der katholischen Kirche in Preußen und im Deutschen Reich zurückzudrängen, etwa durch Verbot des Jesuitenordens, die Einführung der Zivilehe und den »Kanzelparagrafen«, der es untersagte, die Predigt für politische Agitation zu nutzen. Priester wurden in hoher Zahl inhaftiert, darunter sogar zwei Bischöfe, bis es 1878 zu einer Annäherung und 1887 schließlich zu einer diplomatischen Beilegung des Konflikts kam.

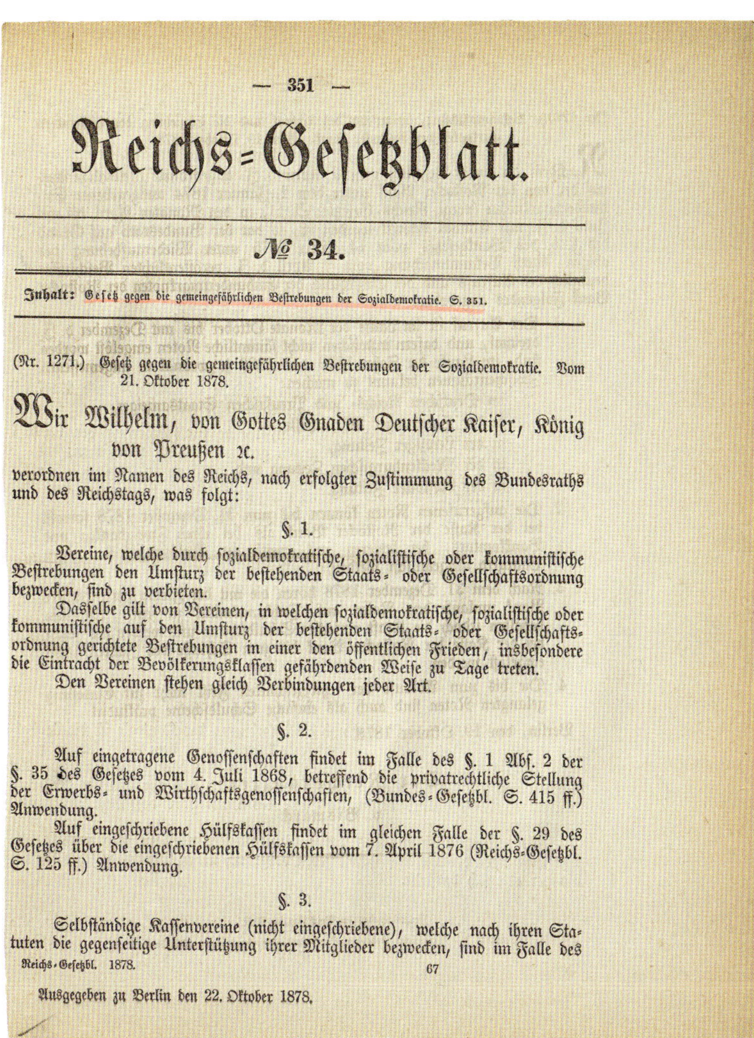

— 351 —

Reichs-Gesetzblatt.

№ 34.

Inhalt: Gesetz gegen die gemeingefährlichen Bestrebungen der Sozialdemokratie. S. 351.

(Nr. 1271.) Gesetz gegen die gemeingefährlichen Bestrebungen der Sozialdemokratie. Vom 21. Oktober 1878.

Wir Wilhelm, von Gottes Gnaden Deutscher Kaiser, König von Preußen 2c.

verordnen im Namen des Reichs, nach erfolgter Zustimmung des Bundesraths und des Reichstags, was folgt:

§. 1.

Vereine, welche durch sozialdemokratische, sozialistische oder kommunistische Bestrebungen den Umsturz der bestehenden Staats- oder Gesellschaftsordnung bezwecken, sind zu verbieten.

Dasselbe gilt von Vereinen, in welchen sozialdemokratische, sozialistische oder kommunistische auf den Umsturz der bestehenden Staats- oder Gesellschaftsordnung gerichtete Bestrebungen in einer den öffentlichen Frieden, insbesondere die Eintracht der Bevölkerungsklassen gefährdenden Weise zu Tage treten.

Den Vereinen stehen gleich Verbindungen jeder Art.

§. 2.

Auf eingetragene Genossenschaften findet im Falle des §. 1 Abs. 2 der §. 35 des Gesetzes vom 4. Juli 1868, betreffend die privatrechtliche Stellung der Erwerbs- und Wirthschaftsgenossenschaften, (Bundes-Gesetzbl. S. 415 ff.) Anwendung.

Auf eingeschriebene Hülfskassen findet im gleichen Falle der §. 29 des Gesetzes über die eingeschriebenen Hülfskassen vom 7. April 1876 (Reichs-Gesetzbl. S. 125 ff.) Anwendung.

§. 3.

Selbständige Kassenvereine (nicht eingeschriebene), welche nach ihren Statuten die gegenseitige Unterstützung ihrer Mitglieder bezwecken, sind im Falle des

Reichs-Gesetzbl. 1878. 67

Ausgegeben zu Berlin den 22. Oktober 1878.

Kat. 562

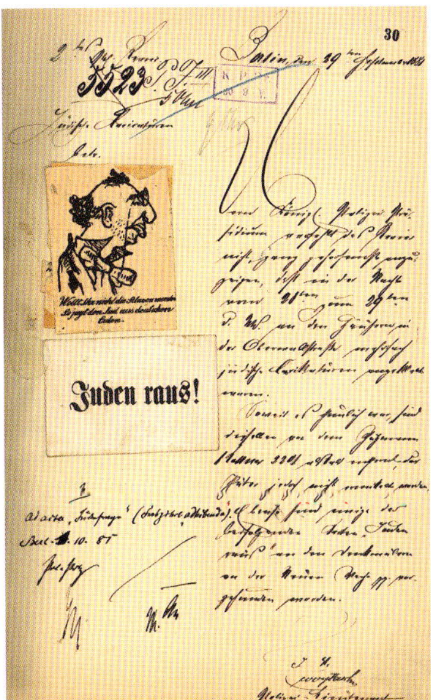

30

Juden raus!

Kat. 563

Kat. 564

»Gesetz gegen die gemeingefährlichen Bestrebungen der Sozialdemokratie«

Reichsgesetzblatt, Nr. 34, Berlin, 22. Oktober 1878
Kat. 562

Auf Initiative Bismarcks waren zwischen 1878 und 1890 »sozialdemokratische, sozialistische und kommunistische« Vereinigungen verboten worden. Die Kriminalisierung großer Teile der Arbeiterbewegung ging mit der Einführung staatlich reglementierter Kranken-, Unfall-, Alters- und Invaliditätsversicherungen einher. Da Sozialdemokraten als Einzelpersonen weiter für den Reichstag kandidieren konnten, hatten sie trotzdem erheblichen Einfluss erlangt, als Wilhelm II. eine weitere Verlängerung des Sozialistengesetzes ablehnte.

Von der Polizei am 28./29. September 1881 aufgefundenes judenfeindliches Agitationsmaterial

Aus einer Akte des Königlichen Polizeipräsidiums, Berlin, zur »Judenfrage«, 1881–1883
Kat. 563

»Mittheilungen aus dem Verein zur Abwehr des Antisemitismus«

Probenummer, Berlin, 21. Oktober 1891
Kat. 564

Bereits Ernst Moritz Arndt, ein früher Protagonist der Nationalbewegung, hatte die Reinheit des deutschen Volkes beschworen und in merkwürdiger Verquickung Hass auf alles Französische und alles Jüdische gepredigt. Demokratisch-liberale Teile der Nationalbewegung setzten sich dagegen für eine Gleichberechtigung Deutscher jüdischer Konfession ein. Diese hatten nach der Gleichstellung der Konfessionen im Norddeutschen Bund 1869 zwar meist nicht mehr mit rechtlichen Benachteiligungen zu kämpfen, sahen sich aber seit der Wirtschaftskrise 1873 wieder vermehrt Anfeindungen ausgesetzt. Zu einer Verschärfung der Angriffe kam es am Ende der liberalen Ära des Kaiserreichs im Berliner »Antisemitismusstreit« 1879/81, ausgelöst von dem Historiker Heinrich von

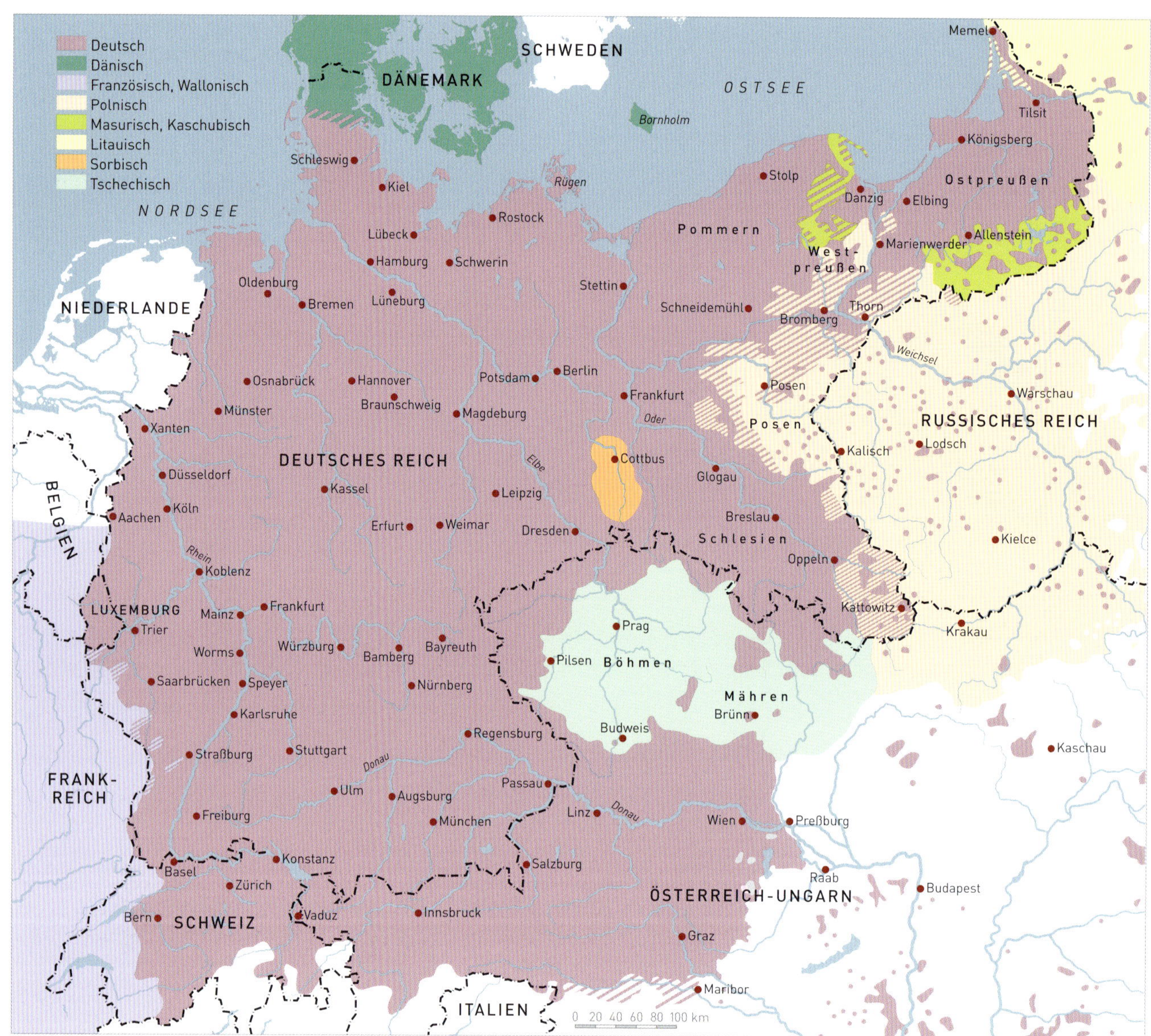

Karte zu den Sprachen im Deutschen Reich

Treitschke. Angeblich um eine nüchterne Beurteilung bemüht, brandmarkte er das Judentum als fremdes, nicht zu integrierendes Element, das die nationale Einheit bedrohe. Im Umkreis des Journalisten Wilhelm Marr entstand gleichzeitig der Begriff Antisemitismus, der pseudowissenschaftlich Juden als fremde, »semitische« Rasse ausgrenzen sollte – eine Vorstellung, die auch im liberalen Bildungsbürgertum an Boden gewann. Rassismus, Nationalismus und Militarismus verbanden sich in ihrer radikalsten Form in der völkischen Bewegung, zu der Agitationsverbände wie der 1891 noch unter anderem Namen gegründete Alldeutsche Verband gehörten. Bereits während des Antisemitismusstreits bezogen aber ebenso jüdische und nichtjüdische Deutsche, darunter der Historiker Theodor Mommsen und der Pathologe Rudolf Virchow, scharf gegen die Äußerungen Treitschkes oder auch die Auslassungen des Berliner Hofpredigers Adolf Stoecker Stellung. 1890 wurde der Verein zur Abwehr des Antisemitismus ins Leben gerufen, der bis 1933 existierte.

Karte zu den Sprachen im Deutschen Reich

Peter Palm, 2020

Im Deutschen Reich lebten besonders in den Grenzregionen nationale Minderheiten, die dem neuen Nationalstaat meist ungewollt angeschlossen worden waren. Den größten Anteil machte dabei die polnische Minderheit mit zu dieser Zeit ungefähr 2,5 Millionen aus, die seit den Teilungen des späten 18. Jahrhunderts zu Preußen, aber nicht zum Deutschen Bund gehört hatte. Richteten sich Germanisierungsbemühungen, die nach der Reichsgründung und verstärkt seit den 1880er Jahren einsetzten, meist auf die Verdrängung der einheimischen Sprache, etwa durch die Einführung von Deutsch als Schulsprache, gingen hier die Maßnahmen wesentlich weiter und erfuhren große öffentliche Aufmerksamkeit. Im Kulturkampf stand der polnische Klerus dieser überwiegend katholischen Landesteile im Fokus, während sich antisemitische Hetze besonders gegen die ländliche jüdische Bevölkerung richtete. Ab 1885/86 wurden nicht eingebürgerte Polen und Polinnen aus Russland und Österreich ausgewiesen, ein entsprechendes Einwanderungsverbot erlassen und Ansiedlungsanreize für Deutsche gesetzt, wenn auch mit mäßigem Erfolg. Elsässer und Lothringer, die oft schon traditionell einen deutschen Dialekt sprachen, wurden dagegen als »verlorene Söhne« (Treitschke) betrachtet, die zurückgewonnen werden sollten. Trotzdem mussten sie als »Reichslande« lange auf einen eigenen Landtag verzichten. Wie in Nordschleswig blieb in Elsass-Lothringen das Verhältnis zum Deutschen Reich gefangen in einem sich gegenseitig aufschaukelnden Wechselspiel aus Germanisierungsversuchen und Separationsbestrebungen (siehe auch den Beitrag von Østergård/Østergaard in diesem Band, S. 72–87, sowie S. 244–245).

Demonstration für Frauenwahlrecht in Berlin, 12. Mai 1912

Gebrüder Haeckel, Berlin

Kat. 566

Das Wahlrecht im Deutschen Reich war ausgesprochen progressiv: allgemein, gleich, geheim und direkt. Fast jeder Mann über 25 Jahren konnte eine Stimme abgeben. Allerdings galt auf Landesebene in Preußen weiter das Dreiklassenwahlrecht und, damals eine Selbstverständlichkeit, Frauen durften überhaupt nicht wählen. In den 1890er Jahren wurde diese Selbstverständlichkeit zunehmend infrage gestellt. Besonders nachdem Frauen ab 1908 Mitglied einer politischen Partei werden durften, war das Wahlrecht eine zentrale Forderung der frühen Frauenbewegung. Durchgesetzt werden konnte es jedoch erst nach der Revolution von 1918/19. Französinnen, die für die kurze Phase der Pariser Kommune 1871 zumindest dort volle Bürgerrechte genossen hatten, durften sogar erst ab 1944 wählen.

Kat. 566

Die Fahnen nieder

Versuch über Symbole und Symptome der Nation

ANDREAS PLATTHAUS

In Orange County im US-Bundesstaat Kalifornien liegt ein kleines Areal mit dem Anspruch der Selbstverwaltung. Als Walt Disney hier 1955 seinen eigenen Vergnügungspark errichtete, gab er ihm einen recht staatstragenden Namen: Disneyland. Und als »Magic Kingdom«, ein »bezauberndes Königreich«, weil hier nur die Fantasie herrschen sollte, wurde bald die ganze Anlage charakterisiert. Für deren Repräsentation aber auf die gängigen Symbole wehrhafter Eigenständigkeit zurückgegriffen wurde: ein Schloss in der Mitte und eine am üblichen Militärzeremoniell orientierte tägliche Parade durch die Hauptstraße. 1959 kam in Gestalt einer Attraktion namens »Submarine Voyage«, deren Design Anleihen bei der Disney-Verfilmung »20 000 Meilen unter dem Meer« (1954) des gleichnamigen Romans von Jules Verne von 1869/70 machte, sogar eine eigene U-Boot-Flotte hinzu. Sie stand mit der Zahl ihrer Schiffe weltweit an siebter Stelle und konnte zur Jungfernfahrt immerhin den amerikanischen Vizepräsidenten Richard Nixon als Ehrengast begrüßen, nachdem bei der Eröffnung des Parks vier Jahre zuvor nur der Gouverneur von Kalifornien teilgenommen hatte, um dem Königreich mitten in der Republik seine Reverenz zu erweisen. Aber mit der Eigenständigkeit von Disneyland war es dann doch nicht so weit her: Jeden Nachmittag marschiert bis heute gleich hinter dem Eingang, in der »Staatsterminologie« von Disneyland also gleich nach der Grenze, eine Ehrengarde auf, um feierlich die Flagge der Vereinigten Staaten einzuholen. Auch dies eine Form der Fantasie, die der Staatsmacht huldigt.

Für deutsche Augen und Ohren ist das martialische Gepränge der Flaggenzeremonie im als kindlich-künstlich empfundenen Disneyland befremdlich. Es wird dabei die Nationalhymne gespielt und von den amerikanischen Gästen des Vergnügungsparks mitgesungen, aber vor allem werden zufällig im Publikum vertretene Angehörige der fünf US-Streitkräfte – Army, Air Force, Navy, Coast Guard und Marines – aufgefordert vorzutreten, um den Dank für ihren aktuellen oder früheren Dienst an der Nation entgegenzunehmen. Mit einem Mal erweist sich das märchenhafte Leben in Disneyland als ganz realpolitisch amerikanisch und die Tradition der Gleichsetzung von Staat und Militär als ungebrochen. Man bekommt bei dieser Zeremonie eine Ahnung davon, wie es im Deutschen Reich nach 1871 zugegangen sein muss, in jenem Land, das damals der ganzen Welt als Verkörperung des Militarismus galt. Einen Eindruck hiervon vermittelt das berühmte Foto vom 1. Januar 1913, das Kaiser Wilhelm II. mit seinen sechs Söhnen nach dem diplomatischen Neujahrsempfang im Berliner Schloss auf dem Weg zum Zeughaus zeigt, wo er wie an jedem ersten Tag des Jahres die Parole an die Streitkräfte ausgibt – alle sieben Hohenzollern in Uniform. Und man darf vermuten, dass sie so auch schon beim festlichen Empfang für die Vertreter der anderen Staaten erschienen waren.

Kaiser Wilhelm II. mit seinen sechs Söhnen auf dem Weg zum Zeughaus
Berlin, 1. Januar 1913
Abb. 44

Das martialische Deutschland war ein zeitgenössisches Klischee, vielfach dokumentiert in ausländischen Karikaturen, die Pickelhauben und Stechschritt als typische Attribute Deutschlands aufgriffen. Die Reichseinigung war nach Bismarcks notorischen Worten durch »Eisen und Blut« erfolgt, also auf den Schlachtfeldern der preußischen Kriege mit Dänemark, Österreich und Frankreich, bei denen die Zahl der deutschen Verbündeten immer weiter anstieg, bis am Schluss jener neue kaiserlich regierte Staatenbund entstanden war, dessen Mitgliedsländer aber immer noch so viel Selbstständigkeit genossen, dass nur im Militär eine übergreifende Klammer gefunden wurde. Darin glichen sich das amerikanische und das deutsche Selbstverständnis, die jeweils nicht auf die Bindekraft eines Zentralstaats setzen konnten. Und die jahrhundertealte Kultur war für die kleindeutsche Lösung, die die deutsche Frage gefunden hatte, kein taugliches Bindemittel mehr.

Zumal Deutschland sich selbst als verspätete Nation betrachtete und deshalb für die »lange Dauer«, die sehr allmähliche Entwicklungsform gemeinsamer Kultur nur Spott übrighaben konnte: Hatte man nicht lange genug gewartet, ehe endlich gewaltsam Fakten geschaffen wurden? Die Nationenbildung durch Krieg hatten andere viel früher betrieben; sie war ein Resultat des revolutionären 18. Jahrhunderts und seiner Kulmination in der Französischen Revolution. Aber als Modell war sie ungeeignet, denn ihre beiden Musterfälle, die Vereinigten Staaten und Frankreich, unterschieden sich drastisch voneinander: eine ganz neu gegründete Nation auf dem amerikanischen Kontinent und eine seit dem Mittelalter existierende in Europa. Den Zusammenhalt Frankreichs hatten lange nur Kirche und König verbürgt, kein modernes Nationalbewusstsein, wie es die Französische Revolution in ihrer Abgrenzung von einer Welt absolutistischer Feinde hervorbrachte. Sie erzwang als Verteidigung die Levée en masse, die aus der Bevölkerung Frankreichs Franzosen und Französinnen machte. Die Bürgerinnen und Bürger der Vereinigten Staaten von Amerika dagegen schöpften ihr nationales Zusammengehörigkeitsgefühl weniger aus dem noch defensiv geführten Unabhängigkeitskrieg von 1775 bis 1783 als aus der anschließenden permanenten Offensive infolge des eigentümlichen amerikanischen Sendungsbewusstseins (Manifest destiny), das die Erschließung und vor allem Eroberung des nordamerikanischen Kontinents vom Atlantik bis zum Pazifik legitimierte. Eine vergleichbar expansive Energie besaß das französische Volk ungeachtet der napoleonischen Eroberungszüge nicht; in Europa sollte die Doktrin des Manifest Destiny erst in der »Volk-ohne-Raum«-Parole des aggressivsten deutschen Nationalismus ein Äquivalent finden. Diese letztere Aggression war entscheidend durch die Niederlage im Ersten Weltkrieg gespeist worden, dessen Brutalität jeglicher althergebrachten Rücksichtnahme auf andere Staaten, die nunmehr alle als Nationen und daher als feindlich angesehen wurden, ein Ende gesetzt hatte. Nie waren die Egoismen der europäischen Staaten so ausgeprägt wie in der Zwischenkriegszeit, während sich die Vereinigten Staaten im außenpolitischen Isolationismus einzurichten versuchten. Wer seine nordamerikanischen Territorien nicht freiwillig gegen Bezahlung aufgab, wie Frankreich im Fall Louisianas oder Russland im Fall Alaskas, der wurde bekämpft: die indigenen Völker Amerikas sowieso, die gar keinen Begriff von europäischem Territorialverständnis hatten, aber auch Spanien und dessen ehemalige Kolonie Mexiko.

Allein gegenüber Großbritannien und seinem Dominion Kanada ließ die kontinentale Führungsmacht Rücksicht walten, weil die Grenze zu Kanada das Resultat des ersten amerikanischen Einigungskriegs gewesen war. Von Norden war danach keine Bedrohung mehr zu erwarten, so wie auch Dänemark durch die Niederlage von 1864 als Rivale Preußendeutschlands dauerhaft ausfiel. Der zweite amerikanische Einigungskrieg wurde dann von 1846 bis 1848 gegen Mexiko geführt und entsprach in der Erzrivalität der Gegner dem Deutsch-Französischen Krieg von 1870/71, während der dritte, der Amerikanische Bürgerkrieg von 1861 bis 1865, ein Gegenstück zu dem 1866 ausgefochtenen »Bruderkrieg« Preußens mit Österreich bildet, durch den das Habsburgerreich aus Deutschland verdrängt wurde. Erneut also eine Konzentration nationalen Gefühls und nationalen Territoriums in Europa gegenüber einer Expansion von beidem in Amerika. Zum Bruch dieser Konzentrationstradition kam es 1871 durch die Annexion Elsass-Lothringens im Frankfurter Frieden, dem Geburtsfehler des Deutschen Reichs.

Die drei siegreich geführten und umgehend mythisch (Düppeler Schanzen, Königgrätz, Sedan) verbrämten Einigungskriege ließen in Deutschland eine militärische Hybris entstehen. Sie basierte auf dem seit der Zeit des Großen Kurfürsten gepflegten preußischen Selbstverständnis als Soldatenstaat, das durch die Feldzüge Friedrichs des Großen und die Befreiungskriege von 1813/14 noch einmal erheblich gestärkt worden war. In den Vereinigten Staaten ist das identifikatorische Verhältnis zwischen der Bevölkerung und den Streitkräften zwar bis heute ungebrochen, aber es war auch nie so sehr Grundlage des Staatsverständnisses wie in Deutschland. Umso desaströser wurde hierzulande der Ausgang des Ersten Weltkriegs empfunden, aber erst mit der dann auch moralischen Katastrophe des Zweiten Weltkriegs ist den Deutschen der Militarismus ausgetrieben worden. Dagegen überstand die amerikanische Bewunderung für die eigenen Streitkräfte das Debakel von Vietnam, weil dieser Krieg nie erklärt worden war und sich weit entfernt und zum Großteil unter Stellvertretern abspielte. Es war ein individuelles Leid der gefallenen oder verkrüppelt und traumatisiert zurückgekehrten eigenen Soldaten, nicht wie im deutschen Fall kollektives Versagen, das in den Vereinigten Staaten sichtbar wurde, und es führte vielmehr zu einem noch vertieften Kult um militärische Pflichterfüllung, der sich etwa in der ubiquitären Wendung »Thank you for your service« gegenüber aktiven Militärs oder Veteranen artikuliert. Das ist der Hintergrund für Zeremonien wie die eingangs geschilderte tägliche Flag Retreat in Disneyland.

Einholung der Flagge
Tägliche Zeremonie vor Sonnenuntergang in Disneyland, Anaheim, Kalifornien 2014
Abb. 45

Eine vergleichbare Manie um nationale Symbole und Pflichterfüllung hatte sich im »Dritten Reich« herausgebildet, und es ist diese gespenstische Ähnlichkeit symbolischer Handlungen in der aktuellen Führungsmacht der demokratischen Welt und in der totalitären Macht schlechthin, die die Irritation beim deutschen Publikum hervorruft. Ein unschuldig empfundenes Verhältnis zum Krieg scheint ihm nicht mehr vorstellbar, während sich Amerikaner und Amerikanerinnen nicht nur materiell, sondern auch moralisch auf der Siegerseite der Geschichte wähnen: Und mit ihnen steht dort die Nation. Erschüttert wurde dieses stolze Selbstbild erst in jüngster Zeit durch die Präsidentschaft Donald Trumps, der einem amerikanischen Nationalismus das Wort redet, den der liberale Teil des Landes als beschämend ansieht. Erst im vergangenen Jahr machte die in Harvard lehrende Historikerin Jill Lepore Furore mit ihrem kleinen Buch »This America – The Case for the Nation«, in dem sie versucht, den Begriff der Nation gegen seine chauvinistische Usurpierung wieder positiv zu besetzen, indem sie ihn als Gegenstand der vielfältigen amerikanischen Emanzipationsbestrebungen identifiziert. Ein solcher historischer Rettungsversuch setzt indes voraus, dass der Gedanke der Nation und die Rede von ihr nicht bereits derart kontaminiert wurden, wie es im nationalsozialistischen Deutschland geschehen ist. Man mag es mögen oder nicht – mit der Nation ist bei uns kein Staat mehr zu machen.

Das macht die Deutschen aber für den Rest der Welt, der keinen vergleichbaren moralischen Bankrott erlebt hat, ähnlich rätselhaft, wie wir den amerikanischen Nationalstolz empfinden. Der Appell anderer Staaten an Deutschland, international wieder Verantwortung zu übernehmen, setzt ja voraus, dass es sich überhaupt als Nation begreift. Dazu gehört jedoch, wie das abschreckende Beispiel Trumps belegt, mehr als nur eine regierungsamtliche Beschwörung. Verlangt ist ein identifikatorisches Verständnis der klassischen staatlichen Institutionen als gemeinnützige Einrichtungen, also als solche, die der ganzen Gemeinschaft dienlich sind (»Thank you for your service ...«). Genau das befördert Trumps strategisch spalterische Politik nicht, und deshalb ist ein Umschlag des amerikanischen Selbstverständnisses ins rein Chauvinistische zu befürchten, wenn es Verteidigerinnen des nationalen Interesses im aufklärerischen Sinn wie Jill Lepore nicht gelingen sollte, das aufgeblasene Selbstbild platzen zu lassen. Während es in Deutschland vonnöten wäre, den Nationenbegriff nach 75 Jahren nur zu verständlicher Verdrängung wiederzubeleben: nicht als Rückkehr zum gescheiterten Konzept eines sich gegen andere abgrenzenden deutschen Nationalismus, sondern als Selbstvergewisserung bestimmter Werte, die eine Nation erworben und ausgearbeitet hat, die jene Achtung vor der wechselseitigen Souveränität ermöglicht, die Nationen gleichwertig nebeneinander bestehen lässt. Und im Idealfall dadurch miteinander verbindet. Sodass irgendwann die Flaggen ein letztes Mal eingeholt werden könnten, weil man sie am Folgetag gar nicht wieder aufziehen würde. Nicht einmal in Disneyland.

Anhang

Objektverzeichnis

DER AUSSTELLUNG

FOYER

Kat. 1
Die Schlacht von Mars-la-Tour
Zinnfiguren-Diorama
Leipzig, 1980
60 × 180 × 270 cm
MHM BAAQ8496

PROLOG: NATION – WELCHE NATION?

Raumton
»Des Deutschen Vaterland«, gelesen von Schülerinnen und Schülern

Kat. 2 → S. 30–31
Flugblatt mit Ernst Moritz Arndts Gedicht »Des Deutschen Vaterland«
Druckerei U. Klopf sen. und Alexander Eurich
Wien, 1848
Stiftung Deutsches Historisches Museum, Berlin, 1988/1012.22

Kat. 3
Flugblatt mit Ernst Moritz Arndts Gedicht »Des Deutschen Vaterland«
Verlag Fr. Weidle
Berlin, 1848
Landesarchiv Berlin, F Rep. 310, Nr. 336

Kat. 4
Fahne der Groitzscher Kommunalgarde
Groitzsch, Königreich Sachsen, 1848
157 × 172 cm
MHM XBAA4525

Kat. 5
Flugblatt mit Carl Heinrich Schnauffers Gedicht »Deutschlands Wiedergeburt / Schwarz, Roth, Gold«
Großherzogtum Baden, Mannheim, 1848
MHM BBAO8286

NATION UND REVOLUTION

Kat. 6 → S. 30–31
»Zur Erinnerung an das Jahr 1848«
Prämienblatt als Jahresendbeilage der Zeitschrift »Der Familienfreund«
Neusalza, um 1848/49
Lithografie
MHM BAAG3184

Kat. 7 → S. 31
»Die Deutsche Nationalversammlung in der Paulskirche zu Frankfurt a/M«
Stahlstich nach Heinrich Hasselhorst von J. M. Kolb und F. Giersch
Verlag von G. G. Lange
Darmstadt, um 1850
MHM BBAY0000

Kat. 8 → S. 32–33
»Grundrechte des Deutschen Volkes«
Schriftplakat
Frankfurt, 27. Dezember 1848
MHM BBAK0571

Kat. 9 → S. 33
Manifest der Kommunistischen Partei
Karl Marx und Friedrich Engels
London, Februar 1848
Druck: Office der Bildungs-Gesellschaft für Arbeiter
Bundesarchiv, Bibliothek

Kat. 10
Kokarde in National- und Bundesfarben
Königreich Sachsen, 1848–1852
Durchmesser 3,5 cm
MHM LU 628

Kat. 11 → S. 22
Barrikadenkampf im Mai 1849 in Dresden
Julius Scholtz, 1849
Öl auf Leinwand, 23 × 34 cm
Städtische Galerie Dresden – Kunstsammlung Museen der Stadt Dresden

Kat. 12 → S. 34
»Die Reaction am Baum der Freiheit«
Holzstich nach Wilhelm Scholz aus dem humoristisch-satirischen Wochenblatt »Kladderadatsch«,
19. Januar 1850
MHM BAAX4938

Kat. 13 → S. 145
Kaminuhr anlässlich der österreichischen Märzverfassung von 1849
Um 1850
Dr. Rudolf Novak

Kat. 14
Brief des britischen Prinzgemahls Albert an den späteren österreichischen Außenminister Alexander Graf von Mensdorff-Pouilly
18. Mai 1861
Mährisches Landesarchiv in Brünn (Moravský zemský archiv v Brně)

Kat. 15 → S. 36–37
Infanterieoffizier-Degen
Geschenk Wilhelms, Prinz von Preußen, an Premierleutnant Heinrich Haering
Überreicht am 22. September 1848
MHM BBAD0034

Kat. 16 → S. 36–37
Dankschreiben Wilhelms, Prinz von Preußen
Babelsberg, 22. September 1848
MHM BBAC8053

Kat. 17 → S. 37
Kartätschkugel
Erinnerungsstück des Messerschmieds David Reuschle an die Märzrevolution 1848
Museum für Stadtgeschichte Templin

Kat. 18 → S. 37
Hinrichtung Johann Ludwig Maximilian Dortus (1826–1849) am 31. Juli 1849
Tusche auf Papier, 14,8 × 17,9 cm
Stiftung Deutsches Historisches Museum, Berlin, Kg 54/274

Kat. 19 → S. 33
Umgearbeiteter dänischer Dragonerhelm
Herzogtümer Schleswig und Holstein, 1848
MHM BBAT9125

Kat. 20
Helm für Offiziere der Infanterie
Herzogtümer Schleswig und Holstein, 1848
MHM BBAT9124

Kat. 21 → S. 33
Segelfregatte »Eckernförde«
1844 in Dänemark als »Gefion« in Dienst gestellt
Modell 1:100, um 1960er Jahre
60 × 86 × 42 cm
MHM BAAL5293

Kat. 22 → S. 34
Talisman »Faltbrief mit Stofffetzen vom dänischen Linienschiff Christian VIII«
MHM BAAG9807

Kat. 23
Kanonenkugel aus der Schlacht bei Idstedt am 24./25. Juli 1850
Durchmesser 12,5 cm
MHM BBAW5532

KRIEG ODER FRIEDEN?

Kat. 24 → S. 35
Einladung und Programm zum »Congress der Friedensfreunde«, 22.–24. August 1850
Frankfurt am Main, 1850
Institut für Stadtgeschichte, Frankfurt am Main, ISG_Impressen_01449

Kat. 25 → S. 34–35
»Die Völkerschlacht bei Bronzell«
Holzstich (Reproduktion) aus dem humoristisch-satirischen Wochenblatt »Kladderadatsch«, 17. November 1850
Universitätsbibliothek Heidelberg / Kladderadatsch: Humoristisch-satyrisches Wochenblatt — 3.1850 / 192 (public domain)

Kat. 26
William Howard Russell (1820–1907)
Roger Fenton, um 1854
Fotografie (Reproduktion)
Library of Congress, LC-USZ4-9183

Kat. 27 → S. 317
Florence Nightingale (1820–1910) in einem Lazarett in Scutari
Holzstich aus der »Illustrated London News«, 24. März 1855, S. 176
MHM BBAU8706

Kat. 28
»The Valley of the Shadow of Death«, 1855
Roger Fenton
Fotografie (Reproduktion)
The J. Paul Getty Museum, Los Angeles

Kat. 29 → S. 166–167
»Allgemeine Ansicht der grossen Schlacht bei Solferino«
Kolorierte Lithografie nach Hector Giacomelli, New York
MHM BBAW0152

Kat. 30 → S. 326
»Bersaglieri Kugel aus der Schlacht bei Solferino 24. Juni 1859«
Königreich Sardinien, 1859
Deformierte Bleifragmente
Sächsisches Rot-Kreuz-Museum Beierfeld

Kat. 31 → S. 318
Henri Dunant (1828–1910), um 1855
Fotografie (Reproduktion)
Bildarchiv Preußischer Kulturbesitz

Kat. 32 → S. 167
Camillo Benso Graf von Cavour (1810–1861)
Verlag Goupil & Co., Paris/London/Berlin, und M. Knoedler, New York
Lithografie
MHM

Kat. 33 → S. 167
Das Treffen von General Garibaldi und König Viktor Emanuel II. von Sardinien am 16. Oktober 1860 bei Teano
Holzstich aus der »Illustrated London News«, 29. Dezember 1860, S. 622–623
MHM BBAU8879

Kat. 34
»An die Oesterreicher!«
Gedicht von Bernhard Endrulat
Flugblatt aus der Berliner Volks-Zeitung vom 29. Mai 1859
MHM BBAJ6493

Kat. 35 → S. 168–169
»Das Schillerfest in Hamburg am 11., 12. und 13. November 1859«
Bernhard Endrulat,
mit 12 Illustrationen von Otto Speckter
Hamburg 1860
MHM FISt 00120730750

Kat. 36
Transport gefangener polnischer Aufständischer auf dem Weg von Warschau nach Moskau
Holzstich aus »Le Monde Illustré«,
6. Februar 1864
MHM BBAY0275

FORTSCHRITT

Kat. 37
Zwei Schreiben an den preußischen Prinzregenten Wilhelm wegen Reform der vaterländischen Wehrverfassung
Abgeordnete aus Blasheim, 4. April 1860 /
Abgeordnete aus Herford, Provinz Westfalen, April 1860
MHM BBAU4995; BBA08441

Kat. 38 ➔ S. 27
Flügelmütze für Mannschaften der Landwehrhusaren
Königreich Preußen, eingeführt 1842
MHM BBAM1061

Kat. 39 ➔ S. 41
Wilhelm I. (1797–1888)
Carte-de-Visite-Fotografie, 1860er Jahre
MHM BBAM8627

Kat. 40 ➔ S. 40–41
Graf Albrecht von Roon (1803–1879)
Carte-de-Visite-Fotografie, vor 1879
MHM BAAN5442

Kat. 41 ➔ S. 49
Otto von Bismarck (1815–1898)
G. Linde, Hoffotograf des Kronprinzen und der Kronprinzessin von Preußen
Putbus (Insel Rügen)
Carte-de-Visite-Fotografie, um 1862
MHM BAAW6954

Kat. 42 ➔ S. 50–51
Fotoalbum mit Offiziersporträts des mobilen 7. schweren Landwehr-Reiter-Regiments
Geschenk an Otto von Bismarck
Halberstadt und Quedlinburg,1866
MHM BBAW0706

Kat. 43 ➔ S. 38–39
Rudolf Virchow (1821–1902)
Carte-de-Visite-Fotografie
MHM BBAY0262

Kat. 44 ➔ S. 38–39
Messingmikroskop, wie es zur Trichinenschau genutzt wurde
Firma Wasserlein, nach 1860
25 × 8,4 × 10,9 cm
Berliner Medizinhistorisches Museum der Charité

Kat. 45 ➔ S. 39
Dankadresse des Bezirksvereins Alt-Cölln an Rudolf Virchow wegen der Ablehnung eines Duells mit Bismarck
Berlin, 11. Juni 1865
Berliner Medizinhistorisches Museum der Charité

Kat. 46 ➔ S. 40
Werner von Siemens (1816–1892)
Carte-de-Visite-Fotografie (Reproduktion)
Siemens Historical Institute

Kat. 47 ➔ S. 40
Zeigertelegraf
Telegraphen-Bauanstalt von Siemens & Halske
Berlin 1847
20 × 35 × 35 cm
Nachrichtentechnische Sammlung Aachen, Institut für Nachrichtentechnik, Aachen, RWTH Aachen

Kat. 48
Seetelegrafenkabelstück der Strecke Arkona (Rügen) – Trälleborg (Trelleborg, Schweden)
Hersteller vermutlich Norddeutsche Seekabel Werke (NSW), 1865
Stiftung Deutsches Technikmuseum Berlin

Kat. 49
Theodor Mommsen (1817–1903)
Carte-de-Visite-Fotografie (Reproduktion)
Stiftung Deutsches Historisches Museum, Berlin, Ph 90/49

Kat. 50
Römische Geschichte
Theodor Mommsen
Bde. I-III , Leipzig 1854–56
MHM FISt 00122161750

Kat. 51 ➔ S. 40–41
Adolph Diesterweg (1790–1866)
Carte-de-Visite-Fotografie
MHM BBAY0264

Kat. 52
»Wegweiser zur Bildung für deutsche Lehrer«
Bearbeitet und herausgegeben von Adolph Diesterweg
Essen 1844 (1. Aufl. 1835)
MHM FISt 00121729750, 00121730750

Kat. 53 ➔ S. 295
Alfred Krupp (1812–1887)
Carte-de-Visite-Fotografie (Reproduktion)
Historisches Archiv Krupp, Essen

Kat. 54 ➔ S. 294–295
Mittelteile des Panoramas der Kruppschen Gussstahlfabrik
Hugo van Werden,
Oktober 1864
Fotografie (Reproduktion)
Historisches Archiv Krupp, Essen

Kat. 55 ➔ S. 294
Krupp-Stand mit Eisenbahnradreifen auf der Londoner Weltausstellung 1862
Fotografie (Reproduktion)
Historisches Archiv Krupp, Essen

Kat. 56 ➔ S. 296–297
Ausstellungsstand der Gußstahlfabrik Friedrich Krupp auf der Internationalen Ausstellung in Dublin 1865
London Stereoscopic & Photographic Company
Fotografie (Reproduktion)
Historisches Archiv Krupp, Essen

Kat. 57 ➔ S. 295
Kleinbahn-Schiene, Breitfuß
Fried. Krupp A. G., Essen 1879
Stiftung Deutsches Technikmuseum, Berlin

Kat. 58 ➔ S. 282
Schreiben vom Chef des Ingenieurkorps, General Wilhelm von Radziwill, an Kriegsminister Albrecht von Roon wegen Entsendung eines Beobachters in die USA
Briefentwurf, Berlin, 16. Januar 1863
MHM BAAP5747

Kat. 59 ➔ S. 283
Unfall auf der Alexandria & Orange Eisenbahnlinie, ausgelöst von Rebellen 1862
Andrew Joseph Russell
Fotografie (Reproduktion)
The J. Paul Getty Museum, Los Angeles

Kat. 60 ➔ S. 283
»A Harvest of Death« / »Wenn der Tod Ernte hält«
Das Schlachtfeld von Gettysburg am 4. Juli 1863
Timothy H. O'Sullivan
Aus »Alexander Gardner's Photographic Sketch Book of the Civil War«
Fotografie (Reproduktion)
The J. Paul Getty Museum, Los Angeles

Kat. 61 ➔ S. 74
»Nationalitäten- und Sprachenkarte des Herzogthums Schleswig. Der Deutschen Nationalversammlung gewidmet«
Hermann Biernatzki, 1849
Karte (Reproduktion)
Schleswig-Holsteinische Landesbibliothek, Y 11:15

Kat. 62 ➔ S. 88–89
»Aufgefundenes Schiff aus dem Nydammer Moor in Schleswig« Das sogenannte Nydamboot auf dem Dachboden des Flensburger Gerichtsgebäudes
Holzstich von Ludwig Burger aus einer illustrierten Zeitung
Arkivet ved Dansk Centralbibliotek for Sydslesvig

Kat. 63 ➔ S. 89
Riemenfragmente, wahrscheinlich des sogenannten Kiefernholz-Bootes
Um 300 n. Chr.
Ahorn, 5 × 20 cm
Museum für Archäologie Schloss Gottorf, Landesmuseum Schleswig-Holstein

Kat. 64 ➔ S. 89
Schwertriemenhalter
2. Hälfte 4. Jahrhundert n. Chr.
Kupferlegierung, 12,6 × 11 cm
Museum für Archäologie Schloss Gottorf, Landesmuseum Schleswig-Holstein

Kat. 65 ➔ S. 89
Lanzenspitze
Mitte 3. Jahrhundert n. Chr.
Eisen, 3,1 × 26,5 cm
Museum für Archäologie Schloss Gottorf, Landesmuseum Schleswig-Holstein

Kat. 66
Axt
1. Hälfte 5. Jahrhundert n. Chr.
Eisen, 4,7 × 14,4 cm
Museum für Archäologie Schloss Gottorf, Landesmuseum Schleswig-Holstein

Kat. 67 ➔ S. 75
»Der Dänische Spion Blaunfeldt. Wie man ›Dänisches Ungeziefer‹ fängt, von dem Schleswig-Holstein geplagt wurde.«
Lithografie, Hamburg 1864
MHM BAAH0679

Kat. 68 ➔ S. 90–91
»Mein Recht ist Eure Rettung« Gedenkblatt auf die Proklamation Herzog Friedrichs VIII. von Schleswig-Holstein
Lithografie P. Grosenich, Hamburg 1863
Schleswig-Holsteinische Landesbibliothek

Kat. 69 ➔ S. 76
Büste Christians IX. (1818–1906), König von Dänemark
Höhe 33 cm
Schleswig-Holsteinische Landesbibliothek

Kat. 70 ➔ S. 76
Ditlev Gothard Monrad (1811–1887), königlich dänischer Ministerpräsident
Holzstich aus der »Illustrirten Zeitung«
MHM BBAY0259

Kat. 71 ➔ S. 90–91
Einzug sächsischer Exekutionstruppen in Altona unter dem Jubel der Bevölkerung am 24. Dezember 1863
August Beck, 1864
Bleistift auf Papier, 20,8 × 25,7 cm
MHM BAAH0377

Kat. 72 ➔ S. 91
Bataillonswagen des Königlich Sächsischen 4. Jäger-Bataillons mit Bataillonsarzt Dr. Reichel und Oberleutnant Lehmann, Wirtschaftsoffizier, nebst Trainsoldat und Offiziersdienern, 1864
Fotografie
MHM BBAR9008

Kat. 73 ➔ S. 91
Strandbatterie in Neustadt/Holstein, 7. Batterie des Königlich Sächsischen Fußartillerie-Regiments, 1964
Fotografie
MHM BBAR9009

Kat. 74 ➔ S. 92
Generalfeldmarschall Friedrich von Wrangel (1784–1877) und das preußische Hauptquartier
Photographische Anstalt von Friedrich Brandt
Fotomontage, Flensburg 1864
Schleswig-Holsteinische Landesbibliothek

Kat. 75 ➔ S. 92
Feldmarschallleutnant Ludwig von Gablenz (1810–1874) und das österreichische Hauptquartier
Photographische Anstalt von Friedrich Brandt
Fotografie, Flensburg 1864
Schleswig-Holsteinische Landesbibliothek

Kat. 76 ➔ S. 92–93
Generalleutnant Helmuth von Moltke (1800–1891), 1864
Carte-de-Visite-Fotografie (Reproduktion)
The History Collection/ Alamy Stock Foto

Kat. 77 ➔ S. 93
Prinz Friedrich Karl von Preußen (1828–1885) als Oberstinhaber des österreichischen Husarenregiments Nr. 7, 1864
Carte-de-Visite-Fotografie (Reproduktion)
Sammlung Wolfgang K. Hamann, Berlin

Kat. 78
Waffenrock, Mannschaften, Infanterie Königreich Dänemark
Königreich Dänemark, Modell 1889, gestempelt 1863
MHM BBAT9926

Kat. 79 → S. 78
Generalleutnant Christian Julius de Meza (1792–1865), Oberkommandierender der dänischen Truppen am Danewerk
Holzstich aus der »Illustrated London News«, 23. Januar 1864
MHM BBAY0274

Kat. 80
Ziegelsteine des Danewerks
1160–1180
Danevirke Museum

Kat. 81 → S. 79
Dänische Soldaten retten eine Kanone während des Rückzugs vom Danewerk am 5./6. Februar 1864
Holzstich nach einem Gemälde Niels Simonsen, 1865
Schleswig-Holsteinische Landesbibliothek

Kat. 82
Die Toten aus den Gefechten bei Oberselk und Jagel am 3. Februar 1864 im Spritzenhaus von Bustorf
Holzstich nach einer Zeichnung von August Beck aus der »Illustrirten Zeitung«, 2. April 1864
Schleswig-Holsteinische Landesbibliothek

Kat. 83 → S. 81
Sprengung des verschanzten Lagers von Fredericia durch österreichische Einheiten im Mai 1864
August Beck, 1864
Bleistift auf Papier, 23,9 × 34,6 cm
MHM BAAH0374

Kat. 84 → S. 94–95
Belagerungsplan der Düppeler Schanzen
Pietsch, Feuerwerker in der preußischen 4. Artilleriebrigade und Zeichner bei der kombinierten Artilleriebrigade des 1. preußisch kombinierten Armeekorps für Schleswig-Holstein
Berlin, um 1864
87 × 78 cm
Schleswig-Holsteinische Landesbibliothek

Kat. 85 → S. 94
In den Laufgräben vor Düppel
Adolf Northen, 1867
Öl auf Leinwand, 59 × 95,5 cm
Schleswig-Holsteinische Landesbibliothek

Kat. 86 → S. 96–97
Sprenggranate mit Bleimantel für 12-Pfünder-Feldgeschütze
MHM BAAH2253

Kat. 87 → S. 96–97
Sprengstücke von Granaten für 6-, 12- und 24-Pfünder-Feldgeschütze
Bodenfunde an den Düppeler Schanzen
Historiecenter Dybbøl Banke

Kat. 88 → S. 96
Spatenblatt
Bodenfund an den Düppeler Schanzen
Museum Sønderjylland Sønderborg Slot

Kat. 89 → S. 96
Faschinenmesser M 1855 mit Sägerücken, wie es preußische Pioniere 1864 bei Düppel verwendeten
MHM BAAA2039

Kat. 90 → S. 96–97
Feldflasche eines dänischen Soldaten
Museum Sønderjylland Sønderborg Slot

Kat. 91
Notizbuch von Unteroffizier Gustav Schade, 5./8. Kompanie des preußischen 18. Infanterie-Regiments, 1864–1866
MHM BAAV8975

Kat. 92
Offiziere der 3. Kompanie des preußischen 4. Garde-Regiments zu Fuß im Feldzug 1864
Fotografie
Schleswig-Holsteinische Landesbibliothek

Kat. 93 → S. 97
»Prost, Danske!« Ein preußischer und ein dänischer Soldat trinken zusammen
Wilhelm Camphausen, 1864
Bleistift auf Transparentpapier, 12 × 10 cm
Schleswig-Holsteinische Landesbibliothek

Kat. 94
»Ein Maler auf dem Kriegsfelde« Illustriertes Tagebuch
Wilhelm Camphausen
Bielefeld 1865
MHM FISt 00099998750

Kat. 95
Aufräumungsarbeiten auf dem Schlachtfeld
Wilhelm Camphausen
Holzstich in »Ein Maler auf dem Kriegsfelde«
Bielefeld o. J. [1913]
MHM 00099998750

Kat. 96 → S. 98
»Gade i Sönderborg under Bombardementet« / Eine Straße in Sonderburg unter Bombardement
Carl Frederik Aagaard
Lithografie
Schleswig-Holsteinische Landesbibliothek

Kat. 97
»Düppel 18. April 1864. Schanze II. Innere Ansicht«
Charles Junod, Hamburg
Fotografie (Reproduktion), nach dem 18. April 1864
Schleswig-Holsteinische Landesbibliothek, Album Ka 62

Kat. 98 → S. 99
»Düppel 18. April 1864. Schanze IV. Eingang«
Charles Junod, Hamburg
Fotografie, nach dem 18. April 1864
MHM BAAN7537

Kat. 99 → S. 99
»Düppel 18. April 1864. Schanze IV. Innere Ansicht mit dem Blockhaus«
Charles Junod, Hamburg
Fotografie, nach dem 18. April 1864
MHM BAAN7541

Kat. 100 → S. 80
»Düppel 18. April 1864. Schanze VIII. Innere Ansicht«
Charles Junod, Hamburg
Fotografie, nach dem 18. April 1864
MHM BAAN7536

Kat. 101
»Düppel 18. April 1864. Schanze IV. Äussere Ansicht«
Charles Junod, Hamburg
Fotografie, nach dem 18. April 1864
MHM BAAN7540

Kat. 102
Preußische Schiffsbrücke in Sonderburg
Charles Junod, Hamburg
Fotografie (Reproduktion), nach dem Übergang nach Alsen am 29. Juni 1864
Dansk Centralbibliotek for Sydslesvig e. V., Flensburg

Kat. 103 ➔ S. 101
Rathaus und Apotheke in Sonderburg
Charles Junod, Hamburg
Zwei Fotografien (Reproduktionen), nach dem Übergang nach Alsen am 29. Juni 1864
Schleswig-Holsteinische Landesbibliothek, Album 6, ZA 95

Kat. 104 ➔ S. 98
Prinz Friedrich Karl und sein Stab vor der Düppeler Mühle
Heinrich Graf oder sein Mitarbeiter Adolf Halwas, Berlin
Fotografie, nach dem 18. April 1864
MHM BAAN7533

Kat. 105 ➔ S. 100
Betontrümmer des zersprengten Pulvermagazins auf Schanze VI
Heinrich Graf oder sein Mitarbeiter Adolf Halwas, beide Berlin
Fotografie (Reproduktion), nach dem 18. April 1864
Wehrgeschichtliches Museum Rastatt

Kat. 106 ➔ S. 100
Kriegshospital des Johanniterordens in Wester Schnabek bei Ulderup
Fotografie (Reproduktion), 1864
Schleswig-Holsteinische Landesbibliothek

Kat. 107 ➔ S. 102
Turmschiff »Rolf Krake«
Modell 1:50, angefertigt von der Marinestation Sonderburg für die Düppel-Gedächtnisausstellung in der Exerzierhalle bei Schloss Sonderburg 1914
65 × 129 × 23 cm
Museum Sønderjylland Sønderborg Slot

Kat. 108 ➔ S. 103
Die Mannschaft des preußischen Flaggschiffs SMS Arcona
Fotografie (Reproduktion), 1864
Schleswig-Holsteinische Landesbibliothek, Album 6, ZA 95

Kat. 109 ➔ S. 103
Der österreichische Konteradmiral Wilhelm von Tegetthoff (1827–1871) auf dem Flaggschiff SMS Schwarzenberg
Fotografie (Reproduktion), 1864
Schleswig-Holsteinische Landesbibliothek, Album 25, 6388-6378

Kat. 110 ➔ S. 93
»Die Schleswig-Holsteinische Volksversammlung zu Rendsburg am 8. Mai 1864«
Johann Friedrich Fritz
Lithografie
Schleswig-Holsteinische Landesbibliothek

Kat. 111 ➔ S. 81
Übergang nach Alsen am 29. Juni 1864
Ulrich von Salpius, 1864
Aquarell, weiß gehöht, auf blaugetöntem Papier, 25 × 32 cm
Schleswig-Holsteinische Landesbibliothek

Kat. 112 ➔ S. 104–105
»Pionier Klinke öffnet der Sturmkolonne den Weg zur Schanze II, am 18. April 1864«
Postkarte aus dem Verlag Th. Lau, Sonderburg
Schleswig-Holsteinische Landesbibliothek

Kat. 113 ➔ S. 104–105
Tafel für Carl Klinke (1840–1864) vom Gedenkstein für die bei Düppel gefallenen preußischen Pioniere
Deutsches Museum Nordschleswig

Kat. 114 ➔ S. 105
»Aufgefundener Degen«
Suchanzeige im »Militair-Wochenblatt« vom 25. April 1871, Nr. 62, S. 407
MHM 00027433750

Kat. 115 ➔ S. 105
Offiziersdegen, graviert zur Erinnerung an die Aufpflanzung der ersten preußischen Sturmfahne auf den Düppeler Schanzen
Königreich Preußen, 1864
Privatbesitz

Kat. 116 ➔ S. 107
»›Uebermuth thut selten gut!‹ Beseitigung des Idstedter Löwen durch schleswig-holsteinische Patrioten am 28. Februar 1864«
S. Hamburger, 1864
Lithografie
Schleswig-Holsteinische Landesbibliothek

Kat. 117 ➔ S. 107
Idstedt-Löwe
Gipskopie des Flensburger Denkmals von Herman Wilhelm Bissen
Höhe 48,5 cm
Museum Sønderjylland Sønderborg Slot

Kat. 118 ➔ S. 106
»Erinnerung an die Einzugsfeier in Berlin am 7. December 1864«
Gedicht von Theodor Fontane
Druck Fr. Wassermann, Templin 1864
Theodor-Fontane-Archiv Potsdam

Kat. 119 ➔ S. 106
Schreiben Theodor Storms an Theodor Fontane
Husum, 19. Dezember 1864
Schleswig-Holsteinische Landesbibliothek

Kat. 120 ➔ S. 84
Milchkännchen mit dänischen Flaggen und der Aufschrift »Vergiss mich nicht«
Nach 1864
Museum Sønderjylland Sønderborg Slot

Kat. 121 ➔ S. 82
Kostenlose Ausgabe von Pflanzen zur Kultivierung von Heideflächen in Jütland, 1889
Fotografie (Reproduktion)
Hedeselskabet, Dänemark

Kat. 122 ➔ S. 82
Vortragssaal der Volkshochschule Testrup in Mårslet südlich von Aarhus, ca. 1890er Jahre
Fotografie (Reproduktion)
Martin Bo Nørregård, Flensburg

Kat. 123 ➔ S. 83
Fredrik Bajer (1837–1922) in Uniform und in Zivil
Zwei Fotografien (Reproduktionen)
Det Kongelike Bibliotek, Kopenhagen

Kat. 124 ➔ S. 85
»Stem Dig Hjem!« / Stimm Dich heim!
Plakat, 1920
Museum Sønderjylland Sønderborg Slot

Kat. 125 ➔ S. 86
Rückzug dänischer Streitkräfte aus Afghanistan
Karikatur von Roald Als (geb. 1948) für die dänische Tageszeitung Politiken vom 21. Juli 2013
Signierter Computerausdruck, 2019
MHM

1866 – DEUTSCHER KRIEG

Kat. 126
Gedenkblatt mit Franz Joseph I. von Österreich und Wilhelm I. von Preußen zum Deutsch-Dänischen Krieg 1864
Lithografie
Schleswig-Holsteinische Landesbibliothek

Kat. 127 ➔ S. 147
Spielkarten von einer gemeinsamen Eisenbahnfahrt Kaiser Franz Josephs I. und König Wilhelms I. im August 1865
Französisches Blatt
MHM BBAV7974

Kat. 128 ➔ S. 146
Brief Queen Victorias an ihren Cousin, den österreichischen Außenminister Alexander Graf von Mensdorff-Pouilly
Osborne, 4. August 1865
Mährisches Landesarchiv in Brünn
(Moravský zemský archiv v Brně)

Kat. 129
Brief von Ernst II. von Sachsen-Coburg und Gotha, an den österreichischen Außenminister Alexander Graf von Mensdorff-Pouilly
Gotha, 10. März 1866
Mährisches Landesarchiv in Brünn
(Moravský zemský archiv v Brně)

Kat. 130 ➔ S. 52
Attentat auf Bismarck am 7. Mai 1866
Extra-Beilage zu Nr. 106 der Deutschen Allgemeinen Zeitung, 9. Mai 1866
MHM BAAX4967

Kat. 131 ➔ S. 51
Seidenhemd Bismarcks mit geflickten Einschusslöchern
1866
Bismarck-Museum, Friedrichsruh

Kat. 132
Waffe des Attentäters, die Bismarck in seinem Schreibtisch aufbewahrte
Sechsschüssiger Bündelrevolver mit Elfenbeingriff
Länge 13 cm
Kaliber 7 mm
Bismarck-Museum, Friedrichsruh

Kat. 133
»Der Krieg und die Bundesreform«
Preußische Jahrbücher 17 (Juni 1866)
Heinrich von Treitschke
Zentrum für Militärgeschichte und Sozialwissenschaften der Bundeswehr

Kat. 134 ➔ S. 112–113
»An Mein Volk!«
Aufruf Wilhelms I. vom 18. Juni 1866
Druck F. Bär, Neisse
Stiftung Deutsches Historisches Museum, Berlin, Do 2007/3544

Kat. 135 ➔ S. 112–113
Büste Wilhelms I., König von Preußen, ab 1871 deutscher Kaiser
Carl Keil, Ems, nach 1871
Metallguss von Hermann Gladenbeck, Berlin, Höhe 35,5 cm
MHM BBAD3802

Kat. 136 ➔ S. 113
Büste Franz Josephs I., Kaiser von Österreich
Ca. 1860
Höhe 30 cm
Dr. Rudolf Novak

Kat. 137 ➔ S. 113
»An Meine Völker!« Aufruf Franz Josephs vom 17. Juni 1866
K. k. Hof- und Staatsdruckerei, Wien
Österreichische Nationalbibliothek, Sammlung von Handschriften und alten Drucken, F 311140E-E.Alt-Flug

Kat. 138 ➔ S. 121
Friedrich Ferdinand Freiherr von Beust (1809–1886)
Holzstich in der »Illustrirten Zeitung«, 8. Dezember 1866
MHM BBAY0268

Kat. 139
Lederhelm mit Spitze (»Pickelhaube«) für Mannschaften von Linieninfanterie-Regimentern
Königreich Preußen, Modell 1857, genutzt 1860/67
MHM BBAT7764

Kat. 140 ➔ S. 114–115
Lederhelm mit Spitze (»Pickelhaube«) für Mannschaften der Garde du Corps
Königreich Hannover, 1846/66
MHM BAAP3076

Kat. 141 ➔ S. 114–115
Tschako (Käppi) für Mannschaften der Linieninfanterieregimenter
Königreich Hannover, 1859/67
MHM BBAS5518

Kat. 142 ➔ S. 115
Waffenrock eines Sergeanten des 1. Infanterie-(Leib-)Regiments
Königreich Hannover, 1858/67
MHM BAAZ3264

Kat. 143 ➔ S. 115
Feldflasche (»Kantine«) der 7. Kompanie des 1. Infanterie-(Leib-)Regiments
Königreich Hannover, 1858/67
MHM BAAA8564

Kat. 144
Säbel mit Scheide für Unteroffiziere und Mannschaften der 2. Eskadron des Garde-Kürassier-Regiments
Königreich Hannover, 1859/66
Länge 110 cm
MHM BAAA2472

Kat. 145 → S. 116
Schlacht bei Langensalza am 27. Juni 1866
Johann Bernhard Schmelzer
Lithografie
MHM BAAH0651

Kat. 146 → S. 117
Signalhorn des hannoverschen 2. Jäger-Bataillons, mit dem bei Langensalza das letzte Signal gegeben wurde
Historisches Museum Hannover

Kat. 147
Übersichtskarte für die Main-Armee
MHM BAAR2672

Kat.148 → S. 140–141
Preußische Soldaten in Felduniform
Philipp Hoff, Frankfurt am Main 1866
Fotografie
Wehrgeschichtliches Museum Rastatt

Kat. 149 → S. 141
Porträts bayerischer Soldaten und Offiziere 1866
9 Carte-de-Visite-Fotografien auf Karton aufgezogen
Wehrgeschichtliches Museum Rastatt

Kat. 150 → S. 141
Schwarz-rot-goldene Armbinde
Großherzogtum Baden, 1866
Wehrgeschichtliches Museum Rastatt

Kat. 151 → S. 119
Lederhelm mit Spitze (»Pickelhaube«) für das Infanteriebataillon
Fürstentum Reuß jüngere Linie, um 1845
Vogtlandmuseum Plauen

Kat. 152 → S. 119
Waffenrock eines Hornisten der 2. Kompanie der Jägerabteilung
Fürstentum Reuß ältere Linie, 1865
Vogtlandmuseum Plauen

Kat. 153 → S. 122
Die Meißner Elbbrücke nach der Sprengung vom 15./16. Juni 1866
Lithografie
MHM BAAG3669

Kat. 154 → S. 122240
Einmarsch preußischer Truppen in Löbau am 16. Juni 1866
Adolph Göhde, Löbau
Lithografie
MHM BBAW3674

Kat. 155 → S. 126–127
König Johann und Kronprinz Albert von Sachsen überschreiten am 18. Juni 1866 bei Hellendorf die Landesgrenze nach Böhmen
Fotografie nach einem Gemälde von Theodor von Götz
MHM BAAN7425

Kat. 156 → S. 149
Österreichische Kavallerie im Kampf gegen preußische Truppen bei Nachod am 27. Juni 1866
Johann Baptist Heinefetter, 1877
Öl auf Leinwand, 77 × 103 cm
MHM BBAT2891

Kat. 157 → S. 138
Treffen am 29. Juni 1866 (Schlacht bei Gitschin)
Ansicht von Dilec und Eisenstadtl mit den Burgen Těšín, Kumburg und Bradlec
Hugo Tichý, Jičín/Gitschin
Fotografie
MHM BAAN0893

Filmstation Königgrätz
Oberstleutnant Dr. Thorsten Loch, Oberstleutnant Lars Zacharias (Konzept), MAT-Autorenteam der Offizierschule des Heeres, Dresden (gestalterisch-technische Umsetzung)

Kat. 158 → S. 137
Telegramm von Feldzeugmeister Benedek an Kaiser Franz Joseph, Königgrätz, 1. Juli 1866, 11 Uhr 30
Österreichisches Staatsarchiv, Kriegsarchiv

Kat. 159 → S. 137
Telegramm von Kaiser Franz Joseph an Feldzeugmeister Benedek, Wien, 1. Juli 1866, 14 Uhr 30
Österreichisches Staatsarchiv, Kriegsarchiv

Kat. 160 → S. 148
Waffenrock eines Oberleutnants der Infanterie
Kaisertum Österreich, 1859–1868
Wehrgeschichtliches Museum Rastatt

Kat. 161 → S. 127
Tschako eines Offiziers des 6. Infanterie-Bataillons der 2. Infanterie-Brigade »Prinz Friedrich August«
Königreich Sachsen, um 1866
MHM BBAT7607

Kat. 162 → S. 287–288
Preußisches Zündnadelgewehr für Infanterie M 1841
System Dreyse
Länge 142 cm
Kaliber 15,4 mm
MHM BAAL5440

Kat. 163 → S. 287–288
Österreichisches Perkussionsgewehr für Infanterie M 1854 II
System Lorenz
Länge 133 cm
Kaliber 13,9 mm
MHM BAAE2825

Kat. 164 → S. 135
Helmuth von Moltke (1800–1891)
Carl Schuler, 1881
Höhe 23,6 cm
MHM BAAV6249

Kat. 165 → S. 134
Feldzeugmeister Ludwig von Benedek (1804–1881), Oberbefehlshaber der österreichischen Nordarmee
Holzstich von Charles Maurand nach einer Fotografie von M. Angerer, Wien, aus einer französischen Illustrierten, 1866
MHM BBAY0269

Kat. 166 → S. 131
Oberstleutnant Luitbert von Friesen wird verwundet vom Schlachtfeld bei Königgrätz getragen
G. v. Bauck, um 1866
Aquarell, 20 × 28,5 cm
MHM BBAJ9795

Kat. 167 → S. 131
Luitbert von Friesens blutiges Schnupftuch
Königreich Sachsen, 1866
MHM BBAJ4031

Kat. 168 ➔ S. 160–161
Kaiserin Elisabeth von Österreich (1837–1898), genannt »Sisi«
Wiederholung des Gemäldes der Kaiserin in Hofgala mit Diamantsternen im Haar als Brustbild
Werkstatt Franz Xaver Winterhalter, um 1865
Öl auf Leinwand, 106 × 91 cm
Landessammlungen Niederösterreich, LK2239

Kat. 169 ➔ S. 157
Kinderuniform eines Obersts der k.k. Artillerie, getragen 1865 von Kronprinz Rudolf
Kaisertum Österreich, 1865
Schloss Schönbrunn Kultur- und Betriebsges. M.b.H.

Kat. 170 ➔ S. 157–158
Brief von Rudolf an seinen Vater Kaiser Franz Joseph (Kopialbuch)
Ischl, 17. Juni 1866
Österreichisches Staatsarchiv, Abteilung Haus-, Hof- und Staatsarchiv

Kat. 171 ➔ S. 157, 159
Brief von Kaiserin Elisabeth an ihren Sohn Rudolf
Wien, 29. Juni 1866
Österreichisches Staatsarchiv, Abteilung Haus-, Hof- und Staatsarchiv

Kat. 172 ➔ S. 158–159
Kopie eines Briefes von Rudolf an seine Mutter Kaiserin Elisabeth
Wien, 9. Juli 1866
40 × 25 cm
Österreichisches Staatsarchiv, Abteilung Haus-, Hof- und Staatsarchiv

Kat. 173 ➔ S. 152–153
Ratifikationsurkunde zum Prager Friedensvertrag zwischen Preußen und Österreich vom 23. August 1866
Unterzeichnet von König Wilhelm und Bismarck am 28. August 1866
Österreichisches Staatsarchiv, Abteilung Haus-, Hof- und Staatsarchiv

Kat. 174 ➔ S. 150–151
Einzug der preußischen Truppen in Berlin am 20. September 1866: Am Brandenburger Tor, 1866
F. Jamrath und Sohn
Fotografie
MHM BAAN7077

Kat. 175
Garde Corps. Ein Denkmal den gefallenen Kameraden. Erinnerung an den glorreichen Feldzug des Jahres 1866
L. Haase & Co., Berlin, Breslau, Köln
Fotografie
MHM BAAN0603

Kat. 176 ➔ S. 162
Tischplatte aus einem Gasthaus in Königgrätz, in das Kaiser Franz Joseph am 4. November 1866 einkehrte
71 × 102 × 4 cm
Stefan Rest, Wien

Kat. 177
Diarium der Reise des Kaisers nach Mähren, Schlesien und Böhmen
18. Oktober bis 9. November 1866
Österreichisches Staatsarchiv, Haus-, Hof- und Staatsarchiv

Kat. 178 ➔ S. 159
Briefbeschwerer zum Andenken an Königgrätz mit Fragment eines Granatkopfes und zwei Granatsplittern
Neu Joachimsthal, 1875
Bundesmobilienverwaltung Hofmobiliendepot – Möbel Museum Wien

Kat. 179 ➔ S. 162–163
Souvenir mit geweihter ungarischer Krönungserde und Scharnierdeckel in Form der Stephanskrone
Szendrik (Hersteller), Ungarn, um 1867
Messing vergoldet, graviertes Monogramm »FJI«, 6,2 × 2,8 cm
Landessammlungen Niederösterreich, LK1944

Kat. 180 ➔ S. 163
Georg Klapka (1820–1892), Banater Schwabe mit tschechischen Vorfahren und ungarischer General
Holzstich nach einer Fotografie von Disdéri & Co., Paris, um 1861/65
MHM BBAY0266

Kat. 181 ➔ S. 163–164
Attila eines Unterführers der Honvéd-Husarenregimenter
Königreich Ungarn, um 1900
MHM BAAL7509

Kat. 182 ➔ S. 164
Szene in einer Dorfschule – der Schulmeister
Johann Peter Hasenclever, nach 1840
Öl auf Leinwand, 38 × 51 cm
Stiftung Deutsches Historisches Museum, Berlin, Kg 59/91

Kat. 183 ➔ S. 165
»Die Einquartierung«
Lithografie aus dem Sammelwerk »Erinnerungs-Blätter aus dem Feldzuge in Böhmen und Mähren im Sommer 1866« von Calixt Prinz Biron von Curland und Alfred Hindorf
Berlin, um 1867
MHM BBAK2304

Kat. 184
Telegramm vom Kriegsschauplatz (Südarmee), Bulletin Nr. 2 und 3
Linz, 25. Juni 1866
MHM BAAX5012

Kat. 185 ➔ S. 169
Erinnerungsbild an Mathäus Berner, gestorben bei Custoza am 24. Juni 1866
Öl auf Leinwand, 29,5 × 26 cm
Salzburger Wehrgeschichtliches Museum

Kat. 186 ➔ S. 168–169
Schärpe, getragen von einem österreichischen Offizier in der Schlacht bei Custoza
Erinnerungsstück von 1866 der österreichischen Offiziersfamilie Marinelli
MHM BBAT9149

Kat. 187 ➔ S. 170–171
»Roth – Weiss – Roth. Erinnerung an den 20. Juli 1866«
Gedicht von Hermann Stricker über die Seeschlacht bei Lissa
Nach Angabe des Dichters gezeichnet von Georg Weineiss
Graz, um 1890
Lithografie
Österreichische Nationalbibliothek, Bildarchiv und Grafiksammlung, Pk 847

Kat. 188 → S. 171
»La rivincita di Lissa« / Rache für Lissa
Science-Fiction-Roman von Yambo
(d. i. Enrico de' Conti Novelli da Bertinoro)
Rom, 1909
MHM FISt 00122146750

Kat. 189
Denkmünze für die Verteidiger der Stadt Rom
Römische Republik, 1849
Weißmetall, Durchmesser 24,2 mm
BBAT9487, Sammlung Major Rübke

Kat. 190
Erinnerungsmedaille der Tausend bei Marsala Gelandeten
Königreich Italien, 1860
Buntmetall
Durchmesser Münze 30 mm
MHM BBAT9484, Sammlung Major Rübke

Kat. 191 → S. 171
Verdienstmedaille in Bronze für die Befreier der Stadt Rom
Königreich Italien, 1870
Buntmetall
Durchmesser Münze 32 mm
MHM BBAT9488, Sammlung Major Rübke

Kat. 192
Einheitsmedaille
Königreich Italien, 1865
(verliehen bis nach 1871)
Silber
Durchmesser Münze 32 mm
MHM BBAT9483, Sammlung Major Rübke

Kat. 193 → S. 117
Nachbildung der hannoverschen Königskrone von 1843
Metallblech, Glas
Historisches Museum Hannover

Kat. 194 → S. 117
Hannoversche Offiziere der Welfenlegion 1868 in Paris
Fotografie (Reproduktion)
gemeinfrei, Wikimedia Commons

Kat. 195 → S. 142
Die Verfassung des Norddeutschen Bundes
Berlin 1867
Zentrum für Informationsarbeit der Bundeswehr

Kat. 196 → S. 142
Helm für Mannschaften der Infanterie
Königreich Sachsen, 1867/71
MHM BBAT7400

Kat. 197 → S. 143
Uniformierung der Königlich Sächsischen Armee vor der Reorganisation, März 1867
Hanns Hanfstaengl, Dresden 1867
MHM BAAN0579

Kat. 198 → S. 143
Besichtigung des sächsischen Lehrbataillons durch König Wilhelm von Preußen und König Johann von Sachsen in der Neustädter Reiterkaserne, Dresden, 20. Februar 1867
August Beck
Radierung, 25,7 × 31,6 cm
MHM BAAU3926

Kat. 199 → S. 61
Steckspiel
Gesellenstück von August Bebel
Elfenbein, geschnitzt um 1857
2,4 × 2,4 × 2,4 cm
Stiftung Deutsches Historisches Museum, Berlin, MK 83/398.1, MK 83/398.2

Kat. 200 → S. 61
Siegelring August Bebels mit Schatulle
1864
Gold, 2,3 × 1,5 cm
Stiftung Deutsches Historisches Museum, Berlin, K 54/62

Kat. 201 → S. 59
August Bebel (1840–1913)
Fotografie (Reproduktion), um 1865
bpk/adoc-photos

Kat. 202 → S. 143
»Der Militarismus als Ursache der Massenverarmung in Europa und die europäische Union als Mittel zur Überflüssigmachung der stehenden Heere«
Eduard Loewenthal
Potschappel, Februar 1870
MHM 00109712750

Hörstation
Tausend Takte Nationalgefühl
Patriotisch inspirierte Kompositionen des 19. Jahrhunderts von Gottfried Piefke bis Giuseppe Verdi

1867 – GLANZ UND KRISE DES ZWEITEN KAISERREICHS

Kat. 203 → S. 177
Büste Napoleons III. während des Italienischen Unabhängigkeitskriegs 1859
Albert-Ernest Carrier-Belleuse, um 1859
Bronze, Höhe 41,2 cm
Stiftung Deutsches Historisches Museum, Berlin, Pl 97/9

Kat. 204 → S. 185
Helm für Mannschaften der Escadron des Cent-Gardes
Kaiserreich Frankreich, 1854–1870
Bayerisches Armeemuseum Ingolstadt

Kat. 205
Pallasch und Scheide zum Mousqueton (Karabiner) M. 1854 der Escadron des Cent-Gardes
Kaiserreich Frankreich, 1856–1870
Länge 118 cm
MHM BAAA1977

Kat. 206 → S. 177
Spenzer für Reitknechte des Kaiserlichen Marstalls
Kaiserreich Frankreich, 1852–1870
MHM BAAL8581

Kat. 207 → S. 177
Napoleon III. als Nussknacker
Deutsch, um 1860
30 × 20 × 25 cm
Erstes Nussknackermuseum Europas, Inhaber Uwe Löschner

Kat. 208 → S. 176
Napoleon I., Napoleon II. und Napoleon III.
Dresden, nach 1852
Lithografie
MHM BAAU3708

Kat. 209
Denkmünze auf die Hochzeit Napoleons III. mit Eugénie de Montijo (1826–1920) am 30. Januar 1853 in Notre Dame de Paris
Robineau, Paris 1853
Buntmetall, Durchmesser 3,5 cm
MHM BAAB6233

Kat. 210 ➔ S. 180
Napoleon III., Kaiser der Franzosen
William Holl nach einer Fotografie, 1870
Stahlstich
MHM BBAU2331

Kat. 211 ➔ S. 178
Ansicht des Geländes der Pariser Weltausstellung von 1867
Numa Fils (i. e. Christophe Emile Haering), Fotoreproduktion einer Grafik im Carte-de-Visite-Format, Paris 1867
MHM BBAY0270

Kat. 212 ➔ S. 178
Eintrittskarte Bismarcks für die Pariser Weltausstellung 1867
Archiv der Otto-von Bismarck-Stiftung, Friedrichsruh

Kat. 213 ➔ S. 296–297
»Bilder von der Internationalen Ausstellung in Paris: Die Krupp'sche Riesenkanone«
Holzstich aus der Illustrierten Zeitung, 25. Mai 1867
Kölnisches Stadtmuseum

Kat. 214 ➔ S. 178–179
Festungsplan von Luxemburg
H. Baumann, 1854
53 × 71,5 cm
MHM BBAA6375

Kat. 215 ➔ S. 179
»To be sold« / Zu verkaufen. Karikatur zur Luxemburg-Krise, 4. Mai 1867
Aus der Beilage »Punch and the Prussian Bully 1857–1914« zu »Punch«, London, 14. Oktober 1914, S. 8
MHM BBAX7560

1870/71
DEUTSCH-FRANZÖSISCHER KRIEG

Kat. 216 ➔ S. 181
Fürst Leopold von Hohenzollern-Sigmaringen (1835–1905)
Holzstich, 1875
MHM BBAV1542

Kat. 217 ➔ S. 54 ➔ S. 181
»Emser Depesche«
Extrablatt. Kölnische Zeitung. Telegraphische Depesche
13. Juli 1870
Kölnisches Stadtmuseum

Kat. 218 ➔ S. 183
Nachricht über die Aufforderung Frankreichs an die süddeutschen Staaten, neutral zu bleiben
Extra-Beilage zu Nr. 146 der Magdeburgischen Zeitung, 18. Juli 1870
MHM BBAR7210

Kat. 219 ➔ S. 183
»An mein Volk!«
Aufruf König Wilhelms I. von Preußen, Berlin, 31. Juli 1870
Landesarchiv Berlin, A_Pr_Br_Rep.030_11034_Bl.44

Kat. 220 ➔ S. 183
Kaiser Napoleons III. an das französische Volk
Aufruf (Reproduktion), Paris, 23. Juli 1870
Bibliothèque de documentation internationale contemporaine, Nanterre, AFF11924

Kat. 221
Die Franzosen in Deutschland
Verlag Cäsar Fritsch
München Juli 1870
MHM BBAY1997

Kat. 222
Eisernes Kreuz 1870, Großkreuz, Ausführung für Fahnenspitzen
Königreich Preußen, 1870/1871
5,8 × 5,8 cm
MHM BBAT9686

Kat. 223 ➔ S. 182–183
»Untersuchungsacten des Kgl. Sächs. Bezirksgerichts Leipzig gegen Wilhelm Obermueller/Staatsverrath etc. 1870«
Königliches Bezirksgericht Leipzig, Nr. 24.
Sächsisches Staatsarchiv – Staatsarchiv Leipzig

Kat. 224 ➔ S. 182–183
»Müssen denn die Sachsen sich auch totschießen lassen?«
Artikel aus Sächsischer Zeitung, 16. Juli 1870
Sächsisches Staatsarchiv – Staatsarchiv Leipzig

Kat. 225 ➔ S. 182–183
Steckbrief Wilhelm Obermüller
Leipziger Tageblatt, Nr. 17
Sächsisches Staatsarchiv – Staatsarchiv Leipzig

Kat. 226 ➔ S. 190–191
Rohr einer Mitrailleuse, System Reffye
Frankreich 1869/1871
Länge 185 cm
Bayerisches Armeemuseum Ingolstadt

Kat. 227
Patronenkasten (Ladeblockbehälter) einer Mitrailleuse des Systems Reffye
Frankreich, 1869–1871
Kölnisches Stadtmuseum

Kat. 228
13 mm Patrone für Mitrailleusen des Systems Reffye
Frankreich, 1869–1871
Länge 11,7 cm
MHM BAAT8637

Kat. 229 ➔ S. 191
»Siegesbulletin des Mitrailleur an seine Mitrailleuse«, Flugblatt 3 einer Folge zum Deutsch-Französischen Krieg
Kölnisches Stadtmuseum

Kat. 230 ➔ S. 186
Hauptfeldwebel des 28. Linieninfanterie-regiments
Uniformfigurine
Kaiserreich Frankreich, 1867–1870
Musée de l'Armée, Paris

Kat. 231 → S. 287–288
Zündnadelgewehr Chassepot
Kaiserreich Frankreich, 1866
Länge 130 cm
Kaliber 11 mm
MHM BAAG5842

Kat. 232
»Yatagan«, Bajonett für französische Infanterie-Gewehre mit Scheide
Kaiserreich Frankreich, 1866
Länge 72 cm
MHM BAAA0029

Kat. 233 → S. 187
Helm und Waffenrock für Musketiere des 2. Thüringischen Infanterie-Regiments Nr. 32
Königreich Preußen, um 1870/71
Stiftung Deutsches Historisches Museum, Berlin, U 53/498

Kat. 234
Helm für Mannschaften der Linieninfanterieregimenter
Königreich Preußen, 1867/1871
Stiftung Deutsches Historisches Museum, Berlin, U 1254

Kat. 235
Koppel mit Kastenschloss M 1847
Königreich Preußen, ab 1847
Stiftung Deutsches Historisches Museum, Berlin, U 73/173.a

Kat. 236
Seitengewehrtroddel für Unteroffiziere
Königreich Preußen, ab 1860
Stiftung Deutsches Historisches Museum, Berlin, U 1611

Kat. 237
Feldflasche mit Korken
Königreich Preußen,1867/1880
Stiftung Deutsches Historisches Museum, Berlin, U 2018/70.a-b

Kat. 238
Brotbeutel für Unteroffiziere und Mannschaften
Königreich Preußen, um 1867/1890
Stiftung Deutsches Historisches Museum, Berlin, U 53/500

Kat. 239
Granatensammler auf dem Schlachtfelde von Spicheren
Holzstich nach Ph. Müller
aus »Über Land und Meer«, Nr. 47, 1871
MHM BBAY0272

Kat. 240 → S. 191
Fernglas, Geschenk von Captain J. L. Seton an Julius von Rosen, Hauptmann im I. Bataillon des Hohenzollernschen Füsilierregiments Nr. 40
Um 1870
Familienarchiv von Rosen

Kat. 241
Fotografie aus einem auf dem Schlachtfeld von Spicheren gefundenen Tornister
Ludwigsburg, 1870/71
Wehrgeschichtliches Museum Rastatt

Kat. 242
Quartiermeister, 2. Algerisches Schützen-Regiment
Uniformfigurine
Kaiserreich Frankreich, 1870
Musée historique de la ville de Strasbourg

Kat. 243 → S. 192
Preußischer Dragoner im Kampf mit französischen Zuaven
Wilhelm Alexander Meyerheim
1871
Öl auf Leinwand, 47 × 57 cm
MHM BBAU8296

Kat. 244 → S. 192
»Die erste Kriegsbeute. Ein toll und voll getrunkener Zuave wird in einem auf deutschen Grund und Boden gelegenen Wirthshause von einer deutschen Patrouille gefangen genommen u. nach Saarbrücken abgeliefert«
Nach einer Skizze von Eduard Harburger, Feldmaler für die Gartenlaube
Bleistift und Tusche auf Papier, 28 × 20,7 cm
MHM BBAX8315

Kat. 245
»Drei bei der Vertheidigung eines Gartenhäuschens in dem Treffen bei Weißenburg am 4. August 1870 gefallene Turcos der französischen Armee, in einer schattigen Gartenlaube liegend«
Nach einer Originalzeichnung von Professor Paul Thumann aus Weimar, Feldmaler der Gartenlaube
Bleistift und Tusche auf Papier, 28 × 31,5 cm
MHM BBAX8316

Kat. 246 → S. 193
Marketenderin des 92. Linieninfanterieregiments
Uniformfigurine
Französische Republik, 1885
Musée historique de la ville de Strasbourg

Kat. 247 → S. 193
Schnapsfässchen einer Marketenderin des 16. Bataillons, Chasseurs à Pied
Kaiserreich Frankreich, 1863
Wehrgeschichtliches Museum Rastatt

Kat. 248
»Feld der Todten« hinter dem Gaisberg bei Weißenburg
Gereon Pape
Tusche auf Papier, 42,5 × 57,8 cm
Kölnisches Stadtmuseum

Kat. 249
Quartiermeister des 3. Kürassierregiments
Uniformfigurine
Kaiserreich Frankreich, 1870
Musée historique de la ville de Strasbourg

Kat. 250 → S. 194
Pistole, geführt bei Mars-la-Tour von einem Angehörigen des Altmärkischen Ulanen-Regiments Nr. 16
Königreich Preußen
Länge 39 cm
Kaliber 15,2 mm
Privatbesitz

Kat. 251 → S. 194
Koller für Mannschaften des Magdeburgischen Kürassierregiments Nr. 7
Königreich Preußen, 1870/71
MHM BAAZ3179

Kat. 252 ➔ S. 194
Helm für Unteroffiziere und Mannschaften der Linienkürassierregimenter, mit Hiebspuren
Königreich Preußen, 1867/1871
Stiftung Deutsches Historisches Museum, Berlin, U 2507

Kat. 253
Pallasch für Mannschaften der Regimenter der schweren Kavallerie
Kaiserreich Frankreich, 1854–1870, Französische Republik 1870–1882
Länge 117 cm
MHM BAAA0531

Kat. 254 ➔ S. 195
Leibfahne des 8. Königlich Sächsischen Infanterieregiments Nr. 107
Königreich Sachsen, 1867–1918
120 × 109 cm
MHM BAAA5340

Kat. 255 ➔ S. 195
Versilberter Fahnenring der Leibfahne des 8. Königlich Sächsischen Infanterieregiments Nr. 107 graviert mit den Namen der Träger bei St. Privat und Sedan
Königreich Sachsen
8 × 4,5 cm
Privatbesitz

Kat. 256 ➔ S. 196
»Hundemüde!« Ruhende Soldaten nach der Schlacht von Gravelotte bzw. St. Privat
Zeichnung von Kaspar Kögler für »Die Gartenlaube«, 1870, Nr. 45, S. 752
Bleistift auf Papier, 20,4 × 28,8 cm
MHM BBAX8326

Kat. 257 ➔ S. 55 ➔ S. 195
Telegramm Bismarcks über den Ausgang der Schlacht bei Mars-la-Tour an seine Ehefrau Johanna von Puttkammer, 17. August 1870
Archiv der Otto-von-Bismarck-Stiftung, Friedrichsruh

Kat. 258
»Wilhelm I. koning van Pruisen in den slag bij Gravelotte op den 18den Augustus 1870« / Wilhelm I. König von Preußen in der Schlacht bei Gravelotte am 18. August 1870
Binger van Emrik
Lithografie
MHM BAAH0383

Kat. 259 ➔ S. 196
»Königliche Hoheit Kronprinz Albert, der Sieger von Beaumont«
Theodor von Götz, Dresden 1881
Aquarell, 29,3 × 50,1 cm
MHM BBAR8624

Kat. 260 ➔ S. 187
Helm für Mannschaften der Infanterie-Regimenter
Königreich Bayern, 1868–1886
MHM BBAB3260

Kat. 261 ➔ S. 197
Abgetrennter Ärmel vom Uniformrock eines Quartiermeisters der Marineinfanterie
Kaiserreich Frankreich, 1870
Comité national des traditions des Troupes de marine

Kat. 262 ➔ S. 197
»A Bazeille[s] 1er Septembre 1870 soir« / Gefallene in den Ruinen von Bazeilles, Abend des 1. September 1870
Auguste Lançon, 1871/1876
Radierung, 39,7 × 56,5 cm
Musée de l'Armée, Paris

Kat. 263
Ruine von Bazeilles mit davor hockenden und stehenden Zivilisten, 1870
Fotografie
Wehrgeschichtliches Museum Rastatt

Kat. 264 ➔ S. 198
Einwohner von Bazeilles werden von bayerischen Truppen zur Hinrichtung abgeführt
Postkarte nach einem Holzschnitt von A. Lanson [Auguste Lançon?], 1912
MHM BBAB0434

Kat. 265 ➔ S. 199
Ansicht des Zimmers in Donchery, in dem am 2. September 1870 Otto von Bismarcks Unterredung mit Napoleon III. stattfand
Gereon Pape
Tusche auf Papier, 40,8 × 54,1 cm
Kölnisches Stadtmuseum

Kat. 266 ➔ S. 200–201
Losungsbuch, in dem Bismarck die Schlacht von Sedan und das Treffen mit Napoleon III. vermerkt hat
1870
Bismarck-Museum, Friedrichsruh

Kat. 267 ➔ S. 201
»Pax Morientibus!« / Friede den Sterbenden!
Wilfrid-Constant Beauquesne
Öl auf Leinwand, 53,4 × 39,7 cm
Bayerisches Armeemuseum Ingolstadt

Kat. 268
Erstürmung der Porta Pia in Rom, 20. September 1870
Fotografie (Reproduktion)
Archivio del Museo Centrale del Risorgimento di Roma (MCRR)

Kat. 269 ➔ S. 201
Jacke eines Offiziers der Légion des Volontaires de l'Ouest
Republik Frankreich, 1870/71
MHM BBAQ7588

Kat. 270 ➔ S. 202
Weste zur Uniform eines Offiziers der Légion des Volontaires de l'Ouest mit Einnäher mit dem Herzen Jesu im Futter
Republik Frankreich, 1870/71
MHM BBAQ7587

Kat. 271 ➔ S. 202
Chechia für Mannschaften der Zuaven- und Algerischen Schützenregimenter
Republik Frankreich, um 1900
MHM BAAZ3528

Kat. 272 → S. 203
Gottesdienst am Versöhnungstage des Jahres 1870 bei der Belagerungsarmee vor Metz
Instruktionstuch, signiert »GM«, nach 1870
Baumwolle, bedruckt
67,7 × 69,2 cm
MHM BBAW0750

Kat. 273 → S. 205
Leutnant des 4. Bataillons der Mobilgarde des Niederrhein-Departements
Uniformfigurine
Kaiserreich Frankreich, 1870
Musée historique de la ville de Strasbourg

Kat. 274 → S. 205
Fahne der Nationalgarde
Frankreich, um 1850
152 × 149 cm
MHM BBAM7092

Kat. 275 → S. 204
Léon Gambetta (1838–1882), von September 1870 bis Januar 1871 Innenminister der Regierung der Nationalen Verteidigung
1885
Bronze, Höhe 38 cm
Bayerisches Armeemuseum Ingolstadt

Kat. 276 → S. 205
Spottmünze auf Napoleon III. mit aufgravierter Narrenkappe
Kursmünze 10 Centimes
Buntmetall, Durchmesser 30 mm
MHM BBAT9687

Kat. 277 → S. 205
Spottmünze auf Napoleon III. mit aufgravierter Pickelhaube
Kursmünze 10 Centimes
Buntmetall, Durchmesser 30 mm
MHM BBAT9688

Kat. 278 → S. 205
Spottmünze auf Napoleon III. mit aufgraviertem Zylinder
Kursmünze 10 Centimes
Buntmetall, Durchmesser 30 mm
MHM BBAT9689

Kat. 279 → S. 205
Spottmünze auf Napoleon III. mit Schlafmütze
Kursmünze 10 Centimes
Buntmetall, Durchmesser 30 mm
MHM BBAT9691

Kat. 280
Spottmünze auf Napoleon III. mit Adler, um dessen Hals eine Schlange aufgraviert ist
Kursmünze 10 Centimes
Buntmetall, Durchmesser 30 mm
MHM BBAT9690

Kat. 281 → S. 62–63
»Kettenbild«
Fotocollage in Wilhelm Brackes Buch »Der Braunschweiger Ausschuß der socialdemokratischen Arbeiter-Partei in Lötzen und vor dem Gericht«, Braunschweig 1872
Bibliothek der Friedrich Ebert Stiftung, Bonn

Kat. 282 → S. 206
»Capt. E Hilbot, sa femme et son chien«/Hauptmann E Hilbot, seine Frau und sein Hund
L. Pierson
Carte-de-Visite-Fotografie (Reproduktion)
Musée de l'Armée, Paris

Kat. 283
Soldat mit Frau in weißer Haube
Carte-de-Visite-Fotografie (Reproduktion)
Musée de l'Armée, Paris

Kat. 284
Zwei Soldaten mit einer älteren Frau
Carte-de-Visite-Fotografie (Reproduktion)
Musée de l'Armée, Paris

Kat. 285 → S. 206
Sapeur und Marketenderin eines unbekannten Truppenteils
Antonin, Paris
Carte-de-Visite-Fotografie (Reproduktion)
Musée de l'Armée, Paris

Kat. 286 → S. 206
Ein Freiwilliger oder Nationalgardist und eine Marketenderin, an einem Fass lehnend
Dolivet, Paris
Carte-de-Visite-Fotografie (Reproduktion)
Musée de l'Armée, Paris

Kat. 287 → S. 206
Ein Mann und eine Frau in Uniform, vermutlich Angehörige eines Freiwilligenverbands
Carte-de-Visite-Fotografie (Reproduktion)
Musée de l'Armée, Paris

Kat. 288
Leutnant Faure, ein weiblicher Offizier der Nationalgarde
Carte-de-Visite-Fotografie (Reproduktion)
Musée de l'Armée, Paris

Kat. 289
Marie-Antoinette Lix (1839–1909) in Leutnantsuniform, vermutlich eines Freiwilligenverbands
Reproduktion einer malerisch überarbeiteten Fotografie
Musée de l'Armée, Paris

Kat. 290
Marie Favier, geb. Demigneux
Capitaine adjudant-major aux franc-tireurs du Doubs, bataillon Nicolaï, 1870
Charles Joussaune, 1912
Fotografie
Musée de l'Armée, Paris

Kat. 291 → S. 206–207
»Hamon père« / Vater Hamon in der Uniform der Nationalgarde
L. Pierson
Carte-de-Visite-Fotografie (Reproduktion)
Musée de l'Armée, Paris

Kat. 292 → S. 206–207
»Hamon fils« / Sohn Hamon in der Uniform der Nationalgarde
L. Pierson
Carte-de-Visite-Fotografie (Reproduktion)
Musée de l'Armée, Paris

Kat. 293
Nationalgardist mit Mädchen
Carte-de-Visite-Fotografie (Reproduktion)
Musée de l'Armée, Paris

Kat. 294
Sitzender Soldat mit Gewehr und stehendem Mädchen in Kleid mit Handtasche
Carte-de-Visite-Fotografie (Reproduktion)
Musée de l'Armée, Paris

Kat. 295
Stehender Soldat mit Gewehr und einem auf einer angedeuteten Mauer sitzenden Kind
Carte-de-Visite-Fotografie (Reproduktion)
Musée de l'Armée, Paris

Kat. 296 → S. 206–207
Junger Trommler in Uniform
Lefévre, Paris
Carte-de-Visite-Fotografie (Reproduktion)
Musée de l'Armée, Paris

Kat. 297
Junger Soldat mit Gewehr an einem Fass lehnend
Champs, Paris
Carte-de-Visite-Fotografie (Reproduktion)
Musée de l'Armée, Paris

Kat. 298 → S. 208–209
»Enfants déguisés« / Verkleidete Kinder
Zwei Jungen in der 1867 vorgestellten Uniform der Franctireurs des Vosges
Carte-de-Visite-Fotografie (Reproduktion)
Musée de l'Armée, Paris

Kat. 299 → S. 227
»Un de siege (!!!) Excuare aliquis nostris ex ossibus ultor!« / Eines aus der Zeit der Belagerung (!!!) Ein Rächer wird aus meinem Staub erstehen
Carte-de-Visite-Fotografie (Reproduktion)
Musée de l'Armée, Paris

Kat. 300 → S. 209
Franctireur des Vosges
Uniformfigurine
Republik Frankreich, 1870/71
Musée de l'Armée, Paris

Kat. 301
»Kampf gegen Franctireurs bei Raon am 6. Oktober 1870«
Bilderbogen Nr. 27 aus der Folge »Der Krieg Deutschlands gegen Frankreich. Bilderzeitung der Gegenwart«,
Otto Kraffert & Co., Dresden
MHM BBAW4819

Kat. 302
Parole-Buch
Unbekannter deutscher Truppenteil, 1870
MHM BBAT5652

Kat. 303
»Eine alte Frau wurde von Soldaten erschlagen, weil sie den Verwundeten die Augen sollte ausgestochen haben«
Tagebuch des Kgl. Sächs. 12. Feldlazaretts, Eintrag am 20. August 1870
MHM BBAL4643

Kat. 304 → S. 344–345
Das als Lazarett genutzte Gehöft Mogador, das während der Schlacht bei Gravelotte abbrannte
Gereon Pape nach Skizze, 2. Oktober 1870
Bezeichnet verso: »Bei Gravelotte. Lazarett wo die Verwundeten verbrandt sind. 2.10.70. (Nach Skizze.)«
Tusche auf Papier, 33,5 × 51,1 cm
Kölnisches Stadtmuseum

Kat. 305 → S. 344
»Nemesis«
Gereon Pape
Tusche auf Papier, 42 × 58 cm
Kölnisches Stadtmuseum

Kat. 306 → S. 210
Tschapka für Mannschaften der Linien-Ulanenregimenter
Königreich Preußen, 1867–1889
MHM BAAY9718

Kat. 307
Ulanka, Lithauisches Ulanen-Regiment Nr. 12
Königreich Preußen, 1860–1868
Stiftung Deutsches Historisches Museum, Berlin, U 138

Kat. 308 → S. 210
Kavallerielanze, Modell 1856
Königreich Preußen
Länge 315 cm
MHM BAAF6240

Kat. 309 → S. 210–211
»La Charge des Uhlans« / Ulanenangriff, 1870/71
Alphonse de Neuville
Vorlage für eine Abbildung in Quatrelles (d. i. Ernest-Louis-Victor-Jules L'Épine): « À coups de fusil », mit Illustrationen von Alphonse Neuville
Paris, 1877
Federzeichnung, 36,5 × 41 cm
MHM BBAU2998

Kat. 310 → S. 210–211
»Franc-tireur brûlé vif par les Prussiens« / Von preußischen Soldaten lebendig verbrannter Franctireur, Pouilly-lès-Dijon, 23. Januar 1871
Guipet, Dijon 1871
Photoglyptie (Reproduktion)
bpk / RMN – Grand Palais / Emilie Cambier

Kat. 311
Arthur Erhardt: Kleinkrieg. Geschichtliche Erfahrungen und künftige Möglichkeiten
Potsdam 1942
MHM 00002840750

Kat. 312
Arthur Erhardt: Kleinkrieg. Geschichtliche Erfahrungen und künftige Möglichkeiten
Potsdam 1944
MHM 00031651750

Kat. 313 → S. 259
Straßburg vom Steintor aus gesehen am Tag nach der Kapitulation der belagerten Stadt
Charles Winter / Paul Sinner
Fotografie (Reproduktion)
Wehrgeschichtliches Museum Rastatt

Kat. 314 → S. 212–213
Deutsche Stellung mit vier 12-cm-Kanonen vor Straßburg, 1870
Ernst Lucke & Co, Berlin
Fotografie
MHM BAAW7121

Kat. 315 → S. 214
Die Hauptstraße in Kehl nach französischem Beschuss, 1870
Paul Sinner
Fotografie
Wehrgeschichtliches Museum Rastatt

Kat. 316 → S. 213
Zerstörte Brauerei hinter der I. Parallele in Bischheim, 1870
Ernst Lucke & Co, Berlin
Fotografie
MHM BAAY0541

Kat. 317 → S. 214
»The Porte Blanche Strasburg. 30th Sep. 1870«
Aus dem Skizzenbuch des Kriegskorrespondenten William Simpson mit Bleistift- und Aquarellskizzen, 1870
8,9 × 14,9 cm
MHM BBAR4524

Kat. 318
Fragment einer Glocke aus dem Fort Mortier
Straßburg, 1870
21 × 13 × 9 cm
Wehrgeschichtliches Museum Rastatt

Kat. 319 → S. 215/265
Trümmerstück einer Fiale des Straßburger Münsters
Straßburg, geborgen 1870
7 × 17 × 9,5 cm
Musée historique de la ville de Strasbourg

Kat. 320 → S. 215
Verschmolzene eiserne »Krähenfüsse« aus der Zitadelle von Straßburg
Straßburg, geborgen 1870
14 × 24 × 15 cm
Musée historique de la ville de Strasbourg

Kat. 321 → S. 267
Angesengte Buchseiten aus der von deutscher Artillerie in Brand geschossenen städtischen Bibliothek im Temple Neuf
Straßburg, geborgen 1870
Musée historique de la ville de Strasbourg

Kat. 322 → S. 215
Handschriftlicher Bericht der Kapitulation von Straßburg und zwei der Unterschriftsfedern, 1870
Wehrgeschichtliches Museum Rastatt

Kat. 323 → S. 216
Degen eines Marschalls von Frankreich
François-Achille Bazaine (1811–1888) zugeschrieben
Französisches Kaiserreich, 1864
Länge 97 cm
MHM BAAA2778

Kat. 324 → S. 217
Der bei Metz erbeutete Fahnenadler des französischen 4. Linieninfanterie-regiments
Kaiserreich Frankreich, 1870
25,3 × 9,5 × 28,5 cm
Stiftung Deutsches Historisches Museum, Berlin, Fa 77/15

Kat. 325 → S. 217
»Au Maréchal Bazaine, la France reconnaissante« / Marschall Bazaine gewidmet, das dankbare Frankreich
Faustin Betbeder, genannt Faustin
Farblithografie
MHM BBAW0166

Kat. 326 → S. 229
Seegefecht bei Havanna am 9. November 1870
Holzstich aus Frank Leslies's Illustrated Newspaper, 3. Dezember 1870, S. 185
MHM BBAY0271

Kat. 327 → S. 218–219
Das belagerte Paris aus der Vogelperspektive 1870/71 mit eingezeichneten deutschen und französischen Stellungen
J. (oder F.) Stiel, Karlsruhe, unter Verwendung einer reproduzierten Grafik, 30 × 42 cm
Wehrgeschichtliches Museum Rastatt

Kat. 328
Brief Bismarcks an die Gattin zur Beschießung von Paris
Versailles, 28./29. Oktober 1870
Archiv der Otto-von-Bismarck-Stiftung, Friedrichsruh

Kat. 329 → S. 220
»Auf Vorposten in Maison-rouge, dem Schlosse des Herzogs von Orleans, während der Belagerung von Paris im Feldzug 1870/71«
Friedrich Wilhelm Heine, 1870
Aquarellierte Federzeichnung, 19,1 × 19,8 cm
MHM BBAX8241

Kat. 330 → S. 220
»Auf Vorposten in Gagny, während der Belagerung von Paris im Feldzug 1870/71, Feldwache der 2. Kompagnie des 7. Infanterie-Regiments ›Prinz Georg‹ No. 106«
Friedrich Wilhelm Heine
Federzeichnung, 18,7 × 19,3 cm
MHM BBAX8242

Kat. 331
Titelblatt: Erinnerungsblätter aus der Vorpostenzeit der Königl. Preuss. XI. Division gesammelt vor Paris
Lithografie von A. Pettinger, Breslau, um 1875
MHM BAAH0682

Kat. 332 → S. 220–221
Holzholen in Choisy le Roi
Lithografie nach Salzmann von A. Pettinger aus dem Mappenwerk »Erinnerungsblätter aus der Vorpostenzeit der Königl. Preuss. XI. Division gesammelt vor Paris«, Breslau, um 1875
MHM BAAH0683

Kat. 333
Stillleben Choisy le Roi
Lithografie nach Salzmann von A. Pettinger aus dem Mappenwerk »Erinnerungsblätter aus der Vorpostenzeit der Königl. Preuss. XI. Division gesammelt vor Paris«, Breslau, um 1875
MHM BAAH0691

Kat. 334 → S. 220–221
Feldwache II-Choisy le Roi
Lithografie nach Höber von Haun aus dem Mappenwerk »Erinnerungsblätter aus der Vorpostenzeit der Königl. Preuss. XI. Division gesammelt vor Paris«, Breslau, um 1875
MHM BAAH0805

Kat. 335
Kochszene auf dem Kirchhof in Thiais
Lithografie nach Salzmann von Agaten aus dem Mappenwerk »Erinnerungsblätter aus der Vorpostenzeit der Königl. Preuss. XI. Division gesammelt vor Paris«, Breslau, um 1875
MHM BAAH0806

Kat. 336
Der Füsilier im Damenboudoir
Lithografie nach Baumbach von A. Pettinger aus dem Mappenwerk »Erinnerungsblätter aus der Vorpostenzeit der Königl. Preuss. XI. Division gesammelt vor Paris«, Breslau, um 1875
MHM BAAH0813

Kat. 337
Auf der Demarkationslinie in Ivry
Lithografie nach Horstig von Knust aus dem Mappenwerk »Erinnerungsblätter aus der Vorpostenzeit der Königl. Preuss. XI. Division gesammelt vor Paris«, Breslau, um 1875
MHM BAAH0819

Kat. 338
Füsilier Pochziol 7te Compagnie Schlesisches Füsilier-Regiment No. 38
Lithografie nach Baumbach von A. Pettinger aus dem Mappenwerk »Erinnerungsblätter aus der Vorpostenzeit der Königl. Preuss. XI. Division gesammelt vor Paris«, Breslau, um 1875
MHM BAAH0828

Kat. 339 → S. 222
Gefechtsgelände mit aufgereihten Leichnamen französischer Soldaten vor dem Fort la haute Bruyere des VI. Armeekorps, aufgenommen von Chevilly aus, 30. September 1870
Calixt Prinz Biron von Curland
Aquarell, 26,9 × 47,7 cm
MHM BBAW0128

Kat. 340 → S. 222–223
»Straßenkampf in Le Bourget bei der Erstürmung dieses Dorfes während der Belagerung von Paris am 30. October 1870 durch Truppen des Königlich Preußischen Gardecorps«
Friedrich Wilhelm Heine
Bleistiftzeichnung, 25,1 × 19,3 cm
MHM BBAW0195

Kat. 341 → S. 188
Feldmütze für Mannschaften der Infanterieregimenter
Königreich Württemberg, 1864–1870
Wehrgeschichtliches Museum Rastatt

Kat. 342 → S. 188
Tschako eines Fähnrichs des Schützen-Regiments Nr. 108
Königreich Sachsen, 1867–1897
MHM BAAQ4009 und BAAQ4010

Kat. 343 → S. 206
Amerikanisches Spencer-Gewehr, von badischen Truppen am 18. Dezember 1870 erbeutet
Länge 120 cm
Kaliber 13 mm
Stiftung Deutsches Historisches Museum, Berlin, W 59/2719

Kat. 344 → S. 219
Blick auf die Befestigungen von Paris während der Belagerung
Entwurf von Félix Philippoteaux, 1872, für das Panorama »Die Belagerung von Paris«
Öl auf Leinwand, 85 × 88 cm
Musée de l'Armée, Paris

Kat. 345 → S. 224
Korb eines aus Paris aufgestiegenen Ballons
Republik Frankreich, 1870
110 × 135 × 125cm
Musée de l'Air et de l'Espace – Le Bourget

Kat. 346 → S. 309
Liste der aus dem belagerten Paris aufgestiegenen Ballons
Verlag E. Pichot, Paris, um 1871
Farblithografie, 51,7 × 68,6 cm
MHM BBAX9662

Kat. 347 → S. 224
Protokollbuch der Freiwilligen Feuerwehr Zwiesel mit Eintrag zur Bergung des Pariser Ballons »Général Chanzy« vom 20. Dezember 1870
Stadt Zwiesel

Kat. 348 → S. 225
Preußische Zietenhusaren bei der Verfolgung eines französischen Ballons
Wilhelm Alexander Meyerheim
1871
Öl auf Leinwand, 57,5 × 47 cm
MHM BBAU8297

Kat. 349 → S. 225
3,7-cm-Ballonabwehrkanone der Firma Krupp
Essen, Königreich Preußen, 1870
Stiftung Deutsches Historisches Museum, Berlin, W 544

Kat. 350 → S. 227
»Historisches Andenken« an die Belagerung von Paris und die Kommune
E.J.F.S., Lithografische Werkstatt J. Bigal & Cie., Paris 1871
25 × 26,8 cm
MHM BBAS9077

Kat. 351
Geschossfragment als Souvenir der Beschießung des Forts Issy
5,5 × 14 × 9,2 cm
MHM BBAT2668

Kat. 352
Brief Bismarcks an die Gattin über die Zerstörungen in St. Cloud
Versailles, 3. Februar 1871
Archiv der Otto-von-Bismarck-Stiftung, Friedrichsruh

Kat. 353
»Environs de Paris. Strasse von St. Cloud, Besuch am 22. Febr. 1870«
Fotografie
MHM BAAN0645

Kat. 354 → S. 227
Die Hörner des letzten während der Belagerung von Paris geschlachteten Rindes
56 × 136 × 34 cm
Musée Bouilhet Christofle, en dépôt au musée d'art et d'histoire Paul Eluard de Saint-Denis

Kat. 355
Ein Baum wird auf dem Boulevard d'Enfer gefällt, um Feuerholz zu gewinnen, Januar 1871
Auguste Lançon
Radierung, 47 × 30 cm
Musée de l'Armée, Paris

Kat. 356 ➔ S. 226
Einschlag eines deutschen Geschosses auf der Place de l'Observatoire, Januar 1871
Auguste Lançon
Radierung, 39 × 55, 6 cm
Musée de l'Armée, Paris

Kat. 357 ➔ S. 226
Warteschlange vor einem Laden auf dem Boulevard Montparnasse, Januar 1871
Auguste Lançon
Radierung, 40 × 57 cm
Musée de l'Armée, Paris

Kat. 358 ➔ S. 226
Nachtlager in einem Keller, Gonesse, Februar 1871
Auguste Lançon
Radierung, 40 × 57 cm
Musée de l'Armée, Paris

DIE GRÜNDUNG DES DEUTSCHEN REICHS

Kat. 359
Aufruf der Regierung der Nationalen Verteidigung an die Einwohner von Paris
Schriftplakat (Reproduktion)
Paris, 18. Januar 1871
Kat. 27741

Kat. 360 ➔ S. 47
Die Proklamierung des deutschen Kaiserreichs am 18. Januar 1871
Friedrichsruher Fassung
Anton von Werner, 1885
Öl auf Leinwand, 167 × 202 cm
(verkleinerte Reproduktion)
Kat. 27788

Kat. 361 ➔ S. 56
Brief Bismarcks über die Kaiserproklamation an seine Ehefrau Johanna
Versailles, 21. Januar 1871
Archiv der Otto-von-Bismarck-Stiftung, Friedrichsruh

Kat. 362 ➔ S. 234–235
»Comment un trône s'écroule! – Comment un trône s'élève!« / Der eine Thron stürzt! – Der andere wird errichtet!
Holzstich von Smeeton aus der Zeitschrift »L'Illustration. Journal Universel«, 1871, Nr. 1454 (Reproduktion)
© Look and Learn

Kat. 363
Eduard von Simson mit zwei deutschen Kaiserkronen.
Titelblatt »Über Land und Meer«
Ausgabe für Österreich-Ungarn, 41. Jg., Nr. 34 (1899)
Holzstich
MHM BBAX2399

Kat. 364 ➔ S. 232–233
Reliefbild von Schloss Neuschwanstein
Vermutlich Ende 19. Jahrhundert, Rahmen 1. Hälfte 19. Jahrhundert
Durchmesser 35 cm
MHM BBAX7998

Kat. 365 ➔ S. 233
Gedenktafel mit den Namen der 48 Abgeordneten, die am 21. Januar 1871 gegen die Verträge stimmten
Aus einem Erinnerungsalbum, angelegt von Moritz Ratzinger, 1870/71 Leutnant im 1. Königlich Bayerischen Feldartillerie-Regiment
Bayerisches Armeemuseum Ingolstadt

Kat. 366 ➔ S. 235
»Das ganze Deutschland soll es sein. 1870«
Ein Gedenk-Album in 50 Photographien
Weißensee, Leipzig, Berlin, 3. Auflage
MHM BAAG8748

Kat. 367 ➔ S. 240–241
Extrablatt zum Magdeburger Correspondenten mit der Ankündigung des deutschen Einmarsches in Paris
Magdeburg, 28. Februar 1871
MHM BBAR7210

Kat. 368 ➔ S. 241
Barrikade am Eingang zum Fauborg du Temple
Paris, 18. März 1871
Fotografie (Reproduktion)
© Archives Charmet / Bridgeman Images

Kat. 369 ➔ S. 242–243
Selbstgefertigte Waffe
Paris, 1871
Metall und Holz
Länge: 79 cm
Saint Denis – musée d'art et d'histoire Paul Eluard

Kat. 370 ➔ S. 242
Aufruf des »Wohlfahrtsausschusses« der Kommune von Paris
Paris, 22. Mai 1871
Musée de l'Armée, Paris

Kat. 371 ➔ S. 241
Denkmünze auf Adolphe Thiers
Republik Frankreich, 1871
Buntmetall, 27,8 × 23,55 mm
MHM BBAT9321, Sammlung Major Rübke

Kat. 372 ➔ S. 241
Denkmünze zur Erinnerung an die Verteidigung von Paris
Republik Frankreich, Commune de Paris, 18. März 1871
Buntmetall, 16,5 × 13,2 mm
MHM BBAT9324, Sammlung Major Rübke

Kat. 373 ➔ S. 242–243
In Gefangenschaft gestickte Tasche von Louise Michel
2. Hälfte 19. Jahrhundert
12 × 5 cm
Saint Denis – musée d'art et d'histoire Paul Eluard

Kat. 374 ➔S. 239
Rechnung für die Überführung der Leiche des Leutnants d. R. Ernst Rube in die Heimat
Darmstadt, 8.Februar 1871
MHM BAAN0914

Kat. 375 ➔ S. 251
Gedenktafel für 1870/71 in Frankreich gestorbener Beierfelder
55,5 × 47,8 × 1,9 cm
Sächsisches Rot-Kreuz-Museum Beierfeld

Kat. 376
Unsere vermißten Soldaten
Die Gartenlaube, Leipzig 1872, Heft 8, S. 130 (Reproduktion)
SUB Göttingen/Signatur 4 SVA II, 2058:1872

Kat. 377 ➔ S. 238
Die Albertstadt (die neuen Kasernenbauten) bei Dresden aus der Vogelschau
Holzstich nach Adolf Eltzner von Bruno Strassberger
aus der Leipziger Illustrirten Zeitung, 21. April 1877, S. 328 f.
MHM BBAL2828

Kat. 378 ➔ S. 237
Velarium auf der Prager Straße, 11. Juli 1871
Hoffmann & Römler, Dresden, 1871
Fotografie
MHM BAAN0654

Kat. 379 ➔ S. 237
Ehrenpforte am Albertplatz in der Neustadt, 11. Juli 1871
Hoffmann & Römler, Dresden, 1871
Fotografie
MHM BAAN7049

Kat. 380
Einlass-Karte zu einer Tribüne für die Dauer der Siegesparade der deutschen Truppen in Berlin
Berlin, 16. Juni 1871
MHM BBAK0578

Kat. 381 ➔ S. 238
Eisernes Kreuz I. Klasse aus dem Besitz von Hermann von Wichmann (1820–1886)
Königreich Preußen,
gestiftet am 19. Juli 1870
42,2 × 42,42 mm
MHM BBAT9039

Kat. 382
Erinnerungsmedaille, gefertigt aus Granatsplittern
Deutsches Reich, 1871
Eisen, 14,5 × 16,2 mm
MHM BBAT9511, Sammlung Major Rübke

Kat. 383 ➔ S. 239
Kriegsdenkmünze für die Feldzüge 1870/71, Ausführung für Nichtkombattanten
Deutsches Reich, gestiftet am 20. Mai 1871
Eisen, Durchmesser 39,8 mm
MHM BBAT9510, Sammlung Major Rübke

Kat. 384
Gedicht »Dem Deutschen Heere« von Richard Wagner
Archiv der Otto-von-Bismarck-Stiftung, Friedrichsruh

Kat. 385
Denkmal für Volkskämpfer
Die Gartenlaube, Heft 37, Leipzig 1872, S. 609–612 (Reproduktion)
SUB Göttingen/Signatur 4 SVA II, 2058:1872

Kat. 386 ➔ S. 244
Preußische Parole-Ausgabe auf dem Marktplatze der französischen Festung Belfort während der deutschen Besetzung, 1873
Fotografie
Wehrgeschichtliches Museum Rastatt

Kat. 387 ➔ S. 245
Feder, mit der 1872 ein Vertrag zur Abtretung des Geländes für die Neubefestigung von Straßburg unterzeichnet wurde
Verglaster Holzkasten, 24,3 × 48,8 × 5,8 cm
MHM BBAO2554

Kat. 388 ➔ S. 245
Ein Paar Epauletten eines Hauptmanns im Königs-Infanterie-Regiment (6. Lothringisches) Nr. 145
Königreich Preußen, 1893–1915
MHM BAAY4772

Kat. 389 ➔ S. 245
»Notre drapeau quand même! Épisode historique – Strasbourg 1871« / Trotz allem unsere Fahne! Historische Episode – Straßburg 1871
Lithografie
Wehrgeschichtliches Museum Rastatt

Kat. 390 ➔ S. 246
Gewicht zu 20 Zollpfund
1839–1856 abgekürzt »ZP«,
danach nur noch »P«
20 × 12 × 12 cm
Deutsches Zollmuseum

Kat. 391 ➔ S. 247
Münzhumpen zur Reichsgründung 1871
Firma Sy & Wagner, Berlin 1873
Silber (800/1.000)
34 × 19,5 cm
Deutsche Bundesbank, Frankfurt am Main

Kat. 392
Vollständiges Orthographisches Wörterbuch der deutschen Sprache
Konrad Duden
Leipzig 1897
Zentrum für Informationsarbeit der Bundeswehr

AN DER SCHWELLE ZUM MODERNEN KRIEG

Kat. 393
Reisesekretär für einen sächsischen Stab in Frankreich
Königreich Sachsen, 1870/71
130 × 102 × 50 cm
Wehrgeschichtliches Museum Rastatt

Kat. 394
Schuber mit sächsischen Generalstabskarten
1863
BAAX2340-BAAX2368, BAAX5494

Kat. 395
Brief von Generalstabschef Helmuth von Molkte an die Generalinspektion des Ing.-Korps betr. Generalstabskarten
Berlin, 1. Feburar 1868
MHM BAAP5724

Kat. 396
Anweisung des preußischen Kriegsministers Albrecht von Roons, die Bibliothek und Modellsammlung der Militärschule Saint Cyr sicherzustellen
Versailles, 23.Oktober 1870
MHM BAAV8986

Kat. 397
Souvenier mit Text v. H. Dehmel und Zeichnung v. Baron von Moltke im Lederbehälter
1827/1866
12 × 14 × 1 cm, Zeichnung: 11 × 13,2 cm
MHM BAAV8937

Kat. 398
Gipsabdruck von Moltkes Hand, ein Schreibutensil haltend
11 × 10,5 × 20 cm
MHM BAAV6252

Kat. 399 ➔ S. 274
»Übersichtskarte über die im Kriege 1870/71 durch die Deutschen in Betrieb genommenen französischen Eisenbahnen«
Aus Hermann Buddes
»Die Französischen Eisenbahnen im deutschen Kriegsbetriebe 1870/71«,
Berlin 1904
Österreichisches Staatsarchiv, Kriegsarchiv

Kat. 400 ➔ S. 274
Von deutschen Pionieren repariertes Eisenbahnviadukt bei Cartigny, Frankreich 1870/71
Fotografie (Reproduktion)
Wehrgeschichtliches Museum Rastatt

Kat. 401
Güterwaggons in Metz, Malardot, Metz, 1870
Fotografie (Reproduktion)
Wehrgeschichtliches Museum Rastatt

Kat. 402 ➔ S. 275
Dampflokomotive »Main« auf einem französischen Bahnhof, 1870/71
Fotografie (Reproduktion)
Bayerisches Armeemuseum Ingolstadt

Kat. 403 ➔ S. 286
Johann Nikolaus von Dreyse (1787–1867), Entwickler des Zündnadelgewehrs
Carte-de-Visite-Fotografie, um 1860
MHM BAAN5492

Kat. 404 ➔ S. 286
Georg Heinrich von Priem (1794–1870) als Oberstleutnant
Um 1844/47
Öl auf Leinwand, 36,5 × 31,5 cm
MHM BBAT2862

Kat. 405
Perkussionsschloß für Infanteriegewehr M 1839/55
Länge 14,1 cm
Kaliber der dazugehörigen Waffe 18 mm
MHM BAA01901

Kat. 406
Schloss für Zündnadelgewehr M 1841
Länge 23 cm
Kaliber der dazugehörigen Waffe 15,43 mm
MHM BAA01901

Kat. 407 ➔ S. 285
Schnittmodel eines Dreyse'schen Zündnadelgewehrs M 1841
Länge 52 × 3,6 cm
Kaliber 15,43 mm
MHM BAAU7821

Kat. 408
Schloss für Zündnadelgewehr – Chassepot M 1866
Länge 19,5 cm
Kaliber der dazugehörigen Waffe 11 mm
MHM BAAX0200

Kat. 409 ➔ S. 289
Bronzerohr einer Vorderladerkanone, die auf Hinterladesystem umgerüstet wurde
Königreich Preußen, 1842, aptiert 1868
Länge 194 cm
Kaliber 120 mm
MHM BAAL7966

Kat. 410
Alfred Krupp (1812–1887)
Carte-de-Visite-Fotografie (Reproduktion)
Historisches Archiv Krupp, Essen

Kat. 411 ➔ S. 299
4-cm-Ballongeschütz der Firma Krupp 1870, vorgeführt von einem Angehörigen der Werksfeuerwehr
Fotodruck aus der dreisprachigen, in Leder gebundenen Mappe »Friedrich Krupp Essen A/R.« mit einer Produktschau zu Rüstungsgütern des Unternehmens, nach 1877
MHM BAAI3106

Kat. 412
21 cm Belagerungskanone der Firma Krupp in Lafette, 1871
Fotodruck aus der dreisprachigen, in Leder gebundenen Mappe »Friedrich Krupp Essen A/R.« mit einer Produktschau zu Rüstungsgütern des Unternehmens, nach 1877
MHM BAAI3106

Kat. 413 ➔ S. 299
Modell im Maßstab 1:10 einer 6,5-cm-Ballonabwehrkanone der Firma Krupp von 1909
Um 1970
20 × 40 × 27 cm
MHM BAAE5310

Kat. 414 ➔ S. 292
Fonderie et Ateliers de Construction H. Gruson
Grusonwerk Magdeburg-Buckau, 1879
Broschüre
MHM BBAQ4831

Kat. 415
Die Fanale von Salzbrunn
Lithografie nach Alfred Hindorf aus dem Mappenwerk von Prinz Biron von Curland und Alfred Hindorf »Erinnerungs-Blätter aus dem Feldzuge in Böhmen und Mähren im Sommer 1866«, Berlin, Blatt 7
MHM BBAK2315

Kat. 416 ➔ S. 277
Schreibtelegraf
C.F. Lewert Telegraphen-Bauanstalt Berlin
Königreich Preußen, um 1860
18 × 23 × 30 cm
MHM BBAW5276

Kat. 417 ➔ S. 277
Schreibetelegraf
Königreich Preußen, 1870
22 × 32 × 36 cm
MHM BBAD5571

Kat. 418
Morsestreifenschreiber für die Militärtelegrafie
Frankreich, C.G.R. Paris
60 × 37 × 48 cm
MHM BBAF3671

Kat. 419
Kriegserinnerungen des Obertelegrafisten Carl Louis Bernroth vom September 1870 bis Mai 1871
Carl Louis Bernroth, Manuskript um 1871
MHM BBAX7558

Kat. 420
Telegramm mit der Bitte, Quartiere für drei Ordonnanzoffiziere des Werderschen Korps zu beschaffen
Telegraphie des Norddeutschen Bundes, unterzeichnet von Carl Louis Bernroth, Gray, 27. Dezember 1870
MHM BBAX7558

Kat. 421
Preußen zapfen eine französische Telegrafenleitung an
Holzschnitt nach E.B., Titelblatt von »The Graphic«, 5. November 1870
MHM BBAY0200

Kat. 422 ➔ S. 302
Generalquartiermeister Theophil von Podbielski (1814–1879)
Fotografie aus »Das ganze Deutschland soll es sein. 1870. Ein Gedenk-Album in 50 Photographien«
MHM BAAG8748

Kat. 423
Büchlein, Kriegs-Depeschen 1870–1871 (unvollständig) vom 31. 7. 1870 – 2. 3. 1871
Berlin 1914
10,4 × 6,6 × 0,7cm
MHM BAAX5153

Kat. 424/1 ➔ S. 314
»Correspondenz-Karte« des Unteroffiziers Friedrich Weidner an seine Ehefrau Karoline
Biwak Billigheim, 3. August 1870
MHM BAAX5225

Kat. 424/2 ➔ S. 314
Brief von Karoline Weidner an ihren Ehemann Friedrich
Berlin, 5. August 1870
MHM BAAX5267

Kat. 425 ➔ S. 315
Schreiben von Karoline Weidner an das Regiment ihres Ehemanns Friedrich
Berlin, 18. Oktober 1870
MHM BAAX5224

Kat. 426 ➔ S. 313
Brief von Benedikte von Rosen an ihren Ehemann Julius
Trier, 26. August 1870
Familienarchiv von Rosen

Kat. 427 ➔ S. 314
Brief von Julius von Rosen an seine Ehefrau Benedikte
K.Q. Coin les Cuvry, Frankreich, 15. September 1870
Familienarchiv von Rosen

Kat. 428 ➔ S. 313
Medaillon mit Porträt und Haaren von Julius von Rosen (1827–1891), als Hauptmann
4,5 × 3 × 0,4 cm
Familienarchiv von Rosen

Multimediastation
Briefe der Familien von Rosen und Weidner

Kat. 429 ➔ S. 318
Eine Erinnerung an Solferino
Henry Dunant, Basel 1863
Sächsisches Rot-Kreuz-Museum Beierfeld

Kat. 430 ➔ S. 320
Österreichische Beitrittserklärung zur Genfer Konvention, 1866
Österreichisches Staatsarchiv, Abteilung Haus-, Hof-und Staatsarchiv

Kat. 431 ➔ S. 321
Rotkreuzarmbinde für einen Angehörigen der Freiwilligen Krankenpflege
Königreich Preußen, 1870/71
MHM BBAS5010

Kat. 432 ➔ S. 319
»Unter dem rothen Kreuz. Fremde und eigene Erfahrungen auf Böhmischer Erde und den Schlachtfeldern der Neuzeit, gesammelt von Dr. Julius Naundorff, Hauptmann und gewesenem Feldhospitalcommandanten«
Leipzig 1867
Sächsisches Rot-Kreuz-Museum Beierfeld

Kat. 433
»Denkschrift der vom 22. bis 27. April 1869 gehaltenen internationalen Conferenz von Delegierten der der Genfer Konvention beigetretenen Regierungen und der Vereine zur Pflege im Felde verwundeter und erkrankter Krieger«
E. Gurlt, Berlin 1869
Sächsisches Rot-Kreuz-Museum Beierfeld

Kat. 434 ➔ S. 230–231
»Übertritt der Bourbaki'schen Armee in die Schweiz«
Bilderbogen Nr. 1568, Verlag C. Burckhardt's Nachf., Weißenburg (Elsass)
MHM BBAW4808

Kat. 435 ➔ S. 327
Bayerischer Feldverbandsplatz 1870/71
Louis Braun
Öl auf Leinwand, 115 × 104 cm
Bayerisches Armeemuseum Ingolstadt

Kat. 436 ➔ S. 327
Dreiecktuch nach Friedrich von Esmarch (1823–1908)
Nach einer Zeichnung von Johann Heinrich Wittmaack gestochen von Karl Becker, Kiel 1868
123 × 60 cm
Deutsches Medizinhistorisches Museum Ingolstadt

Kat. 437
Chirurgisches Feldbesteck
Königreich Preußen
18 × 48 × 17 cm
Sanitätsakademie der Bundeswehr

Kat. 438 ➔ S. 328
Maske, Tropfflasche und Zungenzange, verwendet im preußischen Militärsanitätswesen
Königreich Preußen, 1869
18 × 12 × 23 cm
Sammlung Ronnie Strauch, Sindelsdorf

Kat. 439 ➔ S. 331
Transportkiste des französischen Militärsanitätsdienstes
Kaiserreich Frankreich, 1870
45,3 × 42,5 × 86 cm
Stiftung Deutsches Historisches Museum, Berlin, W 77/61

Kat. 440 ➔ S. 328
Pockenwarnschild
1871
12 × 28 × 1 cm
Deutsches Medizinhistorisches Museum Ingolstadt

Kat. 441 ➔ S. 328–329
Lazarett »Amtshaus« 1864 in Flensburg
Fotografie
Schleswig-Holsteinische Landesbibliothek

Kat. 442
Dänische und preußische Verwundete im Hof des Gymnasiums zu Flensburg 1864
Fotografie
Schleswig-Holsteinische Landesbibliothek

Kat. 443 ➔ S. 328–331
Deutsche Verwundete und Sanitätspersonal in einem Gang des Schlosses von Versailles
Fotografie aus der Serie »Ansichten des Kriegsschauplatzes«
München/Berlin 1870
Wehrgeschichtliches Museum Rastatt

Kat. 444 ➔ S. 330–331
Personal des Reservelazaretts N° 1 in Dresden-Neustadt, 1870/71
Fotografie
MHM BAAN6930

Kat. 445
Sanitätsbericht über die Deutschen Heere 1870/71, Band 4
Medizinal-Abtheilung des Königlich Preussischen Kriegsministeriums (Hrsg.)
Berlin 1884 ff.
Sanitätsakademie der Bundeswehr

Kat. 446
Ganzseitiger Bericht über den Abmarsch der Ambulanzen der »Société de Secours aux Blessés« / Gesellschaft für Verwundetenhilfe
Le Monde Illustré, 13. 8. 1870
MHM BBAP8370

Kat. 447 ➔ S. 323
Madame Marie Simon – The Friend of the Wounded
Holzstich aus »Cassell's History of the War between France and Germany, 1870 to 1871«, 1874
MHM BBAV4171

Kat. 448
Prinzessin Carola und Prinz Albert von Sachsen
Lithografie, um 1871
Sächsisches Rot-Kreuz-Museum Beierfeld

Kat. 449 ➔ S. 323
Ehren- oder Mitgliedsabzeichen des Königlich Sächsischen Albertvereins für Krankenpflege
Königreich Sachsen, nach 1873
Silber, vergoldet, 41 × 33 mm
MHM BAAB5926

Kat. 450 ➔ S. 322
Damen aus Adel und Bürgertum verpacken Lebensmittel und Wäsche für die preußischen Armeen in Böhmen und die Mainarmee, Gardes-du-Corps-Kaserne, Berlin 1866
Kamrath & Sohn, Berlin
Fotografie
Wehrgeschichtliches Museum Rastatt

Kat. 451
Die Galerie des Batailles im Schloss von Versailles als Magazin für Liebesgaben, 16. Dezember 1870
»Ansichten des Kriegsschauplatzes«, Nr. 97
München und Berlin, 1870
Carte-de-Fotografie
Wehrgeschichtliches Museum Rastatt

Kat. 452 ➔ S. 324
Los der Deutschen National-Lotterie
Berlin, 20. Februar 1871
Sächsisches Rot-Kreuz-Museum Beierfeld

Kat. 453 ➔ 325
Sidonien-Orden, Großkreuz, verliehen an Großherzogin Luise von Baden am 24. Juli 1881
Königreich Sachsen, gestiftet am 30. Dezember 1870
Gold, emailliert, 83,33 × 61,31 mm
MHM BBAU4919

Kat. 454 ➔ S. 325
Olga-Orden
Königreich Württemberg, 1871
Silber, emailliert, 39,81 × 35,35 mm
MHM BAAB4994

Kat. 455
Silbernes Militär-Sanitätsehrenzeichen
Königreich Bayern, 1812–1918
Silber, 48,85 × 40,7 mm
MHM BAAV3747

Kat. 456
Allgemeines Ehrenzeichen, 2. Klasse für Mitglieder der Freiwilligen Krankenpflege
Königreich Preußen, 1871
Silber, 40,52 × 29,03 mm
MHM BAAC6842

Kat. 457 ➔ S. 325
Verdienstkreuz für Frauen und Jungfrauen
Königreich Preußen, gestiftet am 22. März 1871
Silber, emailliert, 37,56 × 33,64 mm
MHM BAAB7916

Kat. 458
Erinnerungsmedaille für die Weihnachten 1870 in Hamburger Lazaretten untergebrachten Verwundeten
Freie und Hansestadt Hamburg, 1871
Buntmetall, vergoldet, 42,71 × 37,06 mm
MHM BAAB6738

Kat. 459 ➔ S. 333
Sammelrahmen mit Uniformknöpfen französischer Kriegsgefangener
1870/71
Kölnisches Stadtmuseum

Kat. 460 → S. 334–335
Ansicht des Kriegsgefangenenlagers am Brückenkopf in Ingolstadt und Typen französischer Kriegsgefangener
Zwei Lithografien aus einem Erinnerungsalbum, angelegt von Moritz Ratzinger, 1870/71 Leutnant im 1. Königlich Bayerischen Feldartillerie-Regiment
Bayerisches Armeemuseum Ingolstadt

Kat. 461 → S. 332–333
»Barakenlager auf dem Alaunplatz in Dresden. Erinnerung an 1870/71«
Lithografie, 1872
MHM BAAH0632

Kat. 462 → S. 332
Aus dem französischen Lager in Mainz, 1870/71
Philipp Hoff, Frankfurt am Main
Fotografie
Wehrgeschichtliches Museum Rastatt

Kat. 463
Algerische Schützen oder »Turkos« als Kriegsgefangene in Ingolstadt, 1870
Lichtdruck nach Originalaufnahme von Fr. Sölch, Ingolstadt, um 1870
15 × 12,5 cm
MHM BAAT4767

Kat. 464 → S. 334
Algerische Schützen oder »Turkos« als Kriegsgefangene in Ingolstadt, 1870
Lichtdruck nach Originalaufnahme von Fr. Sölch, Ingolstadt
MHM BAAT4765

Kat. 465 → 334
Drei kriegsgefangene französische Unteroffiziere in der bayerischen Landesfestung Ingolstadt, 1870
Photographische Anstalt Fr. Sölch, Ingolstadt
Fotografie
MHM BAAT4770

Kat. 466 → S. 334–335
Der Tod des Sergeanten Gombault
George Moreau de Tours, 1892
Öl auf Leinwand, 225 × 285 cm
(verkleinerte Reproduktion)
Musée de Dinan – Ville de Dinan

BILDERGALERIE

Kat. 467 → S. 358–359
Die Erstürmung der Düppeler Schanze Nr. II durch das Brandenburgische Füsilier-Regiment Nr. 35 am 18. April 1864
Wilhelm Camphausen, 1864/65
Öl auf Leinwand, 158 × 252 cm
Stiftung Preußische Schlösser und Gärten Berlin-Brandenburg

Kat. 468 → S. 73
»Fra forposterne i 1864« / Auf Vorposten 1864
Vilhelm Rosenstand, 1896
Öl auf Leinwand, 126,5 × 189,5 cm
Museum Sønderjylland/Sønderburg Slot/ Statens Museum for Kunst

Kat. 469 → S. 368
Der sterbende Soldat
Adolph Menzel, 1866
Aquarell über Bleistiftzeichnung, 10,2 × 12,8 cm (vergrößerte Reproduktion)
Sammlung Georg Schäfer, Schweinfurt
akg-images

Kat. 470 → S. 132–133
Anmarsch der preußischen 2. Armee unter Kronprinz Friedrich Wilhelm am Morgen der Schlacht von Königgrätz, 3. Juli 1866
Otto Heyden, 1870
Öl auf Leinwand, 165 × 283 cm
MHM BBAT2892

Kat. 471 → S. 123–124
Der sächsische Kronprinz Albert in der Schlacht bei Königgrätz
Theodor von Götz, 1868
Öl auf Leinwand, 85 × 113,5 cm
MHM BAAU3899

Kat. 472
Eroberung der Batterie von der Gröben durch das preußische I. Garde-Regiment
Carl Röchling, um 1906
Gouache über Bleistift auf Pappe, 101 × 131 cm
MHM BAAS9679

Kat. 473
Kronprinz Friedrich Wilhelm an der Leiche des Generals Abel Douay
Kunstdruck nach Anton von Werners Gemälde von 1890
61,5 × 76,5 cm
MHM BBAW3877

Kat. 474 → S. 354
Fragment aus dem Panorama der Schlacht von Rezonville
Edouard Detaille, um 1883
Öl auf Leinwand, 143 × 169 cm
MHM BBAU2997

Filmstation
»Bombardement d'une maison« / Das Haus zur letzten Patrone
Stummfilm von Georges Méliès
Frankreich, 1897
© Lobster Films Collection

Kat. 475 → S. 198–199
Sächsische Artillerie in der Schlacht bei Sedan 1870, Höhen ostwärts von La Moncelle
Georg von Boddien, 1896
Öl auf Leinwand, 164 × 303 cm
MHM BAAU3916

Kat. 476 → S. 278–280
»Graf Moltke und sein Generalstab vor Paris (19. September 1870)«
Anton von Werner, 1873
Öl auf Leinwand, 190 × 316 cm
Kunsthalle zu Kiel

Kat. 477 → S. 364–365
»Die Deutschen in Versailles«
Louis Braun, 1877
Öl auf Leinwand, 165 × 283 cm
MHM BBAW 3875

Kat. 478 → S. 236
Otto von Bismarck, Festdekoration für Siegesparade
Adolph von Menzel, 1871
Öl auf Leinwand, 395 × 158 cm
(Reproduktion: Menzel, Adolph von: Otto von Bismarck, 1871, GK I 10202
Stiftung Preußische Schlösser und Gärten Berlin-Brandenburg / Daniel Lindner. Das Original hängt als Leihgabe in der Dauerausstellung des MHM.)

Kat. 479 ➔ S. 236
Helmut von Moltke, Festdekoration für Siegesparade
Adolph von Menzel, 1871
Öl auf Leinwand, 395 × 158 cm
(Reproduktion: Menzel, Adolph von: Graf Moltke, GK I 10203
Stiftung Preußische Schlösser und Gärten Berlin-Brandenburg / Daniel Lindner.
Das Original hängt als Leihgabe in der Dauerausstellung des MHM.)

Kat. 480
Einzug Kaiser Wilhelms durch das Brandenburger Tor
Ferdinand Keller, um 1888
Entwurf, Öl auf Leinwand, 132 × 155 cm
Eigentum des Hauses Hohenzollern, SKH Georg Friedrich Prinz von Preußen

Kat. 481
König Albert von Sachsen
Um 1874
Öl auf Leinwand, 76 × 63,5 cm
MHM BAAG6756

Kat. 482
Porträt eines Leutnants im 2. Westfälischen Husaren-Regiment Nr. 11
C. Blanc (vermutl. Célestin-Joseph Blanc)
1871
Öl auf Leinwand, 118 × 84,5 cm
MHM BBAT2890

Kat. 483
Porträt eines jungen Soldaten
Robert Krausse, Leipzig 1870
Öl auf Leinwand, 46,5 × 58 cm
MHM BBAW3878

Kat. 484 ➔ S. 367
»Entrée des parlementaires allemands dans Belfort, le 16 février 1871« / Deutsche Verhandlungsführer kommen nach Belfort, 16. Februar 1871
Alphonse de Neuville, 1884
Öl und Gouache auf Leinwand, 82 × 119 cm
Paris, musée d'Orsay, dépôt au musée de l'Armée, Paris, achat par l'État, 1886

Kat. 485 ➔ S. 366
»Kriegsgefangen (Oktober 1870)«
Kunstdruck nach Anton von Werners Gemälde von 1886
106 × 157 cm (Maße des Originals)
MHM BAAU9848

Kat. 486
Communarden
Bernhard Heisig (1925–2011)
Öl auf Leinwand, 116,5 × 164 cm
MHM BAAJ1218

PANORAMA

Die Erstürmung von St. Privat am 18. August 1870
Auftaktinszenierung des zweiten Ausstellungsteils mit einer verfremdeten Rekonstruktion des historischen Panoramas in kleinerem Maßstab nach Kat. 487

Kat. 487 ➔ S. 351–354
»Die Erstürmung von St. Privat am 18. August 1870«
Gemalt vom Schlachtenmaler Prof. Louis Braun
Aufnahme und Druck Johann Baptist Obernetter in München, deponiert 1883
Schmuckmappe »Panorama Dresden« mit 10 Lichtdrucken
MHM BAAN7462–BAAN7471

Kat. 488 ➔ S. 357
»3 Schlachtenmaler 1870/71«
Carte-de-visite-Fotografie, 1870/71 (Reproduktion)
Privatbesitz

Kat. 489 ➔ S. 350–351
Louis Braun (1836–1916) im Atelier, um 1900
Fotografie (Reproduktion)
Privatbesitz

Kat. 490
Gefallene Offiziere des Kgl. Sächsischen Schützen-Füsilier Regiment Nr. 108, 1870
Fotografie
MHM BAAN0595

Kat. 491
»Liste der sächsischen Verluste bei Gravelotte / Saint Privat. Die Betheiligung des 12. (kgl. Sächsischen) Armee-Corps bei Gravelotte-Saint-Privat am 18. August 1870«
MHM BAAX5158

»ALS OB MAN DEN KRIEG ZIVILISIEREN KÖNNTE!«

Kat. 492 ➔ S. 331
Verbandmittelwagen mit Feldapotheke
1868–1917
Länge 355 cm
Sanitätsakademie der Bundeswehr

Kat. 493 ➔ S. 298–299
Mitrailleuse des Systems Christophe-Montigny
Österreich-Ungarn, 1867
MHM BAAO3300

Kat. 494
8-läufiges Salvengeschütz
Frankreich
Kaliber 18 mm
MHM BBAA9596

Kat. 495
MG 08/15 auf Zweibein
Deutsches Reich, 1915, genutzt 1918
Kaliber 7,92 mm
MHM BAAT8669

Kat. 496
Maschinengewehr MG 42
Deutsches Reich, 1942
Kaliber 7,92 mm
MHM BAAQ7433

Kat. 497
Maschinengewehr MG 4
Bundesrepublik Deutschland, 2005
Kal. 5,56 × 45 mm
MHM BBAU5577

Kat. 498 ➔ S. 299
Bordkanone M61 Vulcan
USA 1963–1990
Kaliber 20 mm
MHM AAAG2259

Kat. 499
Manschettenknöpfe »1870« in Lederschatulle
2,7 × 7,6 × 4,3 cm
Wehrgeschichtliches Museum Rastatt

Kat. 500
Porzellan-Figurengruppen »Einzug der Sieger«
Emrich Otfried Andresen,
Manufaktur Meißen
Höhe 27,5 cm
MHM BBAV6533

Kat. 501/ Kat. 502 ➔ S. 290
Zwei Vier-Pfünder-Feldkanonen C/67 der 2. Leichten Feld-Batterie des Rheinischen Feldartillerie-Regiments Nr. 8, genannt »Batterie Leo«
Königreich Preußen, 1867–1872
Hersteller: Krupp, Essen
Kölnisches Stadtmuseum

Kat. 503 ➔ S. 371
Kartusche einer von der Batterie Leo des Rheinischen Feldartillerie-Regiments Nr. 8 am 2. Januar 1871 verschossenen Granate
Kölnisches Stadtmuseum

Kat. 504
Gedenkplatte für die Angehörigen der Batterie Leo (2. Leichte Feldbatterie) des Rheinischen Feldartillerie-Regiments Nr. 8
23,5 × 22,2 cm
Kölnisches Stadtmuseum

Kat. 505 ➔ S. 371–372
Der 3. Zug der Batterie Leo in Bovelles, Nordfrankreich, Anfang April 1871
Fotografie (Reproduktion)
Kölnisches Stadtmuseum

Kat. 506 ➔ S. 371–372
Die Batterie Leo mit Feldwebel Otto und Sergeant König in Bovelles, Nordfrankreich, Anfang April 1871
Fotografie (Reproduktion)
Kölnisches Stadtmuseum

Kat. 507
Offiziere und Unteroffiziere der Batterie Leo 1870/71
Fotografie (Reproduktion)
Kölnisches Stadtmuseum

Kat. 508 ➔ S. 373
Premierleutnant Dannhauer bei der Batterie Leo
Fotografie (Reproduktion)
Kölnisches Stadtmuseum

Kat. 509
Portepeefähnrich Schott
Fotografie (Reproduktion)
Kölnisches Stadtmuseum

Kat. 510 ➔ S. 573
Max Droz, 1870/71
Fotografie (Reproduktion)
Kölnisches Stadtmuseum

Kat. 511 ➔ S. 370–371
»Batterie Leo auf dem Marsche im Feldzuge 1870–1871« / »Hauptmann Leo 1871« / »Die Angehörigen der Batterie Leo bei einer Zusammenkunft i. J. 1880«
Fotografie (Reproduktion)
Kölnisches Stadtmuseum

Kat. 512 ➔ S. 374
Aufnahme der Batterie am 5. April 1900
Fotografie (Reproduktion)
Kölnisches Stadtmuseum

Kat. 513 ➔ S. 374–375
»Die Grabstätte unseres unvergesslichen Hauptmanns Leo in Florenz«
Fotografie (Reproduktion)
Kölnisches Stadtmuseum

Kat. 514
Reservistenkrug »Fest steht und treu die Wacht am Rhein«
1897
MHM BAAG7760

Kat. 515
Reservistenkrug »Fest steht und treu die Wacht am Rhein«
Hersteller Reinhold Merkelbach, 1914
MHM BAAF9430

Kat. 516
Reservistenkrug eines Angehörigen des 2. Königlich Bayrischen Fußartillerie-Regiment
1903
MHM BAAT6627

Kat. 517
Reservistenkrug eines Angehörigen des Königlich Preußischen Eisenbahnregiments Nr. 2
1910
MHM BAAF6779

Kat. 518
Reservistenkrug eines Angehörigen des 11. Königl. Sächs. Infanterie-Regiments Nr. 139
MHM BAAF9433

Kat. 519
Reservistenkrug eines Angehörigen des 15. Königl. Sächs. Infanterie-Regiments Nr. 181
Firma G. Wiesinger sen., München 1902
MHM BAAF9432

Kat. 520
Reservistenkrug eines Angehörigen des 2. Königl. Sächs. Grenadier-Regiments Kaiser Wilhelm I., König von Preussen Nr. 101
1907
MHM BAAF9722

Kat. 521
Reservistenkrug eines Angehörigen des Königlich Preußischen 1. Garde-Ulanen-Regiments
MHM BAAF9723

Kat. 522
Reservistenkrug für einen Angehörigen des 1. Königlich Sächsischen Pionier-Bataillons Nr. 12
MHM BAAF9431

Kat. 523
Reservistenkrug für einen Angehörigen des 2. Königlich Sächsischen Grenadier-Regiments Kaiser Wilhelm I., König von Preussen Nr. 101
Hersteller Firma Georg Wiesinger sen.,
München, 1906
MHM BAAF9720

Kat. 524
Reservistenkrug für einen Angehörigen des 5. Königlich Sächsischen Infanterie-Regiments Kronprinz Nr. 104
Hersteller Firma Georg Wiesinger sen., München, 1906
MHM BAAF9721

Kat. 525
Reservistenkrug für einen Angehörigen des Königlich Preußischen Fußartillerie-Regiments General-Feldzeugmeister Nr. 3
1899
MHM BAAG5562

Kat. 526
Reservistenkrug für einen Angehörigen des 3. Niederschlesischen Infanterie-Regiments
Hersteller Wilhelm Imhoff, Kassel, 1905
MHM BAAG3286

Kat. 527
Reservistenkrug für einen Angehörigen des Königlich Sächsischen Fußartillerie-Regiments Nr. 12
1910
MHM BAAG7772

Kat. 528
Reservistenkrug für einen Angehörigen des Königlich Sächsischen Fußartillerie-Regiments Nr. 12
1911
MHM BAAG5853

Kat. 529
Reservistenkrug für einen Angehörigen des 5. Königlich Sächsischen Feldartillerie-Regiments Nr. 64
1913
MHM BAAG7766

Kat. 530
Reservistenkrug für einen Angehörigen des Königlich Preußischen Eisenbahn-Regiments Nr. 1
Firma Merkelbach & Wick, 1906
MHM BAAG7771

Kat. 531
Reservistenkrug für einen Angehörigen der 7. Königlich Sächsischen Kompanie des Eisenbahn-Regiments Nr. 1
1912
MHM BAAG0745

Kat. 532
Reservistenkrug für einen Angehörigen des 1. (Königlich Sächsischen) Regiments Leib-Grenadier-Regiments Nr. 100
1907
MHM BAAG9237

Kat. 533
Reservistenkrug für einen Angehörigen des 1. Ober-Elsässischen Infanterie-Regiments Nr. 167
1906
MHM BAAG7770

Kat. 534
Reservistenkrug für einen Angehörigen des 4. Königlich Sächsischen Infanterie-Regiments Großherzog Friedrich II. von Baden 103
1911
MHM BAAG7765

Kat. 535
Reservistenkrug für einen Angehörigen des 19. Königlich Bayerischen Infanterie-Regiments König Viktor Emanuel II. von Italien
Hersteller Jakob Maier, München, 1904
MHM BAAG9120

Kat. 536
Reservistenkrug für einen Angehörigen des 3. Königlich Sächsischen Ulanen-Regiments Nr. 21 Kaiser Wilhelm II., König von Preußen
MHM BAAC7773

Kat. 537
Reservistenkrug für einen Angehörigen des Kurmärkischen Dragoner-Regiments Nr. 14
1904
MHM BAAG7764

Kat. 538
Reservistenkrug für einen Angehörigen des Königlich Sächsischen Karabinier-Regiments (2. Schweres Regiment)
1914
MHM BAAG7768

Kat. 539
Reservistenkrug für einen Angehörigen des 4. Badischen Feldartillerie-Regiments Nr. 66
1910
MHM BAAH9949

Kat. 540
Reservistenkrug für einen Angehörigen des 7. Thüringischen Infanterie-Regiments Nr. 96
1898
MHM BAAP0592

Kat. 541
Reservistenkrug für einen Angehörigen des Infanterie-Regiments Kaiser Wilhelm, König von Preußen (2. Württembergisches) Nr. 120
1902
MHM BAAP7765

Kat. 542
Reservistenkrug für einen Angehörigen des Königlich Preußischen 2. Garde-Regiments zu Fuß
1909
MHM BAAQ8757

Kat. 543
Reservistenkrug für einen Angehörigen des 3. Badischen Dragoner-Regiments Prinz Karl Nr. 22
MHM BAAT6608

Kat. 544
Reservistenkrug für einen Angehörigen des 4. Unterelsässichen Infanterie-Regiments Nr. 143
MHM BAAT6614

Kat. 545
Reservistenkrug für einen Angehörigen des Braunschweigischen Husaren-Regiments Nr. 17
1911
MHM BAAT6601

Kat. 546
Reservistenkrug für einen Angehörigen des 11. Königlich Bayerischen Infanterie-Regiments von dem Tann
1900
MHM BAAT6624

Kat. 547
Reservistenkrug für einen Angehörigen des 6. Königlich Bayerischen Chevaulegers-Regiments Prinz Albrecht von Preußen
1913
MHM BAAT6622

Silhouettenfigur Theodor Fontane (1819–1898)

Kat. 548
Der Schleswig-Holsteinische Krieg im Jahre 1864
Theodor Fontane
Erstmals Berlin 1866
MHM FISt

Kat. 549
Der deutsche Krieg von 1866, 2 Bde.
Theodor Fontane
Erstmals Berlin 1870/71
MHM FISt

Kat. 550
Kriegsgefangen. Erlebtes 1870
Theodor Fontane
Erstmals Berlin 1871
MHM FISt

Kat. 551
Aus den Tagen der Okkupation. Eine Osterreise durch Nordfrankreich und Elsaß-Lothringen 1871
Theodor Fontane
Erstmals Berlin 1871
MHM FISt

Kat. 552
Der Krieg gegen Frankreich 1870–1871, 2 Bde.
Theodor Fontane
Erstmals Berlin 1873–1876
MHM FISt

Silhouettenfigur Friedrich Engels (1820–1895)

Silhouettenfigur Karl May (1842–1912)

Kat. 553
Die Liebe des Ulanen, 5 Bde.
Karl May
Erstmals 1883–1885
MHM FISt

Silhouettenfigur Bertha von Suttner (1843–1914)

Kat. 554
Die Waffen nieder!
Bertha von Suttner
Erstmals Dresden 1889
MHM FISt

Filmstation
Ausschnitte aus »Ned med vaabnene!« / Die Waffen nieder!
Dänemark, 1914
Stummfilm, schwarzweiß
Det Danske Filminstitut / Danish Film Institute

Silhouettenfigur Émile Zola (1840–1902)

Kat. 555
La Débâcle
Émile Zola
1895
MHM FISt

Silhouettenfigur Paul von Hindenburg (1847–1934)

Silhouettenfigur Georges Clemenceau (1841–1929)

Silhouettenfigur Kaiser Wilhelm II. (1859–1941)

Kat. 556
Geständerter Pfeifenkopf mit den Porträts der drei deutschen Kaiser
Großherzogtum Baden, 1889
MHM BAAY9122

Kat. 557
»Der neue Kurs«
Postkarte, Stengel & Co., Dresden, gestempelt 5. Dezember 1914
MHM BBAB1055

Kat. 558
»Wenn ich der Kaiser wär' – Politische Wahrheiten und Notwendigkeiten«
Daniel Frymann (d. i. Heinrich Claß)
2. Aufl., Leipzig 1912
MHM FISt 00122145750

Silhouettenfigur Alexandrine Gravelotte von Rosen (1870–1946)

Kat. 559
Armreif mit Eisernem Kreuz des Großvaters aus den Befreiungskriegen in Schatulle
Geschenk für Alexandrine Gravelotte von Rosen zur Konfirmation 1887
10 × 9 × 9 cm
Familienarchiv von Rosen

Kat. 560
Alexandrine mit Armreif
Fotografie

Modul Kulturkampf

Kat. 561 → S. 376
»Zwischen Berlin und Rom«
Karikatur aus dem humoristisch-satirischen Wochenblatt »Kladderadatsch«, 16. Mai 1875 (Reproduktion)
bpk

Modul Sozialistengesetze

Kat. 562 → S. 377
»Gesetz gegen die gemeingefährlichen Bestrebungen der Sozialdemokratie«
Reichsgesetzblatt, Nr. 34, Berlin, 22. Oktober 1878 (Reproduktion)
© Deutsches Historisches Museum / I. Desnica

Modul Antisemitismus

Kat. 563 ➔ S. 377
Von der Polizei am 28./29. September 1881 aufgefundenes judenfeindliches Agitationsmaterial
Aus einer Akte des Königlichen Polizeipräsidiums, Berlin, zur »Judenfrage«, 1881–1883 (Reproduktion)
Landesarchiv Berlin, A. Pr. Br. Rep. 030 15223, S. 30

Kat. 564 –S. 377
»Mittheilungen aus dem Verein zur Abwehr des Antisemitismus«
Probenummer, Berlin, 21. Oktober 1891 (Reproduktion)
Bayerische Staatsbibliothek München, 4 Jud. 53 c-1/2, Ausgabe Nr. 1 vom 21. Oktober 1891

Modul Nationale Minderheiten

Kat. 565 ➔ S. 378
Karte zu den Sprachen im Deutschen Reich
Peter Palm, Berlin

Modul Frauenwahlrecht

Kat. 566 ➔ S. 379
Demonstration für Frauenwahlrecht in Berlin, 12. Mai 1912
Gebrüder Haeckel, Berlin
Fotografie (Reproduktion)
akq-images

Mobile mit Postkarten von deutschen Nationaldenkmälern
(Reproduktionen)

Kat. 567
Das Kaiser-Bilderbuch
Hermann Hoffmeister
2., verbesserte Aufl., Leipzig 1877
(Reproduktionen von Auszügen)
MHM 00120238750

Kat. 568
Monsieur le Hulan et les trois couleurs. Conte de Noël
Paul Déroulède
Paris 1884 (Reproduktionen von Auszügen)
MHM FISt 00121040750

Kat. 569
Martha's Tagebuch
Nach dem Roman »Die Waffen nieder« von Bertha von Suttner für die reifere Jugend
Bearbeitet von Hedwig Gräfin Pötting, illustriert von Adrienne Gräfin Pötting
Dresden/Leipzig/Wien, 1897
(Reproduktionen von Auszügen)
MHM FISt 0020321152

Kat. 570
Der Trommler von Düppel. Erzählungen aus der Nordmark
Johannes Dose
München 1907 [1902?]
(Reproduktionen von Auszügen)
MHM FISt 00122126750

Kat. 571
»La Guerre franco-allemande 1920« / Der Französisch-Deutsche Krieg 1920
Pierre Baudry (1897–1918) und Lucien Sinard (Lebensdaten unbekannt), 1909
Kreide, Tusche und Aquarell auf Papier
(Reproduktionen von Auszügen)
Musée de l'Armée, Paris

Kat. 572
L'histoire d'Alsace. Racontée aux petits enfants d'Alsace et de France par l'oncle Hansi avec beaucoup de jolies images de Hansi et de Huen
Jean-Jacques Waltz
Paris 1913 (Reproduktionen von Auszügen)
MHM FISt 00122045750

Kat. 573
Aus großer Zeit. Eine Erzählung für junge Mädchen
Henny Koch
Stuttgart, 1914 (Reproduktionen von Auszügen)
MHM FISt 00122045750

Kat. 574
»Le Moblot«
Gedicht aus Jean Richepins »Allons Enfants de la Patrie«, 1920
(Reproduktionen von Auszügen)
MHM FISt 00101185750

Kat. 575
Schuhbürste mit eingeritzten Daten der Kriege 1870/71 und 1914/18
5 × 20 × 2 cm
Kölnisches Stadtmuseum

EPILOG: NATION – WELCHE NATION?

Kat. 576
Bismarck-Büste, in zwei Teile zerbrochen, mit Spuren von Gewalteinwirkungen
Nach W. Uhlm
Höhe 43 cm
MHM BBAD0577

Filmstation
Journal 1870/71
7-teilige Fernsehserie, Süddeutscher Rundfunk, 1970
Ausschnitt aus Folge 4: Interview in Versailles mit Legationsrat Lothar Bucher, Mitarbeiter Bismarcks, über die Reichsgründung
Vorführung mit freundlicher Genehmigung des SWR

Filmstation
Historikerinnen und Historiker aus fünf Ländern im Gespräch
Uffe Østergård, Aarhus/Dänemark, Universität Aarhus
Miloš Řezník, Prag/Tschechien, Leiter Deutsches Historisches Institut Warschau
Birgit Aschmann, Berlin/Deutschland, Humboldt-Universität zu Berlin
Monique Fuchs, Straßburg/Frankreich, Leiterin Historisches Museum Straßburg
Manfried Rauchensteiner, Wien/Österreich, ehem. Direktor Heeresgeschichtliches Museum Wien
Produktion: kursiv | text – objekt – raum GmbH / TIME PRINTS KG – Film & Medien

Mitmach-Mobile
Was wünscht Du Dir, was wünschen Sie sich für Deutschlands Zukunft?

Personen

A

B

T

U

V

W

Z

Ausgewählte Literatur

A

Jens Ahlers (Hg.): Mennesker i krigen – 1864 – Menschen im Krieg, Ausst.-Kat. Schleswig-Holsteinische Landesbibliothek/ Museum Sønderjylland – Sønderborg Slot, Kiel 2014

Pierre Allorant/Walter Baderer/Jean Garrigues (Hg.): 1870, entre mémoires régionales et oubli national. Se souvenir de la guerre franco-prussienne, Rennes 2019

Wolfgang Altgeld: Vorlesung. Die nationale Einigung Italiens und Deutschlands 1848–1871, 2. überarb. Aufl., Bonn 2015

Beate Althammer: Das Bismarckreich 1871–1890, 2., aktualisierte Aufl., Paderborn 2017

Eric Anceau: Ils ont fait et défait le Second Empire, Paris 2019

Benedict Anderson: Die Erfindung der Nation. Zur Karriere eines erfolgreichen Konzeptes, 2. Aufl. mit einem Nachwort von Thomas Mergel, Frankfurt am Main 2005

Magret Lavinia Anderson: Lehrjahre der Demokratie. Wahlen und politische Kultur im Deutschen Kaiserreich, Stuttgart 2009

Jürgen Angelow: Von Wien nach Königgrätz. Die Sicherheitspolitik des Deutschen Bundes im europäischen Gleichgewicht (1815–1866), Oldenburg 1996

Tobias Arand: 1870/71. Die Geschichte des Deutsch-Französischen Krieges erzählt in Einzelschicksalen, Hamburg 2018

Birgit Aschmann: Preußens Ruhm und Deutschlands Ehre. Zum nationalen Ehrdiskurs im Vorfeld der preußisch-französischen Kriege des 19. Jahrhunderts, München 2013

Oliver Auge/Ulrich Lappenküper/Ulf Morgenstern (Hg.): Der Wiener Frieden 1864. Ein deutsches, europäisches und globales Ereignis, Paderborn 2016

B

Dominik Bartmann: Anton von Werner. Geschichte in Bildern, Ausst.-Kat. Berlin Museum/Deutsches Historisches Museum, Berlin, München 1993

Richard Basset: For God and Kaiser. The Imperial Austrian Army, New Haven/ London 2016

Winfried Baumgart: König Friedrich Wilhelm IV. und Wilhelm I: Briefwechsel 1840–1858, Paderborn u. a. 2013

Frank Becker: Bilder von Krieg und Nation. Die Einigungskriege in der bürgerlichen Öffentlichkeit Deutschlands 1864–1913, München 2001

Frank Becker (Hg.): Zivilisten und Soldaten. Entgrenzte Gewalt in der Geschichte, Essen 2015

Jean-Jacques Becker/Stéphane Audoin-Rouzeau: La France, la nation, la guerre: 1850–1920, Domont 2012

Robert Belot (Hg.): 1870. De la guerre à la paix. Strasbourg – Belfort, Paris 2013

Mathilde Benoistel/Sylvie Le Ray-Burimi/ Christophe Pommier (Hg.): France Allemagne(s) 1870–1871. La guerre, la commune, les mémoires, Ausst.-Kat. Musée de l'armée, Paris 2017

Bismarck – Preußen, Deutschland und Europa, Ausst.-Kat. Deutsches Historisches Museum im Martin-Gropius-Bau, Berlin 1990

Bettina Brand: Germania und ihre Söhne. Repräsentation von Nation, Geschlecht und Politik in der Moderne, Göttingen 2010

Klaus-Jürgen Bremm: Von der Chaussee zur Schiene. Militärstrategie und Eisenbahnen in Preußen von 1833 bis zum Feldzug von 1866, München 2005

Klaus-Jürgen Bremm: 1866. Bismarcks Krieg gegen die Habsburger, Darmstadt 2016

Klaus-Jürgen Bremm: 70/71. Preußens Triumph über Frankreich, Darmstadt 2019

Tom Buk-Swienty: Schlachtbank Düppel. 18. April 1864. Die Geschichte einer Schlacht, Berlin 2011

Ken Burns: The Civil War – Der Amerikanische Bürgerkrieg, München 1992.

Nikolaus Buschmann: Einkreisung und Waffenbrüderschaft. Die öffentliche Deutung von Krieg und Nation in Deutschland 1850–1871, Göttingen 2003

Annett Büttner: Die konfessionelle Kriegskrankenpflege im 19. Jahrhundert, Stuttgart 2013

C

Konrad Canis: Bismarcks Außenpolitik 1870–1890. Aufstieg und Gefährdung, Paderborn 2004

Konrad Canis: Die bedrängte Großmacht. Österreich-Ungarn und das europäische Mächtesystem 1866/67–1914, Paderborn 2016

Jean-François Chamet u.a. (Hg.): D'une guerre à l'autre. Que reste-t-il de 1870–1871 en 1914?, Paris 2016

Francis Choisel: La Deuxième République et le Second Empire au jour le jour. Chronologie érudite détaillée, Paris 2015

Christopher Clark: Preußen. Aufstieg und Niedergang. 1600–1947, München 2007

Carl von Clausewitz: Vom Kriege, hg. von Werner Hahlweg, 19. Aufl., Bonn 1980

Laurence Cole (Hg.): Different Paths to the Nation. Regional and National Identities in Central Europe and Italy, 1830–70, Basingstoke u.a. 2007

Gordon A. Craig: Königgrätz. Eine Schlacht macht Weltgeschichte, München 1992

D

Ute Daniel: Augenzeugen. Kriegsberichterstattung vom 18. zum 21. Jahrhundert, Göttingen 2006

Iwan-Michelangelo D'Aprile: Fontane. Ein Jahrhundert in Bewegung, Reinbek bei Hamburg 2018

Klaus Deinet: Napoleon III.: Frankreichs Weg in die Moderne, Stuttgart 2019

Richard Dietrich (Hg.): Europa und der Norddeutsche Bund, Berlin 1968

Christoph Dipper/Ulrich Speck (Hg.): 1848. Revolution in Deutschland, Frankfurt am Main 1998

E

Matthias Eberle: Im Spiegel der Geschichte. Realistische Historienmalerei in Westeuropa 1830–1900, München 2017

Jörg Echternkamp/Sven Oliver Müller (Hg. im Auftrag des Militärgeschichtlichen Forschungsamtes): Die Politik der Nation. Deutscher Nationalismus in Krieg und Krisen 1760–1960, München 2002

Michael Epkenhans/Gerhard P. Groß (Hg. im Auftrag des Militärgeschichtlichen Forschungsamtes): Das Militär und der Aufbruch in die Moderne 1860–1890, München 2003

Michael Epkenhans: Die Reichsgründung 1870/71, München 2020

Richard J. Evans: Das europäische Jahrhundert. Ein Kontinent im Umbruch 1815–1914, München 2018

F

Gerd Fesser: Sedan 1870. Ein unheilvoller Sieg, Paderborn 2019

Karin Feuerstein-Praßer: Die deutschen Kaiserinnen, Regensburg 2008

Orlando Figes: Krimkrieg. Der letzte Kreuzzug, Berlin 2011

Roland G. Foerster (Hg.): Generalfeldmarschall von Moltke. Bedeutung und Wirkung, Oldenburg 1991

Theodor Fontane: Der Schleswig-Holsteinsche Krieg im Jahre 1864, Berlin 1866

Theodor Fontane: Der deutsche Krieg von 1866, 2 Bde., Berlin 1870/71

Theodor Fontane: Der Krieg gegen Frankreich 1870–1871, 2 Bde., Berlin 1873–1876

Stig Förster/Markus Pöhlmann/Dierk Walter (Hg.): Schlachten der Weltgeschichte. Von Salamis bis Sinai, München 2001

Stig Förster/Jörg Nagler (Hg.): On the Road to Total War. The American Civil War and the German Wars of Unification, 1861–1871, Cambridge/New York 1997

Friedrich Forstmeier u.a. (Hg. im Auftrag des Militärgeschichtlichen Forschungsamtes): Handbuch zur deutschen Militärgeschichte. 1648–1939, 6 Bde., München 1979–1981

Ute Frevert: Die kasernierte Nation. Militärdienst und Zivilgesellschaft in Deutschland, München 2001

Daniel Fulda: »Ich lasse alle Nationalitäten gelten«? Karl Mays Re-Narration der deutsch-französischen Geschichte im Kolportagemodus (Die Liebe des Ulanen), in: Wolfram Pyta/Jörg Lehmann (Hg.): Krieg erzählen – Raconter la Guerre. Darstellungsverfahren in Literatur und Historiographie nach den Kriegen von 1870/71 und 1914/18, Berlin 2014, S. 29–47

G

Lothar Gall: Bismarck. Der weiße Revolutionär, Frankfurt am Main/Wien/Berlin 1980

Lothar Gall: 1848. Aufbruch zur Freiheit, Ausst.-Kat. Deutsches Historisches Museum, Berlin/Schirn Kunsthalle, Frankfurt am Main, 2. Aufl., Berlin 1998

Lothar Gall: Europa auf dem Weg in die Moderne 1850–1890, 5. Aufl., Stuttgart 2002

Jan Ganschow/Olaf Haselhorst/Maik Ohnezeit: Der Deutsch-Dänische Krieg 1864. Vorgeschichte – Verlauf – Folgen, Graz 2013

Jan Ganschow/Olaf Haselhorst/Maik Ohnezeit: Der Deutsch-Französische Krieg 1870/71. Vorgeschichte – Verlauf – Folgen, 2. Aufl., Graz 2013

Manfred Görtemaker: Geschichte Europas. 1850–1918, Stuttgart 2002

Dieter Gosewinkel: Einbürgern und Ausschließen. Die Nationalisierung der Staatsangehörigkeit vom Deutschen Bund bis zur Bundesrepublik Deutschland, Göttingen 2001

Alain Gouttman: La grande défaite 1870/71, Paris 2015

Gerhard Groß: Mythos und Wirklichkeit. Operatives Denken im preußisch-deutschen Heer von Moltke d. Ä. bis Heusinger, Paderborn 2012

Wolf D. Gruner: Der Deutsche Bund 1815–1866, München 2010

Dominik Gügel/Christina Egli: Napoleon III. Der Kaiser vom Bodensee, Konstanz 2008

Wolfgang Gülich: Die Sächsische Armee zur Zeit des Deutschen Bundes. 1815–1867, Beucha/Markkleeberg 2017

Wolfgang Gülich: Die Sächsische Armee im Norddeutschen Bund und im Kaiserreich. 1867–1914, Beucha/Markkleeberg 2017

H

Rüdiger Hachtmann: 1848 – Epochenschwelle zur Moderne, Tübingen 2002

Hans-Werner Hahn: Geschichte des deutschen Zollvereins, Göttingen 1984

Jürgen Hannig: Im Schatten von Spichern. Militarismus und Nationalismus im Saarrevier vor dem Ersten Weltkrieg, in: Georg Jenal (Hg.)/Stephanie Haarländer (Mitarb.): Gegenwart der Vergangenheit. Festgabe für Friedrich Prinz zu seinem 65. Geburtstag, München 1993, S. 257–276.

Dieter Hein: Die Revolution von 1848/49, 6. Aufl., München 2019

Winfried Heinemann/Lothar Höbelt/Ulrich Lappenküper (Hg.): Der Preußisch-Österreichische Krieg 1866, Paderborn 2018

Heinz Helmert/Hansjürgen Usczeck: Preußischdeutsche Kriege von 1864 bis 1871. Militärischer Verlauf, 5. Aufl., Berlin (Ost) 1984

Mark Hewitson: The People's Wars. Histories of Violence in the German Lands, 1820–1888, Oxford 2017

Eric J. Hobsbawm: Nationen und Nationalismus. Mythos und Realität seit 1780, 2. Aufl., München 1998

Lothar Höbelt: 1848. Österreich und die deutsche Revolution, Wien/München 1998

Lothar Höbelt: Franz Joseph I.: Der Kaiser und sein Reich. Eine politische Geschichte, Wien 2009

Michael Hochgeschwender: Der amerikanische Bürgerkrieg, 2., durchgesehene Aufl., München 2013

Karl Holl: Pazifismus in Deutschland, Frankfurt am Main 1988

Alistair Horne: Paris ist tot – es lebe Paris! Der Deutsch-Französische Krieg 1870/71 und der Aufstand der Kommune in Paris, Bern/München/Wien 1967

J

Carsten Jahnke/Jes Fabricius Møller (Hg.): 1864 – og historiens lange skygger/1864 – und der lange Schatten der Geschichte: Den dansk-østrigsk-preussiske krig i 1864 og dens betydning i dag/Der Krieg von 1864 und seine Gegenwartsbedeutung, Husum 2011

Christian Jansen (Hg.): Der Bürger als Soldat. Die Militarisierung europäischer Gesellschaften im langen 19. Jahrhundert: ein internationaler Vergleich, Essen 2004

Christian Jansen/Henning Borggräfe: Nation – Nationalität – Nationalismus, Frankfurt am Main/New York 2007

Christian Jansen: Gründerzeit und Nationsbildung 1849–1871. Seminarbuch Geschichte, Paderborn 2011

Alexander Jordan/Thomas Madeja/Winfried Mönch (Bearb): Von Kaiser zu Kaiser. Erinnerungen an den Deutsch-Französischen Krieg 1870/71, Ausst.-Kat. Wehrgeschichtliches Museum, Rastatt 2008

Pieter M. Judson: Habsburg. Geschichte eines Imperiums, 2. Aufl., München 2017

K

Stefan Kaufmann: Kommunikationstechnik und Kriegführung 1815–1945. Stufen telemedialer Rüstung, München 2006

Nils Klawitter/Dietmar Pieper (Hg.): Das Reich der Deutschen. Wie wir eine Nation wurden, München 2018

Uwe Klußmann/Joachim Mohr (Hg.): Das Kaiserreich. Deutschland unter preußischer Herrschaft. Von Bismarck bis Wilhelm II., München/Hamburg 2014

Peter Kolmsee: Unter dem Zeichen des Äskulap. Eine Einführung in die Geschichte des Militärsanitätswesens von den frühen Anfängen bis zum Ende des Ersten Weltkrieges, Bonn 1997

Hans-Christof Kraus: Bismarck. Größe – Grenzen – Leistungen, Stuttgart 2015

Christine G. Krüger: »Sind wir denn nicht Brüder?« Deutsche Juden im nationalen Krieg 1870/71, Paderborn 2006

Wolfgang Kruse: Die Erfindung des modernen Militarismus. Krieg, Militär und bürgerliche Gesellschaft im politischen Diskurs der Französischen Revolution 1789–1799, München 2003

L

Dieter Langewiesche: Der gewaltsame Lehrer. Europas Kriege in der Moderne, München 2019

Ulrich Lappenküper (Hg.): Otto von Bismarck und das »lange 19. Jahrhundert«. Lebendige Vergangenheit im Spiegel der »Friedrichsruher Beiträge« 1996–2016, Paderborn 2017

Ulrich Lappenküper (Hg.): Das Bismarck-Problem in der Geschichtsschreibung. Biographische Perspektiven seit 1970, Paderborn u. a. 2017

Ulrich Lappenküper/Ulf Morgenstern/Maik Ohnezeit (Hg.): Auftakt zum deutschen Nationalstaat: Der Norddeutsche Bund 1867–1871, Friedrichsruh 2017

Ullrich Lappenküper: Bismarck und Frankreich 1815–1898. Chancen zur Bildung einer »ganz unwiderstehlichen Macht?«, Paderborn 2019

Ulrike Laufer/Hans Ottomeyer (Hg.): Gründerzeit 1848–1871. Industrie und Lebensträume zwischen Vormärz und Kaiserreich, Ausst.-Kat. Deutsches Historisches Museum, Berlin, Dresden 2008

Jörn Leonhard: Bellizismus und Nation. Kriegsdeutung und Nationsbestimmung in Europa und den Vereinigten Staaten 1750–1914, München 2008

Thorsten Loch/Lars Zacharias (Hg.): Wie die Siegessäule nach Berlin kam. Eine kleine Geschichte der Reichseinigungskriege von 1864 bis 1871, Freiburg 2011

Jan Luckszat: Der Weg zur Reichseinigung. Hilfen für die historische Bildung. Unter Mitarbeit von Dierk Kähler, Potsdam 2008

Heinrich Lutz: Zwischen Habsburg und Preußen. Deutschland 1815–1866, Berlin 1985

M

Georg Maag/Wolfram Pyta/Martin Windisch (Hg.): Der Krimkrieg als erster europäischer Medienkrieg, Berlin 2010

Xavier Mauduit/Corinne Ergasse: Flamboyant Second Empire! Et la France entre dans la modernité ..., Malakoff 2018

James McPherson: Für die Freiheit sterben. Die Geschichte des Amerikanischen Bürgerkriegs, Köln 2009

Heidi Mehrkens: Statuswechsel. Kriegserfahrung und nationale Wahrnehmung im Deutsch-Französischen Krieg 1870/71, Essen 2008

Andreas Metzing: Kriegsgedenken in Frankreich (1871–1914). Studien zur kollektiven Erinnerung an den Deutsch-Französischen Krieg von 1870/71, Freiburg 2002

Wolfgang Mommsen: Das Ringen um den nationalen Staat. Die Gründung und der innere Ausbau des Deutschen Reiches unter Otto v. Bismarck 1850–1890, Berlin 1993

Klaus Müller: 1866: Bismarcks deutscher Bruderkrieg. Königgrätz und die Schlachten auf deutschem Boden, 2. Aufl., Graz 2016

Thankmar von Münchhausen: 72 Tage. Die Pariser Kommune 1871 – die erste »Diktatur des Proletariats«, München 2015

Frank Lorenz Müller: Die Thronfolger. Macht und Zukunft der Monarchie im 19. Jahrhundert, München 2019

N

Shlomo Na'aman: Der Deutsche Nationalverein. Die politische Konstituierung des deutschen Bürgertums 1859–1867, Düsseldorf 1987

Sönke Neitzel: Die Kriegsbücher Fontanes, in: Bernd Heidenreich/Frank-Lothar Kroll (Hg.): Theodor Fontane – Dichter der Deutschen Einheit, Berlin 2003, S. 121–131

Sönke Neitzel/Daniel Hohrath (Hg.): Kriegsgreuel: Die Entgrenzung der Gewalt in kriegerischen Konflikten vom Mittelalter bis ins 20. Jahrhundert, Paderborn 2008

Thomas Nipperdey: Deutsche Geschichte 1800–1918, Neuausg., München 2013

Christoph Nonn: Bismarck. Ein Preuße und sein Jahrhundert, München 2015

Lars Nowak (Hg.): Medien – Krieg – Raum, München 2018

O

Georg Ortenburg: Waffen der Einigungskriege 1848–1871, Bonn 1990

P

Susanne Parth: Zwischen Bildbericht und Bildpropaganda. Kriegskonstruktionen in der deutschen Militärmalerei des 19. Jahrhunderts, Paderborn u. a. 2010

Hélène Puiseux: Les Figures de la Guerre. Représentations et sensibilités 1839–1996, Paris 1997

R

Mike Rapport: 1848. Revolution in Europa, Stuttgart 2011

Walter Rauscher: Die fragile Großmacht. Die Donaumonarchie und die europäische Staatenwelt 1866–1914, Frankfurt am Main 2014

Dieter Riesenberger: Für Humanität in Krieg und Frieden. Das Internationale Rote Kreuz 1863–1977, Göttingen 1992

Jörg Requate (Hg.) : Das 19. Jahrhundert als Mediengesellschaft, München 2009

François Roth: La Guerre de 1870, Paris 1990

Gian Enrico Rusconi: Cavour und Bismarck. Der Weg zur deutschen und italienischen Einigung im Spannungsfeld von Liberalismus und Cäsarismus, München 2013

S

Erwin A. Schmidl (Hg.): Freund oder Feind? Kombattanten, Nichtkombattanten und Bürgerkrieg seit dem 18. Jahrhundert, Frankfurt am Main 1995

Daniel Marc Segesser: Recht statt Rache oder Rache durch Recht? Die Ahndung von Kriegsverbrechen in der internationalen wissenschaftlichen Debatte 1872–1945, Paderborn u. a. 2010

Alexander Seyferth: Heimatfront 1870/71. Wirtschaft und Gesellschaft im deutsch-französischen Krieg, Paderborn u. a. 2007

Dennis Showalter: The Wars of German Unification, 2. Aufl., London u. a. 2015

Wolfram Siemann: Vom Staatenbund zum Nationalstaat. Deutschland 1806–1871, München 1995

Marco Sigg: Der Unterführer als Feldherr im Taschenformat. Theorie und Praxis der Auftragstaktik im deutschen Heer 1869–1945, Paderborn 2014

Matthias Steinbach: Abgrund Metz: Kriegserfahrung, Belagerungsalltag und nationale Erziehung im Schatten einer Festung 1870/71, München 2002

Jonathan Steinberg: Bismarck. Magier der Macht, 2. Aufl., Berlin 2012

Willibald Steinmetz: Europa im 19. Jahrhundert, Frankfurt am Main 2019

Dieter Storz/Daniel Hohrath (Hg.): Nord gegen Süd. Der Deutsche Krieg 1866, Ingolstadt 2016

Michael Stürmer: Die Reichsgründung. Deutscher Nationalstaat und europäisches Gleichgewicht im Zeitalter Bismarcks, Neuaufl., München 1997

T

Francesco Traniello/Gianni Sofri: Der lange Weg zur Nation. Das italienische Risorgimento, Stuttgart 2012

U

Volker Ullrich: Fünf Schüsse auf Bismarck. Historische Reportagen 1789–1945, München 2002

Volker Ullrich: Die nervöse Großmacht. 1871–1918. Aufstieg und Untergang des deutschen Kaiserreichs, 2., überarbeitete Aufl., Frankfurt am Main 2013

Veit Valentin: Geschichte der deutschen Revolution 1848–1849, 2 Bde., Berlin 1930/31

W

Peter Walkenhorst: Nation – Volk – Rasse. Radikaler Nationalismus im Deutschen Kaiserreich 1890–1914, Göttingen 2007

Franz Walter: Die SPD. Biographie einer Partei von Ferdinand Lassalle bis Andrea Nahles, Reinbek bei Hamburg 2018

Dierk Walther: Preußische Heeresreform 1807–1870. Militärische Innovation und der Mythos der »Roonschen Reform«, Paderborn u. a. 2003

Hans-Ulrich Wehler: Nationalismus. Geschichte, Formen, Folgen, 2. Aufl., München 2001

Hans-Ulrich Wehler: Deutsche Gesellschaftsgeschichte. Bd. 3: Von der »Deutschen Doppelrevolution« bis zum Beginn des Ersten Weltkrieges 1849 – 1914, 2. Aufl., München 2007

Roland Wenzlhümer: Connecting the Nineteenth-Century World. The Telegraph and Globalization, Cambridge 2015

Wolfram Wette: Militarismus und Pazifismus. Auseinandersetzung mit den deutschen Kriegen, Bremen 1991

David Wetzel: Duell der Giganten. Bismarck, Napoleon III. und die Ursachen des Deutsch-Französischen Krieges 1870/71, Paderborn 2005

Johannes Willms: Napoleon III. Frankreichs letzter Kaiser, München 2008

Rolf Wirtgen (Bearb.) u. a.: Das Zündnadelgewehr. Eine militärtechnische Revolution im 19. Jahrhundert, Herford/Bonn 1991

Heiner Wittmann: Napoleon III. Macht und Kunst, Frankfurt am Main 2013

Z

Hannah Zindel: Belagerung von Paris. 69 Freiballons, 381 Tauben und fast elf Tonnen Post, in: Lars Nowak (Hg.): Medien – Krieg – Raum, Paderborn u. a. 2018, S. 141–160

Autorinnen und Autoren

Gerhard Bauer
Dr. phil. (geb. 1963)

studierte Geschichte, Kunstgeschichte und Anglistik an den Universitäten Erlangen und Edinburgh und promovierte über den Mythos Napoleons im 19. und frühen 20. Jahrhundert. Er ist Sachgebietsleiter Uniform/Feldzeichen am Militärhistorischen Museum der Bundeswehr in Dresden und hat dort wissenschaftliche und Ausstellungsverantwortlichkeit für Themen von 1300 bis 1918. Er hat an der Neukonzeption des Museums mitgearbeitet und kuratierte die Ausstellungen »Blutige Romantik. 200 Jahre Befreiungskriege gegen Napoleon« (2013) sowie »14 – Menschen – Krieg« (2014) über den Ersten Weltkrieg. An der Hochschule für Bildende Künste Dresden unterrichtet er in Intervallen als Lehrbeauftragter Kostümgestalterinnen und Kostümgestalter in Uniformkunde.

Frank Becker
Prof. Dr. phil. (geb. 1963)

ist seit 2011 Professor für Neuere und Neueste Geschichte an der Universität Duisburg-Essen. Arbeitsschwerpunkte sind Kulturtransferforschung, Sozialgeschichte des Krieges, europäischer Kolonialismus sowie Körper- und Sportgeschichte. Derzeit gehört er zum Leitungsgremium des DFG-Graduiertenkollegs 1919 »Vorsorge, Voraussicht, Vorhersage: Kontingenzbewältigung durch Zukunftshandeln« und ist Mitglied der DFG-Forschungsgruppe 2600 »Ambiguität und Unterscheidung. Historisch-kulturelle Dynamiken« an der Universität Duisburg-Essen. Publikationen zur Geschichte des Krieges u. a.: Bilder von Krieg und Nation. Die Einigungskriege in der bürgerlichen Öffentlichkeit Deutschlands 1864–1913, München 2001; (Hg.) Der Erste Weltkrieg und die Städte. Studien zur Rhein-Ruhr-Region, Duisburg 2015; (Hg.) Zivilisten und Soldaten. Entgrenzte Gewalt in der Geschichte, Essen 2015.

Michael Epkenhans
Prof. Dr. phil. (geb. 1955)

ist außerplanmäßiger Professor an der Universität Hamburg und Leitender Wissenschaftler sowie Stellvertretender Kommandeur am Zentrum für Militärgeschichte und Sozialwissenschaften der Bundeswehr in Potsdam. Von 1996 bis 2009 war er Gründungsdirektor und Geschäftsführer der bundesunmittelbaren Otto-von-Bismarck-Stiftung in Friedrichsruh. Er hat zahlreiche Monografien und Editionen zur Militärgeschichte des 19. und 20. Jahrhunderts publiziert.

Frank Hagemann
Oberst, Dr. phil. (geb. 1968)

ist Leiter der Abteilung Bildung und Beauftragter für Angelegenheiten des militärischen Personals am Zentrum für Militärgeschichte und Sozialwissenschaften der Bundeswehr in Potsdam. Ausbildung zum Offizier der Panzergrenadiertruppe, Teilnahme am Lehrgang General-/Admiralstabsdienst International, Studium der Geschichts- und Sozialwissenschaften an der Universität der Bundeswehr Hamburg. Promotion an der Universität Potsdam, Master of Arts in Security Studies an der U. S. Naval Postgraduate School in Monterey/CA. Verwendungen u. a. als Zugführer und Kompaniechef, Dozent für Militärgeschichte an der Offizierschule des Heeres in Dresden, G3-Dezernent beim Deutschen Militärischen Vertreter EU/NATO in Brüssel sowie als Referent im Bundesministerium der Verteidigung in Bonn und anschließend in Berlin. Er veröffentlichte u. a.: Geschichtsbewusstsein als Kernkompetenz. Historische Bildung in der Bundeswehr, hg. gemeinsam mit Sven Lange, Potsdam 2020.

Alma Hannig
M. A. (geb. 1977)

ist seit 2008 wissenschaftliche Mitarbeiterin und Lehrbeauftragte für Neuere und Neueste Geschichte für verschiedene Universitäten und wissenschaftliche Einrichtungen. Seit 2013 ist sie außerdem als Ausstellungskuratorin in Wien tätig. 2018/19 war sie freie wissenschaftliche Mitarbeiterin für das Militärhistorische Museum der

Bundeswehr. Ihre Forschungsschwerpunkte sind Politik- und Diplomatiegeschichte der Habsburger Monarchie und Deutschlands im langen 19. Jahrhundert, Erster Weltkrieg sowie Geschichte des Populismus in Österreich. Jüngste Publikationen u. a.: »I do not believe in the use of war to benefit arts«: Austrian arts and artists in the last year of the war, in: Jean-Paul Bled/Jean-Pierre Deschodt (Hg.): 1918. Demain la paix?, Paris 2019, S. 249–266; »Le plus brillant Congrès«? La Monarchie des Habsbourg et la paix européenne en 1914, in: Vincent Chambarlhac u. a. (Hg.): Veilles de guerre. Précurseurs politiques et culturels de la Grande guerre, Villeneuve d'Asqc 2018, S. 17–194.

Christian Jansen
Prof. Dr. (geb. 1956)

war nach einem Studium der Geschichte und Mathematik und einigen Jahren in einem Druckereikollektiv wissenschaftlicher Mitarbeiter an den Universitäten Heidelberg (Promotion 1989) und Bochum (Habilitation 1998). Anschließend viele Jahre auf befristeten Professuren in Konstanz, Bochum, Jerusalem, Berlin und Münster. 2013 Berufung auf die W3-Professur für Neuere Geschichte (Schwerpunkt 19. Jahrhundert) an der Universität Trier. Wichtige Publikationen zum Thema: Gründerzeit und Nationsbildung 1849–1871, Paderborn 2011; Die Fortschrittspartei – ein liberaler Erinnerungsort? Größe und Grenzen der ältesten liberalen Partei in Deutschland, in: Jahrbuch zur Liberalismusforschung 24 (2012), S. 43–56; (mit Henning Borggräfe) Nation – Nationalität – Nationalismus, Frankfurt am Main 2007, überarb. Aufl. 2020. Weitere Publikationen unter www.uni-trier.de/index.php?id=50400.

Eva Langhals
M. A. (geb. 1983)

studierte Geschichtswissenschaft und Russistik in Berlin. Wissenschaftliche Mitarbeit an zeithistorischen Ausstellungen, u. a.: Inhaftiert in Hohenschönhausen. Zeugnisse politischer Verfolgung 1945–1989 (2013), Gedenkstätte Berlin-Hohenschönhausen; »Alles nach Plan«. Formgestaltung in der DDR (2016), Haus der Geschichte, Bonn; Der Rote Gott. Stalin und die Deutschen (2018), Gedenkstätte Berlin-Hohenschönhausen. Seit 2018 ist sie freie wissenschaftliche Mitarbeiterin für das Militärhistorische Museum der Bundeswehr. Publikationen u. a.: Eine Deutsche in Belgien zur Zeit des Ersten Weltkriegs. Aus den Tagebüchern der Thea Sternheim, in: 14 – Menschen – Krieg (Ausst.-Kat.), hg. von Gerhard Bauer u. a., Dresden 2014, S. 375–382, sowie: Die Stalinorgel, in: Der Rote Gott. Stalin und die Deutschen (Ausst.-Kat.), hg. von Andreas Engwert u. a., Berlin 2018, S. 50/51.

Ulrich Lappenküper
Prof. Dr. (geb. 1959)

ist Historiker, Geschäftsführer und Mitglied des Vorstands der Otto-von-Bismarck-Stiftung in Friedrichsruh sowie außerplanmäßiger Professor für Neuere Geschichte an der Helmut-Schmidt-Universität der Bundeswehr in Hamburg. Seine Forschungen befassen sich insbesondere mit der Geschichte der internationalen Beziehungen im 19. und 20. Jahrhundert, mit den deutsch-französischen Beziehungen im 19. und 20. Jahrhundert sowie mit Leben und Wirken Otto von Bismarcks. Zu seinen jüngsten Veröffentlichungen gehören: (Hg.) Das Bismarck-Problem in der Geschichtsschreibung. Biographische Perspektiven seit 1970, Paderborn u. a. 2017; Bismarck und Frankreich 1815 bis 1898. Chancen zur Bildung einer »ganz unwiderstehlichen Macht«?, Paderborn u. a. 2019.

Sylvie Le-Ray Burimi
M. A. (geb. 1970)

ist Hauptkonservatorin für das Kulturerbe und verantwortlich für die Abteilung für Schöne Künste und Kulturerbe des Armeemuseums im Hôtel national des Invalides in Paris. Sie war Kuratorin der Ausstellungen »Napoléon III et l'Italie. Naissance d'une Nation« (2011), »Vu du front. Représenter la Grande Guerre« (2014), »France-Allemagne(s). 1870–1871: la guerre, la Commune, les mémoires« (2017) sowie »Photographies en guerre« (2020). Arbeitsschwerpunkte sind Darstellungen des Krieges, Fragen des Kulturerbes und Künstlerlebens in Kriegszeiten. Sie ist Mitherausgeberin von »Saint-Louis des Invalides. La cathédrale des Armées françaises« (Paris/Straßburg 2018) sowie des Katalogs zur Ausstellung »France-Allemagne(s). 1870–1871: la guerre, la Commune, les mémoires« (Paris 2017).

Thorsten Loch
Oberstleutnant, Dr. phil. (geb. 1975)

ist Referent im Bundesministerium der Verteidigung. Zuvor Verwendungen als Kompaniechef, Dozent für Militärgeschichte sowie wissenschaftlicher Mitarbeiter am Militärgeschichtlichen Forschungsamt/Zentrum für Militärgeschichte und Sozialwissenschaften der Bundeswehr. Er ist Lehrbeauftragter an der Universität Potsdam und der Helmut-Schmidt-Universität/Universität der Bundeswehr Hamburg und Preisträger des 1. Preises des Förderpreises für Militärgeschichte und Militärtechnikgeschichte 2019. Jüngere Publikationen u. a.: Deutsche Generale 1945 bis 1990. Profession, Karriere, Herkunft, Berlin 2020 (= Deutsch-Deutsche Militärgeschichte, 2); mit Markus Vette (Hg.): Friedrich Clauson von Kaas, »Potsdam ist geschlagen«. Briefe aus dem Deutsch-Französischen Krieg 1870/71. Im Auftrag des Zentrums für Militärgeschichte und Sozialwissenschaften der Bundeswehr, Freiburg 2016.

Heidi Mehrkens
Dr. phil. (geb. 1974)

ist Lecturer in Modern European History an der University of Aberdeen, wo sie unter anderem zur Kulturgeschichte des Politischen und zur Militärgeschichte des 19. Jahrhunderts forscht und lehrt. Zu ihren jüngsten Veröffentlichungen zählen: Ein Opfer des Krieges und der Kriegsgesetze? Die Beschießung von Bazeilles im Deutsch-Französischen Krieg 1870, in: Benoit Majerus/Thomas Kolnberger/M. Christian Ortner (Hg.): Krieg in der industrialisierten Welt (Krieg und Gesellschaft Bd. 4), Wien 2017; Heroic Heirs. Monarchical Succession and the Role of the Military in Restoration Spain and France (mit Richard Meyer Forsting), in: Michael Broers/Ambrogio A. Caiani (Hg.): A History of the European Restorations. Governments, States and Monarchy, London/Oxford 2019.

Ulf Morgenstern
Dr. phil. (geb. 1978)

ist wissenschaftlicher Mitarbeiter der Otto-von-Bismarck-Stiftung und Lehrbeauftragter an der Universität Hamburg. Er forscht zur Geschichte des 19. Jahrhunderts und zur sächsischen Landesgeschichte, zuletzt als Bearbeiter und Herausgeber der Editionen: Otto von Bismarck, Gesammelte Werke. Abt. III 1871–1898 Schriften, Bd. 7: 1886–1887 (Neue Friedrichsruher Ausgabe), Paderborn 2018; »Ach ist das schön hier!« Privatbriefe Walther Schückings aus der Versailler Friedensdelegation 1919, in: Jahrbuch zur Liberalismus-Forschung, 30. Jg. (2018), S. 299–335.

Uffe Østergård
Prof. em. (geb. 1945)

lehrte europäische und dänische Geschichte an der Copenhagen Business School und war Professor an der Universität Aarhus. Zuvor hatte er eine Jean-Monnet-Professur an der Universität Aarhus inne und leitete das Dänische Institut für Holocaust- und Genozidstudien in Kopenhagen. Schwerpunkte seiner Forschung sind politische Kultur und Nationalismus in Europa und in der EU.

Bjørn Østergaard
M. Sc. (geb. 1963)

studierte Biologie und ist seit 1992 am Museum Sønderjylland-Historiecenter Dybbøl Banke beschäftigt. Seit 2004 ist er Leiter des Historiecenters, seit 2005 auch Leiter der Dybbøl Mühle.

Andreas Platthaus
(geb. 1966)

studierte Rhetorik, Philosophie, Geschichte und Betriebswirtschaftslehre. Seit 1997 ist er Feuilletonredakteur der »Frankfurter Allgemeinen Zeitung« und leitet dort das Resort Literatur und Literarisches Leben. Zuletzt publizierte er die historische Studie »Der Krieg nach dem Krieg – Deutschland zwischen Revolution und Versailles«; weitere Bücher widmeten sich der Leipziger Völkerschlacht, dem Bankier Alfred Herrhausen sowie Geschichte und Ästhetik des Comics. 2017 ernannte ihn die Französische Republik zum Chevalier de l'Ordre des arts et lettres, 2018 erhielt er den Hessischen Kulturpreis, 2019 war er Fellow im Thomas Mann House in Pacific Palisades. Während dieses Aufenthalts schrieb er den Band »Auf den Palisaden – Amerikanisches Tagebuch«, der in Kürze bei Rowohlt Berlin erscheinen wird.

Katja Protte
M. A. (geb. 1967)

ist seit 2003 Sachgebietsleiterin Kunst und Ausstellungskuratorin am Militärhistorischen Museum der Bundeswehr in Dresden. Sie hat an der Neukonzeption des Museums mitgearbeitet und verschiedene Kunst- und Fotoausstellungen kuratiert. Von 1995 bis 2003 arbeitete sie als wissenschaftliche Mitarbeiterin am Deutschen Historischen Museum (DHM), Berlin, und am Haus der Geschichte der Bundesrepublik Deutschland, Bonn. Publikationen u. a.: Deutungsmacht und Eigensinn. Das MHM – ein Museum für Menschen mit und ohne Uniform, in: Regine Falkenberg/Thomas Jander (Hg.) für das DHM: Assessment of Significance, Berlin 2018; Mauerspringer. Großplastik der DDR im MHM, in: Jürgen Danyel u. a. (Hg.): Kommunismus unter Denkmalschutz?, Worms 2018; Krieg und Kunst – Das Beispiel Verdun, in: Michael Hörter/Diego Voigt (Hg.): Verdun 1916, Münster 2016.

James Retallack
Prof. Dr. phil. (geb. 1955)

studierte als Rhodes-Stipendiat Neuere Geschichte an der Universität Oxford und ist University-Professor für Geschichte an der Universität Toronto. Forschungsschwerpunkte sind Konservatismus, Antisemitismus, Regionalismus, Wahlpolitik und das Königreich Sachsen. Er ist Herausgeber von »Reichsgründung: Bismarcks Deutschland 1866–1890«, Bd. 4, Deutsche Geschichte in Dokumenten und Bildern, Deutsches Historisches Institut (DHI) Washington, und arbeitet derzeit an einer neuen Bebel-Biografie. Jüngste Publikationen u. a.: »August Bebel: A Life for Social Justice and Democratic Reform«, in: Archiv für Sozialgeschichte 58 (2018) sowie die mit dem Hans-Rosenberg-Preis 2019 ausgezeichnete Monografie »Red Saxony. Election Battles and the Spectre of Democracy in Germany, 1860–1918«, Oxford 2017 (erscheint als überarbeitete Ausgabe in deutscher Übersetzung in Düsseldorf 2020).

Dieter Storz
Dr. phil. (geb. 1958)

ist Hauptkonservator am Bayerischen Armeemuseum in Ingolstadt. Er studierte nach dem Grundwehrdienst Geschichte und Germanistik an der Ludwig-Maximilians-Universität in München, wo er 1990 mit der Dissertation »Kriegsbild und Rüstung vor 1914. Europäische Landstreitkräfte vor dem Ersten Weltkrieg« promoviert wurde. Er kuratierte Ausstellungen zum Ausbruch des Ersten Weltkriegs (»Dieser Stellungs- und Festungskrieg ist scheußlich«, 2014), dem Krieg von 1866 (»Nord gegen Süd«, 2016) sowie zur Revolution in Bayern und dem Ende der bayerischen Armee (»Friedensbeginn? Bayern 1918–1923«, 2018). Publikationen u. a.: Deutsche Militärgewehre vom Werdergewehr bis zum Modell 71/84, Wien 2011; Artillery, http://encyclopedia.1914-1918-online.net/article/artillery, 2014; mit Daniel Hohrath (Hg.): Nord gegen Süd. Der Deutsche Krieg 1866, Ingolstadt 2016.

Armin Wagner
Oberst, Dr. phil (geb. 1968)

ist Historiker und Direktor des Militärhistorischen Museums der Bundeswehr in Dresden. Verwendungen u. a. am Militärgeschichtlichen Forschungsamt in Potsdam, als Dozent für Militärgeschichte an der Offizierschule des Heeres in Dresden, als Referent im Bundespräsidialamt und im Bundesministerium der Verteidigung, Berlin. Jüngste Publikationen u. a.: »Der Führer Adolf Hitler ist tot.« Attentat und Staatsstreich am 20. Juli 1944, Berlin 2019 (Hg. zusammen mit M. Pahl); Spione und Nachrichtenhändler. Geheimdienst-Karrieren in Deutschland 1939–1989, Berlin 2016 (Hg. zusammen mit H. Müller-Enbergs).

Lars Zacharias
Oberstleutnant, M. A. (geb. 1976)

ist 1995 in die Bundeswehr eingetreten. Nach dem Studium der Geschichte und Sozialwissenschaften in Hamburg sowie diversen Truppen- und Stabsverwendungen war er u. a. Dozent für Militärgeschichte und absolvierte einen ISAF-Einsatz in Mazar-e-Sharif/Afghanistan. Seit 2016 ist er tätig als Subject Matter Expert J3 und Officer of Primary Responsibility for Pre-Deployment Training/Current NATO Operations am NATO Joint Force Training Center in Bydgoszcz/Polen. Publikationen u. a.: mit Thorsten Loch: Mythos Königgrätz: Zum politischen Konstrukt der Schlacht von 1866. Eine operationsgeschichtliche Analyse, in: Winfried Heinemann u. a. (Hg.): Der preußisch-österreichische Krieg 1866, Paderborn 2018, S. 161–188; mit Thorsten Loch (Hg.): Wie die Siegessäule nach Berlin kam. Eine kleine Geschichte der Reichseinigungskriege 1864 bis 1871. In Zusammenarbeit mit dem MGFA, Potsdam, und dem Napoleonmuseum Thurgau, Freiburg 2011.

Abbildungen

akg-images
S. 363, 368 unten, 379

Archiv der Otto-von-Bismarck-Stiftung, Friedrichsruh
S. 55, 56, 178 oben, 195 oben

© Archives Charmet / Bridgeman Images
S. 241 oben links

Arkivet ved Dansk Centralbibliotek for Sydslesvig
S. 82 unten, 88

Bayerisches Armeemuseum
S. 233 unten, 275 unten

Bayerische Staatsbibliothek München, 4 Jud. 53 c-1/2, Ausgabe Nr. 1 vom 21. Oktober 1891
S. 377 unten rechts

bpk
S. 318 rechts

bpk / adoc-photos
S. 59, 261

bpk / Coll. O. Calonge / adoc
S. 243 oben

bpk / Deutsches Historisches Museum / Arne Psille
S. 360–361

bpk / Franz Kühn
S. 381

bpk / Hermann Buresch
S. 42–43, 47

bpk / RMN – Grand Palais
S. 206 oben mittig links, 219, 367

bpk / RMN – Grand Palais / Emilie Cambier
S. 197 unten, 206 oben mittig rechts, 206 oben rechts, 207 oben mittig rechts, 207 oben rechts, 207 unten links, 207 unten rechts, 208, 211 oben, 226 oben, 226 mittig, 226 unten, 227 unten rechts

bpk / RMN – Grand Palais / Hervé Lewandowski
S. 254

bpk / RMN – Grand Palais / image musée de l'Armée
S. 209

bpk / RMN – Grand Palais / Pascal Segrette
S. 242 mittig links

bpk / RMN – Grand Palais / Pierre-Louis Pierson
S. 206 links, 207 oben links, 207 oben mittig links

bpk / RMN – Grand Palais / Philippe Fuzeau
S. 186

Bismarck-Museum, Friedrichsruh
S. 52 unten, 53, 200

Bundesarchiv, Bibliothek
S. 33 oben links

Bundesbank, Frankfurt am Main
S. 247

© Bundesmobilienverwaltung, Hofmobiliendepot, Möbel Museum Wien, Foto: Edgar Knaack
S. 159 unten

Camphausen, Wilhelm: Erstürmung der Düppeler Schanzen, GK I 50397 / Stiftung Preußische Schlösser und Gärten Berlin-Brandenburg / Wolfgang Pfauder
S. 358–359

coll. Musée de Dinan – Ville de Dinan
S. 335 unten

Collections La contemporaine/AFF11924
S. 183 oben rechts

Det Kgl. Bibliotek / Royal Danish Libray
S. 83

© Deutsches Historisches Museum
S. 30 links, 194 rechts, 263

© Deutsches Historisches Museum / A. Psille
S. 61, 164

© Deutsches Historisches Museum / I. Desnica
S. 112 links, 377 oben

© Deutsches Historisches Museum / S. Ahlers
S. 37 oben, 66–67, 177 oben rechts, 187 links, 206 unten, 217 unten, 331 oben

Deutsches Museum Nordschleswig
S. 104 rechts

Deutsches Medizinhistorisches Museum, Ingolstadt / Foto: Hubert P. Klotzeck
S. 327 unten, 328 unten

Digital image courtesy of the Getty's Open Content Program.
S. 283 oben und unten

Dorotheum Wien, Auktionskatalog 7. 5. 2015
S. 162 oben, 162 unten

gemeinfrei, Wikimedia Commons
S. 117 rechts

Hermann Biow, Jacob Venedey, Abgeordneter von Homburg in der Nationalversammlung von Frankfurt a. M., 1848, Museum für Kunst und Gewerbe Hamburg (Public Domain)
S. 25

Hedeselskabet, Dänemark
S. 82 oben

Historisches Archiv Krupp, Essen
S. 294 oben, 294–295, 295 oben links, 296 oben

© Historisches Museum Hannover / Foto: R. Gottschalk
S. 117 unten links

© Historisches Museum Hannover / Foto: Ulrich Pucknat (HMH)
S. 117 oben links

HHStA, AUR 1866 VIII 23
S. 152

HHStA, HausA Selekt Kronprinz Rudolf Kt. 12–1
S. 158

HHStA, HausA Selekt Kronprinz Rudolf Kt. 12–2
S. 159 oben rechts

HHStA, HausA Selekt Kronprinz Rudolf Kt. 18
S. 159 oben links

HHStA, MdÄ AR F 42/109
S. 320

Historiecenter Dybbøl Banke
S. 77

ID 119438082 © Michael Gordon | Dreamstime.com
S. 383

IMAGNO/Wiener Stadt- und Landesb / Süddeutsche Zeitung Photo
S. 156

Institut für Stadtgeschichte, Frankfurt a. M.
S. 35 unten

INTERFOTO / Sammlung Rauch
S. 316

© Kunsthalle zu Kiel, Foto: Sönke Ehlert
S. 278–279

Landesarchiv Berlin, A. Pr. Br. Rep. 030, Nr. 11034.
S. 183 unten

Landesarchiv Berlin, A. Pr. Br. Rep. 030 15223, S. 30
S. 377 unten links

© Landessammlungen NÖ
S. 161, 163 oben links

© Look and Learn
S. 234 unten

Kölnisches Stadtmuseum / Foto: Hendrik Strelow
S. 373 oben

Mährisches Landesarchiv in Brünn (Moravský zemský archiv v Brně)
S. 146 (G. 140, K. 611)

Menzel, Adolph von: Graf Moltke, GK I 10203 / Stiftung Preußische Schlösser und Gärten Berlin-Brandenburg / Daniel Lindner
S. 236 links

Menzel, Adolph von: Otto von Bismarck, 1871, GK I 10202 / Stiftung Preußische Schlösser und Gärten Berlin-Brandenburg / Daniel Lindner
S. 236 rechts

MHM
S. 21, 24, 27, 30 rechts, 31, 32, 34 unten, 38 links, 39, 41, 49, 50–51, 62, 75, 76 unten, 78, 81 oben, 90 rechts, 91, 98 unten, 99 oben, 100, 105 unten, 116, 121, 122–123, 126, 128, 131 oben, 134, 138, 139–140, 141 oben, 143 mittig, 143 unten rechts, 150, 151, 163 unten, 165, 166–167, 167 oben, 167 unten rechts, 168 oben, 171 oben, 176, 178 unten, 179 unten, 180, 183 oben links, 189, 192 unten, 196, 198 oben, 211 unten, 214 oben, 214–215, 217 oben, 220 oben, 220–223, 224 unten, 227 oben, 228–231, 233 oben, 234 oben links und oben rechts, 235, 237, 238 oben, 239 oben rechts, 240, 244, 245 unten, 249, 250, 251 oben, 252, 259, 260, 273, 274, 276, 282 links, 282 rechts, 286 oben, 292, 297, 299 mittig, 301, 302–307, 313 unten links und unten rechts, 314, 315, 317, 318 links, 319, 322, 323 unten, 324, 329 oben, 330, 332, 333, 334 links, 334 unten rechts, 342–343, 351–354,

MHM/Andrea Ulke
S. 33 oben rechts, S. 33 unten, 34 oben, 36, 37 unten, 38 rechts, 80, 96 oben, 97, 99 unten, 105 oben, 112 rechts, 113 oben, 114–115, 119, 124–125, 127, 131 unten, 132–133, 135, 141 unten, 142 rechts, 143 oben und mittig, 145, 147–149, 154, 163 oben rechts, 168 unten, 169, 171 unten, 177 links und unten rechts, 179 oben, 185 rechts, 187 rechts, 188, 190, 191 unten, 192 oben, 193 unten, 194 oben links, 194 unten links, 195 unten links und rechts, 197 oben, 198 unten, 201 oben, 201–204, 205 oben links, 205 unten, 210, 212–213, 213 unten, 214–215, 216, 218, 225, 232, 238 unten, 239 unten, 241 rechts oben und unten, 245 oben und mittig, 246, 251 unten, 253, 268, 277, 285, 286 unten -289, 298, 299 unten, 308–309, 312, 313 oben links und oben rechts, 321, 323 oben, 325–327 oben, 328, 331 unten, 334–335 oben, 337, 355, 362, 364–366, 368 oben

MHM Flugplatz Berlin-Gatow,
Foto: Ralf Walter Heldenmaier
S. 299 oben

musée d'art et d'histoire Paul Eluard – Saint Denis, Cliché: Irène Andréani
S. 227 unten rechts, 242 oben, 242–243 unten

Musée de l'Air et de l'Espace – Frédéric Cabeza
S. 224

Museen der Stadt Dresden – Stadtmuseum Dresden, SMD PhG 04507
S. 346–347, 357 oben

Musee Historique de Strasbourg/ Photo Musees de Strasbourg, M. Bertola
S. 185 oben, S. 193 oben links und oben rechts, 205 oben rechts, 215 unten rechts, 265, 266

Museum für Archäologie Schloss Gottorf, Landesmuseen Schleswig-Holstein
S. 89 oben, 89 mittig, 89 unten

Museum Sønderjylland – Sønderborg Slot
S. 73, 84, 85, 96 unten, 97 unten links, 102, 107 unten

Nachrichtentechnische Sammlung Aachen, Institut für Nachrichtentechnik, RWTH Aachen
S. 16–17, 40 rechts

ÖNB/Wien, PK 847
S. 170

Österreichische Nationalbibliothek, Sammlung von Handschriften und alten Drucken, F 311140E-E.Alt-Flug
S. 113 unten

Österreichisches Staatsarchiv, Abt. Kriegsarchiv Wien, KA AhOB MKSM HR Akten K. 343 (1866) 69/9
S. 137 oben und unten

Österreichisches Staatsarchiv, Abt. Kriegsarchiv Wien, KA KS (Kartensammlung) H IV c 270–9
S. 275 oben

Peter Palm, Berlin
S. 70–71, 110–111, 174–175, 378

Privatbesitz
S. 350, 357 unten

© Rheinisches Bildarchiv, Patrick Schwarz
S. 54 (rba_d053098), 181 unten (rba_d053098), S. 191 oben (rba_d053097), 199 (rba_d053100), 296 unten (rba_d053096), 333 unten (rba_d052228), 344 oben (rba_d053101), 344 unten (rba_d053101), 370–371 unten (rba_d053094), 371 oben (rba_d052226_01), 372 oben (rba_d053094), 372 unten (rba_d053094), 373 unten (rba_d053094), 374 (rba_d053094), 375 (rba_d053094)

© Rheinisches Bildarchiv, Sabrina Walz
S. 290 (rba_d037898)

Roald Als, published in Politiken on 21 July 2013
S. 86

Sächsisches Staatsarchiv, Staatsarchiv Leipzig, 20080 Königliches Bezirksgericht Leipzig, Nr. 24. 1870 – 1876. Wilhelm Obermüller
S. 182

Sammlung Wolfgang K. Hamann, Berlin
S. 93 oben rechts

© Schloß Schönbrunn Kultur- u. Betriebsges.m.b.H./Fotograf: Christoph Mühlbauer
S. 157

© SDTB/Foto: C. Kirchner
S. 295 oben rechts

SHLB, Handschriftenabt., Nachlass Theodor Storm
S. 106 rechts (Sign.: Cb50.51:39)

SHLB, Landesgeschichtliche Sammlung
S. 74 (Sign.: Y 11:15), 76 oben, 79 (Sign.: 4193 [a], 1865:166), 81 unten (Sign.: 5132), 90 links (Sign.: P4-F-42 1864), 92 oben, 92 unten, 93 unten (Sign.: Album 6, ZA 95), 94 (Sign.: 18-1956), 95 (Sign.: II Kb 15 Nr. 6), 97 unten rechts (Sign.: 4a-b, 4574), 98 oben (Sign.: 4639), 101 oben (Sign.: Album 6, ZA 95), 101 (Sign.: Album 6, ZA 95), 103 oben (Sign.: Album 6, ZA 95), 103 unten (Sign.: Album 25, 6388-6378), 104 links, 107 oben (Sign.: 5897), 329 oben (Sign.: 5486 (a))

Siemens Historical Institute
S. 40 links

Städtische Galerie Dresden – Kunstsammlung, Museen der Stadt Dresden, Foto: Franz Zadnicek
S. 23

SUB Göttingen/Signatur 4 SVA II, 2058:1872
S. 239 oben links

The History Collection/Alamy Stock Photo
S. 93 oben links

Theodor-Fontane-Archiv Potsdam
S. 106 links

Universitätsbibliothek Heidelberg/ Kladderadatsch: Humoristisch-satyrisches Wochenblatt — 3.1850/192 (https://digi.ub.uni-heidelberg.de/diglit/kla1850/0192/)/public domain
S. 35 oben

Zentrum Informationsarbeit Bundeswehr, Bibliothek
S. 142 rechts

Titelabbildung/Klappenbroschur: Camphausen, Wilhelm: Erstürmung der Düppeler Schanzen, GK I 50397 (Detail)/ Stiftung Preußische Schlösser und Gärten Berlin-Brandenburg/Wolfgang Pfauder
Karten Klappenbroschur: Peter Palm, Berlin

KRIEG MACHT NATION

Wie das deutsche Kaiserreich entstand

9. April 2020 bis 31. Januar 2021

MILITÄRHISTORISCHES MUSEUM DER BUNDESWEHR

BUNDESWEHR

Direktor
Oberst Dr. Armin Wagner

Kommissarischer Leiter Abteilung Museumsbetrieb und Leiter Ausbildung
Oberstleutnant Peter Haug

Leiter Abteilung Führung
Oberstleutnant Jens Körner

Leiter Ausstellung
Sven Birke

Leiter Kommunikation
Wissenschaftlicher Oberrat Jan Kindler

Leiter Restaurierung
Dr. Lutz Strobach

Leiter Sammlung
Wissenschaftlicher Oberrat Götz Ulrich Penzel

Leiter Zentrale Fachangelegenheiten
Regierungsamtsrat Carsten Linne

KATALOG

Herausgeber und Herausgeberin
Wissenschaftlicher Oberrat Dr. Gerhard Bauer, Wissenschaftliche Oberrätin Katja Protte, Oberst Dr. Armin Wagner

Redaktion
Katja Protte, Eva Langhals, Steffen Jungmann

Bildredaktion
Steffen Jungmann

Wissenschaftliches Lektorat
Annette Wunschel, Eva Langhals, Thomas Pasche

Verlagslektorat
Sina Volk, Sandstein Verlag

Karten
Peter Palm, Berlin

Gestaltung
Michaela Klaus, Sandstein Verlag

Satz und Reprografie
Christian Werner, Sandstein Verlag

Druck
FINIDR s.r.o., Český Těšín

Schrift
Diamante, Din Pro

Papier
LuxoArt Samt New 135 g/m²

Dieser Katalogband erscheint
in der Reihe:

FORUM MHM
Schriftenreihe des Militärhistorischen Museums der Bundeswehr, Band 15
Herausgegeben von Armin Wagner

Die Deutsche Nationalbibliothek verzeichnet diese Publikation in der Deutschen Nationalbibliografie; detaillierte bibliografische Daten sind im Internet über http://dnb.dnb.de abrufbar.

www.sandstein-verlag.de
ISBN 978-3-95498-545-6

AUSSTELLUNG

Kurator und Kuratorin

Wissenschaftlicher Oberrat Dr. Gerhard Bauer, Wissenschaftliche Oberrätin Katja Protte

Ausstellungsgestaltung

Thomas Ebersbach, Leipzig

Ausstellungsgrafik

Försterwerbung Chemnitz, Pigmentpool, Picto GmbH

Wissenschaftliche Mitarbeit und Recherche

Alma Hannig, Eva Langhals, Dr. Elmar Heinz,Thomas Pasche, Nicole Thiele-Schulze

Praktikantinnen, Praktikanten und Wehrübende

Christian Alberts, Lisa Baldauf, Nora Pauline Berg, Alexander Gatzsche, Michael Körbs, Romain Poudray, Alexander Reindl, Martin Schinken, Sophia Stöllinger, Florian Wegen

Objektdisposition und Transportorganisation

Katja Friedrich, David Pfeffer

Leiterin Musealer Bestandsnachweis

Regierungsamtfrau Antje Hucke-Melkus

Leiter Zentrale Fachangelegenheiten

Regierungsamtsrat Carsten Linne

Lagezentrum

Sven Birke, Jens Wohllebe, Heiko Herzog

Ausstellungstexte

Dr. Gerhard Bauer, Katja Protte, Alma Hannig, Eva Langhals

Lektorat

Annette Wunschel, Nicole Thiele-Schulze, Eva Langhals

Übersetzung

Bundessprachenamt SMD 14, Mareike Sedlmeier

Bildredaktion

Steffen Jungmann

Fotografin

Andrea Ulke

Karten

Peter Palm, Berlin

Textgestaltung und Bildbearbeitung

Katrin Korritter, Katrin Micklich, Katja Springer

Konservatorische Betreuung

Dr. Lutz Strobach (Leitung), Steffen Fuhrmann, Elisabeth Härtel, Ingrid Naumann, Sebastian Neubert, Bettina Schlecht, Derya Wieser, Karoline Zakaszewski

Museumspädagogisches Programm

Alexander Reindl, Ines Schnee, Wissenschaftliche Oberrätin Avgi Stilidis, Erik Zimmermann

Führungsteam

Carsten Bleßmann, Dr. Verena Böll, Barbara Brugger, Dr. Christine Bücher, Randi Hamann, Franz-Josef Hille, Heinrich Hofer, Dr. Alexander Klein, Alexander Paulick, Stefanie Preißler, Samira Rog, Katja Smirnowa, Angelina Vollenweider, Marcus Weber

Führungsmanagement

Anja Dinter, Claudia Rose

Hörführung

Ines Schnee, Wissenschaftliche
Oberrätin Avgi Stilidis,
Erik Zimmermann (Texte)
Romanus Fuhrmann, Dulcie Smart
(Sprecher)
K13 Studios Berlin GmbH (Produktion)
Isabell Bretsch (technische Realisierung)

Begleitprogramm

Wissenschaftlicher Oberrat
Jan Kindler, Kai-Uwe Reinhold

Presse- und Öffentlichkeitsarbeit

Hauptbootsmann Jörg Binsack,
Hauptmann Fabian Friedl

Marketing und Vertrieb

Christoph Lehmann,
Almut Hoffmann

Medientechnik

Tilo Meissner

Lichtgestaltung

Michael Schneider

Elektrik und Beleuchtung

Mirko Dinter, Rene Horn,
Michael Schneider

Technische Medienkoordinatorin

Isabell Bretsch

Interaktive Ausstellungsmedien

Isabell Bretsch, Daniel Finke

Schnitt Ausstellungsmedien

Tilo Meissner

Ausstellungsproduktion und -aufbau

Hofmann & Großmann, Möbelwerkstätten
Härtig, Steinbach-Wagner,
kursiv | text – objekt – raum GmbH,
Phillipp Hornig, Heiko Herzog

Einbringeteam/Arthandling

vienna arthandling